英汉汉英词典

ENGLISH-CHINESE CHINESE-ENGLISH DICTIONARY

全新版
NEW EDITION

李德芳　姜兰 ◎ 主编

四川辞书出版社

图书在版编目(CIP)数据

英汉汉英词典:全新版/李德芳,姜兰主编.—
成都:四川辞书出版社,2024.1

ISBN 978-7-5579-1420-2

Ⅰ.①英… Ⅱ.①李… ②姜… Ⅲ.①英语—词典
②词典—英、汉 Ⅳ.①H316

中国国家版本馆 CIP 数据核字(2023)第 218159 号

英汉汉英词典（全新版）
YINGHAN HANYING CIDIAN（QUANXINBAN）

主　编　李德芳　姜兰

责任编辑 /	袁一丹　雷　敏	
封面设计 /	李其飞	
版式设计 /	王　跃	
责任印制 /	肖　鹏	
出版发行 /	四川辞书出版社	
地　　址 /	成都市锦江区三色路 238 号	
邮政编码 /	610023	
印　　刷 /	成都国图广告印务有限公司	
开　　本 /	787 mm×1092 mm　1/32	
版　　次 /	2024 年 1 月第 1 版	
印　　次 /	2024 年 1 月第 1 次印刷	
印　　张 /	24	
书　　号 /	ISBN 978-7-5579-1420-2	
定　　价 /	39.80 元	

· 本书如有印装质量问题,请寄回出版社调换。
· 制作部电话:(028)86361826

出版说明

Preface

　　本词典是一部内容丰富的英汉汉英双向词典。适合大、中学生及具有中级或中级以上英语水平的各类读者使用,既可以用作查阅的工具,也可以作为翻译或写作的帮手。

　　本词典的英汉部分收词8 000余条,连同扩展词汇实际共收词约15 000条,基本上涵盖了我国教育部颁布的《初中英语新课程标准》词汇表、《高中英语新课程标准》词汇表和《大学英语教学大纲》词汇表中所列词汇。本词典还针对英语学习和英语教学的实际需要,将一些英语知识进行了归纳和提炼,词典中共设有用法说明和辨析千余条,有助于读者从多层次、多角度学习、掌握和运用英语词语。

　　本词典的汉英部分收词25 000余条。除一般词和大量新词外,还收入一些常见的方言、成语、谚语及自然科学的常用词语。汉语词语的选择注重科学性和规范性,英语释义地道准确,原汁原味,简明易懂。所收的汉语词语涵盖面广,在日常学习、生活与社交活动中使用频率高,搭配能力强,可供读者口头交际和书面表达时使用。

　　随着时代的发展,人们的日常语言中不断涌现出反映时代面貌的新词语或新义项。因此在本词典编纂过程中,编纂人员选收了数千条在报刊、影视、网络等媒体上使用频率较高的新词语,使本词典具有鲜明的时代特色。

　　参加本词典编纂工作的人员,既有权威的语言学专家,又有长期在英语教学第一线工作的经验丰富的教师,这为本词典的高质量提供了可靠的保障。然而,由于时间所限,词典中也难免会存在疏漏或不足。我们欢迎广大读者不吝赐教,以便使本词典更加完善。

编　者

目 录

Contents

出版说明

.... 1

凡例

.... 5

略语表

.... 6

英汉词典正文

.... 1—394

汉英词典正文

.... 395—740

汉语拼音音节索引

.... 741—756

国际音标分类表

.... （后衬）

新版国际音标发音表

.... （后衬）

凡　例

Guide to the Use of the Dictionary

本词典由英汉和汉英两部分组成。

英汉部分

1. 词条：单词用黑正体按字母顺序突出两个字母排列。拼写相近、词义相同的单词列为一条，如：analyze(-se)或 colo(u)r；拼写相同、词源和词义不同者，原则上另列词条，并在右上角标以 1，2…数码。例中出现词条词用"～"代替，但词尾有变化的或词头大写的，则全词写出。

2. 注音：本词典采用新版国际音标。主重音注在左上方，次重音注在左下方，单词的同一词性有不同发音的同时放入斜括号内用逗号分开，如：always /ˈɔːlweɪz，ˈɔːlweɪz/。

3. 词性：本词典词性用白斜体缩写形式表示，一个词的不同词性前冠罗马数字Ⅰ，Ⅱ，Ⅲ 等。动词只写 v.，表示既可作及物也可作不及物动词，若写明 vt.，表示只作及物动词，写明 vi.，表示只作不及物动词；名词只写 n.，表示既可作可数也可作不可数名词，标有[C]表示只作可数名词，标有[U]表示只作不可数名词。

4. 屈折变化：不规则的动词和形容词、副词分别按过去式、过去分词、现在分词(如有不规则的)和比较级、最高级的顺序，注上音标，放入圆括号中；名词复数不规则的注明 pl. 后标出不规则形式，放入圆括号中。

5. 词义：多义词的不同义项用 ❶，❷，❸…排列。同一义项如有两个或两个以上的汉语释义时，意思相近的用逗号隔开，否则用分号隔开。

6. 同义词和反义词：词条义项后有同义词和反义词，同义词前用"同"标出，反义词前用"反"标出。

7. 派生词和短语：本词典的派生词前用"派"标出。短语用黑体，短语有多义的分别用①，②，③…区别。短语中出现词条词用"～"代替。

8. 用法和辨析：凡有这两项均放在框内列在该词条最后。

汉英部分

1. 本词典所收条目分单字条目和多字条目，并按汉语拼音字母顺序排列次序。

2. 单字条目及多字条目若有多个义项，用 ❶，❷，❸…标注顺序，并在序号后先提供用法提示，再提供英文译文。

3. 某些单字条目为多音字时，在单字条目的下方，以"另见…"标示其另外的读音。

4. 例证中出现词条词用"～"代替。可用作替换或省略的词则放在圆括号之内。

5. 条目的释义与例证之间加冒号"："；例证如有不同的英文译文，则用分号"；"隔开；例证与例证之间用单竖线"｜"隔开。

6. 为方便查阅，正文后备有汉语拼音音节索引。

略 语 表

Abbreviations Used in the Dictionary

1. 词类

adj adjective 形容词

adv. adverb 副词

art. article 冠词

aux. v. auxiliary verb 助动词

[C] countable noun 可数名词

conj. conjunction 连词

int. interjection 感叹词

n. noun 名词

prep. preposition 介词

pron. pronoun 代词

[U] uncountable noun 不可数名词

v. verb 动词

vi. intransitive verb 不及物动词

vt. transitive verb 及物动词

2. 修辞色彩及用法

〈褒〉褒义　　　　　　〈贬〉贬义　　　　　　〈方〉方言

〈古〉古时用语　　　　〈讳〉忌讳语　　　　　〈敬〉敬语

〈旧〉旧时用语　　　　〈口〉口语　　　　　　〈口令〉口令语

〈量〉量词　　　　　　〈谦〉谦语　　　　　　〈书〉书面语

〈俗〉俗语　　　　　　〈叹〉感叹语　　　　　〈套〉套语

〈婉〉委婉　　　　　　〈文〉文学用语　　　　〈象〉象声词

〈谚〉谚语　　　　　　〈喻〉比喻

3. 学科

〈地〉地理学　　　　　〈电〉电学　　　　　　〈电影〉电影学

〈动〉动物学　　　　　〈法〉法律　　　　　　〈纺〉纺织

〈佛教〉佛教　　　　　〈工艺〉工艺美术学　　〈化〉化学

〈机〉机械　　　　　　〈计〉计算机　　　　　〈建〉建筑

〈交〉交通运输　　　　〈解〉解剖学　　　　　〈经〉经济学

〈军〉军事　　　　　　〈林〉林学　　　　　　〈逻〉逻辑学

〈农〉农业　　　　　　〈气〉气象学　　　　　〈商〉商业

〈摄〉摄影学　　　　　〈生〉生物学　　　　　〈生理〉生理学

〈食〉食品;食品工程　〈史〉历史　　　　　　〈数〉数学

〈体〉体育　　　　　　〈天〉天文学　　　　　〈心〉心理学

〈药〉药理学　　　　　〈冶〉冶金学　　　　　〈医〉医学

〈音〉音乐　　　　　　〈印〉印刷　　　　　　〈语〉语言学

〈哲〉哲学　　　　　　〈植〉植物学　　　　　〈中医〉中医学

〈自〉自动化　　　　　〈宗〉宗教

英汉词典

English-Chinese Dictionary

A a

a / eɪ,ə / , **an** / æn,ən / *art.* ❶一(个、本、件、把…) ❷某个：A Mr Smith came to see you this morning. 今天早上有一位史密斯先生来看你。❸任何一个：A dog is a faithful animal. 狗是忠实的动物。

用法
❶a 用在以辅音音素开始的词前面，an 用在以元音音素开头的词前面：a man 一个男人；a book 一本书；an ox 一头牛；an hour 一小时。❷a,an 与可数单数名词连用，表示"一类"的意思。❸a 不能和指示形容词（this,that 等）人称代词的所有格（my,your,his,her 等）连用。❹只限一个人担任的职务的词（如主席、总统、校长等）作为 elect,choose,appoint 等动词的补语时，不用冠词，如：He was elected chairman. 他被选为主席。但不限定一个人担任的职务的词通常要用 a 或 an,如：I was chosen (as) a member of the team. 我被选为该队队员。❺两个名词用 and 连接起来视为一个整体时，第二个名词不用冠词 a 或 an,如：a knife and folk（一副）刀叉。

aback / ə'bæk / *adv.* 向后,朝后：be taken ～（被…）吓了一跳；大吃一惊 圆 backward 反 forward

abacus / 'æbəkəs / *n.* [C]（*pl.* abaci / 'æbəsaɪ / 或 abacuses / 'æbəkəsɪz /）算盘：use（operate）an ～ 打算盘

abandon / ə'bændən / *vt.* 抛弃；遗弃：～ one's family（one's country,one's post,a ship）抛弃家人（背弃祖国,放弃职位,弃船）

abate / ə'beɪt / *vt.* 减少,减弱；减轻,减退：～ sb's enthusiasm 挫伤某人的热情/drugs to ～ pain 镇痛药 圆 decrease —*vi.* 减小,减弱；减轻,减退：The wind ～d in fury. 风力减弱了。

abbey / 'æbi / *n.* [C]大修道院；大寺院

abbreviation / ə,briːvi'eɪʃn / *n.* ❶[U]缩写；简略 ❷[C]缩写词

abdomen / 'æbdəmən / *n.* [C]腹(部)

abduct / æb'dʌkt / *vt.* 诱拐；绑架；劫持：～ a

child for ransom 诱拐儿童以勒索赎金 派 abduction *n.*

abhor / əb'hɔː(r) / *vt.* (-horred;-horring)憎恶；厌恶；痛恨：We all ～ cruelty to animals. 我们都憎恨虐待动物。

abide / ə'baɪd / (abode 或 abided) *vi.* ❶遵守（法律、诺言、决定等）：～ disciplines 遵守纪律 圆 obey,observe 反 disobey ❷坚持(意见等) 圆 keep,observe —*vt.* 忍受,容忍；顶住：Nobody can ～ such a cruel person. 没有人能够容忍这种残忍的人。圆 endure,tolerate 反 break,violate 派 abidance *n.*

ability / ə'bɪləti / *n.* ❶[U]能力：the ～ to speak English 说英语的能力/ One's writing ～ grows by practice. 一个人的写作能力靠实践来提高。圆 power,capacity,competence ❷才能；本事：He is a man of abilities. 他是一位有才干的人。圆 skill,capability

able / 'eɪbl / *adj.* ❶有能力的：an ～ man 有才干的人/ **be ～ to do sth.** 有能力(办法、机会)做某事：She was ～ to catch an early bus. 她赶上早班公共汽车。圆 capable 反 unable,incapable ❷有才干的；聪明的；能干的：The woman is particularly ～. 那个女子特别能干。圆 qualified,competent 反 incompetent

辨析
able 意为"有才能的",指人的才智,作表语形容词时后接不定式：You are more able to do it than she is. 你比她更有能力做此事。He said he was able to finish his work in time. 他说他能及时完成任务。**can** 意为"能；会",指体力、知识、技能等方面的能力,是情态动词：Can you lift the suitcase? 你能举起这口箱子吗？I told them I would come as soon as I could. 我告诉他们我将尽早来。**capable** 意为"有能力的；能胜任的",指能力的拥有,作表语形容词时后接介词 of：Show your teacher what you are capable of. 向你的老师展示你的才能。A man like him is capable of anything. 像他那样的人什么事都能干。

A

abnormal / æb'nɔːml / adj. 不正常的；反常的：It is absolutely ～ behavior. 这完全是反常的行为。反 normal 派 abnormally adv.

aboard / ə'bɔːd / adv. & prep. 在（车、船、飞机）上；上（车、船、飞机）：The captain is ～. 船长在船上。/Welcome ～! 请上船（上车，上飞机）!

abolish / ə'bɒlɪʃ / vt. 废除（法律、旧风俗、旧习惯）；消灭（战争等）：The bad customs have been ～ ed. 这些不良风俗业已废除。派 abolition n.

aborigine / ˌæbə'rɪdʒɪni / n. [C] ❶土著居民：The Eskimos are among the ～s of North America. 爱斯基摩人属北美土著居民。❷（常作 A-)澳大利亚土著居民

abortion / ə'bɔːʃn / n. 流产；堕胎：Her mother asked her to have an ～ at once. 她母亲要求她立即做人工流产。

abound / ə'baʊnd / vi. ❶（物产）丰富 ❷富于；盛产；多：～ in opportunities 有很多机会/～ with rain 多雨 反 lack, want

about / ə'baʊt / Ⅰ prep. 关于；在周围：What do you know ～ him? 关于他，你知道些什么? / He was tired of walking ～ the street. 他讨厌在街上走来走去。同 concerning, around Ⅱ adv. 周围；到处；大约：She must be somewhere ～. 她一定在附近某处。/ be ～ to 正要；将要：She is ～ to start. 她正要动身。同 around, nearly, almost

<u>用法</u>
be about to 句型中的 to 为不定式符号，其后接动词原形：We were about to leave when he came. 他来的时候我们正要离开。

<u>辨析</u>
be about to 表示正要发生的动作：The train is about to leave. 火车马上就要开了。be to 表示按计划、安排将要发生的动作：The boys are to go to school next week. 孩子们下周要上学了。be going to 表示打算进行或有迹象表明将要发生的动作：It's going to rain. 快下雨了。

above / ə'bʌv / Ⅰ prep. 在…之上；超过：～ sea level 高出海平面；海拔 / We flew ～ the clouds. 我们在云层之上飞行。/ ～ all 首先；尤其是：And ～ all, don't tell him about it. 最重要的是不要将此事告诉他。同 over, beyond 反 below, under Ⅱ adv. 在上面：Her bedroom is just ～. 她的卧室就在上面。同 overhead

<u>辨析</u>
❶表示"正上方"时，above 和 over 两词可互换：Some birds are flying above (over) the lake. 一些鸟在湖上飞翔。❷表示"在…上方"而不明确指示是"正上方"时，不用 over：The sun rose above the horizon. 太阳从地平线上升起。❸above 和 over 都可用来表示数量上"超过…"，above 比 over 更常用：There is nothing in this shop above (over) 10 yuan. 这个店的货物没有一件超过 10 元。

abridge / ə'brɪdʒ / vt.（在保留主要内容的同时）精简…的篇幅，删节，节略：～ a novel 缩写一部小说

abroad / ə'brɔːd / adv. 在国外；到国外：at home and ～ 国内外/ study ～ 留学/ His brother went ～ last year. 他的兄弟去年出国了。/ Her father has returned from ～. 她父亲已从国外回来。同 overseas 反 home

abrupt / ə'brʌpt / adj. ❶突然的；出其不意的：～ departure 突然的离去 同 sudden ❷陡峭的；险峻的：～ slope 陡峭的山坡 同 steep 反 level ❸粗鲁的；无礼的：～ manner 粗鲁的态度；唐突的举止 同 rough 反 polite ❹（讲话、文章等）不连贯的；支离破碎的

absence / 'æbsəns / n. 缺席；不在：an ～ of two years 离开两年/ I didn't notice his ～. 我没注意到他缺席。反 presence

absent / 'æbsənt / adj. 缺席的；不在的：He is ～ from class today. 他今天缺课。同 missing 反 present

absolute / 'æbsəluːt / adj. 绝对的；完全的：majority 绝对多数/ ～ truth 绝对真理/ A child has ～ trust in his mother. 孩子绝对信赖母亲。同 pure, complete 反 relative 派 absolutely adv.

absorb / əb'sɔːb / vt. ❶吸收（水、热、光等）：Plants ～ energy from the sun. 植物从太阳吸取能量。反 discharge, release ❷吸引；使全神贯注于：be ～ed in 被…迷住；专心于：He is ～ed in study. 他专注于学习。同 engage, attract

abstain / əb'steɪn / vi. 戒；避免；避开：～ from wine (drinking) 戒酒

abstract Ⅰ / 'æbstrækt / adj. 理论上的；抽象

A

的;深奥的:～ art 抽象艺术/ ～ concept 抽象概念/ His plan was too ～ to put into operation. 他的计划太抽象,无法付诸实施。Ⅱ / ˈæbstrækt / n. ❶摘要;概括:～s information 文摘信息/ ～s paper 文摘报 同 brief, summary ❷抽象;抽象概念 Ⅲ / æbˈstrækt / vt. ❶提取;抽取:～ metal from ore 从矿石中提取金属 ❷摘录…的要点:write an ～ of ...写…的摘要 派 abstraction n.

absurd / əbˈsɜːd / adj. 不合理的;荒唐可笑的;愚蠢的:an ～ idea 荒谬的想法/ an ～ novel 荒诞小说/ an ～ suggestion 荒谬的建议 派 absurdity n.

abundance / əˈbʌndəns /n. 丰富;充裕;大量:live in ～生活富裕/ year of ～ 丰年 同 richness, plenty

abundant / əˈbʌndənt / adj. 丰富的;充裕的:China is ～ in (with) natural resources. 中国的自然资源丰富。同 rich, plentiful 反 poor, scarce 派 abundantly adv.

abuse / əˈbjuːs / Ⅰ vt. ❶滥用;虐待:Don't ～ your power. 不要滥用你的权力。同 misuse, mistreat ❷辱骂 同 curse, insult Ⅱ n. ❶滥用;虐待:～ of children 虐待儿童 ❷辱骂:personal ～人身攻击 同 curse, insult

academic / ˌækəˈdemɪk / Ⅰ adj. 大学的;高等教育的;学术的:～ authority 学术权威/ ～ circles (world) 学术界/ ～ degree 学位/ ～ exchange 学术交流/ ～ paper 学术论文/ ～ research 学术研究 Ⅱ n. [C]大学生;大学教师;学究式人物

academician / əˌkædəˈmɪʃən / n. [C] 院士

academy / əˈkædəmi / n. [C] 高等专科学校;研究院;学院;学会:a military ～ 陆军军官学校/ an ～ of fine arts 美术学院/an ～ of music 音乐学院/ the Chinese ～ of Sciences 中国科学院

accede / ækˈsiːd / vi. ❶答应,同意;应允,依从(与 to 连用):～ to a demand 答应要求 ❷就职,就任;即位;继承(与 to 连用):～ to an office 就职

accelerate / əkˈseləreɪt / v. 加速;促进:～ capital turnover 加速资金周转 反 decelerate 派 acceleration n.

accelerator / əkˈseləˌreɪtə(r) / n. [C](汽车等的)加速踏板,油门踏板;油门拉纽

accent / ˈæksent / n. [C] ❶口音;腔调:He speaks English with an American ～. 他讲英语带有美国口音。❷重音;重读:In the word "begin", the ～ is on the second syllable. "begin"这个词的重音在第二个音节上。

accept / əkˈsept / vt. 接受;承认;答应:I ～ed his presents. 我接受了他送的礼物。/ The boy ～ed full responsibility for breaking the window. 这男孩对打坏窗户之事负全责。同 take, receive, admit 反 refuse, oppose 派 acceptable adj.

辨析

accept 意为"接受;接纳",通常指经过自己考虑,主观上同意收取别人提供的东西:She accepted his invitation. 她接受了他的邀请。receive 意为"接到;收到",仅指收到某东西的客观行为,如收到信件、请帖、礼物等:When did you receive her letter? 你什么时候收到了她的信? He received a gift, but did not accept it. 他收到一份礼物,但未接受。

acceptance / əkˈseptəns / n. ❶接受;接收;领受;验收:～ a test 对一项试验进行验收 同 reception ❷承认;认可:meet with general ～ 得到广泛的承认 同 recognition

access / ˈækses / n. [U] ❶通路;入口:This is the only ～ to the library. 这是到图书馆的唯一通路。同 way, entrance ❷有进入(或接触、接近、会面)的机会(或权利):gain (get, have) ～ to 有…机会(或权利):Students must gain ～ to books. 学生们必须有读书的机会。同 approach, admission 派 accessible adj.

accessory / əkˈsesəri / Ⅰ n. [C] ❶附件;附属品:auto (car) accessories 汽车配件 ❷同谋;帮凶:an ～ to a crime 从犯 Ⅱ adj. ❶附属的;附加的:an ～ school 附属学校 ❷同谋的

accident / ˈæksɪdənt / n. [C] 意外事故;偶发事件:a traffic ～ 交通事故/ an unfortunate ～不幸事故/ He had a bad ～. 他出了大事故。/by ～ 偶然;意外地:I met him in the street by ～. 我偶然在街上遇见了他。without ～ 安全地:The night passed without ～. 一夜平安无事。同 event, misfortune 派 accidental adj; accidentally adv.

A

辨析

accidental 强调事件的偶然性：His teacher discovered an accidental error in his pronunciation. 他的老师在他的发音中发现了一个无意之间犯的错误。**incidental** 强调事件的伴随性，表示较与一事物次要：Fish is incidental in our meals. 在我们的饮食中鱼不是主食。

acclaim / əˈkleɪm / Ⅰ v. 欢呼；喝彩：warmly ～ the success 热烈欢呼取得成功 同 cheer Ⅱ n. [U] 欢呼；喝彩；称赞

accommodate / əˈkɒmədeɪt / v. ❶容纳；接纳；提供；供给，供应：～ sb. with lodging 给某人提供住宿 同 receive, board ❷适应；迁就；调节：～ oneself to new conditions 适应新情况 同 adjust

accommodation / əˌkɒməˈdeɪʃn / n. ❶招待设备；膳宿；住宿：seek ～s 寻找住处 同 lodging ❷适应；调节 同 adjustment

accompany / əˈkʌmpəni / vt. ❶陪伴：He always accompanied his mother wherever she went. 他母亲走到哪里，他就陪伴到哪里。❷为…伴奏：The pianist accompanied her singing. 她唱歌，钢琴家为她伴奏。同 play

accomplish / əˈkʌmplɪʃ / vt. 完成；达到；实现：～ one's purpose 达到某人的目的 / The task will not be ～ed in one generation. 这任务不是一代人所能完成的。同 achieve, finish 派 accomplishment n.

accord / əˈkɔːd / n. [U] ❶一致；协调：in ～ with 与…一致：His words are in complete ～ with his thoughts. 他心口如一。同 agreement, harmony ❷自愿；主动：I did it of my own ～. 我是自愿做这件事的。派 accordance n.

according / əˈkɔːdɪŋ / adv. 按照；根据：～ **to** 根据…：from each ～ to his ability 各尽所能 / The books are placed on the shelves ～ to authors. 这些书是按作者姓名排序摆在书架上的。派 accordingly adv.

accordion / əˈkɔːdɪən / n. [C] 手风琴：play the ～ 拉手风琴

account / əˈkaʊnt / Ⅰ v. ❶说明原因；解释：～ **for** 解释：He could not ～ for his absence from school. 他无法解释他缺课的原因。同 explain ❷以为；认为：He ～s himself lucky to be alive after that accident. 他认为在那次事故

中能活下来是他的幸运。同 consider Ⅱ n. [C] ❶账户；账目：open an ～ 开账户 / settle the ～ 结账 / current ～ 活期存款账户 / fixed ～ 定期存款账户 / bill, check ❷描写，叙述；报道：a false ～ 虚假报道 / a trustworthy ～ 一篇内容可靠的报道 同 description, statement ❸重要性；价值：take sth. **into** ～ 考虑；重视：You must take this into ～. 你必须考虑到这一点。**on** ～ **of** 因为；由于；归于：She could not come on ～ of her illness. 她因病不能来。**on no**（**not on any**）～ 决不；毫不；无论如何不：I will not do such a thing on any ～. 无论如何我也不会做这样的事。同 significance, consideration

accountant / əˈkaʊntənt / n. [C] 会计；会计师：certified public ～ 持证会计师 / work as ～ 做会计

accounting / əˈkaʊntɪŋ / n. [U] 会计学；清算账目：～ control 会计监督 / the public ～ firm 会计事务所 / ～ statement 会计报表

accumulate / əˈkjuːmjəleɪt / v. 积累；积聚；堆积：～ a fortune 积累财富 / ～ funds for … 为…积累资金 同 collect, gather, pile 派 accumulation n.

accuracy / ˈækjərəsi / n. [C] 精确；精确度：test the ～ of …检测…的精确度 / with accuracy 精确地 同 exactness, precision

accurate / ˈækjərət / adj. 精确的；准确的：His information is quite ～. 他的消息相当准确。同 exact, precise 派 accurately adv.

辨析

accurate 意为"准确的；精确的"，强调与客观事实相符：This is an accurate watch. 这是一只走时准确的表。**correct** 意为"正确的"，指按照一定的标准衡量是否正确：Is this sentence correct? 这句子没错吧？**exact** 意为"确切的"，强调在数量、质量等方面与某物完全吻合：What is the exact meaning of the word? 这个词的确切含义是什么？**precise** 有"确切而不模棱两可"之意：I can't tell you the precise date of the birth of the poet. 我无法告诉你这位诗人确切的出生日期。

accusation / ˌækjuˈzeɪʃn / n. [U] 指控，控告；指责，谴责：by false accusation 根据诬告 / eyes full of accusation 满是指责的目光

accuse / əˈkjuːz / vt. 控告；指责：falsely ～ sb. 诬告某人 / ～ sb. **of sth.** 就某事控告某

人：We ～d him of his immoral conduct toward her. 我们指责他对她的不道德行为。同 charge，blame

accuse 意为"控告；指责"，指官方或个人较正式地对某项罪行提出控告，或对某个错误进行尖锐的批评，后接介词 of：He was falsely accused of stealing. 他被错误地指控犯有偷窃罪。charge 意为"指控；控告"，指被正式指控犯有某一罪行，或被指责犯下某一严重错误，后接介词 with：People charged me with neglecting my duty. 人们指责我玩忽职守。/He was charged with bribery. 他被控告收受贿赂。

accustom / əˈkʌstəm / vt. 使习惯：～ sb. to (doing) sth. 使某人习惯于…/～ oneself to the environment 适应环境 同 habituate

accustomed / əˈkʌstəmd / adj. ❶通常的，惯常的：Pauline went to her accustomed restaurant for lunch. 波林到她常去的那家餐馆里吃午饭。❷习惯了的；适应了的（与 to 连用）：She is accustomed to working late. 她习惯于工作到深夜。

ace / es / n. [C] ❶（纸牌、骰子的）一点；A 牌 ❷（开赛车或飞机的）王牌驾驶员；空中英雄；能手；专家：football ～ 足球球王

ache / eik / I n. [C]疼痛：She had ～s and pains all over. 她感到周身疼痛。同 pain II vi. 痛：My head ～s badly. 我头痛得厉害。同 pain

achieve / əˈtʃiːv / vt. 实现；完成；达到：～ success 成功/ ～ one's purpose 达到目的/All this cannot be ～d overnight. 所有这一切不是一夜之间就能实现的。同 complete，realize，obtain

achievement / əˈtʃiːvmənt / n. ❶[U]完成；达到 同 realization，completion ❷[C]成就；成绩；功绩：His ～s are worthy of record. 他的功绩值得记载。/ heroic ～s 英雄业绩/ scholarly ～s 学术成就/ scientific and technological ～s 科技成果 同 accomplishment

acid / ˈæsɪd / I adj. 酸性的 II n. 酸

acknowledge / əkˈnɒlɪdʒ / v. ❶承认：～ defeat 认输/ He openly ～d his fault. 他公开承认了他的过失。同 recognize，admit ❷致谢：～ with thanks 感激；谢谢 同 thank 派 acknowledgement n.

acknowledge 指承认所隐瞒的事：He would not acknowledge his fault. 他不会认错。admit 指只承认所说的事实本身而不一定接受与事实有关的看法或观点：He admitted he had been in prison. 他承认他蹲过监狱。confess 意为"供认；招认"，语气较强，指正式地承认自己的罪行、过失、弱点，或公开自己的秘密：He confessed that he had committed theft three times. 他承认他曾三次偷窃。own up 指承认与自己有关的事。own up 是俚语，含有爽快承认之意：I own up that I do not know much about Russian. 我承认我不大懂俄文。

acquaint / əˈkweɪnt / vt. 使熟悉；使了解：I ～ed him with my intention. 我让他了解我的意图。/ **be (get) ～ed with** 对…熟悉：I am not personally ～ed with him. 我个人和他并不熟悉。

acquaintance / əˈkweɪntəns / n. 相识，熟悉；熟人：make the ～ of sb. 结识某人 / I have a nodding ～ with her. 我和她是点头之交。同 understanding，familiarity，colleague

acquire / əˈkwaɪə(r) / v. 学得（知识、技术）；获得（财产、权利）：～ a knowledge of 学到（获得）…的知识 同 gain，obtain 派 acquirement n.

acquisition / ˌækwɪˈzɪʃn / n. ❶[U]获得，取得；占有：The ～ of knowledge is a social process. 知识的获取是一种社会性的活动。❷[C]获得物；增添的人（或物）（尤其有特别长处或价值者）：Our museum's latest ～ is a Picasso. 我们博物馆最近添了一幅毕加索的画。/He is a valuable ～ to the team. 他是该球队不可多得的新队员。

acquit / əˈkwɪt / vt. (-quitted;-quitting) ❶宣告…无罪；无罪释放：John Campell was ～ted on all charges. 约翰·坎贝尔被宣告在所控罪行上是无辜的。❷使（自己）做出某种表现；使（自己）履行（或完成）He ～ted himself well at the interview. 面试时，他表现得不错。

acre / ˈeɪkə(r) / n. [C] 英亩

acrid / ˈækrɪd / adj. ❶（气味等）辛辣的，苦的；刺激的，呛人的：～ smoke from burning rubber 橡胶燃烧的呛鼻烟雾 ❷（言辞、性格等）刻薄的；讥讽的：an ～ disposition 刻薄的性格

acrimony / ˈækrɪməni / n. [U]（脾气、言辞、态度等的）尖刻；严厉；辛辣：attack sb. with great

A

～ 以极其激烈的言辞攻击某人

across / ə'krɒs / Ⅰ *prep.* ❶横过;穿过:～ the country 全国各地 回 through ❷在…的另一边:There is a forest ～ the rive. 河对岸有一片森林。回 opposite,beyond Ⅱ *adv.* 横过,穿过;从一边到另一边:I'll row you ～. 我将把你渡到河对岸去。

act / ækt / Ⅰ *v.* 做;表演;起作用:His son ～ed badly in school. 他儿子在学校表现不好。/ She ～ed in this play. 她演出此戏。回 conduct,perform,work,play / ～ **as** 担任;扮演;充当:He ～ed as conductor. 他担任指挥。～ **(up) on** 对…起作用;按照…行动:This medicine ～s on the heart. 这种药对心脏病有效。/ You should ～ on others' advice. 你应该按照别人的建议去做。～ **out** 表演;比划着表达:He tried to ～ out a story he had read. 他试图把读过的故事表演出来。Ⅱ *n.*[C] ❶举动;行为:He did another noble ～. 他又做了一件高尚的事。回 action,deed ❷法令;条例

action / 'ækʃn / *n.*[U] ❶行动;行为;活动:go into ～ 开始行动 / take ～ 采取行动 / in ～ 在活动;在运转 回 act,effect,performance ❷作用:put out of ～ 使失去作用 回 work,function

activate / 'æktɪveɪt / *vt.* 使活动;使激活:～ public opinion 活跃舆论 / be ～d by economic interests 为经济利益所驱使 回 stimulate,arouse

active / 'æktɪv / *adj.* ❶主动的;积极的;活跃的:～ defense 积极防御 / ～ remedy 速效药物 回 vigorous,lively 反 inactive ❷在活动中的;现行的;现役的:～ volcano 活火山 / ～ capital 流动资本 / ～ military unit 现役军队 回 running,working

activist / 'æktɪvɪst / *n.*[C] 积极分子 回 enthusiast

activity / æk'tɪvəti / *n.*[C] 活动;所做的事情:reading activities 读书活动 / social activities 社会活动;社交活动 / terrorist activities 恐怖活动 / take part in an ～ 参加活动 回 action

actor / 'æktə(r) / *n.*[C] 男演员;celebrated ～ 名演员 / the best ～ 最佳男主角 / the best supporting ～ 最佳男配角

actress / 'æktrəs / *n.*[C] 女演员:the best ～ 最佳女主角 / the best supporting ～ 最佳女配角

actual / 'æktʃʊəl / *adj.* 实际的;现实的:～ state

现状 / This is an ～ step. 这是一个实际的步骤。回 real,true,current 派 actually *adv.*

acute / ə'kjuːt / *adj.* ❶尖锐的;敏锐的:～ angle 锐角 / ～ eyesight 敏锐的眼光 回 sharp,sensitive ❷剧烈的;严重的:～ pain 剧痛 回 sharp,keen

ad / æd / *n.* (＝ advertisement)[C]广告

AD,A. D. (拉丁文 Anno Domini 的缩写) 公元(放在年代之前或之后)

adage / 'ædɪdʒ / *n.*[C]谚语,格言

adapt / ə'dæpt / *v.* ❶使适应;使适合:She lacks the ability to ～ easily. 她的适应能力不太强。回 adjust,suit / ～ **oneself to** 适应:Can you ～ yourself to the new job? 你能适应新工作吗? ❷改编;改写:～ a film from a novel 把小说改编成电影 回 rewrite

辨析

adapt 指作适当的改变以适应新环境:She can't adapt herself to the cold weather in Beijing. 她无法适应北京寒冷的天气。**adjust** 意为"调整;调节",指精加调整以达到协调一致:These desks and chairs can be adjusted to the height of any child. 桌椅的高度可根据儿童身高调节。**fit** 指事物适合某一用途:Your clothes fit well. 你的衣服很合身。**suit** 常指符合某种特定场合、情况、地位的要求:The title of the book is well suited to its contents. 这本书的书名与内容很相称。

add / æd / *v.* 加;添加;增加:Add five to nine. 把 5 与 9 相加。回 increase,attach 反 subtract / ～ **to** 补充;增添:That will only ～ to our difficulties. 那只会给我们增加困难。～ **up to** 总计达:The costs ～ed up to 20 million American dollars. 费用总计达 2000 万美元。

addict Ⅰ / ə'dɪkt / *vt.* ❶使沉溺;使醉心:be ～ed to work 工作入迷 回 devote ❷使成瘾:be ～ed to smoking 吸烟成瘾 Ⅱ / 'ædɪkt / *n.*[C]有瘾的人:a drug ～ 吸毒上瘾的人

addition / ə'dɪʃn / *n.*[U]加法;增加:in ～ to 除…之外(在后部分包括在总数内):In ～ to English,he has to study a second foreign language. 除英语外,他还得学第二门外语。回 increase 反 subtraction

additional / ə'dɪʃən)1 / *adj.* 附加的;追加的;另外的:～ investment 追加投资 / ～ tax 附加税 回 extra,added

additive / 'ædətɪv / Ⅰ *n.* 添加剂;添加物;加

A

法：food ～ 食品添加剂/ free from chemical ～ 无化学添加剂 Ⅱ *adj.* 添加的；附加的 同 additional

address / ə'dres/ Ⅰ *n.* [C] ❶住处；通讯处：Can you tell me your ～? 你能告诉我你的住址吗？同 residence ❷ 演讲：The president made an ～ over the radio. 总统发表了广播演讲。同 speech, lecture Ⅱ *v.* ❶写地址：This letter was wrongly ～ed. 这封信的地址写错了。❷讲话；演讲 同 speak, lecture

adequate / 'ædɪkwət/ *adj.* ❶充分的；足够的；适当的：His wages are ～ to support four people. 他的工资足够养活四口人。/ take ～ measures 采取适当措施 同 enough, sufficient, suitable ❷胜任的：**be ～ to** 胜任；对…适应：Though a bit too old, he is ～ to the work. 虽然他年龄大了一点，但仍能胜任这份工作。同 capable, competent 派 adequately *adv.*

adhere / əd'hɪə(r) / *v.* ❶黏附：Wax ～s to the fingers. 蜡粘在手指上。同 stick ❷坚持（与…连用）：～ to one's ideas 坚持自己的观点/ He said he should ～ to the original plan. 他说他应该坚持原计划。同 hold

adherent / əd'hɪərent / *n.* [C]追随者，支持者；拥护者；信徒

adjacent / ə'dʒeɪs(ə)nt / *adj.* ❶邻近的，毗连的：the city square and the ～ streets 都市广场及其邻近街道/The house ～ to yours has been sold. 与你家毗邻的房子已经卖掉了。❷（或前或后）紧接着的，相接触的：a map on an ～ page 紧接在前面（或后面）一页的地图

adjective / 'ædʒɪktɪv / *n.* [C] 形容词

adjourn / ə'dʒɜːn/ *v.* 暂停；休会：～ for an hour 休会一小时

adjust / ə'dʒʌst / *vt.* 调整；使适合：I must ～ my watch. 我必须将手表调一下。同 adapt, regulate 派 adjustable *adj.*；adjustor, adjuster *n.*

adjustment / ə'dʒʌstmənt / *n.* [U]调整；调节；校准；校正：～ of exchange rate 汇率调整/ of salary 工资调整/ ～ tax 调节税/ make a price ～ 调整价格 同 adaptation

administer / əd'mɪnɪstə(r) / *v.* ❶管理；支配：～ a government department 管理一个政府部门 同 manage, direct ❷执行；施行；实施：～ justice (laws)执法 同 execute

administration / əd,mɪnɪ'streɪʃn / *n.* [U] ❶管理；经营：have experience in ～ 有行政管理经验/ a master of business ～ (MBA)工商管理硕士 同 management, direction ❷管理部门；行政机关；政府 同 department

administrative / əd'mɪnɪstrətɪv / *adj.* 行政的；管理的：simplify the ～ structure 精简机构/ ～ objective management 行政目标管理/ ～ interference 行政干预 同 executive

admirable / 'ædmərəbl / *adj.* 可钦佩的；令人羡慕的；极好的：His honesty is ～. 他的诚实令人钦佩。同 estimable, fine

admire / əd'maɪə(r) / *vt.* 钦佩；赞美，夸奖：I ～ your frankness. 我钦佩你的坦率。/ We ～ him for his bravery. 我们佩服他的勇敢。同 esteem, praise, appreciate 派 admiration *n.*

admission / əd'mɪʃn / *n.* ❶[U]（进入、入学、入会的）许可：～ notice 录取通知书/ office 招生办公室/ ～ ticket 入场券/ ～ by ticket 凭票入场/ An ～ is limited to the invited guests. 入场限于应邀来宾。同 access, allowance ❷[C]承认；自白 同 by one's own ～ 据某人自己承认 同 affirmation

admit / əd'mɪt / *vt.* (-mitted;-mitting) ❶允许进入：He opened the door and ～ted me into the room. 他打开门让我进屋。同 permit, receive ❷承认：He finally ～ted himself beaten. 他终于认输了。同 acknowledge 反 reject

adolescence / ,ædə'les(ə)ns / *n.* 年轻人；青少年；青春期：Adolescence is a beautiful time in one's life. 青少年时期是人生的美好时期。同 teenager, youth

adolescent / ,ædə'les(ə)nt / Ⅰ *adj.* 青春期的 同 young Ⅱ *n.* 青少年：～ psychology (psychology of the ～) 青春期心理 同 youth, teenager

adopt / ə'dɒpt / *vt.* ❶采纳；采取；采用：～ a bill 通过议案/ ～ a measure 采取措施 / I'll ～ your teaching method in my school. 我将在我校采用你的教学方法。同 take, accept ❷收养：one's ～ed son (daughter) 某人的养子(养女)/ ～ a child 收养孩子

adoption / ə'dɒpʃn / *n.* ❶采纳；采取：move the ～ of the bill 提议；通过议案 同 acceptance ❷收养：put a child up for ～ 把孩子送给人抚养

adore / ə'dɔː(r) / v. ❶崇拜(上帝);敬慕:～ sb. for ... 因为…而崇拜某人 圊 worship, respect ❷很喜欢:～ one's wife (parents) 疼爱妻子(父母) 圊 love, treasure

adorn / ə'dɔːn / vt. 装饰,装点;佩带;装扮:They ～ed their hair with garlands of flowers. 她们头上戴着花环。/a book ～ed with numerous excellent illustrations 配有大量精美插图的书籍

adult / 'ædʌlt, ə'dʌlt / Ⅰ n. [C]成年人:He is an ～ now. 他现在已是一个成年人了。圊 grownup Ⅱ adj. 成年的;成熟的:～ education 成人教育/ ～ examination for higher education 成人高考 圊 grown, mature

adulthood / 'ædʌlthʊd / n. 成年:enter one's ～ 进入成年期 / in one's ～ 在成年时期

advance / əd'vɑːns / Ⅰ v. 推进;进展:They ～d toward the castle. 他们朝着城堡前进。圊 march, promote Ⅱ n. 前进;增长:You can't stop the ～ of aging. 人总是要变老的。圊 progress, increase / **in** ～ 预先,事先;在前面:Everything has been fixed in ～. 一切都预先安排好了。 派 advancement n.

advanced / əd'vɑːnst / adj. 先进的;高级的:～ English 高级英语/Shanghai is an technologically ～ city in China. 上海是中国一个技术先进的城市。

advantage / əd'vɑːntɪdʒ / n. ❶[C]益处;优点,优势:Each has his ～s. 各有各的优点。反 disadvantage ❷[U]利益;好处:It has no ～ to me at all. 这对我没有任何好处。圊 benefit, profit/**take** ～ **of** 利用;乘机:I can't take ～ of your good nature. 我不能因你性情善良而占你的便宜。派 advantageous adj.

advent / 'ædvent, 'ædv(ə)nt / n. [C](重要人物或事物的)出现;来临,到来:the ～ of a new era 新时代的来临/at the ～ of spring 在春天到来时

adventure / əd'ventʃə(r) / n. [U]冒险;奇遇:I've read the novel *The Life and Strange Adventures of Robinson Crusoe*. 我已读过小说《鲁滨孙漂流记》。圊 risk 派 adventurous adj.

adverb / 'ædvɜːb / n. [C]副词

adverbial / ædvɜːbɪəl / Ⅰ adj. 副词的;状语的 Ⅱ n. 状语

adversary / 'ædvəsəri / n. 敌手;对手:a worthy

(well-matched) ～ 劲敌 圊 opponent, enemy

adverse / 'ædvɜːs / adj. ❶逆的;相反的;敌对的:～ circumstances 逆境/ ～ current 逆流/ ～ psychology 逆反心理 圊 opposite, hostile ❷不利的;有害的:be ～ to sb. 不利于某人 圊 unfavorable 派 adversity n.

advertise(-ze) / 'ædvətaɪz / Ⅰ v. 登广告,为…做广告 Ⅱ n. 广告;公告(略作 ad):～ design 广告设计 / ～ fee 广告费/ a wanted ～ 一则招聘广告 / common wealth ～ 公益广告 / the ～ agency 广告公司

advertisement / əd'vɜːtɪsmənt, ˌædvə'taɪzmənt/ n. [C]广告;公告;启示:If you want a job, put an ～ in the newspaper. 如果你想找工作,在报上登一则广告好了。

advertising(-zing) / 'ædvətaɪzɪŋ / Ⅰ n. 广告业;(总称)广告;登广告;广告宣传:outdoor ～ 户外(室外)广告 / TV ～ 电视广告 Ⅱ adj. 广告的:～ affairs 广告业务

advice / əd'vaɪs / n. [U] 劝告,忠告;意见:seek ～ from sb. 向某人请教 / If you take his ～ and study harder, you'll pass the examination. 要是你听他的劝告,更加努力学习,你就会考试及格。圊 warning, suggestion

advise / əd'vaɪz / v. 劝告,忠告;建议:Which book would you ～ me to buy? 你建议我买哪本书? 圊 recommend, suggest

advisable / əd'vaɪzəbl / adj. 明智的;可取的 圊 desirable, sensible

adviser(-or) / əd'vaɪzə(r) / n. [C] 劝告者;顾问:～ on economic policy 经济政策顾问 / technical ～ 技术顾问 圊 counselor, counsel

advocate / 'ædvəkeɪt / Ⅰ n.[C]提倡者;辩护者;鼓吹者:consumer ～ 消费者权益维护者 圊 promoter, supporter Ⅱ vt. 提倡;拥护;主张;鼓吹:firmly ～ social security 坚决提倡社会保障 圊 promote, support 反 oppose

aerial / 'eərɪəl / Ⅰ adj. 空中的;空气的;航空的:～ chart 航空图/ ～ attack 空袭/ ～ transportation 空运 Ⅱ n. (= antenna)[C](无线电的)天线

aerobics / eə'rəʊbɪks / n. 健身操;健美操;韵律操

aeroplane / 'eərəpleɪn / n. (= airplane)[C](英)飞机 圊 plane, airplane

aerospace / 'eərəˌspeɪs / Ⅰ n.[U]航空航天空

A

间,宇宙空间 Ⅱ *adj.* 航空航天(空间)的;航空航天器的:～ research 航空航天研究

aesthetic(al) / iːsˈθetɪk(əl) / *adj.* 美学的;审美的;艺术的:～ education 美育(美学教育)/ ～value 审美价值

aesthetics / iːsˈθetɪks / *n.* 美学

affair / əˈfeə(r) / *n.* [C]事情:It's an ～ of great importance. 这是一件很重要的事情。/ ～s of state 国家大事/ public ～s 公事/ private ～s 私事/ ～s review 时事评论 回 matter,thing,business

辨析

affair 意为"事情;事务",指实际进行着的事,复数表示正在进行中的重大事件:They have no right to interfere the internal affairs of China. 他们无权干涉中国内政。**business** 意为"事务;业务;商业;生意",多指公务,是口语常用词:I have some business which prevents me from going out this evening. 我今晚有事不能外出。**matter** 常指需要考虑和处理但具体内容不明确的事:The matter cannot be decided in this way. 这件事不能就这样决定。**thing** 含义更加模糊,最为常用:We can't always have things in our own way. 不可能事事总如我们所愿。

affect / əˈfekt / *v.* ❶影响:Whatever she says will not ～ my decision. 无论她说什么都不会影响我的决定。回 influence ❷感动;打动:His speech ～ed the audience deeply. 他的讲话深深打动了听众。/ All the people in the room were ～ed to tears. 屋里所有的人都感动得流下了眼泪。回 move,impress,touch

affection / əˈfekʃn / *n.* 爱;感情:the ～ of parents for their children 父母对儿女的爱 回 love,passion

affirm / əˈfɜːm / *vt.* 断言;肯定;证实:～ one's judgement 证实某人的判断 回 declare,confirm

affirmative / əˈfɜːmətɪv / *adj.* 肯定的:an ～ answer 肯定的答复 回 confirmative,positive 反 negative

afflict / əˈflɪkt / *vt.* 折磨;使苦恼,使痛苦:The pangs of conscience ～ed him. 一阵阵良心的责备使他痛苦不已。/ She is continually ～ed by headaches. 她经常为头痛病所苦。

affluence / ˈæfluəns / *n.* [U]❶富裕;富足:live in ～生活优裕 ❷大量;丰富;充裕:～ of rain 大量的雨水

affluent / ˈæfluənt / *adj.* ❶富裕的;富足的:an ～ family 富裕的家庭/live in ～ times 生活在富足的年代 ❷大量的,充沛的,丰富的;富饶的:florid and ～ fancy 丰富多彩的想象力/a land ～ in natural resources 自然资源丰富的地区

afford / əˈfɔːd / *vt.* ❶买得起;负担得起:He said he couldn't ～ a car. 他说他买不起汽车。❷提供;给予:I can hardly ～ the time for I'm very busy. 我很忙,抽不出时间。回 offer,provide

afraid / əˈfreɪd / *adj.* ❶害怕的:Don't be ～. 别害怕。/ She is ～ of dogs. 她怕狗。回 fearful,frightened ❷担心;唯恐:She was weak and ～ that she could not do the job. 她体弱,担心干不了这活儿。

用法

afraid 可用于以下三种句型:❶be afraid of (后接名词或代词):There is nothing to be afraid of. 没什么可怕的。❷be afraid to do sth.:The boy was afraid to come in. 那男孩不敢进来。❸be afraid that(后接从句):I am afraid that I'll be late. 恐怕我要迟到了。

Africa / ˈæfrɪkə / *n.* 非洲

African / ˈæfrɪkən / Ⅰ *adj.* 非洲的 Ⅱ *n.* [C]非洲人

after / ˈɑːftə(r) / Ⅰ *prep.* 在……之后;在后面:We shall leave ～ breakfast. 我们吃完早饭就走。回 behind 反 before/～ a while 过一会儿;不久;即刻:He will be here ～ a while. 他即刻就到。～ all 毕竟;到底;终归:After all, he is a boy of five. 毕竟,他只是一个五岁的孩子。Ⅱ *conj.* 在……以后:After his father died, he lived with his aunt. 他父亲死后,他就和婶婶住在一起。

afternoon / ˌɑːftəˈnuːn / *n.* 下午;午后:this ～ 今天下午/ on Monday ～ 星期一下午 / have ～ tea 喝下午茶

用法

❶表示"在下午",介词常用 in;若表示"在某一天的下午",或当 afternoon 前后有定语时,则要用介词 on:on Sunday afternoon;on a cloudy afternoon;on the afternoon of March 28. ❷表示"今天下午;昨天下午;明天下午",只能用 this afternoon, yesterday afternoon 和 tomorrow afternoon。

A

afterward(s) / ˈɑːftəwəd(z) / *adv.* 后来；以后 圓 later

again / əˈɡeɪn / *adv.* 又；再：Please say it ~. 请再说一遍。圓 repeatedly / ~ **and** ~ 再三地；反复地；I warned him ~ and ~. 我一再警告他。**now and** ~ 时时：The couple quarreled now and ~. 这对夫妇时时吵架。**once** ~ 再一次：You may try it once ~. 你可再试一次。

against / əˈɡeɪnst / *prep.* 对着；紧靠着；逆；反对：The house is ~ the hospital. 房子在医院对面。/ He always advances ~ difficulties. 他总是迎着困难前进。/ They are ~ the plan. 他们反对这个计划。

age / eɪdʒ / Ⅰ *n.* 年龄；岁数；时代：~ ago 很久以前 / for ~s 很长时间；长期 / over ~ 超龄 / under ~ 未成年 / What's your ~? 你多大年龄？**at the** ~ 在…岁时：He went abroad at the ~ of eighteen. 他 18 岁出国。Ⅱ *v.* 变老；老化；成熟 圓 mature, ripen

aged / eɪdʒd / *adj.* 年老的：an association of ~ people 老年人协会 / a society of the ~ 老年型社会 圓 old, elderly

ag(e)ing / ˈeɪdʒɪŋ / *n.* 变陈；成熟；老化：the ~ of the population 人口老化 圓 ripen, mature

agency / ˈeɪdʒənsi / *n.* 经办；代办(处)；代理(处)：travel ~ 旅行社 / sales ~ 销售代理 圓 operation, bureau

agenda / əˈdʒendə / *n.* (agendum 的单数) [C] 议事日程；记事本：put (place) sth. on the ~ 把…列入议事日程 / draw (make) up an ~ 制订议事日程 圓 program, schedule

agent / ˈeɪdʒənt / *n.* [C] 代言人；代理人：the right of ~ 代理权 / the sole ~ 独家代理 圓 representative

aggravate / ˈæɡrəˌveɪt / *vt.* ❶加重，加剧；使恶化，使更坏：~ an illness 使病情加重/A lie will only ~ you guilt. 撒谎只会使你错上加错。❷使恼火；激怒：The whispering in class ~s our teacher. 课堂上的窃窃私语使我们的老师很恼火。

aggregate Ⅰ / ˈæɡrɪɡət / *adj.* 聚合的；总的，合计的：the rate of growth of aggregate demand 总需求量的增长率/newspapers with an aggregate circulation of 6 million 总发行量为 600 万份的报纸 Ⅱ / ˈæɡrɪɡət / *n.* [C] 合计：He spent an aggregate of fifteen years in various jails. 他在不同的监狱里总共待了 15 年。/ **in the** ~, **on** ~ 总共；作为整体；take things on ~ 从整体上把握事物 Ⅲ / ˈæɡrɪɡeɪt / *vt.* ❶总计达：The money collected will ~ $1,000. 募集到的款项总额达 1000 美元。❷(使)聚集，(使)积累：~ riches 积累财富

aggression / əˈɡreʃn / *n.* [U] 侵略；侵犯：a war of ~ 侵略战争 圓 invasion, attack

aggressive / əˈɡresɪv / *adj.* ❶攻击性的，侵略的；好与人争吵的：an ~ war 侵略战争 / an ~ weapon 进攻性武器 圓 offensive ❷有进取心的；积极的：an ~ salesman 有干劲的推销员

aggressor / əˈɡresə(r) / *n.* [C] 侵略者；侵略国

aghast / əˈɡɑːst, əˈɡæst / *adj.* 惊呆的；惊骇的，惊愕的：He stood, with his mouth wide open, ~ with wonder. 他吓得目瞪口呆，站在那里摸不着头脑。

agitate / ˈædʒɪˌteɪt / *vt.* ❶搅动，搅拌；摇动，拨动：A mixer ~s the cement until it is ready to pour. 搅拌器搅拌水泥，直至可以用来灌注。/ ~ one's fan 扇扇子 ❷鼓动；煽动：~ strongly for a piece of legislation 极力鼓动支持一项法律

agony / ˈæɡəni / *n.* [U;C] (肉体或心灵上极度的) 痛苦；剧痛：The accident victim spent hours in mortal ~ before dying. 事故的受害者临死前几个小时一直处于极度的痛苦之中。/ The loss of her husband filled her with ~. 失去了丈夫，她痛不欲生。

ago / əˈɡəʊ / *adv.* 以前：He left five minutes ~. 他五分钟前离开的。/ long, long ~ 很久以前 圓 before, past

agree / əˈɡriː / *vi.* 同意，赞同；应允：I don't ~ with you on this point. 在这一点上，我不同意你的意见。/ Everybody agreed to the plan at the meeting. 在会上，所有的人都同意这个计划。圓 grant, approve

用法

❶agree with 指同意某人的说法、看法，后常接 sb.：I did not quite agree with what you said. 我不完全赞同你所说的。They finally agreed with us. 他们终于同意了我们的看法。❷agree to 指同意某人的建议、计划、条件等，后常接 sth.：She agreed to the arrangement. 她同意了这一安排。❸agree on 指"对…意见一致"：We agreed on making an early start. 我们已一致同意早些动身。

agreeable / ə'gri:əbl / *adj.* 同意的,欣然同意的;惬意的,令人愉快的 同 pleasing,pleasant / ～ voice 悦耳的声音 / ～ weather 舒适的天气

agreement / ə'gri:mənt / *n.* ❶ [U] 一致;同意:The two sides reached ～ at once. 双方马上达成了一致协议。反 disagreement ❷ [C] 协定;协议;契约:an ～ concerning sci-tech 科技合作协定 / arrive at (come to,make,reach) an ～ 达成协议/ a verbal ～ 口头协定/ violate an ～ 违反协议 同 bond,contract

agricultural / ˌæɡrɪ'kʌltʃərəl / *adj.* 农业的;农艺的:～ tax 农业税/ ～ ecological environment 农业生态环境/ ～ modernization 农业现代化

agriculture / 'æɡrɪkʌltʃə(r) / *n.* [U] 农业;农艺;distribution of ～ 农业布局/ go in for ～ 务农

aha / ɑ:'hɑ: / *int.* 啊哈(表示惊奇、满意等)

ahead / ə'hed / *adv.* 在前面;在前头:Walk ～ of me. 走我前面。/ go ～ 前进;干吧/ ～ of time 提前 同 before,forward 反 behind,backward

aid / eɪd / Ⅰ *vt.* 帮助;援助:I will ～ him in the matter. 我愿意帮助他处理这件事。/ ～ the poor 扶贫 同 help,assist Ⅱ *n.* [U] 帮助;援助;救助:first ～ 急救/ provide ～ 提供援助 同 help,assistance

AIDS / eɪdz / *n.* 艾滋病:the World ～ Day 世界艾滋病日

ailment / 'eɪlmənt / *n.* [C] 疾病(常指小病);病痛(尤指慢性疾病):a skin ～ 皮肤病/Children often have minor ～s. 小孩子常常闹些小病小灾。

aim / eɪm / Ⅰ *v.* ❶对准;瞄准:He ～ed the gun at the target. 他举枪瞄准目标。同 point,direct ❷立志:He ～s to be a scientist. 他立志当一名科学家。同 try,attempt Ⅱ *n.* [C] 目的;目标;愿望:He does everything without ～. 他做事毫无目标。/ accomplish (realize) one's ～ 实现目标/achieve one's ～ 达到目标 同 good,target,direction

air / eə(r) / *n.* [U] ❶天空;空气;大气:disaster 空难/ ～ fare 机票(价)/ ～ pollution 空气污染/ **by** ～ 乘飞机:Are you going to travel by ～? 你打算乘飞机旅行吗? **in the** ～ 在空中;悬而未决 **on the** ～ 广播;播音 ❷外观;神态;样子:put on ～s 摆架子;装腔作势 / with the ～ of 带着…神情 同 look,attitude

aircraft / 'eəkrɑ:ft / *n.* [C] 飞机;航空器;飞艇:an ～ carrier 航空母舰 / pilot (fly) an ～ 驾驶飞机 同 plane,airplane

airline / 'eəlaɪn / *n.* [C] 航空公司;航线:domestic ～ 国内航线 / overseas ～ 国外航线 同 airway

airmail / 'eəmeɪl / *n.* 航空邮寄件;航空邮政 同 air-post

airplane / 'eəpleɪn / *n.* [C](美)飞机 同 plane,aeroplane

airport / 'eəpɔ:t / *n.* [C] 机场;航空站:I'll meet him at the ～ this afternoon. 今天下午我去机场接他。同 airfield

airy / 'eəri / *adj.* ❶通风的;通气的:an ～ room 通风的房间 ❷不切实际的;虚幻的:空洞的;～ dreams 梦幻/an ～ title 虚衔/an ～ plan 不切实际的计划

aisle / aɪl / *n.* [C] 走廊;通道;走道:an ～ seat 靠过道的座位 / clear an ～ 疏通走道 同 passageway,corridor

alarm / ə'lɑ:m / Ⅰ *n.* [U] 警报;惊慌:sound the ～ 发警报 / His condition gave his friends the deepest ～. 他目前的状况使他的朋友们极为惊慌。/ ～ bell 警钟 / ～ clock 闹钟/ in ～ 惊慌地 同 fear,terror Ⅱ *vt.* ❶恐吓,使害怕:She was terribly ～ed. 她极度惊恐。同 scare ❷向…报警

alas / ə'læs / *int.* 唉;哎呀(表示悲哀或惋惜)

album / 'ælbəm / *n.* [C] 相册;集邮册;专辑

alcohol / 'ælkəhɒl / *n.* [U] 酒;酒精;含酒精的饮料:abstain from ～ 戒酒

alcoholic / ˌælkə'hɒlɪk / Ⅰ *adj.* (含有)酒精的 Ⅱ *n.* [C] 酗酒者;酒鬼 同 drunk,drunkard

alert / ə'lɜ:t / Ⅰ *adj.* 警惕的;警觉的:be ～ to ... 对 …警觉;对…敏感 同 watchful Ⅱ *n.* [C] 警报;警戒:sound out an air ～ 发出空袭警报

algebra / 'ældʒɪbrə / *n.* 代数(学):do ～ 做代数题

alien / 'eɪliən / Ⅰ *adj.* ❶外国的;外国人的;陌生的 同 foreign,strange 反 native ❷异己的;相异的 同 unlike,different Ⅱ *n.* [C] 外侨

A

外国人 foreigner

alienate / ˈeɪlɪəneɪt / vt. 使疏远；离间：～ oneself from one's friends 疏远朋友 同 estrange 反 unite

align / əˈlaɪn / vt. ❶使成一直线；使排成一行；使排齐；对准，校直：His books were neatly ～ed in two rows on the shelf. 他的书整整齐齐地在书架上排成两侧。❷校正，调准；调整：～ the lenses of a tel scope 调准望远镜的镜头 ❸使结盟：～ nations against warfare 联合国一致反对战争 派 alignment n.

alike / əˈlaɪk / adj. 相同的；相像的：He and his brother are very much ～. 他和他哥哥长得很像。同 same, similar

alive / əˈlaɪv / adj. 活着的；有活力的：I fear the dog is no longer ～. 恐怕那只狗已死亡了。/ He is very much ～. 他充满活力。同 living, active 反 dead, inactive

all / ɔːl / Ⅰ adj. 所有的；整个的；全部的：All the children will be asleep before nine o'clock. 所有孩子9点钟前都会入睡。同 total, whole Ⅱ pron. 所有一切；全体：Is that ～ you can carry? 你就能提那么多吗？/ All of us are here except John. 除约翰外，我们全都在这儿。同 everything, everybody 反 none, nothing, nobody Ⅲ adv. 完全地；彻底地：This shirt is ～ worn out. 这件衬衣全破了。同 totally, wholly/～ along 一直，自始至终：I know that ～ along. 自始至终我都知道那事。～ alone 独自：She is ～ alone in the house. 她独自一人在家。～ at once 突然：The storm broke out ～ at once. 暴风雨突然来临。～ but 差不多；除了…全：We found them ～ but two. 除两个外，其他的我们全找到了。～ in 疲乏到极点（多用于口语）：I am ～ in. 我累得要死。～ over 到处，遍布：He has traveled ～ over the country. 他周游过全国。～ right 好，行：Everything is ～ right. 一切正常。

allegation / ˌælɪˈgeɪʃn / n. [C]断言；宣称，声称：He made an ～ that Jon has stolen ＄300. 他声称乔恩偷了300美元。/ I thought their ～s but reasonable. 我认为他们的断言毫无道理。

allege / əˈledʒ / vt. 断言；宣称，声称：Jack ～d that she stole the money. 杰克声称她偷了钱。/ Nothing particular could be ～d against him. 他的为人无懈可击。

alley / ˈæli / n. [C]小路；巷 同 lane

allergic / əˈlɜːdʒɪk / adj. 过敏性的；变应性的；对…过敏的：have an ～ to milk 对牛奶过敏

alliance / əˈlaɪəns / n. 结盟；同盟；联盟：in ～ with 与…结盟 / offensive and defensive ～ 攻守同盟 同 union, league 反 separation

allied / ˈælaɪd / adj. 联合的，结盟的，联盟的；联姻的：China, France, Great Britain, Russia, and the United States were ～ nations during World War Ⅱ. 在第二次世界大战期间，中国、法国、英国、苏联及美国为同盟国。

allocate / ˈæləkeɪt / vt. ❶分配；分派；派给：～ funds to schools 把经费分给各校 同 assign, distribute ❷把（物资、资金等）划归：～ money for research 拨款进行科研 同 assign

allocation / ˌæləˈkeɪʃn / n. ❶[U]分配；分派；拨给：～ of communication and transportation 交通布局 / fixed direction ～ 定向分配 同 distribution, assignment ❷[C]分配物；配给物 同 assignment

allot / əˈlɒt / (-lotted;-lotting) vt. ❶分配给：a task to sb. 给某人分配一项任务 同 distribute ❷拨给：～ money for a park 拨款修公园 同 assign

allow / əˈlaʊ / v. 允许；给；让…得到：Smoking is not ～ed in the cinema. 不准在电影院内吸烟。/ I can't ～ you to go out. 我不允许你出去。同 let, approve 反 forbid, refuse

allowance / əˈlaʊəns / n. [C] ❶容许；准许 同 permission, approval ❷津贴；补贴；补助（费）：government ～ 政府津贴 / traffic ～ 交通费 同 grant

alloy / ˈælɔɪ / n. 合金

ally Ⅰ / ˈælaɪ / n. [C]同盟者；同盟国 Ⅱ / əˈlaɪ / vt. 使结盟 同 unite

almost / ˈɔːlməʊst / adv. 差不多；几乎：It's ～ eleven o'clock. 差不多快11点钟了。同 nearly, approximately

aloe / ˈæləʊ / n. [C]芦荟

alone / əˈləʊn / Ⅰ adj. 单独的：She was ～ in the room. 她一个人待在屋子里。同 single Ⅱ adv. 单独地；独自地：He went to cincma ～. 他独自去看电影。反 together

along / əˈlɒŋ / Ⅰ prep. 沿着：There are many new houses and shops ～ the street. 沿街有许

多新房子和商店。**Ⅱ** *adv.* 向前；一道；Come ~! 来吧！/ ~ **with** 借同：She will go ~ with her dog. 她将带狗一同去。**get ~ with** 相处；进展：These boys get ~ with each other quite well. 这些男孩子彼此相处得很好。回 forward, together

alongside / ə,lɒŋ'saɪd / **Ⅰ** *prep.* 在…旁边；与 …并肩：~ a river 在河边 回 along **Ⅱ** *adv.* 并 排地；并肩地

aloud / ə'laʊd / *adv.* 大声地；高声地：I asked her to read the text ~. 我要她朗读课文。回 loudly, noisily 反 quietly, silently

alphabet / 'ælfəbet / *n.* [C]字母表

already / ɔːl'redi / *adv.* 已经；早已：They had ~ arrived home when I called. 我打电话时他 们已经到家了。回 beforehand

also / 'ɔːlsəʊ / *adv.* 也；同样；还：She likes swimming, and I ~. 她喜欢游泳,我也喜欢。**not only …but …** 不但…而且…：I not only saw him but ~ had supper with him. 我不但见到 了他,还和他一起共进晚餐。回 likewise, besides

辨析
also 通常用在肯定句中,位置常在助动词后、行为动词前,偶尔也可置于句末：I can also do it myself. 我自己也能干此事。There's also a film about Dr. Bethune. 也有一部关于白求恩大夫的影片。**too** 用于肯定句中,在口语中更常见,位置常在句末(其前可用逗号),有时也可置于主语后：I can do it myself too. (＝I, too, can do it myself.)我自己也能干此事。**either** 常用于否定句中,置于句末：She cannot go with us either. 她也不能同我们一道去。

alter / 'ɔːltə(r) / *vt.* 改变；变更：~ for the better (worse)变好(坏)回 change, transform

alteration / ,ɔːltə'reɪʃn / *n.* ❶[U]改动；更改：This green coat needs ~. 这件绿色的外套需要改一下。❷[C]变化；调整；变动：There have been a few ~s to the winter courses. 冬季的课程有一些变动。

alternate **Ⅰ** / 'ɔːltəneɪt / *v.* 交替；轮流 回 interchange/, alter **Ⅱ** / ɔːl'tɜːnət / *adj.* ❶交替的；轮流的;间隔的;交错的:~ current 交流电/ write in ~ lines 隔行书写 回 interchanging ❷供选择的;供替换的;预备的;候补的:~ routes 可供选择的路线/ ~ sources of energy

替代能源 派 alternation *n.*

alternative / ɔːl'tɜːnətɪv / **Ⅰ** *n.* [C]替换物 回 choice, selection **Ⅱ** *adj.* 两者择一的;选择的: have no ~ but …除了…外别无选择 回 alternative

although / ɔːl'ðəʊ / *conj.* 虽然;尽管;纵使:Although he is very old, he tries his best in building socialism. 他虽然老了,但仍在为建设社会主义尽心竭力。回 tough, while

用法
如果从句以 although, though 引导,全句就不能有 but 出现,但可用 yet 来表示转折:Although it is raining hard, (yet) he is going out. 虽然雨下得很大,但他还是打算出去。

altitude / 'æltɪtjuːd / *n.* [C]❶高;高度;海拔:at an ~ 在某一高度/ reach an ~ of …达到…的高度 回 height 反 depth ❷(*pl.*)高地;高处 回 heights

altogether / ,ɔːltə'geðə(r) / *adv.* 总共;完全;总之:There are ten computers in our classroom ~. 我们教室里总共有 10 台计算机。回 totally, wholly, entirely

aluminium / ,æljə'mɪniəm / *n.* [U]铝

always / 'ɔːlweɪz, 'ɔːlweɪz / *adv.* 无例外地;总是:I ~ work hard at English. 我一直努力学英语。回 continually 反 never, seldom

AM, a. m. (拉丁文 ante meridiem 的缩写)午前;上午

am / æm, əm / *v.* (我)是(见 be)

amass / ə'mæs / *vt.* ❶积聚(尤指财富);积累;聚集:During the past two years alone, be ~ed a staggering $ 1.5 billion in profits for himself. 单单在过去的两年里,他就为自己聚集了达 15 亿元之巨的利润。/~ political power 积聚政治权力 ❷堆积,把…聚成堆:He ~ed his papers for his memoirs. 他把文件汇集起来,准备写回忆录。

amateur / 'æmətə(r) / **Ⅰ** *adj.* 业余的;外行的 反 professional **Ⅱ** *n.* [C]业余爱好者:music ~ 业余音乐爱好者

amaze / ə'meɪz / *vt.* 使惊奇:I was ~d at his conduct. 我对他的行为感到惊奇。回 surprise, astonish

amazement / ə'meɪzmənt / *n.* [U]惊奇;诧异:to one's ~ 使某人感到吃惊的是/ He looked at us in ~. 他惊奇地看着我们。回 surprise, astonishment

A

amazing /ə'meɪzɪŋ/ *adj.* 令人惊异的：The story is very ～. 这故事令人感到惊奇。

ambassador /æm'bæsədə(r)/ *n.* [C]大使；使节：exchange ～s 互换大使/American ～ to China (Beijing)美国驻华(北京)大使/ appoint an ～ 任命大使/ recall an ～ 召回大使

ambiguous /æm'bɪɡjʊəs/ *adj.* 模棱两可的；含糊不清的：～ answer 含糊的答复 同 vague, uncertain

ambition /æm'bɪʃn/ *n.* 雄心；野心；抱负；志向：have a high ～ 胸怀大志/怀有野心/ realize one's ～ 实现某人的抱负/She is clever but lacks ～. 她很聪明，但胸无大志。派 ambitious *adj.*

ambulance /'æmbjələns/ *n.* [C]救护车：call an ～ 叫救护车

ambush /'æmbʊʃ/ Ⅰ *n.* [U,C]埋伏；伏击：lay an ～ for sb. 设埋伏以待某人/The enemy fell into the ～. 敌人中了埋伏。Ⅱ *vt.* 伏击：An entire platoon was ～ed during a patrol and wiped out. 整整一个排在巡逻中遭到伏击，全被歼灭。

amend /ə'mend/ *vt.* ❶修改，修订(法律、议案等)：～ the constitution 修改宪法 ❷改进；改善；改良：～ conditions in the slums 改善贫民窟的境况/～ one's life 革心洗面 派 amendment *n.*

America /ə'merɪkə/ *n.* 美洲；美国：the United States of ～ (U. S. A.；USA)美利坚合众国/ Central ～ 中美洲/ Latin ～ 拉丁美洲/ North ～ 北美洲/ South ～南美洲

American /ə'merɪkən/ Ⅰ *adj.* ❶美洲的；美国的 ❷美国人的 Ⅱ *n.* [C]美国人

amiable /'eɪmɪəbl/ *adj.* 和蔼可亲的；亲切友好的；悦人的：an ～ tone of voice 悦耳的语调/an ～ greeting 亲切的问候/She has an ～ disposition. 她性情温柔。

amid /ə'mɪd/ *prep.* 在…中；在…当中 同 among

amidst /ə'mɪdst/ *prep.* (＝amid)在…中；在…当中 同 among

ammonia /ə'məʊnɪə/ *n.* [U]氨；氨水

ammunition /ˌæmjʊ'nɪʃn/ *n.* ❶[U]弹药；军火：live ～ 真枪实弹 ❷[U](喻)子弹，炮弹(指可用来攻击别人或为自己辩护的材料、证据等)：The scandal provided ～ for press attacks against the government. 这起丑闻向新闻界提供了攻击政府的炮弹。

among /ə'mʌŋ/ *prep.* 在…中间；在…之中：She is sitting ～ the children. 她坐在孩子们中间。同 amidst

辨析

among 指在三个或三个以上的人或东西中间：The apple will be divided among the three boys. 这个苹果将分给这三个小孩。**between** 指在两者之间：There is some disagreement between us and him. 我们和他之间存在着某种分歧。

amongst /ə'mʌŋst/ *prep.* (＝among)在…之中；在…中间 同 amidst

amount /ə'maʊnt/ Ⅰ *n.* [C] ❶总额；总数 同 total, sum ❷数量；数额：We only want a small ～. 我们只要少许。同 quantity/**a large ～ of** 大量的：He has spent a large ～ of money on books. 他花了很多钱买书。**in (great, large) ～s** 大量地 Ⅱ *vi.* 总共；总计：What you have spent ～s to more than fifty yuan. 你花的钱总共有 50 多元。同 reach

用法

amount 常与不可数名词连用：a large (great) amount of money 很多钱 / a small amount of money 少量的钱

ampere /'æmpeə(r)/ *n.* 安培：～-hour 安培小时 / ～-meter 电流计；安培计

amphibian /æm'fɪbɪən/ *n.* [C]两栖动物；水陆两用飞机

ample /'æmpl/ *adj.* ❶大量的；充裕的；富裕的：a man of ～ means 富裕阔绰的人/Stocks are ～. 存货充足。❷面积(或空间)大的；宽敞的：an ～ lawn 大草坪/The flat's ～ for a family of five. 这个单元住五口之家还是宽宽绰绰的。

amplify /'æmplɪfaɪ/ *vt.* 放大；扩大；增强：～ on (upon)引申;进一步阐述/ ～ radio signals 增强无线电信号 同 enlarge,expand

amplitude /'æmplɪtjuːd/ *n.* [U] ❶广大；广阔：an island of some ～颇为广阔的岛屿 ❷丰富；充裕；充足：an ～ of money 巨额钱财

amuse /ə'mjuːz/ *vt.* 娱乐；使感到有趣：His answer ～d me very much. 他的回答使我觉得很好笑。同 delight, entertain/ **～ oneself by doing sth.** 做某事以自娱：The boys ～d themselves by drawing. 男孩子们以画画取乐。

amusement / ə'mjuːzmənt / n. 娱乐;消遣;乐趣;娱乐活动;a~ park (grounds)游乐场 / to one's ~ 令…感到有趣 圆 entertainment, recreation, pastime

analeptic / ˌænə'leptɪk / n. 兴奋剂;~ inspection center 兴奋剂测试中心

analog(ue) /'ænəlɒg / n. [C] ❶类似物;模拟;~ pattern 模拟系统/ ~ simulation 模拟仿真/ be ~ to (with)类似于 ❷同源语

analogous / ə'næləgəs / adj. 类似的;相似的;~ with each other 两者相似 圆 similar

analogy / ə'nælədʒi / n. 相似;类似;类推;by ~ 照此类推 / on the ~ of … 根据…类推 圆 similarity

analyse(-ze) /'ænəlaɪz / vt. 分析;分解;We ~d the causes of our failure. 我们分析了失败的原因。圆 examine

analysis / ə'næləsɪs / n. (pl. analyses / ə'næləsiːz /)分析;分解;We made a careful ~ of the problem. 我们仔细分析了那个问题。圆 examination

anarchy /'ænəki / n. [U] ❶无政府(状态);(由于无政府而产生的)政治混乱;After its defeat in war the country was in a state of. 战败之后,该国处于无政府动乱状态。❷混乱,无秩序;Intellectual and moral ~ followed the loss of faith. 信仰的失落导致思想和道德的混乱

ancestor /'ænsestə(r) / n. [C]祖先;祖宗

ancestry /'ænsestri / n. ❶祖先;列祖;trace one's ~ (to)... 追溯祖先(到…) ❷世系;血统;be born of good ~ 出身名门

anchor /'æŋkə(r) / I n. [C]锚;raise (weigh) the ~ 起锚;起航 Ⅱ v. 抛锚;停泊;~ one's hope on sb. 把希望寄托在某人身上圆 attach

ancient /'eɪnʃənt / adj. 古代的;古老的;~ Rome 古罗马 / ~ times 古代 圆 old, aged

and / ænd, ənd / conj. ❶和,又(表示并列关系);a book ~ a pen 一本书和一支笔 / read ~ write 读和写 / my father ~ I 我和我父亲 / ~ **so on** 等等;诸如此类 ❷于是;而且 圆 also, moreover

anecdote /'ænɪkdəʊt / n. 轶事;amusing (funny) ~ 趣闻轶事 / literary ~ 文坛轶事 圆 tale, story

anew / ə'njuː / adv. 重新;再;repent and start ~ 悔过自新 圆 again, newly

angel /'eɪndʒl / n. [C]天使;安琪儿;守护神;enough to make the ~ weep 惨不忍睹 圆 saint, spirit

anger /'æŋgə(r) / n. [U]生气;愤怒;He was filled with ~. 他满腔怒火。圆 rage

angle /'æŋgl / n. [C] ❶角;角的度数;external (internal) ~ 外(内)角 ❷角度 view sth. from a different ~ 从不同的角度看问题 圆 viewpoint

angry /'æŋgri / adj. 发怒的;生气的;狂暴的;They were very ~ at what she had done. 他们对她所做之事很生气。/ He was very ~ with me when I was late. 我迟到了,他对我大发脾气。/ ~ winds 狂风 圆 enraged 派 angrily adv.

anguish /'æŋgwɪʃ / n. [U](身体上的)剧痛;(尤指精神上的)极度痛苦;the ~ of grief 悲痛欲绝/The parents were in deep mental ~ at what might have happened. 想到可能发生的事儿,做父母的精神上痛苦不已。

angular /'æŋgjələ(r) / adj. 有角的;尖的

animal /'ænɪml / n. [C] 动物;牲畜;wild ~s 野生动物/ domestic ~s 家畜

animate I /'ænɪmeɪt / vt. ❶使有生命,赋予…以生命;the mysterious force that ~s the cells of the body 使身体细胞具有生命的神奇力量 ❷激励;鼓舞;使活泼;使有生气;He was able to ~ a lecture on a dull subject with witty remarks. 他妙语连珠,能把一个枯涩的题目讲得妙趣横生。❸把…摄制(或绘制)成动画片;~ a film sequence 制作系列动画片 Ⅱ /'ænɪmɪt / adj. ❶活着的;有生命的;Plants are part of ~ nature. 植物是生物界的组成部分。❷活泼的;有活力的;生气勃勃的;an ~ expression of joy 喜笑颜开

ankle /'æŋkl / n. [C]踝

annihilate / ə'naɪəleɪt / vt. 消灭;歼灭;毁灭;The epidemic ~d the population of the town. 这场流行病夺走了全镇人的生命。/The invasion force was ~d to the last man. 入侵者被一个不剩地歼灭了。

anniversary / ˌænɪ'vɜːsəri / n. [C]周年;周年纪念日;celebrate the 10th ~ of … 庆祝…的10周年纪念日

annotate /'ænəʊteɪt / vt. 给…注释(或评注)

This new edition has been elaborately ～d by the author. 作者对这本新版书做了详尽的注解。派 annotation n.

announce /ə'naʊns/ vt. 宣告；宣布；发表：It has been ～d that the meeting will be held next week. 下周开会的事已经宣布了。同 declare, publish 派 announcer n.

announcement /ə'naʊnsmənt/ n. [C]宣布；通知；告示：make (issue) a public ～ 发布公告／An ～ will be made next Monday. 通告将在下星期一发出。同 declaration, forecast

> **辨析**
>
> **announce** 意为"宣布；通告；预告"，指首次宣布一件众人期待的并和他们有关的事，含有预告之意：The news was announced by Radio Beijing. 这消息被北京广播电台公布了。**declare** 常指公开和明确地宣布，多用于正式场合：The result of the examination has been declared. 考试结果已宣布。**publish** 特指以印刷品的方式向公众宣布：The news was published yesterday. 这条消息已于昨天公布。

annoy /ə'nɔɪ/ vt. 使人烦恼：She was ～ed because she missed the bus. 她因没赶上公共汽车而感到烦恼。同 trouble, bother 派 annoyance n.

annual /'ænjuəl/ adj. 每年的；一年一度的：～ budget 年度预算／～ income 年收入／～ pay (salary) 年薪／～ output 年产量 同 yearly 派 annually adv.

anonymous /ə'nɒnɪməs/ adj. ❶匿名的；无名的：an ～ letter phone call 匿名信电话／The giver of the prizes wished to remain ～. 奖金设立者不希望自己的姓名被披露。❷出自无名氏之手；来源不明的：This book was written by an ～ author. 这本书出自无名氏作者之手。／an ～ donation 不具名的捐赠

another /ə'nʌðə(r)/ adj. & pron. 又一(个)；再一(个)：one ～ 相互／Will you have ～ cup of tea? 再来一杯茶，好吗？

answer /'ɑːnsə(r)/ Ⅰ vt. 回答；答复：We must ～ his letter right away. 我们必须立即给他回信。同 reply, respond／～ for ① 负责：We must ～ for her safety. 我们必须对她的安全负责。② 接受处罚：You'll ～ for your wrong doing one day. 总有一天你会为所做的错事受到惩罚。Ⅱ n. [C]回答；答复；答案：

find an ～ to the question 找出问题的答案／His ～ to the question is correct. 他对这个问题的回答正确。同 reply, key

ant /ænt/ n. [C] 蚂蚁

antagonist /æn'tæɡənɪst/ n. [C] ❶对抗者；对手：His ～ in the debate was smarter than he. 他的辩论对手比他精明。❷(戏剧、小说等中主角的)对立面；反面人物：Iago is the ～ of Othello. 伊阿古是奥赛罗的对立面。

Antarctic /æn'tɑːktɪk/ Ⅰ adj. 南极的；南极区的：the ～ Circle 南极圈／the ～ Zone 南极地带 Ⅱ n. 南极(地区)；南极圈

Antarctica /æn'tɑːktɪkə/ n. 南极洲

antenna /æn'tenə/ n. (pl. antennae 或 antennas) (= aerial) 天线：community ～ 共用天线／internal ～ 室内天线／master ～ TV system 共用天线电视系统 同 aerial

anthem /'ænθəm/ n. 赞美诗；颂歌

anthropologist /ˌænθrə'pɒlədʒɪst/ n. [C]人类学家

anthropology /ˌænθrə'pɒlədʒi/ n. [U]人类学家

anti- /'ænti/ (前缀) (放在名词或形容词之前)表示"反""抗""阻""排斥"等：～-dumping policy 反倾销政策／～ dumping duty 反倾销税／～-riot police 防暴警察／～-unfair-competition 反不正当竞争／～-corruption 反腐败

antipathy /æn'tɪpəθi/ n. [U]反感，厌恶，憎恶：There is a great deal of ～ between them. 他们之间的嫌隙甚深。／I can't overcome my ～ for hypocrisy. 我无法克制自己对虚伪的厌憎。

antibiotics /ˌæntɪbaɪ'ɒtɪks/ n. 抗菌素；抗生素

anticipate /æn'tɪsɪpeɪt/ vt. 预料；预先；预期：～ one's wages 提前使用工资／～ the rival 抢在对手之前／～ doing sth. 期望做某事 同 expect, predict 派 anticipation n.

antique /æn'tiːk/ Ⅰ adj. 古时的；古代的；旧式的：an ～ shop 古玩店 同 ancient, old Ⅱ n. [C]古物；古器；古玩：a genuine ～ 一件珍稀古董

antonym /'æntənɪm/ n. [C]反义词 反 synonym

anxiety /æŋ'zaɪəti/ n. [U] ❶忧虑；担心：I feel great ～ about the boy's safety. 我对男孩

A

的安危感到非常担忧。同 worry, concern ❷
渴望 同 longing

anxious / ˈæŋkʃəs / *adj.* 焦急的；急切的；渴望
的：He is ～ to know the exam result. 他急着
想知道考试结果。同 worried, uneasy, concerned / **be ～ for** 渴望：I am ～ for a change.
我渴望换个环境。**be ～ about** 担心；担忧：He
is ～ about her health. 他担心她的健康。派
anxiously *adv.*

any / ˈeni / Ⅰ *adj.* 任何的；无论什么：Any
book will do. 任何一本书都行。/ If you see
～ interesting book, please buy a copy for me.
如果你看到有趣的书，请帮我买一本。Ⅱ
pron. 一个；无论哪个；一些：Have you ～
books? 你有书吗？

anybody / ˈenibɒdi / *pron.* 任何人；无论谁 同
anyone

anyhow / ˈenihaʊ / *adv.* 无论如何 同 anyway

anymore / ˈeniˈmɔː(r) / *adv.* 而今再也：Sally
doesn't work here ～. 萨莉不再在这儿工作
了。/Do you play tennis ～? 你还打网球吗？

anyone / ˈeniwʌn / *pron.* (＝anybody)任何人

anything / ˈeniθɪŋ / *pron.* 任何事物；任何事
情，一切：I don't find ～ in the room. 在房间
里我什么也没找到。/ He is ～ but a good
teacher. 他根本不是一位好老师。同 everything

anyway / ˈeniweɪ / *adv.* (＝anyhow)无论如
何；不管怎样：Anyway, I finished the job. 不管
怎样，我把那事做完了。

anywhere / ˈeniweə(r) / *adv.* 任何地方；无论
何处：You may go ～ you want. 你想去哪儿就
去哪儿。

apart / əˈpɑːt / *adv.* 分别；相距：～ from 除
了/ He stood far ～ from me. 他远离我站着。
同 separately

apartment / əˈpɑːtmənt / *n.* [C]公寓；住宅 同
flat

ape / eɪp / *n.* [C]猿

apex / ˈeɪpeks / *n.* [U] (*pl.* apexes 或 apices/
ˈeɪpɪˌsiːz/) ❶顶；顶点；最高点：the ～ of a tri-
angle 三角形的顶点/at the ～ of a mountain
在山顶/the ～ of a career 事业的顶点 ❷(心、
肺、树叶等的)尖端：the ～ of a leaf 树叶的尖
端/the ～ of the tongue 舌尖

apologise(-ze) / əˈpɒlədʒaɪz / *vi.* 道歉；认

错：～ **to sb. for sth.** 因某事向某人道歉：She
～d to her teacher for coming to school late.
她因上学迟到向老师道歉。

apology / əˈpɒlədʒi / *n.* [C]道歉；谢罪：**make
an ～ to sb.** 向某人道歉：You should make an
～ to her. 你应该向她道歉。

appal(l) / əˈpɔːl / *vt.* (-palled;-palling)使惊
骇；使胆寒：I was ～ed at how ill he looked. 见
他一脸的病容，我不觉惊呆了。/We are ～ed
to see the misery around us. 我们看到周围一
片凄凉的景象，不觉大为愕然。

apparatus / ˌæpəˈreɪtəs / *n.* [C] (*pl.* apparatus 或 apparatuses / ˌæpəˈreɪtəsɪz /)仪器；装
置；器官：chemical ～ 化学仪器/ digestive ～
消化器官 同 instrument, organ

apparent / əˈpærənt / *adj.* 明显的；外表的 同
obvious, evident 派 apparently *adv.*

appeal / əˈpiːl / *vi.* & *n.* 恳求；呼吁；上诉：
～ to arms 诉诸武力 / reject an ～ 驳回上诉
～ **to sb. to do (for) sth.** 恳求某人做某事：
The old man ～ed to us for help. 这位老人恳
求我们帮助他。

appealing / əˈpiːlɪŋ / *adj.* 有感染力的；吸引
人的；动人的；媚人的：an ～ sense of humor
极富感染力的幽默感/What an ～ little baby!
好一个逗人喜爱的小宝宝！

appear / əˈpɪə(r) / *vi.* ❶ 出现；显得；好像：
She ～s older than she is. 她看起来比她实际
年龄大。同 show, emerge ❷来到；露面：～
in person 亲自到场 同 show, present

appearance / əˈpɪərəns / *n.* [C]❶出现；显露；
来到；露面：～ to all 一目了然 / enter an ～ 到场
同 show, emergence ❷仪容；外观；外表：in ～
表面上；在外表上 / Never judge by ～. 不可
以貌取人。同 look

appease / əˈpiːz / *vt.* ❶使平静；平息；抚慰：
She tried to ～ the crying baby by giving him
the breast. 她给啼哭的婴儿喂奶使他不哭。/
～ sb.'s anger 使某人息怒 ❷解(渴)；充
(饥)；满足：～ one's thirst with a watermelon
吃西瓜解渴/He ～d his curiosity by asking a
few questions. 他问了几个问题，满足了他的
好奇心。❸姑息；对…作出让步：The boy
～d his father and got up from television to
finish his homework. 那男孩听从父亲的劝说，
离开电视机做作业去了。

append / əˈpend / *vt.* 附加；增补：～ a note to

A

a letter 在信上加注/a chart ～ed to statement 附在文字说明上的图表

appendix /ə'pendiks/ n. (pl. appendices 或 appendix) ❶附录；附录；附属物：consult the ～ 查阅附录 ❷阑尾：remove the ～ 切除阑尾

appetite /ˈæpitait/ n. ❶食欲；胃口：He has a good ～. 他胃口好。/ She lost her ～. 她食欲不振。同 stomach, hunger, taste ❷欲望；兴趣；爱好：It is to my ～. 这很合我的胃口。同 taste, passion

applaud /ə'plɔːd/ v. 鼓掌；赞许：When he finished his speech, the audience warmly ～ed. 他演讲完毕时，观众热烈鼓掌。

applause /ə'plɔːz/ n. [U]掌声；热烈鼓掌；喝彩；称赞；赞成：greet sb. with warm ～ 热烈鼓掌欢迎某人/ win the ～ of ...得到…的赞扬 同 cheer, praise

apple /ˈæpl/ n. [C] 苹果

appliance /ə'plaiəns/ n. [C] ❶用具；器具；器械；装置：household electrical ～ 家用器具/ medical ～ 医疗器械/ office ～ 办公用具 同 tool, apparatus, device ❷应用；适用 同 applications

applicable /ˈæplikəbl/ adj. 能应用的；可适用的；合适的：The treaty will be ～ from Oct. 1. 条约从 10 月 1 日起生效。/ ～ to ...可适用于… 同 fit, suitable

applicant /ˈæplikənt/ n. [C]申请人：an ～ for a scholarship 奖学金申请人

application /ˌæpliˈkeiʃn/ n. [C] ❶申请；申请书；申请表：an ～ form 一份申请表 / an ～ for employment 求职申请书 ❷应用；适用；运用 同 use, appliance ❸(计算机)应用程序

apply /ə'plai/ v. 应用；申请：～ for a visa 申请护照 / ～ a theory to practice 把理论运用于实践 /～ to sb. for sth. 向某人申请某样东西：He applied to the shop for a job. 他向商店求职。/ ～ oneself to 致力于；专心于：She applied herself to English teaching. 她致力于英语教学。同 use, employ

appoint /ə'pɔint/ v. 指定；任命；委派：～ sb. to a post 委派某人任某职/ He was ～ed mayor of the city. 他被任命为该市市长。同 assign, name, order

appoint 意为"任命""委任"，指不经选举，由当权者经过仔细考虑后进行委派、分派：They appointed her to be head of the department. 他们委任她当系主任。**assign** 意为"指派""委派"，指一般意义上的分派、分配：The duty was assigned to her. 那项任务分派给了她。**name** 意为"任命""指定""提名"：They named her as president. 他们提名她担任主席。

appointment /ə'pɔintmənt/ n. ❶任命；选派；职位：a letter of ～ 聘书 /accept an ～ 接受任命 / take up an ～ 就任 同 assignment, position ❷约定；约会：make an ～ with sb. 与某人约会/ keep (break) an ～ 守(违)约 同 date, engagement

apportion /ə'pɔːʃn/ vt. 分派；分摊；按比例分配：The execution of the will ～ed the property equally to each heir. 遗嘱执行是将财产平分给每个继承人。/～ expenses among the three men 叫三个人分担费用

appositive /ə'pɔzitiv/ n. [C]同位语

appraise /ə'preiz/ vt. ❶评价；鉴定：～ ability and achievement in students 对学生的能力和成绩作评估 ❷估计；估价：Property is ～d for taxation. 为报税而估价财产。/ a painting ～d at $1 million 一幅估价 100 万美元的画

appreciate /ə'priːʃieit/ vt. 感激；欣赏；鉴赏：～ sb. for sth. 为某事感激某人：I ～ you for your timely help. 真感谢你的及时帮助。同 thank, esteem

appreciation /əˌpriːʃiˈeiʃn/ n. ❶ 欣赏；鉴赏；赏识：have an ～ for 有鉴赏力 同 esteem, admiration ❷评价；估价；鉴别 同 assessment, judgment ❸感谢；感激：show (express) one's ～ for... 对…表示感谢 同 thank

apprehend /ˌæpriˈhend/ vt. ❶逮捕；拘押：The thief was ～ed and put in jail. 小偷被逮捕，并被关进监狱。❷理解；领会；领悟；明白；懂得：～ the meaning of your words. 我懂你说的话的意思。/It was ～ed at a glance by everyone. 大家对它一目了然。

apprentice /ə'prentis/ n. [C]学徒；初学者；生手：take an ～ 收徒弟 同 beginner, learner

approach /ə'prəutʃ/ Ⅰ v. 临近；逼近：Christmas is ～ing. 圣诞节即将来临。Ⅱ n.

[C]途径；方法；通路：This is the ～ to the cinema. 这是去电影院的路。/ When you are learning a foreign language, the effective ～ is to study the spoken language. 学习外语的有效方法是学口语。

appropriate / əˈprəʊprɪət / *adj.* 适当的；恰如其分的：at an ～ time 在适当的时间 / take ～ measures 采取恰当的措施 同 proper, suitable 反 unsuitable

approval / əˈpruːv(ə)l / *n.* [U]赞成；认可：The manager gave his ～ for my plan. 经理同意了我的计划。同 favor, agreement

approve / əˈpruːv / *v.* 赞同；允许（与 of 连用）：We ～ of your choice. 我们赞同你的选择。同 favor, agree, praise

approximately / əˈprɒksɪmətli / *adv.* 大约；近似 同 nearly, roughly 反 precisely

April / ˈeɪprəl / *n.* (略作 Apr.)四月

apron / ˈeɪprən / *n.* [C] 围裙

apt / æpt / *adj.* ❶有…倾向的；易于…的：He was ～ to behave impulsively. 他好感情用事。/ When one is tired one is ～ to make mistakes. 人疲倦时容易出差错。❷适当的；恰当的：an ～ observation 中肯的意见 / an ～ metaphor 贴切的比喻

aptitude / ˈæptɪtjuːd / *n.* ❶自然倾向 同 tendency ❷能力；才能：develop one's ～ to negotiate 培养谈判才能 / special (peculiar) ～ 特长 同 ability, capability

Arab / ˈærəb / *n.* [C] 阿拉伯人

Arabian / əˈreɪbɪən / Ⅰ *adj.* 阿拉伯的；阿拉伯人的：The ～ Nights《天方夜谭》Ⅱ *n.* [C] 阿拉伯人

arbitrary / ˈɑːbɪtrəri / *adj.* 武断的；专横的；任意的：an ～ decision 武断的决定 同 self-willed, willful

arc / ɑːk / *n.* ❶弧；弓形；拱 ❷弧光：～ light 弧光；弧光灯

arch / ɑːtʃ / Ⅰ *n.* [C]弓形；拱门；桥洞：～ bridge 拱桥 Ⅱ *v.* 拱；成弓形 同 curve, bend

archaeologist / ˌɑːkɪˈɒlədʒɪst / *n.* [C]考古学家；考古学者

archaeology / ˌɑːkɪˈɒlədʒi / *n.* [U]考古学

archetype / ˈɑːkɪtaɪp / *n.* [C] ❶原型：That little engine is the ～ of huge modern locomotives. 那台小发动机是现代大机车的原型。❷

典型；范例：an ～ of the American rags-to-riches dream 典型的从一贫如洗到万贯家财的美国梦

architect / ˈɑːkɪtekt / *n.* [C]建筑师；缔造者 同 creator, founder

architecture / ˈɑːkɪtektʃə(r) / *n.* [U] 建筑；建筑学

Arctic / ˈɑːktɪk / Ⅰ *n.* 北极；北极圈；北极区 Ⅱ *adj.* 北极的；北极区的：the ～ Circle 北极圈 / the ～ Ocean 北冰洋 / the ～ Regions 北极地区

ardent / ˈɑːdənt / *adj.* ❶热烈的；强烈的；激动的：one's ～ desire for freedom 某人对自由的热望 ❷热情的；热切的；忠诚的：an ～ theatre-goer 戏迷 / an ～ longing 热切的企盼

are / ɑː(r) / *v.* (你，你们，我们，她们，它们)是(见 be)

area / ˈeərɪə / *n.* ❶[C]地区；地域；范围：high and new tech ～ 高新技术开发区 / ～ code (电话)区号 同 district, zone ❷面积：coverage ～ 覆盖面积 同 size

argue / ˈɑːgjuː / *v.* 辩论；争论：～ **with sb. about (on, over, upon) sth.** 与某人辩论某事：It is no use ～ing with him about the matter. 和他辩论此事是徒劳。～ **sb. into (out of) doing sth.** 劝某人做(不做)某事：Do you want to ～ me into agreeing to your plan? 你想说服我同意你的计划吗? 同 discuss, debate

辨析
argue 指以说理的方式阐明自己的观点，有时可指以激烈的方式进行的辩论：Don't argue with me. 不要与我争论。debate 指争论双方在有人公断的情况下正式、公开地进行辩论：They are debating whether war can be abolished. 他们正在辩论战争能否被消灭的问题。

argument / ˈɑːgjumənt / *n.* 辩论；争论；论战；论点：get into an ～ 卷入一场争论 / beyond ～ 无可争辩 / put forward an ～ 提出一个论点 同 discussion, debate, proof

arise / əˈraɪz / *v.* (arose / əˈrəʊz /, arisen / əˈrɪzn /) 出现；起来；升起：Problems have ～n 问题出现了。/ The children arose from their seats. 孩子们从座位上站了起来。同 rise, ascent 反 fall, sink

aristocrat / ˈærɪstəkræt / *n.* [C](一个)贵族 派 aristocratic *adj.*

A

arithmetic /ə'rɪθmətɪk/ *n.* [U] 算术：do ~ 做算术题

arm /ɑːm/ Ⅰ *n.* [C] ❶手臂；胳膊：~ **in** ~ 肩并肩；手挽手：The two children are walking ~ in ~. 这两个孩子挽臂而行。❷(*pl.*)武器：~s race 军备竞赛 Ⅱ *v.* 武装；装备：~ed forces 武装部队／look with folded ~s 袖手旁观／They have been ~ed with new weapons. 他们已经配备了新武器。

armo(u)r /'ɑːmə(r)/ *n.* [C]❶装甲兵；装甲兵部队 ❷盔甲

army /'ɑːmi/ *n.* ❶军；军队：join the ~ 参军／serve in the ~ 服兵役／~ construction 军队建设／the Army Day (August 1)(中国人民解放军)八一建军节 圓 military, troops ❷大群；大批：an ~ of ... 一群… 圓 host

around /ə'raʊnd/ Ⅰ *prep.* 在…周围；环绕着；到处；整整一圈：all ~ 周围；到处／the world ~ 遍及全世界／all the year ~ 一年到头／~ the clock 日夜；24 小时 圓 round, about, encircling／There are many trees ~ the building. 大楼周围有很多树。Ⅱ *adv.* 四处；周围；大约：~ ten o'clock 十点钟左右／We looked ~ but saw nothing. 我们环顾四周,什么也没看见。圓 round, about, almost

arouse /ə'raʊz/ *vt.* 唤醒；引起；激起：Don't ~ my anger. 不要惹我生气。／His words ~d our suspicion. 他的话引起了我们的怀疑。圓 rouse, stir

arrange /ə'reɪndʒ/ *vt.* 整理；安排：It is all ~d. 这事全都安排好了。／~ **for** 预先准备：The room has been ~d for the evening party. 开晚会的房间已安排妥当。圓 prepare, plan, adjust

用 法
arrange 作不及物动词时,其后不跟 that 从句,若要表示安排某人做某事,用句型 arrange for sb. to do sth.：The leadership has arranged for Mr. Smith to attend the meeting. 领导已安排史密斯先生参加会议。

arrangement /ə'reɪndʒmənt/ *n.* ❶整理；排列；布置：by ~ 安排次序 圓 display, adjustment ❷安排；准备：make ~s for... 为…做准备 圓 preparations, plans

array /ə'reɪ/ *n.* ❶队列；排列：in battle ~ 成战斗队形／an ~ of 一批；一列 圓 display, arrangement ❷衣服；盛装：in holiday ~ 穿着节日盛装 圓 dress

arrest /ə'rest/ *vt. & n.* ❶逮捕；扣留：house ~ 软禁／resist ~ 拒捕 圓 seize, capture ❷停止；阻止

arrival /ə'raɪvl/ *n.* 到达；到来；到达者：a new ~ 新来的人；新到的货／an ~ form 来客登记表／on one's ~ …一到达；…到达时 圓 reaching, approach, visitor 反 departure

arrive /ə'raɪv/ *vi.* 到达；达到：~ **at** (**in**)到达某地：They ~d in Beijing yesterday. 他们昨日到达北京。／It was about 12 o'clock when they ~d at the village. 他们到达村里时大约 12 点钟。／~ **at a conclusion** 得出结论：They can't ~ at a conclusion at this meeting. 在这次会议上他们不可能得出结论。圓 reach, come, conclude

用 法
arrive 为不及物动词,表达"到达某地"之意时后面必须接介词。习惯上较大的地方用 in,较小的地方用 at。

arrogance /'ærəgəns/ *n.* [U]骄傲自大；傲慢：We should guard against ~ at any time. 任何时候我们都要力戒骄傲自大。圓 overpride 反 modesty 派 arrogant *adj.*；arrogantly *adv.*

art /ɑːt/ *n.* ❶美术；艺术：~ gallery 美术馆／~ show 美术展览／fine ~s 美术／~-work *n.* 工艺品 ❷技术；技艺：martial ~s 武术 圓 craft, skill ❸(*pl.*)人文学科：Bachelor of Arts 文学士／Master of Arts 文学硕士／liberal ~s 人文学科

artery /'ɑːtəri/ *n.* ❶干线：economic arteries 经济命脉／traffic ~ 交通干线 圓 trunk, trunk-line ❷动脉

article /'ɑːtɪkl/ *n.* [C] ❶文章；论文：He published an ~ on space travel last month. 上个月他发表了一篇有关太空旅行的文章。圓 essay, thesis ❷冠词 ❸物品；商品：household ~s 家庭用品／toilet ~ 盥洗用品 圓 object, thing

artificial /ˌɑːtɪ'fɪʃl/ *adj.* 人造的；人工的：~ flower 人造花／~ silk 人造丝／~ rainfall 人工降雨 圓 man-made, false

artist /'ɑːtɪst/ *n.* [C]艺术家；艺人；能手

artistic(al) /ɑː'tɪstɪk(əl)/ *adj.* ❶艺术的；美术的：~ creation 艺术创作／~ criticism

艺术批评/ ～ effect 艺术效果 ❷艺术家的；美术家的

as / æz,əz / Ⅰ *conj.* 当…时；因为，由于；如，像：She sang ～she worked. 她一边工作，一边唱歌。/ As you are tired,you'd better rest. 你已疲倦,最好休息一下。/ He does not speak ～ other people do. 他说起话来不像其他人。/ ～**if** 好像：She spoke ～ if she had known everything. 听她说起来就好像她什么都知道。～ **it were** 似乎：You are,～ it were,a naughty boy. 可以说你是个很调皮的孩子。～ **long** 只要：You may go ～ long ～ you have finished your job. 只要任务完成了,你就可以走。～ **soon** ～…就…：Call to me ～ soon ～ you get home. 一到家就给我来电话 Ⅱ *prep.* 作为；：～ **a result** 因此；结果：Tom didn't work hard enough and he failed the exam ～ a result. 汤姆努力不够,因此考试没及格。～ **a rule** 通常：He comes on Sunday ～ a rule. 他通常星期天来。Ⅲ *adv.* 同样地；他和你一样关心此事。/ ～ **usual** 通常,照常：The shops are open ～ usual. 商店照常营业。～ **well** 也：Please take this ～ well. 这个也请拿去。

ascend / əˈsend / *v.* ❶攀登；登上；升高：～ a hill 登山/ ～ the throne 登上王位 同 climb, mount ❷追溯(到某个时间) 同 trace

ascent / əˈsent / *n.* [C] 登高；上升；斜坡：his first ～ of Mount Tai 他的首次登泰山/ rapid ～ 急坡；陡坡/ We saw the ～ of a balloon in the air. 我们看到了一只气球升上空。

ascribe / əˈskraib / *vt.* ❶把…归因(于)(与 to 连用)：～ one's wealth to hard work 认为其财富乃是勤劳所得/He ～s beauty to that which is simple. 他认为,美自质朴出。❷认为…属(于)；认为…源(自)(与 to 连用)：For many years these poems were wrongly ～d to Marlowe. 多少年来这些诗曾被误认为是马洛的作品。

ash / æʃ / *n.* ❶灰,灰烬(不与数字连用)：Don't drop cigarette ～ on the floor. 不要让烟灰落在地板上。❷(*pl.*)骨灰

ashamed / əˈʃeimd / *adj.* (表语形容词)羞愧的;耻辱的：You should be ～ of what you have done. 你应该为你的所作所为感到羞愧。同 shamed,shy

ashore / əˈʃɔː(r) / *adv.* 向岸;向陆地;上岸;上

陆地：The schooner was driven ～. 那条帆船被冲上了岸。/This ship got ～ on a rock. 那条船搁在礁石上搁浅了。

Asia / ˈeiʃə / *n.* 亚洲：Southeast ～ 东南亚

Asian / ˈeiʃn,ˈeiʒn / Ⅰ *adj.* 亚洲的 Ⅱ *n.* [C]亚洲人

aside / əˈsaid / *adv.* 在一边；向一边：move ～ 移开 同 sidewise,sideways

ask / ɑːsk / *v.* 问；请；要：May I ～ you a question? 我可以问你一个问题吗？/ He ～ed me to come on time. 他叫我准时来。/ ～ for leave 请假/ ～ the way 问路 / ～ for trouble 自寻烦恼 同 question,request,invite/～ **after** 询问；问候：They ～ed after their sick classmate. 他们问候生病的同学。～ **for** 要：The girl ～ed for some new books. 这个女孩要买几本新书。

ask 可用于以下几个句型：❶ask sb. sth.：He asked me a question. 他问了我一个问题。❷ask sb. for sth.：She asked her mother for a new pen. 她向她母亲要了一支新钢笔。❸ask sb. to do sth.：The teacher asked me to sit down. 老师要我坐下。❹ask for sth.：Oliver asked for more food. 奥列弗请求再给点吃的。

ask 是普通用词,指向某人表示自己的需要、愿望：The boy asked his father for some money. 这男孩向他父亲要钱。**request** 是较为客气和正式的用词：He requested me to be more patient. 他要求我再耐心些。

asleep / əˈsliːp / *adj.* (表语形容词)睡着的：fall ～ 入睡/ fast ～ 熟睡/ He is not ～ yet. 他还没有睡着。同 sleeping 反 awake

aspect / ˈæspekt / *n.* 局面；看法；样子；方面：from an ～ 从一个方面/You've only considered one ～ of the problem. 你只考虑到这问题的一个方面。/ Our maths teacher is a man with a serious ～. 我们的数学老师是一个外貌严肃的人。同 side,view,outlook

aspiration / ˌæspəˈreiʃn / *n.* 志气；抱负；渴望：noble (lofty) ～ 崇高的志向 / cherish (have) high ～ 胸怀大志 / He realized his ～ at last. 他终于实现了他的抱负。同 ambition,desire

aspire / əˈspaiə(r) / *vi.* 渴求；追求(知识、名

A

誓等）：～ for knowledge 渴求知识/ ～ for truth 追求真理/ ～ after independence 渴望独立 同 desire

ass / æs / n. [C] 驴子

assassination / əˌsæsɪˈneɪʃn / n. ●暗杀；行刺 同 murder, kill ❷恶意中伤；破坏（名誉等）同 harm

assault / əˈsɔːlt / Ⅰ n. [C]攻击；袭击；突击：They carried out an ～ against the fortress. 他们向那座堡垒发动攻击。Ⅱ vt. 攻击；袭击；突击：Two lads of nine were accused of ～ing a boy of there. 有人告状说两个9岁的孩子殴打一个3岁的小孩。/A crowd of critics ～ed his verse. 一批评论家群起攻击他的诗歌。

assemble / əˈsembl / v. ●聚集；会集；集合：～ forces 调集兵力 / The pupils ～d on the field. 学生们聚集在运动场上。同 gather ❷装配；组装：～ a machine 组装一台机器/assembling workshop 装配车间

assembly / əˈsembli / n. [C] ●（特殊目的的）集会，会议：an ～ hall 会议厅 / freedom of speech and ～ 言论和集会自由/ hold an ～ 举行集会 同 meeting, gathering ❷（机械的）装配；配件；部件：～ line 装配线，生产线

assent / əˈsent / Ⅰ vi. 同意；赞成；赞同：Everyone ～ed to the plans for the dance. 大家都同意对舞会的安排。Ⅱ n. [U]同意；赞成；赞同：a nod of ～点头表示同意/by common ～ 一致同意

assert / əˈsɜːt / vt. ●(坚决)主张；坚持；维护：The dominant American ideology ～ed a faith in individual advancement. 美国的主导思想坚决主张个性的提高。❷坚称；力陈；断言：We encouraged him to ～ his own view of the matter. 我们鼓励他明确地说出自己对此事的看法。/He ～ed that he shot the bird. 他一口咬定他打中了鸟。/～oneself 坚持自己的权利(或意见)：A leader must ～ himself sometimes in order to be followed. 领袖有时必须坚持自己的主张才能赢得民众。

assess / əˈses / vt. ●评价；估价：They ～ed the house at a million dollars. 他们估价那房屋值100万美元。同 estimate, evaluate ❷征收(税款、罚款等)：～ a fine against(upon) sb. 对某人进行罚款 同 tax, charge

assessment / əˈsesmənt / n. [U]估价；评价；(价格的)评定 同 estimate, evaluation

asset / ˈæset / n. [C] ●财产；资产：～s revaluation 资产重估/current ～s 流动资产/ fixed ～s 固定资产/ the loss of state-owned ～s 国有资产流失 同 property, possessions ❷宝贵的人(或物) 同 treasure

assign / əˈsaɪn / vt. 指定；分配：These rooms have been ～ed to them. 这些房间已分配给他们。同 appoint, distribute

assignment / əˈsaɪnmənt / n. 分配(任务、作业、工作等)；What's today's ～ in English? 今天的英语作业是什么？

assimilate / əˈsɪmɪˌleɪt / vt. 吸收；吸取：The mind ～s knowledge 大脑吸收知识。/Plants ～ food from the earth. 植物土壤中吸收养分。

assist / əˈsɪst / v. 帮助；协助：I'll ～ her in this task. 我要协助她完成这项任务。同 help, support, aid

assistance / əˈsɪstəns / n. [U]帮助；援助：be of ～ to sb. 有助于某人/give ～ to sb. 给某人以帮助 同 help, aid, support

assistant / əˈsɪstənt / Ⅰ n. 助手；助理：He is ～ manager of our company. 他是我们公司的副经理。同 aide, helper Ⅱ adj. 助理的；辅助的：～ professor 助理教授/ ～ manager 副经理/ special ～ 特别助理/ shop ～ 营业员 同 helping, aiding

associate Ⅰ / əˈsəʊʃieɪt / v. 联系；联合；联想：The little girl always ～s cake with her birthday. 小女孩总是把蛋糕和她的生日联想在一起。同 relate, connect Ⅱ / əˈsəʊʃiət / n. [C]伙伴；合伙人；同事：business ～ 合伙经商人 / ～ in crime 同案犯 同 colleague, partner Ⅲ / əˈsəʊʃiət / adj. 副的：～ professor 副教授 同 vice

association / əˌsəʊsiˈeɪʃn / n. ●[U]联合；联系；交往：bring up ～ 引起联想 同 alliance, union, connection ❷[C]协会；社团：establish an ～ 建立协会 同 organization, union

associative / əˈsəʊʃiətɪv / adj. 联合的；联想的：～ memory 联想记忆/ ～ thinking 联想思维/ ～ Chinese Character Cards 联想式汉字卡 同 united

assume / əˈsjuːm / v. ●假装；假定；设想：Let's ～ the young man to be innocent. 让我们设想这年轻人是无罪的吧。同 suppose ❷担任；承担：You should ～ the responsibility. 你应当

承担这个责任。同 undertake 派 assumption n.

assurance / əˈʃʊərəns / n. ❶保证；断言 同 guarantee ❷保险 同 insurance

assure / əˈʃʊə(r) / vt. ❶使确信；使放心：He checked the machine carefully to ～ that it was in good condition. 他仔细检查了机器，直到确信一切正常为止。同 ensure, convince ❷对…进行保险 同 insure

astonish / əˈstɒnɪʃ / vt. 使吃惊，使惊讶：I was ～ed at the news. 听到这个消息，我感到震惊。同 surprise, shock

astonishment / əˈstɒnɪʃmənt / n. [U]惊讶：she watched the boy with ～. 她吃惊地望着那男孩。同 surprise, shock

astound / əˈstaʊnd / vt. 使震惊，使惊骇，使大吃一惊：She was ～ed at (by) the news that she had won the contest. 她听到自己在竞赛中获胜的消息后感到吃惊。/I was ～ed that he was preparing to give me a job. 他准备给我一份工作，这使我大吃一惊。

astride / əˈstraɪd / prep. 跨在…上：The naughty boy sat ～ his grandpa's cane. 那个小淘气把他祖父的拐杖当马骑。

astronaut / ˈæstrənɔːt / n. [C]太空人；宇航员

astronomy / əˈstrɒnəmi / n. [U]天文学

astronomer / əˈstrɒnəmə(r) / n. [C]天文学家

at / æt, ət / prep. 在，于(表示时间或空间的一点)：She is an English teacher ～ a middle school. 她在一所中学当英语教师。/ At that time she was in Shanghai. 那时她在上海。

athlete / ˈæθliːt / n. [C]运动员：track and field ～s田径运动员/ all-round ～ 全能运动员

athletic / æθˈletɪk / adj. 运动的；体育的：～ sports 体育运动；竞技

athletics / æθˈletɪks / n. (pl.)体育运动；竞技 同 sports, games, gymnastics

Atlantic / ətˈlæntɪk / Ⅰ adj. 大西洋的 Ⅱ n. (the Atlantic)大西洋

atmosphere / ˈætməsfɪə(r) / n. [U] 空气；大气：～ pollution 大气污染/ ～ pressure 大气压力

atmospheric / ˌætməsˈferɪk / adj. 大气的；大气层的；空气的：～ pollution 大气污染

atom / ˈætəm / n. [C]原子：～bomb 原子弹

atomic / əˈtɒmɪk / adj. 原子的；原子能的：～

age 原子时代/ ～ reactor原子反应堆/ ～ power station 原子能发电站

attach / əˈtætʃ / v. 系；附上；使隶属于：He ～ed his horse to a tree. 他把马拴在一棵树上。/ This hospital is ～ed to the college. 这医院附属于那所学院。同 tie, fasten connect

attachment / əˈtætʃmənt / n. [C] ❶依附；(计算机的)附件：～s of a contract 合同附件 同 addition ❷依恋：feel ～ to one's parents 依恋父母

attack / əˈtæk / Ⅰ v. 进攻；攻击：The village was ～ed by the enemy. 这个村子遭到敌人的袭击。反 defend, guard Ⅱ n. 进攻；攻击；(疾病)侵袭：a surprise ～ 突袭 / a heart ～ 犯心脏病

attain / əˈteɪn / v. 达到；获得：He ～ed success through hard work. 他经过艰苦努力获得了成功。/ I can never hope to ～ to his height. 我从不敢企望达到他的高度。同 reach, win

attempt / əˈtempt / Ⅰ vt. 试做；企图：They are ～ing a difficult task. 他们正在试干一项艰难的工作。同 try Ⅱ n. [C]企图；努力 同 try, effort/**make an ～ at doing sth.** 试图做某事：The young man made an ～ at saving this child. 这位青年人试图拯救这小孩。**make an ～ on** 向某人进攻；夺取：The thief made an ～ on the old woman's life. 盗贼想杀死这位老太太。

attend / əˈtend / v. ❶照顾；照料：The nurses ～ed to the wounded day and night. 护士们日夜护理伤员。同 nurse, serve ❷出席；参加：We'll ～ the meeting. 我们将出席这次会议。/ Children should ～ school. 孩子们应该上学。同 visit ❸注意；留心：Are you ～ing to what is being said? 你在注意听人家说话吗?

attendance / əˈtendəns / n. ❶ 到场；出席：book 签到簿 同 presence, participation 反 absence ❷出席人数；出勤率：check the ～ 检查出席人数 ❸护理；照顾：a doctor in ～ 护理医生 同 care, nursing

attendant / əˈtendənt / n. [C] ❶出席者；侍者；服务员：lift ～ 电梯服务员 同 waiter, servant ❷随从：an ～ to an ambassador 大使随员 同 follower, companion

attention / əˈtenʃn / n. [U]专心；注意；注意力：A good teacher must know how to secure the ～ of his pupils. 一个好教师必须懂得如

A

何吸引学生的注意力。同 care,concern

attentive / ə'tentɪv / adj. 注意的；周到的：The pupils are very ～ to their teacher's. 学生们很注意听老师讲课。派 attentively adv.

attitude / 'ætɪtjuːd / n. [C]态度；看法：a matter-of-fact ～ 求实精神／We should take an active ～ to it. 对这事我们应采取积极的态度。同 view,position

attract / ə'trækt / vt. 吸引；引诱：Bees are ～ed by flowers. 蜜蜂为花所吸引。同 draw, pull,drag

attraction / ə'trækʃn / n. 吸引；吸引力；诱惑力：personal ～s 个人魅力 同 charm,fascination

attractive / ə'træktɪv / adj. 有吸引力的；有迷惑力的：goods ～ in price 价格诱人的货物 同 charming,fascinating

attribute / ə'trɪbjuːt / vt. 把…归因于；把…归咎于：～... to ... 把…归因于…；He ～d his failure to bad luck. 他把失败归因于运气不好。同 credit

auction / 'ɔːkʃn / Ⅰ n. 拍卖：～ shop 拍卖行／sell a curiosity by ～ 拍卖一件古董 同 sale, bargain Ⅱ vt. 拍卖：～ off a building 拍卖掉一栋楼房 同 sell

audible / 'ɔːdɪbl / adj. ❶可听见的：～ whisper 听得见的低语 同 hearable ❷音响的：～ signal 音响信号

audience / 'ɔːdiəns / n. [C]听众；观众：television ～ 电视观众／There was a large (small) ～. 听众(观众)很多(少)。 同 viewers,listeners,readers

audio / 'ɔːdiəʊ / adj. 听觉的；声音的；音频的：～ frequency 音频／～ system 组合音响

audio-visual / ˌɔːdiəʊ'vɪʒuəl / adj. 视听的：～ education 视听教育／～ center 视听中心／～ equipment 视听设备／～ teaching materials 视听教材

audit / 'ɔːdɪt / Ⅰ v. 审计；查账 同 check,examine Ⅱ n. 审计；查账：～ program 审计程序／an ～ report 审计报告 同 checking,examination 派 auditor n.

auditorium / ˌɔːdɪ'tɔːriəm / (pl. auditoria) n. 大会堂；礼堂：lecture ～ 演讲大厅／main ～ 大礼堂 同 hall

August / 'ɔːgəst / n. (略作 Aug.)八月

aunt / ɑːnt / n. [C]伯母；婶；舅母；姑；姨

aural / 'ɔːrəl / adj. 听觉的；耳的：～ comprehension 听力理解／～ surgeon 耳科大夫

Australia / ɒ'streɪliə / n. 澳大利亚

Australian / ɒ'streɪliən / Ⅰ adj. 澳大利亚的 Ⅱ n. [C]澳大利亚人

Austria / 'ɒstriə / n. 奥地利

Austrian / 'ɒstriən / Ⅰ adj. 奥地利的 Ⅱ n. [C]奥地利人

authentic / ɔː'θentɪk / adj. ❶真的；真正的；名副其实的：Are your documents ～ or faked? 你的这些文件是真的还是仿造的？❷可靠的；可信的；确实的：an ～ news report 可靠的新闻报道／give ～ oral testimony 拿出过硬的口头证据

author / 'ɔːθə(r) / n. [C] ❶作者：a contemporary ～ 当代作家 同 writer ❷网页制作人

authoritative / ɔː'θɒrəteɪtɪv / adj. 有权威的；官方的：～ information 官方消息／an ～ person 权威人士 同 authorized,official

authorize(-se) / 'ɔːθəraɪz / vt. 授权；委托；允许：～ an agent 指定代理人／～d by usage 约定俗成／be ～d to do sth. 被允许做某事 同 empower,permit

authority / ɔː'θɒrəti / n. ❶权威；权限；职权；专家：academic ～ 学术权威／abuse one's ～ 滥用职权 同 power ❷(通常用 pl.)当局，官方；有关方面：authorities concerned 有关当局

auto / 'ɔːtəʊ / n. (＝automobile)(pl. autos)汽车；机动车

autobiography / ˌɔːtəbaɪ'ɒgrəfi / n. [C]自传

autograph / 'ɔːtəgrɑːf / n. [C]亲笔；(尤指名人的)亲笔签名：Many people collect the ～s of celebrities. 许多人收藏名人的亲笔签名。

automate / 'ɔːtəmeɪt / vt. 使自动化：～ the procedures 使程序自动化 派 automation n.

automatic / ˌɔːtə'mætɪk / adj. ❶自动的；自动装置的：～ control system 自动控制系统 同 self-acting ❷机械的；无意识的；习惯性的 同 mechanical

automobile / 'ɔːtəməbiːl / n. (＝auto)[C]汽车(主要用在美国英语中)：～ industry 汽车工业

autonomous / ɔː'tɒnəməs / adj. 自治的；自治权的：an ～ region 自治区／～ investment 自主投资／an ～ port 自由港

A

autonomy / ɔːˈtɒnəmi / n. 自治;自治权;自主

autumn / ˈɔːtəm / n. (=fall)秋季;秋天

auxiliary / ɔːɡˈzɪljəri / adj. ❶附属的;从属的;several ～ branches of the library 该图书馆的几个分馆 ❷辅助的;当助手的;Some sailboats have ～ engines. 有些帆船装有辅助发动机。/an ～ nurse 助理护士 ❸备用的;后备的;The hospital has an ～ power system in case of blackout. 这家医院装有备用发电系统以防灯火管制。

avail / əˈveɪl / Ⅰ v. 有用;有益;有助;This proud tradition now ～s them well in their present struggles. 这一光荣传统在他们目前的斗争中起着很大作用。/ ～(oneself) of 利用;There's moral in everything, if we would only ～ ourselves of it. 只要我们善于吸取,从每件事中都可以吸取教训。Ⅱ n. [U]效用,用途;好处,帮助;His efforts were of little ～. 他的种种努力不起作用。/He tried to revive her but to no ～. 他极力想让她苏醒过来,但是没有成功。

available / əˈveɪləbl / adj. 可利用的;可得到的;有效的;Can this kind of washing machine ～ in this shop? 在这家商店能买到这种型号的洗衣机吗? / The ticket is ～ only today. 此票只有今天有效。

avenge / əˈvendʒ / vt. 复仇;报仇;报复;He said he would ～ his parents. 他说他定要为他的父母报仇。

avenue / ˈævənjuː / n. [C]大街;林荫大道;途径;手段;That is a good ～ to success. 那是通往成功的佳径。同 road, street, way

average / ˈævərɪdʒ / Ⅰ n. 平均;平均数;above (below)～ 超过(低于)平均数/ on an ～ 平均起来;一般说来 Ⅱ adj. 平均的;一般的;the ～ age 平均年龄/ the ～ rate of growth 平均增长率 Ⅲ v. 均分

avert / əˈvɜːt / vt. ❶转移(目光、注意力等);She ～ed her eyes from the wreck. 她转移目光不再看失事飞机的残骸。❷防范,避免,消除(灾难、危险等);The driver ～ed an accident by a quick turn of the steering wheel. 司机急忙掉转方向盘,从而避免了一起车祸。

avoid / əˈvɔɪd / vt. 避免;逃避;回避;She told her child to ～ talking with a stranger. 她告诉孩子不要和陌生人讲话。

用法 avoid 后只跟名词或动名词,不跟不定式;Fortunately, we were able to avoid the accident. 幸好我们躲过了那场事故。I cannot avoid seeing him. 我难免要和他见面。

await / əˈweɪt / vt. 等候;期待;He has ～ed your coming for a week. 他等候你的到来已有一周了。同 wait, expect

awake / əˈweɪk / Ⅰ vt. (awoke / əˈwəuk /, awoke 或 awaked)醒来;叫醒,唤醒;I awoke with a start. 我从梦中惊醒。同 wake, arouse 反 sleep Ⅱ adj. 醒着的;She is ～ now. 她现在是醒着的。反 sleep

awaken / əˈweɪkən / vt. 使醒,使觉醒;Please ～ me at six. 请6点钟叫醒我。/ His honesty ～ed my sympathy. 他的诚实唤起了我的同情。同 arouse, excite

award / əˈwɔːd / Ⅰ n. 奖;奖金;奖学金;grant an ～ 授奖/ receive an ～ 获奖/ sci-tech results~s 科技成果奖同 prize Ⅱ vt. 授予;奖给同 grant, present

aware / əˈweə / adj. 知道的;意识到的;Are you ～ that you have hurt her feelings? 你有没有觉察到你已经伤害了她的感情? / I became ～ how he might feel. 我意识到他会有怎样的感受。同 conscious, informed / **be ～ of** 觉察到;意识到;He wasn't ～ of the danger. 他没意识到有危险。

away / əˈweɪ / adv. 远离;离开;走开;do ～ with 废除;去掉/ She went ～. 她走开了。

awe / ɔː / n. [U]敬畏;敬佩;Deep ～ fell upon them all. 众人不禁凛然敬畏。/The book is worth our ～. 这是一本值得我们肃然起敬的书。/ **in ～ of** 敬畏;They stand in ～ of Charles. 他们非常敬畏查尔斯。

awful / ˈɔːfl / adj. 非常的;极坏的;A million dollars is an ～lot of money. 100万美元是非常大的一笔钱。同 great, bad 派 awfully adv.

awkward / ˈɔːkwəd / adj. 笨拙的;为难的;尴尬的;in an ～ situation 处境尴尬/ an ～ problem 棘手的问题同 trying, tough

ax(e) / æks / n. [C] ❶斧头 ❷(经费、人员等的)削减;give sb. the ～解雇某人/ His father got the ～ last month. 上月他的父亲被解雇了。同 dismiss, reduce

axis / ˈæksɪs / n. (pl. axes)轴;轴线;中心线;on an ～在轴心上/ ～ of communication 交通干线

axle / ˈæksl / n. [C]车轴;轮轴同 axis

B

B b

baby / ˈbeɪbi / n. [C] ❶婴儿;～hood n. 婴儿期/ ～ish adj. 孩子气的 同 infant ❷幼畜

baby-sit / ˈbeɪbɪˌsɪt / (-sat; -sitting) vt. 代人临时照看小小孩:～ with sb's children during church service 教堂做礼拜时为某人照看孩子

bachelor / ˈbætʃələ(r) / n. [C] ❶学士;学士学位:～'s degree 学士学位/Bachelor of Arts 文学士(简作 BA)/ Bachelor of Science 理学士(简作 BS) ❷未婚男子;单身汉

back / bæk / Ⅰ adv. 回;向后:Please put the book ～ on the shelf. 请把书放回书架上。❷backward forth, forward Ⅱ n. 背,脊背,后面:If you lie on your ～, you can see the sky. 你若仰卧,就能望见天空。同 rear 反 front/～ and forth (= backwards and forwards)来回:She walked ～ and forth along the shore. 她在岸边来回走动。Ⅲ adj. 后面的;背面的:Please go out through the ～ door. 请从后门出去。同 rear 反 front Ⅳ v. 支持:Many of his friends ～ed his plan. 他的很多朋友支持他的计划。同 support/～ up 支持:Don't worry. They will ～ us up. 别着急,他们会支持我们的。

backache / ˈbækeɪk / n. 背痛

backbone / ˈbækˌbəʊn / n. ❶[C]脊,脊骨,脊柱 ❷[U]骨气;勇气;毅力:He showed real ～ in the crisis period. 在危机时期他表现出真正的骨气。❸[C]骨干;栋梁;支柱;基础:Agriculture is the ～ of the economy. 农业是经济的基础。

background / ˈbækɡraʊnd / n. [C]背景;经历:in the ～暗中;幕后 同 setting, experiences

backing / ˈbækɪŋ / n. [U]支持;后盾;帮助;资助:financial ～财政上的支持

backspace / ˈbækspeɪs / Ⅰ vt. 退后一格 Ⅱ n. 退格:～ key (计算机的)退格键

backward / ˈbækwəd / Ⅰ adj. ❶向后的 同 back, rearward 反 forward ❷倒的;相反的 同 back, reversed ❸落后的;(进展)缓慢的 同 undeveloped, slow 反 advanced, fast

Ⅱ adv. ❶向后:He looked ～ to see if his mother was following him. 他向后看看是不是妈妈跟在后面。同 back 反 forth, forward ❷倒;逆:go ～ 倒退;退步 同 back 反 forward

backyard / ˌbækˈjɑːd / n. [C]庭院;后院

bacon / ˈbeɪkən / n. 咸猪肉;熏猪肉

bacteria / bækˈtɪərɪə / n. (bacterium 的复数)细菌:harmful ～有害细菌/ destroy(kill) ～消灭细菌

bacteriology / bækˌtɪərɪˈblədʒi / n. 细菌学

bacterial / bækˈtɪərɪə / n. 细菌的;细菌引起的:～ infection 细菌感染

bad / bæd / (worse, worst) Ⅰ adj. ❶坏的;恶劣的;不道德的:We hate ～ people and things. 我们讨厌不道德的人和事。同 evil, immoral 反 good, moral ❷(价值、质量等)低劣的:This kind of tea is very ～. 这种茶质量极差。同 poor, inferior ❸有害的;不利的:Smoking is ～ for health. 吸烟有害健康。同 harmful, hurtful 反 harmless, beneficial ❹严重的;厉害的:She had a ～ cold yesterday. 昨天她患了重感冒。同 serious, severe ❺病的;痛的;不舒服的:He had a ～ nose. 他鼻子疼。同 ill, sick 反 healthy, well ❻(食物等)腐败的:The food went ～. 食物坏了。同 decayed, rotten 反 fresh ❼错误的;不适当的:It's a ～ idea. 这主意不好。同 wrong, unsound 反 right, sound ❽使人不愉快的;讨厌的:～ manners 没有礼貌 同 unpleasant, unwelcome 反 pleasant, welcome Ⅱ adv. (= badly)恶劣地;拙劣地;严重地

badge / bædʒ / n. [C]徽章;像章:a school ～校徽/ a police ～警徽

badly / ˈbædli / (worse, worst) adv. ❶坏;恶劣地;卑鄙地 同 basely, meanly 反 well ❷有缺点地;拙劣地:He writes ～. 他书写很糟。同 poorly, unskillfully 反 well ❸严重地;非常:She is ～ ill. 她病得厉害。同 greatly, terribly

badminton / ˈbædmɪntən / n. 羽毛球

baffle / ˈbæfl / *vt.* 使困惑,使迷惑;使为难;难倒;It ~d me that they rejected our offer. 他们居然拒绝我们的建议,我百思不得其解。/Her disease had long ~d the skill of her physicians. 她的病早就使她的医生感到束手无策。

bag / bæg / *n.* [C]提包;口袋;书包:a travelling ~ 旅行袋 / a money ~ 钱袋

baggage / ˈbæɡɪdʒ / *n.* (＝[英]luggage)[U](美)行李:~ train 行李车/ ~ office 行李房/ claim one's ~ 认领行李 同 luggage,suitcases

bait / beɪt / Ⅰ *n.* 饵;引诱物;诱惑;Little boys are easy to take (swallow,rise to) the ~. 小男孩很容易上当。同 lure,attraction Ⅱ *vt.* 引诱;诱惑 同 lure,attract

bake / beɪk / *vt.* 烘,焙(面包等):The cook ~s bread and cake in the oven. 厨师用烤箱烤面包和饼。同 toast

balance / ˈbæləns / Ⅰ *n.* ❶天平;秤 同 scales ❷平衡;均衡:~ beam 平衡木/ ~ development 均衡发展 Ⅱ *v.* 用天平称;权衡,对比 同 weigh,compare

balcony / ˈbælkəni / *n.* [C]阳台;露台

bald / bɔːld / *adj.* ❶(头)秃的;秃头的:He went ~ very young. 他很年轻时就秃顶了。同 bald-headed,hairless 反 hairy ❷无毛的;无树的;光秃的:The hill became ~ only within three years. 仅仅三年时间,那小山就变得光秃秃的了。同 hairless,featherless,treeless ❸毫不掩饰的;赤裸裸的:It is just a ~ lie. 这简直是赤裸裸的谎言。同 bare,naked

bale / beɪl / *n.* [C](货物捆扎成的)大包,大捆:a ~ of cotton 一大包棉花/a ~ of hay 一大捆干草

ball / bɔːl / *n.* [C] ❶球:a ~ game (match)一场球赛 ❷舞会:They had a ~ after work. 下班后他们举行了一场舞会。

ballet / ˈbæleɪ / *n.* 芭蕾(舞);芭蕾舞剧团:dance a ~ 跳芭蕾舞/ a ~dancer 芭蕾舞演员/ water ~ 水上芭蕾

balloon / bəˈluːn / *n.* [C]气球:an ad. ~ 广告气球

ball(-)point / ˈbɔːlpɔɪnt / *n.* [C]圆珠笔,原子笔

bamboo / ˌbæmˈbuː / *n.* [U]竹

ban / bæn / Ⅰ *n.* [C]禁止;禁令:There is a ~ on shouting here. 禁止在此高声喧哗。同 prohibition Ⅱ (banned;banning)*vt.* 禁止;取缔:He ~ned the workers from smoking in the workshop. 他禁止工人们在车间里吸烟。同 forbid,prohibit 反 allow

banana / bəˈnɑːnə / *n.* [C] 香蕉:a hand of ~s 一串香蕉

band[1] / bænd / *n.* [C] ❶管乐队:string~ 管弦乐队/ military~ 军乐队/ rock-~ 摇滚乐队/ jazz ~ 爵士乐队 同 orchestra,company ❷一帮;一伙:a ~ of robbers 一帮(伙)土匪 同 party,gang ❸(收音机)波段

band[2] / bænd / Ⅰ *n.* [C]带;带状物:He always wears a ~ round his head. 他总是在头上扎一根带子。同 strip,belt Ⅱ *vt.* (用带子)绑,扎 同 bind,tie 反 untie,loosen

bandage / ˈbændɪdʒ / Ⅰ *n.* [C]绷带:put on a ~ 包扎 Ⅱ *vt.* 用绷带包扎

bang / bæŋ / Ⅰ *v.* ❶猛敲;猛撞;猛地关上:Don't ~ at (on) the door. 不要砰砰打门。同 strike,hit ❷砰砰作响 Ⅱ *n.* 猛敲;猛撞;砰砰的声音:with a ~ 砰的一声

bandit / ˈbændɪt / *n.* [C]土匪;强盗:~ and tyrant on road 车匪路霸 同 thief,robber

banish / ˈbænɪʃ / *vt.* ❶流放;放逐:~ sb. from a country 驱逐某人出境 同 exile,expel ❷消除;排除(顾虑、恐惧等):~ worries from heart 排除心中的忧虑 同 remove,dismiss 派 banishment *n.*

bank[1] / bæŋk / *n.* [C] ❶(河、海、湖的)岸;堤:construct a ~ 修筑河堤/ His company is on the south ~ of the river. 他的公司在河的南岸。/ I often take a walk along the ~ after supper. 晚饭后我常沿着河岸散步。同 shore ❷埂;垄;堆:a ~ of snow 一堆雪 同 ridge,mass,pile

bank[2] / bæŋk / *n.* [C] ❶银行:a ~ account 银行账户/ a book 银行存折/ ~ deposit 银行存款/an investment ~ 投资银行/ a commercial ~ 商业银行 ❷库;库房:a talents ~ 人才库/ a blood ~ 血库/ a gene ~ 基因库/ a data ~ 信息库/ a question ~ 试题库 同 store,storehouse

banker / ˈbæŋkə(r) / *n.* [C]银行家

banking / ˈbæŋkɪŋ / *n.* 银行业;银行学;金融:~ hours 银行营业时间/ ~ service 银行服务

banknote / ˈbæŋknəut / *n.* [C]纸币;钞票 同 bill

B

bankrupt / ˈbæŋkrʌpt / Ⅰ *n.* [C]破产者 Ⅱ *adj.* 破产的;无力偿还的:go ～ 破产/ The company is to be declared ～. 那家公司即将宣告破产。同 broke,ruined

bankruptcy / ˈbæŋkrʌptsi / *n.* 破产;倒闭:～ law 破产法 / file for (declare) ～ 申请(宣布)破产

banner / ˈbænə(r) / *n.* [C]旗,旗帜;横幅:welcoming ～ 欢迎条幅 同 flag

banquet / ˈbæŋkwɪt / *n.* [C]宴会;盛宴:state ～ 国宴/ wedding ～ 婚宴/ ～hall 宴会厅/ farewell (welcome) ～ 告别(欢迎)宴会 同 dinner,feast

bar / baː(r) / Ⅰ *n.* [C] ❶小酒店;酒吧:They went to the ～ together. 他们一道去了酒吧。同 pub,saloon ❷条;杆;棒:～ code 条码;条形码/ There are seven iron ～s across his window. 他的窗子上钉有七根铁条。同 rod,pole ❸栏;栅;障碍物:It is the ～ to success. 这就是成功的障碍。同 barrier Ⅱ *vt.* (barred,barring)闩上;阻挡:Please ～ the door after you. 请把门闩上。

barbarous / ˈbɑːbərəs / *adj.* ❶野蛮的;残暴的;未开化的 同 brutal,cruel,uncivilized

barbecue / ˈbɑːbɪkjuː / *n.* [C]烧烤:have a ～ 举行烧烤野餐

barber / ˈbɑːbə(r) / *n.* [C]理发师:I had a haircut at the ～'s yesterday. 我昨天在理发店理了发。

bare / beə(r) / *adj.* 赤裸的;光秃秃的:The hill is ～ of trees. 这座山上没有树。

barely / ˈbeəli / *adv.* 好容易才;几乎不能;勉强:He ～ has money to support his family. 他几乎没钱养活家人。同 hardly,only

bargain / ˈbɑːgən / Ⅰ *n.* [C] ❶合同;买卖契约;交易:black market ～s 黑市交易/ We made a ～ at last. 我们终于达成交易。❷廉价品;特价品 Ⅱ *v.* 谈判;订合同;讨价还价:He doesn't know how to ～ in the market. 他不知道在市场上买东西如何讨价还价。

barge / bɑːdʒ / *n.* [C]驳船;游艇

barium / ˈbeəriəm / *n.* [U]钡

bark¹ / bɑːk / *n.* 树皮

bark² / bɑːk / Ⅰ *vi.* (狗)吠,叫:The dog ～s at him. 这狗对着他叫。Ⅱ *n.* 狗或狐狸的叫声:She cannot endure the ～ of that dog. 她不能

忍受那条狗的叫声。

barley / ˈbɑːli / *n.* [U]大麦

barn / bɑːn / *n.* [C] ❶谷仓 ❷(美)马房;牛舍

barometer / bəˈrɒmɪtə(r) / *n.* [C]晴雨表;气压表

baron / ˈbærən / *n.* [C] ❶男爵;贵族 同 nobleman ❷巨商:a ～ of industry 工业巨子/ an oil ～ 石油大王 / a coal ～ 煤炭大王

barrel / ˈbærəl / *n.* [C]大桶

barrier / ˈbæriə(r) / *n.* [C]障碍;阻碍;关卡:set up ～s on the road 设立路障/overcome language ～s 克服语言障碍 同 bar,obstacle

base / beɪs / Ⅰ *n.* [C]底部;基础;基地:a ～ for export and foreign exchange earning 出口创汇基地/ Shanghai is one of the most important industrial ～s in China. 上海是中国最重要的工业基地之一。同 basis,foundation Ⅱ *v.* 基于:～ **on** 基于;以……作根据:Socialism ～s itself on materialism. 社会主义以唯物论为基础。同 place,establish

baseball / ˈbeɪsbɔːl / *n.* 棒球;棒球运动

basement / ˈbeɪsmənt / *n.* 地下室;底层;基部 同 foundation

bash / bæʃ / Ⅰ *vt.* 猛击;猛撞:～ a door in 把门撞开/ ～ one's head on the wall 用头猛撞墙 Ⅱ *n.* [C]猛击;重击;猛撞:a ～ in the face 脸上重重地挨了一拳

basic / ˈbeɪsɪk / *adj.* 基本的;基础的:a ～ principle 基本原则/a ～ problem 基本问题/ the ～ vocabulary 基本词汇/ ～ state policy 基本国策/ ～ subject 基础学科 同 fundamental,essential

basin / ˈbeɪsn / *n.* [C] ❶水盆;面盆 ❷盆地;流域

basis / ˈbeɪsɪs / *n.* [C](*pl.* bases / ˈbeɪsiːz /)基础;根据:economic ～ 经济基础/ theoretical

～理论依据 圊 base,foundation

basket / ˈbɑːskɪt / *n.* [C]篮子;筐:a ～ of fruit 一篮水果

basketball / ˈbɑːskɪtbɔːl / *n.* 篮球;篮球运动: play ～ 打篮球

bass¹ / beɪs / Ⅰ *n.* 男低音:sing ～ 唱男低音/ sing in ～ 用男低音唱 Ⅱ *adj.* 低音的

bass² / bæs / *n.* 鲈鱼

bastard / ˈbæstəd / *n.* [C]私生子

bat¹ / bæt / Ⅰ *n.* [C]球拍 Ⅱ *v.* 击球 圊 strike,hit

bat² / bæt / *n.* [C]蝙蝠:as blind as a ～ 和蝙蝠 一样瞎的;有眼无珠

batch / bætʃ / *n.* [C]批;批次;整批(货);～ number 批号/ in ～ es 成批;分批 圊 bunch,lot

bath / bɑːθ / *n.* [C]洗澡:Have a hot ～. 洗一 个热水澡吧!

bathe / beɪð / *vi.* 洗澡:～ in cold water 洗冷 水浴/ ～in sweat 汗流浃背/ ～in tears 泪流 满面/ I often ～ in the river in summer. 我夏 天常去河里洗澡。圊 wash

baton / ˈbætən,bəˈtɒn / *n.* ❶(乐队、歌唱队指 挥用的)指挥棒 ❷短棍;短棒;警棍 ❸(接力赛 跑用的)接力棒

batter / ˈbætə(r) / *v.* 持续打击;(以连续猛 击)捣毁,砸烂;重创:Blizzards ～ ed Britain for the third day. 暴风雨连续三天袭击英 国。/They have been known to ～ their children. 大家都知道,他们经常殴打孩子。

battery / ˈbætəri / *n.* [C]电池(组):dry ～ 干 电池/ charge a ～ 给电池充电

battle / ˈbætl / *n.* [C]战役;战斗;会战:We should fight a ～ against pollution. 我们应当 与环境污染作斗争。圊 fight,combat

辨 析

battle 意为"战役;战斗;拼搏",指有组织的 部队之间的战役,通常持续时间较久,也指 短兵相接的战斗:The battle lasted ten years. 这场战争打了 10 年。a hand-to-hand battle 一场短兵相接的战斗。**engagement** 意 为"战斗;交战",指实际交战:The admiral tried to bring about an engagement. 海军上 将设法使战斗打响。**war** 意为"战争",指规 模和影响都较大的武装斗争:The Second World War ended in 1945. 第二次世界大战 于 1945 年结束。

bay / beɪ / *n.* [C]海湾 圊 gulf,harbor

bayonet / ˈbeɪənət / *n.* [C]刺刀

BBC (= British Broadcasting Corporation) 英 国广播公司

BC,B.C. (= Before Christ)公元前(写在年 代之后)

be / biː,bɪ / *v.* (现在式 am,is,are;过去式 was, were;过去分词 been;现在分词 being) ❶ *vi.* 是;成为;存在;有:Horses are animals. 马是动 物。/ Knowledge is power. 知识就是力量。/ Has the postman been here yet? 邮递员来 过了吗?/ He was a doctor. 他当过医生。❷ *aux. v.* (助动词,帮助构成时态、语态):English is taught in our school. 我们学校教英语。 / I was lying in bed when the teacher came. 老 师来时,我正躺在床上。

beach / biːtʃ / *n.* [C]海滩;海滨;bathing ～ 海 滨浴场 圊 coast,seashore

bead / biːd / *n.* [C] ❶(有孔的)小珠:the ～ s of a necklace 项链上的珠子 ❷(汗、血等的)小 滴;水珠:～ s of sweat 滴滴汗珠/ ～ s of dew 露珠/ draw a ～ on 瞄准:The marksman drew a ～ on his garget. 神枪手瞄准了靶子。

beak / biːk / *n.* [C](鸟的)嘴;喙

beam / biːm / *n.* [C] ❶(光线的)束,柱: a ～ of hope 一线希望/ a laster ～ 一束激光 圊 ray ❷梁;横梁;横木:The ～s can bear the weight of the roof. 横梁能够承受屋顶的重量。

bean / biːn / *n.* [C]豆

bear¹ / beə(r) / *n.* [C]熊

bear² / beə(r) / *vt.* (bore / bɔː /,borne 或 born / bɔːn /) ❶忍受;支持;负担:I cannot ～ wet weather. 我受不了潮湿的天气。圊 stand,tolerate ❷生(孩子):She was born in 1958. 她生 于 1958 年。❸怀有;抱有:I'll ～ your advice in mind. 我将记住你的忠告。圊 hold

beard / bɪəd / *n.* [C] 胡 子;须 圊 mustache,whisker

bearing / ˈbeərɪŋ / *n.* ❶支撑 圊 support ❷忍 受;忍耐:beyond ～ 难以忍受 圊 enduring ❸ 生产;结果;结实 圊 production

beast / biːst / *n.* [C]兽:wild ～ 野兽 圊 animal

beat / biːt / *v.* (beat,beaten / ˈbiːtn /)打,敲; (心脏)跳动:Stop ～ing him. 不要打他了!/ Her heart ～ madly with fright. 由于惊吓她 的心狂跳不已。/ ～ the record 打破纪录 圊 strike,hit 派 beating *n.*

B

beat 通常指连续地敲打,也指有意识的举动:The thief beat his head. 这贼击打他的头。**hit** 指瞄准目标给予重击:We hit the enemy hard one after another. 我们给敌人一次又一次的沉重打击。**strike** 是普通用语,常指突然用刀、手或其他东西打击:He hit me. I struck him back. 他打中了我,我也还手打了他。

beautiful / ˈbjuːtɪfl / *adj.* 美丽的;优美的:the true, the good, the ～ 真善美 / The girl is ～. 这女孩真美。同 pretty, attractive 派 beautifully *adv.*

beautiful 意为"美丽的",普通用语,一般用以形容女性,也可形容事物,偶尔也用来形容男性外貌,但有贬义:She is too beautiful for words. 她的美无法用言语来形容。**fair** 多用于形容女性,常用于诗歌或古语中:a fair lady 美丽的少女。**handsome** 意为"英俊的;漂亮的",可形容人或物,主要用于形容英俊、健壮的男人。若形容女性,常指健康、举止大方的漂亮成年女性:What a handsome building! 多么美的建筑物! He is a handsome fellow. 他是个英俊的小伙子。**lovely** 意为"好看的;可爱的",多指在个人感情因素影响下认为可爱、好看:What a lovely day it is! 今天天气真好! She is such a lovely girl. 她如此可爱。**pretty** 意为"漂亮的;可爱的",常指文雅、有魅力的人,也指伶俐、活泼的少女或小孩,也可形容事物:What a pretty girl! 多么漂亮的女孩! a pretty house 漂亮的房子。

beautify / ˈbjuːtɪfaɪ / *v.* 使美丽;美化;装饰:～ our life 美化生活 / ～ the environment 美化环境 同 decorate

beauty / ˈbjuːti / *n.* ❶[U]美;美丽:wholesome ～ 健康美 / ～ culture 美容术(业)❷[C]美人;美的东西:choose the ～;a ～ pageant 选美比赛

because / bɪˈkɒz / *conj.* 因为:He didn't come ～ he was ill. 他病了,所以没来。同 as, since / ～ **of** 由于;因为:He didn't attend the meeting ～ of his illness. 他因病没来开会。

beckon / ˈbekən / *v.* (以招手、点头等)示意;召唤:The guide ～ed us to follow him. 导游示意我们跟着他。/ He ～ed and the girl came over. 他招了招手,那姑娘就走了过来。

become / bɪˈkʌm / *vi.* (became / bɪˈkeɪm /, become) 变成;成为:China will ～ a modern and strong socialist country. 中国将成为现代化的社会主义强国。同 grow, turn

bed / bed / *n.* [C] ❶床;床位:go to ～ 睡觉;就寝 / make the ～ 整理床铺 / double (single) ～ 双(单)人床 ❷苗床;苗圃:seed ～ 苗圃 / a flower ～ 花坛 ❸河床;海底;湖底:You can see the river ～ under the water there. 在那里你可以看到水下的河床。同 river-bed, sea-bed, lake-bed

bedding / ˈbedɪŋ / *n.* [U]被褥;卧具 同 bed-clothes

bedroom / ˈbedruːm / *n.* [C]寝室;卧室:His ～ is under mine. 他的寝室就在我楼下。

bedtime / ˈbedtaɪm / *n.* 就寝时间;睡觉时间:My ～ is about eleven o'clock. 我就寝的时间大约是 11 点。

bee / biː / *n.* [C]蜜蜂

beef / biːf / *n.* [C](*pl.* beeves / biːvz /)牛肉;菜牛:～-steak 牛排

beer / bɪə(r) / *n.* [U]啤酒

beet / biːt / *n.* 甜菜;糖萝卜

beetle / ˈbiːtl / *n.* [C] ❶甲虫 ❷眼睛近视的人

befall / bɪˈfɔːl / *vt.* (-fell/-ˈfel/, -fallen /-ˈfɔːlən/)(通常指不幸的事)发生于;降临于:Bad luck and ill health ～ him throughout his life. 他一生都不走运,而且病魔缠身。

before / bɪˈfɔː(r) / Ⅰ *prep.* 在…以前:Must I be home ～ eight o'clock? 我 8 点钟前必须在家吗? Ⅱ *conj.* 在…以前:Think well ～ you decide. 决定之前应好好想想。反 after Ⅲ *adv.* 以前:I haven't seen her ～. 我以前没有见过她。/ ～ **long** 不久:I'll get the dictionary ～ long. 我不久就会得到这本词典。**long** ～ 很久以前:I saw her long ～. 我很久以前看见过她。

❶before 作为连词引导时间状语从句时,从句中的时态用现在时代替将来时,用过去时代替过去将来时:I must finish my work before I go home. 我必须完成工作后再回家。❷before 作副词时常置于句末,句子用完成时态:I haven't done it before. 我以前从未做过此事。

beforehand / bɪˈfɔːhænd / *adv.* 预先;事先;提前地:You should tell me the news ～. 你应当事先把那个消息告诉我。同 previously

B

befriend / bɪˈfrend / *vt.* 友好对待；亲近；与…交朋友：The children ～ed the lost dog. 孩子们亲近迷了路的狗。/She ～ed the new girl in class. 她与班上新来的女同学交上了朋友。

beg / beg / *v.* (begged；begging) 请求；乞求 同 ask，request；"I ～ your pardon" 请某人再说一遍 ～ **sb. to do sth.** 请求某人做某事。/ I ～ged him to excuse me for doing such a foolish thing. 我请求他原谅我做的蠢事。～ **for sth.** 请求得到某物：He ～ged for my help. 他恳求我的帮助。

beggar / ˈbegə(r) / *n.* [C] 乞丐；穷人

begin / bɪˈgɪn / *v.* (began／bɪˈgæn／，begun／bɪˈgʌn／；beginning) 开始：Classes ～ at eight in the morning. 早上 8 点钟开始上课。/ When did you ～ to study English? 你什么时候开始学英语的？同 start 反 end，stop

> **辨析**
>
> **begin** 是常用词，意义广泛(反义词为 end)：We'll begin our work soon. 我们马上开始工作。**commence** 较 begin 更正式，多用于书面语中，表示研究工作、仪式、典礼等的开始：The evening party will commence right after the dinner. 宴会一结束，晚会就开始。**start** 强调做某事的第一步：They started for Shanghai last night. 昨晚他们起程去上海了。

beginner / bɪˈgɪnə(r) / *n.* [C] ❶初学者；生手：This is a book for ～. 这是一本初学者的入门书。同 green-hand ❷创始人：They said that he was the ～ of the impressionist. 他们说他是印象派的创始人。同 founder

beginning / bɪˈgɪnɪŋ / *n.* 开始；开端；起源：at the ～ (of) 在开始时；起初/ from the ～ to the end 自始至终；从头到尾/ I'll read the book from the very ～ to see if I can find something useful for me. 我要从头读读这本书，看看能否找到有用的东西。同 start，origin

behalf / bɪˈhɑːf / *n.* 为帮助某人；支持 同 sake，benefit／**on ～ of** 代表；为了：The lawyer spoke on ～ of his client convincingly. 那位律师代表他的当事人所说的话令人信服。

behave / bɪˈheɪv / *v.* 行为；举止；为人：He ～d well. 他为人好。/ Behave yourself. 放规矩点。同 act，conduct

behavio(u)r / bɪˈheɪvjə(r) / *n.* [U] 行为；举止；表现：Her good ～ deserves praise. 她的良好表现值得称赞。同 act，conduct，manner

behind / bɪˈhaɪnd / **Ⅰ** *prep.* 在…后面：The

clock is a little ～ time. 这钟走得稍微慢了一点。同 after 反 before **Ⅱ** *adv.* 在后；向后：Please look ～. 请向后看。

being / ˈbiːɪŋ / (be 的现在分词形式) *n.* ❶[U] 存在；生存；**come into ～** 形成；产生：We do not know when the world came into ～. 我们不知道世界是何时产生的。同 existence ❷[C] 生物；存在物：a human ～ 人/. living ～s 生物 同 creature，human

belief / bɪˈliːf / (*pl.* beliefs) *n.* 信心；信念；信仰：religious ～ 宗教信仰/ I don't think it is right to laugh at other's ～. 我认为嘲笑别人的信仰是不对的。同 confidence，trust

> **辨析**
>
> **belief** 多指宗教信仰：He decided to give up his personal belief. 他决定放弃个人的信仰。**faith** 指坚定不移的信念，也可指宗教信仰：I have faith in his ability to succeed. 我相信他有取得成功的能耐。**trust** 意为"信任；信赖"：He is never the sort of man to be trusted. 他根本不是一个可信任的人。**confidence** 指根据经验、证据证实某人或某事可靠，值得信任：Don't put too much confidence in what he said. 不要过分相信他说的话。

believe / bɪˈliːv / *v.* 相信；认为：I ～ what you said. 我相信你说的话。同 trust，accept／～ **in** 相信；信任；信仰：I ～ in his honesty. 我相信他的诚实。

belittle / bɪˈlɪtl / *vt.* 轻视；小看；贬低：～ sb's merits 贬低某人的优点/～ sb's achievements 贬低某人的成就

bell / bel / *n.* [C]钟；铃：door～ 门铃；sound the ～ 敲钟/ The ～ rings. 铃声响了。

bellicose / ˈbelɪkəʊs / *adj.* 好战的；好争斗的；好吵架的：a ～ people 好战的民族/His facial expression was unpleasantly ～. 他脸上露出一副气势汹汹的样子，令人讨厌。

bellow / ˈbeləʊ / **Ⅰ** *v.* 怒吼；吼叫：Don't ～ at little children. 别对小孩大吼大叫。同 shout，roar **Ⅱ** *n.* 怒吼声；吼叫声 同 cry，roar

belly / ˈbeli / *n.* [C]腹部；肚子；胃：have a large ～ 大腹便便

belong / bɪˈlɒŋ / *vi.* 属于：～ **to** 属于：That dictionary ～s to her. 那本词典是她的。/ Li Ning ～s to our team. 李宁是我们队的队员。

belongings / bɪˈlɒŋɪŋz / *n.* 附属物；所属物；财产：personal ～ 个人财产/ After they packed up

B

their 〜, they left the room. 收拾好自己的东西后，他们便离开了房间。同 property, possessions

beloved / bɪ'lʌvd / adj. 敬爱的；受到爱戴的：The teacher is 〜 by all. 这位老师受到大家的爱戴。同 loved 反 disliked

below / bɪ'ləʊ / I adv. 在下方：Is it above or 〜? 它在上面还是在下面？同 under, beneath 反 above, over II prep. 在…下面：The Dead Sea is 〜 sea level. 死海的海面低于海平面。同 under, beneath 反 above, over

辨析

below 表示某物位置低于所提及的事物（反义词为 above）：The sun sinks below the horizon. 太阳落到地平线下。under 表示某物处于垂直向下的位置（反义词为 over）：The cat was under the table. 猫在桌子下面。beneath 是比较正式的用语，多为文言或诗歌用词，表示"低于；在…之下"之意时与 below, under 同义、同用法：We shall have a rest beneath the tree. 我们要在树下休息一会儿。beneath 表示"在…底下"之意时，则指面与面的接触（反义词为 on）。

belt / belt / n. [C]带子；皮带：life 〜 安全带；救生带 同 string, ribbon

bench / bentʃ / n. [C]长凳：warm on the 〜（体育比赛中）当替补队员 / work 〜 工作台

bend / bend / v. (bent/bent/, bent) 弯曲；弄弯；屈身：His head was bent so low. 他的头垂得很低。同 curve, bow 反 stretch, straighten

beneath / bɪ'niːθ / I prep. 在…之下：〜 the average 在平均值以下 同 under II adv. 在下方 同 under, below 反 above, over

beneficial / ˌbenɪ'fɪʃl / adj. 有益的；有利的；有助的：Eating apples is 〜 to health. 吃苹果有益健康。同 helpful, useful 反 harmful, useless

benefit / 'benɪfɪt / I n. 利益；好处：Your advice is of good 〜 to me. 你的劝告对我很有益。同 profit, advantage 反 loss, disadvantage II v. 得益；有益于：We 〜ed greatly by this frank talk. 我们从这次坦率的谈话中获益匪浅。同 profit, gain

benevolence / bə'nevələns / n. [U] ❶仁慈；善行：He gave the little girl 10 dollars out of 〜. 出于仁慈之心，他给了那小女孩 10 美元。同 kindness, charity ❷捐助物；捐款：A lot of people contributed 〜 after the tsunami. 海啸发生后，很多人都去捐款。同 beneficence, gift 派 benevolent adj.

benign / bɪ'naɪn / adj. ❶善良的；和蔼的；亲切的：a 〜 old man 和蔼的老人/the 〜 features of Mr. Potts 波茨先生慈祥的面容 ❷（疾病）对生命不构成危险的；（肿瘤等）良性的：a 〜 illness 不危及生命的疾病/a 〜 tumour 良性肿瘤

bent / bent / I v. (bend 的过去式和过去分词) 弯曲 II adj. 弯曲的；曲背的：The old farmer's back was 〜 from years of toil. 这位老农因长年劳累而驼了背。同 curved, twisted 反 straight

benumbed / bɪ'nʌmd / adj. 僵冷的；僵硬的；失去知觉的：fingers 〜 with the cold 冻僵的手指

berry / 'beri / n. [C]浆果；莓

beside / bɪ'saɪd / prep. 在…旁；在…附近；在…之外：the point 离题；The young man is 〜 the bus. 那位年轻人站在汽车旁。同 next, beyond

besides / bɪ'saɪdz / I prep. 除…之外，还有：There are many other places to visit in China 〜 Suzhou. 除苏州外，中国还有许多地方可游览。II adv. 而且；此外：She doesn't like it. Besides, she can't afford it. 她不喜欢也买不起它。同 moreover, furthermore

besiege / bɪ'siːdʒ / vt. ❶包围；围攻；围困：They were 〜d for six months but refused to surrender. 他们已被围困了 6 个月，但仍拒绝投降。❷挤在…的周围；围住：Employment agencies were 〜d by the jobless. 职业介绍所被失业者围了个水泄不通。

best / best / (good, well 的最高级形式) I adj. 最好的：She is my 〜 friend at school. 她是我学生时代最好的朋友。同 excellent, supreme 反 worst II adv. 〜 the point 离题；Which book do you like 〜? 你最喜欢哪本书？同 excellently, most III n. 最佳；全力 同 first, top / **do one's** 〜 尽力；努力：I'll do my 〜 to study English well. 我将尽全力把英语学好。**make the** 〜 **of** 充分利用：You should make the 〜 of this valuable opportunity. 你应该充分利用这个宝贵的机会。

bestow / bɪ'stəʊ / vt. 把…赠与；把…给予：〜 a doctorate on sb. 给某人授博士学位/Several gifts were 〜ed on the royal visitors. 谒见国王的人被赠与一些礼物。派 bestowal n.

best-seller / 'best'selə / n. [C]畅销书：His new book became the 〜 that year. 他的新书成了那年的畅销书。

bet / bet / I n. [C]打赌；赌金；赌注：Let's

make a ～. 让我们打个赌。圆 gamble Ⅱ v.
(bet 或 betted；betting)赌；打赌；敢断定：I ～
she will come. 我敢断定她会来的。圆 gamble

betray / bɪ'treɪ / vt. ❶不忠；She ～ed her
promises. 她未遵守诺言。❷出卖：They ～ed
their country. 他们出卖了自己的国家。❸泄
露；暴露：What you said ～ed your ignorance.
你所说的话暴露出了你的无知。圆 expose，reveal 派 betrayal n.

better / 'betə(r) / (good，well 的比较级形式)
Ⅰ adj. 较好的；更好的：Milk is ～ for babies
than soybean milk. 对婴儿来说，牛奶比豆奶
好。圆 finer 反 worse Ⅱ adv. 较好地；更好地：
She swims ～ than her brother does. 她游泳比
她弟弟游得好。Ⅲ v. 改善：They tried to ～
their living conditions. 他们努力改善生活条
件。圆 improve，refine 反 worsen/ had ～最好
(后接动词原形)：You'd ～ put on your coat.
你最好穿上外衣。

between / bɪ'twiːn / prep. 在…之间(一般指
两者之间)：～ the lines 在字里行间(体会言
外之意)/ What's the difference ～ this and
that? 这个和那个之间有什么区别?

beverage / 'bevərɪdʒ / n. [U]饮料(如牛奶、茶、
咖啡、啤酒等)：alcoholic ～ 含酒精饮料/
cooling ～ 清凉饮料

beware / bɪ'weə(r) / v. 谨防；当心：～ of fire
当心火烛；当心失火 圆 mind

bewilder / bɪ'wɪldə(r) / vt. 迷惑；弄糊涂；使
发愣；使为难：He was so ～ed that he didn't
know what to do. 他茫然不知所措。圆 puzzle，
confuse

辨析

bewilder 语气比 confuse 强，有因困惑而不知
所措之意。confound 强调由于惊吓或其他原
因而不知所措：His behaviour confounded us.
他的所作所为让我们感到困惑。confuse 指
思绪混乱，动作不听使唤：I am absolutely
confused by the noise. 这噪声弄得我心烦意
乱。puzzle 常指因问题复杂而产生的"迷惑"
"迷乱"：The letter puzzled me. 这封信让我
迷惑不解。

bewitch / bɪ'wɪtʃ / vt. 使入迷；使着魔；使神
魂颠倒：be ～ed by a glorious sunset 为壮丽
的日落景象所陶醉/Shirley Temple ～ed a
generation of moviegoers. 秀兰·邓波儿倾倒
了一代电影观众。

beyond / bɪ'jɒnd / prep. 超出…(的范围)：

This is ～ my capacity. 这非我能力所及。圆
over，exceeding

biannual / baɪ'ænjuəl / adj. 一年两次的：～
congress 两年召开一次的大会

bias / 'baɪəs / Ⅰ n. [C] ❶斜线 ❷偏见；倾向
性；癖好：He always has a ～ against his son.
他总是对自己的儿子有偏见。Ⅱ vt. 对…有偏
见；有倾向性 圆 prejudice，incline 派
biased adj.

Bible / 'baɪbl / n. (the Bible)《圣经》；swear on
the ～ 手按《圣经》发誓

bibliography / ˌbɪblɪ'ɒɡrəfi / n. ❶[C]书目提
要；文献目录 ❷[U]目录学；文献学

bicycle / 'baɪsɪkl / n. [C]自行车

bid / bɪd / (bade 或 bid，bidden 或 bid)Ⅰ v. ❶
报价；出价；投标：public ～ding 公开招标/
They bid against each other for the building of
the main stadium of Beijing Olympic Games. 他
们相互竞争投标北京奥运会主运馆的修建。
圆 offer ❷(打桥牌时)叫牌 圆 declare Ⅱ n.
[C] ❶出价；投标：call for invite ～ s 招标/
make a～ for 出价；投标 圆 offer，proffer ❷叫
牌 圆 declaration

big / bɪg / (bigger，biggest) adj. 大的；重大
的：Shanghai is a ～ city. 上海是一座大城
市。/The ～ news of today is the election of
President. 今天的重大新闻是总统竞选。圆
large，great，important 反 little，small

bike / baɪk / n. (＝bicycle)[C]自行车

bikini / bɪ'kiːni / n. 比基尼(女式泳装)

bilateral / ˌbaɪ'lætərəl / adj. ❶两边的；双边
的：～ talks 双边会谈 圆 two-sided，mutual ❷
互惠的；对等的：～ trade agreement 互惠贸易
协定 圆 mutual

bilingual / ˌbaɪ'lɪŋɡwəl / Ⅰ adj. 熟悉两种语
言的；使用两种语言的：a ～ dictionary 双语
词典/～ education 双语教育 Ⅱ n. [C]能使用
两种语言的人

bill / bɪl / n. [C] ❶账单；settle a ～ 结账/ pay
a ～ 付账(单)/ Tom paid the ～ for repairing
his car. 汤姆付了修车的账单。圆 account ❷
单子；清单：a ～ of fare 菜单；节目单 圆 list
❸ 招贴；广告；传单：post a ～ 张贴海报/
Post no ～s on the fence. 此栏杆上不准张贴
广告。圆 poster，advertisement ❹纸币；钞票：
He found a dollar ～ under the desk. 他在桌
下发现一张一美元的钞票。圆 banknote ❺议

B

案;法案: draft (pass) a ～ 草拟(通过)一项议案 圃 proposal

billboard / ˈbɪlbɔːd / n. [C](户外)广告牌;告示牌;招贴板

billiards / ˈbɪlɪədz / n. (pl.)台球;play ～ 打台球

billion / ˈbɪljən / num. (美)十亿;(英)万亿

billionaire / ˈbɪljəˈneə(r) / n. [C]亿万富翁

billow / ˈbɪləʊ / Ⅰ vi.(波浪)翻腾;波浪般起伏 圃 wave, surge Ⅱ n. 巨浪;波涛;～s of smoke 滚滚浓烟 圃 wave, surge 派 billowy adj.

bin / bɪn / n. [C]容器;箱子;垃圾箱:a grain ～ 粮仓/a litter ～ 杂物箱/a rubbish (dust) ～ 垃圾箱 圃 box, container, dustbin

bind / baɪnd / vt. (bound, bound) ❶捆;扎;绑:He bound the girl with a piece of rope. 他用绳子捆住这个女孩。 圃 tie, fasten ❷装订:The workers use machines to ～ the pages into books. 工人们用机器把书页装订成册。 圃 fasten

bingo / ˈbɪŋɡəʊ / n. 宾戈游戏(一种凭运气的赌博游戏)

biochemistry / ˌbaɪəʊˈkemɪstri / n. 生物化学

biological / ˌbaɪəˈlɒdʒɪkl / adj. 生物的;生物学的:～ clock 生物钟/～ chain 生物链/～ laboratory 生物学实验室/～ science 生物科学/～ technology industry 生物技术产业

biologist / baɪˈɒlədʒɪst / n. [C]生物学家

biography / baɪˈɒɡrəfi / n. [C]传记;传记文学

biology / baɪˈɒlədʒi / n. [U]生物学

bionics / baɪˈɒnɪks / n. 仿生学;～ techniques 仿生技术

biosphere / ˈbaɪəʊˈsfɪə(r) / n. [C] ❶生物圈 ❷生命层

bird / bɜːd / n. [C]鸟;禽:a flock of ～s 一群鸟/migratory ～s 候鸟/water ～s 水禽/kill two ～s with one stone 一石二鸟;一举两得

bird's-eye / ˈbɜːdzaɪ / adj. 俯视的,鸟瞰的;远眺的:From the plane we had a ～ view of London. 我们从飞机上俯瞰了伦敦的全景。

birth / bɜːθ / n. [U] ❶诞生;出生:birth control program 生育控制计划;计划生育/The exact date of the ～ of Tom is January 1st. 汤姆出生的准确日子是1月1日。/give ～ to 生产(婴儿);(喻)产生,造成

She gave ～ to twin girls. 她生了一对双胞胎女孩。 ❷起源;血统;出身:He is a man of noble ～. 他出身高贵。

birthday / ˈbɜːθdeɪ / n. [C] 生日;～ card 生日贺卡/～ party 生日聚会/～ present 生日礼物/ They celebrated Ann's ～ in the park. 他们在公园里庆祝安的生日。

birthplace / ˈbɜːθpleɪs / n. 出生地;故乡:Tianjin is my ～. 天津是我的故乡。

biscuit / ˈbɪskɪt / n. [C](英)饼干;(美)小面包,小点心

bishop / ˈbɪʃəp / n. [C](基督教)主教

bit¹ / bɪt / v.(bite 的过去式形式)叮;咬

bit² / bɪt / n.一点儿;少许:a ～ of meat 一小片肉 圃 piece / ～ by ～ 一点一点地;渐次:Bit by ～ she understood his words. 她逐渐理解了他说的话。 **do one's ～** 尽某人一份力量: We should do our ～ for our nation. 我们应该为国家尽一份力量。

bite / baɪt / v.(bit, bitten)咬;叮:He was bitten by a snake. 他被蛇咬了。 圃 sting

biting / ˈbaɪtɪŋ / adj. ❶严寒的;刺痛的,刺骨的;凛冽的:～ winter 严冬/a ～ east wind 凛冽的东风 ❷(言辞)刻薄的,尖刻的;讽刺的,挖苦的:a ～ comment 尖刻的评论

bitter / ˈbɪtə(r) / adj. ❶苦的;苦味的:Good medicine tastes ～. 良药苦口。 反 sweet ❷难受的;令人悲伤的;痛苦的:Her failure to pass the examination was a ～ disappointment to her parents. 她考试失败是一件令其父母极为失望的事。 圃 harsh, painful 派 bitterly adv.; bitterness n.

bizarre / bɪˈzɑː(r) / adj. 奇形怪状的;古怪的;怪诞的;异乎寻常的:～ behaviour 古怪的行为/a ～ series of events 一连串的怪事

black / blæk / adj. 黑的;黑暗的:He was ～ in the face. 他脸色发紫。/The sky grew ～ with clouds. 乌云使天空暗下来。 圃 dark 反 white/～ **and blue** 遍体鳞伤:青一块、紫一块:He was beaten ～ and blue. 他被打得遍体鳞伤。

blackboard / ˈblækbɔːd / n. 黑板;～ newspaper 黑板报/A student cleaned off the ～ after class. 下课后一位学生把黑板擦干净了。

blacken / ˈblækən / vt. ❶使变黑;使发脏:Soot ～ed the snow. 煤灰将雪弄黑了。/ Smoke ～ed the sky. 浓烟遮黑了天空。 ❷破

坏,败坏(名誉等);诋毁:～ sb.'s reputation 败坏某人的声誉

blacklist / ˈblæklɪst / n. [C]黑名单:The police drew up a ～ed for political reasons 因政治原因而被列入黑名单

blackmail / ˈblækmeɪl / n. &vt. 敲诈;勒索;讹诈:The young man committed ～. 那年轻人犯了敲诈罪。同 bribe

blade / bleɪd / n. 刀刃;刀片:sword with two ～s 双刃剑 同 knife,edge

blame / bleɪm / Ⅰ vt. 责备;责怪;埋怨:Bad workmen often ～ their tools. 拙匠常怪工具差。同 condemn,criticize Ⅱ n. 责任;过失 同 responsibility / throw (lay,put,take)(a) ～ on (upon) sb. 把某人之错归咎于某人:He often throws ～s on his brother. 他常把过失推给他的兄弟。

blameless / ˈbleɪmlɪs / adj. 无可指责的;无过错的,无过失的:Although the boy had not broken the window himself,he was not entirely ～. 尽管窗户不是那男孩打破的,但他也不是完全没有过错。

blank / blæŋk / Ⅰ n. [C]空白;空格;空白表格:an application ～ 申请表/ Please fill in the ～ with a proper word. 请用恰当的词填空。同 space,vacancy Ⅱ adj. 空白的,未写字的;无表情的:a ～ sheet of paper 一张白纸 同 empty,unmarked

blanket / ˈblæŋkɪt / n. [C]毯子;羊毛毯

blast / blɑːst / v. 炸毁;摧毁;炸裂:The roof was ～ed off. 屋顶被炸毁了。同 explode,destroy

blaze / bleɪz / Ⅰ n. [C]火焰;火光:He put some wood on the fire and it soon burst into a ～. 他放了些木柴在火上,木柴很快就燃起来了。同 fire,flame Ⅱ vi. 发光;冒火焰:A fire was blazing well in the fireplace. 炉子中的火在熊熊燃烧。同 burn,flame

辨析 blaze 指较大的火焰或强光:A lively blaze was under way. 火烧得正旺。**flame** 意为"火焰;火苗",常指火上部温度最高、呈红黄色的那一部分,或指一团大火吐出的火舌:The house was in flames. 房子失火了。**flash** 指一闪而过的光。**glare** 常指太阳、利刃等发出的强烈而刺目的光。**glow** 指熔铁等发出的热光或萤火虫发出的冷光。**glimmer** 指微弱的光。**glitter** 指金、黄金、金刚石等发出的明亮夺目的光。**lightning** 指闪电的光。

bleach / bliːtʃ / Ⅰ vt. 晒白;漂白;使脱色:～ the linen napkins in the wash 漂洗亚麻布餐巾 Ⅱ n. [U]漂白剂:a strong household ～ 高效家用漂白剂。

bleed / bliːd / v. (bled / bled /,bled)流血;失血:His hand was ～ing. 他的手在淌血。

blend / blend / Ⅰ vt. 使混合,使混杂;使交融;混合成:～ the eggs and milk(together)把鸡蛋和牛奶拌和 Ⅱ n. [C] ❶混合物,混合体,混成品:This coffee is a ～ of three varieties. 这种咖啡是由三个品种混合配制而成的。❷缩合词:Smog is a ～ of smoke and fog. smog 是 smoke 与 fog 的缩合词。

bless / bles / v. (blessed 或 blest)祝福;保佑;保护…免于(灾祸等):They married with their parents' ～ing. 他们的结婚得到父母的祝福。

blind / blaɪnd / adj. 瞎的;盲目的:～ import 盲目进口/ ～ investment 盲目投资/ ～ worship 盲目崇拜/ ～ go 失明/ He is ～ in the right eye. 他的右眼是瞎的。/ He is ～ to his own weakness. 他看不到自己的弱点。同 sightless,thoughtless

blink / blɪŋk / Ⅰ v. 眨眼睛;闪烁 同 wink,sparkle Ⅱ n. ❶眨眼睛;闪光:You can see the ～ of the lighthouse along the riverside. 在河边你会看见灯塔的闪光。同 twinkle ❷一瞬间:He ran out in a ～ of an eye. 一瞬间工夫他就跑了出去。同 instant,moment

block / blɒk / Ⅰ n. [C] ❶块;木块;石块:stumbling ～ 绊脚石/ wood ～ 木刻 ❷街区;街段:Walk two ～s ahead and you'll find the hospital. 朝前走过两个街区,你就可以找到那家医院。❸阻塞;障碍物:traffic ～ 交通阻塞 同 obstacle,barrier Ⅱ v. 堵塞;阻塞:A severe storm ～ed up the railways. 一场猛烈的暴风雨使铁路中断。

blockade / blɒˈkeɪd / n. [C]封锁;堵塞

blond(e) / blɒnd / adj. ❶亚麻色的;淡黄色的 ❷白肤金发碧眼的 同 fair,fair-skinned

blood / blʌd / n. [U] ❶血;血液:～ pressure 血压/ ～ test 验血/ ～ transfusion 输血/ ～ type 血型/ ～ bank 血库/ ～vessels 血管/donate ～ 献血/ ～ donor 献血者 ❷血统;种族;flesh and ～ 血肉关系;亲骨肉 ❸血气;气质:He is a person of hot ～. 他是个火暴脾气的人。同 spirit,temperament

bloodstream / ˈblʌdstriːm / n. [U] ❶血流;体内循环的血液 同 blood,circulation ❷主流:the economic ~ of the society 社会经济的主流

bloody / ˈblʌdi / *adj.* ❶出血的；流血的：It is a ~ fight. 这是一场流血的斗争。同 bleeding ❷血腥的；残忍的：~ murder 血腥的谋杀 同 cruel，savage

bloom / bluːm / Ⅰ *vi.* 开花：The rose ~s beautifully. 开放的玫瑰很漂亮。同 flower Ⅱ *n.* [C]花：The cherry trees have beautiful ~s. 樱花开得很美。同 flower / **in** ~ 在开花中：The tulips are in full ~ now. 郁金香花正盛开着。

> **辨析**
>
> **bloom** 常指不结果实、只供观赏的花。**blossom** 指果树花。**flower** 是常用词，可指各种类型的花。

blossom / ˈblɒsəm / Ⅰ *vi.* 开花：The plum trees began to ~. 李子树开始开花。同 flower，bloom Ⅱ *n.* [C](尤指果树的)花：**in** ~ 在开花中；开着花 同 flower，bloom

blot / blɒt / [C] Ⅰ *n.* ❶污染；墨渍；(道德上的)污点：Don't make any ~ on the form. 别把墨水溅到表格上。同 stain Ⅱ *v.* (blotted；blotting)抹脏；弄上污渍 同 stain，dirty

blouse / blauz / *n.* [C](妇女或儿童穿的)短上衣；(宽大的)工作服

blow / bləu / Ⅰ *vi.* (blew/bluː/，blown /bləun/) ❶吹：The papers were blown away by the wind. 报纸被风吹走了。❷爆炸：The ship blew up. 船爆炸了。同 blast，explode Ⅱ *n.* [C]打；打击：This battle dealt the enemy hard ~s. 这一仗狠狠地打击了敌人。同 strike，hit

blue / bluː / Ⅰ *adj.* ❶蓝色的；青的：a ~ collar worker 蓝领工人/ His face was ~ from the cold. 他的脸冻得发紫。❷下流的：Children are not allowed to see ~ films. 小孩是不允许看黄色电影的。❸沮丧的；忧郁的：Her mother looks ~. 她妈妈神情忧郁。同 depressed，sad Ⅱ *n.* [U]蓝色：He was dressed in ~ yesterday. 昨天他穿的是蓝色衣服。

blueprint / ˈbluːprɪnt / *n.* 蓝图；行动计划 同 outline，plan

bluff / blʌf / *n.* 陡岸；悬崖；峭壁 同 cliff

blunder / ˈblʌndə(r) / Ⅰ *n.* [C]大错，大娄子：Signing the agreement was a major ~ on the Prime Minister's part. 签订该条约是首相的一大失策。Ⅱ *vi.* 犯大错误；出大娄子：Just pray that he doesn't ~ again and get the names wrong. 但愿他别再出洋相，把名字又弄错了。

blunt / blʌnt / *adj.* ❶(刀或刀口)不锋利的，钝的；(铅笔等)不尖的：sharpen a ~ knife 把钝刀磨快 ❷率直的，坦率的；不客气的，生硬的：a ~ speech 没遮没拦的言辞

board / bɔːd / Ⅰ *n.* [C] ❶木板；纸板；布告牌；甲板：I saw a note on the ~. 我看见布告牌上贴着通知。/ **on** ~ 在船上；在飞机上：The passenger has come on ~. 那位乘客已上船。❷委员会；董事会：He is a member of our school ~. 他是我们学校董事会的成员。Ⅱ *v.* 上船；上飞机：The passengers ~ed the plane at noon. 旅客们中午上的飞机。

boast / bəust / *v.* 自夸；自吹；说大话：John ~s that he is the best man alive. 约翰自夸天下第一。/ He often ~s of his deeds，learning and cleverness. 他常夸耀自己的业绩、学识与智慧。同 exaggerate

boat / bəut / *n.* [C]小船；艇；小轮船：When we are in danger，we should be in the same ~. 在危难中，我们应当同舟共济。

body / ˈbɒdi / *n.* [C] ❶身体；躯体：We wear clothes to keep our bodies warm. 我们穿衣是为了保暖。❷团体：governing ~ 行政机构 同 orgnization ❸尸体

boil / bɔil / *v.* 沸腾；(液体)煮开：The water is ~ing. 水开了。/ She's ~ing the milk for her baby. 她正在给婴儿烧牛奶。反 freeze 派 boiling *adj.*

bold / bəuld / *adj.* ❶勇敢的；大胆的；冒失的：May I make so ~ as to ask your name? 我可以冒昧地问您的姓名吗？同 courageous，brave ❷粗大的；醒目的：~ headlines 醒目的大标题 派 boldly *adv.*

bolt / bəult / Ⅰ *n.* [C]螺栓；插销；门闩 同 bar Ⅱ *v.* 闩(门)：Don't ~ a child alone in the room. 别把小孩一人关在屋子里。同 bar，fasten

bomb / bɒm / *n.* [C]炸弹：atom ~ 原子弹/ nuclear ~ 核弹 / time ~ 定时炸弹

bond / bɒnd / Ⅰ *n.* ❶联结；黏合 同 link ❷公债；债券：treasury ~s 国库债券/ issue a ~ 发行一种债券 Ⅱ *vt.* 结合；黏合：They ~ed the two different materials together. 他们把两种不同的材料黏合在一起。同 bind，connect

bondage / ˈbɒndidʒ / *n.* [U]奴役；束缚；羁绊：celebrate one's escape from ~ 庆祝自己摆脱了奴役苦

bone / bəun / *n.* [C]骨骼；骨头：Dogs like

～s. 狗喜欢吃骨头。

bonfire / ˈbɒnfaɪə(r) / n. [C]篝火;营火

bonus / ˈbəʊnəs / n. [C]奖金;津贴;红利:annual ～ 年度奖金/distributing ～es improperly 滥发奖金/ wrapped ～ 红包/ ～ dividend 股息红利 同 reward, allowance

bony / ˈbəʊni / adj. 多骨的;骨瘦如柴的 同 skinny, thin

book / bʊk / I. n. [C]书;书籍:E～s 电子图书/children's ～s 儿童读物/ reference ～s 参考书/ I can keep the ～ for two weeks. 这本书我可以借两周。II. vt. 预订:Tickets can be ～ed one week in advance. 票可以提前一周预订。

bookcase / ˈbʊkkeɪs / n. [C]书橱;书柜:He has a big ～ in his room. 他房里有一个大书橱。

bookmark / ˈbʊkmɑːk / n. [C]书签:I always use a piece of paper for my ～. 我常用一张小纸片做书签。

bookshelf / ˈbʊkʃelf / n. [C]书架:He put a clock on his ～. 他在书架上放了一只钟。

bookshop / ˈbʊkʃɒp / n. [C]书店:There is a new ～ near our school. 我们学校附近有一家新书店。

booking / ˈbʊkɪŋ / n. 预约;预订;订货:a ～ note 订单/ make a ～ 预订/ a ～ clerk 售票员/a ～ office 售票处 同 ordering, reservation

booklet / ˈbʊklət / n. [C]小册子 同 pamphlet

boom / buːm / I. vi. 迅速发展;繁荣;兴旺 同 expand, prosper II. n. [C]繁荣;兴旺:business ～ 商业繁荣/population ～ 人口激增/ In recent years, there has been a travel ～ (tourist ～) throughout the country. 近年来全国掀起了一股旅游热。同 prosperity, thriving

boost / buːst / I. vt. ❶促进,激励;提高;增强:～ local business 促进当地商业的发展 ❷增加,使增长;help to ～ profits 有助于提高利润 II. n. [C] ❶推动,促进;激励:The promotion was a big ～ to his ego. 这一提升促使他更为自负。❷增加,增长,提高:receive a pay ～获得一次加薪/a ～ in exports 出口的增加

boot / buːt / n. [C]长筒靴

booth / buːð / n. [C]货摊;摊位;电话亭 同 store, stand

border / ˈbɔːdə(r) / n. [C]边缘;边界:～ trade 边境贸易/ You must go through the customs in order to pass across the ～. 你要过

境就必须在海关办理手续。

bore / bɔː(r) / vt. 使厌烦;使厌倦:We were ～d by his talk. 他的讲话使我们感到厌烦。同 tire, weary

boring / ˈbɔːrɪŋ / adj. 令人厌烦的;枯燥乏味的;无聊的:The film is ～. Nobody likes to see it. 这部电影很无聊,没人爱看。同 dull, tiresome

born / bɔːn / adj. 天生的,生来的: He said that the boy was a ～ athlete. 他说那小男孩是个天生的运动员。同 innate, inborn

borrow / ˈbɒrəʊ / v. 借;借用:a ～ed word 外来词/ May I ～ your Chinese-English dictionary? 我可以借用你的汉英词典吗? 反 lend

bosom / ˈbʊzəm / n. 胸,胸部;胸怀;内心:take sb. to ～ 视某人为知己/ After that they made ～ friends with each other. 那以后他们就成了知心朋友。同 affection, mind

boss / bɒs / n. [C]老板;上司;当家人:Who's the ～ in the house? 谁是这里的一家之主? / She is the ～ of a clothing store. 她是一家服装店的老板。同 employer, manager

botanical / bəˈtænɪkl / adj. 植物的;植物学的:There is a big ～ garden near our school. 我们学校附近有一个很大的植物园。

botany / ˈbɒtəni / n. [U]植物学

both / bəʊθ / I. pron. 两个;两者;双方:Both (of them) are teachers. 他们两人都是教师。II. adv. ～ ... and ... 两个都;既……又…:Both he and I are from Shanghai. 我和他都是上海人。

bother / ˈbɒðə(r) / v. 打扰;麻烦:He is always ～ing me. 他老是打扰我。/ It's not important. Don't ～ your head about it. 这并不重要,不要为它费心思。同 trouble, disturb 派 bothersome adj.

辨析

bother 意为"打扰",表示不太严重的烦扰:I can't bother him with my little affairs. 我不能拿这些小事去麻烦他。**disturb** 语气较强,指长久地使人不能安静或妨碍工作的进行:I am sorry to disturb you so early. 很抱歉,我这么早就来打扰你。**trouble** 意为"使烦恼;使费心;折磨",常用词,语气比 bother 强,比 disturb 弱:He was troubled about his son's behavior. 他为他儿子的行为感到烦恼。**worry** 常指没有必要的担心:Don't worry yourself about the children. They are old enough to look after themselves. 别为孩子们操心。他们已长大,可以自己照顾自己了。

B

bottle / ˈbɒtl / n. [C]瓶子：There is a ～ of ink on the desk. 桌子上有一瓶墨水。

bottom / ˈbɒtəm / n. [C]底部：at the ～ of the garden 在花园的尽头/ at the ～ of the mountain 在山脚下

bottomless / ˈbɒtəmlɪs / adj. ❶无限的，无穷无尽的：millionaires with ～ purses 财源滚滚的百万富翁 ❷不见底的，深不可测的，极深的：a ～ gorge 深不见底的峡谷

bough / baʊ / n. [C]树枝；(树的)主茎，主干：slender ～细树枝

bounce / baʊns / v. 反弹；跳 回：Striking a rock, the bullet ～d off. 子弹打在岩石上反弹开了。同 spring, leap

bouncy / ˈbaʊnsi / adj. ❶(指球等)富有弹性的，弹力足的：An old tennis ball is not as ～ as a new ball. 旧网球的弹力没有新的足。❷生气勃勃的，精神饱满的；轻快活泼的：a ～ personality 活泼的个性 ❸跳跃的；颠弹的：Hard ground makes balls more ～. 坚硬的地面使球颠弹得更厉害。

bound¹ / baʊnd / Ⅰ vt. (bind 的过去式和过去分词形式)束缚；捆绑 Ⅱ n. [C]跳跃；弹跳：advance by leaps and ～s飞跃前进，突飞猛进 同 jump, spring Ⅲ vi. 跳跃；弹回：Her heart ～ed with joy. 她高兴得心头怦怦直跳。同 jump, spring

bound² / baʊnd / adj. 必定一定：be ～ to do 一定，必然；负有义务，负有责任：Your plan is ～ to succeed. 你的计划一定会成功。/ We are ～ to obey the law. 我们有义务守法。同 sure, certain 反 uncertain

bound³ / baʊnd / adj. 准备到…去的；开往(驶往)…的：He entered a train ～ for Beijing. 他登上一辆开往北京的火车。同 going, destined

bound⁴ / baʊnd / n. (pl.)边界；界限；范围：out of ～s 越界；禁止入内/ There are no ～s to her ambition. 她的野心是无止境的。同 limit, boundary 派 boundless adj.

boundary / ˈbaʊndri / n. [C]边界；分界线：beyond the ～ 超越界线/A river forms the ～ between the two countries. 一条河成了两国的分界线。同 bounds, border

boundless / ˈbaʊndlɪs / adj. ❶无边无际的，广阔的：Outer space is ～. 宇宙空间是无边无际的。❷无限的，无穷无尽的：be ～ in one's gratitude 感激不尽

bourgeois / ˈbʊəʒwɑː / Ⅰ adj. 资产阶级的 Ⅱ n. [C]资产阶级分子

bow¹ / bəʊ / n. [C](射箭用的)弓；弓形物：Draw not your ～ till your arrow is fixed. 箭要搭好别拉弓(三思而后行)。同 arc, curve

bow² / baʊ / v. ❶鞠躬；点头：The host ～ed his guest in. 主人鞠躬迎接客人进屋。同 nod, bend ❷屈服；使弯曲：We shall never ～ down to our enemies. 我们决不向敌人屈服。/ The branches were ～ed down with the weight of the snow. 树枝被积雪压弯了。同 yield, surrender Ⅱ n. [C]鞠躬；点头：He gave her a ～ for it. 他为此事向她鞠躬。同 nod, bend

bowel / ˈbaʊəl / n. (pl.)肠：The girl had loose ～s yesterday. 那女孩昨天腹泻。

bowl / bəʊl / n. [C]碗；大杯；钵：He broke his ～. 他把碗打破了。/ She ate three ～s of rice. 她吃了三碗米饭。

bowling / ˈbəʊlɪŋ / n. 保龄球：play ～ 打保龄球/ a ～ alley 保龄球场(馆)

box¹ / bɒks / n. [C] ❶盒子；箱子：a ～ of matches 一盒火柴/ a tool ～ 工具箱/ black ～ 黑匣子 同 case, chest ❷包箱；专席：a press ～ 记者席/a witness ～ 证人席 同 stall, compartment

box² / bɒks / Ⅰ v. 拳击；打拳：They will ～ each other for the championship. 为争夺冠军他们将进行拳击比赛。同 slap, bowl Ⅱ n. [C]一拳；一巴掌

boxing / ˈbɒksɪŋ / n. 拳击(术)；拳击运动：They like to go in for ～ after work. 下班后他们常去击拳。

boy / bɔɪ / n. [C]男孩；少年：The ～ likes swimming. 那男孩很喜欢游泳。同 lad, youth 派 boyish adj.

boycott / ˈbɔɪkɒt / Ⅰ vt. 联合抵制；拒绝参加：Products from that country are ～ed. 人们都抵制那个国家的产品。同 reject, exclude Ⅱ n. 联合抵制；拒绝参加：economic ～ 经济抵制/trade ～ 贸易抵制 同 rejection, exclusion

brace / breɪs / n. [C]支架；支撑物 同 support

bracelet / ˈbreɪslət / n. [C]手镯；手铐 同 handcuffs

bracket / ˈbrækɪt / n. [C] ❶托架；支架 (pl.)括号：Please put the words between the ～s. 请把单词写在括号里。

braid / breɪd / n. (pl.)辫子: She has beautiful ～s . 她的辫子很漂亮。

braille / breɪl / n. [U](供盲人写作、阅读,用手触摸的)点字法,布莱叶盲文

brain / breɪn / n. ❶[C] 头脑;脑子: He blew out his enemy's ～ with an axe. 他用斧头把敌人的脑袋砍开了花。 ❷(pl.)智慧;智力: beat one's ～s 绞尽脑汁/Use your ～s before you act. 行动之前动动脑筋。同 mind,intelligence

brake / breɪk / Ⅰ n.[C]闸;刹车;制动器: hand ～ 手刹/ foot ～ 脚刹/ You should first learn how to apply the ～ suddenly to avoid an accident. 首先你得学会如何为避免意外事故而紧急刹车。Ⅱ v. 制动;刹车: The driver had to ～ hard when he saw a woman was in front of his car. 看到车前有一位妇女,司机不得不紧急刹车。同 check,shop

branch / brɑːntʃ / n.[C] ❶枝杈;树枝: He cut down all the ～es of that tree. 他把那棵树的枝条全都砍了下来。同 limb ❷支流;部分;部门: English is a ～ of the Germanic language family. 英语是日耳曼语系中的一个分支。/ the Party ～ 党支部/ the League ～团支部/ open up a ～ 开分店(开分公司)同 section,part,department

brand / brænd / Ⅰ n.[C]品牌;商标;烙印: ～-name 名牌/ ～-name and quality products 名优产品/ ～-name strategy 名牌战略/ This ～ of tinned beans is welcome by all. 这种品牌的青豆罐头受到大家的欢迎。同 trademark,label Ⅱ vt.打烙印;印商标

brandy / 'brændi / n.[U]白兰地酒

brass / brɑːs / n.[U]黄铜;铜器

brave / breɪv / adj. 勇敢的: He is a ～ soldier. 他是个勇敢的士兵。同 courageous,fearless 派 bravely adv.

bravery / 'breɪvəri / n. [U]勇敢;英勇: The policeman showed great ～ in saving the drowning child. 那位警察在抢救落水儿童时,表现极为勇敢。

breach / briːtʃ / Ⅰ n. ❶[C]裂口,豁口,缺口: A cannon ball made a ～ in the castle wall. 一发加农炮弹把城堡墙轰开一个缺口。/ There's a ～ in our security. 我们的安全措施尚有罅隙。 ❷[U;C](对诺言、义务等的)违背;(对法律、协议等的)违反,违犯: serious ～es of discipline 种种严重违纪行为 ❸[U;C]

(友好关系的)破裂;疏远;裂痕:heal the ～ between the two parties 弥合两党间关系的裂痕 Ⅱ vt. 攻破,突破;打开缺口: ～ the enemy barbed wire 突破敌人的铁丝网

bread / bred / n. [U]面包: a loaf of ～ 一块面包/ buttered ～涂黄油的面包/dry ～ 没涂黄油的面包/ He had to earn his ～ when he was very young. 他很小就不得不自己谋生。

> **用法**
>
> **bread** 为不可数名词,若要表示一块面包,习惯上说 a piece of bread,a slice of bread 或 a loaf of bread。

breadth / bredθ / n. ❶宽度;广度: Do you know the ～ of this room? 你知道这个房间有多宽吗?同 width ❷(心胸等的)宽容;大量: ～ of mind 胸怀宽广/ We all admire his ～ of view. 我们都很羡慕他的见多识广。同 greatness

break / breɪk / Ⅰ v. (broke/brəʊk/,broken/brəʊkn/) ❶打破;折断;破裂: Billy broke his coloured pencil. 比利把他的彩色铅笔弄断了。/ Who broke the cup? 谁打烂了杯子? 同 split,crush ❷损坏;破坏: She broke her watch by winding it too tightly. 她把发条上得太紧,因而把表弄坏了。同 destroy ～ **away** (**from**) 逃脱;脱离: The prisoner broke away from his guards while being taken to another gaol. 那个囚犯在转狱途中挣脱看守逃走了。 ～ **down** ①(机器)损坏: The power generator broke down. 发电机坏了。②(健康或精神)垮掉: He has completely broke down in health. 他的身体彻底垮了。 ～ **in** ①打断;插话: Don't ～ in while others are speaking. 别人说话时别插话。②闯入;强行进入: The thief broke in. 贼破门而入。 ～ **into** 闯入;破门而入: The burglar broke into my house and stole my gold watch. 盗贼破门而入,盗走了我的金表。 ～ **off** ①突然中断;暂停: The conference broke off at noon. 会议中午暂停。②折断: A branch of the tree broke off. 一根树枝断了。 ～ **out** 突然发生;爆发: When did the World War Ⅱ ～ out? 第二次世界大战什么时候爆发的? ～ **through** 克服;制胜;冲破;突破: Our troops had little difficulty in ～ing through the enemy's line. 我们的军队毫不费力地突破了敌人的防线。 ～ **up** 拆散;打破;结束: When does your school ～ up for the summer holidays? 你们学校何时放暑假? Ⅱ n. ❶[C]破

B

裂；决裂：How do you think about the ～ between the two countries? 你对两国的绝交有何看法？圆 burst, split ❷[U]破晓：They left the village at the ～ of day. 天破晓时他们离开了村子。圆 dawn, daybreak ❸[C]中止；停顿：He always writes in his study without a ～. 他总是不停地在书房里写作。圆 pause ❹[C]（课间或工间）休息时间：It's time for lunch. Let's take a ～ for twenty minutes. 该吃午饭了，我们休息 20 分钟吧。圆 pause, interval 派 breakable adj.；breakagen.

breakaway / ˈbreɪkəweɪ / Ⅰ n. [C]脱离，退出：Two new opposition parties were formed in a ～ from the United Party. 从联合党脱离的过程中形成了两个新的对立政党。Ⅱ adj. 脱离组织（或团体）的；闹分裂的，（主张）独立的：a ～ political party 分裂出来的政党

breakdown / ˈbreɪkdaʊn / n. ❶崩溃，倒塌；（机器等的）损坏：～ in health 身体垮了 / have a ～ 出故障 / in health，精神）崩溃 圆 collapse, failure ❷失败；挫折；停顿 圆 failure, pause

breaker / ˈbreɪkə(r) / n. [C]破坏者；开拓者：a law ～ 不法分子

breakfast / ˈbrekfəst / n. 早饭；早餐

break-in / ˈbreɪkˌɪn / n. [C]（持不法动机）破门而入，非法闯入；盗窃（行为）：investigate a ～ at the local bank 调查一起闯入当地银行的盗窃案

breakout / ˈbreɪkˌaʊt / n. [C]❶逃脱（尤指集体使用暴力的）越狱：a ～ from a mental institution 从精神病院逃脱 ❷（疾病等）突然爆发；突然发生

breakthrough / ˈbreɪkθruː / n. 突破；突围；重大成就：They have made a great technological ～in recent years. 这些年以来，他们在技术上取得了重大的突破。

breakup / ˈbreɪkˌʌp / n. ❶分散；分裂；分离：the ～ of a marriage 离婚 ❷解散，解体，瓦解，崩溃：They are on the brink of a ～ of the two party system. 他们处于两党制濒于崩溃的边缘。

breast / brest / n. [C]胸膛；胸部；乳房

breath / breθ / n. [U]呼吸：**out of** ～ 喘不过气；上气不接下气：He ran so fast that he was out of ～. 他跑得太快，以至于喘不过气来。**give out**（**take in**）～ 吐气（吸气）：Taking in a deep ～, he dived into the water. 他深吸一口

气潜入水里。

breathe / briːð / v. 呼吸：The doctor asked Mary to ～ deeply to check her health. 医生让玛丽做深呼吸以检查她的健康状况。

breathless / ˈbreθləs / adj. 无声无息的；喘气来的：There was a ～ silence when the police came in. 警察进来时，房里安静得令人大气都不敢出。

breathtaking / ˈbreθˌteɪkɪŋ / adj. 惊人的；激动人心的：a ～ match 一场激动人心的比赛

breed / briːd / n. 品种；种类：fine ～ 优良品种 圆 species, kind Ⅱ vt.（bred / bred /，bred）饲养：They ～ cattle for market. 他们饲养牲口以供应市场。圆 raise, grow ❷生育；繁殖：Rabbits ～ rapidly. 兔子繁殖迅速。圆 reproduce, bear ❸教养；培养：He was born and bred in China. 他在中国土生土长。圆 train, educate

breeze / briːz / n. 微风；和风：cool ～ 凉风 / on the ～ 迎风招展/ in the spring ～ 沐浴春风 圆 blow, movement

brevity / ˈbrevɪti / n. [U]（讲话，行文等的）简洁，简练，简短：send a telegram in its ～发一份文字简练的电报 / essays written with clarity and ～ 文笔清晰简洁的散文

brew / bruː / Ⅰ v. 酿酒，酝酿：～ beer 酿造啤酒 / They are ～ing a plot. 他们正在酝酿一起阴谋。圆 plan Ⅱ n. 酿造

brewery / ˈbruːəri / n. [C]酿造厂；酿酒厂：The ～ is famous all over the country. 那家酿酒厂全国有名。

bribe / braɪb / Ⅰ v. 贿赂；收买：He ～d himself into the committee. 他通过贿赂混进了委员会。圆 corrupt Ⅱ n. [C] 贿赂；行贿物：He says that he will never take ～s. 他说他决不受贿。

brick / brɪk / n. [C]砖

bride / braɪd / n. [C]新娘

bridegroom / ˈbraɪdgruːm / n. [C]新郎

bridge / brɪdʒ / Ⅰ n. [C] ❶桥：an arched ～ 拱桥 / a cross-over ～ 天桥 / a draw（suspension）～吊桥 / a railway ～ 铁路桥 / a highway ～ 公路桥 / They are going to build（construct, lay, throw）a ～ across the river. 他们要在河上架桥。❷桥牌：He likes to play ～. 他喜欢打桥牌。Ⅱ vt. 联结；跨过（障碍）：The parents and children are trying hard to ～

their generation gap. 父母和子女都在尽力缩小他们之间的代沟。同 link, connect

brief / briːf / *adj.* 简短的；简洁的：He is ～ of speech. 他说话简洁。/ In ～, we should take action at once. 简而言之，我们必须马上采取行动。

bridle / 'braɪdl / *n.* [C]马勒；缰绳

bright / braɪt / *adj.* ❶明亮的；晴朗的；辉煌的：The garden is ～ with sunshine. 花园里阳光明媚。/ If you want to have a ～ future, you should work still harder. 想要有美好未来，你得更加努力地工作。同 clear, splendid ❷聪明的：She is ～ beyond her years. 她年纪不大，人却很聪明。同 clever, intelligent

briefcase / 'briːfkeɪs / *n.* [C]公文包 同 bag, folder

brigade / brɪ'geɪd / *n.*[C]旅；队：a fire ～ 消防队/ a rescue ～ 急救队 同 unit, team

brighten / 'braɪtn / *v.* ❶发光；发亮：Her face ～ed up with joy. 她的脸上露出了兴奋的神情。同 shine, lighten 反 darken, blacken ❷使快活；使活跃：To be with their grandson ～ed up the old couple. 和孙子在一起使老两口非常快活。同 gladden, cheer 反 sadden

brightness / 'braɪtnɪs / *n.* [U]❶明亮；亮度 同 light, shine 反 darkness, gloom ❷聪明；机灵：Not long after that I found her ～. 那以后不久就发现她很聪明。同 intelligence, cleverness

brilliant / 'brɪliənt / *adj.* ❶光辉的；辉煌的：～ sunshine 灿烂的阳光/ The lights are far too ～. 灯光太耀眼了。同 bright, shining 反 gloomy, dim ❷卓越的；英明的；才华横溢的：His brother is a ～ student. 他的哥哥是一个很有才华的学生。/ We watched their ～ performance in the theatre. 我们在剧院里看了他们的卓越表演。同 intelligent, talented 反 dull 派 brilliantly *adv.*

brim / brɪm / *n.* [C](茶杯、碗等容器的)边；(帽子的)沿 同 edge, border

bring / brɪŋ / *vt.* (brought/brɔːt/, brought)带来；拿来：Please ～ a dictionary with you. 请随身带本词典来。同 carry, convey 反 take/～ **about** 带来；造成：It may ～ about a good result. 这可能带来好的结果。～ **sb. around to** (**doing**) **sth.** 说服某人做某事：I'll try to ～

him around to your views. 我将努力劝说他同意你的观点。～ **forth** 提出；使产生；引起：He brought the plan forth to our consideration. 他提出计划让我们考虑。/ March winds and April showers ～ forth May flowers. 三月的春风、四月的阵雨催开五月的鲜花。～ **into** 使…进入(某种状态)：She brought me into touch with everything. 她使我接触到一切。～ **out** 使清楚；显示出来：He was so excited that he could hardly ～ out a "thank you". 他激动得连一声"谢谢"都说不出来。～ **to** 使…恢复知觉：She will soon be brought to. 她很快就会苏醒过来。～ **to light** 发现；揭发：His enemies brought to light some foolish things he had done. 他的敌人揭穿了他干的一些蠢事。～ **to pass** 促成：By much planning, the mother brought the marriage to pass. 这位母亲花了很多心思促成这桩婚事。～ **up** ①抚养；养育；教养：He paid much attention to ～ing up his children. 他花了很多心思抚养孩子。②停止：Bill started to complain, but I brought him up short. 比尔开始抱怨，但我很快让他停止下来。③提出；谈及：At the meeting, he brought up the idea of a picnic. 在会上，他提出了野餐的事。

> **辨析**
> **bring** 意为"带来；拿来"：Bring me the book. 把书给我拿来。**carry** 意为"携带；搬运"，指用运输工具或靠人力，将物体从一处送到另一处：These books are too heavy to carry. 这些书太重，不好携带。**take** 意为"拿走"，指把物品拿离说话者：Who has taken my pen? 谁把我的钢笔拿走了？

brink / brɪŋk / *n.* [C]❶(陡峭处的)边缘，边沿(河、池等的)边，边沿；陡岸；滨：the ～ of the pond 池塘边 ❷顶点；始发点；边缘：beyond the ～ of sb.'s endurance 超出某人忍耐的限度/ be on the ～ of war 处于战争边缘

brisk / brɪsk / *adj.* ❶敏捷的；轻快的；精力充沛的：She passed us at a ～ walk. 她步履轻捷地从我们身边走过。/ a ～ old man 精神矍铄的老汉 ❷(天气等)干冷的；清新的：a ～ day 天气干冷的一天/ The air was ～. 空气清新。

bristle / 'brɪsl / *n.* 硬毛；鬃毛 同 hair

Britain / 'brɪtn / *n.* 英国：the United Kingdom of Great ～ and Northern Ireland 大不列颠及北爱尔兰联合王国(英国的正式名称)

B

British / ˈbrɪtɪʃ / Ⅰ adj. 英国的 Ⅱ n. (the ～) 英国人民

brittle / ˈbrɪtl / adj. 硬而脆的；易碎的，易损坏的：～ porcelain 易碎的瓷器

broad / brɔːd / adj. ❶宽的；宽阔的；广大的：The lake is a mile ～ here. 这里的湖面有一英里宽。/ We should serve the masses of the ～ people. 我们应该为广大人民群众服务。同 wide, vast ❷宽宏的：He is a man of ～ views. 他是一个宽宏大量的人。同 open-minded 反 narrow-minded 派 broadly adv.

broadcast / ˈbrɔːdkɑːst / Ⅰ v. (broadcast 或 broadcasted)广播；播音；传播：～ live 现场广播 / This station ～s sports news at seven. 这个台七点钟播体育新闻。/ You shouldn't ～ my secret to the whole class. 你不该向全班同学散布我的秘密。/ The news was ～ at eight o'clock last night. 这消息是昨天晚上八点钟播出的。Ⅱ n. ❶广播；播音：a ～ station 广播站/ the Central People's Broadcasting Station 中央人民广播电台 同 televise, radio ❷播音节目：The blind girl listens to news ～ every evening. 那盲人女孩每天晚上收听新闻节目。同 program, radio

broaden / ˈbrɔːdn / v. 放宽，变阔；扩大：～ one's interests 拓宽兴趣/ The workers are ～ing the street. 工人们正在加宽街道。/ The stream ～s into a river here. 小溪流到这儿宽了，成为一条河。同 widen, expand, enlarge 反 narrow

brochure / ˈbrəʊʃə(r) / n. [C]小册子：a holiday ～ 假日指南/ a sales ～ 商品推广手册

broil / brɔɪl / vt. ❶烤，炙，焙 ～ a steak 烤牛排 ❷使灼热；把…烤焖，将…烧焦：We turned back, much ～ in the hot sun. 我们返回时,在烈日下被晒得灼热不堪。

broken / ˈbrəʊkən / Ⅰ v. (break 的过去分词形式)破碎 Ⅱ adj. 破碎的：The bowel was ～. 这碗是破的。同 burst, smashed 反 undamaged, complete

broker / ˈbrəʊkə(r) / n. [C](股票、公债等)经纪人；掮客；代理人；中间人：a ～ office, a ～ house 经纪人事务所/a real-estate ～ 地产经纪人/ He became an insurance ～ after graduation. 毕业后他当了保险经纪人。同 a-gent, stockbroker, middleman

bronze / brɒnz / n. 青铜，青铜制品；青铜色：

He won a ～ medal at the sports. 在运动会上他获得一枚铜牌。/ They are setting up a ～ statue in the garden. 他们正在花园里竖一尊铜像。

brook / brʊk / n. [C]小溪；小河

broom / bruːm / n. [C]扫帚

brother / ˈbrʌðə(r) / n. [C]兄弟：blood ～s 亲兄弟/ cousin ～s 堂兄弟；表兄弟/elder ～ 哥哥 / younger ～ 弟弟/ half ～(异父或异母)弟兄/ twin ～s 孪生兄弟 派 brotherly adj.

brotherhood / ˈbrʌðəhʊd / n. 兄弟(般的)关系；兄弟情谊

brow / braʊ / n. [C](通常用 pl.)眉毛：Knit the ～s and you will hit upon a stratagem. 眉头一皱，计上心来。

brown / braʊn / adj. 褐色的；棕色的：There is a room with ～ glass windows near my dormitory. 我的宿舍旁有一间带褐色玻璃窗的房间。

browse / braʊz / v. ❶随便翻阅；游览：～ through a market 逛市场/He spent the afternoon browsing in the bookstores. 他整个下午都泡在那些书店里翻阅书刊。❷看橱窗(里的)商品

brunch / brʌntʃ / n. 早午饭；晚早饭(该词由 breakfast 和 lunch 合成,指吃得比早饭晚而比午饭早的一顿饭)：They got up too late and had to have a ～. 他们起得太晚,只好吃一顿晚早饭。

brush / brʌʃ / Ⅰ v. 刷；擦；拂：The light wind gently ～ed his cheeks. 和风轻拂他的面颊。/ Please ～ your shoes. 请把鞋子擦一擦。同 rub, wipe Ⅱ n. [C]刷子；画笔：a Chinese ～ 毛笔/tooth ～ 牙刷

brushup / ˈbrʌʃʌp / n. [C]温习；复习；复习期：He gave his Spanish a ～ before his trip to Mexico. 去墨西哥之前,他温习了一下西班牙语。/The orchestra needed a good deal of ～ before the performance. 演出之前,这个管弦乐队需要进行大量的反复排练。

brutal / ˈbruːtl / adj. 残忍的；野蛮的；严酷的：～ winter 严冬/ He is not accustomed to the ～ heat of Nanjing. 他很不适应南京的酷热天气。同 cruel, cold-blooded, severe 反 kind, pitiful 派 brutally adv.

brutality / bruːˈtæləti / n. [U]残忍；残暴；暴行：In this film you can know about the concentration camp ～ at that time. 在这部电影里你可以了解到那时候集中营里的残暴行为。

brute / bru:t / n. [C] 禽兽；畜生；残忍的人 同 beast, animal, savage

bubble / 'bʌbl / I n. [C] 水泡；气泡；soap ～s 肥皂泡 同 foam II v. 吹泡；起泡

buck / bʌk / n. (pl. buck 或 bucks) [C] ❶雄鹿 ❷公羊

bucket / 'bʌkɪt / n. [C] 桶；吊桶

buckle / 'bʌkl / I n. [C] (皮带等的)扣子，搭扣，搭钩 II v. ❶搭扣把…扣上 (或扣住、扣紧)：～ one's shoes 扣上鞋带/He ～d on his revolver. 他用搭扣把左轮手枪扣紧。❷变形；弯曲；鼓起：Chopsticks of celluloid ～ easily in hot water. 赛璐珞筷子在热水中容易变形。/ Her knees ～d with exhaustion. 她累得腿都直不起来。/～down 倾全力(于)；专心致志(于)；开始认真从事(于)：～ down to writing a book 全力以赴地写书 ～ up 扣紧皮带(安全带，搭扣)：Please ～ up now, we're about to land. 请系好安全带，我们就要着陆了。

bud / bʌd / n. [C] 芽；花苞：Trees put forth ～s in spring. 树在春天发芽。同 sprout

Buddhism / 'budɪzəm / n. 佛教

Buddhist / 'budɪst / I n. [C] 佛教徒 II adj. 佛教的

budget / 'bʌdʒɪt / n. [C] 预算；预算案：annual ～ 年度预算/defence ～ 国防预算 同 estimates

buffalo / 'bʌfələu / n. [C] ❶水牛；野牛 ❷水陆坦克

buffet n. [C] ❶ / 'bʌfeɪ / 碗橱 ❷ / 'bu-feɪ / 自助餐；快餐：He always goes to have a ～ after work. 下班后他总爱去吃自助餐。

bug / bʌg / n. [C] 臭虫

bugle / 'bju:gl / n. [C] 号角；喇叭：blow the ～ 吹喇叭/ ～ born 号角 同 trumpet

build / bɪld / I v. (built / bɪlt /, built) 建立；创立；增强：The school was well built. 这所学校建造得很好。/ Sports and games ～ our bodies. 体育运动增强我们的体质。同 establish, construct II n. [U] 构造；体格：He is a man of strong ～. 他是一个体格壮健的人。同 structure, physique

building / 'bɪldɪŋ / n. [C] 建筑；建筑物；大楼：～ materials 建筑材料/ a public ～ 公共建筑/ a teaching ～ 教学楼/ Many of my

classmates removed to new apartment ～s. 我的很多同学都搬进了新的公寓楼。同 house, construction

buildup / 'bɪldʌp / n. [C] ❶增长，增强，增进；发展：a ～ of pressure 压力的增大/The ～ of the national industry is vital. 发展民族工业至关重要。❷捧场；渲染；宣传攻势：She received a big ～ in the media. 她在传媒大界大受好评。

built-in / ˌbɪlt'ɪn / adj. 内置的：My father's radio has a ～ aerial. 我父亲的收音机带内置天线。

bulb / bʌlb / n. [C] ❶(植物的)球茎，鳞茎 ❷电灯泡；电灯；白炽灯；日光灯：Only a few of the ～ s were working. 只有几只电灯泡还亮着。

bulk / bʌlk / n. [U] 大块；大批；大量：in ～ 大批，大量/ a man of large ～ 一个身材魁伟的人 同 mass, volume, size, body 派 bulky adj.

bull / bul / n. [C] 公牛：～ in a china shop 鲁莽/ ～fight 斗牛/ ～fighter 斗牛士

bullet / 'bulɪt / n. [C] 子弹：The soldier fired a ～ at the enemy. 战士向敌人开枪。同 shell, shot

bulletin / 'bulɪtɪn / n. [C] 公示；公告；新闻简报：a ～ board 布告牌/ news ～ 新闻简报 同 notice, announcement

bullish / 'bulɪʃ / adj. ❶(像)公牛的；牛脾气的；执拗的 ❷(证券等行情)上涨的，看涨的：a ～ market 牛市/There was a ～ trend in the stock market. 股市行情看涨。

bully / 'buli / n. [C] 恶霸；暴徒：play the ～ 横行霸道

bump / bʌmp / I v. 碰撞；击：The two cars ～ed together. 两辆车撞在一起了。/ ～ into 偶遇：We ～ed into an old friend yesterday. 昨天我们意外地遇到了一位老朋友。同 knock, strike II n. ❶碰撞 同 knock ❷肿块 同 swelling, bulge

bumper / 'bʌmpə(r) / I n. 满杯；丰盛 同 a-bundance, plenty II adj. 丰盛的：a ～ harvest 大丰收/ They hope to have a ～ year. 他们希望迎来一个丰收年。同 abundant

bun / bʌn / n. [C] 圆面包；馒头

bunch / bʌntʃ / n. [C] 束；串：a ～ of flowers 一束花/ a ～ of keys 一串钥匙 同 bundle

bundle / ˈbʌndl / Ⅰ n. [C]包;捆;束:a ～ of clothes 一包衣服/ a ～ of banknotes 一扎钞票 同 bunch,package Ⅱ v. 捆;包;把…乱塞入:He ～d everything into a drawer. 他把所有东西都塞进抽屉里。同 pack

bunk / bʌŋk / n. [C](车、船上的)床铺;铺位 同 bed

buoy / bɔɪ / n. [C]浮标;航标;救生圈;救生衣:a life ～ 救生圈/ a light ～ 浮标灯 同 float

buoyant / ˈbɔɪənt / adj. ❶能浮起的,能漂起的;有浮力的:Cork is a very ～ material. 软木是一种浮力很大的材料。❷能使物体浮起的,有托浮力的:Balloons can float because air is ～. 气球能飘浮,是因为空气有托浮力。

burden / ˈbɜːdn / Ⅰ n. 担子;负担:His ～s have lightened a little. 他身上的担子已减轻了些。同 load,weight Ⅱ v. 使负重担;使劳累:They are not ～ed with families. 他们没有家庭拖累。/ Middle school teachers are so ～ed with teaching that they cannot engage themselves in research work. 中学教师教学负担太重,无暇顾及学术研究。同 load

bureau / ˈbjʊərəʊ / n. [C](pl. bureaus 或 bureaux / ˈbjʊərəʊz /)局;处;所:the Federal Bureau of Investigation (美)联邦调查局(缩写为FBI)/ the Political Bureau of the Central Committee of the Communist Party of China 中国共产党中央委员会政治局/ the Public Security Bureau 公安局/ the Tax Bureau 税务局/ travel ～ 旅行社

bureaucracy / bjʊəˈrɒkrəsi / n. 官僚;官僚主义;官僚政治:overcome ～ 克服官僚主义

bureaucrat / ˈbjʊərəkræt / n. [C]官僚主义者

bureaucratic / ˌbjʊərəˈkrætɪk / adj. 官僚的;专断的:～ government 官僚政府

burglar / ˈbɜːglə(r) / n. [C]窃贼;盗贼:The police caught a ～ last night. 昨夜警察抓住了一个盗贼。同 housebreaker,robber

burglary / ˈbɜːgləri / n. 盗窃(行为);盗窃罪:The young man committed (a) ～ and was sentenced to five years. 那年轻人犯了盗窃罪,被判刑五年。同 housebreaking,robbery

burial / ˈberɪəl / n. 安葬;埋葬;葬礼:His ～ will take place next Sunday. 他的葬礼下星期日举行。同 funeral

burn / bɜːn / v. (burnt / bɜːnt / 或 burned /

bɜːnd /)点燃;燃烧:Some materials do not ～. 有些物质不会燃烧。同 light 反 extinguish/ ～ daylight 白昼点灯,徒劳无益/ ～ midnight oil 熬夜,开夜车/ ～ up 烧尽;烧毁:We shall ～ up all the garden rubbish. 我们要将花园里的垃圾全部焚烧掉。派 burning adj.

burst / bɜːst / Ⅰ v. (burst,burst) 冲破,破裂;爆炸:The sun ～ through the clouds and shone over the earth. 太阳冲破乌云,阳光普照大地。/ ～ into tears 突然大哭 同 break,split,explode/ ～ forth (out) 爆发:A cry of horror ～ forth from the crowd. 人群中爆发出恐怖的叫声/ "Don't hit me!" she ～ out. 她大声呼叫:"不要打我!" Ⅱ n. 爆发;迸发:a ～ of laughter 爆发出一阵笑声 同 explosion,blast

bury / ˈberi / v. 埋葬;掩盖:He was buried alive by the enemy. 他被敌人活埋了。同 entomb,hide,cover 反 unearth,uncover

bus / bʌs / n. [C]公共汽车:We missed the school ～ and had to take a taxi. 我们没有赶上校车,只好乘出租。/ by ～ 乘公共汽车:Shall we walk or go by ～ ? 我们是步行还是乘公共汽车去?

bush / bʊʃ / n. [C]灌木;丛林:a clump of ～es 一片灌木林 同 shrub,jungle

bushy / ˈbʊʃi / adj. ❶丛林密布的,灌木丛生的:a ～ garden 灌木丛生的花园 ❷茂密的,浓密的:a ～ beard 浓密的胡须/ ～ eyebrows 浓眉

business / ˈbɪznəs / n. ❶[U]商业;业务;生意;事:～ letters 商业信函 / E-～ 电子商务/ retail ～ 零售业/ wholesale ～ 批发业/ We do not do much ～ with them. 我们与他们没有多少生意上的往来。同 commerce,trade,affair/ on ～ 因公;因事:He went to Shanghai on ～. 他因公去上海。none of one's ～ 与某人无关:Go on with your work. It is none of your ～. 继续干你的工作,那不关你的事。**have no ～ to do sth.** 无权做某事:You have no ～ to say things about me. 你无权谈论我的事。❷[C]商号;公司:He started a new ～ after he settled down in Guangzhou. 在广州定居下来后,他开办了一家新公司。同 firm,company

bust / bʌst / n. [C]胸部;半身塑像:measure one's ～ 给某人量胸围/ In front of our teach-

B

ing building there is a ～ of a poet. 我们教学楼前有一座诗人的半身塑像。**同** bosom, chest, breast

busy / ˈbɪzi / *adj.* (-ier,-iest) ❶ 忙的：Autumn is a ～ season. 秋天是一个繁忙的季节。**同** engaged,working **反** free, idle ❷ 占用的；没空的：He can't see you right now. He is ～ with an important meeting. 他现在无法接见你。他正在开一个重要的会议。**同** occupied **反** free **派** busily *adv.*

用法
形容词 busy 可用于以下两种句型：❶ be busy with ＋名词(代词),意为"忙于某事"：He is busy with his work day and night. 他日夜忙于工作。❷ be busy doing sth.,意为"忙于做某事"：The students are busy preparing for the final examination. 学生们正忙于准备期末考试。

but / bʌt,bət / Ⅰ *conj.* 可是；但是：She would like to go ～ she is too busy. 她想去,但太忙。/ It never rains, ～ it pours. 不雨则已,一雨倾盆。**同** however, nevertheless Ⅱ *adv.* 不过；只：She left ～ half an hour ago. 她离开不过才半小时。**同** only, just Ⅲ *prep.* 除了：There was nothing ～ water. 除了水以外,什么也没有。**同** except /～ **for** ～是：But for your advice, I should have made a big mistake. 要是没有你的劝告,我已经犯大错了。

用法
but (*prep.*)前有动词 do 时,其后接不带 to 的不定式,如：I did nothing but go home. 我除了回家之外,别无办法。She did nothing but cry all day. 她整天只是哭。若 but 前用的是 do 以外的动词,but 后就接带 to 的不定式,如：They desire nothing but to enjoy the present moment. 他们只希望今朝有酒今朝醉。

butter / ˈbʌtə(r) / *n.* [U]奶油；黄油

butterfly / ˈbʌtəflaɪ / *n.* [C]蝴蝶

button / ˈbʌt(ə)n / Ⅰ *n.* [C] ❶纽扣：You should sew on a ～ here. 你应该在这里缝上一个纽扣。❷按键：a forward ～ 快进键/ a rewind ～ 倒退键/ a pause ～ 暂停键/ Press this ～ and you'll see the film. 按一下这个键,你就会看到那部电影。Ⅱ *v.* 钉扣子；扣子：Button (up) your coat. 把外衣纽扣扣上。**同** fasten

buy / baɪ / *v.* (bought / bɔːt /, bought)买；购

买：I bought the tickets yesterday. 我昨天买的票。/ He will ～ his brother a new book. 他将给他弟弟买一本新书。**同** purchase **反** sell

辨析
buy 为普通用语,意义较广,指日常生活中购买东西,可用于借喻：buy a man 向某人行贿,收买某人。**purchase** 通常表示购买大件的东西,指正式的交易：He has purchased a house. 他买了一幢房子。

buzz / bʌz / Ⅰ *v.* (蜂等)嗡嗡叫：The bees are ～ing among flowers. 蜜蜂在花丛中嗡嗡叫。**同** hum Ⅱ *n.* 嗡嗡声；蜂鸣声 **同** hum, murmur

by / baɪ / Ⅰ *prep.* ❶靠近；在…旁：There is a middle school ～ the church. 教堂旁有一所中学。**同** near, next ❷不迟于；到…为止：Be back ～ ten o'clock. 十点钟以前回来。**同** before ❸经过；由；沿：He walked right ～ me. 他正好从我身边走过。**同** past, along ❹靠；用；通过；乘坐(交通工具)：～ air (train, bus, spaceship, ship)乘飞机(火车、汽车、宇宙飞船、轮船)/ He will go to Beijing ～ air (airplane). 他将乘飞机去北京。**同** through, with/～ **and** 不久：She will be here ～ and ～. 她很快就到这儿。～ **far** …得多：This pen is better ～ far. 这支笔好得多。～ **hand** 用手：The letter was delivered ～ hand. 此信是靠人工递送的。～ **the end of** 到…为止：By the end of last term,we had learned 2,000 words. 到上学期末,我们已学了 2 000 个单词。Ⅱ *adv.* 在近旁；经过：A group of children passed ～. 一群孩子走过去了。/ The Smiths live close ～. 史密斯一家住得很近。**同** near, nearby

bye / baɪ / *int.* (＝goodbye)再见

byname / ˈbaɪneɪm / *n.* 别名；绰号：Don't use your ～ in formal meeting. 在正式会议上不要用别名。

bypass / ˈbaɪpɑːs / Ⅰ *n.* 旁路；旁道 **同** detour, byway Ⅱ *vt.* 忽视；绕过：The bus ～ed the city and arrived at a small village. 汽车绕过城市开到一个小村子。**同** ignore, neglect **反** face, confront

bystander / ˈbaɪstændə(r) / *n.* [C]旁观者；局外人；看热闹的人：The police asked some of the ～s about the accident. 警方向一些旁观者了解出事的情况。

byte / baɪt / *n.* [C] (计算机)字节

C c

cab / kæb / n. [C]出租汽车：call（hail）a ～ （举手）叫出租车/You may take a ～ to see your old friend. 你可以乘出租车去看你的老 朋友。同 taxi, taxicab

cabbage / ˈkæbɪdʒ / n. 白菜；卷心菜

cabin / ˈkæbɪn / n. [C] ❶机舱；舰长室：a ～ boy 客舱服务员/ the ～ class（客轮）二等舱 同 compartment ❷小房 同 hut

cabinet / ˈkæbɪnət / n. [C] ❶橱柜，壁柜：She put some bowls into the kit-chen ～. 她把几只 碗放进橱柜里。同 cupboard ❷（the ～）内阁： The Cabinet Minister is having a meeting. 内 阁部长正在开会。

cable / ˈkeɪbl / n. [C]缆索；电缆；越洋电报：a ～car 缆车/ a ～way 索道/ a ～ gram 越洋 电报/ The workers are laying a ～. 工人们正 在铺设电缆。同 wire, line

cactus / ˈkæktəs / n.（pl. cacti ˈkæktaɪ 或 cactuses）仙人掌

CAD（＝computer-aided design）计算机辅助 设计

cadre / ˈkɑːdə(r) / n. [C]干部：Cadres of all ranks should pay special attention to such problems. 各级干部都应特别重视这样的问 题。同 officer, official

cafe / ˈkæfeɪ, kæˈfeɪ / n. [C]咖啡馆；酒吧

cafeteria / ˌkæfəˈtɪərɪə / n. [C]自助餐馆： Most students take meals in the school ～. 大 多数学生在学生食堂就餐。同 restaurant

caffeine / ˈkæfiːn / n. [U]咖啡因，咖啡碱

cage / keɪdʒ / n. [C]鸟笼；笼：A bird escaped from the ～. 有一只鸟从笼子里飞走了。

cake / keɪk / n. [C]面包；蛋糕；饼：a piece of ～ 一块蛋糕/ She bought her son a birthday ～ this morning. 今天上午她为儿子买了一 个生日蛋糕。

calamity / kəˈlæməti / n. [C]灾难；不幸事 件：A tsunami is a disastrous natural ～. 海啸 是一种毁灭性的自然灾害。同 disaster, mis-fortune

calcify / ˈkælsɪfaɪ / v.（使）石灰质化，（使）钙 化；（使）骨化：Cartilage often calcifies in older people 老年人体内的软骨常常会钙化。/This calcium salts work to ～ the bones. 钙盐有使 骨骼钙化的功效。

calcium / ˈkælsɪəm / n. [U]钙

calculate / ˈkælkjuleɪt / v. 计算：I must have ～d wrongly. 我一定算错了。同 figure, com-pute/～ **on** 依赖；依靠；指望：We ～ on a hundred people attending the meeting. 我们指 望有 100 人参加这个会议。

calculation / ˌkælkjuˈleɪʃn / n. 计算；计算结 果：The boy learned mathematical ～s at five. 那男孩五岁就学会了数学运算。/ My ～ is different from yours. 我的计算结果与你的不 相同。同 computation, figuring

calculator / ˈkælkjuleɪtə(r) / n. [C]计算器； 计算者：a pocket ～ 袖珍计算器

calculus / ˈkælkjuləs / n. [U]微积分（学）：dif-ferential ～ 微分（学）/integral ～ 积分（学）

calendar / ˈkælɪndə(r) / n. [C]日历；历书：a desk ～ 台历/a wall ～挂历 / a school ～ 校 历 同 timetable

calf / kɑːf, kæf / n.（pl. calves/kɑːvz, kævz）❶ [C]小牛，牛犊 ❷[C]（大型哺乳动物的）仔，幼 兽：The children saw the new seal ～es at the zoo. 孩子们在动物园看到了新生的小海狗。

call / kɔːl / Ⅰ v. ❶喊；叫：When the teacher ～s you, please stand up. 老师叫你时，请站起来。 同 cry, shout ❷命令；召集，召回：Call the chil-dren in for supper. 叫孩子们进来吃晚饭。同 assemble, invite ❸打电话：I'll ～ you when I arrive in Beijing. 一到北京，我就打电话给你。 同 telephone, phone ❹命名；称呼：She is ～ed Lucy. 她叫露西。同 name, entitle/～ **back** 使 回想；召回；回电话：Please ask her to ～ back as soon as she comes. 她一来就请她回个电

话。～ **down** 祈求；责骂，斥责：He was ～ed down by his mother for being late for class. 他因上课迟到而受到母亲的责骂。～ **for** ①来取；来接：I will ～ for you at your home. 我将去你家接你。②需要；需求：Success in school ～s for much hard study. 要想学习成绩好，需要多用功。～ **forth** 唤起；振作起；鼓起勇气（精神等）：April showers ～ forth May flowers. 四月的阵雨浇出五月的鲜花。～ **off** 停止；取消：The basketball game was ～ed off because of rain. 篮球赛因雨取消。～ **on** / **upon** ①恳求；请求；要求：We ～ed on our English teacher for a song. 我们请英语老师唱一首歌。②访问，拜访：She ～ed on an old friend when she was in the city. 她来该市时拜访了一位老朋友。～ **out** 大声叫喊：The old woman ～ed out with pain. 老太太痛得叫了起来。～ **up** ①提醒；使回忆起：The picture ～ed up memories of our class trip. 这张照片使我们回忆起班上旅行的事。②召唤，动员：He was ～ed up for military service. 他应征入伍。③打电话：She ～ed up a friend just for a chat. 她给朋友打电话聊天。Ⅱ n. 喊；信号；要求；通话；拜访：a dial-direct ～ 直拨电话/ a house ～ 上门出诊；上门维修/ a reporting ～ 举报电话 圙 cry, shout , visit, phone, telephone/ **make (give) sb. a ～** 打电话给某人：If I have something important, I'll make you a ～. 如有重要事情，我会打电话给你。**make (pay) a ～ on sb.** 访问某人：They said they were going to make a ～ on you the next day. 他们说第二天去拜访你。

calligraphy / kəˈlɪɡrəfi / n. [U](尤指好看的)字迹，笔迹；书法：practise ～ after a master sheet 临帖练习法

calm / kɑːm / Ⅰ adj. 平静的；镇定的：The sea was ～. 海面平静。/ Though she was very frightened, she answered my question with a ～ voice. 尽管她很惊恐，但仍以平静的声音回答我的问题。圙 quiet, still, peaceful Ⅱ v. 使平静；使镇定：Calm yourself! 请安静！/ He stayed ～ at the meeting. 在会上他一直很镇定。 㴋 calmly adv.

calorie / ˈkæləri / [C] n. 卡，卡路里(热量单位)

Cambridge / ˈkeɪmbrɪdʒ / n. 剑桥(英格兰东南部城市，剑桥大学所在地)

camel / ˈkæməl / n. [C]骆驼：Camels live in

hot district. 骆驼生活在炎热地区。

camera / ˈkæmərə / n. [C]照相机；摄影机：an auto focus ～ 傻瓜相机/ I like a color digital ～. 我喜欢彩色数字摄像机。

cameraman / ˈkæmərəˌmæn / n. [C](尤指电影或电视的)(专业)摄影师，摄像师

camouflage / ˈkæməflɑːʒ / n. [U]伪装，掩饰；(动物的)(天然)保护色：natural ～ 天然保护色/The soldiers covered their helmets with heaves as ～. 士兵用树叶遮盖钢盔作伪装。

camp / kæmp / n. [C]野营地：They set up their ～ near the top of the mountain. 他们在靠近山顶的地方扎营。圙 tent, campsite

campaign / kæmˈpeɪn / n. [C]战役；运动：a patriotic public health ～ 爱国卫生运动/ a ～ for contributions 募捐运动/ The students launched an anti-smoking ～ on campus. 学生们在校园里发起一场戒烟运动。圙 battle, movement

campus / ˈkæmpəs / n. [C]校园：We have colorful ～ culture and life. 我们有丰富多彩的校园文化和校园生活。

can¹ / kæn, kən / aux. v. (could / kʊd /) ❶能，会：She ～ speak French. 她会说法语。❷可能：What he said couldn't be true. 他说的不可能是真的。❸(口语)可以(表示许可)：The boy asked whether he could go for an outing. 小男孩问他是否可以去郊游。

can² / kæn / n. [C]罐头；听：a coffee ～ 咖啡罐头/ an oil ～ 油桶/ a water ～ 水桶/ an ash ～ (美)垃圾桶/ a ～ of beer 一听啤酒

Canada / ˈkænədə / n. 加拿大

Canadian / kəˈneɪdjən / Ⅰ adj. 加拿大的；加拿大人的 Ⅱ n. [C]加拿大人

canal / kəˈnæl / n. [C]运河；沟渠；水道：the Suez Canal 苏伊士运河/ China's Grand Canal 中国大运河 圙 channel, waterway

cancel / ˈkænsl / vt. ❶取消；撤销：The teacher called to ～ tomorrow's class meeting. 老师打电话说取消明天的班会。圙 abolish ❷删去；划掉：He ～ed an incorrect figure in his plan. 他把计划中的一个错误数字划掉。圙 erase, remove

cancer / ˈkænsə(r) / n. 癌：His grandfather died of lung ～. 他的祖父死于肺癌。

candid / ˈkændɪd / adj. 直率的，坦诚的，直言不讳的：a candid reply 坦诚的回答/a ～ excitement 毫不掩饰的兴奋/a ～ critic 直言不讳的评论家

candidate / ˈkændɪdɪt / n. [C]候选人；应试者；应征者：There are ～s for president of the university. 有 8 名候选人竞选校长。/ The twenty ～s for the job all came from Shanghai. 20 名求职者都是上海人。同 competitor, applicant

candle / ˈkændl / n. [C]蜡烛：The old fisherman lit a ～ to see what was happening. 老渔夫点燃一支蜡烛看看发生什么了。/ We seldom use ～s now. 现在我们很少使用蜡烛。

candy / ˈkændi / n. (美)糖果

cane / keɪn / n. [C]手杖；棍；棒；茎：sugar ～ 甘蔗/ The old man was walking with a ～. 老人拄着拐杖走路。同 stick

cannon / ˈkænən / n. [C](pl. cannon 或 cannons)大炮；机关炮；火炮：The soldier fired a ～ at the enemy. 战士向敌人开炮。

canoe / kəˈnu / n. [C]独木舟

canteen / kænˈtiːn / n. [C](工厂、公司、学校等的)食堂；小卖部：Most students have meals at the student ～. 多数学生在学生食堂用餐。同 cafeteria

canvas / ˈkænvəs / n. ❶[U]帆布 ❷[C]画布；油画

canyon / ˈkænjən / n. [C]峡谷

CAO(= chief administrative officer)首席行政官

cap / kæp / n. [C]帽子；盖头：take off one's ～ 脱帽

capability / ˌkeɪpəˈbɪləti / n. 能力；才能：Can you prove your ～ for the job? 你能证明你有能力胜任这项工作吗？/ It was beyond her capabilities. 那是她力所不能及的。同 ability, skill

capable / ˈkeɪpəbl / adj. 有能力的；有技能的：She is a ～ girl. 她是一个很能干的女孩。同 able, competent 反 unable, incompetent/ **be ～ of doing sth.** 有能力做某事：He is ～ of doing anything. 他什么事都能做。

capacious / kəˈpeɪʃəs / adj. 宽敞的；容量大的：a ～ storage bin 大(容量)储藏柜/a man of ～ mind 心胸宽大的人

capacity / kəˈpæsəti / n. ❶能力；才能：The boy has a great ～ for mathematics. 那男孩很有数学才能。同 ability, capability ❷容量；容积：The classroom has a seating ～ of 80

students. 这间教室可坐 80 名学生。同 volume, size

cape / keɪp / n. [C]海角；岬：The Cape of Good Hope is in the south of Africa. 好望角在非洲南端。同 headland, point

capillary / kəˈpɪləri, ˈkæpɪləri / n. [C]毛细(血)管

capital / ˈkæpɪtl / n. [C] ❶首都；省会；首府；都市；中心：Beijing is the ～ of China. 北京是中国的首都。同 center, headquarters ❷资本；本钱：The company has a ～ of 3,000,000 dollars to improve its equipment. 这家公司用 300 万美元资金来改进设备。同 cash ❸大写字母；(句子的)第一个字母：He wrote his name in ～s. 他用大写字母写名字。

capitalism / ˈkæpɪtəlɪzəm / n. [U]资本主义

capitalist / ˈkæpɪtəlɪst / Ⅰ adj. 资本主义的 Ⅱ n. [C]资本家

capsule / ˈkæpsjuːl / n. [C] ❶胶囊：The patient must have three ～s at a time. 病人须一次服用三粒胶囊。❷密封舱；航天舱：a space ～ 航天舱；太空舱/ They recovered the ～ successfully. 他们成功地回收了太空舱。同 satellite, spaceship, spacecraft

captain / ˈkæptɪn / n. [C]队长；长官：the ～ of a football team 足球队长/ the ～ of a ship 船长 同 leader, commander

caption / ˈkæpʃn / n. [C]标题；说明；字幕：He read the ～ under the photo carefully. 他仔细读了照片下面的说明。同 heading, title, explanation

captivate / ˈkæptɪveɪt / vt. 使着迷；使倾倒；迷惑：The children were ～d by her story. 孩子们被她的故事迷住了。/The prima donna ～d the audience. 女主角使观众们着了迷。

captive / ˈkæptɪv / n. [C]俘虏：They took 17 ～s in the battle. 战斗中他们活捉了 17 名俘虏。同 prisoner

capture / ˈkæptʃə(r) / Ⅰ vt. 捕捉；捕获；俘房：The police ～d the robber soon. 警察很快抓住了抢匪。同 seize, catch, arrest Ⅱ n. 捕获；战利品；捕获物：With the ～ of the escaped criminal he was praised greatly. 由于捕获了逃犯,他受到高度赞扬。同 arrest

car / kɑː(r) / n. [C]小汽车；车；车厢：a restaurant (dining) ～餐车/ a touring ～游览车/ sleeping ～卧铺车厢/My colleagues bought a

～ one buy one recently. 最近我的同事们一个接一个地买了小汽车。同 vehicle, auto

carat / 'kærət / n. [C]克拉,公制克拉(钻石等珠宝的重量单位,等于 200 毫克;略作 c,ct)

carbohydrate / ˌkɑːbəʊ'haɪdreɪt / n. 碳水化合物:The food you eat everyday should have some ～ in. 你每天吃的食物中应当含有碳水化合物。

carbon / 'kɑːbən / n. [U]碳:～ dioxide 二氧化碳/～ monooxide 一氧化碳

card / kɑːd / n. [C]❶卡片;名片:identification ～身份证/ a post ～ 明信片/ a calling ～ 名片/ a student ～ 学生证/ a New Year's ～ 新年贺卡/ a membership ～ 会员证/ He was given a red (yellow) ～ in the football match. 在这场足球赛中他得了一张红(黄)牌。❷纸牌:They play ～s after work. 下班后他们打牌玩。

cardboard / 'kɑːdbɔːd / n. [U]纸板:He put his books in a ～ box. 他把书放在一个厚纸盒里。

cardinal / 'kɑːdɪnl / adj. 主要的;基本的:four ～ principles 四项基本原则/ Being kind to others is her ～ virtue. 对人友善是她的主要美德。同 major, chief, basic 反 minor, secondary

care / keə(r) / Ⅰ v. ❶关心;担心:A good teacher always ～s about his students. 一个好老师总是关心他的学生。同 mind, concern 反 disregard ❷关怀;照顾:She ～s a lot for children first. 她总是首先照顾孩子们。同 concern, watch ❸喜欢;愿意:I don't ～ to go shopping with you; I'd rather stay home reading. 我不愿意跟你去购物,我宁愿待在家里看书。同 like, want 反 dislike ❹介意;计较:I don't ～ what she said at the meeting. 我并不介意她在会上说了些什么。同 mind / ～ about:①喜欢,爱好;介意:I don't much ～ a-bout going. 我并不很想去。/ She doesn't ～ about the matter. 她对此事毫不介意。②关心;重视:He often thinks only of himself. He doesn't ～ about other people. 他常常只想到自己,从不关心别人。/ ～ for 喜爱;想;照料:Would you ～ for some tea? 你想喝点茶吗? Ⅱ n. 照料;关心;小心谨慎:You should drive with great ～ in the town. 在市里开车你得十分小心。/ The little patient was left in my

～. 小病人留给我来照顾。同 concern, re-gard, caution / take ～ of 照料,护理;看管:Let me take ～ of the cleaning. 让我来打扫吧。/ You should take good ～ of your books. 你应好好爱惜书。

career / kə'rɪə(r) / n. [C]职业;生涯;经历:She planned to make acting her ～. 她打算把表演作为她的职业。/ People are interested in his long diplomatic ～. 人们对他长期的外交官经历很感兴趣。同 profession, occupation

careful / 'keəfl / adj. 小心的;细致的;关切的:She is ～ at her work. 她工作细心。/ Be ～ not to drive too fast. 小心别把车开得太快。同 watchful, attentive 反 careless 派 carefully adv.

careless / 'keələs / adj. 粗心的;漫不经心的:Don't be ～ with your pronunciation. 不要对你的发音不准漫不经心。同 unconcerned, thoughtless 反 careful, attentive

caretaker / 'keəˌteɪkə(r) / n. [C]照看者;照看者;(大楼的)看管人;(学校等的)看门人

cargo / 'kɑːgəʊ / n. 货物:The workers are ship-ping the ～ at the part. 工人们在港口装货。同 goods

caring / 'keərɪŋ / adj. 有同情心的;一心一意的;为公民提供福利的:the ～ professions, such as nursing and social work 照料别人的职业,如看护和社区工作

carnation / kɑː'neɪʃn / n. [C](麝)香石竹,康乃馨

carnival / 'kɑːnɪvl / n. ❶[U]狂欢节,嘉年华会 ❷[C](流动)游艺团,游艺场(有各种游戏、杂耍等)

carnivorous / kɑː'nɪvərəs / adj. 食肉的:Ti-gers and lions are ～ animals. 老虎和狮子都是食肉动物。

carrier / 'kærɪə(r) / n. [C]❶搬运人;携带者;邮递员;运输工具:a public ～ 公共运输工具 ❷运输公司;运输企业者;邮件运输商行 ❸(保险业的)承保单位 ❹带菌者;病邮;病原携带者;传病媒介

carpenter / 'kɑːpəntə(r) / n. [C]木工;木匠

carpet / 'kɑːpɪt / n. [C]地毯;地毡:The floor is covered with a ～. 地板上铺着地毯。

carriage / 'kærɪdʒ / n. [C]车;四轮马车;(铁路)客车厢

carrot / 'kærət / n. 胡萝卜

carry / ˈkæri / v. 携带;运送;传送;支持:He carries his changes in his pocket. 他把零钱放在他口袋里。/ She was ~ing a box on her shoulder. 她肩上扛着一只箱子。/ These pillars ~ the weight of the roof. 这些柱子支撑着屋顶。/ The pipes ~ oil to cities. 这些管子把油送往城市。同 take, bring, transport, convey/~ **away** ①冲走;刮去:The bridge was carried away by the flood. 洪水冲走了桥。②使失去自制力;吸引住:The music carried her away. 这音乐吸引了她。~ **off** ①劫持,劫走:Cancer carried him off. 癌症夺走了他的生命。②意外成功:She carried off the palm in both tennis and swimming. 她在网球和游泳两项运动中获胜。~ **on** ①从事,进行:They carried on business for many years in Shanghai. 他们在上海经商多年。②继续:He carried on in spite of the difficult conditions. 尽管条件艰苦,他仍坚持下去。~ **out** 实施;执行;完成:We must ~ out reforms in education. 我们必须进行教育改革。/ We should ~ out the plan to the full. 我们应该不折不扣地执行计划。~ **through** 完成;结束:He carried his project through despite the opposition. 尽管有人反对,他还是完成了自己的项目。

carsick / ˈkɑːsɪk / adj. 晕车的:They had to stop because Billy got ~. 因为比利晕车,他们不得不两次停车。

cart / kɑːt / n. 大车;手推车:She put the goods she chose into the shopping ~. 她把选好的商品放进购物车里。

cartoon / kɑːˈtuːn / n. 卡通,动画片;漫画:The little boy draw ~s well. 小男孩漫画画得很好。

carve / kɑːv / v. 雕刻:He ~d a boat of ivory. 他雕了一条象牙船。同 cut

case¹ / keɪs / n. [C] ❶情况;状况:Do you know what we should do in this ~? 你知道在这种情况下我们该做什么吗?同 situation, condition, state ❷事实;实情:She thinks that her mother would be healthy forever but that is not the ~. 她认为她母亲会永远健康,但事实并非如此。同 fact ❸事例;实例:a ~ in point 恰当的例子/ Please cite a ~ to explain the problem. 请举例解释这个问题。同 example, instance ❹病症;病例;病人:He asked the doctor to explain his ~ to him carefully. 他要求大夫向他详细说明他的病情。同 disease, illness ❺诉讼;案件:This is a civil (criminal) ~. 这是一桩民事(刑事)案件。同 suit, trial | **in any** ~ 无论如何:In any ~ I shall return in a day or two. 总之,我一两天内就回来。**in** ~ 如果,万一:He doesn't dare to leave the room in ~ he should be recognized. 他不敢出门,生怕被人认出来。**in no** ~ 绝不,毫不:In no ~ can she go out. 她绝不能出去。

case² / keɪs / n. [C]箱(子);盒(子):a book ~ 书橱/ a brief ~ 公文包/ a note ~ 皮夹子/ a suit ~ 手提箱/ Please put it back in the ~. 用完请放回盒子里。同 box, chest

cash / kæʃ / I n. [C]钱;现金;现款:She paid the TV set in ~. 买电视机她用现金付费。/ Cash or charge, please? 请问是付现金或是记账? / Sorry, I have no ~ with me. 很抱歉,我没带现金。同 money, banknote, bill II vt. 把…兑现:You'd first ~ your check before you go to that small shop. 去那家小店之前,你得把支票兑换为现金。同 change, exchange

cashier / kæˈʃɪə(r) / n. [C]出纳员:A ~ should work very carefully. 出纳员应非常细心地工作。同 teller, treasurer

casino / kəˈsiːnəʊ / n. [C]赌场;夜总会;俱乐部

cassette / kəˈset / n. [C]盒式录音带

cast / kɑːst / v. (cast, cast) 投,掷,抛:~ a vote 投票/~ seeds 播种/~ a net 撒网/~ a glance (a look, an eye) at (over, on) sb. 向某人瞧了瞧 同 throw, toss/~ **about** (**around**) ①寻找:They are ~ing about for an experienced teacher to take Mr. Chen's place. 他们正在找寻一位有经验的老师代替陈先生。②思考;考虑:I am ~ing about how to get my bike back from John. 我正考虑怎样从约翰那里取回我的自行车。~ **aside** 抛弃:Cast your worries aside. 抛开你的顾虑吧! ~ **away** 抛弃;浪费:He will ~ away this money just as he has done in the past. 他会像以往一样把这笔钱浪费掉。~ **out** 赶走;驱逐:After the scandal, he was ~ out of the best society. 自那件丑闻后,他已被上流社会除名。

castle / ˈkɑːsl / n. [C]城堡:It is an ancient ~. 这是一座古城堡。同 stronghold

casual / ˈkæʒʊəl / adj. ❶偶然的;碰巧的:I had a ~ meeting with Mr. Smith at the airport. 在机场我和史密斯先生不期而遇。同 accidental, unplanned 反 fixed, arranged ❷随便的;非

正式的；不拘礼的：You are not right to take a ～ attitude toward your teacher. 对老师态度随便是不对的。/ May I wear ～ clothes here? 在这里我可以穿便服吗? 同 informal 反 formal ❸临时的；不定期的：The company employs him as a ～ laborer. 公司雇他为临时工。同 random, occasional 派 casually adv.

casualty / ˈkæʒjuəlti / n. [C] 严重伤亡事故；(事故中的) 伤亡人员；受害者：There were heavy casualties in the accident. 那场意外事故造成了惨重伤亡。同 accident, killed, wounded

cat / kæt / n. [C] 猫

catalog(ue) / ˈkætəlɒg / n. [C] 目录；目录册：I looked up the author ～ and found the book I wanted. 我查作者目录找到了我要的书。同 list, file

catalyst / ˈkætəlɪst / n. [C] ❶催化剂：The enzyme was a ～ in that reaction. 酶是那个反应的催化剂。❷促进(或刺激)因素；起促进作用的人

catastrophe / kəˈtæstrəfi / n. [C] 大灾难；大祸；糟糕的结局：They survived a ～ in the tsunami. 他们逃脱了海啸这场大灾难。/ What caused the ～ of the party? 是什么使晚会的结局这么糟糕? 同 disaster, misfortune

catch / kætʃ / v. (caught / kɔːt /, caught) 捉；抓；捕；赶上；染上：He caught the ball. 他接住了球。/ They were caught in the rain last night. 昨晚他们被雨淋了。同 seize, arrest, overtake, contract／～ **(a) cold** 感冒；伤风：Put on more clothes or you'll ～ (a) cold. 穿暖和些，否则你会着凉的。～ **fire** 着火：Paper ～es fire easily. 纸容易着火。～ **hold of** 抓住；握住：Please ～ hold of the rope. 请抓住绳子。～ **sight of** 一眼看见；突然看见：I suddenly caught sight of a thief behind the door. 我突然看见门后有个贼。～ **up with** 赶上；追上：You have to work hard in order to ～ up with the rest of the class. 你必须努力学习以赶上班里其他人。

catching / ˈkætʃɪŋ / adj. ❶传染性的：Measles is very ～. 麻疹传染很快。❷有感染力的；迷人的，吸引人的：a ～ time 迷人的时刻／The singer has a ～ style. 那位歌手演唱的风格很吸引人。

categorize / ˈkætɪgəraɪz / vt. ❶将…分类，把…分类：We ～d the snowflakes into several shapes. 我们把雪花的形状分成几种。❷命名；

描述：He was ～d as a slow reader. 他被认为是一个阅读慢的人。

category / ˈkætəgəri / n. [C]种类；类目；类型：Does Botany belong to the ～ of biology? 植物属于生物学类吗? 同 division, class

cater / ˈkeɪtə(r) / vi. 供应伙食；满足(需要)；投合：A restaurant is difficult to ～ to all tastes. 一家餐馆很难满足所有人的口味。/ The hospital should ～ to the need of its patients. 医院应当满足病人的需要。同 satisfy, please

caterpillar / ˈkætəpɪlə(r) / n. [C]毛虫；蝎(蝴蝶、蛾等鳞翅目昆虫的幼虫)

cathedral / kəˈθiːdrəl / n. [C]大教堂

cathode / ˈkæθəʊd / n. [C]阴极；负极

Catholic / ˈkæθlɪk / Ⅰ adj. 天主教的 Ⅱ n. [C]天主教徒

cattle / ˈkætl / n. (总称)牛；家畜：The man raised ～ in the countryside. 那人在农村养牛。

cauliflower / ˈkɒlɪflaʊə(r) / n. [C]花椰菜，花菜

cause / kɔːz / Ⅰ v. 引起；给…带来：What ～d his failure? 什么致使他失败? / His carelessness ～d the accident. 他的粗心大意造成了这次意外事故。同 make, produce Ⅱ n. 原因，理由；目标；理想；事业：Don't stay away without good ～. 不要无故离开。/ We are engaged in a great and glorious ～. 我们正从事一项伟大而光荣的事业。同 reason, aim, goal

caution / ˈkɔːʃn / n. ❶[U]小心；谨慎：He lifted the box with ～. 他小心地提起那只箱子。同 care, carefulness ❷警告；告诫：The policeman gave the driver a ～ for illegal parking. 因违章停车警察警告了那位司机。同 warning, alarm

cautious / ˈkɔːʃəs / adj. 小心的；谨慎的：She is ～ when riding across the street. 骑车过街时她非常小心。同 careful, watchful, attentive 反 careless, rash

cave / keɪv / n. [C]岩洞；洞穴

CD (＝compact disk)激光唱片；光盘

CD-ROM (＝compact disk read-only memory) 信息储存光盘

cease / siːs / v. 停止；中止；结束：The heart will ～ to beat when life ～s. 生命结束，心脏就会停止跳动。/ My joy shall never ～. 我的快乐

永无休止。同 stop,end 反 begin,start

辨析

cease 可作及物动词用，也可作不及物动词用，后面接名词或接不定式，强调逐渐结束某种状态：The music ceased suddenly. 音乐戛然而止。stop 强调突然中止某种行为或动作，或状态的突然结束：Stop! Or I'll shoot. 站住！否则我要开枪了。The boy stopped crying quite suddenly. 那小孩突然不哭了。We stopped to have a rest. 我们停下来休息了一会儿。

ceaseless / ˈsiːslɪs / adj. 不停的,不间断的;无休无止的: ~ effort 不懈的努力/the ~ stream 奔腾不息的溪流

cede / siːd / vt. 放弃;割让;出让: ~ territory to a country 把土地割让给某个国家/~ one's stance in debate 在辩论中放弃立场

ceiling / ˈsiːlɪŋ / n.[C]天花板 同 roof 反 floor

celebrate / ˈselɪbreɪt / vt. 歌颂;庆祝: They warmly ~d this festival. 他们热烈地庆祝这个节日。His courage was ~d in all newspapers. 他的英勇行为为赢得所有报纸的颂扬。同 commemorate,praise 派 celebration n.

celebrity / səˈlebrəti / n. ❶[U]著名;名声: He teaches well and won ~ among students soon. 他书教得好,很快在学生中赢得名声。同 fame,reputation 反 disgrace ❷[C]名人;著名人士: He often says that he knows many celebrities. 他常说他认识很多名人。同 noble,worthy

celery / ˈseləri / n.[U]芹菜

cell / sel / n.[C] ❶细胞: The doctor wrote an article on ~ division. 那位大夫写了一篇论细胞分裂的文章。❷小牢房: The criminal was shut in a ~ jail. 罪犯被关在一间单人牢房里。同 ward,prison ❸电池: He put a dry ~ in the radio. 他在收音机里放进一只干电池。同 battery

cellar / ˈselə(r) / n.[C]地下室;地窖 同 basement

cello / ˈtʃeləʊ / n.[C](pl. cellos)大提琴

cellular / ˈseljʊlə(r) / adj. 细胞的,由细胞组成的;细胞状的: ~ structure 细胞结构/ the transport of ~ products to the rest of the body 细胞产品往身体其他部分转送

cement / sɪˈment / n.[U]水泥

cemetery / ˈsemətri / n.[C]公墓;墓地

同 graveyard

censor / ˈsensə(r) / I n.[C](书刊、报纸、电影、电视等的)审查员,检查员: military ~s 军事审查员 II vt. ❶检查,审查;监察: a heavily ~ed editorial 一篇经过严格审查的社论 ❷删除;修改: The figure has been ~ed from a report published today. 今天出版的报道中这个数字被删除了。

census / ˈsensəs / n.[C]人口普查;人口调查: They carry out a ~ every two years in this district. 在这个地区他们每两年进行一次人口普查。同 registration

cent / sent / n. ❶[C]分;分币: The color pencil cost sixty ~s. 这支彩色铅笔卖六角钱。❷[U]一百: five per ~ 百分之五,5%

centennial / senˈteniəl / I n.[C]一百周年;一百周年纪念(日): We celebrated the ~ of our teacher's birth last Saturday. 上星期六我们为老师庆祝了一百周年诞辰。同 centenary,century II adj. 一百年的;一百周年纪念的: This is a ~ tree. Let's take a picture in front of it. 这是一棵百年老树,我们在它前面照张相吧。

centigrade / ˈsentigreid / adj. 摄氏温度的(略为 C): The highest temperature here is thirty-five degrees ~. 这里的最高温度是摄氏 35 度(35℃)。

centigram(me) / ˈsentigræm / n.[C]厘克

centimeter / ˈsentimiːtə(r) / n.[C]厘米(略作 cm)

centipede / ˈsentipiːd / n.[C]蜈蚣;马陆

central / ˈsentrəl / adj. ❶中心的;中央的;中枢的: the ~ government 中央政府/ Their office building is in the ~ part of the city. 他们的办公大楼位于市中心。同 middle,midway 反 local,outer ❷主要的,核心的: The ~ problem of today's discussion is how to reduce pollution. 今天讨论的主要问题是如何减少污染。同 major,fundamental 派 centralize vt.; centrally adv.

centre(-er) / ˈsentə(r) / n.[C]中心;中央: a financial ~ 金融中心/ a shopping ~ 购物中心/a training ~ 培训中心/ The boys and girls often play around the fountain in the ~ of the park. 孩子们常在公园中央的喷水池四周玩耍。同 middle, heart, core 反 exterior,outside

century / ˈsentʃəri / n. 世纪;百年: The city

changed a lot in the 90's of the 20th ～. 在 20 世纪 90 年代这座城市发生了很大的变化。/ He was a famous writer in the sixteenth ～. 他是 16 世纪的著名作家。

CEO (＝chief executive officer) 首席执行官

ceramics / sɪˈræmɪks / *n.* 陶瓷制品;陶瓷器; 陶瓷艺术:pieces of smashed ～陶瓷品碎片

cereal / ˈsɪərɪəl / *n.* 谷类;五谷;谷类食物:I went to buy some breakfast ～ in the supermarket. 我去超市买了一些早餐吃的谷类食品。同 grain

ceremonial / ˌserɪˈməʊnjəl / *adj.* 礼仪的;典礼的;正式的;适于正式场合的:a ～ occasion 正式场合/～ dress 礼服

ceremony / ˈserəməni / *n.* [C]典礼;仪式:a wedding ～ 婚礼/the opening ～ 开幕式/ the closing ～ 闭幕式/ His father spoke at the graduation ～. 他的父亲在毕业典礼上讲了话。

certain / ˈsɜːt(ə)n / *adj.* ❶(作表语)确定的, 无疑的: It is ～ that this team will win the game. 可以肯定这个队会赢。同 sure, undoubted 反 uncertain, doubtful ❷(作表语)确信的,深信的: I am ～ that he won't come. 我确信他不会来。/ Are you ～ of that? 你对那事确信无疑吗? ❸(作定语)某一,某种: He did it for a ～ purpose. 他干此事是为了某种目的。同 some 派 certainty *n.* ; certainly *adv.*

> 辨析
> **certain** 比 **sure** 语气更强。如果确定是事实, 用 certain,若认为是事实,通常用 sure。主语是 it 时,通常用 certain,不用 sure: It is certain that he will come. 他肯定会来。

certificate / səˈtɪfɪkət / *n.* [C]证(明)书;执照:a birth ～ 出生证明/ a death ～ 死亡证明/ a marriage ～ 结婚证书/ a medical ～ 诊断书/ They issued a ～ to him. 他们给他颁发了执照。同 document, license

certification / ˌsɜːtɪfɪˈkeɪʃn / *n.* [C]证明;证明书

certify / ˈsɜːtɪfaɪ / *vt.* 证明;发证书;发执照: The doctor certified the boy as healthy. 大夫证明小男孩身体健康。/ This is to ～ that he studied in our school five years ago. 兹证明他五年前在我校读书。同 prove, testify, assure

chain / tʃeɪn / *n.* [C] ❶链条;锁链:shake off ～s 摆脱枷锁/a watch ～ 表链/ Please don't

keep the dog on a ～. 请别把狗拴在铁链上。 ❷一连串;一系列;连锁:He runs a ～ store near our school. 他在我们学校附近经营一家连锁店。/ After a ～ of events she knew a lot. 经过一连串的事件,她懂得了很多东西。同 series, string

chair / tʃeə(r) / *n.* [C]椅子

chairman / ˈtʃeəmən / *n.* [C](*pl.* chairmen)主席;议长: He was elected ～ of the meeting. 他被选为会议主席。

chalk / tʃɔːk / *n.* [U]粉笔:coloured ～s 彩色粉笔/ a piece of ～ 一支粉笔

challenge / ˈtʃælɪndʒ / Ⅰ *n.* 挑战;激励:give a ～ 提出挑战/accept a ～ 接受挑战/ a letter of ～ 挑战书 Ⅱ *v.* 向…挑战;要求: ～ the limits 挑战极限/ He ～d me to play basketball. 他向我挑战比赛篮球。同 claim, dare

chamber / ˈtʃeɪmbə(r) / *n.* [C] ❶室,房间; (尤指)寝室:She retired to her ～. 她退进了她的卧室。❷会议厅;立法机关;司法机关:the council ～议事室 ❸(动植物体内的)室,腔: The heart has four ～s. 心脏有四室。

champagne / ʃæmˈpeɪn / *n.* [U]香槟酒:We always have ～ in our party. 我们总在聚会上喝香槟酒。

champion / ˈtʃæmpɪən / *n.* [C]冠军;优胜者: He won the ～of the world cup. 他赢得了世界杯赛的冠军。

chance / tʃɑːns / Ⅰ *n.* ❶[U]运气;偶然:take (stand, try) one's ～ 碰运气/It was pure ～ that I won the match. 我在那场比赛中获胜纯属偶然。❷机会;可能;侥幸:There is no ～ of his becoming a doctor. 他不可能成为医生。同 opportunity/ **by** ～ 偶然;意外地:I met him by ～. 我偶然碰见了他。Ⅱ *v.* ❶碰巧;偶然发生:Perhaps you might ～ on (upon) the dictionary at some old bookstall. 或许你会碰巧在哪家旧书摊上买到这本字典。同 happen, occur ❷冒险;碰运气:It may be risky, but we'll ～ it. 这可能有风险,但我们要碰碰运气。

chancellor / ˈtʃɑːnsələ, ˈtʃænsələ / *n.* [C] ❶ (奥地利、德国等的)总理,首相 ❷(大学的)名誉校长;(美国某些大学的)校长

change / tʃeɪndʒ / Ⅰ *v.* ❶改变;变化:She ～d her opinion. 她改变了看法。/ The city has ～d a great deal. 这座城市变化很大。❷更换;

C

互换；Shall we ～ seats? 我们交换座位好吗？ 同 exchange/～ ... into ... 把…变成…：Water is ～d into steam by heat. 水加热变成蒸气。 Ⅱ n. ❶变化：Great ～s have taken place in our country. 我们国家发生了巨大的变化。同 exchange ❷[U]零钱，找头：I have no ～ for an ice-cream. 我没有零钱买冰激凌。同 exchange 派 changeable adj.

channel / ˈtʃæn(ə)l / n. [C] ❶海峡；水道，渠：They cut a ～ to bring water to their fields. 他们挖了一条水渠把水引入农田。❷频道；波段：He changed ～s to find the program he liked. 他不停地换频道找他喜欢的节目。

chant / tʃɑːnt / n. [C]歌；圣歌；赞美诗 同 song, chorus

chaos / ˈkeɪɒs / n. [U]混乱；无秩序的；混沌：The whole district was in ～ after the fire. 火灾后整个地区一片混乱。同 disorder, confusion 反 order, peace

chaotic / keɪˈɒtɪk / adj. 混乱的：The city traffic was ～. 城市交通乱糟糟的。

chapter / ˈtʃæptə(r) / n. [C]章；回：The sentence is at Chapter 4. 那个句子在第四章。同 part, section

character / ˈkærəktə(r) / n. ❶[U]特性，特征；品格：He has a noble ～. 他有高尚的品格。/ She is firm in ～. 她性格坚强。同 nature, quality ❷(小说、戏剧中的)角色，人物：He appears in the ～ of Hamlet. 他扮演哈姆雷特的角色。同 part, person

characteristic / ˌkærəktəˈrɪstɪk / Ⅰ adj. 特有的；独特的 同 typical Ⅱ n. [C]特征；特性；特点：Everybody has his own individual ～. 每个人都有自己的个性。同 quality, feature

charcoal / ˈtʃɑːkəʊl / n. [U]木炭

charge / tʃɑːdʒ / Ⅰ n. ❶[C]费用；价钱：His ～s are not very high. 他收费不高。/ The tea in this hotel is free of ～. 这个宾馆里的茶水是免费的。同 fee, cost ❷[U]管理；主管；看管：We let him ～ of our children. 我们请他照看我们的孩子。/ The museum is under the ～ of the city government. 这个博物馆由市政府主管。同 control, management ❸[C]控告；指控：She withdrew the ～ against her boss. 她撤回了对老板的指控。同 accusation /in～ of 主管：Who is in ～ of study? 谁管学习？ take

～ of 负责；管理：It is he who takes ～ of the key to the classroom. 是他管教室的钥匙。 Ⅱ v. ❶承担；使负荷：We ～d him with heavy responsibilities. 我们让他担当重任。同 assign ❷控告；指控：The manager was ～d with bribery. 经理被控告受贿。同 accuse / ～ **sb. with sth.** 指控，控告：They ～d him with murder. 他们指控他犯了谋杀罪。❸充电

charity / ˈtʃærəti / n. ❶慈善，仁慈；施舍；慈善团体：The poor here live on ～. 这里的穷人靠救济生活。同 help, humanity

charm / tʃɑːm / n. [U]魅力；妩媚：It shows the ～ of nature. 它显示了大自然的魅力。同 attraction, beauty

charming / ˈtʃɑːmɪŋ / adj. 迷人的；可爱的；令人神往的：Her little stories are very ～ indeed. 她的小故事确实非常吸引人。同 attractive, pleasing

chart / tʃɑːt / n. [C]图表：The expert is studying a weather ～. 专家正在研究一份天气图。同 map, graph

charter / ˈtʃɑːtə(r) / Ⅰ n. ❶包租(交通工具)：We'll take a ～ flight to Hong Kong. 我们将乘包机去香港。同 rent, hire ❷宪章：Have you ever read *the Charter of the United Nations*? 你读过《联合国宪章》吗？同 constitution Ⅱ vt. 包租：You'd better ～ a bus to the airport. 你们最好包一辆车去机场。同 rent, hire

chase / tʃeɪs / v. 追逐；追求：Stop chasing about and sit down. 不要跑来跑去，坐下来！同 follow, hunt /～ **after** 跟踪；追逐：Chase after her and ask her to come earlier. 追上她，叫她早点来！

chat / tʃæt / Ⅰ v. (chatted; chatting)闲谈；聊天：After supper we ～ted for an hour. 晚饭后我们闲聊了一个小时。同 talk Ⅱ n. 闲谈；聊天：I'd like to have a ～ with my parents. 我想和我父母聊聊天。同 talk

chatter / ˈtʃætə(r) / vi. ❶喋喋不休，饶舌，唠叨：He was ～ing on about his new car. 他喋喋不休地谈论他的新车。❷(牙齿)打战：His teeth ～ed with cold. 他的牙齿因寒冷而直打战。

cheap / tʃiːp / adj. 廉价的；便宜的：These books are ～. 这些书价格便宜。/ Things in a supermarket are ～. 超市里的东西很便宜。

同 low-priced, inexpensive 反 expensive

cheat / tʃiːt / Ⅰ n. 骗子；欺骗；欺诈：He is a ～. 他是一个骗子。同 trick, cheater Ⅱ v. 欺骗；骗取；行骗：She ～ed him of his money. 她骗了他的钱。/ He always ～s at examinations. 他考试总是作弊。同 trick, deceit

check / tʃek / Ⅰ n. ❶[C]支票；账单：He gave his son a ～ for two hundred dollars. 他给儿子一张 200 美元的支票。/ "The ～, please!" said the man to the boss. 那人对老板说："(请结账)买单！" 同 bill ❷检查；核对：If we both add up the figures, your result will be a ～ on mine. 如果我俩同时加上这些数字，你的得数就可以用来核对我的得数。同 examination, inspection Ⅱ v. 检查；核对：Please ～ these figures. 请将这些数字核实一下。同 examine, inspect / ～ **in** 报到；办理登记手续：Everyone has to ～ in at the factory by nine o'clock. 所有人都得在 9 点钟到工厂签到上班。～ **off** 核对做记号于某物(表示已查无误)：Have these bills been ～ed off? 这些账核对过了吗？～ **out** 结账离开：Mr. Wang ～ed out five minutes ago. 王先生五分钟前就结账走了。

cheek / tʃiːk / n. [C]脸颊：Before she left, she kissed her mother on the ～. 临走前她吻了吻母亲的脸颊。

cheer / tʃɪə(r) / v. 欢呼；使振奋：The students ～ed when they heard that there would be a party this weekend. 听说这个周末有聚会，学生们都欢呼起来。/ He was ～ed by the good news. 这个好消息使他感到振奋。同 shout, encourage/～ **up** (使)愉快起来：He ～ed up at the thought of seeing his old friend. 他一想到要见老朋友，心里就高兴。派 cheerful adj.

cheers / tʃɪəz / int. 干杯；谢谢；再见

cheese / tʃiːz / n. [U]奶酪

chef / ʃef / n. [C]厨师：He is a famous ～ in France. 他是法国的著名厨师。同 cook

chemical / ˈkemɪkl / adj. 化学的：a ～ change 化学变化/～fertilizer 化肥/ a ～ formula 化学公式/ ～ reactions 化学反应

chemist / ˈkemɪst / n. [C]化学家；药剂师

chemistry / ˈkemɪstri / n. [U]化学：physical ～ 物理化学/warfare ～ 军事化学/ applied ～应用化学/ organic (inorganic) ～ 有机(无机)化学

chemo- / ˈkeməʊ / (前缀)意为"化学的"：～

synthesis 化学合成/～ therapy 化学疗法；化学治疗/ ～sphere 臭氧层

cheque / tʃek / n. [C]支票

cherish / ˈtʃerɪʃ / vt. ❶爱护；珍视：Support the army and ～ the people. 拥军爱民。同 love, treasure ❷怀有(感情)；抱有(希望)：The old soldier ～s a deep love for his motherland. 老战士十分热爱自己的祖国。同 harbor, entertain

cherry / ˈtʃeri / n. [C]樱桃；樱桃树

chess / tʃes / n. [U]棋；国际象棋：play ～ 下象棋/a ～ master 象棋大师

chest / tʃest / n. [C] ❶柜子；箱子；橱：I put my ID card in the ～ but I didn't find it. 我把身份证放在柜子里了，但是我没有找到。同 box, case, cabinet ❷胸；胸膛：The doctor said that she suffered from ～ disease. 大夫说她患了胸部疾病。同 breast, bosom

chestnut / ˈtʃesnʌt / n. ❶[C]栗子；栗树 ❷[U]栗色 同 brown

chew / tʃuː / v. 咀嚼；咬碎：She told her son to ～ thoroughly when eating. 她告诉儿子吃东西要细嚼慢咽。/ ～ (**upon, over**) sth. (喻)沉思，细想：Just ～ those facts over and let me know your opinion. 你细想一下这些事实，然后将你的意见告诉我。

chick / tʃɪk / n. [C]小鸡；小鸟；小孩

chicken / ˈtʃɪkɪn / n. 小鸡；鸡；鸡肉：They feed some ～s in the yard. 他们在院子里养了几只鸡。/ The ～ is delicious. 鸡肉美味可口。

chief / tʃiːf / Ⅰ adj. 主要的；首要的：The ～ news is printed on the front page of the newspaper. 主要新闻登在报纸的头版。同 main, major, leading Ⅱ n. [C] 首领；领袖：a commander in ～总司令/the ～ of a police station 警察局局长/ the ～ of the delegates 首席代表 同 head, leader 派 chiefly adv.

child / tʃaɪld / n. [C] (pl. children / ˈtʃɪldrən/) 小孩；孩子：The ～ is interested in swimming. 那小孩对游泳很感兴趣。同 adult

childbirth / ˈtʃaɪldbɜːθ / n. [U;C]分娩；生产

childhood / ˈtʃaɪldhʊd / n. [U]童年；幼年；童年时期：My mother often recalls her happy ～ now. 现在我妈妈经常回忆她快乐的童年。/ He lived a poor life in his ～. 幼年时期他过着贫困的生活。同 boyhood, girlhood 反 adulthood

childish / ˈtʃaɪldɪʃ / *adj.* 孩子的；幼稚的：
Looking at her ～ face, I felt happy too. 看着
她孩子气的脸蛋，我也高兴起来。/ I don't
like such ～ games. 我不喜欢玩这种幼稚的游
戏。同 childlike, foolish 反 mature, grown-up

chill / tʃɪl / *n.* [C] ❶寒冷；寒气：the ～ of a
fall day 秋日寒峭/She turned on the fire to
take the ～ from the air. 她生火驱寒取暖。❷
受凉；感冒；(由风寒引起的)发烧：catch a ～
着凉

chilli / ˈtʃɪli / *n.* [U] (干)辣椒：People in Sichuan and Hunan like ～ pepper very much.
四川人和湖南人都非常喜欢吃辣椒。

chilly / ˈtʃɪli / *adj.* 寒冷的：I felt rather ～
outside the house. 在屋子外边我感到很冷。
同 cold

chimney / ˈtʃɪmni / *n.* [C]烟囱；烟道：You can
see few big ～s in our city now. 现在你很难在
我们这个城市里看到大烟囱了。/ He smokes
like a ～. 他抽烟非常厉害。同
smokestack, stovepipe

chimpanzee / ˌtʃɪmpæn'zi: / *n.* [C]黑猩猩

chin / tʃɪn / *n.* [C]下巴，颏：The man hit her
on the ～. 那人打着她的下巴。

China / ˈtʃaɪnə / *n.* 中国：the People's Republic
of ～ 中华人民共和国/ The machine is made
in ～. 这台机器是中国制造的。

china / ˈtʃaɪnə / *n.* [U]瓷器：She presented me a
set of ～ as my birthday gift. 她送我一套瓷
器做生日礼物。同 chinaware, earthenware

Chinese / ˌtʃaɪ'ni:z / I *adj.* ❶中国的；中国人
的：More and more foreigners are interested in
～ food now. 现在越来越多的外国人对中国
饮食感兴趣。/ I'm glad that you can understand ～ Beijing operas now. 我很高兴你现在
能看懂京剧了。❷中国话的；汉语的：～ Card
汉卡/ ～Character 汉字/ ～ Character information processing 汉字信息处理 II *n.* ❶[C]中
国人：The ～ are hardworking people. 中国人
民是一个勤劳的民族。❷[U]中国话；汉语：
Jack can speak a little ～ after two months'
learning. 学了两个月，杰克能说一点中文了。
/ Many foreigners think that ～ is difficult to
learn. 许多外国人认为汉语很难学。

chip / tʃɪp / I *n.* [C]薄片；碎片；(*pl.*) 炸土豆
片：The girl likes potato ～s very much. 小女
孩很喜欢吃炸土豆片。同 slice, bit II *vt.*

(chipped; chipping)切成细条状

chlorine / ˈklɔ:ri:n / *n.* [U]氯(符号 Cl)

chlorophyl(l) / ˈklɒrəfɪl / *n.* [U]叶绿素

chocolate / ˈtʃɒklət / *n.* 巧克力

choice / tʃɔɪs / *n.* 选择；抉择：I found it difficult to make a correct ～. 我发现要做出正确
的选择是很难的。同 selection, decision

choir / ˈkwaɪə(r) / *n.* [C]合唱团；(尤指教堂
的)唱诗班；圣乐团

choke / tʃəʊk / *v.* 窒息；哽噎；阻塞；She ～d up
over the news. 听到这个消息，她哽得说不出
话来。

choose / tʃu:z / *v.* (chose/tʃəʊz/, chosen /
ˈtʃəʊzn/) 挑选；选择：We chose her as our group
leader. 我们选她当组长。/ She chose to be a
teacher. 她选择了当教师。同 select, decide

chop / tʃɒp / *vt.* (chopped; chopping) 砍；劈；
斩；剁：～ wood with an axe 用斧劈柴/～
down a tree 砍倒一棵树/ ～ up 剁碎，切细：
～ up cabbage for coleslaw 为凉拌把卷心菜切
成丝

chopstick / ˈtʃɒpstɪk / *n.* [C]筷子：Mike uses
～s well. 迈克能很熟练地使用筷子。

chord / kɔ:d / *n.* [C] ❶和弦；和音 ❷心弦：His
story struck a ～ of pity in the listeners 他的
遭遇触动了听众的怜悯心。

chore / tʃɔ:(r) / *n.* [C] ❶琐事；例行工作：the
administrative ～s of the office 办公室的日常
工作 ❷家庭杂务：the daily ～s of cleaning,
cooking and shopping 打扫、做饭、购物这些日
常家庭事务

Christ / kraɪst / *n.* 救世主(特指耶稣基督)：be-
fore ～ (略作 B. C.)公元前：That happened in
265 B. C. 那事发生在公元前 265 年。

Christian / ˈkrɪstʃən / I *n.* 基督教徒 II *adj.*
基督教的

Christmas / ˈkrɪsməs / *n.* 圣诞节：～ Day 圣
诞节(12 月 25 日)/ ～ Eve 圣诞前夜(12 月 24
日)/ a ～ card 圣诞卡/at ～ 在圣诞节/ Father ～ 圣诞老人/ a ～ tree 圣诞树

chromosome / ˈkrəʊməsəʊm / *n.* [C]染色体：
The scientists have won great achievements in
studying ～. 在对染色体的研究中，科学家们
取得了很大的成就。

chronic / ˈkrɒnɪk / *adj.* ❶长期的，一贯的：～
financial problems 长期的金融问题 ❷惯性的；
恶习难改的：a ～ liar 一贯撒谎的人 ❸(疾病)

慢性的,顽固的:～ hepatitis 慢性肝炎/ a ～ patient 慢性病患者

chronology / krə'nɒlədʒi / n. [C](大事)年表;(事件、资料等)按发生年月顺序的排列

chrysanthemum / krɪ'sænθəməm / n. 菊花

chuckle /'tʃʌkl / vi. 咯咯声;轻声笑;暗自笑:The little girl ～d happily over a cartoon. 小女孩边看动画片边高兴得咯咯笑. 同 giggle

chunk / tʃʌŋk / n. [C]厚片,大片,大块:a ～ of meat 一大块肉

church /tʃɜːtʃ/ n. [C]教堂:Jack and his family often go to ～. 杰克和家人常去教堂做礼拜.

cicada / sɪ'keɪdə / n. [C](pl. cicadas 或 cicadae/sɪ'keɪdiː/)蝉,知了

cigar / sɪ'gɑː(r) / n. [C]雪茄烟

cigarette / ˌsɪgə'ret / n. [C] 香烟:a pack of ～s 一包香烟/ Cigarettes are not good for health. 香烟对健康无益.

cinema / 'sɪnəmə / n. [C]电影院;电影:They met with an old friend in the ～. 在电影院他们遇到一位老朋友. / Let's go to the ～. 咱们去看电影吧! 同 movie, film

circle / 'sɜːkl / Ⅰ n. [C] ❶圆;圆圈;环状物:Please draw a ～ with A for its centre. 以 A 为圆心画一个圆. 同 ring, cycle ❷圈子;集团:He is famous in academic ～. 在学术界他很有名. 同 group/**all ～s of life** 各行各业;各阶层人士 Ⅱ v. 环绕;盘绕:The fence ～s the yard. 院子四周围着篱笆. / The good news soon ～d around. 喜讯很快传开了. 同 encircle, surround

circuit / 'sɜːkɪt / n. [C] ❶电路;线路:closed ～ TV(CCTV)闭路电视/ integrated ～集成电路 同 route, course ❷环行;巡回:The moon takes a month to make its ～ around the earth. 月球绕地球一周要一个月时间. 同 circle, course, orbit

circular / 'sɜːkjələ(r) / adj. 圆形的;循环的

circulate / 'sɜːkjəleɪt / v. 循环;流通:Blood ～s through the boy. 血液在体内循环. 同 circle, distribute

circulation / ˌsɜːkjə'leɪʃn / n. ❶[U]循环;血液循环;流通:The doctor said that the old man had a bad ～. 大夫说老人血液循环不好. / The authority decided to put some new coins into ～. 当局决定发行一些新硬币. 同 circling, distribution ❷[C]发行量;销售量:Her novels have a large ～. 她的小说发行量很大.

同 distribution

circumference / sə'kʌmfərəns / n. 圆周;周长:Do you know the ～ of the earth? 你知道地球的周长是多少吗?

circumstance / 'sɜːkəmstəns / n. [C]事实;详情;环境:If ～s permit, I'll go abroad to study. 如果情况允许,我将要出国读书. 同 situation, condition, detail / **in (under) no ～** 决不:Under no ～ will I go with you. 无论怎样我也不跟你走.

circus / 'sɜːkəs / n. [C]马戏;马戏团

cite / saɪt / vt. 引用;引证;举(例):The judge ～d a few cases in the court. 法官在法庭上提出了几个案例. / He often ～s Lu Xun in his articles. 他在文章中常常引用鲁迅的话. 同 quote, refer

citizen / 'sɪtɪzn / n. [C]公民;市民;居民:The teacher asks us to be a law-abiding ～. 老师要求我们做一个守法的公民. / He is an honorary ～of our city. 他是我们市的荣誉市民.

city / 'sɪti / n. [C]城市;都市:an ancient ～古城/ the Forbidden City (北京的)紫禁城/ He spent half a month visiting a few coastal-line open cities. 他花半个月时间访问了几个沿海开放城市. 同 town 反 countryside

civic / 'sɪvɪk / adj. ❶城市的,都市的:the new ～ centre 新的市中心 ❷公民的;市发的:～ duties 公民的义务 ❸民事的;平民的

civil / 'sɪvl / adj. ❶公民的;市民的;民用的:We have not only ～ rights but also ～ duties. 我们不仅有公民权利,也有公民义务. 同 public ❷国内的:The ～ war lasted for eight years. 那场内战持续了八年之久. 同 domestic ❸文明的;有礼貌的:a ～ society 文明社会/ His father asks him to be a ～ person. 他父亲要求他做一个有礼貌的人. 同 civilized, polite 反 uncivil, ill-mannered

civilian / sə'vɪliən / Ⅰ n. [C]平民;老百姓;非军事人员:～s and soldiers 军民 同 citizen, commoner Ⅱ adj. 平民的;民间的:The Queen dreamed to live a ～life. 女王渴望过平民生活. 同 unmilitary

civilization(-sation) / ˌsɪvəlaɪ'zeɪʃn / n. 文明;文化:ancient ～古代文明/ modern ～现代文明/ materials ～物质文明/ spiritual ～精神文明/ The ～ of China has a long history. 中国文化有悠久的历史. 同 culture

civilize(-se) / 'sɪvəlaɪz / vt. 使文明;使开化:a

~d neighborhood 文明街道/ a ~d school 文明学校/The development of education helped to ~ the people of that district. 教育的发展帮助那个地区的人文明起来。圆 educate, refine

claim / kleɪm / v. ❶声称,宣称:He ~ed to have finished his task without help. 他声称是在没有帮助的情况下完成任务的。圆 declare, insist ❷要求,认领:Nobody come to ~ the luggage. 没有任何人来认领行李。圆 demand, require

clamo(u)r / ˈklæmə(r) / I n. ❶[C;U]吵闹声,喧器声,喧嚷:He was interrupted in a speech by ~s of disapprobation. 他的演讲被人们大声的指责声打断了。❷[C;U]提出要求的呼声:a ~ against the new bill 反对新法案的呼声 II vi. ❶嚷嚷,吵闹,喧嚷 ❷嚷着要求(或反对):a crowd of demonstrators ~ing to see the minister 嚷要要见部长的一群示威者

clamp / klæmp / I n. [C]夹钳,钳;夹具:He used a ~ to hold the arm on the chair. 他用夹钳把扶手固定在椅子上。II vt. (用夹钳等)夹紧,紧紧抓住;固定:A picture frame must be ~ed together while the glue is drying. 照片镜框用胶接好后,胶水未干前必须用夹子夹紧。/He ~ed his hand over her mouth to stop her from screaming. 他用手紧紧捂住她的嘴,不让她发出尖叫声。/ ~ down(对…)实行限制;(对…)进行压制:The government has promised to ~ down on criminal activity. 政府已承诺要严厉打击犯罪活动。

clap / klæp / v. (clapped; clapping)喝彩;拍(手):The audience ~ped the singer. 观众为歌唱家鼓掌。圆 applaud

clarify / ˈklærɪˌfaɪ / vt. ❶澄清,阐明,使清楚明了:The teacher's explanation clarified the difficult rules. 老师的解释阐明了难懂的规则。❷澄清(液体),消除(杂质),净化: ~ syrup 使糖浆澄清

clash / klæʃ / I vi. ❶(金属等)发出碰撞声:The bell of St. Paul's ~ed out. 圣保罗教堂的钟叮当当地响。❷发生冲突:Her wedding ~ed with my exam so I couldn't go. 她的婚礼与我的考试时间冲突,所以我不能去参加。❸不协调;不相配;不一致:Those red shoes ~ violently with that orange dress and purple hat. 那双红鞋同橘色衣服、紫色帽子极不相配。II n. [C]❶(金属等的)碰撞声 ❷冲突,矛盾;不协调,不一致:a verbal ~ 口角/a border ~ between two countries 两国边境冲突

clasp / klɑːsp / v. 紧握;扣住:She ~ed his hand tight in both of hers. 她紧紧握住他的双手。圆 pin, fasten, hold

class / klɑːs / n. ❶[C]种类;等级:These problems fell into three main ~es. 这些问题分成三大类。/ We have the first- ~ equipment in our school lab. 我们学校实验室有一流的设备。圆 sort, kind ❷[C]课;上课:She conducted an English ~ for Chinese students. 她给中国学生上英语课。圆 lesson ❸[C]班;班级;年级:He is studying in a beginner's ~. 他正在初级班学习。❹[U]社会等级;阶级:He thinks that he belongs to the middle~. 他认为他属于中产阶级。圆 status

classic / ˈklæsɪk / I n. [C]名著;杰作;经典(著作):I like to read Chinese ~s after class. 课余我喜欢读中国名著。圆 masterpiece, masterwork II adj. (文学艺术等)第一流的;最优秀的;古典的:It is one of the greatest ~ myths. 这是最优秀的古希腊神话之一。圆 first-class, excellent, traditional

classical / ˈklæsɪkl / adj. 古典的;经典的:~ architecture 古典建筑/ Beethoven contributed greatly to the west ~ music. 贝多芬对西方古典音乐做出了极大贡献。圆 traditional, classic

classification / ˌklæsɪfɪˈkeɪʃn / n. 分类;分级;类别;等级:job ~ 职业分类/ social ~ 社会等级 圆 class, sort, grade

classified / ˈklæsɪfaɪd / adj. 分成类的:You'd better first look up the ~ catalog. 你最好先查一查分类目录。圆 arranged, grouped

classify / ˈklæsɪfaɪ / vt. 把…分类;把…分级:Apples here are classified according to size. 这里的苹果依大小分等级。圆 class, grade, group, arrange

classmate / ˈklɑːsmeɪt / n. [C]同班同学:A ~ of mine won the first prize. 我的一位同班同学获得了一等奖。

classroom / ˈklɑːsruːm / n. [C]教室;课堂:She hurried out of the ~ with a book in her hand. 她手里拿着一本书匆匆忙忙地走出教室。

clause / klɔːz / n. [C]❶分句,从句,子句:a subordinate ~ 从句 ❷(正式文件或法律文件的)条款:a most-favoured nation ~ 最惠国待

遇条款

claw / klɔː / n. [C] 脚爪：A hawk has sharp ～s. 鹰有锋利的爪子。

clay / kleɪ / n. [U] 黏土：Bricks are made from ～. 砖是泥做的。同 mud, earth

clean / kliːn / Ⅰ adj. 干净的；整洁的：The room is very ～. 房间很干净。/ Wash your hands ～ before dining. 吃饭前把手洗干净。反 dirty Ⅱ v. 弄整洁；打扫；洗涤：She is ～ing the blackboard. 她正在擦黑板。同 sweep, wash, dust 反 dirty, soil / ～ **out** 清扫；花光；抢光：The thieves ～ed out the store. 盗贼将商店洗劫一空。～ **up** 收拾；打扫；肃清：Can you ～ up the desks? 你能将这些书桌扫干净吗？

clear / klɪə(r) / adj. ❶明亮的；清澈的；明朗的：The day was beautifully ～. 那天碧空如洗。/ You can see the top of the mountain on a ～ day. 在晴朗的日子你可以看到山顶。同 sunny, bright ❷清楚的；明白的：I am not ～ about what happened there. 我不清楚那里发生了什么事情。派 clearly adv.

clench / klentʃ / v. 咬紧牙关；握紧拳头：He ～ed his jaws and said not a single word. 他紧咬牙关，一声不吭。同 grip, grasp

clerk / klɑːk, klɜːrk / n. [C] 办事员；职员：She is a bank ～. 她是银行职员。

clever / ˈklevə(r) / adj. (-er, -est) 聪明的；灵巧的；机灵的：Tom was very ～ about such things. 汤姆在这类事情上挺精明。同 bright, smart 反 stupid / **be** ～ **at** 擅长于：He is ～ at writing comedies. 他擅长于写喜剧。

click / klɪk / Ⅰ n. [C] 咔嗒声 Ⅱ v. ❶(使)发出咔嗒声：The lock ～ed shut. 锁咔嗒一声锁上了。❷点击(鼠标)

client / ˈklaɪənt / n. [C] 客户；顾客；委托人：He serves the ～s wholeheartedly. 他全心全意为顾客服务。同 buyer, customer, trustor

cliff / klɪf / n. [C] 峭壁；悬崖：He was brave to stand on the edge of the ～ to overlook the beautiful scene. 他很勇敢，站在悬崖边上俯视下边的美景。

climate / ˈklaɪmət / n. 气候：How do you like the ～ of Beijing? 你觉得北京的气候怎样？/ I like a mild ～. 我喜欢温和的气候。同 weather

climax / ˈklaɪmæks / n. [C] 高潮；顶点：She missed the ～ of the play. 她没有看到话剧的高潮部分。/ He is at the ～ of his business. 他正处于事业的顶峰。同 peak 反 bottom

climb / klaɪm / v. 爬；攀登：They ～ed out through the window. 他们从窗子爬出去了。同 mount

cling / klɪŋ / v. (clung/klʌŋ/, clung) 黏住；依附；坚持；抱住不放：The wet T-shirt clung to the boy's body. 湿湿的 T 恤衫紧紧地贴在小男孩身上。/ Don't always ～ to your own views. 别总是固执己见。同 stick, hold

clinic / ˈklɪnɪk / n. [C] 诊所；门诊部

clinical / ˈklɪnɪkəl / adj. ❶诊疗所的：～ treatment 门诊治疗 ❷临床实习的；临床教学的：～ medicine 临床医学/ a ～ diagnosis 临床诊断

clip¹ / klɪp / n. [C] 夹；回形针

clip² / klɪp / vt. 剪，剪短；修剪；剪辑：～ one's hair short 剪短发/ He ～s some articles from the newspaper for his son. 他常常为儿子从报上剪下一些文章。同 cut 派 clipper n.

cloak / kləʊk / n. [C] 外套；斗篷

clock / klɒk / n. [C] 时钟：Please advance the ～ one hour. 请把时钟拨快 1 小时。/ The ～ struck eleven. 钟已敲过 11 点。/ **round the** ～ 日夜：The workers often work round the ～. 工人们时常不分昼夜地工作。

clone / kləʊn / v. 无性繁殖；克隆

cloning / ˈkləʊnɪŋ / n. [U] 无性繁殖；克隆技术

close / kləʊz / Ⅰ v. 关，闭；封闭；结束：Please ～ the door. 请关门。/ The meeting ～d at half past eleven. 会议 11:30 结束。同 shut, end, stop Ⅱ adj. 接近的；附近的；靠近的：Winter is ～. 冬天已近。/ The store is ～ to the school. 商店在学校附近。同 near, nearly Ⅲ adv. 接近；靠近：Come ～ so I can see you. 走近点，好让我看见你。同 near, nearly 派 closely adv.

closet / ˈklɒzɪt / n. [C] 小房间；橱：a clothes ～ 衣橱/ a water ～ (WC) 盥洗室

C

close-up / ˈkləusˌʌp / n. [C] ❶特写镜头：❷详尽的描写：a ～ of modern society 现代社会的详细写照

cloth / klɒθ / n. [U]布；衣料：This ～ wears well. 这种布耐穿。/ Do you like this kind of ～? 你喜欢这种布料吗？

clothe / kləuð / vt. 给…穿衣；覆盖：He was thickly ～d. 他穿得很厚。/ The sun ～s the earth with light. 阳光普照大地。圆 dress

clothes / kləuðz / n. (pl.)衣服；服装：holiday ～ 节日盛装/ night ～ 睡服；睡衣/ work (working) ～ 工作服/ sports ～ 运动服/ make ～ 做衣服 put on ～ 穿衣服/ take off ～ 脱衣服

clothing / ˈkləuðɪŋ / n. [U](总称)衣服

cloud / klaud / n. 云；云状物：We watched a sea of ～s at the top of the mountain. 我们在山顶观看到了云海。圆 fog, vapor, smoke

cloudy / ˈklaudi / adj. ❶多云的：It was ～ this morning but it turned out fine now. 今天早上天空多云，但是现在转晴了。圆 clouded 反 clear ❷模糊不清的；不明了的：I have only a ～idea about it. 对于这事我只有一个模糊的想法。圆 unclear, vague 反 clear, obvious

clown / klaun / n. [C]小丑；丑角：He plays the ～ in a circus. 他在一个马戏团里演小丑。圆 fool, joker

club / klʌb / n. [C]俱乐部：a book ～ 读书会/ a night～ 夜总会

clue / ˈklu: / n. [C]线索；暗示：He said he could provide some ～s to help the police find the criminal. 他说他可以给警察提供一些线索帮助他们找到罪犯。圆 sign, hint, trace

clump / klʌmp / n. ❶一簇(树或灌木丛)；一群；一束：a little ～ of buildings 一小群建筑物/The boy hid in the ～ of tress. 那男孩躲藏在树丛中。❷一团，一块：a ～ of muddy fur 一团脏兮兮的毛发

clumsy / ˈklʌmzi / adj. 笨拙的；愚蠢的：He is ～ in speaking. 他是个笨嘴拙舌的人。圆 un-skilled

cluster / ˈklʌstə(r) / I n. [C] ❶一组，一丛，一束，一簇：～s of purple flowers 一束束紫色花 ❷一组，一批，一群：There was little ～ of admirers round the guest speaker. 只有寥寥几个仰慕者围在客座演讲人的四周。II (使)聚

集；(使)成簇；(使)成群：a hill where the white buildings ～ed together 一个白色建筑物聚集成群的小山丘

co- / kəu / (前缀)表示"共同""一起""相互"：～-owner 共同拥有者/ ～-pilot (飞机)副驾驶员/ ～-author 合著者/ ～-worker 同事

coach / kəutʃ / n. [C] ❶客车；长途汽车：They traveled around by ～. 他们坐长途客车四处旅行。❷教练；私人教师：He is our new foot-ball ～. 他是我们的新足球教练。圆 trainer

coal / kəul / n. [U] 煤：～ gas 煤气/ mine ～ 采煤/ a ～ miner 煤矿工人

coarse / kɔ:s / adj. 粗糙的；粗鲁的：～ cloth 粗布/～skin 粗糙的皮肤/～ manners 粗鲁的举止

coast / kəust / n. [C]海岸：The city is on the south ～. 该城位于南岸。/ The ship sailed a-long the ～. 轮船沿海岸航行。圆 shore, sea-side

辨析

coast 意为"海岸"，指海边的长条陆地，是地理学用语：The land is barren on the east coast. 东海岸的土地贫瘠。**beach** 意为"滩"，指由江水、河水冲刷形成的并覆盖着鹅卵石或沙的土地，常用做日光浴的场所：The children are lying on the beach. 孩子们躺在海滩上。**shore** 意为"滨""岸"，指与洋、湖、江等水域相连的任何陆地，常为避暑之地：They shouted to a man on the shore. 他们向岸上的人呼叫。

coat / kəut / n. [C]上衣；外套：She put on her ～ and went away. 她穿上外套走了。

coating / ˈkəutɪŋ / n. [C]涂层，外膜，外层：e-lectric wire with a plastic ～外包塑料皮的电线/a ～ of dust 层灰

cocaine / kəuˈkein / n. [U]可卡因

cock / kɒk / n. [C] ❶公鸡：Cocks crow in the morning. 公鸡清晨打鸣。❷(水管、煤气管等的)旋塞；龙头：Please turn on (off) the ～. 请打开(关上)龙头。圆 tap, knob

cockroach / ˈkɒkˌrəutʃ / n. [C]蟑螂

cocktail / ˈkɒkteil / n. [C]鸡尾酒：make (pre-pare, mix) a ～ 调制鸡尾酒/ They held a ～ party in the hall. 他们在大厅举行鸡尾酒会。

cocoa / ˈkəukəu / n. [U]可可粉；可可茶

coconut / ˈkəukənʌt / n. [C]椰子

cocoon / kəˈkuːn / n. [C]茧

code / kəud / n. [C]❶代号；密码；电码：a bar ～ 条形码/ an area dialing ～ 电话区号/ a postal ～ 邮政编码 ❷法规，法典；准则：the civil ～ 民法/ the criminal ～ 刑法/ the moral ～ 道德准则 圖 laws, rules, principles

coffee / ˈkɒfi / n. [U]咖啡饮料；咖啡：black ～咖啡/ white ～ 加奶咖啡

coffin / ˈkɒfin / n. [C]棺材；灵柩

cognition / kɒɡˈniʃn / n. [U]认知，认识；理解；感知：in full ～ of the facts 充分认识事实/The brain waves fluctuate during ～. 脑电图在认知活动中会发生波动。

cohere / kəuˈhiə(r) / vi. ❶黏合，附着；凝聚，团结：The two materials can ～ without special glue. 这两种材料不用特殊的胶水就可以黏合。❷(论证、话语等)有条理，连贯，前后一致：Your arguments ～ nicely. 你的论点前后连贯。

coherent / kəuˈhiərənt / adj. ❶(逻辑上)连贯的，有条理的，前后呼应的：a ～ theory 脉络清晰的理论 ❷(在说话、思路等方面)清晰的，明了的：When he went crazy he would be not ～. 他发疯时就会语无伦次。❸和谐的；融洽的：a ～ design 和谐的设计

cohesion / kəuˈhiːʒn / n. [U]黏合(性)；聚合(性)；凝聚力：The organization lacked ～. 这个组织缺乏凝聚力。

coil / kɔil / Ⅰ vt. ❶卷，缠，盘绕：She ～ed her scarf around her neck. 她把围巾缠在脖子上。/The dog ～ed round his legs. 狗盘缩着腿。/Thick smoke ～ed up the chimney. 浓烟在烟囱上方升腾起来。Ⅱ n. [C](一)卷，(一)圈，(一)匝；盘状物：a ～ of rope 一卷绳子/ Coil of smoke rose from the accident site. 滚滚烟雾从出事地点上空盘旋着升起。

coin / kɔin / n. [C]硬币：～phone 投币式电话/ toss a ～ 投币决定(某事)

coincide / ˌkəuinˈsaid / vi. 同时发生；相符合；相一致：We didn't ～ in opinion. 我们的见解不同。圖 meet, agree

coke / kəuk / n. [U]焦炭：People there use ～ for fuel. 那里的人们用焦炭作为燃料。

cold / kəuld / Ⅰ adj. ❶冷的，寒冷的：Most children like ～ drink very much. 大多数孩子都喜欢喝冷饮。/ Yesterday was the ～est day

of this winter. 昨天是今年冬天最冷的一天。圖 cool, chilly 反 hot, warm ❷冷淡的；不热情的：You shouldn't be so ～ toward others. 你不应该对他人这么冷淡。圖 indifferent, uncaring ❸冷静的；冷酷的；无情的：He had to accept the ～ facts. 他不得不接受那严酷的事实。圖 cool Ⅱ n. ❶[U]冷；寒冷：I really can't stand the ～here. 我真不能忍受这儿的寒冷气候。圖 coldness, chill 反 heat, warmth ❷[C]伤风；感冒：She cannot come to the meeting because she caught (a) bad ～. 因患重感冒她不能来开会了。/catch a ～感冒：Most people ～ two or three ～s a year. 大多数人每年要患两三次感冒。get (suffer) a bad (heavy, severe) ～ 患重感冒：She was suffering a bad ～. 她患了重感冒。派 coldly adv.

collaborate / kəˈlæbəˌreit / vi. ❶(尤指在艺术创作上)合作；协作：The director has ～d with the playwright. 这位导演曾经和这位剧作家合作。❷ 勾结，通敌：～ with the enemy 与敌人狼狈为奸

collapse / kəˈlæps / Ⅰ v. 倒塌；崩溃；垮台：The hut ～d under the weight of snow. 小木屋因承受不了雪的重量而倒塌。圖 fall Ⅱ n. 倒塌；崩溃；(价格)暴跌：We hope to see the ～ of the oil price. 我们希望看到油价暴跌的局面。圖 fall, decline

collar / ˈkɒlə(r) / n. [C]衣领

colleague / ˈkɒliːɡ / n. [C]同事；同僚：Uncle Li is my father's old ～. 李叔叔是我父亲的老同事。圖 associate, partner

collect / kəˈlekt / v. 搜集；聚集：A crowd of pupils ～ed at the school gate. 一群学生聚集在校门口。/ She ～ed all their exercise books. 她将他们的练习本都收了起来。圖 gather, assemble

collection / kəˈlekʃn / n. ❶收集；采集：The large ～ of coins took him about ten years. 他花大约十年时间收集了大量的钱币。圖 gathering, assembly ❷[C]收藏品；收集物：This museum has a fine ～ of modern pictures. 这家博物馆收藏一些珍贵的现代绘画。圖 assemblage ❸征收；收款；募捐：All students in his class made a ～ for the disabled child. 全班同学为那位残疾儿童募捐。圖 collecting, receiving

collective / kəˈlektiv / adj. 集体的；共同的；集体的：～ economy 集体经济/ the ～ leader-

C

ship 集体领导/the ～ ownership 共同所有权/ His father works in a ～-owned enterprise. 他父亲在一家集体企业上班. 同 joint, gathered, united 反 individual 派 collectively *adv.*

college / ˈkɒlɪdʒ / *n.* [C]学院;专科学校: a junior ～ 专科学校/ a literature ～ 文学院/a medical ～ 医学院/a normal training ～ 师范学院/ at (in) ～ 在大学/ go to ～ 上大学/ pass (go) through ～ 读完大学

collide / kəˈlaɪd / *vi.* ❶碰撞,冲撞;相撞: The two cars ～d at a high speed. 这两辆汽车相撞时速度很快. ❷ 冲突,抵触,不一致: Their views often ～d. 他们的观点经常相左.

collision / kəˈlɪʒn / *n.* [U;C]❶碰撞;相撞;碰撞事件 a head-on ～ between a bus and a car 公共汽车和轿车之间的迎头相撞 ❷(利益、意见等的)冲突,抵触: a ～ of principles 原则上的冲突

collocate / ˈkɒləˌkeɪt / *v.* ❶排列;并列,并置: ～ the dishes on the table 将碟子并排放在饭桌上 ❷(词语)组合,组配,搭配: The word "see"～s with "off"in the phrase"see off". "see"这个词同"off"在"see off"这个词组里搭配在一起.

colon / ˈkəʊlən / *n.* [C]冒号: You should use a ～ here. 你该在这儿用一个冒号.

colonial / kəˈləʊnɪəl / *adj.* 殖民地的;殖民的

colonist / ˈkɒlənɪst / *n.* [C]殖民者;移民

colony / ˈkɒləni / *n.* [C]殖民地

colo(u)r / ˈkʌlə(r) / *n.* 颜色;色彩: What ～ do you like best? 你最喜欢什么颜色?/ Red, yellow and orange are called warm ～s. 红、黄、橙称为暖色.

colo(u)rful / ˈkʌləfl / *adj.* 丰富多彩的;颜色鲜艳的: They are living a ～ life after retirement. 退休后他们过着多姿多彩的生活./ Old foreign women like ～ dresses. 外国老太太喜欢穿色彩鲜艳的衣服.

column / ˈkɒləm / *n.* [C] ❶柱;支柱;圆柱: The roof is supported by four ～s. 屋顶由四根圆柱支撑. 同 support, pillar, post ❷(报刊的)专栏(文章): the advertising ～ 广告专栏/ the sports ～ 体育专栏/ He lives on writing ～s for the newspaper. 他靠给报纸撰写专栏文章为生. 同 division, section, article ❸ 纵队;小分队:a tank ～ 坦克纵队

columnist / ˈkɒləmnɪst / *n.* [C]报刊专栏作者: The boy wants to become a sports ～. 那男孩想当一名体育专栏作家.

comb / kəʊm / *n.* [C]梳子

combat / ˈkɒmbæt / *n.* 战斗;斗争: Her son was killed in ～ many years ago. 许多年前她的儿子作战阵亡了.

combination / ˌkɒmbɪˈneɪʃn / *n.* 结合;联合;化合 同 union

combine Ⅰ / kəmˈbaɪn / *v.* 联合;结合;化合: We should ～ theory with practice. 我们应该把理论与实践结合起来. 同 unite, join Ⅱ / ˈkɒmbaɪn / *n.* [C]联合收割机;结合体

come / kʌm / *vi.* (came / keɪm /,come) 来,到达;发生;出现;变成: Please ～ here. 请到这儿来. / The hare came to a small tree. 兔子来到一棵小树前. / May ～s between April and June. 5月在4月与6月之间. / Bad luck always ～s to me. 我总碰到倒霉的事. 同 arrive,approach,appear 反 go,leave/～ about 发生;出现: Sometimes it is hard to tell how a quarrel ～s about. 有时很难说明争吵发生的原因. ～ across 碰到;偶然见到: The other day I came across a book that you might like. 日前我偶然看到一本你可能喜欢的书. ～ along 快点: Come along, it's nearly 12 o'clock. 快点,已经快12点了. ～ around 复原;苏醒: You need not worry; this boy will ～ around very soon. 不必担心,这小孩不久即可痊愈. ～ back 回来: When will you ～ back? 你什么时候回来? ～ (back) to life 苏醒;复活: We thought he was drowned, but after an hour's artificial respiration he came (back) to life. 我们认为他已经淹死了,但经过一个小时的人工呼吸,他又活了. ～ by ①经过: They came by three great cities on their journey. 旅途中,他们经过了三个大城市. ②获得: He seemed to have ～ by a large fund of knowledge. 他似乎已获得丰富的知识. ～ down 下降;下来: We saw them coming down the stairs. 我们看见他们下楼来. ～ in 进入: That is where you ～ in. 那是你进来的地方. ～ into being (事物、局面的)形成,产生: The committee came into being in 1969. 委员会于1969年成立. ～ into power 当权;上台: Tom came again into power. 汤姆再度执政. ～ on ①赶快;快点: Come on, or we'll be late. 赶快;不然我们就迟了. ②出现;登台: He felt a cold coming on. 他觉

得感冒了。**～ out** ①出现：The sun came out. 太阳出来了。②结果；结束，完成：How did the story ～ out？故事是怎样结束的？**～ over** 走过来：They came over. 他们走过来了。**～ to** ①复苏：She didn't ～ to until two days later. 她两天后才苏醒过来。②总计；达到：The expense ～s to a hundred dollars. 开支共计 100 美元。**～ to a conclusion** 得出结论；做决定：They have ～ to a conclusion upon this case. 关于这件案子，他们已得出结论。**～ to an agreement** 达成协议：We have ～ to an agreement with the workers in that factory. 我们已和那个工厂的工人达成了协议。**～ to an end** 结束：The story suddenly came to an end. 故事突然结束。**～ to one's rescue** 援救；营救：The dog was chasing our cat when Mary came to its rescue. 狗正在追我们的猫，这时玛丽跑去救猫。**～ true** 实现：His wish will ～ true. 他的愿望会实现。**～ up** ①接近；走近：We saw a big black bear coming up. 我们看见一只大黑熊走过来。②发芽：The seeds haven't ～ up yet. 种子还未发芽。**～ up with** 赶上；追上：Let's go slowly so that the others may ～ up with us. 我们走慢些以便其他人能赶上来。

comedian /kə'miːdiən/ n. [C]喜剧演员；喜剧作家

comedy /'kɒmədi/ n. [C]喜剧；喜剧性事件：She is writing a ～. 她正在创作一部喜剧。同 humor, fun 反 tragedy

comet /'kɒmət/ n. [C]彗星：Do you know anything about Halley's Comet? 你了解哈雷彗星吗？

comfort /'kʌmfət/ Ⅰ vt. 安慰；使舒适：Try to ～ him! 尽力安慰他吧！He ～ed his back with soft cushions. 他放上软垫使背部舒适。同 ease 反 trouble, discomfort Ⅱ n. [U]安慰，慰问；安逸，舒适：Her money and goods are not her only ～. 金钱与财产并不是她唯一的安慰。同 ease, relief 反 trouble, discomfort

comfortable /'kʌmftəbl/ adj. 舒适的；愉快的；自在的：The beds and chairs are fairly ～. 这些床和椅子让人觉得相当舒适。派 comfortably adv.

comic /'kɒmɪk/ Ⅰ adj. 喜剧的；滑稽的：The ～ performances of the comedians amused us greatly. 喜剧演员们的滑稽表演逗得我们十分开心。同 funny, humorous Ⅱ n. [C]喜剧演员；滑稽人物 同 comedian

comma /'kɒmə/ n. [C]逗号；小停顿

command /kə'mɑːnd/ v. 命令；指挥：If you ～ wisely, you'll be obeyed cheerfully. 指挥有方，人人乐从。

commander /kə'mɑːndə(r)/ n. [C]司令官；指挥员：～ in chief 总司令 同 leader, chief

commemorate /kə'meməreɪt/ vt. ❶纪念：a festival ～ the 200th anniversary of the event 纪念这个事件发生 400 周年的节日 ❷庆祝，庆贺：～ the arrival of the new millennium 庆祝新千年的到来

commend /kə'mend/ vt. ❶表扬，称赞，嘉许；推崇：～ a soldier for bravery 嘉奖一位表现英勇的士兵／～ sb. upon his diligence 表扬某人勤奋 ❷推荐：～ an applicant to the company 向这家公司推荐一名申请人

comment /'kɒment/ Ⅰ n. 评论；意见：Have you any ～s to make on this problem? 你对此问题有何评论？／Her strange behaviour caused a good deal of ～s. 她的反常行为引得人们议论纷纷。同 criticism, remark Ⅱ v. 评论；评述：He often ～s on how different the two things are. 他常谈论这两件东西的不同之处。同 criticize, remark

commerce /'kɒmɜːs/ n. [C]商业；贸易：He began to engage in ～ two years ago. 两年前他开始经商。同 business, trade

commercial /kə'mɜːʃ(ə)l/ Ⅰ adj. 商业的；商务的：He graduated from a ～ college. 他毕业于一所商学院。／This is a big ～ city. 这是一座大的商业城市。同 trading Ⅱ n. 商业广告：I don't like TV ～s. 我不喜欢电视广告节目。

commission /kə'mɪʃn/ n. ❶委任；委托；代办：He is going to execute some ～s for his company in Hainan. 他将代公司在海南办几件事情。同 authorization ❷[C]任务；职权：He tried his best to carry out his ～. 他尽力完成了任务。❸[C]委员会：the Military Commission 军事委员会／the Commission for Inspecting Discipline 纪律检查委员会同 committee, council, board ❹[C]佣金；回扣：You can get a 15% ～ on the goods you sell. 你可以从你销售的商品中抽取 20%的佣金。同 fee

commit /kə'mɪt/ vt. (-mitted；-mitting) ❶犯罪；犯错：He was accused of ～ting robbery. 他被指控犯了抢劫罪。同 do, execute ❷交付；托付：She ～ted her daughter to the care

C

of her parents. 她把女儿托付给父母照顾。同 entrust /~ **oneself to sth.** 答应对某事负责:I have ~ted myself to helping him. 我答应过帮助他。

commitment / kə'mɪtmənt / n. ❶[C;U]承诺,允诺;保证:fulfill one's ~s 履行承诺/ They reaffirmed their ~ that they would help. 他们重申了他们将给予帮助的许诺。❷ [U]致力;献身;投入:~ to a cause 为事业而献身/a professor with a real sense of ~ to his job 真正一心扑在工作上的教授

committee / kə'mɪti / n. [C]委员会;全体委员:The ~ is made up of nine members. 这个委员会由九人组成。/ The ~ are discussing a very important proposal. 委员们正讨论一份重要的提案。同 committee, council

commodity / kə'mɒdəti / n. [C]日用品;商品:She was angry that she bought some fake commodities. 买到假冒商品使她非常生气。同 product, goods

common / 'kɒmən / adj. 共同的;普通的,一般的:English is often used as the ~ language at international conferences. 在国际会议上英语被当作共同语言使用。/ The boy has made a ~ mistake. 小男孩犯了一个常见的错误。同 public, general 反 private, rare / **in** ~ 共有的;公用的:They had nothing in ~. 他们没什么共同之处。派 commonly adv.

> **辨析**
> **common** 意为"普通的;平常的",常指许多人共同拥有或某物共同具有:Colds are common in winter. 感冒在冬天很常见。**general** 意为"普通的",指在特定的人或物中流行,很少有例外:The typewriter has been in general use for many years. 打字机已流行多年了。**ordinary** 意为"常见的,平凡的",指事物无特别之处:This is quite an ordinary event. 这是一件极平常的事。**universal** 意为"普遍的;通用的;全然没有例外的":There is no language on earth that is completely universal. 世界上没有一种语言是完全通用的。

commonplace / 'kɒmənpleɪs / n. [C]平凡的事;平常话:Traveling abroad has become a ~ for him. 出国旅游对他来说已是司空见惯的事情。

commonwealth / 'kɒmənwelθ / n. [C]共和国;联邦;共同体:Do you know when the Commonwealth of Independent Nations was

founded? 你知道独联体是哪年成立的吗?同 republic, federation, union

communal / 'kɒmjunəl / adj. 共有的;集体的;公用的;公共的:a ~ television room in a hotel 旅馆里的公共电视室/~ property 公共财产

communicable / kə'mjuːnɪkəbl / adj. 可传播的;可传送的;(尤指疾病)可传染的,传染性的:a ~ disease 一种传染病/Fear is a ~ emotion. 恐惧是一种可以传染给别人的情感。

communicate / kə'mjuːnɪkeɪt / v. 通信;通话;传递信息:The deaf ~ by the sign language. 耳聋的人靠手语进行交流。/ I immediately ~d with the police. 我立即与警方取得了联系。同 convey, pass, transmit

communication / kə,mjuːnɪ'keɪʃn / n. ❶[U]通信;信息;情报:Language is a major means of ~. 语言是主要的交流工具。/ He is studying the ~ of animals. 他正在研究动物的信息传递方式。同 exchange, information ❷ (pl.)通信设施;交通设施:Our city has excellent ~s. 我们市里有完备的交通设施。

communism / 'kɒmjunɪzəm / n. [U]共产主义

communist / 'kɒmjunɪst / Ⅰ adj. 共产主义的:the Communist Party of China 中国共产党/ the Communist Youth League of China 中国共产主义青年团 Ⅱ n. [C]共产主义者

community / kə'mjuːnəti / n. 社会;社区;共同体:They have set up a new scientific ~ nearby. 他们在附近建起了一个新的科学园区。同 neighborhood, district

compact / kəm'pækt / Ⅰ adj. 紧密的;结实的:This is a ~ organization. 这是一个很严密的组织。同 close, dense 反 loose Ⅱ v. (使)紧密;(使)简洁:a ~ed disk 压缩光盘/ He is ~ing the report for tomorrow. 他正在把明天的报告修改得更简洁。同 compress, press 反 loosen 派 compactly adv.

companion / kəm'pænɪən / n. [C]同事;朋友;伙伴;战友:Bad ~s on the Net led him astray. 在网上交的坏朋友使他误入歧途。/ The book is a ~ to the present volume. 那本书与现在的这一卷是姐妹篇。同 associate, friend, company

companionship / kəm'pænɪənʃɪp / n. [U]交情,友情,友谊;交往:He missed the ~ he'd enjoyed in the navy. 他非常想念他在海军服役时结下的友情。

company /ˈkʌmpəni/ n. ❶[C]公司：There are advantages in working for a large ～. 在大公司工作有很多好处。同 firm, business ❷[U]陪同；同行：He keeps good (bad) ～. 他和好人(坏人)来往。/ I enjoyed his ～. 有他为伴，我觉得很愉快。同 companion / **bear (keep) sb.** ～ 陪伴；陪同：I want somebody to bear me ～. 我想找一个人做伴。**part** ～ **with** 与…分手；分别：On this point I'm afraid I must part ～ with you. 在这一点上恐怕我不能同意你的意见。**in** ～ **with sb.** 与某人一起：He came in ～ with a group of girls. 他与一群女孩同来。

comparable /ˈkɒmpərəbl/ adj. ❶可比较的，有可比性的：His poetry isn't bad, but it's hardly ～ with Shakespeare's. 他的诗不错，但与莎士比亚不可同日而语。❷类似的：from approximately ～ social backgrounds 来自大致相仿的社会背景

comparative /kəmˈpærətɪv/ adj. 比较的；(语法)比较级的：She studies ～ literature. 她研究比较文学。/ You should use a ～ degree here. 这里你应该用比较级。

compare /kəmˈpeə(r)/ v. 比较；对比：Read the two articles and ～ them. 读读这两篇文章，再将它们比较一下。同 contrast, examine / ～ ... **with** ... 把…与…比较；He carefully ～d this book with that one. 他仔细地把这本书与那本书作了比较。/ My English cannot ～ with his. 我的英语不如他。～ ... **to** ... 把…比作…：Life is ～d to a voyage. 人生好比航海。

comparison /kəmˈpærɪsn/ n. [U]比较；比喻：Please make a ～ between the two plans and choose the better. 请把这两个计划比较一下，选出好的一个。同 contrast, examination / **in** ～ **with** 比较；相比：The advanced and the backward only exist in ～ with each other. 先进与落后只有相比较才存在。

compass /ˈkʌmpəs/ n. [C]罗盘；指南针

compassion /kəmˈpæʃn/ n. [U]同情，怜悯：fell great ～ for the starving children 对挨饿的孩子表示深切同情

compel /kəmˈpel/ v. (-pelled;-pelling)强迫，迫使：The boss ～led the workers to work 12 hours a day. 老板强迫工人们每天工作 12 小时。同 force, drive

辨析

compel 意为"迫使；使不得不"，指强迫别人做某事：He compelled her to stay at home. 他强迫她在家待着。**force** 意为"强迫；迫使"，指使他人屈从于个人的意志或慑于某种权威而做某事：The enemy was forced to give up his arms. 敌人被迫放下武器。**oblige** 意为"迫使"，指因某种需要使某人做某事，或迫使某人对客观情况作出反应：Your bad behaviour obliges me to dismiss you. 你的恶劣行为迫使我不得不解雇你。**impel** 指被强烈的愿望、情感驱使做某事：His hunger impelled him to beg. 饥饿驱使他行乞。

compensate /ˈkɒmpenseɪt/ v. 补偿；赔偿：The boss should ～ workers for their injuries during work. 工作期间工人受伤，老板应给予赔偿。同 pay

compensation /ˌkɒmpenˈseɪʃn/ n.[U]补偿，赔偿；赔偿金，补偿金：He had to live on unemployment ～ then. 那时候他不得不靠失业补助金过日子。同 repayment

compete /kəmˈpiːt/ vi. 竞争；比赛：Whom are you competing against for the championship? 你将和谁争夺冠军？He is going to a-gainst (with) his old rival in the second round. 第二回合时他将与老对手竞争。同 contest, vie

competence /ˈkɒmpɪtəns/ n. [U]能力；胜任，称职：The insane woman lacked the ～ to manage her own affairs. 那个神志不清的女人没有自理能力。/Dose she have the necessary ～ for the position? 她能胜任这项工作吗？

competent /ˈkɒmpɪtənt/ adj. ❶有能力的，胜任的，称职的；合格的：be fully ～ at one's work 完全胜任工作/A doctor should be ～ to treat many diseases. 医生应有能力治疗多种疾病。❷有效的；足够的；恰当的：a ～ answer 有力的回答/a ～ salary 丰厚的薪金

competition /ˌkɒmpəˈtɪʃn/ n. ❶[U]竞争；角逐：They were in ～ with each other for the prize. 他们为得奖而互相竞争。❷[C]比赛；竞赛：They held an open ～ last Friday. 上周五他们举行了一场公开赛。同 contest

competitor /kəmˈpetɪtə(r)/ n. [C]比赛者；竞争者；对手：Class Three is our strong ～ in the game. 三班是我们这次比赛的强大竞争对手。同 rival, opponent

compile /kəmˈpaɪl/ vt. 编辑；汇编：He is

C

planning to ~ a new Chinese -English dictionary. 他正计划编写一本新的汉英词典。同 collect,edit

complain / kəm'pleɪn / v. 抱怨；诉苦；发牢骚；叫屈：They ~ed that there was not enough hot water. 他们抱怨热水不够。同 criticize 反 praise / ~ **about** (**of**) **sth.** 向某人抱怨某事：They ~ed of being short of reading materials. 他们抱怨缺乏阅读材料。/ She is always ~ing about the weather. 她老是抱怨天气不好。

complaint / kəm'pleɪnt / n. 抱怨；不满：The manager seldom gets letters of ~ from the customers. 经理很少收到顾客的投诉信。同 criticism 反 praise / **make** (**lay**, **bring**) **a ~ against sb. of** (**about**) **sth.** 就某事对某人进行控告、控诉：A ~ was brought against him about the matter. 他因此事被控告了。

complement / 'kɒmplɪmənt / Ⅰ n. [C] ❶ 补充，补充物；互补物；配对物：A fine wine is a ~ to a good meal. 佳肴须得美酒配。/ The lexicon is not a ~ of syntax. 词汇不是句法的补充。❷ 足数，全数；足额；全套：the aircraft's full ~ of crew 飞机的全体机组人员 ❸ 补(足)语 Ⅱ vt. 补足；补充；使完整：The two books ~ each other nicely. 这两本书互为补充，相得益彰。

complete / kəm'pliːt / Ⅰ adj. 完全的；全部的；彻底的：The year is now ~. 今年到此结束。/ This is the *Complete Works of Shakespeare.* 这是《莎士比亚全集》。同 entire, full, thorough, finished 反 incomplete Ⅱ v. 结束；完成：Complete a sentence with the correct word. 用正确的词完成句子。同 finish 反 began, start 派 completely adv.

辨析

complete 意为"完整的；完全的；完成的"，指由许多部分构成的整体，或指一件东西各部分完整：Complete success turned his head. 彻底胜利使他得意忘形。**entire** 意为"整体的；完好的"，语气比 whole 强，用于指形状、数量或时间范围的整体。凡已被分割或破坏的都不能称为 entire：The entire book consists of 20 chapters. 全书共20章。**total** 意为"总的；全部的；全额的"，指数量或程度完全：His total income amounts to 2,000 yuan. 他一年总收入为2 000元。**whole** 意为"全体的；全部的"，指一件东西的各部分齐全且完整无损：The boy wanted the whole cake for himself. 这小孩想独吃整块蛋糕。

complex / 'kɒmpleks / Ⅰ adj. 合成的；复杂的；综合的：This is a ~ sentence. 这是一个复合句。/ I didn't understand the ~ argument. 我没有弄懂那个复杂的论点。同 complicated, confusing 反 simple, easy Ⅱ n. [C] 复合物；综合体 派 complexity n.

complicated / 'kɒmplɪkeɪtɪd / adj. 复杂的；难懂的；错综的：This problem is too ~ to explain to a child. 这问题太复杂，难以向一个孩子讲清楚。同 mixed, confusing 反 simply, easy

compliment / 'kɒmplɪmənt / Ⅰ n. [C] ❶ 称赞，恭维(话)；敬意：pay a ~ to sb. on sth. 为某事赞美(恭维)某人 / We did him the ~ of visiting him. 我们拜访他以示敬意。同 praise, commendation 反 insult, slander ❷ (pl.) 问候，祝贺：exchange ~s互相问候(祝贺) / Give my ~s to your parents. 代我向双亲问候。同 greetings, tribute Ⅱ v. 夸奖，恭维；祝贺：~ sb. on sth. 夸奖某人某事 同 praise acclaim 反 slander

comply / kəm'plaɪ / vi. 遵从，服从；顺从；听从：~ with the doctor's order 遵从医嘱/With some reluctance he complied. 他有些不情愿地服从了。

component / kəm'pəʊnənt / Ⅰ n. [C]组成部分；部件；元件：The engineer checked the ~s of the machine carefully. 工程师对机器的部件进行了仔细检查。同 part, element Ⅱ adj. 组成的；成分的：He stopped his car by a shop and bought some ~ parts. 他把车停在一家商店旁，买了一些零部件。

compose / kəm'pəʊz / v. ❶ 构思；写作；构成；作曲：The music was ~d by Beethoven. 这首乐曲是贝多芬创作的。同 write, create ❷ 组成，构成：Water is ~d of hydrogen and oxygen. 水由氢和氧组成。同 make, form

composed / kəm'pəʊzd / adj. 镇静的；沉着的：the doctor's ~ nature 医生的稳健性情/ a small, beautiful and ~ blonde 一位娇小、美丽又文静的金发女郎

composer / kəm'pəʊzə(r) / n. 作曲家；创作者；设计者：She became a popular ~ soon. 她很快成为一名受欢迎的作曲家。同 writer, creator, devisor

composition / ˌkɒmpə'zɪʃn / n. ❶组成；构成；成分：He is analysing the ~ of the soil. 他正在分析土壤成分。同 construction, formation

❷作文，文章；乐曲：We learn 〜 at school. 我们在学校学习写作。/ She wrote a very good 〜. 她写了一篇好作文。 同 work, theme, music

compound Ⅰ/ kəm'paund / v. 混合组成：The word is 〜ed of a preposition and a verb. 这个词是由一个介词和一个动词合成的。 同 mix Ⅱ / 'kɒmpaund / adj. 混合的：This is a 〜 word. 这是一个复合词。 同 mixed, combined

comprehend / ˌkɒmprɪ'hend / vt. 理解；了解

comprehension / ˌkɒmprɪ'henʃn / n. 理解；理解力：The teacher had no 〜 of the boy's problem at home. 老师不了解这男孩在家里出现的问题。/ Reading 〜 is very important in learning English. 阅读理解在学习英语中是很重要的。 同 understanding /above (**beyond**, **past**) 〜 不可理解，难以理解：This is quite above (beyond) my 〜. 这是我完全不能理解的。

comprehensive / ˌkɒmprɪ'hensɪv / adj. 综合的；包含内容多的：a 〜 development 综合发展/ a 〜 planning 全面规划/a 〜 university 综合大学/ At the end of the term he took a 〜 view of his study. 学期末他对自己的学习进行了全面的检查。 同 inclusive, overall

compress / kəm'pres / vt. ❶紧压，挤压：The fuel mixture is 〜ed in the chamber by the piston. 活塞将混合燃料挤压在燃烧室。❷压缩：〜 a story into a few short sentences 把故事浓缩成几个简单的句子

comprise / kəm'praɪz / vt. ❶包含，包括；由…组成，由…组成：The advisory board 〜s six members. 咨询委员会由 6 名成员组成。/Cave art 〜d an astonishing variety and mastery of techniques. 洞穴艺术中表现出技巧的多样性及其运用的娴熟让人叹为观止。❷构成，组成：Seminars and lectures 〜d the day's activities. 专题讨论和讲座是这一天的全部活动内容。/The essays 〜d his total work. 这几篇文章就是他的全部著作。

compromise / 'kɒmprəmaɪz / vi. 妥协；让步：We have to 〜 with him on this point. 我们只好就这一点与他妥协。

compulsory / kəm'pʌlsəri / adj. 强制性的；义务的；(学科)必修的：〜 education 义务教育/ We have five 〜 subjects this term. 本学期我们上五门必修课。 同 enforced, required

compute / kəm'pjuːt / v. 计算；估算：Their losses in the accident are 〜d ＄500,000. 他们在这次意外事故中的损失估计达 50 万美元。 同 count, calculate

computer / kəm'pjuːtə(r) / n. [C]计算机：a personal 〜 (PC)个人电脑/ a multi-media 〜 多媒体计算机/ The 〜 communication is widely used now. 现在计算机通信得以广泛运用。 同 electro-computer, calculator

comrade / 'kɒmreɪd / n. [C]同志；同事：He said he should stay with his 〜 in time of danger. 他说危险时刻他应和自己的同志在一起。 同 colleague, partner

concave / 'kɒnkeɪv / Ⅰ n. 凹面；凹面体 Ⅱ adj. 凹的；凹面的：a 〜 mirror 凹面镜 反 convex

conceal / kən'siːl / vt. 隐藏；隐瞒：She 〜ed her picture in an old dictionary. 她把照片藏在一本旧字典里。 同 hide, cover 反 reveal, expose/〜 **sth. from sb.** 向某人隐瞒某事：I didn't 〜 anything from him. 我对他没隐瞒什么。

concede / kən'siːd / vt. ❶承认：I'm willing to 〜 that he's a good runner. 我愿意承认他是一名优秀的赛跑运动员。❷授予；给予；让与；放弃：The defeated nation 〜d some of their territory to the enemy. 战败国把一部分领土割让给了敌国。❸(比赛中)让(球)；(故意)打输(比赛)：They 〜 d two more goals to the other side in the first half. 在上半场他们给对方让了两个球。 派 conceded adj.

conceit / kən'siːt / n. [U]自负；自大；骄傲自满：He is full of 〜. 他极其自负。Everybody should guard against 〜. 每个人都应该防止骄傲自满。 同 vanity 反 modesty

conceive / kən'siːv / v. 想出；构思 同 think, imagine/〜 **of** 想象；设想，构想出：It is impossible to 〜 of anything better than this. 想象不出比这更好的东西了。

concentrate / 'kɒnsntreɪt / vt. 集中；聚集 同 focus/〜 **on** 集中：You'll solve the problem if you 〜 on it. 要是全神贯注，你会解决这个问题的。

concentric / kən'sentrɪk / adj. 同中心(或圆心)的；共轴的：a 〜 circle 同心圆/〜 annual rings 同心年轮 派 concentrically adv. ; concentricity n.

concept / 'kɒnsept / n. [C]概念；观念；思想：You are late again. Do you have any 〜 of what time it is? 又迟到了,你究竟有没有时间概念? 同 idea, thought

concern / kənˈsɜːn / vt. ❶与…有关;涉及:The event ~ed us greatly. 这事与我们关系极大。同 relate, affect/~ **oneself with** 关心:Don't ~ yourself with other people's affairs. 少管别人的闲事。❷担心;忧虑:I'm ~ed at the condition of my sick friend. 我为朋友的病情担忧。同 care, worry, regard 派 concerned adj.

用法

❶concern with 表示"参与;与…有关":They could not prove that he was concerned with the crime. 他们无法证明他与此罪有关。❷ concern for (about) 表示"关怀;忧虑":Everybody is concerned about the future of his country. 人人都关心自己国家的前途。

concerning / kənˈsɜːnɪŋ / prep. 关于:The officials are discussing problem ~ agriculture. 官员们正在讨论有关农业的问题。同 about, regarding

concert / ˈkɒnsət / n. [C] 音乐会;演奏会:go to a ~去听音乐会/ attend a ~出席音乐会

concerto / kənˈtʃeɪtəʊ / n. (pl. concerti 或 concertos)协奏曲:a piano ~ 钢琴协奏曲

concession / kənˈseʃn / n. [C;U]让步,退让;承认,认可(物);让予(物):make no ~s to terrorists 发誓绝不向恐怖主义者让步/make no ~ to caution 不听从告诫

concise / kənˈsaɪs / adj. 简洁明了的;扼要的:a ~ style 简洁的文体/a ~ panorama of the city 城市概貌

conclude / kənˈkluːd / v. ❶结束:The story ~d tragically. 这故事结局悲惨。同 end, finish 反 begin, start ❷作结论:The jury ~d from the evidence that the accused man was not guilty. 陪审团依据证据作出结论,认定被告无罪。同 decide, determine ❸缔结:~ a treaty with ... 与…订立条约 同 settle, arrange

conclusion / kənˈkluːʒn / n. [C]结尾;结局;结论:Please tell me the ~ of the movie. 请把电影的结局告诉我。同 end, finish, decision/ **come to a** ~ 得出结论:You should not come to ~s at once. 你不应立即作结论。

concrete / ˈkɒnkriːt / Ⅰadj. 具体的;有形的;实在的:You should make ~ analysis of ~ problems. 你应当具体问题具体分析。同 spe-

cific Ⅱn. [U]混凝土

concur / kənˈkɜː(r) / vi. [C](-curred;-curring) ❶(碰巧)同时发生,His graduation day ~red with his birthday. 毕业典礼日适逢他的生日。❷同意;保持一致;赞同:The judges all ~red in giving me the prize. 裁判一致同意给我发奖。/We ~ with you in this respect. 在这方面,我们同意你们的意见。

condemn / kənˈdem / vt. ❶谴责;指责:He was ~ed smoking in public. 他在公共场所吸烟受到谴责。同 blame 反 praise ❷判…刑;宣告…有罪:The manager was ~ed for bribery and sent in prison. 他受贿被判刑入狱。同 sentence, convict 反 release

condense / kənˈdens / vt. ❶压缩;浓缩;使密集;使凝聚,使凝结:~ a gas into a liquid 把气体浓缩成液体/be ~d into thick soup 熬成浓汤 ❷使紧凑;简缩;使简洁;简要表达:a re-worded , ~d articles 重新措辞并简缩的文章/~ a paper into a few paragraphs 把一篇论文减缩成几个段落

condition / kənˈdɪʃn / n. [C]情况;状况;条件:The ~ is rapidly changing. 情况正在急速变化。/ That is China's actual ~. 这就是中国国情。同 state, situation /**on ~ that** 如果…;在…条件下:You may use my camera on ~ that you return it next saturday. 你可以用我的相机,条件是下周六必须归还。

condolence / kənˈdəʊləns / n. [U]吊唁,慰唁;慰问:a letter of ~吊唁信/I sent her an expression of ~ over the loss of her father. 我对她父亲的去世发了慰唁。

conduct Ⅰ / ˈkɒndʌkt / n. [U]品行;行为:wrong ~ 错误行为/ dishonourable ~ 可耻行为/ violent ~ 暴行/ I'm glad to see your ~ at school has improved. 我很高兴看到你在学校的表现有所改进。同 behavior, deeds Ⅱ / kənˈdʌkt / v. ❶引导;带领;指挥;指导:A girl ~ed him into the hall. 一位姑娘把他引入大厅。/ Though she is young, she is able to ~ an orchestra well. 尽管她很年轻,但她能把一支管弦乐队指挥得很好。同 guide, lead, direct ❷实施;处理;经营:His father ~ed his company successfully. 他父亲经营公司很成功。同 handle, manage, operate ❸传导;传(热、电):Most metals ~electricity well. 大多数金属都导电良好。同 transmit, convey

conductor / kənˈdʌktə(r) / n. [C] ❶导体；导线：A tall building needs a lightning ～. 高楼需要安装避雷针。圖 wire, transmitter ❷售票员；列车员：a bus ～ 公共汽车售票员/a train ～ 列车员 ❸(乐队、合唱队的)指挥：She is an excellent orchestra ～. 她是一名优秀的管弦乐队指挥。圖 director

cone / kəun / n. [C]圆锥；锥体

confederation / kənˌfedəˈreɪʃn / n. [C]联盟，同盟；政治联合体

conference / ˈkɒnfərəns / n. [C]会议；讨论会：A news (press)～ will be held next Monday. 下周一召开新闻发布会(记者招待会)。圖 meeting, discussion

confess / kənˈfes / v. 招认，供认；自白，坦白：At last he had to ～ himself to be guilty. 最终他不得不承认自己有罪。圖 admit, acknowledge 派 confession n.

> **用法**
> confess (to)后一般跟名词或动名词，不跟不定式：The suspect confessed (to) his crime. 嫌疑人供认了他的罪行。The boy confessed (to) breaking the window. 那男孩坦白是他打破了窗子。

confidence / ˈkɒnfɪdəns / n. [U]信任；信心：He had no ～ in himself. 他失去了信心。/ I have full ～ that I shall pass the exam. 我完全有把握通过这次考试。圖 trust, belief

confident / ˈkɒnfɪdənt / adj. 确信的；有信心的：The little girl gave her mother a ～ smile. 那小女孩自信地对她母亲微笑。/ We are ～ of winning the game. 我们确信我们会赢得那场比赛。圖 sure, certain, trusting

> **用法**
> confident 后接：❶介词 of：We are confident of success. 我们相信能成功。❷that 从句：We are hopefully ～ that we can overcome the difficulties. 我们满怀希望地相信我们能克服困难。

configuration / kənˌfɪɡjʊˈreɪʃn / n. [C] ❶结构，架构；构造：a ～ of small social units 小型社会单位的构成体/the ～ of stars in the sky 天空中星星的布排构图 ❷外形，构形；轮廓：～ of mountains 群山的轮廓

confine / kənˈfaɪn / vt. ❶限制，使局限：Please ～ your remarks to the subject under discussion. 请把发言局限在讨论的问题上。❷控制，使不流传(或扩散)；禁闭：be ～d to one's bed with illness 因病卧床/Efforts are made to ～ the epidemic to the farm where it has broken out. 做出努力将传染病控制在它所爆发的那个农场。

confirm / kənˈfɜːm / vt. 证实；确认；批准：You'd better phone the chairman to ～ the time and place of the meeting. 你最好给主席打个电话确认一下开会的时间和地点。圖 prove, verify 派 confirmation n.

conflict Ⅰ / ˈkɒnflɪkt / n. 斗争；争论；抵触；冲突 Ⅱ / kənˈflɪkt / vi. 争执；相冲突；矛盾：Their stories ～ed with each other. 他们的说辞相互矛盾。圖 dispute, disagree 反 agree

conform / kənˈfɔːm / vi. ❶遵照；服从：～ to directions 遵照指示/Most of us tend to conceal our teal selves by ～ing to the norm. 我们中的大部分人倾向于用遵循规成的方式来掩盖真实的自我。❷一致；相符；适合，适应：He ～s with my idea of a teacher. 他与我心目中的老师一样的。/Your design doesn't ～ with the regulations. 你们的设计不符合规定。

confront / kənˈfrʌnt / vt. ❶面对，正视；与…对峙：The two armies ～ed each other along the border. 两军在边界上相互对峙。/I don't understand your refusal to ～ reality. 我不明白你为什么不肯正视现实。❷面临；遭遇：The President ～s attacks from both reformers and conservatives. 总统面临来自改革派和保守派的双重抨击。

confucian / kənˈfjuːʃən / Ⅰ adj. 孔子的；儒家的：The overseas students are visiting the ～ temple. 留学生们正在参观孔庙。Ⅱ n. [C]孔子的门徒；儒家 派 confucianism n.

confuse / kənˈfjuːz / v. 使混乱，使糊涂：He is always confusing sugar with salt. 他老是糖盐不分。/ We are always confusing the twin brothers. 我们总是辨认不清这对双胞胎兄弟谁是谁。圖 mistake, puzzle /be (become, get) ～d about (at, with) sth. 混淆，搞糊涂：He was ～d at her sudden appearance. 她突然出现使他手足无措。派 confusion n.

congratulate / kənˈɡrætʃuleɪt / vt. 祝贺；庆贺：His colleagues came up to ～ him. 他的同事们都过来向他表示祝贺。/ ～ sb. on (upon) sth. 向某人祝贺某事：We ～d him on having passed the examination. 我们祝贺他通过

了考试。派 congratulation *n.*

congregate / ˈkɒŋgrɪ geɪt / *vi.* 聚集，集合；云集：The crowds ～d in the town square. 人群聚集在镇上的广场上。

congress / ˈkɒŋgres / *n.* [C]代表大会；国会：an annual ～ 年会/ the National People's Congress 全国人民代表大会/ the United States Congress 美国国会

conjunction / kənˈdʒʌŋkʃn / *n.* ❶[U]结合；联合；联系 ❷连接词

connect / kəˈnekt / *v.* 连接；联系：The two towns are ～ed by a railway. 两市由铁路相连。/ It is closely ～ed with this matter. 它与此事密切相关。同 join, link, relate 派 connected *adj.*

connection / kəˈnekʃn / *n.* 连接；联系：Is there any ～ between the two cases? 这两件案子之间有联系吗？同 link, relation

connective / kəˈnektɪv / Ⅰ *adj.* 联结的，连接的：～ remarks between chapters 章节之间的过渡语 Ⅱ *n.* [C]❶联结物，结合物 ❷连接词，关联词

connotation / ˌkɒnəʊˈteɪʃn / *n.* [C]内涵义，隐含义；引申义：a letter with sinister ～s 含义恶毒的信/A possible ～ of "home" is a place of warmth, comfort and affection. "家"的一个可能的含义是温暖、舒适并且充满爱的地方。

conquer / ˈkɒŋkə(r) / *v.* 征服；战胜；克服：We have never been ～ed by a foreign foe. 我们从未被外敌征服过。同 defeat, overcome 派 conqueror *n.*

conquest / ˈkɒŋkwest / *n.* [U]征服；克服；获得：They made a ～ of the land by armed force. 他们以武装夺得了那块土地。同 defeat, gain

conscience / ˈkɒnʃəns / *n.* 道德心；良心：He had a guilty ～. 他感到内疚。/ A guilty ～ is a thousand witnesses. 做贼心虚。同 morals

conscious / ˈkɒnʃəs / *adj.* 有意识的；神志清醒的；自觉的：Is the patient ～ yet? 病人清醒了吗？/ He was ～ that he had made a foolish mistake. 他意识到自己犯了一个愚蠢的错误。同 awake, aware, knowing/ **be ～ of** 清楚知道：I'm quite ～ of my responsibility as a teacher. 我十分清楚作为一个教师的责任。

consciousness / ˈkɒnʃəsnəs / *n.* [U]知觉；觉悟；意识：Man's social being determines his

～. 存在决定意识。同 sense, awareness/ **lose** (**recover**) **one's ～** 失去(恢复)知觉：Jim recovered his ～ three hours later. 三个小时后吉米恢复了知觉。

consensus / kənˈsensəs / *n.* [C](意见等的)一致：by the ～s of expert opinion 根据专家一致意见

consent / kənˈsent / *vi.* 同意；允许：Her parents wouldn't ～ to her staying out at night. 她的父母不允许她在外过夜。同 agree, approve 反 disagree

用法

consent 后可接带 to 的不定式或介词 to 加名词(动名词)：Will you consent to give (giving) him another chance? 你同意再给他一次机会吗？ He readily consented to my request. 他欣然同意我的请求。

consequence / ˈkɒnsɪkwəns / *n.* ❶[C]后果；结果：The boss had to fire him in ～ of his laziness. 由于他的懒惰，老板不得不把他解雇。同 result ❷[U]重要；重要性：The loss of his books is a matter of great ～ to a student. 书的遗失对学生来说是件大事。同 importance

consequently / ˈkɒnsɪkwəntli / *adv.* 因此；必然地：She got up at nine and ～ she was late. 她九点钟才起床，因此迟到了。同 therefore

conservation / ˌkɒnsəˈveɪʃn / *n.* [U](尤指对自然资源等的)保护：measures for the ～ of mineral resources 矿产资源保护措施/～ area 自然(或历史)保护区

conservative / kənˈsɜːvətɪv / *adj.* ❶保守的；保守主义的；守旧的：Are old people always more ～ than the young? 老年人总是比年轻人更保守吗？同 traditional ❷保守的人；保守主义

conserve / kənˈsɜːv / *vt.* 保存，保藏；保护：～ the energy for the last lap 为最后一圈保持体力/～ electricity 节电/We must ～ our forests and woodlands for future generations. 我们为了子孙后代保护好我们的森林和林地。

consider / kənˈsɪdə(r) / *vt.* 思考，考虑，认为，把…看作：He always ～ed carefully before he acted. 他总是三思而后行。同 think, weigh, regard /～ **doing sth.** 考虑做某事：We are ～ing doing it. 我们正考虑做此事。～ **as …** 把…当作(看作)…：We ～ed him as a fool. 我们认为他是一个傻瓜。

considerable / kənˈsɪdərəbl / *adj.* 相当大的；相当多的；重要的：The general manager has ～ income every year. 那位总经理每年的收入可观。/ The mayor is a ～ person in the city. 市长是一个城市中的重要人物。同 large，great，plentiful 反 small，insignificant

considerate / kənˈsɪdərət / *adj.* 体贴的；考虑周到的：She is ～ of（to，toward）old people. 她对老人很体贴。同 concerned，thoughtful

consist / kənˈsɪst / *v.* ❶由…组成（与 of 连用）：The paper ～s of eight pages. 该论文共有八页。同 contain，include ❷在于；依赖于（与 in 连用）：Happiness ～s in contentment. 知足常乐。同 lie ❸与…一致；符合（与 with 连用）：His actions do not ～ with his words. 他言行不一。同 harmonize

consistency / kənˈsɪstənsi / *n.* ❶[U；C]浓度，稠度：yogurts of varying ～ 不同稠度的酸奶 ❷[U]一致；符合；协调：～ and continuity in government policy 政府政策的一致性和连贯性／Your behaviour lacks ～—you say one thing and to another！你言行不一，说一套，做一套。

consistent / kənˈsɪstənt / *adj.* ❶一贯的，始终如一的；坚持的：a ～ policy 一贯方针／The last five years have seen a ～ improvement in the country's economy. 近五年来，该国经济持续增长。❷和谐的；一致的；符合的，可共存的：a report that is not ～ with the facts 与事实不符的报告／His views and actions are ～. 他言行一致。

console / kənˈsəʊl / *vt.* 安慰，慰问：Only his children could ～ him when his wife died. 妻子死后，只有孩子们能够给他以安慰。

consolidate / kənˈsɒlɪdeɪt / *vt.* 巩固，加强：The company has ～d its hold on the market. 公司巩固了自己对市场的控制。/The party ～d itself in a remote rural area. 该党在边远地区加强了自己的力量。

consonant / ˈkɒnsənənt / *n.* [C]辅音；辅音字母（略作 cons）：a ～ cluster 辅音连缀

conspire / kənˈspaɪə(r) / *vi.* （共同）密谋，搞阴谋：～ against sb. 密谋反对某人／The two men ～d to steal the jewels. 那两个人密谋偷珠宝。派 conspiracy *n.*

constant / ˈkɒnstənt / *adj.* 不变的；不断的；忠实的：He is ～ to the communist ideals. 他忠

于共产主义理想。/ Three days of ～ rain made her depressed. 连续三天的阴雨使她很沮丧。同 steady，continual，loyal 派 constantly *adv.*

constitute / ˈkɒnstɪtjuːt / *vt.* 组成；构成：Seven days ～ a week. 七天构成一个星期。同 form，make，compose/ **be ～d of** 由…组成：A baseball team is ～d of nine players. 棒球队由 9 名球员组成。

constitution / ˌkɒnstɪˈtjuːʃn / *n.* ❶[U]组成，构造：The scientist thinks that we should know more about the ～ of life. 科学家认为我们应当更多地了解生命的构造。同 structure，make-up ❷体格，体质：He is a good student with a strong ～. 他是一个体格强壮的好学生。同 health，build ❸宪法；章程；法规：Presidential elections are held every four years according to the American ～. 按照美国宪法，总统每四年选举一次。同 laws

constrain / kənˈstreɪn / *vt.* ❶强迫，迫使：be ～ed to admit the offense 被迫承认过错/I felt ～ed to do what he told me. 我照他的话去做是身不由己。❷关押，禁闭；限制；束缚：be ～ed in chains 身陷囹圄/Our research has been ～ed by lack of cash. 我们的研究苦于经费不足。

construct / kənˈstrʌkt / *v.* 建造；构思；创立：The house was ～ed out of wood. 这房子是用木头建造的。/ The whole story is skilfully ～ed. 整个故事构思巧妙。同 make，create，build

construction / kənˈstrʌkʃn / *n.* 建设，修建；建筑物：socialist ～ 社会主义建设/ a ～ site 建设工地/ capital ～ 基本建设/ The new railway is under construction. 新铁路正在修建中。同 building，creating

constructive / kənˈstrʌktɪv / *adj.* 建设性的；有积极作用的，有助益的：a very ～ attitude 非常积极的态度/During the experiment the teacher gave some ～ suggestions that prevented accidents. 试验中，老师提出了一些建议，防止了了事故发生。

consul / ˈkɒnsl / *n.* [C]领事：a ～ general 总领事

consult / kənˈsʌlt / *v.* ❶请教；咨询；商量；协商：I ～ed my teacher on how to write English composition well. 我请教老师如何写好英语作文。/ They are ～ing about the way to solve the problem. 他们正商量解决问题的办法。同 discuss, interview, confer ❷ 查阅；查看：You can ～ the telephone book for her new address. 你可以查阅电话簿找她的新住址。同 refer 派 consultation n.

consultant / kən'sʌltənt / n. [C] 顾问；提供咨询的专家：You may go and ask your legal ～ on this problem. 就这个问题你可以去咨询你的法律顾问。/ Some experts set up a firm of ～s in the centre of the city. 几位专家在市中心成立了一家咨询公司。同 adviser

consume / kən'sjuːm / vt. 消费；消耗；花费；耗尽：He ～d much time and energy in writing his thesis. 他花费了很多时间和精力写论文。/ His new refrigerator ～s a lot of electricity. 他的新冰箱很耗电。同 use, exhaust, waste 反 preserve, save

consumer / kən'sjuːmə(r) / n. [C] 消费者；用户：a ～ council 消费者委员会 / ～ goods 消费品 / A government should try hard to protect the legal rights of ～s. 政府应尽力保护消费者的合法权利。同 customer, buyer, user, shopper

consumption / kən'sʌmpʃn / n. [U] 消耗；消费(量)：high-level ～ 高消费／～ ahead of time 超前消费 / We are glad to see that the ～ of wine is decreasing year by year. 我们很高兴看到酒的消费量正逐年减少。同 use, exhaustion, waste 反 saving, preservation

contact / 'kɒntækt / Ⅰ n. 接触；联系；交往：Talking with young people, you can come into ～ with many new ideas. 与年轻人交谈，你能接触到许多新思想。/ I haven't been in ～ with my brother for a long time. 我好长时间没有和我哥哥保持联系了。同 touch, connection Ⅱ v. 与…联系，与…接触：We ～ each other by telephone. 我们常通过电话相互联系。同 touch, connect

contain / kən'teɪn / v. 容纳；包含：The suitcase ～ed nothing but dirty clothes. 箱子里除了脏衣服外，什么都没有。同 hold, include

contemporary / kən'tempərəri / Ⅰ adj. 当代的；同时代的；同年龄的：He is a ～ outstanding poet. 他是当代著名诗人。同 modern, up-to-date, current 反 old, out-of-date Ⅱ n. [C] 当代人；同龄人：He met with his contemporaries at college yesterday. 昨天他遇到了大学时代的几个同学。同 peer

contempt / kən'tempt / n. [U] 鄙视；蔑视：～ for a traitor 对卖国贼的蔑视 同 disgust 反 respect

content[1] / 'kɒntent / n. ❶ 容纳的东西；容量：The oxygen ～ of the air here is thin. 这里空气中的含氧量很少。同 capacity, volume ❷ 内容，要旨；(pl.)(书籍)目录：I like both the style and the ～ of this book. 这本书的风格和内容我都喜欢。/ He read the ～s of the textbook first. 他先看了看教科书的目录。

content[2] / kən'tent / adj. 满意的；满足的：The old lady is ～ to spend her weekends with her grandson. 老太太很乐意和孙子一起度周末。同 satisfied 反 dissatisfied / ～ with 满足于：She is ～ with the meal. 她对这顿饭感到满意。

contest Ⅰ / 'kɒntest / n. [C] 竞赛；比赛：An English writing ～ was held in our school. 我们学校举行了英语写作比赛。同 competition, match Ⅱ / kən'test / v. 争夺；角逐；比赛：She ～ed against the last opponent for the championship. 她和最后一个对手角逐冠军。同 compete

context / 'kɒntekst / n. 上下文；前后关系：I always guess the meaning of an unknown word from the ～. 我总是从上下文猜一个不认识的词的意义。

continent / 'kɒntɪnənt / n. 大陆；陆地；大洲：the ～ of Asia 亚洲大陆 同 mainland

continental / ˌkɒntɪ'nentl / adj. 大陆的；大陆性的：～ climate 大陆性气候

continual / kən'tɪnjʊəl / adj. ❶ 频繁的，反反复复的：～ bus departures 公共汽车频繁的发车 ❷ 不停的，从不间断的：Life is a ～ struggle. 人生即不断拼搏的过程。

continue / kən'tɪnjuː / v. 持续；继续；依旧：The rain ～d for three days. 雨连续下了三天。/ She still ～s in low spirit. 她依然情绪低落。同 last, remain

用法

continue 后可接不定式，也可接动名词：He continued to point (pointing) out my spelling mistakes. 他进一步指出我的拼写错误。We continued watching them. 我们继续监视他们。

continuous / kən'tɪnjʊəs / adj. 不断的；连续的：A man's brain needs a ～ supply of blood.

人的大脑需要不断的血液供给。同 lasting, unbroken 派 continuously *adv.*

contort / kən'tɔːt / *vt.* 扭曲，把…弄弯；歪曲：～ the truth 歪曲真相／Her face was ～ed with anger. 她的脸气得变了形。

contract Ⅰ / 'kɒntrækt / *n.* [C]合同；契约；承包：The clerk had a two-year ～ of employment with the company. 那位职员与公司签了两年的雇用合同。同 agreement Ⅱ / kən'trækt / *v.* 签合同；承包：The two countries ～ed a trade agreement three years ago. 两国在三年前签订了一项贸易协议。／Do you know which firm did they ～ the project to? 你知道他们把这项工程承包给了哪家公司吗？

contraction / kən'trækʃn / *n.* ❶[U;C]收缩；缩小；缩短：Cold causes the ～ of liquids, gases, and solids. 冷却会使液体、气体和固体收缩。／The ～ of mercury by cold makes it go down in thermometers. 水银遇冷收缩，在温度计中下降。❷[C]缩约形式，缩约词；缩约："Can't" is a ～ of "cannot". "can't"是"cannot"的缩约形式。

contradict / ˌkɒntrə'dɪkt / *vt.* 与…相矛盾；与…相反：His statements ～ with the facts. 他的话与事实相矛盾。同 counter, conflict

contradiction / ˌkɒntrə'dɪkʃn / *n.* 矛盾：She fell into ～s. 她陷入矛盾之中。同 counter, conflict

contrary / 'kɒntrəri / Ⅰ *n.* 相反；反面：He expected to pass the exam, but the result was the ～. 他希望能通过考试，但结果正相反。同 opposite／**on the** ～反之，相反；另一方面：We thought the weather would be bad, but on the ～ we had fine sunshine. 我们原以为天气会很糟，但结果相反，那天阳光灿烂。Ⅱ *adj.* 相反的：His opinion is ～ to mine. 他的看法与我的相反。同 opposite.

contrast Ⅰ / 'kɒntrɑːst / *n.* 对立；对照；对比：There is a great ～ between life of the present and the past. 现在的生活和过去的生活有天壤之别。同 differences, comparison Ⅱ / kən'trɑːst / *v.* 对比，与…对照：It's very interesting to ～ birds and fishes. 把鸟和鱼进行对比是很有趣的。同 compare

contribute / kən'trɪbjuːt / *v.* ❶捐助；贡献：They ～d food and clothing to the orphans. 他们为孤儿捐献食物和衣服。同 offer, donate, help ❷投稿：My classmates often ～ articles to newspapers and magazines. 我的同学们经常向报刊投稿。❸(与 to 连用)有助于：Physical exercise ～s to good health. 身体锻炼有助于健康。同 benefit, help

contribution / ˌkɒntrɪ'bjuːʃn / *n.* ❶捐助；贡献：They received a lot of charitable ～s. 他们收到大量慈善捐款。同 help, donation ❷投稿：She sent a ～ to a magazine. 她向一家杂志社投稿。

control / kən'trəʊl / Ⅰ *vt.* (-trolled; -trolling)控制；支配；克制：The machine is automatically ～led. 这台机器是自动控制的。同 manage Ⅱ *n.* 控制；支配；克制：He has good ～ of his class. 他对他的班级具有良好的控制能力。同 management / **in** ～ 在控制之中；在掌握之中：The next moment he had himself in ～. 他很快就控制住自己。／She is in ～ of the store. 这家商店由她管理。

controversy / 'kɒntrəvɜːsi, kən'trɒvəsi / *n.* [U;C]争论；辩论：a violent ～ over a commercial treaty 关于一项商业条约的激烈辩论

convenience / kən'viːnɪəns / *n.* 方便；便利设施：The apartment has all the modern ～s. 这套房子拥有一切现代化设施。／**at your** ～ 在你方便的时候：Come to me at your earliest ～. 在你方便时马上来找我。**for** ～**'s sake** 为方便起见：I live near the school for ～'s sake. 为方便起见，我住在学校附近。

convenient / kən'viːnɪənt / *adj.* 方便的；合适的：Will it be ～ for you to start the work tomorrow? 明天开始工作你行吗？同 handy, suitable 派 conveniently *adv.*

convention / kən'venʃn / *n.* ❶[U;C](对社会行为等的)约定俗成；习俗：～s of daily life 日常习俗／abandon the formal ～s of the past 摒弃旧日拘泥的习俗 ❷[C](正式的)会议；(定期的)大会：a teachers' ～ 教师代表大会／a ～ on human rights for Africa 非洲人权问题大会 ❸[C;U]常规，惯例；传统：It is a matter of ～ that businessmen should wear suits. 商人穿西装是一种惯例。

conversation / ˌkɒnvə'seɪʃn / *n.* 谈话；会话；会谈：We had several ～s with him. 我们已和他谈过几次。同 chat, talk

converse / kən'vɜːs / *v.* 交谈；谈话：My uncle who just came back from America often ～s in two languages with me. 我叔叔刚从美国回来，常常用两种语言和我交谈。同 talk

C

convert / kən'vɜːt / v. ❶变换；转换；改变：
These machines ～ cotton into cloth 这些机器
将棉花加工成布。/a sofa that ～ s into abed
一款可改变成床的沙发 ❷使改变信仰（或立
场、观点等）；使皈依，使归附

convex / 'kɒnveks / I n. 凸面；凸面体 II adj.
凸的；凸面的：a ～ mirror 凸面镜 反 concave

convey / kən'veɪ / vt. 运输，运送；传达：He
～ed the message to the premier. 他把信息呈
送给总理了。/ Words failed to ～ my feeling.
用言语不能表达我的感情。同 tell, communicate, transport

convince / kən'vɪns / vt. 使相信；说服：She
tried to ～me that she was innocent. 她尽力想
让我相信她是无辜的。同 persuade /～ sb. of
sth. 说服某人相信某事；I couldn't ～ him of
his mistake. 我无法说服他认识自己的错误。

用法
convince 后除接介词 of 外，还可接 that 从
句：He cannot convince himself that his best
friend has betrayed him. 他无法让自己相信
他最好的朋友背叛了他。

coo / kuː / vi.（鸽子）咕咕地叫

cook / kʊk / I n. [C]厨师：Too many ～s spoil
the broth. 厨子多了煮坏汤。II v. 烹调；煮：He
～ed his meals on a gas ring. 他在煤气灶上做
饭。同 make, prepare

cookie / 'kʊki / n. [C] ❶（小）甜饼干；choco-
late-chip ～s 巧克力饼干 ❷〈俚〉人，家伙：a
smart ～机灵鬼/some tough ～s 一些难对付
的家伙 ❸〈贬〉勾人的女人：That's the way the
～ crumbles.〈口〉结果事情成了这个样子。

cool / kuːl / I adj. 凉快的，凉爽的；冷静的：
The evening is delightfully ～. 晚间凉爽宜人。
/ He kept ～ in the face of danger. 面临危险
他很镇静。同 cold, calm 反 warm, excited II
vt. 使冷却；使凉快；使冷静下来：What he said
～ed her anger. 他的话使她不再生气。/ Some
rain would ～ us off. 下点雨会使我们感到凉
快。同 freeze, calm 反 warm, excite

cooperate / kəʊ'ɒpəreɪt / vi. 合作；协作；配合：
We are cooperating toward a common goal. 我
们正为一个共同的目标而合作。/ He ～d
with the company happily. 他与那家公司愉快
地合作。同 unite, join 反 conflict, compete

cooperation / kəʊ,ɒpə'reɪʃn / n. [U]合作；协
作：technological ～ 技术合作/ international
～国际合作 反 conflict, competition

cooperative / kəʊ'ɒpərətɪv / I adj. 合作的；
协作的：～ development 合作开发/ We made
a ～ effort to finish the task. 我们共同努力完
成了任务。II n. [C]合作社；合作团体 同 association 派 cooperatively adv.

coordinate / kəʊ'ɔːdɪneɪt / vt. 整理；调节；协
调：A swimmer should ～ the movements of
his arms and legs. 游泳者应该协调双臂和双
腿的动作/We must ～ our operations with
theirs. 我们必须使自己的行为和他们的行动
协调一致。II / kəʊ'ɔːdɪnət / n. [C]坐标

cop / kɒp / n. [C]（美俚）警察；警员 同 policeman

cope / kəʊp / vi. 应付；对付（与 with 连用）：I
know how to ～ with a complicated situation.
我知道怎样对付复杂的局面。同 handle, deal

copper / 'kɒpə(r) / n. 铜；铜币；铜制品

copy / 'kɒpi / I v. 抄写；仿制；复印：He cop-
ied the passage in his notebook. 他把那段文字
抄在笔记本上。/ Never ～ foreign things
blindly. 绝不要盲目照搬外国的东西。同 reproduce, imitate II n. [C]抄本；册；本（电影）
拷贝：I made two copies of this poem. 这首诗
我抄了两份。/ How many copies of the book
have you published? 这本书你们印制了多少
册? 同 reproduction, imitation

copyright / 'kɒpɪraɪt / n. 版权；著作权：The
～ law is to protect the right of the author. 版
权法是保护作者著作权的法律。

coral / 'kɒrəl / n. [C]珊瑚：a ～ island 珊瑚岛

cord / kɔːd / n. 绳；索；粗线；电线：the electric ～ 电
线/ the flexible ～ 花线；皮线 同 rope, string

core / kɔː(r) / n. [C]果实的核；核心；要点：
The professor pointed out the ～ of the problem. 教授指出了问题的核心。同 heart, es-
sence

cork / kɔːk / n. [U]软木；[C]软木塞：I helped
to pull out the ～ of the bottle. 我帮他拔
出了瓶子的软木塞。同 stopper, plug

corn / kɔːn / n. [U]谷类；（美）玉蜀黍：Little
children like pop ～. 小孩喜欢吃爆米花。

用法
corn 一般情况下是不可数名词，但作"谷粒"
讲时是可数名词。如要表示"一粒米"，可以
说：a corn of rice.

corner / 'kɔːnə(r) / n. [C]角落：The boy fell

and hit his head against the ～ of a desk. 小男孩摔倒了，头撞上书桌角。/ Turn the ～, you'll find the hospital. 转过街角你就会找到那家医院。同 angle,turn /**round the** ～ 即将来临;靠近:Christmas is round the ～. 圣诞节即将来临。**from all** ～**s** 各地:People have come from all ～s of the country to watch the game. 人们从全国各地赶来观看比赛。

用法

❶corner 前用介词 at, on, round 或 around 表示180°以上的角:I'll meet you at (on) the corner of the Smith Street. 我将在史密斯街的拐角处与你见面。❷corner 前用介词 in 表示180°以下的角:They are sitting in the corner of the classroom. 他们坐在教室的角落里。

corporation / ˌkɔːpəˈreɪʃn / n. [C] (股份有限)公司,社团;法人,法人团体:a trading ～ 贸易公司/ a multinational ～ 跨国公司 同 company,business,organization

corrode / kəˈrəud / vt. ❶腐蚀;侵蚀:Moist air ～s iron. 潮湿的空气使铁生锈腐蚀。/Money sometimes ～s people's minds. 金钱有时会腐蚀人的灵魂。❷(渐渐)损害,损伤:It was sad to see him ～ with suspicion. 看到他因多疑而扭曲了性格,真让人伤心。

correct / kəˈrekt / Ⅰ vt. 改正;校正;修改:Please ～ the mistakes in my exercises. 请把我练习中的错误改一下。同 repair, remedy, improve Ⅱ adj. 正确的;恰当的:This sentence is ～. 这句话正确。同 right, proper 反 wrong,improper 派 correctly adv.

correction / kəˈrekʃn / n. [U]改正;修改:The ～ of the essay took two hours. 修改论文花了两小时。

correspond / ˌkɒrəˈspɒnd / vi. ❶相当于;一致;～ **to** (**with**)... 与...一致,相当于:The house ～s with my needs. 这房子符合我的要求。/ His expenses do not ～ to his income. 他的开支与他的收入不相符。同 agree,match ❷通信:They ～ every month. 他们每月都通信。同 communicate/～ **with** 通信:I ～ed with her at that time. 那段时间我一直与她通信。

correspondence / ˌkɒrəˈspɒndəns / n. [U]通信;信件;相符:By yesterday I had received a great deal of ～. 到昨天为止,我已收到大量信件。同 letters, communication

correspondent / ˌkɒrəˈspɒndənt / n. [C]通信员;记者:He is a ～ for (on, of) the *People's Daily*. 他是《人民日报》的记者。同 journalist,newsman

corridor / ˈkɒrɪdɔː(r) / n. [C]走廊;过道

countdown / ˈkauntdaun / n. [C]倒计数;倒计时(阶段):The (ten-second) ～ began at 16:00 hours. 16 时开始(10 秒钟的)倒计时。

corrupt / kəˈrʌpt / Ⅰ adj. 腐败的;贪污的;道德败坏的:Honest people are disgusted with ～ officials. 正直的人们厌恶贪官污吏。同 dishonest,wicked 反 virtuous, honest Ⅱ v. 败坏;腐蚀;贿赂,收买:The businessman tried to ～ the tax official but was refused. 那商人企图贿赂税务官员但遭到拒绝。同 decay,bribe

corruption / kəˈrʌpʃn / n. [U]腐败;败坏;贿赂;Official ～ should be stopped. 官场腐败应当制止。同 decay,bribery

cosmetic / kɒzˈmetɪk / Ⅰ n. [C]化妆品;Girls always like ～s. 女孩们总是喜欢化妆品的。同 makeup,beautifier Ⅱ adj. 化妆用的;整容的;～ surgery 整容手术

cosmos / ˈkɒzmɒs / n. 宇宙:in the ～ 在宇宙中 同 universe

cost / kɒst / Ⅰ v. (cost, cost) 花费;消耗(钱、劳动、时间、生命等):This coat ～ me much money. 这件外套花了我很多钱。/ Careless driving may ～ you your life. 粗心驾车可能使你丧命。同 require Ⅱ n. 价格,价值;费用;代价:The ～ of the used computer is only $50. 那台二手电脑的价格仅 50 美元。同 price, charge,loss / **at all** ～**s** 无论如何;不惜任何代价:We are determined to obtain our rights at all ～s. 我们决心不惜一切代价来取得我们的权利。**at the** ～ **of** 以...为代价,以...为牺牲(后接表示生命、健康、金钱、时间等的词):The young man saved the old man at the ～ of his own life. 那位年轻人以牺牲自己的生命为代价救了这位老人。

costly / ˈkɒstli / adj. ❶昂贵的;豪华的:He bought a ～ fur coat to his wife her birthday present. 他买了一件昂贵的毛皮大衣作为生日礼物送给妻子。同 expensive,high-priced ❷牺牲重大的;代价高的:You have made a ～ mistake. 你犯了一个代价极高的错误。

cottage / ˈkɒtɪdʒ / n. [C]村舍,茅舍;别墅 同 hut

C

cotton / 'kɒtn / n. [U]棉花;棉布:a ～ field 棉田/～ clothes 棉布衣

couch / kaʊtʃ / n. [C]长沙发;睡椅

cough / kɒf / Ⅰ v. 咳嗽:The old man ～ed badly at night. 老人晚上咳得厉害。Ⅱ n. 咳嗽:She was caught in the rain and had a bad ～. 她淋了雨,咳得厉害。

could / kʊd / aux. v. (can的过去式和过去分词形式)能;可以

council / 'kaʊnsl / n. [C]大会;委员会;议事机构:an advisory ～ 顾问委员会/ a cabinet ～ 内阁会议/ a world ～ 国际会议/ the Security Council 联合国安全理事会/ the State Council (中国)国务院

辨析

council 意为"政务会;理事会",常指政治团体、国际代表或地方代表参加的会。**assembly** 是正式用语,指为一共同目的预先安排的众多人参加的集会,也指议会:The U. N. General Assembly passed a new measure. 联合国大会通过了一项新议案。**conference** 是正式用语,指讨论问题或交换意见的会议,也可指运动方面的联合会或协会:a football conference 足协。**congress** 意为"代表大会",指政府机关、立法机构派代表参加决策的会议,也可指学术讨论会:a medical congress 医学会议。**meeting** 是普通用词,常指两个或两个以上的人进行的任何聚会:Their meeting is held on the third floor. 他们的会议在三楼召开。

council(l)or / 'kaʊnsələ(r) / n. [C]议员;顾问;评议员 回 adviser

counsel / 'kaʊnsl / n. ❶商议;评议;审议:They took ～ with each other on the problem. 他们就一问题共同商议。回 discussion, deliberation ❷忠告;劝告:He followed his father's ～ to work as a lawyer. 他听从父亲的忠告,当了一名律师。回 advice ❸[C]律师;辩护人:He is ～ for the defense. 他是辩方律师。回 lawyer, attorney

count / kaʊnt / v. 数;计算:Count from one to a hundred. 请从1数到100。回 number, calculate /～ **in** 包括:Count me in. 算我一个。～ **on** 依靠;指望:Don't ～ on him to come. 别指望他会来。～... **as** ... 把…看作…:We ～ her as a friend. 我们把她看作朋友。～ **up to** 共计:It ～s up to more than fifty yuan. 共计50多元。

counter[1] / 'kaʊntə(r) / n. [C]柜台:After putting 100 yuan on the ～, she went out of the restaurant. 在柜台上放了100元钱后她离开了餐馆。/ The service ～ is inside the hall. 服务台设在大厅里。回 bar, table

counter[2] / 'kaʊntə(r) / Ⅰ adj. 相反的;对立的;反对的:Obviously your idea is ～ to mine. 很明显你的想法与我的正好相反。回 opposite, contrary, converse Ⅱ adv. 反方向地;相反地:What he did went ～ to what the teacher hoped for. 他所做的与老师所希望的背道而驰。回 contrarily, conversely

counterfeit / 'kaʊntəfɪt / Ⅰ n. [C]冒牌货;赝品:The expert said that the oil painting was a ～. 专家说那幅油画是赝品。回 imitation, forgery, fake Ⅱ adj. 伪造的;仿造的;假冒的:a ～ trade-mark 冒牌商标/～ and shoddy commodities 假冒伪劣商品 回 false, forged

country / 'kʌntri / ❶[C]国土,国家;领土;故土:Asian countries 亚洲国家 / One ～, two systems, 一国 两制。/ The young man traveled all over the ～ by bicycle. 那年轻人骑车环游全国。回 nation, state ❷乡间;田野:They are living in the ～. 他们住在乡下。回 countryside

辨析

country 强调一国的领土:We love our country. 我们爱我们的国家。**nation** 强调一国的人民:the Chinese nation 中华民族。**power** 强调一国的实力和影响:a great power 一个强国。**state** 强调一国的政府机构:the State Council 国务院。

countryside / 'kʌntrɪsaɪd / n. 乡下;农村:I prefer to live in the ～ than (to) live in the city. 我宁愿住在农村而不愿住在城市。回 country

county / 'kaʊnti / n. [C](美国的)县(州以下最大的行政区划);(英国的)郡(最大的地方行政区划,相当于中国的省);(中国等的)县:the local ～ government 地方县政府

couple / 'kʌpl / n. [C]一对,一双;夫妇;几个,几件事物:I found a ～ of socks in the bedroom, but they don't make a pair. 我在卧室里找到一双袜子,但不配对。/ a ～ of days (months, years) 几天(几月,几年) 回 pair, several

coupon / 'ku:pɒn / n. [C](附在货物上的)赠券;(连在广告上的)礼券;购物优惠券

courage / ˈkʌrɪdʒ / n. [U] 勇敢；胆量：The boy had the ～ to jump down from the truck. 小男孩很勇敢，从卡车上跳下来。 同 bravery, daring 反 fear / **lose** ～ 失去勇气，灰心：Cheer up! Don't lose ～. 振作起来，不要灰心丧气。 **take** ～ 鼓起勇气：I took ～ to say "no". 我鼓起勇气说了声"不"。

courageous / kəˈreɪdʒəs / adj. 勇敢的；英勇的：You should be ～ enough to tell us the truth. 你应该勇敢地把真相告诉我们。

course / kɔːs / n. ❶[C]航线，路线：The ship is not on her right ～. 船未按正确航线航行。 ❷进程；过程：He knew something about the ～ of the event. 他了解一些这个事件的过程。 同 process ❸[C]课程；elective ～s 选修课/ evening ～s 夜校课程/ self-teaching ～ 自修课/ short-term ～s 短训班/ **in the ～ of** 在…期间：in the ～ of discussion 在讨论过程中 **of** ～ 当然，一定：—May I use your dictionary? —Of ～. —我可以用一下你的字典吗？—当然可以。

court / kɔːt / n. ❶法院；法庭：He will be brought to ～ for trial. 他将被带进法庭接受审判。 ❷庭院；院子：There is a small ～ in front of her house. 她的房前有一个小院。 同 courtyard ❸场地；球场：Our school has two twins ～s. 我们学校有两个网球场。

courtesy / ˈkɜːtəsi / n. ❶[U]礼貌；谦恭有礼；殷勤周到：He could at least have had the ～ to say sorry. 他连起码说声对不起的礼貌都没有。 ❷[C]谦恭有礼的举止（或言辞）：an exchange of ～互相致礼/show sb. every ～ of the house 在家盛情款待某人/ **by ～ of** 蒙…的好意（或惠允）；蒙…提供（或赠送）：By ～ of the exhibitor, we have taken a number of photos of the art products on display. 承蒙展出者许可，我们拍摄了若干艺术陈列品的照片。

courtyard / ˈkɔːtjɑːd / n. [C]庭院；院子 同 court, yard

cousin / ˈkʌzn / n. [C]堂兄弟，表兄弟；堂姐妹，表姐妹：I have three ～s on my father's (mother's) side. 我有三个堂(表)兄妹。

cover / ˈkʌvə(r) / Ⅰ v. ❶掩；盖：Dust ～ed your desk. 灰尘布满了你的书桌。 同 wrap, over lay / **be ～ed with** 被…覆盖：The hills are ～ed with thick snow. 山上覆盖着厚厚的白雪。 ❷占用(时间、空间)；包含，包括：His speach ～ed all aspects of the problem. 他的发言谈及了问题的各个方面。 同 include, contain Ⅱ n. 封面；盖子；套子：The book needs a new ～. 需要给这本书换上新的封面。 同 covering, lid

covering / ˈkʌvərɪŋ / n. 覆盖物；套，罩

cow / kaʊ / n. [C] 母牛；乳牛

用法

各种牛的英文表示法：cattle(总称) 牛；bull 公牛；calf 牛犊；ox 公牛，黄牛；buffalo 水牛，(美)野牛。

coward / ˈkaʊəd / n. [C] 懦夫

cowboy / ˈkaʊbɔɪ / n. [C] 牧童；牛仔：Young people like ～ suits. 年轻人喜欢穿牛仔服。

CPU (= central processing unit)(计算机)中央处理器

crab / kræb / n. 螃蟹；蟹肉

crack / kræk / Ⅰ n. [C]裂缝；裂纹；爆裂声：The ～s in the wall were caused by the earthquake. 墙上的裂缝是地震造成的。/I heard the ～ of fireworks outside. 我听到外边有鞭炮声。 同 split, snap, pop Ⅱ v. 爆裂；破裂；发出爆裂声：The glass bottle ～ed suddenly. 玻璃瓶突然裂了。 同 split, break, clap

cracked / krækt / adj. 有裂缝的，破裂的；碎的：A ～ vessel is known by its sound. 碗破听音。/ ～ wheat 碾成碎粒的小麦

cracker / ˈkrækə(r) / n. [C] 爆竹；鞭炮：The children are setting off ～s in the courtyard. 孩子们在院子里放鞭炮。 同 firecracker, fireworks

cradle / ˈkreɪdl / n. [C]摇篮；(喻)发源地，策源地：A man may meet with a lot of difficulties from the ～ to the grave. 人的一生会遇到许许多多的困难。/ The Jinggang Mountains are the ～ of the Chinese revolution. 井冈山是中国革命的摇篮(发源地)。 同 birthplace, source

craft / krɑːft / n. ❶工艺；手艺：She likes the making of potter's ～ very much. 她非常喜欢陶艺制作。 同 art, skill ❷[C]行业；职业；手工业：People seldom practise the carpenter's ～ now. 现在很少有人从事木匠业了。 同 trade, occupation ❸船；航空器 同 spaceship, aircraft

craftsman / ˈkrɑːftsmən / n. (pl. craftsmen)手艺人；工匠：The factory needs master craftsmen. 工厂需要能工巧匠。

C

crane / kreɪn / n. [C] ❶鹤 ❷起重机；吊车：She operates the ～ in the factory. 她在厂里开吊车。同 lifter

crash / kræʃ / Ⅰ v. ❶碰撞；坠落；坠毁：The truck ～ed into a wall. 卡车撞上一堵墙上。同 fall, dash, smash ❷（计算机）死机：I don't know why the computer ～ed suddenly. 我不知道为什么计算机突然就死机了。Ⅱ n. [C] ❶碰撞；坠落；坠毁：The plane ～ caused the death of more than one hundred passengers. 飞机坠毁造成一百多人死亡。同 fall, collapse ❷破裂声：The glass fell to the floor with a ～. 玻璃杯哗的一声摔到地上。同 crack, clap ❸（计算机）死机

crawl / krɔːl / v. 爬；爬行；匍匐前进：The snake ～ed into a cave. 蛇爬进了洞里。同 creep, inch

crayon / 'kreɪən / n. [C]蜡笔；颜色笔：colored ～s 彩色蜡笔／a picture in ～ 蜡笔画

crazy / 'kreɪzi / adj. (-ier, -iest) ❶ 疯狂的，发疯的：The noise is driving me ～. 这声音吵得我快发疯了。同 insane, mad 反 sane, sensible ❷热衷的：He is ～ about football. 他对足球着了迷。同 very fond, wild 反 cool, indifferent ❸愚蠢的，荒唐的：a ～ idea 荒唐的想法 同 foolish, absurd 反 smart, wise

creak / kriːk / vi. 吱吱嘎嘎作响

cream / kriːm / n. [U]奶油：Most children like icecream. 大多数孩子都喜欢吃冰激凌。

create / krɪ'eɪt / vt. 创造；引起；造成；产生：Do you believe that God ～d the world? 你相信上帝创造了世界吗？／We've ～d a beautiful new house out of an old ruin. 我们在废墟上建造了一栋漂亮的新屋。同 make, cause, invent

creation / krɪ'eɪʃn / n. 创造；创作；作品 同 invention, production, writing

creative / krɪ'eɪtɪv / adj. 创造性的；有创造力的：That is a ～ idea. 那是一个很有创意的想法。同 imaginative

creature / 'kriːtʃə(r) / n. [C]动物；生物：the wild ～ 野生物／a good ～ 一个好人／a poor ～ 一个可怜的人／a weak ～ 一个软弱的人／a human ～ 人 同 animal, human, being

credible / 'kredəbl / adj. ❶（人或言论等）可信的；值得相信的：a ～ witness 可靠的见证人／That boy's excuse for being absent was hardly ～. 那孩子缺席的理由几乎不可信。❷

有效的；有威力的：They haven't produced any ～ policies for improving the situation. 他们尚未拿出改善局势的行之有效的对策。

credit / 'kredɪt / n. [U] ❶信任，相信：The manager gave ～ to what he said. 经理相信了他说的话。同 trust, belief 反 distrust, disbelief ❷信誉；声望；荣誉：Her success does her great ～. 她的成功给她带来极大的荣誉。／Telling lies would hurt your ～. 说谎会使你的名声受到损害。同 recognition, honor 反 dishonor ❸信用；信贷：He drew some money with his ～ card. 他用信用卡取了一些钱。❹学分：English Ⅱ is a 4-～ course. 英语二级是四个学分的课程。

creek / kriːk / n. [C]（河的）支流；小河溪

creep / kriːp / vi. (crept/ krept /, crept)（身体贴着地面）爬行；悄悄地行进；（枝条）蔓生：The cat crept toward the mouse. 猫悄悄地靠近老鼠。／The ivy crept up all over the wall. 常青藤爬满了墙壁。同 crawl, inch

crew / kruː / n. 全体乘务员：The ship has a ～ of twenty. 这艘船上有二十名船员。

cricket / 'krɪkɪt / n. ❶[C]蟋蟀 ❷[U]板球：play ～ 打板球

crime / kraɪm / n. 罪；犯罪：Crime is on the rise in many big cities. 在许多大城市里犯罪正在增加。／He committed a ～ and was sent to prison. 他犯了罪被关进监狱。同 offense, lawbreaking

criminal / 'krɪmɪn(ə)l / Ⅰ adj. 犯罪的；犯法的；刑事的：a ～ act 犯罪行为／a ～ case 刑事案件 同 illegal 反 legal Ⅱ n. [C]犯人；刑事犯：The ～ was sentenced to five years' imprisonment. 犯人被判五年徒刑。同 lawbreaker, convict

crinkle / 'krɪŋkl / v. (使)起皱；(使)起波纹：His face ～ into a smile 他满脸皱纹地笑了起来。／My clothes were all ～ when I got them out of the case. 我把衣服从箱子里拿出来时，它们全部起皱了。派 crinkly adj.

cripple / 'krɪpl / n. [C]跛子；伤残人：The soldier was brave. 那位跛脚士兵很勇敢。同 lamer

crisis / 'kraɪsɪs / n. (pl. crises)危机；难关；危险期：The family united as one to ride out their economic ～ smoothly. 全家人团结一致顺利渡过了经济危机。同 emergency, urgency

crisp / krɪsp / adj. 易碎的；脆的：The snow

was ～ underfoot. 脚下的雪踩起来松脆。
反 hard

critic / ˈkrɪtɪk / n. [C]批评家；评论家：a drama (literary, music) ～ 戏剧(文学、音乐)评
论家 同 judge, reviewer

critical / ˈkrɪtɪkl / adj. ❶批评的；批判的：
The editor is writing an important ～ essay. 编
辑正在写一篇重要的评论文章。同 judging,
reviewing ❷紧要的；关键性的；危急的：The
wounded is now in ～ condition. 伤员现在情
况危急。/ He is always the first to help others
at ～ moment. 在危急关头他总是第一个出
来帮助别人。同 decisive, urgent, dangerous
反 uncritical, safe 派 critically adv.

criticism / ˈkrɪtɪsɪzəm / n. [U]评论；批评

criticize / ˈkrɪtɪsaɪz / vt. 批判；批评：The
teacher ～d the student by name because of his
lack of responsibility. 老师点名批评了那位学
生的不负责任。反 praise /～ sb. for sth. 因
某事批评某人：She's always criticizing her
husband for being lazy. 她总是批评她丈夫
懒惰。

crocodile / ˈkrɒkədaɪl / n. [C]鳄鱼

crook / krʊk / n. [C]❶(一头有弯钩的)手杖；
曲柄杖 ❷臂弯：She held the baby in the ～ of
her left arm. 她用左胳膊的臂弯抱着婴儿。❸
弯曲物；弯曲部分；钩子：have a ～ in one's
back 背驼/the ～ of a cane 手杖弯头

crop / krɒp / n. [C]庄稼，作物；收成，收获：a
big (rich, bumper, good) ～ 丰收/ a bad
(poor) ～ 歉收/ gather ～s 收庄稼/ raise
～s种庄稼

cross / krɒs / Ⅰ vt. 穿越；横过：Be careful
when ～ing the street. 过街时要小心。同 pass
Ⅱ n. 十字架；十字形物品：the Red Cross (Society)红十字会 Ⅲ adj. 相反的：It was ～ to
our design. 它与我们的计划相反。

crossing / ˈkrɒsɪŋ / n. [C] 交叉点；十字路口：
The car stopped at the ～. 小车在交叉路口停
下。同 crossroads

crossroad / ˈkrɒsˌrəud / n. ❶岔路，支路 ❷十
字路口：a store at the ～在十字路口的商店/
Traffic stalled at a ～. 交通在十字路口堵塞
了。❸紧要关头，关键时刻：be at the ～s 面临
重大抉择的关头

crow[1] / krəʊ / n. [C] 乌鸦

crow[2] / krəʊ / vi. ❶(雄鸡)啼 ❷(婴儿)欢叫

❸自夸；洋洋自得，幸灾乐祸：～ over sb. 's
failure 因某人遭失败而幸灾乐祸 同
brag, boast

crowd / kraʊd / Ⅰ n. [C]人群；大众：A big ～
gathered on the street. 街上聚集了一大群人。
/ The writer often says that his books are for
the ～. 那位作家常说他的书是为大众写的。
同 group Ⅱ v. 拥挤；挤满：The pupils ～ed
round the teacher to ask questions. 学生们围
着老师问问题。同 jam, stuff / **be ～ed with**
挤满；充满；塞满：His mind is ～ed with
whys. 他脑子里满是问号。

crown / kraʊn / Ⅰ n. ❶[C]王冠 ❷(the ～或
the Crown)王位，王权；君主，国王 Ⅱ vt. 为…
加冕，立…为王；授予荣誉：He ～ed his son
King. 他立他的儿子为国王。

crucial / ˈkruːʃ(ə)l / adj. 至关重要的；决定性
的，关键的：a ～ moment 紧要关头/a ～ bat-
tle 决定性的战役

crude / kruːd / adj. ❶天然的；未加工的；未成
熟的：That's only my ～ idea. 那只是我不成
熟的想法。/ The price of ～ oil is on the rise.
原油价格不断上涨。同 raw, natural, immature ❷粗糙的；粗鲁的：His ～ manners made
me angry. 他的粗鲁态度使我很生气。同 rude

cruel / krʊəl / adj. 残酷的：She told the child
not to be ～ to animals. 她告诉孩子不要虐待
动物。同 inhuman 反 kind 派 cruelly adv. ;
cruelty n.

cruiser / ˈkruːzə(r) / n. [C] 巡洋舰；游艇 同
warship, yacht

crush / krʌʃ / vt. 压，挤；压碎，粉碎：Be careful
not to ～ the glass. 小心别压碎玻璃。/ They
are trying to ～ into the front seats. 他们尽力
想挤进前排的座位上去。同 mash, grind

crust / krʌst / n. 硬外皮；外壳：He knows little about the earth's ～. 他不了解地壳的情
况。同 shell

crutch / krʌtʃ / n. [C]拐杖；支柱：The patient
can only walk on ～es. 那病人只能拄着拐杖
走路。同 support, post

cry / kraɪ / Ⅰ vi. 哭；叫，喊：Little children always ～ when hurt. 小孩受伤时总是哭叫。/
～ **down** 诋毁；看不起：He stood up to speak,

C

but his audience cried him down. 他站起来说话,但听众把他轰了下去。～ **for** 迫切要求:The strikers cried for a raise of pay. 罢工者要求提高工资。～ **out** 大声叫喊:As soon as I went in, she cried out with pleasure. 我一进屋,她就高兴得叫了起来。Ⅱ *n.*[C]叫声;哭声:We heard a ～ of "Help!" 我们听到有人喊"救命!" 同 shout,plea

crystal / 'krɪstl / Ⅰ *n.* 水晶;水晶制品 Ⅱ *adj.* 水晶般的;清澈的,透明的:It's wonderful to swim in a ～ stream. 在清澈见底的溪水里游泳真棒。

cube / kju:b / *n.* 立方体;立方形;立方;三次方

cubic / 'kju:bɪk / *adj.* 立方体的;立方形的;立方的;三次方的

cuckoo / 'kʊku: / *n.*[C]杜鹃;布谷鸟

cucumber / 'kju:kʌmbə(r) / *n.* 黄瓜

cue / kju: / *n.*[C]提示;暗示:I don't know how to answer this question. Can you give me some ～s? 我不知道怎么回答这个问题。你能给我点提示吗? 同 hint, suggestion

cuff / kʌf / *n.*[C] ❶袖口:Your ～ is dirty. 你的袖口脏了。同 band, hem ❷(*pl.*)手铐:The criminal didn't wear ～s at the court. 罪犯在法庭上没有戴手铐。同 handcuff

cultivate / 'kʌltɪveɪt / *vt.* ❶耕作;栽培;养殖:They ～d flowers and earned a lot of money. 他们种花挣了许多钱。同 grow, farm ❷培养;教养:He ～s the sort of people who can be useful to him in his business. 他培养对他的业务有用的人。同 educate, teach

culture / 'kʌltʃə(r) / *n.* 文化;教养;修养:The doctor studies ancient Greek ～. 那位博士研究古希腊文化。/ Professor Li is a man of considerable ～. 李教授是一个文化修养很高的人。同 learning, civilization

cup / kʌp / *n.*[C] 杯子;优胜杯;奖杯:a ～ of tea 一杯茶/a ～ of coffee 一杯咖啡/ They won the world cup. 他们赢得了世界杯。

cupboard / 'kʌbəd / *n.*[C] 碗橱

cure / kjʊə(r) / *vt.* 医治;治愈:The medicine ～d my stomachache. 这药治好了我的胃痛。/ Time ～d him of his grief. 时光流逝消除了他的悲伤。同 heal, remedy

辨析

cure 意为"治疗",强调病后恢复健康:The medicine cured her toothache. 这种药治好了她的牙痛。**heal** 意为"复原;治愈",指伤口愈合:The wound heals rapidly. 这伤口好得快。**remedy** 意为"医治;补救",指改变身心方面不正常,不理想的状况:Aspirin may remedy a headache. 阿司匹林可医治头痛。**treat** 意为"治疗",含义最广,包括对伤员进行诊断、制订治疗方案,开药方等整个过程:Cancer is difficult to treat. 癌症很难医治。

curiosity / ˌkjʊərɪ'ɒsəti / *n.*[U]好奇;好奇心:The crowd looked at them with great ～. 众人非常好奇地看着他们。/ To satisfy her ～, I told her the secret. 为满足她的好奇心,我把秘密告诉了她。同 interest, concern

curious / 'kjʊərɪəs / *adj.* 好奇的;稀奇的;奇妙的:Don't be too ～ about things you are not supposed to know. 对于你不应该知道的事别太好奇。同 interested, odd

curl / kɜ:l / Ⅰ *n.* 卷毛;鬈发 Ⅱ *v.* (使)蜷曲;蜷缩:Does her hair ～ naturally? 她的头发是天然鬈发吗? / The frost ～ed up the leaves. 严霜使叶子卷起来。同 curve, spiral

currency / 'kʌrənsi / *n.* ❶通货;货币:The government issued some new ～. 政府发行了一些新货币。同 money, banknote, bill ❷[U]通用;流通;流传:Very soon her novels got ～ among young students. 很快她的小说就在年轻学生中流传开来。同 circulation

current / 'kʌrənt / Ⅰ *adj.* 通用的;流行的;当前的;现时的:The ～ situation is very complicated. 当前形势很复杂。同 present, up-to-date 反 past, out-of-date Ⅱ *n.*[C]水流;电流;潮流;倾向:the cold (warm) ～ in the sea 寒(暖)流/ He turned off the ～ to check the machine. 他切断电流查看机器。/ This type of mobile phones is no longer in ～. 这种型号的手机已不再流行了。

curry / 'kʌri, 'kɜ:ri / *n.*[C;U]咖喱;咖喱饭;咖喱菜肴

curse / kɜ:s / Ⅰ *v.* 诅咒;咒骂:She ～d her neighbors with anger. 她生气地咒骂她的邻居。同 swear, abuse Ⅱ *n.*[C] ❶咒骂,诅咒之词;be under a ～ 被诅咒的 同 swearing, oath ❷祸根,祸害;受诅咒的东西(人) 同 burden, misfortune

cursor / ˈkɜːsə(r) / *n.* (计算尺)游标;(计算机)光标

curtain / ˈkɜːtn / *n.* [C]窗帘;幕;幕布：raise the ～启幕/drop the ～ 落幕/ She opened the ～ to see if it was raining outside. 她拉开窗帘看看外边是不是在下雨。

curve / kɜːv / *n.* [C]曲线;弯曲：Draw a ～ here. 在这里画条曲线。/ The automobile has to slow down to go around a sharp ～ in the road. 汽车急转弯时得减速。同 bend,turn

cushion / ˈkʊʃn / *n.* [C]垫子;坐垫

custody / ˈkʌstədi / *n.* [U]照看;监护;保管;(离婚状态下孩子的)监护权：The files are in the secretary's ～. 这些文件是由秘书保管的。/Parents have the ～ of their young children. 父母对自己年幼的儿女尽有监护义务。

custom / ˈkʌstəm / *n.* ❶ 习惯;风俗;惯例：This ～ has been kept up for 2,000 years. 这一风俗已经保持了两千年。/ It is not my ～ to take off my shoes when I get into the hall. 我不习惯进入门厅脱鞋。同 habit,convention ❷(常用 Customs)海关;关税：It will take us over an hour to pass the Customs. 我们办完海关手续要一个多小时。同 customhouse,duty

辨析

custom 意为"风俗;习惯",主要指一国或一个社会的风俗,有时也可指一个人的习惯：Social customs vary in different parts of the world. 世界各地的风俗习惯各不相同。It was his custom to rise early. 早起是他的习惯。habit 通常指个人长期以来形成的自然习惯：He can never get rid of the bad habit of smoking. 他永远也不能改掉抽烟的恶习。convention 指人们约定俗成的规则、习惯：It is silly to be a slave to social convention. 做社会习俗的奴隶是愚蠢的。manners (*pl.*)意为"礼貌;规矩",指某一特定时期盛行的礼仪或风俗：She has written a book on the manners and customs of the ancient Egyptians. 她写了一本关于古埃及人风俗习惯的书。practice 意为"习惯;常例",指行为举止的一般方式,强调因个人选择形成的习惯：The old practice still prevails. 旧习俗仍然盛行。

customer / ˈkʌstəmə / *n.* [C]顾客;主顾：Customers First. 顾客第一。/ The old lady is a regular ～ of the shop. 老太太是这家商店的老主顾。同 shopper,client

cut / kʌt / *v.* (cut,cut;cutting) 切;割：Please ～ the bread into two. 请把面包一分为二。/ ～ **across** 走捷径：They ～ across an empty lot. 他们取捷径穿过一块空地。～ **away** 砍掉;剪掉：We should ～ away all the dead branches from the tree. 我们应该砍掉树上所有枯枝。～ **down** 减低;缩减;限制：The doctor told Mr. Wang to ～ down his consumption of cigarettes. 医生吩咐王先生少抽烟。～ **in** 插嘴;打断：While we were watching the show,a man ～ in to tell who won the election. 我们在看节目时,一个人突然插进来宣布谁竞选将胜。～ **off** 切断;割掉：The television show was ～ off by a special news report. 电视节目被特别新闻报道打断。～ **up**(口语)使伤心：She was ～ up at the news. 听到这个消息,她很伤心。

cyber / ˈsaɪbə(r) / *n. & adj.* 网络(的);网络空间(的);计算机：～ affairs 网恋/ a ～ cafe 网络咖啡屋,网吧/ a ～ citizen(cult) 网民(网虫)/ a ～ message board 网络浏览者/ ～ space 网络空间;虚拟现实 同 network

cycle / ˈsaɪkl / *n.* ❶ [C]自行车：I saw him ride on a ～ at the corner of the street. 我在街角看见他骑着自行车。同 bike,bicycle ❷循环;周期：He is studying the life ～ of insects. 他在研究昆虫的生活周期。同 circulate

cylinder / ˈsɪlɪndə(r) / *n.* [C]❶圆柱状物;圆柱体 ❷(发动机的)汽缸;泵体

cynical / ˈsɪnɪkl / *adj.* 挖苦的;讽刺的;愤世嫉俗的 同 sarcastic,sneering

D d

dad / dæd / *n*. [C](口语)爸爸

daddy / ˈdædi / *n*. (＝dad)[C](口语)爸爸

dagger / ˈdægə(r) / *n*. [C] 匕首；短剑：The thief drew a ～ at a customer. 那小偷拔出匕首向一位顾客刺去。同 knife

daily / ˈdeɪli / Ⅰ *adj*. 每日的 Her ～ life is simply. 她的日常生活非常简朴。同 everyday Ⅱ *n*. 日报：In order to improve his Chinese, Jim reads *the People's Daily* everyday. 为了提高汉语水平,杰米天天读《人民日报》。

dairy / ˈdeəri / *n*. [C]牛奶场；乳品店

dam / dæm / *n*. [C]堤；水闸；坝：There are several ～s across the Nile. 尼罗河上有好几个水坝。

damage / ˈdæmɪdʒ / Ⅰ *v*. 损害；毁坏：The crops were badly ～d this year. 今年庄稼遭损严重。同 harm, spoil Ⅱ *n*. ❶[U]损害；伤害：The snowstorm caused (did) heavy ～ to the crops. 那场暴风雪使农作物受损严重。同 destruction, harm ❷(*pl*.) 赔偿金：He claimed 50,000 dollar ～s from the company. 他向那家公司索要 5 万美元赔偿费。

damn / dæm / *vt*. 诅咒：Damn you! (God ～ you!)真该死! / Damn it (all)! (口)见鬼! 真糟糕! 同 abuse, curse

damp / dæmp / Ⅰ *adj*. 潮湿的；有潮的：If you put on ～ clothes, you'll probably catch a cold. 要是穿湿衣服,你会着凉的。同 wet, humid Ⅱ *n*. [U] 湿气；潮湿：There is too much ～ here. 这儿太潮湿。

dance / dɑːns / Ⅰ *vi*. 跳舞：The girl ～d with joy after she won the praise. 受到称赞,小女孩高兴得手舞足蹈。/ He ～s here every night. 他每晚都在这儿跳舞。Ⅱ *n*. 舞蹈；舞会：I like classical (modern, popular) ～. 我喜欢古典 (现代,流行)舞。/ We'll hold a ～ next Saturday. 下周六我们将举行舞会。同 ball, party

danger / ˈdeɪndʒə(r) / *n*. [U]危险；威胁：Smoking too much causes ～ to health. 吸烟过多威胁身体健康。同 risk, hazard 反 safety / **in ～** 在危险中：The wounded soldier is in ～. 那位伤员有生命危险。**out of ～** 脱险：The doctor said that his father was out of ～. 医生说他的父亲已脱离危险。

用法

danger 后面常接介词 of,不接动词不定式：(正)There is danger of his being late. (误) There is danger for him to be late.

dangerous / ˈdeɪndʒərəs / *adj*. 危险的；不安全的：It's very ～ to do such a thing. 做这样的事很危险。同 risky 反 safe, secure 派 dangerously *adv*.

用法

dangerous 意为"危险的;使人有危险的",表示某人做某事有危险,习惯上用：It is dangerous for him to do such a thing. 或 He is in danger to do such a thing. 不说 He is dangerous to do such a thing.

dangle / ˈdæŋgl / *v*. (使)悬垂,(使)悬挂;悬荡：a bunch of keys dangling at the end of a chain悬挂在链端的一串钥匙/The children sat on the bridge dangling their feet in the water. 孩子们坐在桥上,把脚悬垂在河水中。

dare / deə(r) / Ⅰ *v. aux*. 敢,竟敢 Ⅱ *v*. 敢,敢于：～ hardships and danger 敢于面对艰难/He ～d to tell the truth. 他敢于说出真相。同 venture

用法

❶dare 无论作及物动词还是不及物动词都可用于陈述句、否定句或疑问句中：He dares to go. 他敢去。He did not dare to go. 他不敢去。Will he dare to go? 他敢去吗? ❷ dare 作情态助动词只有 dare 和 dared 两种形式,而且通常用在否定句、疑问句或条件句中：Dare he swim across? 他敢游过去吗? She dared not come in. 她不敢进来。❸how dare you (she, he...)含"胆大妄为"的意思：How dare you say such things to her! 你怎敢对她说这样的话!

daring / ˈdeərɪŋ / *adj.* 大胆的；勇敢的：Be more ～! 勇敢些! 同 brave, bold 反 timid, cowardly

dark / dɑːk / Ⅰ *adj.* ❶黑暗的；暗的：It was nearly ～ when we came home. 我们到家时，天已快黑了。同 dim, gloomy ❷黑色的；深色的：She coloured the leaves ～ green. 她把树叶涂成深绿色。同 black 反 bright Ⅱ *n.* 黑夜；黑暗；暗处：She couldn't see anything clearly in the ～. 黑暗中她什么东西也看不清。同 night, darkness 派 darkness *n.*

darling / ˈdɑːlɪŋ / *n.* [C]亲爱的人；宠儿：My ～! 亲爱的!/ Mary is her father's ～. 玛丽是她父亲的心肝宝贝。同 love, lover, sweetheart

dart / dɑːt / *n.* [C] 标枪；飞镖；掷镖游戏：The boys are playing ～s. 男孩们在玩掷镖游戏。

Darwinism / ˈdɑːwɪnɪzm / *n.* [U] 达尔文学说；进化论

dash / dæʃ / Ⅰ *v.* 冲；短跑；奔跑；突进：The horse ～ed away. 那匹马飞快地跑开了。同 rush Ⅱ *n.* [C] 急奔；猛冲；短跑：The cavalry rode off at a ～. 骑兵队急驰而去。同 rush

data / ˈdeɪtə / *n.* （datum 的复数）❶资料；材料：We collected a lot of ～ for our research. 我们为研究工作收集了很多资料。/ Can you get the first-hand ～ for us? 你能为我们找到一些第一手资料吗? 同 information, statistics ❷数据：～ analysis 数据分析/a ～ band (base) 数据库/Please give us some raw ～. 请给我们一些原始数据。同 figures, statistics

database / ˈdeɪtəbeɪs / *n.* [C] 资料库；(计算机)数据库：Very soon he set up a ～ for his own. 他很快建立起了自己的数据库。同 databank

date[1] / deɪt / *n.* [C] 枣

date[2] / deɪt / Ⅰ *n.* [C] ❶日期：What is the ～ today? 今天几月几日? / Your application is out of ～. 你的申请已经过时。同 time, day ❷约会：She called off the ～ with her classmate because of her illness. 因为生病，她取消了与同学的约会。同 appointment Ⅱ *v.* ❶注明日期；记日期：That would ～ back to ten years ago. 那事应当追溯到 10 年以前。/ The E-mail is ～d October 12. 那封电子邮件的日期是 10 月 12 日。❷(与 …)约会；交往：The two have been dating each other for about half

a year. 两人彼此交往已经有半年左右。/ **out of** ～ 过时的；不时髦的：The fashion is getting out of ～. 这式样逐渐过时。**up to** ～ 现代的；最新式的；时兴的：You must have up-to-～ ideas. 你的思想必须跟上时代。

用法
❶date 前的介词可以用 at, on：at an early date；on that date。❷"What's the date today?"的答语只能是具体日子，而不是星期几：What's the date today? It's January 2nd. 今天几月几日? 今天是 1 月 2 日。关于星期的问答，应为：What day is it today? It's Monday. 今天星期几? 星期一。❸英美记载日期的顺序不同，如 1998 年 10 月 20 日用数字表示，美国表示为 10/20/1998，英国则表示为 20/10/1998。

datum / ˈdeɪtəm / *n.* (*pl.* data) 资料；数据；情报

daughter / ˈdɔːtə(r) / *n.* [C]女儿：He brought up his ～s in great strictness. 他管教女儿们很严格。/ She is the only ～ of the family. 她是家里的独生女。

dawn / dɔːn / *n.* 黎明；曙光；拂晓：Dawn shows a new day. 黎明预示着新的一天开始了。同 daybreak, daylight / **at** ～黎明时：They get up at ～. 他们黎明时分起床。**from** ～ **till dusk** 从早到晚：They worked very hard from ～ till dusk. 他们从早到晚拼命工作。

day / deɪ / *n.* ❶[C]一天，一日：What ～ is today? Today is Monday. 今天星期几? 今天星期一。/ There are seven ～s in a week. 一个星期有七天。/ She goes to have dinner with her grandmother every other ～. 她每隔一天去陪她的祖母吃晚饭。同 date ❷白昼，白天：Most animals look for food in the ～. 大多数动物在白天觅食。同 daytime, daylight 反 night, night-time ❸(*pl.*) 日子；时代：Today's children know little about the old ～s. 现在的孩子很少了解旧社会。/ I was very happy in my school ～s. 在学生时代我非常快乐。同 times ❹节日：Children's Day 儿童节/ Christmas Day 圣诞节/ May Day 五一国际劳动节/ National Day 国庆节/ New Year's Day 元旦/ Teachers' Day 教师节/ Tree-Planting Day 植树节/ World Environment Day 世界环境日/ **all** ～ 全天：He worked all (the) ～ (long). 他全天工作。**and night** (**night and** ～)日日夜夜：He often

works ～ and night. 他时常不分昼夜地工作。
all ～ and all night 整日整夜 ～ **after** ～ 每
天;一天又一天

用法

❶今天、昨天、明天、前天、后天对应的英语
说法分别是:today (this day), yesterday, tomorrow, the day before yesterday, the day
after tomorrow. ❷one day 可指过去或将来
的某一天:I met her in the street one day. 有
一天我在街上见过她。I may meet her again
one day. 我总有一天会再见到她。

daylight / 'deɪlaɪt / n. [U]白昼;日光;黎明:
They started before ～. 他们黎明前出发。同
sunlight, daytime

daze / deɪz / Ⅰ vt. ❶使发昏,使呆住;使茫然:
A blow on the head ～d him. 当头一击把他打
晕了过去。❷使目眩,使眼花缭乱: The splendour of the palace ～d her. 这座富丽堂皇的宫
殿使她眼花缭乱,目不暇接。Ⅱ n. [C]晕眩;恍
惚;茫然

dazzle / 'dæzl / Ⅰ vt. ❶使目眩,使眼花,刺
(目),耀(眼): The sun shone clear, and the
reflection ～d our eyes. 那时烈日当空,反光使
我们睁不开眼。❷使晕眩,使惊奇;使倾倒: He
was ～d by the success of his first book. 他的
处女作的成功冲昏了他的头脑。/She was ～
d by his wit. 她为他的聪慧才智倾倒。Ⅱ n.
[U]❶耀眼的光,灿烂的光辉;令人赞叹的东
西: the ～ of powerful electric lights 大功率电
灯耀眼的光 ❷昏眩,迷乱: the ～ of fame 被
名誉迷惑 派 dazzling adj.

dead / ded / adj. 死的;无生命的: The cat has
been ～ for 3 days. 那只猫已死三天了。/
This street is ～ at night. 这条街晚上寂静无
声。同 lifeless 反 alive, living

deadline / 'dedlaɪn / n. [C]最后期限;极限:I
must finish the article within two days to meet
the ～. 我必须在两天内写完这篇文章以赶上
截止日期。

deadlock / 'dedlɒk / n. 僵持;僵局: The match
was at a ～. 比赛处于僵持之中。/ In order to
break the ～, he began to speak slowly. 为了
打破僵局,他开始发言。同 standstill

deadly / 'dedli / adj. 致命的: Fog is the
sailor's deadly enemy. 雾是航海者致命的敌
人。同 fatal

deaf / def / adj. 聋的;不愿听的: He is ～ in

(of) one ear. 他一只耳朵聋了。/ He was ～
to any advice. 他听不进任何劝告。同 earless,
stubborn 派 deafen v.

用法

如果表示"聋哑的",应该说:deaf-and-dumb;
表示"聋哑人",则应该说:deaf mute; stone
deaf 表示"完全聋的"。

deal / diːl / Ⅰ v. (dealt/delt/, dealt) ❶处理,
应付(与 with 连用): She can ～ properly with
all kinds of complicated situations. 她能恰当地
应付各种复杂的局面。同 treat, handle ❷分
发;分配;发牌: The apples must be dealt out
fairly. 这些苹果必须公平分配。同 give, deliver ❸做买卖: We've dealt with that firm for
many years. 我们和那家公司做买卖多年了。
同 trade, bargain Ⅱ n. ❶大量,许多: She spent
a great ～ of money on clothes. 她把大量的钱
花在买衣服上。同 plenty ❷交易;协议: He
made a ～ with the company. 他和那家公司做
生意。同 bargain, trade

用法

a great (good) deal of 意为"很多的;大量
的",后只跟不可数名词: A great deal of
money was spent on the project. 那项工程耗
费了大量的金钱。

dealer / 'diːlə(r) / n. [C] 商人;贩子: a car
～ 汽车商/a real estate ～ 房地产商/ a special
sales ～ 特约经销商/ In order to save money,
he often buys goods from a wholesale ～. 为了
省钱,他常常从批发商处购买商品。同 trad-
er, merchant, businessman

dealing / 'diːlɪŋ / n. [C]交易;商业往来: a ～
in stock and shares 股票交易/ a fair ～ 公平
交易/ black-market ～s 黑市交易/ business
(commercial) ～s 商业来往 同 trade, business

dean / diːn / n. [C](大学的)学院院长,教务
长,系主任: His father is ～ of a university. 他
父亲是一所大学的教务长。

dear / dɪə(r) / Ⅰ adj. ❶亲爱的;可爱的: My
～ daughter is waiting for me at the gate. 我亲
爱的女儿正在门口等我。❷beloved ❷昂
贵的: This coat seems rather ～. 这件上衣看起
来相当昂贵。同 costly, expensive 反 cheap Ⅱ
int. 哎呀(表示焦急、伤心或惊奇) Ⅲ adv. 昂
贵地;高价地: He sells his goods very ～. 他的
货物卖得很贵。反 cheaply

辨析

dear 意为"高价的",指商品的价格过高：This book is too dear. 这本书太贵了。**expensive** 意为"昂贵的；奢华的",指价格超过物品所值，或指价格高过购买者的财力：This coat is very beautiful, but it is too expensive for me. 这件外衣很漂亮，但对我来说太贵了。**costly** 意为"值钱的；昂贵的",指由于稀罕、精致而十分昂贵：He bought a costly diamond necklace. 他买了一条非常值钱的钻石项链。

death / deθ / n. 死；死亡：Death comes to all men. 人皆有死。/ The criminal was shot to ～. 罪犯被击毙。反 birth, life, existence

deathblow / 'deθbləʊ / n. [C] ❶ 致命一击：The soldier received a ～ early in the battle. 战斗打响不久，那个战士便遭到致命的一击。❷（尤指突发的）导致事物失败的因素：The sudden withdrawal of grant money was the ～ to the project. 资助款的突然撤销使这项计划化作泡影。

debit / 'debɪt / Ⅰ n. [C] ❶ 借方；借记；借入 ❷ 借项；借项总金额 Ⅱ vt. 把…记入账户的借方；记入（账户）的借方；记入（某人）账户的借方

debate / dɪ'beɪt / Ⅰ v. 争论，辩论；讨论：The subject was hotly ～d. 这个问题曾被激烈地辩论过。同 discuss, argue Ⅱ n. 争论；辩论；讨论：After a heated ～, they came to an agreement. 经过激烈辩论，他们达成了一致意见。同 discussion, argument

debt / det / n. [C] 债务；欠款：He spent little money until his ～s were paid off. 在债还完之前他很少花钱。/ in ～ 欠债：He is over head and ears in ～. 他债台高筑。out of ～ 不欠债：Out of ～, out of danger. 无债一身轻。have（get into, run into, fall into）～ 借债，负债：It's easier to get into ～ than get out of it. 借债容易还债难。pay（back）the ～ 偿还债务：He was unable to pay his ～s. 他无力还债。

decade / 'dekeɪd / n. [C] 十年：Our school was founded there ～s ago. 我们学校是三十年前建立的。

decay / dɪ'keɪ / v. 腐烂；腐朽；衰退：Too much sweet ～s children's teeth. 吃过多甜食会使小孩牙齿腐坏。/ The wooden door of his room began to ～. 他房间的木门开始腐烂了。同 decline, rot, corrupt 反 flourish 派 decayed adj.

deceive / dɪ'siːv / vt. 欺骗；使弄错：He has entirely ～d us. 他完全欺骗了我们。同 cheat, fool, mislead / ～ **sb. into doing sth.** 骗某人做某事：We were ～d into buying that house. 我们受骗买下了那幢房子。

decelerate / diː'seləreɪt / vt. 降低…的速度，使减速，使减缓：efforts to ～ inflation 降低通货膨胀的种种努力/He ～ the truck. 他使卡车减速。

December / dɪ'sembə（r）/ n. 十二月（略作 Dec.）

decent / 'diːsnt / adj. 体面的；正派的；得体的；合乎礼仪的：She is always in ～ clothes. 她总是穿着得体。同 proper, suitable

decibel / 'desɪbel / n. [C] 分贝（表示声音强度和功率比的单位，略作 dB, db）：Most people speak in a range between 45 and 75 ～. 大多数人讲话时的声音强度是在 45 至 75 分贝之间。

decide / dɪ'saɪd / v. 下决心；决定：She ～d to go. 她决定去。/ I ～ on having my holiday next month. 我决定下月休假。同 determine 派 decided adj.

decimal / 'desɪməl / adj. 小数的；十进制的；以十为基础的：～ fraction 小数/ a ～ point 小数点/ a ～ system 十进制

decision / dɪ'sɪʒən / n. 决定；决议；决心：They passed the ～ at the meeting. 他们在会上通过了那项决议。同 determination / **make（came to, arrive at）a** ～ 作出决定：I made（came to）a ～ to accept the job after the debate. 经过争论，我决定接受这项工作。/ We'd better arrive at a ～ at once. 我们最好马上作出决定。

decisive / dɪ'saɪsɪv / adj. ❶ 决定性的：a ～ factor 决定性因素/ a ～ battle 决定性的战役 同 determining ❷ 果断的；明确的：Please give us a ～ reply as soon as possible. 请尽快给我们一个明确的答复。同 definitive, resolute 派 decisively adv.

deck / dek / n. [C] 甲板

declaration / ˌdeklə'reɪʃn / n. ❶ 宣告，宣布；宣言 ❷（关税的）申报

declare / dɪ'kleə（r）/ v. ❶ 声称，声明；宣布；公布：He ～d that it was true. 他宣布这是真

的。/ The war was ～d over. 战争宣告结束。
同 proclaim, announce ❷（向税务机关、海关
等）申报：Do you have anything to ～? 你有什
么要报税的吗?

decline / dɪˈklaɪn / v. ❶拒绝；谢绝：He ～d
the invitation. 他辞谢了邀请。/ I invited her
to dine, but she ～d. 我请她吃饭, 可她婉言谢
绝了。同 refuse, deny 反 accept ❷倾斜；衰落；
下跌：The sun ～d toward the west. 太阳已西
斜。/ His mother's health is declining. 他母亲
的健康状况越来越差。/ The prices of daily
necessities are declining. 日常用品的价格在下
降。同 sink, decrease

decompose / ˌdiːkəmˈpəʊz / v. ❶（使）分解；
（使）分离：～ a chemical compound 分解化合
物 ❷（使）腐烂；（使）腐败：The old fruits and
vegetables ～ quickly in the heat. 在热天, 不
新鲜的水果和蔬菜烂得快。

decorate / ˈdekəreɪt / vt. 装饰, 装潢；布置：The
hall is ～d with colorful balloons. 礼堂装饰有
五颜六色的气球。/ It cost him about 8,000
yuan to ～ his room. 他花了 8000 元装修
房间。

decoration / ˌdekəˈreɪʃn / n. ❶装饰, 装潢 ❷
[C]（常用 pl.）装饰物, 装饰品

decrease I / dɪˈkriːs / v. 减少, 减小：His interest in this subject gradually ～s. 他对这门学
科的兴趣逐渐减弱。/ The number of traffic
accidents has ～d greatly in this district. 这个
地区的交通事故次数已极大减少。同 drop,
reduce 反 grow, increase II / ˈdiːkriːs / n. 减
少；降低：A big ～ in sales caused the store to
close. 销售量大减使这家商店倒闭。同 reduc-
tion 反 growth, increase

decree / dɪˈkriː / n. [C] ❶法令, 政令；敕令：is-
sue a ～ 颁布法令 / ignore a ～ 无视法令 ❷判
决；裁定：a divorce ～ 离婚判决

dedicate / ˈdedɪkeɪt / vt. 奉献；献身：～ oneself
to 献身于；致力于：They ～d themselves to the
cause of scientific research. 他们献身于科研事
业。同 give, devote

deduce / dɪˈdjuːs / vt. 演绎, 推断, 推论：～ a
conclusion from premises 从前提断出结论/
From the height of the sun, I ～ that it was a-
bout ten o'clock. 我从太阳的高度推测出时间
大约是 10 点钟。

deduct / dɪˈdʌkt / vt. 减去, 扣除：The teacher
～ed fifteen marks for his misspelling. 因拼法

错误, 老师扣了他 15 分。/ Income tax is normally ～ed from a person's wages. 一般来说,
所得税是从个人的工资收入中扣除。

deed / diːd / n. [C]行为；事迹：Their ～s did
not agree with their words. 他们言行不一致。
/ He did good ～s for passengers on the train.
他在火车上为乘客做好事。同 action,
achievement / in ～ 事实上；真正地：A friend
in need is a friend in ～. 患难之交是真交。

deep / diːp / adj. ❶深的；深厚的：The well is
ten feet ～. 这口井 10 英尺深。反 shallow ❷
深情的；深切的：The teacher showed ～ concern for her pupils. 这位老师深切地关心自己
的学生。同 intense / be ～ in 专心于；全神贯
注于：He is ～ in reading. 他正在专心读书。
派 deepen v.；deeply adv.

deer / dɪə(r) / n. [C]（pl. deer）鹿

defame / dɪˈfeɪm / vt. 破坏…的声誉；说…的
坏话；诋毁, 诽谤, 中伤：She accused him of de-
faming her good name. 她控告他诽谤她的好
名声。

default / dɪˈfɔːlt / I n. [U] ❶（职责、义务等
的）未履行：He lost his job by sheer ～ of duty. 他完全由于疏于职守而丢了工作。❷弃
权：He progressed into the finals because of his
opponent's ～. 由于对手的弃权, 他进入了决
赛。❸（计算机）系统设定（值）, 系统预置；默
认设定：～ program 系统设定程序 II vi. ❶不
履行义务；不履行债务, 拖欠：～ on one's
commitments 违背承诺 ❷弃权, 放弃比赛：She
～ed in the tennis tournament. 她在网球锦标
赛中弃权。

defeat / dɪˈfiːt / I vt. 击败；使受挫折：Our
school team ～ed the team of the Second Middle School at football. 我校足球队在比赛中打
败了二中的球队。同 beat, conquer 反 win II
n. 失败；击败：He is a man who knows no ～.
他是个不服输的人。同 conquest 反 victory

defect / dɪˈfekt / n. [C]缺点；缺陷：The little
girl has an inborn ～ in eyesight. 小女孩先天
视力不足。同 fault, weakness 派
defective adj.

defence(-se) / dɪˈfens / n. [U]保卫；防御：
The soldiers built up a strong ～. 战士们筑起
了坚固的防御工事。同 protection, safeguard

defend / dɪˈfend / vt. 保卫；防守：The country
is ～ed with a strong navy. 这个国家有强大

的海军保卫。同 protect, safeguard/～ **from**
保护,保卫,使不受…伤害:The bank was built
to ～ the road from being washed away by the
floods. 建造这座堤是为了保护这条路不被洪
水冲垮。

辨析

defend 意为"防卫;防护;保卫",常指用武力
或其他防御措施抵挡当前受到的攻击,是一
时的举动:The soldiers defended their country with bravery. 这些士兵勇敢地保卫他们
的国家。**protect** 意为"保卫;保护",指设置
保护物以防可能发生的危险:This coat will
protect you from the cold. 这件外衣将使你
不受冻。**guard** 意为"防守",指不让危险发
生,有"小心预防"的意思:The city was
guarded by about 1,000 people. 这座城由
1000 人守卫着。

defendant / dɪ'fendənt / n. [C]被告:The ～
prevailed in the case. 被告在本案中胜诉。

defensive / dɪ'fensɪv / Ⅰ adj. ❶防御(性)的;
保卫(性)的:～ warfare 防御战/～ armament
weapons 防御性武器/a ～ position 防御阵地
❷防守的;(人的态度等)防备的,自卫的:a ～
attitude 守势/The expression on his face was
resentful and ～. 他的神色含着怨恨,如临大
敌似的。

defer / dɪ'fɜː(r) / vt. (-ferred;-ferring) 使推
迟,使延期;拖延:As no one could agree,the
decision was ～red. 由于大家都不同意,决定
迟迟未能作出。

defiance / dɪ'faɪəns / n. [U] ❶(公然的)蔑视,
藐视;反抗,违抗:a ～ of regulations 违反规
章制度/He shouted ～ at the policeman. 他向
警察大叫大嚷表示反抗。❷挑战,挑衅:an ac-
tion of ～ against nature 向大自然挑战的行
动/ **in ～ of** 违抗;不顾,无视:He acted in ～
of public opinion. 他不顾公众舆论,仍旧我行
我素。

deficiency / dɪ'fɪʃ(ə)nsi / n. ❶[U;C]缺少,
短缺,匮乏,不足:deficiencies in personnel and
equipment 人员和设备的匮乏/ She was vitamin ～. 她身体里缺乏维生素。❷[C]缺点;缺
陷;毛病:His deficiencies for the job are only
too clear. 对这项工作来说,他的不足之处是
显而易见的。

deficient / dɪ'fɪʃ(ə)nt / adj. ❶缺少的;缺乏
的,匮乏的,不足的:a ～ supply of nutrients
营养供应不足 ❷有缺陷的,有缺点的:a men-

tally ～ person 心理(或智力)上有缺陷的人/
Our knowledge of the subject is ～. 我们对该
课题的了解是不全面的。

deficit / 'defɪsɪt,dɪ'fɪsɪt / n. ❶[C]不足额;短
缺额:a ～ of £ 250 250 英镑的缺额/trade
～s 贸易逆差 ❷[C;U]赤字;逆差;亏空;亏
损:The country has a ～ on its balance of payments. 这国收支上出现了赤字。

define / dɪ'faɪn / vt. ❶给…下定义,释(义)
解释:The dictionary not only ～s words but
also shows the user how to use them. 这部词
典不但解释词义,而且告诉使用者如何使用词
汇。❷详解,详述;使明确,使清楚:～ one's
position on a subject 表明自己在某个问题上
的立场/Please listen while I ～ your duties.
请听我详细说明你的任务。

definite / 'defɪnət / adj. 明确的;肯定的;限定
的:His attitude was not very ～ at that time.
那时他的态度还不很明确。/ Please give me a
～ answer soon. 请尽快给我一个肯定的答
复。同 exact,positive 派 definitely adv.

definition / ,defɪ'nɪʃn / n. 定义;解释:He
looked up the ～ of the difficult word in a dictionary. 他在字典里查那个难词的定义。同
meaning,explanation

deformity / dɪ'fɔːməti / n. [U]畸形;变形

defrost / dɪ'frɒst / v. 除霜;解冻:～ a refrigerator 给冰箱除霜/ Mother ～ed some meat for
dinner. 妈妈把肉解冻了做晚饭。

deft / deft / adj. 娴熟的;灵巧的;巧妙的:the
～ fingers of pianist 钢琴家灵巧的手指/a ～
performance 技艺娴熟的表演

defy / dɪ'faɪ / vt. ❶(公然)违抗,反抗,蔑视
藐视:～ public opinion 藐视公众舆论/I felt
Jimmy was waiting for an opportunity to ～
me. 我觉得吉米在等待时机跟我作对。❷激
挑:Defy you to prove that I cheated in the examination. 我倒看看你能不能证明我考试
作过弊。❸经受得起;顶得住:The problem
defies all attempts to solve it. 这个难题怎么也
解决不了。

degrade / dɪ'ɡreɪd / vt. ❶降级,罢免,黜,谪
贬:be ～d from public office 被解除公职 ❷使
受侮辱,使丢脸;降低(身份等):films that ～
women 糟践妇女的影片 ❸〈化〉使降解

degree / dɪ'ɡriː / n. ❶[U]程度:The two problems differ from each other in ～ and nature.

D

这两个问题在程度和性质上都不尽相同。同 extend, class, rank, status ❷[C]度，度数：The highest temperature here is only 28 〜s Centigrade (28℃) in summer. 这里夏天的最高温度只有 28 摄氏度。/ He drew an angle of 30 〜s. 他画了一个 30 度的角。❸[C]学位；学衔：a bachelor's 〜 学士学位/ a doctor's 〜 博士学位/ He received a master's 〜 in London in 2006. 2006 年他在伦敦获得硕士学位。

delay / dɪ'leɪ / Ⅰ v. 推迟；延误：I 〜ed answering you owing to pressure of work. 我因工作忙没有及时答复你。/ The train was 〜ed by a heavy snow. 火车因大雪误点了。/ We will 〜 the meeting for a week. 我们将把会议推迟一个星期。同 postpone Ⅱ n. 耽搁；延误：After a 〜 of one hour, we continued our journey. 耽搁一个小时之后，我们又继续旅行了。同 interval

delegate / 'delɪgeɪt / n. 代表；委员；特派员：a 〜 to a conference 会议代表/ an official 〜 正式(官方)代表/ a chief 〜 首席代表/ a 〜 without power to vote 列席代表/ They appointed a 〜 to the congress. 他们派了一名代表参加大会。同 representative, deputy

delegation / ˌdelɪ'geɪʃn / n. 代表团：They sent a 〜 to the United Nations. 他们向联合国派出自己的代表团。同 mission, commission

delete / dɪ'liːt / vt. 删掉；擦掉：He saw that the teacher 〜d his name from the list. 他看到老师从名单上删掉了他的名字。同 cancel, erase 反 add

deliberate / dɪ'lɪbərət / Ⅰ adj. ❶故意的，存心的，蓄意的：a 〜 attempt to injure sb. 对某人的故意伤害/He wondered if her silence was 〜. 他疑惑她是否故意缄默不语。❷从容的，慢条斯理的，悠闲的：Jane has a slow, 〜 way of talking. 简讲起话来总是慢条斯理，不慌不忙。Ⅱ v. 仔细考虑，斟酌：He is slow to answer, deliberating over each question. 他总是仔细考虑每一个问题，从不轻易作答。派 deliberately adv.

delicacy / 'delɪkəsi / n. ❶[U]精致，精美；优雅，雅致：the 〜 of lace 花边的精美 ❷[U]柔软；细嫩；清秀；娇美：the 〜 of her features 她身材的绰约多姿 ❸[C]美味，佳肴：the delicacies of the season 应时的珍馐美味 ❹[U]纤弱，娇弱：the 〜 of her health 她身体的纤弱

delicate / 'delɪkət / adj. ❶精致的，精美的；优雅的，雅致的：a 〜 pattern on the wallpaper 壁

纸上的精美图案 ❷(光、色等)柔和的；淡(雅)的：a 〜 shade of pink 淡粉红色 ❸(食物)鲜美的，清淡可口的；(气味)清淡的：〜 food 清淡可口的食物/Roses have a 〜 fragrance. 玫瑰散发出一股幽幽的清香。❹脆的，易碎的；易损坏的；娇贵的：〜 procelain 易碎的瓷器/〜 flowers 娇嫩的鲜花 ❺灵敏的，敏锐的；敏感的；精密的：a 〜 sense of hearing 灵敏的听觉/〜 scientific instruments 精密的科学仪器

delicious / dɪ'lɪʃəs / adj. 美味的；可口的：Sichuan food is 〜. 四川菜很好吃。同 tasty

delight / dɪ'laɪt / Ⅰ n. [U]欢喜；高兴：To the boy's 〜, his father bought him a new computer. 令这男孩高兴的是，父亲给他买了一台新的计算机。/ **take 〜 in** 喜爱，以…为乐：He takes much 〜 in his studies. 他从学习中得到极大乐趣。同 joy, pleasure 反 displeasure Ⅱ v. 使高兴；感到高兴：He was 〜ed at (by) the news. 听到这个消息他很高兴。/ I 〜ed in doing good. 我以做好事为乐。同 amuse, please 反 displease 派 delightful adj.

辨析

delight 意为"欢喜；高兴"，指一种强烈的愉悦感，也指一种短暂的喜悦情绪：To his delight, his novel was accepted for publication. 使他高兴的是，他的小说被接受出版了。pleasure 意为"愉快；满足"，常用词，语气较弱，表示没有不愉快的感觉：It's a pleasure to work with you. 和你一起工作是件令人高兴的事。joy 意为"欢乐；高兴"，语气比 pleasure 强：He was filled with joy when he heard the good news. 听到这个好消息，他心里非常高兴。

deliver / dɪ'lɪvə(r) / vt. ❶递送；移交；表达，讲述：The thief was 〜ed into the police. 小偷被交给了警察。同 hand, transmit ❷表达；讲述：She 〜ed herself well. 她表达能力不错。/He 〜ed an address at the opening ceremony. 他在开幕式上致辞。同 proclaim, utter ❸分娩；接生：The young mother 〜ed a boy. 这位年轻妈妈生了一个男孩。同 produce 派 delivery n.

delta / 'deltə / n. [C](河流的)三角洲：the Yangtze (＝Changjiang) Delta 长江三角洲

demand / dɪ'mɑːnd / Ⅰ v. 要求；需要：He 〜ed that he should be told everything. 他要求将一切都告诉他。/ Her aunt told her that the work 〜ed care and patience. 婶婶告诉她做

那项工作需要细心和耐心。同 need, require

Ⅱ n. 要求；需求：The supply of food does not meet the ～ in that district. 在那个地区食品供不应求。同 need, claim

辨析

demand 意为"要求；需要"，指坚持要得到某物或坚持要做某事：The prisoner demanded a new trial. 那囚犯要求重新审判。**require** 意为"需要；要求"，普通用语，含有"必要、不可缺"之意：He required a couple of days of rest. 他需要休息几天。**need** 意为"需要"，不如 require 正式：Plants need sun. 植物需要阳光。**want** 意为"想要；缺少"，指对个人所缺少的东西表达直接的欲望：We can supply all you want. 我们能提供你所需要的一切。

demanding / dɪˈmɑːndɪŋ / adj. 要求高的；苛求的；需要技能的；需要花气力的，费劲的：a ～ but worthwhile job 费力但值得一干的工作/The school is a ～ one. 那个学校是个要求很严格的学校。

democracy / dɪˈmɒkrəsi / n. [U] ❶民主：the sense of ～ 民主意识/ socialist ～ 社会主义民主 反 autocracy ❷民主国家；民主制：They are determined to establish a ～ for their own. 他们决心建立一个自己的民主国家。

democratic / ˌdeməˈkrætɪk / adj. 民主的；民主政体的：～ election 民主选举 / ～ consultation 民主协商 / ～ parties 民主党派 反 autocratic

democratize / dɪˈmɒkrətaɪz / v. (使)民主化

demolish / dɪˈmɒlɪʃ / vt. ❶拆除(建筑物等)；摧毁；爆破：The fire ～ed the area. 那场大火把这地区烧成一片废墟。❷终止，撤销(机构等)；废除(制度等)：～ a commission 撤销委员会/～ a feudal agrarian system 废除封建土地所有制 ❸推翻；驳倒(论点、理论等)：～ a theory 推翻一种理论

demonstrate / ˈdemənstreɪt / v. ❶表明；证明：He cited a lot of examples to ～ the truth of his theory. 他引用了大量事例证明他的理论是正确的。同 prove, explain ❷示范；演示：The salesman ～d the new washing-machine to the customer. 销售人员向顾客演示新型洗衣机如何使用。同 show, display ❸示威：The citizens ～d against the rising of taxes. 市民们示威游行反对提高税收。同 parade 派 demonstration n.

den / den / n. [C] ❶兽穴(或窝)；洞穴：The bear's ～ was in a cave. 那头熊的窝做在洞中。❷私室，密室；书斋

denial / dɪˈnaɪəl / n. ❶[U;C]否认；反对：give a ～ to the rumour 辟谣/The colonel issued a ～ of any wrongdoing. 那位上校发表声明否认他干过任何坏事。❷[U]拒绝(给予)；回绝：His ～ of petition caused the students to rebel. 他不准学生们请假，这激起了他们的反抗。

denote / dɪˈnəʊt / vt. ❶预示，是…的征兆；标志着：A smile often ～s pleasure. 微笑常常表示愉悦。/Frost ～s the coming of winter. 霜冻现象预示冬季的来临。❷本义为，意思是：The word "stool" ～s s small chair without a back. "凳子"一词的本义是没有靠背的小椅子。❸(符号)等代表，表示，是…的标记；是…的名称：In algebra, the sing "X" usually ～s an unknown quantity. 在代数里，符号 X 常常表示未知数。

denounce / dɪˈnaʊns / vt. (公开)谴责，斥责，指责：Smith ～s drug abuse roundly in his speeches. 史密斯在发言中痛斥滥用毒品的行为。/The new government ～d the old treaty as a mere scrap of paper. 新政府谴责旧条约不过是一纸空文而已。

dense / dens / adj. 稠密的；密集的：The crowd was so ～ that we could hardly move. 人群密集，我们几乎不能动弹。同 thick, crowded 反 thin

density / ˈdensəti / n. [U] 密集；浓密；密度：The population ～ of this area is great. 这个地区的人口密度很大。

dentist / ˈdentɪst / n. [C] 牙科医生；She went to see a ～ last Friday. 上周五她去看牙病。

deny / dɪˈnaɪ / vt. 否认；拒绝：The man denied knowing the truth. 那人不承认他知道事实的真相。/ She failed in the examination and denied herself to all visitors. 她考试失败，谢绝会见所有来客。反 admit, allow

用法

deny 后跟名词、动名词或从句，不跟不定式：He denied all charges. 他否认所有指控。She denied having said so. (= She denied that she had said so.)她否认说过这样的话。

depart / dɪˈpɑːt / vt. 离开；出发：The train ～s at 6:30 am. 这列火车早上 6:30 开出。/ They ～ed in tears. 他们挥泪而别。同 go, leave 反 stay, arrive

D

department / dɪ'pɑːtmənt / n. [C] 部；司；局；处；科；系：the Education Department 教育部/ the Health Department 卫生部/the Department of the Treasury 财政部/the Department of Foreign Languages 外语系/a ～ store 百货公司/ the Emergency Department 急诊部

departure / dɪ'pɑːtʃə(r) /n. 离开；出发；起程：It suddenly rained at his ～. 他出发时突然下起雨来。同 going, leaving 反 arrival, return

depend / dɪ'pend / vi. 依靠；依赖；信任(多与 on 连用)：A man's success ～s chiefly on himself. 一个人的成功主要靠自己。/ All ～s on the weather. 一切取决于天气。同 rely, rest

dependant / dɪ'pendənt / n. [C] ❶靠别人生活的人 ❷从属；侍从：army ～s 军属/ family ～s 家眷 同 subordinate, servant

dependence / dɪ'pendəns / n. [U]依靠；依赖；信任：Young people should reduce economic ～ on their parents gradually. 年轻人应当逐渐减少对父母的经济依赖。同 reliance, trust

dependent / dɪ'pendənt / Ⅰ adj. 依靠的；依赖的：Most college students are ～ on their parents in our country. 在我国多数大学生依靠父母生活。同 liable 反 independent Ⅱ n. [C]受赡养者；从属

deploy / dɪ'plɔɪ / vt. ❶部署，调遣：～ a battery of new missiles 部署一批新式导弹 ❷利用；调动；施展：～ one's resources as efficiently as possible 尽可能有效地利用自己的聪明才智/～ one's argument 施展自己辩才

deposit / dɪ'pɒzɪt / Ⅰ vt. ❶沉淀；沉积：The flood ～ed a layer of mud on the ground. 洪水过后地面沉积了一层泥土。❷存放；寄存：He ～ed his suitcase with me. 他把他的手提箱寄放在我处。/ People ～ their money in the bank. 人们把钱存银行里。同 place, store, bank Ⅱ n. ❶沉积物；矿床 ❷存款：draw out one's ～ 提取存款/ make a large ～ 存入巨款/ a current (fixed) ～ 活期存款(定期存款) 同 savings

depress / dɪ'pres / vt. ❶沮丧；消沉：The bad weather ～ed her. 坏天气使她情绪低落。同 upset 反 inspire ❷使不景气：The market is ～ed. 市场萧条。

depressed / dɪ'prest / adj. 压抑的；沮丧的；没精打采的：Don't be ～ about your failure. 别为失败而沮丧。/ She looks ～ because of

headache. 因为头疼她看起来没精打采。同 discouraged, sad 反 joyful, cheerful

depression / dɪ'preʃn / n. [U]沮丧；消沉；萧条：He is in a state of deep ～ on account of his failure to pass the examination. 他因考试不及格深感沮丧。同 sadness, decline

deprive / dɪ'praɪv / vt. 剥夺；使丧失：The accident ～d him of his left arm. 那场意外事故使他失去了左臂。/ His death ～d China of one of its greatest poets. 他的逝世使中国失去了一位最伟大的诗人。同 rob, strip

depth / depθ / n. [U] 深；深度：An ancient tomb was found at a ～ of 50 feet. 古墓是在50英尺深处发现的。/ His thesis shows the ～ of the young scholar. 论文体现了年轻学者渊博的学识。

deputy / 'depjuti / n. [C] ❶代理人；代表：He was the ～ while our manager was on vacation. 我们经理休假时由他代理工作。同 agent, delegate ❷副职：a ～ mayor 副市长 同 vice

derive / dɪ'raɪv / v. 得到；取得；追溯…起源：A lot of English words ～ from Latin. 很多英语词语来源于拉丁语。同 gain, obtain, trace

descend / dɪ'send / vi. 下降；下来；传给：The sun ～ed behind the hills. 太阳落到山后面去了。/ This house ～ed from my grandfather. 这房子是我祖父传下来的。同 drop, decline, pass 反 rise

descendant(-ent) / dɪ'sendənt / n. [C]子孙；后裔：We are all ～s of the Yellow Emperor. 我们都是炎黄子孙。同 successors, children 反 ancestor

describe / dɪ'skraɪb / vt. 叙述；描述；形容：The landscape was vividly ～d in her composition. 她在作文中生动地描写了这一景色。同 define, narrate

description / dɪ'skrɪpʃn / n. 描写；叙述：Can you give me a ～ of your teacher? 你能给我描述一下你们老师的模样吗? 同 narration, account

desert¹ / 'dezət / n. 荒地；沙漠：the Gobi Desert 戈壁滩/ the Desert of Sahara 撒哈拉沙漠 同 wasteland

desert² / dɪ'zɜːt / vt. 抛弃；丢弃：He was ～ed by his friends. 他遭朋友抛弃。/ How can a man ～ his wife and children? 一个男人怎么

能抛妻离子呢? 同 abandon,leave

deserve / dɪˈzɜːv / v. 值得；应受：The place ～s a visit. 那地方值得一游。同 merit,rate

用法

❶deserve 后通常接被动形式的不定式或主动形式的动名词(表被动意义)，偶尔也可接 that 从句(从句用虚拟语气)：He deserves to be punished. 他该受惩罚。The boy deserves warning. 该给这小孩警告。Does he deserve that you should treat him like that? 他值得你那样对他吗? ❷deserve 后接名词时不需加介词 of,但如果用 deserving 则需加 of：He deserves praise. (＝He is deserving of praise.) 他该受表扬。

deserved / dɪˈzɜːvd / adj. 应得的，理所应当的：It was a well-～ victory. 那是一场理所应当的大胜仗。

deserving / dɪˈzɜːvɪŋ / adj. ❶有功的，应赏的：A decoration of bravery was awarded to the ～ police officer. 那名立功的警官被授予一枚英勇勋章。❷值得的，该得的；理所应当的：He is ～ of the highest praise for his conduct. 他应该因其所作为而得到最高表彰。

design / dɪˈzaɪn / Ⅰ n. [C] 图样；设计；计划：I think it necessary to carry out our ～ at once. 我认为有必要马上执行我们的计划。/ These buildings are after his ～s. 这些大楼是照他的设计建造的。同 pattern,plan Ⅱ v. 计划；谋划；设计；预定：This is a book ～ed mainly for use in middle schools. 这是一本中学阶段使用的书。/ The room is ～ed as a children's play-room. 这房间计划用作儿童娱乐室。同 plan,intend,devise 派 designer n.

desirable / dɪˈzaɪərəbl / adj. 合乎需要的；称心的；令人满意的：She wants to find a ～ job in the city. 她想在城里找一份满意的工作。同 advisable

desire / dɪˈzaɪə(r) / Ⅰ v. 向往；渴望；要求：The children ～d to visit the Summer Palace. 孩子们渴望参观颐和园。/ We ～ a room for the night. 我们希望有个房间过夜。同 want,seek,request Ⅱ n. 愿望；心愿：She has a strong ～ to travel the West Europe. 她极想去西欧旅游。同 want,wish

用法

desire 作"要求"讲时后可接 that 从句(从句用虚拟语气)：I desire that he (should) go. 我请求他去。

desk / desk / n. [C] 书桌；办公桌；工作台：an information ～ 问询处/ a reception ～ 服务台；接待处/ He was sitting at the ～ when I went in. 我进去时他正在办公。

desktop / ˈdesktɒp / adj. (尤指微型计算机)适合书桌上用的，台式的：a ～ computer 台式计算机

desolate / ˈdesələt / adj. ❶不毛的；荒芜的；荒凉的；无人烟的：a ～ hillside 光秃秃的山坡/ a ～ industrial landscape 工业凋敝的景象 ❷被遗弃的；孤苦无依的，孤凄的：a ～ life 孤独的一生/When her husband died, she was left ～. 丈夫去世后，她孤苦无依。

despair / dɪˈspeə(r) / Ⅰ n. [U] 失望；绝望：He gave up the attempt in ～. 他绝望地放弃了尝试。Ⅱ vi. 绝望；丧失信心：So long as you help me, I shall never ～. 只要你帮助我，我就不会绝望。同 discourage 反 hope,desire

desperate / ˈdespərət / adj. 令人绝望的；拼死的；不顾一切的：He became ～ after his wife's death. 妻子死后他非常绝望。同 hopeless,wild 反 hopeful

desperation / ˌdespəˈreɪʃn / n. [U] 绝望；冒险；自暴自弃：The death of her son drove her to ～. 失去儿子使她感到绝望。同 despair 反 confidence

despise / dɪˈspaɪz / vt. 瞧不起；轻视；蔑视：Don't cheat at the examination, or you'll be ～d by your classmates. 考试不要作弊，否则你的同学会瞧不起你。反 respect,appreciate

despite / dɪˈspaɪt / prep. 不管；尽管：Despite their objections, I will do it just the same. 虽然他们反对，但我照样会去做。

辨析

despite 后直接跟名词或从句：I shall have a try despite the difficulty. 尽管有困难，我仍将一试。We went despite that they advised us not to. 尽管他们劝我们不去，但我们还是去了。for all, regardless of 和 with all 都用于比较正式的书面语中：For all you say, I still like you. 虽然你说了这些话，但我仍然喜欢你。We won regardless of our injuries. 虽然我们受了伤，但还是赢了。With all her faults the teacher still liked her. 尽管她有许多缺点，但老师仍然喜欢她。in spite of 后接名词、代词，不能直接跟 that 从句，但可用 the fact that：We went in spite of the rain. (＝We went in spite of the fact that it was raining.) 尽管天在下雨，但我们还是去了。

D

despoil / dɪˈspɔɪl / vt. 掠夺，抢劫；剥夺：The bandits ～ed the villages. 土匪们把一座座村庄洗劫一空。/ She fell into evil company and was soon ～ed of her innocence. 她交上了坏朋友，很快她的纯洁天真就无迹可寻了。

dessert / dɪˈzɜːt / n. 甜食，点心；尾餐：I like to have some icecream for ～. 我喜欢吃些冰激凌当作饭后的甜点。同 sweet，cake

destination / ˌdestɪˈneɪʃn / n. [C]目的地；终点：Where is the ～ of your traveling? 你们旅行的目的地是哪儿。同 aim，goal

destiny / ˈdestəni / n. 命运：He believed that he could grasp his own ～. 他相信他能掌握自己的命运。同 fate，fortune

destroy / dɪˈstrɔɪ / vt. 破坏；摧毁；消灭：The house was ～ed in the big fire. 房子在那场大火中给烧毁了。/ His hope to become a lawyer was ～ed. 他要当一名律师的希望破灭了。同 break，ruin，kill

destruction / dɪˈstrʌkʃn / n. [U]破坏；毁灭；消灭：War usually means ～，not construction. 战争通常意味着破坏而不是建设。同 ruin，killing 反 creation，construction

detach / dɪˈtætʃ / vt. 使分开，使分离：～ the key from the ring 从钥匙圈上取下钥匙／ Please ～ the coupon and send it with your money to the following address. 请撕下购物优惠券，连同你的贷款一起寄往下列地址。

detail / ˈdiːteɪl / n. [C]细节；琐碎的事：Every ～ of the plan is important. 这份计划的每个细节都很重要。同 point，element **in** ～ 详细地：Tell me what has happened in a few words，don't go in ～. 扼要地告诉我所发生的事，不要讲得过细。**enter (go) into ～(s)**详细说明；详细描述：It will take up too much space to go into ～s. 详细描述太占篇幅。

detect / dɪˈtekt / vt. ❶察觉，发觉：Two pupils helped the police ～ the robber. 两个小学生帮助警察发现了那个抢匪。同 notice，discover ❷侦察；探测：The machine can ～ the escape of gas. 这台机器可以测出天然气泄漏。同 disclose，expose 派 detection n.

detective / dɪˈtektɪv / n. [C]侦探；密探：a police ～ 警探／ The film star hired a private ～ to protect him. 那位影星雇了一名私人侦探保护自己。同 investigator

detector / dɪˈtektə(r) / n. [C]发觉者；探测器：

Do you believe a lie ～? 你相信测谎仪吗？/ A smoke ～ is helpful. 烟雾探测器很有用。同 indicator，discoverer

determination / dɪˌtɜːmɪˈneɪʃn / n. [U]决定；决心：You must carry out your plan with ～. 你必须坚定不移地实施你的计划。同 decision，resolution

determine / dɪˈtɜːmɪn / v. 断定；决定；决心：Our plans must be ～d by circumstances. 我们的计划必须视情况而定。同 decide，resolve

determined / dɪˈtɜːmɪnd / adj. 坚决的；有决心的：We are ～ to go and nothing will stop us. 我们决心去，什么也阻挡不了我们。同 firm，decided，resolute

detest / dɪˈtest / vt. 憎恶，讨厌：She ～ed having to get up early. 她讨厌早起而又不得不早起。同 hate

develop / dɪˈveləp / v. ❶发展，开发：a ～ed country 发达国家／ a ～ing country 发展中国家／ The situation ～ed rapidly. 形势发展迅速。/ The new product they ～ed is welcome. 他们开发的新产品很受欢迎。同 advance，improve ❷发育；成长：He has ～ed into a strong man. 他成长为一个健壮的人。同 grow ❸显影；冲洗(胶片等)：He went to ～ some films in the darkroom. 他到暗室去冲洗胶卷去了。

development / dɪˈveləpmənt / n. [U]进展；发展：The art received its greatest ～ in that period. 这种艺术在那段时期获得了最大的发展。同 advance，improvement

deviate / ˈdiːvɪeɪt / vi. 偏离；背离(与 from 连用)：～ from the subject under discussion to minor issues 偏离主题而去讨论许多次要问题／ ～ from the course of routine 打破常规

device / dɪˈvaɪs / n. [C]设计；装置，设置：They are setting up a new safety ～ in the workshop. 他们正在车间安装一种新的安全装置。同 instrument，apparatus

devil / ˈdevl / n. [C]魔鬼；恶人 反 angel

devise / dɪˈvaɪz / vt. ❶设计，发明：The boy often says that he will ～ a new TV set when he grows up. 小男孩常说他长大了要设计一种

新的电视机。同 design, invent ❷策划;（精心）设计;想出:~ a foolproof plan getting rid of termites 想出一个消灭白蚁的简易方案/ The novelist ~d a number of incidents to illustrate the character he had created. 小说家炮制了若干故事来刻画其创造的人物。

devote / dɪˈvəʊt / *vt.* 专心;献身:~ **oneself to** 献身于;致力于;专心于:It is wrong to ~ yourself only to amusement. 你只专注于娱乐是不对的。同 give, dedicate

辨析

devote 意为"献身;奉献",强调认真而专心地做某事,不顾及其他任何事物:He is devoted to his studies. 他专注于他的学习。**dedicate** 强调热切或庄重地奉献:The scientist dedicated his life to science. 那位科学家献身于科学事业。

devoted / dɪˈvəʊtɪd / *adj.* 热爱的;专心的;忠诚的;忠实的:a ~ friend 忠实的朋友 同 faithful, loyal / be ~ **to** 忠实于;致力于;专心于:We are ~ to our country. 我们忠于我们的国家。/ She is ~ to her studies. 她专心于她的学业。

devotion / dɪˈvəʊʃn / *n.* [U]献身;忠诚,忠实:His ~ to the Party is unquestion-able. 他对党的赤胆忠心不容置疑。同 loyalty, dedication

devout / dɪˈvaʊt / *adj.* 虔诚的,虔敬的:a ~ Catholic 虔诚的天主教徒/She is sincere, loyal, ~ toward the body, the flesh. 她真挚、忠诚,守身如玉。

dew / djuː / *n.* [U]露水

diagnose / ˈdaɪəgnəʊz / *vt.* 诊断(疾病):The old doctor ~d his illness as flu. 老大夫诊断他患了流感。同 determine, identify

diagnosis / ˌdaɪəgˈnəʊsɪs / *n.* (*pl.* diagnoses) 诊断:I am afraid that the doctor has made an erroneous ~ of her disease. 我担心大夫误诊了她的病。同 determination, identification

diagonal / daɪˈægən(ə)l / Ⅰ *adj.* ❶对角(线)的:a ~ line 对角线/The path is ~ to the edge of the field. 这条小路与田边成对角。❷斜的:a ~ stripe in cloth 布上的一条斜条纹 Ⅱ *n.* [C] ❶对角线 ❷斜线:cut bread on a ~ 沿对角线切开面包

diagram / ˈdaɪəgræm / *n.* [C]图解;图表;简图:The young engineer draws ~ well. 那位年轻的工程师绘图很好。同 chart, sketch

dial / ˈdaɪəl / Ⅰ *n.* 钟(或表)面;标度盘;拨号盘:I cannot see the figures on the ~ clearly. 我看不清楚表面上的数字。Ⅱ *v.* (dialed 或 dialled; dialing 或 dialling)拨(电话号码);打电话(给…):Mother taught her son how to ~ 110 in case of emergency. 妈妈教儿子如何在紧急时拨打 110 电话。同 ring, telephone, call

dialect / ˈdaɪəlekt / *n.* [C]方言:The old lady speaks Shanghai ~. 那位老太太讲上海话。同 accent, tongue

dialog(ue) / ˈdaɪəlɒg / *n.* 对话:Listen to the ~ and then fill in the blanks. 听对话填空。同 talk, conversation

diameter / daɪˈæmɪtə(r) / *n.* [C] 直径

diamond / ˈdaɪəmənd / *n.* 金刚石;钻石

diary / ˈdaɪəri / *n.* [C]日记;日记簿:She often keeps a ~ in English. 她时常用英语写日记。/ His travel ~ is very interesting. 他的旅行日记写得很有趣。同 record, journal

dictate / dɪkˈteɪt / *v.* 听写;口授;口述:Our teacher often ~s to us in class. 上课时老师经常让我们做听写练习。同 deliver

dictation / dɪkˈteɪʃn / *n.* 听写:How many mistakes are there in your ~? 你的听写中有多少错误? 同 record, notes

dictator / dɪkˈteɪtə(r) / *n.* [C] ❶独裁者;专制者 ❷口授者

dictatorship / ˌdɪkˈteɪtəʃɪp / *n.* [U]专政:the people's democratic ~ 人民民主专政

dictionary / ˈdɪkʃənəri / *n.* [C]字典;词典:look up a word in the ~ 查字典/ We can buy convenient electronic dictionaries now. 现在我们能买到各种方便的电子词典了。

die / daɪ / *v.* 死;死亡;灭亡:Plants would ~ without water. 植物无水会枯死。反 live, exist /~ **away** 渐渐地消失:The colour of the sunset ~d away. 落日的余晖渐渐消失了。~ **from** 因(疾病以外的原因而)死亡:He ~d from overwork (loss of blood, a wound, an accident, drinking too much). 他死于过度劳累(失血,外伤,事故,过量饮酒)。~ **of** 因(病、悲伤、饥饿、营养不良、焦虑、羞愧等)死亡:He ~d of cancer. 他死于癌症。~ **out** 逐渐消失:Many old customs are dying out. 许多旧习俗逐渐消失。

D

用法

❶"他死了"对应的英文表达是：He is dead. 一般不用"He has died."这种表达方式。❷ die 是终止性动词，故不说：He has died for two years. 应说：He has been dead for two years. 或 It is two years since he died. 或 He died two years ago.

did / dɪd / v. 做（do 的过去式形式）

diet / 'daɪət / n. 食物；饮食：She is on a low-fat ～. 她正在接受低脂肪饮食疗法。同 food / **go on a** ～节食

differ / 'dɪfə(r) / vi. 不同；相异；有分歧：If you don't agree with me, I'm afraid we shall have to ～. 如果你不同意，恐怕我们只好保留不同的意见了。同 disagree 反 agree/～ **from** 不同于：I'm sorry to ～ from you. 很遗憾，我的看法和你的不同。

difference / 'dɪfrəns / n. 不同；差别；差异；差额：Please tell the ～ between the two. 请说出这两者的差异。/ The ～ between 9 and 4 is 5.9 和 4 之差为 5。同 distinction 反 agreement

different / 'dɪfrənt / adj. 不同的；有差异的；各种的：They are studying in ～ classes. 他们在各自的班上学习。/ The two sisters are ～ in character. 两姐妹性格不同。同 distinct, varying 反 same, alike / ～ **from (to)** ... 与…不同：My house is ～ from yours. 我的房子与你的不同。

difficult / 'dɪfɪkəlt / adj. 困难的；艰难的；难对付的：～ days 艰难岁月 / He found it ～ to stop smoking. 他发觉戒烟很难。/ The place is ～ to find. 那个地方很难找。同 hard 反 easy, simple

difficulty / 'dɪfɪkəlti / n. 困难；困境：avoid the ～ 回避困难/clear away the ～ 排除困难/ conquer the ～ 战胜困难/ face the ～ 正视困难，面对困难/ They are trying hard to settle the ～. 解决困难。/ **have much (great) ～ in doing sth.** 做某件事有困难：I have much ～ in falling to sleep. 我难以入睡。

diffuse¹ / dɪ'fjuːs / v. (光、热、气等)扩散，散发；传播：to ～ knowledge 传播知识

diffuse² / dɪ'fjuːs / adj. 扩散的；啰唆的；冗长的：His speech was too ～ for me to catch his point. 他的讲话冗长，我难以抓住要点。同 wordy

dig / dɪg / v. (dug / dʌg /, dug; digging) ❶挖；掘：The fields need to be dug up. 这些田土需要翻挖。/ The workers dug a tunnel through the mountain. 工人们在山里挖了一条隧道。反 bury ❷探究：He is ～ging away at his English. 他在刻苦钻研英语。同 search

digest Ⅰ / daɪ'dʒest / v. 消化；领会，领悟：This food ～s ill (well). 这种食物难(易)消化。/ He read the report for the second time to ～ the important points of it better. 他又读了一遍那份报告，以便能更好地领会其中的要点。同 absorb, understand Ⅱ / 'daɪdʒest / n. 文摘；摘要：I like to read *Reader's Digest*. 我喜欢看《读者文摘》。

digestion / daɪ'dʒestʃən / n. [U]消化；消化力：Rice is easy of ～. 米饭很容易消化。/ Though the old man is over sixty, he has a good ～. 虽然老人六十多岁了，但他的消化力却很强。

digit / 'dɪdʒɪt / n. [C] 阿拉伯数字：The number 2008 contains four ～s. 2008 是个四位数。

digital / 'dɪdʒɪtl / adj. 数字的；数字显示的；记数的：a ～ camera 数码相机/～ coding 数字编码/～ display 数字显示/ image processing 数字图像处理 / an optical ～ disk 数字光盘/ a ～ library 数字图书馆

dignify / 'dɪgnɪfaɪ / vt. 使有尊严；使变得庄严(或崇高)；为…增光，给…添彩：～ sb.'s departure with a ceremony 为某人举行仪式以壮行/The low farmhouse was dignified by the great elms around it. 那低矮的农舍四周有高大的榆树环绕，平添了几分庄严。

dignity / 'dɪgnəti / n. [U]尊严；高贵：lose one's ～ 有失体面(掉价)/ pocket one's ～ 放下架子/ stand on one's ～ 摆架子 同 honor, elegance

dilemma / dɪ'lemə / n. [C]困窘；困境；进退两难：To work or to retire put (placed, threw) him in a ～. 究竟是工作还是退休，这使他进退两难。同 difficulty

diligence / 'dɪlɪdʒəns / n. [U]勤勉；勤奋：He succeeded in his studies by ～. 他通过勤奋获得了学习上的成功。同 effort, industry 反 laziness

diligent / 'dɪlɪdʒənt / adj. 勤奋的；刻苦的：He is ～ at (in) his lessons. 他学习勤奋。派 diligently adv.

dilute / dɪ'l(j)uːt, daɪ'l(j)uːt / vt. ❶使变稀；使变淡；稀释，冲淡：This dye must be ～d in a bowl of water. 这颜料必须放入一碗水中加以稀释。❷削减；降低；减轻：The high price of a new car ～d our enthusiasm for buying one. 一辆新车的价格这么高，大大降低了人们的购买欲。Ⅲ adj. 稀释的，冲淡了的：～ whisky 掺水威士忌 派 dilution n.

dim / dɪm / adj. 昏暗的；暗淡的；朦胧的：The light is ～ here; I can't read anything. 这儿光线太暗，什么也无法读。同 dark, obscure 反 bright

dimension / dɪ'menʃn / n. [C]尺寸；长（宽、厚、深）度；大小：They measured the ～s of the room. 他们测出了屋子的大小。同 size, measurements

dimensional / dɪ'menʃənl / adj. …维的；空间的；立体的：a three-～ film 立体电影

dimple / 'dɪmpl / n. [C]酒窝，(笑)靥

dine / daɪn / vi. 吃饭；进餐：He often ～s on fish. 他经常吃鱼。同 eat, feed / ～ out 外出吃饭：They decided to ～ out for a change. 他们决定外出吃饭换换口味。/ a dining-room 食堂/饭厅/ a dining car 餐车/ a dining table 餐桌

dinner / 'dɪnə(r) / n. (一日间的)主餐；正餐：at ～ 在吃饭/ a nice ～ 美餐/ a plain ～ 家常便饭/ a state ～ 国宴/The engineer gave a ～ at a hotel in honor of his old friends. 工程师在宾馆设宴款待他的老朋友们。同 supper, banquet

dinosaur / 'daɪnəsɔː(r) / n. [C]恐龙：Dinosaurs died out many years ago. 恐龙在许多年前就绝种了。

dip / dɪp / v. (dipped; dipping) 汲取；浸：The water is too cold to swim, so I'll just ～ a toe in. 水太冷，不能游泳，所以我只将脚打湿了一下。/ I can't give you any opinion because I only ～ped into the book. 我只是稍稍翻阅了一下这本书，不可能给你提供什么意见。同 soak, plunge

dioxide / daɪ'ɒksaɪd / n. 二氧化物：Do you know the difference between carbon ～ and carbon monoxide? 你知道二氧化碳和一氧化碳的区别吗？

diploma / dɪ'pləumə / n. (pl. diplomas 或 diplomata)毕业文凭；学位证书；执照：a ～ for prize 获奖证书/ He gained a ～ in history after four years' study. 在学习四年后他获得了历史学文凭。同 degree, certificate

diplomacy / dɪ'pləuməsi / n. [U]外交；交际手段：They settled the problem by using ～. 他们运用外交手段解决了问题。

diplomat / 'dɪpləmæt / n. [C]外交家；外交官：His father is a career (professional) ～. 他的父亲是一位职业外交官。

diplomatic / ˌdɪplə'mætɪk / adj. 外交的：The two countries resumed ～ relations three years ago. 三年前两国恢复了外交关系。

direct / dɪ'rekt / Ⅰ vt. 管理；指导；指挥：One's thinking ～s one's actions. 思想指导行动。/ They ～ed me wrongly. 他们给我指错了方向。同 instruct, guide, lead Ⅱ adj. 直接的；坦率的：Please give me a ～ answer. 请明确答复我。同 straight, frank, face-to-face 反 indirect Ⅲ adv. 直接地：The train goes there ～. 火车直接去那里。同 straightly, frankly

direction / dɪ'rekʃn / n. ❶管理；指挥；指导：follow ～s 遵照指示/ obey ～s 服从指挥 同 instruction, command ❷(pl.)用法说明：～s for use 使用说明/ instructions ❸方向；方位：in all ～s 四面八方 同 way

directly / dɪ'rektli / Ⅰ adv. 立即；马上；直接：I'll be there ～. 我马上就去那里。同 quickly, straightly Ⅱ conj. (＝as soon as)(口语)一…就：We get up ～ the bell rings. 铃声一响我们就起床。

director / dɪ'rektə(r) / n. [C] ❶指导者；主管：a music ～ 音乐指挥/ a factory ～ 厂长 同 instructor, administrator ❷董事；理事：The board of ～s made a decision to hire a sales-manager at the meeting. 董事会在会议上决定雇用一名销售部经理。同 trustee, manager ❸导演：He became a film ～ after graduation. 毕业后他成为一名电影导演。

directory / dɪ'rektəri / n. [C]姓名地址录；(电话)号簿：You can find his new number in the telephone ～. 你可以在电话号簿上查到他新的电话号码。同 list

dirt / dɜːt / n. [U]污物；灰尘：His clothes were covered with ～. 他衣服上满是脏东西。同 dust, mud

dirty / 'dɜːti / adj. 脏的；不干净的；下流的；不正当的：His face was ～. 他的脸很脏。/ Dirty books and magazines are not allowed in schools. 学校不允许兜售黄色书刊。同 unclean, immoral 反 clean, moral

disability /ˌdisəˈbiliti/ n. ❶[U]无能力；无力；丧失能力：a learning ～学习困难/～ of raising one's head 抬头乏力 ❷[C]伤残，残废：physical ～生理残伤

disable /disˈeibl/ vt. 使丧失能力，使伤残：He was ～d in the war. 他在战争中受伤致残。同 damage/～ sb. from doing sth. 使某人丧失做某事的能力：An accident ～d him from walking. 一场事故使他再不能走路了。

disadvantage /ˌdisədˈvɑːntidʒ/ n. 不利条件，损失；缺点：The ～s overweigh advantages. 不利条件超过有利条件。/ His poor English put him at a ～ at the international conference. 他的蹩脚英语使他在国际性会议上处于不利地位。同 harm,drawback 反 advantage,benefit

disagree /ˌdisəˈɡriː/ vi. 不同意；不一致；不适宜：Even friends sometimes ～. 即使是朋友，有时也会意见不合。/ I disagree with you about that. 在那个问题上我不同意你的看法。同 differ 反 agree 派 disagreement n.

disagreeable /ˌdisəˈɡriːəbl/ adj. ❶令人不愉快的；不合意的讨厌的：a ～ job 不合意的职业/His remarks sound very ～ to the ear. 他的话不堪入耳。❷不友善的；脾气坏的，难相处的：be ～ towards sb. 对某人不友好/He gave his answers short and ～. 他只是爱理不理地回答个三言两语。派 disagreeably adv.

disappear /ˌdisəˈpiə(r)/ vi. 消失；失踪：He ～ed into the night. 他消失在夜色之中。同 vanish,fade 反 appear 派 disappearance n.

disappoint /ˌdisəˈpɔint/ vt. 使…失望；使落空：What she said ～ed me greatly. 她说的话令我大失所望。/ The failure in the exam ～ed my hope. 考试失败令我的希望落空。同 fail,sadden 反 encourage / **be ～ed at (in)** 对…感到失望：I was greatly ～ed in that affair. 那件事令我大失所望。派 disappointed adj.

用法
be disappointed of 指因得不到而感到失望：She was disappointed of the book. 她因得不到那本书而感到失望。be disappointed with 指对…感到失望，后面常接指人的词：The boss was disappointed with his new secretary. 老板对新来的秘书感到失望。

disappointment /ˌdisəˈpɔintmənt/ n. 失望，沮丧：She went home in ～ because she didn't find her lost son. 因为没有找到失踪的儿子，

她失望地回到家里。同 dissatisfaction,misfortune 反 satisfaction,success 派 disapproval n.

disapprove /ˌdisəˈpruːv/ v. 不赞成，不许可；不同意：I wholly ～ of what you say. 我完全不赞成你说的话。同 oppose,refuse 反 approve

disarm /disˈɑːm/ v. ❶缴…的械，解除…的武装：The police captured the robber and ～ed him. 警察抓住了那个抢劫犯，并缴了他的械。❷使没有杀伤(或伤害)力；使(言论)不具说服力：The lack of logic ～ed his argument. 由于缺乏逻辑性，他的论点不能使人信服。❸裁军：The superpowers are unlikely to ～ completely. 超级大国是不可能彻底裁军的。

disaster /diˈzɑːstə(r)/ n. 灾难；大祸：an air ～ 空难/ a traffic ～ 车祸/ Only a six-year-old survived the ～. 只有一个六岁大的男孩从那场灾难中活了下来。同 accident,misfortune

disastrous /diˈzɑːstrəs/ adj. 灾难性的；不幸的：The ～ floods caused great losses. 那次特大洪水造成了极大的损失。同 ruinous,destructive,unfortunate

disband /disˈbænd/ vt. 解散，散伙，解体；遣散：～ an organization 解散一个组织/The group ～ed after a few months. 几个月后该团体即被解散。

disc /disk/ n. [C]圆盘；磁盘；唱片

discard /disˈkɑːd/ vt. 扔掉，丢弃，抛弃：～ an empty bottle 丢弃空瓶子/～ one's old friends 抛弃自己的老朋友

discharge I /disˈtʃɑːdʒ/ vt. ❶允许…离开；释放；解雇：The doctor ～d the patient from the hospital yesterday. 昨天大夫让病人出院了。/ The young worker was ～d for his laziness. 那年轻工人因懒惰而被解雇。同 dismiss,fire,release ❷排出；放出：The big chimneys of the factory ～d thick smoke. 那家工厂的几个大烟囱排出浓烟。同 emit,release II /ˈdistʃɑːdʒ/ n. [U] ❶获准离开；释放：He is over sixty and has got his ～ from the company. 他六十多了，已从公司离退。同 release ❷排出；流出：The ～ of dirty water from the factory ruined the crops. 从工厂排放的污水毁了庄稼。同 emitting,release

disciple /diˈsaipl/ n. [C]门徒；信徒：a devoted ～ 忠实的信徒 同 follower,believer

discipline / ˈdɪsəplɪn / n. [U] ❶训练；锻炼：He was under perfect ～ when he was young. 他很小就受到良好的训练。囲 training, exercise ❷纪律：the military ～ 军纪/ the Party ～ 党纪/ the school ～ 校纪/ The school is strict in ～. 这所学校纪律严明。囲 rules, regulation

disclaim / dɪsˈkleɪm / vt. 否认；不承认：He ～ed all knowledge of the matter. 他矢口否认知道此事。/The planner ～ed responsibility for the consequences. 计划制定者拒绝对此后果承担责任。

disclose / dɪsˈkləʊz / vt. 揭发；揭开；泄露：She ～d the information to the press. 她把消息泄露给了新闻界。囲 tell, expose

disco / ˈdɪskəʊ / n. [C] 迪斯科舞厅；迪斯科舞曲：The young couple often go to a ～ on weekends. 那对年轻夫妻常在周末去迪斯科舞厅跳舞。

discolo(u)r / dɪsˈkʌlə(r) / vt. & vi. (使)褪色；(使)变色；(被)玷污：The heat would ～ the paint. 高温会使油漆褪色。/Many materials fade and ～ of exposed to sunshine. 许多材料一旦暴露在阳光下就会褪色或变色。派 discoloration n.

discomfort / dɪsˈkʌmfət / n. [U] 不舒适；不安；不自在：One has to bear a little ～ while travelling. 人旅行时总要忍受一点小小的不适。反 comfort

discontent / ˌdɪskənˈtent / n. [U] ❶不满：They tried to stir up ～ among the employees. 他们企图在雇员中间挑起不满。❷不满意；不满足：Her ～ with her job is making her parents very unhappy. 她不满意自己的工作，这使她的父母极为不快。

discontinue / ˌdɪskənˈtɪnjuː / v. 中断；终止；中止；停止：～ one's work 停止工作/This evening newspaper will ～ next month. 这份晚报将于下月停刊。

discount Ⅰ / ˈdɪskaʊnt / n. 折扣：He sold the goods at a ～ of ten percent. 他卖九折出售商品。囲 cut Ⅱ / dɪsˈkaʊnt / vt. 打折卖：The air tickets are ～ed at 20% now. 现在机票打八折出售。

discourage / dɪsˈkʌrɪdʒ / vt. 阻止，劝阻；使气馁：Don't let one failure ～ you. 别因一次失败而气馁。囲 depress 反 encourage /～ **sb. from**

doing sth. 劝阻某人不做某事：We tried to ～ him from climbing the mountain without a guide. 我们试图劝他无向导不要爬山。

discover / dɪsˈkʌvə(r) / vt. 发现；找到；看出：We often ～ our mistakes when too late. 我们发现自己的错误时，往往为时已晚。囲 find, realize

discovery / dɪsˈkʌvəri / n. 发现；发觉；被发现的事物：Man has made many new discoveries in science since last century. 上个世纪以来人类在科学上做出了许多新的发现。囲 finding

discredit / dɪsˈkredɪt / vt. ❶破坏…的名誉；使丢脸：Being caught cheating ～ed the boy among his classmates. 那位学生由于考试作弊被当场抓住而在同学们中间丢尽了脸。/ She's been ～ed by the scandal. 她被这起丑闻弄得声名扫地。❷使不可置信；使不可信赖：The insurance investigator ～ed his claim. 保险公司调查员证实他的索赔要求不可信。

discrepancy / dɪsˈkrepənsi / n. [U] 差异；不符，不一致：The ～ in their interests did not the least affect their friendship. 他们之间在兴趣爱好上的差异丝毫不影响他们的友谊。/ There is (a) considerable ～ between the two accounts. 这两种说法有很大出入。

discriminate / dɪˈskrɪmɪneɪt / v. ❶歧视；分别对待：Does this factory ～ between men and women? 这家工厂有性别歧视吗？❷区别；辨别：Can't you ～ good from bad? 难道你不能分辨好坏吗？囲 separate, distinguish 派 discrimination n.

discus / ˈdɪskəs / n. [C] 铁饼：throw the ～ 掷铁饼

discuss / dɪˈskʌs / vt. 讨论；议论：～ a question with sb. 与某人讨论问题/ The students are ～ing how to protect our environment. 学生们正在讨论如何保护我们的自然环境。囲 talk, argue, debate 派 discussion n.

disease / dɪˈziːz / n. 病；疾病：Depression has become a common ～ among the group. 抑郁症已成为这群人中的一种常见病。/ Doctors are trying hard to bring his heart ～ under control. 大夫们正尽力控制他的心脏病。囲 illness, sickness

disgrace / dɪsˈɡreɪs / n. [U] 耻辱；丢脸：He who is sent to prison brings ～ on himself. 蹲监狱的人给他自己带来耻辱。囲 dishonor, shame 反 grace, honor

disguise / dɪsˈgaɪz / vt. 伪装；假装；掩饰（事实、意图、感情等）：John ～d himself as a policeman. 约翰把自己伪装成一名警察。同 mask, hide

disgust / dɪsˈgʌst / vt. 令人厌恶；令人作呕：We are ～ed at（by, with）what we heard and saw here. 我们对在这里的所见所闻感到厌恶。同 dislike 反 please

dish / dɪʃ / n. [C] 盘，碟；一道菜：I ate two ～es of ice-cream. 我吃了两份冰激凌。/ The cold ～ was delicious. 那道凉菜味道很好。

dishearten / dɪsˈhɑːtn / v. 使沮丧；使泄气：She felt ～ed at her failure. 她因失败而感到沮丧。同 discourage

dishonest / dɪsˈɒnɪst / adj. 不老实的；不诚实的；不正直的：He doesn't want to make friends with a ～ man. 他不愿意和不诚实的人交朋友。反 honest

dishono(u)r / dɪsˈɒnə(r) / n. 不光彩；丢脸；不名誉：They fired the man who brought ～ on their company. 他们解雇了败坏公司名誉的那个人。同 shame, disgrace 反 honor

disinfect / dɪsɪnˈfekt / vt. 为（伤口、房屋、衣物等）消毒（或杀菌）：～ dental instruments 给牙科器械消毒/They had to ～ the soil before a new crop could be planted. 在种上新庄稼以前，他们必须对土壤进行杀菌。

disinterested / dɪsˈɪntrɪstɪd / adj. ❶公正的；无私的；不偏不倚的：make a ～ed decision 作出公正的裁决/a ～ed diplomatic observer 不带偏见的外交观察家 ❷不感兴趣的，漫不经心的，不关心的：discuss sth. in a ～ed way 无动于衷地谈论某事

disk / dɪsk / n.（＝disc）[C] ❶圆盘：The moon is like a big bright ～. 月亮像一个明亮的大圆盘。❷唱片：The composer keeps a lot of old video ～s. 那位作曲家保留了很多旧唱片。❸磁盘：a floppy ～ 软盘/ a hard ～ 硬盘/ a back up ～ 备份盘/ ～ operating system（DOS）磁盘操作系统

dislike / dɪsˈlaɪk / Ⅰ vt. 不喜爱；厌恶：I ～ being interrupted at the meeting. 我讨厌在会上发言时被人打断。同 hate 反 like Ⅱ n. [C]不喜爱；厌恶：She shows a ～ for her job. 她不喜欢她的工作。同 distaste, hatred, disgust 反 liking, delight

dismal / ˈdɪzməl / adj. ❶忧郁的；凄凉的：a ～ expression 忧郁的表情/Her voice sounds ～. 她的声音听上去郁郁不乐。❷沉闷无趣的；差劲的；乏味的：a ～ performance 沉闷乏味的演出

dismay / dɪsˈmeɪ / Ⅰ vt. 使失望；使气馁；使绝望：She was ～ed to learn of her husband's disloyalty. 她得知丈夫对她不忠，心里感到很失望。Ⅱ n. [U]失望，气馁；绝望：The results of exam filled us with ～. 这次考试成绩使我们感到气馁。

dismiss / dɪsˈmɪs / vt. 开除；解雇；解散：The boy was ～ed from school. 那男孩被学校开除了。/ Our teacher always ～es the class ahead of time. 我们老师总是提前下课。/ He was ～ed for his stealing. 他因偷盗被解雇。同 fire, discharge, release 反 hire, accept, gather 派 dismissal n.

disobey / ˌdɪsəˈbeɪ / vt. 不服从；违反：Don't ～ school discipline. 别违反学校纪律。反 obey

disorder / dɪsˈɔːdə(r) / n. [U] 无秩序；混乱，杂乱；小病：Her room is always in ～. 她的房间总是乱糟糟的。/ Affairs in that district are in great ～. 那个地区的态势极端混乱。

dispatch Ⅰ / dɪˈspætʃ / vt. 派遣；发送：～ a telegram 发电报/The captain ～ed a boat to bring a doctor on board ship. 船长调了一艘小艇去接医生上船。Ⅱ / dɪˈspætʃ, ˈdɪspætʃ / n. ❶（部队、信使等的）派遣；（信件等的）发送：demand for the ～ of an envoy 要求派遣一名使节/the date of the ～ of the parcel 包裹寄出的日期 ❷ [C]（公文）快信，急件；快讯，（新闻）报道：send a ～ from New York to London 从纽约发往伦敦的急件/The correspondent rushed ～es to his newspaper in New York about the fire in Seoul. 那名记者赶紧给他纽约的报社发去了有关首尔大火的几则快讯。

dispel / dɪˈspel / vt.（-pelled; -pelling）驱散（云、雾等）；使消失，消除，消释：The sun soon ～led the mist. 太阳很快驱散了雾霭。/The fears were ～led. 这些忧虑烟消云散了。

disperse / dɪˈspɜːs / vt. ❶使散开；赶散；疏散：A thunderstorm ～ the picnickers. 一场雷雨使很野炊的人们四散而去。❷消散；驱散：The chill night air ～ with the dawn. 夜间的寒气随着黎明的到来消散了。

display / dɪˈspleɪ / Ⅰ vt. 陈列；展出；显示；

The oil painting which is ～ed in the museum is famous. 正在博物馆展出的那幅油画非常著名。/ He ～ed no fear in front of the robber. 面对抢匪他显得毫无畏惧。同 exhibit, show Ⅱ n. 显示；展示；(计算机)显示屏，显示器：They went to watch a fashion ～ last Sunday. 上周日他们去观看了时装展。同 exhibition show

displease / dɪsˈpliːz / vt. 使不愉快；使生气：His rudeness ～d all the guests. 他的粗暴无礼令所有客人不快。反 please 派 displeased adj.

disposable / dɪˈspəʊzəbl / adj. 一次性(使用)的，用后即扔的：～ plastic spoons 一次性塑料勺

disposition / ˌdɪspəˈzɪʃn / n. ❶性情；性格：a cheerful ～开朗的性情/In this ～ of mind, I began my new life. 我以这种心情开始了新生活。❷排列；布置；配置：the ～ of furniture in a room 房间里家具的布置

dispute / dɪˈspjuːt / v. 辩论；争吵；怀疑：They ～d with us for a prize. 他们为奖品和我们争论。同 argue, quarrel

disregard / ˌdɪsrɪˈɡɑːd / vt. 不理；不顾；漠视：It is not to be lightly ～ed. 这事不能等闲视之。同 neglect, ignore 反 regard

用法
disregard 用作名词时，其后可接介词 for, of 或 to：That driver was arrested for his complete disregard of the traffic laws. 那位司机因完全违反交通规则而被捕。

disrupt / dɪsˈrʌpt / vt. ❶搅乱；扰乱：The news ～ed their conference. 这则消息搅乱了他们的会议。❷使中断；破坏…的完整性：Telephone service was ～ed for hours. 电话通信中断了数小时。

dissatisfy / dɪsˈsætɪsfaɪ / vi. 使不满；使不平：We were dissatisfied with his impolite blame toward our teacher. 他对老师的无礼指责令我们感到不满。同 discontent, disappoint 反 satisfy

dissertation / ˌdɪsəˈteɪʃn / n. [C](研究)报告；(学术)论文：He finished his master's ～ a week ago. 一周前他写完了他的硕士论文。同 thesis

dissolve / dɪˈzɒlv / v. ❶分解；(使)溶解；(使)融化：Salt and sugar ～ easily in water. 盐和糖很容易溶于水。同 melt, evaporate ❷解散；取消(契约等)；解除(婚约等)：They ～d their business partnership because they couldn't agree with each other. 由于意见不合，他们解除了生意合伙关系。同 dismiss, divorce

distance / ˈdɪstəns / n. 距离；远处：at a ～ 隔开一些/ from a ～ 从远处/in the ～ 在远处/The ～ from my home to my school is not far. 从我家到学校的距离不远。同 length, extent, span

distant / ˈdɪstənt / adj. 遥远的；远处的；疏远的：It is very ～ from the truth. 这与事实相差很远。/ Our school is three *li* ～ from the railway station. 我们学校离火车站有三里路。同 far, remote 反 near

distil(l) / dɪsˈtɪl / (-tilled; -tilling)vt. ❶蒸馏；用蒸馏法提取：～ fresh water from sea water 从海水中蒸馏出新鲜淡水 ❷净化；提炼；浓缩；吸取…的精华：useful advice ～ed from a lifetime's experience 从一生经验中提炼出的有用的忠告/A proverb ～s the wisdom of the ages. 一则谚语浓缩了成百上千年的智慧。

distinct / dɪˈstɪŋkt / adj. ❶不同的；有区别的：Beijing opera is ～ from our local drama. 京剧与我们地方戏截然不同。同 different, extraordinary ❷清楚的；清晰的；明显的：They achieved a ～ improvement in their experiment. 他们的实验取得了明显的进展。同 plain, clear, obvious 反 vague, unclear 派 distinctly adv.

distinction / dɪˈstɪŋkʃn / n. ❶[U]差别；区别；区分；辨别：First we should draw a clear ～ between right and wrong. 首先我们应当分清是非。同 difference, separation ❷[C]荣誉；名声：The mayor is going to interview the scientist who won many ～s. 市长将接见那位获得过许多荣誉的科学家。同 fame, repute

distinctive / dɪˈstɪŋktɪv / adj. 有特色的；与众不同的：He comes from the south and has a ～ accent. 他来自南方，有着特别的口音。同 outstanding, extraordinary 反 ordinary, common

distinguish / dɪˈstɪŋɡwɪʃ / vt. 区别；辨别；使杰出：He can readily ～ those two objects. 他很容易地把那两个物体区别开来。/ The girl ～ed herself by winning the champion. 那姑娘因获得冠军而出名。同 identify, signalize/～ ... and ... (... from ..., between ... and ...) 区

别…和…：We must ～ friends from foes. 我们必须分清敌友。

distinguished / dɪˈstɪŋɡwɪʃt / *adj.* 著名的；杰出的：The Chinese nation is ～ for its diligence and courage. 中华民族以勤劳、勇敢著称。同 famous，outstanding

distort / dɪˈstɔːt / *vt.* 歪曲；曲解；扭曲：How can you ～ the facts in broad daylight? 在光天化日之下你怎么能歪曲事实呢？同 bend，twist，deform 派 distortion *n.*

distract / dɪˈstrækt / *vt.* 分散（思想、注意力等）；使分心（和介词 from 连用）：Reading ～s the mind from grief. 读书能使人分心而减轻痛苦。

distress / dɪˈstres / Ⅰ *n.* [U]苦恼；悲痛；危难；不幸：His death caused his relatives great ～. 他的去世令亲人们感到非常悲痛。同 grief，misfortune Ⅱ *vt.* 使苦恼，使痛苦：She was ～ed to find that her brother had got lung cancer. 她痛苦地发现她哥哥患了肺癌。同 upset，trouble

distribute / dɪˈstrɪbjuːt / *vt.* 分配；分给；分发；分类：It is said that the professor's property was ～d among his students. 据说那位教授的财产分配给了他的学生们。/ The books in the library were ～d according to subjects. 图书馆里的书按科目分类。同 divide，deliver

distribution / ˌdɪstrɪˈbjuːʃn / *n.* ❶分发；分配；发行：a ～ network 发行网/ Who has the ～ right of this film? 谁有这部电影的发行权？同 division，delivery ❷分布；散布：The population ～ in this district is wide. 这一地区的人口分布很广。同 spread，scattering 反 collection

distributor / dɪˈstrɪbjətə(r) / *n.* [C] 分发者；分配者；发行商

district / ˈdɪstrɪkt / *n.* [C] 区；(行政)区域；He lives in different ～ from his mother. 他和母亲住在不同的地区。同 area，region

distrust / dɪsˈtrʌst / *vt.* 怀疑；不信任：I couldn't ～ my own eyes to face what he was doing. 面对他的所作所为，我简直不敢相信自己的眼睛。同 doubt，disbelieve 反 believe

disturb / dɪˈstɜːb / *vt.* 打扰；扰乱：I am sorry to have ～ed you a lot. 对不起，太打扰你了。同 bother，trouble 派 disturbance *n.*

ditch / dɪtʃ / *n.* [C] 沟；渠：They are digging a drainage ～ to let dirty water out. 他们正挖一条排水沟把脏水引出去。同 canal，channel

dive / daɪv / (dived 或 dove /dəʊv/，dived) 俯冲；跳水：～ into water 跳入水中/～ into books 埋头读书 Ⅱ *n.* 跳水；潜水；I like to watch fancy ～ game. 我喜欢观看花样跳水比赛。

diverse / daɪˈvɜːs / *adj.* ❶不同的，相异的：A great many ～ opinions were expressed at the meeting. 会议上众说纷纭，莫衷一是。❷ 多种多样的，种类繁多的：a culturally ～ population 文化多元的民族

diversity / daɪˈvɜːsɪti / *n.* ❶[U]差异(性)：～ of dispositions 禀性的差异/There was considerable ～ in the style of the reports. 这几篇报道的文笔各不相同。❷多种多样；多样性：The ～ of food on the table made it hard for him to choose. 桌上菜肴品种多得让他不知道该吃哪种才好。

divert / daɪˈvɜːt / *vt.* ❶使偏离，使转向：～ a stream from its natural course to a farm for irrigation 把小溪改道引进农场灌溉田地/～ the subject into a side issue 把话题扯向一个枝节问题 ❷转移；盗用，挪用(资金) ❸转移(注意力等)：She pointed to the left to ～ the child's attention while she old the cake. 她用手指向左边转移那孩子的注意力，同时把蛋糕藏了起来。

divide / dɪˈvaɪd / *v.* 分，分开；除；分配；分摊：Ten ～d by two is five. 10 除以 2 等于 5。同 separate，share /～…from… 把…和…分开：The Red Sea ～s Africa from Asia. 红海把非洲和亚洲分开来。～… into …把…分成…：Let's ～ ourselves into groups. 咱们分成几个小组吧。

dividend / ˈdɪvɪdend / *n.* [C] ❶红利；股息：He pays a ～ of five percent each time. 他每次付 5%的股息。同 interest，profit ❷被除数

divider / dɪˈvaɪdə(r) / *n.* [C] 除数

division / dɪˈvɪʒn / *n.* [U]分割；分裂

divorce / dɪˈvɔːs / Ⅰ *n.* [U]离婚；离异：He got a ～ from his wife three years ago. 三年前他和妻子离婚了。同 separation 反 marriage，wedding Ⅱ *v.* 离婚：The boy said that his parents were ～d last month. 小男孩说上个月他的父母离婚了。同 separate 反 marry

DIY (＝Do it yourself.)自己动手做

dizzy / ˈdɪzi / *adj.* 头晕眼花的；眩晕的：The smell made me ～. 那气味令我感到头晕。Don't be ～ with success. 别让胜利冲昏头脑。同 confused

do / duː/ *v.* (did/dɪd/, done /dʌn/)；一般现在时第三人称单数 does/dʌz/) ❶助动词：①用于构成现在或过去时：Does he work in a middle school? 他在中学工作吗？/ I didn't go to see the film last night. 昨晚我没去看电影。②用以加强肯定句语气：But I ～ want to go. 可是真想去。③用于祈使句以加强语气：Do come on time. 务必准时来。❷代替动词：①用在肯定句中：She writes better than I ～. 她写得比我好。②用于问句和回答中：He loves his work, does he? Yes, he does. 他喜欢他的工作，是吗？是的。❸做；做完：She did all the work. 她做了全部工作。/～ a good deed 做好事～ / do harm to 对…有害 / honour to sb. 向某人表示敬意；给某人带来荣誉 / one's best 尽全力 / **away with** 废除；消灭：The law did away with slavery. 这项法令废除了奴隶制。～ **by** (口语) 对待：He did very well by me. 他待我很好。～ **for** 料理；挫败；毁灭；杀死：If Jim fails in that test, he is done for. 若吉姆考试不及格，他就完了。～ **in** 杀；谋害；毁灭；劳累：I felt done in after a long day's work. 苦干了一整天，我感到疲惫不堪。/ His business was done in by a big fire. 他的商行被一场大火烧毁了。～ **out** 扫除；整理：Do out the desk drawer. 把书桌抽屉整理一下。～ **up** 修整；恢复；筋疲力尽：Can you ～ up my shirt before tomorrow? 你能在明天以前把我的衬衫熨好吗？/ The house needs to be done up. 这房子需要重新装修。～ **with** 利用；处置；控制：It's difficult to ～ with her. 和她相处不易。/ The children didn't know what to ～ with themselves for joy. 孩子们高兴得难以控制自己。～ **can (could)** ～ **with** 可利用；满足于；相容；忍受：I can't ～ with her insolence. 我不能容忍她的傲慢。/I could ～ with a cup of tea. 我喝杯茶就行了。**have sth. (much, nothing) to** ～ **with** 与…有 (有很大，没有) 关系：Hard work had much to ～ with his success. 工作努力与他的成功有很大的关系。～ **without** 将就；没有…也行：If there's no sugar, you'll have to ～ without it. 如果没有糖，你就只好将就了。

dock / dɒk / Ⅰ *n.* [C] 码头；船坞；(*pl.*) 港区：He worked at the ～s two years ago. 两年前他在港区工作。同 harbor Ⅱ *v.* 停靠码头：The ship ～ed in Qingdao for repairs. 那艘船停靠在青岛码头维修。同 anchor, land

doctor / ˈdɒktə(r) / *n.* [C] ❶医生；大夫：He feels not well. You'd better send for a ～ soon. 她不舒服，你最好马上请大夫。/ Mother often sees a ～ on Monday morning. 妈妈常在星期一上午去看病。同 physician, surgeon ❷博士：Her son is a ～ of Philosophy (PhD). 她的儿子是哲学博士。

doctoral / ˈdɒktərəl / *adj.* 博士的：He has finished his ～ dissertation. 他已经做完了他的博士论文。

doctrine / ˈdɒktrɪn / *n.* [C;U] 教条,教义；信条；主义：the Christian ～s 基督教教义 / strange and false ～s 异端邪说

document / ˈdɒkjumənt / *n.* [C] 公文；文件；文献：a ～ center 文献中心/ official ～s 官方 (正式) 文件；公文/ He was drawing up a ～ when I came in. 我进去时他正在草拟一份文件。同 paper 派 documental *adj.*

documentary / ˌdɒkjuˈment(ə)ri / Ⅰ *adj.* 记录的；纪实的；文献的；根据文件的：The ～ TV programs are moving. 纪实性电影节目很感人。/ I like ～ TV programs. 我喜欢看纪实性电视节目。Ⅱ *n.* [C]纪录片；纪实片；纪实小说：a full-length ～ 大型纪录片 同 film, program

dog / dɒg / *n.* [C] 狗；犬：The family keeps a guide ～. 这家人养了一只导盲犬。

doll / dɒl / *n.* [C] 洋娃娃；玩具娃娃：The little girl sat on the floor playing with a ～. 小女孩坐在地板上玩洋娃娃。

dollar / ˈdɒlə(r) / *n.* [C](货币单位)元；美元 ($)：a Canadian ～ 加元/ a Hong Kong ～ 港元/ He exchanged five thousand American ～s for traveling abroad. 为出国旅游他兑换了5 000美元。

dolphin / ˈdɒlfɪn / *n.* [C] 海豚：They are watching a school of ～s in the pool. 他们在观看水池里的一群海豚。

domestic / dəˈmestɪk / *adj.* ❶本国的；国内的：gross ～ product (GDP) 国内生产总值/ He is especially interested in TV programs of ～ news. 他对国内新闻电视节目特别感兴趣。同 internal, home, native 反 foreign ❷家(庭)

的；家用的：She should be fully responsible for 〜 troubles. 她应对这场家庭纷争负全责。同 homely ❸ 驯养的；家养的：The farmer keeps some 〜 animals. 那农夫养了一些家畜。同 tame, home-bred 反 wild

dominate / ˈdɒmɪneɪt / v. 统治；支配：His new view is dominating over the academic circles. 他的新观点在学术界占领着支配地位。同 rule, direct

donate / dəʊˈneɪt / vt. 捐；捐赠；捐款：The old professor 〜d a large sum of money to build a school for the children. 老教授捐了一大笔钱为孩子们修建学校。同 give, grant 派 donator n.

donation / dəʊˈneɪʃn / n. 捐赠；捐款；捐赠物；赠品：make financial 〜s to help develop education 捐资助学／ Soon the people of the flooded area received a large 〜 from all over the country. 很快灾区的人民就收到了来自全国各地大量的捐赠物。同 offering, gift, grant

donkey / ˈdɒŋki / n. [C] 驴；笨蛋：drive a 〜 赶驴子／If I brays at you, don't bray at him. 别和蠢人一般见识。同 mule, fool

door / dɔː(r) / n. [C] 门；门口：at the 〜 在门口／ knock at the 〜 敲门／ next 〜 隔壁／ from 〜 to 〜 挨家挨户／ Please open the 〜 to the visitor. 请为客人开门。同 entrance, gate

dormitory / ˈdɔːmətri / n. [C] (集体)宿舍(口语中亦可简称为 dorm)：The boy students' 〜 is on the hill. 男生宿舍在小山坡上。同 dorm

dose / dəʊs / n. [C] ❶(服药的)(一次)剂量；一剂，一服：take a 〜 of cough medicine 服一剂咳嗽药／take medicine in small 〜s 小剂量服药 ❷(不愉快经历的)一次，一份：a 〜 of flattery 一通马屁

dot / dɒt / I n. [C] 小圆点；小数点 同 spot, point II v. 打点于…

dote / dəʊt / vi. 溺爱；过分宠爱(与 on 连用)：〜 on classic music 特别喜欢古典音乐／They 〜 on their youngest daughter. 他们溺爱小女儿。

double / ˈdʌbl / adj. 两倍的；双的：He does 〜 work to earn his tuition. 为挣学费他做两份工作。／ The students in this school are now 〜 what they were five years ago. 这所学校现在的学生人数是五年前的两倍。

doubt / daʊt / I v. 怀疑；不相信：I 〜 whether it is true. 我怀疑这是否真的。同 suspect, disbelieve 反 believe II n. 怀疑；疑虑：arouse 〜s 引起怀疑／ destroy 〜s 消除疑虑／ There is not the least 〜 that we shall win. 我们会取胜是毫无疑问的。同 suspicion 反 belief／ **beyond**(**past**) 〜 毫无疑问：Beyond 〜, you'll recover soon. 你会很快恢复健康，这是毫无疑问的。**in** 〜 怀疑的；未确定的：The result of the election is still in 〜. 选举结果尚未确定。**no** 〜 无疑地：You have no 〜 heard the news. 你无疑已听到这消息了。**without** 〜 无疑地；毫无问题：Without 〜 he is the best singer among us. 无疑他是我们中最好的歌手。

用法

❶doubt 作名词的常用句型是 there is no doubt that ...，而不用 it is no doubt that ...：There is not much doubt about it. 这没有什么可怀疑的。❷doubt 作动词词的句型，在肯定句中常用 whether, if 引导的宾语从句，在否定句或疑问句中常用 that 引导的宾语从句：I doubt whether he will come. I do not doubt that he will come. Do you doubt that he will come?

doubtful / ˈdaʊtfl / adj. 令人怀疑的；可疑的：We are 〜 about the weather for tomorrow. 我们说不准明天的天气会如何。／ He is 〜 of the news. 他怀疑那条消息不可靠。同 uncertain, suspicious 反 certain, doubtless

dove / dʌv / n. [C] 鸽子：The little girl draw 〜s of peace well. 小女孩画和平鸽得很好。

down / daʊn / I adv. 向下；下降：Put it 〜, please. 请把它放下来。／ The oil price is 〜. 油价降了。反 up II prep. 由上向下；沿着：The children ran 〜 the hill. 孩子们跑下山。／ He was walking 〜 the street. 他正沿着街道行走。反 up III v. 打倒；击落；放下：He is 〜ed with flu. 他因患流感病倒了。

downfall / ˈdaʊnfɔːl / n. [U] 垮台；衰落；毁灭：the 〜 of the government. 这项丑闻导致了该国政府的倒台。

download / ˌdaʊnˈləʊd / v. (计算机)下载：He 〜ed a great amount of information from the Internet. 他从因特网上下载了大量的资料。

downstairs / ˌdaʊnˈsteəz / I adj. 楼下的：The 〜 room is empty. 楼下的房间是空着的。反

upstairs Ⅱ *adv.* 在楼下；往楼下：He didn't know who lives ～. 他不知道谁住在楼下。 **反** upstairs

downtown / ˌdaʊnˈtaʊn / Ⅰ *adj.* (闹)市区的；商业区的：The ～ areas are developing rapidly. 城市商业区发展迅速。**同** mid-city, midtown, urban **反** suburban, rural Ⅱ *adv.* 在市区；向市区：Generally speaking, old people don't like to live ～. 一般说来，老年人不喜欢住在闹市区。

downward / ˈdaʊnwəd / Ⅰ *adj.* 向下的；下行的：There is a ～ slope in front of the house. 房屋前面有一个斜坡。**同** down **反** upward Ⅱ *adv.* 向下；下行：He pulled the rope ～. 把绳子往下拉。**同** down **反** upward

doze /dəʊz/ Ⅰ *v.* 瞌睡；打盹：She was too tired and ～d off over reading. 她太疲倦，看书时都打瞌睡了。**同** nap Ⅱ *n.* 瞌睡；打盹：You may have a ～ here. 你可以在这儿打打盹。**同** nap

dozen / ˈdʌzn / *n.* [C] (一)打；十二个：Eggs are sold by the ～in this district. 这个地区鸡蛋论打卖。/ A ～ of pencils is twelve. 一打铅笔是十二枝。/ ～s of 几十；许多：We need to choose ～s of excellent stamps more for the show. 我们还需要挑选几十张优秀邮票参展。

draft / drɑːft / Ⅰ *n.* [C]草稿；草案；草图：The secretary was making a ～ of (for) a speech when I went in. 我进去时秘书正在起草一份讲话稿。**同** sketch, outline Ⅱ *v.* 起草；草拟：He ～ed a letter to the president. 他草拟了一封给校长的信。**同** design, outline

drag / dræg / *v.* (dragged; dragging) 拉；拖：The horse was ～ging a heavy load. 马拖着重载。/ The workers ～ged the river for a sunken boat. 工人们在那条河里打捞沉船。**同** draw, pull **反** push

dragon / ˈdrægən / *n.* [C] 龙；a ～ boat 龙船；龙舟/ a ～ lantern 龙灯/Dragon Well tea 龙井茶

drain / dreɪn / *n.* ❶[C]排水；下水道；排水系统：She asked the worker to clear the ～. 她请工人帮她疏通下水道。**同** ditch, pipe ❷消耗；负担：Teaching his grandson English was a great ～ of his energy. 教孙子学英语消耗了他很大的精力。**同** exhaust

drama / ˈdrɑːmə / *n.* 戏剧；剧本：They are students of ～. 他们是攻读戏剧的学生。/

The young man wrote a very good motion picture ～. 那年轻人写了一个很好的电影剧本。**同** play, script

dramatic / drəˈmætɪk / *adj.* 戏剧的；戏剧性的：He told us that the whole event was really ～. 他告诉我们整个事件很富戏剧性。

dramatist / ˈdræmətɪst / *n.* [C] 剧作家

drank / dræŋk / *v.* 喝，饮(drink 的过去式形式)

draw / drɔː / *v.* (drew /druː/, drawn /drɔːn/) 拉，拖；吸引；画：The boy is ～ing a plane. 男孩正在画飞机。/ The lecture drew a large audience. 那场讲座吸引了许多听众。/ She drew the curtain before she went to bed. 睡觉前她拉上窗帘。**同** drag, pull, paint **反** push/～ **a conclusion** 得出结论：A conclusion has been ～n. 结论已得出。～ **a deep breath** 深深吸气：The doctor told him to ～ a deep breath. 医生要他深吸一口气。～ **back** 收回：He will not ～ back from what he has said. 他说过的话是不会收回的。～ **in** 引诱；缩短：She is ～n in to buy this coat. 她受骗去买这件外套。～ **near** 接近；临近：Christmas is ～ing near. 圣诞节即将来临。～ **off** 脱去；放掉：Please ～ off your socks. 请把袜子脱去。～ **on** 穿上；吸收：The man drew on his trousers hurriedly. 那个人匆匆穿上裤子。～ **out** 取出；引出；拉长：She drew two hundred dollars out of the bank to buy her mother a present. 她从银行取出 200 元钱给母亲买礼品。～ **up** 起草；草拟：The two countries drew up a peace treaty after the war ended. 两国在战争结束后草拟了和平条约。

辨析 draw 意为"引；拉；牵"，一般用语：He drew me aside and whispered in my ears. 他把我拉到一边，对我说悄悄话。drag 意为"拖；拽"，指在某一平面牵引沉重的东西：The thief was dragged out of the hiding place. 有人把贼从躲藏的地方拖了出来。haul 意为"拖；拉；拽"，指向任何方向费力地拖拉，也指拖重载的运输：The fisherman hauled the fish into the boat. 渔夫把鱼拖到了船上。pull 意为"拉"，指在水平方向费力地拖拉：The horse was pulling a cart steadily. 这匹马平稳地拉着大车。

drawback / ˈdrɔːbæk / *n.* [C]不利；缺点；障碍：I think that watching TV has both benefits and ～

s. 我认为看电视有利也有弊。/ He decided to remove the ～s on his way to success. 他决心要除掉通往成功道路上的各种障碍。同 disadvantage, trouble, handicap

drawer /'drɔː(r)/ *n.* 抽屉：She put her diary in the ～. 她把她的日记本放在抽屉里。

drawing /'drɔːɪŋ/ *n.* [U] 绘画：Our monitor is good at ～. 我们班长擅长绘画。同 picture

dread /dred/ *v.* 害怕；恐惧；担心：Do you ～ a visit to the zoo? 你害怕去动物园吗？同 fear, worry 派 dreadful *adj.*

dream /driːm/ Ⅰ *v.* 梦想；想象：Do you ～ at night? 你晚上做梦吗？/ He ～ed a dreadful dream last night. 昨晚他做了一个噩梦。同 fancy, imagine/～ **of** 想象；向往；渴望：Little did I ～ of succeeding so. 我做梦也想不到会这么成功。Ⅱ *n.* 梦；梦想；幻想：He has a beautiful ～ to sail around the world. 航海环游世界是他的美好梦想。同 desire 反 reality 派 dreamer *n.*; dreamy *adj.*

dress /dres/ Ⅰ *v.* 替…穿衣；打扮：She is ～ing her baby. 她正在给小孩穿衣。/ You are finely ～ed today. 你今天穿得真漂亮。同 wear 反 undress Ⅱ *n.* 衣服；服装：evening ～ 晚礼服/ He is in informal ～ today. 今天他穿便服。同 clothes

> **辨析**
> **dress** 和 **clothe** 均为及物动词，后常接 sb. 或反身代词：He dressed (clothed) himself in blue. 他穿着蓝色衣服。**put on** 表示穿衣服的短暂动作，与 take off 相对：It is snowing outside, put on more clothes. 外面在下雪，多穿点衣服。**wear** 常表示一种持续的状态：She never wearsgreen. 她从不穿绿色衣服。She was wearing a red flower in her hair. 她头上戴着一朵红花。

dressing /'dresɪŋ/ *n.* ❶[U;C](拌制色拉等的)调料：salad ～ 色拉调料 ❷[C]敷药；包扎：apply a ～ to a wound 对伤口敷药包扎

drift /drɪft/ Ⅰ *v.* (使)漂流；漂泊：The boat was ～ing down the river. 小船顺着河流往下漂去。同 float, drive Ⅱ *n.* 漂流；漂泊：The ～ of this current is to the south. 这股水流向南方。派 droplet

drill /drɪl/ *n.* ❶练习；操练：class ～s 课堂练习/ daily ～s 日常训练/ oral ～ 口头操练：They conducted a fire ～ last weekend. 上周末他们进行了消防演习。同 training, exercise ❷

[C]钻头；钻床

drink /drɪŋk/ Ⅰ *v.* (drank/dræŋk/, drunk/drʌŋk/) 喝，饮：～ a toast 敬酒/ Let's ～ to Mother's health. 让我们为妈妈的健康干杯。同 suck, absorb/～ **in** ①吸收(水分)：The soil ～s in rain. 土壤吸收雨水。②全神贯注地倾听：The girl drank in every word of the sailor's story of adventures. 这姑娘全神贯注地倾听水手所讲述的冒险故事，一个字也没漏掉。Ⅱ *n.* 饮料，酒；cold ～ 冷饮/ have a ～ 喝一杯

drip /drɪp/ Ⅰ *v.* (dripped; dripping)滴下；漏下：Sweat was ～ping down his face. 汗水从他脸上滴下来。同 drop Ⅱ *n.* [C]水滴；点滴：He is put on a ～ in the hospital. 他正在输液。同 drop

drive /draɪv/ *v.* (drove/drəʊv/, driven /'drɪvn/) 驱赶；迫使；驾驶：Her husband ～s her to office everyday. 她丈夫每天开车送她上班。同 ride, force/～ **away** 驱逐；驱车离开：The enemies are driven away. 敌人被驱逐出去了。～ **off** 赶走：They drove the attackers off. 他们击退了进攻者。～ **sb.** **mad** 使某人发疯：What he said drove her mad. 他说的话使她发疯。派 driver *n.*

droop /druːp/ *v.* 低垂，下垂；发蔫：The flowers were ～ing for want of water. 花因缺水而发蔫。

drop /drɒp/ Ⅰ *v.* (dropped; dropping) 掉下；滴下；下降；降落：The apple blossoms are beginning to ～. 苹果花开始掉了。/ His voice ～ped to a whisper. 他的声音降低成耳语。/ The price of eggs ～ped quickly. 鸡蛋的价格很快降下来了。同 lower, fall, reduce 反 rise, raise/～ **in** 顺便拜访：Drop in some time tomorrow. 明天随便什么时候来玩一一玩。～ **off** 散出；打瞌儿；下车；降低：His friends ～ped off one by one. 他的朋友一个个走了。/ He ～ped off. 他打了个盹。～ **out** 退出：Three runners ～ped out. 三名赛跑运动员退出了比赛。Ⅱ *n.* [C] 水滴；水珠：The rain is falling in large ～s. 雨下得很大。同 drip/～ **at the** **of a hat** 有机会就……；随时；马上：He used to blush at the ～ of a hat. 他以前动辄就脸红。～ **by** ～ 一点一点地；一滴一滴地：The water leaks from the tap ～ by ～. 水一滴一滴地从龙头里漏出来。

dropout /'drɒpaʊt/ *n.* [C] 退学者：The school is trying hard to reduce its ～s. 学校正

尽力减少流失生。 同 truant

drought / draʊt / n. 旱灾；长期干旱：The prolonged ～ brought difficulties to villagers. 持久的干旱给村民带来很多困难。 反 flood

drown / draʊn / v. 淹死，淹没：Do cats ～ easily? 猫容易被淹死吗？ / My voice was ～ed by the noise of the machinery. 我的声音被机器声所淹没。

drug / drʌg / n. [C] 药；药物；(pl.) 麻醉药：an acting ～ 速效药/ sleeping ～ 安眠药/ a ～ store 药房/ International Anti-Narcotic Drugs Day 国际禁毒品日 同 remedy, medicine

drum / drʌm / n. [C] 鼓

drunk / drʌŋk / Ⅰ v. 喝，饮(drink 的过去分词形式) Ⅱ adj. 喝醉的；沉醉的；陶醉的：The little boy got ～ on excessive beer. 小男孩喝了过多的啤酒而醉了。/ They were ～ with joy after winning the champion. 他们陶醉在赢得冠军后的喜悦之中。

dry / draɪ / Ⅰ adj. 干的；口干的；枯燥无味的：It's very ～ for this season of the year. 就这个季节来说，气候要算很干燥的。/ These books are as ～ as dust. 这些书读起来枯燥无味。 同 dried, rainless, dull Ⅱ v. 晒干；弄干：She dried her hair. 她把头发弄干。 反 wet

dual / 'djuːəl / adj. ❶双的，两的；二元的：the ～ law which accounts for negative and positive electricity 解释正负电的二元法则 ❷双倍的；两重的：～ nationality 双重国籍/have a ～ function 具有双重作用

dubious / 'djuːbɪəs / adj. ❶怀疑的：I'm still ～ about the wisdom of that plan. 我对那个计划是否明智仍抱有怀疑。❷有问题的；不可靠的：a rather ～ character 可疑分子/a ～ account of what happened 对所发生的事情的不可靠说法 ❸犹豫的；迟疑的：She feels ～ as to what to do. 她犹豫不决，不知该怎么办。

duck / dʌk / n. [C] 鸭子

duckling / 'dʌklɪŋ / n. [C] 小鸭：Have you ever read *The Ugly Duckling* by Hans Andersen? 你读过安徒生写的《丑小鸭》吗？

due / djuː / adj. 合适的，应得的；预定的；约定的：The bus is ～ at nine. 公共汽车预定 9 点钟到。同 expected, deserved, scheduled/～ **to** 因为；由于：The credit is due to you. 荣誉应该归你。

due to 常用作表语：The accident was due to your carelessness. 事故是由于你的粗心大意造成的。**because of, owing to** 常用作状语：Because of his bad leg, he couldn't walk so fast. 他的腿有毛病，不可能走那么快。They delayed owing to the bad weather. 由于天气不好，他们们迟到了。**thanks to** 常作状语，含有感谢之意，常位于句首：Thanks to your help, we succeeded. 多亏你的帮助，我们才获得了成功。

duke / djuːk / n. [C] 公爵；君主

dull / dʌl / adj. ❶钝的：a ～ knife 一把钝刀 反 sharp ❷迟钝的；愚笨的：a ～ mind 愚钝的头脑 同 slow, stupid ❸(天气) 阴沉的；阴暗的：～ color 暗淡的颜色/a ～ day 阴沉的天 同 gloomy 反 bright ❹单调的；枯燥乏味的：a ～ story 一个乏味的故事 同 boring, dry

dumb / dʌm / adj. 哑的；无言的：He was born ～ but he is clever. 虽然他生下来就是哑巴，但他很聪明。同 mute, speechless

dump / dʌmp / Ⅰ n. [C]垃圾堆；垃圾场 Ⅱ v. 倾倒；倾销：No ～ing. 禁止倒垃圾。/ They ～ed surplus goods abroad. 他们向国外倾销过剩货物。

dumpling / 'dʌmplɪŋ / n. [C] 饺子：She treated us to ～s yesterday. 昨天她请我们吃饺子。

duplicate Ⅰ / 'djuːplɪkɪt / n. [C]副本，抄件；复制品：make a ～ of the original 做一份原件的副本 Ⅱ/'djuːplɪkeɪt/ vi. ❶复制；复写；复印：Can you ～ the key for me? 你能帮我复一把这样的钥匙吗？❷重复；依样重做：He ～d his father's way of standing with his hands in his pockets. 他模仿其父两手插在口袋里站着的样子。

duration / djʊə'reɪʃn / n. [U]持续，延续；持续期间：a play of short ～ of life 寿命/ **for the** ～长期地，持续地：He was drafted for the ～ plus six. 他要再服六年兵役。

during / 'djʊərɪŋ / prep. 在…期间：I was in the army ～ the war. 战争期间我在部队当兵。

dusk / dʌsk / n. [U]黄昏，薄暮：They arrived home at ～. 黄昏时他们到家了。同 sunset 反 dawn

dust / dʌst / Ⅰ n. [U] 灰尘，屑，粉末：The ～ was blown about by the wind. 风吹得尘土到

处飞扬。同 dirt,ash Ⅱ vt. 去掉灰尘：She ~ed the furniture. 她掸去家具上的灰尘。同 clean 派 dusty adj.

Dutch / dʌtʃ / Ⅰ n. ❶荷兰人 ❷荷兰语 Ⅱ adj. ❶荷兰人的 ❷荷兰语的

dutiful / ˈdjuːtɪf(ʊ)l / adj. 尽职的，守本分的，恭敬的，恭顺的；顺从的，服从的：~ citizen 本分公民/She is a ~ daughter to her parents. 她是父母的孝顺女儿。/He was ~ to his mother. 他对他母亲恪尽孝道。

duty / ˈdjuːti / n. ❶义务；责任；职责：It's my ~ to show respect to my teachers. 尊敬老师是我的本分。/ It is our ~ to obey the laws. 遵纪守法是我们的义务。同 task, responsibility/**on** ~ 值日：Who's on ~ today? 今天谁值日？❷(pl.)税，关税：customs duties 海关关税/ import duties 进口税/Duties on cars are reducing. 小汽车的关税在下降。同 tax

DVD(＝digital video disk) 数字光盘；数码影碟

dwarf / dwɔːf / n. [C] 矮子；侏儒 反 giant

dwell / dwel / vi. (dwelt/dwelt/或 dwelled, dwelt 或 dwelled) ❶居住；居留：The old couple have dwelt in the town for 25 years. 老两口在这个小镇上住了 25 年了。同 live, reside ❷凝思；细想：He often ~s on his past. 他常常细想过去的事。同 think, consider 派 dwelling n.

dye / daɪ / Ⅰ vt. 染色；把…染上颜色：She ~d her curtain light blue. 她把窗帘染成淡蓝色。同 color Ⅱ n. [U] 染色；染料：This kind of cloth takes ~ well (badly). 这种布料(不)容易染上色。同 color

dying / ˈdaɪɪŋ / adj. 垂死的；临终的：The patient told his doctor his ~ wish. 病人把临终心愿告诉了他的大夫。/ **be** ~ **for** 渴望：He said he was ~ for a hot bath. 他说他真渴望洗个热水澡。同 mortal, passing

dynamic(al) / daɪˈnæmɪk(əl) / adj. 动力的；动态的；有活力的：The housing market in our country is a ~ market. 我国的住房市场是一个很有活力的市场。同 driving, powerful, energetic

dynamics / daɪˈnæmɪks / n. 动力；动力学

dynamo / ˈdaɪnəməʊ / n. [C] 电动机；发电机：an alternating current ~ 交流发电机/ a direct current ~ 直流发电机 同 generator

dynasty / ˈdɪnəsti, ˈdaɪnəsti / n. [C] 王朝；朝代：the Ming Dynasty 明朝

E e

each / iːtʃ / Ⅰ *adj.* 每；各；各自的：Each boy may try three times. 每个男孩可以试三次。同 every, any, all Ⅱ *pron.* 各个；每个：Each of the students has a new book. 每个学生都有一本新书。同 every, any, all／～ **other** 彼此；互相：They often talk to ～ other in English. 他们常常用英语交谈。

用法

each other 用于两者之间，one another 用于三者以上之间。在现代英语中 each other 和 one another 可以互换。

辨析

❶ **each 与 every** 作形容词时，**each** 强调整体中的个体，**every** 则强调总体，表示其中没有例外：Each dog there has a name. 那里的每条狗都有它自己的名字。Every dog has a name. 所有的狗都有名字。❷ **each** 可作代词，**every** 只能作形容词：Each of them has a book. 他们中每个人都有一本书，不能说 Every of them has a book.

eager / ˈiːɡə(r) / *adj.* 热切的；渴望的：She was ～ to go abroad. 她渴望出国。同 keen, longing／**be ～ for**（**about, after**）渴求某事：She is ～ for success. 她渴望成功。派 eagerly *adv.*

eagle / ˈiːɡl / *n.* [C] 鹰

ear / ɪə(r) / *n.* [C] ❶耳，耳朵：**all ～s** 专心听：She was all ～s when the teacher spoke. 老师讲话时，她全神贯注地听。**give ～s to** 注意；留神：Please give ～s to his report. 请注意听他的报告。**go in (at) one ～ and out (at) the other** 左耳进，右耳出；当作耳边风：My repeated warning to her went in one ～ and out the other. 她把我的一再警告当作耳边风。❷听说；听力：The old woman is over sixty but has a keen ～. 尽管六十多岁了，老太太的听觉却很灵。同 hearing ❸(稻、麦等的)穗

early / ˈɜːli / (-ier, -iest) Ⅰ *adj.* 早的；早期的：My grandfather is an ～ riser. 我爷爷是个早起的人。／ Mother likes to buy ～ vegetables. 妈妈喜欢购买时鲜蔬菜。同 first, primitive 反 late Ⅱ *adv.* 早；在早期；在初期：Don't come too ～. 不要来得太早。反 late

earn / ɜːn / *vt.* 挣得；赢得；获得：How much did John ～ last month? 约翰上个月挣了多少钱？／ He ～ed respect by his fair dealing. 他因为公正而赢得了人们的尊敬。同 make, gain, achieve

earnest / ˈɜːnɪst / *adj.* 热心的；热切的；认真的：Parents are always ～ about their children's education. 父母对孩子的教育总是非常热心。同 sincere, serious 反 careless／**be ～ for** 渴望：He is ～ for greater achievements. 他渴望取得更大的成就。派 earnestly *adv.*

earnings / ˈɜːnɪŋz / *n.* ❶(*pl.*)工资；收入：The family live on his ～ only. 全家人仅靠他的工资过活。同 income, wages 反 expenses ❷收益；利润：The total ～ of the factory will be about 30 million dollars a year. 这家工厂一年的总赢利将达到 3000 万美元。同 profits, reward 反 cost

earphone / ˈɪəfəʊn / *n.* [C] 耳机：The students put on their ～s and listened to the record attentively. 学生戴上耳机认真听录音。

earth / ɜːθ / *n.* (the ～) 世界；地球：How far is the ～ from the sun? 地球离太阳多远？同 globe, planet／**on ～** 究竟；到底：How on ～ did you know it? 你到底是怎么知道这事的？

earthen / ˈɜːθn / *adj.* ❶泥土制的：an ～ dam 土坝 ❷陶制的：an ～ flowerpot 陶制花盆

earthly / ˈɜːθli / *adj.* 尘世的，世俗的：～ passions 世俗的欲望／She believed that our ～ life is all that matters. 她认为我们的现世生活至关重要的。

earthquake / ˈɜːθkweɪk / *n.* [C] 地震；大震荡：Many buildings collapsed in the devastating ～. 许多房屋在那次破坏性地震中倒塌了。同

quake, shock

earthworm / ˈɜːθwɜːm / *n.* [C] 蚯蚓, 曲蟮, 地龙

ease / iːz / Ⅰ *n.* [U] 安逸; 容易: They led a life of ～ in the countryside after they retired. 退休后他们在农村过着悠闲的生活。 同 comfort, rest 反 discomfort, difficulty/at ～ 自由自在; 悠闲, 无拘束: His smile put us at ～. 他的微笑使我们感到无拘无束。 with ～ 容易地: The soldiers marched twenty miles with ～. 士兵们轻而易举地行进了 20 英里。Ⅱ *v.* 使舒服; 放松; 减轻 (疼痛): This medicine will ～ the pain. 这药镇痛。/ The belt is too tight, ～ it a little. 皮带太紧, 放松一点。 同 relieve, lessen, lighten

east / iːst / Ⅰ *n.* 东; 东方: Japan is in the ～ of Asia. 日本位于亚洲的东部。 反 west Ⅱ *adj.* 东部的; 来自东方的: They live in the ～ side of the city. 他们住在城市东区。 反 western Ⅲ *adv.* 在东方; 向东方: My room faces ～. 我的房间朝东。 反 west

Easter / ˈiːstə(r) / *n.* 复活节: An ～ egg is a very good gift. 复活节彩蛋是一份很好的礼物。

eastern / ˈiːstən / Ⅰ *adj.* 东方的; 东部的: He knows little about ～ provinces. 他对东部省份了解不多。 同 east, oriental 反 western Ⅱ *n.* [C] 东方人

eastward / ˈiːstwəd / Ⅰ *adj.* 向东的; 朝东的: There is a temple on the ～ slope of the hill. 在小山上的东面斜坡上有一座庙宇。 反 westward Ⅱ *adv.* (～ s) 向东; 朝东: They traveled ～s. 他们向东旅行。 反 westwards

easy / ˈiːzi / *adj.* (-ier, -iest) ❶ 容易的; 不费力的: It is not very ～ to write a diary in English. 用英语写日记不太容易。 同 simple 反 difficult ❷ 舒适的; 安逸的: He is leading an ～ life. 他过着舒适的生活。 同 comfortable, relaxed ❸ 随和的; 易顺从的: He is ～ to get along with. 他平易近人。 反 hard 派 easily *adv.*

用法
take it (things) easy 中的 easy 为副词, 意为 "不紧张; 从容": Take it easy. 别着急。

eat / iːt / *vt.* (ate/et/, eaten / ˈiːtn/) 吃; 吃饭: They are ～ing tomatoes. 他们在吃西红柿。/ The young couple often ～ out on weekends. 这对年轻夫妻周末常常去餐馆吃饭。 同 take, have/～ one's words 食言: She often ～s her words. 她经常食言。 ～ one's heart out 沮丧; 悲伤: He ate his heart out over the defeat. 他因那次失败而感到沮丧。 ～ up 吃光; 耗尽: He ate up his savings to buy a flat in the city. 他耗尽积蓄在市区买了一套房子。

ebb / eb / Ⅰ *n.* [U] 退潮; 衰退: The tide is on the ～. 退潮了。 同 decline, decrease 反 flow, rise Ⅱ *vi.* 退潮; 退, 落: The boys and girls were playing on the beach when the tide ～ed. 退潮时孩子们在海滩上玩耍。 同 decline, decrease 反 flow, rise

eccentric / ɪkˈsentrɪk / Ⅰ *adj.* 古怪的; 怪僻的; 不合常规的: an ～ conduct 古怪的行为/ It's ～ to wear a mismatched pair of socks. 穿上一双不配对袜子真古怪。Ⅱ *n.* [C] 古怪的人; 怪僻的人: She was a mild ～. 她这个人有点儿怪。

echo / ˈekəʊ / Ⅰ *n.* 回声: If you shout at the top of the mountain, you'll hear the ～ of your voices. 如果你在山顶上大声喊叫, 你会听到你的声音回荡。 同 reflection Ⅱ *v.* 发回声; 回响: His voices ～ed in the valley. 他的声音在山谷中回响。 同 reflect

eclipse / ɪˈklɪps / *n.* [C] (日、月的) 食: a solar (lunar) ～ 日食 (月食)/a total ～ 全食

ecological / ˌiːkəˈlɒdʒɪkl / *adj.* 生态的; 生态学的: ～ agriculture 生态农业/ ～ balance 生态平衡 / ～ environment 生态环境

ecology / iˈkɒlədʒi / *n.* [U] 生态学

economic / ˌiːkəˈnɒmɪk / *adj.* 经济学的; 经济 (上) 的: the ～ base 经济基础/ the ～ aid 经济援助/ the ～ policy 经济政策/a special ～ zone 经济特区

economical / ˌiːkəˈnɒmɪkl / *adj.* 节省的; 节俭的; 经济的: an ～ person 一个节俭的人/ To buy a second-hand car is ～. 买二手车很合算。 同 saving 反 wasteful 派 economically *adv.*

economics / ˌiːkəˈnɒmɪks / *n.* [C] 经济学: a course in ～ 经济学课程/ He is majoring ～ in Britain. 他在英国主修经济学。

economist / ɪˈkɒnəmɪst / *n.* [C] 经济学 (专) 家

economy / ɪˈkɒnəmi / *n.* 经济: domestic ～ 家庭经济/ national ～ 国民经济/ market ～ 市场经济

ecosystem / ˈiːkəʊsɪstəm / *n.* [C] 生态系统: an

agricultural 〜 农业生态系统

ecstasy / 'ekstəsɪ / n. [U;C]狂喜：one's shrill cries of 〜喜极而尖叫/They were in 〜 at the thought of going home. 一想到回家,他们一个个欣喜若狂。派 ecstatic adj.

edge / edʒ / n. [C] 边;边缘：Sitting on the 〜 of the chair is not comfortable. 坐在椅子边上很不舒服。同 side,border

edible / 'edɪbl / adj. 可以食用的,可以吃的：〜 mushrooms 可食用的蘑菇/All parts of the plants are 〜. 这些植物的所有部位均可食用。

edition / ɪ'dɪʃn / n. [C]版本：a pocket 〜 袖珍版/ They planned to publish a new 〜 of the book. 他们计划出这本书的新版本。同 copy, version,volume

editor / 'edɪtə(r) / n. [C]编辑,编者：the 〜 in chief 总编辑/a chief 〜 主编 同 complier,reviser

editorial / ˌedɪ'tɔːrɪəl / Ⅰ n. [C]社论：publish an 〜 发表社论/ Have you read today's 〜? 你读了今天的社论吗？Ⅱ adj. 编辑的;社论的：〜 staff 编辑人员

educate / 'edʒʊkeɪt / vt. 教育,培养：She was 〜d for the law. 她是学法律的。/ You should 〜 your students to behave well. 你应教导你的学生们守规矩。同 teach,train

education / ˌedʒʊ'keɪʃn / n. 教育,培养：elementary (secondary,high) 〜 初等(中等,高等)教育 / nine-year compulsory 〜 九年制义务教育 / She hopes that her daughter will have a college 〜. 她希望她的女儿接受大学教育。同 teaching,training,instruction

educational / ˌedʒʊ'keɪʃənl / adj. 教育(性)的,有教育意义的：Educational Law 教育法/ 〜 reform 教育改革 同 instructive,educative

educator / 'edʒʊkeɪtə(r) / n. [C] 教育家 同 teacher,instructor

effect / ɪ'fekt / n. 结果;影响：Did the medicine have any 〜? 这药有效果吗？/ Our argument had no 〜 on her. 我们的争论对她没有影响。同 result,influence 反 cause,beginning/ in 〜 事实上;实际上：The two methods are in 〜 identical. 这两个方法实际上是一样的。 of no 〜无效;不中用：The search has been of no 〜. 这次搜查一无所获。give 〜 to 实行;实施;使生效：We decided to give 〜 to his plan.

我们决定实施他的计划。

effective / ɪ'fektɪv / adj. 有效的;生效的：This kind of medicine is 〜 against TB. 这种药对治疗结核有效。/ The rule will be 〜 from May 1. 这个规定将从 5 月 1 日起生效。同 valid, efficient,useful 反 ineffective,invalid,useless 派 effectively adv.

efficiency / ɪ'fɪʃnsɪ / n. 效率;功效;效能：The new machine will improve our 〜 greatly. 这台新机器将极大地提高效率。同 power,productivity,capability

efficient / ɪ'fɪʃnt / adj. 效率高的;有能力的：With an 〜 machine,one can do more work. 使用效率高的机器可以干更多的活。同 effective,competent 反 inefficient,ineffective

effort / 'efət / n. 努力;尽力;艰难的尝试：They finished the project in a common 〜. 在共同的努力下,他们完成了那项工程。/ He carried the big box away with little 〜. 他毫不费力地搬走了那个大箱子。同 pains,attempt

e. g. (＝for example;for instance)例如

egg / eg / n. [C] 蛋;卵

eggplant / 'egˌplɑːnt,'egˌplænt / n. [C]茄;茄子

eggshell / 'egˌʃel / n. [C]蛋壳

ego / 'iːgəʊ,'egəʊ / n. [C] (pl. egos) ❶自我,自己 ❷自尊(心);自我形象：boost sb.'s 〜 提升某人的形象/It was a blow to my 〜. 这件事对我的自尊心是个打击。❸自我中心;自负：feed sb.'s 〜 满足某人的虚荣心

Egypt / 'iːdʒɪpt / n. 埃及

Egyptian / ɪ'dʒɪpʃn / Ⅰ adj. 埃及的 Ⅱ n. [C]埃及人

eh / eɪ / int. 啊,嗯(表示惊奇、疑问或征求同意)

eight / eɪt / Ⅰ num. 八 Ⅱ adj. 八个(的)

eighteen / ˌeɪ'tiːn / Ⅰ num. 十八 Ⅱ adj. 十八个(的)

eighth / eɪtθ / Ⅰ num. 第八;八分之一 Ⅱ adj. 第八的;八分之一的

eighty / 'eɪtɪ / Ⅰ num. 八十 Ⅱ adj. 八十个(的)

either / 'aɪðə(r),'iːðə(r) / Ⅰ adj. (两者之间)任何一个：Either of the girls is ready. 两个女孩都准备好了。/ He may go by 〜 road. 两条路他随便走哪条都行。Ⅱ conj. 或者;要么;either…or… 或者…或者…;不是…就是…：He must be 〜 mad or drunk. 他不是疯了就是喝醉了。Ⅲ adv. 也(用于否定、疑问句)：In the old days there were no factories in the town. There were no hospitals ～. 过去这座城镇既没有工厂,也没有医院。

用法

❶either 通常不指两个以上中间的任何一个,可以说:You may put the chair on either side of the table. 很少说:You may put the ring on either finger of your hand. ❷either 用作形容词时,修饰单数名词,用作代词时谓语动词用单数:Either book is good. ❸either...or...连接两个主语,谓语动词与 or 后面的名词或代词相一致:Either my mother or my sisters are coming. Either my sisters or my mother is coming.

elapse / ɪˈlæps / *vi.* (时间)流逝,消逝,过去:Thirty minutes ～d before the performance began. 过了 30 分钟演出才开始。/ There months have ～d since he left home. 他离家已有三个月了。

elastic / ɪˈlæstɪk / Ⅰ *adj.* 弹性的;灵活的 Ⅱ *n.* [C] 松紧带;橡皮圈

elbow / ˈelbəʊ / *n.* [C] 肘;弯头;弯管:He put his ～s on the desk while he was reading. 看书时他把双肘支在书桌上。

elder / ˈeldə(r) / Ⅰ *adj.* 年长的:～ brother 哥哥/～ sister 姐姐 同 older, senior 反 younger, junior Ⅱ *n.* 年龄较大者;(常用 *pl.*)年长者;长辈:She is my ～ by three years. 她比我大三岁。/ We should respect the ～s. 我们应当尊敬长辈。同 senior

elderly / ˈeldəli / *adj.* 上了年纪的;中年以上的:～ people 上年纪的人

elect / ɪˈlekt / *vt.* 选举;选择:He was ～ed. 他当选了。/ We ～ed him as team leader. 我们选他当队长。同 vote, choose

辨析

elect 指在供选择的有限范围内挑选出人或物:They elected him as their chairman. 他们推选他为主席。**choose** 普通用语,指运用自己的判断力,根据自己的意愿选出自己喜欢的人或物:In choosing friends, we should take every possible care. 在择友时,应特别留心。**pick** 根据自己所知情况认真挑选合适的人或物:He wants to pick an exact synonym. 他想选出一个确切的同义词。**select** 意为“精选”,指经过认真考虑、斟酌,在不同事物中选出最好、最合适的人或物:I'm thinking of selecting some modern stories as your outside reading. 我想选些近代的故事作为你们的课外读物。

election / ɪˈlekʃn / *n.* 选举;选举权:They will hold an ～ at the basic level first. 他们将首先举行基层选举。同 choosing, voting

electric / ɪˈlektrɪk / *adj.* 电的;电动的;带电的:an ～ automobile 电动汽车/ an ～ battery 蓄电池/ an ～ bell 电铃/ an ～ light 电灯 同 power-driven

electrical / ɪˈlektrɪkl / *adj.* 与电有关的:an ～ engineer 电机工程师/ an ～ machine 电机 同 power-driven

electrician / ɪˌlekˈtrɪʃn / *n.* [C] 电工;电学家

electricity / ɪˌlekˈtrɪsəti / *n.* [U] 电;电学;电力:a machine worked by ～ 用电驱动的机器

electrify / ɪˈlektrɪfaɪ / *vt.* 使触电;使充电;使电气化

electro- / ɪˈlektrəʊ / (前缀)表示“电”“电的”“电解”:～lysis 电解 / ～plate 电镀 / ～therapy 电疗法

electrode / ɪˈlektrəʊd / *n.* [C] 电极

electron / ɪˈlektrɒn / *n.* [C] 电子:an ～ microscope 电子显微镜 / an ～ tube 电子管

electronic / ɪˌlekˈtrɒnɪk / *adj.* 电子的:～ books 电子图书/ an ～ dictionary 电子词典 / an ～ clock 电子钟/ ～ music 电子音乐 / an ～ organ 电子琴/ ～ mail 电子邮件(E-mail)/ Most little boys like ～ toys. 大多数小男孩都喜欢电子玩具。

electronics / ɪˌlekˈtrɒnɪks / *n.* 电子学

elegant / ˈelɪɡənt / *adj.* 优雅的;优美的;精致的:an ～ art 高雅的艺术/ Her husband is an ～ middle-aged gentleman. 她的丈夫是一位温文儒雅的中年绅士。同 graceful, fine 派 elegantly *adv.*

element / ˈelɪmənt / *n.* 元素;要素;成分:The teacher asked his students to recite *The Periodic Table of the Elements*. 老师要求他的学生背诵“元素周期表”。/ Honesty is one of the main ～s of success. 诚实是成功的主要要素之一。同 part, factor

elementary / ˌelɪˈmentri / *adj.* 初等的;基本的:～ education 初等教育/a ～ school (美)小学

elephant / ˈelɪfənt / *n.* [C] 大象

elevate / ˈelɪveɪt / *vt.* ❶举起,提高;使上升;抬起,抬高:～ one's eyebrows 扬眉/ a railway above ground level 架高铁路以高出地面

❷提拔,提升…的职位,使晋级：be ～d to a higher rank for bravery 因勇敢而受提拔

elevator / ˈelɪveɪtə(r) / n. (＝[英]lift) [C]（美）电梯

eleven / ɪˈlevn / Ⅰ num. 十一 Ⅱ adj. 十一个（的）

eleventh / ɪˈlevnθ / Ⅰ num. 第十一；十一分之一 Ⅱ adj. 第十一的；十一分之一的

eliminate / ɪˈlɪmɪneɪt / vt. 消灭；排除；淘汰：This game will ～ the losing team. 这场比赛将淘汰输了的球队。/ You must ～ errors in your calculation. 你必须消灭计算中出现的差错。同 extinguish, exclude 反 accept, include

elimination / ɪˌlɪmɪˈneɪʃn / n. 消灭；排除；淘汰：They will hold an ～ match next week. 下周他们将举行预赛(淘汰赛)。同 dismissal, exclusion 反 acceptance, inclusion

ellipse / ɪˈlɪps / n. [C] 椭圆；椭圆形

ellipsis / ɪˈlɪpsɪs / n. 省略法；省略号

eloquent / ˈeləkwənt / adj. 雄辩的；有说服力的：He is an ～ speaker. 他是一位雄辩的演说家。/ The lawyer produced ～ proof at the court. 在法庭上律师提供了有力的证据。同 fluent, persuasive 派 eloquence n.

else / els / adj. & adv. 另外,其他：What ～ do you want? 你还想要什么？/ Is there anything ～ you want to say? 你还有什么话要说吗？同 other, extra

elsewhere / ˌelsˈweə(r) / adv. 在别处：We haven't the book you want；you may go ～ for it. 我们这儿没有你需要的那种书,你可以到别处看看。同 here

email, e-mail / ˈiːmeɪl / n. (＝ electronic mail) [C] 电子邮件：Please tell me your ～ address. 请把你的电子邮件地址告诉我。

emancipate / ɪˈmænsɪpeɪt / vt. 解除…的束缚；使从约束中解脱；释放,使自由；解放：Women have been ～d from many old restrictions. 妇女已从许多旧的束缚中解放出来。派 emancipation n.

embarrass / ɪmˈbærəs / vt. 使窘迫；使为难：He felt ～ed about his foolish mistake. 他为所犯的愚蠢错误感到窘迫。/ Don't ～ her by asking her personal questions. 别提些个人隐私问题为难她。同 upset, distress 派 embarrassment n.

embassy / ˈembəsi / n. [C] 大使馆：He works

in the Chinese Embassy in London. 他在中国驻伦敦大使馆工作。

embellish / ɪmˈbelɪʃ / vt. ❶美化；修饰,装饰：Hampton's office was already ～ed with masterly paintings. 汉普顿的办公室已经用许多幅名画布置了起来。❷添加(叙述)的细节；润色（文章）,润饰；渲染：Joanna ～ed her story by adding a few imaginative details to it. 乔安娜增添了一些想象的细节润饰她的短篇小说。

embody / ɪmˈbɒdi / vt. ❶体现；使具体化：The article embodies the author's ideas. 文章体现了作者的思想。❷包含；收录：The new machine embodies many improvements. 新机器有了不少改进。同 include, contain

embrace / ɪmˈbreɪs / Ⅰ vt. ❶(拥)抱：The police came into the room embracing a baby in his arms. 警察走进房间,怀里抱着一个小婴儿。同 hug, clasp ❷包括；包含：This passage ～s many points. 这段文章包括许多新的要点。同 include, contain 反 exclude ❸包围；环绕：The old lady lives in the house ～d by green trees. 老太太住在一座绿树环绕的房子里。同 encircle, enclose, surround Ⅱ n. [C] 拥抱；怀抱：She gave her husband a tight ～ when she met him again. 再见面时,她紧紧拥抱自己的丈夫。同 hug

embryo / ˈembriəʊ / n. [C] 胚胎：Do you know anything about the human ～? 你了解有关人类胚胎的知识吗？

emend / ɪmend / vt. 校订,校勘；修订,修改（作品等）：～ the text of a book 校订书中正文 / The terms of the agreement should be ～ed to take the new conditions into account. 考虑到新的情况,协议书的条款应该修改。派 emendation n.

emerge / ɪˈmɜːdʒ / vi. 出现；浮现：The moon ～d from behind the clouds. 月亮从云后露出来。同 appear 反 disappear

emergency / ɪˈmɜːdʒənsi / n. 紧急情况；突发事件；非常时期：The state of ～ in that district has ended. 那个地区的紧急状态结束了。/ Please call an ～ ambulance to send her to hospital. 请叫一辆急救车送她去医院。同 crisis, urgency

emigrate / ˈemɪɡreɪt / v. 移居国外：He and the whole family ～d from Japan to America three years ago. 三年前他和他的全家从日本移民到美国去。反 immigrate

eminent / ˈemɪnənt / *adj.* ❶卓越的，杰出的；著名的，有名的；显赫的：The committee has 10 members, each ～ in his or her particular field. 该委员会有 10 名成员，他们在各自的领域内都是出类拔萃的。❷(品质)优秀的，突出的，非凡的；显著的；引人注目的：a man of ～ impartiality 大公无私的人/～ services 显著的贡献

emit / ɪˈmɪt / *vt.* (emitted; emitting) 散发；放射；发射：The dead fish ～ted a terrible smell. 死鱼发出可怕的臭味。/ To ～ black smoke into the sky is not allowed. 向天空排放浓烟是不允许的。同 discharge, release 反 inject, absorb

emotion / ɪˈməʊʃn / *n.* [U] 感情；情绪；激动：deep ～ 深厚的感情/ mixed ～ 复杂的感情/ She was shaking with ～. 她激动得浑身发抖。同 feelings, passion 派 emotional *adj.*

辨析

emotion 为常用词，指情绪上从最微弱到最强烈之间的变化：Love, hatred and grief are emotions. 爱、恨和悲伤都是感情的流露。**feeling** 意为"感情；感觉"，指内在的或表露出来的强烈情感，也可指对某人或某物的感觉，常用复数：Don't hurt her feelings. 不要伤害她的感情。**passion** 意为"激情"，指强烈的情感：She could never put any passion into her singing. 她唱歌从来没有激情。

emperor / ˈempərə(r) / *n.* [C] 皇帝

emphasis / ˈemfəsɪs / *n.* 强调；重点：He spoke with ～ on the importance of learning English well. 他强调学好英语的重要性。同 stress, strength / lay (place, put) ～ on 强调：Some schools lay special ～ on improving the teaching conditions. 有些学校特别强调改善教学条件。

emphasize / ˈemfəsaɪz / *vt.* 强调；着重：She ～d the importance of good health. 她强调身体健康的重要。同 stress

empire / ˈempaɪə(r) / *n.* [C] 帝国：the Roman Empire 罗马帝国

employ / ɪmˈplɔɪ / *vt.* 雇用；使用：She ～s her time wisely. 她善于利用时间。/ He was ～ed in a bank. 他受雇于一家银行。同 hire, engage 反 fire, dismiss 派 employee, employer *n.*

employment / ɪmˈplɔɪmənt / *n.* [U] 职业；工作：an ～ opportunity 就业机会 / the ～ rate 就业率 / a system of ～ under contract (合同)聘用制 / He has find ～. 他已找到工作。同 job, occupation, profession 反 unemployment

empower / ɪmˈpaʊə(r) / *vt.* 授权，准许：I ～ my agent to make the deal for me. 我授权我的代理人处理此项交易。/ His assistant will be ～ed to act on his behalf in less weighty matters. 他的助理被授权代他处理那些次要事务。

empty / ˈempti / Ⅰ *adj.* 空的；未占用的；空虚的：The box is ～. 箱子是空的。/ I found an ～ seat in the bus. 我在公共汽车上找到一个空座位。/ I don't want to hear your ～ talk. 我不想听你讲空话。同 bare, vacant, blank, meaningless 反 full, occupied, meaningful Ⅱ *v.* 倒空；变空：The room emptied very quickly. 房子很快就腾空了。/ The dustbins haven't been emptied for two weeks. 垃圾箱已有两个星期没倒过了。同 clear, discharge 反 fill, pack

辨析

empty 意为"空的"，普通用词：an empty talk 空谈；These are all empty bottles. 这些都是空瓶子。**hollow** 意为"空心的"，指物体中间是空的，也指说话空洞：a hollow tree 一棵空心树；a hollow ball 空心球；hollow promise (talk) 空洞的许诺(空谈)。**vacant** 指房间无人居住，还可表示职位的空缺：He bought a vacant piece of land. 他买了一块空地。a vacant seat 空位；a vacant room 没被占据的房间；fill a vacant position 补空缺职位。

enable / ɪˈneɪbl / *vt.* 使…能够 同 allow, permit/～ sb. to do sth. 使某人能做某事：A fast car ～s them to reach Beijing before midnight. 高速汽车能使他们在午夜前赶到北京。

encircle / ɪnˈsɜːkl / *vt.* 环绕；围绕；包围：The scientist was ～d by hundreds of young students. 科学家被几百名年轻学生围住了。同 surround

enclose / ɪnˈkləʊz / *vt.* ❶围住；圈起：The teacher ～d the wrong words with a circle. 老师把错字圈起来。同 encircle, surround ❷封入；附上：He ～d a check in the letter to his daughter. 他随信给女儿附寄了一张支票。同 envelop, attach 反 open

encounter / ɪnˈkaʊntə(r) / *v.* 遭遇；意外遇见：～ difficulties 遇到困难/ ～ an old friend 偶遇一位老朋友 同 face, meet

encourage / ɪnˈkʌrɪdʒ / *vt.* 鼓励；促进：The

good news of her success ～d me greatly. 她成功的喜讯极大地鼓励了我。同 inspire, urge 反 discourage／～ **sb. to do sth.** 鼓励某人做某事：He always ～s me to do the same. 他总是鼓励我做同样的事。

encyclopedia ／ɪnˌsaɪkləˈpiːdɪə／ n. [C] 百科全书：He needs an ～ of agriculture. 他需要一部农业百科全书。

end ／end／ Ⅰ n. [C] 端；尖；尽头；结束；目的，目标：I have read the book from beginning to ～. 我把那本书从头至尾读了一遍。／ They have traveled through the whole country by the ～ of the year. 到年底为止他们已游遍全国。／ In order to attain his ～, he worked very hard. 为了达到目的，他十分努力地工作。同 tip, finish, conclusion, aim 反 beginning, start／ **in the ～** 最后；终于：I am sure everything will turn out all right in the ～. 我确信最终一切都会好起来的。**no ～** 无穷：That would help us no ～. 那对我们的帮助是无法估量的。**on ～** 竖着；继续地：Place the box on ～. 把箱子竖起来放。／ We stood there for three hours on ～. 我们在那里一连站了三个小时。**put an ～ to** 终止；结束：We must put an ～ to this foolish behavior. 我们必须中止这种愚蠢的行为。Ⅱ v. 结束；终止：Wine ～ed him. 喝酒使他丧了命。／ He ～ed his speech with a proposal. 他以一个建议结束了讲话。同 stop, finish 反 begin, start

辨析

end 意为"终止；终结"，指突然停止，也指自然结束：The young man ended his life in this way. 这位青年以这种方式结束了他的生命。**finish** 意为"完成，结束"，指完成某项任务或达到预定目标：What time does the concert finish? 音乐会几点钟结束？**close** 意为"终结，关闭"，常指结束、关闭，也常用来表示会议、讲话等的结束：He hurriedly closed his speech with a funny joke. 他用一句有趣的笑话匆匆地结束了讲演。

endanger ／ɪnˈdeɪndʒə(r)／ vt. 危及；危害；使危险：Smoking ～s man's health. 吸烟危害人类健康。同 risk, hazard 反 save, protect

endeavo(u)r ／ɪnˈdevə(r)／ Ⅰ vi. 努力；尽力：He ～s to keep things nice about his place. 他努力把他周围的环境整得很优雅。同 try, strive Ⅱ n. [C] 努力；尽力：Her ～s to

persuade him to go with her but failed. 她尽力劝他同她一起去，但失败了。同 effort, attempt

ending ／ˈendɪŋ／ n. [C] 结尾；结局：A good ～ is better than a good beginning. 好的结尾胜过好的开头。同 end, finish 反 beginning, start

endless ／ˈendləs／ adj. 无穷无尽的；没完没了的：～ discussion 无休止的讨论／ ～ talk 冗长的谈话 反 limited

endure ／ɪnˈdjʊə(r)／ v. 忍受；忍耐：I can't ～ her impoliteness. 我不能容忍她的无礼。同 bear, stand

enduring ／ɪnˈdjʊərɪŋ／ adj. 持久的；不朽的：～ peace 永久和平 同 lasting, permanent

enemy ／ˈenəmi／ n. [C] 敌人；仇敌；敌军：The soldiers fired at the ～. 战士们向敌人开火。同 rival, opponent 反 friend, ally

energetic ／ˌenəˈdʒetɪk／ adj. 积极的；有力的；精力旺盛的：To play basketball needs ～ players. 打篮球需要精力旺盛的运动员。同 active, vigorous 反 inactive, idle

energy ／ˈenədʒi／ n. 能量；精力；活力：mental and physical energies 脑力和体力／ solar ～ 太阳能／ youthful ～ 青春活力／ atomic ～ 原子能／ ～ sources 能源／ We welcome ～-saving products. 我们乐意接纳节能型产品。同 power, vigor, strength

enforce ／ɪnˈfɔːs／ vt. 实行；执行；强制：These rules should be ～d strictly. 这些规则应当严格执行。同 execute, urge 派 enforcement n.

engage ／ɪnˈɡeɪdʒ／ v. ❶从事；忙于；参加：be ～d in(on) sth. 忙于；从事于：He has been ～d in foreign trade for eight years. 他从事外贸工作八年了。同 involve, participate ❷占用(时间等)：The line is ～d. (电话)占线。Network games has ～d all his time. 玩网络游戏占去了他的所有时间。同 occupy, take ❸雇用；聘用：They broke a rule to ～ the young man as sales manager. 他们破格录用那位年轻人作为销售部经理。同 employ, hire 反 dismiss, fire ❹订婚：be ～d to sb. 与某人订婚：He is ～d to his secretary. 他和他的秘书订婚了。～ for 担保，保证：That is more than I can ～ for. 我可负不了这么大的责任。派 engagement n.

engine ／ˈendʒɪn／ n. [C] 发动机；引擎：There is something wrong with the fire ～. 消防车出

了点毛病。同 motor

engineer / ˌendʒɪ'nɪə(r) / n. [C] 工程师；技师；火车司机；～s and technicians 工程技术人员 同 designer，operator，driver

engineering / ˌendʒɪ'nɪərɪŋ / n. [U] 工程；工程学：space ～ 航天工程/ genetic ～遗传工程/ system ～ 系统工程/ My brother studies at an ～ college. 我哥哥在一所工学院上学。

England / 'ɪŋɡlənd / n. 英格兰；(泛指)英国

English / 'ɪŋɡlɪʃ / I n. 英语：He speaks ～ well. 他英语说得很好。/ I write diary in ～. 我用英语写日记。II adj. 英国的；英语的：She made friends with an ～ girl. 她和一个英国女孩交朋友。/ I like to read ～ novels. 我喜欢读英语小说。

Englishman / 'ɪŋɡlɪʃmən / n. [C] (pl. Englishmen) 英国人；英国男子 反 Englishwoman

engrave / ɪn'ɡreɪv / vt. ❶雕，雕刻，在…上雕刻：～ the ring in a floral pattern 把戒指刻成花卉图案 ❷使深深印入，铭刻；使铭记：childhood experiences ～d in our memory 深深印在我们记忆中的童年时代的往事

enjoy / ɪn'dʒɔɪ / vt. 享受…的乐趣；喜爱；欣赏：Children ～ swimming in summer. 孩子们夏天喜爱游泳。/ We ～ sports very much. 我们非常喜爱运动。同 have，hold，like/ ～ **oneself** 过得快乐：Did you ～ yourselves during the winter vacation? 你们寒假过得愉快吗? 派 enjoyment n.

用法
enjoy 后面接动名词，不接不定式。(正) He enjoys dancing. (误) He enjoys to dance.

enlarge / ɪn'lɑːdʒ / vt. 扩大；放大；增大：～ a photograph 放大照片/ ～ one's views 开阔视野 同 broaden，expand，widen 反 decrease，shrink 派 enlargement n.

enlighten / ɪn'laɪtn / vt. 启发，启迪；指导，教育；使明白，使领悟：Radio should ～ the listener as well as entertain him. 无线电广播应该使听众既得到娱乐又受到教育。/ Can you ～ me on the nature of your research project? 你能不能给我讲讲你的研究项目的性质? 派 enlightenment n.

enmity / 'enmɪti / n. [U；C] 敌意，憎恨，仇恨；敌对，不和：be at ～ with 与…不和/ have ～ against 对…怀有仇恨(或敌意)

enormous / ɪ'nɔːməs / adj. 巨大的；庞大的：They held the meeting in an ～ hall. 他们在一个庞大的礼堂里开会。/ Where did you get such an ～ sum of money? 你从什么地方弄到了这么一大笔钱? 同 huge，vast，tremendous 反 small，little 派 enormously adv.

enough / ɪ'nʌf / I adj. 足够的；充足的：Five men will be quite ～. 五个人就足够了。/ Do you have ～ time to help me with my lessons? 你有时间帮助我复习功课吗? 同 plenty，sufficient II pron. 充足；足够：I have ～ to do. 我有好多事情要做。III adv. 足够地；充分地：The children are old ～ to go to school. 孩子们已到上学的年龄了。同 sufficiently

用法
enough 作形容词时可置于所修饰词之前或之后，若作副词则只能置于所修饰的词之后：We have enough time. 我们有足够的时间。This room is big enough to hold 200 people. 这房间很大，足以容纳 200 人。He writes well enough. 他写得够好了。

enquire / ɪn'kwaɪə(r) / v. 询问，调查 (见 inquire)

enquiry / ɪn'kwaɪəri / n. 询问，调查 (见 inquiry)

enrich / ɪn'rɪtʃ / vt. ❶使富裕；使丰富：Our government has issued a lot of good policies to ～ the people. 我们的政府颁布了许多富民的好政策。/ She studied hard to ～ the mind with knowledge. 她努力学习知识以增长才智。同 improve，refine ❷使(土地)肥沃：They ～ed the soil with fertilizer. 他们施肥使土壤肥沃。同 fertilize 派 enrichment n.

enrol(l) / ɪn'rəʊl / vt. (-rolled；-rolling) 登记；招收：The school is going to ～ 300 new students this year. 今年学校要招收 300 名新生。同 register，enlist —vi. 参军；注册；成为会员：Her son ～ed himself in the army two years ago. 她儿子两年前参军了。/ I have ～ed for three new courses. 本期我注册修三门新课。同 join，register 派 enrollment n.

enslave / ɪn'sleɪv / vt. 使做奴隶；奴役：The captures there were ～d and ill-treated. 那里的战俘们受到奴役和虐待。

ensure / ɪn'ʃʊə(r) / vt. ❶保证；担保：The doctor often tells his patients that a good rest ～s quicker recovery. 大夫常常告诉病人好好休息能保证身体早日康复。同 assure，guarantee

❷保护;使安全:A teacher should have the responsibility to ～ his students against danger. 教师应当有责任保护学生免遭危险。同 protect,secure

entangle / ɪn'tæŋɡl / vt. ❶缠绕,缠住;使纠缠:The bird got ～d in the net. 鸟给网圈套住了。❷使卷入;使陷入(困难等);牵涉,牵连:He ～d himself in the activities of a group of criminals. 他卷入了一伙罪团伙的活动中。

enter / 'entə(r) / v. 进入;参加;加入:She ～ed the room. 她进了房间。/ My brother ～ed university two years ago. 两年前我哥哥上了大学。/ Their products have ～ed the international market. 他们的产品已跻身国际市场。同 insert,join 反 leave

enterprise / 'entəpraɪz / n.[C]事业;企业

entertain / ,entə'teɪn / v. 使娱乐;使欢乐;使有兴趣;招待;款待:The Smiths ～ a great deal. 史密斯家常招待客人。/ The performance ～ed us very much. 我们饶有兴趣地看了那场演出。同 amuse,please,treat

entertainment / ,entə'teɪnmənt / n. ❶[U]招待;款待:He is busy preparing for the ～ of his old friend. 他正忙着准备接待老朋友。同 reception,treatment ❷[C]招待会:They will give a farewell ～ to the graduates next Monday. 他们下周一将为毕业生举行欢送会。同 reception ❸表演会;文娱:Young people like ～ films. 年轻人喜欢看娱乐片。同 performance,show

enthusiasm / ɪn'θjuːziæzəm / n. 热情;热心;热忱:The retired old man has a great ～ for fishing. 那位退休老人热衷于钓鱼。同 warmth,craze 反 indifference

enthusiastic / ɪn,θjuːzi'æstɪk / adj. 热情的;热心的:My classmates are all ～ football fans. 我的同班同学都是热心的足球球迷。/ She is ～ over the part-time job. 她对那份兼职工作充满热情。同 eager,passionate 反 cold,uninterested 派 enthusiastically adv.

entire / ɪn'taɪə(r) / adj. 全部的;整个的;完全的:She spent the ～ day reading the novel. 她花了一整天时间读那本小说。/ He has ～ confidence that his son will pass the college entrance examination. 他对儿子考上大学有完全的信心。同 all,complete,total,whole 反 incomplete,partial 派 entirety n.

entirely / ɪn'taɪəli / adv. 完全地;彻底地;全部

地;I agree to your plan ～. 我完全同意你的计划。同 totally,wholly,completely 反 partially

entitle / ɪn'taɪtl / vt. ❶ 给…权利(或资格):The disabled are still fully ～d to higher education. 残疾人也有充分的权利享受高等教育。同 authorize,qualify ❷给(书、文章)题名;给…称号:The writer ～d the book *Challenge*. 作者为那本书取名为《挑战》。同 name,label

entrance / 'entrəns / n. ❶[C] 入口;门口:They are talking at the ～ to the building. 他们在大楼门口交谈。同 door,entry 反 exit ❷进入;入学;入会:No ～. 禁止入内。He didn't take the ～ examination because he was ill. 由于生病他没有参加入学考试。同 access,admission

entreat / ɪn'triːt / vt. 恳求;乞求:He ～ed the judge for another chance. 他请求法官再给他一次机会。/I ～ your pardon. 请您原谅。

entrepreneur / ,ɒntrəprə'nɜː(r) / n.[C]企业家:The report was made by a successful ～. 报告由一位成功的企业家所作。

entrust / ɪn'trʌst / vt. 委托;信托;托管:Before leaving for London, she ～ed her house to her aunt. 去伦敦之前,她把房屋托付给她的婶婶代管。同 trust,leave

entry / 'entri / n. ❶[C]入口处;门口;通道:Don't stop your car at the ～ of the teaching building. 别在教学楼的入口处停车。同 entrance,doorway 反 exit ❷进入;入场;参赛:He is applying for the ～ to Harvard. 他正在申请进哈佛大学。/ Do you know when was China's first ～ into the Olympic Games? 你知道中国首次参加奥林匹克运动会是什么时候吗? 反 entrance,leaving

envelope / 'envələup / n.[C]信封:a standardized ～ 标准信封 / a pay ～ 工资袋 / She forgot to address the ～. 她忘了在信封上写收信人的姓名地址了。同 cover,wrapper

envious / 'enviəs / adj. 妒忌的;羡慕的:Don't be ～ of other's success. 不要妒忌他人的成功。/ I am ～ of his smartness. 我很羡慕他的精明机灵。同 jealous,green-eyed 反 generous

environment / ɪn'vaɪrənmənt / n. 环境;周围状况;外界:We should protect the ～ from pollution. 我们应当保护环境不遭受污染。/ He who pollutes the ～ should be punished severely. 污染环境的人应当受到严厉的惩罚。/

Everybody wants to have fine working ～. 所有人都希望有良好的工作环境。同 atmosphere, conditions, surroundings

environmental /ɪnˌvaɪrənˈmentəl/ *adj.* 环境的；环境产生的：～ monitoring 环境监测/ ～ program 环境规划/ ～ protection 环境保护

envy / ˈenvɪ / Ⅰ *vt.* 羡慕；妒忌：How I ～ you! 我真羡慕你！/ Don't ～ her good fortune. 不要羡慕她的好运气。Ⅱ *n.* [U]羡慕；妒忌：His success aroused her ～. 他的成功引起了她的妒忌(羡慕)。同 jealousy

enzyme / ˈenzaɪm / *n.* [C]酶

epic / ˈepɪk / Ⅰ *n.* [C] ❶史诗，叙事诗：a folk ～民间史诗 ❷史诗般的文艺作品；可歌可泣的事迹：the ～ of man's first journey to the moon 人类首次登月的可歌可颂的壮举 Ⅱ *adj.* ❶史诗的；史诗般的：an ～ poem 史诗 ❷宏大的，巨大规模的：a banquet of ～ proportions 盛大宴会

epidemic / ˌepɪˈdemɪk / *n.* [C] ❶(疾病的)流行，传播：an ～ of AIDS 艾滋病的蔓延 ❷流行病，传染病：～ s break out, spread, if they are not contained. 如不加以遏制，各种流行病就会爆发并传播开来。

episode / ˈepɪˌsəʊd / *n.* [C] ❶(一连串事件中的)一个事件；(人生的)一段经历：an ～ of one's childhood 某人童年时代的一段经历/an important ～ in our own history 我们历史中的重要篇章 ❷(连载小说中的)一节；连续剧的一出(或一集、一部分)：a TV drama serial of 20 ～s 一部 20 集的电视连续剧

epoch / ˈiːpɒk / *n.* [C]时代；纪元：The use of computers has marked an ～ in language teaching. 计算机的运用开创了语言教学的新纪元。同 era, age, time

equal / ˈiːkwəl / Ⅰ *adj.* 平等的；相等的：The women workers demanded ～ pay for ～ work. 女工们要求同工同酬。/ They are ～ in height. 他们身高相同。同 like, same Ⅱ *n.* 相同的事物；对手：I am not her ～ in swimming. 我游泳不是她的对手。同 match / ～ **to** 等于：Twice two is ～ to four. 二二得四(2 乘以 2 等于 4)。派 equally *adv.*

equality / ɪˈkwɒlətɪ / *n.* [U]等同；相等；平等：Our society should ensure the ～ of opportunity between the sexes in obtaining employment. 我们的社会应当确保男女就业的机会均等。

同 balance, equivalence 反 difference

equation / ɪˈkweɪʒn / *n.* [C]方程式；等式：The chemical ～ is interesting. 这个化学方程式很有趣。

equator / ɪˈkweɪtə(r) / *n.* (the ～) 赤道：The days and the nights are of equal length at the ～. 在赤道白天和夜晚的时间是相等的。

equilateral / ˌiːkwɪˈlætərəl/*adj.* 等边的：an ～ triangle 等边三角形

equilibrium / ˌiːkwɪˈlɪbrɪəm / *n.* (*pl.* equilibriums 或 equilibria) ❶ [U; C]平衡；均衡：maintain ～ on a tight rope 在绷紧的绳索上保持平衡/find an ～ between work and play 在工作和玩乐之间寻求平衡❷[U](心情的)平衡：preserve one's mind in a state of ～保持心境平和/David's ～ has been disturbed. 戴维心绪不宁。

equip / ɪˈkwɪp / *vt.* (equipped; equipping) 装备；配备：The students are fully ～ped for a long journey. 学生们装备齐全准备作一次长途旅行。/ Many offices are ～ped with computers and word processors now. 现在许多办公室都配有计算机和文字处理机。同 provide, furnish, arm

equipment / ɪˈkwɪpmənt / *n.* [U]装备；设备；器材：They installed the complete fire-fighting ～ for the factory. 他们为工厂安装了全套消防设备。同 apparatus, facilities, tools

equivalent / ɪˈkwɪvələnt / Ⅰ *adj.* 相等的；相当的；等量的；等值的：What is 100 dollars ～ to in RMB *yuan*? 100 美元相当于多少元人民币？/ The two sentences are ～ in meaning. 这两个句子意思相同。同 same, equal, similar 反 different, unequal Ⅱ *n.* [C]相等物；等价物；对应物：Please tell the Chinese ～ of this English word. 请说出与这个英语单词相对应的汉语。同 match, equal

er / ɜː(r) / *int.* (表示停顿或说话犹豫)哦

era / ˈɪərə / *n.* [C] 时代；年代；纪元：We have entered an entire new ～. 我们已经进入一个全新的时期。同 age, time, period

eradicate / ɪˈrædɪˌkeɪt / *vt.* 根除；杜绝；消灭：～ crime 杜绝犯罪/～ illiteracy 扫除文盲

erase / ɪˈreɪs / *vt.* 擦掉；删掉；除去：He ～d the wrong word with a rubber. 他用橡皮把错字擦掉。/ The boy asked the teacher not to ～ his name from the list. 男孩请求老师不要

把他的名字从名单上画掉。同 cancel, delete
派 eraser n.

erect / ɪˈrekt / vt. ❶使竖立；使起立：He ~
ed a television antenna on the roof. 他在屋顶
上架了一根电视接收天线。同 raise, elevate
❷ 建造；建立：The statue was ~ed in 2001.
那座塑像是 2001 年建的。同 build, construct
Ⅱ adj. 直立的；竖直的：He sat ~ to listen to
the teacher. 他端坐着听老师讲课。同
straight, upright 派 erection n.

erode / ɪˈrəʊd / vt. ❶腐蚀，侵蚀；蚀去：There
cliffs have been ~d (away) by the sea. 这些
峭壁已被海水侵蚀了。❷逐步毁坏；削弱：The
scandal has ~d his reputation. 这起丑闻使他
的名声不再。派 erosion n.

error / ˈerə(r) / n. [C] 过失；错误：The letter
was sent to him in ~. 那封信错送给他了。/
The teacher pointed his ~s in spelling. 老师指
出了他的拼写错误。同 fault, mistake

辨析

error 意为"过失；错误"，用法比 mistake 正
式，常指因不符合标准、不合规范而出的错：
There are three errors in your composition.
你的作文里有三处错误。**mistake** 意为"错
误；误会"，常指思想、行为不正确或判断、理
解错误：Sorry, I've made a big mistake. 对不
起，我犯了一个大错。**fault** 意为"过失；缺
点"，常指道德修养、个人习惯方面的小缺
点：This is not his fault. 这不是他的错。
shortcoming, weakness 意为"弱点；缺点；短
处"：We all have some shortcomings. 人人都
有缺点。You should admit your weaknesses. 你应该承认你的弱点。

erupt / ɪˈrʌpt / vi. 喷出；爆发：A glowing river
of lava ~ed from the volcano. 炽热的熔岩浆
从火山喷出。同 burst, explode 派 eruption n.

escalator / ˈeskəleɪtə(r) / n. [C]自动扶梯：
She took the ~ to the fifth floor. 她乘自动扶
梯到五楼。

escape / ɪˈskeɪp / v. 逃走；逃跑：He narrowly
~d with his life. 他死里逃生。同 flee, avoid /
~ **from** 逃脱；漏出：Gas ~d from the pipe. 煤
气从管子里漏出来了。

用法

escape 后常接动名词，即 escape doing sth. ，
相当于 avoid doing sth. (避免做某事)：She
escaped being punished. 她逃脱了惩罚。

Eskimo / ˈeskɪməʊ / Ⅰ n. (pl. Eskimo 或 Eskimos)[C] 爱斯基摩人；[U] 爱斯基摩语
Ⅱ adj. 爱斯基摩人的；爱斯基摩语的

especial / ɪˈspeʃl / adj. 特别的；特殊的：They
are discussing a question of ~ importance. 他
们正在讨论一个特别重要的问题。/ The oil
painting is of ~ value. 那幅油画具有特殊的
价值。同 special, particular 反 general, normal

especially / ɪˈspeʃəli / adj. 特别；尤其；格外：
It was ~ cold yesterday. 昨天天气特别冷。/
She writes well, ~ in English. 她的写作很好，
特别是英语写作。同 specially, particularly,
unusually 反 generally, normally

essay / ˈeseɪ / n. [C] 议论文；散文，随笔：I
wrote an ~ entitled My Friends. 我写了一篇
题为《我的朋友》的散文。同 article, thesis

essence / ˈesns / n. [U] 精华；本质；核心：He
didn't seize the ~ of the problem. 他没有抓住
问题的本质。同 spirit, nature, core / **in** ~ 本
质上：The two things are the same in outward
form but different in ~. 这两样东西的外表相
同，但本质不同。

essential / ɪˈsenʃ(ə)l / Ⅰ adj. 基本的；必不可
少的；必要的：Water is ~ to the growth of
crops. 水对庄稼的生长是必不可少的。同
necessary Ⅱ n. 本质；实质；要素：Diligence and
patience are basic ~s to success. 勤奋和耐心
是成功的基本要素。同 essence, element

establish / ɪˈstæblɪʃ / vt. 创立；创办；建立：The
building was ~ed on a solid base. 这幢大楼建立
在坚实的基础上。/ The school ~ed a new course
for students. 学校为学生开设了一门新课程。同
create, found 派 establishment n.

estate / ɪˈsteɪt / n. 房地产；财产；产业：real ~
development 房地产开发 / The young man inherited an ~ of 15 million dollars. 那年轻人
继承了 150 万美元遗产。同 land, property

esteem / ɪˈstiːm / Ⅰ n. [U] 尊敬；尊重：We
have a great ~ for our English teacher. 我们
对我们的英语老师非常敬重。同 respect, admiration 反 contempt Ⅱ vt. 尊敬；尊重：We ~
him for his great achievements in scientific research. 由于他在科研上获得巨大成就，我们
非常尊重他。同 respect, admire 反 contempt

esthetic / iːsˈθetɪk / adj. (=aesthetic)审美的；
美学的：According to my ~ standards, the
room is decorated quite well. 依照我的审美标

E

准看，这房间装饰得相当好。派 esthetics n.

estimate / ˈestɪmeɪt / vt. 估价；估计：He cannot be too highly ~d. 对他的评价再高也不过分。同 value，judge

> **辨析**
>
> **estimate** 指一种猜测性的估价、估计，估计结果可能对，也可能错：I estimate her age at 35. 我估计她有 35 岁。**evaluate** 多指评估人或物的内在价值：She evaluates people by their clothes. 她根据衣着来评价人。**appraise** 多指由专家评定，强调估计的结果是正确的、不容置疑的：Property is appraised for taxation. 估算财产以课其税。**assess** 指对某物进行估价以课税或罚款：They assess his house at 150,000 yuan. 他们给他的房子估价为 15 万元。

etc. / etˈsetərə / (拉丁文 et cetera 的缩写) 等等

eternal / ɪˈtɜːnl / adj. 永久的；永恒的：Do you believe in ~ life? 你相信生命永恒(不朽)吗？同 endless，everlasting，permanent 反 temporary

ethical / ˈeθɪkl / adj. 伦理的；道德的：~ education 伦理教育 / ~ principle 道德原则 同 moral

ethics / ˈeθɪks / n. [U] 伦理(学)；道德(学)：professional ~ 职业道德/ A doctor should have medical ~. 一个医生应当有好的医德。

euro / ˈjʊərəʊ / n. [C] 欧元：People use ~s in that country. 在那个国家人们使用欧元。

Europe / ˈjʊərəp / n. 欧洲

European / ˌjʊərəˈpiːən / Ⅰ adj. 欧洲的 Ⅱ n. [C] 欧洲人

evade / ɪˈveɪd / vt. ❶(巧妙地)逃开，逃脱；躲开：~ the pursuit 逃避追捕 ❷逃避(责任等)；回避(问题等)：He had found a loophole which allowed him to ~ responsibility. 他找到了逃避责任的可乘之隙。派 evasion n.

evaluate / ɪˈvæljueɪt / vt. 评价；估价；把…定值：The manager ~s his ability through his work. 经理通过工作评价他的能力。/ Don't ~ people by clothes. 别以衣着论人。同 estimate，assess，judge

evaluation / ɪˌvæljuˈeɪʃn / n. [U] 估计；评价；评估：an ~ system 评价体系/ the ~ of professional titles 职称评定/ job ~ 工作评估 同 estimation，assessment，judgment

evaporate / ɪˈvæpəreɪt / v. 蒸发；挥发；脱水：The sun ~d the water on the road. 阳光把地上的水蒸发干了。/ They brought some ~d vegetables with them on their journey. 旅行中他们带了些脱水蔬菜。同 dry，steam，dissolve

eve / iːv / n. [C] (节日的)前夜，前夕：on the ~ of 在…前夕/ New Year's Eve 除夕/ They had a big party on Christmas Eve. 在平安夜他们举行了一场盛大的晚会。

even¹ / ˈiːvn / adv. 甚至；还；更：Making model boats is ~ more difficult than making model planes. 做模型船比做模型飞机还要困难。同 still，moreover，much/~ **if** (**though**) 即使：We'll go ~ if he doesn't come. 即使他不来我们也要去。

even² / ˈiːvn / adj. ❶均匀的；平稳的；平坦的：She does an ~ work in the company. 她在那家公司干一份稳定的工作。/ They are going to build an airport on the ~ land. 他们将在那块平地上建造机场。同 regular，steady，flat 反 irregular，uneven ❷相当的；均等的：My desk is ~ with the window. 我的书桌与窗户一般高。同 equal 反 unequal ❸双数的；偶数的：Is 126 an ~ number or an odd number? 126 是偶数还是奇数？反 odd 派 evenly adv.

evening / ˈiːvnɪŋ / n. 晚上；傍晚；黄昏：The ~ draws on. 夜晚来临。/ He writes in the ~. 他在晚上写作。反 morning

> **用法**
>
> 特指在某日的晚上用 on the evening of：I last saw him on the evening of October 25. 我最后一次见到他是在 10 月 25 日晚上。

event / ɪˈvent / n. [C] ❶大事；事件；时事：current ~s 时事/ a national ~ 国内大事/ an ordinary ~ 平常事/ Marriage is quite an ~ to everybody. 对每个人来说婚姻都是一件大事。同 affair，incident/**in any** ~ 不管怎样；反正：In any ~ I'll telephone you before I make a final decision. 不管怎样，我在作出最后决定前都会打电话给你。❷(运动的)比赛项目：field and truck ~s 田径赛/ a team ~ 团体赛 同 game

eventually / ɪˈventʃuəli / adv. 最后；终于：He worked day and night and ~ made himself ill. 他日夜不停地工作，终于病倒了。同 finally

ever / ˈevə(r) / adv. 任何时候；曾经：Have you ~ been to the Great Wall? 你去过长城吗？

evergreen / ˈevəɡriːn / Ⅰ adj. 常绿的：~ foliage 常绿的树叶 Ⅱ n. [C] 常绿植物；万年青：

Most tropical plants are ～s. 大多数热带植物是常绿植物。

everlasting / ˌevəˈlɑːstɪŋ / adj. ❶永恒的，不朽的；无穷无尽的：the ～ beauty of the nature 大自然永恒的美 ❷持久的；不停的：the ～ snows of the mighty Himalayas 雄伟的喜马拉雅山脉的常年积雪

every / ˈevri / adj. 每个的；每一的；所有的：He goes to the school library ～ morning. 他每天上午去学校图书馆。同 each, all/～ other 每隔：I go to see my grandmother ～ other week. 每隔一周我都去看望我的祖母。

everybody / ˈevrɪbɒdi / pron. (= every-one) 每个人；人人：Everybody says it is a good film. 人人都说这是一部好影片。/ Not ～ likes to watch TV. 并不是每个人都喜欢看电视。同 each, all 反 nobody, none

everyday / ˈevrideɪ / adj. 每日的；日常的：～ life 日常生活/ She learned some ～ English. 她学会了一些日常英语。同 daily, common, usual

everyone / ˈevriwʌn / pron. (= every-body) 每人；人人

everything / ˈevriθɪŋ / pron. 一切事物；每件事；I want to teach my students ～ I know. 我要把我所知道的一切都教给我的学生。/ She did ～ carefully. 她把每件事都仔细地做好。同 all 反 nothing

everywhere / ˈevriweə(r) / adv. 处处；到处：Everywhere the delegation went, it was warmly welcomed. 代表团无论走到哪里，都受到热烈的欢迎。/ I looked ～ for my glasses but failed. 我到处找眼镜都没有找到。反 nowhere

evidence / ˈevidəns / n. ❶根据；证据：The corrupted official attempted to destroy the ～ of his guilt. 那贪官企图毁灭罪证。同 proof, witness ❷迹象；征兆：There is ～ that he has arrived at the remote village. 有迹象表明他已经到达那个边远的村庄。

evident / ˈevidənt / adj. 明显的；明白的：It is ～ that she didn't understand what the teacher meant. 很明显她并没有弄清楚老师的意思。同 clear, obvious 反 doubtful 派 evidently adv.

evil / ˈiːvl / Ⅰ n. 邪恶；罪恶；恶行：The teacher should often tell his students the ～s of smoking. 老师应当常给学生讲抽烟的坏处。/ Don't speak ～ of people behind their backs.

不要背后说人坏话。同 sin, mischief 反 good, virtue Ⅱ adj. 邪恶的；坏的；罪恶的：Everybody knows his ～ deeds in the village. 村里所有的人都知道他的罪恶行径。同 cruel, wicked, immoral 派 evilly adv.

evoke / ɪˈvəuk / vt. ❶使回忆起；使产生（共鸣、联想等）：That old film ～d memories of my childhood. 那部老影片使我回忆起童年时代。❷引起，激起：～ reaction 引起反响/His words ～d an angry reply. 他的话引起了愤怒的反应。

evolution / ˌiːvəˈluːʃn / n. [U]进化；发展；演变：The ～ of man took over millions of years. 人类的进化经历了数百万年时间。同 development, progress

exact / ɪɡˈzækt / adj. 正确的；精密的；准确的：His translation is ～ to the letter. 他的翻译非常确切。同 right, correct, precise 反 incorrect, inexact

exactly / ɪɡˈzæktli / adv. 确切地；恰好；正是：That's ～ what I want. 这正是我想要的东西。同 correctly, definitely

exaggerate / ɪɡˈzædʒəreit / vt. 夸张，夸大：It is ～d purposely. 这事被故意夸大了。同 overestimate, overdo

exam / ɪɡˈzæm / n. (examination 的缩写形式) [C]考试

examination / ɪɡˌzæmɪˈneiʃn / n. ❶考试；考查：attend an ～参加考试/ fail in an ～ 考试不及格/ pass an ～ 考试合格/ a final ～ 期终考试同 test, exam, quiz ❷检查；调查：The doctor asked him to have a medical (physical) ～ every year. 大夫要求他每年进行一次体检。同 inspection, investigation

examine / ɪɡˈzæmin / vt. ❶检查；仔细观察：The engineer is examining the machine to see if it has any defects. 那工程师正仔细检查机器是否有什么毛病。同 check, inspect, study ❷对…进行考试（考查）：The teacher ～d his students in mathematics. 老师考查学生的数学学得如何。同 test, exam, quiz

example / ɪɡˈzɑːmpl / n. [C]例子，范例；榜样：A Party member should set a good ～ to others. 共产党员应当为他人树立好榜样。/ Please cite a few ～s to explain the problem. 请举几个例子来说明这个问题。同 case, model/for ～ 例如：She likes sports, for ～, swimming and skiing. 她非常喜欢运动，比如

游泳、滑雪。

exceed / ɪkˈsiːd / vt. 超过；胜过；超出：A driver who ~s the speed limit of 120 miles in this road will be punished. 司机在这段路驾驶超过120英里的时速限制将会受到处罚。同 overtake，surpass

exceedingly / ɪkˈsiːdɪŋli / adv. 极度地；非常地；极大地：He is ~ generous toward his friends. 他对朋友极其慷慨大方。同 extremely

excel / ɪkˈsel / (-celled;-celling) v. ❶超过，胜过；优于：He ~s us all at cooking. 他的烹饪手艺胜过我们大家。/ ~ oneself 超越自我 ❷擅长；(在…方面)突出：He ~s at tennis. 他擅长打网球。

excellent / ˈeksələnt / adj. 优秀的；杰出的；极好的：He was ~ in English. 他英语极好。/ Her ~ composition received high praise. 她的优秀作文受到极大称赞。同 fine，outstanding

except / ɪkˈsept / prep. 除…外：Everybody is ready ~ her. 除她以外人人都准备好了。同 excluding 反 including / ~ for 除…外；除…之外：The film is good ~ for the ending. 除了结尾之外，这部电影很好看。

exception / ɪkˈsepʃn / n. 例外；除外：Most boys like to play football, but Jimmy is an ~. 大多数男孩都喜欢踢足球，但吉米却是个例外。/ Everyone went to swim that afternoon with the ~ of Mike. 除了迈克以外，那天下午大家都去游泳了。同 exclusion 派 exceptional adj.

excess / ɪkˈses / Ⅰ n. 超越；超过；过量；过度：The ~ of rain ruined the crops. 雨水过多毁坏了庄稼。同 exceeding，surplus 反 lack，shortage Ⅱ adj. 过量的；额外的：A passenger must pay for his ~ luggage. 行李超重乘客须付钱。同 extra，additional 反 inadequate 派 excessively adv.

exchange / ɪksˈtʃeɪndʒ / v. 交换；调换；交流；兑换：May I ~ seats with you? 我可以和你调换一下座位吗？/ Our teacher often ~s ideas with us. 我们的老师经常和我们交流意见。/ He ~d Renminbi for foreign money before he went abroad. 出国前他把人民币兑换成外币。同 change，interchange，convert

excite / ɪkˈsaɪt / vt. 兴奋，激动：It's nothing to get ~d about. 这没有什么值得激动的。/ Don't get ~d over such a little matter. 不要为这样的小事情兴奋。同 arouse 反 bore

excitement / ɪkˈsaɪtmənt / n. [U] 兴奋；激动：They jumped in ~ when they knew that they won the champion. 得知赢得了冠军，他们兴奋得跳起来。反 calm，quiet，peace

exciting / ɪkˈsaɪtɪŋ / adj. 令人兴奋的；使人激动的：We were glad when we heard the ~ news. 听到那振奋人心的消息，我们都非常高兴。同 moving，arousing

exclaim / ɪkˈskleɪm / v. 呼喊，惊叫；大声说：The passengers ~ed in despair when the bus was dropping down the bridge. 汽车掉下桥时乘客们都绝望地叫喊起来。同 proclaim，cry，shout

exclamation / ˌekskləˈmeɪʃn / n. ❶[U]呼喊；惊叫；惊叹：She made an ~ of joy when she knew she had passed the examination. 知道考试及格了，她大声欢呼起来。同 cry，shout ❷[C] 感叹词；惊叹语：He used an ~ mark at the end of the sentence. 他在句末用了一个惊叹号。

exclude / ɪkˈskluːd / vt. 把…排除在外；排斥；拒绝：Parents should ~ their children from watching such a horrible film. 父母应拒绝让孩子们看这种恐怖电影。同 ban，reject，refuse 反 admit，allow，include

exclusive / ɪkˈskluːsɪv / adj. 除外的；排他的；专有的：The shop has the ~ right to sell the products of this factory. 该商店有出售这家工厂产品的专卖权。/ The card is ~ to members only. 这种卡只限会员使用。反 inclusive，unshared 派 exclusively adv.

excursion / ɪkˈskɜːʃn / n. 短途旅行；集体游览：The whole family made a day ~ to the suburb of London. 全家人到伦敦郊区一日游。同 trip，outing

excuse Ⅰ / ɪkˈskjuːz / vt. 原谅；宽恕；辩解：Excuse me，may I have a word with you? 对不起，我可以和你谈一谈吗？/ You can't ~ yourself for your mistake. 你不可以为自己的错误辩解。同 forgive，justify Ⅱ / ɪksˈkjuːs / n. [C] 借口；托词：Some students found ~s for not being on time. 有些学生为他们迟到找借口。同 reason

execute / ˈeksɪkjuːt / vt. ❶执行；实行：Your order will be ~d as speedily as possible. 你的命令将尽快被执行。同 enforce，perform ❷处决；处死：He was ~d with fire. 他被处以火刑。同 kill

execution /ˌeksɪˈkjuːʃn/ *n.* [U]执行；行刑：He was perfect in the ～ of his duties. 他执行任务丝毫不差。同performance, killing

executive /ɪɡˈzekjətɪv/ *n.* [C]执行者；总经理；董事：a chief ～ 营业主管/ He is chief ～ officer (CEO) of the company. 他是公司的首席执行官。同director, manager, administrator

exemplify /ɪɡˈzemplɪfaɪ/ *vt.* ❶以示例说明；举例证明：He exemplifies the hopes and confidence we have in the future of the past-cold war world. 他举例说明了我们在冷战后世界的未来里所有的希望和信心。❷作为…的例证(或榜样、典型等)：The novel *Tom Sawyer* exemplifies 19-century life in the United States. 长篇小说《汤姆·索耶历险记》是美国19世纪生活的缩影。

exercise /ˈeksəsaɪz/ *n.* [C]练习；锻炼：morning ～s 早操/ outdoor ～s 户外运动/ The doctor told him to take more ～. 医生告诉他要多运动。同drilling, training, practice

exert /ɪɡˈzɜːt/ *vt.* 运用，行使(权利等)；发挥(作用)；施加(影响)：～ authority 行使权利/ ～ pressure on 对某人施加压力 / ～ **one-self** 使用力，使尽力：If you ～ yourself you can finish the task on time. 如果你加把劲，你就能按时完成任务。

exhaust /ɪɡˈzɔːst/ *v.* 用尽；耗尽：～ one's strength 用尽了力气/Climbing up the mountain ～ed him. (＝He was ～ed by climbing the mountain.)爬山使他筋疲力尽。同tire, consume / **be ～ed with** 因…筋疲力尽：I am ～ed with toil. 我劳累不堪。

exhibit /ɪɡˈzɪbɪt/ Ⅰ *v.* 陈列；展览；显示：The product was ～ed at a World Fair. 这种产品曾在世界博览会上展出。/ She ～ed great interest in pandas. 她对大熊猫表示出极大的兴趣。同show, display, express Ⅱ *n.* [C]展品；陈列品：Do not touch the ～ s. 请勿触摸展品。同show

exhibition /ˌeksɪˈbɪʃn/ *n.* [C]展览；展览会：They will hold a sales ～ at the end of this month in our city. 本月底他们将在我市举办展销会。同show, display

exile /ˈeksaɪl/ Ⅰ *n.* ❶[U]放逐；流放：The court condemned the criminal to ～. 法庭判犯人流放刑。/ He wrote those poems in ～. 那些诗是他流放期间写的。同banishment ❷[C]被放逐者，流亡者：a political ～ 政治流亡者 同outcast, refugee Ⅱ *vt.* 放逐，使充军，支配 同banish, deport

exist /ɪɡˈzɪst/ *vi.* 存在；生存：We cannot ～ without air, food or water. 没有空气、食物和水，我们就不能生存。同live, survive 反die / ～ **on** 靠…生存：She ～s on tea and bread. 她靠茶和面包维生。

existence /ɪɡˈzɪstəns/ *n.* [U]现实；存在；生存；生活：This is the largest ship in ～. 这是全世界现存的最大船只。同being, life, survival 反death

exit /ˈeksɪt/ *n.* [C] ❶出口；安全门；太平门：There are two emergency ～s in this theater. 这个剧场有两个紧急出口。同outlet, doorway 反entrance ❷退场；退出：The actors and actresses made their ～ from the door at the back of the stage. 男女演员们从舞台后面的门退场了。同retreat, departure

exotic /ɪɡˈzɒtɪk/ *adj.* ❶外(国)来的；外国产的，非本地产的：There are many restaurants with ～ foods in this city. 在这座城市里有很多外国风味的餐厅。❷奇异的；异国情调的：He loves ～ clothes and travelling the ～ places. 他喜欢穿奇装异服，到充满异国情调的地方去旅游。

expand /ɪkˈspænd/ *v.* 扩大；扩充；膨胀：As the plant grew, its flowers and leaves gradually ～ed. 随着植物的生长，它的叶子和花朵也逐渐张开了。同enlarge, extend, grow

expansion /ɪkˈspænʃn/ *n.* [U]扩充；膨胀：the ～ of gases 气体的膨胀/ the ～ of business 业务扩展 同enlargement, extension, development

expect /ɪkˈspekt/ *vt.* 期待；指望；预料：The woman is ～ing a telephone call from her son. 那妇女正在等她儿子的电话。同hope, wish, anticipate

用法 expect 后可接名词、不定式、从句，不能接动名词：She is expecting a letter from a friend. 她期待着朋友的来信。Little did I expect to meet him again. 我一点也没料到会再和他见面。I expect that you'll do your duty. 我期望你尽职尽责。

expectation /ˌekspekˈteɪʃn/ *n.* [U]期待；指望；预料：He has not much ～ of success. 他对成功不抱太大希望。同hope, anticipation

expel / ɪk'spel / vt. (-pelled;-pelling) 开除;驱除:He was ～led from school. 他被学校开除了。同 dismiss,drive

expense / ɪk'spens / n.［U］消费;费用;开支:We must keep down ～. 我们必须缩减开支。同 cost,charge /**at the ～ of** 以…为代价:He became a brilliant scholar at the ～ of his health. 他成了知名学者,但牺牲了自己的健康。

expensive / ɪk'spensɪv / adj. 昂贵的;花钱多的:A flat is too ～ for me (to buy). 一套公寓房对我来说太贵了,我买不起。/ She bought her daughter an ～ necklace. 她给女儿买了一条昂贵的项链。同 costly,high-priced 反 cheap,inexpensive 派 expensively adv.

experience / ɪk'spɪərɪəns / n. ❶［U］经验;体验:She has rich ～ in teaching English. 她教英语有丰富的经验。同 undergoing,practice ❷［C］经历;阅历:an pleasant ～ 一次愉快的经历 派 experienced adj.

experiment / ɪk'sperɪmənt / Ⅰ n.［C］实验;试验:make an ～ 做实验/ An interesting ～ is being carried out by Prof. Wang. 王教授正在做一个有趣的实验。同 test,trial Ⅱ vi. 进行试验:They are ～ing with a new drug. 他们正在试验一种新药。同 test 派 experimental adj.

expert / 'ekspɜːt / Ⅰ n.［C］专家;内行;能手:Professor Li is an ～ in economics. 李教授是一位经济学专家。同 master,specialist Ⅱ adj. 熟练的;老练的:He is an ～ driver. 他是一位老练的驾驶员。同 skillful,experienced,trained /**be ～ at (in)**熟练:He is ～ at figures. 他是计算的能手。

expertise / ˌekspɜː'tiːz / n.［U］专门技能(或知识);专长:management ～ 管理技能/ Landing a plane in fog takes a great deal of ～. 雾中降落飞机的技术含量很高。

expire / ɪk'spaɪə(r),ek'spaɪ(r) / vi. ❶期满,届满;(期限)终止;(合同、协议等)到期无效:The trade agreement will ～ at the end of this month. 贸易协定月底到期。❷呼气,吐气:The patient ～d irregularly. 病人的呼吸很不规则。

explain / ɪk'spleɪn / v. 解释;说明:She ～ed why she was late. 她解释了她迟到的原因。同 interpret,illustrate

explanation / ˌeksplə'neɪʃn / n. 解释;说明:I want to know the ～ for her being absent. 我想知道她缺席的理由是什么。同 account,illustration

explicit / ɪk'splɪsɪt / adj. ❶(解释说明)清楚的,明了的;明确的:a product with no ～ instruction 没有给出清楚的使用说明的产品 ❷坦率的,直言不讳的,毫无保留的:She was ～ with me about what she really felt. 她在我面前毫无保留地说出了她内心的真实感受。同 definite,specific

explode / ɪk'spləʊd / v. ❶爆炸;爆发:The country ～d another atom bomb. 那个国家又爆炸了一颗原子弹。同 burst,erupt,blow ❷(人的感情)发作:Hearing that he wanted to fly over the building,we ～d into laughter. 听说他想要从大楼上飞过去,我们哄然大笑起来。同 burst

exploit / ɪk'splɔɪt / vt. ❶剥削:The boss ～ed child labor cruelly. 那老板残酷地剥削童工。同 abuse ❷利用:They ～ed every possibility to develop local agriculture. 他们利用一切可能性发展当地农业。同 use,utilize,employ ❸开拓;开发;开采:The workers ～ed a new oil field. 工人们开采出一个新油田。同 use,utilize

exploration / ˌeksplə'reɪʃn / n. 考察;勘探;探查:He is interested in space ～. 他对太空探索很感兴趣。同 search,inspection,investigation

explore / ɪk'splɔː(r) / v. 探险;勘探;探索:The scientists ～d this district carefully. 科学家们对这一地区进行了仔细勘探。同 search,inspect,investigate

explosion / ɪk'spləʊʒn / n.［C］爆炸;爆发:The gas ～ caused twenty deaths. 瓦斯爆炸造成 20 人死亡。同 burst,outbreak

explosive / ɪk'spləʊsɪv / n. 炸药;爆炸物:They planted 120 packages of ～ at the bottom of the old building. 他们在那栋旧楼底部埋了120 包炸药。同 dynamite,TNT,powder

export Ⅰ / ɪk'spɔːt / vt. 输出;出口:The factory ～s toys to Africa. 这家工厂向非洲出口玩具。反 import Ⅱ / 'ekspɔːt / n. 出口;输出;出口商品:The products of this factory are for ～. 这家工厂的产品供出口。反 import

expose / ɪk'spəʊz / vt. 暴露;揭露:The press ～d the truth of the whole event. 报纸揭露了整个事件的真相。同 reveal,uncover 反 cover, conceal /～ to 暴露：His foolish actions ～d him to ridicule. 他的愚蠢行为使他落为笑柄。

exposure / ɪkˈspəʊʒə(r) / n. 揭露；暴露 同 show, disclosure

express / ɪkˈspres / I vt. (用语言、表情、动作)表达：The film ～es the author's love of his motherland. 影片表达出作者对祖国的热爱。同 say, show, declare II adj. 快的；快捷的：an ～ train 快车/an ～ mail 邮政快件 III n. 快车；快递；快运：He traveled by ～ around the country. 他乘快车游览全国。

expression / ɪkˈspreʃn / n. ❶ 表达；表现；表达方式：This gave ～ to the demands of the people. 这反映了人民的要求。/ Her smiling is an ～ of her pleasure. 她的微笑是她快乐的表现。同 indication ❷ 表情；脸色：There is a happy ～ on her face. 她的脸上带着喜悦的表情。同 look, appearance

expressive / ɪkˈspresɪv / adj. 富于表情的；富于表现力的；意味丰富的：an ～ voice, 富于表现力的嗓音/The girl has large ～ eyes. 那姑娘有一双会说话的大眼睛。

expressway / ɪkˈspresˌweɪ / n. [C]高速公路；(部分立体交叉的)快速干道：a four-lane ～ 一条四车道高速公路

extend / ɪkˈstend / v. 延长；延伸；扩大；扩充：The meeting ～ed late into the night. 会议一直开到深夜。/ The plains ～ far and wide. 平原向四面八方延伸。/ They ～ed the subway to the suburbs. 他们把地铁延伸到郊区。同 stretch, expand, spread

extension / ɪkˈstenʃn / n. ❶ 伸展；扩大；延长(扩大)部分：He asked a three-day ～ to his holidays. 他要求延长三天假期。同 enlargement, broadening, expansion, addition ❷ [C](电话)分机：Could I have ～ 8, please? 请帮我接 8 号分机，好吗？

extensive / ɪkˈstensɪv / adj. 广阔的；广泛的：A lot of ～ reading improved her English comprehension. 大量的泛读提高了她的英语理解能力。同 widespread, wide, vast 反 narrow, small

extent / ɪkˈstent / n. 区域；范围；长度；限度；程度：He has a farm of considerable ～. 他拥有一个相当大的农场。/ The worker is examining the ～ of damage to the machine. 工人在检查机器受损的程度。同 size, degree, limit /

to a certain ～ 部分地；有些；在一定程度上：I agree with you to a certain ～. 我部分同意你的意见。**to what** ～ 到什么程度：To what ～ can he be trusted? 他可靠到什么程度？

exterior / ɪkˈstɪəriə(r) / I adj. ❶外部的；外表的：The ～ walls of the building are old now. 这栋大楼的外墙很旧了。同 external, outer, outside 反 interior, inside ❷ 对外的；外交的：The country insists on its own ～ policy. 该国坚持自己的对外政策。同 foreign 反 domestic II n. 外部；外表：The ～ of the car is beautiful. 这车的外观很好看。同 appearance, outside 反 interior, inside 派 exteriorly adv.

external / ɪkˈstɜːnl / I adj. 外部的；外面的；外用的：This is only the ～ cause of the accident. 这只是这次事故的外因。/ The medicine is for ～ use only. 这药仅供外用。同 outward, outside 反 internal, inside II n. [C]外部；外形：She is kind by ～s. 从外表看她很和蔼。同 appearance, outside 反 internal, inside 派 externally adv.

extinct / ɪkˈstɪŋkt / adj. 绝种的；绝灭的；熄灭了的：Dinosaurs have become ～ for many years. 恐龙已经绝种许多年了。/ The scientists climbed up an ～ volcano. 科学家们爬上了一座死火山。同 extinguished, vanished 反 alive, living 派 extinction n.

extinguish / ɪkˈstɪŋgwɪʃ / vt. 熄灭；扑灭；消灭：They were anxious that they hadn't enough water to ～ the fire. 他们担心没有足够的水灭火。同 destroy, exterminate

extort / ɪkˈstɔːt / vt. 敲诈，勒索；侵吞：～ money from a pedestrian 从一位行人那里勒索钱财

extra / ˈekstrə / I adj. 额外的；外加的：I haven't any ～ time to go shopping with you today. 今天我没有多余的时间陪你去买东西。/ He took an ～ train to Tianjin. 他乘加班车去天津。同 additional, surplus II n. (pl.) ❶额外的人手；额外的事物 同 addition, attachment ❷附加费；另外的收费：The room ser·vice charges no ～s in this hotel. 在这家旅馆房间服务不额外收费。同 surcharge III adv. 特别地；格外地；非常：He has been busy with his thesis recently. 最近他做论文特别忙。同 especially, particularly, extremely

extract I / ɪkˈstrækt / vt. ❶拔出；抽出；取出：～ a bad tooth 拔掉坏牙 同 draw, pull, remove ❷ 提取；榨取：Mother ～ed some juice for the guests. 妈妈榨了一些果汁招待客人。圆 extort，press ❸ 摘要；摘录：He ～ed a good passage from the book as his opening speech. 他从那本书里摘录了一段好文章作为开幕词。Ⅱ / 'ekstrækt / n. [C] 摘录；选录；选段：She makes ～s from newspapers everyday. 她每天都摘录报纸。圆 abstract，excerpt 派 extraction n.

extradite / 'ekstrədait / vt. 引渡：The police ～d the murderer back to his own country for trial. 警方把杀人犯引渡回国接受审判。

extraordinary / ik'strɔːdnəri / adj. 非常的；非凡的；不寻常的：He is a man of ～ genius. 他是一个奇才。/ I don't like the ～ weather here. 我不喜欢这里反常的天气。圆 unusual，uncommon，remarkable 反 usual，common，ordinary

> **辨析**
> **extraordinary** 意为"非凡的；格外的"，指非常不一般的，令人吃惊的人或物：She was a girl of extraordinary beauty. 她是一位美丽非凡的姑娘。**special** 意为"特别的；特殊的"，指在性质、特征或用途等方面不同于一般：Is there anything special in the papers today? 今天报上有什么特殊消息吗？**singular** 意为"非凡的；突出的"，指同类中具有独特之处的人或物：a man of ～ courage 胆识超群的人。

extravagance(-cy) / ik'strævəgəns(i) / n. [U] 奢侈；浪费：We oppose ～ and waste. 我们反对铺张浪费。圆 waste，lavishness

extravagant / ik'strævəgənt / adj. 奢侈的；浪费的；过分的：She is ～ in life. 她生活奢侈。圆 wasteful，excessive 反 saving，economical，reasonable 派 extravagantly adv.

extreme / ik'striːm / Ⅰ adj. 极端的；极度的；末端的；尽头的：That is an ～ case. 那是一个极罕见的例子。/ I have been to the ～ south of the island. 我曾去过这岛的最南端。圆 absolute，farthest Ⅱ n. [C] 极端；极度：She is experiencing the ～ of joy in her life. 她正经历着一生最大的喜悦。/ **go to ～s** 走极端；采取极端手段：She goes to ～ in everything. 她凡事都走极端。**in (to) the (an) ～** 极端地；非常地：The building is magnificent in the ～. 那幢楼极为富丽堂皇。派 extremely adv.

extrude / ik'struːd / vt. 挤出，压出：～ toothpaste from the tube 从管子里挤出牙膏/The machine ～s noodles through holes. 这台机器从孔中把面条挤压出来。

eye / ai / n. [C] 眼睛；视力；视觉：The girl has beautiful blue ～s. 小女孩有一双漂亮的蓝眼睛。/ He has good (weak) ～s. 他的视力很好（差）。圆 sight，eyesight /**catch one's ～** 引人注目：The schoolboy caught his master's ～s. 小学生引起了他老师的注意。**keep an ～ on** 照看；留意；照顾；监视：Please keep an ～ on my suitcase. 请照看一下我的箱子。

eyebrow / 'aibrau / n. [C] 眉毛：She has thick ～s. 她眉毛很浓。

eyesight / 'aisait / n. [U] 视力；目力：I have good (bad) ～. 我的视力很好（不好）。

F f

fable / ˈfeɪbl / n. ❶[C] 寓言：*Aesop's Fables* 《伊索寓言》圃 fiction ❷[U]神话；传说：sort out facts from ～ 从传说中整理事实 圃 legend

fabric / ˈfæbrɪk / n. 织物；纺织品：woolen ～ 羊毛织品 圃 cloth，textile

fabricate / ˈfæbrɪˌkeɪt / vt. ❶制造，制作；组装，装配：～ fine pottery 制造精美的陶器／materials used to ～ electronic components 制造电子元件的材料 ❷伪造(文件等)；杜撰，编造：～ a diploma 伪造毕业文凭

fabulous / ˈfæbjuləs / adj. ❶惊人的，难以置信的；非常的；荒诞的：the ～ treasures of sunken ships 沉船上的稀世珍宝／ ～ rumors 无稽之谣 ❷极好的，绝妙的：That's a ～ idea! 这主意太妙了！

face / feɪs / Ⅰ n. 面孔；脸；(表)面；外貌：The stone struck her on the ～. 石头击在她脸上。／ a care-worn ～ 饱经风霜的脸／ a fair (fine) ～ 漂亮的脸蛋／ a gloomy ～ 阴郁的脸／ a serious ～ 严肃的面孔／ a proud ～ 傲慢的表情 圃 look，appearance ／～ to ～ 面对面：We sent for the man to accuse her ～ to ～. 我们叫那人来当面指控她。**in (the) ～ of** 面临：He remained calm even in the ～ of danger. 即使面临危险，他也镇定自若。**keep a straight ～** 板起面孔：He is so comical that no one can keep a straight ～. 他太滑稽了，人人都忍不住要笑。**make a ～ (faces) at** 向…做鬼脸：The children made ～s at one another. 孩子们互相做鬼脸玩。**put on (draw, pull, wear) a long ～** 愁眉苦脸；拉长了脸：I don't know why she is pulling a long ～ all day. 我不知道她为什么整天愁眉苦脸。**save one's ～** 保全面子：He didn't want to tell her about it in order to save his ～. 为了保全面子，他不想将此事告诉她。Ⅱ v. 面对；正视；朝；向：The

house ～s the street. 这房子面朝街道。圃 meet，confront ／ **be ～d with** 面对；面临：He was ～d with two alternatives — death or submission. 他面临两种选择：死亡或者投降。**～ up to** 勇敢面对：She won't ～ up to the fact that she is getting old. 她不肯承认她老了。

facet / ˈfæsɪt / n. [C] ❶(多面体的)面；(宝石等的)琢面：crystal ～ 水晶界面 ❷(问题、事物等的)一个方面：This case obviously has all sorts of ～ that will affect the trial. 很明显，这个案子牵涉到的方方面面，势必会对审判产生影响。

facial / ˈfeɪʃl / adj. 面部的：Did you notice her ～ expression when she came in? 你注意到她进来时的面部表情了吗？

facility / fəˈsɪləti / n. ❶[C] (通常用 pl.) 设施；设备：We have various transport facilities now. 现在我们有了各种各样的交通工具。圃 means，equipment ❷ [U] 便利；熟练：She played the piano with ～. 她熟练地弹钢琴。圃 ease

fact / fækt / n. [C] 事实；实际；现实；真相：A ～ is something that we know to be true. 事实就是我们认知为真实的事情。／ It is important to distinguish ～ from fiction. 辨别现实与虚构是重要的。圃 truth，reality ／**in ～** 事实上；实际上：I saw him not long ago, in ～, I saw him yesterday. 我不久前见过他，实际上就是昨天见过他。

factor / ˈfæktə(r) / n. [C] 要素；因素：a positive ～ 积极因素 / a negative ～ 消极因素 Diligence is the major ～ for his success. 勤奋是他获得成功的主要因素。圃 element，aspect

factory / ˈfæktəri / n. [C] 工厂：He runs a ～ in the town. 他在镇上经营一家工厂。圃 mill，plant，works

factory 意为"工厂",泛指制造任何物品的工厂:a boiler factory 锅炉厂。**plant** 指与电器或机械相关的工厂:a power plant 发电厂;a bicycle plant 自行车厂。**mill** 指材料加工厂:a cotton mill 纺织厂;a flour mill 面粉厂;a paper mill 造纸厂;a silk mill 丝绸厂。**works** 常指重工业方面的工厂:a steel works 钢铁厂;an iron works 炼铁厂。

faculty / ˈfækəlti / n. [C] ❶才能;能力:The young girl has a ～ for painting. 那位年轻姑娘擅长绘画。同 ability, capacity ❷(大学的)系;科;学院:He is working in the ～ of medicine. 他在医学系工作。同 department, academics ❸全体教学人员:The teaching ～ are having a meeting in the hall. 全体教职人员正在大厅里开会。同 staff

fade / feɪd / v. ❶(使)褪色;凋谢;枯萎:The wallpaper ～d. 墙纸褪色了。/ The newly planted trees ～d. 新栽的小树枯萎了。同 bleach, wither ❷(声音等)逐渐减弱,消失:The sound of the motorcycle ～d away in the distance. 摩托车的声音渐渐消失在远处。同 vanish, disappear

Fahrenheit / ˈfærənhaɪt / adj. 华氏的:Water freezes at 32° ～. 水在华氏 32 度结冰。

fail / feɪl / vi. 失败;不及格:He tried several times, but ～ed. 他试了几次,但都失败了。/ We're glad nobody ～ed in the exam this time. 让我们高兴的是,这次考试没有人不及格。反 success, miss

failure / ˈfeɪljə(r) / n. 失败;失败者:Failure is the mother of success. (＝Failure teaches success.)失败是成功之母。/ He was a ～ as a teacher. 他并不是一位成功的教师。同 defeat, loss 反 success

faint / feɪnt / Ⅰ adj. 模糊的;虚弱的;微弱的;头昏目眩的:He was ～ with hunger. 他因饥饿而十分虚弱。同 dim, weak Ⅱ vi. 昏;晕倒:The boy ～ed in the heat. 小男孩中暑晕倒了。反 recover

fair¹ / feə(r) / Ⅰ adj ❶公平的;公正的:He is ～ to other people. 他对待别人很公正。/ We should be ～ in buying and selling. 我们应当买卖公平。同 just, upright 反 unfair ❷相当的;尚可的:A ～ proportion of the citizens voted against the proposal. 相当一部分市民投票

反对那项提议。❸金发的;白皙的:The girl who has ～ hair is from Italy. 那位金发姑娘是意大利人。同 blond, white-skinned ❹晴朗的:The ～ weather made her pleasant. 晴朗的天气让她心情愉快。同 clear, fine, bright 反 cloudy, bloomy ❺美丽的:All the travelers were attracted by the ～ landscape there. 所有游客都被那儿的美景迷住了。同 pretty, attractive, lovely 反 ugly Ⅱ adv. 明白;公平:If we play ～, I'm sure we will win the match. 如果公平地比赛,我肯定我们会赢。同 clearly, fairly 派 fairness n.

fair² / feə(r) / n. [C] ❶集市:The wife of our Mayor often buys goods in the ～ trade market, too. 我们的市长夫人也常在集贸市场买东西。同 market ❷交易会;博览会:They planned to hold a trade ～ in the center of the city. 他们计划在市中心举行一次商品交易会。同 show, market, exhibition

fairly / ˈfeəli / adv. 公正地;相当:He did not act ～ toward her. 他待她不公平。/ She did ～ good actress. 她是一位相当好的演员。同 justly, rather 反 unjustly

fairy / ˈfeəri / n. [C]仙女;神仙:Grandfather often told ～ tales to me when I was young. 小时候祖父常给我讲童话故事。同 spirit

faith / feɪθ / n. ❶信任;信心;信念:The workers place (put) great ～ in their general manager. 工人们极其信任他们的总经理。/ We have firm ～ that our life will be better and better. 我们坚信我们的生活会越来越好。同 trust, confidence, belief 反 distrust, doubt ❷信仰:One should respect other's ～. 应当尊重他人的信仰。同 religion

faithful / ˈfeɪθfl / adj. 忠诚的;忠实的:Though he is young, he is ～ in his duties. 尽管他年轻,他却忠于职守。同 loyal, trustworthy 反 disloyal, faithless 派 faithfully adv.

fake / feɪk / Ⅰ v. 伪造;假装:Tell us the truth, don't ～ story. 告诉我们真相,不要编造故事。同 forge Ⅱ n. [C]冒牌货;赝品;骗子:The oil painting is a ～. 那幅油画是赝品。同 forge, copy Ⅲ adj. 假的;伪造的;冒充的:Take care not to buy ～ and fault products. 小心别买到假冒伪劣产品。同 forged, false

fall / fɔːl / Ⅰ vi. (fell/fel/, fallen /ˈfɔːlən/) ❶落下;降落:The pen fell from the desk to the floor. 笔从书桌上掉落到地板上。/ The rain was ～ing steadily. 雨不停地下。同 drop 反 rise ❷跌倒;倒下;跌落:Babies often ～ when they are learning to walk. 小儿学步常跌倒。同 drop 反 rise ❸成为;变为:He has ～en ill. 他生病了。/ Do not ～ into bad habits. 不要养成坏习惯。同 become,turn / ～ in love with 爱上;喜爱:He fell in love with an actress. 他爱上了一名女演员。～ back 撤退;后退:Our attack was so vigorous that the enemy had to ～ back. 我们的攻势猛烈,敌人不得不撤退了。～ behind 落后:He always ～s behind when we are going uphill. 我们上山时他总是落在后面。～ in 塌陷;垮:The roof fell in. 屋顶塌陷了。～ in with ①偶遇:On my way home I fell in with our English teacher. 在回家的路上我偶然碰到了我们的英语老师。②同意:He fell in with my views at once. 他立刻同意了我的见解。～ on one's knees 跪下:She fell on her knees and thanked God for his mercy. 她跪下感谢上帝的仁慈。Ⅱ n. [C] ❶落下;跌落:He had a ～ from a horse. 他从马上跌下。同 drop,downfall ❷(美)秋季:She was born in the ～ of 1992. 她是在 1992 年秋天出生的。同 autumn

false / fɔːls / adj. ❶假的;不真实的:His father have a set of ～ teeth. 他父亲戴一副假牙。同 untrue 反 faithful,true ❷仿造的:U-sing ～ coins is illegal. 使用伪币是违法的。同 fake,forged 反 real ❸ 错误的;谬误的:I think it is a ～ argument. 我认为这是一个错误的论点。同 incorrect,wrong

fame / feɪm / n. [U]名声;名望:One cannot only go after (seek) ～ and money. 人不能只追求名利。/ come to ～ 成名;出名:She came to ～ in Beijing eight years ago. 八年前她在北京出了名。同 reputation,honor

familiar / fəˈmɪlɪə(r) / adj. 熟悉的;通晓的:If you write things ～ to you, you'll get very good articles. 如果写熟悉的事物,你就会写出好文章。/ Her uncle has worked in France for twenty years; he is ～ with French. 他叔叔在法国工作了 20 年,法语相当好。同 well-known,intimate 反 strange, unfamiliar / **be on ～ terms with ...** 与…亲密;与…交情很好:He is on ～ terms with the old artist. 他和那位老艺术家交情很好。派 familiarity n.; familiarize v.

family / ˈfæməli / n. [C] ❶家庭;家族;家庭成员:Every ～ in the village has a TV set. 这个村子里家家有电视机。/ Tom is the eldest of the ～. 汤姆是家中最大的孩子。❷(动植物的)科;语系:animals of the cat ～ 猫科动物 / the Germanic ～ of languages 日耳曼语系 同 species,class

famine / ˈfæmɪn / n. [U]饥荒:His grandfather die of ～ in 1927. 他的祖父于 1927 年死于饥荒。同 hunger,starvation

famous / ˈfeɪməs / adj. 著名的;驰名的:a ～ scientist 著名的科学家 / The town is ～ for its hot springs. 该城以温泉驰名。同 noted, remarkable,well-known 反 unknown

fan / fæn / n. [C] ❶扇子 ❷狂热爱好者;迷:He is not only a football ～, but also a film ～. 他不仅是一个足球迷,还是一个影迷。同 lover,admirer,supporter

fancy / ˈfænsi / Ⅰ n. ❶[U]空想;幻想;幻想力:She has a lively ～ like a child. 她像小孩一样有丰富的幻想力。同 dream, imagination ❷[C]爱好;喜爱;迷恋:She has a ～ for Internet shopping. 她热衷于网上购物。同 liking Ⅱ adj. 空想的;精美的,花式的:I don't like ～ ties. 我不喜欢太花哨的领带。/ I like to watch ～ diving. 我喜欢看花样跳水。

fantastic / fænˈtæstɪk / adj. ❶(口语)极好的,很棒的 ❷奇异的

fantasy / ˈfæntəsi / n. [C;U]想象;幻想:make fantasies 胡思乱想/He indulges in fantasies but doesn't act them out. 他沉湎于奇思异想,却没有付诸行动。

far / fɑː(r) / Ⅰ adv. (farther, farthest; further, furthest) ❶(用于疑问句和否定句)远,久远(指空间、时间):How ～ did you go? 你走了多远? ❷(与介词、副词连用)远,久远:～ back in the past 往昔 / ～ in the future 在遥远的未来 / ～ away (off, out, back, in) 遥远;深远 / He reviewed his lesson ～ into the night. 他复习功课直至深夜。同 near,close / ～ **from** 远非;绝非:You are ～ from well. 你一点也不健康。**go (carry) too ～** 过分:Don't carry the joke too ～. 不要把玩笑开得过分了。**～ and near (wide)** 到处:They searched ～ and wide for the missing child. 他们到处寻找那个走失的孩子。**so ～** 到目前为止:So ～ the work has been easy. 到目前为止,这工作是容易的。**as (so) ～ as** ①到,直到:He walked as ～ as the post office. 他走到了邮局。②与…距离相等：We didn't go as (so) ～ as the others. 我们不如其他人走得那么远。③在…以内；就…的（限度）：So ～ as I know,he will be away for three months. 就我所知,他将外出三个月。❸(修饰形容词、副词的比较级)…得多：This is ～ better. 这个要好得多。Ⅱ adj. (farther,farthest；further,furthest)远的；较远的：a ～ country 一个远方的国家 / at the ～ end of the street 在街的那一头 / on the ～ bank of the river 在河的彼岸

fare / feə(r) / n. [C]车船费；票价：A bus ～ is very cheap. 公共汽车票价很便宜。/ How much is the air ～ to Beijing? 去北京的飞机票要多少钱？囘 fee,price,charge

farewell / ˌfeə'wel / Ⅰ int. 再见；告别 Ⅱ n. 再会：**make (bid) a ～ to sb.** 与某人告别：The visitors made their ～s and left. 访问者告别后离开了。囘 goodbye

farm / fɑːm / n. [C]农场：He worked on a ～. 他在农场工作。派 farmer n.

fascinate / 'fæsɪneɪt / vt. 迷住；强烈地吸引住：The children were ～d by the toys in the shop windows. 孩子们被商店橱窗里的玩具迷住了。囘 attract,charm 派 fascination n.

fascinating / 'fæsɪneɪtɪŋ / adj. 迷人的；引人入胜的：What a ～ smile! 多么迷人的微笑啊！囘 attractive,charming

fashion / 'fæʃn / n. 流行；式样；时尚：He walks in a peculiar ～. 他走路的样子奇特。/ Short skirts are the ～ in 2007. 短裙是2007年的流行式样。囘 custom,pattern,style 派 fashionable adj.

fast / fɑːst / Ⅰ adv. ❶快；迅速地：He walks very ～. 他走路很快。囘 quickly,rapidly 反 slow ❷紧；牢固地；可靠地：He held the rope ～. 他紧紧地抓住绳子不放。囘 firmly,tightly Ⅱ adj. ❶快的；迅速的：My watch is ～. 我的表快了。囘 quick,rapid ❷紧的；牢固的；可靠的：He is my ～ friend. 他是我忠实可靠的朋友。囘 firm,tight

fasten / 'fɑːsn / v. 系牢,束紧；闩上：Fasten your seat belt while you're driving. 开车时系紧安全带。囘 tie,fix,bind

fat / fæt / Ⅰ adj. (fatter,fattest) 肥的；胖的：He is getting ～ter. 他长得更胖了。Ⅱ n. [U] 脂肪；肥肉：I do not like ～ (meat). 我不

喜欢吃肥肉。

fatal / 'feɪtl / adj. 致命的；不幸的：a ～ wound 致命伤 / a ～ accident 不幸事件 / Cancer is a ～ disease. 癌症是一种致命的疾病。囘 deadly

fate / feɪt / n. [U] 命运：share the ～ with 与…共命运 / evil ～ 厄运 / We should take our ～ into our own hands. 我们应当掌握我们的命运。囘 fortune,lot

fateful / 'feɪtf(ʊ)l / adj. 决定性的,关键性的；(意义)重大的；影响深远的：a ～ decision 重大决定 / a ～ meeting 具有深远影响的会议

father / 'fɑːðə(r) / n. [C]父亲

fatigue / fə'tiːg / v. 使疲劳；使劳累：He felt ～d with sitting up all night. 他因彻夜不眠而感到疲劳。囘 tire,exhaust

fault / fɔːlt / n. 缺点；错误；过失：This is not her ～. 这不是她的错。/ Parents should know the merits and ～s of their children well. 父母应当很好地了解自己孩子的优点和缺点。囘 mistake,error,weakness 派 faulty adj.

favo(u)r / 'feɪvə(r) / n. [C] 好意；恩惠；帮助：May I ask a ～ of you? 请您帮个忙好吗？囘 kindness,help / **do sb. a ～** 帮助某人：Do me a ～ to come. 务必请光临。/ Could you do me a ～? 你能帮我个忙吗？**in ～ of** 赞成；支持：The students are in ～ of reform. 学生们都赞成改革。**in sb.'s ～** 对某人有利：The situation both at home and abroad is in our ～. 国内外形势对我们有利。

favo(u)rable / 'feɪvərəbl / adj. 有利的；有帮助的：The wind is ～ for setting sail. 风向有利于起航。囘 beneficial,advantageous

favo(u)rite / 'feɪvərɪt / Ⅰ n. [C] 特别喜爱的人；特别喜爱的物：He is a ～ with everybody. 他是人人都喜欢的人。囘 dear,beloved Ⅱ adj. 特别喜爱的：My ～ subject is English. 我最喜爱的科目是英语。囘 best-loved,preferred

fax / fæks / n. 传真；传真机

fear / fɪə(r) / Ⅰ v. 害怕；恐惧：She always ～s mice. 她一向怕老鼠。/ I ～ for his safety. 我为他的安全担心。囘 dread,worry 反 dare Ⅱ n. ❶害怕；恐惧：The boy didn't show any ～ in front of strangers. 在陌生人面前小孩一点也不害怕。囘 dread,horror / **for ～ of** 唯恐；为…担心；生怕：He is for ～ of failure. 他生

怕失败。❷忧虑(与 of 连用)：He is in ～ of his living. 他为他的生计担忧。圆 worry

fearful / ˈfɪəfl / adj. 担心的；可怕的；吓人的：She is ～ of wakening her baby. 她怕吵醒她的孩子。圆 dreadful 反 brave

fearless / ˈfɪələs / adj. 无畏的，大胆的：We are ～ of danger. 我们不怕危险。圆 brave, bold

feasible / ˈfiːzɪbl / adj. 可行的；行得通的；切合实际的：a ～ plan 可行的计划/It is ～ to take his advice. 按他的建议行事是切实可行的。派 feasibility n.

feast / fiːst / n. [C] 宴会；酒席：a noon ～ 午宴 / a festival ～ 节日宴会 / Mr. White makes a ～ tonight. 怀特先生今晚设宴款待。圆 banquet

feat / fiːt / n. [C] 功绩；业绩；事迹：achieve a remarkable ～取得引人注目的业绩/a ～ of engineering 工程学上的壮举 圆 achievement, attainment

feather / ˈfeðə(r) / n. 羽毛：as light as a ～ 轻如鸿毛

feature / ˈfiːtʃə(r) / n. [C] 面貌；特征；特点；特色：Her eyes are her best ～. 她的眼睛是长得最好的部分。/ The key ～ of the poem is simple. 这首诗的主要特点是简朴。圆 looks, characteristic

February / ˈfebruəri / n. (略作 Feb.) 二月

federal / ˈfedərəl / adj. 联盟的；联邦的

federation / ˌfedəˈreɪʃn / n. [C] 联邦

fee / fiː / n. [C] 费；酬金：School ～s are high in England. 英国的学费很高。圆 pay, charge

feeble / ˈfiːbl / adj. 微弱的；虚弱的：a ～ old man 衰弱的老人 / a ～ mind 薄弱的意志 / a ～ cry 微弱的叫声 / a ～ attempt 没有成功的尝试 圆 weak, faint 反 strong, powerful

辨析
feeble 意为"虚弱的，微弱的，薄弱的"，形容人时，常表示因衰老而变得虚弱不堪：He is too feeble to feed himself. 他太虚弱了，不能自己吃饭。形容事物时，表示无效。**weak** 意为"弱的；体力不佳的；微弱的"，常用词，形容人缺乏足够的力量，精力不充沛或物体承受不住压力、攻击，否则就会弯曲、崩溃等：She has weak legs. 她的双腿无力。She grew weaker and weaker. 她变得越来越虚弱。

feed / fiːd / v. (fed /fed/, fed) 吃，喂；饲养；供给：The girl fed the chickens on corn. 小姑娘用玉米粒喂小鸡。/ Pandas ～ chiefly on bamboos. 熊猫主要以竹为食物。/ He fed the data into his computer. 他把那些数据输入计算机。圆 eat, supply /～ **on** 以…为食物；以…维生命：What do you ～ your dog on? 你给狗喂什么食物？ **be fed up with** 讨厌；厌恶：She is fed up with his grumbling. 她讨厌他老发牢骚。

feedback / ˈfiːdbæk / n. 反馈；反应：The shop welcomes the ～ from customers. 这家商店欢迎顾客反馈的信息。圆 reaction, response, reflection

feel / fiːl / v. (felt /felt/, felt) ❶感觉；感到：He felt his heart beating fast. 他感到他心跳得很快。/ I ～ as if it were going to rain. 我觉得好像要下雨了。❷触；摸：She felt the pot and found that it was hot. 她摸了摸那壶，发现壶是烫的。圆 touch/～ **one's way** 摸索着走；谨慎处事：Since the staircase is rather dark, we must ～ our way carefully. 楼梯太黑暗，我们必须小心地摸着走。～ **about** 摸索：He was ～ing about in the dark. 他在黑暗中摸索。～ **for** 探索；摸索：He felt in his pocket for a penny. 他在口袋里摸到一便士。～ **like** 摸起来如何…；有…样的感觉；想要：I ～ like catching cold. 我感觉像是感冒了。/ She ～s like crying. 她真想哭。～ **up to** 能胜任；有能力做：He doesn't ～ up to a long walk. 他没有力气走远路。

feeling / ˈfiːlɪŋ / n. (常用 pl.) 感情；感觉：What he said hurt her ～s. 他的话伤了她的感情。/ She suddenly had no ～ in her left hand. 她的左手突然没有了感觉。圆 emotion, passion, sense

fellow / ˈfeləʊ / Ⅰ n. [C] ❶人；家伙；小伙子：He is a good, honest ～. 他是一个诚实的好人。圆 gay, boy ❷同伴；同辈：He always helps his ～s warm-heartedly. 他常常热心地帮助他的同伴们。圆 partner, associate, colleague Ⅱ adj. 同伴的；同辈的：Her ～ workers didn't know that she was ill. 她的同事们不知道她生病了。圆 related, associate

female / ˈfiːmeɪl / Ⅰ n. [C] 女子；雌性动物：Most teachers in the Primary schools are ～s. 这所小学的老师多数是女的。反 boy, man, male Ⅱ adj. 女性的；雌性的：She raised a ～ cat. 她养了一只雌猫。反 male

F

feminine / ˈfemɪnɪn / *adj.* ❶女性特有的；女人味的：～ intuition 女性特有的直觉/If she puts on a little lipstick, she'll be more ～. 她如果抹点口红，就更有女人味。❷女性的；妇女的：～ staff members 女性职员 ❸(某些语言的语法中)阴性的：a ～ noun 阴性名词(如 queen, tigress)

fence¹ / fens / *n.* [C] 栅栏；围栏；篱笆：She looked out from the garden ～ and saw that her father was coming back. 从花园的栅栏里出去，她看到父亲正走回家。 反 wall, barrier

fence² / fens / *n.* 击剑；击剑术：Many young people like to watch a ～ game. 许多年轻人喜欢看击剑比赛。

ferry / ˈferi / I *n.* [C] 渡船；渡口：The pupils crossed the river by ～. 小学生们乘渡船过河。 II *vt.* 运送；摆渡；渡过：The old man ferries people to and fro everyday. 老人每天用渡船来摆渡行人过河。 同 convey, transport

fertile / ˈfɜːtaɪl / *adj.* ❶肥沃的；富饶的：The family has ～ fields and comfortable houses. 这家人有肥沃的田地和舒适的房屋。 反 barren ❷丰产的；丰富的：This district is ～ of fresh fruits. 这个地区盛产新鲜水果。 同 fruitful, plentiful

fertilizer / ˈfɜːtəlaɪzə(r) / *n.* [U]肥料：They are spreading chemical ～ in the fields. 他们正在田里施肥。 同 manure

festival / ˈfestɪvl / *n.* [C] 节日；喜庆日子：the Spring Festival 春节/ a film ～ 电影节/ the Lantern Festival 元宵节/ the Mid-autumn Festival 中秋节

fetch / fetʃ / *v.* 去拿来；去取来：Please ～ me the dictionary. 请把词典给我拿来。 同 bring

feudal / ˈfjuːdəl / *adj.* 封建的；封建制度的：a volume of ～ studies 一部研究封建制度的书/ a ～ state 封建国家

feudalism / ˈfjuːdəlɪzəm / *n.* [U]封建主义；封建制度

fever / ˈfiːvə(r) / *n.* [U](常与不定冠词连用)发热，发烧；狂热：Her ～ has gone down. 她已经退烧了。/ They were in a ～ of joy when they won the cham-pion. 赢得冠军时他们欣喜若狂。 同 heat, excitement /**have a ～** 发烧：She has a ～. 她发烧了。 派 feverish *adj.*

few / fjuː / I *adj.* 少数的，不多的：Who made the ～est mistakes? 谁犯的错

误最少？/ She is a girl of ～ words. 她是一个少言寡语的女孩。/ We stayed here only a ～ days. 我们在此只待了几天。 同 rare, scarce 反 many II *pron.* 少数：Few knew and ～ cared. 很少有人知道，也很少有人关心。/ I know a ～ of these people. 这些人中我认识几个。 反 many

用法

few 意为"很少；几乎没有"：There are few mistakes in his composition. 他的作文几乎没有错误。a few 意为"几个；颇有几个"：There are a few mistakes in his composition. 他的作文中有几处错误。

辨析

❶few, a few 都必须放在可数名词前，谓语动词用复数；不可数名词前则用 little 或 a little，谓语动词用单数：There is little water in the cup. 杯子里几乎没有水。There is little milk in the glass. 杯子里还有些牛奶。❷ a good few 与 a good many 同义，是"很有几个"的意思。

fiancé / fɪˈɒnseɪ / *n.* [C]未婚夫 反 fiancée

fiancée / fɪˈɒnseɪ / *n.* [C]未婚妻 反 fiancé

fiber(-re) / ˈfaɪbə(r) / *n.* 纤维；纤维质：They use cotton ～s to spin into thread. 他们用棉纤维纺线。

fiction / ˈfɪkʃən / *n.* ❶[C] 小说：He is fond of reading detective ～s. 他喜欢读侦探小说。同 story, novel ❷ [U] 虚构；捏造；编造：The whole story is pure ～. 整个故事纯属虚构。派 fictional *adj.* ; fictionalize *v.*

fictitious / fɪkˈtɪʃəs / *adj.* ❶假的；仿造的：The criminal used a ～ name. 罪犯用了假名。/ a ～ bill 空头支票 ❷不真实的；想象的；虚构的：a ～ character in the novel 小说中一个虚构的人物

field / fiːld / *n.* [C]❶田地，场地：The ～ must be manured. 田里必须施肥了。/ We found him in the football ～. 我们在足球场上找到了他。 同 farm, land ❷领域，界：Many great discoveries have been made in the ～ of science. 科学界已有许多伟大的发现。同 range, scope

fierce / fɪəs / *adj.* 凶猛的；猛烈的；激烈的：The dog is very ～. 那条狗极凶。/ A ～ storm hit the area. 一场狂风暴雨袭击了这个地区。同 cruel, violent

FIFA (= Fédération Internationale de Football Association；International Football Federation)国际足球联合会

fifteen / ˌfɪfˈtiːn / Ⅰ *num.* 十五 Ⅱ *adj.* 十五个(的)

fifth / fɪfθ / Ⅰ *num.* 第五；五分之一 Ⅱ *adj.* 第五的；五分之一的

fiftieth / ˈfɪftɪəθ / Ⅰ *num.* 第五十；五十分之一 Ⅱ *adj.* 第五十的；五十分之一的

fifty / ˈfɪftɪ / Ⅰ *num.* 五十 Ⅱ *adj.* 五十个(的)

fight / faɪt / Ⅰ *v.* (fought / fɔːt /, fought) 战斗；斗争；打仗：They are ~ing for their freedom. 他们在为自由而战。/ England fought with France against Germany. 英法联合对德作战。同 struggle, battle Ⅱ *n.* [C]战斗；斗争：It was a terrible ~. 那是一场可怕的战斗。同 struggle, battle

figure / ˈfɪɡə(r) / Ⅰ *n.* [C] ❶数字：Are you good at ~? 你是否善于计算? 同 number ❷体形；外表：His ~ is small. 他身材矮小。/ This girl has a good ~. 这姑娘身材很好。/ Exercises improve a person's ~. 运动能改善人的体型。同 form, shape ❸人物：a popular ~ 受众人欢迎的人物 / a great ~ in literature 大文豪 同 person, character ❹图形；图表：The blackboard was covered with geometrical ~s. 黑板上画满了几何图形。同 picture, diagram Ⅱ *v.* 计算；估计：I ~ that she will win the first prize. 我估计她会得头等奖。同 estimate /~ **on** 指望；依靠；料到：We ~ on your coming early. 我们指望你早些来。~ **out** 计算出；估计：Figure it out and see what it comes. 把它算出来, 看结果得多少。/ I ~ out we shall reach Beijing on Friday. 我估计我们将在星期五到达北京。

file / faɪl / Ⅰ *n.* [C]档案；卷宗；(计算机)文件：Please put these documents in the ~. 请把这些文件放进卷宗里。/ He deleted some dated ~s. 他删除了一些过时的文件。同 records, documents Ⅱ *v.* ❶把⋯归档：He asked his secretary to ~ the letters in alphabetical order. 他要求秘书把信件按字母顺序归档。同 register, classify ❷排成纵队行进：The children ~d into the hall. 孩子们排队进入大厅。同 march, move

fill / fɪl / *vt.* 使⋯满, 装满；占满：She was ~ed with boiling anger. 她满腔怒火。/ All the streets were ~ed with people. 所有街道都挤满了人。同 block, occupy 反 empty /~ **in** 填满；填充：Fill in the blanks with prepositions. 用介词填空。~ **out** 长得丰满, 长胖；填充：When Jane was nineteen, she began to ~ out. 简 19 岁开始长得丰满起来。/ Please ~ out a check. 请开张支票。~ **up** 装满：Fill up the bottle. 把瓶子装满。~ **...with** 用⋯装满：Fill the glass with milk. 把杯子倒满牛奶。

film / fɪlm / *n.* [C]电影, 影片；胶卷：Let's go to the ~s. 咱们去看电影吧。/ a comic ~ 喜剧片 / a documentary ~ 纪录片 / a feature ~ 故事片 / a wide-screen ~ 宽银幕影片 同 movie, picture, video

filter / ˈfɪltə(r) / *v.* 过滤；渗透：The water for drinking was ~ed. 饮用水是经过过滤的。

filth / fɪlθ / *n.* [U] ❶污(秽)物；(肮)脏物；污垢 ❷猥亵语；脏话；下流话

final / ˈfaɪnəl / *adj.* 最终的；最后的：the ~ examination 期末考试 / the ~ result 最后结果 / His ~ decision was to study abroad. 他的最后决定是去国外留学。同 last, terminal 反 first 派 finally *adv.*

finance / ˈfaɪnæns / Ⅰ *n.* 财政；金融；(pl.)资金：The bank needs an expert of ~. 那家银行需要一位金融专家。Ⅱ *vt.* 提供资金给⋯, 融资：The company ~d ten students through college. 那家公司给 10 位学生提供读完大学的费用。同 fund, capitalize

financial / faɪˈnænʃəl / *adj.* 财政上的；金融的：Do you know the ~ condition of the company? 你了解那家公司的财务状况吗? 同 economic 派 financially *adv.*

find / faɪnd / *vt.* (found / faʊnd /, found) ❶寻得；找到；发现：Did you ~ the pen you lost yesterday? 你找到昨天丢失的那支笔了吗? 同 discover 反 lose ❷发觉, 察觉；知道：I found it difficult to learn English well. 我觉得学好英语很困难。/ We found him dishonest. 我们发觉他不诚实。同 note, realize /~ **fault** (**with**) 抱怨, 挑剔；对⋯吹毛求疵：That is the only fault to be found with him. 那是他身上挑出来的唯一一毛病。~ **out** 发现；找出；查出：How can I ~ out who took my book? 我怎么能查出是谁把我的书拿走了?

finding / ˈfaɪndɪŋ / *n.* 发现(物)；(pl.)调查(或研究)结果：The scientist published his latest ~s in the newspaper. 科学家在报上发表了他

F

的最新研究成果。同 discovery, result

fine¹ /faɪn/ Ⅰ adj. (天气)晴朗的；美好的；优秀的：It is ~ today. 今天天晴。/ What a ~ view! 多么美好的景色！/ He is a ~ scholar. 他是一位优秀的学者。同 nice, excellent, bright Ⅱ adv. (口语)很好，妙：How are you? Fine. Thank you. 你好吗？好，谢谢。

fine² /faɪn/ Ⅰ n. [C]罚金；罚款：He paid a ＄300 ~. 他交了 300 美元的罚款。同 forfeit Ⅱ v. 处…以罚款：The young man was ~d for speeding. 因超速行车那年轻人被处罚款。同 punish

finger /ˈfɪŋɡə(r)/ n. [C]手指：a fore ~ 食指/ a middle ~ 中指/ a ring ~ 无名指/ a little ~ 小指

fingerprint /ˈfɪŋɡəprɪnt/ n. [C]指纹；指纹印：Her ~s on the handle proved she'd been there. 她留在把手上的指纹证明她曾去过那里。

finish /ˈfɪnɪʃ/ vt. 完成，结束：He said he had ~ed his homework. 他说他已完成家庭作业。同 end, complete 反 start

用法

finish 后接动名词，不接不定式：The teacher has finished correcting our compositions. 老师已改完我们的作文。

fire /ˈfaɪə(r)/ Ⅰ vt. ❶开火；射击：We ~d our guns at the enemy. 我们向敌人开火。同 shoot ❷解雇：He was ~d by his boss. 他被老板解雇了。同 dismiss 反 hire Ⅱ n. 火；火灾：He who plays with ~ gets burned. 玩火者自焚。/ a big (great) ~ 一场大火 / a blazing ~ 熊熊烈火

firm¹ /fɜːm/ adj. 坚定的；牢固的；稳固的：I don't think that the chair is ~ enough to stand on. 我觉得这把椅子不够结实，不能站上去。/ as ~ as rock 坚如磐石 / a ~ faith 坚定的信仰 同 hard, strong, resolute 反 soft 派 firmly adv.

firm² /fɜːm/ n. [C] 公司；商行：He is thinking of starting another ~ in Hong Kong. 他正考虑在香港再开一家商行。/ a commercial ~ 贸易公司 /an exporting ~ 出口公司/ a publishing ~ 出版公司 同 company, business

first /fɜːst/ Ⅰ num. 第一 Ⅱ adj. ❶第一的；最早的：January is the ~ month of the year. 一月是一年的第一个月。/ ~ floor (英)二楼，(美)一楼，底层 反 last ❷ 第一流的；最重要的；主要的：He is the ~ violinist of the orchestra. 他是乐队的第一小提琴手。同 first-class, first-rate Ⅲ adv. 第一；最初(常用于强调)：First, I'll tell you a good news. 首先，我要告诉你一个好消息。反 finally Ⅳ n. [C] 最初；第一名：She was the ~ to come to the office. 她是第一个到办公室的人。反 start /at ~ 最初；当初：At ~ he didn't want to come. 他起初不想来。from ~ to last 自始至终，始终，一直：He sat there thinking from ~ to last. 他始终坐在那儿沉思。

firsthand /ˌfɜːstˈhænd/ adj. (资料、经历、来源等)第一手的；亲身体验的；直接的：a ~ experience 亲身经历/book reviews based on ~ research 基于直接研究而写成的书评/Mary gave me a ~ account of the accident. 玛丽告诉我她所目睹的事故发生经过。

fish /fɪʃ/ n. ❶[C] (pl. fish 或 fishes)鱼：catch a ~ 捉到一条鱼 ❷[U] 鱼肉：a ~ dinner 鱼餐

fisherman /ˈfɪʃəmən/ n. [C] (pl. fishermen) 渔夫

fist /fɪst/ n. [C] 拳头

fit /fɪt/ Ⅰ adj. (fitter, fittest) ❶健康的：I am not feeling very ~ now. 眼下我觉得身体不大舒服。同 healthy ❷合适的；恰当的：The weather is not ~ to go out. 这天气不适合出去。同 suitable, proper Ⅱ v. (fit 或 fitted；fitting)适合；适应：That ~s you all right. 那对你很合适。同 suit, match/ ~ in 适应；配合：The house ~s in beautifully with its surroundings. 这座房子和周围的环境非常协调。~ sb. (sth.) out 供给必需品；装备；配备：The soldiers were ~ted out with guns and clothing. 士兵们配发了枪支和服装。~ for 使适合；使胜任：Military training ~s men for long marches. 军事训练使人能适应长途行军。~ up 装备；布置；安装：We ~ted up one of the bedrooms as a study. 我们把卧室中的一间改成了书房。Ⅲ n. [C] 疾病的突然发作；一股，一阵：a ~ of coughing 一阵咳嗽 / a ~ of pain 一阵痛 / a ~ of energy 一股劲 / a ~ of weeping 一阵哭泣 / give sb. a ~ 使某人大吃一惊：What he said at the meeting gave us ~s. 他会上的发言使我们大吃一惊。have (throw) a ~ (口语)大惊；大怒；闷闷不乐：

She had a ～ when she saw the bill. 她看到那张账单时,大吃一惊。**by ～s and starts** 断断续续地;一阵一阵地:This watch of mine goes by ～s and starts. 我这块表走走停停。

five / faɪv / Ⅰ *num.* 五;5 Ⅱ *adj.* 五个(的)

fix / fɪks / *vt.* ❶使固定;钉牢:Please ～ the post in the ground. 请将柱子竖立在地上。圆 fasten,install ❷确定;决定:They ～ed a date for the meeting. 他们已定好开会的日子。圆 decide ❸修理:This watch is easy to ～. 这块表好修。圆 repair,mend/～ **over** 修理:Can the old man ～ over the engine? 那位老人能把发动机修理一下吗? ～ **on**(**upon**)选定:We've ～ed on the date to start. 我们选定了出发的日子。/ They ～ed upon me to do this work. 他们选定由我来做这项工作。～ **up** 安排;确定;安装:We've ～ed up a date for the dance. 我们已定好舞会的日期。派 fixed *adj.*

flag / flæg / *n.* [C]国旗,旗帜:raise (fly) a ～ 升旗 / haul down (lower) a ～ 降旗 / the national ～ 国旗 圆 banner,colors

flake / fleɪk / *n.* [C] 薄片;(雪、羽毛等的)一片:snow ～ 雪片 / wheat ～s 麦片 圆 chip,slice

flame / fleɪm / *n.* 火焰;火苗:The red car burst into ～s suddenly. 那辆红色轿车突然起火燃烧。圆 fire,blaze

flap / flæp / Ⅰ(flapped; flapping) *vt.* ❶拍动;摆动;振(翅):A gust of wind ～ped the tents. 一阵风吹动帐篷。/Grey pigeons ～ped up into the sky when frightened. 一群灰鸽受了惊,纷纷振翅飞向空中。❷拍打,拍击:～ the flies away 把苍蝇赶走 Ⅱ *n.* [C] ❶帽边,鞋舌;(书的护封的)勒口;盖,折盖:the ～ of an envelope 信封的口盖 ❷摆动;飘动;(鸟翼等的)振动 ❸拍动;拍打;拍打声

flare / fleə(r) / Ⅰ *n.* [U]闪烁;闪光:We saw the ～ of a flashlight in the dark. 在黑暗中我们看到了手电筒的闪光。圆 spark,flash Ⅱ *vi.* 闪耀;发光:The torch ～s in the darkness. 火把在黑暗中闪亮。圆 glow,blaze/～ **up** 突然发怒;激动:His anger ～d up when his motives were questioned. 有人对他的动机表示怀疑时,他勃然大怒。

flash / flæʃ / Ⅰ *n.* [C] 闪烁;发光:a ～ of lightning 闪电 圆 blaze,flash / **in a** ～ 即刻:I'll be here in a ～. 我即刻就到。Ⅱ *v.* 闪光;

闪烁:Flash your light around to see if anyone is hiding here. 用你的灯四周照一照,看看有没有人藏在这里。圆 blaze,sparkle /～ **across** 闪现;闪过:The lightning ～ed across the sky. 闪电从天空划过。

flashback / ˈflæʃbæk / *n.* [C;U] ❶倒叙,倒叙情节;闪回,闪回镜头:the ～ to the hero's school days 男主角学生时代的倒叙 ❷再现,重现;回忆,追忆:a sudden ～ of the accident 那次事件在脑海里的突然再现

flat[1] / flæt / Ⅰ *adj.* ❶平坦的;平的:The floor is quite ～. 地很平。圆 plain,smooth ❷无味的;无聊的;枯燥的:The party was very ～. 那次聚会很乏味。圆 boring,dull 反 interesting/**be ～ out** 精疲力竭的:We are all ～ out after lifting the piano. 我们抬了那架钢琴后累得精疲力竭。Ⅱ *adv.* 平直地;断然地

flat[2] / flæt / *n.* [C]一套房间;公寓:He bought a three-room ～ last year. 去年他买了一套有三个房间(一套三)的公寓。圆 apartment

flatten / ˈflætn / *v.* 使平坦,使…平:The workers are ～ing the road. 工人们正在铺平道路。圆 level,even

flatter / ˈflætə(r) / *v.* 奉承,阿谀;使某人高兴:I feel greatly ～ed by your invitation. 承蒙邀请,不胜荣幸。圆 overprize,please / ～ **oneself** 自认为:She ～ed herself that she spoke English quite well. 她自认为英语说得相当好。

flavo(u)r / ˈfleɪvə(r) / *n.* ❶滋味;风味;情趣:I like icecream with different ～s. 我喜欢各种不同口味的冰激凌。/ The houses there have a strong local ～. 那儿的房屋具有很浓的地方韵味。圆 taste,feature ❷香料;调味料

flaw / flɔː / *n.* [C]瑕疵;缺点;缺陷:You can hardly find any ～ in the handicraft. 在这件手工艺品上你简直很难找出什么缺陷来。圆 fault,break

flea / fliː / *n.* [C]蚤,跳蚤

flee / fliː / *v.* (fled /fled/,fled) 逃走;避开:He fled away at the first sight of danger. 他一见到危险就避开了。/ He killed his enemy and fled the country. 他杀死他的敌人后逃离了那个国家。圆 escape,avoid

fleet / fliːt / *n.* [C] 舰队

flesh / fleʃ / *n.* [U] 肉;肌肉;肉体:Are lions and tigers ～-eating animals? 狮子和老虎是

肉食动物吗? 圆 meat, muscle, body / **in the ～** 本人; 亲自: He's nicer in the ～ than in the photograph. 他本人比照片好看。 派 fleshy adj.

flexible / ˈfleksəbl / adj. 柔韧的; 易弯曲的; 灵活的; 可变通的: We should make a ～ plan. 我们应当制订一个灵活的计划。 反 stiff, inflexible

flick / flɪk / vt. ❶轻打; 轻拍; 轻弹; 拂; 甩动: ～ a match into flame 啪的擦亮火柴 / The driver ～ed the horse with his whip to make it go fast. 驾车人用鞭子轻轻抽打马儿, 催它快走。 / He ～ed an ash off his sleeve. 他轻轻拂掉衣袖上的烟灰。 ❷急速移动; 按动; 振动: A grasshopper ～ed its wings. 一只蚱蜢振翅欲飞。

flight / flaɪt / n. ❶[U] 飞行; 飞翔: in the ～ 在飞行中 / A hen is incapable of ～. 母鸡不会飞。 圆 flying ❷[C] 航空旅行; 航程; 航班: a lunar ～ 月球飞行 / the space ～ 宇宙飞行 / a round-the-world ～ 环球飞行 / We took Flight 3127 to London. 我们搭乘 3127 航班飞往伦敦。 圆 journey, airliner ❸[C] 楼梯的一段; I climbed two ～s up to her room. 我上了两段楼梯去她的房间。 圆 stairs ❹逃跑; 溃退: The thief took to ～. 小偷逃跑了。 圆 escape, retreat / **in ～** 逃走: They were in ～ from the flood. 他们避开洪水。 / **make (take) a ～** 逃离: She took a ～ on hearing the terrible sound. 她一听到那可怕的声音就逃走了。

fling / flɪŋ / Ⅰ vt. (flung, flung) ❶(用力地)扔, 掷, 抛, 丢: ～ out a ball 抛球 / They ～ their hats in the air. 他们把帽子抛到空中。 ❷丢下; 抛弃: ～ aside all cares 丢开一切忧虑 / ～ **oneself** 使冲向; 使投身: ～ himself into his work 全身心地投入工作 Ⅱ n. [C] (用力的)扔, 掷, 抛, 丢: An abrupt ～ of his hands threw her on the grass. 他双手突然一丢, 使她摔倒在草坪上。

flip / flɪp / (flipped; flipping) vt. ❶轻拨; 使在空中翻转; 扔; 甩: Let's ～ a coin to decide who should go first. 我们抛硬币来决定谁先去吧。 ❷快速翻动; 突然翻转: ～ the fish on its back 将鱼翻个肚朝天 / The years ～ ped the calendar like dry leaves from a lawn. 岁月催人, 日历一张张撕掉, 犹如落在草坪上的枯枝。 ❸浏览; (很快地)翻书: ～ through a magazine 浏览杂志

float / fləʊt / v. 漂浮; 飘动: The boat ～ed down the river. 小船顺流而下。 / We saw a box ～ing on water. 我们看见一只箱子飘在水上。 圆 drift, swim 反 sink

flock / flɒk / Ⅰ n. [C] 一群; 大量; 众多: a ～ of geese (girls, visitors) 一群鹅 (少女、访问者) / **in ～s** 成群: People came in ～s to see the new bridge. 人们成群结队前来参观这座新桥。 Ⅱ v. 群集; 成群而来: Sheep usually ～ together. 羊通常是成群生活的。 圆 gather, crowd

辨析
a flock of (鸟、兽等的)一群, 尤指羊群: a flock of sheep (goats) 一群羊 (山羊)。 **a crowd of** (杂乱的)一群人: a big crowd of people 一大群人。 **a herd of** 兽群, 尤指牛群: a herd of cows (deer, elephants) 一群牛 (鹿、象)。 **a swarm of** 一群昆虫: a swarm of ants 一群蚂蚁。 **a school of** (鱼或其他水族动物的)群: a school of dolphins 一群海豚。 **a pack of** 行猎动物的一群: a pack of hounds 一群猎犬。 **a party of** 同行的一群人, 共同工作的一组人: a party of travellers 一群同行的旅行者。

flood / flʌd / Ⅰ n. [C] 洪水; 水灾: The house of the peasant was washed away by the ～. 那个农民的房屋被洪水冲走了。 圆 overflow Ⅱ vt. 淹没; 使水泛滥: The river ～ed a lot of fields. 河水淹没了大量农田。 圆 drawn, overflow

floor / flɔː(r) / n. [C] 地面; 地板; 楼层: The baby is sitting on the ～. 小婴孩坐在地板上。 / The old lady lives on the third ～. 老太太住在三楼。 圆 ground, story

用法
❶ floor 着重指地面, 前面习惯用介词 on: on the floor。 storey 着重指空间, 前面常用介词 in。 ❷若要表示第几层上有某样东西, 习惯上用 floor 而不用 storey: There is a lab on the first floor. 第二层楼上有个实验室。

floppy / ˈflɒpi / adj. 松软的: a ～ disk 软磁盘 圆 hard

flora / ˈflɔːrə / n. (pl. floras 或 florae / ˈflɔːriː/) ❶[C;U] 植物群; 植物, 植物区系: ～ and fauna 植物与动物 / the ～s of the West Indies 西印度群岛各种植物群 ❷[U] 细菌群: intestinal ～ 肠菌群

flour / ˈflaʊə(r) / n. [U] 面粉: We use ～ for

making bread. 我们用面粉做面包。

flourish / ˈflʌrɪʃ / vi. 繁荣；茂盛；兴旺：The young man runs a shop and his business is ∼ing. 那年轻人开着一家商店，生意很兴隆。同 thrive, develop 反 decline

flow / fləʊ / vi. 淌；流动：Tears ∼ed from her eyes. 眼泪从她眼里流了出来。/ The river ∼s to south. 河水向南流去。同 move, pour

flower / ˈflaʊə(r) / n. 花；花卉：The ∼s bloom. 花开了。/ The ∼s have faded. 花已凋谢。/ The roses are in full ∼. 玫瑰花盛开。

flu / fluː / n. [U] (influenza 的缩略形式)流行性感冒

fluctuate / ˈflʌktjʊeɪt / vi. ❶(价格、数量等)波动；(意见、行为等)变化不定：The price of vegetables ∼s according to the weather. 蔬菜的价格随天气变化而波动。/Her affections had been continually fluctuating. 她平常的情感极不专一。❷摆动，波动：The electric current ∼s in the same manner. 电流以同样的方式波动。

fluent / ˈfluːənt / adj. 流利的；流畅的：Our teacher speaks ∼ English. 我们老师讲一口流利的英语。同 eloquent

fluid / ˈfluːɪd / n. 流体；液体：Water is a ∼. 水是液体。同 liquid

fluoride / ˈflʊəraɪd / n. [U]氟化物：sodium ∼氯化铵

fluorine / ˈflʊəriːn / n. [U]氟(符号 F)

flush / flʌʃ / v. (脸)变红，涨红：Her face ∼ed with excitement. 她激动得满脸通红。同 blush, redden

flute / fluːt / n. [C]长笛

flutter / ˈflʌtə(r) / v. 拍翅；飘动；颤动：A butterfly was ∼ing in the sunshine. 一只蝴蝶在阳光下翩翩起舞。同 wave, swing

fly[1] / flaɪ / Ⅰ v. (flew /fluː/, flown /fləʊn/) 飞；飞行；飘扬：On Sunday they often ∼ their model planes in the fields. 星期天他们常常在田野里放模型飞机。同 float, pilot/∼ **by** 很快地飞过；(时间)飞逝：The summer flew by. 夏天很快就过去了。∼ **into a great passion (anger, rage)** 勃然大怒：She flew into rage at the news. 她一听到这消息就勃然大怒。Ⅱ n. 飞，飞行，飞行距离

fly[2] / flaɪ / n. [C]蝇；苍蝇

foam / fəʊm / n. [U]泡沫：The ∼ of beer dis-

appeared in a few moment. 不一会儿啤酒中的泡沫就消失了。同 bubble 派 foamy adj.

focus / ˈfəʊkəs / Ⅰ n. (pl. focuses 或 foci /ˈfəʊsaɪ/)[C]焦点；中心：The problem of prices has become the ∼ of argument. 价格问题已经成为人们议论的中心。同 heart, center Ⅱ v. 聚集；集中：He ∼ed his attention on the improvement of his English reading comprehension. 他把注意力集中在提高英语阅读理解能力上。同 concentrate

fog / fɒg / n. [U]雾；浓雾：This city has a very bad ∼ in winter. 这个城市冬季的雾很大。/ His mind is in a hazy ∼. 他如坠云雾中。同 mist, cloud

foil[1] / fɔɪl / vt. 阻挠，阻碍；挫败；击败：Quick thinking by the bank clerk ∼ed the robbers. 银行职员的机智使抢劫犯没能得逞。/I was ∼ed of my purpose. 我未能达到目的。同 frustrate

foil[2] / fɔɪl / [U]箔；金属薄片：aluminum ∼铝箔

fold / fəʊld / v. 折叠，对折：If you ∼ the letter into two, it will fit into the envelope. 你把信对折起来就能放进信封了。反 unfold/ ∼ **one's arms** 交臂；抱臂：When they sit, they often ∼ their arms. 他们一坐下来，就常抱着手臂。

folder / ˈfəʊldə(r) / n. [C]文件夹；(存放散纸的)夹子

folk / fəʊk / n. 人们；家人；亲属：Some ∼s are never satisfied. 有些人永远不满足。/ old ∼s 老乡

follow / ˈfɒləʊ / vt. ❶跟；随着：Tuesday ∼s Monday. 星期二在星期一之后。/ Follow this road until you reach the church. 顺着这条路一直走到教堂。❷注视：We'll ∼ closely the development of the situation. 我们将密切关注形势的发展。同 watch, observe ❸听从：Don't ∼ other's advice blindly. 不要盲目听从别人的劝告。同 obey ❹领会；了解：He spoke so fast that I couldn't ∼ him. 他说得太快，我听不懂他的话。同 understand/∼ **on** 随后；继续：I'll be back soon. Meanwhile you ∼ on. 我马上就回来，你继续干。∼ **up** 跟踪；追查；继续：He thinks the story is worth ∼ing up. 他认为这故事值得连载。∼ **out** 贯彻；推行：We must ∼ out this plan. 我们必须执行这个计划。

following / ˈfɒləʊɪŋ / Ⅰ n. (集合名词)追随者；崇拜者：They have a ～ of their own. 他们有自己的一大批追随者。Ⅱ adj. 随后的；接着的：She stayed with us until the ～ afternoon. 她和我们一直待到第二天下午。同 coming, next 反 previous

用法
❶follow 后不可接不定式作宾语补足语：(误) I followed him to go into the house. (正) I followed him into the house. ❷on the following Wednesday 与 on the Wednesday following 意思完全相同。

fond / fɒnd / adj. 喜爱的；爱好的：be ～ of 喜爱；爱好：He is very ～ of his mother. 他很爱他母亲。同 loving, caring

用法
❶ fond 指一贯的爱好：I am fond of talk. 我喜欢交谈。❷fond 常由副词 very 修饰，不由 much 修饰：I am very fond of flowers. 我很爱花。

food / fuːd / n. [U](指某种特定的食物为可数名词) 食物；食品：Chinese ～ 中餐 / cooked ～ 熟食 / fast ～ 快餐 / mental ～ 精神食粮 / sea～s 海味食品 / Our ～ is running short. 我们的食物快吃完了。

fool / fuːl / Ⅰ v. 愚弄；欺骗；开玩笑：I was only ～ing. 我只是开开玩笑而已。/ You can't ～ me into doing that. 你不能骗我做那事。同 cheat, deceive, trick / ～ away 虚度光阴：They ～ed the whole evening away. 他们把整个晚上的时间都给浪费了。Ⅱ n. [C] 笨人；傻瓜：All Fools' Day 愚人节 / Every man has a ～ in his sleeve. 人人都有糊涂的时候。同 idiot 反 wiseman /make a ～ of sb. 愚弄某人；让某人出丑：You are making a ～ of me. 你在愚弄我。play the ～ with 戏弄，愚弄；糟蹋，损坏：They warn you not to play the ～ with them. 他们警告你不要戏弄他们。

foolish / ˈfuːlɪʃ / adj. 愚蠢的：It was very ～ of you to quarrel with a little girl. 你真傻，竟和一个小姑娘吵架。同 stupid 反 wise, clever 派 foolishly adv.

foot / fʊt / n. [C] (pl. feet /fiːt/) ❶脚；底部：He hurt his left ～. 他的左脚受伤了。/ There is a mistaken sentence at the ～ of Page 21. 在 21 页的下部有一个错句。同 base, bot-

tom /on ～ 徒步；步行：I came on ～. 我是步行来的。on one's feet 站着：He is on his feet for sixteen hours a day. 他每天站 16 个小时。under ～ 脚底下：It is very wet under ～. 脚底下很湿。at the ～ of 在…脚下：There is a hut at the ～ of the mountain. 山脚下有一间茅舍。set sth. on ～ 发动；开始：He set the motor on ～. 他发动了汽车。keep one's feet 站稳：The boy stumbled on the stairs but was able to keep his feet. 这孩子在楼梯上绊了一下，但没有跌倒。find one's feet 学会走路：How old was the baby when it began to find its feet? 这孩子开始走路时多大？put one's ～ down 采取坚定的态度；坚决不退让：John didn't want to practise the piano, but his mother put his ～ down. 约翰不想练钢琴，但母亲坚持要他练。❷英尺：He is five ～ eight. 他 5 英尺 8 英寸高。

football / ˈfʊtbɔːl / n. [C] 足球；足球比赛：a ～ fan 足球迷 / a ～ game(match) 足球比赛 / Most boys like to play ～. 大多数男孩喜欢踢足球。同 soccer

foothold / ˈfʊthəʊld / n. [C] ❶立脚处，立足点：a pair of shallow footholds in the rock 岩石上浅浅的一对立脚处 ❷稳固的地位；优势：chisel a ～ for oneself in the city 为自己在城里打稳基础/We need to get a ～ in the European market. 我们要在欧洲市场上找一个立足点。

footstep / ˈfʊtstep / n. [C] 脚步；脚步声；足迹：I heard ～s on the stairs. 我听到有人上楼的脚步声。

for / fɔː(r), fə(r) / Ⅰ prep. ❶达，计(表时间、空间)：I haven't seen you ～ four years. 我有四年未见到你了。/ ～ ever 永远：I love the city ～ ever. 我永远爱这座城市。❷为了(表目的、意愿)：We study ～ the people. 我们为人民而学习。❸由于，因为(表原因)：For lack of money, he can't go abroad. 因为缺钱，他不能出国。❹赞成：Some people were ～ the plan and others were against it. 一些人赞成此计划，另一些人则反对。❺就…而言：The weather is rather cold ～ March. 就三月的天气而言，这算是很冷的了。Ⅱ conj. 因为：He felt no fear, ～ he was a brave man. 他无所畏惧，因为他是一位勇士。

F

辨析

for 引导表示理由或原因的并列句，用法比较正式，并列句常置于句尾。**as** 常用在理由比较明显或原因已经得知的情况下，多用于口语，少用于书面语，它引导的从句常置于句首。**because** 常用来回答由 why 引起的提问，多用于书面语，位置可在主句前面，也可在主句后面。**since** 也可引导表原因的从句，多用于非正式口语。

forbid / fə'bɪd / vt. （forbad /fə'bæd/或 forbade /fə'beɪd/，forbidden /fə'bɪdn/；-bidding）禁止；不许：Smoking is strictly ～den here. 严禁吸烟。同 ban，prohibit

辨析

forbid 意为"禁止；不许"，普通用语，通常指直接下令禁止，也指制定规则以禁止，比 prohibit 通俗：The doctor forbids him to drink wine. 医生禁止他喝酒。**prohibit** 意为"禁止，不准"，较为正式，指制定正式规章，以法律名义或官方强制执行，多为司法用语，含命令意味：Gambling is prohibited. 禁止赌博。

force / fɔːs / Ⅰ vt. 强迫；迫使；强制：The crowd were ～d back. 人群被迫后退。同 make，drive，urge/～ **sb. to do sth.** 强迫某人做某事：The boss ～d him to work 13 hours a day. 老板强迫他一天工作 13 小时。～ **sb. into doing sth.** 被迫做某事：She was ～d into leaving her country. 她被迫离开了自己的国家。～ **through** 突破：He ～d his way through the crowd. 他从人群中挤了过去。Ⅱ n. ❶[U] 力量；气力；体力：The ～ of gravity makes things fall to the earth. 地球引力使物体向地面下落。/ Her physical ～ was weak, but her mental ～ was very great. 她体质弱，但她的精神力量却很强。同 power，strength，energy ❷[C] （有组织的）武装团体：an air ～ 空军 / The enemy ～s suffered severe death. 敌军伤亡惨重。同 army，troop / **by** ～ 强迫地；以武力：He took her money by ～. 他强行夺走了她的钱。

forearm / 'fɔːrɑːm / n.[C]前臂

forebear / 'fɔːbeə(r) / n. 祖先；祖辈：the land from which one's ～s had been driven 其祖先被赶走的地方

forecast / 'fɔːkɑːst / Ⅰ vt. （forecast 或 forecasted）预报；预测；预言：The station has ～

that it will rain tomorrow. 电视台预报明天有雨。同 predict，foretell Ⅱ n. 预测；预报：What is the ～ about the weather for today? 今天天气怎么样？同 outlook，prediction

forefinger / 'fɔːfɪŋɡə(r) / n.[C] 食指

forehead / 'fɒrɪd / n.[C] 额；前部

foreign / 'fɒrən / adj. 外国的；在国外的：He's thinking of buying a new ～ car. 他想买一辆进口新车。/ They absorbed ～ capital to develop the local industry. 他们引进外资发展地方工业。同 overseas 反 native，domestic 派 n.

foreleg / 'fɔːleɡ / n.[C] （动物的）前腿

foremost / 'fɔːməust / adj. 首要的，最重要的；首位的；最杰出的，最著名的：A computer programmer is first and ～ an interpreter. 计算机程序编制者首先是一位解释者。/ They have become ～ in nearly all the general lines of inland trade, commerce, and industry. 他们摇身一变成为几乎所有内陆贸易及工商业中的佼佼者。

foresee / fɔː'siː / vt. （foresaw /fɔː'sɔː/，foreseen /fɔː'siːn/）预知，预见，预测：Can you ～ your future? 你能预知你的未来吗？同 expect，predict

forest / 'fɒrɪst / n. 森林：preserve ～ 保护森林 / He got lost in the ～. 他在森林里迷路了。同 woods

foretell / fɔː'tel / vt. （foretold /fɔː'təuld/，foretold）预知；预见：Timely snow ～s a bumper harvest. 瑞雪兆丰年。同 forecast，predict

辨析

foretell 意为"预言"，强调对未来事件的宣布，预言是否准确、预言者的能力如何、预言是否有根据等都不太重要：The boatman usually can foretell weather. 船夫常能预言天气。**foresee** 对将要发生的事形成一种概念或作出判断：She foresaw that the train would be delayed by the bad weather. 她预计火车会因天气不好而晚点。**forecast** 主要用于天气预报：The weather forecast on the radio tonight tells of coming storms. 今晚收音机播出的天气预报指告暴风雨将至。**predict** 意为"预言；预示"，常用词，较正式，指根据事实或经验等来推断未来的事情，具有科学准确性：The astronomer predicts the return of comet. 天文学家预言了彗星的重返。

forever / fər'evə(r) / adv. （＝for ever）永

远；常常：We love peace ～. 我们永远热爱和平。同 always 反 never

foreword / ˈfɔːˌwɜːd / n. [C] 序；序言；前言：His teacher wrote the ～ to his newly published book. 他的老师给他新出版的书写了前言。同 preface

forge / fɔːdʒ / vt. 伪造；假造：～d bank notes 伪币；假钞 / He was sent to prison because he ～d passports. 他因伪造护照被关进监狱。同 fake, imitate

forgery / ˈfɔːdʒəri / n. 伪造；[C]伪造物；赝品：The police arrested the man for ～. 警察逮捕了伪造文件的人。/ This is a ～ painting. 这是一幅油画赝品。同 fake, imitation

forget / fəˈget / v. (forgot /fəˈgɒt/, forgotten /fəˈgɒtn/或 forgot；forgetting)忘记；遗忘：They almost forgot what they went there for. 他们几乎忘了去那儿的目的。/ I forgot to give him the key to the door. 我忘了给他钥匙。/ I shall never ～ hearing her singing that song. 我永远忘不了她唱那首歌的情景。反 recall, remember 派 forgetful adj.

用法

❶forget 后接不定式表示"因忘记而未做某事"，接动名词表示"忘记曾经做过某事"：He forgot to tell her about it. 他忘记把这事告诉她。He forgot telling him about it. 他忘记此事告诉了他，但后来忘记了。❷forget 作"遗忘"讲时，后面通常不接表处所的宾语补足语：(误) I forgot my key in the classroom. (正) I left my key in the classroom.

forgive / fəˈgɪv / vt. (forgave /fəˈgeɪv/, forgiven /fəˈgɪvn/)原谅；饶恕：Forgive me for interrupting you. 请原谅我打扰了你。同 excuse, pardon

fork / fɔːk / n. [C]叉；餐叉：She put a knife and ～ on the table. 她在桌上放了一副刀叉。

form / fɔːm / I vt. ❶形成；构成：Steam ～s when water boils. 水沸腾时产生水蒸气。同 constitute, compose ❷建立；组成；养成：Three or four classes ～ a grade. 三四个班组成一个年级。/ She has ～ed a good habit to wash hands before meals. 她已经养成饭前洗手的好习惯。同 build, shape, construct 【 **be ～ed of** 由…组成：The country is ～ed of a few large islands. 这个国家由几个大的岛屿组成。Ⅱ n. [C] ❶形式；方式：This English word has two ～s. 这个英语单词有两种形式。同 man-

ner, formality ❷形状；形态：She has a tall graceful ～. 她有修长优美的体型。同 shape, figure ❸[C] 表格：Please fill in the ～ with your name and address. 请在表上填写你的姓名和住址。同 blank, chart

formal / ˈfɔːm(ə)l / adj. ❶正式的；合乎格式的：A student's ～ education at college usually takes four years. 大学正规教育通常需要四年时间。/ This is a ～ contract. 这是一份正式合同。同 official, approved, regular 反 informal ❷礼仪上的；合乎礼仪的：The prime minister paid a ～ call to his neighbor country last week. 上周首相对他的邻国进行了礼节性的拜访。派 formality n. ; formally adv.

format / ˈfɔːmæt / I n. [C] ❶(出版物的)版式，开本 ❷(程序、步骤等的)安排，计划；设计：The course will follow a seminar ～. 这门课将以讨论的形式进行。❸(计算机中资料存储的)格式 Ⅱ vt. (formatted; formatting) ❶为…设计版式 ❷使(磁盘)格式化：The diskette must be ～ted for the computer being used. 磁盘必须格式化后才能使用。

formation / fɔːˈmeɪʃn / n. [U]形成；构成：She paid great attention to the ～ of children's good habits. 她非常重视孩子们好习惯的养成。/ The ～ of the building is unique. 这幢建筑物的结构非常独特。同 construction, composition

former / ˈfɔːmə(r) / I adj. 以前的；从前的：He was the ～ manager of the department. 他是这个部门的前任经理。同 previous, past Ⅱ pron. (the ～) 前者 反 latter

formula / ˈfɔːmjələ / n. [C] (pl. formulas /ˈfɔːmjələz/ 或 formulae /ˈfɔːmjəliː/) ❶(数学)公式；(化学)分子式 ❷处方；配方：Do you know the ～ of this pill? 你知道这种药丸的配方吗？同 recipe, presciption

forsake / fəˈseɪk, fɔːˈseɪk / vt. (forsook /-ˈsuk/, forsaken /-ˈseɪkən/) ❶遗弃；抛弃；摒弃：～ one's wicked habits 摒弃恶习 / He ～ his wife and children and went off with another woman. 他遗弃妻儿，跟另一个女人私奔了。❷(永久地)离开：The artist ～ his country for an island in the South Pacific. 那位画家离开祖国来到了南太平洋的一个海岛上。

fort / fɔːt / n. [C] 要塞；堡垒：The soldiers took the enemy's ～ in two days. 战士们两天内攻下了敌人的堡垒。同 fortress, camp

forth / fɔːθ / *adv.* 向前；往前：and so ～等等 / He was anxious and walked back and ～ in the corridor. 他非常焦急，在走廊里走来走去。同 forward

fortieth / ˈfɔːtiəθ / Ⅰ *num.* 第四十；四十分之一 Ⅱ *adj.* 第四十的；四十分之一的

fortunate / ˈfɔːtʃənət / *adj.* 幸运的；吉利的；带来好运的：That was ～ for you. 你真幸运。/ She was ～ to have passed the examination. 很幸运，她考试过关了。同 lucky 反 unfortunate 派 fortunately *adv.*

fortune / ˈfɔːtʃuːn / *n.* ❶命运；运气：They had good ～ to win the game. 她非常幸运地在那场游戏中获胜。同 luck, fate ❷财产；巨款：It was said that the boy inherited a large ～. 据说那小男孩继承了一大笔财产。同 property, wealth

forty / ˈfɔːti / Ⅰ *num.* 四十　Ⅱ *adj.* 四十个（的）

forum / ˈfɔːrəm / *n.* [C] 公开讨论会；座谈会

forward / ˈfɔːwəd / *adv.* 向前方；前进：The teacher asked the students to move ～. 老师要求学生向前走。反 backward

fossil / ˈfɒsl / *n.* [C]化石：They are hunting for ～s of dinosaurs. 他们正在寻找恐龙化石。

foster / ˈfɒstə(r) / *vt.* ❶培育，培养；鼓励，促进；(环境等)对…有利：provide opportunity to ～ productivity 创造机会促进生产／He ～ed a feeling of pride over his recent success. 他因最近的成功而变得心高气傲。❷养育，收养(常指非亲生的孩子)：～ a homeless child 收养一个无家可归的孩子

found / faʊnd / *vt.* ❶找到；发现(find 的过去式和过去分词形式) ❷建立；创办；成立：The college was ～ed in 1941. 这所学院是 1941 年创办的。/ This novel was ～ed on some facts. 这本小说是基于某些事实写成的。同 build, construct, establish 派 founder *n.*

foundation / faʊnˈdeɪʃn / *n.* ❶ [U]成立；建立；创办：The ～ of a primary school in the mountain area is their common wish. 在山区创办一所小学是他们的共同愿望。同 establishment ❷地基；基础；根据：He has laid a solid ～ for his future study. 他为未来的研究打下了坚实的基础。/ His report has no ～ of fact. 他的报告缺乏事实根据。同 basis, base ❸[C]基金；基金会：We have a ～ for re-search in our college. 我们学院设有科研基金会。同 funds

fountain / ˈfaʊntən / *n.* 泉水；喷泉；源泉：This ～ is used to drink from. 这眼喷泉是用来提供饮水的。/ Knowledge is the ～ of wisdom. 知识是智慧的源泉。同 spring, source

four / fɔː(r) / Ⅰ *num.* 四 Ⅱ *adj.* 四个(的)

fourteenth / ˌfɔːˈtiːnθ / Ⅰ *num.* 第十四；十四分之一 Ⅱ *adj.* 第十四的；十四分之一的

fourth / fɔːθ / Ⅰ *num.* 第四；四分之一 Ⅱ *adj.* 第四的；四分之一的

fowl / faʊl / *n.* 家禽，禽肉；飞禽

fox / fɒks / *n.* [C] 狐狸

fraction / ˈfrækʃn / *n.* ❶碎片；片段；一小部分：She has finished only a ～ of the work. 她只完成了工作的一部分。同 bit, piece, part ❷(数学)分数

fracture / ˈfræktʃə(r) / Ⅰ *n.* [C;U] ❶骨折；(软骨、软组织的)撕裂，挫伤：a ～ of the arm 臂部骨折/kidney ～ 肾破裂 ❷断裂；破裂；折断：a ～ of the ice 冰裂/a ～ of friendly relations 友好关系的破裂 Ⅱ *v.* (使)骨折；挫伤(软骨或软组织)：The boy fell from a tree and ～d his arm. 那个男孩从树上摔了下来，跌断了手臂。

fragile / ˈfrædʒaɪl / *adj.* 易碎的；脆的；体质弱的：We know that china is ～. 我们知道瓷器是易碎的。/ She looks very ～ but is still working. 她看起来身体虚弱，但她仍然在工作。同 breakable, weak 反 tough, strong

fragment Ⅰ / ˈfrægmənt / *n.* [C] ❶破片；小碎块，碎渣：～s of powdery cloud 几块碎片/ burst into ～s 炸成碎片 ❷不完整(或未完成)的部分；孤立的片段：I heard only a ～ of their conversation. 他们的对话，我只听了个只言片语。Ⅱ / ˈfræɡment / *v.* (使)破碎，(使)成碎片；分裂：The vase was ～ed in shipment. 那个花瓶在运输中被打碎了。/The chair ～ed under his weight. 那张椅子在他身体的重压下散了架。

fragrance / ˈfreɪɡrəns / *n.* [C] ❶芬芳，芳香；香气，香味：the ～ of flowers and the song of birds 花香鸟语/The air was heavy with the ～ of lush wild blooms and fruits. 空气中洋溢着茂盛的野生花草和果实的芳香。❷香料；香气 同 perfume, scent

fragrant / ˈfreɪɡrənt / *adj.* 香的；芬芳的；令人

愉快的：～ memories of the party 对晚会的美好回忆 / She put fresh ～ flowers in the vase. 她在花瓶里插满芬芳的鲜花。同 perfumed,odorous

frame / freɪm / n. [C]框架;架子;结构;I broke the ～s of my glasses. 我把眼镜框打烂了。/ a door ～ 门框 / a ～ for a picture 画框 / the ～ of society 社会结构 同 framework,structure

framework / 'freɪmwɜːk / n. 框架;结构;机构;组织:The bridge has a steel ～. 这座桥是钢结构的。同 frame, construction, organization

France / frɑːns / n. 法国

frank / fræŋk / adj. 坦白的;直率的;Please give me a ～ reply soon. 请尽快给我一个坦率的答复。同 honest,straight 派 frankly adv.

free / friː / Ⅰ adj. ❶自由的;无约束的;未在狱中的;You are ～ to express yourself at today's meeting. 在今天的会上你可以畅所欲言。同 unconfined, unlimited / set ～ 释放:The prisoners were set ～. 那些囚犯被释放。**be ～ from** 不受…约束的:I am ～ from duty today. 今天我不当班。❷免费的;免税的:If your wages are small, they'll be ～ of income tax. 如果你工资低,你可免交所得税。同 cost-free,duty-free ❸有空的;未占据的:Her afternoons are usually ～. 她通常下午有空。同 spare,unoccupied /**make ～ with** 随意使用他人之物:They entered the house and made ～ with whatever they could lay their hands on. 他们进入屋子随便拿东西。Ⅱ vt. 使自由;释放:You should ～ the bird from the cage. 你应当把鸟从笼中放出去。同 release, liberate 派 freely adv.

freedom / 'friːdəm / n. 自由;无拘束:～ of speech 言谈自由 / ～ of religion 宗教信仰自由 / He longed for ～. 他渴望自由。同 liberty,ease /**take(use)～ with sb.** 对某人放肆;对某人无礼:Don't take ～ with her. 不许对她这么无礼。

freeway / 'friːˌweɪ / n. [C] ❶高速公路 ❷免费高速干道

freewill / 'friːˌwɪl / adj. 自愿的:a ～ choice 自由选择

freeze / friːz / v. (froze /frəʊz/, frozen / 'frəʊzn/) ❶冷冻;结冰;Fresh water ～s at 0℃. 淡水在零摄氏度结冰。❷令人愣住;呆住;The child froze at the sight of the snake. 那孩子一看见蛇就吓呆了。

freezing / 'friːzɪŋ / adj. 极冷的;冻结的;What ～ weather it is! 今天天气真冷!

freight / freɪt / n. ❶[U]货运:the volume of ～ 货运量/Nowadays, the railways earn most of their profit from ～. 眼下,铁路的大部分赢利来自货运。❷[U](货运的)货物;Only 40% of ～ moves interstate by truck. 只有四成的货物用卡车在各州间运输。/ a ～ of timber 一车木材

French / frentʃ / Ⅰ adj. 法国的;法国人的:～man n. [C]法国人 Ⅱ n. 法语:She became a teacher of ～ after graduation. 毕业后她成为一名法语教师。

Frenchman / 'frentʃmən / n. [C](pl. Frenchmen)法国人,法兰西人;具法国血统的人;法国男子

frequency / 'friːkwənsi / n. 频率;频繁:The ～ of traffic accidents in this road is high. 这段公路上交通事故的发生率很高。同 repetition

frequent / 'friːkwənt / adj. 频繁的;经常的;屡次的:He made ～ trips to Japan. 他经常去日本。/ Professor Li is a ～ visitor to the library. 李教授是图书馆的常客。同 repeated, constant 派 frequently adv.

fresh / freʃ / adj. ❶新鲜的;新制的:The meat is not very ～. 这肉不是很新鲜。/ I like ～ bread. 我喜欢吃新烤的面包。同 raw,crude ❷不熟练的;无经验的:He is a ～ hand in this field. 在这一领域里他还是个新手。同 inexperienced 派 freshly adv.

friction / 'frɪkʃən / n. [U]摩擦;摩擦力:Oil reduces ～. 油能减少摩擦。同 rubbing

Friday / 'fraɪdi / n. 星期五(略作 Fri.)

fridge / frɪdʒ / n. [C]电冰箱(refrigerator 的缩略形式)

friend / frend / n. [C]朋友;友人:We have ～s all over the world. 我们的朋友遍世界。反 enemy /**make ～s(with)**(与…)交朋友:Better not be so quick to make ～s. 交朋友最好不要太性急。

friendly / 'frendli / adj. 友好的;亲切的:He is very ～ to(towards) me. 他对我很友好。同 kind 反 unfriendly

friendship / 'frendʃɪp / n. 友爱;友情;友谊:He paid a ～ visit to Japan last month. 上个月

他去日本进行友好访问。/I hope our ～ will last forever. 我希望我们的友谊长存。 反 hatred

fright / fraɪt / n. [U] 惊吓；恐怖：He gave me a great ～. 他使我大吃一惊。/ The boy shivered with ～. 那小男孩吓得发抖。 同 alarm, fear, dread 派 frightful adj.

frighten / 'fraɪtn / vt. 吓唬；使害怕；使受惊吓：The child was badly ～ed. 那个小孩吓坏了。 同 alarm, scare/～ sb. into (out of) doing sth. 恐吓某人做(不做)某事：He was ～ed into confessing. 他受惊吓后便招认了。

frightening / 'fraɪtnɪŋ / adj. 令人惊恐的，骇人的：This is a ～ thought. 这个想法令人不寒而栗。/It was a ～ situation to be in. 当时的情景非常可怕。

frigid / 'frɪdʒɪd / adj. ❶寒冷的，酷寒的：The air on the mountaintop was ～. 山顶上的空气很寒冷。❷冷淡的，没有生气的，刻板的：a ～ reaction to the proposal 对提议作出的冷淡反应/a welcome that was polite but ～彬彬有礼但拘谨刻板的欢迎方式

frog / frɒg / n. [C] 青蛙

from / frɒm, frəm / prep. ❶自；从(表示空间的距离)：～ door to door 挨家挨户 / ～ Beijing to London 从北京到伦敦 / ～ under the table 从桌子下 / ～ behind the door 从门后 ❷自，从(表示时间的起始)：～ the first of May 从五月一日起 / ～ one's childhood 自某人童年起 / ～ beginning to end 自始至终/ ～ then on 从那时起 / ～ time to time 不时地 / ～ three o'clock to five o'clock 从三点到五点 ❸由…发出；来自：He received a present ～ his friend. 他收到了他朋友送给他的礼物。❹由，从，据(表示来源)：draw water ～ a well 由井里汲水 / Don't judge a person ～ his appearance. 不要以貌取人。

front / frʌnt / Ⅰ n. ❶前面；正面：Please go in ～. 请前面走。 反 back, rear/**in ～ of** 在…前面；当着…的面：There is a pond in ～ of the house. 房子前面有个池塘。 **in the ～ of** 在…的前部：He is sitting in the ～ of the car with the driver. 他和驾驶员一起坐在汽车前面。❷前线；前方：go to the ～ 上前线 同 /on the production ～ 在生产前线 同 battlefront，frontline Ⅱ adj. 前面的；前部的；正面的：He sat in the ～ row. 他坐在前排。 / The news is in

the ～ page of the newspaper. 这条消息登在报纸的头版。 反 back, last

frontier / 'frʌntɪə(r) / n. [C] ❶边境，边界，国境，边疆：They drove across the ～ between Canada and the United States. 他们驾车驶过加美边界。 / He lives in a small town on the ～. 他住在一个边境小城。 同 border, boundary, margin ❷新领域；尖端领域：The scientists are exploring the ～s of science. 科学家们正在探索新的领域。 同 advance, top

frost / frɒst / n. [U] 霜；霜冻；严寒：The roof was covered with ～ this morning. 今天早晨屋顶上覆盖着一层霜。/ The heavy ～ killed three sheep. 这场霜冻冻死了三只羊。 同 cold, freeze 派 frosty adj.；frosted adj.

frostbite / 'frɒstbaɪt / n. [U] 冻伤；冻疮；霜害

froth / frɒθ / Ⅰ n. [C；U] 泡，泡沫；白沫：a glass of beer with a lot of ～ on it 泛起许多泡沫的一杯啤酒/The ～ of the waves collected on the beach. 浪花泛起的白沫覆涌在海滩上。Ⅱ vi. 起泡沫；吐白沫：The beer ～ed and overflowed the glass. 啤酒泛起泡沫，溢出了杯子。

frown / fraʊn / Ⅰ vi. ❶皱眉，蹙额：He sat at his desk, ～ing as he so often did. 他坐在办公室前，像往常那样蹙眉蹙额。❷表示不悦(或烦恼、不赞成)：He ～ed at my retort. 他见我顶嘴，脸显愠色。Ⅱ n. [C] ❶皱眉，蹙额：She read the letter quickly, a ～ on her face. 她很快看了那封信，一边看一边皱起了眉头。❷不悦(或严肃、沉思等)的表情：His smile turned into a ～ of dismay. 他先是笑容满面，不一会儿变得愁眉苦脸。

frozen / 'frəʊzn / adj. ❶结冰的，冰冻的；冻住的：a ～ river 结了冰的河流 ❷严寒的，极冷的：It's a beautiful day—～ and icy and clear. 天气很好，冰天雪地，晴朗晶莹。❸冻伤的，冻坏的；冻僵的：～ toes 冻伤的脚趾 ❹(行为、态度等)冷淡的，缺乏感情的：He kept chewing the inside of his lip a lot, ～ into complete silence. 他不停咬着内嘴唇，表情冷淡，默默无言。❺冷冻的，冷藏的：～ vegetables 冷冻的蔬菜

fruit / fruːt / n. ❶水果；果实：He eats much ～. 他吃很多水果。/ There are many ～ s in the house. 屋子里有很多种水果。❷(常用 pl.)结果；成果：We are now enjoying the ～ s of our hard work. 我们现在享受着辛勤劳动的

成果。同 result, product 派 fruitful adj.

frustrate / frʌ'streɪt, 'frʌstreɪt / vt. ❶使无用（或无效）；使（计划，希望等）落空，使泡汤：The student's indifference ～d the teacher's efforts to help him. 这个学生无动于衷，老师对他的帮助都白费了。❷挫败，击败；使受挫折：～ an opponent 挫败对手 ❸使失望，使沮丧，使失意：The lack of money and facilities depressed and ～d him. 他因缺乏资金和设备而十分沮丧，一筹莫展。

fry / fraɪ / v. 油煎；油炸：Mother is ～ing fish in the kitchen. 妈妈正在厨房煎鱼。

fuel / 'fjʊəl / n. [U]燃料（如用复数则指不同种类的燃料）：They have used up all their ～. 他们已经用完所有的燃料。

fugitive / 'fjuːdʒɪtɪv / n. [C] ❶逃亡者，亡命者；逃犯：a ～ from a dictatorial regime 逃脱独裁统治的亡命者/a jail ～越狱犯 ❷流亡国外的人；难民：～s from an invaded country 从被入侵国逃出来的难民

fulfil(l) / fʊl'fɪl / vt. (-filled;-filling) 履行；执行；完成：They have ～led their duties admirably. 他们出色地完成了任务。/ You must ～ your promise. 你必须履行你的诺言。同 perform, finish 派 fulfil(l)ment n.

full / fʊl / adj. 满的；完全的；充满的：This bottle is ～. 这只瓶子是满的。/ The hall is ～ of teachers and students. 大厅里坐满了老师和学生。同 filled 反 empty 短 ～ of 充满：This bottle is ～ of water. 瓶子里装满了水。/ Our teacher's conversation is ～ of wits. 我们老师的谈话妙趣横生。派 fully adv.

full-scale / 'fʊlˌskeɪl / adj. ❶（图画、模型等）与实体同样大小的，实比的：a ～ replica 与实物大小一致的复制品 ❷完全的；完整的；全面的：The police have started a ～ murder investigation. 警察已经对谋杀展开了全面侦查。

full-time / 'fʊlˌtaɪm / adj.&adv. 全部时间（的）；专职（的）；全日制（的）：receive ～ education 获得全日制教育/a ～ domestic servant 全职保姆

fume / fjuːm / I n. (刺鼻、浓烈或有害的)烟，气，汽：be thick with the ～s of gunpowder 硝烟弥漫/He breathed whisky ～s all over my face. 他一嘴的酒气喷得我满脸都是。II vi. ❶冒烟（或气、汽），（烟、气、汽等）冒出，散发：Staggering off, he ～d with brandy. 他步履蹒跚地走了，身上散发出白兰地酒味。❷发怒，发火：I ～d at my own inability. 我深为自己的无能恼火。

fun / fʌn / n. [U]娱乐；有趣的事；乐趣：We had a lot of ～ at her birthday party. 在她的生日聚会上我们玩得很开心。/ What ～! 多么有趣！同 amusement, enjoyment 短 **make ～ of** 嘲弄；取笑：Don't make ～ of the little girl. 不要取笑那个小女孩。

function / 'fʌŋkʃn / I n. [C] ❶功能；机能；作用：The ～ of this machine is to cut steel. 这台机器的功能是切割钢铁。/ What is the ～ of the English word in this sentence? 这个英语单词在句中起什么作用？同 use, role, part ❷职务；职责：Her ～ is to take good care of the children. 她的职责是照管好这些孩子。同 duty, task ❸函数：linear ～ 线性函数 II vi. 运行；活动；起作用：The telephone in my office was not ～ing. 我办公室里的那部电话机坏了。/ This noun ～s as an adjective here. 这个名词在这里起形容词的作用。同 work, operate, perform

fund / fʌnd / n. (pl.) 资金；基金；专款：research ～s 科研经费 / welfare ～s 福利基金 / a relief ～ 救济款 / They decided to draw foreign ～s to build the expressway. 他们决定吸引外资来修建这条高速公路。同 capital, foundation

fundamental / ˌfʌndə'mentl / I adj. 基础的；基本的：He learned the ～ rules of English grammar first. 他首先学习了英语语法的基本规则。同 basic, elementary, essential II n. (pl.)基本原则；基本原理：A ～s of good behavior is honesty. 优良品行的一条基本原则就是诚实。

funeral / 'fjuːnərəl / n. [C]葬礼：They held a state ～ for the dead president. 他们为去世的总统举行了国葬。同 burial

funnel / 'fʌnl / n. [C] ❶漏斗 ❷漏斗状物：a long ～ of people 一长队排成扇形的人群 ❸（火车、轮船等的）烟囱；烟道，焰道

funny / 'fʌni / adj. (-ier, -iest)滑稽可笑的；有趣的；稀奇的：He likes ～ movies. 他爱看滑稽电影。/ There is something ～ about the matter. 这事情有点稀奇古怪。同 odd, comic

fur / fɜː(r) / n. 毛皮：He wore a pair of ～ gloves. 他戴着一双皮手套。

furious / ˈfjʊəriəs / *adj.* ❶狂怒的,暴怒的: The ～ man pressed on. 那个怒火中烧的男子步步进逼。/ be ～ with rage 火冒三丈 ❷狂暴的: a ～ storm 狂风暴雨 ❸激烈的;紧张的: a ～ argument 唇枪舌剑

furnish / ˈfɜːnɪʃ / *vt.* 装备;布置;提供: I want to ～ this room better. 我想把这房间好好布置一下。/ He ～ed me with the necessary information. 他向我提供了必要的信息。同 equip, decorate, provide

furniture / ˈfɜːnɪtʃə(r) / *n.* (集合名词)家具: They bought a piece (set) of ～. 他们买了一件(套)家具。

furrow / ˈfʌrəʊ / *n.* [C] ❶犁沟: make ～s for sowing 耕地播种 ❷沟;车辙: deep ～s in the muddy road 泥泞路上的深深车辙 ❸褶皱;皱纹: ～s of worry lined his faces. 他的脸上因忧愁而布满了皱纹。

further / ˈfɜːðə(r) / Ⅰ *adj.* 更远的;更多的;进一步的: We should have a ～ discussion on the problem. 我们应当就此问题进行更深入的讨论。同 farther, more, additional Ⅱ *adv.* 更远;而且;进一步: I can walk no ～. 我不能再往前走了。同 farther, moreover

furthermore / ˌfɜːðəˈmɔː(r) / *adv.* 此外,另外;而且: ～, she has successfully depicted the atmosphere of Edwardian India. 此外, 她出色地描绘了爱德华时期的印度风情。

fury / ˈfjʊəri / *n.* ❶[U;C]狂怒,暴怒: drunken ～ 撒酒疯/Wilde was full of ～. 威尔德怒不可遏。❷[U]狂暴;激烈;猛烈;强烈;剧烈: He close rather to encounter the utmost ～ of the clements abroad. 他宁愿到外面去承受各种恶劣条件的磨炼。

fuse[1] / fjuːz / *n.* [C] ❶导火索,导火线: He lit the ～ and waited for the explosion. 他点燃导火线后,在一旁等着爆炸。/ arm a ～ 装导火索 ❷引信,信管: a time ～ 定时引信 / **have a short ～** 容易激动,动辄发怒: The manager has a rather short ～. 经理脾气暴躁,动不动就发火。

fuse[2] / fjuːz / Ⅰ *n.* [C]保险丝,熔线: This plug uses a 5 amp ～. 这个插座要用一根 5 安培的保险丝。Ⅱ *v.* ❶(使)熔化: ～ metals 熔融金属 ❷(使)熔合,(使)熔接: The intense heat ～d the rocks together. 高温将一块块岩石熔合在一起。/ zinc and copper fuse together to make brass. 锌和铜熔合成黄铜 ❸融合: Sadness and joy are ～d in her poetry. 她的诗歌交织着悲和喜。

fuss / fʌs / *n.* 忙乱;大惊小怪: Don't make a ～ over such a small thing. 不要对这件小事大惊小怪。同 ado, trouble 派 fussy *adj.*

futile / ˈfjuːtaɪl / *adj.* ❶无用的,无效的,徒劳的: a ～ effort 徒劳/It is ～ to continue the investigation. 再继续调查就是白费心机。❷(话语等)空洞的,无意义的: ～ chatter 无聊的嗑牙扯淡 派 futility *n.*

future / ˈfjuːtʃə(r) / *n.* 将来;未来;前途: The teacher often says that the boy has a bright ～. 老师常说这小孩前途无量。同 prospect 反 past / **in (the)** ～ 今后;将来: Try to live a better life in ～. 今后要努力过更好的生活。/ You should be confident in the ～. 你应对未来抱有信心。

G g

gain / geɪn / Ⅰ v. ❶获得；赢得；博得；挣得：～ experience 获得经验 / ～ the audience's attention 吸引观众的注意 / ～ a battle 打了胜仗 / ～ one's living 谋生 / ～ strength 恢复体力 囲 win, obtain, achieve ❷进步；改进；增加：～ in weight 增加重量 / ～ in health 更加健康 / The car is ～ing speed. 车子在加速。囲 improve, increase grow 反 decrease, lose ❸到达；抵达：After battling against the blizzard, we finally ～ed our destination. 在同暴风雪搏斗之后，我们终于到达了目的地。囲 arrive, reach Ⅱ n. ❶[U](因贸易、工作)获得(利益、盈余)：regardless of personal ～ or loss 不计个人得失 / Last year he got a clear ～ of 1,000 *yuan*. 去年他获得净利润 1000 元。囲 profit, return ❷[C]增加；增进：Increase of wealth is not always a ～ to one's happiness. 财富的增加并非总是幸福的增进。囲 growth, increase 反 loss

galaxy / 'gæləksi / n. ❶[C]星系：the existence of galaxies beyond the Milky Way 银河外星系的存在 ❷(令人瞩目的东西或人等的)一群，一族：A ～ of fireworks went up. 焰火升空耀若群星。

gale / geɪl / n. [C]大风：It is blowing a ～. Let's close the windows. 刮大风了，我们把窗户关上吧。囲 wind, typhoon

gallery / 'gæləri / n. [C]画廊；美术馆；美术陈列馆：We visited the National ～ yesterday. 昨天我们参观了国家美术馆。

gallon / 'gælən / n. [C]加仑(液体单位)

gamble / 'gæmbl / Ⅰ n. [C]赌博；投机；冒险：Some people like ～ on horse races. 有些人喜欢赌马。/ Your new plan seems to be a ～. 你的新计划似乎是一次冒险。囲 bet, lottery Ⅱ vt. 赌博；投机；冒险：He has ～d away all his money. 他赌博输光了所有的钱。囲 bet, risk

game / geɪm / n. [C]1. (有规则的)游戏；运动；

比赛：play ～s 做游戏 / Boys always like football ～s. 男孩们总是喜欢足球比赛。囲 play, match ❷(pl.)运动会；竞技赛：the Olympic ～s 奥林匹克运动会 ❸一次，一盘；一场：have a ～ at cards 打一盘牌 / have a ～ of chess 下一盘象棋 / win four ～s in the first set 在第一回合中赢四局

gang / gæŋ / n. [C](一)帮；(一)伙；(一)群：They formed two ～s and fought each other. 村里人已结成两伙相互争斗。囲 band, club

gangster / 'gæŋstə(r) / n. [C]匪徒；歹徒；暴徒：The police caught the ～ this morning. 今天上午警察抓住了那个歹徒。囲 bandit, criminal

gaol / dʒeɪl / n. [C]监狱；监禁：The young man has been sent to ～. 那年轻人已被送进监狱。囲 jail

gap / gæp / n. [C]裂缝；缺口；空白；间隙；差距（close, fill, fill in, fill up, supply）a ～ 填补空白；弥补缺陷；弥合差距 / a generation ～ 代沟 / a wide ～ 巨大分歧 / There is a great ～ between his idea and mine. 他的想法与我的大相径庭。囲 break, crack, difference

garage / 'gærɑːʒ / n. [C]汽车库；汽车修理厂：He parked his car in the ～. 他把车停在车库里。/ My car is under repair in the ～. 我的车正在修车厂维修。

garbage / 'gɑːbɪdʒ / n. [U]垃圾：Don't dump ～ anywhere. 不要把垃圾倒得到处都是。囲 rubbish, waste

garden / 'gɑːdn / n. [C]❶花园；果园；菜园：No ～ without its weeds. 没有不生杂草的花园。/ He is watering his vegetable ～. 他在给菜园浇水。囲 yard, orchard ❷公园：The old couple are having a walk in the public～. 老两口正在公园散步。囲 park

gardening / 'gɑːdnɪŋ / n. 园艺：This book is about farming and ～. 这本书讲到农耕和

garlic / ˈgɑːlɪk / n. [U] 大蒜

garment / ˈgɑːmənt / n. [C] 衣服；外套：second-hand ～ 旧服装 / a sport ～ 运动服 / a woman's upper ～ 女上衣 / a working ～ 工作服 圓 clothes, dress

garrison / ˈɡærɪsn / n.[C]驻军；卫戍部队；警卫部队：the Beijing ～ 北京卫戍区 / the Shanghai ～ 上海警备区 圓 troops, army, post

gas / ɡæs / n. [U](与不定冠词连用指某一种气体，用复数指不同种类的气体)❶气体：end ～ 尾气 / exhaust ～ 废气 / marsh ～ 沼气 / natural ～天然气 ❷ 煤气：burn ～烧煤气 / His sister works in a ～ company. 他姐姐在一家煤气公司工作。

gash / ɡæʃ / Ⅰ n.[C]深长的切口(或伤口)；切痕，砍痕 Ⅱ vt. 在…上划开深长的口子；割开；划伤：She ～ed her arm on some broken glass. 她被一些碎玻璃划伤了胳膊。

gasolene(-ine) / ˈɡæsəliːn / n. [U](美)汽油(口语中简称 gas)：He stopped his car for ～. 他停下车来加油。

gasp / ɡɑːsp / vi. 喘息；喘气：She ～ed with rage. 她气得直喘气。

gate / ɡeɪt / n. [C]大门：Who is the man at the ～? 在门口那里的人是谁?

辨析
gate 指有墙(围墙、篱笆)而无顶的门，不指一般房子的门或门口：The city gate was pulled down. 城门已被拆掉。door 指有顶的建筑物的大门或车辆、橱柜的门：The door was broken. 房门被撞开了。The driver closed the door and started the car. 司机关上了车门，启动汽车。

gather / ˈɡæðə(r) / v. 聚集；收集；采集：We must ～ the people to our side. 我们必须把人民团结到我们这一边。/ A crowd ～ed about the entrance. 一群人聚集在入口四周。/ The teacher asked a student to ～ the papers. 老师让一个学生收试卷。圓 assemble, collect

辨析
gather 意为"采集；聚集"，无论指人或物都含杂乱地聚成、归拢的意思：They are gathering flowers in the garden. 他们在花园里采花。assemble 意为"集中；集合"，指人们为实现共同的目标集合在一起，也指使具有共

同特性的物体聚在一起：We have assembled here to discuss the question. 我们聚集在此讨论这个问题。accumulate 意为"积累；积聚"，指连续不断地、有规律地积累：He accumulated a fortune by buying and selling used cars. 他靠买卖旧车积累了一大笔钱。collect 意为"收集"，指有计划、有选择地把零散的东西汇成有序的整体：She is fond of collecting stamps. 她喜爱集邮。

gathering / ˈɡæðərɪŋ / n. 集会；聚会；聚集：They said that they would have a ～ to celebrate their success. 他们说要举行一个集会来庆祝他们的胜利。圓 assembly, meeting

gay / ɡeɪ / adj. 快乐的；高兴的：They were ～ as little birds at the thought of the coming holiday. 想到假日就在眼前，他们快活得像小鸟一样。圓 happy, cheerful 反 sad

gaze / ɡeɪz / vi. 凝视；注视：～ at (on, upon) 凝视；注视：For hours he sat gazing at the stars. 他坐在那里几个小时凝视天上的星星。圓 look, stare

GDP (= gross domestic product) 国内生产总值

gear / ɡɪə(r) / Ⅰ n. 齿轮；传动装置；(汽车等的)排挡：The largest ～ was broken. 最大的那个齿轮断裂了。/ You should learn to use the reverse ～. 你应当学会使用倒车挡。Ⅱ v. 调整；(使)适合：I have to ～ myself to the new life here as soon as possible. 我得使自己尽快适应这里的新生活。圓 adapt, adjust, match

gel / dʒel / n. [C;U]❶凝胶(体)，冻胶；胶带体 ❷发胶

gem / dʒem / n. [C]❶宝石：a bracelet studded with ～s 一只嵌有宝石的手镯 ❷珍品，精品；宝物：The ～ of his collection was a rare Italian stamp. 他藏品的精华部分是一枚罕见的意大利邮票。❸受人爱戴(或珍视)的人；尤物

gene / dʒiːn / n. [C]遗传因子；基因：a ～ pool 基因库 / ～ engineering 基因工程

general / ˈdʒenrəl / Ⅰ adj. ❶总的；全体的；大概的；笼统的：He is the ～ secretary of the conference. 他是大会的秘书长。/ I learned the ～ idea of the plan after talking with the ～ manager. 在与总经理交谈之后我了解了这个计划的大概内容。圓 overall, chief, main 反 particular ❷一般的；普通的；普遍的：Do you know the ～ attitude of the students towards this decision? 你知道学生对这个决定一般持什么态度吗？/ The price of food is a matter of ～ anxiety. 食品的价格是人们普遍担忧的问题。同 common, usual Ⅱ n. [C]将军：The old ～ has a beautiful granddaughter. 老将军有一个漂亮的孙女。/ in ～一般说来；通常：In ～, your plan is good. 你们的方案总的来说是好的。派 generalization n.；generalize(-se) vt.

generally / ˈdʒenrəli / adv. 一般；通常；大体上：It was once ～ believed that the earth was flat. 曾经人们一般都认为地球是平的。/ Generally speaking, she is friendly to us. 总的来说，她对我们很友好。同 usually, ordinarily, commonly

generate / ˈdʒenəreɪt / vt. 产生；发生：They ～ electricity for citizens. 他们为市民们发电。同 creat, produce

generation / ˌdʒenəˈreɪʃn / n. [C]❶一代：the future ～ 后代 / the last (past) ～上一代 / the young ～ 青年一代 / ～ after ～ 世世代代 / The old man often says that they have the responsibility to educate the younger ～. 老人常说他们有责任教育好年轻的一代。同 age, era ❷产生；发生：This machine is used for the ～ of electricity. 这台机器是用来发电的。同 creation, production

generator / ˈdʒenəreɪtə(r) / n. [C]发电机

generosity / ˌdʒenəˈrɒsəti / n. 慷慨；大方；宽宏大量：Thank you for your ～. 感谢你的慷慨大方。反 selfishness, meanness

generous / ˈdʒenərəs / adj. 慷慨的；大方的；宽容的：He presented a ～ gift to her mother on her birthday. 妈妈生日他送了一份厚礼。/ We all like him because he has a ～ nature to others. 由于他对人宽宏大量，我们都很喜欢他。同 liberal, unselfish, big-hearted 反 stingy, selfish, mean 派 generously adv.

genetic / dʒəˈnetɪk / adj. 遗传的；遗传学的：～ code 遗传密码 / ～ engineering 遗传工程 派 genetically adv.

genetics / dʒəˈnetɪks / n. 遗传学

genius / ˈdʒiːnɪəs / n. ❶天资；天才；天赋：He has shown his wonderful creative ～. 他显示了惊人的创造天赋。/ The little girl has a ～ for languages. 那小女孩极具语言天赋。同 gift, talent ❷天才；才子：a mathematical ～ 数学天才 / Einstein was a great scientific ～.

爱因斯坦是伟大的科学天才。同 talent

gentle / ˈdʒentl / adj. ❶温和的；有礼貌的；文雅的：～ nature 温和的性格 / ～ manners 文雅的举止 / The old lady has a ～ look. 老奶奶有一副和善的面容。同 polite, refined 反 rude, rough, wild ❷轻柔的；徐缓的；不猛烈的：Her ～ voice made us comfortable. 她轻柔的嗓音让我们感到舒服。/ I saw the man went up the ～ slope slowly. 我看见那人慢慢地走上缓坡。同 soft, light, gradual 反 sudden, abrupt

gentleman / ˈdʒentlmən / n. (pl. gentlemen) ❶绅士；有身份的人；有教养的人；彬彬有礼的人：A ～ cannot be so rude to a woman. 有教养的人不会这样粗鲁地对待妇女。同 nobleman ❷先生：Ladies and ～! 女士们，先生们！/ This ～ wishes to visit our school. 这位先生想参观我们的学校。同 man, sir

gentlewoman / ˈdʒentlwʊmən / n. [C] (pl. gentlewomen)女士；有身份的妇女

gently / ˈdʒentli / adv. 温柔地；轻柔地：The nurse said ～ to the patient that she was all right. 护士温柔地对病人说情况很好。/ Speak ～ to the child. 对孩子说话应温和些。同 softly, lightly

genuine / ˈdʒenjuɪn / adj. 真正的；真实的；真诚的：～ pearls 真珍珠 / a ～ signature 亲笔签名 / ～ sorrow 真实的伤感 / This is a ～ picture of Picasso. 这是一幅毕加索的真迹。同 real, true, honest 反 false, artificial

geography / dʒɪˈɒɡrəfi / n. [U]地理学

geologist / dʒɪˈɒlədʒɪst / n. [C] 地质学家；研究地质的学者

geology / dʒɪˈɒlədʒi / n. [U]地质学

geometry / dʒɪˈɒmətri / n. [U]几何学：plane ～ 平面几何学 / solid ～ 立体几何学

geophysics / ˌdʒiːəʊˈfɪzɪks / n. [U]地球物理学

geophysicist / ˌdʒiːəʊˈfɪzɪsɪst / n. [C]地球物理学家

germ / dʒɜːm / n. [C]病菌；细菌：This disease is spread by ～s. 这种疾病是通过细菌传播的。/ A ～ warfare is disastrous. 细菌战是灾难性的战争。

German / ˈdʒɜːmən / Ⅰ n. [C]德国人；德语 Ⅱ adj. 德国的；德国人的

Germany / ˈdʒɜːməni / n. 德国

germinate / ˈdʒɜːmɪneɪt / v. ❶发芽；(使)抽

芽;开始生长:Warmth, moisture, and oxygen ～s seeds. 种子发芽需要温度、湿度和氧气。❷萌发(观点、想法等);(使)产生;形成:The university presses ～d no ideas at all. 这些大学出版社没有拿出一点新的想法。/ Some inventions ～ out of the experiences of daily life. 有些发明源于日常经验。

gesture / ˈdʒestʃə(r) / n. 姿势;姿态;手势:a ～ language 手势语 / Her strange ～ made me puzzle. 她奇怪的手势让我感到困惑不解。 圓 sign, signal

get / get / vt. (got /gɒt/, got 或 gotten /ˈgɒtn/) 得到;获得;取;赢得:Where did you ～ the dictionary? 这本词典你在哪儿买的? / They've got five tickets. 他们买到了五张票。圓 gain, achieve, obtain —vi. ❶ 变得;使:When spring comes, it ～s warmer and warmer. 春天到来了,天气越来越暖和。/ He got very angry. 他很气愤。/ She soon got well. 她不久便复原了。圓 become, turn ❷回到;走到;到达:Let's see who ～s there first. 让我们看看谁先到那里。/ They got to the factory at a quarter to nine. 他们是 8:45 到工厂的。/ He got home at nine last night. 他昨晚 9:00 回到家。圓 arrive, reach ❸达到(某种阶段):How did you ～ to know I was here? 你怎么知道我在这儿? ❹使(成为某种状态):I must ～ (have) the breakfast ready. 我必须把早餐准备好。/ I must ～ (have) my hair cut. 我得去理发了。圓 make / ～ **along** 过活;进展;进步;友善相处:How are you getting along? 你近况如何? / How is your son ～ing along with his school work? 你儿子的功课怎么样? ～ **away** 离去;去度假:The thief has got away. 那贼已逃之夭夭。/ She hopes to ～ away next Monday for a week. 她希望从下星期一起休假一周。～ **away from** 摆脱;回避:It is no use ～ting away from the facts. 这些事实是回避不了的。～ **sth. back** 回来;取回:I'll ～ the book back. 我要收回这本书。～ **down to** 认真着手处理;开始从事:You should ～ down to your work after the holiday. 假期后你应开始工作。～ **hold of** 抓住;握:He got hold of the tail of the dog. 他抓住狗的尾巴。～ **in** (使)进入;到达;收割;认识;插话;收集:He got in by the window. 他从窗口跳进去。/ The peasants are ～ting in the crops. 农民正在收割庄稼。/ I can't ～ him in at all. 我根本不能与他结识。/ May I ～ a word in? 我

可以插一句话吗? ～ **into** 进入;陷入;穿上;升至:～ into trouble (difficulty) 陷入麻烦(困境) / She has got into bed. 她已上床。/ He got into his overcoat quickly. 他迅速穿上大衣。～ **off** 脱下;下车;走脱;离开:The bus stopped and he got off. 公共汽车停了,他便下了车。/ Mother told him to ～ off his wet clothes. 母亲叫他脱下湿衣服。～ **on** 穿上;上车;使进步:～ on the train (a horse, a bike) 上火车(上马,骑上自行车) ～ **out** 出去;传出去;拔出:The news has got out that you are leaving. 传闻你要走了。/ The dentist got her bad tooth out. 牙医帮她拔掉了虫牙。～ **over** 康复;克服;摆脱;越过:It took me a long time to ～ over my cold. 过了好久我的伤风才好。/ It is hard to ～ over the death of my father. 我很难从父亲去世的悲伤中恢复过来。～ **through** 通过;结束;完成;达到目的:Did you ～ through the exam? 你考试及格了吗? / I got through the book in one evening. 我一个晚上就看完了这本书。～ **to** 开始;到达:They will ～ to Beijing tomorrow. 他们明天到北京。/ He got to thinking that she wouldn't come after all. 他开始觉得她肯定不会来了。～ **to one's feet** 站起;站着:Sorry, you have to ～ to your feet. 对不起,你只好站着。～ **up** 起床:I like to ～ up early in the morning. 我喜欢早起。

辨析

get 意为“得到;取得”,常用词,不管通过什么方式弄到手都可用 get:Will you get me a ticket? 你可以帮我弄张票吗? **acquire** 意为“求得;学到”,指靠自己的努力或能力获得,一经获得即成为永久之物:You should try to acquire good habits. 你应努力养成良好的习惯。**gain** 意为“赢得;争取”,指通过竞争或一定的努力才能取得、获得:I hope he'll gain the victory this time. 我希望他这次获胜。**obtain** 意为“获得;找到”,书面用语,比 get 正式。指依靠他人的帮助或自己的努力,经过相当长的时间后得到所渴望的东西:We can obtain knowledge through books. 我们能从书本中获得知识。**attain** 意为“得到;达到”,指达到较为完美的程度:He has attained his goal of being a good singer. 他已达到成为一名优秀歌手的目标。

---

ghastly / ˈɡɑːstli, ˈɡæstli / adj. ❶可怕的,恐怖的,令人毛骨悚然的:The scene after the battle was ～. 战斗过后的场景惨不忍睹。❷极

坏的,糟糕的;令人不快的:a ～ bowl of soup 一碗难喝的汤

ghost / ɡəʊst / n. [C]鬼;幽灵;幻影般的东西: I don't believe in ～s. 我不相信有鬼存在。/ She came in like a ～. 她像幽灵一样进来。同 soul,spirit

giant / ˈdʒaɪənt / Ⅰ n. [C] 巨人;巨物:He became a ～ in the field of finance when he was only thirty-eight. 他 38 岁就成了金融巨头。同 monster Ⅱ adj. 巨大的:We all like ～ pandas. 我们都喜欢大熊猫。/ China is taking ～ steps forward. 中国正以巨人般的步伐前进。同 huge,vast 反 small,tiny,little

gift / ɡɪft / n.[C] ❶礼物;礼品:I want to get some interesting ～s to take home. 我想买一些有趣的礼物带回家。同 present ❷天资;天赋;才能:She has a ～ for music. 她有音乐天赋。/ My uncle is a man of many ～s. 我的叔叔是一个多才多艺的人。同 ability

ginger / ˈdʒɪndʒə(r) / n. [U] 生姜

giraffe / dʒəˈrɑːf / n. [C]长颈鹿:A ～ may grow to 6 meters tall. 一只长颈鹿可以长到六米高。

gigantic / dʒaɪˈɡæntɪk / adj. 巨大的:a ～ net 天罗地网 同 giant,huge

girl / ɡɜːl / n.[C] 女孩,少女,姑娘;女仆;女职员:factory ～ 女工 / a modern ～ 摩登女郎 /the leading ～ 女主角/He sent his ～ to a ～'s school. 他把女儿送进一所女子学校读书。同 miss,maiden

give / ɡɪv / v.(gave /ɡeɪv/,given /ˈɡɪ-vn/) ❶给,给予;赠给:I gave her a pen. 我给了她一支笔。/ Give one to me,please. 请给我一个。同 offer,present 反 take,receive ❷付出:I would ～ a lot to know where she is. 我愿出高价打听她的下落。同 offer ❸供给;供应:The sun ～s us warmth and light. 太阳供给我们光和热。❹致力于;献身于:He would rather die than ～ in. 他宁死不屈。devote /～ off 放出;流出;飞出:～ off vapor (smoke,light) 放出气(烟、光) / Rotten eggs ～ off a bad smell. 腐烂的鸡蛋发出一股臭味。～ out 发出;分发,分配;用尽:The cowboy ～ out a yell. 牛仔大叫一声。～ up ①放弃;屈服;投降:Jimmy is ～ing up his job as a newsboy when he goes back to school. 吉米回校后放弃了送报的工作。②戒除:The doctor told Tom to ～ up smoking. 医生叫汤姆戒烟。③放弃希望;放弃念头:You should ～ up the idea of going abroad. 你应放弃出国的念头。～ rise to 导致;招致:Such conduct might ～ rise to misunderstanding. 这种行为可能导致误解。～ way (to) ①退后;撤退:Our troops had to ～ way. 我们的部队只好撤退。②让出空间;Give way to traffic coming in from the right. 请让右边来的车先走。

given / ˈɡɪvn / Ⅰ v.(give 的过去分词形式)给;给予 Ⅱ adj. 假设的;特定的;已知的:Given his support, I think we will finish the task on time. 如果得到他的支持,我想我们会按时完成任务的。/ You must reach there at a ～ time. 你得在指定的时间到达那儿。同 assumed,stated,specified

glacier / ˈɡlæsɪə(r) / n. [C]冰川;冰河

glad / ɡlæd / (gladder,gladdest) adj. 高兴的;愉快的;乐意的:I am very ～ to help you with your homework. 我很乐意帮助你完成家庭作业。/ We are ～ of your success. 我们为你的成功感到高兴。/ Her mother was very ～ about her arrival. 她的到来令她母亲感到很高兴。同 happy, pleased, willing 反 sad, unhappy, unwilling 派 gladden vt.;gladly adv.

glance / ɡlɑːns / Ⅰ n. [C]一瞥;一眼:They stole a ～ at John. 他们偷偷看了约翰一眼。同 look,glimpse Ⅱ v. 扫视;看一眼;瞧一下:I leaned back in my chair, ～ing about the room. 我靠在椅子上,环视了一下房间。同 look,glimpse / ～ at 瞥;扫视:She ～d at the sleeping boy and then hurried away. 她瞟了一眼熟睡的孩子,随即匆匆离去。

gland / ɡlænd / n. [C]腺:adrenal ～肾上腺

glare / ɡleə(r) / Ⅰ n. ❶[U] 强光:We could see nothing because of the ～ of the car's lights. 由于车灯炫眼,我们什么也看不见。同 flare,blaze ❷[C]怒视;瞪:The boy gave his mother a ～. 那小男孩瞪了他母亲一眼。Ⅱ v.闪耀;怒目而视:The sunlight ～d on the ice. 阳光照在冰上反射出耀眼的光。/ They stood there glaring each other. 他们站在那儿怒目相视。同 stare

glaring / ˈɡleərɪŋ / adj. ❶(光线等)刺眼的,炫目的,耀眼的:a ～ red 炫目的红色/It was a September day, hot and ～. 这是一个九月天,酷热难当,骄阳似火。❷显眼的,明显的,引人注目的:a ～ error in spelling 明显的拼写

错误/a ～ lie 赤裸裸的谎言

glass /glɑːs/ n. ❶[U]玻璃：a piece（bit）of ～一块玻璃/broken ～碎玻璃/sheet ～平板玻璃/Glass breaks easily. 玻璃易碎。❷[C]玻璃杯；玻璃制品：a ～ of milk 一杯牛奶/She put on her ～es to read the letter. 她戴上眼镜读信。

glide /glaɪd/ v.（使）滑动；（使）滑行：Fishes were gliding about in the lake. 鱼儿在湖里轻快地游来游去。/He ～d down from the slope. 他从坡上滑下去。同 slide，drift

glimpse /glɪmps/ n.[C]一瞥；一看：He caught a ～ of the chairman after he came in. 他走进来以后看了主席一眼。同 glance，peep

glitter /ˈglɪtə(r)/ vi. 闪耀，闪烁：Gold ～s brightly. 金子闪闪发光。同 flash，sparkle

global /ˈgləʊbl/ adj. ❶球面的；球形的 ❷全球的；全世界的：a ～ flight 环球飞行/on a ～ scale 在全球范围内/We wish for peace. 我们希望世界和平。/Scientists of all countries are concerning the problem of ～ warming. 各国的科学家都在关注全球性变暖的问题。同 worldwide，international 反 local，regional ❸普遍的；综合的：同 comprehensive 派 globalize v. ；globally adv.

globe /gləʊb/ n.[C] ❶地球；世界：He traveled around the ～ and learned a lot. 他环球旅行，学到了很多东西。同 world，earth ❷球；球体；地球仪：The teacher rotated the ～ and found the location of the small island. 老师旋转地球仪找出了那个小岛的位置。同 ball，sphere

gloom /gluːm/ n.[U] ❶黑暗；阴暗：He walked through the ～ of the thick forest. 他穿过茂密阴暗的森林。同 dark ❷忧愁；沮丧：Don't let defeat fill you with ～. 别因失败而沮丧失望。同 sadness，depression 派 gloomy adj.

glorify /ˈglɔːrɪfaɪ/ vt. ❶给…荣耀，为…增光，使光荣：the names which ～ this country 为这个国家增光添的人们 ❷使更美；美化；为…增色：Sunset glorified the valley. 落日的余晖使山谷更显得绚丽。❸称赞；赞美，颂扬：Her brave deeds were glorified in song and story. 她的英勇事迹被编成歌曲和故事广为传颂。

glorious /ˈglɔːrɪəs/ adj. ❶辉煌的；灿烂的；壮丽的：a ～ view 壮丽的景观/a ～ time 一段

愉快的时光 同 splendid，brilliant 反 plain ❷光荣的：The town has a ～ history. 小镇有着光荣的历史。同 honored

glory /ˈglɔːri/ n.[U] ❶ 光荣；荣誉：He deserves his ～. 他无愧于所得的荣誉。/They fight for ～，not for money. 他们为荣誉而战，不是为金钱而战。同 honor，fame ❷壮丽；灿烂；辉煌：I like the ～ of the sunset very much. 我非常喜欢落日的壮观景象。同 brightness

glossary /ˈglɒsəri/ n.[C]（附于书籍卷末的）词汇表；术语或专门词语汇编：I haven't read the ～ of this book. 我还没看这本书的词汇表。

glove /glʌv/ n.[C]手套：draw（put on）one's ～s 戴手套/a pair of ～s 一双手套

glow /gləʊ/ vi. 灼热；发光：The sunset ～s in the west. 日落西方，红霞满天。/Her face ～ed with delight. 她满脸喜气。同 shine，brighten 派 glowing adj.

glue /gluː/ Ⅰ n.[U]胶；胶水：This kind of ～ sticks fast. 这种胶水黏性强。同 paste Ⅱ v. 胶合；粘贴：He ～d two pieces of wood together. 他把两块木板粘在一起。同 paste，stick

GMT，G. M. T. （＝Greenwich Mean Time）格林尼治标准时间

GNP （＝gross national product）国民生产总值

go /gəʊ/ v.（went /went/，gone /gɒn/）❶去；动身；行走：When did he ～ to Beijing? 他什么时候到北京去的？/～ bathing（shooting，hunting，fishing，mountain-climbing）去沐浴（射击、狩猎、钓鱼、登山）/～ for a walk（ride，swim）去散步（骑马、游泳）/～ on a journey（a trip，a voyage，an outing）去旅行（游览、航海、郊游）/～ to bed 上床睡觉/～ to college 上大学 同 walk，move，leave ❷变得；变成：He went red with anger. 他因愤怒而脸红。同 become，turn ❸（进行时与带 to 的不定式连用）打算；计划干（某事）：I'm ～ing to do it in my own way. 我要按自己的方式去做。❹（进行时与带 to 的不定式连用）将要；即将：I am ～ing to tell you a story. 我这就给你们讲个故事。/～ **about** 四处走动；着手做：Go about your own business. 做你自己的事。～ **abroad** 出国：Many people can afford to ～ abroad now. 现在很多人都有钱出国了。～ **ahead** 有

进展；先走一步：The work is ～ing ahead in good style. 这项工作进展顺利。～ **all out** 全力以赴；尽所能：We should ～ all out to help him. 我们应尽全力帮助他。～ **along** 进行；继续：Things went along smoothly. 事情进展顺利。～ **along with** 陪伴：I'd like to have you ～ along with me. 我要你陪我一起去。～ **away** 离去：～ away from me. 给我走开。～ **back** 返回：He went back home last night. 昨晚他回了家。～ **by** 走过；(时间) 流逝：Time ～es by quickly on vacation. 假期的时间过得很快。～ **down** (船只) 下沉：The ship went down with all people on board. 那条船连同船上的人都沉下去了。～ **down on one's knees** 跪下：Mother asked her son to ～ down on his knees. 母亲要儿子跪下。～ **forward** 前进；进行：If he thinks he is right, he ～es straight forward. 如果他认为他是正确的，他就勇往直前。～ **home** 回家；回国：When did you ～ home last night? 昨晚你什么时候回家的？～ **in** 进入；参加：The thread will not in. 线穿不进针孔。～ **in for** 从事，致力于；参加：What sport do you ～ in for? 你参加哪个体育项目？～ **on** 继续，接着做；发生：He went on talking as though nothing had happened. 他若无其事地继续讲下去。／ I shall ～ on to deal with the gerund. 我现在接着讲动名词。／ Please ～ on with your work. 请继续做你的工作。～ **out** 出去；(灯) 熄灭：He has gone out. 他已出去。／ The candlelight went out itself. 蜡烛自行熄灭了。～ **over** 复习；检查，核对：Let's ～ over this lesson. 咱们把这一课温习一下。／ The teacher is ～ing over the examination papers. 老师正在批阅考卷。～ **through** 通过／完成；检查：The proposal did not ～ through. 这项提议未被通过。～ **to pieces** 精神崩溃；身体衰弱；破碎；瓦解：At the news of her mother's death she went completely to pieces. 听到她母亲去世的消息，她的精神完全崩溃了。～ **up** 上升；升起：The path ～es up the hill. 小径通往山上。～ **with** 相配；配合，陪伴：Her coat doesn't ～ with her shoes. 她的外衣与鞋子不相配。～ **without** 没有…也行：There is no milk for breakfast, so we'll have to ～ without. 早餐没牛奶喝，我们只好凑合着吃。

goal / gəʊl / n. [C] ❶目标；目的：We are fighting for one common ～. 我们正为着一个共同目标而奋斗。同 aim, purpose ❷球门；得分：Team A won by two ～s. 甲队以两球获胜。／ My brother is the ～ keeper of the football team. 我哥哥是足球队的守门员。同 score

goat / gəʊt / n. [C]山羊：He raises a lot of ～s. 他养了许多山羊。

god / gɒd / n. ❶ [C] 神 ❷上帝：God bless you. 愿上帝保佑你。／ God helps those who help themselves. (谚语)自助者天助。

gold / gəʊld / n. [U] 黄金；金子：a ～ watch 金表／ age of ～ 黄金时代／ He won a ～ medal in the match. 在比赛中他获得金奖。

golden / 'gəʊldən / adj. 金色的；珍贵的；极好的：They walked in the field with ～ wheat. 他们行走在金黄色的麦田里。／ It is a ～ opportunity for you. 这是你的一个绝好机会。同 gold-colored, precious

goldfish / 'gəʊldfɪʃ / n. [U]金鱼：Some ～ are swimming freely in the fish-tank. 几条金鱼在鱼缸里自由地游着。

golf / gɒlf / n. [U]高尔夫球运动：I like to play ～. 我喜欢打高尔夫球。

good / gʊd / I adj. (better / 'betə /, best / best/) ❶美好的；良好的；令人快乐的；令人满意的：～ news 好消息／ have a ～ time 过得很快乐／ have a ～ night 睡得好／This is a ～ tool. 这是一把好工具。同 fine, nice, excellent ❷善良的；有道德的：He is a very ～ man. 他是一个非常善良的人。／ It is ～ of you to tell me the news. 把这消息告诉我，你真好。同 kind ❸能胜任的；有能力的：He is ～ at drawing. 他擅长绘画。同 able, skillful ❹相当多的：a ～ deal of money 很多钱／ a many people 很多人／ a ～ way 相当长的路程／ as ... as 实际上；几乎：His promise is as ～ as gold. 他的保证很可靠。II n. [U] ❶善；利益；好处：What's the ～ of doing that? 那样做有什么好处？／ We should do ～all our lives. 我们应一辈子做好事。／ I am telling you this for your ～. 我告诉你这个是为了你好。同 merit, benefit ❷效用；用途；用处：A car is much ～ to him. 汽车对他很有用。It's no ～ doing that. 那样做是没有用的。同 use/ **for** ～ 永久地：I have given up smoking for ～. 我永远不再抽烟了。**do sb.** ～ 对某人有益：Have a glass of beer, it will do you ～.

喝杯啤酒吧,对你有好处。

goodbye / ɡʊdˈbaɪ / *int.* 再见;再会:She kissed her mother ~ at the airport. 在机场她和母亲吻别。/ They said ~ to each other after the conference. 会议结束后他们互相道别。圆 bye,bye-bye

goodness / ˈɡʊdnəs / *n.* 善良;善行;美德:He gave the boy some money out of the ~ of heart. 出自好心他给了小男孩一些钱。/ For ~' sake,I really don't know anything about it. 看在老天爷的分上,对这事我确实一无所知。圆 goodwill,virtue,kindness 反 badness,wickedness

goodwill / ˌɡʊdˈwɪl / *n.* [U]善意;友善;友好,亲善:return sb.'s ~ 报答某人的好心/The old man beamed with ~. 那老汉慈祥地笑了。

goods / ɡʊdz / *n.* (*pl.*) 货物;商品:high-priced ~ 高档商品 / second-hand ~ 二手货 / defective ~ 次品/ smuggled ~ 走私货/ They are sending some consumer ~ to the country-side. 他们正把消费品送往农村。/ This shop supplies easy-to-sell ~ only. 这家商店专供抢手货。圆 commodity,merchandise

goose / ɡuːs / *n.* [C] (*pl.* geese / ɡiːs /) 鹅

gorge / ɡɔːdʒ / *n.* [C]峡;峡谷;山峡:Three Gorges Project 三峡工程 / The foreigners are visiting the Three Gorges. 外宾正在参观三峡。

gorgeous / ˈɡɔːdʒəs / *adj.* ❶光彩夺目的,华丽的;豪华的,辉煌的:a ~ hall 金碧辉煌的大厅/trees in ~ fall colours 披上绚丽秋色的树木 ❷极好的;令人极其愉快的:This cake is ~. 这蛋糕好吃极了。

gorilla / ɡəˈrɪlə / *n.* [C]大猩猩

gossip / ˈɡɒsɪp / *n.* ❶[U]闲话;聊天;流言蜚语:I was having a ~ with our teacher when you came. 你来时我正和老师聊天。/ Do you believe all the ~ you hear? 你会相信你所听的所有闲话吗? 圆 chatter ❷[C]爱说闲话的人;搬弄是非者:Don't be a dreadful ~. 别搬弄是非。

govern / ˈɡʌvn / *v.* ❶管理;统治;支配:Who ~s the country? 谁来统治这个国家? / He has ~ed the country for more than 30 years. 他治理这个国家三十多年了。圆 rule,manage ❷控制;抑制:You should ~ your temper. 你应该克制你的脾气。圆 control

government / ˈɡʌvənmənt / *n.* ❶[C]政府;内阁:a central ~ 中央政府 /People all over the country wish to build a clean and honest ~. 全国人民都希望建设一个廉洁的政府。圆 administration,authorities ❷[U]行政管理;治理;管理;支配:Our monitor is a member of the student ~. 我们班长是学生自治会成员。圆 management,direction,governing,control

governor / ˈɡʌvənə(r) / *n.* [C]❶州长;地方长官;总督:He visited the ~ of Hawaii. 他拜访了夏威夷州的州长。圆 administrator,ruler ❷主管;理事;董事:chief,head,director

gown / ɡaʊn / *n.* [C] 长袍;长外衣:He took a picture in an academic ~. 他穿着学位服照了张相。圆 dress,robe

grab / ɡræb / *v.* (grabbed;grabbing)抢夺;抓牢;急抓:He ~ bed me by the arm. 他抓住我的手臂。/ She ~ bed at the opportunity of going abroad. 她抓住了出国的机会。圆 seize,grasp

辨析
grab 意为"急抓;抢;夺",强调抓住的速度很快:The dog grabbed the meat and ran. 狗抢了肉就跑。grasp 意为"紧抓;紧握;了解",常指用指头、爪等紧紧抓住:She grasped my hand and shook it. 她紧握住我的手握了起来。seize 意为"抓住;夺取",指突然用力抓住某人或某物:The policeman seized the woman and pulled her back from the edge of the cliff. 警察抓住那位妇女,把她从悬崖边上拉了回来。

grace / ɡreɪs / *n.* ❶[U]优美;优雅:She danced with ~. 她舞姿优美。圆 beauty,elegance ❷[C] (*pl.*) 文雅;才艺:Speaking French and playing the piano are social ~s. 讲法语和弹钢琴是两大社交才艺。派 graceful *adj.*

grade / ɡreɪd / *n.* [U]❶班级;年级:An elementary school in America has eight ~s. 美国的小学有8个年级。/ He is a graduate of ~ 2006. 他是2006级毕业生。❷品位;级别;等级:Milk is sold in ~s. 牛奶分等级售出。/ This kind of tea is of the highest ~. 这种茶叶是上等的。圆 class,rank,degree ❸成绩;分数:His ~ on history is "A". 他的历史成绩为"A"。圆 mark,score

gradual / ˈɡrædʒuəl / *adj.* 逐渐的;逐步的:The students are discussing the problem of the ~

increase in population of this district. 学生们正在讨论这一地区人口的逐步增长问题。同 successive,continuous 反 sudden,immediate

gradually / ˈɡrædʒuəli / *adv.* 逐渐地；逐步地：After a month's rest his health ～ improved. 休息一个月之后他渐渐恢复了健康。/ Many people have noticed that prices are going up ～. 很多人都注意到物价在逐渐上涨。同 continuously,steadily 反 suddenly,quickly

graduate Ⅰ / ˈɡrædʒueit / *v.* 毕业：3,500 students ～d from this university last year. 该大学去年有 3500 名学生毕业。Ⅱ/ˈɡrædʒuət/ *n.* [C]获学位者；毕业生：a ～ in philosophy 哲学专业毕业生 / Oxford ～s 牛津大学毕业生

graduation / ˌɡrædʒuˈeiʃn / *n.* ❶[U]毕业；大学毕业时：He was about twenty-two on his ～. 他毕业时大约 22 岁。/ The ～ found an ideal job in a big company. 那位大学毕业生在一家大公司找到了一份理想的工作。❷[C]毕业典礼：Will your parents come to attend the ～? 你父母会出席毕业典礼吗?

grain / ɡrein / *n.* 谷类；谷粒：We shouldn't waste a ～ of rice. 我们不应浪费一粒粮食。同 corn,seed

gram(me) / ɡræm / *n.* [C]克(重量单位)

grammar / ˈɡræmə(r) / *n.* [U] 语法；语法规则：a ～ book 语法书 /There is so much ～ to be learned in the first lesson. 第一课有许多语法知识要学。

grammatical / ɡrəˈmætik(ə)l / *adj.* ❶语法的；文法的：～ analysis 语法分析 ❷(句子)合乎语法的;遵从原则的,符合原理的：～ sentences 合乎语法规则的句子

gramophone / ˈɡræməfəun / *n.* [C]留声机：The old lady has an old ～ and some ～ records. 老太太有一台旧的留声机和一些唱片。

grand / ɡrænd / *adj.* 庄严的;伟大的;雄伟的;豪华的;华丽的：a ～ view 壮丽的景色 /the ～ finale 大结局 / The King lived in a ～ palace. 国王住在宏伟的宫殿里。/ The famous film star lives in ～ style. 那位著名影星过着豪华的生活。同 splendid,magnificent,luxurious

grandchild / ˈɡræntʃaild / *n.* (*pl.* grandchildren)孙子(女)；外孙(女)

granddaughter / ˈɡrændɔːtə(r) / *n.* [C]孙女；外孙女：great ～ 曾孙女;外曾孙女

grandfather / ˈɡrænfɑːðə(r) / *n.* [C]祖父;外

祖父：great ～ 曾祖父;外曾祖父 同 grandpa

grandma / ˈɡrænmɑː / *n.* [C]祖母;外祖母

grandmother / ˈɡrænmʌðə(r) / *n.* [C]祖母;外祖母：great ～ 曾祖母;外曾祖母 同 grandma

grandpa / ˈɡrænpɑː / *n.* [C]祖父;外祖父 同 grandfather

grandparent / ˈɡrænpeərənt / *n.* [C]祖父或祖母;外祖父或外祖母：great ～s 曾祖父母;外曾祖父母 同 grandpa,grandma

grandson / ˈɡrænsʌn / *n.* [C]孙子;外孙子：great ～ 曾孙;外孙

grandstand / ˈɡræn(d)stænd / *n.* ❶[C](体育场、足球场、赛马场等的)大看台,主看台 ❷大看台观众,主看台观众：The entire ～ cheered when our team won. 我队取胜时主看台上所有的观众都欢呼起来。

granny / ˈɡræni / *n.* [C]奶奶;姥姥;老奶奶

grant / ɡrɑːnt / *vt.* 答应;(姑且)承认;给予：I ～ that he has made a certain social success, but I still don't approve of his opinion. 我承认他取得了一定的社会成就,但我还是不赞同他的观点。/ He was ～ed the citizenship of that country. 他获得了那个国家的公民权。同 allow,permit,admit/**take ... for** ～ed 视…为当然;认定：A teacher cannot take it for ～ed that students should completely obey him. 老师不能认为学生完全服从他是理所当然的。

grape / ɡreip / *n.* [C]葡萄：a bunch of ～s 一串葡萄

graph / ɡrɑːf / *n.* [C]曲线图;图表：The student is drawing a line ～. 学生正在画曲线图。同 chart,diagram,table

grasp / ɡrɑːsp / Ⅰ*v.* ❶抓住;握住：I ～ed his right hand firmly. 我紧紧抓住他的右手。同 grip,seize ❷领会;掌握;了解：It is not very easy for me to ～ his meaning. 对我来说,要领会他所说的意思没那么容易。同 understand,master Ⅱ*n.* (通常用单数)紧握;把握;理解：You seem to have a good ～ of English history. 你似乎对英国历史很了解。/ Success is within our ～ now. 现在我们已有取得成功的把握。同 grip,understanding

grass / ɡrɑːs / *n.* [U] ❶ 草：green ～ 青草/rank ～ 杂草/ withered ～ 枯草 同 herb ❷草原;草地：at ～ 在牧场上/ Keep off the ～! 勿踏草坪! 同 lawn,grassland/ ～ land *n.* 牧

场；草地；草原

grasshopper / ˈɡrɑːʃɒpə(r) / n. [C]蚱蜢；蝗虫

grassy / ˈɡrɑːsi,ˈɡræsi / adj. 为草覆盖的；长满草的；草深的：a ～ mound 杂草丛生的土墩

grateful / ˈɡreɪtfl / adj. 感激的；令人愉快的：I'm heartily ～ to you for what you have done for me. 我衷心感谢你为我做的一切。/ He has got a ～ letter. 他收到一封感谢信。同 thankful

gratitude / ˈɡrætɪtjuːd / n.〔U〕感谢；感激：I can hardly express my ～ to you. 我难以表达我对你的感激之情。Her selfless help deserves our ～. 她无私的帮助值得我们感谢。同 thanks

grave¹ / ɡreɪv / n. [C] 坟墓；墓穴：a ～-digger 掘墓人 / a ～ yard 墓地 / The son set up a ～-stone for his parents. 儿子为父母竖了一块墓碑。同 tomb

grave² / ɡreɪv / adj. ❶严重的；重大的：He made a ～ mistake in the project. 在那项工程中他犯了一个严重的错误。/ Nobody knew the ～ consequence. 没有人知道那个严重的后果。同 important,significant 反 light,trivial ❷严肃的；庄重的：a ～ face 庄重的面孔 / He was ～ as he told them about the accident. 在同他们谈到那意外事故时，他非常严肃。同 serious,solemn 反 cheerful,light-hearted

辨析

grave 尤指在表情、态度方面的严肃，也指那些可能造成伤害的重要事物：The sick man's condition is very ～. 这个病人的病情严重。**serious** 强调由于关心重要事情而显得表情和态度严肃、庄重：He became serious when he spoke of finding a job. 谈及找工作，他变得一本正经。**solemn** 指一个人不笑时的严肃表情：He looked at her with a solemn expression. 他满脸严肃地注视着她。

gravel / ˈɡræv(ə)l / I n. [U]沙砾，砾石；石碴 II vt. 用石子铺盖；给…铺上石碴；铺沙砾于…：～ a road 在路上铺沙砾

gravity / ˈɡrævəti / n. [U] ❶重力；重量：The stone rolled down the mountain by ～. 这块石头在重力作用下滚下山。❷严重性；重要性：He knew nothing about the ～ of the present situation. 他对目前形势的严重性一无所知。同 importance

gray / ɡreɪ / (＝grey) I adj. 灰色的；灰白的：～ economy 灰色经济 / ～ expenditure 灰色消费 II n. [U]灰色：dark ～ 深灰色 / light ～ 浅灰色 / Her grandmother likes to dress in ～. 她奶奶喜欢穿灰色衣服。

graze / ɡreɪz / v. (牛、羊等)吃草；放牧：The cows were grazing on the hillside. 牛儿在山坡吃草。同 feed

great / ɡreɪt / adj. ❶伟大的；卓越的；优秀的：Mao Zedong was a ～ man. 毛泽东是一位伟人。同 noble,distinguished ❷重要的；重大的：That is a ～ discovery. 这是一个重大的发现。同 important,significant ❸很，非常：a ～ deal 很多 / a ～ number 很多 / a ～ while ago 很久以前 / a ～ majority 大多数 / We had a ～ time in the countryside. 在农村我们度过了非常愉快的时光。❹(口语)善于；精通：He is ～ at chess. 他下象棋下得很好。同 excellent ❺(口语)极好的；极棒的：That's ～! 棒极了！同 excellent 派 greatly adv.；greatness n.

Greece / ɡriːs / n. 希腊

greed / ɡriːd / n. [U] 贪心；贪婪：We hate his ～ for honors. 我们讨厌他爱慕虚荣。同 longing,hunger 反 generosity

greedy / ˈɡriːdi / adj. 贪吃的；贪婪的；贪心的：The boy is ～ for more knowledge. 小男孩渴求学到更多的知识。/ Don't be ～ for power. You should serve for the people. 不要权欲熏心，要为人民服务。反 generous /be ～ for (after,of) 贪图：He is always ～ for something new. 他总是贪求新的东西。/ She is a woman ～ of money. 她是一个贪图金钱的人。

Greek / ɡriːk / I adj. 希腊的 II n. 希腊人；希腊语

green / ɡriːn / adj. ❶绿色的：a ～ coat 一件绿色上衣 / ～ food 绿色食品 / ～ product 环保型产品 / He is working in the ～ house. 他在温室里干活。❷未成熟的：～ banana 青香蕉 ❸无经验的；没经过训练的；幼稚的：The young man is still ～ to (at) his job. 这个年轻人尚无工作经验。Don't blame him. He is only a ～ hand. 不要责备他,他还只是一个新手。同 inexperienced,young

greenery / ˈɡriːn(ə)ri / n. [U] ❶绿色植物 ❷(装饰用的)青枝绿叶

greenhouse / ˈɡriːnhaʊs / n. [C]温室；花房；

the ～ effect 温室效应 / We can have various ～ vegetables in winter. 冬天我们能吃到各种各样的温室蔬菜。同 hothouse,glasshouse

Greenwich / ˈgrenitʃ / n. 格林尼治(英国伦敦东南一市镇；为本初子午线所经过的地方)：～(Mean) Time 格林尼治标准时间(略为 GMT,G. M. T.)

greet / griːt / vt. 欢迎；致意：His speech was ～ed with loud cheers. 他的演说受到热烈欢迎。/ The students ～ed their teacher politely. 学生们很有礼貌地向老师打招呼。同 welcome,address,solute

greeting / ˈgriːtiŋ / n. [C]欢迎；问候；致意：exchange ～s 互致问候 / wave a ～ 挥手致意 / New Year's ～s 新年祝贺 / the season's ～s 节日祝贺 / Give my ～s to your mother, please. 请代我向你母亲问好。同 welcome, address,solution

grey / grei / Ⅰ adj. 灰色的 Ⅱ n. [U]灰色(见 gray)

grief / griːf / n. [U] 忧伤；悲伤：We had much ～ at (for,over) that matter. 我们对那件事感到很悲伤。同 sorrow,misery 反 job,happiness

grievance / ˈgriːv(ə)ns / n. ❶[C;U]不平(之事),不满(之事)；委屈；冤情：pour ～ 诉苦 / settle ～ quickly 尽快处理冤情 ❷[C]抱怨；诉苦；申诉：A committee was set up to look into the workers' ～. 成立了一个委员会来调查工人们的申诉。

grieve / griːv / v. 悲痛；伤心；哀悼：We feel deeply ～d at your misfortune. 对你的不幸我们深感悲伤。同 sorrow 反 delight

grip / grip / v. (gripped; gripping)紧抓；紧握：Please ～ the stick tightly. 请牢牢抓住这根棍子。同 grasp,seize

groan / grəun / v. & n. 呻吟：She was injured in the accident and ～ed with pain. 她在意外事故中受了伤,痛苦地呻吟着。同 cry,moan

grocer / ˈgrəusə(r) / n. [C] 杂货商；杂货店主：I'll go to the ～'s (shop) to buy some food. 我要去杂货店买些食品。

grocery / ˈgrəusəri / n. ❶杂货业；杂货店 ❷ (pl.)食品杂货

groove / gruːv / Ⅰ n. [C]❶槽,沟：a steel plate with ～s cut in it 里面刻有凹槽的钢盘 ❷(唱片心)纹(道) ❸常规,成规；老一套：His mind

works in a narrow ～. 他的思想囿于常规。Ⅱ vt. 在…上开槽(或沟等)：The sand on the shore has been ～d by the waves. 沙滩被海浪冲击出道道凹槽。

grope / grəup / vi. ❶摸索；摸索着走：He ～d into the kitchen and switched on the light. 他摸索着走进厨房,打开电灯。❷探索,寻求：～ after the truth 探索真理/The two sides are groping towards an agreement. 双方正在寻求达成一项协议。

gross / grəus / adj. 总计的；全部的：～ domestic product (GDP) 国内生产总值/ ～ national product(GNP) 国民生产总值/ ～ weight 毛重 / Her ～ income will very likely exceed 82, 000 dollars this year. 她今年的总收入很可能超过 8. 2 万美元。同 total,whole,entire

ground / graund / n. ❶[U] 地；地面；土地：The ～ is covered with snow. 地上覆盖着雪。/ The boy was lying on the ～. 男孩躺在地上。同 earth,land ❷[C](有特殊用途的)场地：the sports ～ 运动场/ They built a new pleasure ～ near our school. 他们在我们学校附近修了一座新的游乐场。同 spot,area ❸(pl.)(房屋四周的)土地；庭院：The cottage stands in lovely ～s. 小屋坐落在美丽的庭院中。❹理由；根据：There is no ～ for anxiety. 没必要焦虑。/ You have no ～ for complaining of his conduct. 你没有理由控告他的行为。同 reason,basis /above (below) ～ 活的(死的)：I am sure he is still above ～. 我相信他还活着。gain ～ 前进,进展；得势：The patient gained ～ daily. 病人日益恢复健康。give (lose) ～ 退却；让步；失利：Both of them would not give ～, so they quarrelled. 他们两人互不相让,于是吵了起来。hold (stand, keep) one's ～ 坚守；不让步：The referee held his ～ although his decision was hotly contested by the crowd. 尽管人们对裁判的决定提出了强烈抗议,但他仍然坚持他的立场。shift one's ～ 改变立场：He shifted his ～ whenever it was to his advantage. 只要对他有利,他就随时改变立场。

groundless / ˈgraundlis / adj. 无理由的,无根据的：a ～ fiction 毫无根据的杜撰/The fear fortunately proved to be ～. 幸而发现这只是一场虚惊。

group / gruːp / n. [C]队,组,群；团体：a ～ of boys 一群男孩 / The children played in ～s.

孩子们分组游戏。/ We'll hold a ～ discussion on this problem. 对这个问题我们将进行小组讨论。 同 body, crowd

grow / grəʊ / v. (grew/gruː/, grown /grəʊn/) ❶发育；生长；长大；增长：How quickly she is ～ing! 她长得多快呀！/ Cities grew rapidly. 城市发展迅速。/ The rice is ～ing fine. 水稻长势良好。 同 develop, increase ＊ **out of** 长得穿不进；源于；由…而生：～ out of one's clothes 长得穿不下原来的衣服。/ The mistake grew out of his carelessness. 这错误是由于他粗心引起的。＊ **～ up** 长大；成人：He was born in Beijing, but grew up in Shanghai. 他生在北京长在上海。❷(逐渐)变得；～ older 渐老 / ～ small-er 渐小 / It is ～ing dark. 天色渐晚。 同 become, turn ❸ 种植；使生长：We have ～n a lot of flowers this summer. 今年夏天我们种了很多花。 同 plant, cultivate

grown-up / ˈɡrəʊnʌp / n. 成年人

grown / ɡrəʊn / adj. 成年的；长成的；成熟的：a ～ man 成年男子

growth / ɡrəʊθ / n. [U]增长；生长：The rapid ～ in economy of our country is inspiring. 我国经济的快速增长令人鼓舞。/ Her appearance changed a lot with a ～. 随着年龄的增长她的外表发生了很大变化。 同 increase, development, expansion, enlargement

grudge / ɡrʌdʒ / I n. [C]不满；嫌隙；积怨；恶意：a bitter ～深深的积怨 II vt. ❶勉强地给；不情愿地做：She will not ～ doing a bit extra unless it's really needed. 除非确实需要，否则她是不会加班加点的。❷怨恨；嫌恶；妒忌：He ～d me my success. 他嫉妒我的成功。

gruel / ɡruːəl / n. [U]粥；稀饭：I have one bowl of ～ and an egg for breakfast. 我早餐吃一碗稀饭和一个鸡蛋。

grumble / ˈɡrʌmbl / vi. ❶抱怨，发牢骚；挑剔：When his boss would call on Sunday morning he would ～ but go to work. 每当星期天老板打来电话时他总是满肚子怨言，但还是去上班了。❷咕哝，嘟囔；发哼声：Husbands ～ every summer as they dutifully pack the car for the family holiday. 每年夏天丈夫们一面嘟囔，一面却恪尽职守地把全家去度假要用的东西装到车里去。

guarantee / ˌɡærənˈtiː / n. & vt. 保证；担保：the length of ～d service 保修期 / the quality ～ period 保质期 / Buying a train ticket doesn't ～ you a seat. 买到火车票并不保证你能有座位。/ This watch is ～d for two years. 这只表保修两年。 同 promise, assurance

guaranty / ˈɡær(ə)nti / n. [C]❶担保；担保书 ❷担保人，保证金，抵押品

guard / ɡɑːd / I n. [C]哨兵，警卫；警戒：mount ～ 放哨；站岗 同 watch, protector / **relieve** ～ 接班：The ～ is relieved at intervals. 卫兵每隔一段时间换一次班。**stand** ～ 站岗：The dog stood ～ over his wounded master. 这狗看守着它受伤的主人。**on** ～ 值班；当班：Get up. It's your turn to go on ～. 起来，该你值班了。II v. 保卫；看управ；防范：I'll ～ over the luggage while you get the ticket. 你去买票，我来看行李。/ The lunatic was carefully ～ed. 那个疯子被严加看管着。 同 defend, safeguard, protect / ～ **against** 预防：He ～ed against repeating the mistake. 他警惕犯同样的错误。

guardian / ˈɡɑːdɪən / I n. [C] ❶看守者，看护者；守护者；保卫者，捍卫者：the ～ of morals 伦理道德的捍卫者 ❷监护人 II adj. 守护的：a ～ angel 守护者

guerrilla / ɡəˈrɪlə / n. [C]游击战；游击队员：a ～ war (warfare) 游击战 / ～ forces 游击队 / Her grandfather was a ～ during the anti-Japanese war. 在抗日战争期间她的祖父是一名游击队员。

guess / ɡes / I v. 猜测；猜中：～ a riddle 猜谜 / I ～ she'll be back in half an hour. 我猜她半小时后回来。/ If I ～, I often ～ most nearly. 我要是猜，常猜得八九不离十。 同 think, suppose II n. [C]猜测：make a ～ 猜测 / miss one's ～ 没猜中；猜错 / a wrong ～ 错误的推测。/ **at a** ～ 据猜测；凭估计：At a ～, I should say there were 50 people present. 依我估计有 50 人在场。**by** ～ 凭推测：Don't answer by ～, work the problem out. 不要凭猜想回答，把这道题算出来。

guest / ɡest / n. [C] 客人；宾客；房客：We're expecting ～s to dinner. 我们在等候出席宴会的客人。/ This hotel can accommodate 300 ～s at the same time. 这家宾馆可以同时接待 300 位房客。 同 visitor, caller

guidance / ˈɡaɪdəns / n. [U]指导，辅导；率领：The school provides occupation ～ for the students. 学校为学生提供就业指导。/ They

G

are making an experiment under the ～ of the expert. 他们正在专家的指导下做实验。同 direction,leadership

guide / gaɪd / Ⅰ vt. 引导；指导；指引：She ～d the child across the street. 她领着孩子过街。The professor is guiding the postgraduates in research work. 教授在指导研究生进行科研。同 direct,lead Ⅱ n. ❶向导；导游：It would be safer to take a ～. 带个向导安全些。同 conductor ❷指南；手册：a study ～ 学习指南 / a traveller's ～ 旅游指南 同 handbook,instructions

guidebook / ˈgaɪdbuk / n. [C]手册；旅行指南：The eighteen-year-old girl traveled around the world with a ～. 那个十八岁的姑娘带着一本旅游指南环球旅行。同 handbook,instruction

guideline / ˈgaɪdlaɪn / n. [C]指导方针；准则：～ on housing reform 住房改革的指导方针 / lay out economic ～s 制定经济方针 同 guide,principle

guidepost / ˈgaɪdpəust / n. [C]指标；路标；指导方针：The ～ shows the way to our school. 路标指着通往我们学校的路。

guilt / gɪlt / n. [U] ❶有罪；犯罪：The manage denied his ～. 经理否认自己有罪。同 crime, blame 反 innocence ❷内疚：She felt a good deal of ～ because she told a lie to her mother. 由于对母亲说谎，她感到非常内疚。同 regret,shame

guilty / ˈgɪlti / adj. ❶ 有罪的：The man confessed himself ～ of theft. 那人承认自己犯了盗窃罪。同 convicted 反 innocent, blameless ❷内疚的：She felt ～ about being rude toward her parents. 对父母态度粗暴让她感到很内疚。同 ashamed 反 regretful

guise / gaɪz / n. [C]伪装；貌似,相似：in the ～ of a reporter 伪装成记者 / under the ～ of objective journalism 在标榜客观报道的幌子下

guitar / gɪˈtɑː(r) / n. [C]吉他：The boy plays the ～ very well. 小男孩吉他弹得很好。

gulf / gʌlf / n. [C]海湾；深坑；深渊；鸿沟：the Persian Gulf 波斯湾/ This quarrel created a ～ between the old friends. 这次争吵使老朋友之间产生了隔阂。

gum / gʌm / n. [U]口香糖：Many young people like chewing ～. 许多年轻人都喜欢嚼口香糖。

gun / gʌn / n. [C]炮；枪：fire a ～ 开枪/an air ～ 气枪/ an antitank ～ 反坦克炮 / a machine ～ 机关枪 / a long-range ～ 远程炮

gunpowder / ˈgʌnpaʊdə(r) / n. [U]火药：Do you know who invented ～? 你知道是谁发明了火药吗？同 explosive

gust / gʌst / n. [C] ❶阵风；一阵狂风：A ～ of wind blew his hat off. 一阵狂风吹掉了他的帽子。同 blow,gale,blast ❷(感情的)迸发；汹涌：He burst out a ～ of anger when he heard the news. 听到这则消息他勃然大怒。同 eruption,surge

guy / gaɪ / n. [C](美)人；家伙：He is a nice ～. 他是个好人。同 fellow,lad

gym / dʒɪm / n. [C]体育馆；健身房(见 gymnasium)

gymnasium / dʒɪmˈneɪzɪəm / n. (pl. gymnasia 或 gymnasiums)体育馆；健身房：She goes to the ～ every day. 她每天都去健身房锻炼身体。同 gym,stadium

gymnast / ˈdʒɪmnæst / n.[C]体操家；体育家 同 athlete, sportsman

gymnastic / dʒɪmˈnæstɪk / adj. 体操的；体育的：Our school bought some new ～ apparatus. 我们学校买了一些新的体操器械。/ He invited us to watch the ～ exhibition last Saturday. 上周六他邀请我们观看了体操表演。

gymnastics / dʒɪmˈnæstɪks / n. 体操；体育

Gypsy / ˈdʒɪpsi / (pl. Gypsies) n. [C]吉普赛人

H h

ha / hɑː / *int.* （表示惊奇、快乐、怀疑等）哈! 嘿!

habit / ˈhæbɪt / *n.* ❶ [C] 习惯; 惯常的行为: Many people say that smoking is a bad ～. 许多人都说抽烟是一种坏习惯。/ You should form the good ～ of getting up early. 你应该养成早起的好习惯。圆 nature, custom ❷ [U] 脾性; 习性: You'll not be afraid of snakes if you understand their ～. 如果了解蛇的习性，你就不会怕它们了。圆 nature, character

habitat / ˈhæbɪtæt / *n.* [C] （植物的）产地; （动物的）栖息地; 住处: the giant panda ～ 熊猫栖息地 / the ginseng ～ 人参产地 圆 habitation

habitation / ˌhæbɪˈteɪʃn / *n.* 居住; 住处: The town is near the sea and is a place fit for ～. 小镇靠近海边，是一个适宜居住的地方。

habitual / həˈbɪtʃuəl / *adj.* 惯常的; 通常的: He sat down in his ～ seat. 他坐在他常坐的座位上。圆 usual, accustomed

hacker / ˈhækə(r) / *n.* [C] （计算机）黑客: They think that ～s are often young people who are interested in computers. 他们认为"黑客"通常是一些对计算机很感兴趣的年轻人。

hail¹ / heɪl / *n.* [U] 冰雹: The ～ stones are as big as peas. 冰雹像豌豆般大小。

hail² / heɪl / *v.* 向…欢呼: All people there ～ed Liu Xiang as a hero. 所有在场的人都欢呼刘翔为英雄。圆 cheer, applaud

hair / heə(r) / *n.* [U] 毛发（尤指头发）: brush (comb) one's ～ 梳头发 / do one's ～ 做头发 / dye ～ 染发 / have one's ～ cut 理发 / **make one's ～ stand on end** 使毛骨悚然: Her sudden scream made my ～ stand on end. 她突然尖叫，令我毛骨悚然。

haircut / ˈheəkʌt / *n.* [C] 理发; 发式: He had a ～ before the interview. 采访前他去理了发。/ Girls like short ～ this year. 今年姑娘们都喜欢留短发。圆 hairdo

hairdresser / ˈheədresə(r) / *n.* [C] 理发师: Her ～ is a young fellow. 她的理发师是一个年轻的小伙子。

half / hɑːf / Ⅰ *n.* [C] （*pl.* halves /hɑːvz/）一半; 半个: the other ～ 另一半 / the return ～ of a return ticket 往返票的返程票 / the first ～ of a game 比赛的前半场 / Cut it in ～. 把它切成两半。圆 half-share / **by halves** 不完全地; 不完善地: We do nothing by ～. 我们做事从不半途而废。Ⅱ *adv.* 一半; 差不多; 部分地: My work is not ～ done yet. 我的工作尚未完成一半。/ The beggar was ～ dead from hunger. 那乞丐已饿得半死。圆 halfway Ⅲ *adj.* 半个的; 不完全的: A ～ truth is often no better than a lie. 半真半假的话不见得比谎话好。

halftime / ˈhɑːftaɪm, ˈhæftaɪm / *n.* ❶ [U] （足球等比赛中的）半场休息, 中场休息: The Rocket team was leading by two goals at ～. 中场休息时火箭队领先两个球。❷ [U; C] 中场休息时间; 半场休息时间: The coach made instructions to his men during ～. 中场休息时间里教练向他的队员部署打法。

halfway / ˌhɑːfˈweɪ, ˌhæfˈweɪ / Ⅰ *adv.* ❶ 在中途, 半路上, 半途地; We were ～ to Rome. 我们距罗马尚有一半路程。/ The project of the power plant stopped ～. 电厂项目中途搁浅了。❷ 或多或少, 几乎, 大体上: These measures didn't go ～ towards solving our problems. 这些措施根本没能解决我们的问题。Ⅱ *adj.* ❶ 中途的; 位于中途的: The runner reached the ～ mark in the Marathon race after 80 minutes. 马拉松比赛开始 80 分钟后，这位选手便跑到了中点线。❷ 部分的: ～ measures 不彻底的措施 / **meet sb.** ～ 与某人妥协: If you can drop your price a little, I'll meet you ～. 你要是能减点价，我就愿意再让一步。

hall / hɔːl / *n.* [C] 会堂; 大厅; 礼堂: the Great Hall of the People 人民大会堂 / an assembly ～ 会议厅 / a banquet ～ 宴会厅 / a concert ～ 音乐厅 / a dance ～ 舞厅 / a dining ～ 餐厅 / an entrance ～ 门厅 / the examination

～ 考场 / an exhibition ～ 展览厅 / the Hall of Justice 法院 圓 auditorium, lobby

halt / hɔːlt / Ⅰ v. 停止；休息：The soldiers ～ed for a short rest. 士兵们停下来休息一会儿。/ Nobody can ～ the advance of history. 没有人能阻挡历史的前进。圓 stop, cease Ⅱ n. 停止；(短暂的)休息：The car came to a sudden ～. 汽车突然停了下来。圓 stop, pause

ham / hæm / n. [C]火腿：a slice of ～ 一片火腿

hamburger / 'hæmbɜːɡə(r) / n. [C] 汉堡包；牛肉饼

hammer / 'hæmə(r) / Ⅰ n. [C] 铁锤；木槌；榔头：strike with a ～ 用锤敲打 / a stone ～ 石锤 / wooden ～ 木榔头 Ⅱ v. 锤打：When you've packed the box, ～ the lid on. 箱子装好后，就把盖子钉上。

hamper / 'hæmpə(r) / vt. ❶妨碍，使不能自由行动：The snow storm ～ed the efforts to rescue victims from the mountain. 暴风雪使营救山上遇险者的工作无法进行。❷阻碍，影响：Sales are ～ed by wide price fluctuations. 大幅度的价格波动妨碍了销售。

hand / hænd / Ⅰ n. [C] ❶手：It is a good habit to wash ～s before dinner. 饭前洗手是好习惯。/ at ～ 在近处；在手边：I haven't got my picture at ～, but I'll show it to you later. 我的照片没有带在手边，以后再给你吧。at sb.'s ～ 出自某人之手：I did not expect such unkind treatment at your ～s. 我未料到你会如此刻薄。by ～ 手工：The box is made by ～. 这箱子是手工做的。～ in ～ 手拉手；一起：They are walking ～ in ～. 他们手拉着手散步。on (in) ～ 在手上；可用；握有：We have a large supply of goods on ～. 我们现有一大批货物。/ I still have some money in ～. 我手里还有些钱。out of ～ 难以控制；不可收拾：His wrath got out of ～. 他怒不可遏。lend a ～ 帮助：Please lend me a ～ to move the desk away. 请帮我把桌子搬走。shake one's ～, shake ～s with sb. 与某人握手：As soon as she saw me, she shoot my hand warmly. 她一见到我就和我热情地握手。❷人手；雇员：The company is short of ～s. 这家公司缺人手。圓 worker, employee ❸(钟表的)指针：the hour ～ 时针 / the minute ～ 分针 / the second ～ 秒针 圓 pointer Ⅱ v. 交给；传递：Please ～ me the pen. 请把钢笔递给我。圓 give, deliver /～ in 交上：Please ～ in

your exercise books. 请把作业本交上来。～ **on** 依次传递：When you have read this, kindly ～ it on to your friends. 读完后，请将它传给你的朋友们。～ **out** 分发：They are ～ing out leaflets to people. 他们正在向人们散发传单。～ **over** 移交；交出：The offender was ～ed over to the police. 那个罪犯已经被送交警方。

handbag / 'hændbæɡ / n. [C]手提包 圓 bag, purse

handbook / 'hændbʊk / n. [C]手册；指南：a ～ for teachers 教师手册 / a ～ to tourists 旅游指南 圓 guide, guidebook

handful / 'hændfʊl / n. [C] 少数，一把；少量：She took a ～ of sand and played joyfully. 她抓起一把沙子快乐地玩着。

handicap / 'hændɪkæp / n. [C]不利；妨碍；障碍：overcome a ～ 克服不利条件 圓 disadvantage

handicraft / 'hændɪkrɑːft / n. [C]手艺；手工艺品

handkerchief / 'hæŋkətʃɪf / n. [C] (pl. handkerchiefs 或 handkerchieves) 手帕 圓 kerchief, towel

handle / 'hændl / Ⅰ v. ❶拿；摸：Wash your hands before you ～ my books. 请你在拿我的书以前先洗手。圓 touch, feel ❷操纵；管理：An officer must know how to ～ soldiers. 一个军官必须懂得怎样指挥士兵。圓 direct, operate ❸对付；对待；经销：It should be cautiously ～d. 此事应审慎处理。/ This shop doesn't ～ foreign goods. 这个商店不经销外国货。圓 manage, treat Ⅱ n. [C](工具、杯、桶、门、抽屉等的)柄；把手；提手：The ～ is broken off. 门把手断了。圓 knob, handhold

handout / 'hændaʊt / n. [C] ❶施舍物；救济品：The old couple are living off ～s. 老两口靠救济维生。圓 charity ❷讲稿；传单；广告单：The students are reading the ～ carefully. 学生们仔细阅读散发的讲稿。

handrail / 'hændreɪl / n. [C](楼梯的)扶手；(道路的)扶栏

handshake / 'hændʃeɪk / n. [C] ❶握手：The manager welcomed him with a warm ～. 经理同他热情握手，欢迎他的到来。❷(计算机系统中为确保各设备间正常连接而进行的)信号交换

handsome / 'hænsəm / adj. 美观的(男人)俊美的，英俊的；(女人)秀丽的，清秀的：What a ～ old building it is! 多么美观的一座古建筑！/ He's a ～ fellow. 他是一个很英俊的小

伙子。同 attractive,elegant,graceful 反 ugly

handwriting / ˈhændraɪtɪŋ / n. [U]笔迹；笔法：书法：neat（poor）～ 工整（整脚）的书法 / Not many people practise ～ now. 现在练书法的人很少。

handy / ˈhændi / adj. ❶方便的；手边的；便于使用的：Put things you need ～. 把你需要的东西放在随手可取的地方。同 ready,convenient,available 反 inconvenient ❷心灵手巧的：He is ～ at repairing computers. 他很擅长修计算机。同 skillful

hang / hæŋ / v. ❶(hung /hʌŋ/,hung)悬；挂；吊；垂：The pictures are hung on the wall. 那些图画挂在墙上。/ Will you ～ a lamp from the ceiling? 将灯吊在天花板上好吗？/ Don't ～ up. I'll tell you a secret. 别挂断电话，我要告诉你一个秘密。同 drop,suspend ❷(hanged,hanged) 吊死，绞死(常用被动式)：The murderer will be ～ed. 杀人凶手将被处以绞刑。同 execute 派 hanger n.

happen / ˈhæpən / vi. ❶发生：He wondered what was going to ～. 他想知道下一步会发生什么事。同 occur ❷碰巧：It ～ed to be a fine day. 那天恰巧是一个晴天。/ I ～ed to be out when he called. 他来访时，我正好出去了。同 chance ❸ 偶然发现某物(与 on, upon 连用)：He ～ed on the book in a small bookstore. 他在一家小书店偶然发现了这本书。

用法

"他到时我恰巧在那里。"有三种表达方式：
❶ I happened to be there when he arrived. ❷It happened that I was there when he arrived. ❸ It so happened that I was there when he arrived.

辨析

happen 意为"发生"，普通用词，含义最广。除指一般意义上的发生外，还指偶然发生、碰巧遇到：What has happened lately? 最近发生了什么事情？**occur** 意为"发生；出现"，较为正式的用语，所指的时间、事件都较确定，有时也指偶然发生的事：Important elections occur this fall. 今秋举行重要选举。**take place** 意为"发生；举行"，不含偶然之意，常指先布置而后举行：The sports meet will take place on Thursday. 运动会星期四举行。以上三个词都是不及物动词，不能用于被动语态：(正)The accident happened yesterday. (误) The accident was happened yesterday. 事故发生在昨天。

happy / ˈhæpi / adj. (-ier,-iest)幸福的；高

兴的；快乐的：She is very ～. 她很幸福。/ That was the happiest day of my life. 那是我一生中最快乐的一天。同 lucky,glad 反 sad, unhappy 派 happily adv. ;happiness n.

用法

形容词 happy 既可接不定式，也可接 that 引导的从句：He was happy to have been given a chance to go abroad. 令他高兴的是他有了一个出国的机会。也可说成：He was happy that he had been given a chance to go abroad.

harassment / ˈhærəsmənt / n. [U]骚扰：sexual ～ 性骚扰 / She can't bear the noise ～. 她不能忍受噪音骚扰。同 annoyance, trouble

harbo(u)r / ˈhɑːbə(r) / n. [C]港口：The ship entered a safe ～. 船只驶进了安全的港口。同 port,dock

辨析

harbour 意为"港口"，指天然或人造的海港，表示部分或完全封闭的一大片水域，是船只进入或停泊时可以得到安全保障的地方：There are a number of good harbours on the western coast. 在西海岸有很多良港。**port** 意为"港口"，是指人造的商船装卸货物的码头：The ship reached the port. 船已进港。

hard / hɑːd / Ⅰ adv. 努力地，费力地；剧烈地；艰苦地：He studies very ～. 他学习非常努力。/ It's raining ～. 雨下得很大。同 industrially, vigorously Ⅱadj. ❶坚硬的；坚固的(与 soft 相对)：～ currency 硬通货 / The ground is very ～. 地面很坚硬。同 firm,solid 反 soft ❷强烈的；猛烈的：The blow knocked the boxer down. 重重的一击使拳击手倒下了。反 vigorous ❸艰难的；辛苦的；难以理解的；难以解释的：The teacher asked her a ～ question. 老师问了她一个很难的问题。同 difficult 反 easy ❹严厉的；(天气) 恶劣的：a ～ father 严父 / ～ words 严词 / ～ winter 严冬/ Don't be ～ on such a little boy. 别对这么小的孩子太严厉。同 cruel,severe 反 kind 派 handen v.

辨析

hard 意为"艰苦的；困难的"，常指精神上的困苦和肉体上的劳苦，语气比 difficult 强得多，一件 difficult task 非努力不能完成，一件 hard task 非极大的劳苦断难完成。此词含义最广，最通俗：It is hard to tell. 这事很难说。**difficult** 意为"困难的"，多指智力方面遇到的困难：I find it difficult to study English well. 我发现学好英语很困难。

hard-hearted / ˌhɑːdˈhɑːtɪd / *adj.* 硬心肠的，无同情心的：Their anger had made them ∼. 愤怒使他们的心肠变硬了。

hardly / ˈhɑːdli / *adv.* 几乎不；简直不：Her foot is hurt. She can ∼ walk home. 她的脚受伤了，简直走不回家。同 barely, scarcely

用法 ❶ hardly 通常和情态动词 can, could 连用：I can hardly believe my eyes. 我几乎不能相信我的眼睛。❷ hardly 与 when 连用，表示"一……就……"，有时也与 before 连用：I had hardly entered the room when it began to rain. 我一进屋就开始下雨了。如 hardly 放在句首，那么主语和谓语必须倒装：Hardly had I entered the room when (before) it began to rain. 能表达这种含义的还有以下几种结构：①The moment (The instant)＋从句＋主句：The moment (The instant) he comes, let me know. 他一来就通知我。②Scarcely ＋had＋主语＋过去分词＋before：Scarcely had I got there before I telephoned him. 我一到达那里就给他打电话。③No sooner ＋had＋主语＋过去分词＋than：No sooner had we arrived home than he asked us to go out. 我们一到家他就叫我们出去了。④ As soon as：As soon as the bell rang, the pupils ran into the classroom. 铃声一响，孩子们就跑进教室去了。⑤On doing：On hearing the news, he was wild with joy. 他一听到这消息就欣喜若狂。

hardship / ˈhɑːdʃɪp / *n.* [U]艰难；困苦：bear ∼ 吃苦 / suffer ∼ 受苦 / His families endured great ∼ during the war. 他的家人在战争中经受了巨大的苦难。同 difficulty, trouble

hardware / ˈhɑːdweə(r) / *n.* ❶[C] (计算机)硬件 ❷[U]五金器具：The shop sells ∼. 这商店出售五金用品。

hardy / ˈhɑːdi / *adj.* ❶强壮的；坚韧的；能吃苦耐劳的：a ∼ constitution 强壮的体格 / a ∼ people 吃苦耐劳的民族 ❷需要耐力(或勇气)的：the hardiest sports 最能考验人耐力的体育运动 ❸ (植物) 耐寒的：a ∼ perennial 一种耐寒的多年生植物

hare / heə(r) / *n.* [C] 野兔

harm / hɑːm / Ⅰ *vt.* 伤害；损害：The dog hasn't ∼ed you, has it? 那条狗并没有伤害你，对吗？同 hurt, damage, injure Ⅱ *n.* [U] 损害；伤害；危害：It will do you no ∼. 这对你

无害。/ Please don't do any ∼ to your pets. 请勿伤害宠物。同 hurt, damage, injury 派 harmful *adj.*

辨析
harm 可与 injure 换用，指一个人的心智、健康、权利、事业等受到损害：She was afraid that her husband would harm the child. 她担心她丈夫会伤害孩子。**damage** 指事物的价值、用途、外表等遭到破坏：The fire damaged the furniture. 大火把家具烧坏了。**hurt** 普通用词，可指严重的或轻微的伤害，也指感情受到伤害：He fell off the bicycle and got hurt. 他从自行车上摔下来，摔伤了。**injure** 可与 harm 换用，比 hurt 正式，着重指疼痛的感觉：The injured were taken to the hospital. 伤者被送进了医院。

harmonious / hɑːˈməʊniəs / *adj.* 和谐的；和睦的；协调的：We are building up a ∼ society. 我们正在建立一个和谐的社会。反 disharmonious

harmony / ˈhɑːməni / *n.* 和谐；和睦：His idea is in ∼ with mine. 他的想法与我的一致。反 conflict

harp / hɑːp / *n.* [C]竖琴：She played the ∼ in the party. 在聚会上她演奏了竖琴。

harsh / hɑːʃ / *adj.* ❶残酷的；无情的：be ∼ with others 无情地对待他人 ❷严厉的，苛刻的：a ∼ master 严厉的主人 / The punishment was too ∼ for such a minor offence. 对于这样的轻罪，这种惩罚过于严厉了。❸粗糙的；具刺激性的；(声音)刺耳的：His voice has grown ∼. 他的声音变得很刺耳。/ ∼ detergents 强刺激性洗涤剂

harvest / ˈhɑːvɪst / *n.* 收获；收成；成果：a bad (poor) ∼ 歉收 / a good (rich) ∼ 丰收 / the summer ∼ 夏收 / The rice crop bore a plentiful ∼ last year. 去年水稻大丰收。同 gathering, collection

haste / heɪst / *n.* [U]急速；仓促：Haste makes waste. 忙中出错。/ More ∼, less speed. 欲速则不达。/ He went off in great ∼. 他匆匆离去。同 hurry /in ∼ 匆忙地；草率地：He packed his clothes into a trunk in ∼ and went out of the room. 他匆匆地把衣服塞进箱子，走出房间。派 hasten *v.*

hasty / ˈheɪsti / *adj.* 急速的；草率的：The ∼ conclusion of the film made us very unhappy. 这部电影草率的结局令我们深感不快。同

rash, careless 反 cautious

hat / hæt / *n.* [C]帽子：a straw ～ 草帽 / wear a ～ 戴着帽子 / put off one's ～ 脱帽 / put on one's ～ 戴上帽子 同 cap

hatch / hætʃ / *v.* 孵化：Three chicks are ～ed today. 今天有三只小鸡孵出来了。同 bread

hate / heɪt / *vt.* 憎恨；不愿；不喜欢：She ～s me for it. 她因此事而恨我。/ She ～s anyone listening while she's telephoning. 她打电话时讨厌别人听。反 love 派 hateful *adj.*

hatred / 'heɪtrɪd / *n.* [U]憎恨；怨恨：Do you know why he has a deep ～ for (of) English? 你知道他为什么憎恨英语吗？

haughty / 'hɔːti / *adj.* 傲慢的，趾高气扬的：～ aristocrats 傲慢的贵族们/ carry a ～ air 摆出神气活现的架子

haul / hɔːl / Ⅰ *vt.* ❶拖；拉；拽：～ the boat out of water 把船从水中拖上来 ❷(用车等)运送；拖运：haul coal from the mines 从煤矿拖运煤 Ⅱ *n.* ❶拖；拉；拽：Give a ～ at the rope. 拉一下绳子。❷拖运；运送：long ～s by rail 长途铁路运输 ❸一次获得的量：a bumper ～ of fish 一大网鱼/The police said it was the largest ～ of illegal drugs this year. 警察说是今年破获的最大一批非法毒品。

haunting / 'hɔːntɪŋ / *adj.* 萦绕于心头的；难以忘怀的：a ～ melody 萦绕于脑际的乐曲/ ～ memories 难忘的记忆

have / hæv, həv, əv / Ⅰ *vt.* (一般现在时第三人称单数为 has；现在分词为 having；过去式和过去分词为 had) ❶有，拥有（在美语中 have got 常代替 have，在否定句、疑问句中常用助动词 do）：They ～ (got) a car. 他们有一辆汽车。/ Have you a Chinese-English dictionary? (＝Do you ～ a Chinese-English dictionary?) 你有汉英词典吗？/ She has many enemies. 她有很多敌人。/ I ～ only one sister. 我只有一个妹妹。/ The house has four rooms. 这房子有四个房间。❷进行；从事：～ a look (rest, match, swim, test, try, walk) 看一看(休息一会儿,举行一场比赛,游泳,进行测验,试一试,散散步)：Let me ～ a try. 我来试试吧！❸使；让：You'd better ～ your hair cut. 你最好把头发理了。❹经历：Did you ～ a good holiday? 你假日过得愉快吗？❺吃；饮：～ breakfast 吃早饭/ ～ tea 喝茶/ What shall we ～ for breakfast? 我们

早餐吃什么？❻举行：When shall we ～ the meeting? 我们什么时候开会？❼遭受：Do you often ～ colds? 你时常感冒吗？❽(与不定式连用)必须；不得不：I ～ to go now. 现在我得走了。/ The children don't ～ to go to school on weekends. 孩子们周末不必去上学。Ⅱ *v. aux.* (加过去分词构成完成时态)曾经；已经：I ～ seen the film before. 我以前看过这部电影。

hawk / hɔːk / *n.* [C]鹰

hay / heɪ / *n.* [U] 干草：a pile of ～ 一堆干草/ Make ～ while the sun shines. (谚语)晒草要趁太阳好。(做事要抓紧时机。)

hazard / 'hæzəd / *n.* [C]危险；冒险：The policeman put his life in ～ to help the drawn child. 警察冒着生命危险去救溺水儿童。同 danger, risk 反 safety, security 派 hazardous *adj.*

he / hiː, hɪ / *pron.* 他(主格)

head / hed / Ⅰ *n.* [C] ❶头；头部：My ～ aches. 我头痛。/ His ～ swims. 他头晕。/ **keep one's ～** 保持镇静：Whatever happens, you should keep your ～. 无论出现什么情况,你都应该保持镇静。❷首脑；领头人：the family ～ of each household 户主/ a college (university) ～ 学院院长(大学校长) / a department ～ 部门主任/ the ～ of a factory 厂长 / the ～ waiter 领班 / the ～ of a school 校长 ❸(河流的)源头：～ of a lake 湖的源头 ❹上部；上方：the ～ of the page 该页的上方 Ⅱ *v.* ❶向…之首；率领：John's name ～ed the list. 约翰名列榜首。同 lead, command ❷向…方向行进 同 move, process / ～ **for** 向…前进：They are ～ing straight for home. 他们径直向家里走去。

headache / 'hedeɪk / *n.* [C]头痛；令人头痛的人(或事)：The old lady constantly suffers from ～s. 老太太经常头痛。

heading / 'hedɪŋ / *n.* [C]标题；题名：The ～ of the passage is in large letters. 这段文章的标题用的是大写字母。同 headline, name, title

headline / 'hedlaɪn / *n.* (*pl.*) 新闻提要：Have you listened to today's ～s? 你听了今天的重要新闻吗？/ Our manager is busy. He only has time to read the ～s. 我们经理很忙,只有时间读读新闻提要。同 summary, abstract

headmaster / ˌhedˈmɑːstə(r) / *n.* [C](中小学

校长)校长：Jack's father is a ~. 杰克的父亲是校长。

headmistress /ˌhedˈmɪstrəs/ n. [C]女校长

headquarters /ˌhedˈkwɔːtəz/ n. (单数复数同形)司令部；指挥部；总部：They set up their ~ at Tianjin. 他们在天津建立了总部。

heal /hiːl/ v. (伤口)愈合；痊愈；治愈：An old doctor ~ed her wound. 一位老医生治好了她的伤。同 cure

health /helθ/ n. [U]健康；健康状况：be in good (poor) ~ 身体好(不好) / be in broken ~ 体弱多病 / be in strong ~ 身体强壮 / be in weak ~ 身体虚弱/ favour one's ~ 恢复健康 / His ~ failed. 他的健康状况不好。/ She enjoys pretty good ~. 她的身体相当不错。

healthy /ˈhelθi/ adj. 健康的；健壮的：a ~ way of living 健康的生活方式/ He is a very ~ child. 他是一个很健康的孩子。同 well, sound, strong

heap /hiːp/ n. [C]堆；大量；许多：a big ~ of books 一大堆书/ I have ~s of work to do. 我有很多工作要做。同 pile, mass

hear /hɪə(r)/ v. (heard /hɜːd/, heard) ❶听见。We listened but could ~ nothing. 我们听了，可是什么也听不见。/ I ~ her singing in the next room. 我听见她在隔壁唱歌。❷听说；得知：I ~d that she was ill. 我听说她生病了。同 learn /~ **from** 收到信：How often do you ~ from your brother? 你多久能接到你哥哥一封信？~ **of** (**about**) 听说；得知：I've never ~d of the girl. 我从未听说过这个女孩。

用法
hear 后可接不定式或现在分词作宾语补足语。不定式作宾语补足语，强调动作完成的全过程，现在分词作宾语补足语强调动作正在进行：Did you hear him say that? 你听他说那事吗？We heard her playing the piano. 我们听见她在弹钢琴。

辨析
hear 为一般用语，指听的结果：Did you hear the bell ringing? 你听见铃响了吗？listen 意为"倾听"，指有意识地去听，着重于听的动作：He listened with close attention. 他非常注意地听。

hearing /ˈhɪərɪŋ/ n. [U]听；听力：The blind man has sharp ~. 那盲人听觉灵敏。同 listening

heart /hɑːt/ n. [C] ❶心；心脏：Her ~ is beating violently. 她的心在剧烈地跳动。❷内心；心肠：She seems very hard, but has a kind ~. 她看起来很严厉，但却心地善良。同 mind, feeling, soul ❸勇气；精神：Don't lose ~ even if we fail the game. 即使输了比赛也不要丧失勇气。同 courage, mind, spirit ❹中心；实质；要点：Not many people prefer to live in the ~ of a city now. 现在不是许多人都愿意住在市中心。/ You'd better get to the ~ of the problem first. 你最好先谈谈问题的实质吧。同 center, core, soul, essence /**at** ~ 在内心；在感情深处：He was sad at ~. 他很悲伤。**get** (**learn**, **know**) **sth. by** ~ 背出；记住：You should get the poem by ~. 你应该背诵这首诗。**take** ~ 有信心；振作精神：He had taken fresh ~ at the little glimpse of hope. 他看到一线希望后重新振作了起来。派 hearten vt.

hearty /ˈhɑːti/ adj. ❶衷心的；热忱的：I'll give my ~ support to your proposal. 我会衷心支持你的提议。同 wholehearted, warm-hearted ❷(饭菜)丰盛的：a ~ meal 丰盛的一餐 同 rich

heat /hiːt/ I v. 使…热；变热：Water ~s slowly in winter. 冬天水热得很慢。/ Please ~ up the cold soup. 请把冷汤热一热。同 burn, warm II n. [U]热；热度；热烈：body ~ 体温 / ~ energy 热能/ He felt the ~ of the fire on his face. 他感到脸上被火烤得热乎乎的。/ The students are discussing the problem with ~. 学生们正在热烈地讨论问题。同 hotness, excitement 派 heated adj.

heaven /ˈhevn/ n. ❶天堂，天国；天空：go to ~ 死去；上天堂 同 paradise, sky ❷(Heaven)上帝；Thank Heaven! 谢天谢地！/ Heaven knows! 天知道！/ Good Heavens! 天哪！同 God

heavily /ˈhevɪli/ adv. 沉重地：The crime lies ~ on his conscience. 他的罪行使他良心极为不安。反 lightly, gently

heavy /ˈhevi/ adj. ❶重的；难以举起(携带、搬动)的：This suitcase is too ~ for me to carry. 这箱子太重，我提不动。同 weighty 反 light ❷超出一般大小(重量、力量)的：the ~ rain 大雨/ ~ work 繁重的工作/ a ~ blow 重击/ ~ heart 沉重的心情/ ~ sky 阴沉的天空/ ~ sea 汹涌的大海/ ~ food 难以消化

的食物/ a ～ drinker (smoker) 酒鬼 (烟鬼) /
～ traffic 流量大的交通 圆 large, massive, sad

hectare / ˈhekteə(r) / n. [C]公顷(略为 ha.)

heel / hiːl / n. [C]脚后跟;(鞋、袜等的)后跟:
There is a hole in the ～ of his shoe. 他的鞋后
跟上有一个洞。

height / haɪt / n. ❶高度;身高:What's your
～? 你身高多少? / He is six feet in ～. 他
有六英尺高。❷(pl.)高地;高处:We stood on
the ～s overlooking the valley. 我们站在高处
俯瞰整个山谷。圆 highland ❸顶点;最高点:
He retired at the ～ of his career. 他在事业的
巅峰时退休了。圆 top, summit 反 bottom

heighten / ˈhaɪt(ə)n / v. ❶增强,加强;加剧:
use lemon to ～ the flavour 用柠檬增味/～
the tension between the two countries 加剧两
国间的紧张关系 ❷变强;变大:As she waited,
her fears ～ed. 她越等越感到恐惧。

heir / eə(r) / n. [C]继承人;嗣子:He is the
right ～ of the family. 他是这个家族的合法继
承人。

heiress / ˈeərəs / n. [C]女继承人

helicopter / ˈhelɪkɒptə(r) / n. [C]直升机:
Her uncle can fly a ～. 她的叔叔会驾驶直
升机。

helix / ˈhiːlɪks / n. [C](pl. helices 或 helixes)
螺旋结构;螺旋形(物体)

hell / hel / n. 地狱 反 heaven

hello / həˈləʊ / int.(引起人注意或问候)喂!

helmet / ˈhelmɪt / n. [C]头盔;钢盔:a safe ～
安全帽/ a gas ～ 防毒面具

help / help / Ⅰ vt. 帮助;援助;资助:This
book will ～ you (to) improve your English.
这本书能帮助你提高英语水平。/ I can ～
you with your lessons. 我可以帮助你温习功
课。/ My brother ～ed me through the university. 我哥哥资助我读完大学。圆 aid, as-
sist/ ～ **oneself to sth.** 自取;擅自取用:Please
～ yourself to the fruit. 请吃水果。/ Sometimes he ～s himself to my dictionary. 有时他
擅自使用我的字典。～ **sb. with sth.** 帮助某
人做某事:May I ～you with your luggage? 我
帮你拿行李好吗? **can**(**could**)**not** ～ **doing
sth.** 禁不住(忍不住)做某事:I couldn't ～
laughing when I heard such a story. 听到这个
故事,我不禁大笑起来。Ⅱ n. 帮助;助手,帮

手:Thank you for your ～. 谢谢你的帮助。/
The ～ hasn't come this morning. 助手今早
还没来。/ With the ～ of the teacher, I've
made great progress. 在老师的帮助下,我取
得了很大的进步。圆 aid, assistant 派
helpful adj.

hemisphere / ˈhemɪsfɪə(r) / n. [C]半球:Asian
is in the Northern Hemisphere. 亚洲位于北
半球。

hen / hen / n. [C]母鸡:Hens lay eggs. 母鸡
生蛋。

hence / hens / adv. 因此,所以;今后:He said
that he would be in London a month ～. 他说
一个月后他会在伦敦。/ It is raining hard.
Hence, I have to stay. 正在下大雨。因此,我
不得不留下来。圆 so, therefore

henceforth / ˌhensˈfɔːθ, ˈhensfɔːθ / adv. 从今
以后,今后;从此以后:Henceforth, parties which fail
to get 50% of the vote will not be represented
in parliament. 从此得票率不超过 50%的党派
在国会中不再有议席。

her / hɜː(r); hə(r) / pron. 她。(she 的宾格);
她的(形容词性物主代词)

herb / hɜːb / n. [C]草本植物;药草:Chinese
medical ～s 中草药

herd / hɜːd / n. [C]兽群:a ～ of elephants 一
群大象 圆 crowd, flock

here / hɪə(r) / adv. 在这里;向这里:Come
～! 到这里来! Look ～! 看这里。/ Here
comes the bus! 车来了。/ Here he comes. 他
来了。/ Here you are. 这是你要的东西。/
～ **and there** 到处:You can see new buildings
～ and there in this city. 在这座城市里,你四
处可见新的楼房。

hereabout(s) / ˌhɪərəˈbaʊt(s) / adv. 在这一
带,在附近:There is a post office somewhere
～. 这附近有个邮局。

hereby / hɪəˈbaɪ, ˈhɪəˌbaɪ / adv.(用于公文、布
告等)以此方式,特此;兹:He is ～ licensed to
drive motor vehicles of groups A and E. 他将
有资格驾驶 A 照和 E 照的机动车辆,特发此
证。/I ～ resign. 我特此请辞。

heritage / ˈherɪtɪdʒ / n. [C]遗产;继承物;传
统:cultural ～ 文化遗产 / historical ～ 历史
遗产 / We should preserve our national ～s
well. 我们应当保护好我们的民族遗产。圆
legacy, tradition

hero / ˈhɪərəʊ / n. [C](pl. heroes)❶英雄

He was an unknown ～. 他是一位无名英雄。
反 coward ❷男主人公：He is the ～ of the
film. 他是这部电影的男主角。同 character

heroic / hə'rəʊɪk / adj. 英勇的；英雄的：～
deeds 英雄行为 / ～ poems 英雄史诗

heroin / 'herəʊɪn / n. 海洛因

heroine / 'herəʊɪn / n. [C]女英雄；女主角

hers / hɜːz / pron. 她的(名词性物主代词)：
It's my pen；～ is on the desk. 这是我的钢
笔,她的在桌上。

herself / hɜː'self / pron. 她自己(反身代词)：
She hurt ～. 她伤了自己。/ She ～ told me
about the news. 她亲自把这个消息告诉了
我。/ I saw Mary ～. 我看见玛丽本人。/
Can she do it by ～? 她自己能做吗?

hesitate / 'hezɪteɪt / vi. 犹豫；踌躇：He ～d a-
bout what to do next. 他对下一步做什么犹豫
不定。/ If you ～ too long,you'll miss the opportunity. 如果你老是犹豫不决,你就会错失
良机。同 waver,delay 派 hesitation n.

hey / heɪ / int. (引起注意或表示惊讶)
嘿! 喂!

hi / haɪ / int. (＝hey)嗨!

hibernate / 'haɪbəneɪt / vi. (动物)冬眠：
Snakes ～ in winter. 蛇在冬季冬眠。派 hiber-
nation n.

hiccup / 'hɪkʌp / n.[C]打嗝(声)；呃逆：In the
middle of the ceremony there was a loud ～
from his son. 在仪式进行中间他的儿子打了
个响嗝。

hide / haɪd / v. (hid /hɪd/,hidden/'hɪdn/或
hid) ❶躲藏；隐藏：Where is he hiding? 他躲
在哪里? / You'd better ～. 你最好躲起来。
同 conceal,cloak 反 expose ❷隐瞒；遮掩：
She hid her face in her hands. 她用手遮住她
的脸。He hid this from his mother. 此事他瞒
着他母亲。同 cover,mask 反 reveal,expose Ⅱ
n. (观察动物的)隐藏之处

high / haɪ / Ⅰ adj. ❶高的：He is six feet ～.
他身高六英尺。同 tall,towering 反 low,short
❷高级的；主要的：～ education management
高等教育管理 / ～ -priced goods 高档商品 /
Last year she studied in a ～ school in America. 去年她在美国一所高中读书。同 superior,
chief,eminent 反 lowly,cheap ❸高度的；强烈
的：～ fidelity (Hi-Fi)music 高保真音乐 / in
～ spirits 高兴；兴高采烈。精神饱满 同 great,

intense,strong 反 weak,mild ❹高尚的；良好
的：goods of ～ quality 高质量产品 / He is
determined to be a man of ～ character. 他决
心做一个品德高尚的人。同 noble,lofty 反
base,shameful Ⅱ adv. 高；高度地：pay ～ 付
高价 /fly ～ (喻) 有雄心 同 highly

highlight / 'haɪlaɪt / n.[C]最精彩部分(场
面)：He went out for a while and missed the
～ of the competition. 他出去一会儿,没有看
到比赛的最精彩场面。同 focus,climax

highly / 'haɪli / adv. 高；高度地；高尚地；很,
非常：They spoke ～ of him. 他们高度赞扬
他。/ This is a ～ amusing film. 这是一部非
常有趣的影片。同 greatly,very,considerably

highway / 'haɪweɪ / n.[C]公路；大路：High-
ways are built in the city. 这座城市正在修建
许多公路。/ They met with an accident on
312 national ～. 他们在312国道上出了车
祸。/ It is a ～ to fortune for peasants. 这是
农民的一条致富之路。同 highroad,super-
highway

hijack / 'haɪdʒæk / vt. 劫持；劫机：～ a plane
劫持飞机 派 hijacker n.

hike / haɪk / vi. & n. 远足；徒步旅行：They
decided to ～ to the country. 他们决定步行去
乡下。同 walk,journey 派 hiker n.

hill / hɪl / n.[C]丘陵,小山；斜坡；土堆：The
sun was rising over the ～. 太阳正从山冈上
升起。/ They arrived at the top of a ～ half
an hour later. 半小时后他们到达山顶。
同 mound

hillside / 'hɪlsaɪd / n.[C](小山)山腰；山坡：
There is a temple on the ～. 山腰上有一座寺
庙。/ The child couldn't climb the steep ～.
小孩爬不上那个陡坡。同 slope

him / hɪm / pron. (he 的宾格)他：I saw ～
yesterday. 我昨天看见他了。

himself / hɪm'self / pron. (反身代词)他自
己：He cut ～. 他割伤了自己。/ He will go
there by ～. 他亲自去那里。

hind / haɪnd / adj. (成对的分布前后的东西)在
后的,后面的：the ～ legs of a horse 马的后
腿/ the ～ wheels of a car 汽车的后轮

hinder / 'hɪndə(r) / vt. 妨碍；阻碍；阻止：
Don't let me ～ you from going. 不要因为我
而妨碍你去。/ Don't ～ him in his study. 不

要妨碍他学习。/ She was ～ed by the heavy
traffic. 拥挤的交通耽误了她的时间。同
block, obstruct

hint / hɪnt / n. [C]提示；暗示：a broad ～ 明
白的暗示/ a gentle ～ 委婉的暗示/ helpful
(good) ～s 有益的提示/ ～s about letter-
writing 写信须知/～s for beginners 初学者须
知同 implication, indication

hip / hɪp / n. [C]臀部；髋

hire / ˈhaɪə(r) / Ⅰ vt.雇用；租：The girls are
never ～d to do servant's work. 这些姑娘从
不受雇去做服务员的工作。同 rent, employ
反 dismiss Ⅱ n. 租用；雇用；租金，工钱：Are
there any bicycles for ～? 有供出租的自行车
吗？/ He has horses on ～. 他有马匹出租。
同 rent, employment

his / hɪz / pron. ❶(形容词性物主代词)他
的：His pen is on the desk. 他的笔放在桌上。
❷(名词性物主代词)他的东西：That book is
～, not yours. 那本书是他的，不是你的。

historic / hɪˈstɒrɪk / adj. 历史上著名的：a
～ spot (speech) 历史上著名的地点(演说)/ a
～ city of art and culture 文化艺术名城/ a ～
event 有历史意义的事件同 memorable, notable

historical / hɪˈstɒrɪkl / adj. 历史上的；有关历
史的：～ facts 历史事实/ ～ documents 历史
文件/ ～ novels 历史小说/ a ～ play (film,
painting)历史题材的戏剧(影片、绘画)/ ～
events 历史事件/ ～ people 历史人物/～
studies 历史研究同 factual, past

history / ˈhɪst(ə)ri / n. [U]历史学；历史：
ancient ～ 古代史/ general ～ 通史/ contemporary ～ 现代史/ modern ～ 近代史/ world
～ 世界史/ the science of ～ 史学/ People
make their own ～. 人民创造自己的历史。

hit / hɪt / v. (hit, hit) ❶击；打；碰；撞：I ～
my head against the wall. 我的头碰到了墙。/
The stone ～ the window. 石头击中了窗
户。/ Mother ～ the child on the head. 母亲
打孩子的头部。同 beat, knock, strike ❷伤
害…的感情；使受到打击：He was heavily ～ by
his financial losses. 他因财产损失受到重大打
击。同 hurt, blow

hitch / hɪtʃ / Ⅰ vt. ❶(用环、绳等)捆，系；拴；
套：～ the horse to the post 把马拴到柱子上

❷急拉，猛拽；(猛地)移动：～ up one's trouser legs 挽起裤管/He ～ed the pillow to a
comfortable position. 他把枕头移到舒适的位
置。Ⅱ n. [C] ❶捆，系；拴；套 ❷(向上的)急
拉，猛拽；(猛地)移动：He gave his belt a ～.
他把皮带向上拉了一下。❸(临时)故障；突然
停止；障碍：a ～ in the conversation 谈话中出
现的小小问题

hive / haɪv / n. [C](木、草等制成的)蜂房；
蜂箱

hoarse / hɔːs / adj. (声音)嘶哑的：She had a
～ voice because she caught cold. 由于着凉她
声音嘶哑。同 harsh

hobby / ˈhɒbɪ / n. [C]业余爱好：My ～ is
collecting stamps. 我的业余爱好是集邮。同
recreation, pastime

hockey / ˈhɒkɪ / n. [U]曲棍球：play ～ 打曲
棍球

hoe / həʊ / n. [C]锄头

hold / həʊld / Ⅰ vt. (held/held/, held) ❶抓
住；握住；拿住：She held her father's hands
tightly. 她紧紧地抓住父亲的双手。/ The
young woman held a little boy in her arms. 那
年轻妇女怀里抱着一个小男孩。同 grasp,
clasp ❷拥有；持有：Our manager ～s 50%
share in the company. 我们经理在公司拥有
50%的股份。同 keep, own ❸举行；主持：
They'll ～ a poll to know the opinions of the
masses. 他们将举行一次民意调查来了解群众
的意见。/ When shall we ～ the meeting? 我
们什么时候开会？/ The Olympic Games will
be held in Beijing in 2008. 奥运会将于2008
年在北京举行。同 conduct ❹托住；支持：The
roof was held up by four big pillars. 屋顶由四
根大柱子支撑。同 support, sustain ❺容纳；装
得下：The hall ～s 300 people at least. 这大厅
至少容纳300人。/ Will this box ～ all your
things? 这箱子装得下你所有的东西吗？同
contain, include Ⅱ vi. ❶持续；保持；坚持：
How long will the fine weather ～? 好天气能
持续多久？同 keep, adhere ❷有效；适用：The
headmaster said that the rule would ～ in all
cases. 校长说这条规定在任何情况下都有效。
同 apply /～ **back** 走开；退缩：No difficulty
can ～ us back. 任何困难都不能阻挡我们前
进。～ **off** 延期；迟滞：She held off from answering directly. 她迟迟不作直接回答。～

out 坚持；维持；伸出；提出：Hold out the hand of friendship. 伸出友谊之手。/ You should ～ out for a higher price. 你应坚持要更高的价格。～ **over** 延期(决定)：The matter was held over until the next meeting. 此事拖延到下次会议解决。～ **together** 结合在一起：This old coat hardly ～s together now. 这件旧上衣几乎没连在一起了。～ **up** 举起；支持；停顿；延期：John held up his hand. 约翰举起手来。/ The government decided to ～ up the prices of farm produce. 政府决定维持农产品价格。/ They held up at the gate. 他们在大门口停了下来。Ⅱ *n.* ❶抓住；握住：Please take a firm ～ of my hand. 请抓紧我的手。圆 grasp ❷控制；掌握：Our monitor has got a good ～ of the subjects he is learning. 我们班长对所学学科都掌握得很好。圆 control

hole / həʊl / *n.* [C]洞；孔；坑：drill ～s 钻洞/ fill up a ～ 填洞/ There is a ～ in the tooth. 牙齿上有个洞。

holiday / ˈhɒlədeɪ / *n.* [C]假日；节日：Our school had a half-day ～. 我们学校放了半天假。/ I plan to spend the summer ～s here. 我计划在这儿度暑假。/ Tom always takes a job in his ～s. 汤姆总是在他的假期里干零活。圆 break，leave，vacation

Holland / ˈhɒlənd / *n.* 荷兰

hollow / ˈhɒləʊ / *adj.* ❶空的；中空的：a ～ tree 空心树 圆 empty 反 solid ❷空洞的；空虚的；虚假的：What he said were only ～ words. 他说的只不过是些假话。圆 empty，meaningless 反 real

holly / ˈhɒli / *n.* [U]冬青树

holy / ˈhəʊli / *adj.* 神圣的；圣洁的；虔诚的

home / həʊm / Ⅰ *n.* 家；家庭；家乡：He left ～ at the age of 13 他 13 岁离开家。/ They have a comfortable little ～. 他们有一个舒适的小家庭。/ **at** ～ 在家；在国内：She had to stay at ～ to care for her daughter. 她不得不待在家里照顾女儿。/ The next match will be held at ～. 下次比赛将在国内举行。**be (feel, make) oneself at** ～ 无拘束：Make yourself at ～. 请别拘束。Ⅱ *adv.* 在家，到家；在国内，到国内：I saw him on my way ～. 我在回家的路上看见了他。/ Her mother isn't ～ yet. 她的母亲还没回到家里。

homeless / ˈhəʊmlɪs / Ⅰ *adj.* 无家可归的；居无定所的：a ～ tramp 一位无家可归的流浪汉 Ⅱ *n.* 无家可归者；流浪者

homogeneous / ˌhɒməʊˈdʒiːniəs / *adj.* ❶同种类的；同性质的；有相同特征的：～ cell population 同源细胞群体 ❷均匀的；均一的：a ～ distribution 均匀分布/ ～ light 单色光

honest / ˈɒnɪst / *adj.* 诚实的；忠实的；坦白的：He has an ～ face. 他有一副诚实的面孔。/ I shall be quite ～ with you. 我会对你很坦白。/ To be ～, he is a good boy. 老实说，他确实是一个好孩子。圆 frank，true 派 honestly *adv.*

honesty / ˈɒnɪsti / *n.* [U]老实，诚实；正直：Honesty is the best policy. 诚实才是上策。

honey / ˈhʌni / *n.* [U]蜂蜜；甜蜜：have ～ on one's lips and murder in one's heart 口蜜腹剑

hono(u)r / ˈɒnə(r) / *n.* [U]光荣，荣幸；荣誉：I had the ～ of attending her evening party. 我有幸参加她的晚会。圆 glory /**do** ～ **to sb.** 向某人表示敬意；给某人带来光荣：His contributions to science did ～ to our country. 他在科学上的贡献为我们国家增了光。/ Will you do me the ～ of dining with me this evening? 今晚你肯赏光与我共进晚餐吗? **in** ～ **of** 庆祝；纪念：We are planning a big birthday party in your ～. 我们正筹划为你举行一场盛大的生日晚会。

hono(u)rable / ˈɒnərəbl / *adj.* 光荣的；尊敬的；高尚的：an ～ duty 荣誉职位/ ～ conduct 高尚行为/ The hospital gave the nurse an ～ task. 医院给了护士一个光荣的任务。圆 glorious，noble，respectable 反 dishonorable

hoof / huːf / *n.* (*pl.* hoofs 或 hooves)蹄；马蹄

hook / hʊk / Ⅰ *n.* [C]钩；钩状物：Look! The fish has got ～ed. 看! 鱼上钩了。圆 curve，fishhook Ⅱ *vt.* 钩；钩住；引诱…上钩：The boy was glad that he ～ed a fish. 钓到一条鱼,小孩非常高兴。 同 catch, trap

hoop / huːp / n. [C]箍;箍状物;篮圈:Hula ～ 呼啦圈 同 circle, circlet

hooray / huˈreɪ / int. (＝hurrah)好哇!

hop / hɒp / v. (hopped; hopping)单足跳;跳过;跳跃:He got hurt in the left leg and had to ～ along. 他的左腿受了伤,只得单脚跳着走。 同 leap, jump / ～ **on** (**onto**) (口语)上车:He ～ped on a red car. 他跳上一辆红色小车。

hope / həup / I v. 希望;期望:I ～ to see you soon. 我希望很快见到你。 / Will it be fine tomorrow? I ～ so. 明天会晴吗? 我希望会。 / It is ～d that he will come on time. 希望他能准时来。 / The teacher ～d that the students would learn English well. 老师希望学生们把英语学好。 同 wish, expect II n. ❶希望;信心:There is a ray of ～. 有一线希望。 / He was disappointed in all ～s. 他完全失望了。 / We have a ～ of success. 我们有成功的希望。 / She has lost all ～s of victory. 她已失去取胜的信心。 同 wish, expectation / **past** (**beyond**) ～ (成功、痊愈等)无望;不可救药:His little son seems past ～. 他的小儿子似乎是无救了。 ❷被寄托希望的人(或事):He was the ～ of the school. 他是学校的希望。 / You are my last ～. 你是我最后能指望的人。 派 hopeful adj.

horizon / həˈraɪzn / n. [C]地平线;水平线:The sun was rising over the ～. 太阳从地平线上升起。

horizontal / ˌhɒrɪˈzɒnt(ə)l / adj. ❶水平的,与地平线平行的;横(向)的:～ distance 水平距离 ❷平的,平坦的:～ surface 平坦的表面

hormone / ˈhɔːməun / n. 激素;荷尔蒙

horn / hɔːn / n. ❶[C](牛、鹿等动物的)角 ❷号角;喇叭:a motor ～ 汽车喇叭

horrible / ˈhɒrəbl / adj. 可怕的 ;(口语)令人不愉快的;让人讨厌的:the ～ weather 让人讨厌的天气 同 dreadful, terrible

horror / ˈhɒrə(r) / n. [U]恐怖;极端厌恶:Little girls don't like ～ fiction or films. 小女孩不喜欢读恐怖小说和看恐怖电影。 / The girl has a ～ of spiders. 小女孩怕蜘蛛。 同 dread, dislike

horse / hɔːs / n. [C]马:a herd of ～s 一群马

horsepower / ˈhɔːspauə(r) / n. [C]马力:～-hour 马力小时

hospitable / ˈhɒspɪtəbl / adj. ❶款待周到的;好客的;殷勤的:The villagers were ～ to every visitor. 乡亲们殷勤接待每一位客人。 ❷热情的,诚挚的:a ～ smile 热情的微笑 ❸(对新思想等)愿意接受的,思想开明的:He is ～ to new ideas. 他思想开明。愿意接受新观念。

hospital / ˈhɒspɪtl / n. [C]医院:go to ～ 上医院 / enter (go into) (a) ～入院 / leave a ～ 出院 / He is still in ～. 他仍然在住院。 / This is a ～ of Chinese medicine. 这是一所中医院。

hospitality / ˌhɒspɪˈtæləti / n. [U]好客;殷勤:My sister is known for her ～. 我姐姐以好客著称。 同 entertainment, generosity

host / həust / n. [C]主人;节目主持人;东道主:Beijing is the ～ city of the 2008 Olympic Games. 北京是 2008 年奥运会的主办城市。 / I don't know who is the ～ of the evening party. 我不知道晚会的主持人是谁。 同 master, presenter

hostage / ˈhɒstɪdʒ / n. [C]人质;抵押品:exchange ～s 交换人质 / In this event, five girl students were taken ～. 在这次事件中有五名女学生被扣作人质。 / The authority asked to free the ～s. 地方当局要求释放人质。 同 captive, guarantee

hostess / ˈhəustəs / n. [C]女主人;女主持人;女东道主

hostile / ˈhɒstaɪl / adj. 敌意的;敌对的;不友好的:a ～ country/Don't be ～ to your step mother. She is kind to you. 别对你的继母不友善,她对你很好。 同 opposed, unfriendly

hot / hɒt / I adj. (hotter, hottest) ❶热的:a well ～ 温泉 / a ～ dog 热狗;红肠面包 / set up a ～ line 建立热线 / The weather here is not too ～ in summer. 这儿夏天不太热。 / You'd better have a ～ bath after running. 跑步后你最好洗个热水澡。 同 heated, burning, fiery 反 cold ❷辣的;刺激的:Most Sichuan people like ～ pepper very much. 多数四川人都非常喜欢吃辣椒。 同 pungent, peppery ❸热衷的,热切的;热情的:The old professor is ～ on the research of archaeology. 老教授热衷于考古学的研究。 同 ardent, passionate 反 cold ❹激动的;急躁的:The doctors had a ～ debate on the special case. 大夫们就这个特殊的病例进行了激烈的争论。 / The young man has a ～ temper. 这年轻人性情急躁。 同 excited, furious 反 calm, peaceful II vt. (hotted;

hotting)变热；加温：Please ～ the rice up. 请把米饭加热一下。圆 heat

hotel ／ həʊˈtel ／ *n.* [C]旅馆：operate（run）a ～ 经营旅馆／ put up（stay）at a ～ 住旅馆／ They check out of the ～ at 10 o'clock. 十点钟他们结账离开了那家旅馆。

hour ／ ˈaʊə(r) ／ *n.* [C] ❶小时；钟头：two ～s' journey 两小时的旅行／ for an ～ or so 大约一小时／ in an ～ or two 过一两个小时／ a couple of ～s 两三个小时／ every ～ or two 每隔一两个小时／ Clocks call out the ～. 时钟报时。❷时刻；时间：office ～s 办公时间／ play ～s 娱乐时间／ rush（peak）～s 交通高峰时间／ business ～s 营业时间／ the closing ～ 下班时间／ keep good ～s 按时作息／ We should keep early ～s . 我们应当早睡早起。圆 moment, time

hourly ／ ˈaʊəli ／ *adj.* ❶每小时（一次）的：an ～ news broadcasts 每小时一次的新闻广播 ❷按钟点计算的，以小时计算的：～ wages 计时工资

house ／ haʊs ／ *n.* [C] ❶房屋；住宅：a hen ～ 鸡舍／ a cow ～ 牛栏／ a store ～ 仓库／ a bake ～ 面包厂／ I have bought a new ～. 我买了一幢新房子。❷议会；议会大楼：the House of Commons 下议院／ the House of Lords 上议院／ Lower House 下议院，众议院

household ／ ˈhaʊshəʊld ／ Ⅰ *n.* [C]家庭；户；全家人：My father is head of my ～. 我父亲是我家的户主。圆 family, house Ⅱ *adj.* 家庭的；家常的；普通的：～ articles 家庭用品／ ～ expenses 家庭开支／ ～ duties 家务 圆 domestic

housewife ／ ˈhaʊswaɪf ／ *n.* [C]家庭主妇 圆 wife, housekeeper

housework ／ ˈhaʊswɜːk ／ *n.* [C]家务事 圆 housekeeping

housing ／ ˈhaʊzɪŋ ／ *n.* 住房建设；（总称）房屋；住房：～ loan 住房贷款／ ～ reform 住房改革／Our ～ condition has been greatly improved. 我们的居住条件已得到极大的改善。圆 house-building, house

hover ／ ˈhɒvə(r) ／ *vi.* （鸟、飞机等）盘旋：A hawk is ～ing over. 一只鹰在高空中盘旋。圆 fly, float

how ／ haʊ ／ *adv.* ❶怎样；如何：Please tell me ～ to spell the word. 告诉我怎样拼这个词。／ How are you? 你好吗？／ How do you do? 你好！／ How about going for a walk? 去

散散步怎么样? ❷多么；何等：How nice the picture is! 这幅画真美!

however ／ haʊˈevə(r) ／ Ⅰ *conj.* 然而；可是：His wife asked him not to go out hunting, ～, he insisted on going. 他妻子劝他别去打猎，然而他坚持要去。圆 nevertheless Ⅱ *adv.* 无论如何：He will never succeed ～ hard he tries. 无论如何努力，他也不会成功。

howl ／ haʊl ／ *vi.* ❶（狼等）凄厉地长嗥；（狗）狂吠：The coyote was ～ing at the moon. 一只山狗对月狂叫。❷（因疼痛、悲伤等而）号哭；哀号；（因愤怒而）吼叫，咆哮，怒吼：She ～ed as the dentist began to pull the bad tooth. 牙科医生开始拔那颗蛀牙时，她直嚷嚷。❸（风等）呼啸，怒号：I lay in bed, listening to the wind ～ing. 我躺在床上，听着风的呼啸声。

hue ／ hjuː ／ *n.* [C] ❶色泽；色调；色度：a warm ～ 暖色调 ❷颜色，色彩：all the ～ of the rainbow 彩虹的七彩颜色 派 hued *adj.*

hug ／ hʌɡ ／ *vt.* （hugged；hugging）紧抱；搂抱：The child was ～ging her doll. 那小孩紧紧抱住她的洋娃娃。／ They ～ged each other when they met again. 再次见面，他们相互紧紧拥抱在一起。圆 clasp, embrace

huge ／ hjuːdʒ ／ *adj.* 巨大的；庞大的：There are many ～ ships on the river. 河上有许多大轮船。／ We have won ～ success. 我们获得了巨大的成功。圆 giant, vast, enormous 反 little, small 派 hugely *adv.*

human ／ ˈhjuːmən ／ Ⅰ *adj.* 人的；人类的：a ～ being 人／ the ～ nature 人性／ ～ affairs 人事／ ～ race 人类／ ～ rights 人权／ She is not willing to talk about the ～ relationship in her company. 她不愿谈论她公司里的人际关系问题。Ⅱ *n.* （＝ human being）人 圆 man, person

humane ／ hjuːˈmeɪn ／ *adj.* ❶仁慈的；仁爱的；人道的；富有同情心的：be ～ in the treatment of the prisoners 人道地对待囚犯／a more ～ world 一个更具仁爱的世界 ❷人文（学科）的：～ studies（learning）人文科学 派 humanely *adv.*；humaneness *n.*

humanity ／ hjuːˈmænəti ／ *n.* ❶人类；人性 圆 man, mankind ❷（*pl.*）人文科学：departments in the humanities 文科各系

humble ／ ˈhʌmbl ／ *adj.* ❶谦逊的；谦恭的：In my ～ opinion, the machine should be improved. 依本人拙见，这台机器应当改进。／ He is ～ toward his superiors. 他对上司很谦

恭。圖 modest 反 proud ❷地位(或身份)低下的；卑贱的：There isn't any ～ occupation in our society. 在我们的社会中没有卑下的职业。/ He is a man of ～ birth but he has won great success through his hard work. 他出身卑微，但通过努力获得了巨大的成功。圖 low, lowly, inferior 反 noble 派 humbleness n.; humbly adv.

humid / 'hjuːmɪd / adj. 潮湿的：～ air 潮湿的空气 圖 wet, damp 反 dry

humidity / hjuːˈmɪdəti / n. [U]湿气；湿度：They are measuring the ～ of the room. 他们在测房间的湿度。圖 moisture, wetness, dampness 反 dryness

humiliate / hjuːˈmɪlɪeɪt / vt. 使丢脸；羞辱，使蒙羞：She ～d me in front of my friends. 她当着我朋友的面羞辱我。

humorous / 'hjuːmərəs / adj. 幽默的；可笑的：He is good at telling ～ stories. 他擅长讲幽默故事。圖 funny 派 humorously adv.

humo(u)r / 'hjuːmə(r) / n. [U]幽默；可笑；滑稽：We like him because he is a man with a sense of ～. 我们喜欢他，因为他是一个有幽默感的人。圖 amusement, comedy

hump / hʌmp / n. [C]圆形隆起物；驼峰；驼背

hundred / 'hʌndrəd / num. 百：two ～ and five boys 205 个男孩／a few ～ people 几百人／～s of people 数以百计的人

Hungarian / hʌŋˈɡeəriən / I adj. 匈牙利的；Ⅱ n. 匈牙利人；匈牙利语

Hungary / 'hʌŋɡəri / n. 匈牙利

hunger / 'hʌŋɡə(r) / n. [U] ❶饥饿；饿：suffer ～ 挨饿／satisfy one's ～ 充饥／She is fainting with ～. Please give her something to eat. 她饿昏了，请拿点东西给她吃。圖 starvation, hungriness ❷渴望；欲望(与 for 连用)：Little children always have a ～ for knowledge. 小孩总是渴望知识的。圖 desire, longing

hungry / 'hʌŋɡri / adj. ❶饥饿的，感到饿的：I am ～. 我饿了。/ He felt ～ after a day's work. 一天工作之后，他感到很饿。圖 starved, starving ❷渴望的(与 for 连用)：Young people are ～ for (after) truth. 年轻人渴求真理。圖 eager, desirous 派 hungrily adv.

hunt / hʌnt / v. 狩猎；搜寻；搜索：go out ～ing 去打猎／～ the big game 狩猎大猎物／～ **for** 寻找；搜索：～ for fame and game 追名逐

利／He is ～ing for a job. 他正在找工作。派 hunter n.

hurl / hɜːl / vt. ❶猛投，用力掷：～ a pebble through the window 把小石子扔进窗子里／The boys ～ed themselves against the door. 孩子们用身体使劲撞门。❷大声地说出(或喊出)：～ abuse at sb. 大声辱骂某人

hurrah / həˈrɑː / int. 好哇；万岁

hurricane / 'hʌrɪkən / n. [C]飓风；十二级风：blow a ～ 刮飓风／a ～ of applause 暴风雨般的掌声／A ～ swept the whole district. 飓风横扫整个地区。圖 typhoon, storm

hurry / 'hʌri / I v. 使匆忙；赶快：Let's ～ or we'll be late. 赶快，否则我们要迟到了。圖 rush, urge／～ **up** 赶快：Ask him to ～ up with those letters so that we can send them off today. 叫他们赶快把那些信写好，以便我们今天发出去。Ⅱ n. [U]匆忙(用于否定句、疑问句中)：**in a** ～ 匆忙地；仓促地：Nothing is ever done in a ～. 匆匆忙忙是办不好事的。圖 rush, haste 派 hurried adj.

hurt / hɜːt / v. (hurt, hurt) ❶使受伤；使疼痛；伤害：He ～ his shoulder when he fell. 他跌倒时伤了肩。圖 injure, wound ❷使伤心；伤害感情：They will be ～ at our not going to pay a visit to them. 我们不去看他们，他们会难过的。圖 distress

husband / 'hʌzbənd / n. [C]丈夫

hush / hʌʃ / int. 嘘，别响；别作声

hut / hʌt / n. [C](简陋的)小屋；棚屋：a bamboo ～ 小竹屋 圖 cabin, cottage

hydrogen / 'haɪdrədʒən / n. [U]氢

hygiene / 'haɪdʒiːn / n. 卫生；卫生学：Middle school students should learn about some knowledge of public and private ～. 中学生应当学习一点公共卫生和个人卫生知识。

hyphen / 'haɪfən / n. [C]连字符

hypnosis / hɪpˈnəʊsɪs / n. [U](pl. hypnoses / hɪpˈnəʊsiːz/) ❶催眠状态：be under deep ～ 处于催眠后的昏睡状态中 ❷催眠；催眠术

hypothesis / haɪˈpɒθəsɪs / n. [C](pl. hypotheses / haɪˈpɒθəsiːz/)假设；假说

hysterical / hɪˈsterɪkl / adj. 歇斯底里的：I really don't know what caused her ～ laughter? 我真的不知道是什么引起了她歇斯底里的大笑？派 hysteria n.

I i

I / aɪ / *pron.* (第一人称代词的主格)我

ice / aɪs / *n.* [U] 冰：In winter the lake is covered with ～. 冬天湖面上结了一层冰。a block of ～ 一块冰／ ～ cream 冰激凌 派 icy *adj.*

icon / ˈaɪkɒn / *n.* [C] (*pl.* icons 或 icones /-kəˌniːz/) ❶圣像 ❷形象，图像，画像，雕像 ❸图标

idea / aɪˈdɪə / *n.* ❶思想；概念：We should fit our ～s to the new conditions. 我们应该使自己的思想适应新情况。／ I have no ～ (as to) what you mean. 我一点儿也不明白你的意思。同 concept ❷意见；建议：He opposed the ～. 他反对这个意见。／ You shouldn't force your ～ on other people. 你不应把自己的意见强加给别人。同 opinion, attention ❸计划；计策；主意：a fine (good) ～ 好主意／Then a bright ～ came to him. 然后他想到一个好主意。同 attention, plan

ideal / aɪˈdɪəl / *I adj.* 理想的；完美的：an ～ society 理想社会／ an ～ state 理想的国家／ It was an ～ day for a picnic. 这是个外出野餐的好日子。同 perfect *II n.* [C] 理想的人或物：She is afraid that she will not realize (fulfil) her ～s. 她担心她实现不了自己的理想。／ He is determined to establish high ～s. 他决心树立崇高的理想。

identical / aɪˈdentɪkl / *adj.* 完全相同的；同一的：They have ～ views on this problem. 在这个问题上他们看法一致。同 alike 反 different

identification / aɪˌdentɪfɪˈkeɪʃn / *n.* 辨认；鉴定；身份证明：a car ～ plate 汽车牌照／He showed his ～ when the police came. 警察到来时，他出示了自己的身份证明。同 recognition, equation

identify / aɪˈdentɪfaɪ / *vt.* ❶认出；鉴定；验明：The girl said that she couldn't ～ the man who robbed her. 女孩说她辨认不出那个抢劫她的人。同 recognize, distinguish ❷等同；和…认

同：You cannot ～ beauty with good manners. 你不能把漂亮等同于礼貌。同 equate

identity / aɪˈdentəti / *n.* 身份；特征：an～ card 身份证／ Are you certain of the murderer's ～? 你能确认那个杀人犯的身份吗？同 character, personality

ideology / ˌaɪdiˈɒlədʒi / *n.* 思想(体系)；思想意识；意识形态：socialist ～ 社会主义思想／ in the realm of ～ 在思想领域里 同 beliefs, philosophy

idiom / ˈɪdiəm / *n.* [C] 成语；习惯用语：This expression is against ～. 这一表达方式不合乎语言习惯。同 phrase, expression

idiot / ˈɪdiət / *n.* [C] 智力低下者 同 fool

idle / ˈaɪdl / *I adj.* ❶懒散的；无所事事的：He is too ～ to do anything. 他太懒了，什么事也不干。同 lazy 反 diligent ❷闲着的；空闲的：～ machines 闲置的机器／ stand ～ 袖手旁观 同 inactive, unused *II v.* 懒散；闲逛；无所事事：Don't ～ away your time. 不要虚度光阴。派 idleness *n.*

idol / ˈaɪdl / *n.* 偶像；崇拜对象：Many young students like to worship singing ～s. 许多青年学生喜欢崇拜偶像歌星。同 image

i. e. (拉丁语 id est 的缩写)(＝ that is)即，那就是

if / ɪf / *conj.* ❶假设；如果：If you can't finish the book in time, you may come and renew it. 假如你不能及时看完这本书，你可以来续借。／ If I were you, I would not go. 如果我是你，我就不去。同 providing, provided ❷是否(在口语中，if 可代替 whether)：Do you know ～ (whether) he is in the library? 你知道他是否在图书馆吗？同 whether/ **even** ～ 即使；纵然：Even ～ he did say that, I am sure he didn't intend to hurt your feelings. 即使他真的那么说，我也相信他无意伤你的感情。／ I'll do it even ～ it takes me all the afternoon. 虽然做这件事要花我整个下午的时间，但我还是

要做。**as** ～ 好像；仿佛：He talks as ～ (as though) he knew all about it. 他谈起话来好像这事他全知道。～ **only** 要是…多好；但愿(常表示对现在或将来的期望)：If only he could dance. 要是他会跳舞该多好。

ignite / ɪɡˈnaɪt / vt. 点燃；燃烧；着火：He ～d the match by scratching it on the box. 他从盒子上划着了火柴。/Gas oline ～s easily. 汽油易燃。**派** ignition n.

ignorance / ˈɪɡnərəns / n. 无知；愚昧：He committed a crime out of his ～ of the law. 他由于不懂法而犯罪。**同** blindness, innocence **反** wisdom

ignorant / ˈɪɡnərənt / adj. ❶无知识的，无知的；愚昧的：If you don't want to be an ～ person, you must study hard. 如果你不想做一个愚昧无知的人，你就必须努力学习。**同** uneducated, illiterate **反** knowledgeable, wise ❷不知道的：He is ～ of the whole thing. 对于整件事，他完全不知道。**同** uninformed, unaware **反** informed, knowing

ignore / ɪɡˈnɔː(r) / vt. 不理；不顾；忽视：He entirely ～d his personal danger. 他完全不顾自己的安危。**同** overlook, neglect **反** notice

il- / ɪl / (前缀)表示"不"或"缺少"：～legal 非法的/ ～literate 未受过教育的；文盲/ ～logical 不合逻辑的

ill / ɪl / **I** adj. (worse/wɜːs/, worst/wɜːst/) ❶生病的；不健康的：You look ～ these days. 近来你气色不好。/ He has been ～ for a long time. 他病了很久了。/ She was suddenly taken ～. 她突然病了。**同** sick, unhealthy **反** well, healthy ❷坏的；邪恶的：That is ～ news to her. 对她来说，那是坏消息。/ The fellow is famous for his ～ temper. 这家伙以其坏脾气著名。**同** bad, evil, wicked **反** good **II** adv. 坏；不利地：Don't think (speak) ～ of others. 别把他人想(说)得太坏。**同** badly, evilly

用法
ill 作"生病的"讲，通常用作表语。一个病人习惯上说 a sick man，而不说 an ill man。如果 ill 用作定语，它相当于 bad (恶劣的，坏的)的意思：ill luck 厄运；ill temper 坏脾气。

illegal / ɪˈliːɡl / adj. 非法的；不合法的

illegible / ɪˈledʒɪbl / adj. (字迹)难以辨认的，

无法看清的，难读的：an ～ signature 难以辨认的签字/This letter is completely ～. 这封信根本没法读

illicit / ɪˈlɪsɪt / adj. ❶非法的；违法的；违禁的：the ～ drug business 非法毒品交易 ❷违反习俗的；道德不允许的；不正当的：achieve one's success through ～ means 通过不正当的手段获得成功

illiterate / ɪˈlɪtərət / **I** adj. 文盲的；未受教育的 **II** n. [C]文盲

illness / ˈɪlnəs / n. 病；疾病：He suffered from a serious ～ but recovered soon. 他患了重病，但很快就好了。**同** sickness, disease **反** health

illuminate / ɪˈluːmɪneɪt / vt. 阐明；解释；启发：Our teacher ～d the theory with examples. 我们的老师用例子解释那个原理。**同** enlighten, clarify

illusion / ɪˈluːʒn / n. [C]幻想；错觉；假象：cast away one's ～ 丢掉幻想 / They say that safety is only an ～ in America. 他们说在美国安全只是一种幻想。**同** fancy, delusion **反** reality, disillusion

illustrate / ˈɪləstreɪt / vt. (以实例、图表等)说明；加插图：Each verb in this dictionary is ～d with a sentence. 这本词典的每一个动词都用一个例句来加以说明。/ This book is well ～d. 这本书的插图配得很好。

illustration / ˌɪləˈstreɪʃn / n. 说明；例证；图解；插图：Please offer more ～s to explain the problem. 请多提供一些实例来说明这个问题。/ The ～s will help you understand the article. 这些插图将帮助你理解文章的意思。**同** explanation, example, picture

im- / ɪm / (前缀)表示"否定"：～patient 不耐烦的；急躁的/ ～possible 不可能的/ ～proper 不适当的

image / ˈɪmɪdʒ / n. [C] ❶像；肖像；影像；图像：a TV ～ 电视图像 / We saw his ～ on the wall. 我们看到墙上挂着他的肖像。**同** picture, impression ❷形象；印象：The mayor is trying hard to improve his ～ in public. 市长努力提高他在公众中的形象。**同** conception

imaginable / ɪˈmædʒɪnəbl / adj. 可想象的；能想象到的(放在被修饰词之后)：We had the greatest difficulty ～. 我们遇到了想象到的最大困难。

imaginary / ɪˈmædʒɪnəri / adj. 想象中的；不

真实的;虚构的;幻想的: It's not real — it's only ~. 那不是真的,只不过是想象中的事情。 反 real, actual

imagination / ɪˌmædʒɪ'neɪʃn / n. ❶[U] 想象;想象力;创造力: have a good (poor) ~ 有(缺乏)想象力/He is a writer of rich ~. 他是一个想象力丰富的作家。❷[C]想象的事物: You didn't really see a ghost— it was only the ~. 你并没有真正见到过鬼——那只是你想象的东西。 同 fancy, illusion

> **辨析**
>
> imagination 着重强调创造、想象新形象的能力,指重新组合或解释已知事物,也指创造不存在之物并使其完善: Novelists are good at using their imagination. 小说家善于运用想象力。 **fancy** 常指创造虚幻而不真实、不可信事物的能力,凭空想象: Children usually have a lively fancy. 儿童往往有丰富的想象力。

imaginative / ɪ'mædʒɪnətɪv / adj. 富于想象的;想象力的;虚构的: / He is an ~ actor. 他是一位富于想象的演员。 同 creative

imagine / ɪ'mædʒɪn / v. 想象;设想;认为: I ~d her as a big tall woman. 我以为她是个身材高大的女人。 / I can ~ the scene clearly in my mind. 我可以清楚地想象出那个情景。 / He never ~d this would happen. 他绝没料到会发生这种事情。 同 picture, guess, suppose

imbalance / ɪm'bæləns / n. [C]不平衡,失衡;失调: correct an ~ 纠正不平衡的局面/a population ~ 人口中男女比例失调

imitate / 'ɪmɪteɪt / vt. 模仿;仿效: ~ a diamond with crystal 用水晶仿造钻石/ Young people always ~ great actors they like. 年轻人总爱模仿他们喜欢的大明星。 同 follow, copy 派 imitation n.

immature / ˌɪmə'tjʊə(r), ˌɪmə'tʃʊə(r) / adj. ❶发育未完全的;未成熟的: ~ fruit 没熟透的水果/for the wellbeing of ~ babies 为了胎儿的健康 ❷不成熟的,不够老练的;孩子气的: emotionally ~ adults 感情上还未成熟的成年人/It was ~ of her to do that. 她那样做太孩子气了。

immeasurable / ɪ'meʒərəbl / adj. 无法度量的;无边无际的;无限的: the ~ vastness of the universe 宇宙的浩瀚无际/China is a market of ~ potential. 中国是一个具有无限潜在

商机的大市场。

immediate / ɪ'miːdɪət / adj. ❶立即的;即刻的: They said that they would take ~ action to settle the problem. 他们说要采取迅速行动解决这个问题。 / Please send us an ~ reply. 请立即答复我们。 同 instant, prompt 反 delayed ❷直接的;最接近的: The ~ cause of his mistake is that he was too careless. 他犯错误的直接原因是他太粗心大意。 同 direct, nearest 反 distant immediately adv.

immense / ɪ'mens / adj. 无限的;广大的;无边的: an ~ body of water 一片汪洋/Don't be hard on me. I have made ~ improvement. 别苛求我,我已经做出巨大改进了。 同 large, vast, enormous 反 tiny, small

> **辨析**
>
> immense 意为"极大的",指一般标准无法衡量: immense amount 巨额。 **enormous** 常指超出比例,超过通常的限度,有时可与 immense 换用: Long ago enormous animals lived on the earth. 很久以前,巨大的动物生活在地球上。 **huge** 着重指体积或数量极大: It's a huge elephant. 这是一头巨象。

immerse / ɪ'mɜːs / v. ❶使浸没,使浸透: ~ one's feet in water 把双脚浸到水里 ❷使沉浸在;使深陷于;使埋头于: Little by little she became ~d in Moscow life. 她渐渐融入莫斯科的生活。/be ~d in work 废寝忘食地工作/~ oneself in contemplation 陷于沉思

immigrant / 'ɪmɪɡrənt / Ⅰ n.[C]移民;侨民: Canada has many ~s from China. 加拿大有很多中国移民。 同 incomer, newcomer, settler Ⅱ adj. 移民的;移来的: His grandfather was an ~ to the United States from India. 他祖父是美籍印度移民。

immigrate / 'ɪmɪɡreɪt / v. (使)移居入境;(从国外)移来: They ~d from Africa into Spain many years ago. 多年前他们从非洲移居到西班牙。 同 migrate, colonize 反 emigrate

imminent / 'ɪmɪnənt / adj. 临近的;附近的;就要发生的: the ~ general election 即将举行的大选/Civil war there was ~. 那儿的内战迫在眉睫。

immoderate / ɪ'mɒdərət / adj. 不适度的;过度的;无节制的;极端的: They were dead by ~ labour and ill food. 他们因为操劳过度和饮食恶劣而死。/~ eating habits 无节制的大吃的习惯

immoral / ɪˈmɒrəl / *adj.* ❶不道德的；邪恶的；缺德的，败坏道德的：～ habits of behaviour 不道德的行为习惯/～ earnings 收受贿赂所得 ❷放荡的，淫荡的

immortal / ɪˈmɔːtl / *adj.* 不朽的；永生的；永久的：an ～ hero 不朽的英雄圆 lasting, deathless

immune / ɪˈmjuːn / *adj.* ❶免疫的；(有)免疫力的；有抵抗力的：an ～ reaction 免疫反应/ The blood test shows you are not ～. 血检表明你不具免疫力。❷受到保护的；不受影响的：～ to new ideas 不受新思想的影响 ❸免除的，豁免的(与 from 连用)：～ from taxes 免税/To be ～ from error is humanly impossible. 作为人，不犯错误是不可能的。

impact / ˈɪmpækt / *n.* ❶影响；作用：The Internet makes a great ～ on our life. 因特网对我们的生活产生了巨大的影响。圆 influence, effect ❷冲击；碰撞：I saw the ～ of a car crashing into the pole beside the street. 我看见一辆汽车撞到路边的一根电杆上。圆 shock, crash

impart / ɪmˈpɑːt / *vt.* ❶告知，通知；透露：～ a secret to a friend 向朋友透露一个秘密/I have no news to ～. 我没有消息可以透露。❷给予(尤指抽象事物)；分给；传授：The new furnishings ～ed an air of newness to the old house. 新家具给这旧房子带来了新气象。/ There is a general consensus that schools do indeed ～ values. 人们普遍认为学校确实要传授价值观念。

impartial / ɪmˈpɑːʃl / *adj.* 不偏不倚的，中立的；公平的，无偏见的：an ～ judge 公正的法官/What I needed was totally ～ advice. 我需要的是丝毫不带偏见的建议。

impatience / ɪmˈpeɪʃns / *n.* [U]不耐烦；性急；急躁：His ～ made him unreasonable. 他的急躁情绪使他变得不讲道理。圆 restlessness, haste 反 patience

impatient / ɪmˈpeɪʃnt / *adj.* 不耐烦的；急躁的：We don't like teachers who are ～ with children. 我们不喜欢对孩子不耐心的老师。/ He was ～ to finish the game. 他急于结束那场比赛。圆 restless, hasty 反 patient, cool

impede / ɪmˈpiːd / *vt.* 阻碍，妨碍；阻止：The deep snow ～d travel. 厚厚的积雪阻碍了交通。/ Many a man is ～d in his career by a lack of belief in himself. 许多人因为缺乏自信而影响了自己事业的发展。

impel / ɪmˈpel / *vt.* (-pelled; -pelling) ❶驱策，激励；迫使：～ sb. into action 激励某人行动起来 ❷推进，推动：The wind ～led the boat toward the shore. 风把船吹向岸边。/～ developments and innovations 推动发展和革新

imperialism / ɪmˈpɪərɪəlɪzəm / *n.* [U]帝国主义

imperialist / ɪmˈpɪərɪəlɪst / Ⅰ *adj.* 帝国主义的 Ⅱ *n.* [C]帝国主义者

impermanent / ɪmˈpɜːmənənt / *adj.* 转瞬即逝的；短暂的；非永久性的：an ～ unofficial arrangement 非官方的暂时性安排/Magnetic media are notoriously ～. 磁性媒质是最不能持久的。

implant Ⅰ / ɪmˈplɑːnt / *vt.* ❶把…嵌入；埋置(与 in 连用)：a ruby ～ in a gold ring 嵌在金戒指里的一颗红宝石 ❷灌输，注入；使充满：～ respect for democracy in the younger generation 向青年一代灌输尊重民主的意识 ❸种植，种下：～ the seeds 播种 ❹移植；植入：an artificial heart 植入人造心脏 Ⅱ /ˈɪmplɑːnt/ *n.* [C]植入物；移植片；种植体

implement / ˈɪmplɪmənt / *n.* [C]工具；器材：farm ～s 农具/ kitchen ～s 厨房用具/ writing ～s 书写工具 圆 tool, instrument

implication / ˌɪmplɪˈkeɪʃn / *n.* [C]含义；暗示；暗指：Mother smiled and I knew the ～ was that she wouldn't agree with me. 妈妈笑了，我知道这暗示着她并不同意我的意见。/ When reading a novel, I try to understand the cultural ～s in it. 读小说时，我尽力去理解其中的文化内涵。圆 indication, hint

implicit / ɪmˈplɪsɪt / *adj.* ❶暗示的；暗含的，含蓄的：an ～ answer 含蓄的回答/Her silence gave ～ consent. 她用沉默表示赞同。❷绝对的；毫无保留的；毫不怀疑的：He has ～ confidence in hi friends. 他毫无保留地信任自己的朋友。/A soldier must give ～ obedience to his officers. 士兵必须绝对服从上司。

implore / ɪmˈplɔː(r) / *vt.* 恳求；哀求；乞求：She ～d mother to give permission for her to go on the trip. 她恳求母亲允许她去旅行。/～ aid form sb. 乞求某人援助

imply / ɪmˈplaɪ / *vt.* 暗示；意指：Silence often implies consent. 沉默常意味着同意。/ What do you ～ by that statement? 你那句话是什么

意思? 同 mean,indicate

impolite / ˌɪmpəˈlaɪt / *adj.* 不礼貌的;无礼的,失礼的;粗鲁的:grossly ~ eating habits 极其粗鲁的吃相/Take care not to be ~ to customers 注意不要对顾客失礼。派 impolitely *adv.*

import Ⅰ / ɪmˈpɔːt / *vt.* 输入;引入;进口:They ~ wool from Australia. 他们从澳大利亚进口羊毛。/ He ~ed his personal feelings into a discussion. (喻)他把个人的感情带进讨论中。同 introduce 反 export Ⅱ / ˈɪmpɔːt / *n.* [C] 输入品;进口货:~ and export trade 进出口贸易/~ duty(tax)进口税/ ~ license 进口许可证/ Our ~s fall short of our exports. 我们的进口商品少于出口商品。

importance / ɪmˈpɔːtəns / *n.* [U] 重要;重大:It is of no ~. 这事无关紧要。/ He hasn't realized the ~ of studying English. 他还未意识到学习英语的重要性。同 value, significance 反 insignificance

important / ɪmˈpɔːtənt / *adj.* 重要的,重大的:It is very ~ for you to study English well. 学好英语对你来讲很重要。同 great, significant 反 insignificant

impose / ɪmˈpəʊz / *vt.* 征税:We should ~ more duties on tobaccos and wines. 我们应当对烟酒多征税。同 charge

impossible / ɪmˈpɒsəbl / *adj.* 不可能的;办不到的:It is ~ for us to accomplish that task without their help. 没有他们的帮助,我们不可能完成那项任务。/ Nothing is ~ to a willing mind. 世上无难事,只怕有心人。同 unlikely, unachievable

impractical / ɪmˈpræktɪkəl / *adj.* ❶不切实际的;无用的;不现实的:an ~ plan 不切实际的计划/advice of a totally ~ nature 完全脱离实际的建议 ❷不注重实际的;无动手能力的:He is intelligent but too ~ for commercial work. 他人很聪慧,但不善做实际工作,不能经商。

impress / ɪmˈpres / *v.* ❶(以一物)压(另一物);印;盖记号:an ~ed stamp 盖了邮戳的邮票 同 print, mark ❷给…以深刻印象;使铭记:She repeated the words to ~ them in her memory. 她反复重述那些词以便将它们铭记在心。/ He ~ed me favourably. 他给我的印象不错。同 imprint, print

impression / ɪmˈpreʃn / *n.* 印象;感想:What are your ~s of (about) Beijing? 你对北京有何印象?/ What he said makes a lasting ~ on us. 他的话给我们留下了不可磨灭的印象。同 memory, imprint

impressive / ɪmˈpresɪv / *adj.* ❶给人以深刻印象的;感人的,打动人的;令人敬佩的:an ~ building 宏伟的建筑物/an ~ storm 震撼人心的风暴/ Economic development is even more ~. 经济上的发展就更令人瞩目。❷威严的;使人肃然起敬的:an ~ figure 一个令人肃然起敬的人物/an equestrian statue of ~ dignity 庄严而惹人注目的骑士雕像 派 impressively *adv.* 异常地;令人敬佩地

imprint Ⅰ / ˈɪmprɪnt / *n.* ❶[C]印记,戳记,印痕;痕迹:Your foot made an ~ in the sand. 你在沙地上留下了一个脚印。❷深刻的印象;影响;特征,标记:The performance made a deep ~ on our minds. 那场演出给我们留下了深刻的印象。/He left the ~ of his thought on all succeeding scholars. 他的思想对所有后来的学生都产生了影响。Ⅱ/ɪmˈprɪnt/ *vt.* ❶印,压印;盖(印、邮戳等)于:~ a postmark on an envelope 在信封上盖邮戳 ❷铭刻于;使牢记:a scene ~ed on sb.'s memory 深深地铭刻在某人记忆中的一幕

imprison / ɪmˈprɪzn / *vt.* 关押,监禁:The criminal was ~ed for life. 罪犯被终身监禁。同 jail 反 free, release 派 imprisonment *n.*

improper / ɪmˈprɒpə(r) / *adj.* 不适当的;不适合的:Shouting aloud here is ~. 在这儿高声大喊是很不恰当的。同 unfit, unsuitable 反 proper, suitable

improve / ɪmˈpruːv / *v.* 改善;提高:She is improving in health. 她的健康状况正在好转。/ How much you have ~d! 你进步真大! / The government is trying to ~ the living conditions of the people. 政府正在努力改善人民的生活条件。同 better, promote 反 worsen

improvement / ɪmˈpruːvmənt / *n.* 改善;改进:Much ~ has been made in the safety construction of the factory. 工厂的安全设施有了很大的改进。同 betterment

impulse / ˈɪmpʌls / *n.* 冲力;冲动;刺激:The new treaty has given an ~ to trade between the two countries. 新签订的条约推动了两国之间的贸易往来。/ Our manager is a man of ~. 我们的经理是一个容易冲动的

人。/ He resisted a sudden ～ to beat the stealer. 他克制了一时的冲动没有揍那小偷。
同 urge, drive, instinct

impure / ɪmˈpjʊə(r) / *adj.* 不纯洁的；不纯的；掺杂的：The water in that city is often ～. 那座城市里的水常常是不清洁的。/ This kind of salt is ～. 这种盐不纯。 同 mixed, unclean 反 pure 派 impurity *n.*

in- / ɪn / (前缀) 表示"不"或"缺少"：～accessible 达不到的；难以得到的 /～capable 无能的

in / ɪn / *prep.* ❶ (表示地点、场所、部位) 在…里；在…中：～ China 在中国 / ～ the world 在世界上 / ～ the village 在村子里 / ～ the sky 在空中 / ～ the classroom 在教室里 / ～ the corner of the room 在房子的角落里 / ～ the newspaper 在报纸上 / ～ one's mouth 在嘴里 / ～ bed 在床上 / ～ one's hand 在某人的手里 ❷ 进入…中：He put his hands ～ his pockets. 他把手放进口袋里。/ Please throw it ～ the fire! 把它扔进火中！❸ (指时间) 在：～ the 21st century 在 21 世纪 / ～ 1990 1990 年 / ～ the morning(afternoon, evening) 在上午(下午、晚上)/ ～ January 在一月 / ～ spring (summer, autumn, winter) 在春季(夏季、秋季、冬季)/ ～ the daytime 在白天 / ～ the past 过去 / ～ (the) future 将来 ❹ 过(若干时间)；在(若干时间)内：I'll be back ～ a moment. 我过一会儿就回来。/ Can you finish this job ～ a very short time? 你能在很短的时间内完成这项工作吗? ❺ 穿着；戴着：the girl ～ red 穿红衣服的姑娘 ❻ (表示所处环境)在：sitting ～ the sun(sunshine) 坐在阳光下 / ～ the open 在露天 / ～ the shade 在阴凉处 / ～ the dark 在黑夜中 / ～ the moonlight 在月光里 / ～ the rain 在雨中 ❼ (指表达的方法或使用的手段、原料等)用，以：speak English 用英语说 / written ～ ink 用墨水写 / painted ～ oils 油彩画的 ❽ (表示情况或状态)处在…中：～ a troubled state 处在烦恼中 / ～ good order 整齐，情况良好 / ～ a rage 盛怒地 / ～ despair 绝望地 / ～ poverty 处在贫困中 / ～ love 恋爱中 / ～ secret 秘密地 / ～ a loud voice 大声地 / ～ the end 最后

inaccessible / ˌɪnækˈsesəbl / *adj.* 达不到的；难以到达的；不可(或难以)进入的：an ～ butte 一座无法攀登的孤峰 / The place is ～ by

road. 无路通达该地。

inactive / ɪnˈæktɪv / *adj.* ❶ 不活动的；不活跃的；缺乏活力的：an ～ volcano 不活动的火山 / an ～ market 缺乏活力的市场 / Nearly half the men between 55 and 65 are now economically ～ through early retirement. 由于提前退休，55 至 65 岁的男人将近有一半现已不再活跃在经济生活中了。❷ 非现役的，预备役的；后备的 同 idle, passive

inadequate / ɪnˈædɪkwət / *adj.* 不足的；不够的：There are only more than eight hundred books in this small library and is ～ to meet the need. 小图书馆里只有 800 多本书，不足以满足需要。 同 insufficient, short 反 enough, sufficient

inappropriate / ˌɪnəˈprəʊprɪət / *adj.* 不恰当的，不适合的：～ remarks 不得体的话 / It is ～ that he (should) be present. 他出席是不适宜的。

inaugurate / ɪˈnɔːɡjəreɪt / *vt.* 使(某人)就职(通常用被动语态)：He was ～d as President. 他就任总统。

inborn / ˈɪnbɔːn / *adj.* ❶ 天生的，与生俱来的：an ～ sense of rhythm 天生的节奏感 / Many mammals have an ～ fear of poisonous snakes. 许多哺乳动物天生就害怕毒蛇。/ an ～ talent 天才 ❷ 先天的，遗传的：There is an ～ component in human intelligence which is genetically heritable. 人的智力中某种先天因素是可以遗传。

incapable / ɪnˈkeɪpəbl / *adj.* 无能力的；不会的：No boss is willing to hire ～ workers. 没有老板愿意雇用无能的工人。/～ of 不能的，不会的；没有资格的：He is a good boy and is ～ of telling a lie. 他是个好孩子，不会撒谎。/ Is a foreigner ～ of becoming president of that country? 外国人就没有资格当国家的总统吗? 同 unable, incompetent 反 able, capable

incense / ɪnˈsens / *n.* [U]香；香气：the ～ of flowers 花香 同 perfume

incentive / ɪnˈsentɪv / *n.* [C;U]刺激；鼓励；奖励；动机：material ～ 物质刺激 / tax ～s for investing in depressed areas 鼓励向萧条地区投资的税收优惠 / Competition is the strongest ～ to industry. 竞争最能激发勤奋。

inch / ɪntʃ / *n.* [C]英寸(略作 in.)

incident / ˈɪnsɪdənt / *n.* 事件(尤指不太重要的小事件)；插曲；事变：the July Seventh Incident of 1937 1937 年七七事变 / That was one of the strangest ～s in my life. 那是我一生中遇到的最奇怪的事情之一。/ There were several ～s on the frontier. 边境上发生了几起事件。同 event, happening 派 incidentala *adj.*

incite / ɪnˈsaɪt / *vt.* 刺激；激起；煽动；激励：organisms that readily ～ antibody formation 容易激发抗体生成的有机物/She ～d her son to greater efforts. 她激励儿子更加发奋。

incline Ⅰ / ɪnˈklaɪn / *v.* 使倾向；使倾斜：She was ～d to go there by ship. 她倾向于乘船去那里。/ Do you feel ～d for swimming? 你想去游泳吗？/ The man ～d toward me to hear more clearly. 那人向我俯过身来以便更清楚地听到我说的话。同 lean, bent Ⅱ / ˈɪnklaɪn / *n.* [C]斜面；斜坡；倾斜

include / ɪnˈkluːd / *vt.* 包括，包含：She ～s eggs in the list of things to buy. 她把鸡蛋列在购物单上。同 contain 反 exclude

辨析

include 意为"包括；包含；算入"，强调包括的人或物是整体的一部分：There were five people, including two children. 一共五人，包括两个孩子。**comprise** 强调由很多部分组成，所包括的人或物是构成整体的全部成分：The list comprised the names of those who passed. 这个表是由考试及格的人的名字组成的。**contain** 常指多种物体为一较大物体所容纳，这些物体可以是构成整体的部分：The house contains five rooms. 这房子有五个房间。**involve** 常指由整体的性质所决定的成分，含有必然包括之意：Housekeeping involves cooking, washing, sweeping and cleaning. 家务必然包括烹饪、洗衣、扫地及洗刷。

including / ɪnˈkluːdɪŋ / *prep.* 如果包含…在内，算上…的话：There are altogether six members, ～ the chairman. 算上主席一共 6 位成员。/ Your total expenses, ～ these bills, are $300. 你的总开销，包括这些账单，是 300 美元。

inclusive / ɪnˈkluːsɪv / *adj.* 包含的；包括的；范围广的：The group consists of 12 people, ～ of the monitor. 包括班长在内，他们小组共有 12 个人。/ The rent is 450 yuan a mouth, ～ of the heating and water. 房租 450 元一个月，暖气费和水费包括在内。同 including, full, overall 反 exclusive, narrow

income / ˈɪnkəm / *n.* 收入；所得：an annual ～ 年收入/a large ～ 高收入/a low ～ 低收入/the net ～ 纯收入/ The ～ of the family was cut down one-third. 那家的收入减少了三分之一。

incomparable / ɪnˈkɒmp(ə)rəbl / *adj.* ❶无比的，无双的：a man of ～ genius 绝顶聪明的人/a moment of ～ joy 快乐无比的时刻 ❷无从比较的；无可比性的：Censorship still exists, but now it's absolutely ～ with what is was.(新闻)审查制度依然存在，但是今日的审查制度与昔日的审查制度压根儿就没有可比性。

inconsiderable / ˌɪnkənˈsɪd(ə)rəbl / *adj.* (价值、数量、尺寸等)相对较小的，小的：an ～ sum of money 一笔数目不大的款子/an ～ size 小尺寸/Her not ～ talent is dwarfed by his. 她那并不算小的才华和他一比，可就是小巫见大巫了。

inconsiderate / ˌɪnkənˈsɪdərət / *adj.* ❶不为别人着想的，不体谅别人的：an ～ employer 一个不替别人着想的老板/She is intensely selfish, utterly ～ of others. 她为人非常自私，压根儿就不顾别人。❷考虑不周；轻率的：explore the carvings on display with ～ fingers 用手随便乱摸雕刻展品

inconstant / ɪnˈkɒnstənt / *adj.* ❶(人)反复无常的；不专一的；不坚定的，动摇的：an ～ friend 不忠实的朋友/Weak I may have been, but never ～. 我可能意志薄弱，但是我从不见异思迁。❷(事物)多变折；无规则的：Fortune is ～. 命运无常。同 fickle, unstable 反 constant

incorporate / ɪnˈkɔːpəreɪt / *vt.* ❶包含；加入；吸收：～ new insights or research findings 吸收新见解或新的研究成果/We will ～ you suggestion in this new plan. 我们将把你的建议纳入这个新计划之中。❷把…组成公司(或社团)；把…吸收为公司(或社团)成员：When the businesses became large, the owners ～d it. 企业规模变大以后，老板们把它兼并了。❸使具体化(体现)：～ one's thoughts in an article 把自己的思想体现在一篇文章中

incorrect / ˌɪnkəˈrekt / *adj.* 不正确的；错误的：This is an ～ answer. 这是一个错误答案。/ I would not support your ～ behavior. 我不会支持你的不正当行为。同 wrong, false 反 correct, right

increase I / ɪnˈkriːs / v. 增加；增长；增大：The town is fast increasing in population. 该镇人口迅速增加。/ He ~d the speed of the car. 他加快了汽车的速度。同 grow, expand, rise 反 decrease, reduce II / ˈɪnkriːs / n. 增加；增大；增加量：the natural ~ of population 人口自然增长/ the rate of ~ 增长率 同 growth, expansion, rise 反 decrease 派 increasingly adv.

incredible / ɪnˈkredəbl / adj. 难以置信的；不可思议的：The story he told is ~. 他讲的故事令人难以置信。同 unbelievable, amazing

incurable / ɪnˈkjʊərəbl / adj. 治疗无效的，治不好的；不可救药的；无可矫正的：an ~ disease 不治之症/~ pessimism 不可救药的悲观情绪/~ busy bodies 改不了管闲事脾性的人们

indeed / ɪnˈdiːd / adv. 的确；实在；真正地：It was a wonderful travel ~. 这真是一次很奇妙的旅行。同 truly, really

indefinite / ɪnˈdefɪnət / adj. ❶不确定的；未决定的：He said he would come to see me, but only gave me an ~ date. 他说要来看我，但只给了一个不确定的日期。同 infinite, unlimited 反 definite ❷模糊的；含糊的；不明确的：What he wants to do is rather ~. 他究竟想做什么还很不确定。同 vague, confused, uncertain 反 clear ❸（语法）不定的：an ~ article 不定冠词 / an ~ pronoun 不定代词

independence / ˌɪndɪˈpendəns / n. [U] 独立；自主：The country formally declared ~. 这个国家正式宣布独立。同 freedom, self-government 反 dependence, reliance

independent / ˌɪndɪˈpendənt / adj. 独立的：They are ~ economically. 他们在经济上是独立的。/ It is an ~ country. 这是一个独立的国家。同 self-ruling 反 dependent

index / ˈɪndeks / n. [C]（pl. indexes 或 indices）❶索引：a card ~ 卡片索引 / an author ~ 作者索引 / a subject ~ 分类索引 同 catalog, list ❷指标；标志：the quality ~ 质量指标 / the profit ~ 利润指标 同 indicator, pointer, sign ❸指数：the consumer price ~ 消费品物价指数/ the stock market ~ 股票市场指数

India / ˈɪndiə / n. 印度

Indian / ˈɪndiən / I adj. 印度的；印度人的 II n. [C] 印度人；印第安人；印第安语

indicate / ˈɪndɪkeɪt / vt. ❶标示；表示：The arrow ~s the way to the hospital. 那个箭头符号标示到医院去的路。同 show, denote, signify ❷表明；暗示：The light through the window ~d that Liu Hua was still in. 窗户透出的灯光表明刘华仍然在家。同 express, imply

indication / ˌɪndɪˈkeɪʃn / n. ❶[U] 指示；表示；指出：The teacher taught the students to use different signs for the ~ of different meanings. 老师教学生用不同的符号表示不同的意思。同 denotation, signification ❷[C] 迹象；暗示：Black clouds showed ~s of rain. 乌云滚滚表明有下雨的迹象。同 implication, hint, sign

indifferent / ɪnˈdɪfrənt / adj. 漠不关心的；冷淡的；不感兴趣的：He is ~ to his dress. 他对自己的衣着并不在乎。/ She is ~ of her parents. 她对父母漠不关心。同 cold, uninterested 反 concerned, interested 派 indifference n.

indigestion / ˌɪndɪˈdʒestʃn / n. [U] 消化不良，不消化；消化不良症：chronic ~ 慢性消化不良症

indignant / ɪnˈdɪgnənt / adj. 愤慨的；愤愤不平的：We were ~ at his suggestion at the meeting. 对他在会上的提议我们感到愤慨。同 angry, furious 派 indignation n.

indirect / ˌɪndəˈrekt / adj. 间接的：~ speech 间接引语 反 direct

indispensable / ˌɪndɪˈspensəbl / adj. 必需的；不可缺少的：Air, food and water are ~ to life. 空气、食物和水对于生命来说是不可缺少的。同 necessary, essential

individual / ˌɪndɪˈvɪdʒuəl / I adj. ❶个人的；个别的；独自的：~ income tax 个人收入所得税 / That is only an ~ opinion. 那只是个人意见。同 single, personal, private 反 collective, public ❷独特的；个性的：She's grown up and has an ~ style of dressing. 她已经长大了，拥有自己独特的穿着方式。同 particular, special, unusual 反 common, ordinary II n. 个人；个体：Many people say that he is an odd ~. 很多人都说他是一个古怪的人。同 person, fellow, man

indivisible / ˌɪndɪˈvɪzɪbl / adj. ❶不可分的：~ entity 不可分的统一体 ❷不能被整除的，除不尽的：8 is ~ by 3. 8 不能被 3 整除。

indolent / ˈɪndələnt / adj. 懒惰的，怠惰的，好

逸恶劳的；懒散的：an ～ person 懒汉/He is naturally ～ and without application to any kind of business. 他生性懒惰，做什么事都不专心。派 indolence n.

indoor / 'ɪndɔ:(r) / adj. 室内的；室内进行的：an ～ antenna 室内天线 / The boys and girls are having ～ games. 小朋友们在做室内游戏。同 inside 反 outside, outdoor

indoors / ˌɪn'dɔ:z / adv. 在屋里；进入室内：The old lady always stays ～ alone. 老太太总是一个人待在屋里。反 outdoors

induce / ɪn'dju:s / vt. ❶引诱；劝服：～ a patient to take medicines prescribed by the doctor 连哄带骗地劝病人服用大夫开的药/Our price is competitive enough to ～ business. 我们价格具有足够的竞争力以招来业务。❷导致；引发：an illness ～d by overwork 工作过重而引起的疾病/The song ～d a nostalgia for Scotland in us. 这首歌引起了我们对苏格兰的怀乡之愁。

indulge / ɪn'dʌldʒ / v. ❶沉溺；放纵；肆意从事：He did not let himself ～ in hopeless thoughts. 他没有让自己一味地做一些无望的空想。❷纵容；迁就：the daughter whom he ～d 他娇生惯养的女儿/We often ～ a sick person. 我们常常迁就病人。

industrial / ɪn'dʌstrɪəl / adj. 工业的；产业的；实业的：～ developing strategy 工业发展战略 / ～ production 工业生产/ ～ revolution 工业革命 / They live in an ～ city. 他们居住在一个工业城市。

industrialize(-se) / ɪn'dʌstrɪəlaɪz / v. (使)工业化：Japan is an ～d country. 日本是一个工业化国家。

industrious / ɪn'dʌstrɪəs / adj. 勤劳的；刻苦的

industry / 'ɪndəstri / n. ❶工业；产业：heavy ～ 重工业/ light ～ 轻工业/ the ～ of national defence 国防工业 ❷勤奋

inevitable / ɪn'evɪtəbl / adj. 不可避免的；必然发生的：the ～ course of history 历史的必然进程 / The result is ～. 这个结果是必然的。同 unavoidable 反 avoidable 派 inevitably adv.

inexpensive / ˌɪnɪk'spensɪv / adj. 花费不多的；廉价的：The student was glad that he bought an ～ computer. 那学生很高兴他买到了一台廉价的计算机。同 cheap, economical,

low-priced 反 expensive, dear, costly

infamous / 'ɪnfəməs / adj. 声名狼藉的；不名誉的：The young man is ～ in his neighborhood. 那年轻人在四邻中声名狼藉。同 disgraceful, ill-famed 反 famous, graceful

infant / 'ɪnfənt / n. [C]婴儿，幼儿；(法律用语)未成年者：The nurse held an ～ in her arms. 护士怀里抱着一个婴儿。同 child 反 adult

infect / ɪn'fekt / vt. ❶传染；感染：Her daughter was ～ed with TB. 她的女儿感染上了肺病。/ I'm afraid that you will ～ me with your bad cold. 我担心你会把重感冒传染给我。同 affect, influence ❷使受影响：It is a fact that students would be ～ed with all sorts of social ideas. 学生会受各种社会思想的影响，这是事实。同 affect, influence 派 infectious adj.

infection / ɪn'fekʃn / n. ❶传染；传染病：She caught eye ～ while swimming. 游泳时她染上了眼病。/ The doctors took quick action to prevent ～ in this area. 医生们采取迅速行动预防传染病在这个地区传播。❷影响；感染：The ～ of his thoughts is great. 他的思想影响是巨大的。同 influence

infer / ɪn'fɜ:(r) / vt. 推断；判断：We should ～ a conclusion from facts. 我们应当根据事实来推断结论。同 conclude, reason

inference / 'ɪnfərəns / n. [U]推理；推论：I got the conclusion by ～. 通过推理我得到这个结论。同 reasoning, deduction

inferior / ɪn'fɪərɪə(r) / Ⅰ adj. ❶(阶级、身份等)下级的；下等的；低下的：Her husband is an ～ officer. 她的丈夫是一名下级军官。/ His position is ～ to his wife. 他的地位比他妻子低。同 low, humble 反 superior ❷(质量、程度等)劣等的，低劣的，差的，次的：In order to save money, the old woman always buys ～ goods. 为了省钱，老太太总是买低档商品。同 poor, second-rate 反 excellent, superior Ⅱ n. [C] ❶下级；晚辈：An experienced worker shouldn't look down upon his ～s. 老工人不应当看不起晚辈。同 junior 反 superior, senior ❷次品：I found that his TV set was a ～. 我发现他的电视机是次品。同 secondary

infinite / 'ɪnfɪnət / adj. 无限的，无穷的；无边无际的：The universe seems to be ～. 宇宙是广大无边的。/ Such a mistake would cause

~ damage. 这样的错误会带来极大的损害。同 limitless 反 finite, limited 派 infinitely *adv*.

infinitive / ɪnˈfɪnɪtɪv / Ⅰ *n*. [C]原形(动词);不定式 Ⅱ *adj*. 原形的;不定式的:an ~ clause 不定式短语/an ~ marker 不定式标记

inflation / ɪnˈfleɪʃn / *n*. [U]通货膨胀;物价飞涨:The government is trying to put the brakes on ~. 政府正在尽力遏制通货膨胀。同 rise, expansion 反 deflation

inflexible / ɪnˈfleksɪbl / *adj*. ❶不可弯曲的;刚性的:~ plastic 刚性塑料/I felt the boots were rather narrow and ~. 我觉得这双靴子太紧,而且太硬不跟脚。❷坚定的;强硬的;不屈服的;不可动摇的:an ~ will to succeed 百折不挠的意志/They're so ~ with their program! 他们对自己的计划寸步不让! ❸不可改变的:an ~ law 不可变更的法律

influence / ˈɪnfluəns / *n*. 影响;影响力:The president has succeeded in establishing an ~ over his people. 总统在人民中成功地树立了威信。/ A teacher has great ~ over his pupils. 教师对学生有很大影响。

inform / ɪnˈfɔːm / *vt*. 通知;告诉:Keep me ~ed of the fresh developments. 随时告诉我新的进展。/ Can you ~ me where he lives? 你能告诉我他的住处吗? 同 notify, tell

informal / ɪnˈfɔːməl / *adj*. ❶非正式的,非正规的:an ~ talk 非正式会谈/~ education 非正规教育 ❷不拘礼节的,随便的:an ~ person 不拘礼节的人/try to make discussions more ~ 努力使讨论的气氛更为随意 ❸合适于日常谈话的;口语体的:~ spoken English 日常使用的英语口语

information / ˌɪnfəˈmeɪʃn / *n*. [U]消息;情报;信息:an ~ age 信息时代 / ~ industry 信息产业 / How did you get the ~? 你是如何得到这个消息的? / His father is working in the Information Bureau. 他的父亲在情报局工作。/ The ~ conference will be held at 3 o'clock p. m. 下午三点钟召开信息发布会。同 news, date

infrared / ˌɪnfrəˈred / Ⅰ *n*. 红外线 Ⅱ *adj*. 红外线的:~ rays 红外线 / ~ radiation 红外线辐射

ingredient / ɪnˈɡriːdɪənt / *n*. [C] ❶(混合物的)组成部分,成分;(烹调用的)原料:the ~s of a cocktail 鸡尾酒的调配成分/Olive oil is the classic ~ for so many fine dishes. 橄榄油是许多佳肴最重要的烹饪原料。❷(构成)要素,因素:Trust is an essential ~ in a successful marriage. 信任是美满婚姻中至关重要的因素。/Good management is the key ~ of success. 良好的管理是成功的关键。

inhabit / ɪnˈhæbɪt / *vt*. 居住于;栖息于:I don't think that many people ~ the small island. 我认为很少有人住在这个小岛上。同 reside, dwell

inhabitant / ɪnˈhæbɪtənt / *n*. [C]居民;住户:The town has about more than 900 ~s. 这个镇子大约有900多个居民。/ I live in a city of more than 300,000 ~s. 我住在一个有30多万居民的城市里。同 resident, dweller, citizen

inherent / ɪnˈhɪərənt / *adj*. 固有的;天生的;内在的:She has ~ love of beauty. 她天生爱美。同 innate, inborn, natural 派 inherently *adv*.

inherit / ɪnˈherɪt / *vt*. 继承:He ~ed a fortune from his uncle. 他从叔父处继承了一笔遗产。/ The little girl ~ed her mother's kind characters. 小女孩继承了母亲善良的性格。同 get, acquire, receive 派 inheritance *n*.

initial / ɪˈnɪʃl / Ⅰ *adj*. 开始的;最初的;词首的:the ~ issue 创刊号/ Headache is the ~ symptom of the disease. 头痛是这种疾病最初期的症状。/ Please capitalize the ~ letter of this word. 请大写这个词的第一个字母。同 first, primary, original 反 final, last Ⅱ *n*. [C]首字母:The ~ of this word is "W". 这个词的首字母为"W"。派 initially *adv*.

inject / ɪnˈdʒekt / *vt*. 注射;注入;插进:The nurse ~ed her with some medicine. 护士给她注射了一些药物。同 shoot, insert 派 injection *n*.

injure / ˈɪndʒə(r) / *vt*. 伤害;损伤;损害:The driver was slightly ~d in the accident. 车祸中司机受了轻伤。/ What you said ~d her pride. 你说的话伤了她的自尊心。/ Drinking too much will ~ a man's health. 酗酒会损害人的健康。同 damage, hurt, harm

injury / ˈɪndʒəri / *n*. 损伤;伤害;损害:The Smiths escaped ~ in the fire. 火灾中史密斯一家幸免受伤。/ It is an ~ to his reputation. 那是对他名誉的损害。同 damage, hurt, harm

injustice / ɪnˈdʒʌstɪs / n. ❶[U]不公正,不公平;非正义:the victim of ～执法不公的牺牲品/a suffocating sense of ～一阵令人窒息的委屈 ❷[C]不公正的行为;非正义行为:It is an ～ to send an innocent man to jail. 把无辜的人投入监狱是不公正的。

ink / ɪŋk / n. [U]墨水;油墨:Please write in blue ～. 请用蓝墨水写。

inland Ⅰ / ˈɪnlænd / adj. 内陆的;远离海洋的;国内的:She lives in an ～ city. 她住在一个内地市。/ I received an ～ telegraph. 我收到一封国内电报。 圊 interior Ⅱ / ˈɪnlænd / n. [U]内陆;内地 Ⅲ ɪnˈlænd / adv. 在内陆;在内地:He often goes ～. 他常到内地去。

inlet / ˈɪnlet / n. [C]进口;入口;小湾:You can see the ～ of the stream on the top of the mountain. 在山顶上你可以看到那条小溪的入口处。圊 entrance,bay 反 outlet

inn / ɪn / n. [C]客栈;小旅馆;小酒馆:We stayed in a village ～ that night. 那天晚上我们住在一家乡村客栈。圊 hotel

inner / ˈɪnə(r) / adj. 在内的;内部的:an ～ room 内室/an ～ part 内部 圊 inside,interior 反 outside,exterior

innocent / ˈɪnəsnt / adj. ❶无罪的;清白的(与 of 连用):Is he guilty or ～ of the crime? 他是无罪还是有罪? 圊 guiltless 反 guilty ❷天真无邪的;幼稚的:as ～ as a new-born baby 像初生婴儿般天真无邪 圊 childlike,simple ❸头脑简单的;无知的:He is ～ about life in a big city. 他对大城市的生活一无所知。反 experienced

innovate / ˈɪnəveɪt / v. 革新,改革,创新;引入新事物:The fashion industry is always desperate to ～. 时装行业总是渴望不断创新。～ in products 更新产品/～ a computer operating system 改进计算机操作系统 派 innovation n. ;innovative adj.

input / ˈɪnpʊt / Ⅰ n. ❶输入;投入:～ and output 输入和输出 圊 insert 反 output ❷投入的资金(或物):The project calls for more ～. 工程要求更多的投入。圊 investment Ⅱ v. 输入;投入:～ of data into a computer 向计算机输入信息 圊 insert 反 output

inquire / ɪnˈkwaɪə(r) / v. 询问;调查:We should ～ what he wants. 我们应该一问他

想要什么。圊 ask,question/ ～ after 问候:I called at his house to ～ after his health. 我到他家去问候他。～ about 查问;打听;了解:This led us to ～ about his past. 这促使我们去了解他的历史。～ for 查找;询问:He is the person you ～ for. 他就是你要找的人。

inquiry / ɪnˈkwaɪəri / n. ❶打听;询问:an ～ office 问询处/ She made an ～ of the doctor about her health. 她向大夫询问她的健康事宜。圊 question,request ❷调查;查问:The police held an ～ into the case. 警察对那桩案件进行了调查。圊 investigation

insane / ɪnˈseɪn / adj. ❶(患有)精神病的;精神失常的;疯狂的:You must be ～ to go out in this weather. 这种天气还要出去你真是发神经! ❷愚蠢的;荒唐透顶的:an ～ plan for crossing the ocean in a canoe 划独木舟穿越大海的愚蠢计划

inscription / ɪnˈskrɪpʃn / n. [C]铭刻;铭文;碑文;匾额(铸币、图章、勋章等上的)刻印文字:bear an ～刻有铭文/an ～ on a monument 纪念碑上的碑文

insect / ˈɪnsekt / n. [C]昆虫:a swarm of ～s一群昆虫/a beneficial ～ 益虫/destructive ～s 害虫

insert / ɪnˈsɜːt / vt. 插入;嵌入:They always ～ commercials in a TV program. 他们总是在电视节目中插播广告。/ He ～ed a few words while his mother was speaking. 妈妈讲话时他插了几句。

inside / ɪnˈsaɪd / Ⅰ prep. 在…内,在…里面:The purse is ～ the drawer. 钱包在抽屉里。Ⅱ adv. 在里面;在内部:There is nothing ～. 里面什么也没有。圊 indoors 反 outside,outdoors

insight / ˈɪnsaɪt / n. 洞察力;眼光:The writer has a keen ～ into character. 那位作家对人物性格有敏锐的洞察力。/ The headmaster is a man of great ～. 校长是一位很有眼光的人。

同 vision, wisdom

insist / ɪnˈsɪst / v. 坚持；坚决主张（与 on, upon 连用）：The teacher ~ed on the importance of studying English. 老师强调学习英语的重要性。/ He ~ed that he had never seen the criminal. 他坚持说他从来没见过那个罪犯。同 claim, persist

inspect / ɪnˈspekt / v. 检查；视察；检阅：The conductor was ~ing her luggage. 列车员正在检查她的行李。/ The commander will come to ~ the troops. 指挥官要来检阅部队。同 examine, review 派 inspection n.

inspector / ɪnˈspektə(r) / n. [C]检查员；视察员：She is a health ~ of our class. 她是我们班的卫生检查员。同 checker, investigator

inspiration / ˌɪnspəˈreɪʃn / n. ❶[U]灵感：He received his ~ in his dream. 他在梦中获得了灵感。同 idea, impulse ❷[C]鼓舞人心的人或物：What an ~ she was to all around her! 她对她周围的人是一种多么大的鼓舞啊！同 encouragement

inspire / ɪnˈspaɪə(r) / vt. 激励；鼓励；鼓舞：Success ~s us for fresh efforts. 成功激励我们去做新的努力。/ I guess you have been ~d by somebody else. 我想你一定受了别人的鼓舞。同 encourage, excite

instal(l) / ɪnˈstɔːl / vt. 安装；设置：She ~ed a telephone in her bedroom. 她在卧室里装了一部电话。/ My father decided to ~ a new computer for me. 我父亲决定给我安装一台新计算机。同 set, equip, establish 派 instal(l)ation n.

instal(l)ment / ɪnˈstɔːlmənt / n. [C]分期付款：He bought an apartment in (by)~s. 他以分期付款购买了一套公寓房。同 portion, payment

instance / ˈɪnstəns / n. [C]例子；实例；事例：He gave an ~ to explain the question. 他举了一个例子讲解这个问题。同 example, case, sample / for ~例如；比如；举例说：I like animals, for ~, cats, dogs and pandas. 我喜欢动物，例如猫、狗和熊猫。

instant / ˈɪnstənt / Ⅰ n. [C]即时，即刻；瞬间，刹那：He may arrive any ~. 他随时都可能到达。同 moment, minute/ in an ~ 立刻，马上：He answered the teacher's questions in an ~. 他立即回答了老师的问题。Ⅱ adj. (食品)速

溶的；方便的：I like ~ coffer. 我喜欢喝速溶咖啡。同 ready 派 instantly adv.

instead / ɪnˈsted / adv. 代替；更换：They aren't going to have a meeting this Sunday. They'll have a singing competition ~. 本星期日他们不打算开会，而是举行歌咏比赛。/ ~ of 代替：They went there on foot ~ of by bus. 他们没乘公共汽车而是步行到那里去的。/ Instead of Jane, Mary came to help us. 来帮助我的是玛丽，而不是简。

instinct / ˈɪnstɪŋkt / n. 本能；直觉；天性：I trust my ~. 我相信我的直觉。/ She is only five and shows an ~ for painting. 她才五岁，却显示出绘画的天性。同 sense, gift, nature

institute / ˈɪnstɪtjuːt / n. [C]协会；学会；学院；研究所，研究院：an art ~ 艺术学院／ an ~ of foreign languages 外国语学院／ an ~ of technology 理工学院 同 college, academy

institution / ˌɪnstɪˈtjuːʃn / n. [C]机关；社会公共机构：an educational ~ 教育机构／ a business ~ 商业机构／ a scientific ~ 科学协会／ a teaching ~ 教学机构／ a charity ~ 慈善机构 同 organization, institute

instruct / ɪnˈstrʌkt / vt. ❶教；教育；指导：An old teacher ~s us in history. 一位老教师教我们历史课。/ It is my mother who first ~ed me in the correct use of dictionaries. 我妈妈最先教我正确使用字典。同 teach, educate ❷指示；命令：The doctor ~ed me to stay at home. 大夫命令我待在家里休息。同 direct, order ❸通知；告知：He has been ~ed to start at once. 他被告知立即出发。同 tell, inform, notify

instruction / ɪnˈstrʌkʃn / n. ❶(pl.)命令；指示；用法说明：You should follow the ~s. 你应当遵循操作指南。/ He gave me ~s to finish the work before dark. 他指示我天黑前做完工作。同 order, directions ❷[U]教学；教训；教导：I learned how to swim through her ~. 她指导我学会了游泳。同 teaching

instructive / ɪnˈstrʌktɪv / adj. ❶有教育意义的；启迪性的：an ~ and entertaining essay 既有教育意义又有娱乐性的文章/Great books are the most ~. 名著最有启发教益。❷增长知识的；教训开导的：The lecture on eating rituals and their cultural ramifications is ~ as well as amusing. 有关各种饮食礼仪及其文化渊源的讲座既增长知识又有趣味。

instructor / ɪnˈstrʌktə(r) / n. [C]指导者；教员；讲师：a political ～ 政治指导员 / a driving ～ 汽车驾驶教练 圓 teacher,lecturer

instrument / ˈɪnstrəmənt / n. [C] ❶工具；器具；仪器：medical ～s 医疗器具/ scientific ～s 科学仪器/ This factory produces all kind of teaching ～s. 这家工厂生产各种教学仪器。圓 tool,device,apparatus ❷乐器：musical ～s 乐器/ orchestra ～s 管弦乐器/ a string (stringed) ～弦乐器/ a wind ～ 管乐器

insult Ⅰ / ˈɪnsʌlt / n. 侮辱；侮辱的言行：Don't shout ～ at others even if your are angry. 即使是生气你也不要辱骂他人。圓 abuse,offense Ⅱ / ɪnˈsʌlt / vt. 侮辱：He ～ed me by saying that. 他说那种话来侮辱我。圓 abuse,offend

insurance / ɪnˈʃʊərəns / n. [U]保险；保险业；保险费：an ～ company 保险公司 / medical ～ 医疗保险 / social old age ～ 社会养老保险 / He took out ～ on his house. 他为他的房屋保了险。

insure / ɪnˈʃʊə(r) / vt. 给…保险；保证；确保：He ～d his car for 100,000 yuan. 他投保了 10 万元车险。圓 assure,guarantee

intangible / ɪnˈtændʒɪbl / adj. 触摸不到的；无(定)形的：～ personal property 个人的无形资产/Air is ～. 空气是触摸不到的。

intellectual / ˌɪntəˈlektʃuəl / Ⅰ adj. 智力的；知识的：the ～ faculties 智能 / ～ work 脑力劳动 / ～ youth 知识青年 圓 mental, intelligent 反 ignorant Ⅱ n. [C]知识分子：young ～s 青年知识分子 圓 intellect,scholar

intelligence / ɪnˈtelɪdʒəns / n. [U] ❶智力；理解力；～ difference 智力差异 / ～ quotient 智商(IQ) / We should care for the child who is weak in ～. 我们应该爱护弱智儿童。圓 intellect,understanding, brightness ❷情报；谍报：He is responsible for collecting classified ～. 他负责收集保密情报。圓 information, report,secret

intelligent / ɪnˈtelɪdʒənt / adj. 有才智的；聪明的：an ～ child 聪明的孩子/ ～ answers 巧妙的回答 圓 bright,wise

intend / ɪnˈtend / vt. 想要；打算；企图：What do you ～ to do today? 你今天打算做什么？

plan,mean／～ sb. to do sth. 要某人做某事：We ～ them to do it. 我们打算让他们做此事。

intended / ɪnˈtendɪd / adj. ❶故意的；有预谋的：He told no one of his ～ flight but his friend Tom. 除了他的朋友汤姆，他再没把他逃跑的事告诉别人。❷打算中的，预期中的；未来的：the ～ destination 计划的目的地 /an ～ bride 准新娘

intense / ɪnˈtens / adj. ❶强烈的；剧烈的：～ heat 酷热/ ～ pain 剧痛 / I really can't bear the ～ sunlight here. 我真不能忍受这里的烈日暴晒。圓 violent,strong ❷热情的；热心的：In a strange place, you always want to ask an ～ person for help. 在陌生地方，你总是想找一个热心人来帮助你。圓 earnest, warm-hearted

intensity / ɪnˈtensəti / n. [U]强烈；紧张；强度：current ～ 电流强度 / labor ～ 劳动强度/ She showed the ～ of her anger. 她表示出强烈的愤怒。圓 strain,strength

intensive / ɪnˈtensɪv / adj. 加强的；集中的；精细的：They are having an ～ course in English. 他们正在上英语强化课程。/ I like ～ reading very much. 我非常喜欢精读。圓 intense,concentrated,thorough 反 extensive

intent / ɪnˈtent / n. [U] ❶意图，目的：It was not done by ～. 这件事不是故意而为的。/ He declared his ～. 这件事不是故意而为的。/He declared his ～ to run in the election. 他声明自己要出马参加竞选的意向。/ She approached the old man with ～ to defraud. 她怀着诈骗的目的接近那个老头儿。❷意思，含义：The ～ of the article escaped me. 我看不出那篇文章的含义。/ **to (for) all ～s and purposes** 实际上，事实上：His speech was to all ～s and purposes a declaration of love. 他这番话实际上是在表达他的爱情。

intention / ɪnˈtenʃn / n. 意图；目的；打算：He went to London in the ～ of Learning English. 他去伦敦就是为了学英语。/ She didn't say anything at the meeting by ～. 在会上她故意一言不发。圓 purpose,aim,plan

interact / ˌɪntərˈækt / vi. 相互影响；相互作用；互动：Teachers and students ～ on each other. 教学双方相辅相成。/These two chemicals ～ to form a gas. 这两种化学物质相互作

用,形成一种气体。

interest / ˈIntrəst / Ⅰ vt. 使发生兴趣;引起…注意:That will certainly ~ you. 那肯定会引起你的兴趣。同 attract, fascinate Ⅱ n. ❶[U]兴趣;关心:feel a great (no) ~ in 对…有很大兴趣(不感兴趣)/ He takes no ~ in English. 他对英语不感兴趣。同 care, concern ❷[C](常用 pl.)利益;福利:We should put the ~s of the people before all else. 我们应把人民的利益置于其他一切之上。同 benefit / **in the ~s of** 为了…的利益:He works in the ~s of his company. 他为公司的利益干活。❸[U]利息:The bank charges low ~ on all money borrowed from it. 这家银行实行低息贷款。同 profit

interested / ˈIntrəstId / adj. 感兴趣的;关心的:He is ~ in fishing. 他对钓鱼很感兴趣。同 concerned 反 indifferent

interesting / ˈIntrəstIŋ / adj. 有趣的;令人感兴趣的:I don't think he is ~. 我认为他不是一个有趣的人。同 attractive, absorbing 反 dull, boring

inter- / ˈIntə / (前缀)表示"在…中"或"互相":~ action 相互作用 / ~ national 国与国之间的

interfere / ˌIntəˈfIə(r) / vi. ❶(指人)干预(他人之事);干涉(与 in 连用):Don't ~ in other people's business. 少管闲事。同 intervene, intrude ❷(指事件)妨碍;打扰(与 with 连用):You shouldn't let pleasure ~ with business. 你不该让玩乐妨碍事业。同 block, hinder

interference / ˌIntəˈfIərəns / n. [U]干预;干涉;妨碍;干扰:His ~ spoiled our travel. 他的干涉破坏了我们的旅游。/ No one had the right to give ~ in the affairs of another nation. 没有人有权干涉他国内政。同 intrusion, obstruction

interior / InˈtIərIə(r) / Ⅰ adj. 内部的;里面的;内在的:My brother likes ~ design. 我哥哥喜欢室内设计。同 internal, inner 反 exterior, outside ❷内地的;国内的:The delegation visited the ~ cities of the country. 代表团访问了该国的一些内地城市。同 inland, domestic 反 foreign Ⅱ n. ❶内部:The ~ of the hall was beautifully decorated. 大厅内部装饰得很漂亮。同 inside ❷内地:travel in the ~ 国内旅游 同 inland

internal / Inˈtɜːnl / adj. 内部的;国内的;内政的:~ organs 内脏;内部器官 / ~ bleeding 内出血/ ~ trade 国内贸易 / ~ affairs 内政;内部事务 同 interior, domestic, inner 反 external, outside, foreign

international / ˌIntəˈnæʃnəl / adj. 国际的;世界的(性)的:~ trade 国际贸易/ customary ~ practice 国际惯例 / The United Nations is an ~ organization. 联合国是一个国际组织。/ The old lady knows the ~ situation very well. 老太太非常了解国际形势。同 world-wide, global 反 domestic, national

Internet / ˈIntənet / n. 因特网;互联网:an ~ bar 网吧 / Our teacher taught us how to search the ~. 我们老师教我们检索因特网。/ You can find a lot of information on the ~. 你可以在互联网上查到许多资料。

interpreter / InˈtɜːprItə(r) / n. [C]口译者;译员:She wants to be an ~. 她想当一名口译员。同 translator

interrupt / ˌIntəˈrʌpt / vt. 中断;打断;阻止;打扰:Traffic was ~ed by the snowstorm. 交通被暴风雪阻断。/ Don't ~ him in his work. 不要干扰他的工作。同 break, cut, intervene 反 continue 派 interruption n.

intersect / ˌIntəˈsekt / v. 贯穿,横穿;相交,交叉:The garden was ~ed by gravel paths. 花园有石子路贯穿其中。/The two roads ~ at the castle. 这两条路交汇于城堡。

interval / ˈIntəvl / n. [C]间隔时间;间隙(尤指戏剧两幕间、音乐会上下两半场间的间隔):There is a two hours' ~ to the next train. 下一班火车还要过两个小时才来。/ He likes to have a smoke in the ~. 幕间休息时他喜欢抽支烟。同 break, gap, pause / **at ~s** 不时,每隔…(时间或距离):There was a rain falling at ~s. 每隔一段时间就下一阵雨。/ Trees are planted at ~s of five meters. 每隔五米种一棵树。

interview / ˈIntəvjuː / Ⅰ n. [C]接见;会见;面试;采访:The president gave an ~ on television last night. 总统昨晚在电视上接受了采访。/ Your ~ for the job is tomorrow. 你求职的面试定在明天。同 meeting, consult Ⅱ vt. 接见;会见;会谈:The mayor ~ed the foreign investors yesterday afternoon. 昨天下午市长会见了外国投资商。同 meet, see

intestine / ɪnˈtestɪn / n. [C](常用 pl.)肠

intimate / ˈɪntɪmət / adj. 亲密的；私人的：an ～ friend 亲密朋友 / ～ affairs 私事 / an ～ diary 个人日记 圊 close, personal, private

into / ˈɪntʊ, ˈɪntə / prep. ❶进入…之内；向内：Come ～ the room. 进屋来。/ Don't get ～ trouble. 不要惹麻烦。❷变成(…的状况)：When heated, water can be changed ～ vapor. 水加热可变成蒸气。

intonation / ˌɪntəˈneɪʃn / n. [U]语调，音调：The boy is good at imitating others' ～. 小男孩很擅长模仿他人的声调。圊 tone, accent

introduce / ˌɪntrəˈdjuːs / vt. ❶提出：He ～d a question for debate. 他提出一个问题进行辩论。圊 propose ❷介绍：He ～d me to your friends. 他把我介绍给你的朋友。圊 present ❸引进；输入：He ～d a new theory in his report. 他在报告里引入了一种新理论。The president ～d new ideas into education. 校长给教育引进了新的思想。圊 import

introduction / ˌɪntrəˈdʌkʃn / n. ❶介绍 ❷引进；传入：a letter of ～ 介绍信 / ～ of technology 技术引进 圊 presentation ❸导言；绪论；入门：The ～ to this book is well-written. 这本书的序言写得很精彩。圊 preface, foreword

intrude / ɪnˈtruːd / vi. 侵入；闯入：A stranger ～d into our meeting. 一个陌生人闯入了我们的会场。/ You'd better not ～ your opinions on others. 你最好不要把你的意见强加到别人头上。圊 invade, violate 添 intrusion n.

intuition / ˌɪntjuˈɪʃn / n. [U]直觉；直觉力：know sth. by ～ 凭直觉感知某事物 / act on one's ～ 凭自己的直觉行事 / It is said that females have more ～ than males. 据说女性的直觉力比男性强。❷[C]直觉感知的事物；直觉知识：I have an ～ that my friends is ill. 我凭直觉感知朋友病了。/ Our ～s may fail in moments of panic. 在紧张的瞬间我们的直觉认识或许靠不住。

invade / ɪnˈveɪd / vt. 侵略；侵犯；侵害：These countries were ～d in 1938. 这些国家在1938年都遭到了侵略。圊 attack, intrude 添 invasion n.

invalid / ɪnˈvælɪd / adj. ❶无效果的；不得力的；无价值的：an ～ argument 站不住脚的论点/The operation was deemed ～ and value-

less. 有人认为这个行动方案不得力，毫无价值。❷无效(力)的；作废的：an ～ check 无效的支票/He claimed that the referendum is legally ～. 他宣布这次公民投票没有法律效力。

invaluable / ɪnˈvæljuːəbl / adj. 极其宝贵的；非常贵重的；无法估价的：～ experience 宝贵的经验/Self-discipline is an ～ acquisition. 自我约束是一种无价之宝。/a book ～ for reference 很有参考价值的书

invent / ɪnˈvent / vt. 发明；创造：Watt ～ed the steam engine. 瓦特发明了蒸汽机。/ The new machine was ～ed by a young worker. 这部新机器是一个年轻工人发明的。圊 creat

> **辨析**
>
> **invent** 意为"发明"，指创造前所未有的东西：The phonograph was invented by Edison. 留声机是爱迪生发明的。**discover** 意为"发现"，指发现已存在的东西，只是以前不为人所知：Columbus discovered America in 1492. 哥伦布1492年发现了美洲。

invention / ɪnˈvenʃn / n. 发明；创造；发明物：The ～ of a space rocket took many years. 宇宙火箭的发明花了许多年时间。/ That is an ～ of Edison. 那是爱迪生的一项发明。添 inventor n.

inverse / ɪnˈvɜːs / Ⅰ adj. ❶相反的；反向的；倒转的，翻转的：an ～ order 逆序/The results are just ～ to the amount of effort put in. 结果与付出的努力正好相反。❷反的，逆的：Addition and subtraction are ～ operations. 加法与减法是逆运算。Ⅱ n. 相反；颠倒；反面：Dividing by three is ～ of multiplying by three. 除以3和乘以3正好互逆。

invert / ɪnˈvɜːt / vt. ❶使反向；使倒置；使颠倒：～ the glass over a fly 把杯子倒过来罩住苍蝇/Skilled farmers believe that it is never wise to ～ the topsoil. 种庄稼的老把式们认为，把土地的表土翻从来就不是个明智的做法。❷使(词序)倒装：In this language the word order in questions is ～ed. 在这种语言中，疑问句的词序是倒装。

invest / ɪnˈvest / vt. 投资；投入(资金、时间等)：～ funds in stocks 投资股票 / He ～ed all his savings in real estate. 他把所有的存款投资于房地产。/ Our teacher ～ed a lot of time and effort in the new teaching method. 我们的老师投入许多时间和精力研究新教学法。圊 devote, finance

investigate / ɪnˈvestɪgeɪt / *vt.* 调查；调查研究：Scientists ～d the national resources of this area. 科学家们调查了这个地区的自然资源。/ The students ～d the market and learned a lot. 学生们进行了市场调查，学到了很多东西。近 research,examine

investigation / ɪnˌvestɪˈgeɪʃn / *n.* 调查；审查：Let's go out to welcome the ～ group. 走，我们去欢迎考察团。近 research,examination / **make an ～ on (of, into) sth.** 对某事进行调查：He is making a thorough ～ on this matter. 他正对此事进行彻底调查。

investment / ɪnˈvestmənt / *n.* ❶[U;C]投资；投资额；投资物：open up to foreign ～ 对外国投资实施开放政策/They believe education is a good ～ for life. 人们认为教育是个终生值得投资的项目。❷[C](时间、精力、思考等的)投入：A happy marriage requires an ～ of time and energy. 美满的婚姻是需要付出时间和精力的。

invisible / ɪnˈvɪzəbl / *adj.* 看不见的；无形的；不露面的；看不见的：Germs are ～ to our eyes. 我们的肉眼看不见细菌。/ The little girl kept herself ～ in the room. 那小姑娘躲在房里不露面。近 hidden 反 visible

invitation / ˌɪnvɪˈteɪʃn / *n.* 邀请；招待；请柬：The manager accepted an ～ to attend a reception. 经理应邀出席招待会。近 call

invite / ɪnˈvaɪt / *vt.* 邀请；请求：He didn't ～ me in. 他没请我入内。/ She is ～d out to a meal. 她应邀外出吃饭。近 request,ask,call

用法 ▶
invite 通常指请人做不很辛苦而又令人高兴的事(如唱歌、跳舞、聚餐、演讲、参加婚礼等)：He invited us to a party. 他邀请我们参加宴会。

invoice / ˈɪnvɔɪs / *n.*[C]发票；发货清单；服务费用清单：a purchase ～ 购货发票/issue an ～ 签发发货单/Please write out your ～ in quadruplicate. 发票请开一式四份。

involve / ɪnˈvɒlv / *vt.* 包含；牵连；卷入：A foolish mistake can ～ you in a great deal of trouble. 一次愚蠢的错误可使你陷入极大的麻烦之中。近 include,connect,associate

ion / ˈaɪən,ˈaɪɒn / *n.* (电)离子

IQ (＝intelligence quotient)智商

ir- / ɪr / (前缀)表示"不"或"非"：～regular 不

规则的；无规律的 / ～responsible 不负责的；无责任感的

Irish / ˈaɪrɪʃ / Ⅰ*adj.* 爱尔兰的 Ⅱ*n.* 爱尔兰人

iron / ˈaɪən / Ⅰ*n.* ❶[U]铁：crude ～ 生铁/cast ～ 铸铁 / Strike while the ～ is hot. 趁热打铁。❷[C]烙铁；熨斗：She bought a steam ～. 她买了一个蒸气熨斗。Ⅱ*v.* ❶熨；烫：a coat 熨烫衣服 / Mother is ～ing out her shirt. 妈妈正在熨衬衫。❷消除(困难、误解等)：After an hour's talk, they ～ed their misunderstandings. 经过一个小时的交谈，他们消除了误解。近 press,smooth,flatten

ironic(al) / aɪˈrɒnɪk(1) / *adj.* 冷嘲的；讽刺的；挖苦的；令人啼笑皆非的：An ～ smile indicated that she didn't agree with me. 一丝冷笑表明她并不赞同我的意见。派 ironically *adv.*

irony / ˈaɪrəni / *n.* 冷嘲；反讽；反话

irrational / ɪˈræʃənl / *adj.* ❶不合逻辑的；不合理的；荒谬的：I felt a wave of ～ guilt and fear. 我突然产生了一阵莫名其妙的犯罪感和恐惧心。/Superstitions are ～. 迷信是荒谬的。❷没有理性的；失去理性的：～ creatures 无理性的动物/be ～ in one's attitude to one's own child 在对自己的孩子的态度上不明智 ❸(数学)无理的：～ equation 无理方程式

irregular / ɪˈregjələ(r) / *adj.* 不合常规的；不规则的：～ verbs 不规则动词 / an ～ army 非正规军 / The fields are ～ in shape. 这些田地的形状很不整齐。近 disorderly 反 regular

irrigate / ˈɪrɪgeɪt / *v.* 灌溉(田地、作物等)：They ～d their crops with water from this river. 他们用这条河的水浇灌庄稼。近 water 派 irrigation *n.*

irritate / ˈɪrɪteɪt / *v.* 激怒；使发怒；引起恼怒：His letter ～d me a little. 他的信使我有点恼怒。近 annoy

is / ɪz / *v.* (他、她或它) 是(见 be)

Islam / ˈɪzlɑːm / *n.* ❶伊斯兰教；回教 ❷(总称)伊斯兰教徒

island / ˈaɪlənd / *n.* [C]岛，岛屿：a lonely 孤岛/ an uninhabited ～ 荒岛/Taiwan is the largest ～ of China. 台湾是中国最大的岛屿。

isolate / ˈaɪsəleɪt / *vt.* ❶隔离；孤立 ❷分离；分解

isolation / ˌaɪsəˈleɪʃn / *n.* [U]隔离；分离；脱

离;单独;孤立;孤独:～ of the infected person is necessary. 隔离受感染者很有必要。/live in ～ from other nations 闭关锁国/You can't consider one sentence in ～. 你不能孤立地考虑一个句子。

issue / ˈɪsjuː, ˈɪʃuː / Ⅰ v. ❶出来;流出:His blood ～d from the cut. 他的血从伤口流出。同 emit ❷发出;发布;发表;发给:Orders were ～d from the headquarters. 命令从司令部发出。/ This magazine is ～d monthly. 这种杂志每月发行一期。/ Each student was ～d with textbook. 每个学生发了一本教科书。同 release,publish,broadcast Ⅱ n. [C]❶(引起争论的)问题,争端:Inflation is a hot ～ of the day. 通货膨胀是当今的热门问题。同 problem,question ❷发行(物);(报、刊的)期:I have read the latest ～ of *China Daily*. 我已读了最近一期的《中国日报》。同 publication

it / ɪt / pron. ❶它(指无生命的东西,性别不明或性别不重要的动物,性别不明或性别无关紧要的婴儿):Where is the cat? It's under the table. 猫在哪里? 在桌下。❷用作句子形式上无意义的主语:①指天气状况:It's fine today. 今天天晴。②指时间:It's six o'clock now. 现在六点钟。③指距离:It's a long way from here. 距离这里很远。❸模糊地指一般情形,或指由上下文可以了解的事物:Whose turn is ～? 现在轮到谁了? ❹用以强调某一句子成分:①主语:It was he who wrote this article. 是他写的这篇文章。②动词的宾语:It was John that I met in the street yesterday. 我昨天在街上碰到的是约翰。③状语:It was on Sun day that I saw him. 我看见他的那一天是星期天。❺作先行代词,指代短语或从句:①不定式短语:Is ～ difficult to learn English well? 学好英语很困难吗? It is very hard for me to do ～. 我来做这事太艰难了。②动词短语:It's no use going to see him. 去看他无用。③从句:It doesn't matter whether we start now or later. 我们现在开始还是以后开始都没关系。

IT (=information technology)信息技术

Italian / ɪˈtæljən / Ⅰ adj. 意大利的 Ⅱ n. 意大利人;意大利语

Italy / ˈɪtəli / n. 意大利

itch / ɪtʃ / Ⅰ v. ❶发痒,使人发痒:He's ～ing all over. 他浑身发痒。/This T-shirt ～es. 这件T恤衫穿在身上使人发痒。❷热望,渴望:～ for the work to end 急煎煎地巴望工作快结束/I am ～-ing to tell you the news. 我巴不得马上就把消息告诉你。Ⅱ n. ❶痒;have an ～ on one's (the) back 背部发痒 ❷热望,渴望:have an ～ to go around the world 渴望周游世界

item / ˈaɪtəm / n. ❶[C]条;条款;项目;细目:He read the treaty ～ by ～. 他逐条阅读那份条约。/ They discussed many ～s about the design last week. 上周他们对有关设计的很多项目进行了讨论。同 piece,article ❷(新闻等的)一条;一则:I read an interesting ～ in today's newspaper. 在今天的报上我读到一条很有趣的新闻。同 piece,article

iterate / ˈɪtəreɪt / vt. 重申,重述:～ a warning 一再警告/Wise men do not ～ mistakes. 聪明的人不会重复犯错。派 iteration n.

its / ɪts / pron. 它的(it 的所有格;形容词性物主代词):The dog wagged ～ tail. 狗摇尾巴。

itself / ɪtˈself / pron. ❶(反身代词)它自己;它本身:This novel is a history in ～. 这部小说本身就是一部历史。/ Put it by ～. 这东西单独放。❷(表示强调)自身;本身:The book ～ is worth reading. 这书本身就值得一读。/ The problem ～ is not important. 这问题本身并不重要。

ivory / ˈaɪvəri / n. [U]象牙;象牙制品;象牙色:～ tower 象牙塔

J j

jack / dʒæk / n. [C]起重器；千斤顶：an automobile ～ 汽车千斤顶

jacket / 'dʒækɪt / n. [C]短上衣；夹克：A man
in ～ came in. 一个穿夹克的人走进来。

jaguar / 'dʒægjʊə(r) / n. [C](产于南美洲的)
美洲虎，美洲豹

jade / dʒeɪd / n. [U]玉；翡翠

jail / dʒeɪl / n. [C]监牢；牢狱圊 prison, cell

jam¹ / dʒæm / n. [U] 果酱：a jar of apple
(peach, strawberry) ～ 一瓶苹果(桃子、草
莓)酱 / She spread some apple ～ on the
bread. 她在面包上涂了一些苹果酱。

jam² / dʒæm / Ⅰ n. [C]❶堵塞；阻塞；拥挤：We
got in a traffic ～ on the way. 路上我们遇到
堵车。圊 crowding, blocking ❷困境；困难：He
told me that he really want to get out of the
～ soon. 他告诉我他真想马上摆脱困境。圊
difficulty, trouble Ⅱ v. (jammed; jamming) 堵
塞；塞满；挤进：She ～med all her clothes into
a suitcase. 她把所有的衣服塞进一个手提箱
里。/ As soon as he ～med onto the bus, it
started. 他一挤进汽车，汽车就开动了。圊
crowed, block

January / 'dʒænjʊəri / n. 一月(略作 Jan.)

Japan / dʒə'pæn / n. 日本：The car is made in
～. 这辆车是日本造的。

Japanese / ˌdʒæpə'niːz / Ⅰ adj. 日本的；～
clothes 和服 / ～ goods 日货 Ⅱ n. (单复数同
形)日本人；日语

jar / dʒɑː(r) / n. [C]坛子；罐子；缸：a jam ～
果酱瓶 / a ～ of water 一罐水 圊 pot, mug

jasmin(e) / 'dʒæzmɪn / n. [U]❶素馨；茉莉，
素方花 ❷淡黄色，素馨色

jaw / dʒɔː / n. [C]颚：the lower ～ 下颚 / the
upper ～ 上颚

jazz / dʒæz / n. [U]爵士音乐；爵士舞曲：
Young people like modern ～. 年轻人喜欢现
代爵士乐。/ The boy is a ～ fan. 小男孩是个

爵士乐迷。/ ～ist n. 爵士乐爱好者/ ～-man
n. 爵士乐演奏者

jealous / 'dʒeləs / adj. 羡慕的；妒忌的：She is
bitterly ～ of his success. 她极妒忌他的成
功。圊 envious, green-eyed 派 jealousy n.

jeans / dʒiːnz / n. 牛仔裤：He always wears
～. 他总爱穿牛仔裤。

jeep / dʒiːp / n. [C] 吉普车：We visited a ～
factory. 我们参观了一家吉普车生产厂。

jelly / 'dʒeli / n. [U]冻；果子冻：apple (cherry, orange) ～ 苹果(樱桃、橘子)冻

jeopardy / 'dʒepədi / n. [U]危险，危难，危境：
The spy was in constant ～ of being discovered. 该
间谍处于随时都有可能暴露的危险境地。

jerk / dʒɜːk / Ⅰ n. [C]猛推；急拉：He gave the
rope a ～ and it broke. 他猛拉绳子，绳子断
了。圊 jog, pull, thrust Ⅱ v. 猛推；猛扯；急拉：
A car ～ed to a stop in front of him. 一辆小车
猛然停在了他的跟前。/ The girl ～ed her
head around to see that a stranger was after
her. 女孩猛地转过来看到一个陌生人跟着她。
圊 jog, pull, thrust

Jesus / 'dʒiːzəs / n. 耶稣

jet / dʒet / n. [C]喷射机；喷气客机：Have you
any experience of travelling by ～? 你有过乘
喷气机旅行的经历吗？

Jew / dʒuː / n. [C]犹太人；犹太教徒

jewel / 'dʒuːəl / n. [U] ❶宝石：The ring set
with a ～ is very beautiful. 那枚镶宝石的戒指
真漂亮。/ She often says that her favorite ～
is a ruby. 她常说她最喜欢红宝石。圊 stone,
pearl ❷贵重饰物；宝石饰物圊 treasure

jewelry / 'dʒuːəlri / n. [U](总称)珠宝；珠宝
饰物；首饰：They missed some valuable ～ in
their shop last night. 昨天晚上他们商店丢失
了一些贵重的珠宝。/ I don't like to wear ～
in my daily life. 在日常生活中我不喜欢佩戴
珠宝饰品。圊 treasure, jewels

jewish / 'dʒuːɪʃ / adj. 犹太人的；犹太教的

jingle / ˈdʒɪŋgl / Ⅰ *vi.* 发出叮当声；叮当作响；响着铃铛行进：The sleigh bells 〜d as we rode. 我们划雪橇时，雪橇上的铃铛叮当直响。/ 〜 the coins in one's pocket 把口袋里的硬币弄得丁零当啷直响 Ⅱ *n.* ❶叮当声；发出叮当声的东西 ❷（广播或电视中的）广告短诗（或歌），配乐广告短诗（或歌）：a chewing gum 〜 推销口香糖的配乐广告短歌

job / dʒɒb / *n.* [C]职业；工作：He has done a thorough 〜 of it. 他把这件事做得很彻底。/ Jim does odd 〜s in his spare time. 吉姆在空余时间干些零活。Jobs are not easy to get. 工作不好找。/ He is out of 〜. 他失业。同 occupation, work

jog / dʒɒg / *vi.* (jogged; jogging) ❶慢跑：My roommate goes 〜ging in the park after getting up. 我的室友起床后在公园里慢跑。同 run ❷（用手、臂等）轻推；推撞：He 〜ged my elbow. 他轻轻地撞了一下我的胳臂。同 push 派 jogger *n.*

join / dʒɔɪn / *v.* ❶连接；结合：Please 〜 two points by a straight line. 用直线把两点连起来。/ The new highway has 〜ed our school to the city. 这条新公路把我们学校与城市连接起来了。同 unite, combine ❷参加；加入；成为……的成员：〜 the Party 入党 / 〜 the League 入团 / 〜 the army 参军 / 〜 the battle 参战 同 enter, associate ❸与……在一起；伴随（某人做某事）：Will you 〜 us in singing? 你和我们一块儿唱歌好吗？同 associate, enter

joint / dʒɔɪnt / Ⅰ *n.* [C]❶接头；接缝；接合处；接口：The pipe was broken at the 〜s. 这条管子的接口处破了。同 union, link, connection ❷关节；骨节：My mother has a pain in the elbow 〜. 我妈妈的肘关节痛。同 junction, juncture Ⅱ *adj.* ❶共有的；联合的；共同的：She said that was their 〜 property. 她说那是他们的共有财产。/ Many young people want to find a job in a 〜 venture enterprises. 许多年轻人想在合资企业找份工作。同 united, combined 反 individual 派 jointly *adv.*

joke / dʒəʊk / Ⅰ *v.* 开玩笑；说笑话：I am not serious, but joking with you. 我并没有当真，只是和你开开玩笑罢了。同 fool, kid Ⅱ *n.* 笑话：The table laughed at the 〜. 一桌人听到这个笑话都笑了起来。同 fun, game, play

jolly / ˈdʒɒli / *adj.* 快活的；令人高兴的：Our teacher answered our questions with a 〜

laugh. 老师愉快地笑着回答了我们的问题。同 joyful, merry, cheerful 反 sad, unhappy

jolt / dʒəʊlt / Ⅰ *v.* ❶震动；摇动；颠簸：She 〜ed his arm. 她抓住他的臂膀直摇。/ The car 〜ed across the rough ground. 汽车颠簸着驶过崎岖不平的道路。❷使震惊；惊扰，使慌忙：His sudden death 〜ed us all. 他溘然去世，使我们大家大为惊愕。Ⅱ *n.* [C]❶震动，摇动；颠簸：The car gave a 〜 and started. 汽车一震便启动了。❷震惊；引起震惊的事物：The news was a 〜 to me. 这消息对我是一个打击。

journal / ˈdʒɜːnl / *n.* ❶日报；杂志；期刊：a weekly (monthly) 〜 周(月)刊 / a bimonthly 〜 双月刊 / an academic 〜 学术期刊 / This is an influential 〜. 这是一份很有影响的杂志。同 newspaper, magazine, periodical ❷日志；日记：He has the habit to keep a work 〜. 他习惯记工作日记。同 diary, record

journalist / ˈdʒɜːnəlɪst / *n.* [C]新闻工作者；报界人士：He worked as a 〜 in our city after graduation. 毕业后他在我们市当了一名新闻记者。同 reporter, news-writer

journey / ˈdʒɜːni / *n.* [C]旅行（尤指远距离的陆上旅行）；旅程：a 〜 of 3 days 三天的行程 / the 〜 to success 成功之道 / a 〜 on duty 出公差 / a single 〜 单程 / life's 〜 人生旅程 / a 〜 on foot 徒步旅行 / He made a 〜 across the country. 他做了横跨全国的旅行。/ Wish you a good 〜. 祝你一路顺风。同 tour, trip, travel

joy / dʒɔɪ / *n.* [U] 欢乐；高兴；喜悦：Success brought him 〜. 成功给他带来了欢乐。/ To our great 〜 we won the match at last. 使我们高兴的是我们终于赢了比赛。/ He jumped with 〜. 他高兴得跳了起来。同 delight, pleasure

joyful / ˈdʒɔɪfl / *adj.* 充满快乐的；高兴的；十分喜悦的：a 〜 heart 愉快的心情 / 〜 news 令人欣欢的消息 / a 〜 look 高兴的样子 同 happy, merry

judge / dʒʌdʒ / Ⅰ *n.* [C]❶审判官；法官：The 〜 was very kind. 这法官很仁慈。❷仲裁人；裁判员：He acted as a 〜 at the race. 他在赛跑中担任裁判。❸鉴定人；鉴赏家：He is a good 〜 of the fine arts. 他是一位美术鉴赏行家。Ⅱ *v.* ❶审判，审理(案件)：The man was 〜d not guilty. 那人被判无罪。同 try, sentence ❷评判；评介；判断：I can't 〜 whether he was

right or wrong. 我不能断定他是对还是错。/
Don't ~ a person by his appearances. 不要以貌
取人。同 determine

judg(e)ment / 'dʒʌdʒmənt / n. ❶ 审判；(法
官或法庭的)判决：Sit in ~ on a case. 法庭听
审。/ The ~ of the court is reported in all
newspapers. 各报都对法院的判决做了报道。
❷[U] 评判；判断：I let the readers form their
own ~. 我让读者自己去判断。/ That is an
error of ~. 那是一个判断的失误。同 decision

judicial / dʒuː'dɪʃəl / adj. ❶ 司法的；审判
(上)的：the ~ system 司法系统/go through
proper ~ procedures 履行正当的诉讼程序 ❷
法庭的；法庭裁决的；法院判决(或规定)的：
She got a ~ separation from her husband. 她
通过法院判决正式与丈夫分居。

judo / 'dʒuːdəʊ / n. [U]现代柔道(或柔术)

jug / dʒʌg / n. [C]壶；大罐：a ~ of beer 一罐
啤酒 同 container

juggle / 'dʒʌgl / v. 玩杂耍；变戏法；耍花招：
My grandfather can ~ with three bottles. 我
爷爷能用三个瓶子耍把戏。/ He ~d the lit-
tle boy into telling his truth. 他骗小男孩
说出了真相。同 deceive 派 juggler n.

juice / dʒuːs / n. 果汁；菜汁；肉汁：I would like
a glass of vegetable ~. 我想喝一杯蔬菜汁。
同 liquid，fluid

July / dʒuˈlaɪ / n. 七月(略作 Jul.)

jumbo / 'dʒʌmbəʊ / Ⅰ n. [C]体大而笨拙的人
(或动物、物体)；庞然大物Ⅱadj. 特大(号)的；
巨型的：a ~ ice-cream cone 巨型蛋卷冰激凌/a
~ packet of soap powder 大号袋装洗衣粉

jump / dʒʌmp / v. ❶跳；跃；蹦：~ over a
fence 跳过篱笆 / ~ up and down 跳上跳下 /
~ off 跳下；跳离 / ~ into a car 跳进汽车 /
~ onto the floor 跳到地板上 同 leap，bounce
❷(因兴奋、喜悦等)跳动，惊跳：~ for joy 高
兴得跳起来 / Her heart ~ed when she heard
the news. 她听到这个消息时心怦怦直跳。同
leap，beat

junction / 'dʒʌŋkʃn / n. [C]连接点；(公路、道
路等的)交叉口；(铁路)枢纽站；(河流的)汇
合处：at the ~ of two hills 在两座小山的连
接点/Our train waited for long time in a siding
at a ~. 我们的列车在一个枢纽站的岔道上等
候了好长时间。

June / dʒuːn / n. 六月(略作 Jun.)

jungle / 'dʒʌŋgl / n. 丛林，密林：I have never
been to the tropical ~. 我从来没去过热带丛
林。同 forest

junior / 'dʒuːnɪə(r) / Ⅰ n. [C] ❶年少者；较
年幼的人：She is your ~ by two years. 她比
你小两岁。反 senior ❷等级较低者；晚辈：
The old worker often helps his ~. 老工人常
常帮助自己的晚辈。反 senior Ⅱ adj. ❶年少
的；较年幼的：She is ~ to you by two years.
(She is two years ~ to you.)她比你小两岁。
同 younger，minor 反 older，elder，senior ❷资
历较浅的；等级较低的：a ~ class 初级班 / a
~ clerk 低级职员 / He is studying at a ~
high school. 他在一所初中读书。同 inferior，
lower 反 senior，superior

Jupiter / 'dʒuːpɪtə(r) / n. ❶木星 ❷丘比特

jury / 'dʒʊəri / n. [C] 陪审团；全部陪审员(或
评委)：The ~ decided the man was guilty. 陪审
团作出决议那人有罪。/ The ~ is (are) about
to announce the winner. 评委即将宣布获胜者。

just / dʒʌst / Ⅰ adv. ❶刚才；方才：They have
~ gone. 他们刚走。❷ 正好；恰好：It is ~
six o'clock. 现在正好六点。同 exactly ❸ 仅，
只：I've come here ~ to see you. 我是专程来
看你的。同 only，merely Ⅱ adj. 公平的；公正
的；正义的；正直的：The teacher is ~ to us
all. 老师公正地对待我们所有人。/ A judge
must be ~. 法官必须公正。同 fair，right
反 unfair

justice / 'dʒʌstɪs / n. [U]公平，公正；合理：a
sense of ~ 正义感/ I say，in ~ to him，that
he is a good teacher of English. 秉公而论，我
认为他是位优秀的英语教师。同 fairness，
justness 反 injustice

justify / 'dʒʌstɪfaɪ / vt. 证明(人的言论、行动
等)为正当(或有理)：He is fully justified in
doing so. 他这样做是完全有道理的。同 ex-
plain，defend

juvenile / 'dʒuːvənaɪl / Ⅰ n.[C]少年；青少年：
Juveniles should be more concerned for the
whole society. 青少年应当受到全社会更多的
关注。Ⅱ adj. 青少年的；少年特有的：Her
mother bought her some ~ books. 妈妈给她
买了几本适合青少年读的书。同 young，
youthful 反 old，older，elderly

K k

kangaroo / ˌkæŋɡə'ruː/ *n.* [C]大袋鼠

keen / kiːn/ *adj.* ❶热心的；渴望的：~ listeners 热心的听众 / be ~ on (doing) …渴望(做)… 同 eager, enthusiastic 反 cold, uninterested ❷激烈的；强烈的：~ competition 激烈的竞争 / ~ sense of responsibility 强烈的责任感 同 strong ❸敏锐的；敏捷的：~ sight (eye) 敏锐的眼光 同 sensitive ❹锋利的；刺人的：~ criticism 尖锐的批评 / ~ knife 锋利的刀 同 sharp, pointed

keep / kiːp/ *vt.* (kept /kept/, kept) ❶保持；保留；保存：How long may I ~ the book? 这本书我可以借多久？/ ~ **in touch with** 与…保持联系：We ought to ~ in touch with him. 我们应当和他保持联系。~ **sth. in mind** 记住：Please ~ this in your mind. 请将此事牢记在心。~ **sb. in good health** 保持健康：Cold bath ~s me in good health. 冷水浴使我身体保持健康。~ **sb.** (**sth.**) **out of** 不让…进来：The cook always ~s the students out of the kitchen. 厨师总是不让学生进厨房。~ **up with** 跟上；跟…齐头并进：I can't ~ up with you. 我跟不上你。同 continue, maintain ❷遵守；忠于：The Chinese people always ~ their word. 中国人民说话是算数的。/ ~ the law 遵守法律 / ~ regular hours 遵守作息时间 同 abide, observe ❸记入，记录：~ a diary 记日记 / ~ accounts 记账 ❹(使)保持(某种状态或关系)：I am sorry. I've kept you waiting. 对不起，让你久等了。/ Please ~ silent. 请保持安静。❺阻止；防止：~ back 阻止…向前；不告诉：The policemen had to ~ the spectators back. 警察不得不阻止群众上前围观。~ … from me. 他什么都不瞒我。~ **sb.** (**sth.**) **from** (**doing**) **sth.** 阻止：The rain kept us from going out. 这场雨使我们不能外出。同 prevent ❻

抑制(与 from 连用)：I couldn't ~ from laughing. 我不禁大笑起来。❼继续做，不断反复做(某事)(接动名词)：Why does the baby ~ crying? 为什么这婴儿不断地哭？~ **on** 继续，持续，不停：The boy kept on talking even though the teacher asked him to stop. 虽然老师叫这男孩停止讲话，但他还是讲个不停。同 continue

keeper / 'kiːpə(r)/ *n.* [C] ❶看护人 同 caretaker ❷饲养员 同 raiser ❸保管员 同 storeman

ken / ken/ *n.* 认知范围；知识范围：beyond my ~在我的知识范围之外

kernel / 'kɜːnl/ *n.* [C] ❶核，仁 ❷粒；谷粒

kerosene / 'kerəsiːn/ *n.* [U] 煤油：a ~ lamp 煤油灯

kettle / 'ketl/ *n.* [C] 水壶；茶壶：boil a ~ 用水壶烧水 / The ~ is singing. 水烧开了。同 pot

key / kiː/ Ⅰ *n.* [C] ❶钥匙：a ~ for opening a lock 开锁的钥匙/ the ~ of a clock 给钟上发条的钥匙 / the ~ to a door (strongbox) 开门(开保险箱)的钥匙 ❷题解；答案：a ~ to the question 问题的答案 / a ~ to a puzzle 谜底/ the ~ to success 成功的窍门 同 answer, clue ❸(琴、计算机等的)键：strike the ~s of a computer 在计算机上打字 Ⅱ *adj.* 主要的，关键的；基本的：~ factor 主要因素 / ~ point 要点 / ~ issue 关键问题

keyboard / 'kiːbɔːd/ *n.* 键盘

keynote / 'kiːnəut/ Ⅰ *n.* [C] ❶(音乐中的)主音；主调音 ❷(演说等的)主旨，要旨，基调；(行动、政策等的)基本方针，主导原则；(情绪等的)基本倾向，主要动向：the ~ of a speech 演说的中心意旨/Economic expansion was the ~ of the nation's foreign policy. 经济扩张是该国对外政策的主导方针。Ⅱ *vt.* 给…定基调：The governor will ~ the convention. 州长将在会上做基调演说。

kick / kɪk / v. 踢：The child ～ed the ball into the river. 小孩把球踢进了河里。/ The camel ～ed the poor man out. 骆驼把这可怜的人踢了出去。/ corner ～（足球的）角球/ spot ～ 点球 / ～ **off** 开球：John ～ed off and the football match started. 约翰开球，足球赛开始。

kickback / ˈkɪkˌbæk / n. [C]酬金；回扣；贿赂：He denied that he had received any ～s from contractors. 他矢口否认从承包商那里收取过佣金。/ Her employer demanded a ～ on her wages. 雇主要从她的薪水中收取回扣。

kid / kɪd / n. [C] ❶ 小山羊 ❷（俚）小孩：school ～s 学童 同 child, lad

kidnap / ˈkɪdnæp / vt. 诱拐；绑架 同 capture, seize

kidney / ˈkɪdni / n. ❶[C]肾脏：transplant a ～ 移植肾脏 ❷脾气：a man of the right ～ 脾气好的人

kill / kɪl / v. ❶杀死，弄死：The young man was ～ed by an accident. 那位年轻人死于事故。/ ～ **off** 消灭，杀光：The invaders ～ed off all the people of the town. 侵略者把全城人都杀光了。同 murder ❷扼杀；毁灭：～ a bill (proposal) 否决一个议案（建议）同 destroy, abolish ❸消磨（时间等）：～ time 打发（消磨）时光 同 spend, pass 派 killer n.; killing adj.

kilogram(me) / ˈkɪləgræm / n. [C]千克（略作 kg）

kilometre / ˈkɪləmiːtə(r) / n. [C]千米；公里（略作 km）

kilowatt / ˈkɪləwɒt / n. 千瓦（略作 kw）：～-hour 千瓦小时

kin / kɪn / Ⅰ n. 家族；亲属 同 relative Ⅱ adj. 有亲属关系的 同 relative

kind / kaɪnd / Ⅰ n. [C]种类：another ～ of cat 另一种猫 / all ～s of books 各种书籍 / the human ～ 人类 / This ～ of thing shouldn't be allowed. 此类事是不允许的。同 class, sort, type Ⅱ adj. 仁慈的；友好的；和蔼的：Please give my ～ regards to her. 请代我向她问好。/ It is very ～ of you to help us. 承蒙帮助，不胜感激。/ He was ～ with his children. 他对他的儿女很好。同 gentle, friendly, kind-hearted 反 cruel, unfriendly 派 kindly adj.&adv.

kindergarten / ˈkɪndəɡɑːtn / n. [C]幼儿园

kindle / ˈkɪndl / v. ❶ 点燃；使燃烧 同 light ❷引起，激起：～ the interest of 激起…的兴趣

kindness / ˈkaɪndnəs / n. [U]亲切，和蔼；仁慈；好心的行为：out of ～ 出于好心 / with (without) ～（不）友善地 / Thank you for your ～ to me. 谢谢你对我的关心。同 friendliness, mercy, favor

king / kɪŋ / n. [C]国王；君王：an oil ～ 石油大王 / King's English 标准英语 / He is a ～ in name, but not in reality. 他是一位有名无实的国王。

kingdom / ˈkɪŋdəm / n. [C] ❶王国：the United Kingdom 英国 ❷界，领域：the ～ of science 科学领域 / the animal ～ 动物界

kiss / kɪs / Ⅰ v. 接吻（表示亲爱或致意）：The two lovers ～ed passionately. 那对情侣热烈地相吻。Ⅱ n. [C]接吻：～ sb. goodbye 吻别

kitchen / ˈkɪtʃɪn / n. [C]厨房

kite / kaɪt / n. [C]风筝：draw in a ～ 收风筝 / let up a ～ with the wind 放风筝

kitten / ˈkɪtn / n. [C]小猫

knee / niː / n. [C]膝盖：He was wounded in the ～ by a fall. 他跌伤了膝盖。/ **fall on one's** ～**s** 跪下：The children have already fallen on their ～s. 孩子们已跪下。

kneel / niːl / vi. （knelt/nelt/, knelt 或

kneeled) 跪下；跪倒：～ on the ground 跪在地下 / ～ to sb. 向某人下跪 / The girl knelt down to look for a pen. 那姑娘跪下找钢笔。

knife / naɪf / n. [C] (pl. knives) 小刀；餐刀；菜刀：a butcher ～ 屠刀 / a folding ～ 折刀 / a table ～ 餐刀 / a surgeon's ～ 手术刀 / a dull ～ 钝刀 / a sharp ～ 快刀 / **get one's ～ into sb.** 欲伤害某人：Be careful with George, he wants to get his ～ into you. 注意提防乔治,他想伤害你。

knight / naɪt / n. [C] ❶(中古时的)骑士 ❷(英)爵士 派 knightly adj. & adv.

knit / nɪt / v. (knit 或 knitted；knitting) ❶编织(毛衣等)：～ a sweater 织毛衣 /～ up friendship 编织友谊 ❷使接合 同 connect, unite

knitting / 'nɪtɪŋ / n. 编织物；针织品

knitwear / 'nɪtweə(r) / n. 针织品,针织物(指针织的袜子、内衣、外套等)

knob / nɒb / n. [C] 门把；旋钮 同 handle

knock / nɒk / Ⅰ vi. 击；打；敲；碰撞；撞击：He ～ed his head against (on) the wall. 他的头撞在了墙上。/ Who is ～ing at the door? 谁在敲门? / ～ **against (up)** 偶然遇上：Who do you think I ～ed against in the office this morning? 你猜今天早晨我在办公室碰见谁了? / ～ **down** 击倒,打倒：A bus ～ed her down. 一辆汽车把她撞倒了。/ ～ **sth. out** 敲空：You should ～ the pipe out. 你的烟斗应磕干净。同 hit, strike Ⅱ n. 敲,打(的声音)；碰撞,撞击：get a hard ～ 受到沉重打击

knot / nɒt / n. [C] 结：make a ～ 打结 / ～ of a matter 问题的症结 / ～s in the mind 思想疙瘩

know / nəʊ / v. (knew /njuː/, known /nəʊn/) ❶知道；懂得；理解；了解：The students ～ how to answer these questions. 学生们知道怎样回答这些问题。We don't ～ whether he is here or not. 我们不知道他是否在此。同 understand, comprehend ❷认识；认出；熟悉：Do you ～ Mr. White? 你认识怀特先生吗? / I got to ～ him a few years ago. 几年前我认识了他。同 recognize, realize ❸听说：I knew a-bout that last week. 我上周才听说那件事。**be ～n to** 为…熟知：London is ～n to us all. 伦敦是我们大家都熟知的。**be ～n as** 以…而著称：She was ～n as an excellent dancer. 大家公认她是一位出色的舞蹈家。**be ～n for** 称作,叫作：Guilin is ～n for its beautiful scenery. 桂林以山水风景优美而闻名。**～ sb. (sth.) from sb. (sth.)** 辨别,识别：～ a friend from an enemy 分清敌友 / We should ～ right from wrong. 我们应明辨是非。**make oneself ～n** 做自我介绍：You'd better make yourself ～n to the host. 你应向主人做自我介绍。派 known adj.

knowing / 'nəʊɪŋ / adj. ❶有知识的；有见识的；通晓的,熟谙的：a ～ scholar 知识渊博的学者/Both of them were ～ in astronomy. 他们俩在天文学方面都颇有造诣。❷心照不宣的,会意的：He joined in the laugh and looked ～. 他随他人一同大笑,显出一副心领神会的样子。❸故意的,蓄意的：indiscriminate classi-fication of innocent with ～ activity 不分青红皂白将有无意和有意的活动混为一谈 派 know-ingly adv.

knowledge / 'nɒlɪdʒ / n. [U] ❶ 了解；知道；理解：A baby has no ～ of good and evil. 婴儿不知道善恶。同 acquaintance ❷知识；学识：absorb ～ 吸收知识 / acquire ～ 获取知识 / broaden the scope of ～ 扩大知识面 / enlarge ～ 丰富知识 / build up ～ 积累知识/ basic ～ 基础知识 / business ～ 商业知识 / ～ in-dustry 知识产业 / My ～ of English is very poor. 我的英语很差。/ I have no ～ of Lon-don. 我对伦敦一无所知。/ Knowledge originates in practice. 认识来源于实践。派 knowledgeable adj.

knuckle / 'nʌkl / n. 指；指关节

Korea / kə'rɪə / n. 朝鲜：the Democratic People's Republic of ～ 朝鲜民主主义人民共和国 / the Republic of ～ 韩国

Korean / kə'rɪən / Ⅰ n. 朝鲜人；朝鲜文 Ⅱ adj. 朝鲜(人)的

kungfu / 'kʊŋ'fuː / n. [U]功夫；武术；武艺：a ～ movie 功夫(或武打)片

L l

lab / læb / *n.* （口语）实验室（laboratory 的简写形式）

label / ˈleɪbl / Ⅰ *n.* [C]标签；标记：There is a "poison" ～ on the box. 盒子上贴有"有毒"标记。 圃 mark Ⅱ *vt.* 贴标签；做记号：They ～ goods with price before they sell them. 出售前他们给商品贴上售价签。 圃 mark, tag

laboratory / ləˈbɔrətri / *n.* [C]实验室：a chemistry ～ 化学实验室/ a physics ～ 物理实验室/ a language ～ 语言实验室 圃 lab, workroom

laborious / ləˈbɔːrɪəs / *adj.* 费力的；艰辛的；需坚持不懈的：～ and futile negotiations 艰苦而无结果的谈判/a long, ～ road 一条漫长而艰辛的道路

labo(u)r / ˈleɪbə(r) / Ⅰ *n.* ❶[U]劳作；劳动：Labor creates the world. 劳动创造世界。 / They earn their living by manual ～. 他们靠体力劳动谋生。 圃 work ❷[C]工作：They have succeeded by their own ～s. 他们靠自己的艰苦工作获得了成功。 圃 job, employment Ⅱ *v.* ❶工作；劳动：They are ～ing for the happiness of the mankind. 他们正为人类的幸福工作着。 ❷(缓慢、吃力地)做某事：We ～ed for an hour but could not convince them. 我们花了一个小时仍未能说服他们。 / The ship ～ed through the rough seas. 船在波涛汹涌的海上艰难航行者。 派 labo(u)rer *n.*

labyrinth / ˈlæbərɪnθ / *n.* [C]❶迷宫；曲径：a ～ of narrow, twisting alleyways 迷宫般的狭窄曲折的小胡同 ❷复杂局面；(事物的)错综复杂：a ～ of rules and regulations 繁杂的规则和条例

lace / leɪs / *n.* [U]花边；饰带；鞋带：tie one's ～s 系鞋带 / ～ for a dress 连衣裙的花边

lack / læk / Ⅰ *n.* [U]缺乏；缺少；不足：The plant died for ～ of water. 那些植物因缺水而枯死了。 圃 want, need 反 plenty, abundance Ⅱ *v.* 缺乏；缺少：I ～ the words with which to express my gratitude. 我无法用言语来表示我的感谢。 / Your statement ～s details. 你的叙述不够具体。 圃 want, need/ **be ～ing in** 缺乏；缺少：Humour is ～ing in his speech. 他讲话缺乏幽默。

> **辨析**
> **lack** 意为"缺乏；不足"，指完全没有或有而不充分，所缺乏的东西可好可坏：Your failure is simply due to the lack of courage. 你的失败只因缺少勇气。 **need** 指缺少必要的或必需的事物：She needs more help. 她需要更多的帮助。 **want** 指缺乏值得拥有的或希望拥有的事物：For want of practice, he can't speak English very fluently. 因缺少练习，他不能讲流利的英语。 **shortage** 意为"不足；缺少"，常指需要或规定的东西数量不足：Food shortage often occurred in time of war. 战时常常发生粮食匮乏。

lad / læd / *n.* [C]少年；小伙子 圃 boy, child, youth

ladder / ˈlædə(r) / *n.* [C]梯；阶梯：He who would climb the ～ must begin at the bottom. 千里之行，始于足下。 / Please place (rest) the ～ against the wall. 请把梯子靠墙放。

laden / ˈleɪdən / *adj.* 装满的，载货的：a ～ ship 满载货物的船/He returned ～ with honours. 他载誉归来。

lady / ˈleɪdi / *n.* [C]❶贵妇；女士(对所有妇女的称呼)：a young ～ 未婚少女，小姐 / Ladies and Gentlemen! 女士们，先生们！ ❷(*pl.*)女厕所，女盥洗室(复数形式，单数意义)：Is there a Ladies nearby? 附近有女厕所吗?

lake / leɪk / *n.* [C]湖

lamb / læm / *n.* 小羊，羔羊；羔羊肉

lame / leɪm / *adj.* 跛的，瘸的：The worker is ～ from a wound. 那工人因伤而跛足。 圃 crippled, disabled

lament / ləˈment / Ⅰ *v.* ❶悲痛，恸哭；哀悼：Mothers ～ for their missing children. 母亲们为失踪的孩子恸哭不已。 ❷为…感到遗憾；为

…感到惋惜：We ～ the fact that this company cannot continue to make a profit. 这家公司不能继续盈利了，对此我们深感遗憾。Ⅱ n. [C] 悲痛；哀悼；恸哭：a ～ for lost youth 对逝去的青春的哀叹

lamp / læmp / n. [C] 灯：an electric ～ 电灯 / a desk (table) ～ 台灯 /a neon ～ 霓虹灯

land / lænd / Ⅰ v. 着陆；登陆；登岸：The plane ～ed safely. 飞机安全着陆。/ We ～ed in a beautiful bay. 我们在一个美丽的海湾处上了岸。同 ground,dock Ⅱ n. ❶[U] 陆地：Some came by ～ and some by water. 一些人由陆路来，一些人从水路来。同 ground, earth ❷[U] 土地；田地：He has ～ of his own. 他有自己的土地。❸(pl.) 地产：He lives on his own ～ s. 他靠自己的地产过日子。❹国土；国家：China is my native ～. 中国是我的祖国。同 territory nation

landscape / ˈlændskeɪp / n. [C] 风景；景观；风景绘画 同 view,scenery

landslide / ˈlænd,slaɪd / n. [C] 山崩；滑坡；崩塌，塌方：Slight noise might set of a ～. 细微的响声也会引发崩塌。

lane / leɪn / n. [C] 小巷；小路；胡同 同 foot-path,way

language / ˈlæŋgwɪdʒ / n. ❶[U](总称)语言：The ～ we write will always differ somewhat from the ～ we speak. 我们所用的书面语与口头语总是有些差别的。❷[C](一个国家或种族的)语言：acquire (command,master) a ～ 掌握一种语言 /speak (talk) a ～ 讲一种语言 /a common ～ 共同语言 / the finger (gesture,hand,sign) ～ 手语 / native ～ 本族语 / A foreign ～ is a weapon in the struggle of life. 外国语是人生斗争的一种武器。

lantern / ˈlæntən / n. [C]手提灯；灯笼：a sig-nal ～ 信号灯 / light a ～ 点灯 / Lantern Festival 元宵节

lap / læp / Ⅰ vt. (lapped;lapping)舔食(与 up 连用)：The cat quickly ～ped up all the milk. 小猫很快将所有牛奶舔光了。Ⅱ n. ❶膝部：She held her son in her ～. 她把儿子抱在膝上。同 knees ❷(跑道的)一圈：He overtook all the other runners on the last ～. 他在跑最后一圈时超过了其他的运动员。同 course,round

lapse / læps / Ⅰ n. [C] ❶(道德等的)沦丧；背离，偏离：a ～ of principle 背离原则 /a ～ in good judgement 未能作出的正确判断 ❷小错，差错，疏忽，失误：a ～ of memory 记错/a ～ of the tongue 口误 ❸(时间的)流逝，逝去,过去：a ～ of six weeks between letters 书信一来一往六个星期 Ⅱ vi. ❶(地位、水平等)降低,下降；(状况)恶化；(兴趣、信心等)减退：Their zeal upon the work ～d. 他们对工作的热情有所减退。❷进入；陷入：When back home,he ～d into native language. 回到家他就又说起了当地方言。❸(时间)流逝，逝去：Years, just like the river, ～d onward day and night. 岁月就像河流一样不舍昼夜地流逝而去。❹背离正道；偏离标准：The communica-tion satellite ～d from its orbit because it had run out of energy. 通信卫星的能量用尽，因而偏离了轨道。

large / lɑːdʒ / adj. 庞大的；巨大的；大规模的；众多的：He has a ～ family. 他有一大家人。/ A ～ number of new teachers came to our school. 一大批新教师来到我们学校。同 big, huge, large-scale 反 little, small 派 largely adv.

large 不如 big 通俗，也不如 great 感情色彩浓,如果用它形容人，就指人的身体肥胖。它常用来修饰表示面积、体积、范围、数量方面的词：China is a large (big) country. 中国是一个大国。His mother gave him a large (big, great) sum of money to travel around the country. 他母亲给他一大笔钱去周游全国。She is a large girl. 她是个胖女孩。**big** 比 large 通俗，可指物体的重量、事物的程度，也可指人的体格大小、辈分高低，特别强调体积、重量：a big man 大人物 / It is a big tree. 这是一棵大树。He has made a big de-cision. 他做出了一个重大决定。The child is big for his age. 就年龄来说,那孩子长得够高大了。**great** 带有较强的感情色彩，用以形容体积、面积之大(此时与 big, large 同义),主要用以表达意义比较抽象的"伟大", What a great clock it is! 那只钟多大啊! Na-poleon was a great soldier. 拿破仑是一个伟大的军人。Shanghai is a great city. 上海是个大城市。

laser / ˈleɪzə(r) / n. [C]激光；激光器：a ～ disc 光盘 / a ～ printer 激光打印机 /～ trea-ting 激光治疗

last¹ / lɑːst / Ⅰ adj. ❶最后的；末尾的(与 first

相对）：the ～ month of the year 一年的最后
一个月 同 final 反 first ❷刚过去的（与 next 相
对）：～ night（week, month, summer, year）昨
夜（上周、上个月、去年夏天、去年）/ in（for）
the ～ few years 在过去的几年中 同 latest　Ⅱ
n. 最后；末尾；最后的人：I want to hear the ～
of his report. 我想听到他报告的结尾部分。/
Who is the ～ out? 是谁最后离开的？ /at ～
最后，终于；毕竟，到底：At ～ man has
reached the moon. 人类终于登上了月球。

last² / lɑːst / v. 持续，耐久：The cloth ～s well.
这布很耐穿。The left water can ～ him for
seven days. 剩下的水能够让他维持七天。同
continue, endure

> **辨析**
>
> **last** 意为"最后的，末尾的"，指一连串的人、
> 事、物依顺序排列到最后的那一个：I took a
> seat in the last row. 我坐在最后一排。**final**
> 不强调次序的先后，而着重于结局：We have
> made the final decision. 我们已作出最后决
> 定。

lasting / ˈlɑːstɪŋ, ˈlæstɪŋ / adj. 持久的，永久
的；耐久的：maintain a ～ peace 维持长久的和
平/have a ～ effect on 对···产生持久的效力

late / leɪt / Ⅰ adj.（later, latest）❶迟的，晚的
（与 early 相对）：Don't be ～ for school. 上学
不要迟到。It's never too ～ to mend. 改过不
嫌晚。同 delayed 反 early ❷近末尾的，将尽
的：in the ～ afternoon 在下午将尽的时候/ in
～ summer 夏末 同 final, last ❸近来的；新近
的：the ～ novel 新近出版的小说　Ⅱ adv. 迟，晚（与
early 相对）：get up（arrive home）～ 起床很
晚（到家很晚）/ It rained ～ in the afternoon.
近黄昏时下雨了。派 lately adv.

latent / ˈleɪtnt / adj. 隐藏的；潜在的；潜伏的：
～ energy 潜能 同 hidden, potential

later / ˈleɪtə(r) / adv. 后来；以后：See you ～!
再见！

lateral / ˈlætərəl / adj. ❶（位于）侧面的；朝侧
面的；从侧面的：The lungs are ～ to the
heart. 肺位于心脏的两侧。❷平级的；相似的：
The company offered her ～ move but not a
promotion. 公司给她进行了平级调动，职务没
有升迁。❸边音的，旁流音的：The sound "l"
is a ～ sound in English. 英语中的"l"为舌
侧音。

latest / ˈleɪtɪst / adj. 最近的；最晚的；

the ～ news 最新消息/ The old man reads the
～ newspaper everyday. 老人每天都读最新出
版的报纸。

Latin / ˈlætɪn / Ⅰ n. [U]拉丁语　Ⅱ adj. 拉丁
人的；拉丁语的：～ America 拉丁美洲

latitude / ˈlætɪtjuːd / n. 纬度：The city is at a
～ of 40 degrees north. 那城市位于北纬
40 度。

latter / ˈlætə(r) / adj. 后者的；最近的；末尾
的：the ～ half of the year 下半年/ in these
～ days 在最近这些日子里/ I agree to the
～ point. 我赞成后一个论点。反 former

laugh / lɑːf / Ⅰ v. 笑；发笑：The joke made
everyone ～. 那笑话使大家都笑了。He ～s
best who ～s last. 别高兴得太早。(最后笑的
人笑得最好。) / ～ at 发笑；嘲笑；取笑：What
are you ～ing at? 你们在笑什么？　Ⅱ n. 笑声；
笑；cause（create, excite）a ～ 引人发笑 / She
～ed a hearty ～. 她纵情大笑。

> **辨析**
>
> **laugh** 意为"笑；发笑"，指笑时不但有面部表
> 情，还有声音、动作：I couldn't help laughing
> when I heard what he said. 听了他的话，我
> 不禁大笑起来。**smile** 意为"微笑"，常指好
> 意的笑，其后接介词 on, upon, 也可指恶意
> 的冷笑，后接介词 at：She went away with a
> sweet smile. 她嫣然一笑而去。The master
> smiled at my request but said nothing. 对我
> 的请求，主人一笑置之。

laughter / ˈlɑːftə(r) / n. [U]笑；笑声

launch / lɔːntʃ / vt. ❶使（船）下水：They ～
ed a ship from a shipyard. 他们让船从船坞下
水。❷发射（飞弹、火箭等）；发动：～ a spaceship into space. 把宇宙飞船发射到太空 /
The satellite was ～ed in a rocket. 这颗卫星
是装在火箭上发射的。/ They ～ed an attack
on the enemy. 他们向敌人发起进攻。同
start, send

launder / ˈlɔːndə(r) / v. ❶（被）洗熨：He has
his shirt ～ed every day. 他每天都叫人洗熨衬
衫。/The cloth didn't ～ well. 这种布不经
洗。❷洗（黑钱等）

laundry / ˈlɔːndri / n. ❶[C]洗衣店；洗衣房
❷[U]待洗衣物；所洗衣物

lavatory / ˈlævətri / n. [C]厕所；洗手间；盥洗
室 同 washroom, toilet

lavish / ˈlævɪʃ / Ⅰ adj. ❶丰富的；无节制的；

大量的：～ gifts 丰厚的礼物/be ～ with money 花钱大手大脚 ❷非常大方的，毫不吝啬的：the ～ hospitality of the local inhabitants 当地居民的过于好客/～ display of affection 感情的过分表露 Ⅱ vt. 挥霍，浪费；滥施：～ one's love upon sb. 对某人百般爱抚/He rejects the praise that his colleagues ～ed on him with indifference. 他的同事对他滥加赞扬，但他却无动于衷。

law / lɔː/ n. ❶法律；法令：abide by the ～ 守法 / administer the ～ 执法 / break the ～ 犯法 / go to ～ 诉诸法律 / the civil ～ 民法 / the criminal ～ 刑法 /the traffic ～ 交通规则 / Does the ～ allow you to do so? 法律允许你那样做吗? ❷[U]法律系统；法律学，法学：He is reading ～ at Harvard. 他在哈佛大学攻读法律。 ❸自然法则；定律：Newton's Law 牛顿定律 / the ～s of motion 运动定律

lawful / ˈlɔːfl/ adj. 合法的；依法的；法定的：～ rights and interests 合法权利 / ～ business operation 合法经营 / ～ property 合法财产 / He has ～ earned income in this country. 他在这个国家有合法收入。

lawn / lɔːn/ n.[C]草地；草坪：lie on the ～ 躺在草地上/ walk over the ～ 在草坪上行走 同 grassland

lawsuit / ˈlɔːs(j)uːt/ n.[C]诉讼：bring a ～ against sb. 对某人提起诉讼

lawyer / ˈlɔːjə(r)/ n.[C] 律师：They hired a ～ to help them. 他们聘了一位律师来帮助他们。

lay / leɪ/ Ⅰ vi. 躺；位于(lie 的过去式形式)Ⅱ vt. (laid /leɪd/, laid) ❶置放；搁；摆：Please ～ these glasses along, not across. 这些玻璃杯竖着放，不要横放。He laid his hand on my shoulder. 他把手放在我肩上。同 put, place ❷(鸟或昆虫)产卵：Hens ～ eggs. 母鸡下蛋。同 produce ❸打赌：I'll ～ you that he will not come. 我和你赌，他不会来的。❹铺，铺设；覆盖：Lay colours on the canvas. 涂颜料于画布上。They are going to ～ a cable under the river. 他们将在河底铺设电缆。同 set, place / ～ **aside** 放在一边；留作别用：Please ～ your book aside. 请把书搁在一边。/ ～ **down** ①放下；使躺下：She laid herself down gently. 她轻轻地躺下来。/ He laid the box down. 他把箱子放下。②投降；放弃：Lay down your arms! 放下武器！③牺牲：He laid down his life for

truth. 他为真理而献身。 ～ **out** 陈列，展览；安排，布置；设计：Lay the table out for supper. 摆桌子吃晚饭。/ The hill has been laid out as a small park. 这小山被设计成了一座小公园。 ～ **up** 贮藏；储蓄：They are ～ing up enough money to buy a car. 他们正存钱买车。

辨析

lay 意为"放；平放；横放"：He laid down his pen and seemed lost in thought. 他把笔放下来陷入沉思。**place** 意为"放；放置"，多指有规则地放处，不强调动作，而强调把东西放到某一确定地点：Place your dictionary on the shelf. 请把你的词典放在书架上。**put** 为普通用词，强调把某物移放到某处：He put his hands in his pockets. 他把手放在口袋里。**set** 意为"竖放"，强调把某物置于某一确定位置：Set it up. 将它竖起来。

layer / ˈleɪə(r)/ n.[C]层：The workers are putting a ～ of small stones on the road. 工人们在道上铺上一层小石头。

layman / ˈleɪmən/ n.[C]外行；门外汉：We don't need a ～ in our company. 我们公司不需要外行。同 layperson, nonprofessional 反 expert, specialist

lay-off / ˈleɪɒf/ Ⅰ n. 解雇：The company provided several jobs for ～ workers. 这家公司为下岗工人提供了好几份工作。同 unemployment 反 employment Ⅱ vt. 解雇：The boss ～ed her from her job without any reason. 老板无故把她解雇了。同 fire, dismiss 反 employ

layout / ˈleɪaʊt/ n. 布局；安排；设计：They are discussing the ～ of their factory. 他们正在讨论工厂的布局。同 design, plan, arrangement

lazy / ˈleɪzi/ adj. 懒惰的；懒散的：Don't be so ～. 不要这样懒惰。同 idle 反 hardworking

lead¹ / liːd/ Ⅰ vt. (led/led/, led) ❶ 引导；指引：The servant led the visitors in. 仆人将客人领进来。The girl led her little brother to school. 那个女孩领着她的小弟弟去上学。/ ～ **the way** 引路；带路：Our guide led us the way to the library. 我们的向导把我们带到图书馆。同 direct ❷领导；率领；指挥：The Party ～s us from victory to victory. 党领导我们从胜利走向胜利。The commander led the army against the city. 指挥官率领军队攻城。同 guide, commend ❸(使某人)过(生活)：They are ～ing a happy life. 他们过着幸福的生活。同 live ❹导致(某种结果)；通，达：This road

～s to wealth. 这是一条致富之路。/ I don't think it will ～ to a good result. 我认为这事不会有什么好结果。同 come Ⅱ n. 领袖；领路；领先：They always hold the ～ in the scientific researches. 在科研中，他们总是保持领先地位。同 leadership,precedence

lead² / led / n. [C]铅

leaded / ˈledɪd / adj. (汽油)含铅的

leader / ˈliːdə(r) / n. [C]领袖；领导者：They are going to interview the top ～s of the country next month. 下月他们将采访国家高层领导人。同 director,chief 反 follower

leadership / ˈliːdəʃɪp / n. 领导：Under the ～ of the Party, the Chinese people are becoming richer and richer. 在党的领导下，中国人民越来越富裕。

leading / ˈliːdɪŋ / adj. ❶领导的；指导的：a ～ cadre 领导干部 / a ～ body 领导机关 同 directing,governing ❷最主要的；首位的：a ～ article 社论 / He played a ～ actor in the film. 他在那部电影里担任主角。同 highest,first,primary,chief

leaf / liːf / n. [C] (pl. leaves /liːvz/) ❶(树的)叶子：The trees come into ～ in spring. 树木在春季长叶。❷(书籍杂志的)一张：A book of 100 pages has 50 leaves. 一本100页的书有50张。同 sheet

leaflet / ˈliːflət / n. [C]传单；活页：The girl is handing out some advertising ～s. 那女孩正在散发广告单。同 handbill

league / liːɡ / n. [C]同盟；联盟：the Communist League 共产主义者同盟 / the Communist Youth League 共青团 / a ～ member 团员 / the ～ between two powers 两个强国之间的联盟 / The young fellows wanted to form a football ～. 年轻小伙子们很想建立一个足球联合会。同 union,association

leak / liːk / n. [C]漏洞；裂缝：The roof has a bad ～. 屋顶有个大的裂缝。同 crack Ⅱ v. 漏出；泄露：Who ～ed the news out to the public? 谁把消息泄漏给公众了？同 discharge,disclose

leakage / ˈliːkɪdʒ / n. 漏，泄漏；漏出物：He stopped a ～ of the secret successfully. 他成功地阻止了那个秘密的泄露。同 leaking,percolation

lean / liːn / v. (leaned 或 leant/lent/) ❶倚，

靠：Lean a ladder against the wall. 把梯子靠在墙上。同 rest,rely ❷倾斜：It ～s to one side. 它向一边倾斜。同 slant/～ **on** 依赖于；信赖：We'll ～ on others for guidance. 我们将依靠别人的指导。～ **over** 俯身于…之上：～ over a fence 将身子探过篱笆

leap / liːp / Ⅰ v. (leapt / lept /或 leaped)跳；跃；迅速运动：The boy ～ed a ditch and ran away. 小男孩跳过一道沟跑掉了。/ You should look before you ～. 做事前你得三思而后行。同 bounce,hop,rush Ⅱ n. [C]跳跃；飞跃；跃进：a big ～ forward 大飞跃 / take a ～ over an obstacle 跃过障碍 同 jump,spring,hop

learn / lɜːn / vt. (learned, learned 或 learnt/lɜːnt/, learnt) ❶学习；学会：We will ～ to speak English. 我们将学讲英语。同 study,attain/～ **sth. by heart** 记住；背诵：You should ～ this poem by heart. 这首诗你应背诵。～ **from** 向…学习：Learn from Comrade Lei Feng. 向雷锋同志学习。❷闻知；获悉；知道：We haven't ～ed whether he arrived safely. 我们还不知道他是否安全到达了。同 hear 派 learner n.

learned / ˈlɜːnɪd / adj. 有学问的；博学的：～ periodical 学术期刊 / He is a ～ man. 他是一位学者。同 scholarly,profound

learning / ˈlɜːnɪŋ / n. ❶学习：If you want to be successful, you should be good at ～. 如果你想获得成功，你必须善于学习。同 study ❷学问；知识：a man of ～ 有学问的人 / That is only book ～. 那仅仅是书本知识。同 knowledge

lease / liːs / Ⅰ n. [C]❶租约，租契：sign a ～ 签订租约 ❷租赁期限。Ⅱ vt. ❶租出：He ～d his apartment to a friend. 他把自己的公寓租给了一位朋友。❷租入；租得：The company ～s its cars from a local supplier. 该公司从当地的供应商那里租来汽车。

least / liːst / (little 的最高级形式)Ⅰ adj. 最小的；最少的(与 most 相对)：Do you know the ～ distance between these two cities? 你知道这两座城市间的最小距离吗？同 minimum 反 maximum Ⅱ n. [U]最小；最少：He was the one who did the ～ of the work. 他就是那项工作干得最少的人。/ **at (the)** ～ 至少：The trip will take three days at (the) ～. 这一趟旅行至少得三天。**not in the** ～ 毫不：I was not surprised in the ～. 我一点也不感到惊奇。Ⅲ *adv.* 最小；最少：He did the hardest work but was paid the ～. 他干最苦的活，但得的报酬却最少。反 most

leather / ˈleðə(r) / *n.* [U]皮革；皮革制品

leave / liːv / Ⅰ *v.* (left/left/, left) ❶离开；出发；动身：Leave the room at once. 请马上离开房间。She is leaving for Beijing. 她即将动身去北京。同 go, depart 反 come, arrive ❷留下，剩下；忘记：I left my books on the table. 我把书忘在桌子上了。～ **sb.** (**sth.**) **alone** 不要干涉某人（某事）；Leave the cat alone. 不要动那只猫。❸交托；委托：We should ～ this problem to our monitor. 我们应当把这事交给班长处理。同 entrust Ⅱ *n.* 离去；告别；假期：The guest took his ～ at ten. 客人十点钟告辞。/ If you want to go out, you must ask for ～ first. 如果你想出去，你得先请假。

lecture / ˈlektʃə(r) / *n.* [C]演讲；讲课：attend a ～ 听演讲(讲课) / deliver (give) a ～ 讲演(讲课) 同 address, lesson

left / left / Ⅰ (leave 的过去式和过去分词形式)离开；留下 Ⅱ *adj.* 左边的；左侧的：There are many big buildings on the ～ side of the river. 在河的左岸有许多高楼。/ Not many people write with the ～ hand. 没有多少人用左手写字。反 right Ⅲ *adv.* 往左；向左：Left turn (face). 向左转。反 right Ⅳ *n.* 左边；左部；turn to the ～ 向左转 / She sat on my ～. 她坐在我的左边。/Cars in some countries keep to the ～. 在一些国家汽车靠左行驶。反 right

leg / leg / *n.* [C]腿：We should learn to stand on our own ～s. 我们应当学会自立。

legacy / ˈlegəsi / *n.* [C]遗赠物；遗产：cultural ～ 文化遗产 / intellectual ～ 精神遗产 / His father left him a ～ of a million but he refused. 他的父亲给他留下百万遗产，但是他拒绝接受。同 heritage, inheritance

legal / ˈliːgəl / *adj.* 法律(上)的；合法的；法定的：～ action 法律行为 / ～ age 法定年龄 / ～ consulting (法律咨询 / ～ consultant (adviser) 法律顾问 / ～ education 法制教育 / ～ holiday 法定假日 同 constitutional, lawful 反 illegal, unlawful

legend / ˈledʒənd / *n.* 传说；传奇文学；传奇人物

legendary / ˈledʒəndəri / *adj.* 传奇(式)的；传奇中的；具有传奇色彩的：a ～ instead of real character 传奇而非真实的人物/a ～ dragon 传说中的龙

legible / ˈledʒəbl / *adj.* (字迹、印刷等)清晰的，容易辨认的：a book in large ，～ type 一本用易认的大号字体印刷的书籍/His cursive handwriting is hardly ～. 他那潦草的字迹几乎无法辨认。派 legibility *n.*

legislation / ˌledʒɪsˈleɪʃn / *n.* 立法；法规 同 law, regulation

leisure / ˈleʒə(r) / *n.* [U]空闲；闲暇；悠闲：He is busy with his business and hardly has ～ for swimming. 他在忙自己的生意，没有空游泳。/ The old couple are living a life of ～. 老夫妻过着悠闲的生活。同 ease, relaxation

lemon / ˈlemən / *n.* ❶柠檬；柠檬树 ❷柠檬色

lemonade / ˌleməˈneɪd / *n.* 柠檬水

lend / lend / *vt.* (lent/lent/, lent) 借给；租出：Will you ～ your knife to that man? 你可以将小刀借给那个人吗？/～ **sb. a hand** 帮助：Please ～ him a hand in copying the sentences. 请帮助他抄写这些句子。

> **辨析**
> **lend** 意为"借出"：They will lend us some books. 他们愿借些书给我们。**borrow** 意为"借进；从…借"，所指方向与 lend 相反：We'll borrow some books from them. 我们将从他们那里借书。

length / leŋθ / *n.* (空间的)长度；(时间的)长短，在…期间：The bridge has a ～ of about 1,000 metres. 这桥长约 1000 米。/ The ～ of my stay there was about two weeks. 我在那儿大约待了两周。同 extent

lengthen / ˈleŋθən / *v.* 延长；变长：She ～ed her stay in London to a month. 她把在伦敦停留的时间延长为一个月。同 expand, extend 反 shorten, reduce

lens / lenz / *n.* [C](眼镜的)镜片；(相机的)镜头

leopard / ˈlepəd / *n.* [C]豹

less / les / Ⅰ (little 的比较级形式)Ⅰ *adj.* (与more 相对)少量的，较少的(与不可数名词连用)：～ food 较少的食物 / Eat ～, drink ～, sleep more. 少吃，少饮酒，多睡眠。/ The road was something ～ than smooth. 这条路不平坦。Ⅱ *adv.* 更少地；较少地：Tom is ～ clever than John. 汤姆不如约翰聪明。/ She was ～ hurt than frightened. 她没受到什么伤害,却吓坏了。反 more

辨析

less 意为"较少的",常指数量、价值、程度等不足,与不可数名词连用;**fewer** 一般与可数名词连用:less money, fewer friends, less water, fewer books, less education, fewer pens。

lessen / ˈlesn / v. 减少;减轻:They are trying hard to ～ the costs of goods. 他们正尽力降低商品的成本。同 reduce, decrease

lesson / ˈlesn / n. [C] ❶课题;一课;课程:history ～s 历史课 / oral ～s 口语课 / postal ～s 函授课 / I gave them a ～ in English. 我给他们上了一堂英语课。/ We have four ～s this morning. 今天早上我们有四节课。❷教训:All of us should draw a ～ from the accident. 我们都应从这次意外事故中吸取教训。

let / let / vt. (let, let) ❶允许,让(其后跟不带 to 的不定式,通常不用于被动句中):Will you ～ your children go to the cinema tonight? 你让你的孩子们今晚去看电影吗? / Her father won't ～ her go to dance. 她父亲不让她去跳舞。/ Let me see. 让我想想。❷(与第一人称或第三人称的代词连用,形成间接祈使句)让:Let's begin to sing, shall we? 咱们开始唱歌,好吗? / Let us both have a try. 让咱们两个都试一试吧。/ Let her do it at once. 让她马上去做这事。/ ～ **sb.**(**sth.**)**alone** 不理;不管:Let her alone. 别理她。～ **sb.**(**sth.**)**out** 放出;发出;说出:The woman ～ out a sigh. 那妇女叹了一口气。

let-down / ˈletˌdaun / n. [C] ❶失望,沮丧:The book was a bit of a ～. 这本书有些令人失望。❷减少;减弱;减退:the ～ of morale 士气的低落 / I felt a terrible ～ after the party. 聚会后我感到精疲力竭。

lethal / ˈliːθəl / adj. 致死的;足以致命的:ate a ～ dose of amphetamine 服用足以致命的安非他明 / ～ weapons 杀伤性武器

letter / ˈletə(r) / n. [C] ❶字母:26 ～s of the English language 英语的26个字母 ❷信件;函件:answer (reply to) a ～ 回信 / mail (post) a ～ 寄信 / open a ～ 拆信 / write a ～ home 写家信 / an express ～ 快信 / a registered ～ 挂号信

level / ˈlevl / n. ❶水平;标准:Her life has

dropped to a low ～. 她的生活已降到很低的水平。同 standard ❷水平面;水平线:How high are we above sea ～? 我们高出海平面多少? ❸高度;平地:This has attained the world ～. 这已达到世界水平。❹级别,等级:the same educational ～ 同等学力 同 status, position

lever / ˈliːvə(r) / n. [C] 杆,杠杆:economic ～ 经济杠杆

leverage / ˈliːvərɪdʒ / n. [U] ❶使用杠杆;杠杆效率,杠杆作用 ❷(为达目的而使用的)手段,方法;影响:By sending more troops the country wanted to have more political ～ over this area. 该国通过增派部队试图对这一地区施加更多的政治影响力。

levy / ˈlevi / I n. [C] ❶征税 ❷征收的税款:impose 10% ～ on tobacco 对烟草征收 10% 的税款 II vt. 征(税等);收(罚款等):～ a heavy fine for contempt of court 对藐视法庭的行为课以高额罚款 / ～ a duty on imports 对进口商品征收关税

liable / ˈlaɪəbl / adj. (只作表语) ❶有倾向的;易于…的:Take good care of her. She is ～ to colds. 好好照看她,她很容易感冒。同 apt, inclined ❷有责任的;有义务的:You should be ～ for the mistakes you made. 你应对你所犯的错误负责。同 responsible

liar / ˈlaɪə(r) / n. [C] 说谎者

liberal / ˈlɪbərəl / adj. ❶心胸宽大的;开明的;思想开朗的:He is over sixty but he is a man of ～ views. 他已经六十多了,但却是一个思想开朗的人。同 broad-minded, tolerant 反 narrow-minded ❷慷慨的;大方的:～ donation 慷慨捐赠 同 generous 反 mean ❸丰富的;富足的:～ supply 大量的供应 同 plentiful, ample 反 insufficient ❹自由主义的:They say that he has a ～ tongue. 他们说他是一个说话随便的人。派 liberalization n.

liberate / ˈlɪbəreit / vt. 解放;使脱离:Leaders should always think how to ～ the productive forces. 领导人应常考虑如何解放生产力。/ She is trying to ～ herself from worries. 她尽力消除自己的忧虑。同 free, discharge, release 派 liberation n.

liberty / ˈlɪbəti / n. [U] 自由;自由权:gain (get) one's ～ 获得自由 / civil ～ 公民自由权 / Everyone is at ～ to air his view at the meeting. 每个人都可以在会上自由发表意见。 同 freedom

librarian / laɪˈbreərɪən / n. 图书馆馆长(或馆员)

library / ˈlaɪbrərɪ / n. [C]图书馆

licence(-se) / ˈlaɪsns / I vt. 准许;认可:They ~d her to publish her new book. 他们批准她出版新书。同 allow II n. [C]执照;许可证:a bussiness ~ 营业执照 / apply for a ~ 申请执照 / grant (issue) a ~ 颁发执照 / revoke a ~ 吊销执照 / a marriage ~ 结婚许可证 / a driving ~ 驾驶执照 同 permit, certificate

lick / lɪk / vt. 舔:The cat likes to ~ its paws. 这猫老爱舔自己的爪子。

lid / lɪd / n. [C] ❶盖子 ❷眼睑

lie¹ / laɪ / vi. (lay/leɪ/, lain/leɪn/, lying) ❶卧,躺:~ on one's back (side)仰卧(侧卧) / She is lying in bed. 她躺在床上。同 rest 反 stand ❷位于(某地):Japan ~ s to the east of China. 日本位于中国以东。同 sit, exist

用法
> lie 意为"躺",不及物动词,其过去式与 lay (放)的原形相同。

lie² / laɪ / I vi. (lying) 说谎:He ~d to me. 他对我说谎。II n. [C] 谎言;假话:Lies cannot cover up facts. 谎言掩盖不了事实。He never tells ~s to others. 他从不对人说假话。反 truth

life / laɪf / n. (pl. lives/laɪvz/) ❶生命;性命:~ quality 生命质量 / ~ science 生命科学 / ~ space 生活空间/ Where did ~ come from? 生命从何而来? How many lives were lost during the war? 这场战争中有多少人丧生? **take one's own ~** 自杀:She took her own ~ by jumping from the bridge into the river. 她从桥上跳河自杀。❷[C]一生;一辈子;终身:He has made revolution all his ~. 他干了一辈子革命。❸生活;生活方式:city ~ 城市生活 / family ~ 家庭生活/ independent ~ 独立生活 /a miserable ~ 悲惨生活 / a hard ~ 艰难的生活 / We are living a happy ~. 我们过着幸福生活。

lifetime / ˈlaɪftaɪm / I n. [C] ❶一生,终身,一辈子:We've only been here two days, but it seems like a ~. 我们在这里待了才两天,却好像过了一辈子似的。❷长时间,很久:We waited a ~ for the doctor's report. 我们等医生的

报告等了很长时间。II adj. 终身的,一生的:a ~ membership 终身会员/ **of a ~** 终身难遇的,千载难逢的:Winners of the competition will receive the tour of a ~. 这次竞争的获胜者会得到一次千载难逢的旅游机会。

lift / lɪft / I v. ❶举;抬;升高:This box is too heavy for me to ~. 这箱子太重,我抬不动。~ weight 举重 / ~ up one's eyes 向上看 / ~ prices 提高价格 / The airplane ~ed from the airport. 飞机从机场起飞。同 raise, elevate ❷竖立;竖起:The Monument to the People's Heroes ~ s majestically above Tian'anmen Square. 人民英雄纪念碑雄伟地竖立在天安门广场上。II n. ❶ 举起;抬起 ❷电梯:She got the job to operate the ~ in the teaching building. 她得到了在教学楼里开电梯的工作。同 elevator ❸搭便车:**give sb. a ~** 让某人搭车:I asked him to pull up by the side of the road to give me a ~. 我请他把车停在路边让我搭他的车。

light / laɪt / I v. (lit/lɪt/, lit 或 lighted, lighted) 点燃;照亮;使发光:~ a candle(lamp, cigarette)点燃蜡烛(灯、烟)/ ~ a fire 点火 / The streets were brightly lit up. 街上灯光明亮。Their houses are ~ed by the lamps. 他们的房屋用油灯照明。同 fire, burn, brighten 反 extinguish II adj. 轻的;明亮的;淡色的:~ in colour 颜色浅 /~ blue (green, red, brown)浅蓝(浅绿、淡红、浅褐) / The box is surprisingly ~. 这箱子轻得出奇。III n. 光亮;光线;光源;发光物:The sun gives us ~. 太阳给我们带来光明。/ We want more ~ in this room. 我们这个房间需要更多的光亮。/ turn on (off) a ~ 开灯(关灯)/the traffic ~s 交通灯(红绿灯) 同 ray, beam, brightness 派 lightly adv.

lighter / ˈlaɪtə(r) / n. [C]打火机;点火器

lighten / ˈlaɪtn / vt. 照亮;使明亮:There is a lamp on the wall to ~ the path to the toilet. 墙上有一盏灯照亮去厕所的路。同 brighten, shine 反 darken, shade

lightning / ˈlaɪtnɪŋ / n. [U] 闪电:a ~ rod 避雷针 / a ~ war 闪电战 / Lightning plays in the sky. 空中电光闪闪。/ I saw a flash of ~ in the sky. 我看见天空中一道闪电。

light-year / ˈlaɪtjɪə(r), ˌlaɪtˈjɜː(r) / n. [C] ❶ 光年(指光在一年中经过的距离,约合 95 000 亿千米) ❷很大的差距;遥远的距离;很长的

时间：Today's computers are ～s ahead of older ones in power and memory. 现在的计算机在性能和存储方面已遥遥领先于老式的计算机。

like / laɪk / Ⅰ v. ❶喜欢；爱好：She ～s singing and dancing. 她喜欢唱歌跳舞。同 enjoy, appreciate 反 dislike ❷希望；想：I would (should) ～ the problem to be discussed in public. 我希望公开讨论这个问题。同 want, wish Ⅱ adj. 相似的；同样的；像：The two brothers are very ～. 这两弟兄长得很像。/ Like father, ～ son. 有其父必有其子。反 different Ⅲ prep. 像，如：He looks ～ an artist. 他看上去像个艺术家。/ What's the weather ～ today? 今天天气怎样？Ⅳ n. 相似的人或物：Like attracts ～. 物以类聚。/ Like knows ～. 英雄识英雄。/ Like for ～. 以牙还牙。/ We have met the ～s of you before. 我们以前碰到过像你这样的人。

likely / 'laɪkli / adj. 有希望的；有可能的；可能发生的：It's hardly ～ to finish it within a week for me. 我不可能在一周内将这事干完。/ It is ～ that he will win. 他很可能会赢。同 probable, possible

likeness / 'laɪknɪs / n. ❶[C]肖像，画像，照片；相似物：take sb.'s ～给某人画肖像/This statue is a good ～ of the leader. 这座雕像非常逼真地塑造了这位领袖的形象。❷[U]相像，相似：The two sisters bear a striking ～ to each other. 这两姐妹长得一模一样。

likewise / 'laɪkwaɪz / adv. 同样地；照样地：He fulfilled his task and I did ～. 他完成了任务，我也完成了。

lime / laɪm / n. [U]石灰

limestone / 'laɪmstəʊn / n. [U] 石灰石

limit / 'lɪmɪt / Ⅰ vt. 限制；限定：Try to ～ your talk within five minutes. 请尽量在五分钟之内把话说完。同 confine Ⅱ n. 限制；界限：They set a ～ of 35 to the number of passengers. 他们把乘客人数限制在 35 人。同 restriction 派 limitation n.

limited / 'lɪmɪtɪd / adj. 有限的；被限制的：We should make good use of our ～ resources. 我们应当很好地利用我们有限的资源。同 confined, constrained 反 limitless, unlimited

limousine / 'lɪməziːn / n. 大型豪华轿车；高级轿车

limp / lɪmp / vi. 蹒跚；跛行：The wounded soldier ～ed off the battle field. 那位负伤的战士一瘸一拐地离开了战场。

line / laɪn / Ⅰ n. [C] ❶线；绳；线路：the fishing ～ 钓鱼线 / telephone ～s 电话线 / Hang the clothes on the ～. 把衣服晾在绳子上。/ The ～ is busy. Please dial later. 线路正忙，请待会儿再拨。同 thread, string, wire ❷线条：Draw a ～ from A to B. 从 A 到 B 画一条线。❸（人或物的）排，列：a ～ of trees (chairs, people) 一排树（一排椅子，一列人）同 row / in ～ with 与……一致；按照；符合：The behavior of a student should be in ～ with his school's rule. 学生的举止行为应当符合校规。Ⅱ v. 沿……排成行；使……成行：We ～d up to buy tickets. 我们排队买票。

linear / 'lɪniə(r) / adj. ❶线的；直线的；线形的：a ～ arrangement 直线排列 ❷成一直线的；在线上的 ❸长度的：a unit of ～ measure 长度度量单位

linen / 'lɪnɪn / n. 亚麻布；亚麻布制品

liner / 'laɪnə(r) / n. [C]班轮；班机：Which ～ do you take to Shanghai? 你乘哪班飞机去上海？同 plane, ship

linger / 'lɪŋgə(r) / vi. ❶（因不愿离开而）继续逗留，留恋，徘徊：The people ～ed at the door with a long good-bye. 人们在门口依依不舍，久久不肯离去。/ They ～ed over their coffee for a few minutes. 他们又喝了几分钟咖啡。❷继续存留；缓慢消失：Doubts ～ed in my mind. 我始终不能消除心中的疑团。

linguistic / lɪŋ'gwɪstɪk / adj. 语言的；语言学的：a ～ science 语言科学 / Her mother thinks that she has strong ～ competence. 她母亲认为她的语言能力很强。

linguistician / lɪŋgwɪs'tɪʃn / n. [C]语言学家

linguistics / lɪŋ'gwɪstɪks / n. [U]语言学

linkage / 'lɪŋkɪdʒ / n. ❶[U]连接，连合 ❷关联，联系：a ～ between cause and effect 因果关系／develop ～s with the institutes abroad 与外国学术机构建立联系

link / lɪŋk / Ⅰ v. 连接；联系：They ～ed up the two areas by telephone. 他们用电话使两个地区连接起来。/ The new company ～ed itself with several older ones for self-protection. 那家新公司与几家较老的公司联合以保护自己。同 attach, connect Ⅱ n. 联系；连接：I can't find the ～s of connection between the two events. 我找不出这两件事情之间的联系。/ They are building a railway ～ from the port to the interior. 他们正修一条铁路把港口与内地连接起来。同 communication, connection

lion / ˈlaɪən / n. [C] 狮子

lip / lɪp / n. [C] 嘴唇；bite one's ～ 咬嘴唇

lipstick / ˈlɪpstɪk / n. 唇膏；口红

liquid / ˈlɪkwɪd / I n. 液体；The patient could only consume ～s. 那病人只能吃流质食品。同 fluid, water II adj. 液体的；流动的；I have never seen the ～ state of this material. 我从未见过这种物质的液体状态。同 fluid, watery

liquor / ˈlɪkə(r) / n. [U] 酒；汁 同 drink, alcohol

list / lɪst / I n. [C] 名单；目录；一览表；a shopping ～ 购物单 / a name ～ 名单 / a check ～ 清单 / make a ～ 造表 / a ranking ～ 排行榜 / write out a ～ 列表 / He headed the ～ in the examination. 他考试名列第一。同 roll, index II vt. 把…列成表；列举；Li Ming was ～ed as a candidate. 李明被列为候选人。

listen / ˈlɪsn / vi. 倾听；留心听；We ～ed but heard nothing. 我们留心听，可什么也没听见。/ Listen to the teacher. 听老师讲。/ He ～s to the radio at half past six every morning. 他每天早晨六点半听收音机。/ ～ **in to** 听广播；Did you ～ in to the broadcasting programme last night? 你昨晚听广播节目了吗? 派 listener n.

literacy / ˈlɪtərəsi / n. [U] ❶识字，读写能力；有文化；a national agency for adult ～ 国家级成人扫盲机构 ❷了解；通晓；Computer literacy is obligatory for college students. 大学生必须懂电脑。

literal / ˈlɪtərəl / adj. ❶文字(上)的；字面的；There are still some ～ errors in your report. 你的报告中还有一些文字错误。❷忠实于原文的；逐字的；It is a kind of ～ translation. 这是一种直译。同 word-for-word

literally / ˈlɪtərəli / adv. 逐字地；He translated the report into English ～. 他逐字逐句地把报告译成了英语。同 word-for-word

literary / ˈlɪtərəri / adj. 文学上的；书本的；My sister likes ～ works very much. 我姐姐非常喜爱文学作品。His speech is too ～. 他的讲话太书卷子气。

literate / ˈlɪtərət / I adj. 能读会写的；有文化的 同 bookish, cultivated 反 illiterate II n. [C] 有文化的人

literature / ˈlɪtrətʃə(r) / n. [U] 文学；文学作品；Chinese ～ 中国文学 / classical ～ 古典文学 / contemporary ～ 当代文学 / folk ～ 民间文学 / popular ～ 通俗文学 / the Nobel Literature Prize 诺贝尔文学奖 / The girl read a great amount of ～ after class. 那个女孩在课外阅读了大量文学作品。

litre(-er) / ˈliːtə(r) / n. [C] 升(容量单位)

litter / ˈlɪtə(r) / I n. [U] 废物；垃圾；The room is in a ～. 房间一片杂乱。同 rubbish, disorder II vt. 乱扔；乱丢；把…弄得乱七八糟；Please don't ～! 请勿乱丢杂物! 反 tidy

little / ˈlɪtl / I adj. (less 或 lesser, least) ❶小的(与 big 相对)；a pretty ～ house 一所漂亮的小房子 / a poor ～ girl 一个可怜的小姑娘 ❷(指时间、距离等)短的；Won't you stay a ～ while with me? 你不愿意陪我一会儿吗? ❸少许的，少量的(修饰不可数名词)；I have very ～ time for reading. 我很少有时间读书。/ Will you have a ～ water? 你要喝点水吗? / I can speak a ～ English. 我会讲点英语。 II n. ❶少许；少量；She eats ～ for breakfast. 她早餐吃得很少。/ ～ **by** ～ 逐渐；He has become rich ～ by ～. 他渐渐富有起来。❷短时间；短距离；After a ～ while you will feel better. 过一会儿你会觉得舒服些。 III adv. (less 或 lesser, least) 很少；一点；He left ～ more than an hour ago. 他大约一小时前离开的。/ She slept very ～. 她睡得很少。

live¹ / lɪv / v. ❶生存；活着；The patient is still living. 病人还活着。The doctor said he could ～ to a hundred years. 医生说他可活到一百岁。同 exist 反 die / ～ **on** 靠…活着；He still ～s on his parents. 他仍然靠父母生活。/ We ～ on rice, fish and vegetables. 我们以大米、鱼和蔬菜为食。❷居住(与 in, at 连用)；Where do you ～? 你住在哪里? 我住在这条街的 50 号。/ She ～s in London. 她住在伦敦。同 reside ❸度过；过(生活)；They are living a comfortable life. 他们过着舒适的生活。同 lead

live² / laɪv / adj. ❶活的；有生命的；I saw some ～ fish in the basin. 我看到盆里有一些活

鱼。/ Do you know the ～ issue among the young? 你知道年轻人中的热门话题是什么吗？同 active, alive 反 dead ❷现场直播：The game will be televised (broadcast) ～ to the public. 这场比赛将向公众做现场直播。同 real

lively / ˈlaɪvli / adj. ❶生动的；活泼的；有生气的：She's as ～ as a kitten. 她快活得像只小猫。/ He has a ～ imagination. 他的想象力很丰富。同 active, energetic ❷逼真的；栩栩如生的：He can give a ～ description to what he saw. 他能把他见到的东西生动地描述出来。同 vivid

liver / ˈlɪvə(r) / n. [C]肝，肝脏

living / ˈlɪvɪŋ / Ⅰ n. [U]生计；生活：the standard of ～ 生活水平 / The cost of ～ in big cities is very high. 大城市里的生活费用很高。/ He makes (gains, earns, gets) his ～ as a teacher. 他以教书为生。同 existence, income Ⅱ adj. 活着的；现存的：～ languages 现用语言 / ～ beings 生物 同 existing, alive

living-room / ˈlɪvɪŋˈruːm / n. [C]起居室；客厅：He slept in the ～ last night. 昨晚他在客厅里睡觉。同 sitting-room

lizard / ˈlɪzəd / n. [C]蜥蜴

load / ləʊd / Ⅰ v. 装载；把…装上(车、船、飞机等)：The goods were ～ed upon a wagon. 这些货物被装上了车。/ The ship is ～ing for Shanghai. 这船正在上货，准备驶往上海。同 charge 反 unload Ⅱ n. [C] 负荷量；装载量：The aeroplane is capable of carrying a ～ of ten tons. 这架飞机的载重量达十吨。同 weight

loaf / ləʊf / n. (pl. loaves /ləʊvz/)一条面包：a ～ of bread 一条面包 / a white ～ 白面包

loan / ləʊn / n. [C]借出物；借款，贷款：government ～s 公债 / foreign ～s 外债 / domestic ～s 内债 / an agricultural ～ 农业贷款 / an interest-free ～ 无息贷款 / He came here for a ～. 他到这儿来借钱。同 credit

lobby / ˈlɒbi / n. [C](剧场、旅馆等的)前厅，大厅 同 corridor, passage

lobster / ˈlɒbstə(r) / n. [C]虾；龙虾

local / ˈləʊkəl / adj. 地方的；当地的：the ～ doctor 当地医生 / ～ news 地方新闻 / ～ government 地方政府 / Sometimes he writes for the ～ newspaper. 有时候他也为地方报纸写稿。同 district, regional

locate / ləʊˈkeɪt / v. ❶确定…的地点；使…坐落于：The office is ～d in a business centre. 办事处位于商业中心。同 settle, set ❷探明，找出：You'd better ～ the city on a map first. 你最好先在地图上找到那个城市的位置。同 find, detect

location / ləʊˈkeɪʃn / n. [C]位置，场所，地点；(电影的)外景拍摄地：It is a good ～ for reading. 这是一个阅读的好地方。/ You may find the director at the film ～. 你可以在电影外景拍摄地找到导演。同 place, site

lock / lɒk / Ⅰ n. [C]锁：Does the key fit the ～? 这把钥匙能开这锁吗？The ～ won't catch. 这锁锁不上。Ⅱ v. 锁，锁上，锁住：The door ～s automatically. 这门会自动锁上。/ The door will not ～ with his key. 他的钥匙锁不上这扇门。

locker / ˈlɒkə(r) / n. [C]柜，小室；(船上的)储藏室；小舱：You can rent a ～ and put your clothes in it. 你可以租一个保管箱放衣物。同 closet, cabinet

locomotive / ˌləʊkəˈməʊtɪv / n. [C]机车；火车头

locust / ˈləʊkəst / n. [C] 蝗虫

lodge / lɒdʒ / n. [C]门房；传达室；山林小屋

loft / lɒft / n. [C] ❶阁楼；顶楼 ❷(教堂或大厅的)楼厢 ❸(仓库、商业建筑物等的)顶层，天台 ❹天台工作室；天台房屋

log / lɒg / n. [C] ❶原木；木料：The cabin is built with ～s. 小屋是用圆木建造的。同 timber, wood ❷航海(飞行)日志

logic / ˈlɒdʒɪk / n. [U]逻辑；逻辑学：What he said is of great ～. 他所说的很合逻辑。

logical / ˈlɒdʒɪkəl / adj. 逻辑(上)的；符合逻辑的；合乎常理的：We have reached a ～ conclusion. 我们得出了一个符合逻辑的结论。/ What he did is ～. 他所做的是合乎常理的。同 rational, reasonable, coherent 反 illogical, irrational

logician / ləˈdʒɪʃn / n. [C]逻辑学家

lonely / ˈləʊnli / adj. 孤独的，寂寞的；偏僻的，荒凉的：a ～ traveller 孤单的旅行者 / a ～ house 偏僻的屋子 / a ～ village 荒凉的村庄 / a ～ girl 孤寂的女孩 同 alone, deserted

long¹ / lɒŋ / Ⅰ adj. (空间或时间)长的：How ～ is the river? 这条河有多长？/ He hasn't been here for a ～ time. 他好久都没到这儿来了。同 short Ⅱ n. 长时间：The work won't take ～. 这工作不会花太长时间。Ⅲ *adv.* 长久地;长时间地;很久(以前)地:Stay as ～ as you like. 你愿意待多久就待多久。/ I can't wait any ～er. 我不能再等了。 反 short

long² / lɒŋ / *v.* 渴望:We are ～ing for peace. 我们渴望和平。/He has been ～ing to see his son. 他一直渴望见到他的儿子。 同 want, desire

longevity / lɒnˈdʒevɪti / *n.* [U] ❶长寿,长命:A bowl of noodles on one's birthday is a wish for ～. 过生日吃碗面条是祝愿长寿的表示。❷寿命

longitude / ˈlɒndʒɪtjuːd / *n.* 经线;经度:at a ～ of 125 degrees east 在东经 125 度

long-term / ˈlɒŋˈtɜːm / *adj.* 长期的;长期生效的:～ plans 长期计划/Not enough is known about the drug's ～ side effect. 有关此药的长期副作用至今所知不多。

look / lʊk / Ⅰ *v.* 看,瞧,望:We ～ed but saw nothing. 我们看了,但什么也没看见。/ ～ **after** 照料,照管:John's mother told him to ～ after his younger brother. 约翰的母亲叫他照顾弟弟。～ **at** 看:Please ～ at the blackboard. 请看黑板。～ **back** 回顾:As he ～ed back,he felt his life was good. 他回顾过去,觉得日子过得很好。～ **down on** 轻视,不看在眼里:Mary ～ed down on her classmates. 玛丽看不起她的同班同学。～ **for** 寻找,寻求:You are ～ing for trouble. 你在自找麻烦。～ **forward to** 期待,盼望:We are ～ing forward to the vacation. 我们正盼望着假期来临。～ **into** 调查,研究,视察:I'll certainly ～ into that right away. 我一定会马上调查此事。～ **like** 好像,像:He ～s like an honest man. 他看起来像个诚实的人。～ **out** 小心,当心:Look out for the train. 小心火车。～ **over** 检查,视察;观看;研究:Would you mind ～ing over my exercises? 请你检查一下我的作业好吗?～ **through** 浏览,温习,复习:Look through your notes before the examination. 考试前温习你的笔记。～ **up** 查寻:It is a good habit to ～ up new words in the dictionary. 在字典里查生词是好习惯。～ **up to** 尊敬,敬仰:She had taught for many years,and all her students ～ed up to her. 她教了多年书,她的所有学生都尊敬她。Ⅱ *n.* [C]看,望;外表,外观:May I have a ～ at it? 让我看一看好吗? I don't like her ～s. 我不喜欢她的样子。 同

appearance, glimpse

loop / luːp / *n.* [C]圈;环;环形物:The road makes a wide ～ around the building. 那条路围着大楼绕了一大圈。 同 circle, ring

loose / luːs / Ⅰ *adj.* ❶不紧的;宽松的:～-fitting clothes 宽大的衣服 ❷不牢的;松弛的:a ～ tooth 松动的牙齿 / a ～ window 不牢的窗子 Ⅱ *v.* 松开;释放,使无约束;使松弛:Loose the screw. 把螺丝钉松开。派 loosely *adv.* ;loosen *v.*

lord / lɔːd / *n.* (Lord)上帝:She always says,"Lord bless me!"她总爱说" 老天保佑"。

lorry / ˈlɒri / *n.* [C](英)载货卡车:The ～ is driving to the airport. 卡车正驶向机场。 同 truck

lose / luːz / *vt.* (lost /lɒst/, lost) ❶失去;丧失;损失:I have lost my umbrella. 我把雨伞弄丢了。/ He has lost his job. 他失业了。/ Don't ～ your temper. 不要发怒。 反 keep, gain ❷迷失(方向);错过:She lost her way in the strange city and took a taxi back to the hotel. 她在那个陌生的城市里迷失了方向,不得不乘出租车回旅馆。/ I nearly lost the opportunity. 我几乎错失了良机。❸失败;输:Our school basketball team lost the match. 我们的校篮球队比赛输了。 反 win/ ～ **sight of** 看不见:We lost sight of him in the crowd. 我们在人群中看不见他了。

loss / lɒs / *n.* [U]损失;遗失;输:The ～ of health would cause serious result. 失去健康会带来严重的后果。/ Can the company bear the ～ of a million dollars? 这家公司能承受 100 万美元的亏损吗? 同 waste, failure

lot / lɒt / *n.* ❶很多;许多:a ～ of(lots of)大量,许多:I have a ～ of new words to learn. 我有许多新词要记。/ She spent a ～ of time on her homework. 她花了很多时间做家庭作业。 同 many, much 反 little ❷签,阄;抽签:We may draw ～s to decide who will go. 我们可以抽签决定谁去。

辨析
a lot of 既可放在可数名词前,也可放在不可数名词前,表示"许多"之意。**many, a great many, a great number of** 修饰可数名词。**much, a great deal of** 修饰不可数名词。

lotion / ˈləʊʃn / *n.* (医学上的外用)洗剂;(化妆用的)润肤剂

lottery / ˈlɒtəri / *n.* 博彩;抽奖:run a ～ 发行

彩票 / The young man won 20 yuan in the ～. 那年轻人买彩票中了 20 元奖金。

lotus / ˈləʊtəs / n. 莲;荷;a ～ leaf 荷叶 / ～ flowers 荷花/ ～ roots 莲藕 / ～ seeds 莲子

loud / laʊd / Ⅰ adj. 大声的,高声的;喧闹的: He answered the question with ～ voice. 他大声回答问题。/ I can't bear your ～ cries. 你高声吵闹,我真受不了。 同 aloud, noisy Ⅱ adv. 大声地;高声地:Speak ～er, please. 请说大声点。同 loudly 派 loudly adv.

loudspeaker / ˌlaʊdˈspiːkə(r) / n. [C]扬声器

lounge / laʊndʒ / n. [C](旅馆等的)休息室;休息厅:a sun ～ 日光浴廊 / a VIP ～ 贵宾休息室 同 living-room, sitting-room

lovable / ˈlʌvbl / adj. 可爱的,惹人爱的,讨人喜欢的:a ～ child 可爱的孩子/She is really ～. 她确实讨人喜欢。

love / lʌv / Ⅰ vt. ❶爱;热爱:We ～ our country. 我们爱祖国。反 hate ❷喜欢;爱好: He ～s to ride a bike. 他喜欢骑自行车。She ～s playing the piano. 她喜欢弹钢琴。同 like,enjoy 反 hate Ⅱ n. [U] ❶喜爱;热爱;挚爱:a mother's ～ for her children 母爱 / for one's country 爱国 反 hatred ❷爱情;恋爱:**be in** ～ **with** 与…相爱:Mary is in ～ with Tom. 玛丽与汤姆相爱了。

lovely / ˈlʌvli / adj. 美丽的;动人的;可爱的:a ～ view 动人的景色 / ～ weather 好天气 / a ～ girl 可爱的小姑娘 同 beautiful,charming

lover / ˈlʌvə(r) / n. [C] ❶恋人,爱侣 ❷情人(尤指男性),情夫 ❸爱好者:an opera ～歌剧爱好者/He is a ～ of billiards and tall stories. 他喜欢打台球、讲荒诞故事。

low / ləʊ / adj. ❶低的;矮的:The moon was ～ in the sky. 月亮低挂在天空。同 short,反 tall, high ❷(指声音)不高的,低的:He speaks in a ～ voice. 他低声说话。❸(指量、度、价值等)低的,少的:a ～ temperature 低温 / ～ prices 低价

lower / ˈləʊə(r) / v. 放低;降低;减低:～ the flag 将旗降下 / ～ the rent of a house 减低房租 / ～ one's voice 降低声音/ The stocks ～ed in value. 股票跌价了。同 drop, decrease, reduce 反 raise, increase

lowercase / ˌləʊəˈkeɪs / Ⅰ adj. (字母)小写体;小写字母的 Ⅱ n. [U]小号字体

lowly / ˈləʊli / Ⅰ adj. ❶卑微的;地位低下的:a girl of ～ birth 出身卑微的姑娘/a ～ position 低卑的地位 ❷谦卑的;卑恭的;恭顺的: learn to be ～ and reverent 学会待人谦卑恭敬 Ⅱ adv. 谦卑地,恭顺地

loyal / ˈlɔɪəl / adj. 忠诚的;忠心的:He is ～ to his country. 他忠于祖国。/ The students are ～ to their ideals. 学生们忠于自己的理想。同 faithful 反 disloyal

loyalty / ˈlɔɪəlti / n. [U]忠诚;忠心:He pledged his ～ to the company. 他发誓对公司要忠心耿耿。同 faithfulness,devotion 反 disloyalty

lubricant / ˈluːbrɪkənt / n. ❶[C;U]润滑剂;润滑油 ❷[C]用以减少摩擦的东西:a social ～社交润滑剂(指在社交中能起到拉拢关系作用的东西) Ⅱ adj. 润滑的:a ～ additive 润滑添加剂

lubricate / ˈluːbrɪkeɪt / vt. ❶使滑润;加润滑油于:～ the engine 给发动机上油 ❷使顺畅;缓和:～ relations between the warring factions 缓和交战双方间的关系

luck / lʌk / n. [U] (好或坏的)运气,机运:try one's ～, trust to ～ 碰运气 / Good ～ to you! 祝你顺利(或一路平安)! / May you have better ～ next time. 祝你下次走运。/ She has bad (ill, hard) ～. 她运气不佳。同 chance,fortune

lucky / ˈlʌki / adj. 幸运的;侥幸的:How ～ you are to have got the opportunity. 得到这个机会,你真幸运。同 favored, fortunate 反 unlucky, misfortune / I was ～ enough to meet him there. 我很幸运在那儿遇到了他。/ How ～ you are! 你多幸运!

luggage / ˈlʌgɪdʒ / n. [U]行李:He checked his ～ first. 他先寄存了行李。同 baggage, suitcases

lumber / ˈlʌmbə(r) / n. [U](无用的)杂物;木材,木料 同 wood, timber

luminous / ˈljuːmɪnəs / adj. ❶发光的,发亮的;反光的:a pair of ～ brown eyes 一双明亮的棕色眼睛/～ paint 发光漆(或涂料) ❷清楚的;易懂的:a ～ explanation 清楚的解释/She gave a ～ performance of the Mozart piano concerto. 她清晰地演奏了莫扎特的钢琴曲。

lump / lʌmp / n. ❶块;团:a ～ of clay 一块黏土 同 ball, mass ❷瘤;肿块:She has a bad ～ on the head. 她头上肿起一大块。同 swelling

lunar / ˈluːnə(r) / *adj.* 月球的；月亮的：the ～ calendar 阴历 反 solar

lunch / lʌntʃ / *n.* 午餐，午饭：We were at ～ when he called. 他来电话时，我们正在吃午饭。

luncheon / ˈlʌntʃən / *n.* (正式的)午餐，午宴 同 lunch

lung / lʌŋ / *n.* [C] 肺，肺脏

lure / ljʊə(r) / Ⅰ *n.* [C] ❶诱惑物，引诱物；引诱力，吸引力：The ～ of art was too strong to resist. 艺术的魅力让人无法抗拒。❷(诱捕动物等的)诱饵；圈子；鱼饵：Anglers use different ～s to catch different kinds of fish. 垂钓者用不同的诱饵来钓不同的鱼。Ⅱ *vt.* 吸引，引诱，诱惑：Life in the city ～d him away from home. 城里生活诱使他离开了家乡。/ Such prices ～d others into the business. 这样的价格吸引了其他一些人来购买。同 tempt

luxurious / lʌgˈʒʊəriəs / *adj.* 奢侈的；豪华的：He stayed in a ～ hotel. 他住在一家豪华宾馆里。同 costly，expensive

luxury / ˈlʌkʃəri / *n.* [U] 奢侈；豪华：He lives in ～ but works hard. 他生活奢侈，但工作勤奋。

lymph / lɪmf / *n.* [U] 淋巴

lyric / ˈlɪrɪk / Ⅰ *adj.* ❶(古诗)歌一般的；适于吟唱的：a ～ drama 歌剧 ❷(诗歌或歌曲等)抒情的 Ⅱ *n.* [C] ❶抒情诗 ❷歌词

lyricist / ˈlɪrɪsɪst / *n.* [C] ❶歌词作者 ❷抒情诗人

L

M m

ma'am / mæm, mɑːm, məm / *n.* [C]夫人；太太；女士：A gentleman has called , ~. 有位先生打来电话,夫人。

machine / mə'ʃiːn / *n.* [C]机器；机械：a washing ~ 洗衣机 / a vending ~ 自动售货机 / a video-game ~ 电子游戏机

machinery / mə'ʃiːnəri / *n.* (总称)机器；机械：procession ~ 精密仪器 / They installed some new ~ in the lab. 他们在实验室里安装了一些新机器。圆 apparatus, machines

macro / 'mækrəʊ / Ⅰ *adj.* 巨大的；极厚的；大量使用的：~ control 宏观控制 / ~ economy 宏观经济 / ~ education 宏观教育 / ~ management 宏观管理 Ⅱ *n.* 宏指令：~ coding 宏编码

macro- / 'mækrəʊ / (前缀)表示"长"、"大"、"宏"等：~ accounting 宏观会计学/ ~ economics 宏观经济学 / ~economy 宏观经济

macrocosm / 'mækrəʊˌkɒzəm / *n.* [C]❶整个宇宙,全宇宙；宏观世界：a cultural ~宏观文化/He desires , first, to see the spirit of the ~. 他最先渴望了解的是整个宇宙的灵魂。❷全域；大而复杂的整体：No population is absolutely inert in the ~ of humanity. 在人类错综复杂的整体中,没有一个种族是绝对静止不变的。

mad / mæd / *adj.* (madder, maddest) ❶疯狂的；精神错乱的：a ~ dog 疯狗圆 crazy ❷非常激动的；失去理性的：They were ~ (at) missing the train. 他们没赶上火车,气得要命。派 madly *adv.* 疯狂地；极其

madam / 'mædəm / *n.* 夫人,太太,女士(对妇女的尊称)：Madam, will you take my seat? 太太,您坐我的座位好吗? / Madam Lee is from China. 李夫人来自中国。

made-up / ˌmeɪd'ʌp / *adj.* ❶编造的,虚构的：a ~ story 虚构的故事 ❷化妆过的；化了装的：She was heavily ~. 她化了浓妆。

magazine / ˌmægə'ziːn / *n.* [C]杂志；期刊：Most ~ s are published either weekly or monthly. 大多数杂志都是周刊或月刊。圆 periodical, journal

magic / 'mædʒɪk / Ⅰ *n.* [U]魔术；戏法：He is good at performing ~. 他很会表演魔术。Ⅱ *adj.* 有魔力的：a piece of ~ cloth 魔布 / a ~ lantern 幻灯 / This kind of medicine has a ~ effect. 这种药效果神奇。

magician / mə'dʒɪʃən / *n.* [C]魔术师

magistrate / 'mædʒɪstreɪt / *n.* [C]地方行政长官；地方法官：Her father is a ~. 她的父亲是县长。圆 officer, judge

magnet / 'mægnət / *n.* 磁石,磁铁；有吸引力的人或物：~ bar codes 条形码

magnate / 'mægneɪt, 'mægnɪt / *n.* [C]❶显贵,权贵；要人,大人物；富豪；企业巨头：a leading ~ in industrial circles 工业巨头/an oil ~石油大亨 ❷杰出人物,优秀人才：literary ~s 杰出的文人(或文章)

magnetic / mæg'netɪk / *adj.* 磁的；有磁性的：a ~ card 磁卡 / a ~ field 磁场 / a ~ suspension train 磁悬浮列车

magnetism / 'mægnɪˌtɪzəm / *n.* ❶[C；U]磁力,磁性：the mutual relations of the two ~两种磁力的相互关系/weakened ~ 弱化的磁性 ❷[U]魅力,吸引力：Of course any man might have rushed to save her, and reap the reward of her soft and grateful ~. 毫不奇怪,任何男人都会奋不顾身地营救她,并将她温柔、愉悦的迷人魅力当作褒赏。

magnificent / mæg'nɪfɪsənt / *adj.* 宏伟的；堂皇的：They visited the ~ Great Hall of the People when they were in Beijing. 在北京时他们参观了宏伟的人民大会堂。圆 splendid, grand

magnify / 'mægnɪfaɪ / *vt.* 放大,扩大；夸大：It can ~ the word 100 times. 它可以把字放大100倍。圆 enlarger

magnitude / 'mægnɪˌtjuːd / *n.* ❶[C；U](大小

或数量的)巨大，庞大；广大：the height, strength and ～ of a building 建筑物的高大宏伟 ❷[U]伟大；重大；重要(性)；紧迫(性)：two offences of a very different nature and by no means of equal ～两件性质不同、轻重不等的罪名/We could not carry out a project of this ～ without assistance. 没有外援我们无法完成如此重大的项目。/ of the first ～(在某些方面)极出色的，一流的；头等重要的，极其重要的：an affair of the first ～头等大事/an artist of the first ～一流的艺术家

maid / meɪd / n. [C]少女；女仆

mail / meɪl / n. 邮政；邮寄；信件；邮包：send a letter by air ～ 寄一封航空信 / a ～ box 邮箱 / a ～ man 邮递员 / a ～ train 邮件火车/ Is there any ～ this morning? 今上午有邮件吗? 同 post，letters

main / meɪn / Ⅰ adj. 主要的；重要的：Can you grasp the ～ idea of his report? 你能抓住他报告的主要意思吗? / the ～ streets of a town 市内主要街道 / my ～ arguments 我的主要论点 同 chief，principal Ⅱ n. 主要部分：**in the ～** 大体上；就一般而论：In the ～, the book is not interesting. 大体上说来，那本书没趣。派 mainly adv.

mainframe / 'meɪnˌfreɪm / n. [C](计算机的)主机，中央处理机

mainland / 'menˌlænd, 'meɪnlænd / n. [C](the ～) 大陆，本土：I'll go to the ～ from the small island by a ferry. 我将乘轮渡从小岛到大陆去。

mainstream / 'meɪnˌstriːm / Ⅰ n. [C]主要倾向；主流；主流派风格：He is far from the ～ of Russian culture. 他与俄罗斯主流文化相距甚远。Ⅱ adj. 主流的；主要倾向的；主流派的：～ Hollywood products 好莱坞主流产品

maintain / meɪn'teɪn / v. 维持；保持；维修；保养：They ～ friendly relations with each other. 他们相互保持友好关系。/ The police are working hard to ～ public order. 警察努力工作以维持社会秩序。/ He is ～ing a machine. 他正在维修机器。同 keep，preserve

majesty / 'mædʒəsti / n. [U]崇高，尊严；王权：We hope to pay our respects to Her Majesty. 我们希望谒见女王陛下。

major / 'meɪdʒə(r) / Ⅰ adj. 较大的，较重要的：the ～ portion 主要部分 / Your car needs ～ repairs. 你的车需要大修。同 chief，greater Ⅱ n. [C]主修科目；某专业的学生：My sister wants to take economics as her ～. 我姐姐想专修经济学。/ He is a history ～. 他是历史专业的学生。Ⅲ vi. 主修；专攻：He is ～ing in business administration. 他主修工商管理课程。

majority / mə'dʒɒrəti / n. 多数；大多数：His proposition was supported by the great ～ of the students. 他的提议得到大多数学生的支持。同 mass 反 minority

用法
❶majority 主要修饰可数名词，很少修饰不可数名词，可以说 the majority of students，通常不说 the majority of literature。❷majority 作主语时，谓语动词用单数、复数均可：The majority were (was) in favour of the plan. 大多数人赞成这个计划。The majority of doctors believe that smoking is harmful to health. 大多数医生认为吸烟有害健康。

make / meɪk / Ⅰ v. (made/meɪd/，made) ❶造造；制造：Many boys like to ～ model planes. 很多男孩都喜欢制作飞机模型。同 produce ❷获得；挣得；赚：He ～s a profit of 2,500 yuan a month. 他每月赚 2500 元利润。同 gain，win，earn ❸让；使；使得：Experience in the countryside made him know much. 在农村的经历使他懂得了许多。/ **a dive for** 向…猛冲；冲过去拿：The owner made a dive for the rejected clothes. 店主冲向那堆挑剩的衣服。～ **a living** 谋生；度日：He ～s a living as a teacher. 他当教师谋生。～ **a mistake** 犯错误：You made a mistake in trusting him too much. 你错在过分相信他。～ **a noise** 吵闹：It made a noise like a travelling train. 它发出像火车一样的隆隆声。～ **a promise** 答应；许下诺言：He made a promise to help us，but he didn't keep his promise. 他许诺帮助我们，但不遵守诺言。～ **an apology to sb.** 向某人道歉：If you are late for class，you should ～ an apology to the teacher either at the time or after class. 你如果上课迟到，就应在当时或课后向教师道歉。**be made of (from)** 由…制成：The table cloth is made of cotton. 这桌布是棉

制的。～ **faces** (**a face**) 做鬼脸；The sick boy swallowed the medicine and made a face. 这个病孩儿吞下药just做了个鬼脸。～ **friends with** 与…交朋友：Within two days she made friends with everyone on the boat. 两天里她和全船的人都成了朋友。～ **fun of** 取笑：I had thought they were making fun of me. 我原以为他们在取笑我。～ **into** 制成；使转变为：Bamboo can also be made into paper. 竹子也可以造纸。～ **one's mark** 成功；出名：Shakespeare made his mark as a playwright. 莎士比亚是作为戏剧作家闻名于世的。～ **one's point** 阐明观点；证明观点：Darwin made his point by giving a lot of proofs. 达尔文以大量证据证明了他的观点。～ **one's way** 排除困难前进：As soon as he saw us, Henry made his way through the crowd to greet us. 亨利一看到我们就从人群中挤出来欢迎我们。～ **progress** 取得进步：He made such progress that before long he began to write articles in English for an American newspaper. 他进步很快，不久就开始用英文给一家美国报纸写稿。～ **repairs** 修补：The swimming pool will not be open today because some people are making repairs. 游泳池今天不开放，因为一些人正在做修补工作。～ **room for** 给…腾出地方：Can you ～ room for this guest at the dinner table? 您可以在餐桌上为这位客人腾出点地方吗？～ **sentences with** 用…造句：Please ～ sentences with these phrases after class. 请课后用这些短语造句。～ **... to one's measure** 照某人的尺寸做：We have these suits for you to choose from, or I can ～ you one to your measure. 我们有这些衣服供你选择，或者我可以按你的尺寸给你做一件。～ **up** 组成；完成：The committee is made up of seven members. 委员会由七人组成。She had a lot of homework to ～ up yesterday. 她昨天有许多作业要完成。～ **up one's mind** 下决心：They made up their minds to sell the house. 他们下决心把房子卖掉。～ **up for** 弥补：We had to work twice as hard to ～ up for the lost time. 我们不得不加倍努力以弥补失去的时间。Ⅱ *n.* 制造；产品的品牌：They bought a car with the same ～ of mine. 他们买了一辆品牌和我的一样的小汽车。

make 作使役动词时，若它的宾语补足语是不定式就要省略 to，但如果 make 用在被动语态中，不定式作为主语补足语，就要把 to 补充出来：His jokes made her laugh. 他的笑话使她发笑。She was made to laugh by his jokes. 她被他的笑话逗笑了。

辨析

❶**make** 意为"生产；制作"，常用词，指用原料或零件组合成为一件有用的产品：make bricks (bread, a coat, a paper kite) 制砖（制作面包，做衣服，做风筝）。❷**manufacture** 意为"加工；大批量生产"，尤指用机器大量生产：The firm manufactures electrical apparatuses. 这个公司生产电气设备。**produce** 意为"生产"，强调所制造的产品数量，而不像 manufacture 暗示大批生产的程序：Let us use the new methods of producing more crops from the same amount of land. 让我们运用在同样面积的土地上种植更多农作物的新方法。The young writer produces a new novel every two years. 这位年轻作家每两年写一部新小说。❸**make of** 和 **make from** 都表示用原料做成某样东西，一般来说，若原料只发生物理变化就用 make of，否则用 make from：The desk is made of wood. 书桌用木材制成。（仍旧看得出木头）Paper is made from wood. 纸由木材制成。（已经看不出木材）

make-up / ˈmeɪkʌp / *n.* (*pl.* makes-up) ❶[C] 补考：If you didn't pass the examination, you may take a ～ at the end of the term. 如果你考试不及格，你可以在期末参加补考。❷[U] 化妆，化妆品：My sister never wears ～. 我姐姐从来不化妆。❸构造，组成：the ～ of the football team 足球队的组成 ❹性格，气质：It partly depends on your genetic ～. 这部分取决于你的遗传性格。

making / ˈmeɪkɪŋ / *n.* ❶[U] 制作，制造，生产；创作：shoe ～ 制鞋/film ～ 电影摄制/The ～ of a violin requires great skill. 小提琴的制作需要很高的技巧。❷素质，要素；必备条件；潜力，能力：The story has all the ～ of a great movie. 这个故事具备一部优秀影片的所有条件。/ be of one's own ～ 自己造成：The trouble here is of her own ～. 这里的麻烦是她自找的。/ These thoughts are not of his own ～. 这些并非是他自己的想法。**in the** ～ 在制造中；在形成中；在发展中；在酝酿中：The slogans and concepts are everywhere, and they add up to a new American economy in the ～. 口号与理念随处可见,这些都是正在形成的美国新经济的组成部分。

malady / 'mælədi / n. [C](身体的)不适,疾病;(慢性)病,痼病: After years of life in the tropics, he was plagued by one exhausting ～ after another. 他经年累月地待在热带丛林里,要命的疾病接踵而至。/ To be ignorant of one's ignorance is the ～ of the ignorant. 无视自身的无知是无知者的通病。

malaria / mə'leəriə / n. [U]疟疾: Not many people suffer from ～ now. 现在患疟疾的人很少。

male / meil / adj. 男的;男性的: a deep voice 浑厚的男声 圎 manly 反 female

malfunction / mæl'fʌŋkʃn / I n. [C]功能失效,机能失常;故障;事故: The pilot waited for the instruments to regain power, but the ～ continued. 飞行员等待仪表恢复动力,可故障仍旧。II vi. 运转失灵,发生故障;显示功能失常: One of the motors has ～ed. 有一台发动机出了故障。

malice / 'mælis / n. [U]歹念,恶意;怨恨,憎恶: It was not brought about by accident, but by the ～ of Tom. 事情的发生绝非偶然,而是汤姆故意的鬼。/ I bear you no ～. 我对你毫无恶意。 派 malicious adj.

mall / mɔːl / n. [C]大型餐饮购物中心;购物街: People always buy their daily necessities at the shopping ～. 人们总爱在购物中心购买日用品。 圎 shop

malt / mɔːlt, mɒlt / n. ❶[U]麦芽: ～ and wheat 麦芽和小麦 ❷[U;C](一份)麦芽酒 ❸[U;C]麦乳精: a vanilla ～ and a chocolate ～ 一份香草麦乳精和一份巧克力麦乳精

mammal / 'mæml / n. [C]哺乳动物

man / mæn / n. (pl. men/men/) ❶[C]男人: a tall ～ 一个高大的男子 ❷人,人类(不加冠词): Only ～ knows how to cook. 只有人类懂得烹饪。

manage / 'mænidʒ / v. ❶管理;处理: ～ a company 管理公司/ She ～d the problem well. 她把问题处理得很好。 圎 run, handle ❷设法;对付: He ～d to accomplish his work ahead of time. 他设法提前完成了工作。 圎 succeed 反 fail

management / 'mænidʒmənt / n. ❶[U]管理;

经营;处理: ～ fees (costs)管理费/ ～ modernization 管理现代化/ closed ～ 封闭式管理/ goal ～ 目标管理/ They introduced scientific ～ in their factory. 他们公司引进了科学的管理方法。 圎 administration, running ❷[C]管理部门;管理阶层;资方: The ～ held a meeting to discuss the problem. 管理方召开了一个会议讨论这个问题。 圎 executives, managers

manager / 'mænidʒə(r) / n. [C]经理;管理人: a branch ～ 部门经理/ a general ～ 总经理/ a sales ～ 销售经理/ a service ～ 服务部经理 圎 director, administrator

mango / 'mæŋɡəʊ / n. ❶[C;U]芒果 ❷[C]芒果树

manifest / 'mænɪfest / I adj. 明显的,明白的,明了的: be ～ to every man's eye 显而易见的/ An will be made ～, only one answer exists to each question. 很明显,一个问题只有一个答案。/ As ～ in his music, Ives's faith was real and transcendental. 正像他的音乐所明晰表达出的那样,艾夫斯的信念是真实、超脱的。 II vt. 明白显示,清楚表明;表露,流露(情感等): He ～ ed his approval with a hearty laugh. 他用一阵发自内心的笑声清楚地表明了赞同的意思。

manipulate / mə'nipjʊˌleit / vt. ❶(机智、巧妙或狡猾地)安排;处理;利用;影响;控制: ～ the plot 安排情节/ It is a simple matter to ～ such a situation. 应付这样一个局面很简单。 ❷熟练地操作,巧妙地使用: ～ the steering wheel 熟练地操作方向盘/ ～ a pair of scissors 巧用剪刀 派 manipulation n.

mankind / mæn'kaind / n. [U]人类;(总称)人: War is one of the greatest evils of ～. 战争是人类最大的灾祸之一。 圎 man, humankind

manly / 'mænli / adj. 有男子气概的;男人的 圎 manful, manlike 反 female, cowardly

man-made / 'mænˌmeid / adj. 人造的,人的;人为的: a ～ satellite 人造卫星/ ～ accidents 人为事故

manner / 'mænə(r) / n. [C] ❶方式;方法: Do it in this ～. 用这种方法做。 圎 method, means, way ❷态度,举止(用单数): I don't like his ～. 我不喜欢他的态度。 She has a warm and friendly ～ to all of us. 她对我们大家的态度热情友好。 圎 behavior, conduct ❸社交行为;礼貌(常用复数): have good (bad) ～ s

有(没有)礼貌／It is bad ～s to stare at people. 瞪着眼睛看人是不礼貌的。同 behavior,conduct

manpower ／'mænpaʊə(r)／ n. 人力；劳动力：～ resources 人力资源／～ surplus 劳动力过剩 同 labor

mansion ／'mænʃn／ n. ❶[C]豪宅，宅邸；大厦：the governor's ～总督的官邸／I spent two nights in the ～. 我在大厦里过了两宿。❷公寓大厦，公寓楼；公寓楼中的套房：Sloane Avenue ～s 斯隆尼大街公寓楼／In my father's house are many ～s. 我父亲的房子里有多套住房。

manual ／'mænjʊəl／ Ⅰ adj. ❶用手的；人工的；体力的：～ labor 体力劳动 同 hand-operated,physical Ⅱ n.[C]手册，指南：an owner's ～ 用户指南／You'd better first read the instruction ～ of the machine carefully. 你最好先仔细看看这台机器的使用说明书。同 guide,instructions 派 manually adv.

manufacture ／ˌmænjʊ'fæktʃə(r)／ Ⅰ vt. 以机器制造；加工 同 produce,make Ⅱ n.[U]制造；生产：～ industry 制造业／～ with order's materials 来料加工／Have you got a ～ license? 你领到生产许可证了吗？同 production,making

manufacturer ／ˌmænjʊ'fæktʃərə(r)／ n.[C]制造者；制造商；制造厂；制造公司 同 maker,producer

manure ／mə'njʊə(r)／ n.[U]肥料；粪肥

manuscript ／'mænjʊskrɪpt／ n.[C]手稿；原稿；底稿：a novel in ～ 小说手稿／He sent his ～ to a publisher. 他把原稿送交出版商。同 script

many ／'meni／ Ⅰ adj.（more/mɔː/，most /məʊst/)许多的，多的：a good ～ 很多的，相当多的／～ a 很多：Many a man would welcome the opportunity. 许多人要利用这个机会。同 numerous,countless 反 few Ⅱ pron. 许多；～ of them 他们中的许多人 同 lots 反 few

> **辨析**
> **many** 和 **much** 都表示"很多"，many 用来修饰可数名词，much 用来修饰不可数名词；many books 许多书，much water 很多水。

map ／mæp／ n.[C]地图；示意图：There is a world ～ on the wall. 墙上有一幅世界地图。同 chart,graph

maple ／'meɪpl／ n.[C]枫树

marathon ／'mærəθən／ n.[C]马拉松赛跑

marble ／'mɑːbl／ n. 大理石；大理石艺术品：a ～ statue 大理石雕像

March ／mɑːtʃ／ n.(略作 Mar.)三月

march ／mɑːtʃ／ Ⅰ v. 前进；行军：The troops ～ed against the enemy. 部队朝着敌人方向进军。They worked hard and ～ed from victory to victory. 他们辛勤工作，从胜利走向胜利。同 walk,progress Ⅱ n. 前进；行军：the Long March 长征／All of us can sing *March of the Volunteers*. 我们都会唱《义勇军进行曲》。同 advance,parade,walk

margin ／'mɑːdʒɪn／ n. 页边的空白；边缘：There are some notes written in the ～. 书页边缘记有笔记。

marginal ／'mɑːdʒɪnəl／ adj. ❶页边的，页边空白处的；边注的：～ notes 页边注释 ❷边缘的，沿的；边缘地区的：a ～ piece of land 边缘地区的一块地 ❸最低限度的，接近承受边缘的；勉强够格的：a ～ majority 微弱(或勉强)多数

marine ／mə'riːn／ adj. 海的，海产的；航海的：a ～ environmental science 海洋环境科学／～ products 海产品

maritime ／'mærɪtaɪm／ adj. 海(上)的；海事的：Maritime Law 海洋法 同 oceanic

mark ／mɑːk／ Ⅰ n.[C] ❶记号；符号；标志：punctuation ～s 标点符号／the price ～ 价目标签／the trade ～ 商标／While reading he always makes a ～ where he has a question. 读书时他常在有疑问的地方做记号。同 sign,symbol ❷斑点；痕迹；疤痕：There are some dirty ～s on the wall. 墙上有一些污迹。同 stain ❸(考试的)分数：He got a full ～ in the English test. 英语考试他得了满分。同 score,grade Ⅱ v. 加标记，加符号；记分数：The teachers are ～ing examination papers. 老师们正在评阅考卷。同 score,grade 派 marked adj.；markedly adv.

market ／'mɑːkɪt／ n.[C] ❶市场；集市：～ economy 市场经济／～ demand 市场需求／～ easy 市场疲软／～ management 市场管理／There are many small ～s in the town. 镇里有许多小集市。同 mall,shop ❷销售；需求：a ～ department 销售部／～ channel 销售渠道／There is a very large ～ for cars in our city. 我

们城市里小汽车很畅销。同 demand

marketing / 'mɑ:kɪtɪŋ / n. [C] ❶销售学；市场推广：She majored in ～. 她专修市场营销。❷采购食品：Her husband did the ～ on Fridays. 她丈夫星期五负责买食物。

marriage / 'mærɪdʒ / n. 结婚；婚姻：early (late) ～ 早(晚)婚 / a ～ advertisement 征婚广告 / a ～ agent 婚姻介绍所 / Young people like group ～. 年轻人喜欢集体结婚。反 divorce 同 wedding

married / 'mærɪd / adj. 结婚的；已婚的：Is she ～? 她结婚了吗？同 wedded

marrow / 'mærəʊ / n. [U]髓；骨髓；脊髓：bone marrow transplants 骨髓移植

marry / 'mæri / v. 结婚：John is going to ～ Jane. 约翰将和简买结婚。/ Tom and Alice are going to get married. 汤姆和艾丽斯要结婚了。同 wed 反 divorce

Mars / mɑ:z / n. (天文)火星

marsh / mɑ:ʃ / n. 沼泽；湿地：～ gas 沼气

marshal / 'mɑ:ʃəl / n. [C](陆军)元帅

martyr / 'mɑ:tə(r) / n. [C]烈士；受难者：He died a ～ to his belief. 他为自己的信仰而牺牲。同 hero, sufferer

marvel / 'mɑ:vəl / n. [C]奇异的事；令人惊奇的事：It is really the ～s of modern science. 这真是现代科学的奇迹。同 wonder, miracle

marvel(l)ous / 'mɑ:vələs / adj. 奇迹般的，惊人的；了不起的同 astonishing, wonderful 反 awful, ordinary

Marxism / 'mɑ:ksɪzəm / n. 马克思主义

Marxist / 'mɑ:ksɪst / Ⅰ adj. 马克思主义的 Ⅱ n. [C]马克思主义者

masculine / 'mæskjʊlɪn, 'mɑ:skjʊlɪn / adj. ❶男人的，男子的；男性的；男性主导的：She was a woman who spoke her mind in a ～ society. 她是一个男权社会里表达自己想法的女性。❷男子气概的，男子汉的；阳刚的，强壮的：～ strength 男子汉的力量/She loved the ～ aspects of Stanley. 她爱上了斯坦利的阳刚之气。❸阳性的 派 masculinity n.

mask / mɑ:sk / Ⅰ n. [C]面具；面罩：a gas ～ 防毒面具 / She swam with a ～ on. 她戴着面罩游泳。Ⅱ v. 掩饰；掩盖：He talked about some other things to ～ his real purpose. 他说一些别的事情以掩盖他的真实目的。同 hide, disguise 反 expose

mass / mæs / n. [C] 块，堆；大量；群众：The ～es are the makers of history. 人民群众是历史的创造者。/ I have got a great ～ of letters to answer. 我得回大量的信件。同 lump, group, people

massacre / 'mæsəkə(r) / n. [C]大屠杀；残杀

massage / 'mæsɑ:ʒ / n. 按摩；推拿：keep-fit ～ 保健按摩 / There is a ～ center in our town. 我们镇里有一家按摩中心。/ I am tired. Can you give me a ～? 我很疲倦，你能给我按摩一下吗？同 rub, press

massive / 'mæsɪv / adj. 粗大的；大量的；大规模的：There are four ～ pillars in the front of the hall. 大厅的前面有四根粗大的柱子。/ They made ～ efforts but failed. 他们做出了巨大的努力，但没有成功。同 huge, heavy, enormous, large-scale

mast / mɑ:st / n. [C]桅杆；旗杆 同 pole, flag-pole

master / 'mɑ:stə(r) / Ⅰ n. [C] ❶主人；顾主：The ～ likes his dog. 主人很喜欢他的狗。同 owner, boss ❷名家：He is a ～ in literature. 他是一个文学大师。同 expert ❸ a Master of Arts (Science)文科(理科)硕士 / a Master's degree 硕士学位 / a Master's thesis 硕士论文 Ⅱ vt. 成为…的主人；精通：Chinese is a difficult language to ～. 汉语是一门很难掌握的语言。同 learn, grasp

masterly / 'mɑ:stəli / adj. &adv. 娴熟的(地)；熟练的(地)；巧妙的(地)；极好的(地)：a ～ summing-up of the situation. 对局势的精辟评价/At an obvious level, the book is simply a ～ guided tour. 显而易见，这是一本很好的导游手册。

masterpiece / 'mɑ:stəpi:s / n. [C]杰作，代表作；杰出的事 同 masterwork

mat / mæt / n. [C]席子；垫子：She put a welcome ～ in front of her flat. 她在房门前放了一块踏脚垫。

match¹ / mætʃ / n. [C]火柴：a box of ～es 一盒火柴 / strike a ～ 划火柴

match² / mætʃ / Ⅰ n. [C] ❶比赛；竞赛：I like to watch a football ～. 我很喜欢看足球赛。同 game, contest ❷婚姻，匹配：They decided to make a ～. 他们决定结婚。/ It is a high building with no ～ in the world. 这幢高楼举世无双。同 equivalent Ⅱ v. ❶比赛；竞赛；I'm ready to ～ my strength with (against) yours. 我准备跟你比力量。❷(在品质、颜色等方面)相当，相配：The carpets should ～ the curtains. 地毯应该和窗帘相配。/ You should always ～ your words with your deeds. 你应当言行一致。同 fit

mate / meɪt / n. [C]同事；伙伴：class～，school ～ 同学 / room～ 室友 / work～ 工友；同事 / team-～ 队友 同 companion

material / məˈtɪəriəl / Ⅰ n. 原料；材料：dress ～s 布料 / building ～s 建筑材料 / raw ～s 原材料 / reading ～s 阅读材料 / teaching ～s 教材 同 matter，substance Ⅱ adj. 物质的(与 spiritual 相对)：the ～ world 物质世界 / a ～ noun 物质名词 / ～ wealth 物质财富 / ～ benefit 物质利益 同 physical 反 mental

materialism / məˈtɪəriəlɪzəm / n. [U]唯物论；唯物主义：dialectical ～ 辩证唯物主义 / historical ～ 历史唯物主义 反 idealism

maternal / məˈtɜːnəl / adj. ❶母亲的；母亲似的，慈母般的：～ love 母爱/She is very ～ towards her staff. 她对手下的职员都很慈爱。❷母系的；娘家的；母亲遗传的：～ grandmother 外婆/～ aunt 姨妈/Her beautiful long hair was a ～ inheritance. 她那一头漂亮的长发是母亲的遗传。派 maternally adv.

mathematics / ˌmæθəˈmætɪks / n. [U]数学
用法
mathematics 作学科名称时视为单数，如它前面加了 my，the，such 等限定词时视为复数：Mathematics is my weak subject. 数学是我较差的学科。My mathematics are weak. 我的数学不好。

math(s) / mæθ(s) / n. (＝mathematics)数学

matter / ˈmætə(r) / Ⅰ n. ❶[U]物质：She discovered a new kind of ～. 她发现了一种新的物质。同 substance ❷[C] 事务；事件；问题：money ～s 金钱方面的事情 / This is a ～ I know little about. 这件事我不大清楚。/ What's the ～ with you? 你怎么啦? / No ～ what he says or does, we do not believe him. 不管他说什么，做什么，我们都不会相信他。同 affair，business，trouble / **as a ～ of fact** 事实上：As a ～ of fact, he didn't know it. 事实上他并不知道此事。Ⅱ vi. (主要用于疑问句、否定句和条件句中)关系重大，要紧：It doesn't ～ to me what you do and where you go. 你做什么或去什么地方与我无关。同 count

辨析
matter 指占有空间、实际存在的东西：Matter may be gaseous, liquid, or solid. 物质可能是气体、液体或固体。**material** 指制成某些物品的原料：Oil is an important raw material. 石油是重要的原料。**substance** 指存在于物质世界的东西，也指在心中有实际形象的东西：The substance of the plan is good. 该计划的内容是好的。

mattress / ˈmætrɪs / n. [U]床垫

mature / məˈtʃʊə(r) / adj. 成熟的；完全发育的；到期的：Mature fruits taste well. 成熟的水果味道好。/ After years' work, he became a ～ man. 经过多年的工作，他成熟了。同 ripe，experienced

maxim / ˈmæksɪm / n. [C]格言，箴言，警句：座右铭

maximum / ˈmæksɪməm / Ⅰ n. [C](pl. maxima /ˈmæksɪmə/) 最大量；最高点；极点(与 minimum 相对)：It is the ～ temperature recorded in London. 这是有记载的伦敦最高温度。/ The ～ load for this lorry is two ton. 这辆卡车的最大载重量是两吨。反 minimum Ⅱ adj. 最大的；最大量的：～ wage 最高工资 / to the ～ 最大限度地 / The ～ speed of this car is 80 miles per hour. 这辆车的最高时速是每小时 80 英里。同 biggest，greatest，highest 反 minimum，least

May / meɪ / n. 五月：May Day 五一国际劳动节 / the May 4th Movement 五四运动

may / meɪ / aux. v. (might/maɪt/) ❶可能；或许：He ～ have missed the train. 或许他没赶上那班火车。/ She ～ be right in this point. 在这一点上她可能是对的。❷可以(表示许可或请求许可)：May I come in? 我可以进来吗? ❸表示询问：How old ～ (might) she be? 她的年龄会有多大呢? ❹表示愿望或希望：May they long live! 祝他们长寿! / May you succeed! 祝你成功!

maybe / ˈmeɪbi / adv. 大概；或许：Maybe he will come to our party tomorrow. 也许他明天会来参加我们的聚会。同 perhaps

mayor / meə(r) / n. [C]市长

maze / meɪz / n. ❶迷宫，迷径：led sb. through a ～ of caves. 带某人穿过迷宫般的洞穴 ❷错综复杂(的事物)，盘根错节(的事物)：a ～ of interlacing waterpipes 错综复杂的水管/a ～ of disorganized facts 一大堆混乱不堪、毫无头

绪的事实

me / mi / *pron.* 我(I的宾格)

meadow / 'medəʊ / *n.* [C]草地；牧场同 grass-land

meal / miːl / *n.* ［C］一餐；一顿饭；饮食；We always have three ～s a day. 我们总是一日三餐。/ Most families meet together for a big ～ on New Year's Eve. 多数家庭会在除夕夜聚在一起吃丰盛的年夜饭。

mean¹ / miːn / *vt.* (meant/ment/, meant) ❶表示，意指；意欲：He ～s no harm to you. 他不想伤害你。/ What do you ～ by saying that? 说这话你什么意思？同 imply, indicate, intend ❷对…是重要的；对…有价值的：Your friendship ～s a great deal to me. 你的友谊对我极为重要。/ The word doesn't ～ anything here. 这个词用在这里毫无意义。

mean² / miːn / *adj.* ❶自私的；吝啬的；小气的：The fellow is a ～ minded man. 那家伙是一个吝啬自私的人。同 stingy, selfish 反 generous, unselfish ❷卑鄙的；讨厌的：It was ～ of Jack to cheat in the exam. 杰克考试作弊是很卑鄙的。同 low, unpleasant 反 dignified, kind 派 meanly *adv.*

mean³ / miːn / Ⅰ *n.* 平均值；平均数同 average Ⅱ *adj.* 中间的；中等的；平均的：in the ～ time (while)在此期间 / The ～ temperature here in spring is about 12℃. 这里春季的平均温度是摄氏 12 度左右。同 average 反 extreme

meaning / 'miːnɪŋ / *n.* 意义；意思；含义：What's the ～ of this sentence? 这个句子的意思是什么？/ It is a word with many ～s. 这是一个多义词。同 sense, significance 派 meaningful *adj.*

means / miːnz / *n.* ❶[C]方式，方法；手段；工具(复数形式，常作单数使用)：A mobile phone is a new ～ of communication that people like to use. 移动电话是人们喜欢使用的一种新的通信工具。❷(*pl.*)财富，钱财：He has the means to support his family. 他有钱养活家人。/ by ～ of 借助；凭借；依靠：Thoughts are expressed by ～ of words. 思想用语言表达出来。by all ～ 尽一切办法；无论如何；务必：Come to attend the meeting by all ～. 你务必要来参加会议。/ I'll finish it in two hours by all ～. 我尽力在两小时内做完这事。by no ～ 决不；一点也不：These goods are by no ～ satisfactory. 这些货物一点也不令人满意。同 way, method

用 法

❶means 表示"方法；手段"之意时，形式是复数，作单数或复数名词使用均可：A proper communication means hasn't been found. 人们还没有找到合适的交通工具。The means of helping others are never lacking. 要帮助他人是不会没有方法的。❷means 表示"财富"之意时，形式和用法上都是复数：His means permit him to live comfortably. 他拥有的财富使他能过上舒适的生活。

meantime / 'miːntaɪm / *adv.* 同时，其间：Wang Lan is out. In the ～, I answered the telephone twice for her. 王兰出去了，其间我代她接了两个电话。同 meanwhile

meanwhile / 'miːnwaɪl / *adv.* 同时，其间同 meantime

measurable / 'meʒ(ə)rəbl / *adj.* ❶可测量的，可计量的：a quantifiable and ～ market share 可量化并可计量的市场份额 ❷引人注目的；重大的；具有重要意义的：～ improvements in the quality of the products 产品质量的重大提高 / have ～ impact on the lives of the people 对人们的生活产生重大影响 派 measurably *adv.*

measure / 'meʒə(r) / Ⅰ *n.* ❶大小；数量；度量：give full (short) ～ 称量足(不足) / cut to one's ～ 量体裁衣 同 size, amount ❷[C]方法；步骤；措施：They took strong ～s against dangerous drivers. 他们对危害公众安全的司机采取强硬措施。同 action, means Ⅱ *vt.* 量；测量：～ a piece of land 丈量一块土地 / The tailor ～d me for a suit. 裁缝给我量尺寸做套装。同 size, calculate

measurement / 'meʒəmənt / *n.* ❶[U]测定；测量；度量：Without a watch, we cannot make an accurate ～ of time. 如果没有表，我们将无法测得准确时间。同 evaluation, calculation ❷(通常用 *pl.*)(量得的)尺寸；大小：Do you know the ～s of your bedroom? 你知道你卧室的大小吗？同 size

meat / miːt / *n.* [U]肉(不包括鱼肉和禽肉)：～-eating animals 肉食动物 / cold ～ 冷盘 / fresh ～ 鲜肉 / a piece of ～ 一块肉同 flesh, beef, pork

mechanic / mə'kænɪk / *n.* [C]技工；机械工人同 machinist, workman

mechanical / mə'kænɪkl / *adj.* 机械的；力学的同 machinelike 派 mechanically *adv.*

mechanics / mə'kænɪks / *n.* [U]力学；机械

学;Mechanics is a very interesting subject. 力学是一门很有趣的学科。

mechanization / ˌmekənaɪ'zeɪʃn / n. [U]机械化

medal / 'medl / n. [C]奖章;勋章;纪念章;He was awarded a ～ for his bravery. 因表现勇敢,他获得一枚奖章。 同 badge

meddle / 'medl / vi. 干涉,插手;好管闲事;Do not ～ in things that do not concern you . 不要插手那些与你无关的事情。

media / 'miːdɪə / (medium 的复数形式) n. [C]媒介;传导体;mass ～ 大众传媒 / news ～ 新闻媒体 / The television is important ～ of communication. 电视是很重要的传输媒介。 同 means,agency

median / 'miːdɪən / Ⅰ adj. (位于)中间的,居中的;the ～ position 中间位置/a low ～ income 中等偏低的收入 Ⅱ n. [C]❶中间数,平均数❷(三角形的)中线

mediate / 'miːdɪeɪt / vi. 调解,斡旋,充当中间人(与 in, between 连用);The United Nations is trying to ～ between the two warring countries. 联合国正努力调解交战两国之间的争端。/He is appointed to ～ in a legal dispute. 他被指派去调解一起法律纠纷。—vt. 通过调解(或斡旋等)解决(纠纷、冲突等);～ a dispute 调解纠纷 派 mediation n.

medical / 'medɪkl / adj. 医学的;医疗的;内科的;a ～ school 医科学校 / ～ students 医科学生 / ～ examination 体检 / ～ insurance 医疗保险 / They pay more attention to ～ and health work now. 他们现在更加重视医疗卫生工作。

medicine / 'medsɪn / n. ❶[U]医学;医术;内科学: study ～ and surgery 研究内科与外科❷药;药剂: traditional Chinese ～ 中药❷药;西药/He takes too much ～ . 他药吃得太多。/ This is a good (kind of) ～ for a cough. 这是(一种)治咳嗽的良药。 同 drug,pill

辨 析

medicine 是常用词,药物的总称。可引申用于指一切对健康有益的东西;What kind of medicine are you taking? 你在服用什么药物? Sunshine and rest are good medicine for a patient. 阳光和休息对病人是良药。**drug** 也为常用词,指任何可治病的药物。复数形式用 s 时还可指毒品、麻醉剂等;Many drugs have been used in the treatment of cold. 有许多药物用来医治感冒。It's extremely dangerous for one to take drugs. 吸毒是极其危险的。

medieval / ˌmedɪ'iːv(ə)l / adj. 中世纪的,中古(时期)的;中世纪风格的;似中世纪的;仿中世纪的;～ literature 中世纪文学

meditate / 'medɪteɪt / vi. 默念,冥想;He ～s twice a day. 他每天默念两次。/He sat on the grass meditating on his misfortunes. 他坐在草地上冥想自己的不幸。—vt. 计划、打算;谋划;企图;～ revenge 谋划复仇/They are meditating a reimposition of tax on electronics. 他们正计划对电子产品重新征税。 派 meditation n.

Mediterranean / ˌmedɪtə'reɪnɪən / n. 地中海

medium / 'miːdɪəm / Ⅰ n. (pl. mediums 或 media)[C]媒介;传导体(见 media) Ⅱ adj. 中等的;适中的;He hopes to become ～ size. 他希望成为身材中等的人。 同 middle,moderate 反 extreme

meet / miːt / Ⅰ v. (met/met/, met) ❶遇见;相逢;We met by chance. 我们偶然相遇。 同 see,encounter / ～ **with** 遭遇;偶然碰到:～ with an accident 遇到意外 / I met with an old friend in the train. 在火车上我碰到一个老朋友。❷迎接;The hotel bus ～s all the trains. 旅馆的汽车在火车站迎候各班车的旅客。 同 greet ❸满足(需要、要求等);Have we enough money with us to ～ all expenses? 我们身边的钱够付全部的费用吗? 同 satisfy Ⅱ n. [C]集会;会: the sports ～ 运动会 同 assemble

meeting / 'miːtɪŋ / n. [C]会议;集会;聚会:a ～ room 会议室/ The manager spoke at the spot ～. 经理在现场会上发表讲话。 同 assembly

辨 析

meeting 指较正式的"会议",一般有主席,发言按次序,目的是讨论某些问题: Our class will have a meeting this afternoon to discuss this problem. 我们班今天下午将开会讨论这个问题。**party** 指娱乐性或庆祝性的"宴会"或"晚会";a birthday party 生日宴会。

mega- / 'megə / (前缀) ❶表示"巨大的","数量多的","超大量的","超大型";～business 超大型企业 / ～debt 巨额债务 / ～jet 超大型喷气式客机 / ～ dose 超大剂量 ❷表示"兆","百万倍";～bite 兆比特 ❸表示"极…的";"非常…的";～ hit 超级火爆的影片或演出/～ trend 超级流行趋势

megaphone / 'megəˌfəʊn / n. [C]扩音器;传声器;喇叭;话筒;address the crowd through a

～ 用喇叭向人群作演说

mellow / ˈmeləʊ / Ⅰ *adj.* ❶(果实)成熟的;甘美多汁的:～ wine 醇香的美酒/～ grapes 熟透的葡萄 ❷柔和的:a sweet and ～ voice 甜美温柔的声音/～ colours of the dawn sky 拂晓时天空中柔和的色彩 ❸老练的;稳重的;成熟的:He's got ～ as he's got older. 随着年龄的增大,他变得更加成熟了。Ⅱ *v.* ❶(使)(果实)变熟 ❷(使)变得柔和:Gentle sunshine ～ed the old garden, casting an extra sheen of gold on leaves that were gold already. 温柔的阳光柔和地照在老园里,在那已金灿灿的叶子上洒上点点金辉。❸(使)变得老练(或稳重):The years have ～ed him. 这些年的日子使他变得老成了。

melody / ˈmelədi / *n.* 旋律;曲调;歌曲:She played a new ～ at the party. 聚会上她演奏了一首新曲子。同 tune, song

melon / ˈmelən / *n.* 瓜;甜瓜:I'd like to have a slice of water～ after supper. 晚饭后我总要吃一块西瓜。

melt / melt / *v.* (使)融化;(使)熔化:The sun soon ～ed ice. 太阳很快就使冰融化了。同 dissolve

member / ˈmembə(r) / *n.* [C]分子;成员;会员:a ～ of a club 俱乐部会员 / a Party ～ 共产党员 / a League ～ 共青团员 / an honorary ～ 名誉会员 同 element, associate

membership / ˈmembəʃip / *n.* 成员(会员)资格;全体会员;Many students applied for the Party ～. 许多学生申请加入共产党。/ The club has a large ～. 这家俱乐部有很多会员。同 fellowship, members

memento / mɪˈmentəʊ / *n.* [C]令人想起故人(或往事)的东西;纪念物,纪念品:the ～ of sb.'s time in China 那些令人想起在中国的时光的东西/a small gift as a ～ of the journey 作为此次旅行纪念的小礼品

memo / ˈmeməʊ / *n.* (＝memorandum)[C]备忘录

memorandum / ˌmeməˈrændəm / *n.* [C](*pl.* memorandums 或 memoranda)备忘录

memorial / məˈmɔːriəl / *n.* 纪念物,纪念品;纪念馆:In most English villages there is a war ～. 英国大多数村庄都有一个阵亡将士纪念碑。/ They built a ～ to the martyrs. 他们修建了一座烈士纪念碑。同 monument

memorize(-se) / ˈmeməraɪz / *vt.* 记住;熟记:The teacher asks us to ～ new English words as many as possible. 老师要求我们尽量多记英语单词。同 remember 反 forget

memory / ˈmeməri / *n.* ❶记忆;记忆力:He has a bad ～ for dates. 他对日期的记忆很差。/ Can you tell his address from ～? 你能凭记忆说出他的住址吗? ❷(计算机)内存

mend / mend / *v.* ❶缝补;修理:～ shoes 修补鞋子 / a broken window 修理破窗户 同 repair, fix ❷修正;改过;改善:to ～ one's ways 改过自新 同 better, correct

> **辨析**
>
> **mend** 和 **repair** 都有"修补"的意思,但指修补衣服、鞋袜等时只用 mend,不用 repair; repair 指修缮建筑、堤坝,修理机器、车辆等。

mental / ˈmentəl / *adj.* 心理的;精神的;脑力的:～ labour 脑力劳动 / ～ health 心理健康 / ～ disorder 心理障碍 / ～ outlook 精神面貌 同 intelligent 反 physical, material

mentality / menˈtæləti / *n.* 脑力;智力;心理:normal ～ 正常心理(智力)/ try-your-luck ～ 侥幸心理:He is studying how to develop children's ～. 他在研究如何发展儿童智力。同 intellect, mind

mention / ˈmenʃn / Ⅰ *v.* 说到;写到;提及:Don't ～ it. 别客气(不用谢)。/ The event is ～ed in today's newspaper. 该事件在今天的报上被提及。同 cite, hint Ⅱ *n.* [U]提到:He made no ～ of your requests. 他没提到你的请求。同 reference, indication

menu / ˈmenjuː / *n.* [C]菜单:the main ～ (计算机)主菜单 / He didn't look at the ～ before he ordered some fish. 他不看菜单就点了一些鱼。

merchandise / ˈmɜːtʃəndaɪz / *n.* [U](集合名词)商品;货物:They bought some general ～ in the supermarket. 他们在超市买了一些杂货。同 goods, stock

merchant / ˈmɜːtʃənt / *n.* [C]商人 同 businessman, dealer

merciful / ˈmɜːsɪfl / *adj.* 仁慈的;宽大的:We should be ～ to the disabled. 我们对残疾人应当仁慈一些。反 cruel

merciless / ˈmɜːsɪləs / *adj.* ❶毫无同情(或怜悯)之心的,无情的;残忍的:be ～ to one's enemies 对敌人决不留情/He was ～ in his criticism of the newspapers. 他对报纸进行了无情的抨击。❷(风、雨等)强烈的,严重的;肆虐的:～ snowstorms 强暴风雪

Mercury / 'mɜːkjəri / n. 水星

mercury / 'mɜːkjəri / n. [U]水银;汞

mercy / 'mɜːsi / n. 仁慈;宽恕;慈悲心:We should learn to show ～ to others. 我们应当学会宽容他人。/ They showed little ～ to the poor. 他们对穷人毫无怜悯之意。/ **at the ～ of, at one's ～** 任由…摆布,在…掌握中:They are at the ～ of wind and waves. 他们任由风浪的摆布。

mere / mɪə(r) / adj. 仅仅;只不过:Mere words won't help. 光说(不做)无济于事。/ Don't be hard on her. She is a ～ child. 别苛求她,她只不过是个小孩而已。圆 bare,simple

merely / 'mɪəli / adv. 仅仅;只不过:Studying in London is ～ a dream to her. 对她来说,去伦敦读书只不过是一个梦想而已。/ I ～ asked his name. 我只问了他的名字。圆 only,simply

merge / mɜːdʒ / vi. ❶合并;会合:The two firms ～ d. 这两家公司合并了。/The two roads ～ a mile ahead. 这两条路在前面一英里处会合。❷融合在一起,融为一体:The whole scheme, front and back, ～ s well with the garden design. 前后部分的整个规划与庭园设计浑然天成,不露痕迹。

meridian / mə'rɪdɪən / I n. ❶[C]子午线;子午圈 ❷[C]经线:The prime ～ of 0° passes through the old observatory at Greenwich. 零度经线经过格林尼治老天文台。II adj. (有关)子午线的;(有关)子午圈的:～ circle 子午环

merit / 'merɪt / n. 价值;优点;功绩,功劳:It is an old painting of great ～. 这是一幅具有很高价值的古画。/ Frankness is one of his ～ s. 直率是他的优点之一。圆 value, virtue, advantage

merry / 'meri / adj. 愉快的;欢乐的;高兴的:Wish you a ～ Christmas! 祝你圣诞快乐! 圆 happy, cheerful, glad 反 unhappy, sad

mess / mes / n. 混乱,杂乱;肮脏;(狗、猫等的)粪便:Don't make a ～ of your room. 别把你的房间弄得乱七八糟。圆 disorder, confusion/ **in a ～** 杂乱;陷入困境:The children's room was in a ～. 孩子们的房间十分脏乱。添

messy adj.

message / 'mesɪdʒ / n. [C](口头或书面的)通知;信息;消息:Wireless ～ s told us that the ship was sinking. 无线电报传来的消息告诉我们那只船正在下沉。/ If I am out, please leave a ～. 如果我不在家,请给我留言。圆 letter, information

messenger / 'mesɪndʒə(r) / n. [C]报信者;信差;通信员

metabolism / mɪ'tæbəlɪzəm / n. [C;U]新陈代谢,代谢作用:He has a very active ～. 他的新陈代谢功能非常强。/There elements are vital in cell ～. 这些元素在细胞新陈代谢中不可缺少。

metal / 'metl / n. 金属:Gold is a precious ～. 金子是一种贵重的金属。

metaphor / 'metəfə(r) / n. 隐喻;比喻 圆 comparison, simile

meteor / 'miːtɪə(r) / n. [C]流星

meteorology / ˌmiːtɪə'rɒlədʒi / n. [U]气象;气象学

meteorologist / ˌmiːtɪə'rɒlədʒɪst / n. [C]气象学家

meter[1] / 'miːtə(r) / n. [C]计量器;计量仪表:an electric ～ 电表 / a water ～ 水表 / a gas ～ 煤气表 / a parking ～ 停车计时表 圆 measure

meter[2] / 'miːtə(r) / n. (＝metre)[C](公制长度单位)米,公尺:a cubic ～ 立方米 / a square ～ 平方

method / 'meθəd / n. [C] 方法;办法:Our teacher adopted a new ～ to teach maths. 我们的老师用新方法教数学。圆 way, means

metre / 'miːtə / n. [C](公制长度单位)米,公尺(见 meter[2])

metric / 'metrɪk / adj. 公制的;米制的:a ～ ton 一公吨

metro / 'metrəʊ / n. [C;U]地下铁路,地铁:take the ～乘坐地铁/go to work by ～乘地铁上班

metropolis / mə'trɒpəlɪs / n. [C]大都市;主要城市 圆 city, capital

mice / maɪs / n. [C](mouse的复数形式)鼠;耗子

micr(o)- / 'maɪkr(əʊ) / (前缀)表示"小""微""微量":～economy 微观经济 / ～bus 微型汽车 / ～element 微量元素 / ～film 微缩胶卷

microcomputer / 'maɪkrəʊkəmpjuːtə(r) / n.

[C]微机：Her mother bought her a new ～. 她妈妈给她买了一台新的微机。

microorganism / ˌmaɪkrəʊˈɔːgənɪzəm / n. [C] 微生物

microphone / ˈmaɪkrəfəʊn / n. [C] 扩音器；话筒

microprocessor / ˌmaɪkrəʊˈprəʊsesə(r) / n. 微信息处理机；微处理器

microscope / ˈmaɪkrəskəʊp / n. [C] 显微镜：The researcher examined bacteria under a ～. 研究人员在显微镜下观察细菌。

microwave / ˈmaɪkrəweɪv / n. 微波：a ～ stove 微波炉 / ～ technology 微波技术

mid / mɪd / adj. 中间的；中部的：～day 中午 /～night 午夜；半夜

midday / ˌmɪdˈdeɪ / n. 正午；中午：It was ～ when they arrived. 他们到达时正是正午时分。圎 noon，noonday

middle / ˈmɪdl / I n. [C] 中间；中部；中央：in the ～ of the century 本世纪中叶 / standing in the ～ of the street 站在街心 II adj. 中间的；中部的；中央的；中等的：a ～ school 中学 / His father is a man of ～ size. 他父亲是个中等个子的人。

midnight / ˈmɪdnaɪt / n. 午夜；半夜：at ～ 在午夜 / The test is approaching. He had to burn the ～ oil to prepare for it. 考试临近，他不得不熬夜(开夜车)做准备。

midst / mɪdst / n. 中部；中间；当中：There is a lodge in the ～ of the forest. 森林深处有一栋小屋。圎 middle，center

midterm / ˈmɪdtɜːm / I n. ❶[U](任期等的)中期：Our next project is due at ～. 我们的下一个项目将在中期完成。❷[C]〈口〉期中考试 II adj. 中期的，期中的：the congressional ～ election 国会中期选举/～ exams 期中考试

midtown / ˈmɪdtaʊn / I n. [U] 市中心区：Most of the ～ was closed to traffic. 市中心大部分地段的交通已封闭了。II adj. (位于)市中心的：We threaded our way through the traffic in ～ Brighton. 我们穿过布赖顿市中心的车流和人流。

midway / ˌmɪdˈweɪ / n. 中途 圎 halfway

might[1] / maɪt / v. aux. (may 的过去式形式) 可能；也许；可以：I'm afraid it ～ snow tonight. 我看今晚也许会下雪。

might[2] / maɪt / n. [U] 力量；威力；能量：He is working with all his ～. 他正全力以赴地工作。圎 power，strength

mighty / ˈmaɪti / adj. (-ier，-iest) 伟大的；强大的；巨大的：a ～ nation 强大的国家 / the ～ ocean 浩瀚的海洋 圎 strong，powerful

migrant / ˈmaɪgrənt / n. [C] 候鸟，移居者：Swallows are ～s. 燕子是候鸟。

migrate / maɪˈgreɪt / vi. 迁徙；迁移；移居 圎 move，travel，emigrate 猋 migration n.

mild / maɪld / adj. 温和的；和善的；不严厉的：It is ～ today. 今天天气暖和。/ She is ～ in disposition. 她性情温和。圎 gentle，kind，good-tempered

mile / maɪl / n. [C] 英里

milestone / ˈmaɪlstəʊn / n. [C] ❶里程碑，里程标 ❷意义重大的事件，划时代的事件，里程碑：a ～ in one's life 人生中的重要转折点/ The fall of Berlin was one of the ～s of the World War Ⅱ. 攻陷柏林是第二次世界大战中的重要里程碑之一。

military / ˈmɪlɪtəri / adj. 军人的；军用的；陆军的：～ training 军事训练 / in ～ uniform 穿着军服 / ～ ranks 军衔 / He studies in a ～ academy. 他在一所军事学院读书。

milk / mɪlk / I n. [U] 乳；奶 (尤指牛奶)：Milk is of great benefit to children. 牛奶对孩子的健康很有益。II v. 挤(牛、山羊等的)奶：The girl is ～ing a cow. 姑娘正在挤牛奶。猋 milky adj.

mill / mɪl / n. [C] 工厂；工场：a saw (paper，silk，steel) ～ 锯厂(纸厂，丝厂，钢铁厂) 圎 factory，plant，works

millennium / mɪˈleniəm / n. [C] (pl. millenniums) 一千年；千年期

mince / mɪns / I vt. ❶将(肉等)切碎，切细；将(肉等)绞碎：The meat has been ～d. 肉已经切碎了。❷迈着碎步扭捏走(路)：He ～d his way across the room. 他一扭扭地小步走过房间。II n. [U] 碎肉，肉末，肉糜：They had ～ and potatoes for lunch. 他们中饭吃肉末和土豆。

millimeter(-re) / ˈmɪlɪmiːtə(r) / n. [C] 毫米 (略作 mm.)

million / ˈmɪljən / n. [C] 百万：～s of 千百万的；无数的 / She is too young to count from one to a ～. 她太小，不能从 1 数到 100 万。

millionaire / ˌmɪljəˈneə(r) / n. [C] 百万富翁，大富豪

mind / maɪnd / Ⅰ *n.* ❶记忆;回忆圆 memo-ry/ bear (keep) sth. in ～ 记住某事;You must constantly bear (keep) in ～ that haste makes waste. 你须将"欲速则不达"这句话常记在心。**go out of one's** ～ 被忘记;想不起来:I'm sor-ry. It completely went out of my ～. 对不起,我完全忘记那件事了。❷意欲;心意;想法圆 thoughts,opinion/ **make up one's** ～ 下决心;He made up his ～ not to smoke again. 他下决心不再吸烟了。❸头脑;精神;理智:She learns physics easily. She must have a good ～. 她学物理很容易。她一定有一个聪明的头脑。圆 brain,spirit Ⅱ *v.* ❶留心;注意:Mind (out),there's a bus coming. 当心,有辆车开过来了。/ Mind your own business. 少管闲事。圆 care,regard ❷介意;反对:Do you ～ my smoking here? 你介意我在这里抽烟吗? / —Do you ～ my leaving this payment until next year? —Yes,I do ～. 一这笔款项我留到明年再付,你反对吗? 一当然反对。圆 object

> **用法**
> mind 后接动名词或从句,不接不定式作宾语:Would you mind opening the door for me? 请帮我把门打开好吗? I don't mind whether they agree or not. 他们同意不同意我都不在乎。

mindless / ˈmaɪndlɪs / *adj.* ❶不需要动脑筋的:a boring ,～ job 不用脑筋的无聊工作 ❷不注意的,不顾及的,无视的:be ～ of the dangers the workers are faced with 不顾工人们面临的危险 ❸没头脑的;愚笨的;无知的

mine¹ / maɪn / *pron.* 我的(名词性物主代词):She is an old friend of ～. 她是我的一位老朋友。

mine² / maɪn / Ⅰ *n.* [C] ❶矿;矿山:a coal ～ 煤矿 / a gold ～ 金矿 ❷地雷;水雷:They laid a ～ in the road. 他们在公路上布雷。Ⅱ *vt.* 开采(矿物):They live on mining coal. 他们靠采煤为生。圆 dig,unearth

mineral / ˈmɪnərəl / *n.* 矿物:～ ores 矿 石 / ～ deposits 矿藏;矿床 / I prefer ～ water to tea. 我喜欢喝矿泉水,不喜欢喝茶。圆 ore,deposit

mingle / ˈmɪŋgl / *vt.* ❶相互交往,互相往来:He wandered around, trying to ～ with the guests. 他四处转悠,想跟宾客们打成一片。❷

混合:His account ～d truth with exaggera-tions. 他的叙述中事实与夸张的东西混在一起。/She accepted the money with ～d feel-ings. 她怀着复杂的心情接受了这笔钱。

mini- / ˈmɪni / (前缀)表示"小":～ bus 小公共汽车 / ～-disc 微型唱片 / ～-story 微型小说/～-skirt 超短裙

miniature / ˈmɪnətʃə(r) / Ⅰ *adj.* 小型的:a ～ camera 小型照相机圆 small-scale,mini Ⅱ *n.* [C]缩影;缩图;缩版;缩小的模型圆 micro-form,micrograph

minimum / ˈmɪnɪməm / Ⅰ *n.* [C] (*pl.* mini-ma /ˈmɪnɪmə/) 最小量;最低额(与 maximum 相对):a ～ wage 一份最低工资 / The tem-perature in this room reaches a ～ of −5℃ in winter. 冬天这房间的最低温度可达摄氏零下五度。反 maximum Ⅱ *adj.* 最小的;最低的圆 least,smallest 反 maximum

minister / ˈmɪnɪstə(r) / *n.* [C]部长;公使:the Prime Minister 首相;内阁总理 / The ～s are discussing how to improve their work. 部长们正讨论如何改进工作。

ministry / ˈmɪnɪstri / *n.* [C] (政府的)部;部门:the Ministry of Foreign Affairs 外交部 / the Ministry of Education 教育部圆 depart-ment

minor / ˈmaɪnə(r) / *adj.* 较小的;次要的:the ～ planets 小行星 / She plays a ～ part in the film. 她在电影中演配角。圆 smaller,second-ary 反 greater,major

minority / maɪˈnɒrəti / *n.* ❶少数;较小的一部分:They were in the ～ at the meeting. 在会上他们只占少数。圆 few,fewer ❷少数民族 反 majority

mint / mɪnt / *n.* ❶[U]薄荷;薄荷糖 ❷[C]造币厂;制造厂

minus / ˈmaɪnəs / Ⅰ *prep.* 减,减去:How much is twelve ～ two? 12 减 2 等于多少? 反 plus Ⅱ *n.* 负数;负号;减号

minute¹ / ˈmɪnɪt / *n.* [C]分钟;片刻;一会儿:There are 60 ～s in an hour. 1 小时有 60 分钟。/ I'll come back in a ～. 一会儿我就回来。/ Just a ～, please. 请稍等。圆 moment,instant

minute² / maɪˈnjuːt / *adj.* 微小的;极小的:Please tell us the ～ details of the accident. 请把事故的细节告诉我们。圆 small,detailed

miracle / ˈmɪrəkl / n. [C]奇迹；令人惊奇的事；work (work) ~ s 创造奇迹 / drugs 特效药 同 wonder, marvel

mirage / ˈmɪrɑːʒ, mɪˈrɑːʒ / n. [C]海市蜃楼 反 reality

mirror / ˈmɪrə(r) / Ⅰ n.[C]镜子 Ⅱ vt. 反映；反射：The blue sky and white cloud are ~ed in the lake. 蓝天白云映在湖面上。同 reflect, show

mis- / mɪs / (前缀)表示"错"，"误"或"坏"：~understand 误解

misapprehend / ˌmɪsæprɪˈhend / vt. 误解，误会：~ sb.'s intentions 错会某人的意图 派 misapprehension n.

misbehave / ˌmɪsbɪˈheɪv / vi. 行为不当，不守规矩：~ in church 在教堂不守规矩 派 misbehavio(u)r n.

miscalculate / ˌmɪsˈkælkjuˌleɪt / v. ❶误算，错算：~ the amount(how much) one needed in renovating the house 算错了翻新这幢房子所需的费用/He ~d when adding up the figures. 他在加数时算错了。❷错误地估计；对……作出错误的判断：~ the public's mood 错误地判断公众的心态

mischief / ˈmɪstʃɪf / n. [C]顽皮孩子；淘气鬼：The little ~ tore my book into pieces. 那小淘气把我的书撕成了碎片。

miscount / ˌmɪsˈkaʊnt / Ⅰ v. 数错；算错：The shop assistant ~ed the customer's change. 店员算错了找给顾客的零钱。Ⅱ n.[C]计算错误

miser / ˈmaɪzə(r) / n. [C]守财奴；吝啬鬼

miserable / ˈmɪzərəbl / adj. 痛苦的；悲惨的：feel~ from cold and hunger 因饥寒交迫而感到痛苦异常 / The book is about the ~ living condition of the refugees after the war. 这本书写了战后难民们悲惨的生活状况。同 sad, wretched

misery / ˈmɪzəri / n. [U]不幸；悲惨；痛苦；(pl.)不幸事件：Pollution causes great ~ to humankind. 污染带给人类巨大的痛苦。同 suffering, unhappiness

misfortune / ˌmɪsˈfɔːtʃuːn / n. 不幸；灾祸：suffer ~ 遭受不幸 / companions in ~ 患难之交；患难中的伙伴 同 misery, disaster 反 luck, fortune

mislead / ˌmɪsˈliːd / vt. (misled / ˌmɪsˈled /, misled) 带错路；引(某人)入歧途：The boy was misled by bad companions. 小男孩被不良伙伴带坏了 。/ This information ~ s the public. 这个消息误导公众。同 misguide, cheat

Miss / mɪs / n. (对未婚女子的称呼)小姐：See you later, Miss Li. 李小姐再见。

miss / mɪs / v. ❶没赶上(火车、汽车等)；未达到；未看见：The hunter fired at a tiger but ~ed (it). 猎人开枪打虎，但未打中。/ He ~ed the first train. 他没赶上早班车。/ You ~ed a word here. 你在这儿写掉了一个字。/ Wang Ying doesn't come. She ~ed the notice for the meeting. 王英没有来，她未看见开会通知。同 fail, skip, overlook ❷想念：She ~es her mother badly. 她非常想念妈妈。同 want 派 missing adj.

missile / ˈmɪsaɪl / n.[C]导弹；发射物

mission / ˈmɪʃən / n. [C] ❶使团；代表团：Her brother is a member of a trade ~ to America. 她的哥哥是一个赴美贸易代表团的成员。同 delegation ❷使命；任务：The young man was sent on a diplomatic ~. 那年轻人被派去执行外交任务。同 task

missionary / ˈmɪʃənri / n.[C]传教士

mist / mɪst / n. [U]雾：The sun rose. The ~ cleared. 太阳出来了，雾散了。同 fog, smog

mistake / mɪˈsteɪk / Ⅰ n.[C]错误；过失：We all make ~s occasionally. 我们都会偶尔犯错。同 error, fault / by ~ 错误地：You left your umbrella by ~. 我错拿了你的雨伞。Ⅱ v. (mistook/mɪsˈtʊk/, mistaken/mɪˈsteɪkən/) 弄错；误解：Don't ~ my meaning. 别误解我的意思。/ He mistook the hour and so came late. 他弄错了时间，所以来晚了。

mister / ˈmɪstə(r) / n. (通常缩写成 Mr.)先生：Mr. Smith 史密斯先生

mistreat / ˌmɪsˈtriːt / vt. 虐待：The dog's owner ~ed it terribly. 那条狗的主人对它的虐待很严重。

mistress / ˈmɪstrəs / n.[C]主妇；女主人；情妇

misunderstand / ˌmɪsʌndəˈstænd / v. (misunderstood /ˌmɪsʌndəˈstʊd/, misunderstood) 误解，误会：You misunderstood his kindness. 你误解了他的好意。反 understand 派 misunderstanding n.

misuse Ⅰ / ˌmɪsˈjuːs / n. [C;U](词语等的)误用，错用；(职权、金钱等的)滥用：~ of powers (authority)滥用职权/The machine was dam-

aged by ～. 这台机器因操作不当而损坏了。
Ⅱ / ˌmɪsˈjuːz/ v. ❶误用，错用(词语等)；滥用
(职权、金钱)：The minister was accused of
misusing agricultural funds. 那位部长被指控
滥用农业基金。❷虐待；(不公正地)对待：The
employees in this firm got ～d. 这家公司的雇
员遭到了不公正对待。

mix / mɪks/ v. 混合；搅和：～ flour and water
把面粉和水混合在一起 / Oil and water will
not ～. 油和水不相溶。同 combine，blend 反 di-
vide，separate

mixture / ˈmɪkstʃə(r) / n. 混合；混合物：～ of
gases 混合气体 / The ～ is sour. 那种混合液
是酸的。同 combination，fusion

moan / məʊn/ Ⅰ n. [C]呻吟声：We heard the
～s of the wounded under the bridge. 我们听
到桥下有受伤的人在呻吟。同 sob，groan Ⅱ
v. 呻吟；悲叹：The old man fell down and ～ed
out a plea for help. 老人跌倒在地呼唤帮助。
同 groan

mobile / ˈməʊbaɪl / adj. 运动的；活动的；可移
动的：a ～ phone 移动电话 / The ～ medical
team often goes to the countryside. 那支流动
医疗队常常下乡。同 movable，traveling

mobility / məʊˈbɪləti / n. [U]机动性；流动性：
Personnel ～ is popular now. 现在人才流动很
流行。同 flow，movement

mobilize(-se) / ˈməʊbəlaɪz / v. 动员(尤指战
时动员)：We ～ all people to protect our environment. 我们动员所有的人保护我们的环境。
同 activate

mock / mɒk / Ⅰ vt. ❶嘲笑，嘲弄，讥笑：He
was still ～ing his adversaries a few years before his death. 直到临死前的几年他还在嘲弄
他的对手们。❷效仿，模仿(以取笑)：His pet
monkey attempted to ～ his actions. 他的宠物
猴想要模仿他的举止。Ⅱ adj. ❶仿制的，仿
造的；假(冒)的：a ～ sort of shyness 故意装
出的羞涩/one's ～ friends 虚伪的朋友 ❷模
拟的，演习的：～ exam 模拟考试

modal / ˈməʊdəl / Ⅰ adj. ❶形式的，形态的；
方式的 ❷(动词的)语气的；情态的：～ verb
情态动词 Ⅱ n. [C]情态动词

mode / məʊd / n. [C]方法；方式；样式：Every-
one has his own ～ of life. 每个人都有自己的
生活方式。/ Girls always like the latest ～ of
clothes. 女孩总喜欢衣物的最新款式。同
method，style

model / ˈmɒdl / n. [C]❶模型；模式；原型：a
～ plane 模型飞机 / Please make sentences
after the ～. 请照例子造句。同 design，pat-
tern，type ❷典型；模范：a ～ worker 劳动模
范 同 example ❸模特儿

modem / ˈməʊdem / n. [C](计算机)调制解
调器

moderate / ˈmɒdərət / adj. ❶温和的；稳健
的：In discussing the problem he was trying to
be a man of ～ opinions. 在讨论问题时他尽量
做一个不偏激的人。同 temperate，calm 反 ex-
treme，immoderate ❷中等的；适度地；有节制
的；(价格)合理的：The old woman is over sixty and has a ～ appetite. 老太太六十多岁，食
量中等。/ Prices in this supermarket are
strictly ～. 这家超市里的各种价格很公道。/
She has just graduated and can only rent a ～-
price room. 她刚毕业，只能租一间价格适中的
房子住。同 immoderate 反 modest，medium，
reasonable 派 moderately adv.

modern / ˈmɒdən / adj. 现代的；近代的；新式
的：in the ～ world 在当今世界 / ～ inventions and discoveries 现代发明与发现 同 up-
to-date；contemporary

modernization / ˌmɒdənaɪˈzeɪʃn / n. [U]现代
化：management ～ 管理现代化

modest / ˈmɒdɪst / adj. 谦虚的：He is ～ a-
bout his achievements. 他很谦逊地对待自己
的成就。同 humble 反 showy

modesty / ˈmɒdɪsti / n. 虚心；谦逊；端庄：
Though she is excellent，she is in all ～. 尽管
她很优秀，但她很谦逊。同 decency，propriety
反 pride，conceit

modification / ˌmɒdɪfɪˈkeɪʃn / n. ❶缓和；限
制 同 restriction，moderation ❷修改：Here is
our report. Please make a ～ in it. 这是我们的
报告，请帮助修改一下。同 adjustment，revi-
sion

modify / ˈmɒdɪfaɪ / vt. ❶更改；修改；改变：
The manager is ～ing a production plan. 经理
正在修改生产计划。同 alter，change，revise ❷
修饰：Adjectives ～ nouns. 形容词修饰名词。
同 qualify

modulate / ˈmɒdjuleɪt / vt. ❶调节；修整；使适
应…的需要：～ the cabinet's energy policy 调
整内阁的能源政策 ❷使(声音)变得柔和；改
变(说话的语调)；调节(音量)：When the boss

M

entered, she ～d her voice politely. 老板进来时她有礼貌地压低了声音.

moist / mɔɪst / *adj.* 潮湿的;多雨的;(眼睛等)湿润的:I don't like the ～ season here. 我不喜欢这里的雨季. 同 damp, rainy, watery

moisture / 'mɔɪstʃə(r) / *n.* [U]潮湿,湿气:～ capacity (content)湿度;含水量 同 damp, humidity

molecule / 'mɒlɪkjuːl / *n.* [C]分子

moment / 'məʊmənt / *n.* [C]瞬间,片刻:It was done in a ～. 一会儿这事就做好了. 同 minute, instant / the ～ 一……就…:I started the ～ your letter arrived. 你的信一到,我就动身了. **at the** ～ 此刻;那时:He was drawing a picture at the ～. 那时他正在画一幅画.

momentary / 'məʊməntəri / *adj.* ❶一刹那的,瞬间的,眨眼间的:a ～ hesitation 片刻的犹豫 ❷暂时的;短暂的:The ～ smile flicked on his features as he spoke. 他说话的当儿,脸上掠过了一个笑影儿. 派 momentariness *n.*

momentous / mə'mentəs / *adj.* 极为重要的,重大的,具有重要意义的:a ～ occasion 重大场合 / a ～ man 举足轻重的人物 / at a ～ crisis 在千钧一发的紧要关头

monarch / 'mɒnək / *n.* [C]君主;国王

Monday / 'mʌndi / *n.* 星期一(略作 Mon.)

monetary / 'mʌnɪtri / *adj.* 钱的;货币的;金融的:～ crisis 金融危机 / ～ inflation 通货膨胀 / ～ circulation 货币流通 / ～ reform 货币改革 / ～ unit 货币单位 / Europe ～ market 欧洲货币市场 同 financial

money / 'mʌni / *n.* [U]货币;金钱:～ in cash 现金,现款 / deposit ～ 存钱 / draw ～ 取钱 / raise ～ 筹款 / prize ～ 奖金 / make (earn) ～ 挣钱;赚钱 / Mother gives me some pocket ～ every week. 妈妈每周都给我一些零花钱. 同 cash, banknote

monitor / 'mɒnɪtə(r) / Ⅰ *n.* [C]❶(学校的)班长:Our ～ always helps others. 我们的班长总是帮助他人. ❷监听器;检测器;监视器:a heart ～ 心脏监视器 / He used a new ～. 他使用了一种新的检测器. 同 detector Ⅱ *v.* 监听;监视;监控:This instrument is used to ～ planes in the sky. 这种仪器是用来监视空中飞机的. 同 check, detect

monk / mʌŋk / *n.* [C]和尚;僧侣;修道士

monkey / 'mʌŋki / *n.* [C]猴子

monopoly / mə'nɒpəli / *n.* [C] 垄断;独占;专利;专卖:break(up) a ～ 打破垄断 / grant a ～ 授予专利 / hold a ～ 拥有专利 / gain a ～ 得到独家经营权

monotonous / mə'nɒtənəs / *adj.* 单一的,没有变化的;乏味的:a ～ piece of music 一首旋律单调的乐曲 / He considered this work extremely ～. 他认为这项工作极其单调乏味. 派 monotonously *adv.* ; monotony *n.*

monster / 'mɒnstə(r) / *n.* [C]怪物;妖怪:ghosts and ～s 妖魔鬼怪

month / mʌnθ / *n.* [C]月;月份:a baby of three ～s 三个月大的婴孩 / this ～ 本月 / last ～ 上个月 / next ～ 下个月 / He pays the workers by the ～. 他按月给工人们发工资.

monthly / 'mʌnθli / Ⅰ *adj.* 每月的;每月一次的:～ pay 月薪 / ～ ticket 月票 / Young people like the ～ sports magazine. 年轻人喜欢读体育月刊. Ⅱ *adv.* 每月地;每月一次地:Mother goes shopping in the supermarket ～. 妈妈每月一次去超市购物. Ⅲ *n.* 月刊

monument / 'mɒnjumənt / *n.* [C]纪念碑;纪念馆:the Monument to the People's Heroes 人民英雄纪念碑 同 memorial

mood / muːd / *n.* ❶ 心情;情绪:She is a girl of ～s. 她是一个喜怒无常的女孩. / When my grandmother is in a good ～, she would tell me interesting stories. 祖母心情好时会给我讲许多有趣的故事. 同 temper, spirit ❷语气:It is a subjunctive ～. 这是虚拟语气.

moon / muːn / *n.* (the ～) 月亮;月球

moonlight / 'muːnlaɪt / *n.* [U]月光:He followed her out into the silver ～. 他跟着她走出屋外,来到银色的月光下.

mop / mɒp / Ⅰ *n.* [C]拖把;拖布 Ⅱ *vt.* (mopped; mopping)用拖把擦洗:～ the floor 拖地板

moral / 'mɒrəl / Ⅰ *adj.* 道德的;有道义的:～ standards 道德标准 / ～ character 道德品质 Ⅱ *n.* ❶道德,品德:professional ～s 职业道德 / public ～s 公共道德 / a man without ～s 没有道德的人 反 immoral ❷教训,寓意:The ～ of the story is "Knowledge is strength. ". 这个故事的寓意是"知识就是力量". 同 lesson, teaching

morale / məˈrɑːl, məˈræl / *n.* [U;C](个人或集体的)士气,精神风貌,风貌: boost one's ～增强士气/buck up a patient's ～使病人精神振作起来

more / mɔː(r) / Ⅰ *adj.* (many 和 much 的比较级)(数)更多的;(量)更大的;(程度)更高的;附加的: More and ～ people have realized its importance. 越来越多的人认识到它的重要性。/ You should spend ～ time studying. 你应该花更多的时间去学习。同 extra, additional 反 less, fewer Ⅱ *adv.* ❶更(与两个或两个以上音节的形容词或副词构成比较级)❷(much 的比较级)更多地,更大: You need to sleep ～. 你需要更多地睡眠。❸再: Once ～, please. 请再来一次。/ I shall not go there any ～. 我再也不去那儿了。/ We saw him no ～. 我们再也没看到他了。/ ～ and ～ 越来越: The story gets ～ and ～ exciting. 故事越来越动人。Ⅲ *n.* 较多量;较多的人或物: More of us went to see the film. 我们中有较多的人去看了那场电影。/ the ～..., the ～ ...越…,越…: The ～ he reads, the ～ he likes to read. 他书读得越多,他就越喜欢读书。

moreover / mɔːrˈəʊvə(r) / *adv.* 并且,此外: It was dark and ～, it was raining hard. 天黑了,而且正下着大雨。同 besides, furthermore

morning / ˈmɔːnɪŋ / *n.* 早晨,上午: in the ～ 在上午 / this ～ 今天上午 / on Sunday ～ 星期天上午

mortal / ˈmɔːtl / Ⅰ *adj.* ❶(尤指人等生命体)死的;注定要死的,终将死亡的: All human beings are ～. 凡人都要死的。❷极度的,极大的: the ～ hatred 深仇大恨/～ pain 剧痛 ❸致死的,致命的: a ～ disease 致命的疾病 Ⅱ *n.* [C]凡人,普通人: We are all ～s. 我们皆凡人。

Moscow / ˈmɒskəʊ / *n.* 莫斯科

mosquito / məˈskiːtəʊ / *n.* [C](mosquitos 或 mosquitoes) 蚊子: Mosquitoes spread diseases. 蚊子传播疾病。

moss / mɒs / *n.* 苔藓;地衣

most / məʊst / Ⅰ *adj.* (many 和 much 的最高级)最多的;最大程度的: Those who have (the) ～ money are not always the happiest. 最有钱的人不一定最幸福。同 greatest, largest, maximum 反 least, minimun Ⅱ *n.* 最大量;

最高额;大部分;大多数: The ～ I can give you is 100 *yuan.* 我能给你的最大数额是 100 元。/ Most girls like skirts. 大多数女孩爱穿裙子。同 majority 反 minority / at (the) ～ 至多: I can pay only ten yuan at the ～. 我最多只能付 10 元钱。Ⅲ *adv.* ❶(用以构成双音节或多音节形容词和副词的最高级)❷非常,极其,十分: This is a ～ useful book. 这是一本极其有用的书。/ I shall ～ certainly go. 我一定去。派 mostly *adv.*

motel / məʊˈtel / *n.* [C] 汽车旅馆同 hotel, lodge

mother / ˈmʌðə(r) / *n.* [C]母亲: Mother's Day 母亲节 / step-～ 继母 / ～ tongue 本国语言 / ～-in-law 岳母 / ～like 母亲般的 派 motherly *adj. & adv.*

motherland / ˈmʌðəlænd / *n.* 祖国: We all love our ～. 我们都热爱我们的祖国。同 homeland, fatherland

motion / ˈməʊʃn / Ⅰ *n.* ❶运动: ～ and rest 运动与静止 同 move, movement 反 rest, stillness ❷手势;动作;姿态: make ～s with one's hand 打手势 同 gesture ❸提议;动议: make a ～ 提议 同 proposal, suggestion Ⅱ *v.* ❶打手势;示意: The chairman ～ed us (to us) to sit down. 主席做手势示意我们坐下。同 sign, gesture, wave ❷提议;动议: Our monitor ～ed to have a party on Saturday. 我们班长提议星期六聚会。同 suggest, propose 派 motional *adj.*

motivate / ˈməʊtɪveɪt / *vt.* 激励;驱使;促动: ～sb. to take action 促使某人采取行动同 drive, urge, stimulate

motivation / ˌməʊtɪˈveɪʃn / *n.* 刺激;动力;动机: She is good at English because she has strong ～ for learning it. 因为有很强的学习动机,她的英语学得很好。同 stimulation

motive / ˈməʊtɪv / *n.* 动机;目的: The police wanted to find out his ～ for the crime. 警察想弄清楚他的犯罪动机。同 motivation, purpose

motor / ˈməʊtə(r) / *n.* [C]发动机,电动机;马达: a ～ ship 汽船 /a ～ truck 载重汽车 / the ～ industry 汽车工业 同 engine, machine

motorbike / ˈməʊtəbaɪk / *n.* [C]摩托车

motorcar / ˈməʊtəkɑː / *n.* [C]汽车: More and more people want to buy a ～ now. 现在越来越多的人想买汽车。

motorcycle / ˈməʊtəsaɪkl / n. [C]摩托车

motorway / ˈməʊtəweɪ / n. [C]汽车道；高速公路 圆 driveway, highway

motto / ˈmɒtəʊ / n.[C]箴言；座右铭；格言：a school ~ 校训／The teacher often quotes ~es to teach his students. 老师常常引用格言教育学生。

mo(u)ld / məʊld / Ⅰ n. [C]模子；模型；铸模：He is a person in the ~ of Lei Feng. 他是一个雷锋式的人物。 圆 model, pattern Ⅱ vt. 使…成形；浇铸；塑造：She is trying to ~ the children into perfect people. 她正尽力把孩子们塑造成完美的人。／ He ~ed a figure out of clay. 他用模子做了一个泥像。 圆 shape

mount / maʊnt / Ⅰ v. 登上（山、梯等）；增加；上升：He ~ed his horse and rode away. 他骑上马走了。／ Our living expenses are ~ing up. 我们的生活花费正在增加。 圆 climb, ascend Ⅱ n. 山（用于山名前，略写为 Mt.）：Mount Everest 珠穆朗玛峰

mountain / ˈmaʊntən / n.[C]山 圆 hill, peak

mountainous / ˈmaʊntənəs / adj. 有山的；多山的；巨大的：~ wave 巨浪／ He lives in a ~ district. 他住在山区。 圆 hilly, towering

mourn / mɔːn / v. 悲伤；哀悼：The doctor ~ed for the dead child. 医生为死去的小孩感到悲伤。 圆 sorrow, grieve

mournful / ˈmɔːnful / adj. ❶忧伤的，悲伤的，悲痛的：the ~ cry of the wolf 狼的哀嚎／ the ~ look on one's face 脸上流露出的忧伤神情 ❷流露出悲伤之情的；令人悲痛的：~ news 令人悲痛的消息／The music is rather ~. 这首曲子非常忧伤。 派 mournfully adv.；mournfulness n.

mouse / maʊs / n. [C]（pl. mice /maɪs/）❶老鼠：All children like Mickey Mouse. 小孩都喜欢"米老鼠"。／ A cat catches mice. 猫会抓老鼠。 圆 rat ❷（计算机）鼠标

moustache / məˈstɑːʃ / n. [C]（长在嘴唇上面的）胡子

mouth / maʊθ / n. [C]（pl. mouths /maʊðz/）❶嘴：The little baby hasn't any tooth in her ~. 这小婴儿嘴里还没长牙。／ Shut your ~! 闭上你的嘴! ❷（袋、瓶、洞、河流等的）开口处：The town lies near the ~ of Changjiang River. 小城位于长江口附近。

mouthful / ˈmaʊθful / n. [C]一口；满口；少量

move / muːv / v. ❶走动；移动；搬动：Please help me to ~ the old sofa away. 请帮我把这旧沙发搬开。 圆 remove, shift ／~ in 搬进；迁进 ~ out 搬出；迁出：We ~d out on Monday and the new tenants ~d in on Tuesday. 我们星期一迁出，新房客星期二就搬进来。 ~ on 继续向前，朝前走：The officer has given the order to ~ on. 军官已下达继续前进的命令。 ❷感动；激动；打动：I was deeply ~d by the story. 我被故事深深地感动了。 圆 touch, excite

movement / ˈmuːvmənt / n. 动；活动；运动：They launched a ~ against smoking in their school. 他们学校发起一场戒烟运动。 圆 motion, activity

movie / ˈmuːvi / n. [C]影片；电影院：go to see a ~ 去看电影／ a ~ fan 影迷／ a ~ star 影星 圆 film, picture

Mr. , Mr / ˈmɪstə(r) / n. (＝mister)[C] 先生（冠于男子姓或姓名前的称呼）：Mr. Green 格林先生

Mrs. , Mrs / ˈmɪsɪz / n. 夫人，太太（冠于已婚妇女的姓或姓名前的称呼）：Mrs. Green 格林太太

Ms / mɪz / n. 女士，小姐（冠于已婚或未婚女子姓或姓名前的称呼）

much / mʌtʃ / Ⅰ adj. (more, most) 许多的；大量的：He never eats ~ for breakfast. 他早餐从来吃得不多。 圆 abundant 反 little Ⅱ n. 大量；许多：He ate ~ at the dinner. 他在宴会上吃了许多东西。 Ⅲ adv. ❶(more, most)很，非常：I shall be ~ surprised if he succeeds. 假如他成功的话，我会很惊奇的。 圆 very ❷很（修饰比较级或最高级）：He is ~ better today. 他今天好多了。 圆 greatly

mud / mʌd / n. [U]泥；泥浆：He fell down in the ~. 他摔倒在烂泥里。 圆 clay, dirt 派 muddy adj.

muddle / ˈmʌdl / Ⅰ vt. ❶将…弄乱；把…搅和在一起；把（事情等）弄糟：~ an arrangement 打乱安排 ❷使搞混，使弄不清，使糊涂：His thoughts were ~d. 他思维不清。／~ up 将…弄混，混淆：The man ~d up the date of arrival. 那人把抵达日期搞错了。 Ⅱ n. ❶糊涂，混淆：He is in so much of a ~ that he is of no help. 他非常糊涂，根本帮不上忙。 ❷混乱，凌

乱,乱七八糟;混乱的局面,糟糕:the worsening ～ of the company's finances 该公司越来越糟的财政状况

mulberry / ˈmʌlbəri / n. 桑树;桑葚

mule / mjuːl / n. [C]骡子

multi- / ˈmʌlti / (前缀) ❶表示"多的","两个以上的":～ vitamined 含多种维生素的 ❷表示"多方面的","多方位的":～ specialist 多面手

multifunction / ˌmʌltiˈfʌŋkʃn / n. [C]多功能:a ～ system 多功能系统

multimedia / ˌmʌltiˈmiːdiə / Ⅰ n. 多媒体 Ⅱ adj. 多种手段的;多种方式的:a ～ computer 多媒体电脑 / ～ software 多媒体软件

multiple / ˈmʌltɪpl / Ⅰ adj. 多样的;多重的:a ～ choice test 选择法测试 / He is a man of ～ interests. 他是一个兴趣多样的人。同 many, various Ⅱ n. 倍数

multiply / ˈmʌltɪplaɪ / v. ❶乘:6 multiplied by 5 is 30. 6 乘以 5 等于 30。反 divide ❷使增加;使繁殖:The teacher told the child that rabbits ～ rapidly. 老师告诉孩子兔子繁殖很快。同 increase, reproduce

multitude / ˈmʌltɪtjuːd / n. ❶[C]大量,许多:The mass of data available in a ～ of reliable sources makes the conclusion convincing. 大量可靠来源的数据使该结论颇具说服力。❷[C]人群,聚成一堆的人:A large ～ assembled before the auditorium for the occasion. 一大群人聚集在礼堂前等待那个重要时刻。

mum / mʌm / n. [C](儿语)妈妈

mumble / ˈmʌmbl / Ⅰ v. 含糊其词地说:咕哝着说:She was ～ing some indistinct words as she went. 她一面走,一面口中念念有词。同 murmur Ⅱ n. [C]含糊其词的话语,咕哝

mummy / ˈmʌmi / n. [C] (儿语)妈妈

municipality / mjuːˌnɪsɪˈpæləti / n. ❶[C]自治市,自治镇:Small municipalities are looking for financial help from the state. 小的自治市镇正在寻求国家的财政援助。❷市政当局

murder / ˈmɜːdə(r) / Ⅰ n. 谋杀;凶案:The man was declared guilty of ～. 那人被宣判犯了杀人罪。同 killing Ⅱ vt. 谋杀:Do you know when Lincoln was ～ed? 你知道林肯是什么时候遭谋杀的吗?同 kill 派 murderer n.

辨析 murder 指蓄意非法杀死他人:He murdered his friend in order to get gold. 为了得到黄金,他把自己的朋友谋杀了。kill 指某种原因导致人、动物、植物的死亡:Two people were killed in a car accident. 两个人在车祸中死亡。They killed the snake in the garden. 他们在花园里打死了一条蛇。The drought killed our fruit trees. 干旱使我们种的果树枯死了。

murmur / ˈmɜːmə(r) / v. 低语;低声说:The boy came in and ～ed a secret to his mother. 小男孩走进来小声地告诉他妈妈一个秘密。同 whisper

muscle / ˈmʌsl / n. 肌肉:He often goes into physical training by making his ～s. 他常常进行体育锻炼以使肌肉发达。

muscular / ˈmʌskjələ(r) / adj. 肌肉的;肌肉发达的;强健的:He exercises his ～s everyday and becomes a ～ man. 他每天锻炼肌肉,成为一个身体强健的人。同 strong

museum / mjuˈziːəm / n. [C]博物馆;展览馆:the Science Museum 科学博物馆/the History Museum 历史博物馆 / the Palace Museum in Beijing 北京故宫博物院 同 gallery, library

mushroom / ˈmʌʃrʊm / n. [C](食用)蘑菇

music / ˈmjuːzɪk / n. [U]音乐:a ～ cafe 音乐茶座 / a ～ hall 音乐厅 / ～ television (MTV)音乐电视 / classical ～ 古典音乐 / modern ～ 现代音乐 / I like folk ～. 我喜欢民间音乐。同 song, tune

musical / ˈmjuːzɪkl / adj. 音乐的;悦耳的:a ～ instrument 乐器 同 tuneful

musician / mjuˈzɪʃən / n. [C]音乐家 同 artist, composer

Muslim / ˈmuzlɪm, ˈmʌzlɪm / Ⅰ n. [C]穆斯林 Ⅱ adj. 穆斯林的;伊斯兰教的;伊斯兰文化的

must / mʌst, məst / aux. v. ❶必须,应该(表示必要):Everybody ～ obey the laws. 人人都必须遵纪守法。❷必定,必然(表示猜测):You ～ be hungry after a long walk. 你走了那么远的路一定饿了。

mustache / məˈstɑːʃ / n. (=moustache) 髭;小胡子

mustard / ˈmʌstəd / n. [U]芥末,芥子:Mustard is hot but many people like it. 芥末很辣,但很多人喜欢吃。

M

mute / mjuːt / Ⅰ *adj.* 哑的；沉默的 圃 voiceless，silent Ⅱ *n.* ❶[C]哑巴 ❷（乐器的）弱音器

mutter / 'mʌtə(r) / Ⅰ *v.* 咕哝；抱怨 圃 mumble，murmur Ⅱ *n.* 低语；小声抱怨

mutton / 'mʌtn / *n.* [U] 羊肉：instant-boiled ～ 涮羊肉

mutual / 'mjuːtʃuəl / *adj.* 相互的；共同的：～ benefit 互惠 / ～ help and support 互相帮助与支持 圃 two-sided，common

my / maɪ / *pron.* 我的（形容词性物主代词）：It's ～ book. 那是我的书。

myself / maɪ'self / *pron.* 我自己（反身代词）：I hurt ～. 我伤了自己。/ I can do it by ～. 我能独自做。

mysterious / mɪ'stɪəriəs / *adj.* 神秘的 圃 secret，puzzling

mystery / 'mɪstri / *n.* [C] 神秘：disclose a ～ 揭开奥秘 / Don't make a ～ of it. 不要让这事神秘化。圃 secret，puzzle

myth / mɪθ / *n.* [C] 神话；神话式的人（或故事）：I like modern fiction as well as ～s. 我不仅喜欢神话故事，也喜欢现代小说。

mythology / mɪ'θɒlədʒi / *n.* ❶神话：classical ～古典神话/～ book 神话书 ❷[U]神话研究；神话学 ❸神话集：the myth-ologies of primitive races 原始民族神话集 派 mythological *adj.*

M

N n

nail / neɪl / Ⅰ *n.* ❶钉子：draw out a ～ 拔出钉子 / drive（hammer，knock）in a ～ 把钉子敲进去 / **hit the ～ on the head** 击中要害，一针见血 ❷指甲；趾甲：cut ～s 剪指甲 / dye the ～s 染指甲 / **bite one's ～s 咬指甲；束手无策** Ⅱ *vt.* 钉住，钉牢：**～ one's eyes on sth.** 盯住某物看，目不转睛 同 pin，fasten

naive / naɪˈiːv，naɪˈiːv / *adj.* 天真无邪的；轻信的；无经验的 同 innocent

naked / ˈneɪkɪd / *adj.* 裸体的；无遮掩的：～ eye 肉眼 / ～ to the waist 光着上身；赤膊 with ～ fists 赤手空拳地 同 bare，undressed 反 dressed，concealed

name / neɪm / Ⅰ *n.* [C]名字；姓名 Ⅱ *v.* ❶取名：We ～d the baby John. 我们给婴孩取名约翰。❷叫出名字：Can you ～ these trees? 你能叫出这些树的名字吗? ❸提名，任命：Mr. Wang has been ～d for the director-ship. 王先生已经被提名任董事之职。同 choose，appoint

namely / ˈneɪmli / *adv.* 即，就是：Only one boy was absent，～ Harry. 只有一个小孩缺席，就是哈里。同 that is，that is to say

nap / næp / *n.* [C]小睡；打盹：have（take）a ～ after lunch 午饭后小睡片刻 同 rest，sleep

napkin / ˈnæpkɪn / *n.* [C] ❶餐巾 ❷小毛巾 ❸尿布

narrate / nəˈreɪt / *v.* 作解说；叙述 同 tell，state 派 narration *n.*

narrative / ˈnærətɪv / Ⅰ *n.* ❶[C]记叙文；故事 ❷[U]叙述，讲述；记叙体；叙述手法：He essay has too much ～. 他的论文中叙述的成分太多。/ the use of ～ in poetry 诗歌中的叙事手法 Ⅱ *adj.* 叙述的；叙事体的；以故事形式的：a long narrative poem 一首长篇叙事诗

narrow / ˈnærəʊ / Ⅰ *adj.* 窄的；狭的：The road was too ～ for cars to pass. 这条路太窄了，车辆通不过。/ ～ escape from death 幸免于难，死

里逃生 同 tight，small 反 broad，wide Ⅱ *v.* 使变窄 同 tighten，limit 反 broaden，widen 派 narrowness *n.*

narrowly / ˈnærəʊli / *adv.* 仅仅；勉强地：He ～ escaped drowning. 他差一点溺死。

nasal / ˈneɪzəl / *adj.* ❶鼻的：the ～ cavity 鼻腔 ❷鼻音的：～ sound 鼻音

nasty / ˈnɑːsti，ˈnæsti / *adj.* 肮脏的；卑劣的，下流的；令人厌恶的 同 dirty，annoying 反 decent，kind

nation / ˈneɪʃn / *n.* [C] 国家；民族：the United Nations 联合国 / the Chinese ～ 中华民族 同 country，state

national / ˈnæʃnəl / *adj.* 国家的；民族的：～ affairs 国家大事

nationality / ˌnæʃəˈnæləti / *n.* 国籍；民族

native / ˈneɪtɪv / *adj.* 本地的；本土的：your ～ land 你的祖国 / ～ language 母语 同 home，local

natural / ˈnætʃrəl / *adj.* ❶自然界的；天然的：～ gas 天然气 / ～ science 自然科学 / ～ selection 自然淘汰 同 original 反 unnatural，artificial ❷生来的，天赋的：～ gift 天赋才能 / She is a ～ leader. 她是个天生的领导者。同 inborn ❸常情的，通常的：It's ～ to shake hands with someone you've just met. 与初次见面的人握手是常情。同 normal，regular 派 naturally *adv.*

nature / ˈneɪtʃə(r) / *n.* ❶[U] 自然；自然界：Is ～ at its best in spring? 自然界在春天最美吗? ❷性质；本质；天性 同 character，essence

naughty / ˈnɔːti / *adj.* 不听从的；顽皮的；淘气的：a ～ child 顽皮的小孩 同 playful，mischievous 派 naughtily *adv.*；naughtiness *n.*

naval / ˈneɪvəl / *adj.* 海军的；军舰的

navy / ˈneɪvi / *n.* [C] 海军

near / nɪə(r) / Ⅰ *adv.*（nearer，nearest）（时间，空间等）近，邻近：He lives ～ by. 他住在附近。同 close 反 far Ⅱ *adj.*（-er，-est）近

的；接近的：Can you tell me the ～est way to the station? 你能告诉我去车站的近路吗？/ The examination is ～ at hand. 考试快到了。同 close, neighboring 反 far, distant / ～sighted adj. 近视的 Ⅲ prep. 在…附近：Don't go ～ the edge. 不要走近边沿。同 close to, not far from

nearby / ˌnɪəˈbaɪ / Ⅰ adj. 附近的 同 close, near 反 far, distant Ⅱ adv. 在附近 同 close, near 反 distantly

nearly / ˈnɪəli / adv. 几乎；将近：He is ～ ready. 他快准备好了。同 about, almost 反 completely, wholly

neat / niːt / adj. 整洁的；整齐的；精巧的：a ～ desk 整洁的书桌 / a ～ child 爱整洁的孩子 同 clean, tidy 反 untidy, disorderly

辨析

neat 指清洁、整齐的情形，也指做事干净利落：Her house is as neat as a pin. 她的家里非常整洁。He was remarkably neat in his dress. 他穿戴非常整齐。The Minister of Defence was always neat in everything he did. 国防部长每件事都做得干净利落。**orderly** 指物件安排得妥当、不混乱，或指人思路清晰、做事有条理：The room looked orderly. 这间屋子看起来有条理。Mr. Wells has an orderly mind. 韦尔斯先生办事有条不紊。**tidy** 指地方收拾得整洁，物品摆放得整齐，也指人习惯上爱整洁：Their grandmother keeps the house tidy. 他们的祖母把房子收拾得整整齐齐。My son is very tidy and never goes out without combing his hair. 我儿子是一个非常爱整洁的人，出门前总要把头发梳好。

necessary / ˈnesəsəri / adj. 必要的；必需的；必然的；必定的：Sleep is ～ for health. 睡眠对保持健康是必要的。同 needed, essential 反 unnecessary, needless 派 necessarily adv.

用法

❶necessary 作句子谓语时，主语不能指人，可以说：It is necessary to finish the work within this week. 或 The work is necessary to be finished within this week. 或 It is necessary for us to finish the work within this week. （在本周内完成这项工作是有必要的。）但不能说：We are necessary to finish the work within this week. ❷necessary 后面接介词 for 或 to，一般没区别：Food is necessary for life. 食物对生命来说是必要的。

Books are necessary to students. 书对学生来说是必不可少的。但 it is necessary for us to do 等句式里的 for 不可改为 to。❸在 it is (was) necessary ＋ that 句式里，that 引导的从句中，谓语用虚拟语气，即 should 加上动词原形或直接用动词原形：It is necessary that he should come here every Sunday. It is necessary that he come here every Sunday. 他每个星期天来是有必要的。

necessity / nəˈsesəti / n. 必需品；急需品：bare (basic, daily, household) necessities 最低限度的(基本的、日用的、家庭的)必需品 / Food and warmth are necessities. 食物和温暖是不可缺少的东西。/ Necessity is the mother of invention. 需要是发明之母。同 need, demand

neck / nek / n. [C]颈；脖子

necklace / ˈnekləs / n. [C]项链；项圈

need / niːd / Ⅰ aux. v. 需要；必要：You needn't talk so loud. 你不必讲得那么大声。/ Need you go yet? 你还必须去吗？Ⅱ vt. ❶需要：The flowers ～ rain. 这些花需要雨水。Your composition ～s rewriting. 你的文章需要重写。同 want, demand ❷必须(通常用于疑问句和否定句中)：Does he ～ to know? 他必须知道吗？/ He did not ～ to be reminded about it. 不必提醒他那件事。Ⅲ n. 缺乏；需要；必须：A friend in ～ is a friend indeed. 患难朋友才是真正的朋友。/ in (great) ～ of (很)需要 同 want, necessity 反 wealth, excess

用法

❶ need 表示"需要"之意时，接着名词主动形式表示被动含义：His coat needs mending. 如动名词被换为不定式，则要用被动形式：His coat needs to be mended. 他的上衣需要补一下。类似用法的动词还有 want, require 等。❷ there is need 句式后面接 for ＋ 名词的结构：There is need for more money. 需要更多的钱。当 need 前面有 a, the, no, some, any, not much 等修饰时，need 后面接 for 或 of 均可：There is a great need for (of) a book on this subject. 非常需要一本关于这个主题的书。There's no need for (of) anxiety. 用不着急急。

needless / ˈniːdləs / adj. 不必要的；多余的：～ to say 不用说，当然 同 unnecessary, useless 反 essential, useful

needle / ˈniːdl / n. [C]针

negative / ˈnegətɪv / Ⅰ adj. ❶否定的 同 refusing, opposing 反 affirmative, positive ❷(数学)负的;~ sign 负号 / ~ quantity 负数 ❸(电)负的;阴性的 ❹(摄影)底片 Ⅱ n. [C] ❶否定;否认:Two ~s make an affirmative. 否定之否定为肯定。❷(数学)负数 ❸(摄影)底片

neglect / nɪˈglekt / Ⅰ vt. 忽视;忽略:He ~ed his health. 他忽视了他的健康。同 ignore, disregard 反 notice, regard Ⅱ n. [U]怠慢,忽视 同 inattention, idleness 反 attention, regard 派 neglectful adj. ; neglectfully adv.

辨析

neglect 强调对一个人、一件工作或一项任务未给予必要的注意:He neglected his family. 他不顾家庭。He neglected to give back his friend the money. 他(因疏忽)忘记还朋友的钱了。ignore 指故意拒绝考虑某事或完全忽视某一警告:The driver ignored the dangerous signs until he pulled up at the wrecked bridge. 这位司机无视危险信号,一直把车开到破损的桥前才停下来。overlook 强调无心地忽略了应注意的事物:He overlooked the telephone bill. 他忽略了电话缴费单。slight 强调故意忽视一个人、一样东西、一件事或一种责任,也指故意对某人表现出不尊重的态度:The student slighted the midterm test. 这学生轻视这次中期考试。She felt slighted because she was not asked to the party. 因没被邀请参加宴会,她感到遭到轻视。

negligence / ˈneglɪdʒəns / n. [U]疏忽;玩忽职守;不留心,粗心大意:He is very concerned in case his company are sued for ~. 他小心从事,以免公司因玩忽职守而遭起诉。The fire was caused by ~. 大火是因粗心大意而引起的。

negotiate / nɪˈgəʊʃɪeɪt / v. 谈判;协商:They ~d a peace treaty. 他们商订和平条约。同 discuss, debate 派 negotiation n.

Negro / ˈniːgrəʊ / n. [C](pl. Negroes) 黑人(有轻蔑之意,现用 Black, Black people 或 Black American 美国黑人)

neighbo(u)r / ˈneɪbə(r) / Ⅰ n. [C]邻居;邻国 同 borderer Ⅱ vi. 相邻,紧挨着:Their farm ~s on a large stretch of woods. 他们的农场与一大片树林相邻。同 border, touch 派 neighbo(u)rly adj.

neighbo(u)rhood / ˈneɪbəhʊd / n. 邻近地区;附近地方:A house was on fire in our ~ last night. 昨晚我们附近一所房子失火了。同 community, district

neither / ˈnaɪðə(r) , ˈniːðə(r) / Ⅰ adj. (与单

数名词连用)(两者)都不; Neither statement is true. 两种说法都不是真的。Ⅱ pron. (两者)都不:I like ~ of them. 两个我都不喜欢。Ⅲ adv. ~ ... nor ... 既不…也不…:It's ~ pleasant to eat nor good for your health. 它既不好吃,也不利于你的健康。Ⅳ conj. 既不…也不…,任何一个…都不…;Mary doesn't like to sing,~ does she dance. 玛丽既不喜欢唱歌,也不爱跳舞。

用法

❶neither 表示"两人或两物都不": I have two dictionaries, but neither (one) is here. 我有两本字典,但一本也不在这儿。如果表示"两者以上都不",用 none: I have three dictionaries, but none is here. 我有三本词典,但一本也不在这儿。❷在"neither... nor..."句式中动词的人称和数由 nor 后面的名词或代词的人称和数决定:Neither the father nor the sons are wrong. Neither the sons nor the father is wrong. 父亲和儿子们都没错。

nephew / ˈnevjuː , ˈnefjuː / n. [C]侄子;外甥

nerve / nɜːv / n. ❶[C]神经 ❷勇气;胆量 同 courage, strength

nervous / ˈnɜːvəs / adj. ❶神经紧张的;神经过敏的;Some are ~ in the dark. 有些人在黑暗处就神经紧张。同 anxious, fearful 反 steady, calm

nest / nest / Ⅰ n. [C]巢;窝 Ⅱ vi. 筑巢;做窝

net¹ / net / n. [C] ❶网;罗网:a fishing (hair, tennis) ~ 鱼(发,网球)网 同 web ❷网络,通信网,网状系统

net² / net / Ⅰ adj. 净的;纯的:a ~ price 实价 / a ~ profit 纯利;净利 同 clear, pure 反 gross Ⅱ n. 净重;净利;实价 同 gain 反 loss

network / ˈnetwɜːk / n. ❶网络;网状系统 ❷广播网,电视网:TV networks 电视广播网

neural / ˈnjʊərəl / adj. 神经的;神经系统的

neutral / ˈnjuːtrəl / Ⅰ adj. 中立的;中立国的;中性的 Ⅱ n. [C]中立国;中立者

never / ˈnevə(r) / adv. 从未;未曾;决不:I have ~ been there. 我从未到过那里。同 on no account 反 always, forever ; Never mind. 请勿介意。

nevertheless / ˌnevəðəˈles / adv. &. conj. 然而;虽然如此;依然 同 anyhow, however

new / njuː / adj. 新的;从未有过的;初见到的;初听到的:a ~ invention 一项新发明;/ New Year's Day 元旦 / New Year's Eve 除夕

同 fresh,recent 反 old,used 派 newly adv.

newcomer / 'njuːkʌmə(r) / n. [C] ❶新来的人 ❷新出现的事物

news / njuːz / n. [U]新闻,消息:a piece of ～ 一条消息;a ～ report 新闻报道 同 information,message

❶news 只用作单数:News has come. 消息已经传来。❷news 前面不可直接加 a,"一条新闻"的表达法为 a piece (bit) of news,"多条新闻"为 pieces (bits) of news,"一则新闻"为 an item of news 或 a news item,"多则新闻"为 items of news。

newspaper / 'njuːzpeɪpə(r) / n. [C]报纸:I read it in the ～. 我在报纸上看到的。

newsstand / 'njuː(z)stænd / n. [C]报摊,书报亭

next / nekst / Ⅰ adj. 下一个的;其次的:the ～ train 下班火车 / the ～ room 隔壁房间 / ～ Monday 下星期一 同 following,later 反 last,previous Ⅱ adv. 在这以后;其次;然后:What are you going to do ～? 你下一步要做什么呢? Ⅲ prep. 靠近;贴近:May I bring my chair ～ yours? 我可以把我的椅子搬到你的旁边吗? ▷ **to** 相邻;靠近:They live ～ to the post office. 他们住在邮局隔壁。

nibble / 'nɪbl / Ⅰ v. 小口吃;一点点地咬(或吃);啃:She was nibbling her food like a rabbit. 她像兔子一样地小口吃东西/Inflation was nibbling away at her savings. 通货膨胀把她的积蓄一点点地吞噬掉了。Ⅱ n. [C] ❶咬下的少量食物;一口的量;少量:There's not even a ～ left. 甚至连一口吃的都没剩下。❷小口的吃,一点一点地咬(或吃)

nice / naɪs / adj. 令人愉快的;优美的;宜人的;友善的:a ～ face 美丽的面孔 / ～ weather 好天气 / ～ taste 好味道 / He was ～ to us. 他对我们很友善。同 fine,pleasant 反 unpleasant,unfriendly

nickel / 'nɪkl / n. [U]镍(符号 Ni)

nickname / 'nɪkneɪm / Ⅰ n. 绰号;昵称 同 pet name,baby name Ⅱ vt. 给(某人)取绰号;以绰号称呼

niece / niːs / n. [C]侄女;甥女

night / naɪt / n. 夜晚:They worked from morning till ～. 他们从早到晚地干活。同 dark,nighttime 反 day,daytime / **day and** ～

夜以继日地;不断地:travel day and ～ for a week 日夜不停地旅行一个星期 **all** ～ **long** 整夜地;彻夜:We watched all ～ long. 我们彻夜看守。**at** ～ 在夜里:He came home very late at ～. 他夜里回家很晚。**by** ～ 夜间:They don't work by day but by ～. 他们白天不工作,而是夜里工作。

nightmare / 'naɪtmeə(r) / n. [C] 噩梦;梦魇般的经历 同 bad dream,horror

nine / naɪn / Ⅰ num. 九 Ⅱ adj. 九个(的)

nineteen / ˌnaɪn'tiːn / Ⅰ num. 十九 Ⅱ adj. 十九个(的)

nineteenth / ˌnaɪn'tiːnθ / Ⅰ num. 第十九;十九分之一 Ⅱ adj. 第十九的;十九分之一的

nip / nɪp / Ⅰ (nipped;nipping) v. ❶拧,捏,掐;猛咬:The dog ～ped at his heels. 狗咬住了他的脚后跟。/ ～ the tip off the cigar 把雪茄的头掐掉 ❷疾走,跑动:Where did you ～ off to? 你到哪里去了? Ⅱ n. [C]拧捏,掐;咬:The dog gave him a few ～s on the leg. 狗在他腿上咬了几下。/ ～ **and tuck** 势均力敌的,不分上下的:The two runners contested the race closely —it was ～ and tuck all the way. 那两个赛跑选手竞争激烈一在比赛中一直不相上下。

ninetieth / 'naɪntɪəθ / Ⅰ num. 第九十;九十分之一 Ⅱ adj. 第九十的;九十分之一的

ninety / 'naɪntɪ / Ⅰ num. 九十 Ⅱ adj. 九十个(的)

ninth / naɪnθ / Ⅰ num. 第九;九分之一 Ⅱ adj. 第九个的;九分之一的

nitrogen / 'naɪtrədʒən / n. [U]氮

no / nəʊ / Ⅰ adj. 没有的 Ⅱ adv. 不,并非:～ **longer** 不再:He no longer lived here. 他不再住这里。～ **more than** 不过,仅仅:He has ～ more than 10 dollars. 他只有十美元。/ He is ～ more than a puppet. 他只不过是 个傀儡。

No. / 'nʌmbə(r) / n. (＝number)号码;数目:the No. 2 Middle School 第二中学

Nobel / nəʊ'bel / n. 诺贝尔(瑞典化学家,1833—1896;炸药的发明者;根据他的遗言将其遗产作为基金而设立诺贝尔奖):～ prize 诺贝尔奖

noble / 'nəʊbl / Ⅰ adj. ❶高尚的;崇高的:a ～ deed 伟大的事迹 / a man of ～ mind 思想高尚的人 同 great,selfless 反 selfish,dishonest ❷贵族的,高贵的:～ birth 高贵的出身 Ⅱ n. [C](通常用 pl.)贵族

nobody / 'nəʊbədɪ / pron. 没有人;无人

用法

❶nobody 一般被视为单数：There is nobody in the room. 房间里没有人。❷ no-body 一般不和 not 之类的否定词连用，如一般不说：Nobody does not like it. 而说：Everybody likes it. 人人都喜欢它。

nod / nɒd / Ⅰ v. (nodded；nodding)点头(表示同意或打招呼)：I asked if he could come and he ~ded. 我问他是否能来，他点头答应了。同 bow　Ⅱ n. [C]❶点头；点头示意 ❷打盹；打瞌睡

noise / nɔɪz / n. 噪声；嘈杂声；响声：make a big (loud) ~ 大声喧闹 / ~ pollution 噪声污染 同 sound，roar 反 quiet，silence

辨析

noise 指令人讨厌的噪声：She enjoyed the holiday, being away from city noises. 她喜欢去度假，远离城市的喧闹。sound 含义最广，泛指各种声音，无论是乐音还是噪声：She could hear the sound of cars passing outside. 她能听见外面开过的汽车发出的声音。voice 指人说话或唱歌时发出的声音：The human voice can express every possible feelings. 人的声音能表达各种可能的感情。

noisy / ˈnɔɪzi / adj. (-ier,-iest)吵闹的；嘈杂的：a ~ boy 吵闹的孩子 同 loud，deafening 反 quiet，silent

nominate / ˈnɒmɪneɪt / vt. 提名；推荐；任命同 name，appoint 派 nomination n.

nominative / ˈnɒmɪnətɪv / Ⅰ adj. ❶(语法)主格的：the ~ case 主格 ❷被提名的，被推荐的；指定的 Ⅱ n. [C]❶主格 ❷主格词

nonconductor / ˌnɒnkənˈfɔːmɪst / n. 非导体；绝缘体

none / nʌn / pron. 毫无；一个也没有 同 no-body，nothing 反 everybody，everything

用法

❶none (of)后面的谓语动词既可用单数也可用复数：None of these are (is) mine. 这些没有一个是我的。❷none of 后面的名词或代词指两个以上的人或物：None of my three sisters are at home. 我的三个姐姐一个也不在家。❸none 表示"没有一个"时，后面不能用不可数名词，如不能说：None of the water has been spilt. 应该说：No water has been spilt. 一点水也没洒出去。但是当 none (of)只表示否定含义时，后面可用不可数名词：That's none of your business. 那不关你的事。

nonsense / ˈnɒnsəns / n. [U]无意义的话；废话；胡说；愚蠢的行动：That's all ~. 那全是胡说。同 foolishness，rubbish 反 sense，truth

nonstop / nɒnˈstɒp / Ⅰ adj. ❶(火车、飞机等)中途不停的，直达的：a ~ flight from Beijing to New York 从北京直飞纽约的航班 ❷不停顿的，不间断的，连续的：80 minutes of ~ music 连续演奏 80 分钟的音乐 Ⅱ adv. ❶直达地，直飞地：They drove ~ from Los Angeles to New York. 他们从洛杉矶直驶纽约。❷不间断：They are talking ~ for eight hours. 他们连续交谈了 8 个小时。

noodle / ˈnuːdl / n. [C](通常用 pl.)面条：Do you like ~s in chicken soup? 你喜欢吃鸡汤面吗?

noon / nuːn / n. [U]中午；正午 同 midday 反 midnight/ at ~ 在中午：He often has a nap at ~. 他常常在中午睡一会儿。

nor / nɔː(r) / conj. & adv. 也不(用在 neither 或 not 之后)

normal / ˈnɔːml / adj. 正常的；常态的；正规的：~ temperature of the human body 人体的正常温度 / a ~ college 师范学院 同 u-sual，regular 反 abnormal，unusual

north / nɔːθ / Ⅰ n. [U]北部；北方：a room facing ~ 朝北的房子 Ⅱ adj. 北部的；北方的：North China 华北 Ⅲ adv. 在北方；向北方：I am going ~. 我要向北走。

northward / ˈnɔːθwəd / adv. 向北方

northeast / ˌnɔːθˈiːst / Ⅰ n. (the ~) 东北；东北部 Ⅱ adj. 东北的；向东北方的 Ⅲ adv. 向东北；在东北

northern / ˈnɔːðən / adj. 北方的；北部的

northwest / ˌnɔːθˈwest / Ⅰ n. (the ~) 西北；西北部 Ⅱ adj. 西北的；向西北的 Ⅲ adv. 向西北；在西南

nose / nəʊz / n. [C]鼻子：eagle ~ 鹰钩鼻 / flat ~ 扁鼻子 / running ~ 流鼻涕的鼻子 / vegetable ~ 蒜头鼻子

not / nɒt / adv. 不：not ... any longer (not ... any more)不再/ not ... until ... 直到…才…

用法

❶not 用于帮助构成各种否定句：I cannot wait any longer. 我不能再等了。❷not 放在一些动词后面，如 think, suppose, believe, expect, fear, hope, seem, appear, be afraid 等代替一个从句，如：Will he come tomorrow?

他明天要来吗？可以答：I believe not. 我相信他不会来。I think not. 我想他不会来。I suppose not. 我猜他不会来。I am afraid not. 恐怕他不会来。这些句里的 not 代替的是 that he will not come tomorrow. 如果不用 not 代替从句，习惯上把 not 放在主句里，通常是 I do not believe (do not think, do not suppose, do not expect) that he will come tomorrow. ❸not only ... but also ... 着重强调 but also 后的内容：He is not only a scientist but also a fighter for peace. 他不仅是科学家而且是和平战士。not only还可以接 but 或 but...as well: It concerns not only me but you as well. 这事不但与我有关，而且也与你有关。

notable / ˈnəʊtəbl / Ⅰ *adj.* ❶值得注意的；显著的：a ～ moment in the history 历史上重要的一刻 ❷著名的，重要的：His production is ～ for its humor. 他的创作主要以其幽默而著称。Ⅱ *n.* [C]名人，显要人物

note / nəʊt / Ⅰ *n.* [C] ❶笔记；摘记：I didn't take any ～s. 我没有记笔记。同 record ❷短信；便条：write a thank-you ～ 写一张表示感谢的便条同 message ❸钞票；账单同 bill Ⅱ *v.* 注意，留心；记下：The policeman ～d down every word he said. 警察把他所说的每一个字都记了下来。同 notice 反 overlook

noted / ˈnəʊtɪd / *adj.* 著名的；闻名的 同 famous, well-known 反 unknown

nothing / ˈnʌθɪŋ / *pron.* 没什么；没什么东西同 naught, zero / **have ～ on** 什么也没穿 **have ～ to do with ...** 与…无关

notice / ˈnəʊtɪs / Ⅰ *n.* 注意；布告；公告：You have to stay here till further ～. 你得留在这儿直到接到通知为止。同 attention, poster 反 disregard, neglect / **at (on) short** ～ 一接通知马上，立刻 **take no ～ of** 不注意；不理睬：Take no ～ of what they're saying about you. 别理睬他们说你什么。**take ～ of** 注意，留心 Ⅱ *v.* 注意到，留心；正式通知：I ～d a big difference. 我注意到一大差别。同 see, observe 反 ignore, overlook

notify / ˈnəʊtɪfaɪ / *vt.* (正式)通知，告知 同 inform, tell

notion / ˈnəʊʃn / *n.* 观念；想法；意向 同 idea, belief

notorious / nəʊˈtɔːriəs / *adj.* 臭名昭著的；声名狼藉的 同 infamous, dishonor-able 反 famous, noted

noun / naʊn / *n.* [C]名词：a proper ～ 专有名词

nourish / ˈnʌrɪʃ / *vt.* 提供养分；滋养；养育同 nurture, feed 反 starve

nourishing / ˈnʌrɪʃɪŋ / *adj.* (尤指食物)有营养的；滋补的：This kind of food is not very ～. 这种食物营养不太丰富。/a ～ drink 有滋养作用的饮品

nourishment / ˈnʌrɪʃmənt / *n.* [U]滋养品；营养；食物 同 nutrition, food

novel¹ / ˈnɒvl / *n.* [C] 小说

novel² / ˈnɒvl / *adj.* 新颖的；新奇的同 new, unusual 反 usual, common 派 novelty *n.*

November / nəʊˈvembə(r) / *n.* 十一月

now / naʊ / *adv.* 现在：He is here ～. 他此刻在这儿。同 today, present / **～(every) and then (again)** 有时候；时常：She goes to a movie ～ and then. 她时常去看电影。**～ that** 既然：Now that you've grown up, you must stop this childish behaviour. 你既然长大了，就必须停止这种幼稚的行为。

nowadays / ˈnaʊədeɪz / *adv.* 现今；现在

nowhere / ˈnəʊweə(r) / *adv.* ❶哪儿也不 ❷毫无结果

nuclear / ˈnjuːklɪə(r) / *adj.* ❶核能的：～ explosion 核爆炸 / ～ power plant (station)

核能发电站 / ～ test 核试验 ❷核的；核心的 ❸(生物)细胞核的

nucleus / ˈnjuːkliəs / *n.* [C] (*pl.* nuclei / ˈnjuːklaɪ / 或 nucleuses) ❶核，核心 圖 core, heart ❷(生物)细胞核

nuisance / ˈnjuːsəns / *n.* [C]讨厌的人或事 圖 annoyance, pest

null / nʌl / *adj.* ❶没有价值的，无意义的；无效的：It makes the previous agreement ～. 这使得原有的协议失效。/ ～ **and void** 无约束力的，无效的 ❷(集合)空的：a ～ set 空集合

numb / nʌm / Ⅰ *adj.* ❶麻木的，无感觉的(与 with 连用)：My fingers are ～ with cold. 我的手指冻僵了。❷无感情的，冷淡的；表情僵硬的：Nothing could rouse her from a ～ indifference. 没有什么能改变她的麻木不仁。Ⅱ *vt.* ❶使麻木；使失去知觉

number / ˈnʌmbə(r) / Ⅰ *n.* ❶数：even(odd) ～ 偶数(奇数) / five-digit ～ 五位数 / known (unknown) ～ 已知(未知)数 / plural (singular) ～ 复(单)数 / winning ～ (彩票)获奖号 / wrong ～ 错电话号 / His telephone number is 6611224. 他的电话号码是 6611224。圖 figure ❷数量；总数：They were fifteen in ～. 他们总共是 15 个。圖 amount, total Ⅱ *v.* 编号；计数：The students of the school ～ over 2,000. 这所学校的学生人数超过 2000。圖 count, compute

辨析

numbers of(＋名词复数)，后面的谓语动词用复数：Numbers of people are coming to see the exhibition. 许多人要来参观这个展览。**a number of**(＋名词复数)，后面的谓语动词可用复数，也可用单数：A number of boys are in the next room. 一些男孩在隔壁房间里。**the number of**(＋名词复数)，后面的谓语动词一般只能用单数：The number of your fingers is ten. 你的手指总数是 10。

numerous / ˈnjuːmərəs / *adj.* 许许多多的；大批的：～ stars 许多星星 圖 many 反 few

nurse / nɜːs / *n.* [C] ❶保姆 ❷护士

nursery / ˈnɜːsəri / *n.* [C]幼儿室；托儿所：day (night) ～ 日间(夜间)托儿所

nut / nʌt / *n.* [C]坚果

nutrition / njuˈtrɪʃn / *n.* [U]营养；营养物；营养学

nutritionist / njuˈtrɪʃənɪst / *n.* [C]营养学家

nutritious / njuˈtrɪʃəs / *adj.* 有营养的

nylon / ˈnaɪlɒn / *n.* ❶[U]尼龙 ❷(*pl.*)尼龙袜

N

O o

oak / əʊk / n. 橡树；橡木

oar / ɔː(r) / n. [C]桨；橹

oasis / əʊˈeɪsɪs / n. [C] (pl. oases) ❶(沙漠中的)绿洲 ❷令人宽慰(或愉快)的事情；安稳的地方；安定时期，平稳期：He worked six days a week and looked forward to his day off an ～ of rest and relaxation. 他每周工作六天，盼望有朝一日能够度假，作为其尽情休息和娱乐的慰藉。

oat / əʊt / n. [C]燕麦种子；燕麦谷粒；燕麦庄稼

oath / əʊθ / n. [C] ❶誓言；誓约 圁 pledge ❷ (在法庭的)宣誓

obedience / əˈbiːdɪəns / n. [U]听从，服从；顺从；遵从：A soldier must give implicit ～ to his commanding officers. 士兵必须绝对服从他的长官。～ to a strict moral code is central to this society. 严格遵守道德规范是这个社会的宗旨。

obedient / əˈbiːdɪənt / adj. 服从的；顺从的；听话的圁 faithful, devoted 圂 disobedient, stubborn

obey / əˈbeɪ / v. 服从；听从：Soldiers have to ～ orders. 军人须服从命令。圁 observe, follow圂 disobey, refuse

object Ⅰ / ˈɒbdʒɪkt / n. ❶物体；物品：Tell me the names of the ～s in this room. 告诉我这屋里各物的名称。圁 thing, article ❷目标；目的：an ～ of study 研究的对象 圁 subject, target ❸(语法)宾语 Ⅱ /əbˈdʒekt / v. 不赞成；反对；抗议：I ～ to doing it. 我不赞成这件事。圁 oppose, dislike圂 approve, agree

用法

object 作不及物动词时后接介词 to，宾语表示反对的内容，object 作及物动词时后面一般接 that 引导的从句，从句表示反对的理由：He objected that I was not careful enough. 他因我不仔细而提出反对。I object to paying him. 我反对付他钱。Her mother objected to her going out at night. 她母亲反对她晚上出去。

objection / əbˈdʒekʃn / n. 反对；异议；反对的理由：What is your ～ to (against) my plan? 你反对我计划的理由是什么? 圁 disapproval, complaint圂 approval, agreement

objective / əbˈdʒektɪv / Ⅰ adj. ❶客观的；物体的；如实的 圁 impartial, real圂 subjective, personal ❷(语法)宾格的 Ⅱ n. [C] ❶目标；宗旨圁 aim, goal ❷(语法)宾格

obligate / ˈɒblɪɡeɪt / vt. ❶(在道义上或法律上)使受束缚(或制约)：I felt ～d to turn up on time. 我觉得必须准时露面。❷强迫；责成：She feels ～d to make the background of her books as factual and authentic as possible. 她觉得必须使其书中描写的背景尽量真实可信。

obligation / ˌɒblɪˈɡeɪʃn / n. 义务；责任圁 duty, responsibility

oblige / əˈblaɪdʒ / vt. ❶要求：The law ～s parents to send their children to school. 法律要求父母送子女入学。圁 require, demand ❷强迫(尤用被动式)：They were ～d to sell their house in order to pay their debts. 他们被迫卖房子来还债。圁 force, compel

oblique / əˈbliːk / adj. ❶斜的，倾斜的；歪的：an ～ line 斜线 ❷不直截了当的，转弯抹角的；间接的：He took this as an ～ reference to his own affairs. 他认为这是在影射他自己的事情。

obscure / əbˈskjʊə(r) / Ⅰ adj. ❶晦涩的，深奥的；费解的，难懂的：The meaning of this essay is very ～; I really do not understand it. 这篇文章的意思极为深奥，我实在无法理解。❷含糊不清的，不明确的：The ～ words baffled him. 这些含糊不清的话语使他大惑不解。❸黑暗(笔昙)的；昏暗的；模糊的，不明显的：an ～ figure 隐约可见的身影 Ⅱ vt. ❶使模糊，使看不清：Light rain began to fall and ～d the setting sun. 细雨开始降落，使正在沉落的夕阳变得模糊不清了。❷使费解；使混淆不清；隐瞒，掩盖：The management deliberately ～d the real situation from federal investigators. 管理部门故意向联邦调查员隐瞒事件的真相。派 obscurely *adv.*

辨析

obscure，ambiguous，vague 均有"含糊的，不明确的"之意。**obscure** 表示因事物被掩藏或因智力局限而显得意义隐晦深奥，难以理解：Is the meaning still ～ to you? 你仍然觉得意思不清楚吗？**ambiguous** 尤指有意或无意地使用含有多种意义的词语，使人感到含糊不清和难以理解：an ambiguous reply 模棱两可的回答 **vague** 表示因为太笼统、考虑不全而概念不清，带有含糊、不明确的意味：The first letter is very vague，possibly a U or V. 第一个字母很不清楚，可能是 U 也可能是 V。

observation / ˌɒbzəˈveɪʃn / *n.* [U]观察；观察力：escape one's ～ 不为某人所注意 / a man of no ～ 缺乏观察力的人 同 watchfulness，judgment

observe / əbˈzɜːv / *v.* ❶ 看；观察：I ～d nothing queer in his behaviour. 我没发现他的行为有异常之处。同 see，watch ❷遵守(规则等)，庆祝(节日、生日、周年等)：observe the laws 遵守法律 / Do they ～ Christmas Day in their country? 他们国家的人过圣诞节吗？同 obey，celebrate

用法

observe 表示"无意中看到"之意时，作宾语补足语的不定式不带 to：I observed him go out. 我无意中看到他出去了。

obsolete / ˈɒbsəliːt / *adj.* 作废的；过时的 同 outdated

obstacle / ˈɒbstəkl / *n.* [C]障碍；妨碍：clear away ～s 排除障碍 同 block，check

用法

obstacle 后面如有名词或动名词，要用介词 to：This is an obstacle to progress. 这是一个前进中的障碍。

obstinate / ˈɒbstɪnət / *adj.* 顽固的；固执的 同 stubborn，inflexible 反 flexible，undecided

obstruct / əbˈstrʌkt / *vt.* ❶阻塞，使堵塞：After the typhoon many roads were ～ed by collapsed trees. 台风过后，许多道路被倒塌的树木堵塞了。❷妨碍，阻碍；阻挡，阻止，阻拦：He got ten years in prison for ～ing the course of

justice. 他因妨碍司法公正被判十年徒刑。

obtain / əbˈteɪn / *v.* 取；获得；买：～ a prize 得奖 同 get，gain 反 lose

obvious / ˈɒbviəs / *adj.* 显而易见的；清楚的；明白的：It is an ～ advantage. 那是一个明显的好处。同 clear，plain 反 unclear，concealed 派 obviously *adv.*

辨析

obvious 指非常清楚，十分明白，无可争议：Her happiness was obvious. 她的幸福是显而易见的。**apparent** 指极为明显，一目了然，也指看起来是如此，其实未必然的情况：Her anxiety was apparent to everyone. 大家都觉察到她的焦虑情绪。It was an apparent stroke，but the doctors aren't certain yet. 似乎是中风，但医生们还未确定。**plain** 指事情是清楚的、明白的，强调毫无混淆或出错的可能性：The plain fact of the matter was that the man lied. 事实很清楚，这人说了谎。His guilt is plain — the stolen money was found in his pocket. 他的罪行是清楚的，在他的口袋里找到了所偷的钱。

occasion / əˈkeɪʒn / *n.* ❶[C]时机；机会：It is a favourable ～. 这是一个有利时机。同 circumstance，opportunity / **on** ～ 有时：I call on him on ～. 我有时拜访他。**on one** ～ 曾经有一次：I called on him on one ～. 我曾经拜访过他一次。**take** ～ 利用机会：I took ～ to tell him about my work. 我趁机给他讲了我的工作情况。❷[U] 理由；原因：You have no ～ to be angry. 你没有理由生气。同 reason，cause

occasional / əˈkeɪʒənl / *adj.* 非经常的；偶然的：He pays me ～ visits. 他偶尔来看我。同 uncommon，rare 反 constant，usual 派 occasionally *adv.*

occupant / ˈɒkjʊpənt / *n.* [C]占有者；占用者；居住者：There have been many distinguished ～s of the position of executive director. 已经有很多人担任过执行导演这一职位。/ The ～ is unwilling to pay rent. 那个房屋占用者不愿付房租。

occupation / ˌɒkjʊˈpeɪʃn / *n.* [U] ❶占有；占领：military ～ 军事占领 同 control，possession ❷职业：He has no fixed (definite) ～. 他没有固定的职业。同 job，trade

辨析 occupation 泛指任何一种职业：He gave her an occupation as a bus driver. 他给她提供的职业是驾驶公共汽车。John is by occupation a teacher. 约翰是一名教师。**business** 指营利性（常指为自己利益）的工作：My business is real estate. 我的职业是经营房地产。**employment** 指受雇领薪的工作：All this year's graduates of our school have found employment. 今年我校的毕业生都找到了工作。**profession** 指受过专门训练的、从事脑力劳动的职业，如律师、医生、教师等：He is a lawyer by profession. 他的职业是律师。**trade** 指需要熟练技巧的、进行手工劳动的职业：He is a printer（carpenter）by trade. 他的职业是印刷工人（木工）。

occupy / ˈɒkjupaɪ / vt. 占领：The building occupies an entire block. 这幢建筑物占了整整一个街区。同 conquer, possess 反 liberate, free。**be occupied with**（in）忙于：He has been occupied in writing his novel. 他一直忙着写小说。

occur / əˈkɜː(r) / vi.（occurred；occurring）❶发生：A leap year ～s once every four years. 每四年有一次闰年。同 happen ❷想起；想到：An idea ～red to me. 我想到了一个主意。同 strike ❸存在：Misprints ～ on every page. 每一页都有印刷错误。同 appear, arise

occurrence / əˈkʌrəns / n. [U]发生；出现：They have been studying the ～ of heart disease in various countries. 他们一直在研究心脏病在不同国家的发病率。/ This word is of frequent ～s. 我们因一些突发事件而耽误了。

ocean / ˈəʊʃn / n. 海洋：～ floor 海底 / the Arctic（Atlantic, Indian, Pacific）Ocean 北冰（大西，印度，太平）洋

Oceania / ˌəʊʃiˈeɪniə / n. 大洋洲

o'clock / əˈklɒk / n. 钟点：—What time is it now? —It's five ～. —现在几点？—五点整。

October / ɒkˈtəʊbə(r) / n. 十月：the ～ Revolution 十月革命

odd / ɒd / adj. ❶奇数的：Seven is an ～ number. 7是奇数。反 even ❷非固定的；临时的：make a living by doing ～ jobs 靠做零工维生 同 occasional, irregular 反 constant, regular ❸奇异的；古怪的：an ～ person 古怪的人 同 strange, unusual 反 common, usual

辨析 odd 指令人困惑的奇异，强调有别于正常，不同于一般：That is an odd colour. 那是一种奇怪的颜色。**peculiar** 指异乎寻常，有奇异的独特性：The food has a peculiar taste. 这种食物有一种怪味。**strange** 指因以前从未经历过而感到新奇或惊奇：It's strange that we should meet here. 我们会在这里见面，真奇怪。

odds / ɒdz / n. ❶机会，可能性：The ～ on the champion winning are three to two. 夺冠的可能性是三比二。/ The ～ are strongly against his getting here before Saturday. 极有可能他不会在星期六前到达这儿。❷成功的可能性（或希望）

odo(u)r / ˈəʊdə(r) / n. 气味；臭气；香味：It has a pleasant ～. 它有香气。同 smell, scent

of / ɒv, əv / prep. ❶表示空间距离或时间长短：five miles south ～ Chongqing 重庆以南五英里 / within a year ～ his death 他死后一年内 ❷表示来源：a man ～ humble origin 出身低微的人 / the works ～ Shakespeare 莎士比亚的著作 ❸表示原因：His father died ～ hunger. 他父亲是饿死的。❹表示材料：a dress ～ silk 绸衣 ❺表示具有某种性质：a man ～ ability 有才干的人 / How kind ～ you to help me. 你来帮助我，太谢了。/ It was good ～ your brother to come. 你的兄弟来了，真是太好了。

off / ɒf, ɒf / Ⅰ prep. 从…离开：take a book ～ the shelf 从书架上拿走一本书 Ⅱ adv. 在远处；离开：The town is five miles ～. 那城镇在五英里之外。

offence(-se) / əˈfens / n. ❶犯罪；犯规；过错：minor（grave）～ 轻（重）罪 同 crime, wrongdoing 反 innocence ❷冒犯；触怒；伤感情 同 insult, rudeness 反 pleasure, satisfaction

offend / əˈfend / vi. 犯法；犯罪；违反（规则）同 commit, misbehave —vt. 触怒；伤感情；使不愉快 同 insult, annoy 反 please, calm

offensive / əˈfensɪv / Ⅰ adj. ❶冒犯的；无礼的 同 insulting, rude 反 polite, pleasant ❷令人不愉快的；攻击的 同 aggressive, attack 反 defensive, resisting Ⅱ n.（the ～）攻势；进攻

offer / ˈɒfə(r) / Ⅰ v. 提供；提出；提议：She ～ed a few ideas to improve the plan. 她提出数种意见以改进那项计划。同 present, propose 反 refuse, reject Ⅱ n. [C]提供；提议：an ～ of help 援助的建议 同 proposal, invitation 反 refusal

用法

offer 作动词时,后面可接不定式,也可接双宾语:He offered to help me. 他提出要帮助我。 He offered me a cigarette. 他给我一支香烟。

off-hour / ˈɒfˌaʊə(r) / Ⅰ n. [C] ❶业余时间,非工作时间:Tom collects stamps during ～s. 汤姆在业余时间集邮。❷非高峰时间:Only one car is in service in ～. 非高峰时间只有一辆车服务。 Ⅱadj. ❶非工作时间的:～ diversions 业余消遣 ❷非高峰时间的:cut-rate tickets for ～ travelers 非高峰时期乘客车票的减价

office / ˈɒfɪs / n. [C]办公室;办事处:～ hours 营业时间;办公时间 / after ～ 在业余时间 / branch ～ 分行,分支机构 / home ～ 总部,总公司,总店,总局 / in high ～ 身居高位 / the party in ～ 执政党 / the party out of ～ 在野党

officer / ˈɒfɪsə(r) / n. [C]军官;警官;高级船员

official / əˈfɪʃl / Ⅰ adj. 公务的;官方的:～ powers 职权 / ～ duties 公务 Ⅱ n. [C]行政人员;官员;public ～s 公务员 / bank ～s 银行职员 / He is an ～ in the Ministry of Defense. 他是国防部的官员。

offshore / ˌɒfˈʃɔː(r) / Ⅰ adj. 离岸的;近海的;(风等)向海的 Ⅱ adv. 离岸;近海

offspring / ˈɒfsprɪŋ / n. [C]子孙;后代 同 descendant,heir

often / ˈɒfn,ˈɒftən / adv. (比较级和最高级形式分别为 more often,most often;口语中也可用 oftener 与 oftenest) 常常;经常:How ～ does a bus run? 公共汽车多久一班? 同 frequently,constantly 反 never,seldom

oh / əʊ / interj. 啊,嗬(表示惊奇、恐惧等)

oil / ɒɪl / n. [U]油;石油:an ～ field(口语)油田 / an ～ lamp 油灯 / add(pour) ～ on fire 火上加油

ointment / ˈɔɪntmənt / n. [U;C]药膏,软膏:The doctor gave him some ～ to stop the cut from becoming infected. 医生给他配些药膏,防止伤口感染。

OK / ˌəʊˈkeɪ / (= Okay)(口语) Ⅰ adj. 好的;可以的 Ⅱ adv. 好,对,可以

old / əʊld / adj. (older,oldest) ❶…岁的:一How ～ are you? 一I am five years ～. 一你

多大了? 一我五岁了。❷老的;年长的:There is an ～ man in the picture. 画中有一位老人。同 aged,elderly 反 young ❸旧的;古老的;过时的 同 ancient,outdated 反 new,modern

olive / ˈɒlɪv / n. 橄榄;橄榄树;橄榄色:～ branch 橄榄枝(和平的象征) / ～ oil 橄榄油

Olympic / əˈlɪmpɪk,əˈlɪmpɪk / adj. 奥林匹克的;the ～ Games 奥林匹克运动会

omission / əˈmɪʃn / n. [U] ❶省略,删除;删节:The book was shortened by the ～ of two chapters. 此书删除了两个章节,从而缩短了篇幅。❷排除,删除:His ～ from the team cost England the match. 他的落选使英国队输掉了比赛。❸遗漏;疏漏:the ～ of his name from the list 他的名字在名单上的漏列

omit / əˈmɪt / vt. (omitted;omitting) 遗漏;省略:This sentence may be ～ted. 这句可以省略。同 miss,cut 反 include,add

on / ɒn / Ⅰ prep. ❶在…之上(表示所处位置):pictures ～ the wall 墙上的画 ❷在(表示时间):～ National Day 在国庆节 / ～ Monday 在星期一 ❸关于;论及;the speech ～ international affairs 关于国际形势的演讲 ❹接近;靠近:a town ～ the coast 海边的一个城镇 / ～ my right (left)在我右(左)边 ❺进行中(表示状态的保持):～ business 因公;有事 / ～ holiday 度假 / the tour ～ 在旅行 / the way ～ 在途中 Ⅱ adv. 向前;继续:Go ～ with your story. 把你的故事讲下去。The sports meet is still ～. 运动会还在进行。

once / wʌns / Ⅰ adv. 一次,一度;从前:He goes to see his parents ～ a month. 他每月去看他父母一次。 You should try to do it ～ more (again). 你应该再试做一次。 ～ **and again** 一再:He has been told ～ and again not to slam the door. 他一再被叮嘱不得将门砰的一下关上。 ～ **in a while** 有时;偶尔:Once in a while he goes with us to the movies on Saturday night. 他偶尔在星期六晚上同我们一道去看电影。 ～ **upon a time** 从前(用于故事开头):Once upon a time there was a giant with two heads. 从前有个双头巨人。 **all at** ～ 突然:All at ～ we heard a loud noise. 猛然,我们听到一声巨响。 **at** ～①马上;立刻:She told him to leave the room at ～. 她叫他立刻离开那房间。②同

时：Don't speak at ～. 不要同时说。Ⅱ *conj.* 如果；一旦；每当：Once you cross the river you are safe. 你一旦渡过了河，你便安全了。

one / wʌn / Ⅰ *num.* 一；一个同 a(an), single Ⅱ *pron.* 任何人；任何东西：One must love one's country. 任何人都必须爱国。Ⅲ *adj.* (任何)一个的；某一个的：They share one bike. 他们共用一辆自行车。

用法

❶one 作代词时不能用在所有格代词和所有格名词后面，如不可说：Your cat is black; my one is white. (应该把 my one 改成 mine 或 my cat)你的猫是黑色的，而我的(猫)是白色的。也不说：Your horse is larger than John's one. (应该把 one 去掉)你的马比约翰的(马)大。但 one 前面若有形容词，就可以用 one，如：Your cat is black; my young one is white. 你的猫是黑色的，我的小猫是白色的。❷不可用 one, one's 代替 anyone, everyone, someone 或 none，如不可说：Everyone should take care of one's health. (应该把 one's 改成 his)人人都应关心自己的健康。

辨析

❶固定的口语里 one 和 a(an)不可互换：once upon a time(从前)；one day(有一天)；an hour or two, one or two hours(一两小时)。❷a(an)只有"一"的意思，并不跟二、三、四等形成对比，one 才有对比意味：Have you an umbrella? Yes, I have one. 你有雨伞吗? 是的，有一把(没有多的)。Can a boy do this? No, but a man can. Can one boy do this? No, but two boys can. ❸在 dozen, hundred, thousand 和 million 前面，用 a 或 one 意思相同，但在 about 或 nearly 之类的词后不能用 one，要用 a(an)：About a thousand people attended the lecture. 大约一千人出席了报告会。We stayed nearly an hour in the park. 我们在公园里待了约一个小时。

oneself / wʌn'self / *pron.* 自己；自身；亲自(one 的反身代词)：She used to sit by herself and read. 她从前常常独自坐着看书。

one-way / ˌwʌn'weɪ / *adj.* ❶单向(行驶)的：a ～ street 单行道/～ traffic 单向行驶的车辆 ❷单程的：a ～ friendship 单方面的友谊

onion / 'ʌnjən / *n.* [C]洋葱

only / 'əunli / Ⅰ *adv.* 只；仅仅，不过：Ladies ～. 女士专用。/ We can ～ tell you what we know. 我们只能告诉你我们知道的事情。同 singly, merely 反 together, among Ⅱ *adj.* 唯一

的；最佳的：an ～ son 独子 / This is the example John can give you. 这是约翰能给你的唯一一例子。/ He is the ～ man for the position. 他是这个职位的唯一人选。同 single, a-lone

用法

only 放在句首修饰状语时，句子要倒装；修饰主语时，则不用倒装句式：Only by this means can we succeed. 只用这个方法，我们才能成功。Only he knows that. 只有他才知道那件事。

onto / 'ɒntə / *prep.* (= on to)到…上面：The cat jumped ～ the table. 猫跳到了桌上。

open / 'əupən / Ⅰ *v.* 打开；开始：School ～s in September. 学校在 9 月开学。同 unclose, begin 反 shut, end Ⅱ *adj.* 开着的；公共的；开放的：～ to the public 对公众开放的/～ to traffic 通车 / The bank is ～ at eight. 银行 8 点开门营业。/ an ～ competition (championship, scholarship)公开赛(公开锦标赛, 公开奖学金)/ The letter is torn ～. 信被撕开。同 unclosed, uncovered 反 closed, covered 派 openly *adv.*

opening / 'əupnɪŋ / *n.* ❶开始；开口：～ ceremony 开幕式，开学典礼，通车典礼 / ～ speech 开幕词 / ～ time(营业)开始时间；开放时间 同 beginning ❷洞；孔 同 break, hole ❸就业机会，空缺 同 opportunity, position

opera / 'ɒprə / *n.* 歌剧；歌剧艺术

operable / 'ɒpərəbl / *adj.* 可动手术的；可操作的；可实施的

operate / 'ɒpəreɪt / *v.* ❶(使)运转；操作：～ a machine 操作机器 同 perform ❷起作用：The medicine ～d quickly. 药很快起作用了。同 function ❸管理；经营 同 manage, run ❹动手术；开刀：～ on 给…动手术：This famous doctor has ～d on many important people. 这个著名的医生给许多重要人物动过手术。派 operation *n.*

operator / 'ɒpəreɪtə(r) / *n.* [C]操作人员；(电话)接线员

opinion / ə'pɪnjən / *n.* 意见；评价同 idea, judgment / in one's ～ 据某人看来：In my ～, you'd better wait one more day. 依我所见，你最好再多等一天。**have a good** (**high, low, poor**)～ **of sb.** (**sth.**) 对某人(某事)给予好的(高的、低的、坏的)评价

辨析

opinion 是常用词,指对某事的想法,含有"初步的;不十分肯定"的意味:I try to learn the facts and form my own opinions. 我设法了解各种事实,然后确定自己的意见。**view** 多指对影响较广泛的公众问题所持的观点。和 opinion 相比,view 更为全面和系统:Different social classes hold different political views. 不同的社会阶级有不同的政治见解。

opponent / əˈpəʊnənt / n. [C] ❶对手,敌人:a worthy ～ 势均力敌的对手/beat an ～ at an election 在选举中击败对手 ❷ 反对者:a fierce ～ of nuclear arms 核武器的强烈反对者

opportunity / ˌɒpəˈtjuːnəti / n. 机会;时机: have few opportunities of meeting interesting people 遇到有趣的人的机会不多 / have no (little, not much) ～ of hearing good music 没有(很少有,没有许多)机会听到好的音乐同 chance, occasion

oppose / əˈpəʊz / vt. 反对;拒绝:～ a new plan 反对新计划同 fight, resist 反 support, defend

辨析

oppose 是及物动词,指反对一个人或一件事,尤指反对某种观念、计划等:We opposed the plan because of the cost. 因费用问题我们反对这计划。**object** 多指受个人好恶影响而表示反对,通常只用作不及物动词:He objected to being treated as an outsider. 他反对别人把他当外人看。**resist** 指主动地抗拒攻击或诱惑,既可用作及物动词,也可用作不及物动词:resist the enemy 反抗敌人/He could resist no longer. 他无法再抗拒了。

opposite / ˈɒpəzɪt / Ⅰ adj. ❶(位置)对面的,相对的同 facing, reverse ❷完全不同的;相反的:～ directions 相反的方向同 different, contrary 反 same, alike Ⅱ n. 相反的词;相对的事物:I thought quite the ～. 我想的刚好相反。/ "High"is the ～ of "low". "高"是"低"的反义词。同 contradiction, contrary Ⅲ prep. 在……对面:sit ～ each other 彼此相对而坐

用法

❶opposite 作介词时,后面也可用可不用:I live opposite (to) the post -office. 我住在邮局对面。❷当 opposite 作形容词时,后面的 to 不能省略(可用 from 代替):My view is opposite to (from) yours. 我的观点与你的相反。

opposition / ˌɒpəˈzɪʃn / n. ❶[U]反对,对抗:a great deal of ～ to the war 对战争的强烈反对/In spite of his ～, he respected his son's point of view. 他尽管反对,但还是尊重他儿子的观点。❷对手;(政党等中的)反对派:protests from the ～ 反对派提出的抗议/She wanted to know the ～ before signing the contract. 她想先了解一下对手的情况再签订合同。

oppress / əˈpres / vt. 压迫;压制同 burden, depress 反 ease, cheer 派 oppressed adj. ;**oppression** n.

optical / ˈɒptɪkl / adj. ❶视觉的;视力的 ❷光的;光学的

optimism / ˈɒptɪmɪzəm / n. [U]乐观;乐观主义 同 cheerfulness, confidence 反 pessimism, gloom

optimistic / ˌɒptɪˈmɪstɪk / adj. 乐观的;乐观主义的;无忧无虑的 同 cheerful, confident 反 pessimistic, gloomy

option / ˈɒpʃn / n. ❶[C]选择;选择的东西: Many ～s are open to them. 他们有多种选择。/We have three ～s for this term. 这学期我们可选修三门课。❷[U]选择权;选择余地,选择自由:have little ～没有多大选择余地

optional / ˈɒpʃən(ə)l / adj. 可自由选择的;非强制的;(学科)选修的 同 elective, voluntary 反 required, forced 派 optionally adv.

or / ɔː(r), ər / conj. ❶或者:clean ～ dirty 干净或肮脏 ~ either ... or ...或…或…:You must either tell the truth ～ say nothing. 你须实言,不然便不要开口。❷换言之,即,也就是: twelve ～ a dozen 12 个即一打 ❸否则:Hurry up ～ (else) you'll be late. 赶快,否则你会迟到。/～ so 大约:I'd like twenty ～ so. 我想要 20 个左右。

oral / ˈɔːrəl / adj. 口头的:an ～ test 口试同 spoken 反 written

orange / ˈɒrɪndʒ / Ⅰ n. [C] 橙子,橘子;橘树 Ⅱ adj. ❶柑橘的 ❷橙色的;橘色的

orbit / ˈɔːbɪt / Ⅰ n. (天体、人造卫星等的)轨道 Ⅱ v. 绕轨道运行,把(人造卫星等)送入轨道

orchestra / ˈɔːkɪstrə / n. [C]管弦乐队:The ～ was playing in the hall last week. 乐团曾于上周在这个大厅里演出。

ordeal / ɔː'diːl / *n.* [C](对人格和忍耐力等的)严峻考验;磨难,折磨:an ～ such as imprisonment or illness 诸如入狱和疾病的折磨/the ～ of divorce 离婚的痛苦经历

orchard / 'ɔːtʃəd / *n.* [C]果园:apple ～s 苹果园

order / 'ɔːdə(r) / Ⅰ *n.* [C] ❶命令:give ～s 下命令 同 command 反 ❷次序;顺序:list in alphabetical ～ 按字母顺序列出 同 arrangement, system 反 disorder, confusion / in ～ of 照…排列:in ～ of size (importance) 依大小(重要)次序排列 ❸有规则的状况:in good (bad) ～ 整齐(不整齐);工作情况良好(不佳) 同 quiet, control 反 disorder ❹秩序:It is the business of the police to keep ～. 维持秩序(治安)是警察的事. 同 rule, law ❺订购;订单;订货:待交付的货:an ～ for two tons of coal 两吨煤的订单 同 booking, reservation ❻目的;意向 同 purpose / in ～ to 为了,以便:We started early in ～ to arrive before dark. 我们很早出发,以便天黑前到达. in ～ that 为了,以便:In ～ that every student might understand it, the teacher explained the passage again and again. 为了使每个学生都能明白,教师一遍又一遍地讲那篇文章. Ⅱ *vt.* 命令;订购:The doctor ～ed me to (stay in) bed. 医生吩咐我卧床休息. I've ～ed lunch for 12:30. 我已经订了十二点半的午餐. 同 command, book 派 orderly *adj.*

用法 ❶order 在表示"命令"时,其后从句应用虚拟语气,即 should ＋ 动词原形或直接用动词原形:He orders (His order is) that the work (should) be started at once. 他命令(他的命令是)工作必须马上开始. ❷order 为名词且作"命令"讲时,多用复数形式,如 receive orders 接到命令 / obey orders 服从命令;但某些时候也可用单数,如:He is acting by order. 他依照命令行动.

ordinal / 'ɔːdɪnl / Ⅰ *n.* [C]序数(词) Ⅱ *adj.* 序数(词)的;次序的,顺序的

ordinary / 'ɔːdnəri / *adj.* 正常的;通常的;普通的:an ～-looking girl 相貌平常的女孩 / in ～ dress 穿着平常的衣服 同 common, usual 反 special, unusual

辨析 **ordinary** 意为"平凡的;普通的",指某人或某物不具有突出的特性:He says he is just an ordinary man, living in an ordinary house, with ordinary hopes and fears. 他说他只不过是个平凡的人,住在普通的房子里,有着一般人有的希望和担忧. **normal** 指某人或某物没有超越限度,基本合乎标准或达到平均水平:He is a perfectly normal child physically as well as mentally. 他是身体和思维都完全正常的小孩. **regular** 指符合各类规则、标准:He heard the regular sound of the clock 他听见那钟发出规则的滴答声. These are regular verbs. 这些都是规则动词. **usual** 指按照常规、惯例行事:He wore his usual blue uniform. 他穿着他常穿的那套蓝制服. He made the usual mistakes which all beginners would make. 他犯的就是所有初学者老犯的错误.

ore / ɔː(r) / *n.* 矿石;矿物

organ / 'ɔːgən / *n.* ❶(动植物的)器官 ❷机关;机构 ❸风琴

organic / ɔː'gænɪk / *adj.* ❶器官的 ❷有机的:～ life 有机生命 / ～ chemistry 有机化学 同 living, natural

organization / ˌɔːgənaɪ'zeɪʃn / *n.* 组织:An army without good organization may be defeated easily. 缺乏良好组织的军队容易败仗.

organize / 'ɔːgənaɪz / *vt.* 组织;创办:～ an army (a government, a political party) 组织军队(政府、政党) 同 establish, create 反 disorganize, disorder

Orient / 'ɔːrient / *n.* (the ～)东方;亚洲 派 Oriental *adj.*

orient / 'ɔːrient / *v.* ❶定位;定向:The explorer climbed a tree in order to ～ himself. 探险者爬上一棵树以确定自己的位置和方向. / ～ed assignment 定向分配/market ～ed 以市场为导向 同 fix, locate ❷使熟悉;使习惯:The freshman took a while to ～ himself. 该新生花了点时间熟悉新环境. 同 accustom

origin / 'ɒrɪdʒɪn / *n.* 起源;开端;出身:～ of the quarrel 争吵的起源 / words of Latin ～ 源自拉丁文的词 / a man of humble ～ 出身卑微的人 同 beginning, birth 反 end, death

original / ə'rɪdʒən(ə)l / Ⅰ *adj.* 原先的;最初的;创举的:an ～ plan 原先的计划 / an ～ idea 创见 / an ～ design 别出心裁的设计 同

earliest；novel 反 unoriginal，usual Ⅱ n. [C]原作；原文；原物

originate / əˈrɪdʒɪneɪt / v. 起源；发生；首创出；产生出 同 begin，arise 反 end，terminate

ornament / ˈɔːnəmənt / Ⅰ n. ❶[U]装饰；点缀 同 decoration ❷[C]装饰品；点缀品 Ⅱ vt. 装饰；点缀 同 decorate

orphan / ˈɔːfn / n. [C]孤儿

other / ˈʌðə(r) / Ⅰ pron. 其他的人或物；别的人或事：Thirty of them are boys. The ～s are girls. 他们中 30 个是男孩，其余的是女孩。**at ～ times** 平时，在其他时候 / **every ～ day (week，year)** 每隔一天（一周、一年）/ **in ～ words** 换句话说 / **one after the ～（ one after another）**一个接一个地，相继地：They were examined one after the ～. 他们一个一个地被检查。Ⅱ adj. 其他的；别的；**on the ～ hand** 另一方面（多用在 on the one hand 之后）：It's cheap，but on the ～ hand，the quality is poor. 它很便宜，但另一方面，质量很差。**the ～ day** 几天前：I saw him the ～ day. 我几天前看见过他。

❶other 作形容词时，后面一般接复数名词（这是和 another 的主要区别）：We study mathematics，Chinese，English and other subjects. 我们学习数学、语文、英语和其他课程。但 other 前面有 some，any，every，no，the 等词时，后面的名词可用单数：Please come some other time. 请在另外的时间来吧。Any other person would have taken offence at it. 换一个人准会对此事生气的。The postman comes every other day to our village. 邮递员每隔一天来我们村一次。❷other 与数字连用时注意次序与意义的不同，如：Give me two other books. 给我（任何）两本别的书。Give me the other two books. 把其他那两本书给我。后一句中的 the 不能省略。

otherwise / ˈʌðəwaɪz / Ⅰ adv. 不同样地；除此以外 Ⅱ conj. 否则；不然：Put on your raincoat，～ you will get wet. 穿上雨衣，否则你就要淋湿了。同 or

ouch / aʊtʃ / int. ❶（表示突然剧痛）哎哟 ❷（表示愤怒或不悦）哎

ought / ɔːt / aux. v.（后接带 to 的不定式）应该，应当（表示责任、义务）：Such things ～ not to be done. 这样的事不应该做。

ought 没有时态变化，后面可接不定式的完成式，表示"原来应当""本应"；You ought to have locked the door when you went out. 你走的时候本应该锁门。

ounce / aʊns / n. [C] ❶（英制重量单位）盎司（＝28.3495 克）❷一点，少量：He hasn't an ～ of common sense. 他一点常识都没有。

our / ˈaʊə(r) / pron. 我们的（形容词性物主代词）：We have done ～ share. 我们已经做了我们的那一份。

ours / ˈaʊəz / pron. 我们的（名词性物主代词）：The house is ～. 这房子是我们的。

ourselves / ɑːˈselvz / pron. 我们自己（反身代词）：We'd better go and see them ～. 我们最好亲自去见他们。

out / aʊt / adv. 出；在外：go ～ for a walk 出外散步 / He walked ～ of the office. 他走出办公室。/ ～ of breath 上气不接下气：After he finished the long race，he was ～ of breath. 长跑过后，他累得上气不接下气了。～ of work 失业：When his father was ～ of work，he left school. 他父亲失业后，他就退学了。

outbreak / ˈaʊtbreɪk / n. [C]爆发；暴动 同 explosion，conflict

outburst / ˈaʊtbɜːst / n. [C] ❶（情感等的）突然爆发，迸发：an ～ of laughter 放声大笑 ❷（行动、力量等的）突然出现 / ～ of machine gun fire 机枪的猛射 ❸（火山的）喷发；（烟雾、蒸汽等的）外冒：volcanic ～火山喷发/an ～ of steam from the pressure-cooker 高压锅中蒸汽的外冒

outcome / ˈaʊtkʌm / n. [C]结果 同 result，consequence

outdated / ˌaʊtˈdeɪtɪd / adj. 过时的；旧式的；不再流行的 同 obsolete 反 modern，fashionable

outdoor / ˈaʊtdɔː(r) / adj. 户外的；野外的 同 open-air，outside 反 indoor，inside

outdoors / ˌaʊtˈdɔːz / adv. 在户外；在野外 反 indoors

outer / ˈaʊtə(r) / adj. 外的；外部的：a journey to ～ space 太空旅行 / the ～walls 外墙 同 external，outside 反 internal，inside

outgoing / ˈaʊtɡəʊɪŋ / adj. ❶友好的；性格开朗的；善于交际的：an ～ personality 开朗的性格 ❷即将退休的，即将离任的：the ～ government 任期将满的政府 ❸外出的,离去的:an ～ ship 出航的船只

outing / 'aʊtɪŋ / n. [C]外出度假;郊游 同 picnic

outlaw / 'aʊtlɔː / n. [C]逃犯;亡命之徒 同 bandit,criminal

outlet / 'aʊtlet / n. [C]❶出口;出路 同 opening,exit 反 entrance,inlet ❷发泄方法;排泄 同 release,escape ❸电源插座

outline / 'aʊtlaɪn / I n. [C]❶外形;轮廓:an ～ map of Great Britain 英国的轮廓图 同 shape ❷要点;大纲;提纲:an ～ for a lecture 一篇演讲提纲 同 summary,sketch II v. 画…的轮廓;打草图;概述;概括:～ the American Civil War 略述美国的南北战争 同 draft

outlook / 'aʊtlʊk / n. [C]❶展望;远景 同 view,sight ❷眼界;观点;看法:broaden(narrow)one's ～ 扩大(缩小)视野 / optimistic (pessimistic) ～ 乐观(悲观)看法 同 viewpoint,attitude

output / 'aʊtpʊt / n. 产量:the ～ of a gold mine 金矿的产量 同 achievement,production

outright I / aʊt'raɪt / adv. ❶完全地,彻底地;dismiss the information ～ 对这些消息完全不予理会/The young woman was ～ mad. 那名年轻女子彻底疯了。❷公开地,公然地,直截了当地,直率地:say ～ what one means 直接说出想说的话 ❸立刻,马上;当场地:Ten were killed ～. 有 10 人当场被杀。II / 'aʊtraɪt / adj. ❶完全的,彻底的,十足的:a condemnation of the film 对这部电影的全面抨击 ❷公开的,公然的;毫无保留的;直截了当的,直率的:an ～ denial 断然否认

outset / 'aʊtset / n. [C]开始,开端:at the ～(of)在…开始时/from the ～(of)从…起

outside / aʊt'saɪd / I n. 外面;外部:The ～ of the house needs painting. 房子外部需要刷油漆。同 surface,covering 反 inside II adj. 外面的:an ～ seat 露天座位 同 outer,external 反 inner,internal III adv. 在外面:The car is waiting ～. 车子在外面等着。IV prep. 在…外面:～ the house 在屋子外面

outsider / aʊt'saɪdə(r) / n. [C]组织之外的人;局外人:The ～s see the best (most) of the game. 旁观者清。

outskirt / 'aʊtskɜːt / n.(常用 pl.)郊区;郊外;

边缘 同 suburb

outstanding / aʊt'stændɪŋ / adj. 显著的;引人注意的:an ～ person 杰出的人 同 great,extraordinary 反 ordinary,usual

outstrip / aʊt'strɪp / vt. (-stripped;-stripping)胜过;超过:A horse can ～ a man. 马比人跑得快。同 exceed,surpass

outward(s) / 'aʊtwəd(z) / adv. 向外,在外

oval / 'əʊv(ə)l / I adj. 卵形的;椭圆形的:an ～ face 一张鸭蛋形(瓜子)脸/The mirror is ～. 镜子呈椭圆形。II n. [C]卵形(物);椭圆形(物)

oven / 'ʌvn / n. [C]炉,灶;烤炉,烤箱:electric (gas,microwave) ～ 电(煤气,微波)炉

over / 'əʊvə(r) / I adv. ❶在那边;在另一边:～ there 在那边 ❷自始至终:read it ～ 通读一遍 ❸太,过分地(主要与形容词和副词构成复合词):～ anxious 太焦急的,过于忧虑的/～ polite 太多礼的 ❹重复地:～ and ～(again)一再地,许多次:I've warned you ～ and ～ again not to do that. 我已一再警告你不要做那件事。II prep. ❶在上方(未接触的):The sky is ～ our heads. 天空在我们的头顶上。❷在…上面:He spread his handkerchief ～ his face to keep the flies off. 他把手帕盖在脸上以避开苍蝇。❸遍及…的各部分:He is famous all ～ the world. 他是全世界闻名的人。❹超过:He spoke for ～ an hour. 他讲了一个多钟头。❺直到…过后:Can you stay ～ Sunday? 你能待在这儿过星期日吗? III adj. 结束的;完的:Class is ～ 下课了。

overall / 'əʊvərɔːl / I adj. 全面的;综合的 同 total,general 反 narrow,specific II n.(pl.)工装裤

overcoat / 'əʊvəkəʊt / n. [C]大衣;外套

overcome / əʊvə'kʌm / vt. (overcame /əʊvə'keɪm/ ,overcome)胜过;压倒;克服:～ bad habits 改掉恶习 / ～ difficulties 克服困难 / ～ prejudices 消除成见 同 conquer,defeat 反 surrender,give up

overflow / əʊvə'fləʊ / v. 溢出;泛滥:The milk is ～ing the cup. 牛奶从杯中溢出。同 run over,flood

overhead / əʊvə'hed / I adv. 在头顶上;在空中:the stars ～ 天上的星星 II adj. 在头顶上的:an ～ bridge 天桥 / an ～ light 吊灯

overhear / ˌəʊvəˈhɪə(r) / vt. (overheard / ˌəʊvəˈhɜːd / , overheard)偶然听到；从旁听到

overlap / ˌəʊvəˈlæp / v. (-lapped;-lapping)（与…）重叠；(与…)部分同时发生同 cover, coincide

overlook / ˌəʊvəˈlʊk / vt. ❶俯瞰；眺望：From the house on the hillside, we can ～ the whole harbour. 我们能从山腰的房子里俯瞰港口的全景。同 look over, survey ❷忽视；漏看：～ a printer's error 看漏一个排字错误 同 neglect, omit 反 remember

overnight / ˌəʊvəˈnaɪt / Ⅰ adv. 一夜间；一下子；整夜地同 suddenly, all night Ⅱ adj. 一整夜的；过一夜的

overrate / ˌəʊvəˈreɪt / vt. 过高评价(或估计)：He ～d his ability. 他过高地估计了自己的能力/Her beauty is ～d. 她没有评价的那么美貌。

overseas / ˌəʊvəˈsiːz / adj. 海外的：～ trade 海外贸易/～ Chinese 华侨同 foreign, external 反 native, internal

overstep / ˌəʊvəˈstep / vt. (-stepped; -stepping)超越(范围、界限等)：the language that ～s the limits fo what ought to be allowed on television超出了电视上所允许使用范畴的语言/He ～ped his authority when he ordered the prisoner to he released. 他越权下达命令将罪犯释放。

overtake / ˌəʊvəˈteɪk / vt. (overtook / ˌəʊvəˈtʊk / , overtaken / ˌəʊvəˈteɪkən /) ❶追上；赶上；超过同 catch, pass ❷袭击；压倒同 attack, strike

overthrow / ˌəʊvəˈθrəʊ / Ⅰ vt. (overthrew / ˌəʊvəˈθruː / , overthrown / ˌəʊvəˈθrəʊn /)推翻；颠覆同 overturn, destroy 反 preserve, support Ⅱ n. 推翻；颠覆同 defeat, destruction

overtime / ˈəʊvətaɪm / Ⅰ n. [U]加班加点：

He did four hour's ～ yesterday. 昨天他加了四小时的班。/He's on ～ tonight. 他今晚加班。❷加班费；加班时间 ❸加时赛 Ⅱ adv. 超时(工作)地；加班地：The staff have to work ～. 职员们必须要加班加点地工作。/The game went ～. 比赛进入加时阶段。

overturn / ˌəʊvəˈtɜːn / v. (使)颠覆；推翻：The earthquake ～ed the houses. 地震使房屋倾覆。同 upset, overthrow 反 preserve, support

overwhelm / ˌəʊvəˈwelm / vt. 压倒；战胜；征服同 conquer, overcome 反 surrender

overwhelming / ˌəʊvəˈwelmɪŋ / adj. 压倒的；势不可挡的：an ～ majority 压倒性多数

owe / əʊ / v. 欠；应归功于；应感激：We ～ a great deal to our parents and teachers. 我们得大大感激父母及师长。

owing / ˈəʊɪŋ / adj. 欠着的；未付的；未给予的：～ to 因为；由于：Owing to the rain they could not come. 因为下雨，他们不能来。

owl / aʊl / n. [C]猫头鹰

own / əʊn / Ⅰ adj. 自己的(用在形容词性物主代词后)：I saw it with my ～ eyes. 我亲眼看到的。同 personal, private Ⅱ v. 拥有；所有：He ～s much money. 他有许多钱。同 have, possess 派 owner n.

ownership / ˈəʊnəʃɪp / n. 所有权；物主身份：collective (individual) ～ 集体(个人)所有制 / private (public) ～ 私有(公有)制

ox / ɒks / n. [C] (pl. oxen / ˈɒksən /) ❶(总称)牛 ❷公牛

oxide / ˈɒksaɪd / n. [C]氧化物

oxygen / ˈɒksɪdʒən / n. [U]氧；氧气

ozone / ˈəʊzəʊn / n. [U]臭氧

P p

pace / peɪs / Ⅰ n. [C]一步(走或跑一步的距离);(走或跑的)速度 同 step,speed / **keep ～ with** 与…步调一致,跟…同速前进:Scientists have to work hard to keep ～ with new development of modern science. 科学家必须努力工作以赶上现代科学的新发展。**at a good ～**快速地;相当快地:Economy of China is developing at a good ～. 中国的经济正高速发展。**set (make) the ～** 领先;树立榜样 Ⅱ v. 踱步:～ back and forth 来回踱步 同 step,walk

Pacific / pə'sɪfɪk / adj. 太平洋的:the ～ Ocean 太平洋

pacific / pə'sɪfɪk / adj. ❶平静的,宁静的:a ～ tone of voice 平静的语调 ❷求和的,和解的;爱和平的:～ views 期望和平的主张

pack / pæk / Ⅰ n. [C]包;包裹:a ～ of cigarettes 一包香烟 同 packet,parcel Ⅱ v. 打包;包装:Have you ～ed your things? 你的东西装好了没有? 同 bundle,load 反 unpack,empty

package / 'pækɪdʒ / n. [C]包;包裹 同 pack,parcel

packet / 'pækɪt / n. [C]小包;小盒;小捆:a ～ of letters 一捆信件 / a ～ of 20 cigarettes 一包 20 支装的香烟 同 bag,package

packing / 'pækɪŋ / n. [U]包装;包装用品;填料

pad / pæd / Ⅰ n. [C]❶垫,衬垫 同 protection ❷便签本:拍纸簿 同 notebook,notepad Ⅱ vt. (padded;padding)填塞;填充:～ded clothes 棉衣 同 fill,protect

paddle / 'pædl / Ⅰ n. [C]桨:He rowed a boat with ～s. 他用桨划船。Ⅱ v. 划船运送;划桨

page / peɪdʒ / n. [C]页:continue on ～ 15 下接第十五页/turn to ～ 15 翻到第十五页/Open your books at ～8. 请打开书,翻到第八页。

pail / peɪl / n. [C]桶;提桶 同 bucket

pain / peɪn / n. [U]❶疼痛:Does she feel any ～? 她感到疼痛吗? 同 ache,hurt 反 comfort ❷(pl.) 努力;费力;辛苦 同 suffering,grief 反 joy,pleasure / **No ～s,no gains.** 不劳无获。**at ～s** 尽力;用心;下苦功:He is at ～s to find out the truth. 他正尽力了解事实真相。**take ～s** 尽力;努力;下苦功:We took ～s to finish the work in time. 我们努力按时完成任务。

> **辨析**
>
> **pain** 是常用词,指身体或精神上的痛苦:His arm was often in pain after he broke it. 他的手臂折断后,他时常感到疼痛。His unkind behaviour caused his parents a great deal of pain. 他的不良行为使他的父母感到非常痛苦。ache 指身体某部分较长时间的隐痛,而不是短时间的剧痛:The ache in her head was terrific and she couldn't think straight. 她的头痛得厉害,简直不能思考问题。

painful / 'peɪnf(ə)l / adj. ❶疼痛的;痛苦的:Such a thing is ～ to him. 这样的事对他来说是很痛苦的。同 hurtful,distressing 反 painless,relieving ❷费力的;费心的,困难的:They have many ～ problems to solve. 他们有不少棘手的问题要解决。同 difficult 反 easy ❸麻烦的;令人不快的:It is ～ to see him make mistakes. 看到他犯错误,真令人心痛。同 unpleasant 反 pleasant

paint / peɪnt / Ⅰ n. 油漆;涂料 Ⅱ v. ❶漆:I'm going to ～ the desk yellow. 我打算把书桌漆成黄色。❷绘画:She ～s well. 她画得好。

painting / 'peɪntɪŋ / n. ❶[C] 油画;水彩画 ❷[U]绘画:绘画艺术 同 picture,drawing ❸[U] 油漆

pair / peə(r) / Ⅰ n. [C] ❶(一)双;(一)对;(一)副;(一)把:a ～ of shoes 一双鞋 / a ～ of trousers 一条裤子 ❷一对夫妇;一对情侣 同 couple Ⅱ v.(使)成对;配对 同 match

pal / pæl / n. [C]朋友,伙伴,同志:my best ～ 我最好的朋友

palace / 'pæləs / n. [C]皇宫;宫殿;(供娱乐

的) 大厦: the Summer Palace 颐和园 / the Children's Palace 少年宫

pale / peɪl / *adj.* ❶(人的脸色)苍白的,没有血色的:You are looking ～ today. 你今天脸色苍白。同 white, colorless 反 rosy, high-colored ❷(颜色)暗淡的;浅淡的:～ blue 淡蓝色 同 light, light-colored 反 dark, deep

palm / pɑːm / *n.* [C]❶手掌,(手)掌心:sweaty ～s 出汗的掌心 / in the ～ of sb.'s hand 完全受制于某人的,在某人手掌之中的:He's got the whole committee in the ～ of his hand. 他已完全控制了整个委员会。❷[C]棕榈树

pamphlet / 'pæmflət / *n.* [C]小册子

pan / pæn / *n.* [C]平底锅;盘子

pancake / 'pænkeɪk / *n.* [C]薄煎饼

panda / 'pændə / *n.* [C]熊猫:We like ～s very much. 我们非常喜欢熊猫。

panic / 'pænɪk / *n.* 恐慌,惊慌 同 terror, alarm / fall into a ～ 陷人恐慌之中:She fell into a ～ at the news. 她一听到那个消息就惊恐起来。throw sb. into a ～ 使某人陷人恐慌之中:The coming war threw the people into a ～. 即将到来的战争使人们陷入了恐慌之中。

pant / pænt / Ⅰ *v.* 喘气;气喘吁吁地说 同 gasp Ⅱ *n.* [C]喘气 同 gasp

paper / 'peɪpə(r) / Ⅰ *n.* ❶[U]纸:a sheet of ～ 一张纸 / a ～ bag 一个纸袋 / blank ～ 空白纸 / exam ～ 考卷 / toilet ～ 卫生纸 / waste ～ 废纸 ❷[C]报纸 同 newspaper ❸[C]卷:The teacher set us an English ～. 老师给我们出了一张英语试卷。❹[C]论文:a ～ on economy reform 一篇关于经济改革的论文 同 essay, article ❺[C]票据 Ⅱ *vt.* 用纸包装

parachute / 'pærəʃuːt / *n.* [C]降落伞:～ jumping 跳伞

parade / pə'reɪd / Ⅰ *v.* 游行:The performers ～d the streets. 表演者游行于街道中。同 march Ⅱ *n.* [C]游行:hold a ～ 举行游行 同 march

paradise / 'pærədaɪs / *n.* 天堂;乐土 同 heaven, delight 反 hell, misery

paragraph / 'pærəɡrɑːf / *n.* [C]段;节 同 passage

parallel / 'pærəlel / Ⅰ *adj.* ❶平行的:Draw two ～ lines here. 在这儿画两条平行线。同 alongside 反 nonparallel ❷类似的;相对应的:

My idea is ～ to (with) yours. 我的意见和你的相似。同 similar, corresponding 反 different, unlike ❸(电路)并联的:You may make a ～ connection here. 你可以在这里做电路并联。Ⅱ *n.* [C] ❶平行线;平行面 ❷可相比拟的事物;相似处:have (know) no ～ 举世无双;无与伦比 / without ～ in history 史无前例

parameter / pə'ræmɪtə(r) / *n.* ❶参(变)数,参(变)量 ❷限定因素,参数;特点;界限:keep within the ～s of the discussion 限制在这次讨论的范围之内

paraphrase / 'pærəfreɪz / Ⅰ *n.* [C](用简洁明了的语言对某段文字所进行的)重新阐述,意义释译:make a ～ of an English proverb 释译英语谚语 Ⅱ *vt.* 重新阐述,释译:～ the passage in modern Chinese 用现代汉语将这个段落重新阐述一下

parcel / 'pɑːsl / Ⅰ *n.* [C]包裹;小包 同 package, packet / by ～ 用邮包:Mother sent me a lot of clothes by ～. 妈妈用邮包给我寄了许多衣服。Ⅱ *vt.* ❶分;分配 ❷做成包裹

pardon / 'pɑːdn / Ⅰ *n.* 原谅;宽恕:I beg your ～. 请原谅。(礼貌地表示不同意别人的说法或没听清楚、没理解别人说的话,希望别人重复时的用语) 同 forgiveness, mercy 反 punishment, revenge Ⅱ *v.* 宽恕;原谅:Pardon my impatience, but I have to catch a train. 原谅我的性急,我必须赶上火车。同 forgive, excuse 反 punish, revenge

parent / 'peərənt / *n.* [C]父亲;母亲

用法

parent 只能指父母亲中的一人,表示双亲时须用复数 parents。

parentage / 'peərəntɪdʒ / *n.* [U] ❶家系,家族,血统;出身,门第:a girl of mixed American and Chinese ～ 中美混血的女孩 ❷起源,来源:be of different ～ 来源不一

parental / pə'rentl / *adj.* 父母的

park / pɑːk / Ⅰ *n.* [C] ❶公园:amusement ～ 游乐园 / zoological ～ 动物园 ❷停车场:There is a ～ near the shop. 商店附近有一个停车场。Ⅱ *v.* 停放(车辆等):No ～ing here! 此处不准停车!

parliament / 'pɑːləmənt / *n.* ❶[U]英国议会;议会两院;下议院:～ was opened by the British king. 英国国王宣布议会开会 ❷[C](其他国家的)议会;国会:dissolve ～ 解散议会

part / pɑːt / Ⅰ n.[C] ❶部分：Only (a) ～ of his story is true. 他的故事只有一部分是真的。同 section 反 whole, entirety ❷任务；职责；本分 同 role, duty ❸(剧中的)角色 ❹零件：Have you any spare ～s of this machine? 你有这台机器的备用零件吗? ❺(争论、交易等中的)一方 ❻地区；区域：They come from all ～s of the country. 他们来自全国各地。**act (play) a ～(in)** 扮演角色；起作用：She asked to act a ～ in the TV series. . 她要求在电视剧中扮演一个角色。**do one's ～** 尽本分：Whatever happens, I will do my ～. 无论发生什么事情，我都要尽我的本分。**in ～** 部分地；在某种程度上 **take ～ in** 参加：He asked how many of you were going to take ～ in this maths contest. 他问你们有多少人打算参加这次数学竞赛。**take the ～ of** 与…站在一边；袒护；支持：He took the ～ of Team A. 他支持 A 队。Ⅱ v. 分离；分开：The policemen ～ed the crowd. 警察排开众人。同 divide, separate / ～ **with** 和…分手；舍弃：He hated to ～ with his job but had to. 他不愿放弃他的工作，但又不得不放弃。派 partly adv.

partial / ˈpɑːʃl / adj. ❶局部的；不完全的：a ～ success 部分的成功 同 incomplete, unfinished 反 complete, whole ❷偏心的；偏袒的；不公平的：A parent should not be ～ to any of his children. 做父母的不应偏袒任何一个孩子。同 one-sided, unfair 反 impartial

participant / pɑːˈtɪsɪpənt / n.[C] 参加者：Each ～ will get a free ticket. 每位参加者将获得一张免费票。

participate / pɑːˈtɪsɪpeɪt / v. 分享；参加：～ in sb.'s suffering 分担某人的痛苦 同 share, join in 派 participation n.

participle / ˈpɑːtɪsɪpl / n.[C](语法)分词

particle / ˈpɑːtɪkl / n.[C] ❶粒子；微粒 同 atom, bit ❷微量：a ～ of 一点点；少量的：There is not a ～ of truth in what he said. 他所说的没一句实话。

particular / pəˈtɪkjələ(r) / adj. 特别的；值得注意的；突出的：for no ～ reason 没有特别的理由 同 special, peculiar 反 general / **be ～ about** 对…很讲究，对…很挑剔：She is ～ about her clothes. 她对衣着很讲究。**in ～** 特别地：She loves the song in ～, because her mother used to sing it. 她特别喜欢那首歌，因为她母

亲过去经常唱。派 particularly adv.

partition / pɑːˈtɪʃn / n. ❶[U]划分，分开；分裂，分割：the ～ of profits 利润分成/the ～ of the ancient empire into several independent countries 这个古老的帝国分裂成若干独立的国家 ❷[C]隔板，隔墙；分隔物：an open-plan office with ～s between desks 办公桌用隔板隔开的敞开式办公室

partner / ˈpɑːtnə(r) / n.[C] ❶合伙人；合作者 同 co-owner, mate ❷(跳舞、打网球、玩纸牌等的)同伴，同伴 ❸夫；妻 同 husband, wife

partnership / ˈpɑːtnəʃɪp / n.[U]伙伴关系；合伙关系

part-time / ˈpɑːttaɪm / adj. 用部分时间的；兼职的：a ～ clerk 兼职职员/I work here on a ～ basis. 我在这儿干的是兼职。

party / ˈpɑːti / n.[C] ❶团体；党派，政党：the Democratic Party and the Republican Party (美国)民主党和共和党 同 league, team ❷聚会；宴会：a dancing ～ 舞会 同 gathering, reception

pascal / ˈpæskəl / n.[C]帕(斯卡)(压强单位，略作 Pa)

pass / pɑːs / Ⅰ v. ❶通过：The road was too narrow for cars to ～. 这路太窄了，车子不能通过。同 proceed, progress 反 stop, wait / ～ **by** ①走过：He ～ed by me without greeting. 他从我身边走过而没打招呼。②忽略；不过问：I can't ～ the matter by. 我不能对此事置之不理。～ **away** 死；逝世：He ～ed away during the night. 他在晚间去世。❷度过；消磨：How shall we ～ the evening? 我们将如何消磨今晚的时间? 同 spend 反 waste ❸审查通过；考试及格：All of us ～ed the English examination. 我们英语考试都及格了。同 succeed 反 fail ❹传递：Will you please ～ me that book? 请你把那本书递给我好吗? 同 hand, present 反 hold, keep ❺(对某事或某人)表示(意见)；作判决(与 upon 或 on 连用)：I can't ～ an opinion on your work without seeing it. 我没看到你的作品，不能发表意见。/ ～ **sentence on** 判决；判刑：Before I ～ sentence on you, have you anything to say for yourself? 在我给你下判决之前，你还有什么为自己辩护的吗? Ⅱ n.[C] ❶考试及格：get a ～ 及格 ❷通行证；入场许可证；入场券：No one can get in the fort without a ～. 没有通行证，任何人都不能进入要塞。同 passport

passage /ˈpæsɪdʒ/ n. ❶通过;穿过 同 crossing,pass ❷[C]通道;走道;航程 同 channel,route ❸[C](演讲词或文章的)一段,一节:a ～ from the Bible《圣经》中的一节 同 paragraph,chapter

passenger /ˈpæsɪndʒə(r)/ n. [C]乘客

passer-by /ˌpɑːsəˈbaɪ/ n. [C](pl. passers-by) 过路人

passion /ˈpæʃn/ n. ❶激情;热情 同 affection,enthusiasm 反 coldness,unconcern / **arouse (stir up) one's** ～ 激发某人的热情:A bright future aroused her ～. 美好的未来激发了她的热情. **be in a** ～ 在发怒;在发脾气:The boss was in a ～ then. 老板那时在发脾气。**be filled with** ～ 对…充满爱:The old man is filled with a ～ for his hometown. 老人对家乡充满了爱。❷酷爱;热爱:He tried to develop a ～ for poetry. 他努力培养对诗歌的喜爱。/ He has a ～ for football. 他酷爱足球. 同 fancy,love

passionate /ˈpæʃənət/ adj. 热情的;情绪激昂的;易怒的 同 earnest,excited

passive /ˈpæsɪv/ adj. ❶被动的:Your action put yourself in a ～ position. 你的行为使你自己陷入被动。❷消极的,不积极的:It is not useful to make a ～ resistance. 消极抵抗是没有用的。同 in-active,indifferent 反 active,lively 派 passively adv.

passport /ˈpɑːspɔːt/ n. [C]护照

password /ˈpɑːswɜːd,ˈpæswɜːd/ n. [C]口令,密码:enter your ～输入你的口令

past /pɑːst/ Ⅰ adj. 过去的;已过的:for the ～ few days 过去的几天 同 earlier,previous 反 future,present Ⅱ n. 过去;昔日:We cannot change the ～. 我们不能改变过去. 同 history 反 future,today Ⅲ prep. (在时间或空间上)过;经过;在…之后:half ～ two 两点半

paste /peɪst/ Ⅰ n. 糨糊 Ⅱ v. 粘贴:～ things together 把东西贴在一起 同 stick,fix

pastime /ˈpɑːstaɪm/ n. [C]消遣;娱乐 同 amusement,enjoyment 反 business,labor

pasture /ˈpɑːstʃə(r)/ n. [C] 牧场

pat /pæt/ Ⅰ v. (patted;patting)轻拍,轻打:～ a dog 轻拍一条狗 同 tap / **sb. on the back** 轻拍某人的背(表示赞扬或鼓励):My brother ～ted me on the back and said,"Congratulations!"我哥哥拍着我的背说:"祝贺你!"Ⅱ n. 轻拍;轻拍声 同 tap

patch /pætʃ/ Ⅰ n. [C]❶补片;补丁 同 mend,repair ❷小块土地(尤指作菜地用)同 plot,garden Ⅱ v. ❶ 补缀 同 sew up,mend ❷作为…的补片 ❸拼凑

patent /ˈpeɪtnt/ Ⅰ adj. 专利的;特许的 同 trade-marked 反 unpatented Ⅱ n. 专利;专利权:apply for a ～ 申请专利/ The factory got a ～ on (for) its products. 工厂获得了产品专利权。同 invention,certificate

paternal /pəˈtɜːnəl/ adj. ❶父亲的;父亲般的:～ duties 父亲的职责/a ～ reprimand 严父般的训斥 ❷父亲一方的,父系的:～ uncle 叔叔(伯伯)

path /pɑːθ/ n. [C]小路;小径 同 way,road / **clear a** ～ **for** 为…开路;为…扫清道路:A tractor cleared the ～ for us. 一辆拖拉机为我们开路. **pave (smooth) the** ～ **for** 为…铺平道路:Good education will pave the ～ for you. 良好的教育将为你铺平道路. **stand in one's** ～ 挡路;阻碍:Don't stand in his ～ to success. 不要阻挡他走上成功之路. **take the** ～ **to** 走…的道路:He took the ～ to revolution. 他走上了革命的道路.

patience /ˈpeɪʃns/ n. [U]容忍;忍耐;耐心 同 endurance,perseverance 反 impatience / **have** ～ **with (for)sb.** 对某人有耐心:The teacher has ～ with his students. 那位老师对学生很有耐心. **have the** ～ **to do** 有耐心做:I have the ～ to listen to your complaints. 我有耐心听你的怨言. **lose** ～ 失去耐心:Don't lose ～,and you'll be successful. 不要失去信心,你会成功的. **run out of** ～ 失去耐心:The conductor never runs out of ～.那位公共汽车售票员从不失去耐心. **with** ～ 耐心地:She listened to my story with ～. 她耐心地听我讲故事.

patient /ˈpeɪʃnt/ Ⅰ adj. 有耐心的;容忍的:Please be ～. 请耐心些. 同 enduring,persevering 反 impatient / **be** ～ **in** 在…方面有耐心:She is ～ in teaching children. 她教孩子很耐心. **be** ～ **with sb.** 对某人有耐心:He was not ～ with the boy. 他对那男孩很不耐烦。Ⅱ n.[C]病人:The hospital is equipped to handle 500 ～s. 这医院的设备足以接纳 500 个病人. 派 patiently adv.

P

patriot / ˈpætriət, ˈpeitriət / n. [C] 爱国者

patriotic / ˌpeitriˈɒtik / adj. 爱国的

patriotism / ˌpeitriətizəm / n. [U] 爱国主义

patrol / pəˈtrəul / Ⅰ n. ❶[U] 巡逻 圁 guard, defense / **on** — 在巡逻：The policemen are out on —. 警察在巡逻。❷[C] 巡逻者；巡逻队 Ⅱ v. (-trolled; -trolling) 巡逻：The guards — the yard day and night. 卫兵在院里日夜巡逻。圁 guard, inspect

patron / ˈpeitrən / n. [C] 资助人；赞助人 圁 sponsor, supporter

pattern / ˈpætn / Ⅰ n. 模式；样式；图案：sentence — 句型 / new — of life 新的生活方式 圁 model, design / **after (on, upon) the** — **of** 按照…的方式；仿照… **follow the** — 仿效…的样式：The foreigner tried to follow the — of Chinese life. 那外国人试图仿效中国人的生活方式。Ⅱ vt. 仿制, 仿造；模仿

pause / pɔːz / Ⅰ n. 中止；暂停 圁 break, halt continuousness, progress / **without** — 不停地：The speaker talked on without —. 讲演人不停地往下说。Ⅱ vi. 暂停；中止：He —d for a moment. 他暂停了一会儿。圁 break, halt 反 continue, proceed

pave / peiv / vt. 铺，筑（路等）：The road in front of our classroom is —d with bricks. 我们教室前的那条路是用砖头铺成的。圁 cover, floor / — **the way for** 为…铺平道路；为…做准备：Good training —s the way for success. 良好的训练为成功铺平道路。

pavement / ˈpeivmənt / n. [C] (英) 人行道

pavilion / pəˈviljən / n. [C] ❶凉亭；楼阁, 亭子 ❷(演出或展览用的) 大帐篷

paw / pɔː / n. [C] (动物的) 爪

pawn / pɔːn / Ⅰ n. ❶[U] 典当，押；in —典当：My bike was in —. 我的自行车当掉了。❷[C] 抵押物 Ⅱ vt. 当；抵押

pay / pei / Ⅰ v. (paid/peid/, paid) ❶付给；付款 圁 settle, reward 反 owe, receive / — **by check** 用支票支付 — **by (in) installment** 分期付款 — **in cash** 以现金支付 — **in kind** 以实物支付 — **into one's account** 划到某人的账上 — **on delivery** 货到付款 — **off** 全部还 (付) 清：It took them six years to — off that judgment. 他们过了 6 年才还清所判决的债务。❷给予 (注意等) 圁 give, grant 反 receive / —

attention to 注意：Please — more attention to your work. 请更加注意你的工作。— **a visit to** 访问，参观：We decided to — another visit to Mr. Smith the next day. 我们决定第二天再拜访史密斯先生。— **back** ①偿还 (借款等)：You must remember to — the money back to your friend. 你必须记住把钱还给朋友。②回报；报复：— sb. back in his own coin 以其人之道，还治其人之身 / — sb. back blow for blow 对某人以牙还牙 / — **for** ①付款；支付：I paid thirty-two yuan for the dictionary. 我花了 32 元钱买这本字典。②付出…的代价：He will have to — for his foolish behavior. 他得为他的愚蠢行为付出代价。Ⅱ n. 工资：base —基本工资 / daily — 日工资 / fixed (regular) — 固定工资 / overtime — 加班费 / On what day does he receive his —? 他何日领工资？圁 wages, salary

payment / ˈpeimənt / n. ❶[U] 支付；付款：make (a) — 付款 / — on terms 定期付款；按条件付款 ❷[C] 支付的款项：We have not received the — for the goods. 我们还未收到货款。

PE (= physical education) 体育 (课)

pea / piː / n. [C] 豌豆

peace / piːs / n. [U] 和平；安定 圁 calm, quiet 反 disturbance, insecurity / **at** — 处于和平状态：be at — with all countries 和所有国家和平相处 / **make** — (与…) 讲和：The leaders of the two nations decided to make —. 两国的领导决定讲和。

peaceful / ˈpiːsfl / adj. 爱好和平的；和平的；安详的；宁静的：a — evening 宁静的夜晚 圁 calm, quiet 反 disturbed, violent 派 peacefully adv.

peach / piːtʃ / n. [C] 桃子；桃树

peacock / ˈpiːkɒk / n. [C] 孔雀

peak / piːk / Ⅰ n. [C] ❶山峰；山顶：climb a — 攀登高峰 圁 tip, top 反 base, bottom / **at the** — 在顶峰：at the — of one's success 在成功的顶峰 ❷(物体的) 尖端 Ⅱ adj. 最大值的；高峰的：— hours of traffic 交通高峰期

peanut / ˈpiːnʌt / n. [C] 花生

pear / peə(r) / n. [C] 梨；梨树

pearl / pɜːl / n. [C] 珍珠

peasant / ˈpez(ə)nt / n. [C] 农民

pebble / 'pebl / *n.* [C]鹅卵石

peculiar / pɪ'kjuːlɪə(r) / *adj.* 特殊的；奇异的 回 particular，odd 反 common，usual

peculiarity / pɪˌkjuːlɪ'ærəti / *n.* ❶[U]特性；独特性 characteristic ❷[C]独特之处

pedal / 'pedəl / Ⅰ*n.* [C] ❶脚踏，踏板：The ～ has come off your bicycle. 你自行车上的一个脚踏脱落了。❷(钢琴、竖琴等的)踏板：～ bin 脚踏式垃圾桶 Ⅱ*vi.* 骑车；踩踏板 around on bicycles 骑自行车四处转悠

peddler / 'pedlə(r) / *n.* [C]小贩 回 seller，street-trader

pedestrian / pɪ'destrɪən / *n.* [C]行人：The ～ hit by a red car was dead. 红色小车撞上的那个行人死了。/No ～. 禁止行人通过。

pee / piː / Ⅰ*vi.* 〈口〉小便，撒尿：The baby ～d in her pants and was crying. 那个小宝宝尿了裤子，正哭呢。Ⅱ*n.* ❶小便，撒尿：go for a ～ 小便，解手 ❷尿(液)

peek / piːk / Ⅰ*vi.* (很快地)看一眼，瞥一眼，瞥；偷看，窥视：The man was caught while he was ～ing in through the keyhole. 那人透过钥匙孔向里面窥视时被逮个正着。/No ～ing at the present before supper. 吃晚饭之前不准偷看礼物。Ⅱ*n.* (很快的)一瞥，一看；偷看，窥视：He had a quick ～ at the answers. 他快速地扫了一眼答案。

peel / piːl / Ⅰ*v.* 剥，削(水果等的皮) Ⅱ*n.* [U]果皮

pen / pen / Ⅰ*n.* [C] ❶钢笔 ❷围栏 Ⅱ*vt.* (penned；penning) ❶写：～ a letter 写信 回 write ❷把…关在栏里 回 encage，enclose ❸关押，囚禁 回 imprison，shut in

penal / 'piːnəl / *adj.* 处罚的；刑罚的：～ laws 刑法/a ～ sum 罚金

penalty / 'penəlti / *n.* 惩罚；处罚：suffer a ～ 受处罚 / the death ～ 死刑 回 fine，punishment 反 reward

pencil / 'pensl / Ⅰ*n.* [C]铅笔：～-box 铅笔盒 Ⅱ*v.* 用铅笔写或画

pendulum / 'pendjələm / *n.* (钟等的)摆

penetrate / 'penɪtreɪt / *v.* 进入；贯穿；看穿；渗透：A bullet cannot ～ a wall. 子弹不能穿透墙壁。回 enter，cut into

penetration / ˌpenɪ'treɪʃn / *n.* [U]穿入；渗透；洞察力

penguin / 'peŋgwɪn / *n.* [C]企鹅

penicillin / ˌpenɪ'sɪlɪn / *n.* [U]青霉素

peninsula / pə'nɪnsjələ / *n.* [C]半岛

penniless / 'penɪləs / *adj.* 一文不名的；一贫如洗的 回 moneyless，poor 反 rich，wealthy

penny / 'peni / *n.* (*pl.* pence/pens/ 或 pennies / 'peniz /)便士

用法

❶在英国 pennies 用以表示硬币数，pence 用以表示数额，如 fifteen pennies 15 个便士币，fifteen pence 15 便士(数额)；在美国指数额不用 pence。❷表示数额时，从 2 便士到 11 便士数字跟 pence 连写，如 twopence 2 便士，elevenpence 11 便士，20 便士也连写：twentypence，其他的数字与 pence 都分开写，如 twelve pence 12 便士，twenty-one pence 21 便士。

pension / 'penʃn / *n.* 抚恤金；养老金；年金：The old lady lives on a ～. 老太太靠养老金生活。回 benefit，maintenance

pentagon / 'pentəgən / *n.* ❶[C]五边形；五角形 ❷(the Pentagon)五角大楼(美国国防部所在地)

people / 'piːpl / *n.* ❶(单数形式，复数意义，谓语动词要用复数)人；人民；人们：visit one's ～探望家里的人 回 humans，citizens ❷[C]民族：the ～s of Asia 亚洲各民族 / The Chinese ～ is a brave and hardworking ～. 中华民族是一个勤劳勇敢的民族。/ the People's Liberation Army (the PLA) 人民解放军 回 nation，race

用法

❶a people 或 one people 意为"一个民族"。❷表示"全民族"时，people 前面要用定冠词the；如 the English people 英国人民。❸用以表示"家人""家属"之意时，people 前面用所有格代词：My wife's people are staying with us now. 我妻子的家人现在和我们住在一起。

pepper / 'pepə(r) / *n.* [U] ❶胡椒粉 ❷辣椒

per / pə(r)，pɜː(r) / *prep.* 每，每一：～ day 每天 / ～ hour 每小时

perceive / pə'siːv / *vt.* ❶察觉；感知：Have you ～d the danger? 你察觉出危险了吗？回 feel，notice 反 overlook，ignore ❷认识到；意识到；理解：At once，he ～d that he was unwelcome there. 他一下子意识到了自己在那儿不受欢迎的。回 understand，know

percent / pə'sent / n. 百分之一；百分比：Ninety-eight ~ passed the examination. 98％的人通过了考试。

percentage / pə'sentɪdʒ / n. [C]百分数；百分率

perception / pə'sepʃn / n. 感觉；悟性；洞察力 同 sense, understanding

perceptive / pə'septɪv / adj. ❶有领悟力的；有洞察力的，敏锐的：a ~ critic 颇有洞察力的评论家 ❷感知的，感觉的：~ organs 感觉器官

perch / pɜːtʃ / I n. [C](禽鸟的)栖木，栖息处 同 rest, seat II vi. 栖息；停歇 同 sit, rest

perfect I / 'pɜːfɪkt / adj. ❶极好的；完美的；技术精湛的：Practice makes ~. 熟能生巧。同 excellent, faultless 反 imperfect, faulty ❷(语法)完成的 II /pə'fekt / vt. 使完美；使改善 同 finish, complete 派 perfectly adv.；perfection n.

perform / pə'fɔːm / v. ❶执行；履行：~ one's duties 尽责任 同 accomplish, achieve ❷演出(戏剧)；演奏(音乐)；表演(戏法等)：~ in the role of Romeo 扮演罗密欧的角色 同 play, act

performance / pə'fɔːməns / n. ❶ [U]执行；成果，成绩：faithful in the ~ of his duties 忠于职守/ Our team's ~ was excellent in that year. 在那一年中，我们队战绩卓著。同 accomplishment, achievement ❷[C]演出，表演：The evening ~ is at 8 o'clock. 晚场在 8 点。同 show, play

perfume / 'pɜːfjuːm / n. [C;U] ❶香味；香气，芳香：a faint ~ 淡淡的香味 ❷香水：What French ~ are you wearing? 你用的是什么牌子的法国香水？

perhaps / pə'hæps / adv. 可能；也许 同 maybe, possibly

peril / 'perɪl / n. ❶ [U](尤指严重的或致命的)危险：He was in ~ of a mental collapse. 他面临精神崩溃的危险。❷险事；险情，险境：survive the ~ of the expedition 经历探险过程中的艰难险阻而生存下来

period / 'pɪərɪəd / n. [C] ❶时代；时期：the Spring and Autumn Period 春秋时期 / the Warring States Period 战国时期 同 age, time ❷学时；课时 同 course, term ❸周期；一段时间 同 cycle ❹结束；句号 同 end, stop

periodic / ˌpɪərɪ'ɒdɪk / adj. 定期的；周期性的；the ~ motion of a planet 行星的周期性运动 同 repeated, seasonal

periodical / ˌpɪərɪ'ɒdɪkl / n. [C]期刊 同 publication, magazine

perish / 'perɪʃ / vi. ❶死亡，丧生；凋谢：Many people ~ed in the earthquake. 地震中很多人死去了。/The buds ~ed when the frost came. 霜打花蕾凋谢。❷被摧毁；毁灭；消亡：Buildings ~ed in flames. 一栋栋建筑在烈火中焚毁殆尽。

permanent / 'pɜːmənənt / adj. 长久的；持久的；永恒的：a ~ employee 长期雇员 / a ~ job 固定职业 同 lasting, perpetual 反 impermanent, temporary 派 permanently adv.

permission / pə'mɪʃn / n. [U]许可；准许 同 agreement, grant 反 refusal, prevention / **have ~ to do sth.** 得到许可做某事：He has ~ to use this computer. 他使用这台计算机是得到许可的。**with one's ~**经某人同意：We put off the meeting with the teacher's ~. 我们经老师同意将开会日期延后。**without ~** 未经许可：No one can leave without ~. 未经许可任何人不得离开。

permit I / pə'mɪt / v. (-mitted;-mitting) 允许；许可：Smoking is not ~ted in this theatre. 本戏院不许吸烟。同 agree, allow 反 forbid, prohibit II / 'pɜːmɪt / n. [C]许可证；执照：export (import) ~ 出口(进口)许可证 同 license, pass

perpetual / pə'petʃuəl / adj. 永久的；永恒的 同 lasting, permanent 反 temporary, impermanent

perplex / pə'pleks / vt. 使困惑，使茫然；使费解：She behaved in a way that ~ed me. 她的行为方式令我不解。/Don't ~ a child with so many questions! 别弄这么多问题把小孩子搞得晕头转向！

persecute / 'pɜːsɪkjuːt / vt. 迫害；残害 同 illtreat, oppress 反 support, humor

perseverance / ˌpɜːsɪ'vɪərəns / n. [U]毅力；坚韧；不屈不挠：By ～, the lame boy learned to swim. 靠着毅力，这个跛脚儿童学会了游泳. 同 persistence, resolution

persevere / ˌpɜːsɪ'vɪə(r) / vi. 坚持（与 in 连用）：～ in one's studies 孜孜不倦地研究 同 adhere, persist 反 stop, give up

persist / pə'sɪst / vt. ❶坚持；执意：～ in (with) 坚持：He ～s in taking cold baths in winter. 他坚持在冬天洗冷水澡. 同 persevere, insist 反 stop, end ❷持续：The thick mist will ～ here. 大雾将在此持续下去. 同 last, endure 反 fade, die 派 persistence n. ; persistent adj.

person / 'pɜːsn / n. [C] ❶（语法）人称：the first ～ (I, we), the second ～ (you), the third ～ (he, she, it, they) 第一人称(我，我们)，第二人称(你，你们)，第三人称(他，她，它，他/它们) ❷人：Four ～s saw this. 有四人看见此事. 同 individual, human；in ～亲自，本人：The president appeared in ～. 总裁亲自到场.

personage / 'pɜːsɪnɪdʒ / n. 人物；名士；角色：democratic ～s 民主人士

personal / 'pɜːsənl / adj. ❶个人的；私人的：～ needs 个人需要 / ～ rights 个人权利 / ～ opinions 个人的意见 同 private, individual 反 public, general ❷亲自的：make a ～ call 亲自拜访 同 own 派 personally adv.

personality / ˌpɜːsə'nælɪti / n. [C]人格；个性 同 character, nature

personification / pəˌsɒnɪfɪ'keɪʃn / n. 人格化；化身；象征

personify / pə'sɒnɪfaɪ / vt. 把…拟人化，把…人格化

personnel / ˌpɜːsə'nel / n. ❶（集合名词）人员，职员：The company is strict with its ～. 这家公司严格要求它的员工. 同 staff, members ❷[U]人事部门

perspective / pə'spektɪv / n. [C] ❶视角；观点；想法 同 view ❷远景；景观 同 outlook, scene ❸透视画法；透视图

persuade / pə'sweɪd / v. 说服，劝导 同 convince, advise 反 discourage, forbid / ～ sb. of sth. 使某人相信某事：I'm almost ～d of his honesty. 我几乎相信他是诚实的. ～ sb. to do sth. 劝说某人干某事：He ～d me to go. 他劝我去. 派 persuasion n. ; persuasive adj.

pervade / pə'veɪd / vt. ❶弥漫于，渗透于：A haze ～s the park, prompting health concerns. 公园里弥漫着雾霭，引起了人们对健康的关注. /An intense poetic quality ～s her writings. 她的作品中洋溢着浓浓的诗意. ❷遍布于；流行于：When the echoes had fully ceased, a light laughter at once ～d the assembly. 等回声余音止犁，聚会上顿时遍布一片轻松的欢笑声. /Uncertainty ～s the economic life. 不确定性充斥着经济生活.

pessimism / 'pesɪmɪzəm / n. [U] 悲观；悲观主义：Never does he show ～ in face of difficulty. 他面对困难从不悲观.

pessimist / 'pesɪmɪst / n. [C]悲观论者；悲观主义者

pessimistic / ˌpesɪ'mɪstɪk / adj. 悲观的；悲观主义的：We are never ～ about the future. 对于未来，我们从不悲观. 同 depressed, sad 反 optimistic 派 pessimistically adv.

pest / pest / n. ❶讨厌的人或物 同 nuisance, curse ❷害虫，有害动物；疫病 同 destructive insect, plague

pet / pet / Ⅰ n. [C] 宠物；宠儿：have (keep) ～s 养宠物 同 favorite, darling Ⅱ adj. ❶宠爱的；感兴趣的：～ name 昵称；～ phrase 口头禅 同 favorite, fond ❷特别的；得意的：Snakes are my ～ hate. 蛇是我特别讨厌的动物. Ⅲ vt. 爱抚，抚摸，轻按 同 pat, stroke

petal / 'petəl / n. [C]花瓣

petition / pə'tɪʃn / n. & v. 请愿；祈求 同 appeal

petrify / 'petrɪfaɪ / vt. 使石化，硬化；(喻)使无(思考、感觉、行为等)能力；使发呆：He was petrified with fear. 他完全吓傻了. 同 benumb, astonish

petrol / 'petrəl / n. (＝gasoline)(英)汽油：stop at the next ～ station 在下一个加油站停车

petroleum / pə'trəʊliəm / n. [U]石油

petty / 'peti / adj. 小的；小气的 同 small, miner 反 important, major

pharmacy / 'fɑːməsi / n. ❶[U]配药业；制药业 ❷[U]配药学；药剂学；制药学 ❸[C]药店，药铺

phase / feɪz / n. [C] ❶阶段；时期：The work has entered a new ～. 工作已进入了一个新阶段. 同 period, time ❷面；方面：You should look at the other ～ of the problem. 你应当看

看问题的另一方面。同 aspect, side

PhD (＝Doctor of Philosophy)博士学位

phenomenon / fə'nɒmɪnən / n. (*pl*. phenomena / fɪ'nɒmɪnə /) 现象：the phenomena of nature 自然现象 同 happening, occasion

philatelist / fɪ'lætəlɪst / n. [C]集邮家

philately / fɪ'lætəli / n. [U]集邮

Philippines / 'fɪlɪpiːnz / n. 菲律宾

philosopher / fɪ'lɒsəfə(r) / n. [C] ❶哲学家 ❷哲人，贤哲 ❸达观的人，豁达的人；(在逆境中)处世泰然的人：He was a 〜 with a taste for what is called low life. 他为人豁达，喜欢所谓下层阶级的生活。

philosophy / fɪ'lɒsəfi / n. ❶哲学：doctor of 〜 哲学博士 ❷人生哲学；见解，观点：〜 of life 人生哲学

phone / fəun / (＝telephone) Ⅰ n. 电话；电话机，hang up the 〜 挂断电话 / Please answer the 〜. 请接电话。Ⅱ v. 打电话

phonology / fə'nɒlədʒi / n. 语音学

photo / 'fəutəu / n. [C] (*pl*. photos)照片；相片(photograph 的略写形式)：take a 〜 拍一张照片 同 image, picture

photograph / 'fəutəgrɑːf / n. [C]照片；相片：develop a 〜 冲洗照片 / enlarge a 〜 放大照片 同 image, picture

photographer / fə'tɒgrəfə(r) / n. 摄影师

photography / fə'tɒgrəfi / n. [U]摄影术

phrase / freɪz / n. 片语；短语 同 expression, idiom

physical / 'fɪzɪkl / adj. 物质的；物理的；体力的；肉体的；自然规律的：〜 exercises 运动 / 〜 education (PE)体育 同 material, bodily

physician / fɪ'zɪʃn / n. [C]内科医生

physicist / 'fɪzɪsɪst / n. [C]物理学家

physics / 'fɪzɪks / n. 物理学

physiologist / ˌfɪzɪ'ɒlədʒɪst / n. [C]生理学家

physiology / ˌfɪzɪ'ɒlədʒi / n. 生理学

pianist / 'pɪənɪst / n. [C]钢琴弹奏者；钢琴家

piano / pɪ'ænəu / n. [C] (*pl*. pianos)钢琴
用法
> 在美国英语中，乐器名称前可用、可不用定冠词 the：play the piano 或 play piano 弹钢琴，play the violin 或 play violin 拉小提琴。在英国英语中，乐器名称前要用定冠词 the：play the piano 弹钢琴，play the guitar 弹吉他，play the flute 吹笛。

pick / pɪk / v. ❶(用手)采，摘；取去：〜 flowers 采花 / 〜 fruits 摘果 / 〜 sb.'s pocket 扒某人的口袋 同 collect, gather ❷挑选，选择：〜 words 选适当的字眼 同 choose, select / 〜 **out** ①选择：My sister is going with me to help me 〜 out a new suit. 我姐姐要陪我一起去帮我挑一套新衣服。②分辨出：〜 out one's friends in a crowd 在人群中分辨出自己的朋友 ③理解：I can't 〜 out the meaning of this word. 我不能理解这个字的意思。〜 **up** ①捡起：〜 up a stone 拾起一块石头 ②搭载；携带：The train stopped to 〜 up passengers. 火车停下来搭载乘客。③学会；获得：〜 up a foreign language (自然)学得一种外语

pickle / 'pɪkl / n. (常用 *pl*.)腌制食品；泡菜

picnic / 'pɪknɪk / n. [C]野餐：go on a 〜 去野餐 同 outing

pictorial / pɪk'tɔːrɪəl / adj. ❶画的，绘画的：〜 art 绘画艺术 ❷用图说明的，图示的；插图的：〜 writings 带插图的文字作品 ❸形象化的；生动的：a 〜 description of the countryside 对乡村的生动描述

picture / 'pɪktʃə(r) / Ⅰ n. [C] ❶图画；照片：〜 books 图画书 同 drawing, photo / **take** (**snap**) **a** 〜 拍照：Let's have a 〜 taken under the tree. 我们在树下照张相吧。❷影片；电影 同 film, movie ❸景色 同 scene Ⅱ vt. 描绘；想象 同 describe, imagine

pie / paɪ / n. (以肉或水果为馅的)烤饼；馅饼

piece / piːs / n. [C] ❶块，片，部分：a 〜 of paper(wood, glass, chalk, cloth) 一张纸(一块木头，一块玻璃，一支粉笔，一块布) / The teapot fell and was broken to 〜s. 茶壶掉下来摔成碎片。同 bit, part ❷(艺术或音乐作品的)幅；件；首：a 〜 of art work 一件艺术品 / a 〜 of music 一首乐曲 同 selection, work

pierce / pɪəs / v. ❶刺入；刺穿；透入：The arrow 〜d his shoulder. 箭刺入他的肩膀。/ They 〜d into the heart of the forest. 他们进入了森林的中心。❷在…刺孔，在…上戳洞：the canvases 〜d with jagged holes by shrapnel 被弹片刺得千疮百孔的帆布 ❸(声音)刺破；(光亮)穿入；(目光)看穿：A sharp cry escaped Linda's lips, piercing the night. 一声尖叫从琳达嘴里发出，划破了夜幕。❹突破；穿过：Our forces 〜d the enemy's defense. 我军突破了敌军的防线。

piercing / ˈpɪəsɪŋ / adj. ❶(冷风等)刺骨的，锥子般的；(目光等)犀利的：a ～ wind 一阵刺骨的风/With her ～ eyes she could drill the life out of you. 她那炯炯刺人的目光可以把你的魂挖出来。❷(声音)刺耳的，尖厉的；utter a ～ shriek 发出一声刺耳的尖叫

pig / pɪɡ / n. [C]猪；野猪

pigeon / ˈpɪdʒɪn / n. [C]鸽子

pigment / ˈpɪɡmənt / I n. [U;C]颜料；涂料：lay on colour in small strokes of pure ～ 用淡淡的纯色涂抹颜色 ❷色素，色质：～ cell 色素细胞 II vt. 给…着色，染色于

pile / paɪl / I n. [C]堆，叠：a ～ of books (wood)一大堆书(木头) 同 mass, heal II v. 堆起，堆积 同 gather, heap / ～ up 积聚；累积：The snow is piling up. 雪正越堆越高。

pilgrim / ˈpɪlɡrɪm / n. [C]香客；朝圣者

pilgrimage / ˈpɪlɡrɪmɪdʒ / n. 朝圣：Pilgrimage to the West《西游记》

pill / pɪl / n. [C]药丸；药片：compound ～ 合成药 / sleeping ～ 安眠药 / take a ～ 服药丸

pillar / ˈpɪlə(r) / n. [C] ❶柱 同 post, support ❷(喻)台柱；栋梁：Scientists are ～s of a society. 科学家是社会的栋梁。

pillow / ˈpɪləʊ / n. [C]枕头

pilot / ˈpaɪlət / I n. [C]飞行员；飞行器的驾驶员 同 airman, flyer II vt. 驾驶(飞机等)；为(船舶等)引航 同 guide, direct

pin / pɪn / I n. ❶1. 大头针；饰针；别针 ❷(唱机的)唱针 II vt. (pinned; pinning)别住；钉住：～ one's hopes on 把希望寄托于：The old man ～ned his hopes on his son. 老人把希望寄托在他的儿子身上。

PIN(= personal Identification Number)个人身份证号码，个人识别码

pine / paɪn / I n. 松树；松木 II adj. 松树的

pineapple / ˈpaɪnæpl / n. 凤梨；菠萝

ping-pong / ˈpɪŋpɒŋ / I n. [U]乒乓球运动 II v. 被传来传去

pink / pɪŋk / I n. [U]粉红色 II adj. 粉红色的

pint / paɪnt / n. 品脱(液量或干量单位，等于1/2 加仑，或在英国等于 0.568 升，在美国等于 0.473 升)

pioneer / ˌpaɪəˈnɪə(r) / I n. [C]先锋；先驱；拓荒者：a Young Pioneer 一名少先队员 同 founder, leader II v. 当先驱；开辟(道路等)；提倡(新法等)同 found, start

pipe / paɪp / I n. [C] ❶管：water ～s 水管 / gas ～ 煤气管 同 tube, passage ❷烟斗 ❸管乐器 II vt. 用管道输送

pipeline / ˈpaɪplaɪn / n. [C]管道；管线

pirate / ˈpaɪrət / n. [C]海盗

pistol / ˈpɪstl / n. [C]手枪

pit / pɪt / n. [C]坑，洼 同 hole, hollow

pitch¹ / pɪtʃ / I v. ❶投，掷，扔 同 throw, cast ❷搭；架设 II n. [C] ❶投，掷，扔 同 throw, cast ❷宿营地

pitch² / pɪtʃ / n. [U]沥青

pitiful / ˈpɪtɪfəl / adj. 可怜的；令人同情的 同 miserable, merciful 反 angry, cruel

pitiless / ˈpɪtɪlɪs / adj. 无同情心的；无情的；残忍的：a ～ master 铁石心肠的主人/the ～ heat of the desert 沙漠的毒热

pity / ˈpɪti / I n. ❶怜悯；同情 同 mercy, sympathy 反 anger, cruelty / take (have) ～ on 同情；可怜：Mary always takes ～ on some stray cats or dogs. 玛丽总是可怜那些迷途的猫狗。out of ～ 出于同情；出于怜悯：She gave the man some money out of ～. 出于同情，她给了那人一些钱。❷可惜；遗憾：What a ～! 多么可惜啊! / It's a ～(that) he couldn't swim. 真遗憾，他不会游泳。同 regret II v. 同情；可怜 同 forgive, sympathize

place / pleɪs / I n. [C] ❶地方；场所：a ～ of interest 名胜 同 space, spot / in ～ 在合适的位置；适当的；相称的：Everything is in ～. 一切就绪。in ～ of 代替；取代：Jack played in ～ of Tom. 杰克上场替换了汤姆。out of ～ 不在合适的位置；不适当；不相称：What you said was out of ～. 你讲的话不合适。❷住所；寓所：at one's ～ 在某人家里 同 home, house ❸地位；等级；名次 同 position, rank / in the first ～ 第一，首先 take one's ～ ①代替某人的位置 ②就座；就位：take the ～ of 代替；取代：I don't think TV will take the ～ of movies. 我认为电视不会代替电影。take ～ 发生；举行：Great changes have taken ～ in China. 中国发生了巨大的变化。II v. ❶放置；安排 同 put, locate 反 remove, take away ❷发出(订单)：～ an order for books with Smith & Sons 向史密斯父子公司订购书籍

placement / ˈpleɪsmənt / n. ❶[U]放置；布

置;布局;部署:the ～ of furniture 家具的布置 ❷[U](人员的)安插,工作安排;(学生的)编班 ❸[C]就业安排:The university offers a ～ service for its graduates. 这所大学生为毕业生提供就业服务。

plain / pleɪn / Ⅰ adj. ❶明白的;清楚的;易于了解的:～ English 简明英语 同 clear,obvious 反 indistinct,concealed ❷简单的;朴素的;平凡的:in ～ clothes 穿便衣 / ～ food 简单的食物/～ living 简朴的生活 / ～ meal 便饭同 simple,ordinary 反 difficult,sophisticated ❸(指人的思想、行为等)坦率的,直截了当的 Ⅱ adv. 清楚地;明白地 同 honest,open 反 dishonest,disguised Ⅲ n.[C]平原;平地

plan / plæn / Ⅰ n.[C]计划;策略:Have they made any ～s for the holidays? 他们已经制订了假期计划吗? 同 program,design / **carry out a ～** 执行计划:We carried out the new five-year ～. 我们执行了新的五年计划。 **make ～s** 制订计划 **propose a ～** 提出计划:I'll propose a new ～ at its meeting. 我要在会上提出一个新的计划。Ⅱ v. 设计;打算:Where do you ～ to spend your holiday? 你打算在什么地方度假? 同 intend

plane[1] / pleɪn / n.[C]飞机(aeroplane 的略写形式):**by ～** 乘飞机:They went to London by ～. 他们乘飞机去伦敦。

plane[2] / pleɪn / Ⅰ n. 平面;水平面 同 level Ⅱ adj.平面的;平坦的 同 flat

planet / 'plænɪt / n.[C]行星

plant / plɑ:nt / Ⅰ n.[C]❶植物 同 bush,tree ❷工厂 同 factory,works Ⅱ vt. 栽种;种植:They are ～ing trees on the hill. 他们在山上种树。 同 grow

plastic / 'plæstɪk / Ⅰ adj. (物质)可塑的;(物品)由塑料做成的:～ payment 塑料货币支付(即信用卡支付) 同 flexible,soft 反 rigid,hard Ⅱ n.(常用 pl.)塑料;可塑物

plate / pleɪt / n.[C]盘,碟 同 dish

plateau / 'plætəʊ / n. [C](pl. plateaus 或 plateaux / 'plætəʊz /)高原

platform / 'plætfɔ:m / n.[C](火车站的)月台;讲台;台 同 stage,stand

play / pleɪ / Ⅰ v. ❶自娱;玩耍;游乐 同 entertain / ～ **with** 玩;玩弄:Children were ～ing with toys. 孩子们在玩玩具。 **～ truant** 逃学:Schoolboys who ～ truant should be pun-

ished. 逃学的学生应受处罚。 ❷踢(足球等);打(高尔夫球等) ❸扮演:Who is going to ～ Hamlet? 谁将扮演哈姆雷特? 同 act,perform Ⅱ n. ❶[U]玩;游戏:The children are at ～. 孩子们在玩。 同 amusement,fun ❷[C]剧本;戏剧 同 show,performance

player / 'pleɪə(r) / n.[C]❶运动员,运动者;游戏者:seed ～ 种子选手 / star ～明星选手 / Jack is a good chess ～. 杰克是名好棋手。 同 sportsman,athlete ❷演员 同 actor,actress ❸演奏者

playground / 'pleɪgraʊnd / n.(学校的)运动场,操场;游乐场:children's ～ 儿童游乐场 / The students played basketball on the ～ after class. 学生们下课后在操场上打篮球。

plaza / 'plɑ:zə / n.[C]❶(尤指西班牙城市的)广场,集市 ❷购物中心,商业区

plea / pli: / n.[C]请求;恳求 同 appeal,request

plead / pli:d / vt. (pleaded 或 pled)❶恳求 同 beg,appeal to ❷为…辩护;辩解 同 argue,reason

pleasant / 'pleznt / adj. 合意的;愉快的;友好的:a ～ afternoon (taste,companion) 愉快的下午(合意的味道,友好的伙伴) / Whatever happens,try to make yourself ～ to the guests. 无论发生什么,都要努力做到友好地待客。 同 charming,cheerful 反 unpleasant,displeasing / **have a ～ time** 过得(玩得)愉快:Did you have a ～ time at the party? 你在晚会上玩得愉快吗? 派 pleasantly adv.;pleasantness n.

> **辨析**
>
> **pleasant** 指人或物"令人愉快的",它常表示主观上的:pleasant news (weather)令人愉快的消息(天气)。**pleased** 意为"高兴的;满意的",作表语,只能用于形容人,后面一般接介词 with,at,about,不定式或 that 引导的从句:I'm really pleased that you've come. 我真的很高兴你来了。 This is nothing to be pleased about. 这不是件值得欢天喜地的事。 **pleasing** 意为"讨人喜欢的",它常表示客观上的,不如以上两词常用:This is not pleasing to my taste. 这不合我的口味。

please / pli:z / v. ❶请(用在祈使句中,表示客气地要求);Please come in. 请进来。Two coffees,～! 请来两杯咖啡。 ❷使满足;取悦:Please yourself. (Do as you ～.) 请随意。/ It's difficult to ～ everybody. 取悦每个人是困难的。 同 amuse,charm 反 displease,annoy ❸喜好;想要:Take as many as you ～.

你要多少就请取多少。同 like,wish 反 dislike,hate

pleased / pliːzd / *adj.* (感到)愉快的;(感到)满足的 同 happy,satisfactory 反 sad,unhappy / **be ～ with (at)** 对…感到满意(be ～ at 与 be ～ with 意思相近,但 at 后常接动名词): Are you ～ with your new clothes? 你对你的新衣服感到满意吗? / I was ～ at hearing of his success. 获悉他的成功,我很高兴。

pleasing / ˈpliːzɪŋ / *adj.* 合意的;令人喜爱的 同 pleasant,welcome

pleasure / ˈpleʒə(r) / *n.* ❶[U]愉快;满足: Has he gone abroad for ～ or on business? 他出国是为娱乐还是为业务? 同 enjoyment, satisfaction 反 displeasure,sadness ❷乐事;乐趣: He always says that working is his ～. 他总说工作是他的乐趣。同 amusement,joy 反 trouble / **have the ～ of** 有幸:I have the ～ of presenting the guests. 我很荣幸来介绍客人。 **take ～ in** 从…中得到快乐:He takes great ～ in taking pictures of animals. 他从动物摄影中得到极大乐趣。/ I take little ～ in such things. 我对这类事没什么兴趣。**with ～** 愉快地;高兴地: She accepted our invitation with ～. 她高兴地接受了我们的邀请。

pledge / pledʒ / Ⅰ *n.* [U]誓约;承诺;保证 同 promise Ⅱ *v.* 发誓;承诺;保证:be ～d to secrecy 誓守秘密 同 guarantee,swear

plentiful / ˈplentɪfl / *adj.* 丰富的;充足的;富裕的:The field workers have a ～ supply of food. 野外作业的人员食物供应充足。同 abundant,fruitful 反 rare,scarce

plenty / ˈplenti / *n.* [C]许多;大量:There are ～ of eggs at home. 家里有很多蛋。同 lots,enough 反 lack,scarcity/ **in ～** 大量;充实: They are living in ～. 他们生活富裕。

用法
❶plenty of 后面可接可数名词,也可接不可数名词,其前加 a 的用法现在已经过时: There is plenty of food in the kitchen. 厨房里有很多食物。There are plenty of books on the shelf. 书架上有很多书。❷plenty 一般用在肯定句中,在疑问句或否定句中通常用 enough:We have plenty of food for the holidays. 我们为这个假日准备了很多食物。Have you enough food for the holidays? 你们假日的食物够吃吗? We have not enough food for the holidays. 我们假日的食物不够吃。

plot / plɒt / Ⅰ *n.* [C]❶(小的)一块地;a ～ of vegetables 一块菜地 同 field,patch ❷密谋: a ～ to overthrow the government 推翻政府的阴谋 同 design ❸(小说或戏剧故事的)情节 story,plan Ⅱ *vt.* (plotted;plotting)密谋做;策划:They were ～ting to overthrow the King. 他们正在密谋要推翻国王。同 design,plan

plough / plaʊ / Ⅰ *n.* [C]犁 Ⅱ *v.* 犁(田);耕(地):They are ～ing the fields. 他们正在耕地。/ The ship is ～ing the waves. 轮船破浪前进。同 cultivate

pluck / plʌk / *vt.* ❶采;摘:～ some flowers 采一些花 同 pick,draw ❷鼓起(勇气);振作: ～ up courage 鼓起勇气 同 catch,collect

plug / plʌg / Ⅰ *n.* [C]❶塞子 ❷插头:pull out the ～ 拔出插头 Ⅱ *v.* ❶以塞子塞住 ❷插上插头:～ in the wireless set 插上收音机的插头

plum / plʌm / *n.* [C]李子;李子树

plunder / ˈplʌndə(r) / *v.* & *n.* 掠夺;抢劫 同 rob (*v.*),robbery (*n.*)

plunge / plʌndʒ / *v.* (使某物)投入;(使)突入; 陷入(与 into 连用):～ into action 立即投入行动 / ～ a country into a war 使一个国家陷入战争 同 dive,sink

plural / ˈplʊərəl / Ⅰ *adj.* 复数的:The ～ form of "child" is "children". "child"的复数形式是"children"。反 singular ❷多元的:Our world is indeed a ～ one. 我们的世界确实是一个多元的世界。Ⅱ *n.* (名词或动词的)复数 反 singular

plus / plʌs / Ⅰ *prep.* 加上:Two ～ five is seven. 二加五等于七。Ⅱ *adj.* (比所示数量)多的;正的 Ⅲ *n.* 正号;加号

pm,**p. m.** (＝in the afternoon) 午后;下午

pocket / ˈpɒkɪt / Ⅰ *n.* [C]衣袋;口袋 同 bag, purse / **have ... in one's ～** 可以操纵某人,可以任意处置某物 **keep one's hands in one's ～** 不做事,偷懒 **line one's ～**(以非法手段)中饱私囊 **pick ～** 扒窃 Ⅱ *adj.* 袖珍的;小型的:～ money 身上带的零用钱,(给小孩的)零花钱 / a ～ dictionary 袖珍字典 同 small,little 反 large,big Ⅲ *vt.* 把…装入口袋

poem / ˈpəʊɪm / *n.* [C]诗

P

辨析

poem 指某一首诗,是可数名词。**poetry** 是诗歌的总称,是不可数名词。**verse** 指诗的一行、一节,也指诗的总称,但 verse 侧重指诗的形式,poetry 侧重指诗的内容:This is a lyric poem. 这是一首抒情诗。There is poetry in his paintings. 他的画中有诗。a collection of poetry 诗集;a poem of five verses 一首五节诗;written in verse 以诗歌形式写成的。

poet / ˈpəʊɪt / n.[C]诗人

poetess / ˌpəʊɪˈtes / n.[C]女诗人

poetry / ˈpəʊɪtri / n.[U](总称)诗,诗歌

point / pɔɪnt / Ⅰ n.[C]❶(针、铅笔笔等的)尖,尖端 圆 tip ❷点:a decimal ～ 小数点 / four ～ six 4.6 ❸分数:We won by five ～s. 我们赢了5分。圆 mark,score ❹要点;观点;主旨:～ of view 观点圆 purpose / catch the ～ of 抓住……的要点:Only a few people can catch the ～ of what he said. 只有几个人能抓住他说话的要点。**from one's ～ of view** 从某人的观点来看:From my ～ of view it would be better to be decided by himself. 从我的观点来看,这事最好由他自己决定。**off the ～** 离题的;偏离要点:Your criticism is off the ～. 你的批评离题。**to the ～** 中肯;得要领:Her answer was concise and to the ～. 她的回答简洁中肯。**there is little (no) ～ in doing sth.** 做某事没有意义:There is no ～ in complaining about the service. 抱怨服务质量差无济于事。**on the ～** 即将;正要:I was on the ～ of starting when it began to rain. 我正要开始,天就下雨了。Ⅱ v.❶指(方向或位置):The needle of a compass ～s to the north. 罗盘的针指向北方。圆 direct ❷瞄准;对着:～ a gun at sb. 以枪瞄准某人圆 aim,direct ❸指出;使显著:～ out a mistake 指出错误圆 indicate,show

poison / ˈpɔɪzən / Ⅰ n.毒药;毒物 Ⅱ vt.使中毒;放毒于;毒害:～ one's mind 毒害某人的思想

poisonous / ˈpɔɪzənəs / adj.❶有毒的;有毒的:～ plants 有毒植物 / ～ gas 有毒气体圆 deadly,harmful ❷恶毒的:She apologized for the ～ words she said. 她为自己说的那些恶毒的话而道歉。圆 evil

polar / ˈpəʊlə(r) / adj.(南、北)极的

pole / pəʊl / n.❶柱;杆;竿:telegram ～ 电线杆 ❷(南、北)极:the North (South) Pole 北极(南极) ❸磁极;电极

police / pəˈliːs / n.(集合名词)警察当局;警察;the ～ office 警察局 / The ～ have not made any arrests. 警察当局尚未逮捕人。

policeman / pəˈliːsmən / n.[C](pl. policemen)警察;警员:The woman was helped by the ～. 那位妇女得到了警察的帮助。

policewoman / pəˈliːswʊmən / n.[C](pl. policewomen)女警察;女警员

policy / ˈpɒləsi / n.[C](尤指政府、政党、商行等的)政策,方针:the foreign ～ of a country 一个国家的外交政策圆 plan,program

polish / ˈpɒlɪʃ / Ⅰ v.磨光;擦亮;使光滑:～ furniture 擦亮家具/～ shoes 擦鞋圆 shine,smooth 反 discolor,dull Ⅱ n.擦亮;磨光;上光剂:You'd better give the plate a ～. 你最好把盘子擦亮。派 polished adj.

polite / pəˈlaɪt / adj.有礼貌的;客气的:be ～ to sb. 对某人有礼貌 / a ～ reply 有礼貌的答复圆 well-mannered,thoughtful 反 impolite,rude 派 politely adv.;politeness n.

political / pəˈlɪtɪkl / adj.政府的;政治的

politician / ˌpɒləˈtɪʃn / n.[C]政治家;政客

politics / ˈpɒlətɪks / n.[U]❶政治学;政治;政治活动:go in for ～ 从政:He went in for ～ when he was young. 他年轻时就从政了。❷政纲;政见

用法

若 politics 前面没有修饰语,表示"学科"等意义且作主语时,谓语动词一般要用单数;若前面有定冠词或所有格代词修饰,表示"观点""见解""活动"等意义时谓语动词用复数:Politics is a good topic for discussion. 政治是一个讨论的好题目。His politics were a matter of great concern to his friends. 他的政治活动是他的朋友们极为关心的事。

poll / pəʊl / Ⅰ n.投票;民意调查:They conduct a ～ from time to time. 他们不时要进行民意调查。Ⅱ vi.投票

pollen / ˈpɒlən / n.[U]花粉

pollute / pəˈluːt / vt.使……脏;污染:The water at the bathing beach was ～d by refuse from the factory. 海滨浴水被工厂排出的垃圾污染

了。同 dirty, poison 反 clean, purify 派 pollution n.

pond / pɒnd / n. [C]池塘

ponder / ˈpɒndə(r) / v. 思考，考虑：He ~ed his next words thoroughly. 他仔细考虑了下一步要讲的话。/ Mary ~ed over this for a time. 玛丽把这句话琢磨了一会儿。同 consider, meditate

pony / ˈpəuni / n. [C]小马

pool¹ / puːl / n. [C](尤指天然的)水池，水塘：swimming ~ 游泳池 / indoor(outdoor) ~ 室内(室外)游泳池

pool² / puːl / Ⅰ n. [C]共同资金，合伙投资：We bought a horse by the ~. 我们合资买了一匹马。Ⅱ v. 合并；联营：The three boys ~ed their savings and bought a boat. 这三个男孩把他们的积蓄合起来买了一条小船。同 combine, share

poor / pʊə(r) / adj. ❶无钱的；贫穷的：the ~ 穷人 同 needy, penniless 反 rich, wealthy ❷可怜的：The ~ fellow lost both his legs in the war. 这个不幸的人在战争中失掉了双腿。同 miserable, unfortunate 反 happy, lucky ❸ 坏的；质劣的：~ soil 瘠土 / in ~ health 健康不佳 同 bad, worthless 反 excellent, worthy / **be ~ in** 在⋯方面贫乏；在⋯方面很差：The country is ~ in natural resources. 这个国家自然资源贫乏。/ He is ~ in English. 他英语学得很差。

pop¹ / pɒp / Ⅰ n. ❶[U]流行音乐：Carter likes ~ very much. 卡特很喜欢流行音乐。❷[C] 流行歌曲：Most of the young people are fond of ~s. 多数年轻人都喜欢流行歌曲。Ⅱ adj. (音乐、绘画、电影等)流行的：~ music 流行音乐 / ~ singer 流行歌手

pop² / pɒp / Ⅰ n. 砰的一声；啪的一声：The cork flew off with a ~. 瓶塞砰的一声飞了。同 crack, burst Ⅱ v. 发出响声；突然出现；爆(玉米) 同 explode, burst

pope / pəup / n. (常作 the Pope) (罗马天主教的)教皇

popular / ˈpɒpjələ(r) / adj. ❶受欢迎的；有声望的同 preferred, famous 反 unpopular, unaccepted / **be ~ with** 受爱慕的；有名望的：He is ~ with the people. 他受到人民的爱戴和拥护。❷大众的；通俗的：~ science 大众(通俗)科学 同 public, general 派 popularly adv.

popularity / ˌpɒpjuˈlærəti / n. ❶名气：enjoy ~ 享有盛名 同 fame ❷普及；流行

popularize / ˈpɒpjəlaraiz / vt. 推广；普及：A new method was ~d in the factory. 一种新方法在工厂里得到推广。同 spread

population / ˌpɒpjuˈleiʃn / n. 人口；人口数：a fall (rise) in ~ 人口的减少(增加)／ ~ explosion 人口爆炸 / a city of one million ~ 一个拥有百万人口的城市 同 inhabitants, people

populous / ˈpɒpjələs / adj. 人口稠密的 同 crowded

porcelain / ˈpɔːsəlin / Ⅰ n. [U]瓷；瓷器 Ⅱ adj. 瓷的；瓷制的

porch / pɔːtʃ / n. [C]有顶的门廊；(美)走廊 同 entrance-way, gallery

pore / pɔː(r) / n. [C]毛孔；气孔；细孔

pork / pɔːk / n. [U]猪肉

porridge / ˈpɒridʒ / n. [U]粥

port / pɔːt / n. [C]港；港口：commercial ~ 商业港口 / free ~ 自由港 同 harbor, shelter

portable / ˈpɔːtəbl / adj. 轻便的；便于携带的；手提的：a ~ television 便携式电视机 / a ~ radio 便携式收音机 / Do you want to buy a ~ computer? 你想买一台手提电脑吗？同 light, handy 反 heavy, clumsy

portion / ˈpɔːʃn / n. [C] ❶部分：They bought only a small ~ of the goods. 他们只买了一小部分货物。同 part, piece ❷(食品的)一份：distribute food in ~s 按份分发食品 同 share, part

portrait / ˈpɔːtreit / n. [C] ❶(人或动物的)画像 同 picture, paragraph ❷(生动的)文字描写：family ~ 全家福 / full-length ~ 全身像 / group ~ 团体像 同 account, description

portray / pɔːˈtrei / vt. 画；描述；描写 同 describe, paint

Portugal / ˈpɔːtʃugl / n. 葡萄牙

Portuguese / ˌpɔːtʃuˈɡiːz / Ⅰ n.(单复数同形) 葡萄牙人 Ⅱ adj. 葡萄牙人的；葡萄牙语的

pose / pəuz / Ⅰ vi. ❶摆姿势：~ for a painter 摆姿势让画家画像 ❷假装，冒充；作态：He ~d as a plain uneducated man. 他故意装成没有受过教育的平民。—vt. ❶使摆好姿势；摆正位置：He ~d the picture on the wall. 他把墙上的那幅画扶正。❷提出(问题等)：A loan boom ~s problems. 贷款激增提出难题。

P

❸造成,引起:All drugs ~ some side effects. 所有药物都会引起一定的副作用。Ⅱ n.[C] ❶样子,姿势:in a stiff ~ 身子僵直地 ❷(故意装me的)态度,姿态:strike an indifferent ~ toward sth. 对某事故作不屑一顾的样子

position / pə'zıʃn / n. ❶位置;阵地 同 place, location ❷阶段;地位;职位:hold an important ~ 担任一个重要职务 同 status, post ❸形势;状况:The enemy was in a difficult ~. 敌人处于困境中。同 situation, condition ❹主张;立场:What's your ~ on the problem? 在这个问题上你有什么主张? 同 viewpoint

positive / 'pɒzətɪv / adj. ❶肯定的;积极的:give a ~ (negative) reply 给予肯定的(否定的)答复同 sure, firm 反 uncertain, unsure / **be ~ about (of)** 对……肯定:I am not ~ about the result. 我不能肯定结果如何。❷(数学)正的,正数的:the ~ sign 正号 反 negative ❸ (电)正的,阳性的:a ~ charge 正电 反 negative ❹(语法)原级的 派 positively adv.

possess / pə'zes / vt. 具有;占有;拥有 同 own, control

possession / pə'zeʃn / n. ❶[U]拥有,占有;所有权:lawful(unlawful)~ 合法(非法)占有 同 hold, control / **come into ~ of sth.** 占有某物:The young man came into ~ of a large house. 那年轻人得到了一所大房子。**take (get, have) ~ of** 占有;占领:The army took ~ of the city. 军队占领了城市。❷[C](pl.)所有物:personal ~s 个人财产 同 belongings

possessive / pə'zesɪv / Ⅰ adj. 所有的 Ⅱ n. (语法)所有格

possessor / pə'zesə(r) / n.[C]持有者;所有者

possibility / ˌpɒsə'bɪləti / n. ❶[U]可能性:out of the bounds of ~ 在可能的范围外 / within the bounds of ~ 在可能的范围内 / Is there any ~ of your getting to London this week? 本周你有可能到伦敦吗? 同 chance, probability ❷[C]可能的事;可能发生的事:I see great possibilities in this scheme. 我看这计划很可能成功。同 probability

possible / 'pɒsəbl / adj. 可能的:Is it ~ for you to come to dinner this evening? 今晚你来吃饭行吗? 同 likely 反 impossible/ **as ... as ~** 尽可能……:Come as early as ~. 尽可能早点来。**if ~** 有可能的话:I'll see you off at the airport if ~. 有可能的话,我就去机场给你送行。

possibly / 'pɒsəbli / adv. 可能;或许 同 perhaps, maybe

post / pəʊst / Ⅰ n. ❶邮政;邮件;邮局:take letters to the ~ (office)把信件送到邮局 / **by ~** 邮寄:The present came by ~. 礼物是邮寄来的。❷[C]哨所,岗位:The soldiers stood at their ~s. 士兵们各守岗位。同 station ❸[C]职位;工作:be given a ~ as general manager 被授予总经理的职务 同 job, position ❹[C]柱;桩;杆:lamp ~ 灯柱 / sign ~ 标杆 同 column, pole Ⅱ v. ❶邮寄(信件等):I've come out to ~ (mail) some letters. 我出来寄几封信。同 mail, drop ❷贴出(布告、通知等)同 put up, inform

post- / pəʊst / (前缀)在……之后:~graduate 研究生 / ~doctoral 博士后 / ~war 战后

postage / 'pəʊstɪdʒ / n.[U]邮费;邮资:~ free 免付邮资 / ~ paid 邮资已付

postal / 'pəʊstl / adj. 邮政的;邮局的

postcard / 'pəʊstkɑːd / n.[C]明信片

postgraduate / ˌpəʊst'grædʒuət / Ⅰ adj. 研究生的 Ⅱ n.[C]研究生

postmark / 'pəʊstmɑːk / n.[C]邮戳,日戳戳记

postpone / pə'spəʊn / vt. 延期;推迟:~ infinitely (temporarily) 无限(临时)延期/ The football game was ~d because of rain. 足球赛因下雨延期。同 delay, suspend 反 advance

postscript / 'pəʊstskrɪpt / n.(信的)附笔;又及(略写为 P. S.)

postwar / ˌpəʊst'wɔː / adj. 战后的:~ problems 战后问题

pot / pɒt / n.[C]罐;壶;锅 同 kettle, pan

potable / 'pəʊtəbl / adj. 可饮的,适合饮用的:

～ water 饮用水

potato / pəˈteɪtəʊ / n. [C] (pl. potatoes) 马铃薯：baked ～es 烤马铃薯 / sweet ～es 红薯

potent / ˈpəʊtənt / adj. ❶强有力的；有权势的；有影响的：a ～ opposition force 强大的反对派势力/a ～ figure 权势炙手可热的人物 ❷(议论等)有说服力的：Several ～ arguments were in his favour. 一些有说服力的论据对他很有利。❸(药、酒等)有效力的，有效能的；浓烈的，烈性的：a ～ coffee 浓咖啡/a ～ drink 烈酒

potential / pəˈtenʃ(ə)l / Ⅰ adj. 潜在的；可能的：Try to find out the ～ demand of the market. 设法弄清市场的潜在需求。同 possible, concealed 反 actual, real Ⅱ n. [U]潜力；潜能：develop one's ～ 发挥某人的潜力 / tap ～s 发掘潜力 同 ability, possibility

pottery / ˈpɒtəri / n. 陶器；陶器厂

poultry / ˈpəʊltri / n. ❶家禽(谓语动词用复数)：The ～ are being fed. 正在喂家禽。❷家禽肉(谓语动词用单数)：Poultry is expensive this Christmas. 这个圣诞节的禽肉很贵。

pound¹ / paʊnd / n. ❶磅(重量单位，等于0.4536 千克) ❷英镑(英国货币单位，等于100 便士)

pound² / paʊnd / vt. ❶捣碎；舂烂：The ship was ～ed to pieces on the rock. 船在岩石上撞碎了。同 crush, grind ❷(连续)猛击，敲打：Someone is ～ing at the door with fists. 有人在用拳头打门。同 beat, strike

pour / pɔː(r) / v. ❶使流动；灌，注，倒：She ～ed the wine into the glass. 她把酒倒入一个玻璃杯。同 flow, stream / ～ **cold water on** 浇冷水，使沮丧 / **oil on the flames** 火上加油 ～ **out** 倾诉：She ～ed out her tale of misfortunes. 她倾诉自己的不幸遭遇。❷(大雨)倾盆而下：It never rains but it ～s. (谚语)不雨则已，一雨倾盆。同 flood

poverty / ˈpɒvəti / n. [U]贫穷；缺乏：live in ～ 过穷日子 同 need, lack

powder / ˈpaʊdə(r) / n. ❶粉；细粉；粉末：dust ❷火药 同 explosive

power / ˈpaʊə(r) / n. ❶[U]力；能力；精力：water ～ 水力 / the natural ～s 自然力 / Knowledge is ～. 知识就是力量。同 ability, strength ❷[U]权力；势力 同 right, might ❸[C]强国：the great ～s of Europe 欧洲列强 ❹

[U]功率；动力：Running water produces ～ to run mills. 流水产生的动力推磨。同 electricity

powerful / ˈpaʊəfl / adj. ❶强大的；强有力的：We must build up a ～ army. 我们必须建立一支强大的军队。同 mighty, strong 反 powerless, weak ❷效力大的：a ～ engine 功率大的发动机 / a ～ remedy of cold 治感冒的特效药 同 effective, efficient 反 ineffective, inefficient ❸权威的；权力大的：a ～ man 有权势的人 同 commanding, dominating 反 powerless

practicable / ˈpræktɪkəbl / adj. 能实行的；适用的 同 achievable, possible 反 impracticable

practical / ˈpræktɪkl / adj. ❶实际的：a piece of advice with little ～ value 实际价值少的建议 同 factual, realistic 反 impractical ❷有实践经验的 同 experienced, skilled 反 inexperienced ❸有用的；实用的：a ～ method 一种实用的方法 同 useful 反 useless

practically / ˈpræktɪkli / adv. ❶实际地 同 actually ❷实用地 ❸(口语)几乎；差不多：We've ～ had no fine weather this month. 这个月可以说没有好天气。同 almost, nearly

practice / ˈpræktɪs / n. ❶实施；实际；应用 同 operation, performance 反 theory / **put into** ～实践 in ～ 实践中；实际上：The method will not work in ～. 这种方法在实践中行不通。❷练习；实习：Piano playing needs a lot of ～. 弹钢琴需要多练习。同 training, exercise ❸习惯；常例：the ～ of closing shops on Sundays 星期日有休业的常例 同 custom, habit

practise / ˈpræktɪs / v. (美国英语中亦作 practice) ❶练习；实习：～ the piano 练习弹钢琴 同 train, exercise ❷实行；习惯性地进行：～ caution 常常警惕 同 perform, follow ❸开业当(医生，律师)：My father ～s law (medicine). 我父亲开业当律师(医生)。/ ～ as a lawyer (doctor)开业当律师(医生)同 pursue 派 practised adj.

> **用法**
> ❶英国英语中动词是 practise，名词是 practice，但在美国英语中，动词、名词都用 practice。❷practise 后面只接动名词，不接不定式：You must practise speaking English more. 你必须多练习说英语。

praise / preɪz / Ⅰ vt. 称赞；赞美 同 approve, applaud / ～ **sb. for sth.** 为某事赞扬某人：

They ～d the child for her courage. 他们赞扬了那孩子的勇敢。 Ⅱ *n.* [U]称赞；赞扬：His heroism is worthy of great ～（beyond ～）. 他的英勇行为值得大加称赞（是赞美不尽的）。 圆 approval, merit / **in** ～ **of** 歌颂；表扬；称赞：The old man wrote a poem in ～ of his hometown. 老人写了一首诗歌颂他的家乡。

pray / preɪ / *v.* ❶祈祷；祈求 圆 plead：The farmers are ～ing for rain. 农民们在祈雨。 ❷（书面语）乞求；恳求：We ～ you to show mercy. 我们恳求你发发慈悲。 圆 beg, request ❸请（正式请求，相当于 please）：Pray don't speak so loud. 请不要如此大声讲话。

prayer / 'preə(r) / *n.* 祈祷；祈求：The sick man said his ～ for health. 这位病人祈求身体健康。

PRC (＝ the People's Republic of China)中华人民共和国

preach / priːtʃ / *vt.* 说教；布道；鼓吹 圆 teach, argue

precaution / prɪ'kɔːʃn / *n.* ❶[U] 预防；警惕 圆 caution, care ❷[C]预防措施：take every possible ～ 采取一切预防措施 圆 safeguard, provision

precede / prɪ'siːd / *v.* 先于；领先；优先 圆 lead, head 派 precedence *n.*

precedent / 'presɪdənt / *n.* [U]先例；惯例 圆 example, custom

preceding / prɪ'siːdɪŋ / *adj.* 在前的；在先的：～ chapters 前面几章 / ～ years 前几年 圆 prior, previous

precious / 'preʃəs / *adj.* 贵重的；高价的：the ～ metals 贵重金属 / ～ stones 宝石 / ～ words 金玉良言 / ～ **to sb.** 对某人来说很重要 圆 valuable, expensive

precious 指因稀罕而非常值钱，或者由于物品本身品质上乘而具有极大的价值：The original *Declaration of Independence* is a precious document kept in Washington. 《独立宣言》的正本是保存在华盛顿的一份珍贵文件。 **valuable** 指东西很值钱，或对拥有者来说有极大用途：He has a set of valuable stamps. 他有套很值钱的邮票。

precise / prɪ'saɪs / *adj.* 准确的；正确的：～ measurements 精确的尺寸 圆 exact, accurate

反 imprecise, careless / **at the** ～ **moment** 正在那时 ～ **in** 在…方面精确的：Try to be more ～ in your answers. 答案尽量要明确。

precision / prɪ'sɪʒn / *n.* [U]精确(性)；精密(度)：～ instruments 精密仪器 圆 exactness, accuracy

predecessor / 'priːdɪsesə(r) / *n.* [C]❶前辈；前任者 圆 ancestor, elder 反 successor, descendant ❷ 被取代的事物

predict / prɪ'dɪkt / *vt.* 预言；预示；预告：～ a good harvest 预示丰收 圆 forecast, foresee 派 prediction *n.*

predominant / prɪ'dɒmɪnənt / *adj.* ❶有势力的；占主导（或支配）地位的：a ～ member of the city council 市政厅里最有势力的成员 / Fear with me became ～. 恐惧在我心里占了上风。 ❷占优势的；显著的；普遍的：The ～ key of the opera is D minor. 这出歌剧的基调是 D 小调。 / Alice's health was her ～ worry. 艾丽丝的健康是她的一大心病。

predominate / prɪ'dɒmɪneɪt / *vi.* ❶占主导（或支配）地位；统治；控制：Service industries ～ for employment in the island. 服务性行业在该岛就业市场上占主导地位。 ❷占优势，占绝大多数：In the colder regions, pine trees ～. 在寒冷的地带，绝大多数树木是松树。

preface / 'prefəs / *n.* [C]序言；前言；引语：Who wrote the ～ to the book? 谁给书写的序? 圆 introduction

prefer / prɪ'fɜː(r) / *v.* (-ferred; -ferring)更喜爱；宁可；优先选择 圆 favour, choose 反 reject

prefer 有以下句型：❶prefer this to that 喜欢这个而不喜欢那个，如：I prefer tea to coffee. 我宁愿喝茶，而不愿喝咖啡。 ❷prefer doing this to doing that 愿做这事而不愿做那事，如：I prefer walking to cycling. 我喜欢步行而不愿骑自行车。 ❸prefer to do sth. 宁愿干某事，如：He prefers to work alone. 他宁可（喜欢）单独工作。 ❹prefer to do this rather than do that 宁愿做这事而不愿做那事，如：They prefer to die fighting rather than live in enslavement. 他们宁可战死，也不肯活着受奴役。

preferable / 'prefrəbl / *adj.* 更可取的；更合意的；更好的：In such hot weather, swimming is ～ to other sports. 天这样热，游泳比其他运动更好些。 圆 better, superior 反 inferior

preference / ˈprefrəns / n. 偏爱；优先；优先权 同 liking；**have a ～ for** 偏爱：Our monitor has a ～ for novels. 我们的班长特爱读小说。**in ～ to** 宁可…而不…：The Chinese people drink tea in ～ to coffee. 中国人爱喝茶而不爱喝咖啡。

prefix / ˈpriːfɪks / n. [C] 前缀（略为 pref.）

pregnancy / ˈpregnənsi / n. [U；C] 怀孕，妊娠；怀孕期，妊娠期：She kept well throughout her ～. 整个怀孕期间她身体保养得很好。

pregnant / ˈpregnənt / adj. ❶怀孕的 ❷意味深长的

prehistoric / ˌpriːhɪˈstɒrɪk / adj. 史前的；史前时代的：the ～ period 史前期

prehistory / ˌpriːˈhɪstri / n. [U] 史前

prejudice / ˈpredʒudɪs / I n. 偏见；成见 同 injustice 反 fairness，justice / **free from ～** 毫无成见 **break down ～** 消除成见：It is necessary to break down racial ～. 应该消除种族偏见。**have（hold）a ～** 抱有成见（偏见）：I have no ～ against you. 我对你毫无成见。II vt. 使（某人）抱有成见（偏见）：What Tom had said ～d her against her stepmother. 汤姆说的话使她对她的继母产生偏见。

preliminary / prɪˈlɪmɪnəri / adj.（只作定语）预备的；初步的：a ～ examination 初试 / a ～ hearing 预审 / a ～ investigation 初步调查 / make a few ～ remarks 说几句开场白 / ～ work 前期工作 同 first，primary 反 final，following

prelude / ˈpreljuːd / n. ❶序幕；前奏；先兆 同 introduction ❷前奏曲

premature / ˈpremətʃə(r) / adj. 过早的；早熟的：a ～ death 早死；夭折 / a ～ decision 草率的决定 同 untimely，unripe

premier / ˈpremiə(r) / I n. [C] 总理；首相 II adj. 第一的；首位的；首席的

premium / ˈpriːmɪəm / I n. [C] ❶保险费；保险金：property ～s 财产保险费 ❷奖金；红利；津贴，补贴；额外费用：raise the overtime pay ～ 提高超时工资津贴 ❸奖品；奖励：a ～ for good conduct 品行优良奖

preparation / ˌprepəˈreɪʃn / n. ❶[U] 准备，预备：The meal is in ～. 饭菜正在准备中。同 arrangement，readiness / **in ～ for** 为…做准备：We are doing everything in ～ for the outing. 我们正在为出游做准备。❷（通常用 pl.）准备的事物：～s for war 战备 / make ～s for

a voyage 做好航海的准备 / The school is making ～s for the celebration. 学校在为庆祝活动做准备。

preparatory / prɪˈpærətri / adj. 预备的；初步的：～ measures 预备措施 同 preliminary，previous

prepare / prɪˈpeə(r) / v. 准备，预备：～ a meal 预备饭菜 同 arrange，plan / **be ～d for** 为…做准备：Be ～d for bad news. 做好听到坏消息的准备。

prepay / ˌpriːˈpeɪ / vt.（prepaid / ˌpriː'peɪd /，prepaid）预付

preposition / ˌprepəˈzɪʃn / n. [C] 介词

prescribe / prɪˈskraɪb / v. ❶开药方；开处方：The doctor ～d quinine. 医生开了奎宁。❷指示；规定：I have finished reading the ～d reference books. 我已读完了指定的参考书。同 direct，rule

prescription / prɪˈskrɪpʃn / n. 药方；处方

presence / ˈprezəns / n. [U] 出席；在场：Your ～ at the party is expected. 敬请光临晚会。同 attendance，appearance / **in the ～ of sb.（in sb.'s ～）** 在某人面前，当着某人的面：The boy was punished in the ～ of all his classmates. 那男孩在全班同学面前受惩罚。

present¹ / ˈprezənt / I adj. ❶在场的；出席的：Were you ～ at the ceremony? 你出席典礼了吗? 同 attending，near 反 absent ❷现存的；现在的：～ government 现政府 同 current II n. ❶[C] 礼物：a birthday（Christmas）～ 生日（圣诞）礼物 同 gift ❷[U] 现在；目前：the past，the ～ and the future 过去、现在和将来 同 today / **at ～** 现在；当前：We don't need any more at ～. 现在我们不需要什么了。**up to the ～** 到目前为止：She is well up to the ～. 到目前为止她身体很好。

present² / prɪˈzent / vt. ❶呈递；提出：～ an application 呈交申请书 同 hand in ❷赠；给：～ a gift 赠一份礼 同 give，offer ❸介绍；引见：It is my pleasure to ～ the guest to you. 我很高兴向你介绍这位客人。同 introduce ❹上演：The theatre will ～ Tea House next week. 这家剧院下周上演《茶馆》。同 perform，display

presentation / ˌprezənˈteɪʃn / n. ❶[U] 介绍；引见 同 introduction ❷[C] 赠品；礼物 ❸授予仪式 ❹[U] 呈现 ❺上演；演出

presently / ˈprezəntli / adv. 不久；一会儿：I'll

P

be with you ～. 我不久就会陪你。 同
soon,shortly

preservative / prɪ'zɜ:vətɪv / Ⅰ adj. 有保存能
力的;防腐的 Ⅱ n. 防腐剂

preserve / prɪ'zɜ:v / vt. 保护;使不受损失;防
腐;保存;维持:Ice can help ～ food. 冰能帮助保
存食物。同 protect,maintain 派 preservation n.

preside / prɪ'zaɪd / vi. 主持;主管 同 control,
govern / ～ over 主持:The vice-chairman ～d o-
ver the meeting this time. 这次是副主席主持
会议。

president / 'prezɪdənt / n. ❶总统 ❷(公司的)
董事长 ❸(学校的)院长,校长 ❹(协会的)
会长

press / pres / Ⅰ n. ❶(the ～) 定期刊物;杂
志;报界;新闻界:～ conference 记者招待会:
The book was favorably noticed by the ～. 这
本书曾被新闻界看好。❷印刷业 ❸出版社;
通讯社:the Oxford University Press 牛津大学
出版社 Ⅱ v. ❶压,按;压平;熨平:～ the button 按按钮 / ～ a suit (with an iron) (用熨
斗)熨平衣服 同 iron,smooth ❷用力推;推进;
拥挤:The crowd ～ed forward to see what
was happening. 群众挤向前去观看发生了什
么事。同 push,crowd ❸使负重担;压迫:His
responsibilities ～ heavily upon him. 他的责任
沉重地压在他的身上。同 burden,oppress

P **pressing** / 'presɪŋ / adj. 急迫的;迫切的 同
critical,urgent

pressure / 'preʃə(r) / n. 压;压力;强制力;压
强:atmospheric ～ 大气压 同 stress,influence
/ bring (put) ～ on 对…施加压力:They
brought (put) ～ on him to sell his land. 他们
给他施加压力要他卖掉土地。under the ～ of
在…的压力下:Under the ～ of public opinion,he had to leave. 在舆论的压力下,他只得
离开。

prestige / pre'sti:ʒ / n. [U]威望;威信;声望:
The unselfish man is of great ～. 这个无私的
人有很高的威信。同 authority,fame 派 pres-
tigious adj.

presume / prɪ'zju:m / vt. 假定;假设;揣测:
From the way they talked, I ～d that they
were good friends. 我从他们谈话的方式中揣
测他们是好朋友。同 assume,suppose 派 pre-
sumption n.

presuppose / ˌpri:sə'pəʊz / vt. 预先假定;预料

同 assume,presume

pretence(-se) / prɪ'tens / n. ❶[U]假装;掩
饰;do sth. under the ～ of friendship (religion,patriotism) 以友谊(宗教、爱国)为掩饰
而做某事 同 affectation,cloak ❷[C]借口;托
词:It is only a ～ of friendship. 那不过是以友
谊为借口罢了。同 excuse,pretext

pretend / prɪ'tend / v. 假装(有);佯称(有):
～ illness 装病 / ～ ignorance 假装不知情 同
affect,assume

pretend 后接不定式、从句或直接接名词,不
能接动名词:He pretended to be ill. He pretended that he was ill. He pretended illness.
他装病。

pretext / 'pri:tekst / n. [C]借口;托词 同 excuse / on (under) the ～ of 以…为借口:He
didn't help me on the ～ of having to see a
doctor. 他以必须看病为借口不帮助我。

pretty / 'prɪti / Ⅰ adj. (-ier,-iest)悦人的;可
爱的;漂亮的:What a ～ flower! 多美的一朵
花! 同 beautiful, lovely 反 ugly, plain Ⅱ
adv. 相当;颇:It's ～ cold outdoors today. 今
天户外很冷。同 fairly,rather

prevail / prɪ'veɪl / vi. ❶流行;盛行:The custom ～s in the area. 这种风俗在该地区很盛
行。同 exist, widespread ❷胜过;占优势:～
over one's enemies 战胜敌人 同 dominate,suc-
ceed 派 prevailing adj.

prevent / prɪ'vent / v. 预防;阻止;妨碍 同 a-
void,block 反 allow,permit / ～ sb. from doing sth. 阻止某人做某事:The heavy rain ～
ed him from coming. 大雨使他不能来。派 prevention n.

prevent 主语指人时表示事先采取措施防止
或制止某事发生,这些措施可能是强迫性
的,也可能是防备性的;主语指物时表示阻
碍:They tied him up to prevent his escape.
他们把他绑起来,以防他逃跑。Their
prompt actions prevented the fire from
spreading. 他们及时采取行动,阻止了大火
蔓延。**stop** 是常用词,指由于外界的影响而
立即停止,也指行为进行的过程中突然停止
下来:The game was stopped by rain. 比赛因
雨暂停。A fallen tree stopped the traffic. 一
棵倒下的树妨碍了交通。He put his hand out
to stop the bus. 他伸手示意要公共汽车停下。

preview / ˈpriːvjuː / n. [C] ❶预观;预览;预审;预习 ❷(电影的)预映,试映;(戏剧等的)预演,试演;give a ～ of the director's latest film 预映导演的最新电影 ❸预告:a ～ of next week's viewing 下星期收视节目预告

previous / ˈpriːviəs / adj. (时间或顺序上)在前的,早先的:～ to sb.'s arrival 在某人到达之前 / ～ to departure 在出发之前 / The ～ lesson was hard. 前面的一课真难。同 earlier, preceding 反 later, following 派 previously adv.

prevision / ˌpriːˈvɪʒən / n. 先见;预知 同 foresight, foreknowledge

prey / preɪ / Ⅰ vi. 捕获;折磨 同 kill, plunder Ⅱ n. [C]猎获物;(喻)牺牲品:The wolf is eating his ～. 狼在吃猎获物。同 game, victim

price / praɪs / Ⅰ n. ❶[C] 价格;价钱:～ list 价目表 / ～ tag 价格标签 / What's the ～ of this picture? 这幅画多少钱? 同 cost, expense / above (beyond, without) ～ 无价的;非常贵重的 at any ～ 不惜任何代价:It must be done at any ～. 必须不惜任何代价把它做好。❷[U] 价值:pearls of great ～ 极贵重的珍珠 同 value, worth Ⅱ vt. 给…标价;给…定价:All goods should be clearly ～d. 所有商品都应该标明价格。

priceless / ˈpraɪsləs / adj. 无价的;非常贵重的:～ paintings 极贵重的画 同 invaluable

prick / prɪk / Ⅰ vt. 刺(穿)同 stick, sting Ⅱ n. [C]刺孔

pricker / ˈprɪkə(r) / n. [C]针;锥子

pride / praɪd / n. [U] 骄傲;傲慢;自豪;得意 同 boast, satisfaction 反 modesty / in the ～ of 在…的全盛(巅峰)时期:He died in the ～ of his life. 他在年富力强时期去世。take ～ in 对…感到自豪;She took ～ in her son's success. 她对儿子的成功感到自豪。

priest / priːst / n. [C]教士;牧师;神父

primacy / ˈpraɪməsi / n. [U](重要性、级别、次序等中的)首位,第一位;基础:Industrial employment took ～ over agricultural work in some countries. 在一些国家,工业就业的重要性超过了农业

primarily / praɪˈmerəli / adv. 首先;最初地;基本地;主要地:The book is ～ meant for children. 这本书主要是为小孩子写的。同 originally

primary / ˈpraɪməri / adj. 主要的;最初的;基本的:a ～ school 小学 同 first, basic 反 secondary, unimportant

prime / praɪm / adj. ❶主要的;首位的:his ～ motive 他的主要动机 同 primary, main 反 secondary, lowest ❷ 最佳的;第一流的:～ beef 上等牛肉 同 excellent, first-class 反 worst, second-class

primitive / ˈprɪmɪtɪv / adj. ❶原始的;早期的;未开化的:～ men 原始人 / ～ society 原始社会 / ～ forests 原始森林 同 original, savage 反 advanced, modern ❷简单的;粗糙的;Some ～ weapons were found in the cave. 山洞里发现了一些简陋的武器。同 simple, crude 反 sophisticated, artful 派 primitively adv.

prince / prɪns / n. [C]王子;太子

princess / ˌprɪnˈses / n. [C]王妃;公主

principal / ˈprɪnsəpl / Ⅰ adj. 主要的;首要的;重要的 同 chief, leading 反 secondary, minor Ⅱ n. [C]首长;校长

principle / ˈprɪnsəpl / n. ❶原则;原理:the ～s of geometry 几何学原理 同 rule, belief ❷行为准则 / in ～原则上:I agree with you in ～. 我原则上同意你的意见。

print / prɪnt / Ⅰ v. 印;印刷:These books are well ～ed. 这些书印制精良。Ⅱ n. ❶[U]印刷符号:in large (small) ～以大(小)字体印刷 同 mark, stamp / in ～ 已出版;在销售:The writer is glad to see his novel in ～. 这位作家很高兴看到他的小说出版了。out of ～已售完;绝版:Sorry, the book you want has been out of ～. 对不起,你要的那种书已经售完。❷[C] 印迹;痕迹:a finger ～ 指纹 同 mark, impression

prior / ˈpraɪə(r) / adj. 在先的;优先的:Members of the club have a ～ claim to the opportunity. 俱乐部会员对此机会享有优先权。同 previous, earlier 反 following, later / ～ to 先于;优先于:The stadium was finished ～ to the Asian Games. 体育场在亚运会前竣工。

priority / praɪˈɒrəti / n. ❶[U]在先;居前 同 precedence ❷[C]优先权 同 superiority ❸[C]优先考虑的事

prison / ˈprɪzn / n. 监狱;监牢;牢房;监禁 同 jail / put sb. in ～把某人关进监狱:The robber was put in ～. 那盗贼被关进了监狱。

privacy / ˈprɪvəsi, ˈpraɪvəsi / n. [U] ❶隐居;

独处，独守：in the ～ of a living room 在静谧的客厅里 ❷隐私权；私事；私生活：safeguard sb.'s ～ 保护某人的隐私/He can not allow the outside world to penetrate his ～. 他不允许外界介入他私生活。❸私下；秘密；保密：～ system 保密系统/in strict ～完全秘密地

private / ˈpraɪvət / adj. 私人的；私有的；秘密的：a ～ letter 私信 / a ～ school 私立学校 / have ～ information about sth. 得到有关某事的秘密消息 同 personal, concealed 反 public, known

privilege / ˈprɪvəlɪdʒ / n. [C]特权；优惠；diplomatic ～s 外交特权 / enjoy the ～ in trade 享受贸易特权 同 benefit, right

privileged / ˈprɪvɪlɪdʒd / adj. ❶特权的；享有特权的；优先的：a ～ job 美差/a member of a ～ class 特权阶层的一员 ❷特许的；专用的：the three ～ Bible publishers 三家特许的《圣经》出版商/a ～ parking stall 专用停车处

prize / praɪz / Ⅰ n.[C]奖金；奖品：be awarded a ～ for good conducts 因表现良好而获奖 / draw a ～-winning ticket in a lottery 中彩 同 reward, medal Ⅱ vt. 珍视；重视：We ～ honor above money. 我们珍视荣誉更胜于金钱

probability / ˌprɒbəˈbɪləti / n. 可能性；可能发生的事 同 chance 反 improbability

probable / ˈprɒbəbl / adj. 大概的；可能的：It is ～ that the discussion will be put off. 讨论可能会推迟。同 likely, possible 反 improbable, unlikely

probably / ˈprɒbəbli / adv. 大概；或许 同 perhaps, possibly 反 improbably, unlikely

probe / prəʊb / Ⅰ n.[C]❶探索；(深入的)调查；探查：a police ～ into illegal financial dealing 警方对非法金融交易的调查 ❷探测工具；探头 ❸(医用)探针，探子 Ⅱ v. ❶探究；探查；探索；(深入)调查：～ a question of morality 调查一个道德问题/The police are probing into the case. 警方正调查这一案件。❷用探针探测；探查：He ascended to the edge of the snow, stopped and ～d it with his axe. 他爬上了雪坡的边缘，然后停步用冰斧探一下冰层虚实。❸刺穿：The bird's bill ～d the bard crevice. 鸟喙啄入树皮裂缝。

problem / ˈprɒbləm / n.[C]问题；难题：mathematical ～s 数学题 / ～ of food and clothing 吃穿(温饱)问题 同 question, difficulty

procedure / prəˈsiːdʒə(r) / n. 程序；步骤；过程：follow a ～按程序办 同 process, step

proceed / prəˈsiːd / vi. 前进；继续进行：Proceed with your story. 继续讲你的故事。同 advance, move on 反 stop, retreat 派 proceeding n.

process / ˈprəʊses / Ⅰ n. ❶经过；过程：the ～es of digestion, reproduction and growth 消化、生殖和生长的过程 同 course, procedure ❷前进；进展 同 progress / in ～ of time 随着时间的推进：In ～ of time, the house will be finished. 这房子迟早会建成。in the ～ of 在…的过程中：This theory has stood all tests in the ～ of history. 这个理论在历史进程中经受了一切考验。Ⅱ vt. 加工；处理：～ medical herbs 加工中草药 同 treat, deal with

procession / prəˈseʃn / n. ❶[C](人、车辆等的)行列，队伍：a funeral ～送葬的行列 ❷[U]列队进行：walking in ～ through the streets 列队走过街道 同 march, progress 派 processional adj.

processor / ˈprəʊsesə(r) / n. [C]加工者；处理者；(计算机)资料处理机(处理器)

proclaim / prəˈʊˈkleɪm / vt. ❶(公开或正式)宣布，公布；宣告；声明：～ war 宣战/brazenly ～ rebellion 悍然宣称要造反 ❷声称，宣称…为：The Prince ～ed King in succession to his father, who was dead. 国王驾崩，王子被宣告继承王位。

proclamation / ˌprɒkləˈmeɪʃn / n. ❶[U]宣布，公布：the ～ of martial law 宣布戒严 ❷[C]公告，布告；声明：～s of independence 独立宣言

produce Ⅰ / prəˈdjuːs / v. 制造；生产；产生：woolen goods 生产毛织品 同 make, manufacture Ⅱ / ˈprɒdjuːs / n. 产品；(尤指)农产品：garden (farm) ～ 果园(农场)的产品 同 crop, harvest

> **辨析**
>
> **produce** 泛指一切产物，但多指农产品，是不可数名词。**product** 是可数名词，指一件或多件农业或工业产品，但多指工业产品。**production** 指一件或多件文学或艺术作品，是可数名词。

product / ˈprɒdʌkt / n. [C](天然或人造的)产物；产品：industrial ～s 工业产品/ by -～ 副产品 同 goods, production

production / prə'dʌkʃn / *n.* ❶[U]制造;生产;产量:the ~ of crops(manufactured goods)农作物(工业品)的生产 / a fall(an increase)in ~ 产量的减少(增加)同 manufacture,yield ❷[C]制造品;生产成品:his early ~s as a writer 他作为作家的早期作品同 work,product

productive / prə'dʌktɪv / *adj.*(能)生产的;丰饶的;多产的:~ forces 生产力 / a ~ writer 一位多产作家同 producing,plentiful 反 unproductive,fruitless

productivity / ˌprɒdʌk'tɪvəti / *n.*[U]生产能力;生产率 work-rate,output

profess / prə'fes / *vt.* ❶公开声明;声称;表白:All of them ~ed an enthusiasm for the adventures. 他们所有的人都声称热衷于冒险。❷表明忠于;公开宣布(信仰):~ religion 公开表示信教

profession / prə'feʃn / *n.* 职业;(需要接受高等教育或特殊训练的)专门职业同 occupation,employment / by ~ 以…为职业:He is a doctor by ~. 他的职业是医生。

professional / prə'feʃənl / Ⅰ *adj.* 专门的;职业的:a ~ football player 职业足球运动员 / ~ training 专业训练同 well-trained,paid 反 amateur Ⅱ *n.*[C]专业人员反 amateur ❷专家;内行人同 expert,specialist

professor / prə'fesə(r) / *n.*[C]教授:associate(full)~ 副(正)教授 / honourable(visiting)~ 名誉(客座)教授

proficiency / prə'fɪʃənsi / *n.*[U]熟练;精通同 ability,mastery

proficient / prə'fɪʃənt / *adj.* 熟练的;精通的:She was ~ in music. 她精通音乐。同 skilled,able 反 unskilled,incapable 派 proficiently *adv.*

profile / 'prəʊfaɪl / Ⅰ *n.*[C] ❶(尤指人面部的)侧影;侧面像:a ~ relief bust of Washington 华盛顿的侧面半身像浮雕 ❷轮廓;外貌,外观;外形:the ~ of a distant hill 远山的轮廓 ❸梗概;(人物)简介,小传,素描;概貌:Hair analysis can provide a ~ of one's overall nutritional health. 分析头发可以基本上知道一个人的总的营养状况。/ The magazine features celebrity ~s. 这本杂志登载名人简介。Ⅱ *vt.* ❶画…的侧面像 ❷描绘…的轮廓;显示…的轮廓:Skyscrapers are ~d against cloudless skies. 无云的天空衬托出摩天大楼的轮廓。❸写…的简介;对…作介绍;简单描述:a book profiling fourteen great cooks with a selection of their recipes 一本介绍14位大厨师以及他们的菜谱的书

profit / 'prɒfɪt / Ⅰ *n.* ❶利益;益处:gain ~ from one's studies 从学习中获得好处同 advantage,benefit ❷利润:sell sth. at a ~ 有利可图地售出 / do sth. for ~ 为赢利做某事同 gain,return Ⅱ *v.* ❶(指事物)对…有利,对…有益:What can it ~ him? 此事对他有什么益处呢?同 benefit,serve ❷(指人)获利,获益:I have ~ed by your advice. 我从你的劝告中获益。同 reap,utilize

profound / prə'faʊnd / *adj.* 深的;深奥的;博学的;透彻的:a ~ sleep(sigh,bow)熟睡(深长的叹息,深深的鞠躬) / take a ~ interest in sth. 对某事物深感兴趣同 deep,thoughtful 反 shallow,slight 派 profoundly *adv.*

program(me) / 'prəʊɡræm / Ⅰ *n.*[C] ❶节目单;程序表:write a ~ 列节目单同 schedule,timetable ❷计划;规划;方案;大纲;纲要:a political ~ 政治纲领 / a party ~ 党纲同 plan,outline ❸(计算机)程序 ❹(学校的)教学课程:graduate(undergraduate)~ 研究生(本科)课程 Ⅱ *v.* 编制程序;给计算机输入程序:~ a computer 给计算机编程序同 arrange,design

progress Ⅰ / 'prəʊɡres / *n.*[U]进步;进展;发展同 advance,development 反 decline,loss / make ~ 取得进步;取得进展:He has made great ~ in English. 他在英语方面已经取得了很大的进步。in ~ 在进展中:The research is in ~. 研究工作在进行之中。Ⅱ / prə'ɡres / *vi.* 进步;进行:The work is ~ing steadily. 工作正在稳步进行。同 proceed,develop 反 decline 派 progressive *adj.*

prohibit / prə'hɪbɪt / *vt.* 禁止;防止:~ children from smoking 禁止儿童吸烟 / Smoking is strictly ~ed here. 此地严禁吸烟。同 forbid,prevent 反 allow,permit 派 prohibition *n.*

project Ⅰ / 'prɒdʒekt / *n.*[C] ❶方案;计划:The city is drawing up a ~ to develop its industries. 这座城市正在制定发展工业的方案。同 design,plan ❷工程;项目:Project of Expectation 希望工程 / The province has carried out several capital construction ~s. 这个省实施了几个基本建设项目。同 proposal,task Ⅱ / prə'dʒekt / *v.* ❶投射;放映:Please ~ the film on the screen. 请把影片放映出

来。同 cast, throw ❷规划：The county has ~ed a new dam. 这个县规划要修一座新水坝。同 design, plan ❸伸出；突出；凸出：His forehead ~s noticeably. 他的前额明显前凸。同 stand out

prolong / prə'lɒŋ / *vt.* 延长；拖长：~ a visit 延长访问时间 同 extend 反 shorten

prominence / 'prɒmɪnəns / *n.* [U]显著；突出，杰出，重要：gain national ~ 获得突出的国内地位 / achieve ~ in science 在科学界成绩斐然

prominent / 'prɒmɪnənt / *adj.* ❶突出的；杰出的：a ~ statesman and scientist 一位杰出的政治家和科学家 同 remarkable, striking ❷突起的；凸出的 同 swelling, extended ❸重要的：play a ~ part 起重要作用 同 important 反 unimportant

promise / 'prɒmɪs / Ⅰ *n.* ❶[C]诺言；约定：make a ~ 许下诺言 / Mother made a ~ to buy her a toy dog. 妈妈答应给她买只玩具狗。同 guarantee, pledge ❷[U]希望；(有)前途：a writer of ~ 有希望的作家 同 prospect Ⅱ *v.* ❶答应；允诺；约定：They ~d an immediate reply. 他们答应立即回答。同 pledge, agree ❷有…希望；预示：The dark clouds ~ rain. 乌云预示有雨。同 suggest

用法
❶promise 不论作名词或动词，后面都接不定式：She has promised (has made a promise) to return the violin in the evening. 她答应晚上归还小提琴。❷promise 表示"前途""希望"时，含有良好的意味：He is a boy of great promise. 他是个前途无量的孩子。

promising / 'prɒmɪsɪŋ / *adj.* 有希望的：a ~ student 有前途的学生 / ~ crops 长势很好的庄稼 同 favourable, hopeful

promote / prə'məut / *vt.* ❶促进；发扬；使增长；使增进：~ friendships among the students 增进同学之间的友谊 / economic and cultural exchanges 促进经济文化交流 / The factory is successful in promoting the sales of its products. 这家工厂促销产品很成功。同 develop, encourage 反 prevent ❷提拔，提升：The clerk was ~d manager. 那位办事员被提升为经理。同 raise, advance

promotion / prə'məuʃn / *n.* [U]促进；提升；促销：sales ~ 促销 同 advancement, encouragement

prompt / prɒmpt / Ⅰ *adj.* 敏捷的；迅速的；及时的：a ~ medical treatment 及时的治疗 同 ready, quick 反 late, slow Ⅱ *vt.* 促使；推动；激起：The good result ~ed her to new efforts. 好的结果激发她作出新的努力。同 stimulate, urge 反 discourage

prone / prəun / *adj.* ❶平卧的，俯卧的；卧倒的：a ~ position 俯卧姿势 ❷易于…的，倾向于…的；有…癖的：be ~ to fits of rage 动不动就发火 / We are ~ to think of an extroverted person as a gregarious person. 我们容易把外向的人当成爱社交的人。

pronoun / 'prəunaun / *n.* [C]代词

pronounce / prə'nauns / *v.* ❶(尤指正式或官方)宣称，宣布：Has the judgment been ~d yet? 判决已宣布了吗？同 declare, announce ❷发出(字母或词等)的音：Pronounce these words clearly. 把这些词读清楚。同 voice, say

pronounced / prə'naunst / *adj.* ❶显著的，明显的；显眼的：a whiskey of less ~ taste 味道不太浓烈的威士忌酒 ❷断然的，决然的；强硬的：a ~ opinion 强硬的观点

pronouncement / prə'naunsmənt / *n.* [C]❶声明，公告 ❷看法，意见；决定：the ~ of literary critics on the short story 文艺批评家们对短篇小说的看法

pronunciation / prəˌnʌnsɪ'eɪʃn / *n.* [U](一种语言的)发音；发音法

proof / pruːf / *n.* ❶证据：Is there any ~ that the accused man was at the scene of the crime? 有什么证据证明被告在犯罪现场吗？/ We finally got several ~s of her innocence. 我们最后取得数件能证实她无罪的证据。同 evidence ❷证明；证实：Is it capable of ~ that there exists life on the Mars? 能证实火星上有生物存在吗？同 test, trial

propaganda / ˌprɒpə'ɡændə / *n.* [U]宣传；传播：~ instruments 宣传工具 / carry on active ~ 大力宣传

propagandist / ˌprɒpə'ɡændɪst / *n.* [C]宣传员

propagate / 'prɒpəɡeɪt / *vt.* 传播；宣传：~ one's ideas 宣传自己的观点

propel / prə'pel / *vt.*(-pelled；-pelling)推进；推动：The ship is ~led by steam. 这船靠蒸汽动力推动。同 drive, push 反 stop, slow

proper / ˈprɒpə(r) / *adj.* ❶正确的;正当的;适当的: Is this the tool ～ for the job? 这是做那件工作的适当工具? 同 right, suitable 反 improper, wrong ❷专为…的;独特的(与 to 连用): the books ～ to this subject 专论此问题的一些书 同 own, typical 派 properly *adv.*

property / ˈprɒpəti / *n.* ❶[U]财产;资产:personal ～ 个人财产;动产 / immovable ～ 不动产 同 possessions, wealth ❷[U]所有权;所有: There is no ～ in the seashore. (The seashore cannot be privately owned.) 海岸不能据为私有。同 ownership ❸房地产:He has a small ～ in Kentucky. 他在肯塔基州有些房地产。同 land, estate ❹[C]特性;属性;性质:herbs with healing properties 有治疗性能的草药 同 feature, quality

prophecy / ˈprɒfəsi / *n.* 预言;预言能力 同 forecast

prophet / ˈprɒfɪt / *n.* [C]预言家;先知 同 forecaster, foreteller

proportion / prəˈpɔːʃn / *n.* ❶[U]比例 同 amount, rate / **in** ～ **to** 与…成比例: Imports will be allowed in ～ to exports. 进口产品数量将依据出口产品数量的比例而定。**out of** ～ **to** 与…不成比例:The expenditure is out of ～ to the income. 支出和收入不成比例。❷[C]部分:You have not done your ～ of the work. 你没做完你的那份工作。同 part 派 proportional *adj.*

proposal / prəˈpəʊzl / *n.* [C]建议;计划:～s of increasing trade between two countries 促进两国间贸易的计划 同 suggestion, plan

用法

❶proposal 后面接不定式或 for+名词:his proposal to repair the house 他提出的修补房子的建议。❷proposal 作主语时,其后接的表语从句或同位语从句中的谓语动词也用虚拟语气,即 should+动词原形或直接用动词原形;His proposal is (was) that the house (should) be repaired. 他的建议是房屋应进行修缮。

propose / prəˈpəʊz / *v.* ❶提议;建议:I ～ an early start. 我建议早些动身。同 suggest, design ❷提名;推荐:I'd like to ～ Bob for membership of our football team. 我推荐鲍勃为我们足球队的队员。同 present, recommend

用法

❶propose 为动词时,后面接不定式或动名词都可以:We propose to abolish (abolishing) all weapons of mass destruction. 我们建议销毁一切大规模杀伤性武器。❷propose 为动词时也可接 that 引导的从句,但从句的谓语动词应用虚拟语气,即 should+动词原形或直接用动词原形:I propose (proposed) that a series of discussion (should) be started at once. 我建议马上开始一系列讨论。

proposition / ˌprɒpəˈzɪʃn / *n.* [C] ❶命题;主题 同 statement, thesis ❷主张;建议;提议:The ～ was rejected as impractical. 因为不切实际,这个提议被否决了。同 proposal, declaration

prose / prəʊz / *n.* [U]散文:a ～ writer 散文作家

prosecute / ˈprɒsɪkjuːt / *vt.* 起诉;控告:The manager was ～d for accepting bribes. 经理因受贿被起诉。同 sue 派 prosecution *n.*

prospect / ˈprɒspekt / *n.* ❶[C]景色 同 view, scene ❷[C]前景;盼望的事物:The ～s for the wine harvest are poor this year. 今年的葡萄酒收成前景不好。同 expectation, future ❸[U]期望;希望:I see no (little, not much) ～ of his recovering. 我认为他没有(很少有)痊愈的希望。同 hope, promise

prospective / prəˈspektɪv / *adj.* 未来的;可能发生的;即将成为的:verify the resumes of all ～ employees 核查所有雇员人选的个人简历 / a ～ bride 准新娘

prosper / ˈprɒspə(r) / *vi.* 繁荣;昌盛;兴旺:Our country is ～ing with each passing day. 我们的国家蒸蒸日上。同 succeed, thrive

prosperity / prɒˈsperəti / *n.* [U]成功;繁荣;昌盛:a life of happiness and ～ 幸福与成功的一生 同 success, plenty 反 poverty

prosperous / ˈprɒspərəs / *adj.* 成功的;繁荣的;昌盛的:a ～ business 兴隆的生意 / ～ years 繁荣的年代 同 successful, flourishing 反 unsuccessful, poor

protect / prəˈtekt / *v.* 防卫;保护;防护 同 defend, guard 反 attack, threaten / ～ **from** (**against**) … 使不受…的伤害:The army ～ed the country against attack. 军队保卫国家免遭攻击。/ She's wearing dark glasses to ～ her eyes from the sun. 她戴着墨镜,以防阳光

刺眼。

protection / prəˈtekʃn / n. ❶[U]防御;保护;警戒 圊 defence,shelter ❷[C]保护者;保护物:wearing a heavy overcoat as a ～ against the cold 穿厚大衣以御寒

protective / prəˈtektɪv / adj. 保护的;防护的:～ measures 保护措施 圊 defensive

protein / ˈprəʊtiːn / n. [U]蛋白质:animal and vegetable ～ 动物和植物蛋白质 / Milk contains much ～. 牛奶里含有丰富的蛋白质。

protest Ⅰ / prəˈtest / v. 抗议;坚决反对 圊 oppose,complain 反 approve,agree / ～ against (**about,at**)对…提出抗议:Many people ～ed against the environmental pollution. 许多人都抗议环境受到污染。Ⅱ / ˈprəʊtest / n. 抗议:The customer expressed his ～ against the poor quality of the goods. 顾客对商品质量低劣表示抗议。The angry people retired in ～. 愤怒的人们为表示抗议而退场。圊 objection,resistance

prototype / ˈprəʊtətaɪp / n. [C]原型;典型;范例 圊 original,example

proud / praʊd / adj. ❶自尊的;自豪的 圊 independent,satisfied 反 lowly,dishonourable / be ～ of 对…感到自豪:They are ～ of their clever children. 他们为有聪明的孩子而感到自豪。❷傲慢的;狂妄的:He was too ～ to join our party. 他太骄傲,不屑参加我们的集会。圊 boastful,self-important 反 modest,humble 派 proudly adv.

用法

proud 后面接不定式、of 十动名词或 that 引导的从句都可以:I'm proud to be a Chinese. I'm proud of being a Chinese. I'm proud that I am a Chinese. 我为自己是一个中国人而自豪。

prove / pruːv / vt. (proved,proved 或 proven) 证明;证实:Facts have ～d that practice is the sole criterion for testing truth. 事实证明实践是检验真理的唯一标准。圊 confirm,witness 反 disprove

proverb / ˈprɒvɜːb / n. [C]谚语;格言 圊 saying

provide / prəˈvaɪd / v. ❶提供 圊 offer,supply 反 deprive / ～ for 为…提供所需;为…做准备:He has a large family to ～ for. 他需要维持一个大家庭。～ **sb. with sth.** 供给某人某物:～ children with food and clothes 供给孩

子们衣食 / The sun ～s us with energy. 太阳供给我们能量。❷准备;预防:～ against (for)an earthquake 做预防地震的准备 圊 prepare,plan 反 neglect,overlook ❸规定 圊 require,state

provided / prəˈvaɪdɪd / conj. 倘若;只要:Provided there is no opposition,we shall hold the meeting here. 倘若没有人反对,我们就在这儿开会。/ ～ **that** 假如;若是:I'll go,～ that you go too. 如果你去,我就去。圊 if

province / ˈprɒvɪns / n. [C]省;(一个国家的)大行政区:Sichuan Province(the Province of Sichuan) 四川省 圊 area,region 派 provincia adj.

provision / prəˈvɪʒn / n. ❶[U]供应:The ～ of water and gas in the city is rich. 城里水和气的供应充足。圊 supply ❷[U]准备;预备 圊 preparation ❸[C]规定;条款:They have violated the ～s of the contract. 他们违反了合同条款。圊 requirement,term ❹(常用 pl.)给养

provisional / prəˈvɪʒənəl / adj. 临时的;暂时(性)的;暂定的:a ～ government 临时政府 / the signing of the ～ agreement 临时协议的签署

provocative / prəˈvɒkətɪv / adj. 挑衅性的;挑逗的

provoke / prəˈvəʊk / vt. 对…进行挑衅;激发;激怒;激起 圊 annoy,arouse 反 calm,ease

pseudonym / ˈ(p)sjuːdənɪm / n. [C]假名,化名;笔名:Mark Twain was the ～ used by Samuel Clemens. 马克·吐温是塞缪尔·克莱门斯的笔名。

psychiatrist / saɪˈkaɪətrɪst / n. [C]精神病医生;精神病专家

psychiatry / saɪˈkaɪətri / n. [U]精神病学

psychological / ˌsaɪkəˈlɒdʒɪkl / adj. 心理的;心理学的 圊 emotional,mental

psychologist / saɪˈkɒlədʒɪst / n. [C]心理学家

psychology / saɪˈkɒlədʒi / n. [U]心理学;心理:Do you understand his ～? 你了解他的心理吗?

psychosis / saɪˈkəʊsɪs / n. [C](pl. psychoses / saɪˈkəʊsiːz /)精神病;精神错乱

pub / pʌb / n. [C](英)酒吧;酒馆

public / ˈpʌblɪk / Ⅰ adj. ❶公众的;公共的:a ～ library 公共图书馆 / ～ opinion 舆论 圊 common,general 反 private,personal ❷国家的;政府的:a ～ enemy 国民公敌 圊 social 反 private Ⅱ n. 公众,民众(作主语时,谓语动词用单数或复数均可):The ～ is(are)reques-

P

ted not to litter in the park. 要求公众勿在公园里丢弃废物。园 people,nation / **in** 〜 公然地;公开地

publication / ˌpʌblɪˈkeɪʃn / n. ❶[U]公布;出版:date of 〜 出版日期 园 announcement, printing ❷[C]出版物:Among his many 〜 s was a volume of light verses. 在他众多出版物中有一本消遣诗集。

publicity / pʌbˈlɪsɪti / n. [U] ❶公众(或传媒等)的注意,众所周知,闻名;名声:avoid 〜 避免惹人注目/His latest novel received good 〜. 他最近出版的小说大获好评。❷惹人注目的办法;宣传,宣扬:Her novel was published with a lot of 〜伴随着巨大的宣传攻势,她的小说出版了。

publish / ˈpʌblɪʃ / v. ❶公布;宣布:〜 the news 发布消息 园 announce,advertise 反 conceal,hide ❷出版:The book was 〜 ed last year. 这本书是去年出版的。园 print,put out

pudding / ˈpudɪŋ / n. 布丁;甜食;甜点

puff / pʌf / Ⅰ n. [C]喘息;(短而快的)喷送:喷送声:〜 s from an engine 机车喷出的烟/have a 〜 at a pipe 吸一口烟 园 breath,pant Ⅱ v. 喘息;(烟、蒸汽等)阵阵喷出:The engine 〜ed out of the station. 机车喷着阵阵的烟驶出了车站。园 gasp,pant

pull / pul / v. ❶拉;扯;拖:Pull your chair to the table. 把你的椅子拖近桌边。园 drag,draw / 〜 **ahead (of)**跑在前头;超过:The car soon 〜ed ahead of the bus. 小汽车很快就超过了公共汽车。〜 **down** ①拉下(遮帘等):Shall I 〜 down the blinds? 我可以放下百叶窗吗?②拆除;拆毁:The houses had to be 〜 ed down to make way for the new road. 为了让位给新路,这些房屋只有拆除。〜 **on** 穿上;戴上:Help me to 〜 on these boots. They are very tight. 帮我穿上靴子,它们太紧了。〜 **through** ①(使)渡过难关:You will never 〜 through the examination unless you work hard. 你不发奋是过不了考试这一难关的。②(使)恢复健康:He is still sick,but the doctor is sure that he will 〜 through. 他的病还很重,但医生确信他会痊愈。❷(车、船等)行驶:〜 **in** (车)进站:The train 〜ed in at ten sharp. 火车10点整进站。〜 **out** 离开;驶出:When he arrived at the stop, the bus had 〜ed out. 他赶到车站时,公共汽车已经开出站了。〜 **up** 停,使…停止:You must 〜 your car up at a red light. 看到红灯时你必须停车。

pulse / pʌls / n. 脉搏:feel the 〜诊脉

pump / pʌmp / Ⅰ n. [C]泵;抽水机;打气筒 Ⅱ v. 用打气筒打气;用泵抽水

pumpkin / ˈpʌmpkɪn / n. [C]南瓜

punch / pʌntʃ / Ⅰ vt. 打(孔);给…穿孔;用拳猛击 园 strike,hit Ⅱ n. [C]打孔器;一击;一拳 园 blow,knock

punctual / ˈpʌŋktʃuəl / adj. 准时的;守时的:He is 〜 to the minute. 他严守时间。园 exact 反 unpunctual,late

punctuation / ˌpʌŋktʃuˈeɪʃn / n. [U]标点:〜 marks 标点符号

punish / ˈpʌnɪʃ / v. 处罚;惩罚:How would you 〜 liars? 你如何处罚说谎者? 园 beat, sentence ❤ reward 〜 **sb. for sth.** 因某事惩罚某人:You should be 〜 ed for lying. 你说谎,应当受到惩罚。〜 **sb. with (by)…** 用…惩罚某人:He was 〜ed with a fine for spitting. 他因随地吐痰被罚款。派 punishment n.

pupil / ˈpjuːpl / n. ❶[C]学生(尤指中小学生)园 schoolboy,schoolgirl ❷瞳孔

puppet / ˈpʌpɪt / n. ❶傀儡;木偶 园 doll,tool ❷受操纵的人或组织

puppy / ˈpʌpi / n. [C] ❶小狗 ❷幼小的动物

purchase / ˈpɜːtʃəs / Ⅰ n. ❶[U]买 ❷[C]购买的东西;购得物 Ⅱ vt. 买:〜 a house 买一所房子 buy 反 sell

pure / pjuə(r) / adj. ❶纯净的:〜 water (milk,gold)纯水(纯牛奶、纯金)园 natural, neat 反 impure,dirty ❷纯正的;纯洁的:speak 〜 English 讲纯正的英语 / 〜 thoughts 纯洁的思想 园 true,innocent 反 spoiled,untrue 派 purely adv.

purify / ˈpjuərɪfaɪ / vt. 使纯净;提纯;精炼:〜 the mind 使思想纯洁 园 clear 反 pollute

purity / ˈpjuərəti / n. [U] 纯净;纯洁;纯度 园 cleanliness,innocence 反 impurity

purple / ˈpɜːpl / Ⅰ n. [U] 紫色 Ⅱ adj. 紫色的

purpose / ˈpɜːpəs / n. 目的;计划;意向:What was the 〜 of their visit? 他们来访的目的是什么? 园 aim,goal / **for (the)** 〜 **of** 为了:He came for the 〜 of training us in using computers. 他来的目的是训练我们如何使用计算机。**on** 〜故意地:It is evident that someone broke his glasses on 〜. 很明显有人故意摔坏了他的眼镜。派 purposely adv.

P

purse / pɜːs / n. [C]小钱包

pursue / pəˈsjuː / v. ❶追逐;追捕;追杀;~ a robber 追捕盗贼 同 chase, follow ❷ 追求;~ pleasure 寻乐 / ~ one's ideal 追求理想 同 seek, strive for

pursuit / pəˈsjuːt / n. [U]追赶;追求 同 chase, search / **in** ~ **of** 追求;He went here and there in ~ of truth. 他四处寻求真理。

push / pʊʃ / v. 推;We ~ed the boat into the water. 我们把小船推进水里。同 press, drive / ~ **aside** 把⋯推到旁边;That rude man ~ed me aside and got on the bus ahead of me! 那个粗野的男人把我推向一边,他先上了公共汽车。~ **forward(on)** 推进;努力向前;We must ~ forward in spite of the difficulties. 尽管有困难,我们也得努力向前。/ We ~ed on through the woods until we reached an open road. 我们费力地在林中前进,直到走到一条大路上。

put / pʊt / v. (put, put)放;置;Where did you ~ my hat? 你把我的帽子放哪儿了? 同 lay, place 反 remove, raise / ~ **an end to** ①结束;停止;You should ~ an end to the foolish quarrel at once. 你们应该立即结束这场愚蠢的争吵。②消灭;杀死;The dog was seriously ill, and the farmer ~ an end to it. 狗病得厉害,农夫就把它杀掉了。~ **aside** ①搁置一旁;停下;He ~ his work aside and made some coffee. 他停下工作煮咖啡。②把(钱等)存起来;She ~ aside some money for her son. 她为儿子存了一些钱。~ **away** 把⋯收起来;储存;He has ~ a great deal of money away. 他存了很多钱。~ **down** 控制;平息;镇压;The police are trying to ~ down violent crime in the city. 警察正在竭力控制城市里的犯罪。~ ... **down** ① 放下;Just as I ~ the telephone receiver down, the doorbell rang. 我刚放下电话,门铃就响了。②使(乘客等)下车;Please ~ me down at the next corner. 请让我在下一个街角下车。③写下;记入;I ~ down her address. 我记下她的地址。④镇压;取缔;They ~ down the riot. 他们镇压了暴动。~ **forward** 提出(理论、意见等);促进;It was Einstein who ~ forward the theory of relativity. 是爱因斯坦提出了相对论。~ **into** ①放入;输入;Put the vegetables into the pan with very little water, and heat quickly. 把这些菜放进锅里,加少许水,然后很快加热。②变成;译成;Please ~ this sentence into English. 请把这个句子译成英语。/ Every singer ~s his heart into the music, and the effect is wonderful. 每位歌手都全力投入音乐中,所以效果极佳。~ **off** ①脱掉;消除;Will you ~ off your coat, please? 请把外衣脱掉好吗? / Her explanation ~ off my doubts. 她的解释消除了我的疑虑。②延期;Never ~ off till tomorrow what you can do today. 决不要把你今天能做的事拖到明天。~ **on** ①穿上;He ~ on his coat hurriedly and ran out of the house. 他匆匆穿上大衣,跑出了屋子。②上演;They ~ on a fine performance last Sunday. 上周日他们演出了优秀节目。~ **one's heart into** 全神贯注于;He always ~s his heart into what he is reading. 他总是全神贯注地读书。~ **out** ①伸出;It's rude to ~ out your tongue at people. 向人伸舌头是不礼貌的。②熄灭(灯或火);Put out all fires before leaving the camping ground. 离开野营地时把所有的火灭掉。/ Please ~ the lights out before you leave the building. 你离开大楼时请关掉所有的灯。~ ...**to the test** 试验;检验;We can't tell if the product will be successful until we have ~ it to the test. 直到该产品检验后我们才能知道它是否成功。~ ...**to use** 利用;Let's think out a way to ~ the old machine to use. 我们来想个办法利用这台旧机器。~ **up** ①举起;抬起;Put up your hand if you know the answer. 如果你知道答案就请举手。②建造;搭起;Do you know how to ~ up a tent? 你知道怎样搭帐篷吗? / The original college buildings were ~ up in the 16th century. 原学院建筑物是 16 世纪建造的。③张贴;挂起;The examination results will be ~ up on this notice board tomorrow. 考试的结果将于明天在布告牌上张贴出来。~ **up with** 忍受;I can't ~ up with these noises any more. 我再也无法忍受这些噪声了。

puzzle / ˈpʌzl / Ⅰ v. 使苦思;使迷惑;This letter ~s me. 这封信使我迷惑不解。同 confuse, bewilder / ~ **over(about)**... 为⋯伤脑筋;We really ~d over the problem. 我们真为这个问题伤脑筋。Ⅱ n. [C]难题;谜;Can you solve the ~? 你能解决这个难题吗? / UFOs are still a ~ to human beings. 对于人类来说,不明飞行物仍然是一个谜。同 mystery, riddle

pyramid / ˈpɪrəmɪd / n. ❶锥体 ❷(古埃及的)金字塔

Q q

quadrangle / ˈkwɒdˌræŋgl / n. [C]四边形;四方形;矩形;正方形

quake / kweɪk / vi. & n. ❶(指地)震动;摇动 同 shake,move ❷颤抖;哆嗦 同 tremble,shiver

qualification / ˌkwɒlɪfɪˈkeɪʃn / n. [C] ❶资格;合格证明:educational ～s 学历资格 同 ability,requirement ❷限定条件:necessary ～s 必要条件 同 limitation,condition

qualified / ˈkwɒlɪfaɪd / adj. 有资格的;合格的:a ～ engineer 一个合格的工程师 同 able,fit

qualify / ˈkwɒlɪfaɪ / vt. ❶使具有资格;使合格 同 fit,entitle / ～ sb. for sth. (to do sth.) 使有资格做某事:Her education qualified her for the post. 她所受的教育使她有资格担当这个职务。～ sb. as ... 使有资格成为:His training qualified him as a teacher. 他所受的训练使他有资格当一名老师。❷限制;限定;修饰 同 limit,restrict

qualitative / ˈkwɒlɪtətɪv / adj. 质的,质量的;性质的:a ～ change 质变/a ～ judgement 定性

quality / ˈkwɒləti / n. ❶质量;品质;特质:This wool is of high ～. 这羊毛是高质量的。同 value,grade ❷特征;特性;性能:One of pine wood is that it can be sawn easily. 松木的一个特性是它容易锯开。同 character,feature

quantitative / ˈkwɒntɪtətɪv / adj. 量的,数量的:a ～ change 量变/a ～ jump in agricultural production 农业生产的猛增

quantity / ˈkwɒntəti / n. ❶[U]量;数量:I prefer quality to ～. 我重质量胜过数量。同 amount,sum ❷(常用 pl.)大量:We've had quantities of rain this summer. 今年夏天雨多。同 mass,lot / in quantities 大量地;数量上地:buy goods in large quantities 购买大量货物

用法
a quantity of 后用可数、不可数名词均可。

quantum / ˈkwɒntəm / Ⅰ n. [C](pl. quanta) ❶量;份额,部分;a ～ of evidence 少得不能再少的证据 ❷量子:the quanta of gravitational radiation 引力辐射的量子 Ⅱ adj. ❶量子的:～ physics 量子物理学 ❷大的,重大的:a ～ improvement 重大的改进

quarrel / ˈkwɒrəl / Ⅰ vi. (-reled 或-relled;-reling或-relling)吵架 同 argue,disagree 反 agree,coincide / ～ with sb. about sth. 和某人就某事发生争吵:Let us stop ～ling with them about such unimportant matters. 我们不要再和他们为这些小事争吵了吧。Ⅱ n. [C]口角;争论:Mike had a ～ with Tom for a toy. 迈克和汤姆为了玩具而争吵。同 argument,conflict 反 agreement

quart / kwɔːt / n. [C]夸脱(液体单位,英制约等于1.13升,美制约等于0.94升)

quarter / ˈkwɔːtə(r) / n. [C] ❶四分之一;四等份 ❷(任何一小时之前或之后的)一刻钟;a ～ to two 差一刻两点 / a ～ past six 六点过一刻 ❸季度:the third ～ of the year 第三季度 同 season ❹两角五分:one dollar and a ～ 一元两角五分钱 ❺(常用 pl.)寓所,住处:find ～s in the city 在城里找住处 同 apartment,lodgings

quarterly / ˈkwɔːtəli / Ⅰ adj. 按季度的;季度的:～ payment 按季付款 / ～ subscription 按季订阅 Ⅱ adv. 按季地:The committee meets ～. 委员会每季度聚会一次。Ⅲ n. [C]季刊

quartz / kwɔːts / n. [U]石英

queen / kwiːn / n. [C]女王;皇后:beauty ～ 第一美女,选美得头奖者/ campus ～ 校花/ movie ～ 影后 同 princess

queer / kwɪə(r) / adj. 奇怪的;古怪的 同 strange,unusual 反 common,usual

quench / kwentʃ / vt. ❶消除;平息;终止;满足;缓解:～ one's thirst with water 以水解

渴/～ a rebellion 平息叛乱/His thirst for knowledge will never be ～ed. 他的求知欲永无止境。❷扑灭；熄灭：The fire was ～ed by the rain. 火被雨水浇灭了。

query / ˈkwɪəri / Ⅰ n. [C] ❶问题；疑问；质问；询问：The shop assistant accepted my cheque without ～. 那位商店营业员不加询问便收下了我的支票。❷问号(即"?")Ⅱ vt. ❶问(及)；询问：He queried whether (if) the law allowed this sort of procedure. 他询问法律是否允许这种程序。❷对…提出质疑；对…表示疑问：～ a point in sb.'s speech 就某人讲话中的一点提出质疑/He rang the water company to ～ his bill. 他给自来水公司打电话对他的水费账单提出疑问。

quest / kwest / Ⅰ n. [C](历时较久或艰辛的)寻求；寻找；追求；探索：the ～ for treasure 探宝/renew the weary ～ for work 重新登上找工作的艰辛路程/ **in** ～ **of** 寻求；寻找：go to the south in ～ of employment 去南方寻找工作/They fanned out over the mountains in ～ of the lost child. 他们在山上成扇形展开，四处寻找那个走失的孩子。Ⅱ vi. ❶寻求；寻找；追求；探索：～ after truth 探求真理/～ for a cause that would give meaning to one's life 追求一种会给予自己生活意义的事业 ❷探险

question / ˈkwestʃən / Ⅰ n. 问题；询问：He asked me a lot of ～s. 他问了我许多问题 同 problem，inquiry 反 answer，reply / **out of** ～ 毫无疑问：His sincerity is out of ～. 他的诚意毫无疑问的。/ He is out of ～ the best student in the class. 毫无疑问，他是班上最好的学生。**out of the** ～ 毫无可能，办不到：Picnic in storm is out of the ～. 在暴雨中野餐是办不到的。Ⅱ v. 询问；审问：He was ～ed by the police. 他被警方审问。同 ask，test 反 answer，respond

辨析

question 指对某事怀疑或不知而提出问题并期待回答：After the talk, the speaker answered a number of questions. 报告完后，报告人回答了一些问题。**problem** 指客观存在的、等待解决的问题：The problem of how to enlarge the students' active vocabulary still remains to be solved. 如何扩大学生活用词汇量的问题尚待解决。**issue** 指意见不能达成一致而出现的问题：They have repeatedly raised the issue of the country's membership in the United Nations. 他们已经多次提出关于这个国家成为联合国会员国的问题。

questionable / ˈkwestʃənəbl / adj. 可疑的；不可靠的 同 doubtful，uncertain 反 definite，certain

questionnaire / ˌkwestʃəˈneə(r) / n. [C]调查表；征求意见表；问卷 同 answer-sheet，form

queue / kjuː / Ⅰ n. [C]长队：form a ～排成一行 / jump the ～插队/ stand in a ～站成一行 同 line，procession Ⅱ v. 排成长队：～ up for a bus 排长队等公共汽车 / ～ up to buy tickets for the opera 排队买歌剧票 同 line

quick / kwɪk / Ⅰ adj. ❶快的；迅速的：walking at a ～ pace 快步行走 / have a ～ meal 吃一顿快餐 同 fast，rapid 反 slow ❷敏捷的；机敏的：be ～ of understanding 理解力强 / The girl is ～ with her hands. 那女孩手很巧。❸clever，keen 反 stupid，dull Ⅱ adv. 快：Can't you run ～er? 你不能再跑快点吗? 同 fast，rapidly 反 slowly 派 quickly adv.；quickness n.

用法

❶quick 在口语中可代替 quickly，放在动词之后。❷quick 不指运动速度快，而指动作发生迅速。

quicken / ˈkwɪkən / vt. ❶加快，加速：～ the pace of new-product development 加速开发新产品/They felt their breathing ～. 他们感到呼吸加快了。❷刺激，激发；使有生气；使活跃；使复活：The professor's words suddenly ～ed his own memories. 教授那番话蓦地激活了他自己的记忆。/The recent film has ～ed interest in Titanic. 最近上映的影片激起人们对"泰坦尼克号"的兴趣

quiet / ˈkwaɪət / adj. (-er，-est)静止的；安静的；the ～ sea 风平浪静的海面 / Keep ～! 保持安静! 同 silent，calm 反 loud，noisy 派 quietly adv.；quietness n.

辨析

quiet 指人生性文静，不急躁冲动；动物安静，不骚动；环境不喧嚣；生活恬静，无干扰；水面平静：The dog lay quiet at his master's feet. 那条狗安静地躺在主人的脚边。It was so quiet that you could hear a pin drop. 周围寂静得连根针掉下的声音都听得见。**calm** 指人心境平静，不焦虑，不激动；地方不喧嚣；水面平静：He remained calm during the crisis. 在危机时期，他仍保持平静。After the storm, it resumed calm. 风暴过后，一切又变得平静了。**still** 指人或动物静止不动或寂静无声：Keep still while I take your picture. 我给你照相时你别动。

quilt / kwɪlt / n. [C]被子

quit / kwɪt / vt. (quit 或 quitted, quit 或 quitted; quitting) ❶离开; 辞去: ～ office 离职 / Bill ～ his job for advanced studies. 比尔辞职去进修。同 leave, resign 反 remain, stay ❷停止; 放弃: ～ school 弃学 / They ～ work when the bell rang. 铃响后他们停止工作。同 stop, end 反 start, continue

quite / kwaɪt / adv. ❶完全地; 彻底地; 十分: I ～ agree. 我完全同意。She was ～ alone. 她非常孤独。同 completely, entirely / ～ **another thing** 完全是另一回事: Talking is one thing and doing is ～ another. 说是一回事, 做完全是另一回事。～ **right** 很好: "Is he from England?" "Quite right." "她是英国人吗?" "完全正确。" ❷达到某一程度: ～ **a few** 相当多(用于修饰可数名词): Quite a few students like to watch the football match. 相当多的学生喜欢看足球比赛。～ **a little** 相当多(用于修饰不可数名词): He spent ～ a little money on books and newspapers. 他花了不少钱买书和报纸。～ **a lot (of)**许多: There were ～ a lot of people at her birthday party. 很多人参加了她的生日晚会。

quiz / kwɪz / n. [C] (pl. quizzes / 'kwɪzɪz /) 一般知识测验; 小考 同 test

quota / 'kwəʊtə / n. [C] ❶限额; 定额; (分)配额: assign an import ～制定进口配额/The removal of entry ～s encouraged young people to enter universities. 取消招生限额鼓励年轻人上大学。❷份额, (一)份; (一定)数量: have one's full ～ of love 完全拥有自己的一份爱情/His translation has the usual ～ of insidious, unnoticed Americanisms. 他的译文一如旧规, 不知不觉之中掺进了一定数量的美国特色用语。

quotation / kwəʊ'teɪʃn / n. [C] ❶引证; 引文: direct(indirect) ～ 直接(间接)引语 /～ marks 引号 / ～s from Chairman Mao 毛主席语录 / In his talk, the speaker used many ～s from Shakespeare. 演讲者在讲话中引用了许多莎士比亚的话。同 reference, selection ❷报价; 估价: ～ of prices 报价 同 rate, price

quote / kwəʊt / v. ❶引述; 引用 同 name, illustrate ❷报价; 开价 同 rate, estimate

quotient / 'kwəʊʃnt / n. 商; 商数: intelligence ～(＝IQ)智商; 智力商数

Q

R r

rabbit / 'ræbɪt / n. 兔;兔肉

race / reɪs / Ⅰ n. [C] ❶种族;民族:the white ～s 白种人 同 nation, tribe ❷(速度上的）比赛,竞赛:make a ～ against time 和时间赛跑 / horse ～ 赛马 / Did you run the 1,000-meter ～? 你参加了 1000 米赛跑吗? 同 contest, competition;**hold a** ～ 举行比赛:They like swimming and often hold ～s. 他们很喜欢游泳,常常举行比赛。**lose（win）a** ～ 比赛失败(获胜):She lost the ～ last time. 上次比赛她失败了。**run a** ～ 疾走;赛跑:He ran a 800-metre ～ with his classmates. 他和同学们一道进行了 800 米赛跑。Ⅱ v. 赛跑:Race to see what is happening. 跑去看看发生了什么事。同 run, compete

> **辨析**
>
> race 指具有共同起源和相同遗传特征的人群、人种或种族:Race relations in that country are hard to handle with. 那个国家的种族关系难以处理。**nation** 指具有共同生活区域、经济生活、语言,以及表现在共同文化上的共同心理特征的人的共同体,也常作"国家"讲:These people do not live in a state of their own. They regard themselves as a nation. 这些人没有自己的国家,但他们把自己看作一个民族。

racial / 'reɪʃəl / adj. 种族的;人种的:～ customs 种族习俗 / ～ conflicts 种族冲突 / ～ discrimination 种族歧视 同 national, tribal 派 racialism n.

rack / ræk / n. [C]搁物架;(火车、客机上的)行李架 同 frame, shelf

racket / 'rækɪt / n. [C](网球等的)球拍

radar / 'reɪdɑː(r) / n. ❶[U] 雷达 ❷[C]无线电探测器

radial / 'reɪdɪəl / adj. ❶放射的;辐射状的,辐射式的:～ network 辐射(式)网络 /～ avenues 呈辐射状的街道 ❷径向的,(沿)半径的,径向运动的:～ development 径向展开

radiate / 'reɪdɪeɪt / vi. 辐射;发光;放热 同 shine, shed 反 absorb

radiation / ˌreɪdɪ'eɪʃn / n. [U] ❶放射;辐射 ❷[C]放射物;辐射线 同 ray

radical / 'rædɪkl / adj. ❶基本的;根本的;主要的 同 basic, essential 反 superficial, inessential ❷极端的,激进的 同 extreme, rash 反 moderate, conservative 派 radically adv.

radio / 'reɪdɪəʊ / n.(pl. radios)收音机;电台;无线电;无线电广播:Please tune in on Radio Beijing. 请收听北京广播电台的广播。/ We always listen to the ～ at six in the morning. 我们总是在早晨 6 点钟收听广播。/ **on（over）the** ～ 通过无线电广播;在广播中:The president spoke on the ～ last Monday. 总统上周一发表了广播讲话。/ I heard the news over the ～. 我从广播里听到这则消息。**turn on（off）the** ～ 开(关)收音机:He turned on the ～ and listened to the news carefully. 他打开收音机仔细地听新闻。

radioactive / ˌreɪdɪəʊ'æktɪv / adj. 放射性的;放射性引起的:～ dust 放射性尘埃 / ～ element 放射性元素 / ～ substances 放射性物质

raft / rɑːft, ræft / Ⅰ n. [C]筏子;木筏,木排:竹筏 Ⅱ v. ❶用筏子运送:They ～ed the arms down the river. 他们用筏子把军火送往下游。❷划筏子:～ across(through) the river 划筏子过河

radium / 'reɪdɪəm / n. 镭

rag / ræg / n. ❶碎布 ❷(pl.) 破旧衣服:dress in ～s 穿着破烂衣服

rage / reɪdʒ / Ⅰ n. 发怒:**be in a** ～ **with sb.** 生某人的气 **fly into a** ～ 勃然大怒 同 anger, violence Ⅱ v. 发怒:～ **at（against）** 对…发脾气:Father ～d at (against) me for my carelessness. 由于我的粗心大意,父亲对我非常生气。同 roar, flare up

ragged / 'rægɪd / adj. 衣服破烂的:a ～ old

man 一个衣衫褴褛的老人

raid / reɪd / I *n.* [C]袭击,突袭;搜掠:an air ～ 空袭 同 attack,strike / **make a ～ on** 对⋯突然袭击:The enemy made a ～ on the oil field. 敌军突袭油田地带。II *v.* 侵袭,袭击 同 attack,invade

rail / reɪl / *n.* [C] ❶栏杆;横杆;扶手 同 barrier,fence ❷铁轨;铁路 同 railway,railroad

railroad / 'reɪlrəʊd / *n.* (＝railway)[C]铁路

railway / 'reɪlweɪ / *n.* [C] 铁路;铁道:～ station 火车站 /We'll build many new ～s. 我们将修建许多条新铁路。/ **by ～** 通过铁路;乘火车:Will you come by ～ or by sea? 你乘火车来还是乘船来?

rain / reɪn / I *n.* [U]雨:be caught in the ～ 淋雨 / make ～ 人工降雨 /We had plenty of ～ here last month. 上个月我们这儿雨水很多。II *v.* 下雨:I don't know whether it will ～ or not. 我不知道是否会下雨。同 drop,pour

rainbow / 'reɪnbəʊ / *n.* [C]彩虹

raincoat / 'reɪnkəʊt / *n.* [C]雨衣

rainy / 'reɪni / *adj.* 下雨的;多雨的:～ region 多雨地区 / ～ season 多雨季节 同 damp,wet

raise / reɪz / I *vt.* ❶提高;使升高:My wages were ～d. 我的工资提高了。同 increase,lift 反 drop,lower ❷种植(作物);饲养(牛羊等):She ～d chickens. 她养鸡。同 grow,breed ❸抚养:She alone ～s three children well. 她一个人把三个孩子抚养得很好。同 rear ❹筹集;筹措:～ a loan 筹款 /We must ～ funds for the project. 我们得为这个项目筹集资金。同 collect,obtain ❺提出:I'll ～ the question at the meeting. 我将在会上提出这个问题。同 advance II *n.* (＝[英]rise)[C]增加:get a pay ～ 获得加薪 同 increase,promotion 反 decrease,cut

辨析

raise 和 **rise** 都有"上升,增加"的意思,但 raise 是及物动词,rise 是不及物动词:He raised his voice. 他提高了嗓门。The landlord raised the rent of the room. 房东提高了房间的租金。The sun rises in the east. 太阳从东方升起。Prices have risen quickly. 物价已快速上涨。

raisin / 'reɪzən / *n.* [C]葡萄干

rally / 'ræli / I *v.* ❶重新聚集,重新集合;重整:The veterans rallied ten years after the war. 战后10年这些老兵重聚在一起。❷集合;联合,团结:The president tried to ～ the people around the government. 总统试图把人民团结在政府的周围。❸重新鼓起(勇气等);康复,恢复;振作:～ one's energy 恢复精力/～ from heavy disaster 从深重的灾难中恢复过来 ❹(股价等)止跌回升;(证券市场)行情反弹:Index rallied to nearly 500. 指数已经回到涨到近500。II *n.* [C] ❶重整旗鼓:The second ～ was defeated another time after the first defeat. 第一次失败后,重整的军队又被打败了。❷重振精神;(病后的)康复,恢复 ❸集会:a mass ～ 群众集会 ❹止跌回升;行情反弹:The market stage a sudden ～. 市场行情突然回升。

ramble / 'ræmbl / *vi.* 闲逛;漫步 同 stroll,wander

random / 'rændəm / I *n.* 随意;随机:at ～ 随意;随机:Choose any number at ～. 随便选择一个号码吧。II *adj.* 随意的;随机的:Please make a ～ choice among these books. 请在这些书中随意选择一本。同 accidental,casual 反 planned,intended

range / reɪndʒ / I *v.* ❶排列;整理;把⋯分类 同 arrange,classify ❷(在某范围内)变动,变化:Prices range from 20 yuan to 100 yuan. 价格从20元到100元不等。同 vary II *n.* [C]系列:a ～ of mountains 一条山脉 同 rank,row

rank / ræŋk / I *n.* ❶一列;一队;一行 同 range,line ❷等级;(军队中的)官衔:officers of high ～ 高级官员 同 grade,position ❸阶级;社会阶层 同 class,status II *v.* 评定等级;排列:This town ～s among the famous Chinese beauty spots. 这个城市为中国著名风景点之一。同 classify,arrange

ransack / 'rænsæk / *vt.* ❶彻底搜索,仔细搜查:The police ～ed his house. 警方把他的房子搜了一遍。❷洗劫:The bandits ～ed the village. 匪徒将村子洗劫一空。

ransom / 'rænsəm / I *n.* ❶赎回;赎身 ❷[C]赎金:pay a ～ of ＄2 million 交付200万美元的赎金 II *vt.* 赎;赎回:Her ～ed his son for a million dollars. 他花费了100万美元才赎回了自己的儿子。

rap / ræp / I *n.* [C]轻敲声 同 knock,tap II *vt.* (rapped;rapping) 敲击:The chairman ～

R

ped the meeting to order. 主席敲桌子使会场恢复秩序。同 knock,tap

rapid / ˈræpɪd / *adj.* 快的;迅速的:He is making 〜 progress in English study. 他在英语学习上进步很快。同 quick,fast 反 slow 派 rapidly *adv.*

rare / reə(r) / *adj.* ❶罕见的;稀有的:They have taken measures to protect 〜 animals. 他们已经采取措施保护珍稀动物。/ It is 〜 for her to go out at night. 她难得在晚间外出。同 few,scarce 反 many,plentiful ❷稀薄的;稀疏的:They didn't feel well in the 〜 air on the mountain top. 山顶上空气稀薄,他们感到很不舒服。同 thin 反 thick 派 rarely *adv.*

rarity / ˈreərəti / *n.* ❶[U]稀有,珍贵;稀薄,稀疏同 uncommonness,thinness ❷[C]奇物;奇事;珍品:Such a snowstorm was a 〜 in that region. 这样的雪暴在那个地区是很少见的。

rash / ræʃ / *adj.* 匆忙的;轻率的;鲁莽的:It was 〜 of her to make such a promise. 她作出如此承诺真是太轻率了。同 hasty,careless 反 careful,cautious 派 rashly *adv.*

rat / ræt / *n.* [C]鼠

rate / reɪt / I *n.* ❶比率;比例:attendance 〜 出勤率 /crime 〜 犯罪率 / employment 〜 就业率 / The death 〜 has lowered in our country. 我国的人口死亡率已降低。同 proportion ❷速度:walk at the 〜 of 3 miles an hour 以每小时 3 英里的速度走路 同 speed,pace ❸等级 同 grade,rank / **at this** 〜 照此速度;照这样下去:At this 〜, we'll arrive at the village only in two hours. 以这样的速度,我们在两小时内就可以到达那个村子。**at any** 〜 无论如何:You must come to our party at any 〜. 你无论如何得来参加我们的聚会。 II *vt.* ❶以为:Mary was 〜d as the top student in her class. 玛丽被认为是班上最优秀的学生。同 regard ❷估价;评价:He was highly 〜d by his teacher. 他受到老师的高度评价。同 estimate,classify

辨析
rate 指某种情况发生的比率,或两个数量相比后所得的比值。**proportion** 指一个物体与其他物体在数量、大小等方面的比例:The drawings of young children usually lack proportion. 幼儿的绘画经常不成比例。

rather / ˈrɑːðə(r) / *adv.* ❶宁愿;宁可 同 instead,preferably / **had (would) rather …than** 宁愿…而不…:She would 〜 have the small one than the large one. 她宁愿要小的而不要大的。/ She would 〜 die than surrender. 她宁死不屈。**〜 than** 与其…(不如)…;不是…(而是):This kind of change is physical 〜 than chemical. 这种变化是物理变化而不是化学变化。❷相当地:This book is 〜 interesting. 这本书相当有趣。He plays football 〜 well. 他足球踢得很不错。同 somewhat,quite

用法
❶do…rather than do…, would (had) rather do…than (do)…, prefer…to…, would more willingly do…than (do)…都可表示"宁愿干…,不愿干…":He depends on you rather than depend on me. 他宁愿依靠你也不愿依靠我。He was engaged in studying rather than reading the newspaper. 他正忙于学习而不是看报。❷would (had) rather 除了可接省略 to 的不定式外,还可接 that 从句,从句要用虚拟语气,其谓语动词通常用一般过去时:He would (had) rather his children didn't make so much noise. 他宁愿他的孩子们不要这么吵闹。

辨析
rather,fairly,quite 和 **very** 都可作程度副词,它们修饰意味从弱到强分别是 fairly,quite, rather,very:She speaks English fairly (quite,rather,very) well. 她英语讲得还可以(相当不错;相当好;非常好)。四个词中,只有 rather 能和比较级或 too 连用:rather warmer 相当暖和;rather too cold 太冷了。

rating / ˈreɪtɪŋ / *n.* [C] ❶评级,定级;等级:pop music 〜s lists 流行音乐排行榜 ❷(广播节目的)收听率;(电视节目的)收视率:〜s battle 收视率大战

ratio / ˈreɪʃɪəʊ / *n.* [C] (*pl.* ratios) 比率:at a 〜 of three to one 按三比一的比率 / direct (inverse) 〜 正比(反比)同 proportion,rate

ration / ˈræʃn,ˈreɪʃn / *n.* [C] ❶配给量,定量:the daily 〜 of food 每天的食品配给量 ❷(配给的)一份:a 〜 of meat 一份肉 /a petrol 〜 一份配给汽油

rational / ˈræʃnəl / *adj.* 合理的;理性的:〜 suggestion 合理的建议 / 〜 knowledge 理性知识 / Can you make a 〜 explanation to this? 你能对此作出合理的解释吗?同 sound,reasonable 反 irrational, unreasonable

ravage / ˈrævɪdʒ / *vt.* 毁灭,毁坏:a country ～d by bloodshed and war 被战争和杀戮摧残得满目疮痍的国家 Ⅱ *n.* 毁灭;毁坏,彻底破坏:the ～s caused by the epidemic 那场传染病所造成的危害

raw / rɔː / *adj.* ❶生的;未煮过的:～ meat 生肉 同 uncooked, unprepared 反 cooked, prepared ❷未加工的;自然的:～ materials 原料 同 natural, crude 反 manufactured, finished ❸生疏无知的;未经训练的 同 untrained, inexperienced 反 trained, experienced

ray / reɪ / *n.* [C]光线;射线;辐射线:a ～ of hope 一线希望 / X-rays are different from the ～s of the sun. X光和太阳光是不同的。

razor / ˈreɪzə(r) / *n.* [C]剃刀

reach / riːtʃ / Ⅰ *v.* ❶到达:～ London 抵达伦敦 / It will be Christmas Day when my letter ～es. 我的信将在圣诞节到达。The city has ～ed a population of six million. 这个城市的人口已达 600 万。❷伸手取 同 stretch, extend / ～ for 伸手拿:The soldier ～ed for his gun. 战士伸手去拿枪。Ⅱ *n.* [U]能达到的范围或距离:beyond (out of) ～ 拿不到的;达不到的:Please keep the knife out of the ～ of the children. 请把刀子放到孩子们拿不到的地方。/ The book is too difficult. It is beyond my ～ of understanding. 这书太难,我无法理解。**within** ～ 可以拿到的;力所能及的:You should put your dictionary within ～. 你应该把字典放在伸手可拿的地方。

> **辨析**
> 在表达"到达某地"时,reach 是及物动词,直接接表示地点的名词,arrive 是不及物动词,常与 in 或 at 连用,get 后加介词 to;reach Beijing,arrive in Beijing 或 get to Beijing 都表示"到达北京"之意。

react / riˈækt / *vi.* ❶反应(与 to 连用):Have the students ～ed to the proposal? 学生们对这建议有反应吗? 同 respond, answer ❷(化学)反应(与 on 连用):How do acids ～ on metals? 酸对金属起怎样的作用? ❸反抗(与 against 连用):～ against the old system 反对旧制度

reaction / riˈækʃn / *n.* ❶反应;反作用;反作用力:action and ～ 作用与反作用 /chemical ～化学反应 /His suggestion caused a strong ～. 他的建议引起强烈的反应。同 response, answer ❷反动;对抗:The forces of ～ were defeated completely. 反动势力彻底被打垮。

reactionism / riˈækʃənɪzəm / *n.* [U] 反动主义;极端保守主义

reactionist / riˈækʃənɪst / Ⅰ *n.* [C]反动分子 Ⅱ *adj.* 反动分子的

reactionary / riˈækʃənri / Ⅰ *adj.* 反动的 Ⅱ *n.* [C]反动分子

reactor / riˈæktə(r) / *n.* [C]反应器;反应堆:set up a nuclear ～ 建一个核反应堆

read / riːd / *v.* (read/red/, read) ❶阅读;看懂:～ a book (a letter) 读一本书(一封信)/ A driver must be able to ～ traffic signs. 驾驶员必须能看懂交通标志。同 study, understand ❷默读;朗读:Read the text aloud, please. 请朗读课文。同 recite, deliver ❸(指仪器)指示:What does the thermometer ～? 温度计指示多少度? 同 show, indicate / ～ a-bout 读到…的情况:I ～ about the event in the newspaper. 我从报上得悉这件事。～ be-tween (the) lines 读出字里行间的意思:When you read, you should ～ between the lines. 读书就应该读出字里行间的意思来。

reader / ˈriːdə(r) / *n.* [C] ❶读者:*Reader's Digest*《读者文摘》/ My father is a fast ～. 我父亲是一个快速阅读者。❷读物;读本:basic ～s 基础读物 / English ～s 英语读物

readily / ˈredɪli / *adv.* ❶ 不迟疑地;欣然地;乐意地:My friend ～ promised to help. 我的朋友乐意帮忙。同 willingly 反 unreadily ❷ 容易地;无困难地:This kind of computer can ～ be bought anywhere. 这种计算机在任何地方都容易买到。同 easily 反 unreadily

reading / ˈriːdɪŋ / *n.* ❶[U]读;阅读:～ lamp 台灯 / ～ room 阅览室 / ～ intensive ～ 精读 / extensive ～ 泛读 ❷[C]读物;选读:～s in Chinese literature 中国文学读物 / light ～s 消遣读物 ❸[C]读数;仪器指示数:What was the temperature ～ then? 那时的温度是多少?

readjust / ˌriːəˈdʒʌst / *v.* ❶重新适应:It won't take him long to ～ to a new situation. 他不需要花很长时间就能重新适应新的环境。❷ 重新调节,重新调整:～ the observer's position 重新调整观察者的位置

ready / ˈredi / *adj.* (-ier,-iest) ❶准备好的;

R

有准备的;自愿的:Get everything ～ for the journey. 为旅行做好一切准备。/ He's always ～ to help his friends. 他总是自愿帮助朋友。同 prepared,willing 反 unready,unwilling ❷迅速的;立即的:Don't be so ～ to find faults. 不要这么急于挑剔。同 quick,prompt 反 slow ❸事先准备好的:buy ～ food 买煮好的食品 / be(get) ～ to go? 你准备好走了吗?

real / 'riəl / *adj.* 事实上存在的;真实的:Is this ～ gold or something made to look like gold? 这是真金还是做得看起来像金子一样的假东西? 同 actual,true 反 unreal,false 派 really *adv.*

realism / 'riːəlɪzəm / *n.* [U] ❶现实主义:social ～社会现实主义 ❷写实;写实主义:artistic ～艺术写实主义

realistic / ˌriːə'lɪstɪk / *adj.* 现实的;现实主义的:～ novels 现实主义小说 同 natural,practical 反 unrealistic,unnatural

reality / rɪ'æləti / *n.* 真实;逼真;现实:This is not imagination,but ～. 这不是想象的,而是真实的 同 fact,truth 反 fancy / in ～ 实际上;事实上:We are helping you in ～. 我们实际上是在帮助你。

realization / ˌriːəlaɪ'zeɪʃn / *n.* [U] ❶(计划、野心或希望)的实现 ❷理解;认识

realize / 'riːəlaɪz / *v.* ❶了解;认识到:Does he ～ his error yet? 他认识到错误没有? 同 understand,recognize ❷使(希望、计划等)实现:～ the plan 实现计划 同 fulfil,complete

realm / relm / *n.* [C] ❶王国;国度:an independent ～ 独立王国 同 empire,kingdom ❷领域;范围:ideological ～ 思想领域 / the ～ of music 音乐领域 / the ～ of science 科学领域/ in the ～ of economy 在经济领域里 同 field,region

realty / 'riːəlti / *n.* [U]房地产

reap / riːp / *v.* 收割;收获:～ a field of wheat 收割田中的小麦 同 harvest

rear[1] / rɪə(r) / *n.* 后部;背部:The kitchen is in the ～ of the house. 厨房在房子的后部。/ the ～ wheels(lamps)of a car 汽车的后轮(尾灯)/ get down the bus by the ～ entrance 从后门下公共汽车 同 behind,back 反 front

rear[2] / rɪə(r) / *vt.* 抚养;饲养;培植;栽种:～ children 抚养孩子 / ～ crops 培植庄稼 / ～ cattle 养牛 同 raise,train

rearmost / 'rɪəməust / *adj.* 最后部分的,最后面的;最末端的:the ～ car 最后一辆车

reason / 'riːzn / Ⅰ *n.* ❶理由;原因:Is there any ～ why you should not help? 你有不该帮助的理由吗? 同 cause,explanation ❷理智;理性:Only man has ～. 只有人类有理性。同 sense,understanding / by ～ of 由于,因为:The plan failed by ～ of bad organization. 由于组织得不好,这个计划失败了。for ～s of 为了…的缘故:He didn't go to climb mountains with us for ～s of health. 由于健康原因,他没和我们一起去爬山。with ～ 有理由地;合乎情理地 without ～ 没有理由地;不合乎情理地:She would not come late without ～. 没有理由她是不会迟到的。Ⅱ *v.* 推理;说服:The ability to ～ makes man different from animals. 推理能力使人异于禽兽。同 think,conclude / ～ sb. into sth. 说服某人做某事:He ～ed us into adopting his new method. 他说服了我们采用他的新方法。～ sb. out of sth. 说服某人不做某事:He ～ed his mother out of worry. 他说服母亲不要着急。

reasonable / 'riːznəbl / *adj.* ❶合理的;有道理的:You must make a ～ excuse. 你得有个合理的解释。同 logical,sound 反 unreasonable,unsound ❷通情达理的;讲道理的:Please be ～. 请讲点道理。同 thoughtful 反 unreasonable ❸适度的;公道的:at a ～ price 售价公道 同 fair,just 反 unfair,unjust

reasoning / 'riːzənɪŋ / *n.* [U]推断,推理:His ～ on this point was quite wrong. 他在这一点上的推理大错特错。

rebel Ⅰ / 'rebl / *n.* [C]反叛者;造反者;反抗者 同 traitor,deserter Ⅱ / rɪ'bel / *vi.* (-belled;-belling)反叛;反抗:Some tribes ～led against the government. 一些部落武力反抗政府。同 disobey,revolt 反 obey

rebellion / rɪ'beljən / *n.* 反叛;叛乱;叛变:rise in ～ 起而反叛;揭竿而起 同 revolt,resistance

rebellious / rɪ'beljəs / *adj.* 造反的;叛乱的;反抗的 同 disobedient,insubordinate 反 obedient,subordinate

reborn / ˌriː'bɔːn / *adj.* (喻)再生的;新生的

rebuild / ˌriː'bɪld / *vt.* ❶重建;改建:～ a country 重建国家 ❷重组,改组;改造:try to

～ society 试图改造社会/The president ～ his campaign staff. 总统改组了其竞选人员。

rebuke / rɪˈbjuːk / *vt.* 指责；斥责；非难 同 scold, blame 反 praise, approve

recall / rɪˈkɔːl / *vt.* (使)回忆起；(使)想起：She ～ed her childhood at the sight of that doll. 看到那个洋娃娃她便想起了自己的童年。同 re-collect, remember

用法

recall 后面接动名词, 不接不定式：I recall meeting him somewhere. 我想起在哪儿见过他。

辨析

recall 比 recollect 通俗, 比 remember 正式, 指把忘记的东西又想起来, 常与 can, could 等连用：Try as I might, I could not recall where I had left the book. 无论我怎么想, 也想不起把书丢在哪儿了。**recollect** 原意是把已经散失的东西重新收拾在一起, 引申意为把已经遗忘的东西重新想起。recall 强调一次回忆, recollect 强调回忆过程：He recollected the hardships he had once suffered. 他回想起曾受过的痛苦。**remember** 常用词, 指事物自然在记忆中出现：I suddenly remembered I had left the book in the library. 我忽然想起把书忘在图书馆了。**remind** 意为"使想起；提醒", 宾语通常指人, 指在外力的作用下回想某事或联想某事：The film reminded me of those days in the countryside. 这部电影使我回想起在乡村的那些日子。I always remind myself not to arrive late at meetings. 我总是提醒自己开会不要迟到。

recede / rɪˈsiːd / *vi.* ❶退，后退：～ from the eye of 从…的视线中渐渐远去 ❷变得模糊：They went farther and the house ～d. 他们越走越远, 房子也变得模糊不清。/The painful memory began to ～. 痛苦的回忆渐渐地被抹去了。❸向后倾斜, 向后缩：a chin that ～s 向后缩的下巴

receipt / rɪˈsiːt / *n.* ❶[C]收据；收条：sign a ～ 在一张收据上签字 ❷[U]收到；接到：The ～ of your letter ended my anxiety. 收到你的信才消除了我的焦虑。同 reception, taking

receive / rɪˈsiːv / *v.* 收到；接受；得到：When did you ～ the letter? 你什么时候收到这封信的？/ He ～d a good education. 他受过良好的教育。同 get, accept

receiver / rɪˈsiːvə(r) / *n.* [C] ❶(电话)听筒：

Hang up (Put down) the ～ when you finish. 打完电话就挂上(放下)听筒。❷收音机；电视机 ❸收受者；收件人；收款人；接待者：I don't know who is the ～. 我不知道谁是收件人。

recent / ˈriːsnt / *adj.* 最近的：～ news 最近的消息 同 current, up-to-date 反 old, out-of-date 派 recently *adv.*

reception / rɪˈsepʃn / *n.* ❶[U]接待；迎接：The house has a ～ room, a kitchen and three bedrooms. 这所房子有一间接待室、一间厨房和三间卧室。同 acceptance, welcome ❷[C]招待会：There was a ～ after the wedding cer-emony. 结婚典礼之后举行了一场招待客人的宴会。同 party, gathering ❸接收(效果)：Radio ～ is poor here in our bedroom. 我们卧室里的收听效果很差。

recession / rɪˈseʃn / *n.* ❶[C；U]经济的衰退；经济的衰退期：a global ～ 全球性的经济衰退/get out of ～ 走出经济衰退期 ❷[U]后退；退回；(潮水的)退潮

recessive / rɪˈsesɪv / *adj.* ❶后退的；退回的 ❷隐性的：a ～ character 隐性性状

recipe / ˈresəpi / *n.* [C] ❶菜谱；烹饪法 同 cookery ❷处方 同 prescription ❸秘诀；窍门；诀窍 同 secret

recite / rɪˈsaɪt / *v.* 背诵：The child can ～ many poems from memory. 这孩子能够背诵很多诗。同 repeat, describe

reckless / ˈrekləs / *adj.* ❶不顾后果的，冒失的；鲁莽的，轻率的：a very ～ girl 放肆的姑娘/be ～ of one's life 不顾个人安危 ❷粗心的，不注意的：～ spending 无节制的消费 派 recklessly *adv.*；recklessness *n.*

reckon / ˈrekən / *v.* ❶数；算账 同 count, com-pute ❷猜想；以为 同 guess, regard

recognition / ˌrekəɡˈnɪʃn / *n.* [U]认识；认出；承认 同 acceptance, notice / **beyond**（**out of**）～ 认不出：The place has changed beyond ～. 这个地方已经变得让人认不出了。**in** ～ **of** 承认：He said nothing more in ～ of your be-ing right. 他没有再说什么, 承认你是对的。

recognize / ˈrekəɡnaɪz / *vt.* ❶认识；认出：He had changed so much that one could hardly ～ him. 他变得太多, 几乎让人认不出来了。同 accept, know ❷承认；认可：They ～d him as the lawful heir. 他们承认他是合法的继承人。同 acknowledge 反 ignore, overlook

R

recollect / ˌrekə'lekt / *v.* 记起；想起：～ childhood days 记起童年的日子 同 recall, remember

recommend / ˌrekə'mend / *vt.* 推荐；介绍：Can you ～ me a good novel? 你能推荐一本好小说给我吗？ 同 introduce

用法
recommend 作"建议"讲时，后面可跟动名词、不定式和从句。recommend 后跟从句时，从句中应用虚拟语气，即谓语动词用动词原形或 should 十动词原形：He ～ed that we (should) go first. 他建议我们先去。

recommendation / ˌrekəmen'deɪʃn / *n.* ❶推荐，介绍；推荐书，推荐信：give sb. a ～ 推荐某人 / letter of ～ 推荐信 / The chairman spoke for ～ of the new method. 主席发言推荐那种新方法。同 introduction ❷劝告；建议：make a ～ 劝告 同 advice, suggestion

用法
recommendation 后面跟从句时，从句应当用虚拟语气，即谓语动词用动词原形或 should 十动词原形：I like his recommendation that we (should) read more. 我喜欢他的有关多读书的建议。

reconcile / 'rekənsaɪl / *vt.* 使和好；调停；调解 同 reunite, settle

record Ⅰ / 'rekɔːd / *n.* ❶[C] 纪录；记录：make (break) a ～ 创造（打破）一个纪录 / keep a ～ 保持纪录 /equal (tie) a ～ 平一项纪录 / a ～ of road accidents 车祸记录 同 account, list ❷[C] 唱片 同 disc ❸履历；历史：medical ～s 病历 同 experience, history Ⅱ / rɪ'kɔːd / *v.* 写下；记录；录音 同 tape, register

recorder / rɪ'kɔːdə(r) / *n.* [C] ❶记录者；记录员 ❷录音机；录像机 / a video ～ 录像机 / a pocket ～ 袖珍录音机

recording / rɪ'kɔːdɪŋ / *n.* 录音：It wasn't a live performance but a BBC ～. 那不是实况转播，而是英国广播公司的录音节目。

recount / rɪ'kaʊnt / *vt.* ❶叙述，讲述：The novel ～ the life of a pop star. 这部长篇小说讲述了一位流行歌星的一生。❷详述，详细说明：～ one's plan 详细说明某人的计划

recover / rɪ'kʌvə(r) / *v.* ❶寻回；恢复：～ one's sight (hearing) 恢复视觉（听觉）同 re-

gain, repossess ❷复原；康复：He is slowly ～ing from his illness. 他在慢慢复原。同 restore

recovery / rɪ'kʌvəri / *n.* [U] ❶痊愈；复原：We wish you a speedy ～. 我们祝你早日恢复健康。同 cure, restoration ❷重获；复得：～ of a lost thing 找回遗失物 同 regaining, recapture

recreation / ˌrekrɪ'eɪʃn / *n.* 娱乐；消遣：the ～ ground 游乐场 / Reading and walking are his favorite forms of ～. 读书和散步是他最喜欢的消遣方式。同 play, amusement 反 work 派 recreational *adj.*

recrimination / rɪˌkrɪmɪ'neɪʃn / *n.* [C；U] 反责；反诉：Let's make friends, instead of wasting our time on ～. 咱们交个朋友吧，不要再浪费时间互相指责了。

recruit / rɪ'kruːt / Ⅰ *n.* [C] ❶新兵 ❷（社团、组织等的）新成员，新会员：New ～s to our book club are always welcome. 我们的读书俱乐部随时欢迎新会员参加。Ⅱ *vt.* ❶招收…为新兵；招兵，征兵：These Africans were ～ed for military service. 这些非洲人被征召入伍。❷招募，招收：～ employees 招工

rectangle / 'rekˌtæŋgl / *n.* [C] 长方形，矩形

rectify / 'rektɪfaɪ / *vt.* 纠正；调整 同 correct, adjust

recur / rɪ'kɜː(r) / *vi.* (-curred；-curring) ❶再次发生：The mistake ～s in the second paragraph of the review. 这个错误在书评的第二段再次出现。❷（想法、念头等）重新萌生；再次出现：The idea kept ～ring. 这个念头一直在脑海中出现。派 recurrence *n.*；recurrent *adj.*

recycle / ˌriː'saɪkl / *vi.* 再循环；回收再用

red / red / Ⅰ *adj.* 红色的：Red Cross 红十字（会）/ a Red Army soldier 红军战士 Ⅱ *n.* 红色：be in ～ 穿着红衣服 / bright (dark, light) ～鲜（深、淡）红 / go into the ～ 出现赤字；亏本

redeem / rɪ'diːm / *vt.* ❶买回；赎回：She returned to the pawnbroker's to ～ her watch. 她回到当铺赎回她的手表。❷兑现（债券、股票等）：～ bonds 将债券兑现 ❸遵守（诺言）；履行（义务）：The promise was finally ～ed. 这个诺言最终得以兑现。❹补救；弥补；补偿：These failings are ～ed. 这些失误都得到了补救。

reduce / rɪ'djuːs / v. 减少；降低：~ one's expenses 减少开支／~ one's weight 减轻体重 同 decrease, lessen 反 add, increase ／~...to 使…成为；削减至：~ the loss of blood to a minimum 把失血减少到最低量／Fire ~d the house to ashes. 大火使这所房屋化为灰烬。／Misfortune ~d the poor woman to begging. 不幸的遭遇使那个可怜的女人沦为乞丐。

reduction / rɪ'dʌkʃən / n. ❶[U] 缩减 同 decrease 反 increase ❷[C]（图画、地图等的）缩版，缩图

redundant / rɪ'dʌndənt / adj. 多余的，冗余的：remove ~ words in the sentence 删除句子中多余的词语

reed / riːd / n. [C] 芦苇；芦笛

reef / riːf / n. [C] 礁石；暗礁：strike a ~ 触礁

reel / riːl / v. 卷；绕；抽出 同 revolve, roll

refer / rɪ'fɜː(r) / v. (-ferred; -ferring) ❶送交，提交（以处理）（与 to 连用）：The dispute was ~red to the United Nations. 这一争端已提交联合国处理。同 deliver ❷谈及；谈到：Does that remark ~ to me? 那话是针对我说的吗？同 mention ❸参考：The speaker often ~red to his notes. 讲演者常参考他的笔记。同 consult, resort

referee / ˌrefə'riː / n. [C]（足球等的）裁判员 同 judge

reference / 'refrəns / n. ❶送交；谈到；提及；参考：You should make ~ to a dictionary. 你应该参考字典。~ in (with) ~ to 关于：He spoke in ~ to the project. 他就有关这项工程的问题发表了谈话。without (any) ~ to 与…无关；不管；无论：without ~ to age and sex 不论男女老少 ❷证明书；介绍信；证明人：My ~s will prove to you that I am efficient and dependable. 我的保证人将向你证明我有能力而且可靠。❸附注

refill / ˌriː'fɪl / vt. 再装满；再填充

refine / rɪ'faɪn / v. ❶精炼；提纯：~ crude oil into various petroleum products 将原油炼制成各种石油产品 同 purify ❷使文雅；使精美：~ one's language 使语言更文雅同 perfect 派 refined adj.; refinement n.

reflect / rɪ'flekt / v. ❶（指表面）反射（光、热、声等）；（指镜子）映出影像：The mirror ~s

her face. 镜子映出她的脸。同 mirror 反 absorb, keep ❷思考；考虑：She sat there, ~ing on a certain problem. 她坐在那儿思考某个问题。／You should ~ before you do anything. 做任何事之前，你都应该考虑一下。同 think, consider

reflection / rɪ'flekʃn / n. ❶[U] 反射：~ of heat 热的反射 ❷[C] 影像；倒影：~ in the mirror 在镜中的影像／It is difficult to draw the ~ of trees in the water. 画树在水中的倒影是不容易做到的。同 image, view ❸[U] 考虑；思考：She sat there, lost in ~. 她坐在那儿，陷入沉思。同 thought, consideration 派 reflectional adj.

reflexive / rɪ'fleksɪv / Ⅰ adj. ❶（动词）后接反身代词的；（代词）反身的：a ~ pronoun 反身代词 ❷（本能）反应的：a ~ act of self-preservation 自我保护的本能反应 Ⅱ n. [C] 反身代词；反身动词

reform / rɪ'fɔːm / Ⅰ v. ❶改革；改进；改良；改善：~ tools 改良工具／We think it necessary to ~ the economic management system. 我们认为有必要改革经济管理体制。同 correct, improve ❷重新形成 Ⅱ n. 改革；改良：carry out the economic ~ 进行经济改革／the policy of ~ and opening to the outside world 改革开放政策 同 correction, improvement 派 reformatory adj.

reformation / ˌrefə'meɪʃn / n. [U]（社会、政治及宗教事务上的）革新

refraction / rɪ'frækʃn / n. [U] 折射：~ of light-beam 光束折射

refrain / rɪ'freɪn / v. 抑制；忍住 同 avoid 反 continue, persist

refresh / rɪ'freʃ / v. 使恢复；使振作：~ oneself with a cup of tea 喝杯茶以提神 同 renew, restore

refresher / rɪ'freʃə / n. [C] 提神物；提神饮料

refreshment / rɪ'freʃmənt / n. ❶[U]（精神的）恢复 ❷（常用 pl.）点心；零食 同 food, drink

refrigerate / rɪ'frɪdʒəreɪt / vt. 使冷却；冷冻；冷藏

refrigeration / rɪˌfrɪdʒə'reɪʃn / n. 冷藏；冷冻

refrigerator / rɪ'frɪdʒəreɪtə(r) / n. [C] 冰箱；冷冻库

refuge / ˈrefjuːdʒ / Ⅰ n. 庇护；避难；避难所：seek ～ from the floods 躲避洪水 同 protection, shelter 反 exposure, danger Ⅱ vi. 避难；逃难 同 shelter

refugee / ˌrefjuˈdʒiː / n. [C]避难者；流亡者；难民：～ camps 难民营

refund / ˈriːfʌnd / Ⅰ vt. 退还；偿还：The shop ～ed the purchase price to the customer. 商店把货款退还给了顾客。同 repay, return Ⅱ n. 退还；偿还：demand a ～ 要求退款

refusal / rɪˈfjuːzl / n. 拒绝：He met with a flat ～. 他遭到断然拒绝。同 denial, rejection 反 acceptance

refuse[1] / rɪˈfjuːz / v. 拒绝；不愿接受：～ a gift 拒收礼物 / Lei Feng never ～d to help others. 雷锋从不拒绝帮助别人。/ You should ～ his unreasonable request. 你应该拒绝他的不合理要求。同 deny, reject 反 accept, agree

refuse[2] / ˈrefjuːs / n. [U]垃圾；废物：a heap of ～ 一堆垃圾 同 rubbish, waste

regain / rɪˈɡeɪn / vt. 恢复；复得；回收：～ one's freedom 重获自由 同 recover, repossess

regard / rɪˈɡɑːd / Ⅰ vt. ❶视为；认作：～ ... as ... 认为…是…；把…看作…；～ sb. as a hero 视某人为英雄 / Abraham Lincoln is ～ed as one of the greatest Presidents of America. 亚伯拉罕·林肯被人们认为是美国最伟大的总统之一。同 consider, believe 反 disregard ❷尊重；敬重 同 respect 反 disregard, despise ❸注视；留意 同 notice, observe 反 disregard, ignore Ⅱ n. ❶[U]注意；关心；考虑：He has very little ～ for the feelings of others. 他不大考虑别人的感受。同 thought, care ❷(pl.)问候；致意：Please give my kind ～s to your brother. 请代我向你的哥哥问候。/ as ～s 关于；至于：As ～s films, we are too busy to see. 至于电影，我们太忙没时间去看。派 regardful adj.

regarding / rɪˈɡɑːdɪŋ / prep. 关于：Do you have any suggestions ～ the new project? 对于那个新项目，你有什么建议？同 about

regardless / rɪˈɡɑːdləs / adj. 不重视的；不注意的：～ of 不顾；不管：～ of expense 不考虑费用 同 careless, mindless 反 careful, regardful

regenerate Ⅰ / rɪˈdʒenəreɪt / vt. ❶使(精神上)获得新生；使重生；使悔悟 ❷革新；重建；

复兴：The city was soon ～d after the earthquake. 这座城市在地震后很快就完成了重建。❸使(丢失或受伤的器官)重新产生：A lizard can ～ its tail. 蜥蜴的尾巴可以再生。—vi. 再生：Tissue ～s after skin in scratched. 皮肤划伤后组织会再生。Ⅱ / rɪˈdʒenərɪt / adj. ❶(精神上)新生的，重生的 ❷革新的，改造过的 派 regeneration n.

regime / reɪˈʒiːm / n. [C] ❶政体；政治制度；统治：～ of centralism 中央集权统治 ❷特定的政权；特定政权的统治期

region / ˈriːdʒən / n. [C] ❶地方；区域：the Arctic ～s 北极地区 / the forest ～ 林区 同 area, district ❷领域；界：the ～ of literature 文学领域 同 field, sphere

regional / ˈriːdʒənl / adj. ❶地区性的，整个地区的：a ～ library 地区性图书馆 ❷区域的，地方的：a ～ accent 地方口音 派 regionally adv.

register / ˈredʒɪstə(r) / Ⅰ n. [C]记录；名单；登记簿 同 record Ⅱ v. 记录；登记；注册：I want to ～ this letter. 我这封信寄挂号。同 enroll, record / ～ with 向…登记；向…注册：You must ～ your car with the police. 你必须向警方登记你的汽车。

regret / rɪˈɡret / Ⅰ v. (-gretted;-gretting)为…感到遗憾；抱歉；悔恨；惋惜：～ doing sth. 后悔做过某事：He soon began to ～ having run away from home. 他很快就开始后悔不该从家里出走。/ I ～ being unable to help. 我不能帮忙，感到甚为抱歉。Ⅱ n. ❶[U]惋惜；懊悔；抱歉：Much to my ～, I am unable to accept your kind invitation. 我不能接受你的盛情邀请，深感抱歉。同 disappointment, shame 反 satisfaction, pleasure ❷(pl.)歉意：Please accept my ～s at having to refuse. 不能奉约，谨致歉意。派 regretful adj.; regretfully adv.

用法

regret 后接不定式表示"后悔要干某事"，后接动名词表示"后悔干过某事"：I regret to have to trouble you again. 很抱歉，我又得麻烦你。I regret having troubled you again. 我对再一次麻烦了你，深感遗憾。

regrettable / rɪˈɡretəbl / adj. 可惜的；不幸的：～ failure 不幸的失败 同 sorry, sorrowful 反 cheerful, happy 派 regrettably adv.

regular / ˈreɡjələ(r) / *adj.* ❶有规律的;定期的;经常的:～ customers 老主顾 / ～ education 正规教育 / ～ income 固定收入 / ～ people 生活有规律的人们 同 habitual, frequent 反 irregular, rare ❷对称的 ❸(语法)(动词、名词等)变化有规则的:The verb "go" is not ～. 动词"go"的变化不规则。派 regularly *adv.*

regulate / ˈreɡjuleɪt / *vt.* 管理;使遵守规则;规范:～ one's conduct 规范某人的行为 / ～ the traffic 管制交通 同 manage, control

regulation / ˌreɡjuˈleɪʃn / *n.* ❶[U]管理;控制 同 management, control ❷[C]规则;规定;法令;命令:safety ～s 安全条例 / road ～s 道路(交通)规则 同 law, order

rehabilitate / ˌriː(h)əˈbɪlɪteɪt / *vt.* ❶使康复;使恢复原状:exercises for rehabilitating damaged knees 使受伤的膝盖得到康复的活动 ❷恢复…的名誉(或职位、功能等):～ a witness 恢复证人的名誉 / ～ victims by the million 为上百万名受害者平反

rehearse / rɪˈhɜːs / *vt.* 排练;排演;练习:When will you ～ the play again? 你什么时候再排演这出戏? 同 prepare, practise 派 rehearsal *n.*

reign / reɪn / Ⅰ *n.* [C](君主的)统治时期,在位期,执政期 Ⅱ *vi.* ❶统治,执政:The queen ～ed over her subjects for 45 years. 女王对其臣民统治了 45 年。❷当主管;主宰;权配:Let peace ～ over all. 让和平主宰一切。

rein / reɪn / Ⅰ *n.* [C] ❶缰绳 ❷(*pl.*)统治权;支配权;制约手段:hold the ～s of power 驾驭权力 / the ～ s of government 管理权 / give (free) ～ to 放任,对…完全放权:The proposals give farmers more ～ to plant what they want. 这些提议让农民更自由地去种植他们想种植的东西。keep a tight ～ on 对…严加约束;严格控制 Ⅱ *vt.*(用缰绳)勒住(马)

reinforce / ˌriːɪnˈfɔːs / *vt.* 增援;增强:The lawyer ～d his argument with new facts. 律师以新的事实增强自己论点的力度。同 strengthen, support 反 undermine, weaken 派 reinforcement *n.*

reiterate / riːˈɪtəreɪt / *v.* 重申,重述;反复做:He ～d that this sort of behaviour was a major problem. 他一再说这种行为是主要问题。

reject / rɪˈdʒekt / *vt.* ❶抛开;丢弃 同 dismiss ❷拒绝;不接受:～ an offer of help 拒绝接受

帮助 同 decline, refuse 派 rejection *n.*

reject 指拒绝接受没有价值的意见或不恰当的请求:The idea that the earth is flat was rejected centuries ago. 地球是平面的看法在数个世纪之前就被否定了。**decline** 指礼貌地拒绝别人的邀请或提供的帮助,或指在正式场合下拒绝做某事:She declined the invitation to a dinner party. 她谢绝了参加宴会的邀请。The witness declined to answer certain questions put to him. 证人拒绝回答向他提出的某些问题。**refuse** 指坚决甚至粗暴地拒绝做某事,或指不同意某人的请求:The employers refused to recognize the union. 雇主们拒绝承认工会。

rejoice / rɪˈdʒɔɪs / *vt.* 欣喜;高兴;快乐:We ～ to see that you have come back. 看到你回来,我们很高兴。同 delight, joy 反 grieve

relate / rɪˈleɪt / *v.* ❶讲,说(故事等);叙述(事实等):He ～d to his wife some amusing stories about his employer. 他对妻子述说有关他雇主的一些趣事。同 tell, report ❷有联系;有关系;涉及:We must ～ the conclusion with the facts. 我们必须将结论和事实联系起来。/ It is difficult to ～ these results with (to) any known cause. 很难将这些结果与任何已知的原因联系在一起。/ She is a girl who notices nothing except what ～s to herself. 她是一个对一切都漠不关心而只关心自己的女孩。同 connect, refer

related / rɪˈleɪtɪd / *adj.* ❶有关的;关联的;相关的:On most versions of this theory, these many worlds are not causally ～. 按这一理论的大多数说法,这许多的领域没有因果联系。/ The project asks a number of ～ questions. 这一计划提出了许多相关的问题。❷有族系(或血缘、姻亲)关系的:I'm ～ to the guy. 我与那个家伙是亲戚。

relation / rɪˈleɪʃn / *n.* ❶叙述;故事 同 narration, report ❷联系;关系:the ～ between mother and child 母子(女)关系 同 connection, reference / in (with) ～ to 关于;涉及:I have a lot to say in ～ to English study. 关于英语学习,我有很多话要说。❸(通常用 *pl.*)(国家间)交往,关系:public ～s 公共关系 / the friendly ～s between my country and yours 贵国与我国间的友好关系 ❹亲戚;亲属:He is a near ～ of mine. 他是我的一个近亲。同 relative

辨析

relation 和 **relative** 在指具体意义的"亲属""亲戚"时，互换通用；在指抽象意义的"亲属关系"时，用 relation，不可用 relative；He is a relative（relation）of mine on the maternal side. 他是我的母系亲属。What relation is she to you? 她跟你有什么亲戚关系？

relationship / rɪˈleɪʃnʃɪp / n. [C]关系；联系：the ～ between the two countries 两国之间的关系 / the ～ between supply and demand 供需关系 / teacher-student ～ 师生关系

relative / ˈrelɪtɪv / Ⅰ adj. ❶比较的；相对的：They are living in ～ comfort. 他们现在生活得比较舒服。同 comparative 反 absolute ❷关于(与 to 连用)：the facts ～ to this problem 与此问题有关的事实 同 related,connected 反 unrelated ❸(语法) the ～ pronoun 关系代词 / the ～ adverb 关系副词 Ⅱ n. [C]亲戚；亲属：She wanted to receive letters from her ～s when she was studying abroad. 她在国外学习的时候，很想收到亲属们的来信。同 family, relation 派 relatively adv.

relativity / ˌrelaˈtɪvəti / n. [U]❶相互依存 ❷(物理)相对论：the general theory of ～ 广义相对论 / the special theory of ～ 狭义相对论

relax / rɪˈlæks / v. (使)松弛；(使)放松；(使)松懈：～ the muscles 松弛肌肉 / ～ discipline 放松纪律 同 ease,loosen 反 tighten

relaxation / ˌriːlækˈseɪʃn / n. ❶松弛 同 ease, loosening ❷消遣：Fishing and mountain-climbing are his favourite ～s. 垂钓和爬山是他最爱好的消遣活动。同 amusement

release / rɪˈliːs / vt. 放行；释放；免除；解开：be ～d to the press 发布给新闻界 / be ～d from debt 还清债务 / ～ a man from prison 从监狱释放某人 同 free,loose 反 keep,fasten

relevant / ˈreləvənt / adj. 有关的；相应的：What he said is ～ to the question we are discussing. 他所讲的与我们正在讨论的问题有关。同 related,connected 反 irrelevant

reliability / rɪˌlaɪəˈbɪləti / n. [U]可靠性 同 responsibility,truth

reliable / rɪˈlaɪəbl / adj. 可靠的；可信赖的 同 dependable, responsible 反 unreliable, undependable

reliance / rɪˈlaɪəns / n. [U]信任，信赖；信心；依靠：We should place ～ on the strength of the masses. 我们应该依靠群众的力量。同 trust,confidence 反 distrust

relic / ˈrelɪk / n. [C]纪念物；文物；遗俗；遗物 同 remains

relief / rɪˈliːf / n. ❶减轻；解除：The doctor's treatment gave（brought）some ～. 医生的治疗使病情有所缓解。同 ease, remedy 反 anxiety,upset ❷帮助；救济；救济物：provide relief for refugees 赈济难民 同 assistance,support

relieve / rɪˈliːv / vt. 救济；救助；援助；减轻或解除(痛苦)：～ one's feelings 发泄感情 / ～ one's mind 解除某人的忧虑 / The fund is for relieving distress among the flood victims. 这基金是用于赈济水灾灾民的。/ Let me ～ you of your suitcase. 让我替你拿这个手提箱。同 assist,comfort 反 burden,discomfort

relieved / rɪˈliːvd / adj. 宽慰的，宽心的，放心的：He was very ～ when his life recovered. 他妻子痊愈后他甚感宽慰。/ We were ～ to hear the news. 听到这则消息后，我们就宽心了。

religion / rɪˈlɪdʒən / n. ❶[C]宗教 ❷[U]宗教信仰 同 faith,belief

religious / rɪˈlɪdʒəs / adj. ❶宗教的；宗教方面的 ❷(指人)虔诚的，敬畏神的 同 faithful,devotional 反 irreligious

relinquish / rɪˈlɪŋkwɪʃ / vt. ❶放弃(权利、财产、要求等)：～ a claim 放弃索赔 / ～ music as a profession 放弃专业音乐工作 ❷放松，松开：He slowly ～ed his hold on the rope. 他慢慢地松开了紧搂着的绳索。

relish / ˈrelɪʃ / Ⅰ n. [C;U]❶喜好，爱好，兴趣，兴致：have a ～ for fast driving 喜欢开快车 / eat with great ～ 津津有味地吃东西 ❷作料，佐料，调料，调味品：spicy ～es 香辣调料 Ⅱ vt. 对…感兴趣，喜欢，爱好：His war films were critically applauded as well as ～ed by the multitude. 他的战争影片不但为大众喜欢，还受到评论界的赞誉。/ He ～ed telling such jokes. 他喜欢说这一类笑话。

reluctant / rɪˈlʌktənt / adj. 不情愿的；勉强的：He was ～ to go with me. 他不愿意跟我一道去。同 unwilling 反 willing,eager

rely / rɪˈlaɪ / vi. 信赖；依靠(与 on 或 upon 连用)：Don't ～ on others；～ on yourself. 别靠他人，要靠你自己。/ He can always be relied upon. 他是永远可信赖的。同 depend,reckon

remain /rɪ'meɪn/ *vi.* ❶剩下；遗留：After the fire, very little ～ed of my house. 火烧后，寒舍所剩无几。同 last，survive 反 disappear，die ❷依然存在；继续存在；保持：He ～ed silent. 他保持沉默。同 stay，continue 反 go，leave

remainder /rɪ'meɪndə(r)/ *n.* ❶剩余物：Twenty people came in and the ～ stayed outside. 20 个人进来了，余者留在外面。Can the ～ of the food do for next meal? 剩下的食物还够下顿吃吗？ ❷[C] 余数：Take five from twenty and the ～ is fifteen. 20 减 5，余数是 15。

remains /rɪ'meɪnz/ *n.* 残余；余额；遗体；废墟；遗迹：Here is the ～ of a temple. 这里是一座寺庙的遗迹。同 relics，body

remark /rɪ'mɑːk/ Ⅰ *n.* ❶[C] 评论；谈话：make a few ～ s 说几句话；作短评 同 comment，statement ❷[U] 注意：There was nothing worthy of ～ at the Flower Show. 花展中没有值得一看的花。同 notice，attention Ⅱ *v.* ❶谈起；述及；评论（与 on 或 upon 连用）：～ behind sb.'s back 在背后议论／～ on other's shortcoming 议论别人的缺点／He ～ed that he would be absent the next day. 他谈到他次日不来出席。／It would be rude to ～ upon her appearance. 谈论她的外表是不礼貌的。同 comment，state ❷注意：Did you ～ the similarity between them? 你注意到他们之间的相似之处吗？同 notice，observe

remarkable /rɪ'mɑːkəbl/ *adj.* 不平常的；值得注意的：a ～ event 不平常的事件／They have made ～ achievements in their research work. 他们在研究工作中取得了显著成就。同 extraordinary，unusual 反 ordinary，usual／be ～ for 以…著称：The boy is ～ for his courage. 那个男孩以勇敢著称。派 remarkably *adv.*

remedial /rɪ'miːdɪəl/ *adj.* ❶治疗的；治疗上的：a ～ schema 治疗方案 ❷补习的：a ～ course 补习课程／a ～ class 补习班 ❸补救的；弥补性的：take ～ measures 采取补救措施

remedy /'remədi/ Ⅰ *n.* ❶补救办法；纠正法：Your only ～ is to go to law. 你的唯一补救办法是求助于法律。同 assistance，relief ❷治疗；治疗法；药物：effective ～ 有效的药物／This is a good ～ for colds. 这是治疗感冒的良药。同 treatment，medicine Ⅱ *vt.* ❶补救；

纠正：It is necessary for you to ～ the fault. 你必须纠正错误。同 correct，repair ❷治疗；医治 同 treat，cure

remember /rɪ'membə(r)/ *vt.* ❶记得；想起：I ～ having heard you speak on that subject. 我记得听你谈论过那题目。／～ doing sth. 记得做过某事：I ～ having read the novel. 我记得曾经读过这本小说。／～ to do sth. 记住要做某事：Please ～ to call me this afternoon. 请记住今天下午给我打电话。／Remember to turn off the lights before you leave. 记住离开以前要关灯。同 recall，keep in mind 反 forget，ignore ❷（向某人）问候，致意（与介词 to 连用）：Please ～ me to your father. 请代我向您父亲问好。

remind /rɪ'maɪnd/ *vt.* 使某人想起；提醒某人：Please ～ me to phone her on time. 请提醒我准时给她打电话。／Remind the mayor that the visitor is waiting for him outside his office. 提醒市长，来访者正在他的办公室外面等他。／～ sb. of 提醒；使记起；使想起：If I forget, please ～ me of it. 如果我忘了这事，请提醒我。／The old lady ～s me of my grandmother. 看见那老太太，我就想起了我的祖母。

remiss /rɪ'mɪs/ *adj.* 玩忽职守的；疏忽的：be ～ in one's duties 玩忽职守／It was ～ of you to forget to bring your textbook. 你忘带课本来上课，真是粗心。

remit /rɪ'mɪt/ *vt.* 汇寄（钱或支票等），汇（款）：Please ～ balance due us. 请将欠我方的余额汇来。

remnant /'remnənt/ *n.* [C] ❶剩余（物）；残余（物）；遗留物：～s of a meal 残羹剩饭／a defeated ～ 残兵败将 ❷遗存，遗迹；遗风：～s of the city's glory 这座城市昔日繁荣的遗迹

remote /rɪ'məʊt/ *adj.* 遥远的；边远的；偏僻的；疏远的：～ control 遥控／the ～ age 遥远的时代／a ～ mountain village 边远的山村 同 distant，isolated 反 close，nearby

removable /rɪ'muːvəbl/ *adj.* 可移动的；可除去的 同 transferable

removal /rɪ'muːvl/ *n.* 移动；除去；移居 同 movement，transfer

remove /rɪ'muːv/ *vt.* 移动；除去：～ a boy from school for his bad health 因健康不佳让男孩休学／～ doubts 消除疑虑 同 move，transfer

renew / rɪˈnjuː / v. ❶再做;再说;再给:～ a book 续借一本书/ ～ one's complaints 重新投诉 同 refresh, restate ❷更新;(使)恢复原状:～ one's youth 恢复青春 同 continue 反 discontinue

rent / rent / Ⅰ n. (土地、建筑物等的)定期租金;租金总额:owe three weeks' ～ for one's house 欠三个星期的房租 / collect the ～s 收租 同 fee, payment Ⅱ v. 租用,出租(土地、房屋等):Mr. Hill ～s this land to us at £500 a year. 希尔先生把这块土地租给我们,每年租金 500 英镑。同 hire, lease

repair / rɪˈpeə(r) / Ⅰ vt. 修补;修理:～ a watch (road) 修表(修路) 同 fix, mend 反 destroy, ruin Ⅱ n. 修理;补救 同 improvement, adjustment / **beyond** ～ 无法修理:The TV set is broken beyond ～. 这电视机坏得无法修了。/ **under** ～ 在修理中:The road is under ～. 这条路正在修建中。

repay / rɪˈpeɪ / v. (repaid /rɪˈpeɪd/, repaid) ❶付还:If you lend me £50, I'll ～ you next week. 你若借 50 英镑给我,我下星期就还你。同 return, refund ❷报答;回报(与 for 连用):～ sb. for his kindness 报答某人的恩惠 同 compensate, reward 派 repayment n.

repeal / rɪˈpiːl / Ⅰ vt. 撤销(决议等);废除(法令等) 同 cancel, abolish 反 reestablish, confirm Ⅱ n. 撤销;废除 同 cancellation, abolition 反 reestablishment, confirmation

repeat / rɪˈpiːt / v. 重复;重说;重做:Please ～ what I said. 请复述我说的话。同 restate, redo

repeatedly / rɪˈpiːtɪdli / adv. 反复地;再三地 同 again, frequently

repel / rɪˈpel / (-pelled; -pelling) vt. ❶击退;逐退:The foul air of the house almost ～led me. 屋子里臭气扑鼻,我差点退了回来。/The army ～led the invaders. 部队击退了入侵者。❷与…不相融:Water and oil ～ each other. 油水不相融。❸抵拒;抗御:This coat ～s rain. 这件衣服能防雨。❹排斥,相斥:Electrical charges of a similar kind ～ each other and those that are dissimilar attract. 电荷同性相斥,异性相吸。

repetition / ˌrepəˈtɪʃn / n. 重复说;重做:Any ～ of the mistake will be punished. 再犯这种错误就会受惩罚。同 retelling, restatement

replace / rɪˈpleɪs / vt. ❶取代;替换:I don't

think television will ～ movie. 我认为电视不会取代电影。同 substitute ❷把…放回原处:Please ～ the books on the shelf after reading. 阅读后请把书放回书架。同 return 派 replacement n.

replay Ⅰ / riːˈpleɪ / vt. ❶重放(电影、录音等);重演;重奏 ❷重新举行(比赛) Ⅱ / ˈriːpleɪ / n. [C] ❶(录音等的)重播;(电影、像等的)重放;重演;重奏 ❷重赛

replicate / ˈreplɪkeɪt / v. ❶重复做;反复做:～ a chemical experiment 重复做一个化学实验 ❷复制:The virus can ～ itself. 这种病毒可以自我复制。

reply / rɪˈplaɪ / Ⅰ v. 回答;答复:Please ～ at your earliest convenience. 请尽早答复。同 answer, respond 反 ask, demand Ⅱ n. [C] 回答;答复:When can you give me a ～? 你什么时候可以给我一个答复? 同 answer, response 反 question, request / **in** ～ **to** 作为对…的答复:We sent her an interesting novel in ～ to her kindness. 我们送给她一本有趣的小说,作为对她的友好的答谢。

report / rɪˈpɔːt / Ⅰ v. ❶报道(所见或所闻):The discovery of a new planet has been ～ed. 据报道已发现一颗新行星。同 announce, communicate / **it is (was)** ～**ed that ...** 据报道…:It is ～ed that their experiment has succeeded. 据报道他们的实验成功了。❷报到:You must ～ yourself to the school tomorrow. 明天你得到学校报到。同 appear, present Ⅱ n. 报道;报告;记事:an annual ～ 年度报告 同 announcement, record

repository / rɪˈpɒzɪtəri / n. [C] ❶储藏室;存放处;仓库:a vast ～ for digital information 数字信息的巨大仓库 ❷宝库:A book is a ～ of wisdom, mystery, and truth. 书籍乃智慧、奥秘和真理的宝库。

represent / ˌreprɪˈzent / vt. ❶代表:We chose a committee to ～ us. 我们选出一个委员会来代表我们。❷表示;象征:说明 同 mean, symbolize ❸表现;描绘;说成 同 show, describe

representative / ˌreprɪˈzentətɪv / Ⅰ adj. 有代表性的;典型的:The exhibition is ～ of modern Chinese science. 这个展览会代表了现代中国科学。同 symbolic, characteristic Ⅱ n. [C] 代表;代理人:a ～ of the people 人民代表 / a diplomatic ～ 外交代表 / House of Representatives (美国)众议院 同 agent, delegate

reproach / rɪˈprəʊtʃ / I *vt.* 责备;指摘;斥责,申斥;谴责;非难:She had not even ～ed him for breaking his promise. 她甚至对他的不守信用未加责备。II *n.* [U]指摘;训斥;责备:He looked at her with ～. 他满眼责备地看着她。

reproduce / ˌriːprəˈdjuːs / *v.* ❶繁殖;生殖:The plant ～s by seeds. 这种植物靠种子繁殖。同 breed ❷复制;再上演;仿造:The painting is ～d from a magazine. 这幅画从杂志上复制而来。同 duplicate,copy

reproduction / ˌriːprəˈdʌkʃn / *n.* 再生;繁殖;复制;仿制品 同 breeding,duplicate

reprove / rɪˈpruːv / *vt.* 责备,责骂,指责:His father ～d him for his idleness. 他因无所事事而被其父责骂。/He was ～d by the teacher for not finishing the homework in time. 他没有及时完成家庭作业,因而受到老师责备。

reptile / ˈreptaɪl / *n.* [C]爬行动物;(口语)两栖动物

republic / rɪˈpʌblɪk / *n.* [C]共和国:the People's Republic of China 中华人民共和国 派 republican *adj.*

repulse / rɪˈpʌls / *vt.* ❶击退;驱退,赶走:～ an assault 击退进攻/The enemy was ～d. 敌人被击退了。❷拒绝,回绝:They coldly ～d our offers of friendship. 他们冷淡地拒绝了我们友好的表示。

reputation / ˌrepjuˈteɪʃn / *n.* [U]名誉;名声;名望:live up to one's ～ 名副其实 / have a ～ for 以…而闻名 同 fame

request / rɪˈkwest / I *n.* ❶[U]请求:We came at your ～. 我们应你的请求而来。同 demand,asking ❷[C]所求之物:All my ～s were granted. 我所请求的事全被允许了。II *v.* 请求;邀请:Visitors are ～ed not to touch the exhibits. 请观众勿触摸展览品。同 appeal,invite

用法
❶request 一般不用在口语里。❷request 用作名词时,后面接介词 for;a request for help 要求援助;用作动词时是及物动词,后面不能接 for:He requested help. 他要求援助。❸request 后面不可接宾语加 for,如不可说:We requested them for help. ❹request 后可直接接 that 从句,不可接宾语加 that 从句,如不可说:I requested him that he should help me.

require / rɪˈkwaɪə(r) / *vt.* ❶需要:We ～ extra help. 我们需要额外的帮助。同 need,want ❷命令;要求:～d courses 必修课程/They ～d me to keep silent. 他们吩咐我不要作声。同 order,demand 派 requirement *n.*

用法
❶require 后可以接①名词:Since he was involved in the case, the court required his appearance. 由于他和案件有牵连,法院要求他出庭。②名词＋不定式:The university requires all the students to take the physical training course for two years. 学校要求所有学生修两年体育课。③that 从句,从句用虚拟语气,即谓语动词用动词原形或 should＋动词原形:The progress in industry requires that we (should) produce more iron and steel. 工业的发展要求我们生产更多的钢铁。④sth. of sb.:What do you require of me? 你对我有何要求? ❷require 在表示"需要"时,后面用动名词主动形式表示被动意思,也可用不定式被动形式:The whole place requires cleaning (to be cleaned). 整个地方都需要打扫。

rescue / ˈreskjuː / I *vt.* 援救,解救;使免于:～ a man from bandits 从土匪手中救出一个人 同 save,release II *n.* 援救;解救:come (go) to the ～ 援救 / to sb.'s ～ 救助某人 同 release,recovery

research / rɪˈsɜːtʃ / I *n.* 研究;调查;探索:carry out ～es into the causes of a certain cancer 对某种癌症的起因进行研究 同 study,investigation II *vi.* 研究;探索;调查 同 study,investigate

用法
research 后面可接介词 into 或 on,指抽象的东西多用 into,指具体的东西多用 on:her research into Latin literature 她对拉丁文学的研究;their research on guided missiles 他们对导弹的研究。

resemblance / rɪˈzembləns / *n.* 相似;相似性;相似点 同 likeness,similarity 反 difference,unlikeness

resemble / rɪˈzembl / *vt.* 相似;类似:They ～ each other in shape but not in colour. 它们的形状相似,但颜色不同。同 parallel

resent / rɪˈzent / *vt.* 对…不满;怨恨:I ～ the man's deeds. 我对那人的行为不满。同 dislike 反 like, approve 派 resentful *adj.*; resentment *n.*

R

resent 后接动名词，不接不定式；He resents being called a fool. 他对别人叫他傻瓜感到愤恨。

reservation / ˌrezəˈveɪʃn / n. ❶保留；I accept your suggestion without any ～. 我毫无保留地接受你的建议。同 reserve, preserve ❷预定；预约；She made a ～ with her dentist at ten tomorrow. 她跟牙医预约的时间是明天10点钟。同 booking

reserve / rɪˈzɜːv / Ⅰ vt. ❶保留；留存；All rights of the book are ～d. 此书保留版权。/ The first row is ～d for our guests. 第一排座位留给我们的客人坐。同 keep, store ❷预订；You'd better ～ some seats in the theatre. 你最好在剧院预订一些座位。同 book, schedule Ⅱ n. ❶[C]储备；储备物；后备人员；～ of food 食物储备／～ of foreign exchange 外汇储备 ❷保留；with ～ 附带条件地；有保留(顾虑)地；speak with ～ 说话谨慎 without ～ 无条件(保留)地；不客气；坦率地；accept the conditions without ～ 无保留地接受这些条件 ❸特别保留地；保护区；禁猎区；a forest ～ 保护林／a game ～ 禁猎区

reservoir / ˈrezəvwɑː(r) / n. [C]水库；贮水池

reside / rɪˈzaɪd / vi. 居住；驻扎 同 live, inhabit

residence / ˈrezɪdəns / n. 居住；驻扎；住处；住宅；country ～ 乡村住宅／official ～ 官邸／The foreign visitors took ～ in downtown. 外国客人们在市中心下榻。同 house, home

resident / ˈrezɪdənt / n. [C]居民 同 citizen, dweller

residential / ˌrezɪˈdenʃ(ə)l / adj. 居住的；住所的，住房的，locate in a ～ district 位于住宅区／multi-functional commercial and ～ complex 多功能商住区

resign / rɪˈzaɪn / v. ❶放弃；辞去；辞职；Why did you ～ your right? 你为什么放弃你的权利？/ He has ～ed his position as a sales manager. 他已辞去销售经理的职位。同 abandon, quit ❷听从；顺从；It will not do to ～ oneself to fate. 听天由命是不行的。同 reconcile, submit 派 resignation n.

resist / rɪˈzɪst / v. 抵抗；对抗；～ an attack 抵抗攻击 同 fight, oppose 反 yield, submit to

resistance / rɪˈzɪstəns / n. [U] ❶抵抗；抵抗力；

break down the enemy's ～ 粉碎敌人的抵抗 ❷阻力；An aircraft has to overcome the ～ of the air. 飞机必须克服空气的阻力。

resolute / ˈrezəluːt / adj. 有决心的；坚决的；决断的；We are ～ for victory. 我们决心要取得胜利。同 constant, firm 反 weak, feeble

resolution / ˌrezəˈluːʃn / n. ❶[C]决定；决议；adopt (pass) a ～ 通过决议 同 decision, judgement ❷[U]决心；决意；take firm ～ to do sth. 决心做某事 同 determination, intention ❸解决；解答 同 solution, explanation

resolve / rɪˈzɒlv / Ⅰ v. ❶决定；下决心；He ～d to succeed. 他下决心要成功。同 decide, determine ❷解决；解答；～ a contradiction 解决矛盾 同 solve, settle ❸分解；溶解；melt Ⅱ n. [C] 已决定的事；决心；This did not shake his firm ～. 此事未动摇他坚定的决心。同 resolution, determination

resolve 后面接 that 从句时，从句用虚拟语气，即谓语动词用动词原形或 should＋动词原形；We have resolved that our school (should) have a dining room. 我们已下决心在学校建一个食堂。

resort / rɪˈzɔːt / Ⅰ vi. ❶求助；诉诸(与 to 连用)；If other means fail, we shall ～ to force. 如果其他手段都失败了，我们将诉诸武力。同 employ, use ❷常去；～ to the seaside 常去海滨 Ⅱ n. ❶手段；as a last ～, in the last ～ 作为最后的手段 ❷常去之处；胜地；summer ～s 避暑胜地 ❸付诸；求助；He finished the work without ～ to others. 他没有求助别人，自己完成了工作。

resort 不论用作动词或名词，后面都接介词 to＋名词或动名词，不接不定式；He could not escape without resort to lying. 他不撒谎就没法逃掉。

resource / rɪˈsɔːs / n. [C](常用 pl.)资源；We must exploit the natural ～s of our country. 我们必须开发我国的自然资源。派 resourceful adj.

respect / rɪˈspekt / Ⅰ n. ❶[U]尊重；敬重；Children should show ～ for their teachers. 学生应尊敬老师。同 admiration, recognition 反 disrespect, contempt ❷(常用 pl.)敬意；问候；Give him my ～s. 请代我向他问好。同 regards, greetings / **hold sb. in** 〜 尊敬某人：The scholar was held in 〜. 那位学者很受人尊重。**have** 〜 **for sb.** 尊敬某人：You should have 〜 for her feelings. 你应当尊重她的感情。**in** 〜 **of(to)** 关于：In 〜 of this problem, we don't have to discuss it here. 关于这个问题，我们没有必要在这儿讨论。**pay（show）**〜 **to sb.** 尊敬某人：All of us pay 〜 to Professor Smith. 我们都很尊敬史密斯教授。**win one's** 〜 赢得某人的尊重：His sense of responsibility for work has won our 〜. 他对工作的责任感赢得了我们的尊重。**with** 〜 **to** 关于；至于：I don't want to say anything with 〜 to that problem. 关于那个问题，我什么也不想说。Ⅱ vt. 尊敬；敬重：I 〜 your opinions. 我尊重你的意见。同 admire, honor

respectable / rɪ'spektəbl / adj. 值得尊重的；可敬的：She is poor, but quite 〜. 她虽穷，但值得尊敬。同 honorable, worthy 反 dishonorable, unworthy 派 respectably adv.

respectful / rɪ'spektfl / adj. 尊敬的；尊重的（作表语）：The young should be 〜 to the old. 年轻人应该尊重老年人。同 obedient, polite 反 disrespectful, impolite

respective / rɪ'spektɪv / adj. 各自的；各个的：After the meeting we went off to our 〜 classrooms. 会后我们去各自的教室。同 individual, particular 派 respectively adv.

respire / rɪ'spaɪə(r) / vi. ❶呼吸，吸气：Fish 〜 through gills. 鱼靠腮呼吸。❷（植物等）完成呼吸作用 派 respiration n.

respond / rɪ'spɒnd / vi. 回答；答复；响应；有反应：〜 **to** 回答；对⋯作出反应：〜 to the treatment 对治疗有反应 / The class 〜ed to the suggestion with applause. 全班同学对这个提议报以掌声。同 reply, react

response / rɪ'spɒns / n. [C]回答；答复；响应；反应：In 〜 to the call of the school, all the students threw themselves in the activities of the Civil Virtues Month. 同学们响应学校号召，投入到"文明礼貌月"的活动中。同 reply, reaction

responsibility / rɪ,spɒnsə'bɪləti / n. 责任，职责；责任心；责任感：take the 〜 of education 承担教育责任 / Our monitor has a strong sense of 〜. 我们班长有很强的责任感。同 reliability, duty 反 irresponsibility

responsible / rɪ'spɒnsəbl / adj. ❶应负责任的；有责任的；**be** 〜 **(to sb.) for sth.** 应对（某人）某事负责：The pilot of the plane is 〜 for the passengers' safety. 飞机驾驶员对乘客的安全负有责任。同 liable 反 irresponsible ❷可信赖的；可靠的：give a task to a 〜 man 把工作交给可靠的人 同 dependable, reliable 反 irresponsible, unreliable

rest¹ / rest / Ⅰ vi. ❶平静；休息：We 〜ed (for) an hour. 我们休息了一个小时。同 relax, ease 反 unrest, work ❷（委婉语）长眠；安息：He 〜s in the churchyard. 他长眠于教堂墓地中。同 die, sleep ❸停止；暂停：They let the matter 〜. 他们让这事到此为止。同 halt, pause Ⅱ n. [U]休息；宁静；睡眠；**take（have）a** 〜 休息一会儿：Let's take(have) a 〜. 我们休息一会儿吧。同 relaxation, peace 反 unrest

> **用法**
> take rest 或 take one's rest 意为"就寝"，take (have) a rest 意为"休息"。

rest² / rest / n. (the 〜) 剩余；其余：Take what you want and throw the 〜 away. 把你所要的拿去，其余的可丢弃。同 remains, others

> **用法**
> the rest 作主语时，谓语动词用单数或复数视具体情况而定：I have read a large part of the book, and the rest is quite difficult. 我已看了这本书的大部分，其余部分非常难读。I have a hundred books: seventy five are in Chinese and the rest are in English. 我有100本书：75本是汉语书，其余的是英语书。The rest of her life was happy. 她晚年幸福。

restaurant / 'restərɒnt / n. [C]饭店；餐厅 同 dining-room, eating-house

restless / 'restləs / adj. 得不到休息的；不宁静的；静不下来的：〜 night 不眠之夜 / 〜 life 不平静的生活 同 sleepless, nervous 反 calm, relaxed

restore / rɪ'stɔː(r) / vt. ❶归还：〜 borrowed books 归还所借的书 同 compensate, return ❷重新采用；恢复：〜 old customs 恢复古老风俗 同 recover, rebuild ❸使恢复（健康）；复原；痊愈 同 refresh, cure 派 restoration n.

restrain / rɪ'streɪn / vt. 抑制；遏制；阻止：〜 a child from doing mischief 制止小孩胡闹 / 〜 oneself 克制自己 / 〜 tears 忍住眼泪 同 control, prevent

R

restraint / rɪ'streɪnt / n. [U]抑制；遏制；克制 圆 control，check 反 freedom，liberty

restrict / rɪ'strɪkt / vt. 限制；约束：He was ~ ed to three cigarettes a day. 他被限制每天吸三支烟。圆 confine，limit 反 broaden，free 派 restriction n.

restrictive / rɪ'strɪktɪv / adj. ❶限制的，约束的：The project is not able to continue because of ~ budget. 由于预算限制，该项目无法再继续下去。❷（字、词、短语等对修饰对象有）限制性的，起限制作用的：~ clause 限制性从句

result / rɪ'zʌlt / Ⅰ vi. 发生；产生 圆 arise，happen：~ **from** 产生于；来自于：Success ~ s from hard work. 成功是艰苦工作的结果。~ **in** 导致…的结果：Eating too much often ~s in sickness. 吃得太多常会惹出病来。Ⅱ n. 结果；效果：His limp is the ~ of an accident. 他的跛脚是一次事故的结果。圆 outcome，effect / **as a ~** 由于；因此：He has heart disease. As a ~，he cannot take part in the sports meet. 他有心脏病，因此不能参加运动会。**as a ~ of** 作为…的结果：As a ~ of the traffic jam，quite a lot of people were late. 由于交通堵塞，不少人都迟到了。**without ~** 毫无结果地：The investigation finished without ~. 调查毫无结果地结束了。

resume / rɪ'zuːm / v. 重新开始；恢复；继续：~ office 官复原职 / ~ the thread of one's discourse 言归正传 / She ~d writing three years later. 三年后她又重新开始创作。圆 proceed，continue 反 cease

résumé / 'rezjʊmeɪ，'rezæmeɪ / n. ❶摘要；概要；文摘 圆 summary，outline ❷简历；履历

retail / 'riːteɪl / Ⅰ n. [U]零售：sell by（at）~ 零售 反 wholesale Ⅱ adj. 零售的 反 wholesale

retain / rɪ'teɪn / vt. 保持；保留；保有：Our teacher ~s the style of hard work. 我们的老师保持着努力工作的作风。圆 keep，maintain 反 abandon，lose

retard / rɪ'tɑːd / vt. 延缓（或阻碍、妨碍）…的发展（或进展）：Cold may ~ the growth of bacteria. 寒冷可以延缓细菌的繁殖。

retell / ˌriː'tel / vt.（retold/ˌriː'təʊld/，retold）重述；复述：~ the text 复述课文 / The teacher asked him to ~ the story. 老师叫他复述故事。圆 recite

retire / rɪ'taɪə(r) / vi. ❶退休；退职；退役：He

will ~ on a pension at 60. 他将在 60 岁退休，退休后领养老金。圆 depart，resign ❷就寝：She usually ~s at 11 o'clock. 她通常在 11 点就寝。圆 sleep ❸退下；退却；退出：He ~ d hurt in the basketball match. 在篮球比赛中，他受伤退场。圆 retreat，withdraw

retirement / rɪ'taɪəmənt / n. 退休；退职；退役：The old professor felt busier than before after her ~. 退休后老教授感到比以前更忙了。圆 withdrawal，departure

retort / rɪ'tɔːt / v. 反击；反驳 圆 return，respond

retreat / rɪ'triːt / Ⅰ vi. 退却；撤退：force the enemy to ~ 迫使敌人退却 / ~ towards the capital 向首都撤退 圆 retire，withdraw 反 advance Ⅱ n. 退却；撤退：The army was in full ~. 全军在大撤退。圆 retirement，withdrawal 反 advance

return / rɪ'tɜːn / Ⅰ vi. 回来；归去：~ home 回家 圆 reappear 反 disappear -vt. 归还：When will you ~ the book I lent you? 你借的那本书什么时候还我？圆 restore 反 keep，retain Ⅱ n. 返回；归还：~ key（计算机的）回车键 / the ~ of spring 春之归来 / Many happy ~ s of the day.（贺生日用语）祝你长命百岁！圆 reappearance，repayment 反 departure / **in ~ for** 报答：The boy behaved well in ~ for his mother's love. 男孩表现很好，以报答他母亲对他的爱。

reunite / ˌriːjuː'naɪt / v. 再结合；重聚：~ after many years' separation 多年分离后重聚

reveal / rɪ'viːl / vt. ❶揭示；揭露；泄露：He promised not to ~ the secret to anyone. 他答应不把秘密泄露给任何人。圆 expose，uncover 反 conceal，hide ❷展现；显示：The picture ~s to us the farmers' happy life. 图画展现给我们的是农民的幸福生活。圆 display，show

revelation / ˌrevə'leɪʃn / n. ❶显露；泄露 圆 exposure，discovery ❷显示；展示 圆 display，show

revenge / rɪ'vendʒ / Ⅰ vt. 报仇；报复：~ an injustice 对不公平对待进行报复 / ~ one's friend 为朋友报仇 圆 avenge，repay Ⅱ n. [U]报仇；报复：He planned the murder out of ~. 他为报仇而策划了谋杀。/ **take（have）one's ~** 报仇 **take ~ on sb.** 为自己向某人报复

revenue / 'revənjuː / n. [U；C] ❶（国家的）岁

入；税收：sources of ～ 税收来源/the total ～
s fo the government 政府税收总额 ❷收益；收
入：business ～ 企业收入/～s from the sales
of the trees 销售木材所得的收益

reversal /rɪˈvɜːsəl/ n. ❶[U]反向；倒转 ❷[C]
（财气、运气的）逆转，恶化；背运：That's a ～of
his usual position on relations with Iraq. 他在同伊
拉克关系上所持的态度与平时截然不同。

reverse /rɪˈvɜːs/ Ⅰ vt. 颠倒；倒转；倒退：You
may ～ the procedure and begin with the last i-
tem. 你可以颠倒程序，从最后一项开始。同 o-
verturn,overthrow Ⅱ n. ❶相反；相反的情况；
Don't do the ～ of what we expect. 别做与我们
的期望相反的事。同 opposite,contrary ❷背
面；反面：the ～ of a coin 钱币的反面 同 back,
rear Ⅲ adj. 相反的；背面的；倒转的：in ～ order 以颠倒的顺序 同 opposite,contrary

review /rɪˈvjuː/ Ⅰ v. ❶回顾；复习：～ last
week's lesson 复习上星期的功课 同 reexam-
ine ❷（在报纸或期刊上）评论（作品）；Mr.
Hill ～s for The Times. 希尔先生为《泰晤士
报》写评论。同 criticize,survey Ⅱ n. ❶回顾；
复习 同 examination,study ❷评论文章；评论：
write ～s for the monthly magazine 为月刊写
书评 同 criticism,survey

revise /rɪˈvaɪz/ vt. 修订；修改；校订：～ a
plan 修改计划 同 correct,change

revision /rɪˈvɪʒn/ n. ❶[U;C]修改；修订；校
正，勘校，审校：make extensive ～作大量修订/
He made several ～s to his speech. 他多次修改
自己的演讲稿。❷[C]修订本；订正版：publish a
～ of the dictionary 出版该词典的修订版

revival /rɪˈvaɪvl/ n. ❶[U]复兴；再生；再度
流行：a ～ in consumer demand after a period
of slow business 市场一度疲软之后消费需求
的重新活跃/the ～ of old customs 旧传统的
再度盛行 ❷[U]苏醒，复活，复苏：guard a-
gainst the ～ of fascism 警惕法西斯主义复
活/stimulate an economic ～刺激经济复苏

revive /rɪˈvaɪv/ v. (使)苏醒；(使)复兴 同 refresh,renew

revolt /rɪˈvəʊlt/ Ⅰ vi. 反叛；叛乱；反抗；违抗
同 rebel,resist 反 submit Ⅱ n. 叛乱；违抗，反
rebellion,revolution 反 submission

revolution /ˌrevəˈluːʃn/ n. (情况、方式等)彻
底改变；革命 同 revolt,uprising

revolutionary /ˌrevəˈluːʃənəri/ Ⅰadj. 革命的；

革新的；～ cause 革命事业/～ spirit 革命精神
同 rebel,radical Ⅱ n. [C]革命者；革命家：A ～
would rather die on his feet than live on his
knees. 一个革命者宁愿站着死，也不愿跪着生。

revolve /rɪˈvɒlv/ v. (使)旋转：The earth ～s
on its own axis once every 24 hours. 地球每
24 小时绕自己的轴旋转一周。同 rotate,spin

reward /rɪˈwɔːd/ Ⅰ n. ❶[U]报酬；报答：get
very little in ～ for one's hard work 辛苦工作得
到的报酬却很少 同 prize,pay 反 penalty,punish-
ment ❷[C]酬金；赏金：offer a ～ of £100 for
information about a stolen necklace 悬赏 100 英
镑以求获得被盗项链的消息 同 fee,tip Ⅱ v. 报
答；报偿；酬谢：Is that how you ～ me for my
help? 那就是你因为我的帮忙而给我的报答
吗? 同 compensate,pay 反 punish

rewrite /ˌriːˈraɪt/ vt. (rewrote/ˌriːˈrəʊt/, rewrit-
ten/ˈriːˈrɪtn/)再写；重写

rhyme /raɪm/ n. ❶[U]韵；押韵 ❷[C]有韵
的诗；韵文

rhythm /ˈrɪðəm/ n. 韵律；节奏 派 rhythmic
(al) adj.

rib /rɪb/ n. 排骨；肋骨

ribbon /ˈrɪbən/ n. [C]缎带；丝带；带状物：
cut the ～ 剪彩

rice /raɪs/ n. [U]稻；大米

rich /rɪtʃ/ adj. ❶有钱的；富裕的：the ～ and
the poor 富人和穷人 同 wealthy 反 poor,needy
❷富饶的；丰富的；China is ～ in natural resources. 中国有丰富的自然资源。/ She is ～
in love for children. 她对孩子们充满爱心。同
full,abundant 反 rare,lacking ❸盛产的；肥沃
的：a ～ harvest 大丰收 同 fertile, productive
反 unfertile,unproductive 派 richly adv.；rich-
ness n.

riches /ˈrɪtʃɪz/ n. 财产；财富；富有：amass
great ～ 聚敛大量财富 同 wealth,fortune

rid /rɪd/ vt. (rid 或 ridded；rid 或 ridded；rid-
ding)使获自由；解除；免除：It is not easy to
～ a bad habit. 改掉恶习是不容易的。同
free,liberate 反 burden /n/ get (be) ～ of 摆脱；
去掉；get ～ of fear 摆脱恐惧 / You must get
～ of the bad habit of getting up late. 你得改
掉晚起的坏毛病。

riddle /ˈrɪdl/ n. [C]谜；谜语：guess a ～ 猜谜
/ solve a ～ 解谜 同 puzzle,problem

ride /raɪd/ Ⅰ v. (rode /rəʊd/, ridden /ˈrɪdn/)

骑；He jumped on his horse and rode off. 他跃上马背，疾驰而去。同 drive，handle Ⅱ *n*. [C] 骑马；骑车：go for a ～ before breakfast 早饭前骑一会儿自行车 同 drive

ridge / rɪdʒ / *n*. [C] ❶脊；岭；～ of the roof 屋脊 ❷垄；埂

ridicule / 'rɪdɪkjuːl / Ⅰ *vi*. 嘲弄；戏弄 同 mock，tease 反 respect Ⅱ *n*. 嘲笑；挖苦 同 mockery，sneer

ridiculous / rɪ'dɪkjələs / *adj*. 荒谬的；可笑的：～ ideas 荒谬的想法 / He looks ～ in jeans. 他穿牛仔裤的样子很可笑。同 foolish，funny 反 sensible 派 ridiculously *adv*.

rifle / 'raɪfl / *n*. [C]步枪

rift / rɪft / *n*. [C] ❶裂缝；裂口 ❷(人际关系中的)嫌隙，裂痕，不和；After years of harmonious marriage，however，～s began appearing. 经过多年和谐的婚姻生活之后，他们之间开始出现了裂痕。

right / raɪt / Ⅰ *adj*. ❶正确的；对的；满意的；公正的 同 correct，true 反 wrong，incorrect / all ～ ①行了；好吧；可以 ②(病)好了；安然无恙的：Do you feel all ～? 你感觉还好吗？③令人满意的；不错的 put (set) sth. ～ 使恢复正常；使恢复健康：He asked who can put the machine ～. 他问谁能修好那台机器。❷直角的 ❸右面的；右方的：In Great Britain traffic keeps to the left，not the ～ side of the road. 在英国，车辆靠左边而非靠右行驶。反 left Ⅱ *adv*. ❶一直地；直接地：Put it ～ in the middle. 把它放在正中间。/ Go ～ on until you reach the church. 一直往前走，直到教堂。同 directly，straight 反 indirectly / ～ away (now)马上，立即；I'll come ～ away. 我立刻到来。❷ 正确地；满意地；公正地：Have I guessed the answer ～ or wrong? 我猜的答案是对还是错？同 correctly 反 incorrectly Ⅲ *n*. ❶[U]正确；公正：know the difference between ～ and wrong 了解是非的区别 同 justice，fairness ❷[C]权利：children's (women's) ～s 儿童(妇女)的权利 / human ～s 人权 / intellectual property ～s 知识产权 / exclusive sale ～ 专卖权 / He has a ～ to do that. 他有权做那件事。同 privilege，power ❸右边；右方：Take the first turning to the ～. 在第一个转弯处向右转。反 left / on the ～在右边 派 rightly *adv*.

rightful / 'raɪtf(ʊ)l / *adj*. ❶合法的；依法享

有的：the ～ heir 合法继承人 / the ～ status of an independent nation 一个独立国家的合法地位 ❷正当的，正义的：a ～ act 正义的行为

rigid / 'rɪdʒɪd / *adj*. ❶坚硬的；刚性的 同 firm，hard 反 flexible，soft ❷严格的；僵硬的；死板的：～ discipline 严格的纪律 / They are ～ in attitude. 他们态度严厉。同 strict，severe 派 rigidly *adv*.；rigidity *n*.

rigorous / 'rɪgərəs / *adj*. ❶严格的；严厉的：a ～ critique 一篇措辞严厉的评论 ❷精确的，准确的；严谨的：～ science attitude 严谨的科学态度 ❸(气候)恶劣的；严寒的：a ～ climate 恶劣气候

rigour / 'rɪgə(r) / *n*. ❶[U]严格；严厉：be punished with the full ～of the law 受到法律最严厉的惩处 ❷[C]艰苦；恶劣的条件：survive the ～s of winter 挨过寒冷的冬天 ❸[U]准确，精确；严密：the ～ of an argument 论证的严密性

rim / rɪm / Ⅰ *n*. [C] ❶周边，边缘：on the ～ of the glass 在杯子边上 ❷(轮胎套在上面的)轮圈，胎环 Ⅱ *vi*. (rimmed；rimming) ❶给…装边沿，加边于：The garden was rimmed with hedges. 花园周围竖着篱笆。❷(球等)在…的边上打转不进：His last shot ～med the basket. 他最后投出的球在篮圈上打转。

ring / rɪŋ / Ⅰ *v*. (rang/ræŋ/，rung/rʌŋ/) ❶发出(清晰响亮的)声音：Start work when the bell ～s. 铃响便开始工作。同 sound，strike ❷按铃(作为召唤、警告)；She rang for the waiter. 她按铃叫服务员。/ If you want something，you may ～ the bell. 如果你需要什么，可以按铃叫我。同 call，signal ❸响彻(声音等)；(指耳朵)嗡嗡作响：His last words still rang in my ears. 他的遗言仍响在我耳边。/ ～ back 回电话：Ring me back this afternoon，please. 请今天下午给我回电话。～ up 打电话：He rang up Tom to tell him the good news. 他打电话给汤姆，告诉他那个好消息。/ If you see a blue car，～ up the police at once. 如果你看到一辆蓝色的小汽车，马上给警察打电话。～ with 响彻：The country is ～ing with praise. 全国上下一片赞美声。Ⅱ *n*. ❶按铃；铃声 ❷电话；通话：I'll give you a ～ this evening. 今晚我给你打电话。同 phone，call ❸[C]戒指；环形物：diamond ～ 钻石戒指 / wedding (engagement) ～ 结婚(订婚)戒指 同 circle

ripe / raɪp / *adj.* (指水果、谷物等)成熟的 同 mature, timely 反 unripe, immature

ripen / 'raɪpən / *v.* 使…熟；成熟：The sun ～ed the fruits. 阳光使水果成熟了。同 mature, prepare

ripple / 'rɪpl / Ⅰ *n.* [C](水面上的)微波, 涟漪；起伏的声音：A long ～ of laughter passed through the audience. 观众中响起一阵笑声。同 wave Ⅱ *v.* (使)起微波；(使)起伏：The wheat ～d in the breeze. 在微风吹拂下，麦浪起伏。同 wave

rise / raɪz / Ⅰ *vi.* (rose /rəʊz/, risen /'rɪzən/) ❶(指太阳、月亮等)升起：The sun ～s in the east. 太阳从东方升起。同 climb 反 fall, sink ❷起身；起床：He rose to welcome me. 他起身欢迎我。同 stand 反 retire, sit ❸(指河水等)上涨：The river has risen 2 feet. 河水上涨了两英尺。/Prices continue to ～. 物价继续上涨。同 increase, surge 反 decrease, decline ❹升级；晋升：He rose from an errand boy to the president. 他从小差使晋升为总经理。同 promote, succeed ❺反叛；起义：At last the citizens rose up and defeated their cruel rulers. 最后市民们起义了，并且打败了他们残酷的统治者。同 rebel, revolt Ⅱ *n.* ❶进展 同 progress ❷升高；增加：have a ～ in wages 提高工资 同 increase 反 decrease ❸小山 同 hill ❹起源：The river has (takes) its ～ among the hills. 这条河发源于小山中。同 origin, source ● **give ～ to** 引起；导致：Such a conduct might give ～ to misunderstandings. 这种行为可能会导致误解。

risk / rɪsk / Ⅰ *n.* 风险；危险 同 venture, danger 反 certainty, safety / **at the ～ of** 冒…的危险：He was determined to get there even at the ～ of his life. 他决心到那里去，即使冒生命危险也在所不惜。**run (take) a ～ (～s)** 冒险：A businessman has to take ～s in order to make more money. 为了赚更多的钱，商人总是要冒一定风险的。Ⅱ *v.* (使)冒危险：We must ～ getting caught in a storm. 我们必须冒着暴风雨所阻之险。同 venture, gamble

> **用法**
>
> risk 作动词时后面接动名词，不接不定式：I cannot risk losing my comrades. 我不能冒失去同志的危险。

rival / 'raɪvl / Ⅰ *n.* [C]对手；竞争者：business ～s 商业竞争对手 / ～ in chess 棋逢对手 /

～ in love 情敌 同 competitor, enemy 反 helper, friend Ⅱ *adj.* 竞争的 同 competitive, opposing Ⅲ *v.* 与…竞争：with the visiting team for the championship 与客队争夺冠军 同 compete, oppose 反 help, suppose 派 rivalry *n.*

river / 'rɪvə(r) / *n.* [C] 江；河：the Yellow River 黄河 / the Changjiang (Yangtze) River 长江

road / rəʊd / *n.* [C] 路 同 way, avenue

roam / rəʊm / *vi.* 闲逛；漫游；流浪：He ～ed around the world for a few years. 几年来他周游列国。

roar / rɔː(r) / Ⅰ *n.* [C]吼叫；咆哮；隆隆声；咆哮声 同 cry, shout 反 whisper Ⅱ *v.* 吼叫；咆哮：The patient ～ed with pain. 那病人痛得大声喊叫。同 cry, shout 反 whisper

roast / rəʊst / Ⅰ *v.* 烤；烘 同 bake, cook Ⅱ *adj.* 烤的；烘制的：～ beef 烤牛肉 / Beijing Roast Duck 北京烤鸭

rob / rɒb / *v.* (robbed; robbing)抢夺；抢劫；盗窃 同 plunder, steal / ～ **sb. of sth.** 抢夺某人之物：I was ～bed of my watch. 我的手表被抢了。

robber / 'rɒbə(r) / *n.* [C] 抢劫者；强盗；盗贼 同 plunderer, thief

robbery / 'rɒbəri / *n.* 抢夺；剥夺 同 plundering, theft

robe / rəʊb / *n.* [C]宽松长袍；礼袍：a bath ～ 浴袍 同 garment, gown

robot / 'rəʊbɒt / *n.* [C]机器人：A ～ can do many things that a man can not. 机器人可以做很多人不能做的事情。

robust / rəʊ'bʌst, 'rəʊbʌst / *adj.* ❶强健的；健全的；充满生气的：～ good health 强壮的好身板 / The movie business is enjoying a ～ boom. 电影业正处于强盛时期。❷强壮的，健壮的；粗壮的：a ～ police officer 一个膀阔腰圆的警官

rock / rɒk / Ⅰ *n.* 大石头；礁石：as firm as a ～ 坚如磐石 同 stone, pebble Ⅱ *v.* 摇晃；摇动 同 shake, swing

rocket / 'rɒkɪt / Ⅰ *n.* 火筒式烟火；火箭：～ base 火箭基地 / fire a ～ 点火发射火箭 Ⅱ *v.* ❶用火箭运载 ❷迅速增加

rocking / 'rɒkɪŋ / *adj.* 摇动的；摇摆的

rod / rɒd / *n.* [C] 棒；竿：a fishing ～ 钓鱼竿 同 pole, stick

role / rəʊl / *n.* [C] ❶角色：He wants to play

the ～ of Hamlet. 他想扮演哈姆雷特这个角色。同 character,part ❷作用；任务 同 duty,task / **play a ～ in** 在…中起作用：Jack played an important ～ in winning the game. 杰克为赢得比赛起了重要的作用。

roll / rəul / Ⅰ v. (使)滚动；(使)转动：The coin fell and ～ed under the table. 硬币掉到地上，滚到桌下。同 revolve,rotate / **～ over** (使)翻滚：The car hit a lamppost and ～ed over twice before coming to a stop. 那辆汽车碰到一根灯柱，翻滚了两次才停下来。Ⅱ n. ❶卷形的东西 ❷滚动；转动 ❸记录表；(尤指)名单：call the ～点名 同 list,catalog

roller / ˈrəulə(r) / n. [C]滚柱；滚筒；滚轴

roller-coaster / ˈrəuləˌkəustə(r) / n. [C] ❶(游乐园等中的)过山车道，云霄飞车 ❷急剧变化的局面(或事情等)：the ～ of emotions 情感的急剧变化

Roman / ˈrəumən / Ⅰ n. [C] 古罗马人；罗马人 Ⅱ adj. 古罗马的；罗马的

Rome / rəum / n. ❶罗马 ❷(历史上的)罗马帝国

romance / rəuˈmæns, ˈrəumæns / n. ❶传奇文学；浪漫文学 同 fiction,legend ❷爱情故事；风流韵事

romantic / rəuˈmæntik / Ⅰ adj. ❶浪漫的；浪漫主义的；传奇的：Shelley was a famous English ～ poet. 雪莱是英国有名的浪漫主义诗人。同 loving,passionate 反 unromantic ❷好幻想的；不切实际的：You must get rid of all ～ ideas. 你得抛弃一切不切实际的想法。同 impractical,unrealistic 反 unromantic,practical Ⅱ n. [C]浪漫的人；浪漫主义作家 派 romantically adv.

romanticist / rəuˈmæntisist / n. [C]浪漫主义者；浪漫主义作家

roof / ruːf / n. [C] (pl. roofs)(建筑物、帐篷、车等的)顶，顶部 同 ceiling,top

room / ruːm / n. ❶[C]室；房间 同 apartment,lodging ❷[U] 空间：Is there ～ for me in the car? 车子里有我坐的位置吗？同 space,volume ❸[U]机会；余地；范围：There is ～ for improvement in your work. 你的工作还有改进的余地。同 chance,margin / **make ～ for** 给…腾出地方：Please make a little ～ for the car to pass. 请让出点地方让汽车过去。

root / ruːt / Ⅰ n. [C] ❶(植物的)根：pull up a plant by the ～s 把一株植物连根拔起 ❷(发、

齿、舌)根 ❸根源；根基：～ of all evil 万恶之源 / ～of trouble 祸根 同 cause,origin ❹词根 Ⅱ v. (使)生根成长；(使)扎根 同 fix,set

rope / rəup / n. [C]索；绳子 同 cable,cord / **at the end of the ～** 末尾的；末路的：The enemy has been at the end of the ～. 敌人已经日暮途穷了。

rose / rəuz / n. [C]蔷薇；玫瑰：be not all ～s 并非一切尽如人意 / There is no ～ without a thorn. (谚)没有不带刺的玫瑰。(有乐必有苦。)

rostrum / ˈrɒstrəm / n. [C] (pl. rostrums 或 rostra / ˈrɒstrə/)讲台；讲坛 同 platform,stage

rot / rɒt / v. (rotted；rotting)(使)腐烂 同 decay,spoil / **～ away** 渐渐腐烂：The wood of the stairs has ～ted away. 这梯子的木头已渐渐腐烂了。

rotate / rəuˈteit / v. (使)转动；(使)旋转：The moon ～s around the earth. 月球围绕地球转。同 revolve,spin

rotation / rəuˈteiʃn / n. ❶旋转；转动：The ～ of the earth makes day and night. 地球的自转形成白昼和黑夜。同 roll,turn ❷循环；轮流：They have a ～ of duties in the office. 他们轮流值班。同 circulation,round

rotten / ˈrɒtn / adj. ❶腐烂的；变质的 同 decayed 反 fresh ❷道德败坏的；腐化的：～ at the core 烂透了；腐败透顶 同 corrupt,bad 反 good,honest

rough / rʌf / adj. ❶不平的，不光的：～ paper 粗糙的纸 / fruit with the ～ skin 粗皮水果 同 uneven,coarse 反 even,smooth ❷粗暴的；浮躁的：～ behaviour 粗暴的行为 同 violent,rude 反 gentle,polite ❸粗略的；大致的：make a ～ sketch 画张草图 同 general,incomplete 反 complete,perfect 派 roughly adv.

round / raund / Ⅰ adj. 圆形的；环形的：a ～-table conference 圆桌会议 同 circular,spherical 反 square,many-sided Ⅱ prep. ❶(表示动作)环绕：The earth moves ～ the sun. 地球绕着太阳运行。❷(表示位置)围绕：He had a scarf ～ his neck. 他颈上围有一条围巾。❸大约：Come ～ 2 o'clock. 两点左右来。Ⅲ adv. ❶环绕地：A crowd of people soon gathered ～. 一群人不久就围拢来了。❷循环地：Christmas will soon be ～ again. 圣诞节又快到了。/ **all the year ～** 整年；全年；

They worked hard all the year ～. 他们曾一年到头辛勤劳动。**look** ～ (**around**) 环顾：He looked ～ (around) but didn't find the building he was looking for. 他四处张望，但是没有看到他要找的那栋楼房。**show sb.** ～(**around**) 带某人参观：The headmaster showed the guests ～ (around) in the school. 校长带客人们在学校参观。

roundabout / ˈraʊndəbaʊt / *adj.* 迂回的；拐弯抹角的 同 indirect 反 direct, straight

rouse / raʊz / *vt.* ❶唤醒；唤起；使唤起：The noise ～d me from sleep. 闹声把我从睡眠中吵醒。同 call, wake up ❷激起；激怒 同 arouse, stimulate

route / ruːt / *n.* [C]路途；路线；航线：The climbers tried to find a new ～ to the top of the mountain. 登山者试图找到一条到达山顶的新路。同 course, way

routine / ruːˈtiːn / Ⅰ *adj.* 日常的；常规的：a ～ report 例行报告 / a ～ medical examination 例行体检 同 conventional, usual 反 special, unusual Ⅱ *n.* 惯例；常规：do daily ～ 做日常工作 同 custom, practice

row / rəʊ / Ⅰ *n.* [C]一行；一排；一列：a ～ of books 一排书 / a ～ of houses 一排房子 / a ～ of desks 一排桌子 同 line, rank Ⅱ *v.* 划(船等)：Let's ～ a race. 我们来比赛划船吧。

royal / ˈrɔɪəl / *adj.* 王室的；皇家的：the Royal Air Force(英国)皇家空军 / the Royal Society (英国的)皇家学会 同 kingly, grand

royalty / ˈrɔɪəlti / *n.* ❶[U]王位；王权 ❷[U]王族；皇族 ❸[C]特许使用费；版税

rub / rʌb / *v.* (rubbed; rubbing) 擦；搓：He ～bed his hands with the soap. 他给双手涂上肥皂。同 shine, polish

rubber / ˈrʌbə(r) / *n.* ❶[U]橡胶 ❷[C]橡皮

rubbish / ˈrʌbɪʃ / *n.* [U]垃圾；废物 同 garbage, waste

rubble / ˈrʌbl / *n.* [U]碎石；瓦砾：The building was reduced to ～ during the war. 战争期间这幢建筑成了一片碎石乱瓦。

ruby / ˈruːbi / *n.* ❶[C]红宝石 ❷[U]红宝石色；暗红色

rude / ruːd / *adj.* ❶(指人或人的言语、行为)无礼的，粗鲁的：Don't be ～ to your teacher. 不许对师长无礼。/ It is ～ of you to speak with your mouth full. 你满口食物说话是很不

礼貌的。同 impolite, uncivilized 反 polite, decent ❷粗略的；大概的：He gave me a ～ drawing of the city. 他给了我一张城市略图。同 general, rough 反 complete

ruffle / ˈrʌfl / Ⅰ *vt.* ❶使变皱，弄皱；使不平，使波动：The wind began to ～ the calm surface of the sea. 平静的海面上风起浪涌。❷惹恼，使生气：be ～d from all the interruptions 因不断地被打断而大为光火 ❸草草翻阅(书页等)：He picked up a magazine and ～d the pages. 他拿起一本杂志，随便翻阅着。Ⅱ *n.* [C]皱，皱褶；皱纹；(表面的)起伏

rug / rʌg / *n.* [C]小地毯；毛毯

rugged / ˈrʌgɪd / *adj.* ❶(地面)高低不平，崎岖的；(地貌)多岩石的：a ～ volcanic island 岩石嶙峋的火山岛 同 rough ❷(人脸)多皱纹的；粗糙的：a ～ masculine face 男人味十足的棱角分明的脸 ❸(生活等)艰苦的：a ～ life 艰苦的生活 ❹(天气)恶劣的：the most ～ weather 最为恶劣的天气

ruin / ˈruːɪn / Ⅰ *n.* ❶[U]毁灭；严重损坏；完全丧失：the ～ of her hopes 她的希望破灭 同 decay, destruction 反 construction, creation ❷(*pl.*)废墟；遗迹 同 remains, wreckage Ⅱ *v.* 毁灭；破坏；摧毁：The storm ～ed the crops. 暴风雨毁坏了农作物。同 destroy, damage 反 build, construct

rule / ruːl / Ⅰ *n.* ❶[C]法规；规则；条例：Pupils must obey the ～s of the school. 学生必须遵守校规。同 law, regulation / **as a** ～ 通常；一般而言：As a ～, young people like beer. 年青人通常都喜欢喝啤酒。**by** ～(＝**according to** ～)按照规则：She does everything by ～. 她做任何事都照章行事。**make it a** ～ **to do** (**make a** ～ **of doing**) 习惯做；必做：He makes it a ～ to take a walk before breakfast. 他习惯在早餐前散散步。❷[U]管理；统治：～ under law 法治 同 authority, control Ⅱ *v.* 统治；管理：King Charles Ⅰ ～d England for 11 years without a parliament. 查理一世在无国会的情况下统治英格兰 11 年。同 govern, control

ruler / ˈruːlə(r) / *n.* [C]❶统治者：overthrow the reactionary ～ 推翻反动统治者 同 leader, governor ❷尺；直尺

rumble / ˈrʌmbl / Ⅰ *vi.* ❶隆隆作响；发出隆隆声：The thunder ～d through the night. 雷

声隆隆而至，划破夜空。❷隆隆行进；轰鸣着前进：A subway train ～d underneath her. 一列地铁在她脚下轰鸣着驶过。❸声音低沉地说话；嘟哝：～ about the high price 嘟嘟哝哝地说价格太高 Ⅱ n. [C]隆隆声；轰鸣声；辘辘声

rumo(u)r / ˈruːmə(r) / n. 谣言；传闻：start a ～ 造谣 / spread a ～ 散布谣言 / spike a ～ 辟谣 圊 gossip，whisper

run / rʌn / Ⅰ v. (ran / ræn /，run)❶跑 圊 race，rush，walk，crawl ❷管理：～ a business 经营商店 / ～ a theatre 经营戏院 / ～ a bus company 经营公共汽车公司 圊 operate，manage / ～ **across** 偶然遇见：She ran across an old friend in the supermarket. 在超级市场里她偶然遇到了一位老朋友。～ **after** 追赶：The policeman ran after the thief and caught him. 警察追赶小偷并把他抓住了。～ **away**跑掉，逃跑：Don't ～ away. I want to talk to you. 别跑，我有话跟你说。～ **errands (messages) for sb.** 为某人跑腿做信差 ～ **for** 竞选：He ran for manager of the store but failed. 他竞选商店经理，但没有成功。～ **out (of)**用完；耗尽：I have ～ out of my oil. 我的汽油用完了。～ **over** ①溢出；超过：Her speech ran over the time limit. 她的讲话超过了规定的时限。②撞倒并碾过：The truck ran over a six-year-old child. 卡车碾倒了一个 6 岁的孩子。～ **short of sth.** 缺少某物：They said that they had ～ short of money. 他们说缺钱花。Ⅱ n. [C]跑。小车每小时行驶 120 英里。圊 dash，gallop

runabout / ˈrʌnəbaʊt / n. [C]流浪者

runaway / ˈrʌnəweɪ / Ⅰ n. 逃亡者；出逃者 Ⅱ adj. 逃走的；私奔的

run-down / ˈrʌnˌdaʊn / adj. ❶筋疲力尽的，累极的：You're looking ～. 你看起来很疲劳。❷身体虚弱的：He's severely ～ and had bet-ter see a doctor. 他看上去非常虚弱，最好去看医生。❸破败的；衰落的：a ～ neighbourhood 破败不堪的地区

running / ˈrʌnɪŋ / Ⅰ n. [U]❶奔跑，跑步；赛跑：practise ～ 练习跑步/road ～公路赛跑 ❷管理；照看：～ of a business 经营生意 Ⅱ adj. ❶(液体)流动的；流出的；流水的：～ water 流水/a ～ spring which is free of ice all winter long 整个冬天不结冰的喷泉 ❷连续的，持续不断的：a ～ battle 持续的战斗 ❸奔跑的；赛跑的：～ shoes 跑鞋 ❹(节奏、讲话等)顺畅的；流利的；顺利的：a ～ rhythm in music 音乐中流畅的节奏

rural / ˈrʊərəl / adj. 农村的；农业的：～ life 农村生活 / ～ market 农村集市 / ～ policy 农业政策 圊 country，agricultural 囻 urban

rush / rʌʃ / Ⅰ v. 奔，冲：The children ～ed out of the school gate. 孩子们冲出学校大门。圊 dash，run 囻 walk，crawl Ⅱ n. ❶奔，冲，繁忙：I don't like the ～ of the city life. 我不喜欢繁忙的都市生活。❷急需；抢购：the Christmas ～ 圣诞节的购物潮 / a gold ～ 淘金热 / **in a** ～ 匆忙地：He left his office in a ～. 他匆忙地离开了办公室。Ⅲ adj. 急迫的；繁忙的：～ hours 交通高峰期

Russia / ˈrʌʃə / n. 俄罗斯

Russian / ˈrʌʃən / Ⅰ adj. 俄罗斯的 Ⅱ n. ❶[C]俄罗斯人 ❷[U] 俄罗斯语

rust / rʌst / Ⅰ n. [U]铁锈：The watch doesn't gather ～ easily. 这表不易生锈。圊 decay，stain / ～proof adj. 抗锈的 Ⅱ v. (使)生锈：The lock has ～ed. 那锁已经生锈了。圊 decay，rot

rustle / ˈrʌsl / Ⅰ v. (使)发出沙沙声 Ⅱ n. 沙沙声

ruthless / ˈruːθləs / adj. ❶无情的；冷酷的；残忍的 圊 cruel，savage 囻 kind，gentle ❷持久的 圊 lasting ❸坚决的 圊 firm，determined

S s

sack / sæk / Ⅰ *n.* [C] ❶大袋;大包:two ～s of potatoes 两袋马铃薯 同 bag ❷解雇;革职 (the ～):get the ～ 被解雇 / give sb. the ～ 解雇某人 Ⅱ *vt.* ❶把…装进袋里 同 pack, store ❷解雇 同 dismiss,fire

sacred / ˈseɪkrɪd/ *adj.* ❶神圣的;宗教的:～ music 圣乐 / ～ writings 宗教经典 同 holy, religious ❷严肃的;郑重的:a ～ promise 郑重 的诺言 同 solemn

sacrifice / ˈsækrɪfaɪs / Ⅰ *n.* ❶祭品;供品 ❷献 身;牺牲:He made a ～ for his country. 他为 国牺牲了。Ⅱ *v.* ❶供奉;祭祀 ❷牺牲;献身: He ～d his life to save the drowning child. 他 因救落水的孩子而牺牲了生命。

sad / sæd / *adj.* 悲伤的;忧愁的:We are all ～ for his death. 我们都为他的去世感到悲伤。 同 gloomy, painful 反 cheerful, happy 派 sad- den *v.* ; sadly *adv.* ; sadness *n.*

saddle / ˈsædl / *n.* [C]鞍;马鞍

safe / seɪf / Ⅰ *adj.* ❶安全的;无危险的: You'd better keep the knife in a ～ place. 你 最好把刀子放在安全的地方。同 secure, pro- tected 反 unsafe, harmed / ～ and sound 安然 无事;平安无恙:They came back ～ and sound from America. 他们平安地从美国回到 家里。❷牢靠的;可靠的 同 steady, stable 反 unsafe, unreliable Ⅱ *n.* 保险箱 派 safely *adv.*

safeguard / ˈseɪfgɑːd / Ⅰ *n.* 保护;捍卫;保护 措施 同 protection, precaution Ⅱ *v.* 保护;捍 卫:～ state sovereignty 捍卫国家主权 同 protect, guard

safety / ˈseɪfti / *n.* [U]安全;平安:～ devices 安全设施 / ～ measures 安全措施 / a ～ hel- met 安全帽 / ～ in production 生产安全/ personal ～ 人身安全 / public ～ 公共安全 同 protection, security

Sahara / səˈhɑːrə/ *n.* (非洲)撒哈拉沙漠

sail / seɪl / Ⅰ *n.* ❶[C] 航行;帆: set ～起航; 开船 同 voyage ❷船(单复数同形):a fleet of twenty ～ 20 只船的船队 同 boat Ⅱ *v.* 航行: The ship ～ed from Shanghai to Hong Kong. 这船从上海驶往香港。

sailor / ˈseɪlə(r) / *n.* ❶海员;水手:～ hat 水手 帽 ❷乘船者:a good (bad) ～ 不大晕(常晕) 船的人

saint / seɪnt / Ⅰ *n.* [C]基督教圣徒 Ⅱ *adj.* 神 圣的 同 holy

sake / seɪk / *n.* 目的;缘故;理由 同 purpose, reason / **for the ～ of** 为了;由于:We must be patient for the ～ of peace. 为了和平,我们必 须有耐心。**for God's (pity's, mercy's) ～** (用 于加强语气)看在上帝的面上(请可怜,请发 发慈悲)

salad / ˈsæləd / *n.* 沙拉;色拉;生菜;凉拌菜: fruit ～ 水果沙拉 / green ～ 蔬菜沙拉 / mixed ～ 什锦沙拉 / ～ oil 色拉油

salary / ˈsæləri / *n.* 薪水;薪金:draw a ～ 领薪 水 / The general manager earns a ～ of $120,000 per year. 总经理年薪 12 万美元。 同 pay, wages

> **辨析**
> salary 指高级技术人员、教师或行政管理人员 等从事脑力劳动者领取的薪金,常以周、月或 年计算发给:This position offers a weekly sala- ry of $200. 这个职务每周薪为 200 美元。He collects his salary at the end of each month. 他 每月月底领薪水。pay 指长久、固定的工资, 可特指发给海陆空军人员的固定军饷:We are told to draw our pay once a month. 我们得到通 知每月领一次工资。wage 指发给技术工人、 体力劳动者或服务员的工资,常以小时、天、 周或生产定额计算,按天或周发给:A garden- er earns a minimum hourly wage of 255 in the country. 在那个国家一个园丁每小时最少可 挣 255 美元。

sale / seɪl / *n.* 出售;卖;销售额:～s department 门市部,销售部 / ～s tax 营业税 / Is the house for ～? 这房屋出售吗? Sales are up (down) this month. 本月销售额在增加(减少)。同 exchange, trade反 purchase / **on** 〜上市；出售：This type of TV sets will be on 〜 next month. 这种型号的电视机将在下个月上市。

salesgirl / 'seɪlzɡɜːd / *n.* [C] 女店员；女售货员

salesman / 'seɪlzmən / *n.* [C]（*pl.* salesmen）售货员；店员；推销员

saliva / sə'laɪvə / *n.* [U] 唾液，涎

salivate / 'sælɪˌveɪt / *vi.* 分泌唾液，流涎：The dog could 〜 at the sight of food. 这条狗看见食物就会流口水。

salon / 'sælɒn / *n.* ❶（营业性质的）厅；店；院 ❷（定期举行的社交聚会）：a literary 〜 文学沙龙

salt / sɔːlt / Ⅰ *n.* [U] 食盐：fine 〜 精盐 / a grain of 〜 一粒盐 Ⅱ *vt.* 用盐给…调味；用盐腌 派 salty *adj.* 含盐的，咸的；尖锐的

salute / sə'luːt / Ⅰ *n.* 欢迎；致敬；举手礼：give a 〜 of ten guns 鸣礼炮十响 同 welcome，greeting Ⅱ *v.* 行礼；向…致敬：They 〜d （each other）by raising their hats. 他们举帽（相互）致意。同 bow，greet

same / seɪm / Ⅰ *adj.* 同一的；相同的；不变的：We have lived in the 〜 house for fifty years. 我们 50 年来一直住在这所房子里。同 identical，similar反 different，changed / **at the** 〜 **time** ①同时：Don't sing the song at the same time. 不要同时唱那首歌。②然而：I'll forgive you，at the 〜 time you must never do it again. 我会原谅你的，而你决不能再做那种事。**come（amount）to the** 〜 **thing** 结果相同；无差异：You may pay in cash or cheque，it's the 〜. 你可付现金或支票，其结果相同。Ⅱ*pron.* The same I would do the 〜 again. 我愿重做一次。/ **all（just）the** 〜 ①完全一样；无所谓：Tea or coffee is all（just）the 〜 for me. 对我来说，茶或咖啡都是一样的。②仍然；照样：We'll go all（just）the 〜 even if it does rain. 即使下雨，我们也仍然要去。**the** 〜 **as ...** 像…一样；与…相同：In Beijing the weather in summer is usually the 〜 as in my hometown. 夏天，北京的天气通常和我家乡的一样。

用 法

the same ...as 与 the same ...that 有区别，the same ...as 意为"与…相像的"：This is the same watch as I lost. 这块表与我丢失的那块相像。the same ... that 意为"与…同一的"：This is the same watch that I lost. 这就是我丢失的那块表。

sample / 'sɑːmpl，'sæmpl / Ⅰ *n.* [C] 样品；货样；标本：provide 〜s 提供样品 / random 〜 随机取样 / I want to see some 〜s of your products. 我想看看你们的货样。同 example，model Ⅱ *vt.* 从…取样检验 同 taste，test

sanction / 'sæŋkʃn / Ⅰ *n.* ❶ [U] 认可，许可；准许，批准：give 〜 to 允许（批准）❷ [C] 约束（力）；制约（因素）：The best 〜 against wrongdoing is that of conscience. 对不良行为的最佳约束即是良心的约束。❸ 国际制裁：institute economic 〜s against 对…实施经济制裁 / lift 〜s 解除制裁 Ⅱ *vt.* ❶批准，准许，同意：designate Labour Day as a state 〜ed day of rest 把劳动节这一天指定为国家法定休息日 ❷对…实行制裁，对…施以处罚，惩处

sand / sænd / *n.* ❶ [U] 沙：a grain of 〜 一粒沙子 ❷（常用 *pl.*）沙地；沙滩：on the 〜s 在沙滩上 派 sandy *adj.*

sandal / 'sændl / *n.* [C] 凉鞋

sandstorm / 'sæn(d)ˌstɔːm / *n.* [C]（沙漠上的）沙暴，沙尘暴

sandwich / 'sænwɪdʒ / *n.*（中间夹有肉等的）夹心面包片，三明治

sane / seɪn / *adj.* ❶ 心智健全的，神志正常的：a 〜 person 心智健全的人 / be in a 〜 state of mind 处于神志正常状态 ❷ 清醒的，明智的；合乎情理的：a 〜 decision 明智的决定 / keep the mind 〜 保持头脑清醒 派 sanely *adv.*

sap / sæp / *n.* [U]（植物的）液，汁

satellite / 'sætəlaɪt / *n.* 卫星；人造卫星：a 〜 city（在大城市郊区兴建的）卫星城 / the manned 〜 载人卫星 / launch a weather 〜 发射一颗气象卫星

satire / 'sætaɪə(r) / *n.* 讽刺；讽刺作品：It is a bitter 〜 on（upon）such kind of people. 这是对这种人的辛辣讽刺。同 ridicule

satisfaction / ˌsætɪs'fækʃn / *n.* [U] 满意；满足：have the 〜 of being successful 对成功感到满意 同 comfort，pleasure 反 dissatisfaction，grief

satisfactory / ˌsætɪs'fæktəri / *adj.* 令人满意的；令人满足的：The result of the experiment was 〜. 实验的结果令人满意。同 content，sufficient 反 unsatisfactory 派 satisfactorily *adv.*

satisfy / 'sætɪsˌfaɪ / *v.* 使满意；使满足：Riches do not always 〜. 财富并不永远使人满足。同 delight，please 反 dissatisfy，displease / **be sat-**

isfied with 对…感到满意：I'm not satisfied with your work. You must improve it. 我不满意你的工作,你必须要改进。

Saturday / ˈsætədɪ / n. 星期六

sauce / sɔːs / n. [U]调味汁;酱汁：apple ～ 苹果酱 / soy ～ 酱油 / tomato ～ 番茄酱 同 flavor,seasoning

sauna / ˈsɔːnə,ˈsɑːnə / n. [C]❶桑拿浴,蒸汽浴;芬兰浴：have a ～洗桑拿浴 ❷桑拿浴室,蒸汽浴室

sausage / ˈsɔːsɪdʒ / n. [C]香肠;腊肠

savage / ˈsævɪdʒ / Ⅰ adj. ❶野蛮的;未开化的 同 primitive,uncivilized 反 civilized,cultured ❷残酷的;残暴的 同 cruel,ruthless 反 kind, gentle Ⅱ n. 野人;野蛮人

save / seɪv / v. ❶援救;挽救 同 rescue,safeguard 反 endanger,risk / ～ sb. (sth.) from 从…中挽救某人(某物);使某人(某物)免于：Many books were ～d from the fire. 许多书得以从大火中抢救出来。❷储蓄：～ money for a holiday 存钱度假 同 deposite,stock 反 spend ❸节省;省去：～ time 节约时间 / The computer ～s me much time. 计算机让我省很多时间。同 preserve,spare 反 use,waste ❹(计算机)存储 同 store

savings / ˈseɪvɪŋz / n. 储蓄金;存款：～ account 储蓄账户 / deposit one's ～ 存钱 / withdraw one's ～ 提取存款

saw / sɔː / Ⅰ n. [C]锯：a power ～电锯 Ⅱ v. (sawed, sawn /sɔːn/或 sawed) 锯 同 cut,split

saxophone / ˈsæksəfəun / n. [C]萨克斯管,萨克斯风

say / seɪ / Ⅰ v. (said /sed/, said) 说;讲：He said nothing about his friend Tom. 关于他朋友汤姆,他什么也没说。同 express,speak / ～ hello to sb. 向某人问好：He said hello to every teacher he met. 他向碰到的每个老师问好。**go without** ～**ing** 不用说;显而易见：It goes without ～ing that I'll finish the work on time. 不用说我会按时完成工作的。～ **goodbye to sb.** 向某人告别：She went to the station to ～ good-bye to her friend. 她到车站去向朋友告别。～ **sth. about** 谈谈…的情况：Please ～ something about your study in London. 请谈谈你在伦敦学习的情况。～ **to oneself** 心中暗想;思忖 **that is to** ～ 换言之;即：We'll come back three weeks tomorrow, that is to

～, the 30th of March. 我们三个星期后的明天,即 3 月 30 日回来。Ⅱ n. 要说的话;发言的机会;发言权 voice, vote / **have a** (**no, not much**)～ **in** 对…有(没有、没有多少)发言权：At last, he had his ～ in the matter. 最后他得到了关于此事的发言机会。

辨析

say 着重指所说的内容,尤用于直接引语之前："In those days," he said, "tractors were unknown in the countryside.""那时候,"他说,"农村还没有拖拉机呢。"**speak** 着重指说话的动作,一般用作不及物动词,如果用作及物动词,其宾语只能是某种语言或 truth 等少数词,后面不能接 that 从句：I didn't speak on that occasion. 我那一次没有发言。She can speak Japanese fluently. 她日语说得很流利。**talk** 和 speak 用法相近,也着重指说话的动作,一般也只用作不及物动词;如果用作及物动词,其宾语只能是某种语言或 nonsense 等少数词,不能接 that 从句。talk 有较强的交谈、对答、讨论意味：He was talking to (with) a friend. 他在和一个朋友交谈。He went on talking for a long time, but he spoke so fast that few of us could catch what he said. 他滔滔不绝地讲了半天,但他说得太快,我们几乎不知道他在说什么。**tell** 除 tell the truth (讲实话),tell a lie (说谎), tell a story (讲故事) 等惯用法外,一般后面接双宾语：He has told me the news. 他已经把消息告诉我了。He told me that he had finished it. 他告诉我他已经把它完成了。

saying / ˈseɪɪŋ / n. [C]谚语;格言;名言："More haste, less speed," as the ～ is. 常道:"欲速则不达。"同 proverb

scale / skeɪl / n. ❶[C]尺度;刻度：This ruler has one ～ in centimetre and another in inch. 这尺上有厘米刻度和英寸刻度。同 rule, measure ❷[C]有刻度的度量器 ❸[C]比例;比例尺：a ～ of one to a thousand 1：1000 的比例 同 proportion, ratio ❹规模：**on a large** (**small**)～ 大(小)规模：This kind of cars are being produced in their factory on a large (small) ～. 这种小汽车正在他们的工厂里大(小)规模地生产。❺[C]天平盘;秤盘 ❻(pl.)天平;磅秤：The workers weigh the gold in the ～s. 工人在天平上称黄金。

scan / skæn / vt. (scanned; scanning) ❶细看;审视 同 check, inspect ❷扫描;扫掠：The radar ～s the sky day and night. 雷达日夜扫掠天空. 同 sweep ❸浏览:～ newspapers over breakfast 边吃早餐边浏览报纸 同 skim

scandal / 'skændəl / n. [C]丑事;丑闻:uncover a ～ 揭露丑闻 / A ～ burst. 爆出丑闻. 同 disgrace, shame

scanner / 'skænə(r) / n. (计算机的)扫描器

scar / skɑː(r) / n. 伤疤;伤痕;创伤:The soldier's right hand bore a ～. 那个士兵的右手上有一块伤疤. 同 injury, wound

scarce / skeəs / adj. ❶不充足的;供不应求的:Eggs are ～ and dear this month. 本月蛋少而价高. 同 insufficient, lacking 反 sufficient, abundant ❷稀罕的;难得的:a ～ book 珍本 同 rare, unusual 反 usual, common

scarcely / 'skeəsli / adv. ❶仅仅;几乎不;简直不:I could ～ recognize the man. 我几乎认不出那个人来. 同 barely, hardly ❷刚刚;才:Scarcely had we set out when it began to rain. 我们刚出发就开始下起雨来. 同 just, only

用法

scarcely 是否定意义的词,出现在句首时,句子主谓语应当倒装:Scarcely had he finished his poem when the audience applauded. 他刚朗读完诗,听众就鼓起掌来. 如果 scarcely 不在句首,则主谓语不倒装:He had scarcely finished his poem when the audience applauded.

scarcity / 'skeəsəti / n. 缺乏;不足:The ～ of food drew much attention. 食物的不足引起了极大的关注. 同 lack, shortage

scare / skeə(r) / vt. 使恐惧;使受惊吓:The baby was ～d by thunder. 婴儿被雷声惊吓了. / He ～d me. 他把我吓坏了. 同 frighten, shock 反 calm, comfort

scarf / skɑːf / n. [C](pl. scarves 或 scarfs)❶围巾;头巾 ❷领巾;领带

scatter / 'skætə(r) / v. ❶驱散;离散:The police ～ed the crowd. 警察驱散人群. / The crowd ～ed. 人群散去了. 同 disperse, dismiss 反 gather, collect ❷撒播:～ seeds 播种 同 spread 反 collect

scene / siːn / n. [C] ❶事发地点:the ～ of crime 犯罪现场 同 setting, spot ❷(戏剧中的)一场,一景 同 act, part ❸风景;景致:The boats in the harbor make a beautiful ～. 海港中的船形成很美的风景. 同 view, landscape

辨析

scene 指具体某一景致,包含人的活动:a scene of farmers ploughing the fields 农民耕田的情景. scenery 指某一地区的整体景色:the beautiful scenery of the West Lake 西湖地区的美丽风光. view 指从某处看到的景色:a fine view from the hill top 从山顶上看到的宜人景色.

scenery / 'siːnəri / n. [U] ❶舞台布景:set up ～ 布景 同 background, stage setting ❷风景;景色:We enjoy the fascinating mountain ～. 我们很喜欢这迷人的山中景色. 同 landscape, view

scenic / 'siːnɪk / adj. 风景优美的;舞台布景的

scent / sent / n. ❶[U]气味:strong ～ of hay 浓烈的干草味 同 smell ❷[U]香味:～s of flowers 各种花香 同 fragrance ❸[C](野兽的)遗臭:Hunting dogs know how to follow a ～. 猎犬知道如何追踪兽迹. 同 trace, path

schedule / 'ʃedjuːl, 'skedʒuːl / n. [C](英)时刻表;目录表:The train arrived on ～. 火车准时到达. 同 timetable, program / **ahead of** ～ 提前于 / **behind** ～ 迟到;晚点:The train arrived behind ～. 火车晚点了. / **on** ～ 按时间表;准时 II vt. 将…列表;为…做目录;安排:The President is ～d to make a speech tomorrow. 总统定于明日发表演说. 同 plan, fix

schematic / skɪ'mætɪk / I adj. ❶图解的;草图的:It's only a ～ diagram, it doesn't show the details. 这只是个草图,没有标明细节. ❷规划的;大纲的,概要的 II n. [C]图解;草图,略图;(尤指)电路图

scheme / skiːm / n. [C] ❶计划;规划;方案:health insurance ～ 健康保险计划 / make a ～ 制订计划 同 plan, project ❷诡计;阴谋:The enemy's ～ did not work. 敌人的阴谋没有得逞. 同 plot

scholar / 'skɒlə(r) / n. [C] ❶学者 同 intellectual ❷学生;学习者 同 learner, student 派 scholarly adj.

scholarship / 'skɒləʃɪp / n. ❶[U]学问;学识 同 knowledge, education 反 ignorance ❷[C]奖学金:apply for a ～ 申请奖学金 / get (receive, win) a ～ 获得奖学金 / grant a ～ 授予奖学金 / students on ～ 领奖学金的学生

school / skuːl / n. ❶[C]学校:a middle ～ 中

学 ❷[U](不加定冠词)上学：attend ～ 上学 ❸[U]上课时间；上课：School begins at 8 a. m. 八点钟开始上课。❹[C]大学；学院：law ～ 法学院 / medical ～ 医学院 囘 college，institute ❺[C]学派；流派：poets of the Lake School 湖畔派诗人 囘 thought，style

schooling / 'sku ːlɪŋ / n. [U]教育：He has very little ～. 他受的教育很少。囘 education，instruction

science / 'saɪəns / n. [U]科学：social ～ 社会科学 / natural ～ 自然科学 / ～ fiction 科幻小说

scientific / ˌsaɪən'tɪfɪk / adj. 科学的；关于科学的：～ methods 科学方法 / ～ farming 科学耕作 囵 scientifically adv.

scientist / 'saɪəntɪst / n. [C]科学家

scissors / 'sɪzəz / n. 剪刀；剪子：a pair of ～ 一把剪刀

scoff / skɒf / vi. 嘲笑，嘲弄，讥笑：～ at a fanciful notion 嘲笑空想念头

scold / skəʊld / v. 骂；责备：～ a child for being lazy 责备孩子偷懒 囘 blame，criticize 囝 praise，encourage

scoop / skuːp / Ⅰ n. [C]❶勺子；勺形工具；舀子；戽斗：a kitchen ～ 厨房用勺 ❷一勺(或铲、匙等)的量：Just two ～s of mashed potato for me，please. 请给我来两勺土豆泥吧。Ⅱ vt. (用铲等)挖，铲；(用勺等)舀：～ some sugar out on to the plate 舀一点糖放在盘子里

scope / skəʊp / n. [U]❶范围，视野，见识：This subject is beyond the ～ of this book. 这个主题已超越了这本书的范围。/ You should widen your ～ of knowledge. 你应拓宽你的知识视野。囘 range，vision ❷余地；机会：Give your child ～ to show his creativity. 给你的孩子展示创造力的机会。囘 room，opportunity

scorch / skɔːt / vt. 把…烧焦，把…烤焦；烫；炙伤：a face ～ed by tropic sun 被热带太阳晒过的脸 / The west side of the house had been ～ed evenly free of white paint. 房子的西侧被烤得焦黑，白漆一点也没有了。

score / skɔː(r) / Ⅰ n. ❶得分；比分；计分：The ～ at half time was 2 to 1. 上半场的记分为二比一。囘 goal，point ❷二十个；a ～ of people 二十个人 / I've been there ～s of times. 我去那儿很多次了。Ⅱ vt. 得(分)；记分：～ a goal

踢进一球而得分 / ～ a point 得一分 囘 gain，register

scorn / skɔːn / Ⅰ n. [U]轻蔑；蔑视；藐视：express ～ for one's deeds 对某人的行为表示蔑视 囘 contempt，ridicule 囝 affection，respect Ⅱ vt. 轻蔑；蔑视：It is natural for people to ～ liars. 人们蔑视说谎的人是很自然的。囘 despise，mock 囝 admire，accept

scrape / skreɪp / Ⅰ v. ❶刮；擦：～ mud from one's boots 擦去靴上的泥土 / The worker ～d the rust off the machine. 那工人擦去机器上的铁锈。囘 rub，smooth ❷擦伤；擦坏：The bike ～d the left side of my car. 自行车把我的小车左侧擦坏了。Ⅱ n. ❶[U]刮；擦；刮擦声 ❷[C]麻烦，困境：He got into ～s. 他陷入了困境。囘 difficulty，distress

scratch / skrætʃ / Ⅰ v. ❶抓；搔：The cat ～ed me. 猫抓了我。囘 scrape，rub ❷发刮擦声：This pen ～es. 这钢笔写字时发出刮擦声。❸仓促地写；乱涂：～ a few lines to a friend 仓促地写几句话给一位朋友 Ⅱ n. [C]搔痕；抓伤；抓搔声

scream / skriːm / Ⅰ v. (因恐惧、痛苦等)发出尖叫声：She ～ed in anger. 她愤怒地尖声叫喊。囘 shriek，roar 囝 whisper Ⅱ n. 尖叫声：the ～ of a peacock 孔雀的尖叫声 囘 shriek，roar 囝 whisper

screen / skriːn / n. [C]❶幕；帘；帐；屏风 囘 curtain，shutter ❷荧光屏；银幕 囘 movies，cinema

screw / skruː / Ⅰ n. [C]螺丝；螺丝钉：I have tightened the ～s. 我已经拧紧了那些螺丝钉。囘 bolt，nail/～driver n. 螺丝刀；起子 Ⅱ vt. 拧动；拧紧：～ the cap on (off) the bottle 拧紧(拧开)瓶盖 囘 fasten，twist

script / skrɪpt / n. ❶[U]手写体；手书，手迹：write in a tight ～ 字迹细密地书写 ❷[U；C]书写体；italic ～ 斜体字 ❸[C]剧本，脚本；广播稿：He deserves an Oscar for his original ～. 他应该获得奥斯卡原创电影剧本奖

sculpture / 'skʌlptʃə(r) / n. 雕刻；雕刻作品

sea / siː / n. 海，洋：follow the ～ 当海员；当水手 / by ～ 乘船；由海路 / travel by ～ and land 经海路和陆路旅行 囘 ocean / at ～ ①在海上；在航海中：The ship is at ～. 那艘船在航行中。②困惑，不知所措：He seems to be all at ～. 他似乎茫然不知所措。

seal¹ / siːl / Ⅰ n. 加封;封蜡;封铅;火漆;印章 同 stamp, symbol Ⅱ v. 封住:～ a letter 封好一封信/ ～ off the area 封锁这一地区 / ～ off from the outside world 与外界隔绝 同 close, fasten 反 unseal, open

seal² / siːl / n. [C]海豹

seam / siːm / n. [C] ❶缝;线缝:The bag has very strong ～s. 这包缝得很结实。❷接缝,边缝;裂缝:The ship has started at the ～s. 船板的接缝开裂了。❸(地)层;矿层;煤层:a coal ～煤层

search / sɜːtʃ / Ⅰ v. 搜寻;查究;探查:～ for truth 对真理追求/ ～ for the lost book 寻找丢失的书/ The customs officers ～ed the traveller's bags for smuggled goods. 海关人员搜查旅客的行李,看是否有走私的商品。同 examine, explore Ⅱ n. 搜寻;查究:make a ～ for contraband goods 搜查违禁品 同 examination, exploration / **in～ of** 寻找:The secretary looked here and there in ～ of the chairman of the meeting. 秘书到处寻找会议主席。

用法

search 作及物动词后加名词与作不及物动词加 for 或 out 的意思不同:The police are searching the man. 警察们正在搜查(指身)这个人。The police are searching for the man. 警察们正在搜寻这个人。The police have searched out the man. 警察们已经找到了这个人。

season / ˈsiːz(ə)n / Ⅰ n. [C] ❶季;季节:There are four ～s in a year. 一年有四季。同 quarter ❷时节;in ～ 旺季/ out of ～ 淡季/ The football ～ is drawing near. 足球赛季快到了。同 period, term Ⅱ vt. 给…加味;调味:Do you want to ～ the dish with pepper? 你想给菜里加点胡椒粉吗? 同 flavor

seasonal / ˈsiːzənəl / adj. 季节的;随季节变化的;季节性的;highly ～ goods 季节性很强的物品/Seymour's work at the seaside resort is ～. 西摩在海滨胜地工作是季节性的。

seat / siːt / Ⅰ n. [C] 座位:The back ～ of the car is wide enough for three persons. 车子的后座足够 3 个人坐。/ **take a ～**:Won't you take a ～? 你不坐吗? Ⅱ vt. ❶使坐下;使就座:Please be ～ed. 请坐下。❷有…的座位:a hall that ～s 500 有 500 个座位的大厅

辨析

seat 是及物动词,一般和反身代词连用或用过去分词形式:They put down their spades and baskets, and seated themselves on the ground. 他们放下铲子和篮子,坐在地上。I found him seated on the bench. 我发现他坐在凳子上。**sit** 一般用作不及物动词:She was sitting by the fire with her knitting on her lap. 她坐在火炉旁,膝上放着针织活。

seating / ˈsiːtɪŋ / n. [U]座位:My car ～ for five. 我的汽车可以坐 5 个人/The symphony hall has a ～ capacity of 2,000 people. 交响音乐厅可容纳 2 000 人。

second¹ / ˈsekənd / Ⅰ adj. (在地位、时间、次序、重要性等方面)第二的:February is the ～ month of the year. 二月是一年中的第二个月。/～ to 仅次于:She was ～ to her elder sister. 她仅次于她姐姐。**be ～ to none** 不亚于任何人(物) Ⅱ n. ❶第二个人(或物):You are the ～ to ask me the question. 你是第二个向我问那个问题的人。❷二等货:These stockings are ～s and have some slight defects. 这些长筒袜是次等货,有瑕疵。/ ～hand adj. 用过的,旧的;二手的 ❸(时间或角度计量单位的)秒:The winner's time was 1 minute and 5 ～s. 胜者的时间是一分零五秒。派 secondly adv.

second² / ˈsekənd / vt. 支持;赞同;附议:I ～ Bill 's motion. 我支持比尔的提议。同 back, support

secondary / ˈsekəndri / adj. ❶次要的;辅助的:It is a question of ～ importance. 那是个次要问题。同 minor, subordinate 反 superior, major ❷第二位的;中级的:～ education 中等教育/ ～ school 中等学校 同 second, following 反 first, primary

secret / ˈsiːkrət / Ⅰ adj. 秘密的;机密的;保密的:keep sth. ～ from one's family 不把某事告诉家人 / He escaped through a ～ door. 他从暗门逃走。同 private, unrevealed 反 public, open Ⅱ n. 秘密:keep a ～ 保守秘密 / meet in ～ 秘密会见/ state (trade) ～ 国家(商业)机密 / We have no ～s from you. 我们对你不保守任何秘密。同 mystery ❷秘诀;诀窍:What is the ～ of his success? 他成功的秘诀是什么? 同 formula, key 派 secretly adv.

secretary / ˈsekrətri, ˈsekrəteri / n. [C] ❶秘书

同 clerk, assistant ❷书记：the Party branch ～ 党支部书记 ❸大臣；部长；国务卿：Secretary of the State Department (美)国务卿

secrete / sɪˈkriːt / vt. 分泌：～s hormones 分泌激素

section / ˈsekʃn / n. [C] ❶一段；一节：Have you read the second ～ of the chapter? 你读过这一章的第二节吗? 同 chapter, passage ❷切下的部分；切片；截面：cross ～ 横截面 同 slice, part ❸地域；区域 同 area, district 派 sectional adj.

sector / ˈsektə(r) / n. [C] ❶(企业、社团的)部分；部门；(尤指)经济领域：the hi-tech ～s 高科技领域/Not every ～ of the economy was hit by the recession. 并非各个经济领域都受到萧条的冲击。❷地区，区域

secure / sɪˈkjʊə(r) / Ⅰ adj. 无忧的；安心的；安全的；feel ～ about one's future 不担心自己的前途/Are your words really ～ from attack? 你的言辞真的无懈可击吗? 同 safe, sure 反 insecure, unsafe Ⅱ v. 使安全(常与 from 或 against 连用)：By strengthening the embankments they ～d the village against (from) floods. 他们通过加固堤防使村庄免遭洪水之灾。同 guard, protect 反 endanger, harm

security / sɪˈkjʊərəti / n. ❶[U]安全：Security Council of the United Nations 联合国安理会/sense of ～安全感/public ～ bureau 公安局 同 safety 反 danger, insecurity ❷[C]提供安全之物 ❸[C](pl.)债券；证券：government securities 政府债券/issue securities 发行证券

sediment / ˈsedɪmənt / n. [U;C]沉淀(物)，沉积(物)；沉渣：There is (a) brownish ～ in your glass. 你的玻璃杯里有一层棕色的沉淀物。/riverine ～ 河流沉积物

see / siː / v. (saw/sɔː/, seen /siːn/) ❶看见；看到：Seeing is believing. (谚语) 眼见为实。同 notice, observe 反 neglect, overlook ❷了解；领会：He didn't ～ the point of the story. 他不明白那故事的寓意。/ I ～. 我明白了。同 understand 反 misunderstand ❸会见；访问：Can I ～ you on business? 我因公能见你吗? / You'd better go to ～ a doctor at once. 你最好马上去看病。同 meet, visit ❹护送；陪伴：May I ～ you home? 我可以送你回家吗? 同 accompany / ～ **sb. off** 为某人送行：I was seen off by many friends. 许多朋友为我送行。/ ～ **about** 查看；留意：I'll ～ about the notice.

我会查看一下通知的。～ **into sth.** 调查某事：Will you ～ into the matter first? 你先了解一下这件事情的情况好吗? ～ **sb. through** 使某人渡过难关：Don't worry. We'll ～ you through the difficulty. 别着急，我们会帮助你克服困难的。～ **through sb. (sth.)** 看穿；识破 ～ **to it that** 一定注意，务必：See to it that all the windows are closed before you leave. 离开前一定要关好所有的窗户。

用法
不定式作 see 的宾语补足语时 to 不出现，但作主语补足语时要带 to：I saw him walk up the hill. 我看见他步行上了山。He was seen to walk up the hill. 有人看见他步行上了山。

辨析
see 意为"看见；看到"，强调看的结果。look 指看的动作，不强调是否看见：He looked carefully at the blackboard, but didn't see anything on it. 他仔细地看黑板，但什么也没看见。

seed / siːd / Ⅰ n. [C](pl. seed 或 seeds) 种子：spread ～s 撒种 / It is time to sow the ～. 播种的时间到了。Ⅱ v. 挑选…为种子选手：～ed player 种子选手 / ～ed team 种子队

seek / siːk / v. (sought/sɔːt/, sought)寻找；寻求；探索：～ doctor's advice 请教医生 / ～ one's fortune 求发财 / His paintings are much sought after. 他的画被人争相收购。/ My sister is ～ing a job as secretary. 我姐姐正在谋求一份秘书工作。同 explore inspect 同 for (after) 寻找；探索；追求：One shouldn't ～ only for fame and wealth. 人不能只是追名逐利。

seem / siːm / vi. 似乎；好像；仿佛：What ～s easy to some people ～s difficult to others. 对某些人似乎是容易的事可能对另一些人是困难的。同 appear, look 派 seeming adj.；seemingly adv.

seep / siːp / vi. 渗出；渗漏：The boots allowed little water to ～ inside. 这双靴子不渗水。/ Toxins had ～ed into the groundwater. 毒素渗进了地下水。

seesaw / ˈsiːˌsɔː / n. [C] ❶跷跷板：play on a ～ 玩跷跷板 ❷一上一下的动作，拉锯式的动作；此起彼伏的交替过程：a ～ of terror and delight 恐惧和兴奋的交替

segment / ˈseɡmənt / Ⅰ n. [C]部分；部门；片断；环节；(水果的)瓣：tangerine ～s 橘子瓣/

It is an important ～ of our overall business. 这是我们整个生意中重要的一部分。Ⅱ *vt.* & *vi.* 分割,分裂;把…分开:The pieces of an orange ～ easily. 橘子瓣很容易分开。

segregate / ˈsegrɪgeɪt / *vt.* ❶使分开,使分离;把…隔开:～ a patient with scarlet fever 对猩红热病人实行隔离/Boys and girls are ～d into different dining rooms. 男女生被分别安排在不同的饭厅里。❷对…实行种族隔离:It is illegal to ～ people of different races. 对不同种族的人实行隔离属不合法。

seize / siz / *v.* ❶(依照法律)扣押,查封,没收:～ sb.'s goods for payment of debt 扣押某人的货物以偿付债务 ❷强取;抓住:～ a thief by the collar 抓住小偷的衣领 同 capture,grasp

seldom / ˈseldəm / *adv.* 很少;不常:She ～ goes out. 她不常外出。同 rarely,occasionally 反 always,often

select / sɪˈlekt / Ⅰ *v.* 选择;挑选:I want to ～ some novels for reading. 我想选几本小说读。同 choose,pick 反 refuse,reject Ⅱ *adj.* 精选的:～ passages from Shakespeare 从莎士比亚著作中精选的段落 同 chosen,picked 反 random

selection / sɪˈlekʃn / *n.* ❶[U]选择;挑选:～ committee 选拔委员会 / natural ～ 自然淘汰 / seed ～ 选种 同 choice,pick ❷[C]挑选物;选集:We are going to read some poetic ～s. 我们要读一些诗歌选篇。

selective / sɪˈlektɪv / *adj.* 选择的;挑选的;有选择性的:a ～ bibliography of almost 500 references 罗列了将近 500 条的精选参考节目/wealthy lady is very ～ about clothes. 那位阔太太对衣着十分挑剔。

self / self / Ⅰ *adj.* 自己的 Ⅱ *n.* (*pl.* selves / selvz/) ❶本性;特质 ❷私利;私欲

self-confidence / ˌselfˈkɒnfɪdəns / *n.* [U]自信 派 self-confident *adj.*

self-conscious / selfˈkɒnʃəs / *adj.* 自觉的;自我意识的

self-control / ˌselfkənˈtrəʊl / *n.* [U]自控:lose ～ 失去自控

self-defence(-se) / ˌselfdɪˈfens / *n.* [U]自卫:The young man said he killed the thief for ～. 那年轻人说他因自卫杀死了那个小偷。

self-government / ˌselfˈgʌvənmənt / *n.* [U]自治

selfish / ˈselfɪʃ / *adj.* 自私的 同 greedy 反 unselfish 派 selfishly *adv.*

self-made / ˌselfˈmeɪd / *adj.* 自制的;自己做的;白手起家的

self-respect / ˌselfrɪˈspekt / *n.* [U]自尊

self-sacrifice / ˌselfˈsækrɪfaɪs / *n.* [U]自我牺牲

self-service / sefˈsɜːvɪs / Ⅰ *adj.* (商店、餐馆、车库等)自助服务的,自助消费的 Ⅱ *n.* [U]自助服务

self-sufficient / selfsəˈfɪʃənt / *adj.* 自给自足的:Japan is not ～ in raw materials. 日本在原材料方面不能自给。

self-supporting / ˌselfsəˈpɔːtɪŋ / *adj.* 自立的;She was ～ at the age of twelve. 她 12 岁就自立了。

self-taught / ˌselfˈtɔːt / *adj.* 自学(成才)的,自修(学成)的

sell / sel / *v.* (sold / səʊld/,sold)卖;售;销:～ sth. at a good price 高价卖某物 / ～ at bargain 廉价出售;大拍卖 / ～ at a loss 亏本出售 / ～ by dozen (yard) 按打(码)出售 / ～ under the counter 私下(非法)出售 / The new book ～s well. 这本新书很畅销。同 deal,trade 反 buy / ～ out 售完:This edition of the dictionary is sold out. 本版词典已售完。

semester / sɪˈmestə(r) / *n.* [C]半年;半学年;学期:～ examination 期末考试 / The new ～ will begin next Monday. 新学期下周一开始。同 term

semicircle / ˈsemɪsɜːkl / *n.* [C] 半圆

semicolon / ˌsemɪˈkəʊlən / *n.* [C] 分号;

semicolony / ˌsemɪˈkɒləni / *n.* [C] 半殖民地

semiconductor / ˌsemɪkənˈdʌktə(r) / *n.* 半导体

semifinal / ˌsemɪˈfaɪnl / *n.* & *adj.* 半决赛(的)

semimonthly / ˌsemɪˈmʌnθli / *n.*[C]半月刊

seminar / ˈsemɪnɑː(r) / *n.* [C](大学的)研讨班;研讨会

senate / ˈsenət / *n.*[C]参议院

senator / ˈsenətə / *n.*[C]参议员

send / send / *v.* (sent /sent/,sent) 送;寄:～ sb. a message 送消息给某人 / I have two letters to ～. 我有两封信要寄。同 dispatch, convey 反 hold, receive / ～ **for** 派人去请;吩咐做:We had better ～ for a doctor at once. 我们最好立刻把医生找来。～ **in** ①把…请入(领入,迎入);Send in the next person waiting, please, nurse. 护士,请把下一个等着的人领进来。②呈递;提交:Has he sent in his paper yet? 他的论文交了吗? ～ **out** ①发出:The sun ～s out light and heat. 太阳发出光和热。② 生出;长出:The tree ～s out new shoots in spring. 树木在春天长出新芽。～ **up** 使升高:A piece of cake every night will ～ your weight up. 每夜吃一块饼会使你的体重增加。/ Another spaceship has been sent up recently. 最近又有一艘宇宙飞船上天。

用法
send 指通过他人或某种手段把某物送给某人或把某人送到某地,一般不指自己亲自送,如不能说:I'll send the book to your house myself this evening. (应该把 send 改为 bring)

senior / ˈsiːniə(r) / *adj.* 年长的;职位较高的;资深的:～ middle school 高中 / He is ten years ～ to me. 他比我年长十岁。同 elder, superior 反 younger, junior

用法
senior 和 junior 一样,常与介词 to 连用,表示比较级。

sensation / senˈseɪʃn / *n.* 感觉;知觉 同 feeling, perception

sense / sens / Ⅰ *n.* ❶感官;感觉:have a keen ～ of hearing 听觉敏锐 同 feeling, sensation ❷观念;意识:a ～ of humour 幽默感 / a ～ of duty 责任感 同 awareness, impression ❸判断力;判断;见识:He had a poor ～ of the worth of a thing. 他认识事物价值的能力很差。同 judgment, understanding ❹ 含义:a word with several ～s 有几个含义的词 同 meaning, definition 反 nonsense / **come to one's ～s** 恢复理性;醒悟过来(昏迷后)苏醒过来 **in a ～** 从某种意义上说:What he said in a ～ true. 他说的话在某种意义上是正确的。**make ～** 有意义;使理解:What you say does not make ～ to me. 我不理解你说的话。**out of one's ～s** 神志失常;失去理性:Why did you gamble with those persons? Are you out of your ～s? 你为什么和那些人赌博? 你疯了吗? Ⅱ *v.* 感到;意识到:She fully ～d the dan-ger of her position. 她完全感觉得到她处境危险。同 feel, perceive

senseless / ˈsensləs / *adj.* ❶愚蠢的;无意义的:a ～ idea 愚蠢的想法 同 stupid, meaningless 反 clever, meaningful ❷无感觉的;不省人事的:fall ～ to the ground 无知觉地倒在地上 同 unconscious, insensible 反 conscious, sensible

sensibility / ˌsensəˈbɪləti / *n.* ❶[U]感觉(力),感受(力):He has the great ～ of a comedian. 他颇有做喜剧演员的悟性。❷[U]敏感(性),善感(性);感受(性):He has a poetic ～, keen psychological insights. 他有诗人的敏感性,以及敏锐的心理洞察力。❸(*pl.*)感情,情绪:Her sensibilities were greatly injured. 她的感情受到极大伤害。

sensible / ˈsensəbl / *adj.* ❶有判断力的;明智的:a ～ woman 明智的女人 同 reasonable, wise 反 stupid, unwise ❷感知的(与 of 连用):He is ～ of danger. 他觉察到危险。同 aware, conscious 反 insensible, unaware

sensitive / ˈsensətɪv / *adj.* ❶敏感的;易受影响的(与 to 连用):He is ～ to cold. 他极易感冒。同 keen, sensing ❷灵敏的:The ears are ～ to sound. 耳朵对声音都很敏感。同 fine, delicate 反 rough

sensor / ˈsensə(r) / *n.* 传感器;敏感元件

sentence / ˈsentəns / Ⅰ *n.* ❶[C]句子:～ **by** ～ 一句一句地;逐句地:He read the article ～ by ～. 他逐句念完了整篇文章。**make a ～ with** 用…造句:The teacher asked his students to make ～s with the new words. 这位老师要求他的学生用新单词造句。❷[U]判决;宣判:long (short, life) ～ 长期(短期、无期)徒刑 / death (severe) ～ 死(重)刑 同 condemnation, judgment Ⅱ *vt.* 判决;宣判:He was ～d to five years. 他被判刑五年。同 condemn, judge / ～ **sb. to death** 判某人死刑:Murderers are ～d to death in some countries. 在一些国家杀人犯要被判处死刑。

sentimental / ˌsentɪˈmentl / *adj.* ❶多情的,情深的;充满柔情的:～ reminiscences 深情的回忆 ❷感伤的;多愁善感的:a ～ love song 令人怀恋的情歌 / I felt a little ～ and lonely at times. 我时不时感到有些伤感和孤独。

separate / ˈseprət / Ⅰ *adj.* 分离的;分开的:Cut it into three ～ parts. 把它切成三份。同

S

unconnected, single 反 connected, united Ⅱ v. 使分离；把…隔开同 divide, part 反 join, connect / ～ ... from ...把…和…分开：England is ～d from France by the Channel. 英国和法国被英吉利海峡隔开。 ～ sth. into ... 把…分成：The teacher ～ d us into three study groups. 老师把我们分成三个学习小组。派 separately adv.

September / sep'tembə(r) / n. 九月

sequence / 'si:kwəns / n. ❶连续；一连串：They have had a ～ of bumper harvests. 他们已经连续获得大丰收。同 series, procession ❷次序；顺序：Do you know the ～ of those events? 你知道那些事件的先后次序吗？同 order

serf / sɜ:f / n. [C]农奴 同 slave

sergeant / 'sɑ:dʒənt / n. [C]❶士官；中士 ❷警官

serial / 'sɪərɪəl / Ⅰ n. [C]❶连载作品；系列影片；连播节目：a television ～ 电视连续剧/appear as a ～ in a newspaper 以连载的形式刊登在报纸上 ❷期刊；（分期发表的）系列报告 Ⅱ adj. ❶分期连载的，分次连续播映的：a serial publication 分期连载的出版物 ❷连续的；排成系列的：Many firms mark their goods with a ～ number. 很多公司用序列号作为其商品的标记。❸系列的，连环的：～ murders 系列杀人案

series / 'sɪəri:z / n. [C]（单复数同形）❶系列；连续：in ～ 连续地 / TV ～ 电视连续剧 / a ～ of events 一系列事件 / The children asked me a ～ of questions. 孩子们问了我一系列问题。同 sequence, succession ❷套：a ～ of coins 一套硬币 / a ～ of stamps 一套邮票 / I bought a ～ of science books yesterday. 昨天我买了一套科学图书。同 set

serious / 'sɪərɪəs / adj. ❶严肃的；严重的：～ face 表情严肃 / a ～ illness 重病 同 severe, solemn 反 slight, minor ❷认真的；真诚的：Please be ～ about your work. 请认真工作。同 sincere, honest 反 insincere, dishonest 派 seriously adv. ; seriousness n.

servant / 'sɜ:vənt / n. [C]❶仆人；佣人；服务员：dismiss a ～ 解雇服务员 / Do you want to employ a ～? 你要雇服务员吗？/ ～-girl, ～-maid 女仆 同 helper, employee 反 master, employer ❷（政府的）雇员，公务员

serve / sɜ:v / v. ❶做仆人 ❷供职；服务：～ the people 为人民服务 / He ～s as a teacher at school. 他在学校当老师。同 attend, work ❸侍候（顾客等）；供给；上（菜等）；开（饭等）：We are well ～ d with gas（electricity）in this town. 我们这个镇的居民都有足够的煤气（电）供应。/ Dinner is ～d. 饭已上好。同 supply

service / 'sɜ:vɪs / n. [C]❶服务；贡献：His ～s to the State have been immense. 他对国家的贡献很大。同 help, profit ❷公共设施；公共设施的运转：bus（water, gas, telephone）～ 公共汽车（水、气、电话）服务设施 同 facility, utility ❸商业性服务机构；礼拜仪式：attend Sunday ～ s in the church 星期天到教堂做礼拜 同 ceremony ❺（商品的）保养，维修，售后服务：The manufacturer provides good ～ for its products. 那家厂商提供很好的产品售后服务。同 maintenance, repair

session / 'seʃn / n. [C]会议；会期；一届：the spring（autumn）～ 春季（秋季）会议 同 meeting, period

set / set / Ⅰ v.（set, set）❶（指太阳、月亮等天体）落下，下沉：It will be cooler when the sun has ～. 太阳落山后，天气就会凉爽些。同 sink 反 rise ❷置放；摆：She ～ the dishes on the table. 她把菜放在桌上。同 put, place 反 remove, lift ❸树立（榜样等）；创造（记录）：You should ～ a good example. 你应该树立好榜样。❹提出（任务等）；出（题目）：Who will ～ the questions for the examination? 试题由谁出？同 assign, prepare ❺使（某人）做某事；开始从事：It's time we ～ to work. 是我们该开始工作的时候了。❻嵌；镶：a gold ring ～ with gems 镶有宝石的金戒指 同 fix, ornament/ ～ about 开始；着手：They will ～ about a new project. 我们将开始进行一项新的工程。～ apart 拨出；留出：They decided to ～ apart a sum of money for a new classroom building. 他们决定拨一笔钱修新教学大楼。～ aside ① 拨出；留出：Mother ～s aside some money each month. 妈妈每月都存一点钱。② 把…置于一旁；不理会：He ～ aside all objections and went to the mountain area. 他不顾所有人的反对而去了山区。～ back 推迟；延缓；阻碍：The rain ～ back our touring plan. 大雨使我们的旅游计划推迟。～ free 释放：Do as I tell you and you shall be ～ free. 照我吩咐的去做，你就可以获得释放。～ off ①

出发：He ～ off for Shanghai this morning. 他今天早上动身去上海。② 使爆炸：A spark will～ off fireworks. 一点火花就会使烟花爆炸。～ **out** ① 出发 ② 开始（从事）：Setting out in business is not an easy job. 开创一项事业是不容易的事。③ 打算：I ～ out to make the dress by myself，but in the end I had to ask for help. 我本打算自己做这件衣服的，结果还是得求助于人。④ 说明；阐明：Be sure to ～ out the points of your argument in details. 记住一定要详细地阐明你的观点。～ **up** 建立；创立；竖立：He ～ up his tent. 他搭起了帐篷。/ They ～ up a school for children. 他们为孩子们创办了一所学校。Ⅱ n. [C]❶套；组；副：a ～ of silver cups 一套银质茶杯 同 group ❷电子器械：a television ～ 电视机 同 apparatus Ⅲ adj. 不变的；固定的；规定的；约定的 同 definite，firm 反 indefinite

setback / ˈsetˌbæk / n. [C]挫折；失利，失败；倒退；(旧病的)复发：a temporary ～ in one's fortunes 命运中的暂时挫折/face up to innumerable ～s 勇敢面对无数的挫折/ an unexpected ～ in a patient's recovery 病人康复过程中意想不到的反复

setting / ˈsetɪŋ / n. [C]❶安装；调整 ❷环境；背景：social ～ 社会环境 / stage ～ 舞台布景 同 environment，surroundings

settle / ˈsetl / v. ❶安家，定居(与 in，at 连用)；停留(与 on 连用)：～ in Canada 定居加拿大 / The cold has ～d on my chest. 我患了感冒。/ Isn't it time that Tom got married and ～d down? 难道汤姆结婚成家的时候还没到吗？同 inhabit 反 wander，emigrate ❷解决；决定：～ an argument 结束争论 / Nothing is ～d yet. 诸事未定。同 decide，set ❸支付；结算：～ a bill 付账 / I shall ～ (up) with you at the end of the month. 我月底和你结清账。同 pay，clear / **down to sth. (to do sth.)** 安下心来做某事：You should ～ down to your homework. 你应当安下心来做作业。派 settlement n.

set-up / ˈsetʌp / n. [C]❶结构；设置；安排；组织，机构；体制：learn the ～ of a company 了解一个公司的组织情况 / We must rebuild the entire port ～. 我们必须改造整个港口的结构。❷准备，计划，方案

seven / ˈsevn / Ⅰ num. 七 Ⅱ adj. 七个(的)

seventeen / ˌsevnˈtiːn / Ⅰ num. 十七 Ⅱ adj. 十七个(的)

seventeenth / ˌsevnˈtiːnθ / Ⅰ num. 第十七；十七分之一 Ⅱ adj. 第十七的；十七分之一的

seventh / ˈsevnθ / Ⅰ num. 第七；七分之一 Ⅱ adj. 第七的；七分之一的

seventieth / ˈsevntɪəθ / Ⅰ num. 第七十；七十分之一 Ⅱ adj. 第七十的；七十分之一的

seventy / ˈsevnti / Ⅰ num. 七十 Ⅱ adj. 七十个(的)

several / ˈsevrəl / Ⅰ adj. 几个的；数个的：I've read it ～ times. 我已经读过好几次了。同 some Ⅱ pron. 几个；数个 同 some

severe / sɪˈvɪə(r) / adj. ❶严厉的；严格的：be ～ with one's child 对孩子严厉 同 strict，harsh 反 gentle，kind ❷严重的；剧烈的：～ pain 剧痛 同 intense，violent 反 gentle，mild 派 severely adv.

sew / səʊ / v. (sewed / səʊd /，sewn / səʊn / 或 sewed) 缝；缝合：～ a button on 钉扣子 同 stitch，mend 派 sewing n.

sex / seks / n. [C]性别；性：equality of ～es 男女平等 / the female ～ 女性 / the male ～ 男性 / the other ～ 异性 / the third ～ (总称)搞同性恋的人 / school for both ～es 男女生学校

shabby / ˈʃæbi / adj. (-ier，-iest)破旧的；褴褛的：He looks rather ～ in those clothes. 他穿上那些衣服显得很寒碜。同 worn，ragged 反 new，neat

shack / ʃæk / n. [C]简易房屋，棚屋：The old buzzard has lived in the seam ～ for 20 years. 那个老家伙在同一棚屋里住了 20 年。

shade / ʃeid / Ⅰ n. [U]❶阴凉处：Keep in the ～；it's cooler. 待在阴凉处吧，那儿比较凉爽。同 shadow，darkness 反 sunlight，brightness ❷(图画等的)阴暗部分：There is not enough light and ～ in your drawing. 你的图画中明暗色调不够。Ⅱ v. 遮蔽；遮挡：He ～d his eyes with his hand. 他用手遮眼睛。同 darken，cover 反 lighten，uncover

shadow / ˈʃædəʊ / n. [C]影子；阴影：The ～ gets longer when the sun sets. 太阳落山时影子会变长。同 shade，darkness / **be afraid of one's own ～** 胆小得不得了 **beyond the ～ of a doubt** 无可置疑地，一定 **catch at ～s** 捕风捉影 **quarrel with one's own ～** 莫名其妙地无事生气 **under the ～ of** ①在…的庇护之下；因…的

影响 ②被置于…的危险之下

辨析

shadow 指物体在壁面、地面、水面等上形成的阴影，有一定的轮廓。shade 指光线所不及的地方，阴影没有一定的轮廓。通常说 under a shadow 和 in the shade。

shady / ˈʃeɪdɪ / adj. (-ier, -iest) 遮阴的；成荫的；背阴的：the ～ side of the street 街道阴凉的一边 同 shaded 反 sunny, unshaded

shake / ʃeɪk / v. (shook /ʃʊk/, shaken /ˈʃeɪkən/) 摇动；(使)震动；(使)颤抖：～ head over 对…摇头(表不赞成) / ～ leaves from a tree 摇落树上的叶子 / ～ one's fist at sb. 向某人挥拳(表示挑战、威胁等) / ～ one's sides with laughter 捧腹大笑 / He was shaking with cold. 他冷得发抖。/ He shook hands with me. 他和我握手。同 vibrate, tremble / ～ **off** 抖落；摆脱；甩掉：～ off the cold 驱除感冒 / ～ off old ideas 抛弃旧思想

shaky / ˈʃeɪkɪ / adj. 动摇的；不可靠的；发抖的 同 wavering, trembling

shall / ʃæl, ʃəl / aux. v. (should /ʃʊd, ʃəd/) ❶ (用于构成将来时；用于第一人称肯定式、疑问式及第二人称疑问式)会：We ～ arrive tomorrow. 我们将于明日到达。/ Shall we go there tomorrow? 我们明天将去那儿吗？❷ (用以表示说话者的意志或意愿)一定，必定会：If you work well, you ～ have higher wages. 如果你工作好，你就可得到较高的薪水。❸ (用于表示责任、命令或指示)要，应该：Shall I open the window? 要我打开窗子吗？/ You ～ not have it; it's mine. 你不可以拿它，那是我的。

shallow / ˈʃæləʊ / adj. ❶浅的；不深的：～ water 浅水 / a ～ saucer 浅碟 ❷肤浅的；浅薄的 同 superficial, slight

sham / ʃæm / Ⅰ n. 假冒；赝品 同 fake, copy 反 original Ⅱ vt. 假装 同 pretend, imitate

shame / ʃeɪm / Ⅰ n. [U] ❶羞愧，耻辱；羞耻心：feel ～ at having told a lie 因说谎而感到羞愧 / feel ～ at failing in an examination 因考试失败而感到羞愧 同 disgrace, guilt 反 pride, honor ❷ (用不定冠词)不足取的事，可耻的事(口语中相当于 pity)：What a ～ to deceive the girl! 欺骗那女孩是多么可耻的事啊！/ That he missed the boat is a ～. 他没赶上船，太遗憾了。同 disgrace, scandal Ⅱ vt. 使

感到羞愧；使丢脸 同 disgrace, humble 派 shameful adj.

shameless / ˈʃeɪmləs / adj. 无耻的；厚颜的 同 indecent, corrupt 反 decent 派 shamelessly adv.

shampoo / ʃæmˈpu: / Ⅰ vt. 用洗发剂洗(头发) Ⅱ n. (pl. shampoos) 洗发；洗发剂，洗发液

shape / ʃeɪp / Ⅰ n. 样子；外形；形状：My garden is in the ～ of a square. 我的园子是长方形的。同 figure, outline / **in** ～ 形式上；外形上：In ～ the building looks like a ship. 这楼房在外形上像一艘轮船。**get sth. into** ～ 使成形；使有条理：I find it difficult to get my ideas into ～. 我发现很难把思路理顺。**give** ～ **to** 使成形：At last they gave ～ to the plan. 计划终于成形了。**take** ～ 成形：Bit by bit, the idea took ～ in her mind. 主意慢慢地在她的脑子里形成了。Ⅱ v. 成形 同 form, frame 反 destroy, ruin 派 shapely adj.

share / ʃeə(r) / Ⅰ n. [C] ❶ (共有的)一份；部分：Please let me take a ～ in the expenses. 这些费用请让我出一份。同 part, portion / **go** ～**s with sb. in sth.** 与某人分享(分担)某物：I'll go ～s with you in the expenses. 我将与你一起分担费用。**have a** ～ **in** 在…中参与一份：We all have a ～ in the profit of the company. 公司所赚的钱我们都有一份。❷股份：～ index 股票指数 / He holds 200 ～s in the company. 他在公司里持有 200 股。Ⅱ v. ❶分给；分配；分派：He would ～ his last penny with me. 他即使只有一分钱，也会分给我用。同 divide ❷共有；共用；共享：He hated having to ～ the bedroom with a stranger. 他讨厌与陌生人共住这间卧室。同 participate / ～ **sth. out among (between)** 在…中平均分配某物：The group leader ～d the work among us. 组长把工作平均分派给我们。/ ～ **sth. with sb.** 与某人分享(分担)某物：I ～ the book with the monitor. 我和班长共用一本书。

shark / ʃɑ:k / n. [C] ❶鲨鱼 ❷贪婪狡猾的人

sharp / ʃɑ:p / Ⅰ adj. ❶锋利的：a ～ knife 快刀 同 keen, keen-edged 反 dull, round ❷尖声的；刺耳的：a ～ cry of distress 痛苦的尖叫声 同 harsh, high-toned 反 soft, low ❸尖刻的；厉害的：～ words 尖刻的话 / a ～ tongue 利舌 同 cruel, severe 反 gentle, kind Ⅱ adv. ❶准时

地；整：at seven (o'clock) 〜七点整 同 punc-tually, precisely ❷突然：turn 〜 to the left 急向左转 同 suddenly 派 sharply *adv.* ; sharp-ness *n.*

sharpen / ˈʃɑːpən / *v.* 使尖锐；使急剧：〜 a pen-cil 削尖铅笔 / My razor needs 〜ing. 我的剃刀需要磨了。派 sharpener *n.*

shatter / ˈʃætə(r) / Ⅰ *vt.* ❶使粉碎，打碎，砸碎：〜 a vase 打碎花瓶/ The force of the ex-plosion 〜ed the windows. 爆炸的威力把窗户玻璃震碎了。❷破坏，损害，使（希望等）破灭：〜 the world peace 破坏世界和平/Her hopes were 〜ed by the news. 她的希望被那个消息粉碎了。—*vi.* 被打碎；破碎，碎裂：Glassware is liable to 〜. 玻璃器皿容易破碎。Ⅱ *n.*［C］碎片：The broken vase lay in 〜s. 打破的花瓶已成了碎片。

shave / ʃeɪv / *v.* (shaved, shaved 或 shaven) 刮(胡子)；修面：Do you 〜 yourself or go to the barber's? 你自己修面还是到理发店修面？同 trim, cut Ⅱ *n.*［C］刮脸：My father has a 〜 every morning. 我的父亲每天早晨都要刮脸。

she / ʃiː / *pron.* 她

shed[1] / ʃed / *n.*［C］棚；小屋 同 shat

shed[2] / ʃed / *vt.* (shed, shed; shedding) 脱落；流出；散发：〜 tears 哭泣 / The soldiers 〜 their blood for the country. 战士们为国流血牺牲。同 drop, spill 反 suppress, stop

sheep / ʃiːp / *n.*［C］(单复数同形)羊；绵羊：a black 〜 败家子；害群之马 / a wolf in 〜's clothing 披着羊皮的狼

sheet / ʃiːt / *n.*［C］❶被单：put a clean 〜 on the bed 在床上铺干净的床单 ❷一片；一张：a 〜 of paper 一张纸 / as pale(white) as a 〜 脸色苍白如纸 / The book is in 〜s. 这本书尚未装订。同 piece, leaf

shelf / ʃelf / *n.*［C］(*pl.* shelves/ʃelvz/)（食橱、书架、书柜等的）隔板，架：Please replace the books on the shelves after reading. 读完书后请放回书架。

shell / ʃel / *n.*［C］❶(种子、果实等的)壳；(虫的)甲，壳 ❷炮弹

shelter / ˈʃeltə(r) / Ⅰ *n.* ❶［U］庇护，保护；遮蔽：take 〜 from the rain 躲雨 同 refuge, protection 反 exposure ❷［C］庇护物；庇护所；避难所：a bus 〜 公共汽车候车亭 同 refuge, defence Ⅱ *v.* 庇护；保护；掩护：trees that 〜 a

house from cold wind 遮蔽房屋使其不受寒风侵袭的大树 / 〜 an escaped prisoner 窝藏逃犯 同 protect, guard 反 expose

shepherd / ˈʃepəd / *n.*［C］牧羊人

shield / ʃiːld / Ⅰ *n.*［C］❶盾，盾牌 ❷防御物；保护物；保护者：protective 〜 against infec-tion 抵御感染的保护屏障 ❸盾形物：The sun showed half its 〜 above the horizon. 太阳在地平线露出半个盾形。Ⅱ *vt.* ❶(似)用盾挡住；挡护；遮挡：The ozone layer 〜s all living things against harmful ultraviolet rays from the sun. 臭氧层可保护所有生物不受来自太阳有害的紫外线的辐射。❷防御；保护，防护：〜 a state-owned economy from the competi-tive pressures of global market 保护国有经济免受全球市场的竞争压力

shift / ʃɪft / Ⅰ *v.* 移动；变换：〜 the blame (on)to sb. else 诿过于他人 / The wind has 〜ed to the north. 风向转北。同 move, trans-fer Ⅱ *n.* ❶(位置或性格的)改变，变换 同 change, move ❷换班；值班：day（night）〜 日(夜)班 / working in 〜s 轮班工作

shine / ʃaɪn / Ⅰ *v.* (shone /ʃɒn/, shone 或 shined, shined) ❶发光，照耀：His face shone with excitement. 他因兴奋而容光焕发。同 glow, glitter ❷卓越；出众：He does not 〜 in conversation. 他的谈吐并不出众。同 excel ❸磨光，擦亮：〜 shoes 擦鞋 同 polish, brighten Ⅱ *n.*［U］光亮；光泽：rain or 〜 无论晴雨 / Give your shoes a good 〜. 把你的鞋好好擦一下。同 brightness, polish

shiny / ˈʃaɪni / *adj.* (-ier, -iest) ❶发光的；晴朗的 同 bright, clear 反 gloomy, cloudy ❷擦亮的；磨光的 同 polished, glassy

ship / ʃɪp / Ⅰ *n.*［C］轮船；海船：by 〜 乘船 / load(unload) a 〜 装船(卸船) / take a 〜 乘船 / The factory builds sea-going 〜s. 这个工厂造海船。Ⅱ *v.* (shipped; shipping) 装上船；用船运：They 〜ped the goods to Shang-hai. 他们把货物用船运到上海。同 transport, send

shirt / ʃɜːt / *n.*［C］男衬衣；(美)宽松的女上衣

shiver / ˈʃɪvə(r) / Ⅰ *vi.* (尤指因寒冷或恐惧而)颤抖：〜ing all over with cold 冷得全身颤抖 同 shake, tremble Ⅱ *n.* (常用 *pl.*) 颤抖；哆嗦：get (have) the 〜s 发抖/The sight sent cold 〜s down my back. 那景象使我不寒而栗。同 tremble

S

shock / ʃɒk / Ⅰ n. ❶击；打击 同 blow ❷震惊 同 surprise, horror ❸休克 Ⅱ vt. 使休克；使感到震惊；使感到愤恨：I was ～ed at the news of her death. 她去世的消息使我感到震惊。同 astonish, distress

shoe / ʃuː / n. [C]鞋：put on (take off) one's ～s 穿(脱)鞋

shoelace / ˈʃuːˌleɪs / n. [C]鞋带：His ～s have come loose 他的鞋带松了。

shoot / ʃuːt / Ⅰ v. (shot /ʃɒt/, shot) ❶射击；开枪：They were ～ing at a target. 他们在打靶。同 hit, fire ❷发芽；生枝：Rose bushes ～ again after being cut back. 玫瑰丛在修剪后又会萌发新枝。同 sprout ❸拍照；摄影 ❹投(篮)；射门：～ a basket 投篮 / ～a goal 进一球 Ⅱ n. ❶射击 ❷芽，苗；嫩枝 同 bud, sprout

shop / ʃɒp / Ⅰ n. [C]商店 同 store Ⅱ vi. (shopped; shopping) 购物 同 buy, purchase

> **辨析**
> shop 在英国通常指"店"，在美国指"工场"。department store (百货公司)原是美语中的说法，但现在用得很普遍，英国有时称这种公司为 store。

shopping / ˈʃɒpɪŋ / n. [U]购物：do one's ～ 购物 / a ～ bag 购物袋

shore / ʃɔː(r) / n. [C](水域的)岸，滨 同 beach, coast

short / ʃɔːt / adj. ❶短的；短暂的；矮的：a ～ stick 短棍 / a ～ man 个子矮的人 / a ～ holiday 短暂的假期 同 little, small 反 long, tall ❷不足的；缺少的：The shopkeeper was fined for giving ～ weight. 那店主因卖东西缺斤短两而被罚款。同 scarce, lacking 反 abundant, plentiful / **be ～ of** 缺乏：They are ～ of money. 他们缺钱。**in ～**总之；简言之：In ～, we should do something for her. 总之，我们应当为她做点什么。

shortage / ˈʃɔːtɪdʒ / n. 不足，缺少：a ～ of talented people 人才缺乏 / food ～ 食品短缺 / housing ～ 住房紧张 / labor ～ 劳动力匮乏 / teacher ～ 缺乏师资 同 lack, scarcity

shortcoming / ˈʃɔːtˌkʌmɪŋ / n. (常用 pl.)缺点，短处；缺陷：a person with many ～s一个有许多缺点的人/reveal some serious ～s in the safety procedures 暴露安全程序中的一些严重缺陷

shortcut / ˈʃɔːtkʌt / n. [C]捷径；近路：Is there a ～ we can take? 我们有近路可走吗？/ Can you find a ～ to success? 你能找到通向成功的捷径吗？

shorten / ˈʃɔːtn / vt. (使)缩小；(使)减少，使不足：～ one's visit 缩短某人的访问时间 / My coat is too long；I'll have ～ed it. 我的外套太长，我得把它剪短一点。反 lessen, reduce 反 lengthen

shortly / ˈʃɔːtli / adv. ❶立刻；不久：I'll be back ～. 我不久就回来。同 soon, presently / ～ **after** 不久：The doctor came ～ after breakfast. 早饭后不久大夫就来了。❷简短地；简要地：Mr. Zhang explained the problem ～. 张先生简要地解释了这个问题。同 briefly 反 lengthily

shortsighted / ˌʃɔːtˈsaɪtɪd / adj. 近视的；目光短浅的：The girl is ～. 那女孩近视。/ It is ～ of you to give up all efforts. 你放弃一切努力，目光太短浅了。

short-term / ˈʃɔːtˈtɜːm / adj. 短期的，短时间的：cope with the ～ lack of money 处理资金暂时短缺的问题/～ earnings 短期收益

shot / ʃɒt / n. [C] ❶(枪、炮等的)发射，射击；枪炮声：hear ～s in the distance 听到远处的枪声 同 gunfire, explosion ❷射手；枪手；炮手：He's a first-class ～. 他是一流的射手。❸铅球：put a ～ 掷铅球 ❹注射：give sb. a ～ 给某人打针 同 injection ❺镜头

should / ʃʊd / aux. v. ❶shall 的过去式 ❷应当，应该(表示义务、责任)：We ～ do as he said. 我们应照他说的做。/ He should go to see a doctor earlier. 他应该早点去看医生。❸万一，一旦(表示假设)：If he ～ change his mind, let us know. 一旦他改变主意，请告知我们。❹意外：It is strange that you ～ say so. 很奇怪，你竟然这样说。❺想，愿(表示意愿)：I ～ like to have a bath. 我想洗个澡。❻大概，可能(表示推测)：The children ～ be home by now. 孩子们现在应该到家了。

shoulder / ˈʃəʊldə(r) / Ⅰ n. [C]肩：～ to ～ 肩并肩：The soldiers marched forward ～ to ～. 战士们肩并肩向前进。/ **have sth. on one's ～s** 肩负；承担：We young people have a heavy task on our ～s. 我们年轻人重任在肩。Ⅱ vt. 肩负；承担；挑起 同 undertake, carry 反 avoid, neglect

shout / ʃaʊt / Ⅰ v. 大声喊叫；大声说：He ～ed

to me to go there. 他大声喊我过去。～ at sb. 对某人喊叫 同 roar,yell Ⅱ v. 大叫；呼喊：～ s of joy 欢乐的喊叫 同 roar,yell

shovel / ˈʃʌvl / n. [C]铲；锹 同 spade

show / ʃəʊ / Ⅰ u. (showed,shown /ʃəʊn/ 或 showed) ❶给…看；展示：He ～ed his album to all his friends. 他把他的相册给所有的朋友看。同 display 反 conceal / ～up 到场；出席；露面：Nobody knew why Mr. John didn't ～ up at the evening. 没有人知道为什么约翰先生不出席晚会。❷指示；引导；带领 同 lead, guide / ～ around (round) 带领参观：My husband will ～ you around (round) while I get the tea. 我备茶时,我丈夫会带你四周参观一下。～ off 卖弄;炫耀:She is always ～ing off. 她老爱炫耀自己。～ sb. out (in) 领某人出去(进来)：Don't trouble to ～ me out;I know my way. 你不必麻烦带我出去,我知道路。Ⅱ n. [C]❶陈列；展览会：a flower ～花展 / His plane model is still on ～. 他的飞机模型还在展出。同 exhibition,fair ❷表演;演出；节目：Have you seen any good ～s recently? 你最近看什么好的节目了吗? 同 program,performance

showy / ˈʃəʊi / adj. (-ier,-iest)引人注目的；装饰过分的；炫耀的：a ～ dress 花哨的衣服

shower / ˈʃaʊə(r) / Ⅰ n. [C]阵雨；淋浴 同 fall,rain Ⅱ v. 下阵雨；洗淋浴 同 pour

shred / ʃred / Ⅰ n. ❶[C]碎片；细条；破布条 纸片：The violent seas ripped sails to ～s. 汹涌的大海将船帆撕成了碎片。❷少量,些许：Not a ～ of evidence has been produced in support of those accusations. 提交不出任何证据来支持那些指控。/ tear to ～s 将…撕成碎片：She tore all her letters to ～s. 她将所有的信件都撕成碎片了。②彻底驳倒(论点等) Ⅱ vt. (shredding;shredded 或 shred)把…撕碎(或切碎)；把…弄成细条：This machine is used to ～ documents. 这台机器用于切碎文件。

shriek / ʃriːk / Ⅰ vi. 尖叫 同 scream, yell Ⅱ n. [C]尖叫声 同 scream,yell

shrill / ʃrɪl / Ⅰ adj. 尖声的；刺耳的：a ～ whistle 刺耳的哨声 同 sharp,loud 反 soft,low Ⅱ v. 尖声叫 同 shriek,yell

shrimp / ʃrɪmp / n. [C] ❶ (小)虾 ❷(贬)矮小的人

shrine / ʃraɪn / n. [C]❶神龛；圣坛；神殿 ❷圣地,神圣的场所：The location of his grave has become a ～. 他的墓地已成了圣地。

shrink / ʃrɪŋk / vi. (shrank /ʃræŋk/ 或 shrunk /ʃrʌŋk/, shrunk 或 shrunken /ˈʃrʌŋkən/)❶皱缩；使收缩：This cloth does not ～ in the wash. 这种布料洗涤时不缩水。同 condense 反 stretch ❷退缩；畏缩：You should not ～ before difficulties. 你不应该在困难面前退缩。同 retreat,withdraw

shrub / ʃrʌb / n. [C]灌木

shut / ʃʌt / v. (shut, shut)关上；关闭 同 close,lock 反 open,unlock / ～ down 停止营业；停工；关闭：They have ～ down their factory. 他们的工厂已关闭。～ off 切断；停止供应(煤气、水、电等)：He didn't pay for his water so the company ～ it off. 他没付水费,因此公司停止供水。～ out 排除；遮住；关在外面：The curtains ～ out the light . 窗帘遮光。/ Don't ～ the dog out of the room. 别把狗关在门外。～ up (使)闭口；(使)住嘴：Tell him to ～ up. 叫他闭口。

shutter / ˈʃʌtə(r) / n. [C]❶百叶窗 ❷(相机的)快门

shy / ʃaɪ / adj. (-er 或 -ier,-est 或 -iest) ❶(指人)难为情的；怕羞的：John is ～ and dislikes parties. 约翰怕羞,不喜欢参加社交集会。同 timid,fearful 反 bold ❷(指动物等)易被惊走的,易受惊的,胆怯的：A deer is a ～ animal. 鹿是易受惊的动物。同 cautious, fearful 反 bold,fearless 派 shyly adv. ;shyness n.

sick / sɪk / adj. ❶不适的；病的：He has been ～ for two weeks. 他已病了两周。同 ill,unwell 反 healthy,well ❷(仅用作表语)想呕吐的；恶心的：feel ～ 觉得要呕吐 ❸厌倦的；厌恶的：I am ～ of waiting. 我讨厌等待。同 tired,displeased 派 sicken vt. ; sickly adj. ; sickness n.

用法

❶sick 用作定语时,在英国英语和美国英语中都表示"有病的";但用作表语时,美国英语表示"有病的",英国英语表示"呕吐的"：Do you feel sick? (美)你感到不舒服吗? (英)你想要呕吐吗? ❷sick 的比较级和最高级不用 sicker 或 sickest,也不用 more sick 和 most sick,通常用 worse 和 worst。

sickening / ˈsɪkənɪŋ / adj. ❶令人作呕的；使

S

人厌恶的；令人毛骨悚然的：It's 〜 to see the cruel bullfight. 见到那残忍的斗牛场面真叫人毛骨悚然。❷使人厌烦的，恼人的；使人难受的：It's 〜 that I can't go to the party. 不能去参加晚会，真叫人憋气。

sickle / ˈsɪkl / n. [C] 镰刀

side / saɪd / I n. [C] ❶(物体较平的)面：the six 〜s of a cube 立方体的六个面 同 face, surface ❷旁边：〜 effect 副作用/ 〜 issue 枝节问题/〜 walk 人行道/ **by the 〜of** 在…旁边；与…相比较：She looks small by the 〜 of her companion. 她在她的同伴身旁(和她的同伴比较)显得很小。〜 **by** 〜 并肩地；相互持地：They walked 〜 by 〜. 他们并肩而行。**take (stand by) sb. 's** 〜 站在某人一边；支持某人：Whatever happens, I'll stand by your 〜. 无论发生什么事情，我都支持你。II vi. 站在…的一边；支持 同 back, support

side-effect / ˈsaɪdɪfekt / n. [C] 副作用：toxic 〜毒副作用/The 〜 of the drug are loss of hair and difficulty in eating. 这种药的副作用是头发脱落和进食困难。

sideways / ˈsaɪdweɪz / adv. (斜)向一边地；侧向地：You use get the large table through the door 〜. 你要侧着身子才能把大桌子搬进门去。

siege / siːdʒ / n. 包围；围攻；围困 同 blockade, attack

sigh / saɪ / I n. [C]叹气；叹息：utter (heave) a 〜 叹一口气 同 breath, moon II vi. 叹气；叹息：〜 at (about, over) sth. 为某事而叹息 同 breathe

sight / saɪt / n. ❶[U] 视力；视觉：lose one's 〜 失明；变盲 同 eyesight, vision 反 blindness ❷看见；瞥见 同 glimpse, vision / **at first** 〜 乍一看；初看起来：At first 〜, she is like an actress. 初看起来她很像演员。**catch (have, get) (a)** 〜 of 看见；看出：I caught a 〜 of him. 我瞥见了他。**out of** 〜 看不见：The land is out of 〜. 陆地看不见了。/ Out of 〜, out of mind. (谚)眼不见，心不烦。❸(pl.) 值得看的东西；名胜；风景：Come and see the 〜s of London. 来看看伦敦的名胜吧。同 view, scene

sign / saɪn / I n. [C] ❶记号；符号：mathematical 〜s 数学符号 同 mark, symbol ❷迹象；征兆：Are dark clouds a 〜 of rain? 乌云是

下雨的征兆吗? 同 hint, suggestion ❸手势；示意动作：the 〜 language (聋哑人用的)手语 同 signal, gesture ❹痕迹；踪迹：There is no 〜 of him yet. 尚不见他的踪迹。同 trace, indication II v. ❶签字；签名：Please 〜 on the dotted line. 请在虚线上签名。同 subscribe, write ❷做手势：The policeman 〜ed (for) them to stop. 警察做手势叫他们下来。同 signal, gesture

signal / ˈsɪgnl / I n. 信号；暗号：traffic 〜s交通信号 / give the 〜 for a retreat 发出撤退信号 同 sign, gesture II vi. (向…)发信号 同 sign, gesture

signature / ˈsɪgnətʃə(r) / n. [C]签字：send letters to the manager for 〜 把信件送给经理签字

significance / sɪgˈnɪfɪkəns / n. [U]重要性；重大意义：a matter of great 〜 重大的事 同 consequence, importance

significant / sɪgˈnɪfɪkənt / adj. 重要的；意义深远的：a 〜 speech 重要的演说 同 important, vital

silence / ˈsaɪləns / n. [U] ❶寂静；无声：the 〜 of night 夜的寂静 同 quietness, soundlessness 反 sound, noise ❷缄默；无言：listen to sb. in 〜 默默听某人说话 / observe three minutes' 〜 默哀三分钟 / The girl sat there in 〜, but she was thinking something hard. 那女孩默不作声地坐在那儿，但她在认真地思考着什么问题。同 muteness, dumbness / **keep** 〜 保持沉默；保持安静：Keep 〜! The baby is sleeping. 安静! 宝宝正在睡觉。

silent / ˈsaɪlənt / adj. ❶寂静的：〜 film 无声电影 同 quiet, still 反 noisy, excited ❷寡言的；缄默的 同 wordless, mute 反 wordy, noisy / **be** 〜 **about (on)**对…保持沉默：You'd better be 〜 about what happened. 你最好对发生的事保持沉默。派 silently adv.

silicon / ˈsɪlɪkən / n. [U]硅：〜 chip 硅(芯)片

silk / sɪlk / n. ❶[U]丝；丝线 ❷(pl.) 绸衣

silkworm / ˈsɪlkwɜːm / n. [C]蚕

silly / ˈsɪli / adj. (-ier, -iest)愚蠢的；低能的：Don't be 〜! 别犯傻! 同 foolish, stupid 反 clever, wise

silver / ˈsɪlvə(r) / n. [U]银

similar / ˈsɪmələ(r) / adj. 类似的；相像的：My wife and I have 〜 tastes in music. 妻子和

我对音乐有相似的爱好。同 alike, resembling 反 dissimilar, different / **be ～ in** 在…方面相似：The two brothers are ～ in appearance. 这两弟兄相貌相似。**be ～ to** 和…相似：This specimen is ～ to that one. 这个标本与那个相似。

similarity / ˌsɪmɪˈlærəti / n. ❶[U]类似；相似 同 likeness, resemblance 反 difference ❷[C]相似点

simple / ˈsɪmpl / adj. ❶不复杂的；简单的：a ～ sentence 简单句 / written in ～ English 用简单的英文写出的 同 uncomplicated, elementary 反 complicated, advanced ❷朴素的；无装饰的：She lives a ～ life. 她过着简朴的生活。同 plain, natural 反 fancy, decorated ❸单纯的；直率的：She behaves as ～ as a child. 她的举止单纯得像小孩子一样。同 innocent, naive 反 experienced, sly

simplicity / sɪmˈplɪsəti / n.[U] ❶简单；简易：The plan is of ～ itself. 这计划简单。同 easiness 反 difficulty ❷朴素；朴实：～ in dress 衣着朴素 / speak with ～ 谈吐朴实 / The writer is famous for ～ of style. 这位作家以文风朴实著称。同 plainness 反 fanciness

simplify / ˈsɪmplɪfaɪ / vt. 使单纯；使简化：The teacher asked me to ～ the sentence. 老师要我把句子简化。派 simplification n.

simply / ˈsɪmpli / adv. ❶朴素地；朴实地：dress ～ 衣着朴素 同 plainly, naturally ❷完全地；绝对地：His pronunciation is ～ terrible. 他的发音糟透了。同 absolutely, completely 反 relatively, incompletely ❸仅仅；只：It is ～ a matter of working hard. 此事只需努力就做行。同 merely, solely

simultaneous / ˌsɪməlˈteɪniəs / adj. 同步进行（或完成的）；同时发生（或存在）的：a ～ interpreter 同声传译员 / There was a ～ broadcast of the concert on the radio and the television. 电台和电视台同步播出了这场音乐会。派 simultaneously adv.

since / sɪns / Ⅰ adv. 自从…以来：He left home in 1950 and has not been heard of ～. 他在 1950 年离家，以后便杳无音信。Ⅱ prep. 自…以后；自从：She hasn't been home ～ her marriage. 她自结婚以后未曾回过家。Ⅲ conj. ❶自…以后；从…以来：Where have you been ～ I last saw you? 自从上次和你见面

以后，你到哪里去了？❷既然；因为：Since you can't answer the question, we'd better ask someone else. 既然你不能回答这个问题，我们最好还是问别人。同 as, because

sincere / sɪnˈsɪə(r) / adj. 真实的；诚挚的；直率的：Are they ～ in their wish to disarm? 他们是真的希望裁军吗？同 honest, natural 反 insincere, pretended 派 sincerely adv.

sincerity / sɪnˈserəti / n.[U]真诚；诚意；真实：He wrote a letter to show his ～. 他给我写信表示他的诚意。同 honesty, frankness

sing / sɪŋ / v. (sang/sæŋ/, sung /sʌŋ/)唱：～ to the guitar 伴着吉他唱歌 / ～ in the New Year 歌迎新年 / ～ out the Old Year 唱送旧年 / **high praise for** 高度赞扬 派 singing n.

single / ˈsɪŋgl / adj. ❶唯一的；一个的：a ～ ticket 单程票 / walking in ～ file 以一路纵队行进 同 one, sole 反 several, numerous ❷未婚的；独身的：remain ～ 尚未结婚 同 unmarried, unwed 反 married, wed 派 singleness n.

singly / ˈsɪŋgli / adv. 个别地；单独地

singular / ˈsɪŋgjələ(r) / adj. ❶(语法)单数的 反 plural ❷奇特的：～ clothes 奇装异服 同 unusual, unnatural 反 usual, common ❸非凡的；卓越的：a man of ～ courage 非常勇敢的人 同 unique, particular 反 common, familiar

sink / sɪŋk / v. (sank /sæŋk/, sunk /sʌŋk/) ❶下沉；沉没：Wood does not ～ in water. It floats. 木头在水中不沉，它漂浮着。同 fall, drown 反 surface, emerge ❷使陷入；使沉浸于：He was sunk in thought. 他陷入沉思。

sip / sɪp / Ⅰ (sipped; sipping) v. 小口地喝，抿，呷：We sat in the sun, ～ lemonade. 我们一边坐着晒太阳，一边小口小口地喝着柠檬水。Ⅱ n.[C] ❶一小口的量，一啜（或一呷）之量 ❷细嚼、慢饮；抿尝，浅尝：drink brandy in ～s 一口一口地饮白兰地

sir / sɜː(r) / n. ❶(对男子的礼貌称呼)先生，阁下：Dinner is ～. 饭已备好，先生。❷(用于有爵士称号者的名或姓名之前)爵士：Sir Edward 爱德华爵士

siren / ˈsaɪrən / n. 汽笛；警报器

sister / ˈsɪstə(r) / n. ❶姐妹：elder ～ 姐姐 / younger ～ 妹妹 ❷修女

sit / sɪt / vi. (sat /sæt/, sat; sitting)坐：Let's ～ down. 我们就座吧。反 stand, lie / ～ **up late** 睡得晚；熬夜：He sat up late to prepare for the final examination. 他熬夜为期末考试做准备。

site / saɪt / n. [C](建房的)地点,场所;遗址:conference ～会址 / construction (building) ～ 建筑工地 / test ～ 实验场 / Have you fixed the ～ for the new school? 你们选定新校址了吗? / The museum is built on the ～ of an ancient temple. 博物馆修建在一座古庙的遗址上。同 place, location

sitter / ˈsɪtə(r) / n. [C]替人照看孩子的人:Can you get me a baby ～ for the vacation? 你能为我找一个在假期照看孩子的人吗?

situated / ˈsɪtʃʊeɪtɪd / adj.(城镇、建筑物等)坐落于(某处)的,位于(某处)的:The village is ～ in a valley. 这个村庄坐落于山谷中。同 located

situation / ˌsɪtʃʊˈeɪʃn / n. [C]❶(城镇、建筑物等的)位置,地点同 position, location ❷状况;事态;情势:be in an embarrassing ～ 处于窘境 / the international ～国际形势 / under the present ～在目前形势下同 state, circumstance

situp / ˈsɪtʌp / n. [C]仰卧起坐

six / sɪks / Ⅰ num. 六 Ⅱ adj. 六个(的)

sixteen / ˌsɪksˈtiːn / Ⅰ num. 十六 Ⅱ adj. 十六个(的)

sixteenth / ˌsɪksˈtiːnθ / Ⅰ num. 第十六;十六分之一 Ⅱ adj. 第十六的;十六分之一的

sixth / sɪksθ / Ⅰ num. 第六;六分之一 Ⅱ adj. 第六的;六分之一的

sixtieth / ˈsɪkstɪəθ / Ⅰ num. 第六十;六十分之一 Ⅱ adj. 第六十的;六十分之一的

sixty / ˈsɪksti / Ⅰ num. 六十 Ⅱ adj. 六十个(的)

size / saɪz / n. ❶大小;尺寸:a building of vast ～ 巨大的建筑物同 measurement, volume ❷(衣着等的)号,码:What ～ hat do you wear? 你戴几号的帽子?

skate / skeɪt / Ⅰ n. 溜冰鞋 Ⅱ vi. 溜冰:go skating 去溜冰

skeleton / ˈskelɪtən / Ⅰ n. [C]❶骨骼;骸骨;骷髅:the human ～ 人类的骨骼/development of ～骨骼发育 ❷骨架,框架,构架;轮廓:the bared ～ of a house 房子光秃秃的框架/the ～ of a plan 计划的纲要 Ⅱ adj. ❶骨骼的;像骨骼的:a pair of ～ hands 一双骨瘦如柴的手 ❷骨干的;精干的:～ staff 骨干职员

skeptical / ˈskeptɪkəl / adj.(好)怀疑的;持怀疑态度的;不相信的;a ～ expression 怀疑的神情/She says this tree is 800 years old but I'm ～ of it. 她说这棵树有 800 年树龄了,可我不相信。

sketch / sketʃ / n. [C]❶草图;略图;素描:make a ～ of a harbor 画海港的草图 同 drawing, draft ❷简短的记载;概述;大纲:He gave me a ～ of his plans for the expedition. 他对我略述了他远征的计划。同 abstract, outline

ski / skiː / Ⅰ n. [C](pl. skis 或 ski)滑雪板;雪橇:a pair of ～s 一副滑雪板 Ⅱ vi. 滑雪:She went in for ～ing years ago. 数年前她很喜欢滑雪。

skill / skɪl / n. 技能;技艺:The work calls for ～. 这项工作要求一定的技巧。/ He has the ～ to cope with such things. 他很善于对付这一类事情。/ She gained some ～s in handwriting. 她学会了一些书法技能。/ The pianist has great ～s with his fingers. 这位钢琴家有纯熟的指法。同 craft, ability

skilled / skɪld / adj. 经过训练的;有经验的;熟练的:～ workmen 有经验的工人;技工 同 experienced, trained 反 unskilled 派 **be ～ in**(**at**)在…方面灵巧:The little boy is ～ in using chopsticks. 那小男孩使用筷子很熟练。

skil(l)ful / ˈskɪlful / adj. 有技巧的;熟练的:He is not very ～ with chopsticks. 他用筷子不大熟练。同 experienced, proficient 反 unskillful, inexperienced 派 skil(l)fully adv.

skim / skɪm / v.(skimmed; skimming)❶撇(去):～(off)the cream from the milk 撇去牛奶上的奶油 同 remove, scrape ❷掠过;擦过:A bird ～med(over)the calm water of the lake. 一只鸟掠过平静的湖面。同 glide, sweep ❸略读;浏览:～(through)a novel 浏览一本小说 同 scan, glance

skin / skɪn / n. [U](人或动物的)皮,皮肤

skinny / ˈskɪni / adj.(-ier, -iest)瘦得皮包骨的

skip / skɪp / v.(skipped; skipping)❶轻快地跳:The lambs were ～ping about in the fields. 小羊在田野里跳来跳去。同 jump, bounce ❷跳绳

skirt / skɜːt / n. [C]女裙

sky / skaɪ / n.(the ～)天;天空:There wer no clouds in the ～. 天上没有云彩。同 heaven, space 反 earth

用法

❶sky 前一般应加定冠词 the,若有形容词作定语时,可在前面加不定冠词 a,如 a blue sky。❷sky 的复数常指天气或气候:Skies will remain sunny. 天气会持续晴朗。

skyscraper / ˈskaɪskreɪpə(r) / n. [C]摩天大楼:Guangzhou is a modern city with ～s here and there. 广州是一座高楼林立的现代化城市。

skyward / ˈskaɪwəd / Ⅰ adv. 向上地,朝天地;book ～ 仰望天空/The boy threw the ball ～. 男孩把球往上扔去。Ⅱ adj. 朝天的,向上的;a ～ direction 朝天的角度

slack / slæk / adj. ❶松驰的,松弛的,不紧的:We have to tighten these tent ropes first — they are too ～. 我们得先紧紧这些绑帐篷的绳子——它们太松了。/His muscles started to get ～. 他的肌肉开始松弛了。❷疏忽的,粗心的:The auditor found quite a few ～ procedures in cash offices. 审计员在现金出纳处发现了几笔粗心账。❸萧条的,清淡的,不景气的:Travel business is always ～ at this time of year. 每年到了这个时候都是旅游淡季。派 slacken v.

slander / ˈslɑːndə(r) / Ⅰ vt. 诽谤;诋毁;造谣中伤同 abuse 反 praise Ⅱ n. 诽谤;诋毁;诽谤性言论:spread ～ 散布诽谤性言论/ utter ～ about sb. 诽谤某人 同 distortion 反 praise

slang / slæŋ / n. [U]俚语;行话;黑话

slap / slæp / Ⅰ v. (slapped; slapping)掌击;拍打:She ～ped his face. 她打了他一个耳光。同 hit, strike Ⅱ n. [C]掌击;掴;拍:give sb. a ～ on the face 给某人一记耳光 同 blow, hit

slash / slæʃ / Ⅰ vt. ❶砍,劈;挥击,挥舞(刀、剑等):The child was ～ing a plastic sword aimlessly. 那小孩正胡乱地挥舞着一把塑料剑。❷大幅度削减(价格等);裁减;删除:The shop advertisement says "Weekend only, prices ～ed."那个商店的广告上面写着:"周末大减价。" Ⅱ n. [C] ❶劈砍;砍杀,砍击 ❷伤痕,砍痕;鞭痕 ❸斜线,斜杠;斜线号:"6/8" can be read as "six ～ eight". "6/8"可读作"6 斜杠8"。❹大幅度削减,裁减

slaughter / ˈslɔːtə(r) / vt. & n. 屠宰同 massacre, kill

slave / sleɪv / Ⅰ n. [C]奴隶同 serf, servant 反 master, owner / ～-holder n. 奴隶主 Ⅱ v. 干苦活;奴役同 toil, labor

sledge / sledʒ / n. [C]雪橇;雪车:The Eskimos

use ～s pulled by reindeers to cross the Arctic. 爱斯基摩人乘坐驯鹿拉的雪橇穿越北极。

slavery / ˈsleɪvəri / n. [U] ❶奴役 ❷奴隶制度

sleep / sliːp / Ⅰ v. (slept; slept)睡:I slept well (badly) last night. 我昨晚睡得好(不好)。同 slumber, nap /～ing bag n. 睡袋 Ⅱ n. [U]睡眠;睡眠时间:have a short ～ 小睡一会/ He didn't get much ～. 他睡得不多。同 slumber, nap 反 wake

辨析

sleep 表示睡的状态;go to bed 表示睡的动作:I couldn't get to sleep until 2 o'clock last night. 昨晚我直到两点才入睡。I went to bed at 2 last night. 昨晚我是两点上床睡觉的。I slept late yesterday. 我昨天起得晚。(注意不能译成"我昨天睡得晚",那应是"I went to bed late yesterday.")

sleepy / ˈsliːpi / adj. (-ier, -iest) ❶欲睡的;困乏的:feel ～ 觉得困乏 ❷(指地方)静寂的;不热闹的:a ～ little village 静寂的小村庄

sleeve / sliːv / n. [C]衣袖:roll up the ～s of his shirt 卷起他衬衣的袖子/ seize sb. by the ～ 抓住某人的袖子/ have sth. up one's ～ 胸有成竹,暗中已有应急的打算/ laugh up (in) one's ～ 暗暗发笑/ weep up (in) one's ～ 暗中哭泣

slender / ˈslendə(r) / adj. ❶细长的;苗条的:a ～ girl 苗条的姑娘 / ～ legs 修长的双腿同 slim, thin 反 fat, thick ❷微薄的;微弱的;微小的:～ hope 渺茫的希望 / ～ income 微薄的收入 / You have a ～ chance of success only. 你成功的希望很小。同 slight, weak 反 large, strong 派 slenderly adv. ; slenderness n.

slice / slaɪs / Ⅰ n. [C] ❶薄片;切片:a ～ of meat 一片肉同 piece ❷部分;一份同 portion, share Ⅱ vt. 切(片):～ the meat 把肉切成薄片同 cut, split

slide / slaɪd / Ⅰ v. (slid /slɪd/, slid 或 slidden /ˈslɪdən/)(使)滑动:children sliding on the ice 滑冰的孩子们 同 glide / ～ **into** ①溜进;潜入:The dog slid into the garden. 那条狗溜进花园里。②不知不觉陷入(习惯、毛病等):～ into bad habits 不知不觉地沾染上恶习/ ～ **over** 略过;回避 Ⅱ n. ❶滑动 ❷[C]滑梯;滑道;滑坡 ❸[C]幻灯片

slight / slaɪt / Ⅰ adj. ❶苗条的;细长的:a ～

S

figure 苗条的身材 同 slim,slender 反 sturdy ❷细小的;轻微的;不严重的;不重要的:a 〜 error 小错误 / a 〜 headache 轻微的头痛 同 petty,insignificant 反 great,significant Ⅱ v. 怠慢;轻视;蔑视:She felt 〜ed because no one spoke to her. 她觉得受到蔑视,因为没有人和她说话。同 neglect,disregard 反 value,regard 派 slightly *adv.*

slim / slɪm / *adj.* (slimmer,slimmest)细的;苗条的;小的:a girl of 〜 waist 一位细腰女郎 同 slender,slight 反 fat,broad

sling /slɪŋ / Ⅰ *n.* [C] ❶吊索,吊钩,吊带 hanger,hook ❷弹弓;投石器 Ⅱ *vt.* (slung/slʌŋ/,slung) ❶吊,挂;吊运:They slung a hammock between two trees. 他们在两棵树之间挂了吊床。/ We slung the sofa to the six floor. 我们把沙发吊上六楼。同 suspend ❷投,掷:〜 stones into the river 往河里投石头 同 cast,throw

slip / slɪp / Ⅰ *v.* (slipped;slipping) ❶失足;滑倒:He 〜ped on the icy road and broke his leg. 他在结冰的路上滑倒而摔坏了腿。同 fall,slide ❷溜走;悄悄过去:She 〜ped away without being seen. 她悄悄溜走而未被人看见。/ The years 〜ped by. 岁月悄悄流逝。同 steal,pass ❸滑;落;滑脱:The fish 〜ped out of my hand. 鱼从我手里滑脱出去。同 escape Ⅱ *n.* [C] ❶滑倒;失足 同 fall,slide ❷小错;小失误 同 error ❸纸条

slipper / 'slɪpə(r) / *n.* [C]拖鞋;便鞋:a pair of plastic 〜s 一双塑料拖鞋 / No 〜s in class! 上课不准穿拖鞋!

slippery / 'slɪpəri / *adj.* (-ier,-iest)滑的:be on a 〜 slope 在滑坡上;在走向危险的途中 / The road is wet and 〜. 路又湿又滑。同 smooth,oily 反 coarse,rough

slit / slɪt / Ⅰ *n.* [C]狭长切口;长缝;裂缝 同 cut Ⅱ *vt.* (slitted; slitting) 切开;撕开 同 cut,split

sliver / 'slɪvə(r) / *n.* [C] ❶长薄切片;狭长条,窄条:a 〜 of land 一块狭长的土地/a 〜 of cake 一块蛋糕 ❷木片

slogan / 'sləʊgən / *n.* [C]标语;口号:put up 〜s 张贴标语 / shout 〜s 呼口号

slope / sləʊp / Ⅰ *n.* 倾斜面;斜坡:mountain 〜s 山坡 同 incline 反 plane Ⅱ *v.* 倾斜:Our garden 〜s (down) to the river. 我们的花园向河成坡形。同 incline,lean 反 flatten,level

slow / sləʊ / Ⅰ *adj.* ❶慢的;迟缓的:a 〜 train 慢车 同 gradual 反 fast,quick ❷迟钝的;呆笨的:a 〜 child 迟钝的小孩 ❸ poison 慢性毒药 同 dull,stupid 反 bright,smart ❹ be 〜 at …不善于…:She is 〜 at calculating. 她不善于计算。Ⅱ *adv.* 低速地;缓慢地:Tell the driver to go 〜er. 告诉驾驶员开慢些。Ⅲ *v.* (使)缓行;(使)减速:〜 down(up)(使)放慢;减速:Has the economic growth 〜ed up in that country? 那个国家的经济增长速度减慢了吗?/ Slow down before you reach the crossroads. 在你到达十字路口前你应该减速。派 slowly *adv.*;slowness *n.*

辨析

slow 作为副词时和 slowly 同义,但 slowly 可用于限定动词之前、之后或整个句子之首:He slowly walked up (walked slowly up) the path. Slowly he walked up the path. 他沿着小径慢慢行走。slow 除与上述用外,一般用于限定动词之后或一些复合词中:How slow the time passes! 时间过得多么慢啊! slow-going 进行缓慢的;slow-spoken 说得慢慢的。

slum / slʌm / *n.* [C]贫民窟;陋巷:live in a 〜 居于贫民窟

sly / slaɪ / *adj.* (slyer,slyest) ❶狡猾的;狡诈的 同 cunning,tricky 反 open,direct ❷淘气的;顽皮的 同 naughty

smack / smæk / Ⅰ *n.* [C](尤指用手掌或扁平物的)拍击(声),拍打(声);掌掴(声),扇击(声):He gave the ball a bard 〜. 他大力击球。Ⅱ *vt.* ❶击,掴,扇:I'd 〜 his face. 我要扇他一记耳光。❷砰(或啪)地放下(或甩出、扔下等):She 〜ed the cup on the table. 她把杯子砰的一声放在桌子上。

small / smɔːl / *adj.* 小的;少的:a 〜 town 小镇 / a 〜 audience 不多的听众 / a 〜 sum of money 一小笔钱 同 little 反 big,great

辨析

❶small 表示面积、数量等方面"小":These shoes are too small for me. 这双鞋我穿太小了。little 在表示具体事物的"小"时,常有赞赏、爱怜的感情成分,small 有时则有贬低的意味。She is certainly a pretty little girl. 她当然是个漂亮的小姑娘。You needn't thank me for such a small present. 不必为这点小意思谢我。❷small 的比较级和最高级是 smaller 和 smallest,little 的比较级和最高级是 less 和 least。

smart / smɑːt / *adj.* ❶鲜明的；漂亮的；整洁的；衣冠楚楚的：Go and make yourself ～ before we call on the Jonas. 在我们去拜访乔纳斯家以前，你先把自己打扮得漂漂亮亮的。圊 fashionable, neat 反 old-fashioned ❷聪明的，有技巧的，有头脑的 圊 bright, intelligent 反 dull, stupid 派 smartly *adv.* ；smartness *n.*

smash / smæʃ / *v.* 捣碎；打破：The drunken man ～ed up all the furniture. 那醉汉毁坏了所有的家具。圊 break, crash

smell / smel / Ⅰ *n.* ❶[U]嗅觉：Taste and ～ are closely connected. 味觉和嗅觉紧密相关。❷气味：What a nice ～! 多好闻的气味！圊 scent, odor Ⅱ *v.* (smelt /smelt/, smelt 或 smelled, smelled) ❶(不用进行时态，常和 can, could 连用)嗅出：I can ～ something burning. 我闻到什么东西烧着了。/ Do (Can) fishes ～? 鱼类有嗅觉吗? 圊 nose, scent ❷发出…的气味；有…的气味(常与形容词或副词连用；如果没有形容词或副词，通常表示"发出臭味")：The flowers ～ sweet. 花散发出香味。/ The dinner ～s good. 饭菜闻起来很香。/ The meat is beginning to ～. 这肉开始腐烂了。

smelly / ˈsmeli / *adj.* 味道刺鼻的、难闻的；臭的，有臭味的：The slum is horribly ～. 贫民窟里臭不可闻。/ Take your ～ shoes away. 把你那双臭鞋拿开。

smelt / smelt / *vt.* 熔炼，精炼；从(矿石)中炼取金属，从矿石中炼取(金属)：～ iron from its ores 从铁矿石中炼铁

smile / smaɪl / Ⅰ *n.* 微笑：a big (broad) ～ 笑容可掬 /answer(reply) with a ～ 微笑着回答 / force a ～ 强颜欢笑 / wear a ～ 面带微笑 / There was a pleasant ～ on her face. 她的脸上露出悦人的微笑。Ⅱ *v.* 微笑；以微笑表示(愉快、兴趣、同情等)：What are you smiling at? 你在笑什么? / The weather ～d on us. 天公作美(天气晴朗)。

smog / smɒg / *n.* [U]烟雾

smoke / sməuk / Ⅰ *n.* ❶[U]烟：～ pouring from factory chimneys 从工厂囱冒出的烟 / There is no ～ without fire. (= Where there is ～, there is fire.) (谚)无风不起浪(无火不生烟)。❷[C]吸烟；香烟：Will you have a ～? 你想抽支烟吗? Ⅱ *v.* ❶冒烟；起烟雾：That oil-lamp ～s badly. 那油灯冒烟很厉害。❷吸(烟)：～ a pipe 吸烟斗 / You mustn't ～ in this room. 你绝对不许在这房间里抽烟。

smoking / ˈsməukɪŋ / *n.* [U]吸烟：give up ～ 戒烟 / No ～. 禁止吸烟。

smooth / smuːð / Ⅰ *adj.* 光滑的；平滑的；平静的：～ paper 光滑的纸 / a ～ road 平坦的路 圊 even, level 反 rough, uneven / ～ faced *adj.* 表面平滑的 / ～-tongued *adj.* 油嘴滑舌的；能言善辩的 Ⅱ *v.* 使(变)光滑；使(变)平静：～ down one's dress 烫平衣服 / The sea has ～ed down. 海上已风平浪静。圊 flatten, calm / ～ **away** 消除；克服：They ～ed away all kinds of difficulties and finished the task successfully. 他们克服了所有的困难，成功地完成了任务。～ **over** 掩饰；平息；排除：～over one's faults 掩饰某人的过错 / ～ over obstacles 消除障碍 / ～ over a quarrel 平息一场争吵 派 smoothly *adv.* ；smoothness *n.*

smother / ˈsmʌðə(r) / *vt.* ❶使窒息，使透不过气：The crowd ～ed me. 周围的人群挤得我透不过气来。❷把(火)闷熄：He tried to ～ the flames with a damp blanket. 他试图用湿毯子闷熄火苗。❸厚厚地覆盖：She ～ed her cake with cream. 她在饼子上涂了厚厚一层奶油。❹掩饰；抑制；扼杀：～ (up) a scandal 掩盖丑闻

smuggle / ˈsmʌgl / *v.* 私运；偷运；走私：They ～d goods to some undeveloped countries. 他们把货物走私到一些不发达国家。派 smuggling *n.*

snack / snæk / Ⅰ *n.* [C](正餐之间的)点心，小吃：I had a ～ on the train. 我在火车上吃了点心。Ⅱ *vi.* 吃快餐；吃点心：You can ～ on cake at noon. 中午就吃点蛋糕填补一下吧。

snail / sneɪl / *n.* [C] ❶蜗牛 ❷行动迟缓的人

snake / sneɪk / *n.* [C]蛇

snap / snæp / *vt.* (snapped; snapping)猛咬；突然折断 圊 bite, break

snapshot / ˈsnæpˌʃɒt / *n.* [C] ❶快照 ❷概观，简要小结

snatch / snætʃ / Ⅰ *v.* ❶抢；夺取：He ～ed the letter from me. 他从我手中抢去了那封信。圊 grab, seize ❷迅速获得，趁机获取：～ an hour's sleep 趁机睡一小时 圊 catch, take Ⅱ *n.* 抢；夺取；突袭

sneer / snɪə(r) / *vi.* 嘲笑；讥笑(与 at 连用)：～ at a poor girl 嘲笑一个可怜的女孩 圊

scorn,mock

sneeze / sniːz / Ⅰ n. 喷嚏:Coughs and ∼s spread diseases. 咳嗽和喷嚏传播疾病。Ⅱ vi. 打喷嚏:Use a handkerchief when you ∼. 打喷嚏时应用手帕遮掩. / ∼ at 轻视,不认为重要:Is a thousand dollars anything to ∼ at? 1000美元也能随便忽视吗? / John finished third in a race with thirty other runners. That is nothing to ∼ at. 约翰在30名选手中跑第三,成绩不可小视。

sniff / snɪf / v. (嗅嗅地)以鼻吸气:They all had colds and were ∼ing and sneezing. 他们都感冒了,呼嗅呼嗅地吸气,并打喷嚏。

sniffle / ˈsnɪfl / Ⅰ v. 抽鼻子:吸着鼻子说话 Ⅱ n. 抽鼻声

snob / snɒb / n. [C]势利小人

snore / snɔː(r) / vi. 打鼾:打呼噜

snow / snəʊ / Ⅰ n. [U]雪:a heavy fall of ∼ 下大雪 / roads deep in ∼ 积雪很深的道路 Ⅱ v. 降雪:It ∼ed all day. 雪下了一整天. 派 snowy adj.

snowfall / ˈsnəʊfɔːl / n. ❶[C;U]降雪:Heavy ∼s this month relieved the desiccated land. 本月的几次大规模降雪使土地的旱情可以缓解. ❷[U]降雪量:the average ∼平均降雪量

snowflake / ˈsnəʊfleɪk / n. [C]雪花,雪片:He watched the ∼s dancing. 他看着雪花飞舞。

so / səʊ / Ⅰ adv. ❶这么,那么(表示程度):It is not ∼ big as I thought it would be. 它没我想的那么大. / Would you be ∼ kind as to help me? 你能帮助我吗? / He was ∼ ill that we had to send for a doctor. 他病得很厉害,我们必须去请医生. / I'm ∼ glad to see you! 见到你我真高兴! / It was ∼ kind of you! 你真好! ❷像这样,像那样(表示状态):∼ far 至此;Everything is in order ∼ far, 迄今诸事顺遂. ∼ long as(＝as long as)只要:I'll lend it to you ∼ long as you return it next Sunday. 只要你下星期天还我,我就会借给你. ∼ that 为了;以便;以致;结果是:Speak clearly ∼ that they may understand you. 说清楚些,以便他们能听懂你的话. ∼ ... that ...以致:It was ∼ late that I couldn't attend the meeting. 碰巧我无法参加会议. ∼ as to 以便;以致:He rose early ∼ as to be in time for the first lesson. 他早起为的是赶上第一堂课. / I will have everything ready ∼ as not to keep you waiting. 我会准备好一切,不让你等候. **and ∼ on(forth)** 等等 **or ∼** 大约:They arrived at the small town a month or ∼ ago. 他们大约一个月前到达小镇. Ⅱ pron. (常和动词 say, think, hope, suppose, tell 等连用,代替前文的词语和意思):—He has gone to Shanghai. —I believe ∼. —他去上海了. —我想是去了. / —I went to the bookstore to look for that book and found it sold out. —I told you ∼. —我到书店去买那本书,发现已经卖完了. —我早就告诉你了. Ⅲ conj. 因此;所以:The shops were closed ∼ I couldn't get any. 商店都关门了,所以我什么也没买到。

soak / səʊk / v. 浸泡;(使)湿透:be ∼ed to the skin 浑身湿透 / ∼ in sunshine 沐浴在阳光里 / ∼ in happiness 沉浸在幸福之中 / ∼ oneself in the history 专心研究历史 / Soak the clothes in soapy water before washing. 洗之前把衣物放在肥皂水里泡一泡. 同 wet,bathe

soap / səʊp / n. ❶[U]肥皂:a bar of ∼一块肥皂 / flakes 肥皂片 ❷[C]肥皂剧(通俗连续剧,源于以前由肥皂商制商提供)

soar / sɔː(r) / Ⅰ vi. ❶高飞,翱翔;升高,升腾:a wild hawk ∼ing through heaven 搏击长空的鹞鹰 ❷剧增,猛增,飞涨:Banks failed;unemployment ∼ed. 银行倒闭,失业率猛增. Ⅱ n. [C]高飞,猛增,高涨

sob / sɒb / Ⅰ v. (sobbed;sobbing)呜咽;啜泣;哭诉;呜咽着说:She ∼bed out the story of her son's death in a traffic accident. 她呜咽着叙述她儿子死于车祸的经过. 同 cry,weep 反 laugh Ⅱ n. [C]呜咽;啜泣 同 cry

so-called / ˌsəʊˈkɔːld / adj. 所谓的;号称的:We want no more of the ∼ "help". 我们不再想要这种所谓的帮助了。

用法
> so-called 带有贬义,指名不副实的:the so-called superior nation 所谓的优等民族。

soccer / ˈsɒkə(r) / n. [C](美)足球

sociable / ˈsəʊʃəbl / adj. ❶好交际的;合群的:I was never a ∼ fellow. 我本来就极不善交际。❷(场所、场合、活动等)友善的,友好的,融洽的:a ∼ atmosphere 友善的氛围/∼ places to work 气氛融洽的工作场所 派 sociability n.;sociably adv.

social / ˈsəʊʃl / adj. ❶社会的:∼ activity 社交活动 / ∼ club 联谊会 / ∼ customs 社会

习俗 / ～ problem 社会问题 同 public ❷群居的：～ ants 群居的蚂蚁 同 cooperative

socialism / ˈsəʊʃəlɪzəm / n. [U] 社会主义 反 capitalism

socialist / ˈsəʊʃəlɪst / Ⅰ adj. 社会主义的 Ⅱ n. 社会主义者

society / səˈsaɪəti / n. ❶[U] 社会；社会体制 同 community ❷[C]（为某种目的组成的）团体，会，社，协会：a ～ of engineers 工程师协会 同 club, group

sociology / ˌsəʊsiˈɒlədʒi / n. [U] 社会学

sock / sɒk / n. [C] 短袜：a pair of ～s 一双袜子

socket / ˈsɒkɪt / n. [C] 插口；插座；管座

soda / ˈsəʊdə / n. ❶[U] 碳酸钠；苏打 ❷苏打水：a bottle of orange ～ 一瓶橘子苏打水

sodium / ˈsəʊdiəm / n. 钠（符号 Na）

sofa / ˈsəʊfə / n. [C] 沙发

soft / sɒft / adj. ❶软的；柔软的：Warm butter is ～. 温热的奶油是软的。同 yielding, plastic 反 hard, unyielding ❷（指光、颜色等）柔和的：lampshades that give a ～ light 使光线柔和的灯罩 ❸（指声音）轻柔的：～ music 轻柔的音乐 / in a ～ voice 轻声地 同 gentle, sweet 反 loud, noisy ❹（指空气、气候等）温和的，适合的：a ～ breeze（wind）和风 / ～ weather 温和的气候 同 gentle, mild 反 stormy, cold ❺（指饮料）软的（不含酒精的）派 softly adv. ; softness n.

softball / ˈsɒftˌbɔːl / n. ❶[U] 垒球运动 ❷[C] 垒球

soften / ˈsɒfn / v. 使…变软；使…变柔和

software / ˈsɒftweə(r) / n. [U]（计算机的）软件；程序设备

soil / sɒɪl / n. [U] 土地；土壤：good（poor）～ 沃（瘠）土 同 ground, earth

solar / ˈsəʊlə(r) / adj. 太阳的；日光的；与太阳有关的：～ calendar 太阳历 / ～ eclipse 日食 / ～ energy 太阳能 / the ～ system 太阳系 反 lunar

soldier / ˈsəʊldʒə(r) / n. [C]（陆军）军人，士兵；战士：The children were playing at ～s. 孩子们在玩打仗的游戏。派 officer

sole / səʊl / adj. 单独的；唯一的：～ agent 独家代理商 / ～ heir 唯一继承人 同 single, only 反 shared 派 solely adv.

solemn / ˈsɒləm / adj. ❶庄重的；郑重的：The government made a ～ statement yesterday. 政府昨天发表了一项郑重申明。同 grand, sacred 反 gay, lively ❷表情严肃的；无笑容的：a ～ face 表情严肃的脸 同 sincere 反 insincere 派 solemnly adv. ; solemnness n.

solid / ˈsɒlɪd / Ⅰ adj. 固体的：When water freezes and becomes ～, we call it ice. 水冻结成固体时，我们称它为冰。同 dense, hard 反 liquid, gas Ⅱ n. 固体 派 solidly adv.

solidarity / ˌsɒlɪˈdærəti / n. 团结 同 unity

solidify / səˈlɪdɪfaɪ / v. 使团结 同 unify, unite

solo / ˈsəʊləʊ / n. [C]（pl. solos 或 soli / ˈsəʊliː）独唱；独奏；独唱曲：sing a ～ 独唱 / violin ～ 小提琴独奏

soluble / ˈsɒljʊbl / adj. ❶可溶的：a ～ powder 可溶性粉剂 ❷可解决的，能解除的：a ～ powder 可解决的问题 反 insoluble

solution / səˈluːʃn / n. ❶[C]（问题等的）解答；（困难等的）解决办法：The ～ to（of）the problem required much time. 解决这个问题需要很多时间。同 answer, key 反 question, problem ❷溶解：the ～ of sugar in tea 糖溶解于茶中 同 mixture

solve / sɒlv / vt. 解答；解决：～ a problem 解决问题 同 resolve

some / sʌm / Ⅰ adj. ❶一些（用于肯定句中，在疑问句、否定句、条件句以及有疑问、否定含义的句子中通常用 any）：There are ～ books on the table. 桌上有些书。/ Please give me ～ water. 请给我些水。同 several ❷某一个：Some Smith is waiting for you outside. 有一个叫史密斯的人在外边等你。同 certain / ～ **day**（将来）总有一天；有朝一日 ～ other day 改日：We shall discuss it ～ other day. 我们改日再讨论这个问题。～ **time** 在某个时候；日后；有朝一日 Ⅱ pron. 一些：China has ～ of the finest scenery in the world. 中国有一些世界上最佳的风景。Ⅲ adv. 大约：That was ～ twenty years ago. 那大约是 20 年前的事。同 about

用法

some 作"一些"讲时一般用于肯定句中，但如果说话者期望得到肯定的答复，或表示邀请及请求时，some 也用于疑问句中：Didn't he give you some money? 他不是给过你一些钱吗？Will you have ～ cake? 你想吃些饼吗？

S

somebody / ˈsʌmbədi / Ⅰ *pron.* (只用单数)某人；有人(在疑问句、否定句和条件句中用 anybody)：There is ～ at the door. 有人在门口。同 someone 反 nobody Ⅱ *n.* 重要人物；著名人物

辨析

somebody 和 someone 的用法和意思基本相同，都是单数概念，只能用来表示人，表示"某人""有人"，只是 somebody 较为口语化。some one 表示"某人""某物"，后必须与 of 短语连用：Some one of the students lent my dictionary. 某个学生把我的词典借走了。Some one of his books won a prize. 他有一本书获过一次奖。

someday / ˈsʌmdeɪ / *adv.* (今后)有一天；有朝一日

somehow / ˈsʌmhaʊ / *adv.* ❶以某种方式；以某种手段：We must find money for the rent ～. 我们必须设法找到钱付租金。❷由于某种原因；不知为什么；Somehow I don't trust that man. 由于某种原因，我不信任那个人。

someone / ˈsʌmwʌn / *pron.* 某人；有人 同 somebody 反 nobody

something / ˈsʌmθɪŋ / *pron.* (只用单数)某物；某事(在疑问句、否定句和条件句中用 anything)：There is ～ on the floor. 地上有一样东西。/～ else 另外的事；另外的东西：He said ～ else, but I didn't hear clearly. 他又说了些什么，但是我没有听清楚。～ like 大约；有点像：It looked ～ like a bird. 它看起来有点像一只鸟。～ of 在某种程度上；在某种意义上：She is ～ of a poet. 她略懂写诗。have ～ to do with 与…有关系：That has ～ to do with your future. 那和你的前途有关。or ～ 类似的什么；大概：He is a writer or ～. 他大概是个作家什么的。

用法

❶something 只用单数。❷形容词修饰 something 的定语时，该形容词应放其后：There is something new in his speech. 在他的报告中有些新东西。❸something 代作词表示"有某物"时，用法与 anything 对应。something 用于肯定句，anything 用于疑问句、否定句和条件句：Is there anything in the room? 房间里有东西吗？There is something in the room. 房间里有东西。

sometime / ˈsʌmtaɪm / *adv.* 在某一时间；I saw him ～ in May. 我在五月的某个时候见过他。

辨析

sometime 是副词，表示将来的不确定的某个时间，或者过去某个时刻：I'll come to see you sometime. 我改天去看你。I saw him sometime last year. 我去年的某天见到过他。some time 是副词性短语，表示"一段时间"之意：He lived in England some time when he was young. 他年轻时曾在英格兰住过一段时间。sometimes 是副词，表示"有时"之意：It is sometimes very difficult to find an exact translation for a very common expression. 有时一个很普通的说法却很难找到准确的译法。

sometimes / ˈsʌmtaɪmz / *adv.* 有时；不时；间或：Sometimes we go to the cinema and at other times we go for a walk. 有时我们去看电影，有时我们去散步。同 occasionally

someway(s) / ˈsʌmˌweɪ(z) / *adv.* 以某种方式，不知怎么的

somewhat / ˈsʌmwɒt / *adv.* 略；有点；稍：I was ～ surprised. 我有点惊讶。同 rather

somewhere / ˈsʌmweə(r) / *adv.* 在某处；至某处(在疑问句、否定句和条件句中用 anywhere)：It must be ～ near here. 它一定就在附近某处。

用法

somewhere 作副词表示"在某处"时，用法与 anywhere 对应。somewhere 用于肯定句，anywhere 用于疑问句和否定句。

son / sʌn / *n.* [C]儿子：He is the only ～ of the family. 他是家中的独子。/ ～-in-law 女婿

song / sɒŋ / *n.* ❶[U]歌唱；声乐：the ～ of the birds 鸟的鸣唱 ❷[C]歌词；歌曲：a marching ～ 进行曲/ popular ～s 流行歌曲 同 melody, tune

sonic / ˈsɒnɪk / *adj.* ❶声音的：Under water it is mostly a ～ world. 水下大多是声音的世界。❷声速的：aircraft travelling at ～ and supersonic speeds 声速和超声速的飞行器

soon / suːn / *adv.* ❶不久；很快：He will be here very ～. 他很快就到这里来。同 shortly ❷早；快：How ～ can you be ready? 你多久能准备好？／ Must you leave so ～? 你必须如此早就离开吗？同 early, quickly 反 late, slowly / ～ after 在…后不久：He arrived ～

after three. 他在三点后不久到达。**as (so)** ～ **as** 立即；一…就…: He started as ～ as he received the news. 他一得到消息就立即动身了。～**er or later** 迟早；早晚: You will repent it ～er or later. 你迟早会后悔。**no** ～ **er... than...** 刚…就…: I had no ～er left the house than it began to rain. 我刚离开屋子，天就下起雨来了。

用法

❶soon 意为"不久后"，不表示"立刻"之意，如"他听到敲门声就立即去开门"，不该译成 When he heard the knock, he opened the door soon. 应该把 soon 改成 immediately 或 at once。❷as soon as 引导的从句不可用进行时态，如不可说: She opened the door as soon as I was knocking. 或 I shall let you know as soon as she is arriving. 应该把 was knocking 改为 knocked, is arriving 改为 arrives。❸as soon as 引导的从句一般不用将来时，而用一般现在时表示将来的情况: I will write again as soon as I am free. 我一有空就会再写信。❹no sooner 放在句首时，主语和部分谓语需倒装: No sooner had I knocked than she opened the door. 我一敲门她就开了。

soothe / suːð / *vt.* ❶安慰，抚慰，使平静，使镇定: ～ one's nerves 使自己变得心平气和/To ～ himself John read in his library. 约翰在书房读书，借以排愁解闷。❷减轻，缓解，缓和: I use it to ～ headaches. 我常常用它来缓解头疼。

sophisticated / sə'fɪstɪkeɪtɪd / *adj.* ❶老于世故的；富有经验的 同 experienced 反 unsophisticated ❷复杂的；精密的；尖端的 同 complicated 反 simple

sore / sɔː(r) / *adj.* (指身体某部分)疼痛的 同 painful, hurt 反 painless

sorrow / 'sɒrəʊ / *n.* 悲哀；忧愁；悔恨: express ～ for having done wrong 对犯错表示悔恨/to my great ～ 使我极为悲哀的是 同 misfortune, sadness 反 joy, delight 派 sorrowful *adj.*

sorry / 'sɒri / *adj.* (仅作表语)抱歉的；惭愧的；对不起的: We are very ～ to hear of your father's death. 听到你父亲去世的消息，我们甚为难过。/ I felt deeply ～ about (for) his mother's death. 他母亲过世使我深感难过。同 regretful, sorrowful 反 happy, wonderful

sort / sɔːt / Ⅰ *n.* [C](人或物)群，类，种: Dance music is the ～ she likes most. 舞曲是她最喜欢的音乐。They have all ～s of goods. 他们有各种各样的货物。同 kind, type Ⅱ *vt.* 整理: ～ (out) stamps 分类整理邮票 同 arrange

SOS (= save our souls) (国际通用的船舶、飞机等的)无线电紧急呼救信号

so-so / 'səʊsəʊ / Ⅰ *adj.* 不好也不坏的，还过得去的 Ⅱ *adv.* 不好也不坏地，还过得去

soul / səʊl / *n.* ❶灵魂: He eats hardly enough to keep body and ～ together. 他吃的食物几乎不够维持生命。同 spirit, mind ❷热情: He put heart and ～ into the work. 他全身心投入工作。同 inspiration, vitality ❸精髓；要旨；核心 同 essence, core

sound¹ / saʊnd / *adj.* ❶健全的；完好的；未受伤害的: have a ～ mind and a ～ body 有健全的身心 同 good, healthy 反 unsound ❷正确的；合理的: ～ advice 合理的建议 同 sensible, reasonable 反 unsound, unreasonable ❸彻底的；完全的: have a ～ sleep 酣睡 同 deep, untroubled 反 light

sound² / saʊnd / Ⅰ *n.* 响声；声音: ～ controller (计算机的)声卡 Ⅱ *vi.* 听起来；似乎: How sweet the music ～s! 这音乐听起来多悦耳! 同 seem

用法

sound 作为不及物动词表示"听起来"的意思时，后面可接介词 like，连接词 as if (从句中用虚拟语气) 或表语形容词: What he said sounded like a fairy tale. 他说的听起来简直像神话。It sounds as if they were thinking about a change in their plan. 听起来他们仿佛在考虑改变他们的计划。The terms sound quite reasonable. 这些条件听上去倒是挺合理的。

soup / suːp / *n.* [U]汤

sour / 'saʊə(r) / *adj.* 酸的；有酸味的 同 acid 反 sweet

source / sɔːs / *n.* [C] ❶河的源头；水源；泉源: the ～s of the Nile 尼罗河的源头 / Where does the Rhine take its ～? 莱茵河发源于何处? 同 beginning, headwater ❷来源；出处: The news comes from a reliable ～. 这消息来源可靠。同 cause, origin 反 end, conclusion

south / saʊθ / Ⅰ *n.* 南部；南方: Mexico is to

the ～ of the USA. 墨西哥在美国之南。Ⅱ *adj.* 南部的；南方的：*the* ～ entrance 南入口 Ⅲ *adv.* 在南方；在南部

southeast / ˌsaʊθ'iːst / *n.*, *adj.* & *adv.* 位于（向着、来自）东南(的)

southern / 'sʌðən / *adj.* 在(向、来自)南方的：the ～ states of the USA 美国南方各州

southward / 'saʊθwəd / *adv.* 向南

southwest / ˌsaʊθ'west / *n.*, *adj.* & *adv.* 位于（向着、来自）西南(的)

souvenir / ˌsuːvə'nɪə(r), 'suːvənɪər / *n.* [C]纪念品同 relic, reminder

sovereign / 'sɒvrɪn / Ⅰ *n.* [C]最高统治者；君主；元首；领袖；(某一领域的)掌权者；主宰：the eldest son of the ～国王的长子 Ⅱ *adj.* ❶(权力、地位、级别等)最高的，至高无上的；难以超越的：the ～ body 最高权力机构/ maintain ～ power 维持至高无上的权力 ❷拥有主权的；主权独立的；自治的：～ states 主权国家

sovereignty / 'sɒvrɪnti / *n.* [U]❶最高权力；统治权：submit to sb.'s ～服从某人的统治 ❷主权；自治权（与 over 连用）：China restored (resumed) its ～ over Hong Kong in 1997. 中国于 1997 年恢复对香港行使主权。

sow / səʊ / *v.* (sowed /səʊd/, sown /səʊn/或sowed)播(种)：～ a plot of land with grass seeds 在一块地里撒播青草种子同 plant, scatter

soy / sɔɪ / *n.* [U]❶酱油同 soy sauce ❷大豆同 bean, soybean

soybean / 'sɔɪbiːn / *n.* 大豆同 soy

space / speɪs / Ⅰ *n.* ❶[U]空间；太空同 universe, sky ❷空地；余地：clear a ～ on the platform for the speakers 在讲台上为演说者腾出地方。同 room, gap反 limitation Ⅱ *vt.* 把…分隔开

spacecraft / 'speɪskrɑːft, ˌspeɪs'kræft / *n.* 航天飞行器，宇宙飞船，太空船

spacious / 'speɪʃəs / *adj.* 广阔的；广大的；宽敞的同 large, wide反 small, crowded

spade / speɪd / *n.* [C]锹

Spain / speɪn / *n.* 西班牙

Spanish / 'spænɪʃ / Ⅰ *adj.* 西班牙的；西班牙人的；西班牙语的 Ⅱ *n.* ❶(the ～) (总称)西班牙人 ❷西班牙语

span / spæn / Ⅰ *n.* [C]❶一段时间；a ～ of 3 years 3 年期间 / life ～ 一生的时间；寿命同 interval, period ❷跨距；跨度：The arch has a ～ of 50 meters. 这一拱跨度为 50 米。同 distance, stretch Ⅱ *vt.* (spanned; spanning)跨越：A bridge will ～ the river here. 这里将有一座大桥横跨过江。同 cross

spare / speə(r) / Ⅰ *v.* ❶匀出；挤出：We can't ～ the time for a holiday at present. 目前我们匀不出时间来度假。同 afford, give ❷节约；节省：Some will spend and some will ～. 有人愿花钱，有人爱节约。同 save, reserve反 spend, use Ⅱ *adj.* 多余的；剩余的；备用的：I have no ～ time (money). 我没有闲暇(闲钱)。同 extra, surplus

sparing / 'speərɪŋ / Ⅰ *adj.* ❶节省的，节俭的；吝惜的：He's ～ in commendations. 他很少说褒奖的话。/The girl was ～ with her smiles. 那姑娘不苟言笑。❷有节制的；谨慎的：He advised ～ use of melodramatic tactics. 他建议夸张手法要慎用。派 sparingly *adv.*

spark / spɑːk / *n.* [C]火星；火花：The fireworks burst into a shower of ～s. 烟火爆发出一簇火花。同 flash, sparkle

sparkle / 'spɑːkl / Ⅰ *vi.* 发光；闪烁；闪耀：Her diamonds ～d in the bright light. 她的钻石在亮光下闪闪发光。同 shine, twinkle Ⅱ *n.* 火花；闪光同 spark, twinkle

sparrow / 'spærəʊ / *n.* [C]麻雀

sparse / spɑːs / *adj.* ❶稀疏的；稀少的；零散的：～ woodlands 稀少的林地/ ～ population 稀疏的人口 ❷(人或动物)瘦小的；(土地等)不毛的；贫弱的：～ vegetation 贫瘠的植被派 sparsely *adv.*; sparseness *n.*

speak / spiːk / (spoke /spəʊk/, spoken /'spəʊkən/) *vi.* 说话：The baby is learning to ～. 这小孩在学说话。同 talk / ～ highly of 赞扬；称赞：The manager spoke highly of our success. 经理赞扬了我们的成功。～ of 提到；讲到：He often ～s of the old days when he was in the countryside. 他常常谈到他过去在农村的日子。/frankly ～ing 坦白地说/generally ～ing 一般来说；总的来说 ～ out ①大声地说：The teacher told the shy boy to ～ out. 老师叫这害羞的男孩大声说。②毫不犹豫地说：Stand up and ～ out for the President's whole program. 站起来为总统的整个计划发言吧。—*vt.* 说(某种语言)；说明：～

the truth 说实话 / He ~s several languages. 他能说数种语言。 / Is English spoken here? 这里说英语吗? 同 express, say

speaking / ˈspiːkɪŋ / Ⅰ n. 说话;演讲;develop the skill of ~ 发展说话能力 同 talk, lecture Ⅱ adj. 发言的;交谈的

spear / spɪə(r) / n. [C]矛;梭镖

special / ˈspeʃ(ə)l / adj. 特别的;特殊的;特设的;专用的;What are your ~ interests? 你的特殊兴趣是什么? / On holidays the railways put on ~ trains. 在假日,铁路当局加派专车。 同 particular, specific 反 common, ordinary 派 specially adv.

specialist / ˈspeʃəlɪst / n. [C]专家(尤指医科的);a ~ in plastic surgery 整形外科专家

specialization / ˌspeʃəlaɪˈzeɪʃn / n. [U]专门化;专业化

specialize / ˈspeʃəlaɪz / v. 专门研究;专攻;~ in chemistry 专攻化学 同 major 派 specialized adj.

specialty / ˈspeʃəlti / n. 拳头产品,特色产品,特种工艺:The company's ~ is the manufacture of high performance cars. 这家公司的拳头产品是高性能汽车。/They dined on the restaurant ~. 他们吃了这家餐馆的特色菜肴。

species / ˈspiːʃiːz / n. (单复数同形)物种;种类;有共同特点的一群:many ~ of advertisement 许多种类的广告 / Wheat is a ~ of grass. 小麦是草本植物的一种。 同 kind, group

specific / spəˈsɪfɪk / adj. ❶明确的;具体的:Have you made any ~ plan? 你制订具体的计划了吗? 同 definite, exact 反 indefinite, approximate ❷特有的;特定的 同 special, unique 反 common, general

specify / ˈspesɪfaɪ / vi. 详细说明;明确规定 同 define, indicate

specimen / ˈspesɪmən / n. [C]样品;标本:collect insect ~s 采集昆虫标本 /~s of rocks and ores 岩石和矿石标本/The doctor needs a ~ of your blood. 医生需要你的血样。 同 sample, model

spectacle / ˈspektəkl / n. (多用 pl.)眼镜;护目镜 同 eye-glasses, sun-glasses

spectator / spekˈteɪtə(r) / n. 观众;旁观者 同 viewer, watcher

spectrum / ˈspektrəm / n. [C](pl. spectra /-trə/或 spectrums)❶光谱 ❷频谱;射频频谱 ❸电磁波谱 ❹范围;幅度;系列:A broad ~ of topological features creates a pleasant landscape. 各种各样的地貌构成了一幅宜人的风景画。

speculate / ˈspekjuˌleɪt / vi. ❶臆想;推断,猜测:They talked and ~d until after midnight. 他们一直谈论和分析到半夜。 / I wouldn't like to ~ about the price of that car. 我不想对那部汽车的价格作推断。❷思考;沉思;冥想:~ on one's future 考虑自己的前途

speech / spiːtʃ / n. ❶[U]说话;说话的能力:Our thoughts are expressed by ~. 我们的思想通过说话表达。同 talk, conversation 反 silence ❷[C]演说:make a ~ 发表演说 同 address, lecture

辨析
speech 意为"讲话;演说",是普通用语,既指公共场合对公众的正式演讲,也指非正式的发言;**address** 意为"讲话;演说",是正式用语,指重要场合对听众的正式演说,一般有充分的事先准备。

speed / spiːd / Ⅰ n. 迅速;快;速度 同 quickness, rate 反 slowness, delay / **at a** ~ **of** 以…的速度:drive at a ~ of 50 miles an hour 以每小时 50 英里的速度行驶 **at full** (**top**)~ 全(高)速行进 Ⅱ v. (sped /sped/, sped 或 speeded, speeded)❶快速行进:He sped down the street. 他沿街疾步行走。 同 hurry, run 反 crawl, drag ❷使加速;违章超速驾驶:The medicine ~ed her recovery. 这药加速了她的痊愈。同 quicken, accelerate 反 block, slow

speedy / ˈspiːdi / adj. 快的;迅速的 同 swift, rapid 反 slow, gradual

spell¹ / spel / v. (spelled , spelled 或 spelt /spelt/, spelt)拼(字)的字母;拼写:How do you ~ your name? 你的名字如何拼?

spell² / spel / Ⅰ n. [C] ❶一段工作时间;轮班;轮值:He had a ~ in Congress. 他当过一段时间的国会议员。We took ~s (with) doing the painting. 我们轮流刷漆。❷(疾病等的)发作,一阵:a dizzy ~ 一阵突如其来的头晕目眩/a ~ of coughing 一阵咳嗽 ❸一段(较短的)时间,一会儿:I lived in New York for a ~. 我在纽约住过一段时间。❹(一种天气的)一段持续期:an unbroken ~ of wet weather

阴雨连绵的天气 Ⅱ *vt.* 替…的班:I'd like to ～ you at doing the washing. 我想替你刷碗。

spelling / 'spelɪŋ / *n.* 拼读;拼写;拼写法:Do you use English ～(s) or American ～(s)? 你用英式拼写法还是美式拼写法?

spend / spend / *v.* (spent/spent/,spent)❶用(钱);花费:～ a lot of care on sth. 在某事上花了许多心血 / He spent a lot of money in entertaining his friends. 他花了许多钱招待朋友。/ You should ～ more time looking after your child. 你应当多花点时间照顾孩子。Don't ～ too much money on clothes. 不要把太多的钱花在买衣服上。同 expend, pay 反 earn, save ❷度过;消磨:～ a weekend in London 在伦敦度周末 同 pass

用法

❶spend (time or money) in doing sth. 中 in 可省略:He spent the whole evening (in) reading. 他把整晚的时间都花在读书上。在 spend time in sth. 中,in 后面需接表示动作的名词:They spent two hours in discussion without reaching any agreement. 他们花两小时讨论仍未达成协议。❷spend 通常只能以人为主语,如不能说: This new camera only spent me $100. 应把 spent 改为 cost 或改说: I spent only $100 on this new camera. 这架新照相机只花了我 100 美元。❸spend 后面一般不用不定式:I have spent an hour (in) tracing this quotation. 为了找这句话的出处,我花了整整一个小时。

sphere / sfɪə(r) / *n.* [C]❶球(体);地球仪:The teacher showed us China on the ～. 老师在地球仪上指出中国的位置给我们看。同 ball, globe ❷范围;领域:political ～ 政治领域 / widen one's ～ of knowledge 扩大某人的知识面 / within one's ～ 在某人的能力(活动)范围之内 同 field, area

spherical / 'sferɪkl / *adj.* 球形的;球面的 同 round

spice / spaɪs / Ⅰ *n.* ❶[C;U]香料;调料品 ❷情趣;趣味;风味:The story was rather lacking in ～. 这则故事枯燥无味。Ⅱ *vt.* ❶加香料于;给…调味:The cook ～d up tuna fish by adding curry powder to it. 厨师往金枪鱼里面加了咖喱粉调味。❷使增添情趣;给…增加趣味:a book ～d with humour 一部颇有幽默情趣的书

spicy / 'spaɪsɪ / *adj.* ❶加香料的;有香味的:The wood was ～ with the odour of pine and cedar. 树林里散发着松树和杉树的香味。❷辛辣的,刺激性的:Of course you do find ～ bits in Paris. 你当然会在巴黎找到一些刺激。

spider / 'spaɪdə(r) / *n.* [C]蜘蛛

spill / spɪl / Ⅰ *n.* 溢出:Please clean up the soup ～s on the chair. 请把洒在椅子上的汤擦干净。Ⅱ *v.* (spilled, spilled 或 spilt/spɪlt/, spilt)(使)溢出;(使)洒落:The tea has spilt on the tea table. 茶水溢到茶几上了。同 flow, shed

spin / spɪn / *v.* (spun/spʌn/, spun)❶纺纱;纺线 同 twist ❷使(某物)旋转 同 rotate, twist

spinach / 'spɪnɪdʒ, 'spɪnɪtʃ / *n.* 菠菜

spine / spaɪn / *n.* [C]❶脊椎;脊柱 ❷突起结构;刺激 ❸精神;骨气;勇气:No one has the ～ to sound off. 没有人勇气发表意见。❹书脊

spiral / 'spaɪrəl / *adj.* 螺旋形的;盘旋的

spirit / 'spɪrɪt / *n.* ❶精神;心灵:be in high (low) ～s 情绪高昂(低落) / party ～ 党性 / team ～ (组或队成员)的协作(集体、团队)精神 / I shall be with you in ～. 我将从精神上支持你。同 will, soul 反 body ❷幽灵;妖怪;鬼怪 同 ghost, shade

spiritual / 'spɪrɪtʃʊəl / *adj.* 精神的;心灵的:～ civilization 精神文明 / ～ values 精神财富 / ～ outlook 精神面貌 同 mental, moral 反 physical, material

spit / spɪt / *v.* (spat/spæt/, spat 或 spit, spit)(唾液)吐痰:If you ～ in the street, you may be fined. 如果你在街上吐痰,可能被处以罚款。/ ～ out 吐出:The baby spat out the pill. 那小孩吐出了药丸。

spite / spaɪt / *n.* [U]恶意;怨恨:do sth. out of a private ～ 出于个人恶意做某事 同 hatred, resentment 反 love, kindness in ～ of 不管;不顾:I went out in ～ of the rain. 尽管下雨,我还是出去了。

splendid / 'splendɪd / *adj.* 壮美的;壮丽的;辉煌的:a ～ sunset 壮美的夕阳 / a ～ victory 辉煌的胜利 同 beautiful, magnificent 反 plain, ordinary

splendo(u)r / 'splendə(r) / *n.* ❶[U]光彩;光辉;壮观;豪华:the ～ of a sunset 落日的壮丽/The welcoming ceremony was conducted with modest ～. 举行的欢迎仪式虽简单但不失庄严。❷[U](名声等的)显赫;(业绩等的)卓着;the lofty ～ of sb.'s office 某个职位的显赫

split /splɪt/ v. (split, split) ❶(使)裂开;(被)劈开:Some kinds of wood ～ easily. 有些木头容易劈开。同 divide, break 反 unite, join ❷分裂;断绝关系:He ～ with his wife several years ago. 他几年前跟他妻子离婚了。/ The party split up into three small groups. 该党分裂成三个小派别。同 divide, part 反 unite, join

spoil /spɔɪl/ v. (spoilt/spɔɪlt/, spoilt 或 spoiled, spoiled)❶损害;破坏;糟蹋:fruits ～t by insects 被昆虫糟蹋的水果 / holidays ～t by bad weather 被坏天气破坏的假日 同 damage, ruin 反 improve ❷宠坏;溺爱;姑息:parents who ～ their children 溺爱孩子的父母们 同 indulge ❸(指食物等)变坏;腐败:Some kinds of food easily ～. 有些食物很快就腐败了。同 decay, rot 反 preserve, save

spokesman /ˈspəʊksmən/ n. [C](pl. spokesmen)发言人;代言人:He acts as the ～ for the company. 他是公司的代言人。

sponge /spʌndʒ/ n. 海绵;海绵状物

sponsor /ˈspɒnsə(r)/ I n. [C]发起者;主办者;担保人;赞助人:country ～ of a bill 议案的提出者 同 promoter, supporter Ⅱ vt. ❶发起;主办:The flower show was ～ed by a park. 花展由一个公园主办。同 start ❷资助;赞助:The television program is ～ed by an oil company. 这个电视节目由一个石油公司赞助。同 finance, support

spontaneous /spɒnˈteɪniəs/ ❶自发的;非出于强制的:～ volunteers 自发的志愿者/ make a ～ offer of one's services 自动提供服务 ❷无意识的,自动的;不由自主的:a ～ burst of laughter 不由自主发出的大笑 ❸(举止等)自然的,非勉强的;(人)天真率直的:a ～ display of affection 情感的自然流露

spoon /spuːn/ n. 匙;调羹:salt ～ 盐匙 / tea ～ 茶匙 / soup ～ 汤匙 / be born with a silver ～ in one's mouth 出生在富贵人家 派 spoonful n. & adj.

sport /spɔːt/ n.[U]❶娱乐;消遣;玩笑:say sth. in ～ 说着玩 同 play, amusement ❷(户外)运动;游戏:have ～s 进行体育活动 / a ～s meet 运动会 / Fishing is a popular ～ a-

mong the villagers. 钓鱼是这儿村民普遍从事的运动。同 game, exercise

sportsman /ˈspɔːtsmən/ n. [C](pl. sportsmen)运动员:first-grade ～ 一级运动员 同 athlete, player

spot /spɒt/ n. [C] ❶点,斑点;亮点:white dress material with red ～s 有红点的白色衣料 同 mark, stain ❷地点;场所;位置:the ～ where he was murdered 他被谋杀的地点 / on the ～ 当场;在现场 同 place, location

spotlight /ˈspɒtlaɪt/ n. ❶[C](舞台等的)聚光灯;聚光灯照明圈 ❷引人注意的中心;受瞩目的焦点:A young star sprang into the ～. 一位年轻的明星突然备受瞩目。

spray /spreɪ/ I n.[U](因风或喷射器具造成的)水沫;水雾;浪花:sea ～ 海水浪花 同 splash Ⅱ v. 喷射;喷洒:～ the enemy with bullets 用子弹扫射敌人 同 shower, scatter

spread /spred/ I v. (spread, spread) ❶展开;铺开:～ the cloth on a table 把桌布铺在桌上 / The bird ～ its wings. 鸟儿展翅。同 extend, unfold 反 fold ❷撒;播:～ fertilizers 施肥 / ～ butter on bread 将黄油抹在面包上 同 scatter, distribute 反 collect, gather ❸(使)传播;流传:～ knowledge 传播知识 / ～ from mouth to mouth 口口相传 / ～ through the village 传遍全村 / ～ to neighboring countries. 蔓延到了邻国 / Flies ～ diseases. 苍蝇传播疾病。Ⅱ n. 传播;蔓延:have a broad ～ 广为传播 同 publish, communicate 反 conceal, suppress

spring¹ /sprɪŋ/ n. 春天;春季:in (the) ～ 在春天 / Spring Festival 春节 / Spring is the first season of the year. 春季是一年的第一个季节。

spring² /sprɪŋ/ I v. (sprang/spræŋ/, sprung /sprʌŋ/)❶跳;跃;使…弹开:He sprang out of bed. 他从床上跳下来。同 jump, start 反 drop, fall ❷(突然)出现:A storm sprang up. 风暴突然兴起。同 appear, arise Ⅱ n. [C] ❶跳跃 同 jump, leap ❷泉水:hot ～ 温泉 / mineral ～ 矿泉 同 fountain ❸弹簧;发条:a watch spring 表的发条 派 springy adj.

sprout /spraʊt/ I n. [C] (植物的)苗,芽 同 shoot Ⅱ v. 发芽;生枝 同 grow, shoot

spur /spɜː(r)/ I n. [C] ❶踢马刺,马靴刺:Giving ～s to his horse he galloped through the thickets. 他不断地踢刺他的马,在灌木丛

中跳跃前行。❷激发;激励,鼓舞;鞭策:The book is a ～ to imagination. 这本书能够激发想象力。/**on the ～ of the moment** 一时冲动地;不假思索地;当场,即兴地:She could not possibly make such a decision on the ～ of the moment. 她不可能一时冲动做出这样的决定。Ⅱ vt. (spurred; spurring) ❶用踢马刺策(马) ❷刺激,激发(兴趣等);鼓舞,激励;鞭策:on one's efforts 再接再厉/～ scientific interest 激发科学兴趣

spy / spaɪ / Ⅰ n. [C] ❶间谍 同 secret,agent ❷侦探 同 detective,scout Ⅱ v. 侦察:～ upon the enemy's movements 侦察敌人的动向 同 watch

square / skweə(r) / Ⅰ n. [C] ❶正方形;方形物:a ～ of glass 一块方形的玻璃 / draw a ～ 画一个正方形 同 cube ❷平方;二次幂:Four is the ～ of two. 四是二的平方。❸直角尺;丁字尺:Tian'anmen Square 天安门广场 Ⅱ vt. 使成正方形;使方正;调整,改正 Ⅲ adj. ❶正方形的;成直角的:～ table 方桌 ❷平方的 ❸公正的:play a ～ game 公平比赛 同 honest,just 派 squarely adv.

squash / skwɒʃ / Ⅰ vt. 压碎 同 smash,crush Ⅱ n. 鲜果汁

squeeze / 'skwiːz / Ⅰ v. 压榨;榨取;紧握 同 press, extract Ⅱ n. 挤;捏;紧握 同 pressure,hold

squirrel / 'skwɪrəl / n. [C]松鼠

stab / stæb / Ⅰ v. (stabbed; stabbing)刺;戳:The thief ～bed the boy with a dagger. 小偷用匕首刺那男孩。同 prick,stick Ⅱ n. [C]刺;戳 同 prick,thrust

stability / stə'bɪləti / n. 坚定;稳定;巩固:～ and unity 安定团结 / economic ～ 经济稳定 / political ～ 政治稳定 同 firmness,steadiness

stabilize / 'steɪbɪlaɪz / vt. 使稳定:～ prices 稳定物价 / ～ the market 稳定市场

stable[1] / 'steɪbl / adj. 稳定的;不变的:～ life 稳定的生活 / ～ rate of exchange 稳定的汇率 / Prices remain ～. 物价稳定。同 firm,steady 反 unstable,changeable

stable[2] / 'steɪbl / n. [C]马厩;牛棚

stack / stæk / Ⅰ n. [C](整齐的)堆,垛:a ～ of papers 一堆文件 同 heap,pile Ⅱ vt. 把…叠成堆;使堆积:～ up books 把书堆起来 同 gather,pile

stadium / 'steɪdiəm / n. [C](pl. stadiums 或 stadia)体育馆;运动场:the Capital Stadium 首都体育场

staff / stɑːf / n. [C](集合名词)全体职员;全体工作人员:the headmaster and his ～ 校长及其教职员工们 / be on the ～ 为正式职员 / change on the ～ 人事变动 / cut down (reduce) the ～ 裁减人员 同 crew,employees

stage / steɪdʒ / n. [C] ❶舞台 ❷时期;阶段:at an early ～ in history of our country 在我国历史的早期 / a three-～ rocket 三级火箭 同 period,phase

stagger / 'stægə(r) / v. 蹒跚;摇晃:The man ～ed across the room. 那人蹒跚地走过房间。同 sway

stain / steɪn / Ⅰ v. 玷污;染污:a tablecloth ～ed with gravy 沾有肉汁的桌布 同 spot,spoil 反 honor,clean Ⅱ n. 污渍;污点 同 spot,disgrace 派 stained adj.

stair / steə(r) / n. [C]楼梯;阶梯:escape ～ 安全楼梯 / screw ～ 螺旋楼梯 / I passed her on the ～s. 我在楼梯上遇见她。

stale / steɪl / adj. ❶陈腐的;过时的:～ news 过时的消息 / ～ water 死水 / Running water never gets ～. 流水不腐。同 decayed,old 反 new,original ❷不新鲜的:～ fish 不新鲜的鱼 / ～ bread 陈面包 同 flat,sour 反 fresh 派 stalely adv.;staleness n.

stall / stɔːl / n. [C] ❶货摊;书摊 同 booth,stand ❷厩 同 stable

stammer / 'stæmə(r) / Ⅰ vt. 口吃地说 Ⅱ n. 口吃

stamp / stæmp / Ⅰ n. [C] ❶邮票;印花:cancel a ～ 用邮戳盖销邮票 / stick a ～ on a letter 给信上贴邮票 ❷章,图章 同 mark,seal Ⅱ v. ❶贴邮票 ❷印(图案等)于(纸、布上等) 同 mark,seal ❸顿(足);踏:～ the ground 在地上踩脚 / The girl ～ed her feet with anger. 那女孩气得踩脚。同 trample / ～ out ①踏灭;踩熄:He ～ed out the fire. 他将火踏灭了。②消灭;镇压:The invaders were ～ed out at last. 入侵者终于被消灭了。

stand / stænd / Ⅰ v. (stood/stʊd/, stood) ❶站;立:We had to ～ all the way back in the bus. 在回程的公共汽车上,我们只能站着。/ Everyone stood up when the teacher entered. 老师进来时,全体起立。同 rise 反 sit,lie ❷忍

受;忍耐:He can't ~ the hot weather. 他不能忍受这炎热的天气。**同** bear, endure / **~ at attention** 立正:You can't make the men ~ at attention for the whole afternoon. 你不能让这些人整个下午立正站着。**~ by** ①站在旁边:He stood by me at yesterday's gathering. 在昨天的集会上,他站在我旁边。②旁观:How can you ~ by so cruelly? 你怎能如此残酷地袖手旁观呢? ③援助,支持;向…表示友好:I'll ~ by you whatever happens. 不论发生什么事,我都支持你。**~ for** 代表;代替:P. O. ~s for Post Office or postal order. P. O. 代表 Post Office(邮局)或 postal order(邮政汇票)。**~ in the way** 妨碍;挡住去路 / **~ on end** 直立;竖立 **~ out** 清晰地显出;引人注目:The notice ~s out clearly. 那则通知很引人注目。**~ up for** 支持;维护;保卫:He is always ready to ~ up for truth. 他随时准备维护真理。**~ up to** ①勇敢地面对;抵抗 ②经得起(磨难等);顶得住(磨难)经得住任何艰难困苦(严峻考验)Ⅱ *n.* **❶**立足地;立场:take one's ~ at (in) 站在…立场上 / I can't see his ~. 我看不出他的立场是什么。/ **take one's ~ for** (**against**) 表明立场支持(反对):I hope you take your ~ for us. 我希望你表明立场支持我们。**❷**售货台;售货摊 **同** booth, stall

stand 表示"忍受"之意时,后面可跟动名词和不定式,美国英语多用不定式:I cannot stand waiting (to wait) any longer. 我忍受不了,不能再等下去。

standard / 'stændəd / Ⅰ *n.* 标准;规格:below the ~ 低于标准 / up to the ~ 达到标准 / The living ~ of the people has been raised greatly. 人民的生活水平极大地提高了。**同** rule, model Ⅱ *adj.* 标准的:~ time 标准时间 / It is not so difficult to learn to speak ~ English. 学说标准英语并不难。**同** normal, universal **反** abnormal, unusual

standing / 'stændɪŋ / Ⅰ *n.* [C] **❶**站立;站立的位置 **❷**声望;地位;身份;级别:persons of considerable ~ in the academic community 学术界具有很高威望的人 **❸**(成绩)排名;(*pl.*)(体育比赛中的成绩)名次表:on top of the ~s 名列排名榜前列 Ⅱ *adj.* **❶**站立的;直立的;立式的:a ~ electric fan 落地电扇 **❷**确定不变的;长期维持的;常任的:She left her

jobless state as a ~ burden to her parents. 她觉得自己没有工作,成了父母长期的包袱。**❸**停转的;停住的;停顿的:The shortage of materials put the factory in a ~ condition. 由于原材料短缺,这家工厂处于停产状态。**❹**(液体)不流动的,静止的

standpoint / 'stændpɔɪnt / *n.* [C] 立场;观点:We should look at the problem from a historical ~. 我们应当从历史的角度看待这个问题。**同** opinion, viewpoint

standstill / 'stændstɪl / *n.* 停顿;停止;停滞:All train services are at a ~ today in a dispute over pay. 因为工资纠纷,今天所有的火车服务都停顿了。/ The wheels sank in the mud and the car came to a ~. 车轮陷入泥里,轿车开不动了。

star / stɑː(r) / *n.* [C] **❶**星 **❷**明星;主角;名家:Hollywood film ~s 好莱坞电影明星 **同** lead, hero

stare / steə(r) / *v.* 盯,凝视(与 at 连用):~ into the distance 凝视远方 / ~ sb. in the face 盯着某人的脸;就在某人面前 / ~ with surprise 目瞪口呆 / The little girl ~d at the toys in the window. 小女孩盯着橱窗里的玩具。**同** gaze, glare

start / stɑːt / Ⅰ *v.* **❶**开始;着手:It ~ed raining (to rain). 天开始下雨了。**同** begin, undertake **反** end, finish **❷**出发;动身:I shall ~ for Beijing tomorrow. 我明天动身去北京。**同** leave **反** delay **❸**(因痛苦、惊愕、恐惧等)惊起,惊动:He ~ed at the sound of my voice. 他听到我的声音吓了一跳。**同** rouse, jump **❹**发动;使开始:He can't ~ the car. 他不能启动这辆汽车。Ⅱ *n.* **❶**启程;动身;着手:make an early ~ 早些动身(或着手)**同** beginning, opening **反** end, finish **❷**(因惊愕、恐惧等)惊起:He sat up with a ~. 他一惊而起。**同** jump

startle / 'stɑːtl / Ⅰ *vt.* 使大吃一惊:The man ~d to see that his son was jumping down from a truck. 那人吃惊地看见他儿子正从一辆卡车上往下跳。**同** frighten, surprise **反** calm, settle Ⅱ *n.* 吃惊 **同** surprise, alarm

starvation / stɑː'veɪʃn / *n.* [U] 饥饿:die of ~ 饿死 / ~ wages 不能糊口的工资 / struggle on the verge of ~ 在饥饿线上挣扎

starve / stɑːv / *v.* **❶**(使)挨饿;(使)饿死:~ to death 饿死 / The man said he would ~

rather than beg for food. 那人说他宁愿挨饿也不乞食。❷感觉饥饿：Is there anything to eat? I'm starving. 有什么吃的没有？我觉得饿了。

state / steɪt / Ⅰ n. ❶(仅用单数)情形,状态：The house was in a dirty ～. 那栋房子非常脏。同 condition, position ❷(常用 State)国家；领土：Railways in Great Britain belong to the State. 英国的铁路属于国家所有。同 nation, country ❸(常用 State)州；邦：How many States are there in the United States of America? 美国有多少个州？Ⅱ vt. (尤指仔细、详尽地)说,陈述：～ one's view 陈述观点同 express, narrate

statement / 'steɪtmənt / n. 语言表达；叙述,陈述；声明：Clearness of ～ is more important than beauty of language. 陈述清楚比语言优美更重要。/ make (issue) a ～ 发表声明 / a bank ～ 银行报告；银行结单同 account, declaration

statesman / 'steɪtsmən / n. [C] (pl. statesmen)政治家；国务活动家同 politician

station / 'steɪʃn / Ⅰ n. [C] ❶车站；办公室；站,所：gas (service) ～ 汽车加油站 / a space ～ 宇航(空间)站 /bus ～ 公共汽车站 / comfort ～ 公共厕所 /police ～ 警察局／TV ～ 电视台 / weather ～ 气象站同 terminal, location ❷陆军或海军基地；驻扎人员同 base Ⅱ v. 驻扎；安置；配置同 assign, locate

stationary / 'steɪʃənəri / adj. ❶固定的；静止的；停滞的：～ shadows 静止的影子❷原地不动的；非移动式的；落地的：We were ～ at a set of traffic lights when a police car passed by us. 一辆警车从我们身边驶过,我们站在一组交通信号灯边一动不动。

stationery / 'steɪʃən(ə)ri / n. 文具；信笺

statistical / stə'tɪstɪkl / adj. 统计的；统计学的：～ chart 统计图／～ data 统计资料／～ figure 统计数字／～ table 统计表派 statistically adv.

statistics / stə'tɪstɪks / n. 统计；统计学；统计数字；统计资料：analyze ～ 分析统计资料

statue / 'stætʃu: / n. [C]雕像；塑像；铸像：There is a ～ to Dr. Sun Yat-sen in Nanjing. 南京有一座孙中山先生的雕像。同 sculpture, image

stature / 'stætʃə(r) / n. [U] ❶身高；身材：a man of short ～身材矮小的男人 / a girl who

is big in ～ 大个子的姑娘❷声誉,名望；境界；高度,水平：sb.'s ～ in literary world 某人在文学界的声望

status / 'steɪtəs / n. [U]地位；身份；职位：economic (political) ～ 经济(政治)地位同 position, rank

statute / 'stætjuːt / n. [C;U](立法机关通过的)法令,法规,成文法：The salaries of most federal workers are ste by ～. 联邦工人的薪水有明令规定。

stay / steɪ / Ⅰ v. ❶停留；保持(位置或状况)：～ in bed 待在床上 / I can ～ only a few minutes. 我只能停留几分钟。同 remain, keep / ～ **up** 不睡觉；熬夜：He ～ed up late to prepare for the final examination. 他熬夜准备期末考试。❷阻止；延缓；遏制：～ the progress of a disease 阻止疾病蔓延同 block Ⅱ n. ❶停留；逗留时间同 stop, visit ❷延续同 delay

stead / sted / n. [U](职位、身份、作用等的)代替；接替：run the meeting in sb.'s ～ 代替某人主持会议/The publisher appointed someone unknown in his ～. 出版社指定了一位不知名的人来接替他。

steadily / 'stedɪli / adv. ❶坚固地；稳定地；不变地同 constantly反 unsteadily ❷逐步地；不断地：His health gets worse ～. 他的健康状况不断恶化。同 gradually

steady / 'stedi / adj. (-ier, -iest) 坚固的；不动摇的：on a ～ foundation 在牢固的基础上同 constant, resolute反 unsteady, changeable

steak / steɪk / n. (尤指)牛排；猪排；鱼排

steal / stiːl / v. (stole/stəʊl/, stolen /'stəʊlən/) ❶偷；窃取：Someone has stolen my watch. 有人偷了我的手表。同 rob, take ❷溜进；溜走：He stole into the room. 他溜进房间。同 slip

steam / stiːm / Ⅰ n. [U]蒸汽；水汽：a building heated by ～ 有暖气的建筑物同 vapor Ⅱ v. ❶蒸发；冒蒸汽 ❷蒸煮：～ fish 蒸鱼同 boil, cook

steel / stiːl / n. [U]钢

steep / stiːp / adj. 陡的：a ～ roof 陡斜的屋顶／～ rise in output 产量的激增同 sudden反 flat, gradual

steer / stɪə(r) / v. 驾驶；操纵：～ing wheel(船上的)舵轮；(车上的)方向盘同 direct, pilot

stem / stem / n. 茎；树干；(叶)梗同

shoot, trunk

step / step / Ⅰ v. (stepped;stepping)走;跨步;步行:～ onto (off) the platform 走向(离开)平台 / ～ on the gas 踩油门 同 walk, pace / ～ **aside** 让到一旁;避开:Please ～ aside to let me off the bus. 请站开点让我下车。～ **down** ①从(车厢)下来 ②辞职;让位;下台:He is not ready to ～ down yet. 他还不准备辞职。～ **in** ①走进:Step in, please. 请进来。②干涉;介入:The government may have to ～ in to settle the disagreement between the union and the employers. 政府可能不得不介入解决工会和雇主间的争论。～ **up** ①走近;向上走 ②逐步增加:Our trade with the foreign countries is ～ping up. 我们和外国的贸易正在逐步增加。Ⅱ n. ❶脚步;一步的距离;脚步声;步态:He was walking at slow ～s. 他慢步行走。同 pace / ～ **by** ～ 逐渐地;一步一步地:He solved the problem ～ by ～. 他逐步地解决了这个问题。❷[C](达到目的的)步骤,措施:take ～s to prevent the spread of influenza 采取措施阻止流行性感冒的蔓延/We should take immediate ～s to prevent air from being polluted. 我们应当立即采取措施防止空气污染。同 measure, procedure ❸[C]阶梯;台阶:Mind the ～s when you go down into the cellar. 下地窖时注意台阶。同 stair

stepdaughter / ˈstepdɔːtə(r)/ n. [C]妻子与前夫(或丈夫与前妻)所生的女儿;继女

stepfather / ˈstepfɑːðə(r) / n. [C]继父

stepmother / ˈstepmʌðə(r) / n. [C]继母

stepson / ˈstepsʌn / n. [C]妻子与前夫(或丈夫与前妻)所生的儿子;继子

stereo / ˈsteriəʊ / Ⅰ n. 立体声 Ⅱ adj. 立体声的

stern / stɜːn / adj. 严厉的;严格的;严肃的:a ～ master 严厉的主人 / a ～ discipline 严格的纪律 同 severe, strict 反 gentle, kind

stew / stjuː / Ⅰ vt. 煨,炖,焖:a chicken gently in the pot 用罐以文火炖鸡 Ⅱ n. ❶[U;C]煨炖的食物;炖菜:I'd like more beef ～. 我想再来一些炖牛肉。❷(a ～)焦虑;激动;气愤:be in a ～ about the injustice received in work 为在工作中受到不公正待遇而生闷气

steward / ˈstjuːəd / n. [C](轮船、飞机或火车上的)服务员 同 waiter

stewardess / ˌstjuːˈdes / n. [C](轮船、飞机或火车上的)女服务员 同 waitress

stick / stɪk / Ⅰ v. (stuck/stʌk/, stuck) ❶(使)黏着;(使)附着:～ a stamp on an envelope 将邮票贴在信封上 同 attack, paste 反 remove ❷以(尖物)插入;刺;戳:～ a fork into a potato 把叉插入马铃薯 同 stab ❸(尖物)刺入;阻塞:The needle stuck in my finger. 针刺入我的手指。同 thrust ～ **to** ①贴着:Wet clothes ～ to the skin. 湿衣服黏着皮肤。②坚持:If you ～ to practising the piano every day, you could become quite a good musician. 如果你每天坚持练习弹钢琴,你会成为一位优秀的音乐家。Ⅱ n. ❶柴枝;小树枝;gather dry ～s to make a fire 拾干柴生火 同 branch, twig ❷杖;棍;棒:The old man cannot walk without a ～. 那老人没有手杖无法走路。同 cane, pole 派 sticky adj.

stiff / stɪf / adj. 不易弯曲的;僵硬的;僵直的;be ～ in manners 态度生硬 / be ～ with cold 冻僵 同 hard, rigid 反 soft, yielding 派 stiffen v.; stiffly adv.; stiffness n.

still / stɪl / Ⅰ adj. 不动的;静止的:Please keep ～ while I take photograph for you. 在我给你照相时,请勿动。同 motionless, quiet 反 active, noisy Ⅱ adv. ❶仍;尚;还:He is ～ busy. 他仍很忙。同 yet ❷(与比较级连用)更,愈:Tom is tall, but Mary is ～ taller. 汤姆很高,但玛丽更高。同 even ❸然而;不过:He has treated you badly; ～, he's your brother and you ought to help him. 他虽然对你不好,但他总是你的兄弟,你应该帮助他。同 however, nevertheless

stimulate / ˈstɪmjuleɪt / vt. 刺激;激励;激发:The good news ～d the students' enthusiasm. 那个好消息激发了学生们的热情。同 arouse, excite 反 calm, discourage

stimulation / ˌstɪmjuˈleɪʃn / n. [U]刺激作用;激励:The workers need ～ to new efforts. 工人们需要激励以作出新的努力。

stimulus / ˈstɪmjuləs / n. [C](pl. stimuli)刺激物;刺激源;引发物:Parents are trying to provide constant creative, athletic and emotional ～ for their children. 家长们不断培养孩子们在创造性、身体和情感方面的素质。/Only money can not be the ～ to invention. 仅仅有钱是不能激发创造发明的。

sting / stɪŋ / Ⅰ v. (stung/stʌŋ/, stung) ❶刺

伤；蜇伤：A bee stung me on the cheek. 一只蜜蜂蜇了我的面颊。同 prick, stab ❷给…造成剧痛；伤害：He was stung by his enemy's insults. 他被敌人的辱骂伤害了。同 burn, hurt Ⅱ n. ❶[C]（蜜蜂等的）螫针 同 brick ❷（昆虫等造成的）刺痛，刺伤：Her face was covered with ～s. 她脸上满是刺伤。同 bite, hurt ❸（身体或心灵的）剧痛，刺痛：the ～ of defeat 失败的惨痛 / the ～ of a whip 鞭打的剧痛 同 pain, wound

stingy / ˈstɪndʒi / adj. ❶吝啬的，小气的：Their employer was a ～ and idle man. 他们的雇主吝啬小气，游手好闲。同 greedy ❷缺乏的，不足的，极少的

stir / stɜː(r) / v. (stirred; stirring) ❶动；移动：Not a leaf was ～ring. 没有一片树叶在动。同 move, shake ❷搅和；拌：milk into a cake mixture 把牛奶搅和在蛋糕的混合原料中 / ～ the fire with the poker 拨火 同 blend, mix ❸惹起；激起：The story ～red the boy's imagination. 那故事激起了孩子的想象。同 rouse, stimulate 反 calm

stitch / stɪtʃ / Ⅰ n.[C] ❶（缝纫的）一针 ❷缝线；针脚 Ⅱ v. 缝；缝合 同 sew

stock / stɒk / Ⅰ n. 1. 树干的下部 ❷存货；现货：The book is in (out of) ～. 该书现有（没有）存货。同 store, goods ❸股票；公债 同 shares Ⅱ v. 供应；备置；有…存货：～ a shop with goods 以货物供应商店 同 supply, store

stocking / ˈstɒkɪŋ / n.[C]长筒袜

stomach / ˈstʌmək / n. ❶[C]胃；腹部：～ache n. 胃痛，腹痛 ❷[U]食欲；胃口：The film goes against my ～. 这电影不合我意。同 appetite, thirst / have no ～ for 没胃口；不对胃口；不合意：I have no ～ for sweet food. 我不喜欢吃甜食。

stone / stəʊn / n. 石；岩石：sand ～ 沙石 / lime ～ 石灰石 同 rock, pebble

stool / stuːl / n.[C]凳

stop / stɒp / Ⅰ v. (stopped; stopping) ❶阻止；停下：Nothing can ～ us from going. 什么也阻止不了我们去。The train ～ped. 火车停下来了。同 prevent, halt ❷逗留；住：Are you ～ping at this hotel? 你住在这家旅馆吗？同 stay, rest / ～ doing sth. 停止做某事：My father is trying to ～ smoking. 我父亲正努力戒烟。～ sb. (from) doing sth. 防止某人做某

事：The trees will ～ the sand from moving towards the rich farmland in the south. 树木将阻止沙移向南方肥沃的农田。～ to do sth. 停下来去做某事：Now let's ～ to have a rest. 现在我们停下来休息一下。Ⅱ n. ❶停止；中止：The train came to a sudden ～. 火车突然停下。/ ～-watch（赛跑等用的）秒表 同 block, halt / put a ～ to sth., bring sth. to a ～ 使停下；使结束：The red light brought the traffic to a ～. 红灯使来往的车辆停下来。❷（公共汽车等的）车站，招呼站 同 station, terminal

用法

stop 作不及物动词后接不定式时，不定式表示目的或结果：As he was going to school, he met a friend and stopped to talk with him for a while. 他在上学的路上碰到一个朋友，于是停下和他谈了一阵子。stop 作及物动词后直接接名词或动名词：Stop the train! 让火车停下来！When the mother came into the room, the baby stopped crying. 母亲一走进房间，那个婴孩就不哭了。

辨析

stop, cease, pause, halt 都有"停止"的意思。**stop** 是普通用词，多指动作、行为的停止，而且表示这个结束过程是迅速的：All the students stopped talking as soon as the teacher entered the classroom. 老师一走进教室，所有学生都停止了说话。**cease** 是正式用词，多指状态或情况的停止或不再存在，后接宾语既可是动词十ing形式，也可是动词不定式。它表示的停止过程是逐渐的：He has ceased to breathe. 他已经停止呼吸了。**pause** 指暂时停止，并含有"再继续下去"之意，只用作不及物动词：The teacher paused for a second and then read the text again. 老师停顿了一下，然后重新开始读课文。**halt** 指骤然有力的终止，或指同迫于权威或受阻于外力而停止：A young man raised an arm to halt a taxi. 一个小伙子举手拦住了一辆出租车。

storage / ˈstɔːrɪdʒ / n. ❶[U]贮藏；存储；保管：～ life 储藏期限 / a room for ～ 储藏室 / ～ battery (cell) 蓄电池 同 preservation ❷（计算机的）贮存器

store / stɔː(r) / Ⅰ n. ❶贮藏；储备：lay in ～s of coal for the winter 贮藏大量的煤以供冬季使用 同 stock, preservation ❷（有特殊用途的）物品，必需物：military ～s 军需品 同 provision, supply ❸商店；百货店：a clothing ～ 服装店 / large department ～s of London 伦敦的大百货店 回 shop, market ❹仓库；贮藏室：available from ～s 有存货的 回 storehouse, warehouse / ～keeper n. 仓库管理员；零售店店主 Ⅱ vt. 贮藏；储备：Do all squirrels ～ up food for the winter? 所有的松鼠都为冬天储备食物吗? 回 preserve, save 反 spend, waste

storey / ˈstɔːri / n. (房屋的)一层：a house of two ～s 两层楼的房子

storm / stɔːm / n. [C]风暴；暴风雨：a thunder ～ 雷雨 派 stormy adj.

story / ˈstɔːri / n. [C] ❶历史；事迹；小说；传奇；故事：stories of ancient Greece 古希腊历史 / a ～ for children 儿童故事 回 history, account ❷(＝storey)(房屋的)一层

stout / staʊt / adj. ❶矮胖的 回 fat, round 反 skinny, thin ❷牢固的 回 solid, strong 反 fragile, weak

stove / stəʊv / n. [C]火炉；电炉

straight / streɪt / Ⅰ adj. 直的：a ～ line 直线 / a ～ A student 一个全优学生 回 direct 反 indirect, curved Ⅱ adv. 直地；直接地：Keep ～ on. 继续前进。 回 directly 反 indirectly 派 straighten v. ; straightness n.

straightaway / ˈstreɪtəˌweɪ / Ⅰ adj. 直道的；直接的，径直的：a ～ track 直线跑道 / a ～ run of 15 miles 径直奔跑了 15 英里 Ⅱ adv. 立刻，马上：You have to go there ～. 你得马上到那儿去。

straightforward / ˌstreɪtˈfɔːwəd / Ⅰ adj. 老实的；坦率的 回 frank, honest Ⅱ adv. 正直地；坦率地

strain / streɪn / Ⅰ vt. ❶尽力使用：～ one's voice 尽力提高嗓门 回 strive 反 relax ❷拉紧；伸张 回 tighten, stretch 反 loosen ❸耗损；因过分用力而损伤 回 exhaust, injure Ⅱ n. ❶极度紧张；nervous ～ 神经紧张：Can you stand the ～ of the life there? 你受得了那里的紧张生活吗? 回 tension, pressure 反 relaxation ❷张力；拉紧：The rope broke because of ～. 因张力太大绳子断了。回 force, stretch ❸扭伤；拉伤：Jack has got a ～ in the arm. 杰克的手臂给扭伤了。回 wrench, twist

strait / streɪt / n. [C] 海峡：the Taiwan Straits 台湾海峡 / the Gibraltar Straits 直布陀海峡

/ the Magellan Strait 麦哲伦海峡 回 channel

strange / streɪndʒ / adj. ❶奇怪的；奇异的；不可思议的：hear a ～ sound 听到奇怪的声音 回 odd, peculiar 反 normal, ordinary ❷(作表语)陌生的；不习惯的(与 to 连用)：The village boy was ～ to city life. 那个村童不习惯城市生活。 回 unknown, unfamiliar 反 known, familiar 派 strangely adv. ; strangeness n.

stranger / ˈstreɪndʒə(r) / n. [C]陌生人；异乡人；异国人：The dog always barks at ～s. 狗总是向陌生人叫。回 newcomer, foreigner

strangle / ˈstræŋɡl / vt. 扼杀；勒死，绞死；使窒息：This stiff collar is strangling me. 硬衣领把我卡得喘不过气。回 choke, tighten

strategic(al) / strəˈtiːdʒɪk(əl) / adj. 战略的；谋略的：～ principles 战略方针 / global ～ 全球战略

strategist / ˈstrætədʒɪst / n. [C]战略家；谋略家；兵法家

strategy / ˈstrætədʒi / n. 战略；作战计划；对策 回 tactics, scheme

straw / strɔː / n. [U]稻草；麦秸：a ～ mattress 草垫 / ～ man 稻草人 / ～ sandals 草鞋 回 hay

strawberry / ˈstrɔːbəri / n. [C]草莓

stream / striːm / Ⅰ n. ❶[C]河；溪；水流：I crossed a ～. 我蹚过一条小河。回 brook, branch ❷(液体)流出；人潮：Streams of people were coming out of the railway station. 人流正从火车站涌出。回 flow, run Ⅱ vi. 流：Sweat was ～ing down his face. 汗水正从他脸上流下来。回 flow, run

street / striːt / n. [C]街道；meet a friend in the ～ 在街上碰到一个朋友 回 road, avenue

strength / streŋθ / n. [U]力量；力气：exert all one's ～ 竭尽全力 / save ～ 省力 / take great ～ to do sth. 尽力做某事 回 power, vigor

strengthen / ˈstreŋθən / vt. 加强；巩固：～ discipline 加强纪律 / ～ national defense 巩固国防 / ～ unity 加强团结 / ～ up the management 加强管理 回 harden, reinforce

stress / stres / Ⅰ n. [U] ❶压力；压迫：under the ～ of poverty 在贫困的压迫下 回 pressure, oppression ❷[U]重视；强调 回 emphasis, importance 反 neglect, unimportance

❸[C]重读;重音:Stress and rhythm are important in speaking English. 说英语时轻重读和节奏很重要。同 accent Ⅱ v. 着重强调;He ～ed the point that everyone should respect the disabled. 他强调人人都应该尊重残疾人。同 emphasize,repeat 反 ignore,neglect

stretch /stretʃ/ Ⅰ v. ❶伸展;张开;拉长;扩大:～ a rope tight 把绳拉紧 / ～ one's neck 伸长颈子 / ～ one's arms 伸臂 / ～ oneself 伸伸懒腰 同 extend,expand 反 shrink Ⅱ n. ❶伸展;张开;拉长:The cat woke and gave a ～. 猫醒后伸伸懒腰。同 extent ❷连续;绵延:a beautiful ～ of wooded country 一大片美丽的树林覆盖的乡间 同 expanse,spread | **at a** ～ 连续地;不休息地:He worked for 12 hours at a ～. 他连续工作了 12 个小时。**at full** ～ 尽全力:The workers were at full ～. 工人们已尽全力了。

辨析

stretch 指沿某条线向某个方向伸展;**spread** 指在表面上向各个方向伸展。

stretcher /ˈstretʃə(r)/ n. [C] 担架

stricken /ˈstrɪkən/ adj. 患病的;受伤害的;遭不幸的;受打击的:be ～ with measles 患麻疹/ be conscience ～受良心折磨的

strict /strɪkt/ adj. 严厉的;严格的:a ～ father 严厉的父亲 / ～ discipline 严格的纪律/ be ～ with one's child 对孩子要求严格 同 rigid,severe 反 flexible,loose 派 strictly adv.; strictness n.

stride /straɪd/ Ⅰ n. [C] ❶大步;步幅:He walked with long ～s. 他大步流星地走着。同 gait ❷(常用复数)进展,进步:make great ～s in ...在…方面取得长足进步 同 advance,progress Ⅱ vt. (strode /strəʊd/,stridden/ˈstrɪdn/) 迈大步走;跨越:He strode about the room. 他在房间里大踏步踱来踱去。/ ～ over a brook 跨过小河 同 stalk

strike /straɪk/ Ⅰ v. (struck/strʌk/,struck) ❶打;击;敲:He struck me on the head. 他打我的头。同 hit,pound / ～ **at** 动手要打;向…打来:He struck at the cat,but it ran away. 他动手要打那只猫,但它跑开了。～ **in** 插嘴:Here someone struck in with a question. 这时有人插嘴发问。～ **into** 打进;刺入:It's root will ～ deep into earth in a few days. 几天后,

它的根就会深深扎入土中。～ **off** 取消;删去;切除:His name was struck off the football team. 他的名字已从足球队队员名单中删除。～ **out** ①用力打;猛击 ②产生;发明:～ out a new idea 产生一个新的想法 ❷打出;擦出:a match 擦火柴 / The matches are damp;they won't ～. 火柴潮了划不燃。❸(时钟)敲响报时:Six o'clock has already struck. 6 点已经敲过了。同 ring ❹造成…印象;吸引…的注意:How does the idea ～ you? 你对那主意感觉怎么样? 同 impress,affect ❺罢工:～ for higher pay 为争取较高的薪水而罢工 Ⅱ n. [C]罢工:a ～ of bus-drivers 公共汽车司机的罢工/ a sit-down ～ 静坐罢工 / **on** ～ 在罢工:Most miners have gone on ～. 大部分矿工都罢工了。

striking /ˈstraɪkɪŋ/ adj. 引人注意的;激起兴趣的:a woman of ～ beauty 一个美貌惊人的女人 同 remarkable,outstanding

string /strɪŋ/ Ⅰ n. 带;线;细绳:a ball of ～ 一圈线团 / a piece of ～ 一根线 同 cord,thread Ⅱ vt. (strung /strʌŋ/,strung) ❶串起;把…连在一起:They are ～ing beads. 他们正把珠子串起来。/ ～ ideas together 把思想贯穿起来 同 thread ❷吊,悬,挂,绑:We strung up lanterns in the yard. 我们在院子里挂起了灯笼。同 hang ❸给乐器上(调)弦:～ a violin 给小提琴装弦 ❹使紧张,使兴奋:She was highly strung for the game. 她对比赛感到非常紧张。同 make tense ❺扯去筋,除去纤维

strip¹ /strɪp/ v. ❶剥;脱;裸露 同 peel,remove 反 apply ❷夺去;剥夺 同 plunder,rub

strip² /strɪp/ n[C] ❶长条;狭长的一条或一片 同 slip,stripe ❷(飞机着陆时的)跑道 同 air-strip

stripe /straɪp/ n. [C](表面上的)条纹,线条:a white table-cloth with red ～s 有红色条纹的白桌布 同 line 派 striped adj.

strive /straɪv/ vi. (strove/strəʊv/或 strived,striven /ˈstrɪvn/或 strived)努力;奋斗:We are striving for further progress. 我们在为继续进步而努力。同 struggle,fight

stroke¹ /strəʊk/ n. ❶击;敲 同 blow,punch ❷中风 ❸(写字、绘画的)一笔;笔画 同 movement ❹(报时的)钟声 同 striking,ringing

stroke² /strəʊk/ vt.(用手反复地)抚摸 同

brush,pat / ～ **down** 平息怒气：I failed to ～ him down. 我无法平息他的怒气。

stroll / strəʊl / Ⅰ n. 漫步；闲逛：have (go for) a ～散步 同 walk,ramble Ⅱ v. 散步,闲逛 同 walk,ramble

strong / strɒŋ / adj. 有抵抗力的；强大的；强壮的；坚强的：～ in English 擅长英语 / ～ in number 数量上占优势 / a ～ stick 不易折断的手杖 / a ～ will 坚强的意志 同 powerful, mighty 反 powerless,weak / ～-minded adj. 意志坚强的；有决心的 派 strongly adv.

structural / ˈstrʌktʃərəl / adj. 结构的

structure / ˈstrʌktʃə(r) / Ⅰ n. ❶[U]结构；构造：price ～ 价格结构 / wage ～ 工资结构 同 form,framework ❷[C]建筑物：build a ～ 修造建筑物 同 building,construction Ⅱ vt. 建造；建立 同 build,construct

struggle / ˈstrʌɡl / Ⅰ v. 抗争；奋斗；斗争；挣扎：～ against (with) difficulties 与困难做斗争 / ～ for justice 为正义而战 / The thief ～d in the policeman's arms. 那贼在警察怀中挣扎。同 fight,strive 反 yield,surrender Ⅱ n. [C]抗争；奋斗；斗争；挣扎：the ～ for freedom 为争取自由而斗争 / He made many ～s to get a good education. 为了获得良好的教育,他做了很多努力。同 fight,effort

stubborn / ˈstʌbən / adj. 顽固的；倔强的；顽强的；难处理的；难应付的：a ～ resistance 顽强的抵抗 / ～ illness 顽疾 / He's so ～ that nobody can persuade him. 他很顽固,无人能说服他。同 obstinate,unyielding 反 flexible, yielding 派 stubbornly adv.；stubbornness n.

student / ˈstjuːdnt / n. [C] ❶学生：medical ～s 医科学生 同 pupil,learner 反 teacher,professor ❷学者；研究者：a ～ of nature 研究自然的学者 同 scholar,examiner

studio / ˈstjuːdiəʊ / n. [C]工作室；播音室

study / ˈstʌdi / Ⅰ n. ❶读书；研究；学习：case ～ 病历(档案、专题)研究 / make a ～ of the country's foreign trade 研究该国的国际贸易 同 reading,learning ❷[C]书房 同 studio,library Ⅱ v.求学；研究：～ for a degree 攻读学位/He was ～ing for the medical profession. 他在求学,准备将来当医生。同 learn,research / ～ **by oneself** 自学：He studied by himself and became a lawyer. 他靠自学成为一名律师。

用法

study 作名词有不可数和可数之分,作不可数名词时指一般的"学习"或"研究"：The study of foreign languages above all requires constant practice. 外语学习首先需要经常练习。作可数名词时指具体的研究工作或研究成果：He has made a special study of the use of prepositions in the English language. 他对英语介词的用法进行了特别的研究。

stuff / stʌf / Ⅰ n. 材料；原料 同 material,matter Ⅱ v. 塞满,填塞(与 with 连用)；塞进,装入(与 into 连用)：～ a bag with feathers 用羽毛填充袋子 同 fill,pack 反 remove

stuffy / ˈstʌfi / adj. ❶不通风的,不透气的：a smoky ～ office 烟雾弥漫且不通风的办公室 ❷(鼻子)堵塞的,不通的：The cold made my nose ～. 我因感冒而鼻塞。❸单调乏味的,枯燥的；沉闷的：Surprisingly, the magazine became rather ～. 没想到,这本杂志竟变得很乏味了。

stumble / ˈstʌmbl / vi. ❶绊倒,绊跌；失足摔倒：～ against a stump 被树桩绊了一跤／He was drunk and ～d on the bottom step. 他喝醉了,在最后一段阶梯上摔倒了。❷磕磕绊绊地走；踉跄而行：She ～d into the bedroom. 她跌跌撞撞地走进了卧室 ❸吞吞吐吐地讲话；断断续续地演奏：Just relax and be confident, and you won't ～ this time. 放松些,自信一点儿,这次你不会结结巴巴了。/She was nervous and ～d through a piece by Chopin. 她很紧张,断断续续地勉强演奏完了一首肖邦的曲子。

stupid / ˈstjuːpɪd / adj. 笨的；愚蠢的：Don't be ～ to believe that. 不要那么蠢去相信那件事。同 foolish,dull 反 clever,wise

sturdy / ˈstɜːdi / adj. (-ier,-iest) ❶强壮的；结实的：a ～ desk 结实的课桌 同 strong,stout 反 weak,fragile ❷坚定的；坚强的：～ children 坚强的孩子们 同 firm,resolute 反 fearful,irresolute

style / staɪl / n. ❶方式；风格：speak in a delightful ～ 以令人喜欢的方式说话 同 manner ❷(衣服等的)式样,时尚：the latest ～ in hats (in hair-dressing)帽子(发型)的最新式样 同 design,fashion ❸(书面语)称呼；称号：Has he any right to assume the ～ of colonel? 他有权接受上校称号吗? 同 call, name

stylist / 'staɪlɪst / n. [C]时装设计师;装潢设计师;发型设计师

subconscious / sʌb'kɒnʃəs / Ⅰ adj. 下意识的,潜意识的: Nail-biting is often a ～ reaction to tension. 咬指甲往往是心理紧张时的下意识动作。Ⅱ n. [U]下意识,潜意识: Freud's theory of the ～ 弗洛伊德的潜意识论/the confused thoughts of the ～ 下意识的杂乱念头

subdue / səb'dju: / vt. ❶征服;制服: ～ a rebel army 制服叛军/～ a forest fire 扑灭森林大火/Rome ～d Gaul. 罗马征服了高卢。❷克制;抑制: ～ one's tear 忍住泪水/～ one's anger 压住怒火

subject Ⅰ / 'sʌbdʒɪkt / n. ❶主题,题目;科目,学科: an interesting ～ for conversation 有趣的话题 / a ～ for an essay 文章的主题 同 topic, theme ❷(语法)主语 ❸国民;臣民 citizen 反 ruler ❹实验的对象 Ⅱ / 'sʌbdʒɪkt / adj. 易遭…的;受…支配的(与 to 连用): All players are ～ to the rules of the game. 所有选手都要遵守比赛规则。/ Those islands are ～ to typhoons. 那些岛屿易遭台风侵袭。同 liable, obedient 反 independent Ⅲ / səb'dʒekt / vt. 使遭受;使服从 同 expose, submit

subjective / səb'dʒektɪv / adj. ❶主观(上)的;出于主观想法的: Meaning has both an objective component and a ～ component. 意义既有客观成分又有主观成分。❷个人的,私人的: ～ experience 个人经验 ❸出于个人情感的,臆想的: You're too ～ when it comes to judging her work. 当要评估她的工作时,你太感情用事了。

submarine / ˌsʌbmə'ri:n, 'sʌbməri:n / Ⅰ adj. 水下的;海底的: ～ plants 海底植物 Ⅱ n. [C]潜水艇: build a nuclear ～ 建造核潜艇

submerge / səb'mɜːdʒ / vt. ❶浸泡;浸没: Did you ～ the clothes in the sudsy water? 你把衣服泡进肥皂水里了吗? ❷淹没: The fields were ～d by the flood. 农田被洪水淹没了。❸湮灭,埋没;隐藏,隐瞒: Certain facts were ～d by the witness. 有些事被证人隐瞒了。— vi. 潜入水下: The submarine ～d immediately. 潜艇很快下潜了。

submit / səb'mɪt / v. (-mitted;-mitting)(使)归顺;(使)服从;投降: ～ oneself to discipline 服从纪律/～ to the enemy 投降敌人/～ a proposal to the committee 向委员会提交一项建议 / ～ to separation from one's family 忍痛与家人分离 同 surrender, yield 反 fight, resist

subordinate / sə'bɔːdɪnət / adj. 下级的;辅助的 同 inferior, secondary 反 superior, primary

subscribe / səb'skraɪb / v. ❶认捐;捐助: He ～d 500 *yuan* to the flood relief fund. 他向水灾救济基金捐款 500 元。同 pay, contribute ❷订阅(报纸等): ～ for books 订购书籍 ❸签(名)同 sign

subscription / səb'skrɪpʃn / n. ❶认捐;捐助 同 contribution ❷订购;订阅

subsequent / 'sʌbsɪkwənt / adj. 随后的;后来的: ～ events 后来发生的事件 同 following, later 反 previous 派 subsequently *adv*.

substance / 'sʌbstəns / n. 物质;实质: Water, ice and snow are the same ～ in different forms. 水、冰和雪是不同形式的同种物质。同 material, matter

substantial / səb'stænʃəl / adj. ❶大量的,大规模的;数目可观的: a ～ majority 绝大多数/a ～ amount of money 一大笔钱 ❷实在的,真实的,现实的 ❸坚固的,牢固的;结实的,坚实的;壮实的: a ～ physique 健壮的体形

substitute / 'sʌbstɪtjuːt / Ⅰ n. [C]代理人;代用品: She used a paper cup as a ～ in the experiment. 在实验中她用一个纸杯作为代用品。同 agent, replacement Ⅱ v. 用…代替,代以: They ～d plastics for glass. 他们用塑料代替玻璃。同 replace, exchange

subtitle / 'sʌ(b)ˌtaɪtl / Ⅰ n. [C] ❶副标题;小标题 ❷(尤指电影或电视的)对白字幕 Ⅱ vt. ❶给…加副标题(或小标题)❷为…加上对白字幕

subtract / səb'trækt / vt. 减;去掉: 3 ～d from 8 gives 5. 8 减去 3 等于 5。同 remove, take 反 add 派 subtraction *n*.

suburb / 'sʌbɜːb / n. [C]市郊;郊区: the ～s (总称)郊外;郊区 同 outskirt

suburban / sə'bɜːbən / adj. 市郊的;郊区的: ～ shops 郊区商店

subway / 'sʌbweɪ / n. [C] ❶地道: You must

cross the street by the 〜. 你可以从地道过街。同 tunnel ❷ 地铁：People in the city like to take the 〜. 城市居民喜欢乘地铁。

succeed / sək'siːd / *vi.* ❶ 成功(与 in 连用)：〜 in (passing) an examination 考试及格 同 triumph, win 反 fail ❷ 继承(与 to 连用)：〜 to the throne 继承王位 / Under feudal rule only men could 〜 to family property. 在封建统治下，只有男子能继承家产。同 inherit —*vt.* 继续；继任；接着：Who 〜ed Churchill as Prime Minister? 谁继丘吉尔出任首相的? / The announcement was 〜ed by silence. 消息宣布后，全场鸦雀无声。同 follow, replace

success / sək'ses / *n.* ❶ [U] 成功；成就：meet with 〜 获得成功 同 triumph, achievement 反 failure ❷ [C] 成功的人或物；成功例子：The plan was a great 〜. 这项计划极为成功。**make a 〜 of sth.** 做成某事：They made a 〜 of their experiment. 他们的实验成功了。**win (achieve) a 〜** 获得成功；赢得胜利：We have won one 〜 after another in our economy. 我们在经济上已经取得了一个又一个的胜利。

successful / sək'sesfl / *adj.* 成功的；结果良好的：a 〜 attempt 成功的尝试 同 triumphant 反 unsuccessful 派 successfully *adv.*

succession / sək'seʃn / *n.* ❶ 连续：good harvest for three years in 〜 连续三个丰收年 同 series, sequence ❷ 继任；继承；接替：Who was first in 〜 to the manager? 谁是经理职位的第一接任者? 同 inheritance 派 successional *adj.*

successive / sək'sesiv / *adj.* 连续的；接连的：The football team won ten 〜 games. 足球队连续十场比赛获胜。同 sequent, following 派 successively *adv.*

successor / sək'sesə(r) / *n.* [C] 继承人；继任者：〜s to the great cause 伟大事业的接班人

such / sʌtʃ / Ⅰ *adj.* 同类的；同等的；这样的，如此的；no 〜 words 没有这样的词 同 like, so / 〜as (接名词)像，诸如：He visited several cities 〜 as New York, Chicago and Boston. 他参观了几座城市，像纽约、芝加哥和波士顿等。/ 〜... as (接从句)凡是；像是…的，I don't like 〜 books as he recommends. 我不喜欢他推荐的那些书。〜 as to, 〜...as to 会…那般的，会…的地步：Her high blood pres-

sure wasn't 〜 as to cause anxiety. 她的高血压还未到令人担忧的地步。/ I am not 〜 a fool as to believe that. 我不会傻到去相信那种事。〜 that, 〜... that 如此…以至于：His behaviour was 〜 that we all disliked him. 他的行为不像话，以至于我们都讨厌他。/ It was 〜 a cold day that there was nobody on the street. 天气非常冷，以至于街上没任何人。Ⅱ *pron.* 像这样或那样的人或物：I may have hurt her feelings, but 〜 was certainly not my intention. 我可能伤害了她的感情，但我的确不是故意的。Ⅲ *adv.* 如此；那么

用法
❶ such 作形容词时没有比较级和最高级。❷ such 与 no, some, many, all, several, one, few, any 等连用时，放在这些词后面，其后不能再加不定冠词：No such thing has ever happened. 这种事从没发生过。❸ 用了 such 后不可再用关系代词 which, who 或 that, 也不可再用关系副词 where, 如不可说：Don't talk about such things that (which) you do not understand. 应把 such 删去或改成 those 或 any, 或者把 that 或 which 改为 as。

辨析
such 和 so 都表示程度，意思是"这样；如此"，但 such 是形容词，so 是副词，它们在修饰其他成分时顺序不同：such＋a＋*adj.*＋*n.*；so＋*adj.*＋a＋*n.*：I have never read such an interesting book. I have never read so interesting a book. 我从未读过如此有趣的书。

suck / sʌk / *v.* 用嘴吮吸(水等)；喝；自…吸取：〜 the juice from an orange 吸橘子汁 / 〜 poison out of a wound 吸出伤口的毒 / 〜 knowledge 吸取知识 同 drink, absorb

sudden / 'sʌdən / Ⅰ *adj.* 突然的；出乎意料的；急速的：a 〜 shower 骤雨 / a 〜 turn in the road 路上的急弯 同 unexpected, rapid 反 expected, slow Ⅱ *n.* 突然。**all of a 〜** 突然地；出乎意料地：The car stopped all of a 〜. 车子突然停下来。

suddenly / 'sʌdənli / *adv.* 突然；出乎意料地 同 unexpectedly 反 gradually

suffer / 'sʌfə(r) / *v.* 遭受；患病：〜 for one's carelessness 因粗心而自食恶果 / 〜 from cold and hunger 挨饿受冻 / 〜 from the headache 患头痛病 / His business 〜ed while he was ill. 他在生病期间生意蒙受损失。同 undergo, experience

suffering / ˈsʌfəriŋ / Ⅰ *n.* [U]受苦;痛苦:The medicine can ease and relieve the ～. 药能减轻和解除疼痛。/ They were bearing the ～ patiently. 他们耐心地忍受着痛苦。同 pain, misery Ⅱ *adj.* 受苦的;患病的同 miserable 反 happy

sufficiency / səˈfiʃənsi / *n.* 足量;足够:a ～ of fuel 足够的燃料同 adequacy, enough 反 insufficiency, deficiency

sufficient / səˈfiʃənt / *adj.* 足够的;充分的: Have we ～ food for ten people? 我们有够十个人吃的食物吗?同 adequate, enough 反 insufficient, deficient 派 sufficiently *adv.*

sugar / ˈʃʊɡə(r) / *n.* [U]糖

suggest / səˈdʒest / *vt.* ❶提出(意见等);建议:I ～ a visit to the theatre. 我建议去参观戏院。同 advise, propose ❷提醒;暗示:The look on his face ～ed fear. 他的表情表明了他的恐惧。同 hint, imply

> **用法**
> ❶suggest 后面接动名词,不接不定式: I suggest asking her advice. 我建议问问她的意见。❷suggest 表示"建议"时,后可接 that 从句,从句用虚拟语气,即谓语用动词原形或 should＋动词原形:He suggests (suggested)that the regulations(should) be revised. 他建议修订这些规则。

suggestion / səˈdʒestʃn / *n.* ❶[U]建议:at the ～ of my brother 出于我兄弟的建议同 advice, proposal ❷[C]提出的主意、计划等: make ～ 提出建议

> **用法**
> suggestion 引起的同位或表语从句用虚拟语气:His suggestion is that the regulations (should) be revised. 他的建议是修订这些规则。

suicide / ˈsuːɪsaɪd / Ⅰ *n.* 自杀:commit ～ 自杀/ ～ attack 自杀性袭击同 self-murder, self-destruction Ⅱ *v.* 自杀

suit / sjuːt / Ⅰ *n.* 一套;一副:a man's ～ 男子的套装(包括外套、背心和裤子)/ a woman's ～ 女子的套装(包括上衣和裙子)/ ～case *n.* 手提箱 Ⅱ *v.* ❶使满意;适合…的要求;适应:

The seven o'clock train will ～ us very well. 七点的火车很适合我们。She is ～ed for (to) teaching. 她适合教书(当老师)。同 please, satisfy 反 displease, dissatisfy ❷(尤指衣服、发式等)相配;恰当;合适:It doesn't ～ you to have your hair cut short. 剪短发对你不适合。同 match, fit

suitable / ˈs(j)uːtəbl / *adj.* 适合的;恰当的: clothes ～ for cold weather 适合天冷穿的衣服 / a ～ place for a picnic 适合野餐的一处地点同 appropriate, proper 反 unsuitable, inappropriate

suite / swiːt / *n.* [C] ❶(同一类物品的)(一)套;(一)组;(一)系列:a ～ of furniture 一套家具 ❷套房:a bridal ～ 结纸套房/ a hotel ～ 宾馆的套房 ❸成套家具:a new bathroom ～ 一套新的浴室家具/ a bedroom ～ 一套寝具

sum / sʌm / Ⅰ *n.* ❶总数;总和同 amount, total ❷算术题;do a ～ in one's head 心算 Ⅱ *v.* (summed; summing)总结;概括同 summarize, comprehend / ～ **up** ①总计;合计/ ～ up the advantages 算一算好处有多少 ②概括地说: To ～ up, she is a nice girl. 总而言之,她是一个可爱的女孩。

summarize / ˈsʌməraɪz / *vt.* 概括;概述;总结:The monitor ～d our ideas. 班长总结了我们的想法。同 generalize

summary / ˈsʌməri / Ⅰ *adj.* 概括的同 brief, short Ⅱ *n.* [C]总结;摘要;概要:give a ～ 做总结 / news ～ 新闻摘要 / **in** ～ 概括起来,总的说来同 abstract

summer / ˈsʌmə(r) / *n.* 夏季:in the ～ of 1992 1992 年夏季 / the ～ holidays 暑假

summit / ˈsʌmɪt / *n.* [C] ❶山顶;山峰:climb to the ～ 爬上山顶 ❷巅峰,最高点,顶点,极点:reach the ～ of sb.'s career 达到某人事业的顶峰 ❸首脑会议,最高级会议,峰会:at annual economic ～ 在每年一度的经济峰会上

summon / ˈsʌmən / *vt.* 召唤;传唤:～ sb. to appear as a witness 传唤某人出席当证人同 call, gather

sun / sʌn / *n.* ❶太阳:rise with the ～ 早起/ ～set *n.* 日落;傍晚/ ～rise *n.* 日出;黎明 / under the ～ 在地球上;在世界上 ❷阳光: bathe in ～ 做日光浴 / sit in the ～ 坐在阳光

下 / draw the curtains to shut out(let in) the ～ 拉窗帘遮住(放进)阳光

sunken / ˈsʌŋkən / *adj.* ❶沉没的；浸没的：～ ships 沉船 ❷低于表面的，下陷的：In this grounds there is a ～ rose garden. 他庭院里有一个凹下的玫瑰花园。❸(眼睛或双颊)凹陷的：Captain Beard had hollow eyes and ～ cheeks. 比尔德船长两眼空洞，双颊凹陷。

sunny / ˈsʌni / *adj.* (-ier,-iest)向阳的；阳光充足的：a ～ room 向阳的房间 / a ～ side 向阳的一面；乐观(光明)的一面

Sunday / ˈsʌndi / *n.* 星期日；礼拜日

super / ˈsjuːpə(r) / *adj.* 极好的；特级的 同 wonderful

super- / ˈsuːpə(r),ˈsjuːpə(r) / (前缀)❶表示"超级""过于"：～ conductor 超导体/～ man 超人/～ woman 女强人/～ natural 超自然的，不可思议的/～ power 超级大国/～ star 超级明星 ❷表示"上方"：～ structure 上层结构

superficial / ˌsjuːpəˈfɪʃəl / *adj.* 表面的；肤浅的：～ knowledge 肤浅的知识 / ～ wound 表皮的创伤 同 surface, shallow 反 deep, profound 派 superficially *adv.* ; *superficiality n.*

superior / sjuːˈpɪərɪə(r) / Ⅰ *adj.* 优良的；优秀的 同 excellent, fine 反 inferior, worse / ～ **to** 优于；胜过：This cloth is ～ to that. 这种布料比那种布料好。Ⅱ *n.* [C]上司；长官；长辈；前辈；immediate ～ 顶头上司 同 boss, senior 反 inferior, employee

supermarket / ˈsjuːpəmɑːkɪt / *n.* [C]超级市场：Many people go shopping at the ～ on weekends. 许多人周末去超级市场购物。

superstition / ˌsjuːpəˈstɪʃn / *n.* 迷信；迷信行为

supervise / ˈsuːpəvaɪz / *v.* 监督；主管；指导 同 manage, govern

supervision / ˌsuːpəˈvɪʒn / *n.* [U]监督；管理；督导 同 direction, guidance

supervisor / ˈsuːpəvaɪzə(r) / *n.* [C]监督人；管理人；主管人 同 manager, boss

supper / ˈsʌpə(r) / *n.* 晚餐：We always have ～ at half past six. 我们总是在六点半钟吃晚饭。

supplement / ˈsʌplɪmənt / Ⅰ *n.* ❶增补(物)；补充(物)：She earns money as a ～ to the income of the family. 她挣钱增加家里的收入。同 addition, extension ❷(报刊等的)增刊,副刊 同 attachment Ⅱ *vt.* 补充；增补 同 add, increase

supply / səˈplaɪ / Ⅰ *v.* 供给；供应；备办：～ food for children 供给孩子们食物 同 furnish, provide 反 demand / ～ **sb. with sth.** ,～ **sth. to sb.** 给某人提供…：They said that they would ～ us with everything(everything to us) we need. 他们说将给我们提供所需要的一切。Ⅱ *n.* ❶供给；备办；贮藏：～ and demand 供与求 / **in short** ～ 供应不足：Their food is in short ～. 他们的食品供应不足。❷(尤指)公众必需品；生活必需品：medical supplies for the army 军需药品 同 equipment, necessity

support / səˈpɔːt / Ⅰ *vt.* ❶支持；支撑；扶持：Is this bridge strong enough to ～ heavy lorries? 这桥承受得起载重卡车驶过吗? 同 uphold ❷维持；赡养：He has a large family to ～. 他有很多子女要养活。同 maintain, finance ❸拥护；支持；帮助：～ing troops 支援部队 / a ～ing actor 配角 同 back, help Ⅱ *n.* 支持；支撑；扶持 同 backing, help / **in** ～ **of** 支持；拥护：He spoke in ～ of the proposal. 他发言支持那个建议。

suppose / səˈpəʊz / *vt.* ❶假定：Let us ～ (that) the news is true. 让我们假定这消息是正确的。同 presume ❷推测；想象：What do you ～ he wanted? 你推测他想要什么? 同 guess, imagine 派 supposed *adj.*

supposing / səˈpəʊzɪŋ / *conj.* 倘若；假如：Supposing it rains, what shall you do? 假如下雨, 你将怎么办? 同 if

supposition / ˌsʌpəˈzɪʃn / *n.* [U]假定；想象 同 hypothesis, imagination

suppress / səˈpres / *vt.* ❶镇压；平定；压制：～ a rising 镇压起义 同 crush, restrain ❷扣留；查禁；隐瞒：～ a newspaper 查禁一家报纸 同 arrest, conceal 派 suppression *n.*

supreme / sjuːˈpriːm / *adj.* ❶最高的；无上的：the Supreme Court 最高法院 同 highest 反 lowest ❷最重要的；极大的：make the ～ sacrifice 做最大的牺牲 同 foremost, greatest

sure / ʃʊə(r) / *adj.* ❶(仅作表语)肯定的，必定的；确信的，有信心的：Can we be ～ of his honesty? 我们能确定他是诚实的吗? / Do you feel ～ about it? 你对此事有把握吗? / Be

～ not to forget to bring your book with you. 一定不要忘了把书带来。/ I am ～ that the host team will win. 我确信主队要赢。/ We are not ～ whether the professor has arrived. 我们不能肯定那位教授是否已经到达。/ I am not ～ what he wants. 我不能肯定他想要什么。同 certain, definite 反 unsure, uncertain ❷经过证实的;可靠的;稳妥的:a ～ friend 可靠的朋友 同 firm, reliable 反 unsure, unreliable / **make** ～查明;确信:Go and make ～ of the time and place of the meeting. 去落实一下会议的时间和地点。派 surely adv. 无误地;确实地

surf / sɜːf / Ⅰ n. [U]激浪;碎波 Ⅱ vi. 做冲浪运动:～ on the Internet (计算机)上网;网卡冲浪

surface / 'sɜːfɪs / Ⅰ n. [C]表面;水面: Glass has a smooth ～. 玻璃有光滑的表面。The submarine rose to the ～. 潜水艇升至水面。同 outside 反 inside Ⅱ adj. 表面的;肤浅的:～ politeness 表面的礼貌 同 superficial, shallow 反 deep, profound

surge / sɜːdʒ / vi.(浪涛)汹涌, 澎湃:The floods ～d over the valley. 洪水奔腾着涌过山谷。同 wave, rush

surgeon / 'sɜːdʒən / n. [C]外科医师 反 physician

surgery / 'sɜːdʒəri / n. ❶[U]外科;外科手术: qualified in both ～ and medicine 有资格做外科和内科医生 ❷[C]手术室;诊疗室

surgical / 'sɜːdʒɪkl / adj. 外科的

surname / 'sɜːneɪm / n. [C] 姓

surpass / sə'pɑːs / vt. 超越;胜过:～ sb. in strength 在力量上胜过某人 / The beauty of the scenery ～ed my expectations. 风景的优美超出了我的预料。同 exceed, excel

surplus / 'sɜːpləs / n. 过剩;剩余物资 同 excess, oversupply 反 deficiency, shortage

surprise / sə'praɪz / Ⅰ n. ❶惊奇;惊骇;惊愕:To my ～, his plan succeeded. 使我惊奇的是,他的计划成功了。同 amazement, astonishment / **in** ～ 惊奇地;吃惊地:He shouted in ～. 他吃惊地大声叫喊。**take sb. by** ～ 使某人吃了一惊;冷不防捉住:The thief was taken by ～. 那贼冷不防被捉住了。/ We took the thinking boy by ～. 我们使那沉思的

男孩吃了一惊。**to sb's** ～ 使某人惊奇的是:To my ～, the actress is over 50. 使我惊讶的是,那女演员已 50 多岁了。❷突然袭击 同 blow, attack / **take by** ～ 出奇兵攻占;突袭:The city was taken by ～. 那座城市被突然攻陷了。Ⅱ v. ❶使惊奇;使诧异;You ～d me! 你吓我一跳!/ We were ～d at the news. 我们听到那消息很惊讶。同 amaze, astonish ❷不期而遇;撞见;突然袭击:～ a burg-lar breaking into a house 撞见闯入房子的窃贼 同 discover, attack

surprised / sə'praɪzd / adj. 吃惊的;感到惊讶的 同 amazed, astonished / **be** ～ **at** 对…感到惊奇:We were ～ at his being late. 对于他的迟到,我们感到很惊奇。**be** ～ **to do** 对做某事感到吃惊:I was very ～ to learn that you had decided to go to medical school. 得知你决定上医药学校,我感到很吃惊。

surprising / sə'praɪzɪŋ / adj. 惊人的;出人意料的 同 amazing

surrender / sə'rendə(r) / v. ❶投降;自首;投案:We shall never ～ to the enemy. 我们决不向敌人投降。同 submit, yield 反 resist, oppose ❷放弃;让与:We shall never ～ our liberty. 我们永不放弃自由。同 abandon, give up 反 keep, retain

surround / sə'raʊnd / vt. 包围;环绕:a house ～ed with trees 有树木环绕的一栋房子 同 circle, enclose

surrounding / sə'raʊndɪŋ / Ⅰ adj. 周围的: Beijing and the ～ countryside 北京及周围农村 Ⅱ n.(pl.)周围的事物;环境: living in pleasant ～s 生活在美好的环境里 同 circumstance, environment

survey Ⅰ / sə'veɪ / vt. ❶俯瞰;眺望:You can ～ the valley from the top of the hill. 你从山顶可以俯瞰山谷。同 overlook, view ❷测量;勘测:～ a railway 勘测铁路 同 measure, observe ❸全面审视;调查 同 scan, investigate Ⅱ / 'sɜːveɪ / n. [C]俯瞰;测量;考察 同 view, investigation

survive / sə'vaɪv / v. 生存;幸存:～ an earthquake 在地震后仍然活着 / The old lady has ～d all her children. 那老太太的所有孩子都先她去世。同 keep alive 反 die 派 survival n.

survivor / sə'vaɪvə(r) / n. [C]幸存的人;生

还者：send help to the ～s of the earthquake 对地震后的幸存者给予援助

suspect Ⅰ / sə'spekt / vt. 怀疑；猜想：～ the truth of an account 怀疑报道的真实性 / Ⅰ ～ him to be a liar. 我怀疑他是一个说谎的人。He is ～ed of telling lies. 他有说谎的嫌疑。同 doubt，guess　Ⅱ / 'sʌspekt / n. [C]嫌疑人；可疑对象

suspend / sə'spend / vt. ❶悬挂，吊（与 from 连用）：lamps ～ed from the ceiling 天花板上悬吊的灯 同 hang，swing　❷暂停；延缓；悬而未决：～ payment 延期付款 / ～ judgment 延期宣判 同 stop，delay

suspicion / sə'spɪʃn / n. 怀疑；疑心；嫌疑：He was arrested on（the）～ of having stolen the money. 他涉嫌偷钱而被捕。/ He is under the ～ of the police. 他受到警方怀疑。同 distrust，doubt 反 trust

suspicious / sə'spɪʃəs / adj. 怀疑的：be（feel）～ of sb.（sth.）对某人（某事）怀疑 同 distrustful，doubtful 反 unsuspicious，trustful

sustain / sə'steɪn / vt. ❶支撑；承受 同 support，bear　❷维持；供养 同 maintain，support　❸遭受；经受 同 suffer，undergo

swallow[1] / 'swɒləʊ / v. 吞；咽：～ one's food 咽食物 / ～ one's anger 强忍心中的怒火 / ～ one's words 食言

swallow[2] / 'swɒləʊ / n. [C]燕子

swamp / swɒmp / n. 沼泽；湿地 同 marsh

swan / swɒn / n. [C]天鹅

swarm / swɔːm / n. [C]（昆虫、鸟等的）群：a ～ of ants 一群蚂蚁 同 flock，crowd

sway / sweɪ / v.（使）摇摆；（使）摆动：～ between two opinions 在两种意见中摇摆不定 / ～ to the music 随着音乐节奏摇摆 / The branches of the trees are ～ing in the wind. 树枝在风中摇摆。同 rock，swing

swear / sweə(r) / v.（swore / swɔː/，sworn / swɔːn/）❶郑重地说；发誓，宣誓：He swore to tell the truth. 他发誓要说真话。同 pledge　❷咒骂；辱骂：The captain swore at his crew. 船长咒骂船员。同 curse

sweat / swet / Ⅰ n. [U]汗：wipe the ～ off one's face 揩去脸上的汗　Ⅱ v. 出汗：The long climb made him ～. 长时间的攀登使他出

汗了。

sweater / 'swetə(r) / n. [C]（厚）运动衫；毛线衫

sweep / swiːp / v.（swept / swept/，swept）❶扫除；清扫：～ the floor 扫地 同 clean，clear　❷掠过；扫过；疾驰：The wind swept along the street. 风沿街吹过。同 dash，race

sweet / swiːt / Ⅰ adj. ❶甜的：Do you like your tea ～? 你喜欢茶里面加糖吗？同 sugary，tasty 反 sour，bitter ❷芳香的：How the roses smell! 多么芳香的玫瑰花！同 fragrant，fresh 反 stale / ～heart n. 爱人；恋人；情人　Ⅱ n.（＝candy）[C] 糖果；甜食：a box of ～s 一盒糖果 派 sweeten v.

swell / swel / v.（swelled，swelled 或 swollen / 'swəʊlən/）膨胀；肿胀；隆起；增大 同 expand，enlarge 反 shrink，diminish

swift / swɪft / adj. 快的；迅速的；敏捷的：a ～ revenge 迅速报复 同 rapid，keen 反 slow / be ～ to sth. ，be ～ to do sth. 易于，动不动就：My boss is ～ to anger. 我的老板动不动就生气。/ My baby is ～ to fall asleep. 我的宝宝容易入睡。

swim / swɪm / Ⅰ v.（swam / swæm/，swum / swʌm/）游泳：Let's go ～ming. 我们去游泳吧。Ⅱ n. 游泳：have（go for）a ～去游泳

swing / swɪŋ / Ⅰ v.（swung / swʌŋ/，swung）（使）摇摆；（使）摆动：His arms swung as he walked. 他走路的时候手臂在摆动着。同 rock，sway　Ⅱ n. ❶摇摆；摆动 ❷秋千；打秋千：play on the ～ 荡秋千

swirl / swɜːl / Ⅰ vt. & vi.（使）打转，（使）旋转：The old man was ～ed away on the current. 那个老人被水流卷走了。Ⅱ n. [C] ❶（水、大气等的）漩涡 ❷混乱：Things were in a ～ at home. 家里一片混乱。

Swiss / swɪs / Ⅰ n.（单复数同形）瑞士人　Ⅱ adj. 瑞士的；瑞士人的

switch / swɪtʃ / Ⅰ v. ❶接通或关掉（电源等）：～ the light（radio）on（off）开（关）灯（收音机）❷转变；改变：～ the conversation 改变话题 同 change，shift　Ⅱ n. [C] ❶开关；电闸：master ～总开关 / power ～ 电源开关 同 button，handle ❷转换：We had to make a ～ in our arrangement. 我们只好改变安排。同 change，shift

Switzerland / ˈswɪtsələnd / n. 瑞士

sword / sɔːd / n. [C]剑

syllable / ˈsɪləbl / Ⅰ n. [C] ❶音节 ❷片言只字：He did not utter a ～ at all. 他根本就一言未发。Ⅱ vt. 按音节读；清晰地读

syllabus / ˈsɪləbəs / Ⅰ n. [C] ❶(pl. syllabuses 或 syllabi /-ˈbaɪ/)教学大纲；课程大纲；(论文、演说等的)提纲，摘要；考试要求简编

symbol / ˈsɪmbl / n. [C] ❶象征：Rose is a ～ of beauty. 玫瑰是美丽的象征。Some poets regard tree as a ～ of life. 一些诗人把树当作生命的象征。同 sign, figure ❷符号；记号：chemical ～s 化学符号 同 mark, sign 派 symbolize(-se) vt.

symbolic(al) / sɪmˈbɒlɪk(əl) / adj. 象征的；象征性的 同 representative, typical 派 symbolically adv.

symmetry / ˈsɪmɪtri / n. ❶[U]对称(性)：bilateral ～ 左右对称/ His sense of ～ was satisfied. 他终于找到了对称感。❷[U]匀称；对称美：The ～ of his face was spoiled because of great anger. 他本来匀称的脸气歪了。

sympathetic / ˌsɪmpəˈθetɪk / adj. 有同情心的；表示同情心的；同情的：～ looks (words) 表示同情的样子(话语) 同 kind, warm hearted 反 unsympathetic, cold-hearted

sympathize / ˈsɪmpəθaɪz / vi. 同情，怜悯(与 with 连用)：～ with sb. in his sufferings 同情某人的痛苦 同 pity, understand

sympathy / ˈsɪmpəθi / n. 同情；怜悯；同感：

send sb. a letter of ～ 寄给某人一封慰问信 / feel ～ for sb. 对某人表示同情 派 feeling, pity / in ～ with 同意；赞同：We are all in ～ with your proposals. 我们都赞成你的提议。

symphony / ˈsɪmfəni / n. 交响乐；交响乐团

symposium / sɪmˈpəuziəm / n. [C] (pl. symposia)讨论会；座谈会；研讨会；专题研讨会：a theoretical ～ 理论研讨会

synonym / ˈsɪnənɪm / n. [C]同义词，近义词："Shut" and "close" are ～s. shut 和 close 是同义词。

synthesis / ˈsɪnθəsɪs / n. (pl. syntheses /ˈsɪnθɪsiːz/) ❶合成 ❷综合；综合体

synthetic / sɪnˈθetɪk / adj. 合成的，综合的；人造的：～ fiber 合成纤维 / ～ rubber 人造橡胶 同 artificial

system / ˈsɪstəm / n. ❶系统：the digestive ～ 消化系统 / the nervous ～ 神经系统 / a railway ～ 铁路系统 同 constitution ❷(理论、原则等的)体系；制度；政体：a ～ of philosophy 哲学体系 / a ～ of government 政府制度 / under the ～ of 在…制度下 同 organization, structure

systematic / ˌsɪstəˈmætɪk / adj. ❶有系统的；系统化的：make a ～ study 做系统的研究 ❷有计划的；有步骤的：take ～ steps 有计划地采取措施 同 regular, orderly

S

T t

table / ˈteɪbl / n. ❶[C]桌子：a dining ～ 餐桌 / a tea ～ 茶几同 desk / **at** ～ 用餐：They were at ～ when we called. 我们拜访时，他们正在用餐。❷[C]表；目录：a ～ of contents 目录 / a railway time ～ 火车时刻表同 list，chart

tablet / ˈtæblət / n. [C]❶药片同 pill ❷碑匾

taboo / təˈbuː / I n.（pl. taboos）[C]❶忌讳，禁忌；应避忌的事物：place sth. under（a）～将某事定为禁忌 / ～ upon smoking in offices 禁止在办公室抽烟 II adj. 被禁止的，忌讳的：～ words 忌废讳的语言

tack / tæk / I n.[C]❶小的平头钉，宽头钉 ❷（行动或思想的）方向，方法，方针，政策：Without a guide we may of course go off on the wrong ～. 没有导游我们当然会走错路。 II vt. 用平头钉（或图钉）钉住：He moved the table away and ～ed the carpet down. 他把桌子搬开，把地毯用平头钉钉住。

tactics / ˈtæktɪks / n. 策略；战术；兵法：Tactics is subordinate to strategy. 战术从属于战略。同 strategy，scheme

tag / tæg / n. [C]标签；标牌：price ～ 价格标签 / shipping ～ 货运标签 / You'd better stick a name ～ to the box. 你最好在箱子上贴上标签。同 label，mark

tail / teɪl / n. [C]尾巴

tailor / ˈteɪlə(r) / I n. [C]裁缝 II vt. 裁制（衣服）：He always has his suits ～ed in Paris. 他的衣服总是在巴黎做的。

take / teɪk / v.（took/tʊk/，taken /ˈteɪkn/）❶拿；握：～ one's hand 握住某人的手 / ～ sth. on one's back 背东西 同 get，grasp 反 give，put / ～ **hold of** 抓住：The child took hold of my hand when he became nervous. 这孩子在紧张的时候就抓住我的手。❷捕捉；占领；（在竞赛中）获胜：～ a town 占领一城市 / ～ 500 prisoners 抓获 500 名俘房 同 capture，seize 反

surrender，yield ❸利用；自取；偷窃：You should ～（advantage of）this opportunity. 你应利用这个机会。 / Who has ～n my bicycle? 谁把我的自行车拿走了? 同 use，steal ❹携带；带走：Take the luggage upstairs. 把行李拿上楼。同 carry，bring / ～ **away** 拿走：These books can only be read in the library，and may not be ～n away. 这些书只供在图书馆内阅读，不能带走。～ **back** 拿回；收回：I shall ～ these goods back to the shop. 我要把这些货物拿回店去。～ **down** 拿下；取下：We must ～ the curtains down for cleaning. 我们得把窗帘取下来洗一洗。～ **out** 带出；取出：The building is burning，take the horse out quickly. 房子烧起来了，快把马牵出去。❺享有；吃；喝；接受：～ a look（a holiday，a walk，a bath，a deep breath）看一看（休假，散步，沐浴，做深呼吸）/ He asked me to ～ a seat as soon as I entered. 我一进去，他就叫我坐下。 / Will you ～ tea or coffee? 你是喝茶还是喝咖啡? 同 enjoy，have ❻记录：～ notes of a lecture 记课堂笔记/～ sth. down in shorthand 用速记记下 同 record ❼需要：It took us two hours to get there. 到那儿花了我们两小时。同 need，require ❽假定；推断；以为：Do you ～ me for a fool? 你把我当成笨蛋吗? 同 suppose / ～... **for granted** 认为…理所当然；认定：He spoke English so well that I took it for granted that he was an American. 他英语讲得好极了，我理所当然地认为他是美国人。❾（经询问、测量等）找出，量出同 measure / ～ **one's temperature** 量体温：The nurse took my temperature. 护士量了我的体温。～ **after** 像，相似：He ～ s after his father in mathematical ability. 他有与他父亲相似的数学才能。～ **aim** 瞄准：Before the hunter could ～ aim，the deer jumped out of sight. 在猎人瞄准前，鹿就跑掉了。～ **care of** 照顾：She stayed at home to ～ care of the baby. 她留在家里照顾孩子。～ **great trouble to do sth.** 不辞辛劳做某事：He took great trouble to finish the book. 他不辞辛劳地写完了那本书。～ **off** ①除去；脱去：～ off one's hat 脱帽 / Help me to ～ this handle off. 帮我拿掉这把手。②起飞：Three airplanes took off at the same time. 三架飞机同时起飞。③营救出：Before the ship sank, the passengers were all safely ～n off. 船沉之前，所有乘客都被安全营救出来。～ **on a new look** 呈现新面貌：After the students put up Christmas decorations, the classroom took on a new look. 同学们挂上圣诞装饰物后，教室呈现出新面貌。～ **one's place** 代替；取代（某人）：Who will ～ Mr. Smith's place? 谁将代替史密斯先生？～ **one's turn** 轮流（做）：Like the other nuns, they took their turn to do household chores. 像其他尼姑一样，她们轮流做家务。～ **part in** 参加：The Swiss did not ～ part in World War Ⅱ. 瑞士人没有参加第二次世界大战。～ **place** 发生：The accident took place only a block from his home. 事故发生在离他家一条街远的地方。～ **pride in** 以…为自豪；对…感到骄傲：The parents took pride in the boy's success. 父母为他们儿子的成功感到自豪。～ **the side of** 支持：He always ～s the side of the Republic. 他总是支持共和党一方。～ **to** ①喜欢：Tom took to the girl as soon as they met. 汤姆一见到那女孩，就喜欢上了她。②养成（习惯）；染上：Don't ～ to bad habits. 别染上恶习。～ **up** 开始；从事：He recently took up gardening. 他最近开始学园艺。

tale / teɪl / n. [C] 故事；传说；报告：fairy ～s 童话故事；神话故事 / ～s of adventure 冒险故事 同 story, fable

talent / 'tælənt / n. ❶[U]天资；才气；才能：Helen has great ～ for music but not much ～ for painting. 海伦很有音乐天分但少有绘画天分。同 gift, ability ❷[C] 人才：athletic ～s 体育人才

talented / 'tæləntɪd / adj. 有才能的；有天分的：a ～ actor 天才演员 / Mary is a ～ painter. 玛丽是天才画家。同 able, gifted

talk / tɔːk / Ⅰ vi. 说话；谈话 同 utter, speak / ～ **about** 谈到；谈论：We were ～ing about our children, and about how well they are doing at school. 我们在谈论孩子们以及他们在学校的情况。～ **of** 谈到；说到：We were just ～ing of the most interesting books that we have

read recently. 我们刚才谈到我们最近读过的最有趣的书。～ **over** 商议：Come and see me in my office and we'll ～ it over. 到我办公室来，我们商量一下这事。—vt. 说（一种语言）；讲：～ German 说德语 / ～ business 谈正经事 / ～ sense（nonsense）说有意义的话（说无聊的话）同 speak Ⅱ n. ❶谈话；商议：I've had several ～s with the headmaster about my boy. 我已与校长就我儿子的问题进行过数次谈话。～ too much ～ and not enough work. 说得太多，做得太少。同 chat, discussion ❷[C]（非正式的）演讲：He will give a ～ to the students on his travels in Europe. 他将对学生谈他的欧洲之行进行演讲。同 address, lecture ❸（常用 pl.）正式会谈，商谈：arms ～s 军备谈判/bilateral ～s 双边会谈/notes on ～s 会谈纪要 同 negotiation

talkative / 'tɔːkətɪv / adj. 爱说话的，健谈的；话多的，饶舌的：a lively, ～ young man 活泼健谈的小伙子 / She isn't ～, but she is pleasant to be with. 她不爱说话，但是挺好相处。

tall / tɔːl / adj. 高的：She wears high-heeled shoes to make herself look ～er. 她穿高跟鞋使自己显得高些。同 high, big 反 wide, short

tame / teɪm / Ⅰ adj. ❶驯化的，驯服的：a ～ monkey 驯服的猴子/～ birds 家禽 同 domestic, gentle 反 untamed, wild ❷平淡的；乏味的 同 dull, boring 反 exciting, interesting Ⅱ vt. 驯服；驯化 同 train, regulate

tan / tæn / Ⅰ n. [U]棕褐色；棕黄色的 Ⅱ adj. 棕褐色的；棕黄色的 Ⅲ v.（tanned; tanning）晒黑：The boys were ～ned in summer. 孩子们在夏天晒黑了。

tangent / 'tændʒənt / Ⅰ n. [C]切线；切面：正切曲线 Ⅱ adj. 相切的；正切的：be ～ to a circle 与圆相切

tangible / 'tændʒɪbl / adj. ❶可触及的；有形的：Sculpture is a ～ art form. 雕塑是一种有形的艺术形式。❷明确的，清楚的，真实的：～ proof 确凿证据 ❸（资产等）有形的，价值易估计的：～ assets 有形资产 反 intangible 派 tangibility n.

tangle / 'tæŋgl / Ⅰ vt. ❶使缠结，使纠缠：Can you help me straighten out this string? It's become ～d (up). 这条线绕成一团了，你帮我理直好么？❷卷入，使卷入，使陷入：be ～d in a controversy 被卷入争论 Ⅱ n. [C] ❶（一团）缠结的东西；乱七八糟的东西：Her hair was a

～. 她的头发乱蓬蓬的。❷复杂情况；混乱局面：I am in an awful ～ with my work,can you help? 我的工作一团混乱,你能帮帮忙吗?

tank / tæŋk / n. [C] ❶坦克：drive a ～ 驾驶坦克 ❷槽；罐；箱：fish ～ 鱼缸/gas ～ 汽油罐(箱) / water ～ 水箱

tanker / 'tæŋkə(r) / n. [C]油船；空中加油飞机

tap¹ / tæp / I n. [C]塞子；(自来水、煤气等的)龙头：turn the ～ on (off) 打开(关掉)龙头 / Don't leave the ～s running. 别让水龙头开着。II vt. (tapped；tapping) ❶打开龙头放出 ❷开发；开辟 同 use,employ

tap² / tæp / I v. (tapped；tapping) 轻敲；轻拍：～ a man on the shoulder 轻拍一个人的肩膀 同 pat,rap II v. [C]轻敲；轻拍：a ～ on the window (at the door) 敲窗 (门) 同 pat,rap

tape / teɪp / n. [C]❶带子❷线带 ❷(录音或录像的)磁带：～ recorder 磁带录音机 / video ～ 录像带❸终点线：breast the ～ 冲过终点

tar / tɑː(r) / n. [U]❶沥青,柏油 ❷(烟草燃烧产生的)焦油

target / 'tɑːgɪt / n. [C]❶靶；目标：aim at a ～ 瞄准目标 / hit the ～ 击中靶子 / miss the ～ 没有击中靶子 同 mark,aim ❷对象；目标：the ～ of attack 进攻的目标 / The novel became the ～ of criticism. 那本小说成了批评的对象。/ The workers reached the production ～. 工人们完成了生产目标。同 object,victim

tariff / 'tærɪf / n. 关税；税率：impose a ～ on sth. 对某物征收关税 / You have to pay a ～ on the cotton. 你得为这些棉花付关税。

task / tɑːsk / n. [C](尤指困难的)工作,任务：carry out (perform) a ～ 执行任务/ take up (shoulder) a ～ 承担任务 / give the boy a ～ 给这个男孩一项任务 同 work,assignment

辨析
task 可指某一项任务,是可数名词,work 泛指一般工作,是不可数名词。work 可以指正式职业或一贯性的工作,task 则不含此意。

taste / teɪst / I n. ❶味觉；味道：sweet ～ 甜味 同 flavor ❷爱好：He has a ～ for pop music. 他喜欢流行音乐。同 fondness,liking 反 distaste / **to one's** ～ 合某人的口味 II v. 尝；品味：Do you ～ anything strange in this soup? 你尝出这汤有奇怪的味道吗? 同 sam-

ple,test 派 tasteful adj.

tasty / 'teɪsti / adj. (-ier,-iest)味美的；可口的 同 delicious 反 tasteless 派 tastily adv.

tax / tæks / I n. 税；税额：state (local) ～es 国税(地方税) / collect ～es 收税 / evade ～es 偷税 / pay ～es 纳税 / The country imposes heavy ～ on tobacco. 国家对烟草课以重税。同 tariff,duty II v. 征税：～ incomes 征所得税 同 impose

taxation / tæk'seɪʃn / n. [U]税制；征税

taxi / 'tæksi / n. (＝ [美]cab) [C] (pl. taxis 或 taxies)出租汽车；计程车

tea / tiː / n. ❶[U]茶树；茶叶；茶：make ～泡茶；沏茶 ❷茶点

teach / tiːtʃ / v. (taught / tɔːt /, taught)教；授课：～ a child to swim 教小孩游泳 / ～ English 教英语 同 educate,instruct / ～ **sb. a lesson** 教训某人

teacher / 'tiːtʃə(r) / n. [C]教师；老师；先生；导师：Teachers' Day 教师节 / the ～s' office 教师办公室 / a qualified ～ 合格教师 / a practice (student) ～ 实习教师 同 instructor, trainer

teaching / 'tiːtʃɪŋ / n. ❶[U]教学；教导：assistant ～ 助教 / ～ method 教学方法 / give up ～ for business 弃学经商 / go into ～ 投入教学工作 同 instruction,education ❷教义：follow the ～s of the Church 遵循教会的教义

team / tiːm / I n. [C]队；组：Many eyes turned to a tall, 20-year-old girl on the U.S.A. ～. 很多双眼睛都转向美国队一个20岁的高个儿姑娘。/ He is coaching and managing a football ～. 他正训练和管理一支足球队。/ ～ leader 队长 / visiting ～ 客队 / home (host) ～ 主队 / ～-mate 同队队员；队友 同 group,league II vi. 协作；合作 同 combine,unite 反 divide,separate

teamwork / 'tiːmwɜːk / n. [U](卓有成效的)共同行动,集体行动,合作

tear¹ / tɪə(r) / n. [C]泪；眼泪：Her eyes filled with ～s. 她的眼里充满了泪水。/～ bomb 催泪弹 / ～ gas 催泪毒气／**burst (break) into** ～s 突然哭起来 / **in** ～s 流着泪；哭着：She was in ～s over her failure. 她为失败而流泪。**keep back one's** ～s 忍住使眼泪不流下来 派 tearful adj.

tear² / teə(r) / v. (tore/tɔː/, torn /tɔːn/) 撕；扯；撕碎；~ a sheet of paper in two 将一张纸撕成两半/ be torn open 被撕开 同 split, pull 反 mend, repair / ~ **up** 拔出；连根拔起：It's a hard job ~ing up all these unwanted plants in the garden. 要把花园里不要的植物都拔起来是件艰难的工作。

technical / ˈteknɪkl / adj. 工艺的；技能的，技术的；专门的：~ terms 专门术语 / ~ difficulties 技术性困难 派 technically adv.

technician / tekˈnɪʃn / n. [C]（精通某一项专门技术的）技术员；巧匠

technique / tekˈniːk / n. 技巧；技艺；（做事的）方法 同 skill, method

> **辨析**
>
> **technique** 是可数名词，指具体的某种技艺、技巧：modern management techniques 现代管理技术；**technology** 是不可数名词，泛指实用技术：the technology of computer 计算机实用技术。

technological / ˌteknəˈlɒdʒɪkl / adj. 技术的；工艺（学）的

technologist / tekˈnɒlədʒɪst / n. [C] 技术专家；工艺学家

technology / tekˈnɒlədʒi / n. ❶[U] 技术；工艺学：the Federal Institute of Technology 联邦工学院 ❷技术应用：information ~ (IT) 信息技术 ❸应用科学

tedious / ˈtiːdɪəs / adj. 乏味的；沉闷的；冗长的：~ speech 乏味的演说 / ~ story 单调的故事 / The work is ~ but worthy. 那项工作单调,但值得做。同 boring, dull 反 exciting, interesting 派 tediously adv.; tediousness n.

teenager / ˈtiːneɪdʒə(r) / n. [C]（13 岁至 19 岁的）青少年：activity for ~s 青少年的活动 / The course is offered for ~s. 那门课是为青少年开的。

tele- / ˈteli / (前缀) ❶表示"远距离的"：~control 遥控 ❷表示"电视"：~-course 电视教程 ❸表示"电信"，"电报"，"电话"：~graphone 录音电话机

telecommunication / ˌtelikəˌmjuːnɪˈkeɪʃn / n.（利用电信、电视、电话等的）长途电信,远距离通讯

telegram / ˈtelɪgræm / n. [C] 电报：get (receive) a ~ from sb. 收到某人的电报 / send a ~ to 发电报给… / They sent the invitation

by ~. 他们用电报发出邀请。

telegraph / ˈtelɪgrɑːf, ˈtelɪgræf / Ⅰ n. 电报；电报机：~ receiver 收报机 / ~ transmitter 发报机 / ~-operator 报务员 Ⅱ v. 打电报；以电报传达

telegrapher / tɪˈlegrəfə(r) / n. [C]电报员；报务员

telegraphic / ˌtelɪˈgræfɪk / adj. 电报的；以电报传达的；与电报有关的

telegraphy / təˈlegrəfi / n. [U]电报术；电报学

telephone / ˈtelɪfəun / Ⅰ n. 电话；电话机：send a message by ~ 用电话传递消息 / be wanted on the ~ 被要求接听电话 / install a ~ 安装电话 / make (give) sb. a ~ call 给某人打电话 Ⅱ v. 以电话发送消息；打电话给…：I ~d the secretary that I couldn't attend the meeting. 我打电话告诉秘书说,我不能去参加会议。

telescope / ˈtelɪskəup / n. [C]望远镜

televise / ˈtelɪvaɪz / vt. 由电视播送：The Olympic Games were ~d all over the world. 奥运会通过电视向全世界播送。

television / ˈtelɪvɪʒn / n. [U]电视；电视机：He appeared on ~ last night. 他昨晚在电视上出现。black-and-white(color) ~ 黑白(彩色)电视 / turn on (off) the ~ 开(关)电视

telex / ˈteleks / n. 电传

tell / tel / v. (told /təuld/, told) ❶告知；告诉：~ a lie 撒谎/ ~ the truth 说实话 / He told the news to everybody in the village. 他把这消息告诉村里的每一个人。同 inform, notify 反 conceal, hide ❷辨识；区别（尤与 can, could, be able to 连用）同 distinguish, identify 反 confuse / ~ ... from ... 辨别：Can you ~ Tom from his twin brother? 你能辨别汤姆和他的孪生兄弟吗？/ Every one of us should learn to ~ right from wrong. 我们每个人都应该学会明辨是非。

teller / ˈtelə(r) / n. [C] ❶（银行）出纳员：a qualified bank ~ 合格的银行出纳 ❷（故事的）讲述人：a fortune ~ 算命人/ Charlie is also a marvellous ~ of jokes. 查利的笑话讲得也很精彩。

temper / ˈtempə(r) / Ⅰ n. 性情；脾气；心情 同 mood, passion / **in a good (bad)** ~ 心情好(不佳) **get (fly) into a** ~ **(about sth.)** (为某事)发脾气：At the bad news, he flew into a ~. 他一

听到那坏消息就发起火来。**keep one's** ～ 忍住脾气：He kept his ～ despite the provocation. 他虽然受到挑衅，但忍着不发怒。**lose one's** ～(**with sth. or sb.**)(对某事或某人)发脾气：The teacher lost his ～ with my coming late. 老师因我迟到而发火。Ⅱ *vt.* 锻炼：He got ～ed in the storms of life. 他在生活的风暴中得到锻炼。同 harden，strengthen 反 soften，weaken

temperament / ˈtempərəmənt / *n.* ❶[C；U]气质；性情；秉性；性格 a girl with an artistic ～ 颇有些艺术气质的女孩 / The twins look a-like，but in ～ they are different. 这对双胞胎看起来一样，但是性情却不一样。同 disposition ❷[U]活跃的个性：He is full of ～. 他精神饱满。

temperature / ˈtemprətʃə(r) / *n.* ❶温度；体温：absolute (average，constant，normal) ～ 绝对(平均，恒定，正常)温度 / body (room) ～ 体(室)温 / In Hawaii there are no extremes of ～. 夏威夷的气温不特别冷也不特别热。/ The nurse took the ～s of all the patients. 护士为所有的病人量体温。❷发烧：She had a ～ last night. 昨天晚上她发烧了。同 fever

temple / ˈtempl / *n.* [C]庙宇；寺院；神殿

temporary / ˈtemprəri / *adj.* 暂时的；临时的：～ employment 临时的工作同 brief，impermanent 反 lasting，permanent

tempt / tempt / *v.* ❶劝诱，诱惑(做坏事或笨事)：～ away a boy 劝诱某人留下一男孩 / ～ sb. into staying 劝诱某人留下 / ～ sb. off the straight path 把某人引入歧途/His bad companions ～ed him to drink heavily. 他的损友诱使他酗酒。同 incline，charm 反 discourage ❷吸引；引起…的兴趣：The warm weather ～ed us to go for a swim. 暖和的天气引起我们去游泳的兴趣。同 attract，invite 反 disgust

temptation / temp'teiʃn / *n.* ❶[U]吸引；劝诱；诱惑：face ～ 面对诱惑 / resist ～ 抵制诱惑 / yield to ～ 受诱惑 / the ～ of money 金钱的诱惑 同 attraction，charm ❷[C]诱惑物；有吸引力之物：Clever advertisements are ～s for people to spend money. 巧妙的广告诱人花钱。

ten / ten / Ⅰ *num.* 十，10：～s of thousands 好几万 / ～ to one 十之八九；很可能：Ten to one he will arrive late. 他很可能会迟到。Ⅱ

adj. 十个的，十的

tenant / ˈtenənt / *n.* [C]佃户；房客；租户 同 renter，lodger

tend[1] / tend / *vt.* 护理；照料：shepherds ～ing their flocks 照料羊群的牧羊人

tend[2] / tend / *vi.* ❶走向；趋向：They ～ed to the same conclusion. 他们趋向于同一结论。同 lead，aim ❷倾向：～ to be optimistic 倾向于乐观 同 incline，lean ❸有助于：The measure ～s to improve working conditions. 这项措施有助于改善工作环境。

tendency / ˈtendənsi / *n.* [C]趋向；趋势；倾向：resist wrong tendencies 抵制错误倾向 同 inclination，direction

tender / ˈtendə(r) / *adj.* ❶脆弱的；纤弱的；易损坏的：～ blossoms 娇嫩的花 / ～ spot 痛处；弱点 / ～ wound 一触即疼的伤口 同 fragile，weak 反 rough，hard ❷(指肉)易咀嚼的，嫩的：a ～ steak 嫩牛排 ❸温和的；亲切的：a ～ smile 温和的微笑 同 gentle，kind

tennis / ˈtenɪs / *n.* 网球：～ court 网球场

tense / tens / Ⅰ *adj.* 拉紧的；紧张的：～ atmosphere 紧张的气氛 / The mother's face was ～ with worry. 妈妈因担忧而表情紧张。同 tight，rigid Ⅱ *n.* [C](动词的)时态：the present(past，future) ～ 现在(过去、将来)时

tension / ˈtenʃn / Ⅰ *n.* [U]紧张；紧张局势；紧张状况：ease ～ 缓和紧张状况 / heighten (increase)～ 加剧紧张局势 / The policy caused international ～. 那项政策引起了国际局势的紧张。同 strain，stress 反 calmness，ease Ⅱ *vt.* 使拉紧；使紧张 派 tensional *adj.*

tent / tent / *n.* [C]帐篷

tentacle / ˈtentəkl / *n.* [C](动物的)触须；触动；触手

tenth / tenθ / Ⅰ *num.* 第十；十分之一 Ⅱ *adj.* 第十的；十分之一的

term / tɜːm / *n.* [C] ❶期限：a long ～ of imprisonment 长期监禁 同 period，time ❷(指学校、大学等的)学期：at the end of a ～ 在期末 同 semester ❸词语；术语：technical ～s 专门术语 同 phrase，terminology ❹(多用 *pl.*)条件；条款：state (accept) ～s of peace 提出(接受)和平条件 同 condition，provision / **in** ～**s of** 根据；按照 / **make** (**come to**)～**s** (**with sb.**) (与某人)达成协议

terminal / ˈtɜːmɪnl / Ⅰ *adj.* 末端的；终点的；

T

极限的：～ cancer 晚期癌症 / ～ examination 期末考试/ I'll get off at the ～ station. 我在终点站下车。同 final, end 反 first, beginning Ⅱ［C］末端；终端；终点(站)：airline ～ 航空终点站 / computer ～ 电脑终端 / We met at the bus ～. 我们在公共汽车终点站碰面。同 station, stand 派 terminally adv.

terminate / ˈtɜːmɪneɪt / v. 停止；终止同 conclude, stop 反 begin, continue

terminology / ˌtɜːmɪˈnɒlədʒi / n. 术语学；术语同 term

terrible / ˈterəbl / adj. ❶可怕的；极不舒服的：a ～ war 可怕的战争 同 fearful, horrible 反 calming, comforting ❷极度的；厉害的：heat 酷热 / ～ winter 严冬 同 extreme, severe 反 gentle, mild ❸很糟的；极坏的：The weather was ～ when we were there. 我们在那里时，天气糟透了。同 awful, bad 反 good, wonderful

terribly / ˈterəbli / adv. 可怕地；非常地；极度地：It's ～ hot. 天气非常炎热。/ She was ～ tired. 她累坏了。同 horribly, violently 反 wonderfully

terrify / ˈterɪfaɪ / vt. 使感到恐惧；惊吓：The child was terrified of being left alone in the house. 那孩子因单独被留在屋里而感到惊恐。同 frighten, alarm 反 calm, comfort

territorial / ˌterɪˈtɔːriəl / adj. ❶领土的：～ air 领空/ ～ integrity 领土完整 ❷(有)地域性的，区域性的：a ～ economy 区域经济／ These regulations are strictly ～. 这些规定完全是地区性的。

territory / ˈterətri / n. ❶领土；版图：Chinese ～ 中国的领土 / They joined the army to defend the sacred ～ of their motherland. 他们参军保卫祖国的神圣领土。同 state, land ❷［C］领域；范围：There are many new discoveries in the ～ of physics. 物理学领域里有许多新发现。同 realm, region

terror / ˈterə(r) / n. ❶［U］恐怖；惊骇：live in ～ 生活在恐怖之中 同 fear, fright 反 calmness ❷［C］引起恐怖的人或事物：The boss was a ～ to the workers. 老板是工人们惧怕的人。

test / test / Ⅰ n. ［C］试验；测验，考试：blood ～ 验血 / achievement ～ 教学成果测验 / aptitude ～ 能力倾向测验 / intelligence ～ 智力测验 / objective ～ (由是非题、选择题等组成

的)客观性测验/ ～-tube 试管 / The theory can stand the ～ of time. 这个理论能够经受时间的考验。同 examination, quiz Ⅱ v. 试验；检验：have one's eyesight ～ed 检验视力／ ～ ore for gold 检验矿石以找出其中的黄金 / The machine must be ～ed before it is used. 机器在使用前必须检查一下。同 examine, quiz

testify / ˈtestɪfaɪ / v. 证明；证实 同 indicate, show

testimony / ˈtestɪməmi / n. ❶［U］证词，证供：take ～ from the next witness 从下一位证人那里取证词 ❷［C；U］证据，证明：produce ～ 出示证据 / call sb. in ～ 叫某人作证

text / tekst / n. ［C］❶课文 ❷正文 ❸教科书 同 textbook, schoolbook

textbook / ˈtekstbʊk / n. ［C］课本；教科书同 text, schoolbook

textile / ˈtekstaɪl / Ⅰ adj. (只作定语)纺织的，织物的：the ～ industry 纺织工业 Ⅱ n. 织物；纺织品；纺织原料：cotton(silk, wool) ～ s 棉(丝、毛)织品

texture / ˈtekstʃə(r) / n. ［C；U］❶质地，质感；质相：wool of a coarse ～ 粗羊毛 / You can't plant this crop in the soil with a loose sandy ～. 这种作物不能种在质地松散的沙质土里。❷结构，组织；纹理：The chemist is testing for the ～ of the mineral. 那位化学家正在测试该矿物的结构。

than / ðæn, ðən / conj. 比(用于形容词、副词比较级之后)：John is taller ～ his brother. 约翰比他兄弟高。/ no more ～ 仅仅；只是：I need no more ～ five people. 我只需要五个人。**no other** ～ 正是：The speaker was no other ～ our teacher. 演讲者不是别人，正是我们的老师。

thank / θæŋk / Ⅰ v. 谢；感谢：There is no need to ～ me. 不必谢我。Thank you for your help. 感谢你的帮助。Ⅱ n. 感谢 同 gratitude, gratefulness 反 ingratitude, ungratefulness/ ～ s to 由于，因为：Thanks to your help, we succeeded. 由于你的帮助，我们成功了。

thankful / ˈθæŋkfl / adj. 感谢的；欣慰的：W are ～ to the policeman for his timely help. 我们感谢警察的及时帮助。同 grateful

Thanksgiving / ˌθæŋksˈɡɪvɪŋ / n. 感恩节

that / ðæt / Ⅰ adj. 那(后接复数名词时用

those）；Do you know ～ girl? 你认识那女孩吗？<u>反</u> this Ⅱ *pron.* ❶那，那个(指示代词)：Is that your brother? 那是你兄弟吗? That is why she cannot come here. 那就是她不能来这儿的原因。<u>反</u> this　❷(关系代词)：Shakespeare is the greatest poet ～ England has ever had. 莎士比亚是英国历史上最伟大的诗人。Ⅲ *conj.* ❶(引导名词从句)：The trouble is ～ we are short of food. 困难是我们缺粮。❷(引导状语从句，表示目的、结果、原因或让步)：Bring it nearer（so）～ I may see it better. 把它拿近一些，好让我看得更清楚。/ He worried ～ he couldn't go to sleep. 他急得不能入睡。/ We'll let you use the room on condition（provided）～ you keep it clean and tidy. 只要你保持房间的整洁，我们就让你使用这房间。❸(引导强调句型)：It is the Party's leadership ～ makes our country rich and strong. 正是党的领导使我国家富强。Ⅳ *adv.* (口语)如此，那样：I can't walk ～ far. 我走不了那么快。<u>固</u> so / ～ **is to say** 即；换句话说 **in order** ～ 为了：He gave his life in order ～ others live happily. 为了他人能活得幸福，他牺牲了生命。**now** ～ 既然：Now ～ you have finished the task, you may go home. 既然已经完成任务，你们可以回家了。/ Now ～ you are well again, you can travel. 你既然恢复了健康，就可以旅行了。**That'll do.**（**That will do.**）行了，够了。

辨析

that，which，who 作关系代词引导定语从句时区别如下：❶that 可指人和物，which 只指物，who 只指人：This is the poem that（which）the critics praised so highly. 这就是那些批评家极为推崇的那首诗。He is the only one among us that（who）knows French. 他是我们中唯一一懂法文的人。❷that 只能引导限制性定语从句，which 和 who 除了引导限制性定语从句外，还可引导非限制性定语从句：I gave the letter to John, who then passed it to Tom. 我把信给了约翰，他后来又传给了汤姆。At the exhibition we saw many new farm tools, which were all invented by the farmers themselves. 我们在展览会上看到许多新农具，它们都是农民自己发明的。❸everything, anything, nothing, much, little, all 等不定代词作先行词时，其后的定语从句中的关系代词一般用 that：He never says anything that is worth listening to. 他从来没说过值得听的事情。

❹先行词是形容词最高级或被最高级修饰时，关系代词一般用 that：This is the best movie（that）I have seen this year. 这是我今年看到的电影中最好的一部。❺先行词是序数词或 last, next, only, very 等表示唯一性的形容词时，或被这些词修饰时，关系代词一般只用 that：You are the only person that can help me. 你是唯一可帮我的人。❻先行词是疑问代词 who 和 which 时，用 that：Who that have worked with him do not like him? 和他一起工作的人谁不喜欢他呢？Which of us that is over thirty years has not read this book? 我们中 30 岁以上的人哪一位没读过这本书呢？

the / ðiː, ðɪ, ðə / Ⅰ *art.* ❶作 this, these, that, those 的弱式语，用以指已经提到过或正讨论的人、物、事等 ❷与代表独一无二事物的名词连用：～ sun 太阳 / ～ moon 月亮 ❸与形容词最高级连用：～ highest of the five 五人中的最高者 ❹用于海洋、江河、运河或其他复数地理名词前：～ Red Sea 红海 / ～ Atlantic（Ocean）大西洋 / ～ Nile 尼罗河 / ～ Alps 阿尔卑斯山脉 ❺与表示乐器的名词连用：play ～ piano（～ violin）弹钢琴(拉小提琴) ❻与形容词或分词连用表示一类人：～ rich 富人 / ～ poor 穷人 / ～ young 年轻人 / ～ old 老年人 / ～ dead 死者 / ～ dying 垂死者 Ⅱ *adv.*（用于形容词、副词比较级前）愈，更，越：The more he has, ～ more he wants. 他得到的愈多，愈想得到更多。/ Actually, ～ busier he is, ～ happier he feels. 事实上他越忙越高兴。

theater(-re) / 'θɪətə(r) / *n.* [U]戏院；剧场

theft / θeft / *n.* ❶盗窃；偷窃 <u>近</u> burglary, robbery ❷盗窃罪

their / ðeə(r) / *pron.* 他(她，它)们的(形容词性物主代词)：They have lost ～ dog. 他们的狗丢了。

theirs / ðeəz / *pron.* 他(她，它)们的(名词性物主代词)：It's a habit of ～. 那是他们的一种习惯。

用法

theirs 用作主语时，谓语动词的数根据所指的事物来定：Theirs is a large room. 他们的房间是大房间。Theirs are latest books. 他们的书是最新的书。

them / ðəm / *pron.* 他(她，它)们(they 的宾格)

theme / θiːm / *n.* [C](谈话或写作的)题目；主

题 圆 subject, topic

themselves / ðəm'selvz / *pron.* 他（她，它）们自己（反身代词）；They did the work by ～. 他们独自干了这件工作。

用法

themselves 作"他们亲自"讲时，位置可紧跟在所指的人后边：They themselves did the experiment. 他们自己亲自做实验。

then / ðen / *adv.* ❶其时；当时：We were living in Chengdu ～. 当时我们住在成都。/ **by** ～ 到那时：I shall come back ten years from now; you'll be a big boy by ～. 我十年后才回来，到那时你将是个大孩子了。**from** ～ **on** 自那时起 **until** ～到那时 **since** ～ 那时以来 ❷其次；然后：We'll have fish first and ～ roast chicken. 我们先吃鱼，然后吃烤鸡。圆 next, afterwards ❸（通常用于句首或句尾）那么，因此：—It isn't here. 一它不在这儿。—It must be in the next room, ～.—那么它一定在隔壁房间。

theoretic(al) / θɪə'retɪk(əl) / *adj.* 理论的；推理的：～ basis 理论基础／～ knowledge 理论知识 派 theoretically *adv.*

theorist / 'θɪərɪst / *n.* [C] 理论家；空想者

theorize / 'θɪəraɪz / *vi.* 谈理论；推理

theory / 'θɪəri / *n.* ❶理论；原理：Your plan is excellent in ～, but would it succeed in practice? 你的计划在理论上好极了，但在实际上可行吗？ It is necessary for us to combine ～ with practice. 我们必须要理论结合实际。/ **in** ～ 在理论上：In ～, the plan is feasible. 在理论上这个计划是可行的。圆 principle ❷学说：～ of Marxism 马克思主义学说 圆 thesis, supposition ❸见解；看法 圆 idea, view 派 therorize *v.*

therapy / 'θerəpi / *n.* [U;C]（尤指通过锻炼、按摩等方式而非手术的）治疗（方法）：shock ～ 休克疗法／ speech ～ 语言疗法

there / ðeə(r) / *adv.* ❶在那里；往那里：We shall soon be ～. 不久我们就会到那里。❷（用 there is [are]）有…，…在：There is someone at the door. 有人在门口。/ There are some children playing on the street. 街上有些小孩在玩耍。/～ **and then** 当时；当场；立刻：I decided to do it ～ and then. 我决定立刻就做。**over** ～ 在那里：The book you want is over ～. 你要的书就在那儿。❸（there 放在句首加强

语气，如句子主语不是代词，则置于动词之后）瞧，你看：There goes the last bus! 最后一辆公共汽车开走了！／ There they come! 瞧，他们来了！

thereby / ,ðeə'baɪ / *adv.* 因此；从而；由此

therefore / 'ðeəfɔː(r) / *adv.* 因此；所以 圆 hence, so

thermal / 'θɜːml / Ⅰ *adj.* ❶热的；产生热的：～ energy 热能 ❷保暖的；隔热的：～ underwear 保暖内衣 ❸温泉的：～ waters 温泉水 Ⅱ *n.* ❶[C]上升暖气流：Birds and gliders circle in ～s to gain height. 鸟类和滑翔机借助上升热气流上升。❷(*pl.*) 衣服,（尤指）保暖内衣

thermometer / θə'mɒmɪtə(r) / *n.* 寒暑表；温度计

Thermos / 'θɜːməs / *n.* [C]热水瓶

these / ðiːz / *adj. & pron.* 这些（this 的复数）反 those

thesis / 'θiːsɪs / *n.* (*pl.* theses/'θiːsiːz/)[C]论题；论点；论文：He is writing a ～ on American literature. 他正在写一篇关于美国文学的论文。圆 subject, essay

they / ðeɪ / *pron.* 他（她、它）们（he, she 和 it 的复数）

thick / θɪk / *adj.* ❶厚的；粗大的：a ～ slice of bread 一片厚面包 ／a ～ line 粗线 圆 broad, fat 反 thin, slim ❷密集的；稠密的：a ～ forest 密林 圆 condensed, dense 反 light, watery ❸浓的；稠的：～ soup 稠汤 ／ ～ fog 浓雾 圆 cloudy, foggy 反 clear 派 thicken *vt.*; thickly *adv.*; thickness *n.*

thief / θiːf / *n.* [C] (*pl.* thieves/θiːvz/) 贼；小偷：a common ～ 一个惯偷 ／ a gang of ～ 一伙贼／ The police caught a car ～. 警察抓住一个偷车贼。圆 burglar, robber

辨析

thief 含义很广，指秘密地偷取而不是当面抢劫财物的人：When Tom had a lesson, a thief stole his bicycle. 汤姆在上课时，贼偷了他的自行车。**robber** 意为"强盗"，指用暴力或威胁手段抢夺别人财物的人：I fear that he might be attacked by a robber if he walked through the deserted park. 我担心如果他在夜间通过无人的公园时会遭到强盗袭击。

thigh / θaɪ / *n.* [C]股；大腿

thin / θɪn / *adj.* (thinner, thinnest) ❶薄的；细的：a ～ slice of bread 一片薄面包 ／ a ～

piece of string 一根细线 囿 slight, small 反 thick ❷瘦的；a ～ face 一张瘦脸 囿 slim, skinny 反 fat, thick ❸稀疏的：～ audience 稀少的观众 囿 scattered 反 full, plentiful ❹稀薄的；淡的：～ gruel 稀粥 / ～ beer 淡啤酒 / ～ mist 薄雾 囿 watery 反 concentrated

thing / θɪŋ / n. [C] ❶东西；事物：What are ～s on the table? 桌上的那些东西是什么？囿 object, article ❷事件；事情：There's another ～ I want to ask you. 还有一件事我要问问你。囿 event, business ❸(多用 pl.)情况，情形；局势：That only makes ～s worse. 那只会使情况更糟。囿 circumstance / **above all** ～s 最重要的是；尤其 / **among other** ～s 除了别的以外(还有) **as** ～s **are** 照目前的情况 **for one** ～, **for another** …首先…，再者… **of all** ～s 首先

think / θɪŋk / v. (thought/θɔːt/, thought) ❶思索；考虑：Are animals able to ～? 动物能思考吗？囿 reason, reflect ❷认为；以为：—Do you ～ it will rain? 一你认为天会下雨吗？—Yes, I ～ so. 一是的，我想会。囿 consider, regard / **about** ①思考：I'm sorry. I wasn't listening to you. I was ～ing about something else. 对不起，我没听你说，我在想别的事。②认为：What do you ～ about the government's latest decision? 你认为政府的最新决定如何？③考虑：We must ～ about illness health when choosing a home. 选择住家时，我们必须考虑到母亲的健康。/ Are you still ～ing about moving to the south? 你还在考虑搬到南方去吗？ **back to** 回想起：Every time he read the novel, he would ～ back to the days he was living in the countryside. 他每次读到那本书，就会回想起农村生活的日子。～ **highly (well) of** 对…评价很高：We ～ highly of his action. 我们对他的行为评价很高。～ **ill of** 看不起；轻视：Don't ～ ill of him. He is something in the town. 别看不起他，他在镇里是个重要人物。～ **nothing of** 不在乎；不考虑：Lei Feng thought nothing of himself. 雷锋从不考虑自己。～ **of** ①思考；考虑：When I said that, I was not ～ing of her feelings. 我说那事的时候，没考虑到她的感受。/ If you thought of the possible results before you acted, you wouldn't do such a foolish thing. 如果你行动之前想一想可能的后果，你就不会做出这种愚蠢的事。②想起；记住：Will you ～ of me after I've left? 我走后你能记住我吗？③提出；建议：Who ～s of

the plan? 谁提出的这个计划？～ **of** … **as** …把…看作…：He always ～s of others' difficulties as his. 他总是把别人的困难看作是自己的困难。～ **out** 想出：He thought out a solution to the problem. 他想出了一个解决问题的办法。～ **over** 仔细考虑：Think it over and let me have your decision tomorrow. 仔细考虑，明天让我知道你的决定

thinking / 'θɪŋkɪŋ / I adj. 思想的；有思考能力的：Man is a ～ animal. 人是有思维能力的动物。囿 reflecting, reasonable II n. [U]思想，思考：do some hard ～ 深思 / to one's ～ 照某人的看法 / without ～ 不假思索 囿 reflection, thought

third / θɜːd / I num. 第三；三分之一 II adj. 第三的；三分之一的 派 thirdly adv.

thirst / θɜːst / n. [U] ❶渴：They lost their way in the desert and died of ～. 他们在沙漠中迷路而渴死了。囿 dryness ❷(喻)热望，渴望：a ～ for knowledge 求知欲 囿 desire 反 hate

thirsty / 'θɜːsti / adj. (-ier, -iest) ❶渴的：Do you feel ～? 你口渴吗？囿 dry ❷渴望的；渴求的：They are ～ for success. 他们渴望得到成功。囿 eager, longing

thirteen / ˌθɜːˈtiːn / I num. 十三，13 II adj. 十三个(的)

thirteenth / ˌθɜːˈtiːnθ / I num. 第十三；十三分之一 II adj. 第十三的；十三分之一的

thirtieth / 'θɜːtiəθ / I num. 第三十；三十分之一 II adj. 第三十的；三十分之一的

thirty / 'θɜːti / I num. 三十，30 II adj. 三十个(的)

this / ðɪs / adj. & pron. (后接复数名词时用 these)这，这个：early ～ morning 今天一大早 / to ～ day 直到今天 / What is ～? 这是什么？反 that

thorn / θɔːn / n. ❶[C](植物的)刺，棘：a twig covered with ～s 长满刺的细枝 ❷[C]使人苦恼(或生气)的事(或人)：Inflation has been a constant ～ for the Premier. 通货膨胀问题一直使总理很苦恼。

thorough / 'θʌrə / adj. 完全的；彻底的；周到的；缜密的：a ～ person 一个一丝不苟的人 / give the room a ～ cleaning 把房子彻底打扫一番 / be ～ in one's work 工作认真 囿 complete, perfect 反 incomplete, imperfect 派 thoroughly adv.

those /ðəuz/ *pron.* & *adj.* 那些(that 的复数形式)反 these

though /ðəu/ I *conj.* ❶虽然:Though they are poor,they are always neatly dressed. 他们虽然穷,衣着却总是整洁的。同 although / **as ~**好像;似乎:He walked as ~ he had been drunk. 他走路就好像喝醉了似的。**even ~** 即使:The work must be done even ~ there is a storm. 即使有暴风雨,那工作也必须做完。❷即使:He would not give up ~ he might meet with a lot of difficulties. 即使遇到很多困难,他也不会放弃。II *adv.* 可是;不过;然而:The vase isn't pretty,I like it ~. 这花瓶不漂亮,可是我喜欢它。同 however,yet

用法

❶though 作"虽然"讲时只能和 still 搭配,不能和 but 连用,如不能说:Though she is a child,but she acts bravely. 但可以说:Though she is a child,still she acts bravely. ❷as though 引导的从句常用虚拟语气。

thought /θɔːt/ *n.* ❶[U]思想;思考力;思考方式;思潮 同 thinking,reflection / **at first ~**乍一想:At first ~,what he said is reasonable. 乍一想,他说的有道理。**at the ~ of** 想起…:She was excited at the ~ of her success. 她一想起她的成功就激动。/ He often acts without ~. 他常鲁莽行事。**on second ~(s)** 经仔细考虑后 **read sb.'s ~s** 看出某人的心思 **take ~ for** 对…挂念:The mother took ~ for her son. 母亲挂念儿子。**without a moment's ~** 立即;当场 ❷想法;意见:He keeps his ~s to himself. 他不把自己的意见对别人说。同 idea,opinion

thoughtful /ˈθɔːtfl/ *adj.* ❶思考的;沉思的;深思的:She looked ~. 看上去她在沉思。同 thinking,reflective 反 thoughtless,unthinking ❷体贴的;关心的;考虑周到的:It is ~ of you to remind me of the meeting. 提醒我要开会,你考虑得很周到。/ Bill is a ~ man. 比尔是一个关心别人的人。同 considerate,kind 反 thoughtless,cruel

thoughtless /ˈθɔːtləs/ *adj.* ❶疏忽的;粗心大意的 同 careless,unthinking 反 thoughtful,careful ❷考虑不周到的;不顾及他人的 同 inconsiderate,rude 反 considerate,polite

thousand /ˈθauznd/ I *num.* 千 II *adj.* 千个的:~s of 成千上万的 / one in a ~ 千里挑一

的人物;出众的人物 / (a) ~ and one 无数的 / *The Thousand and One nights*《一千零一夜》《天方夜谭》

thousandth /ˈθauznθ/ I *num.* 第一千;千分之一 II *adj.* 第一千的;千分之一的

thread /θred/ I *n.* ❶(一股)线:a reel of silk ~ 一卷丝线 / a needle and ~ 穿了线的针 同 string,cord / **hang by a ~** 千钧一发;濒临危机 ❷[C]头绪;线索;思路:lose the ~ 抓不住论点;失去头绪 / ~s of a story 故事的线索 同 clue II *vt.* 穿(针)

threat /θret/ *n.* ❶恐吓;威胁 同 warning,menace 反 promise / **under ~ of** 在…威胁下:She obeyed his order,but only under ~ of punishment. 只是因为受到严惩的威胁,她才服从了他的命令。❷前兆;预兆:There was a ~ of rain in the dark sky. 乌云密布的天空有下雨的兆头。同 forewarning

threaten /ˈθretn/ *v.* ❶威胁;恐吓:~ to murder sb. 威胁要谋杀某人 同 terrorize,warn 反 protect,defend ❷预示:The clouds ~ rain. 乌云预示着要下雨。同 endanger

three /θriː/ I *num.* 三,3 II *adj.* 三个的

thrill /θrɪl/ I *n.* [C](一阵)激动 同 excitement II *v.* 使激动:It ~ed me to hear of your success. 听说你成功了真让我激动。同 excite,rouse 反 calm

thrive /θraɪv/ *vi.* (thrived 或 throve /θrəuv/,thrived 或 thriven/ˈθrɪvn/)兴旺,繁荣;茁壮成长:~ on hard work 靠勤劳致富(致富)/ ~ with good management 由于管理完善而兴旺 / Markets are thriving, and prices are stable. 市场繁荣,物价稳定。同 flourish, prosper 反 die,fail

throat /θrəut/ *n.* [C]喉咙;咽喉:A bone has stuck in my ~. 一根骨头哽在我的喉咙里。/ clear one's ~ 清嗓子 / cut one another's ~s 相互残杀 / cut one's own ~ 自取灭亡 / have a bone in one's ~ 难以启齿 / take sb. by the ~ 掐住某人的脖子,掐死某人

throb /θrɒb/ I *vi.* (throbbed;throbbing) ❶搏动;悸动;突突跳动:My heart ~bed fast. 我的心怦怦直跳。❷有节奏地震动,有规律地颤动 II *n.* [C]搏动;跳动:A ~ of pain shot through his chest. 他感到胸部一阵剧烈的抽痛。

throne /θrəun/ *n.* [C] ❶宝座;御座 ❷(the

〜)王位：come to the 〜 即位 / succeed to the 〜继承王位

throng / θrɒŋ / Ⅰ *n*. [C]一大群人：a wildly cheering 〜疯狂欢呼的人群/ the worldly 〜芸芸众生 同 crowd Ⅱ *v*. 拥人；(使)挤满，聚集：The sight of the streets were 〜ed with buyers. 街道上熙攘往的尽是购物的人们/ The demonstrators 〜ed over the bridge towards the city hall. 示威者聚集在通往市政厅的大桥上。

through / θru: / Ⅰ *prep*. ❶穿过；越过；经过：The River Thames flows 〜 London. 泰晤士河流经伦敦。同 past, across ❷(指时间)自始至终：He won't live 〜 tonight. 他活不过今晚。同 during, throughout ❸(表示作用或方法)从，通过：I learnt of the position 〜 a piece of newspaper advertisement. 我从一则报纸广告获知有这个职位。同 by Ⅱ *adv*. 从一端至另一端；自始至终；贯穿：They wouldn't let us 〜. 他们不让我们过去。同 throughout

throughout / θru:'aʊt / Ⅰ *prep*. 遍及，在各处；在整个期间：〜 the country 全国各地 / 〜 the war 在整个战争期间 / Qingdao is known 〜 the world for its beautiful beaches. 青岛以其美丽的海滨而世界闻名。同 over Ⅱ *adv*. 一直；各处：The wood house was rotten 〜. 那座木屋已完全烂掉了。同 everywhere

throw / θrəʊ / *v*. (threw /θru:/, thrown/ θrəʊn/) ❶投；抛；掷：He threw the ball to me. 他把球掷给我。同 cast, toss 反 catch ❷摔倒：The wrestler threw his opponent. 摔跤手把对手摔倒在地。同 overturn / 〜 **away** 扔掉；抛弃：Don't 〜 away old newspapers; they may be of some use. 不要把旧报纸扔掉，或许还有什么用处。〜 **doubt on** 怀疑；Don't 〜 doubt on him. What he said is true. 别怀疑他，他说的是真的。/ Everyone was prepared to accept the statement until the chairman threw doubt on it. 在主席对这种说法产生怀疑之前，人人都准备接受它。〜 **light on** 阐明；说明：Have the police been able to 〜 any light on the mystery of the stolen jewels yet? 警察能解开首饰被盗之谜吗？〜 **off** ①匆匆脱掉(衣服)：Throwing off his coat, he jumped into the river to save the drowning child. 他匆匆脱掉大衣跳到河里去救那溺水的孩子。②摆脱：I wish I could 〜 off these newspaper reporters who are following me everywhere. 我真希望能摆脱

这些我走到哪儿就跟到哪儿的新闻记者。③扔掉；抛掉：It's very difficult to 〜 off old habits of thought. 很难丢掉旧的思维习惯。〜 **oneself into** 投身于… 同 **sb. into prison** 把某人投入监狱：The man was thrown into prison for his robbery. 那人因抢劫而被关进监狱。

thrust / θrʌst / Ⅰ *v*. (thrust, thrust)刺；戳；插：He 〜 his hands into his pockets. 他把双手插入衣袋中。/ The young man 〜 a dagger into his enemy's chest. 年轻人将短剑插入敌人的胸膛。/ 〜 one's way through a crowd 从人群中挤过去 / 〜 sb. to death 将某人戳死 / 〜 sb. to the wall 把某人逼至绝境 同 poke, stab Ⅱ *n*. [C]刺；戳 同 poke, stab ❷[U]要点；要旨 同 gist

thumb / θʌm / *n*. 拇指：be all 〜s 笨手笨脚 / put (turn) one's 〜 up 竖起大拇指表示赞成(同意)

thunder / 'θʌndə(r) / Ⅰ *n*. ❶雷；雷声：We haven't had much 〜 this summer. 今年夏天我们没听到什么雷声。❷似雷的响声：a 〜 of applause 掌声如雷 Ⅱ *v*. ❶打雷：It was lightning and 〜ing. 正在闪电打雷。❷发出如雷的声音：The train 〜ed through the station. 火车轰隆隆驶过车站。

thunderous / 'θʌndərəs / *adj*. 打雷的；响声如雷的：〜 applause 雷鸣般的掌声

Thursday / 'θɜːzdeɪ / *n*. 星期四

thus / ðʌs / *adv*. 这样；因而 同 so, therefore

tick / tɪk / *n*. [C](尤指钟表发出的)滴答声 同 click, beat

ticket / 'tɪkɪt / *n*. [C] ❶票；入场券：free 〜 免费招待券 / lottery 〜 彩票 / meal 〜 餐券，饭票 / platform 〜 月台票 / winning 〜 奖(彩)票 / hold the winning 〜 中奖 / Admission by 〜 only. 凭票入场 / Do you want a single or a return 〜? 你要单程票还是往返票? 同 pass, certificate ❷罚款单：The driver was given a 〜 because of driving too fast. 由于车开得太快，司机被处以罚款。

tickle / 'tɪkl / *v*. 搔痒；逗乐 同 tease, amuse

tide / taɪd / *n*. ❶潮；潮汐：at the high (low)〜 高(低)潮时 / The 〜 is rising. 涨潮了。The 〜 is falling. 退潮了。同 current, flow ❷[C]潮流；趋势：go against the 〜 反潮流 / go with the 〜 随大流，赶潮流 / No one can turn the ~ of history. 谁也不能改变历史的潮流。Time and ~ wait(s) for no man. 时不待我。同 tendency, movement 派 tidal *adj.*

tidy / 'taɪdi / Ⅰ *adj.* 整齐的；整洁的：a ~ room 整洁的房间 同 clean, neat 反 untidy, dirty Ⅱ *vt.* 使整洁，使整齐：~ up one's bed (desk) 整理床铺(书桌) 同 clean 反 mess

tie / taɪ / Ⅰ *v.* (tying / 'taɪɪŋ /) ❶(用带、绳等)捆、绑、拴：~ a dog to the street railings 将狗拴在街旁的栏杆上 同 bind, fasten 反 untie, loosen ❷ 与…得同样的分数；不分胜负：The two teams ~ d. 两队打成平手。同 match Ⅱ *n.* [C] ❶带，绳，(喻)纽带；联系；关系：the ~ s of friendship 友谊的纽带 / family ~ s 家庭关系 同 rope, relation ❷(比赛)平局：The game ended in a ~. 比赛以平局结束。

tiger / 'taɪɡə(r) / *n.* [C] 虎；man-eating ~ 吃人虎 / paper ~ 纸老虎

tight / taɪt / Ⅰ *adj.* ❶紧的；不松动的：These shoes are so ~ that they hurt me. 这双鞋太紧，挤得我脚痛。同 firm, stiff 反 loose ❷紧密的；密集的 同 close, dense 反 loose Ⅱ *adv.* 紧紧地；牢牢地 同 closely, firmly 派 tighten *v.*; tightly *adv.*

tile / taɪl / *n.* [C] 瓦片；瓷砖：~ floor 瓷砖地 / Tiles are used to cover roofs. 瓦是用来盖屋顶的。

till / tɪl / Ⅰ *prep.* 直到：I shall wait ~ ten o'clock. 我将等到十点钟。同 until / ~ **now** 直到现在：They have worked hard ~ now. 他们努力工作到现在。Ⅱ *conj.* 直到…之时；在…以前：Let's wait ~ the rain stops. 让我们等到雨停。同 until

辨析
❶till 和 until 作为介词和连接词可通用，until 多用在比较正式的文体里和句首。❷until 和 till 引起的不可用 shall will, would 表示将来时，如不可说：He wil wait till (until) I shall arrive. 他要等我到达。❸ 在 till 或 until 出现的肯定句中，句子或主句的谓语用延续性动词：I remained there till (until) his arrival (he arrived). 我一直留到他到达。而在 not...until (till)句式中句子或主句谓语要用终止性动词：He did not return till (until) ten o'clock (it was ten o'clock). 他到十点钟才回来。

timber / 'tɪmbə(r) / *n.* [U]木材；木料 同 lumber, log

time / taɪm / *n.* ❶钟点；时间；时期：The world exists in space and ~. 世界存在于空间和时间中。同 period, epoch / **have a good** ~ 玩得很高兴，过得很愉快 **behind** ~ ①迟到：The train is ten minutes behind ~. 火车晚点十分钟。②落后；拖欠：He is always behind ~ with his payments. 他总是不能按时付款。**in** ~ ①及时：We were in ~ for the train. 我们及时赶上火车。②早晚；终究：You'll learn how to do it in ~. 你早晚会学会如何做此事。**on** ~ 按时，准时：The train came in on ~. 火车准时到达。**in no** ~ 立即，很快地：I'll be back in no ~. 我很快就回来。**all the** ~ 一直；始终，从头到尾：I looked all over the house for that letter, and it was in my pocket all the ~. 我在整个屋子里找那封信，而它却一直在我的口袋里。/ He's a business-man all the ~. 他一直就是个生意人。**at all** ~ s 始终 **at one** ~ 曾经一个时期：At one ~ I went to mountain-climbing every summer. 曾经一个时期我每年夏天都去爬山。**at the same** ~ 同时；laugh and cry at the same ~ 又哭又笑 **at that** ~ 在那时：He was only ten years old at that ~. 那时他才十岁。**for the** ~ **being** 暂时，目前：For the ~ being you will have to share this room with another person. 你暂时得与另一个人同住这房间。**from** ~ **to** ~, **at** ~ s 间或，有时：I saw Tom at the library from ~ to ~. 我间或会在图书馆里见到汤姆。**keep good** (**bad**) ~ (钟表)走得准(不准)：Does your watch keep good ~? 你的手表走时准确吗？**kill** ~消磨时间：I saw many passengers were killing ~ by reading at the station. 在车站我看到许多乘客以读书来打发时间。**take one's** ~ 不着急：Take your ~. I am waiting for you at the gate. 别着急，我在大门口等你。❷[C] 倍：Yours is ten ~ s the size of mine. 你的是我的十倍大。❸[C] 次：I asked him three ~ s. 我问了他三次。**many a** ~ 屡次 ~ **and again** 多次，反复地

timely / 'taɪmli / *adj.* 及时的；适时的：~ treatment 及时的治疗 同 prompt, punctual 反 untimely, late

timetable / 'taɪmteɪbl / *n.* [C]时间表；(火车、飞机等)时刻表；课程表：the railway ~ 铁路运行时刻表

timid / 'tɪmɪd / *adj.* 胆怯的；羞怯的：That fellow is as ～ as a rabbit. 那家伙胆小如鼠。同 fearful, shy 反 fearless, confident

tin / tɪn / n. ❶[U]锡 ❷[C] 罐头：a ～ of sardines 一罐沙丁鱼

tinkle / 'tɪŋkl / Ⅰ vi. 发出叮当声，发出丁零声：The shop has a little bell that ～s when you open the door. 这家商店有只小铃铛，有人推门时它就叮当叮当响。 Ⅱ n. 叮当声，丁零声

tint / tɪnt / Ⅰ n. [C]色彩；色调：The paint is white with a yellow ～. 这个颜料白中带黄。 Ⅱ vt. 使带上色彩(或色调)；给着色(或染色)：Some fashionable boys had their hair ～ed red. 一些赶时髦的男孩把头发染成淡红色。

tiny / 'taɪni / adj. (-ier, -iest) 极小的 同 minute, small 反 huge, large

tip[1] / tɪp / n. [C] ❶尖；尖端：the ～s of one's fingers 手指尖 / the ～ of one's nose 鼻尖 同 end, peak / ～toe n. 脚尖；脚趾尖 ❷装在末端的小物：cigarettes with filter ～s 末端装有滤嘴的香烟

tip[2] / tɪp / Ⅰ n. [C]小费；赏钱 Ⅱ v. (tipped; tipping)给小费

tire[1] / 'taɪə(r) / v. 使疲倦；使厌倦：The long lecture ～d the audience. 长篇演说使听众厌倦。 / ～ out 使筋疲力尽：I must sit down and rest. I'm ～d out. 我必须坐下歇一会，我筋疲力尽了。同 exhaust, weary

tire[2] / 'taɪə / n. (=[英]tyre)[C]轮胎：change a ～ 换轮胎 / have a flat ～ 车胎漏气 / mount a ～ 装轮胎 / patch a ～ 补轮胎 / pump air in ～ 往车胎里打气 / spare ～ 备用轮胎

tired / 'taɪəd / adj. ❶疲乏的；累的：He is too ～ to go farther. 他太累了，再也走不动了。同 exhausted, weary 反 energetic, fresh ❷厌烦的：I'm ～ of the same kind of food every day. 我讨厌每天吃同一种食物。

tiresome / 'taɪəsəm / adj. 累人的；令人厌倦的；令人讨厌的 同 tedious, boring 反 easy, pleasing

tissue / 'tɪsju: / n. [U]薄纱；手巾纸；卫生纸：face (facial)～ 面巾 / We have run out of toilet ～. 我们的卫生纸用完了。

titan / 'taɪtən / n. [C]巨人；庞然大物：The soft drink ～s are struggling for a bigger share of the market. 生产软饮料的巨头们正在争抢更

大的市场份额。

title / 'taɪtl / n. [C] ❶名称；题目；标题；page ～ 扉页同 name, heading ❷称号；头衔：The school conferred the ～ of "Excellent Student" on Jack. 学校授予杰克"优秀学生"称号。同 rank, status ❸权利；资格：Only the president has the ～ to travel by first-class. 只有校长才有资格坐头等舱旅行。 / Who gave you the ～ to enjoy free medicine? 谁给了你们享受免费医疗的权利？同 right ❹冠军：The girl won the race. 那姑娘赢得了短跑冠军。同 championship

to / tu:, tu, tə / prep. ❶(表示方向)对，至：go ～ the grocer's 前往杂货店 / fall ～ the ground 落到地上 ❷(表示时间)至，到：from beginning ～ end 自始至终 ❸(表示程度)到，至：wet ～ the skin 湿透了 ❹(表示比较)：I prefer walking ～ climbing. 我喜欢步行，不喜欢爬山。

toad / təʊd / n. [C]蟾蜍；癞蛤蟆

toast[1] / təʊst / Ⅰ n. [U]烤面包(片)；吐司：a piece of ～ 一片面包 Ⅱ vt. 烘；烤：～ the bread brown 把面包烤黄同 brown, heat

toast[2] / təʊst / Ⅰ n. 敬酒；干杯；祝酒；祝酒词：exchange ～s 相互敬礼 / We drank a ～ to her health. 我们为她的健康干杯。 Ⅱ v. 提议为…祝酒(干杯)：Let's ～ the friendship between the two countries. 让我们为两国之间的友谊干杯。

tobacco / tə'bækəʊ / n. (pl. tobaccoes 或 tobaccos)烟草；烟叶：This is a mixture of the best ～s. 这是由数种最好的烟叶配制成的。

today / tə'deɪ / Ⅰ n. ❶今天；本日：Have you read ～'s newspaper? 你看过今天的报纸吗？❷现代；当代 Ⅱ adv. 今天；在当代

toe / təʊ / n. [C] 脚趾；脚指头；**from top to** ～ 从头到脚；完全地 **on one's** ～**s** ①踮着脚尖(走)的 ②提高警觉的 **step on sb.'s** ～**s** ①踩着某人的脚尖 ②触怒(得罪)某人

TOEFL / 'təʊfl / (=Test of English as a Foreign Language)托福考试(美国等国的大学对外国学生入学前的英语测试)

together / tə'geðə(r) / adv. ❶一起；共同地：They went for a walk ～. 他们一起去散步。 / We got ～ and discussed the problem of air pollution. 我们聚在一起讨论有关空气污染的问题。同 collectively, unitedly 反 separately /

～ **with** 和,连同:I'll send you a sample, ～ with some details. 我将连同资料一起给你寄一份样品去。❷同时:All his troubles seemed to come ～. 他的一切麻烦似乎同时来临。❸合计地:In front of the classroom building there are twenty trees all ～. 在教学大楼前总共有20 棵树。

toil / tɔɪl / Ⅰ n. 劳苦;辛苦 同 labor, hardship 反 amusement, play Ⅱ v. 辛苦工作 同 labor, sweat 反 play 派 toilful adj.

toilet / 'tɔɪlɪt / n. [C]卫生间;厕所:～ paper 手纸;卫生纸 / go to the ～ 上厕所 同 bathroom, washroom

token / 'təʊkən / Ⅰ n. [C]❶表示;标志;象征;记号:The white flag is a ～ of surrender. 白旗是投降的标志。/in ～ of 作为…的标志(或象征等);表示:The visitors presented us with a banner in ～ of friendship. 客人们赠送我们一面锦旗,以示友好。❷纪念品:She kept the medals as a ～ by which to remember her dead husband. 她保存奖章以悼念她的丈夫。Ⅱ adj. 作为标志的;象征性的;表意的:a small ～ gift 象征性的小礼物 / a ～ woman on the committee 委员会中虚设的女性成员

tolerable / 'tɒlərəbl / adj. ❶(痛苦等)可以忍受的;(错误等)可容忍的,可宽恕的:exceed ～ limits 超过可以容忍的限度 ❷还可以的,差强人意的;过得去的:The goods arrived in a ～ condition with a few cases slightly damaged. 货物到达时除有几箱稍有损坏外,总体情况还过得去。

tolerance / 'tɒlərəns / n. [U]忍受;容忍:It is necessary for us to show ～ towards one another. 我们必须相互忍让。同 endurance, patience 反 anger

tolerant / 'tɒlərənt / adj. 容忍的;有耐力的:One should be ～ of different opinions. 一个人应当容许不同意见。同 forgiving, understanding 反 intolerant

tolerate / 'tɒləreɪt / vt. 容忍;忍受:I won't ～ your impudence. 我不能容忍你的无礼。同 allow, endure 反 forbid, oppose

toll[1] / təʊl / Ⅰ n. [C](道路、桥)通行费:～ bar 收费口 / ～ gate 收费站(处) / ～ road(way) 收费道路 Ⅱ v. 向…收费

toll[2] / təʊl / Ⅰ v. 鸣钟,敲钟 Ⅱ n.(用 a ～,the ～)钟声

tomato / tə'mɑːtəʊ / n. [C] (pl. tomatoes)番茄:～ juice 番茄汁

tomb / tuːm / n. [C]坟墓 同 grave

tomorrow / tə'mɒrəʊ / Ⅰ n. 明天;the day after ～ 后天 Ⅱ adv. 在明天

ton / tʌn / n. [C]吨

tone / təʊn / n. ❶风格;气度 同 mood, manner ❷音调:The piano has a wonderful ～. 那钢琴的音色好极了。同 sound ❸腔调;语气:You should read the sentence with a rising ～. 你应当用升调读这个句子。同 accent, intonation

tongue / tʌŋ / n. [C] ❶舌;舌头:The doctor asked me to put out my ～. 医生要我伸出舌头。❷语言:one's mother ～ 本国语;母语 同 language ❸口才;说话方式:have a bitter ～ 说话刻薄 / have a ready ～ 雄辩,好口才/ hold one's ～ 保持沉默

tonight / tə'naɪt / Ⅰ n. (在)今晚,今夜:～'s radio news 今晚的新闻广播 Ⅱ adv. 在今夜

too / tuː / adv. ❶也;又;加之:She plays the piano, and sings, ～. 她边弹钢琴边唱歌。同 also, moreover ❷过于;太:We've had ～ much rain lately. 最近我们这儿雨下得太多。同 over, extremely / ～ ... to ... 太…而不能…:He is ～ old to work for his bread. 他年纪太老不能赚钱糊口了。/ The book is ～ difficult for me to understand. 这书太难,我读不懂。**cannot be ～** ...怎么也不过分:You cannot be ～ careful. 你无论怎么小心都不过分。**only ～**非常:I am only too ready to help. 我非常乐意帮忙。

tool / tuːl / n. [C]❶工具,用具;方法;手段 同 instrument, means ❷受他人利用者;傀儡;走狗:He was a mere ～ in the hands of the dictator. 他只是独裁者手中的傀儡而已。

tooth / tuːθ / n. [C](pl. teeth /tiːθ/)牙齿:have a ～ out 拔牙 / ～ache 牙痛 / ～brush 牙刷 / ～paste 牙膏

top / tɒp / Ⅰ n. ❶顶部;顶端:at the ～ of the hill 在山顶 / at the ～ of the page 在书页的上端 / Put the red book on (the) ～ of the others. 把红皮书放在其他书上面。同 peak 反 base, bottom **come out at the ～** 名列前茅 **come to the ～** 出名 **from ～ to bottom** (toe) 从头到脚;从上到下;全部地 **on ～ of the world** 感到高兴;That was all, but it sent me home feeling as if I were on ～ of the world! 我听到的就这么多,然而这几句话却使我兴高采烈地回到了家。❷最高的高度;最高地位:shout at the ～ of one's voice 高声喊叫 圆 head, highest position 反 bottom, end Ⅱ *adj.* 顶部的;首位的;最高的;头等的:～ floor 顶楼 / ～ official 高层官员 / Have you read the ～ news today? 你读了今天的头条新闻吗? 圆 highest, best 反 lowest, worst Ⅲ *vt.* (topped; topping) ❶居…之上 ❷高过;超过 圆 excel, surpass

topic / 'tɒpɪk / *n.* 论题;话题;题目:What is the ～ you talked about? 你们谈的是什么话题? 圆 theme, matter

topical / 'tɒpɪkəl / *adj.* ❶有关时事的;时下关注的;成为话题的:The discussion focused on ～ issues in medicine. 讨论集中在一些人们时下关注的医学话题上。/ His wax portraits were always up to date and ～. 他做的蜡像总是当时当地的新闻人物。❷(医学)局部的:a ～ anaesthetic 局部麻醉

torch / tɔːtʃ / *n.* [C]❶火炬;火把:hold aloft a ～ 高举火把 / hand on the ～ to 把火炬传给… / The mayor lit the ～ for the sports meet. 市长为运动会点燃了火炬。❷手电筒:Please turn on (off) the ～. 请打开(关掉)手电筒。

torment Ⅰ / 'tɔːment / *n.* [C;U]痛苦;苦恼;折磨:mental ～ 精神折磨 / She suffered ～s. 她遭受了巨大的痛苦。Ⅱ / tɔː'ment / *vt.* 折磨;使痛苦;使苦恼;烦扰:be ～ed with worry 忧心如焚 / I wanted to ～ her with indifference. 我曾想到要让她尝尝冷遇是什么滋味。

tornado / tɔː'neɪdəʊ / *n.* [C] (*pl.* tornadoes 或 tornados)龙卷风:A ～ struck that area last week. 上周龙卷风袭击了那个地区。圆 storm, hurricane

tortoise / 'tɔːtəs / *n.* [C]乌龟

torture / 'tɔːtʃə(r) / Ⅰ *vt.* 使受剧烈苦痛;折磨:～ sb. to make him confess sth. 折磨某人使他招认某事 圆 abuse, mistreat 反 cheer, comfort Ⅱ *n.* [U]折磨;拷问:put a man to the ～ 折磨某人 圆 cruelty, trial 反 joy, enjoyment

toss / tɒs / Ⅰ *v.* 扔;抛;掷:Jack ～ed a coin to the beggar. 杰克丢给乞丐一枚硬币。/ ～ **sb. for sth.** 掷硬币决定某事:I'll ～ you for the ticket. 我和你掷硬币,看谁赢得这张票。圆 cast,

throw 反 catch, grasp Ⅱ *n.* 扔;抛;掷:lose (win) the ～ 掷硬币时猜错(对)圆 cast, throw 反 catch, grasp

total / 'təʊtl / Ⅰ *adj.* 完全的;全体的:What are your ～ debts? 你的全部债务有多少? 圆 complete, whole 反 incomplete, partial Ⅱ *n.* 总数;总额:Our expenses reached a ～ of $5,000. 我们的支出总额达 5000 美元。圆 sum, whole 反 subtotal, part 派 totally *adv.*

touch / tʌtʃ / Ⅰ *v.* ❶接触;触及:Can you ～ the top of the door? 你能摸到门顶吗? 圆 feel, stroke ❷触动;感动:The sad story ～ed us. 那悲惨的故事感动了我们。/ We were deeply ～ed by his efforts. 我们被他的努力感动了。圆 affect, move ❸涉及;论及:～ **on** 谈及;提及:Do you know the topic he ～ed on at the beginning of the meeting? 你了解他在会议开始时谈到的那个话题吗? 圆 mention, concern 反 ignore, overlook Ⅱ *n.* 接触;联系:I felt a ～ on my arm. 我觉得胳膊上有人碰了一下。圆 contact, communication / **be in (out of)** ～ **with** 与…保持(失去)联系:The family was out of ～ with him. 家人和他失去了联系。**keep** ～ **with** 与…保持联系:He kept ～ with all his friends after graduation. 毕业后他仍然和朋友们保持着联系。**within** ～ **of** 在能触及的地方

touching / 'tʌtʃɪŋ / *adj.* 动人的;感人的:a ～ story 动人的故事 圆 affecting, moving

tough / tʌf / *adj.* ❶(肉类)坚韧的,咬不动的 圆 hard, strong 反 soft, fragile ❷强壮的;坚强的:～ soldiers 坚强的士兵 圆 sturdy, firm 反 weak, delicate ❸(指人)粗暴的,凶恶的:a ～ criminal 凶恶的罪犯 圆 rough, cruel 反 kind, merciful ❹困难的:a ～ job (problem) 棘手的工作(问题)圆 difficult, hard 反 simple, easy

tour / tʊə(r) / Ⅰ *n.* ❶旅行;周游:a round-the-world ～ 环球旅行 ❷巡回演出:The company is on ～ in the countryside. 公司正在农村进行巡回演出。/ 圆 journey, voyage Ⅱ *v.* 旅行;漫游;巡回:～ western Europe 漫游西欧 / The play ～ed the rural areas. 这出剧曾在农村巡回演出。/ The delegation is on a ～ of the Asian branches. 代表团在亚洲的分支机构巡视。圆 journey, voyage

tourism / 'tʊərɪzəm / *n.* 旅游;观光;旅游业:make money from ～以旅游业赚钱

tourist / ˈtʊərɪst / Ⅰ n. [C]旅游者;观光者:attract ～s 吸引游客/ Jane's work is to show ～s around the city. 简的工作是带游客在城里观光。同 traveller Ⅱ adj. 观光的;旅行的:～ agency 旅行社;旅游公司/ ～ attraction 旅游胜地/ ～ car (coach) 观光车;游览车/ ～ guide 导游/ ～ party 观光团

tournament / ˈtʊənəmənt / n. [C]比赛;联赛;锦标赛;巡回赛:a friendship invitational ～友好邀请赛/a chess ～象棋锦标赛

tow / təʊ / v. & n. 拖;牵引 同 drag,pull

toward(s) / təˈwɔːd (z) / prep. ❶向;对;朝…的方向:walking ～ the sea 向海走去 同 to, for ❷对于;关于:Are his feelings ～ us friendly? 他对我们友善吗? 同 regarding, concerning

towel / ˈtaʊəl / n. [C]毛巾

tower / ˈtaʊə(r) / Ⅰ n. [C]塔:control ～(机场的)控制塔/ observation ～ 瞭望塔/ TV ～ 电视塔/ water ～ 水塔 Ⅱ v. 高耸:the skyscrapers that ～ over New York 高耸于纽约市的摩天大楼 同 rise,mount

town / taʊn / n. [C] ❶(市)镇 同 city ❷市内商业区;闹市区:My grandpa lives in another ～. 我爷爷住在另一座小镇。同 downtown

toxic / ˈtɒksɪk / adj. ❶(有)毒的;毒性的;有害的:～ chemicals 有毒化学品/ ～ gases 毒气 ❷中毒的;由毒性引起的:～ symptoms 中毒症状

toy / tɔɪ / n. [C]玩具 同 plaything

trace / treɪs / Ⅰ n. [C]痕迹;踪迹:They have not found any ～ of the murderer. 他们没有发现杀人犯的任何踪迹。同 track,trail Ⅱ vt. 跟踪,追踪;查找:The police ～d the thief to London. 警察追踪窃贼到了伦敦。同 seek, trail / ～ sth. back to 追溯某事到…:The custom can be ～d back to the 17th century. 这种风俗可以追溯到 17 世纪。～ between the lines 可从字里行间看出

track / træk / n. [C] ❶(车辆、行人、动物等经过留下的)痕迹,踪迹:～s in the snow 雪上的痕迹 同 mark, trail ❷踏成的路;小道:a ～ through the forest 穿过森林的一条小径 同 path,way ❸(火车等的)轨道:single (double) ～单(双)轨 同 rail

tractor / ˈtræktə(r) / n. [C]拖拉机:～ driver 拖拉机手

trade / treɪd / Ⅰ n. ❶[U]买卖;交易;贸易:～ agreement 贸易协定/ border ～ 边境贸易/ export ～ 出口贸易/ international ～国际贸易 同 business,commerce /～mark n. 商标 ❷职业;谋生的方式;(尤指)手艺:He's a weaver (mason,carpenter,tailor) by ～. 他是纺织工(石匠、木匠、裁缝)。同 occupation Ⅱ v. ❶做生意;从事贸易活动:They ～ with nearly all the countries in the world. 他们几乎和世界上所有的国家做生意。同 deal ❷交换 同 exchange

tradition / trəˈdɪʃn / n. 传统;惯例:It is still necessary to keep up the fine ～ of plain living and hard work. 保持艰苦奋斗的优良传统仍然是必要的。同 custom,convention 反 novelty

traditional / trəˈdɪʃənl / adj. 传统的;惯例的:～ Chinese medicine 中医;中药 / ～ friendship 传统友谊 / ～ ideas 传统观念 同 established,usual 反 new,modern 派 traditionally adv.

traffic / ˈtræfɪk / n. [U] ❶交通;来往行人或车辆:～ jam 交通拥挤 / ～ lights 交通灯 / heavy (light) ～交通拥挤(畅通)/ There was not much (a lot of) ～ on the roads yesterday. 昨天路上行人车辆不多(很多)。❷(火车、轮船、飞机等的)运输 同 transportation

tragedian / trəˈdʒiːdiən / n. [C]悲剧作家;悲剧演员

tragedy / ˈtrædʒədi / n. ❶悲剧;悲剧作品:He wrote several famous tragedies. 他写了几部著名的悲剧作品。反 comedy ❷惨事;灾难;不幸:His carelessness caused a ～. 他的粗心大意酿成了不幸。同 disaster,misery 反 happiness,joy

tragic / ˈtrædʒɪk / adj. 悲剧的;悲惨的:a ～ drama 悲剧 / a ～ outcome 悲惨的结局 同 dreadful, unfortunate 反 happy, fortunate 派 tragical adj. ; tragically adv.

trail / treɪl / Ⅰ n. ❶踪迹;痕迹 同 track,trace ❷(打猎的)猎迹 ❸小径:崎岖小道 同 path, way Ⅱ vt. 跟踪;追踪:～ along after (behind) sb. 慢吞吞地跟在某人后面走/～ from the chimney(烟)从烟囱里飘出来/ ～ on the floor (衣服)拖在地板上/ ～ over the wall(杂草等)蔓过墙 同 track,trace

train / treɪn / Ⅰ n. [C] ❶火车;列车:passenger (freight) ～s 客车(货车) / catch the ～ 赶上火车 / miss the ～ 没有赶上火车 / express ～ 快车 / slow ～ 慢车 / travel by ～ 乘火车旅行 ❷系列,一串 同 series, chain ❸ 长袍拖曳在地上的部分;拖裙 Ⅱ v. 训练;教养,教育:～ a horse for a race 训练马参加比赛 / They ～ed the workers to use computers. 他们训练工人使用计算机。同 teach, educate

trainee / treɪˈniː / n. [C]受培训者,实习者

training / ˈtreɪnɪŋ / n. [U]训练;锻炼;培养: basic ～ 基本训练 / flight ～ 飞行训练 / military ～ 军事训练 同 drill, instruction

trait / treɪt / n. [C]特征,特点,特性,特质: Generosity is his best ～. 慷慨是他的最大特点。/ One doesn't remember every feature of a face, but only its salient ～. 人们不能记住一张脸的每一特征,而只能记住其主要特征。同 characteristic

traitor / ˈtreɪtə(r) / n. [C]叛徒;卖国贼 同 betrayer, deserter

tram / træm / n. (＝[美]trolley car)[C](有轨)电车;take a ～ 乘电车

transact / trænˈzækt / vt. 办理,处理;商谈,商议;做(生意):～ private business 处理私事/～ some business 成交几笔生意

transcend / trænˈsend / vt. ❶超越,超出(经验、理性、信念等)的范围:～ self 超越自我/ The conflict between the two countries ～ed ideology. 这两个国家之间的冲突超出意识形态的范围。同 exceed ❷优于,胜过,超过;克服:～ natural conditions 战胜自然条件 / transcend obstacles 扫除障碍

transect / trænˈsekt / vt. 横切,横断

transfer Ⅰ / trænsˈfɜː(r) / v. (-ferred; -ferring) ❶转移;转换:～ wasteland into rich fields 变荒地为良田 同 change, shift ❷调动,使…转学;转车:Jack ～red to a new school last term. 上学期杰克转到一所新学校去了。同 move, transport ❸转让 Ⅱ / ˈtrænsfə / n. 转移;转让;转车;转账:～ fee 转让费 / ～ company 转运公司 / make a ～ 转让;转账 / Do you want a ～ at the next station? 下一站你要转车吗? 派 transferable adj.

transform / trænsˈfɔːm / v. ❶使转换;使变换:A steam engine ～s heat into energy. 蒸汽机使热变成能。同 turn, resolve ❷改变,改

造;改革:～ educational system 改革教育制度 / ～ one's world outlook 改造自己的世界观 同 change, reform 派 transformable adj.

transformation / ˌtrænsfəˈmeɪʃn / n. [U]变化,转变;改造,改革:economic ～ 经济改革 / social ～ 社会改革 同 change, reform

transistor / trænˈsɪstə(r) / n. [C](电子)晶体管

transit / ˈtrænzɪt / Ⅰ n. [U]❶载运,运输:～ by rail 铁路运输 / thorough ～ 全程运输 ❷公共交通运输系统;公共交通设备:public ～ 公共运输系统 Ⅱ vi. 通过,经过,越过

transition / trænˈsɪʃn, trænˈzɪʃn / n. 过渡;转变;变迁 同 passing, change

translate / trænsˈleɪt / v. 翻译:～ from English into Chinese 英译汉 同 interpret, turn

translation / trænsˈleɪʃn / n. ❶[U] 翻译: free ～ (literal) 意译(直译) / word-for-word ～逐字翻译 同 version ❷[C]译文;译本: This is the French ～ of the contract. 这是合同的法文译本。/ Have you read the ～ of *Gone with the Wind*? 你读过《飘》的译本吗?

translator / trænsˈleɪtə(r) / n. [C]翻译者

辨析
translator 一般指书面翻译者,**interpreter** 指口头翻译者。

transmission / trænsˈmɪʃn / n. [U]传送;传递;传导 同 sending, delivery

transmit / trænsˈmɪt / vt. (-mitted; -mitting) 传送,传达;发射;播送:～ a disease 传播疾病 / ～ news by radio 用无线电发送消息 / ～ TV programs 传送电视节目 同 send, broadcast

transnational / trænsˈnæʃ(ə)nəl / adj. 超国界的;跨国的:～ ideologies 超越国界的意识形态

transparency / trænsˈpærənsi / n. ❶[U]透明(性);透明度;透光度:atmospheric ～ 大气透明度 / market ～ 市场透明度 ❷[C]透明正片,幻灯片,透明物:a colour ～ 彩色幻灯片

transparent / trænsˈpærənt / adj. ❶透明的,透光的;清澈的,明净的:Those ～ curtains will never keep the light out. 那些透明窗帘根本挡不了光。/ A good vinegar is clear and ～. 优质醋是晶莹剔透的。❷显而易见的,易识破的,易觉察的:After the war, he came to me pretending to be my nephew, but it was a ～ fraud. 战后他来到我跟前，自称是我的侄子，这显然是个骗局。

transplant / træns'plɑːnt / v. 移植；移种 同 remove

transport Ⅰ / træn'spɔːt / vt. 运送；运输：～ goods by lorry 用卡车运输货物 同 transfer, move Ⅱ / 'trænspɔːt / n. [U]运送；运输：lose in ～ 在运输中丢失 / ～ charges 运费 / ～ network 运输网 / ～ system 运输系统 同 transfer, delivery

transportation / ˌtrænspɔː'teiʃn / n. [U]运输；运送：～ company 运输公司 / ～ permit 运输许可证 / air ～ 空运 / water and land ～ 水陆运输

transverse / 'trænzvɜːs, 'trænsvɜːs / Ⅰ adj. 横的，横向的，横断的，横截的，横切的 Ⅱ n. [C] 横向物，横断面

trap / træp / Ⅰ n. 捕捉机；陷阱：caught in a ～ 掉入陷阱 / 落入圈套 / fall into a ～ 堕入圈套 / get out of a ～ 摆脱圈套 / set a ～ 设圈套 Ⅱ v. (trapped, trapping)用捕捉机捕捉；设陷阱捕捉；诱捕 同 catch

travel / 'trævl / Ⅰ v. (travelled 或 traveled; travelling 或 traveling)❶旅行；游历：～ round the world 环球旅行 同 tour, voyage 反 stay, remain ❷移动；行进：Light ～s faster than sound. 光比声音传播快。同 move, go Ⅱ n. [U]旅行；游历：He is fond of ～. 他喜欢游历。同 journey, tour

tread / tred / Ⅰ v. (trod/trɒd/, trodden /'trɒdn/ 或 trod) ❶踏，践踏，踩碎：～ out a fire 把火踏灭 / Don't ～ on the seedlings. 别踏到幼苗。同 stamp ❷行走(于…)同 walk Ⅱ n. 踏步，脚步声 同 pace, step

treasure / 'treʒə(r) / Ⅰ n. ❶宝物；财富：The pirates buried their ～. 海盗们把他们的财宝埋起来了。同 wealth, savings ❷珍品；珍藏品：The National Gallery has many priceless art ～s. 国家艺术馆有许多无价的艺术珍品。同 jewel Ⅱ v. ❶储藏；珍藏：～ sth. up in one's memory 铭记某事 同 store, save ❷重视；珍爱：～ sb. 's friendship 珍视某人的友谊 同 value

treasury / 'treʒəri / n. [C] ❶金库，宝库；库房，珍藏室：financial ～金库 ❷国库：municipal ～市(省)库 ❸(T-)(国家)财政部；财政官

员：Treasury Department(美国)财政部

treat / triːt / Ⅰ v. ❶对待 同 consider, regard/ ～ as 看待，视为 ～ sb. as equals 平等待人，平等相处/Don't ～ me as a guest. 别把我当客人看待。❷治疗：Which doctor is ～ing her for her illness? 哪位医生在为她治病？同 remedy ❸款待；招待：～ sb. to sth. 招待某人吃什么东西(做某事)；He ～ed me to a good dinner. 他请我吃了一顿美餐。/ I'll ～ myself to a bottle of wine. 我自己要享用一瓶酒。/ Father ～ed us to sea food last Sunday. 上星期天爸爸请我们吃海鲜。同 entertain Ⅱ n. 款待；请客 同 entertainment

treatment / 'triːtmənt / n. 对待；待遇；治疗：The wounded are under ～ in hospital. 伤员正在医院接受治疗。/ He soon recovered under the doctor's ～. 经过医生的治疗，他不久就痊愈了。/ medical ～ 药物疗法/ psychological ～ 心理(精神)疗法 同 management, remedy

treaty / 'triːti / n. [C]条约；协定：a peace ～ 和约 / a non-aggression ～ 互不侵犯条约 / break a trade ～ 违反贸易条约 / conclude a ～ with 与…缔结条约 / The two countries signed a peace ～. 两国签署了和平条约。同 agreement, negotiation

tree / triː / n. [C]树木：Christmas ～ 圣诞树/ fruit ～ 果树/ in a ～ 在树上

tremble / 'trembl / vi. ❶(因恐惧、愤怒、寒冷等)发抖，颤抖：His voice ～d with anger. 他的声音因愤怒而发颤。同 shake, shiver ❷摇曳，摇晃；微动：The bridge ～d as the heavy lorry crossed it. 那辆沉重的货车驶过桥时，桥在摇晃。同 rock, vibrate Ⅱ n. 哆嗦；震颤；发抖：There was a ～ in his voice. 他的声音有一点发颤。

tremendous / trə'mendəs / adj. 极大的；巨大的：～ differences 极大的差异 / travel at a ～ speed 高速运行 / We are making ～ efforts to learn English. 我们正做出极大的努力学好英语。同 huge, vast 派 tremendously adv.

trend / trend / Ⅰ vi. 趋向；倾向：The river ～s towards the east. 这条河向东流。My opinion ～s towards his. 我与他的意见趋于一致。同 tend, incline Ⅱ n. [C]倾向；趋势：～ of thought 思潮 / No one can change the ～ of history. 没有人能够改变历史趋势。同 direction, tendency

trial / ˈtraɪəl / n. ❶试用;试验:by ～ and error 反复试验 / give a new typist a ～ 试用新打字员 同 test, experiment ❷磨炼;艰苦 同 suffering, hardship ❸受审:The ～ lasted a week. 审讯持续了一个星期。／**be on ～ for sth.** 因某事受审:He was on ～ for stealing. 他因偷盗而受到审判。

triangle / ˈtraɪæŋgl / n. [C]三角形

tribal / ˈtraɪbl / adj. 部落的

tribe / traɪb / n. [C]部落;宗族 同 family, race

tribute / ˈtrɪbjuːt / n. ❶[C;U](表示敬意的)礼物;颂词,称赞:pay ～ to sb.'s achievements 赞颂某人所取得的成就 / send floral ～ 献花 ❷[C]有效(或有价值)的标志:His victory in the championship was a ～ to his persistence. 他夺冠成功说明他坚持不懈的努力没有白费。

trick / trɪk / Ⅰ n. [C] ❶诡计;计谋;欺诈手段:He got the money from me by a ～. 他使用诡计从我这儿取得这笔钱。同 deceit, trap ❷恶作剧;戏弄:play a ～ on sb. 开某人的玩笑 同 joke Ⅱ vt. 哄骗;欺诈:They ～ed the boy into telling them the truth. 他们哄骗那孩子说出了真相。同 deceive, mislead

trickle / ˈtrɪkl / Ⅰ v. (使)滴流;(使)淌:Blood ～d from the wound. 鲜血从伤口流出。同 drip, drop Ⅱ n. 滴;细流 同 drip, drop

trifle / ˈtraɪfl / n. [C]小事;琐事:Don't quarrel over ～s. 别为小事争吵。

trifling / ˈtraɪflɪŋ / adj. ❶不重要的,无足轻重的;微不足道的,没有多少价值:matters of ～ importance 无足轻重的事务 ❷轻浮的,轻佻的

trilateral / traɪˈlætərəl / adj. ❶三边的:a ～ figure 三边形 ❷三方的;三国的:～ negotiations 三方谈判

trim / trɪm / Ⅰ adj. 整齐的;整洁的 Ⅱ vt. (trimmed; trimming) 修剪;整修:～ one's hair 修剪头发 / ～ the branches off a tree 把树上的枝修掉 / ～ a dress with lace 给衣服饰花边 / The gardener ～med the trees into good shape. 花工把树剪得很美。同 adjust, arrange

trip / trɪp / n. [C]旅行;(尤指)远足:a ～ to the seaside 去海滨远足 / a weekend ～ 周末旅行 / **on a ～** 在旅行:The old couple are on a ～ in France. 那对老年夫妻在法国旅行。同 journey, excursion

triple / ˈtrɪpl / Ⅰ adj. ❶三倍的;三重的:take a ～ dose of the medicine 服三倍剂量的药 / The attention we received had a ～ effect. 我们所受到的关注具有三重作用。❷由三部分组成的:the ～ entrance of a cave 三叠洞口 Ⅱ vi. ❶增至三倍,增加两倍:In four years the property almost ～d in value. 四年内,财产几乎增值了两倍。

triumph / ˈtraɪəmf / Ⅰ n. 成功;胜利:return home in ～ 凯旋 同 success, victory 反 failure, defeat Ⅱ vi. 获胜;成功:She ～ed over evil. 她战胜了邪恶。同 succeed, win 反 fail, lose 派 triumphant adj.

trivial / ˈtrɪvɪəl / adj. 无价值的,不重要的;琐细的,轻微的:His death in 1941 was due to a ～ mishap. 他 1941 年死于一桩不幸的小事故。／ One or two of them are so ～ that really I am ashamed to mention them. 其中有一两点是不值得说的,我提到这些,实在觉得惭愧。

trolleybus / ˈtrɒlibʌs / n. [C]无轨电车

troop / truːp / Ⅰ n. ❶士兵;军队 同 soldiers, army ❷(人或动物的)一群,一队:a ～ of children 一群儿童 同 group, crowd Ⅱ v. (用复数主语)成群结队而行 同 march, parade

tropic / ˈtrɒpɪk / n. ❶(the ～s)热带地区 ❷回归线

tropical / ˈtrɒpɪkl / adj. 热带的;炎热的:～ climate 热带气候 / ～ crops 热带作物

trot / trɒt / vi. & n. (马)小跑;慢跑 同 jog

trouble / ˈtrʌbl / Ⅰ n. ❶忧虑;苦恼;困难;麻烦 同 worry, difficulty / **in ～** 处于苦难中;在困境中:A person with good manners never laughs at people when they are in ～. 一个有礼貌的人决不会嘲笑处于困境中的人们。**ask (look) for ～** 自找麻烦;自讨苦吃 **get into ～** 陷入困境:Be careful or you'll get into ～. 仔细一点,否则你会遇到麻烦的。**get out of ～** 摆脱困境:You may ask your teacher to help you get out of the ～. 你可以请老师帮助你摆脱困境。**make ～** 闹事,捣乱 ❷痛苦;疾病 同 pain, illness ❸动乱;纠纷;风潮 同 disorder, instability 反 calm, peace Ⅱ v. ❶使忧愁;使苦恼;使不适:be ～d by bad news 为坏消息而感到苦恼 / What ～s me is that he is often late for work. 使我感到苦恼的是他总是上班

迟到。同 worry, upset 反 calm, please ❷麻烦；使费神：May I ～ you to post the letter? 麻烦你帮我寄这封信好吗？同 bother, disturb

troublesome / 'trʌblsəm / adj. 令人烦恼的；讨厌的；困难的：a ～ child 使人烦恼的孩子／a ～ problem 让人烦恼的问题同 annoying, difficult 反 calming, simple

trousers / 'traʊzəz / n. (pl.) 裤子：a pair of ～ 一条裤子

truant / 'tru:ənt / n. 逃避责任者；(尤指)逃学者：to play ～ 逃学

truck / trʌk / n. [C]货车；卡车 同 lorry, van

true / tru: / adj. ❶真实的；真正的：be ～ in word 遵守诺言／be ～ to life(nature) 逼真／Is the news ～? 这消息确实吗？同 genuine, real 反 untrue, false / **come** ～ (希望、理想等)实现：At last, his dream came ～. 他的理想终于实现了。❷忠诚的；忠实的：～ hearted adj.忠实的；诚实的 同 faithful, loyal 反 faithless, disloyal ❸准确的：～ judgment 准确的判断 同 accurate, correct 反 inaccurate, incorrect

truly / 'tru:li / adv. 诚实地；真正地：a ～ beautiful picture 一幅真正美丽的图画

trumpet / 'trʌmpɪt / Ⅰ n. [C] ❶吹喇叭；号：blow(sound) a ～ 吹喇叭／～ call 集合号／**blow one's own** ～ (喻)自吹自擂同 bugle, horn ❷喇叭形物；喇叭形扩音器；助听器 ❸ (用单数)(象等发出的)喇叭似的叫声 Ⅱ v. ❶吹喇叭 同 blare, blow ❷大声宣告，到处宣扬 同 announce, noise abroad ❸吹嘘，自夸 同 boast, brag

trunk / trʌŋk / n. [C] ❶树干 同 stem ❷躯干 同 body ❸(建筑的)主要部分 ❹象鼻子 ❺干线：～ line 铁路干线／～ road 干道

trust / trʌst / Ⅰ n. ❶信任；信赖：She doesn't place much ～ in his promises. 她不大相信他的诺言。同 confidence, faith 反 distrust, mistrust ❷责任；义务：a position of great ～ 责任重大的职位 同 duty, responsibility Ⅱ v. 信任；相信：He is not the sort of man to be ～ed. 他不是一个可靠的人。同 believe 反 distrust, mistrust / ～ **in** 相信；信仰／～ **to** 依赖；依靠：You ～ to your memory too much. 你过于依赖你的记忆了。派 trustful, trusty adj.

truth / tru:θ / n. (pl. truths/tru:ðz, tru:θs/) ❶[U]真实性；真相：He didn't tell us the ～. 他没有对我们说真话。／To tell the ～, I for-

got all about your request. 说实话，我把你的要求全忘了。同 reality 反 untruth ❷[C]真理：the ～s of science 科学的真理 同 fact, principle 反 fiction

try / traɪ / Ⅰ v. ❶努力：He tried to finish it, but failed. 他努力要完成它，但失败了。同 strive, endeavour ／ **one's best** 尽某人最大努力：I'll ～ my best to finish it in time. 我要尽最大努力及时完成这事。❷试；试用：Try how far you can jump. 试试看你能跳多远。同 attempt, test ／ ～ **on** 试穿：She tried on several pairs of shoes before she found one she liked. 她试穿了好几双鞋子后才找到一双喜欢的。～ **out** ①试验：The scientists tried out thousands of chemicals before they found the right one. 科学家们试验了数千种化学物品才找到合适的那种。②参加选拔：Shirley will ～ out for the lead in the play. 雪莉将参加选拔主角的演出。❸审问；审判：He was tried and found guilty. 他受审判并被认定有罪。同 inquire Ⅱ n. 尝试；试验；努力：Let me have another ～ at it. 让我再试一次。同 attempt, effort

用 法

try 后跟动名词表示"试试是否行得通；看看效果如何"，强调的是试用某种方法：Try turning it counter-clockwise and see whether it works. 你把它按反时针方向转一下，看行不行。try 后跟不定式表示"试着去做"，强调做某事有困难：He tried to start the machine but failed. 他竭力想开动机器，但失败了。

tsunami / tsu:'nɑ:mi / 海啸，海震

tub / tʌb / n. [C]桶；盆；浴缸，浴盆

tube / tju:b / n. ❶(金属、塑料或橡皮等制的)管；管：a ～ of toothpaste 一管牙膏／test ～ 试管同 pipe ❷电子管；显像管 ❸地铁；Will you go to the station by ～? 你乘地铁去车站吗？／He always takes the ～ to work. 他总是乘地铁上班。同 subway

tuck / tʌk / vt. 把…夹入；把…藏入 同 insert, thrust

Tuesday / 'tju:zdi / n. 星期二

tug / tʌg / Ⅰ v. (tugged; tugging)用力拉，用力拖：We ～ged so hard that the rope broke. 我们用力太猛使得绳子拉断了。同 drag, pull 反 push Ⅱ n. ❶拉，扯，拖：The naughty boy gave her sister's hair a ～. 那顽皮的男孩扯了一下

他姐姐的头发。同 pull 反 push ❷拖船

tuition / tju:'ɪʃn / n. [U] ❶教学；讲授；指导 同 instruction，education ❷学费：pay ～ 交学费

tulip / 'tju:lɪp / n. [C]郁金香

tumble / 'tʌmbl / vi. 摔倒；跌倒：The boy ～d off the bike. 那男孩从自行车上摔了下来。同 fall，drop 反 rise

tumo(u)r / 'tju:mə(r) / n. [C]肿瘤：benign ～ 良性肿瘤 / malignant ～ 恶性肿瘤 / remove a ～ 切除肿瘤

tune / tju:n / Ⅰ n. [C]❶曲，曲子；语调：whistle a popular ～ 用口哨吹流行曲子 / hum a ～ 哼曲子 同 melody / **call the** ～ 发号施令，任意指挥 change one's ～ 改变论调(态度) **in** ～ 音调准确：This piano is in ～. 这架钢琴音调准确。**out of** ～ 音调不准确，走调：He sang out of ～. 他唱走了调。**to the** ～ **of** ... 和着…的曲调 ❷和谐；协调，一致：Bill is in ～ with his classmates. 比尔与同学们和谐相处。同 harmony Ⅱ vt. 调谐，调音；使和谐；使一致 同 adjust，adapt

tunnel / 'tʌnl / n. [C]地道；隧道；坑道：dig a ～ 挖隧道(地道)

turbulent / 'tɜ:bjulənt / adj. ❶骚乱的，骚动的；动乱，动荡的；混乱的：～ political and social conditions 动荡的政治和社会状况 / the ～ years of adolescence 处在青春活力汹涌澎湃的年代 ❷湍流的，紊流的，涡旋的：～ fluctuations 紊动 派 turbulence n.

Turkey / 'tɜ:ki / n. 土耳其

turkey / 'tɜ:ki / n. ❶[C]火鸡：roast a ～ 烤火鸡 ❷[U]火鸡肉

turn / tɜ:n / Ⅰ ❶(使)旋转；(使)移动 同 rotate，spin ❷(使)改变：My hair has ～ed grey. 我的头发变灰白了。同 change，transform 反 remain，stay / **from side to side** (把身体)转过来转过去：He ～ed from side to side and couldn't go to sleep. 他翻来覆去不能入睡。～ **against** 反对；反感：Those who were once for him have turned against him. 那些原来支持他的人现在都转而反对他。～ **down** 拒绝：He tried to join the police but was ～ed down because of poor physique. 他试图加入警察队伍，但因体格差而遭到拒绝。～ **in** ①归还：He ～ed in his badge and quit. 他归还徽章，辞掉职务。②上交，交出：You'd better ～ in the

money that you found. 你最好把捡到的钱上交。～ **into** 变成，翻译成～ **off** 关上(水、气、电等)：The tap won't ～ off，and there's water all over the floor. 龙头关不上，满地都是水。～ **on** 打开(水、气、电等)：Please ～ the light on for me. It's getting dark. 请把灯给我打开，天黑了。～ **over** 翻：I heard the clock，but then I ～ed over and went back to sleep. 我听到了钟声，但我翻过身又睡着了。/ Please ～ over and read the directions on the back. 请翻页，读背后的说明。～ **to** ① 转向：Turn to me a little more. I can't see your eyes in the shadow. 向我这边转一点，在阴暗中我看不清你的眼睛。②翻到：Please ～ to page 33. 请翻到 33 页。③求助于：When he's in trouble，he always ～s to his sister. 他有麻烦时总是求助于他的姐姐。Ⅱ n. ❶旋转；转动：a few ～s of the handle 把手的数次转动 同 roll，swing ❷时机，机会 同 chance，opportunity ❸轮班，轮次：It's your ～ to read now，John. 约翰，现在该你读了。同 shift / **in** ～ 接连地；按顺序地：The boys were summoned in ～ to see the examiner. 男孩子们依次被召去见那位考官。**by** ～**s** 轮流地：He went hot and cold by ～s. 他时而发热，时而发冷。

turnabout / 'tɜ:nəˌbaut / n. [C]转向；转身；向后转：a car capable of a quick ～能急转弯的小汽车 ❷[C](政策、观点等的) 突然转变，突然变化，变卦：a sudden ～ on the policy 政策的突然改变

turnip / 'tɜ:nɪp / n. [C]芜菁；萝卜

turnover / 'tɜ:nˌəuvə(r) / n. ❶营业额；成交量：the ～ of foreign trade 对外贸易额/ The company's ～ has increased by 135%. 公司的营业额增加了 135%。❷(货物或人员等的)流通，流动：high ～ and vacancy rates 很高的流动率和闲置率

turtle / 'tɜ:tl / n. [C]海龟；玳瑁

tutor / 'tju:tə(r) / n. [C]家庭教师；(大学)导师：Do you need a ～? 你需要请家庭教师吗? 同 coach，instructor 反 pupil，student Ⅱ vt. 教，指导同 coach，instruct 反 study，learn

TV / ˌti:'vi: / n. (＝television)电视，电视机：～ play 电视剧 / ～ set 电视机 / ～ festival 电视节

twelfth / twelfθ / Ⅰ num. 第十二；十二分之一 Ⅱ adj. 第十二的；十二分之一的

twelve / twelv / Ⅰ num. 十二，12 Ⅱ adj. 十二

个(的)

twentieth / ˈtwentiiθ / Ⅰ num. 第二十；二十分之一 Ⅱ adj. 第二十的；二十分之一的

twenty / ˈtwenti / Ⅰ num. 二十，20 Ⅱ adj. 二十个(的)

twice / twaɪs / adv. 两倍；两次：I've been there once or ～. 我去过那儿一两次。

twig / twɪg / n. [C]小枝；嫩枝

twilight / ˈtwaɪlaɪt / n. [U]黎明；曙光；黄昏：I like to take a walk at ～. 我喜欢在黄昏时散步。同 dawn,dusk

twin / twɪn / Ⅰ adj. ❶成双的,成对的：They ordered a room with ～ beds. 他们订了一间有两张床的房间。同 double,paired ❷孪生的,双胞胎的：～ brothers (sisters)孪生兄弟(姐妹) Ⅱ n. [C]孪生儿之一

twinkle / ˈtwɪŋkl / Ⅰ v. 闪烁；闪耀：stars that ～ in the sky 天上闪烁的星星 同 flash,shine Ⅱ n. 闪烁；闪亮 同 flash,shine

twist / twɪst / v. ❶转动；旋动 同 spin,rotate ❷捻,搓：She knew how to ～ threads into a rope. 她知道怎样把线搓成绳子。同 wring,curl 反 untwist ❸扭伤；扭曲：I fell and ～ed my ankle. 我摔伤了脚踝。同 wrench,turn ❹歪曲；曲解：Please don't ～ what I said. 请别曲解我说的话。同 distort 派 twister n.；twisty adj.

two / tuː / Ⅰ num. 二,2 Ⅱ adj. 两个(的)

type / taɪp / Ⅰ n. [C] ❶典型；模范 同 model,sample ❷样式；类型：It's a ～ of music I enjoy. 那是一种我喜欢的音乐。同 kind,sort Ⅱ v. 打字：～ a letter 用打字机打一封信

typewrite / ˈtaɪpraɪt / v. (typewrote /ˈtaɪprəʊt/,typewritten/ˈtaɪpˌrɪtn/)打字；用打字机打字

typewriter / ˈtaɪpraɪtə(r) / n. [C]打字机

typhoon / taɪˈfuːn / n. [C] 台风：A ～ hit (struck) the coastal area. 台风袭击了沿海地区。

typical / ˈtɪpɪkl / adj. 有代表性的；典型的：～ character 典型人物 / She is ～ of her generation. 她是她这一代人的典型。同 representative,standard 反 atypical,unusual 派 typically adv.；typicality n.

typist / ˈtaɪpɪst / n. [C]打字员

tyranny / ˈtɪrəni / n. [U]暴政；专制；残暴 同 dictatorship,cruelty

tyrant / ˈtaɪrənt / n. [C]暴君 同 dictator

tyre / ˈtaɪə(r) / n. (＝tire)[C]轮胎；车胎

U u

UFO / ˈjuːfəʊ / n. (= unidentified flying object) [C]不明飞行物：find a ～ 发现不明飞行物

ugly / ˈʌɡli / adj. (-ier,-iest) ❶难看的；丑陋的：～ furniture 难看的家具 / an ～ man 丑陋的人 圆 unbeautiful, unlovely 囻 beautiful, lovely ❷可怕的；讨厌的：～ smell 讨厌的气味 圆 horrible 囻 good 飔 uglily adv.; ugliness n.

UK, U. K. (= the United Kingdom) 英国

ultimate / ˈʌltɪmət / adj. 最后的；最终的：the ～ aim 最终目的 / ～ ends of the world 天涯海角 / ～ strength 极限强度 圆 final, last 囻 initial, first 飔 ultimately adv. 最终；最后

ultrasonic / ˌʌltrəˈsɒnɪk / adj. 超声的；超音速的

ultraviolet / ˌʌltrəˈvaɪələt / I adj. 紫外的 II n. 紫外光；紫外辐射

umbrella / ʌmˈbrelə / n. [C]伞：close (shut) an ～ 收起伞 / open (put up) an ～ 撑开伞 / under the ～ of 在…的庇护下

UN, U. N. (= the United Nations) 联合国

unable / ʌnˈeɪbl / adj. 不能的(只作表语用)：The boy is ～ to walk. 这男孩不会走路。圆 incapable 囻 able, capable

unacceptable / ˌʌnəkˈseptəbl / adj. 难以接受的；不称心的 圆 offensive, undesirable

unaccountable / ˌʌnəˈkaʊntəbl / adj. ❶无法理解的，难以说明的；莫名其妙的：some ～ phenomena 一些难以解释的现象/ For some ～ reason, she did nto attend her daughter's wedding. 不知什么原因，她没有出席女儿的婚礼。❷不负责任的；无责任的：As a subordinate, I am surely ～ for the incident. 作为下属，此事肯定没我什么责任。

unanimous / juːˈnænɪməs / adj. 全体一致的；意见相同的，无异议的：the ～ demand 一致的要求/ The kids were ～ for a picnic. 孩子们一致赞成去野餐。飔 unanimity n.; unanimously adv.

unattached / ˌʌnəˈtætʃt / adj. ❶不联结的，不连接的：an ～ building 独立式的大楼 ❷无隶属关系的，非附属的，独立的：The nursery is ～ to any primary school. 这家幼儿园不附属于任何一所小学。❸未婚的；未订婚的

unavailing / ˌʌnəˈveɪlɪŋ / adj. 无效的；无用的；徒劳的：～ efforts 徒劳

unaware / ˌʌnəˈweə(r) / adj. 没有发觉的；不知道的 圆 ignorant, unconscious

unbalanced / ˌʌnˈbælənst / adj. 不平衡的；不安定的

unbearable / ʌnˈbeərəbl / adj. 难以忍受的；不能容忍的

unbind / ʌnˈbaɪnd / vt. (unbound,unbound) ❶解开；松开：Before going to bed she unbound her hair. 上床之前，她把头发松开。❷使解除束缚，使自由，解放；释放：～ the prisoners 释放囚犯

unburden / ʌnˈbɜːdən / vt. ❶使卸去负担，卸去…的包袱：～ a donkey 卸去驴的驮负 ❷使消除忧愁，使解除思想负担：Talking to a psychiatrist is a good way of ～ing herself of a lot of worries. 同精神病医生交谈是让她摆脱诸多烦恼的一条有效途径。

uncertain / ʌnˈsɜːtən / adj. ❶不肯定的；不确定的：The time of their arrival is ～. 他们到达的时间还未确定。/ I am ～ of (about, as to) his plans for the holiday. 我不确知他度假的计划如何。/ We are ～ that he will come in time. 我们不确定他能否及时来。圆 doubtful, indefinite 囻 certain, definite ❷易变的；无常的；靠不住的：～ weather 变化无常的天气 / Jack's father is a man with ～ temper. 杰克的父亲是个喜怒无常的人。圆 irresolute, wavering 囻 certain, resolute 飔 uncertainly adv.

uncle / ˈʌŋkl / n. [C]伯父；姨父；叔父；舅父；姑父

U

unclear /ˌʌnˈklɪə(r)/ *adj.* 不明白的;不清楚的:It was ～ to us why they lost the game. 他们为什么输了比赛,我们不清楚。

uncomfortable /ʌnˈkʌmftəbl/ *adj.* 不舒服的;不自在的,不安的 同 unpleasant,disturbed 反 comfortable

uncomplaining /ˌʌnkəmˈpleɪnɪŋ/ *adj.* 没有怨言的;不发牢骚的;能忍受的 同 patient,tolerant 反 complaining

unconditional /ˌʌnkənˈdɪʃənəl/ *adj.* 无条件的;无保留的;无限制的;绝对的,完全的:an ～ support 无条件支持/Then the real undertaking at present is the ～ freeing of the people. 那么目前真正要做的是将这些人无条件释放。

unconscious /ʌnˈkɒnʃəs/ *adj.* 失去知觉的;无意识的;不知不觉的:He is still ～ after the accident. 事故后他仍然没有知觉。/ She is ～ of the danger. 她并未意识到危险。/ He is ～ that he has done wrong. 他没有意识到自己做错了事。 同 insensible,senseless 反 conscious 派 unconsciousness *n.*

uncontrollable /ˌʌnkənˈtrəʊləbl/ *adj.* 难以控制的,控制不住的;无法管束的:in ～ fury 怒不可遏/ They mourned their brother with ～ grief. 兄弟之死使他们悲痛欲绝。

uncountable /ʌnˈkaʊntəbl/ *adj.* ❶无数的,数不清的:～ wealth 无法估量的财富/ ～ shingles devastated by white ants 被白蚁咬坏的无数屋顶板 ❷(名词)不可数的,不具数的

uncover /ʌnˈkʌvə(r)/ *v.* 揭开…的盖子;(喻)揭露:The police have ～ed a plot against the President. 警察局已破获一个反对总统的阴谋。 同 open,reveal 反 cover

undecided /ˌʌndɪˈsaɪdɪd/ *adj.* ❶未定的,未决的;The whole question is still ～. 整个问题尚未决定。/ The outcome of the election was left ～. 选举结果尚不明朗。❷犹豫不定的;优柔寡断的:How could he make it, being so ～? 他这样优柔寡断的,怎么能成事呢?

undeniable /ˌʌndɪˈnaɪəbl/ *adj.* ❶不可否认的,无可争辩的;毋庸置疑的;确凿无疑的:an ～ proof 不可否认的证据/ Mr. Jones's good intentions are ～. 琼斯先生的好意毋庸置疑。❷公认优秀的;无可挑剔的:an ～ masterpiece 一部公认的优秀作品

under /ˈʌndə(r)/ *prep.* ❶(表示位置)在…下面,在…底下:～ the table 在桌子下面;私下地,私下买通 / stand ～ a tree 站在树下面 同 below,beneath 反 above,over ❷(表示级别、数量、标准等)低于…,在…之下:students ～ sixteen years of age 不满16周岁的学生 同 lower,inferior 反 higher,superior ❸(表示条件)在…之下:～ such conditions 在这些条件下/ ～ the leadership of the Party 在党的领导下 ❹(表示过程)在…中:problem ～ decision 在考虑中的问题/ bridge ～ construction 建设中的大桥

underdeveloped /ˌʌndədɪˈveləpt/ *adj.* 不发达的;落后的 同 backward 反 developed

underestimate /ˌʌndərˈestɪmeɪt/ *vt.* 低估;看轻 反 overestimate

undergo /ˌʌndəˈɡəʊ/ *vt.* (underwent,undergone) 经历;遭受;忍受:The explorers had to ～ much suffering. 探险者必须忍受许多苦难。 同 suffer,endure

undergraduate /ˌʌndəˈɡrædʒʊət/ *n.* [C]大学生;尚未取得学位的大学生

underground Ⅰ /ˌʌndəˈɡraʊnd/ *adv.* 在地下;秘密地 Ⅱ /ˈʌndəɡraʊnd/ *adj.* 秘密的;(喻)地下的:the ～ activities 地下活动 同 secret Ⅲ /ˈʌndəɡraʊnd/ *n.* 地面下层;地下空间;～ railway 地下铁道 / travel by ～ 乘地铁旅行

underlie /ˌʌndəˈlaɪ/ *vt.* (underlay,underlain; underlying) ❶位于…之下;置于…之下;Shale ～ the coal. 煤层底下是页岩层。❷构成…的基础;是…的潜在根源;使发生;支承;潜存于…之下:It must ～ everything. 一切都必须以此为基础。

underline /ˌʌndəˈlaɪn/ *vt.* 在…下画线:Please ～ the important sentences while reading. 请一边阅读一边在重要的句子下面画线。

undermine /ˌʌndəˈmaɪn/ *vt.* 逐渐损坏:His health was ～d by drinking. 饮酒使他的健康每况愈下。 同 weaken

underneath /ˌʌndəˈniːθ/ *adv.* 在下面;在底下:He went over and found a letter ～ the door. 他走过去发现门下面有一封信。 同 below,under 反 over

understand /ˌʌndəˈstænd/ *v.* (understood /ˌʌndəˈstʊd/,understood) 懂;了解;领会:～ French 懂法语 同 comprehend,see 反 misunderstand

understanding /ˌʌndəˈstændɪŋ/ Ⅰ *n.* ❶[U]

理解力;判断力;beyond one's ～ 超过某人的理解力 同 comprehension,sense 反 misunderstanding ❷谅解;体谅;arrive(come to,reach) an ～ with sb. 取得某人的谅解/ mutual ～ 互相理解 同 forgiveness Ⅱ adj. 了解的;善解人意的;an ～ man 善解人意的人/ He nodded with an ～ smile. 他点点头,会心地笑了。

undertake / ˌʌndə'teɪk / v. (undertook,undertaken) ❶担任;答应,许诺;担保:He undertook to finish the job by Friday. 他答应星期五之前做完那项工作。同 agree,promise ❷开始;着手;进行 同 begin,start 反 drop,stop

undertaking / ˌʌndə'teɪkɪŋ / n. [C] ❶任务;事业;企业:finance a cultural ～ 资助文化事业/ charitable ～s 慈善事业 ❷担保,保证;承诺,许诺:I must have a written ～ from you. 你必须给我写一份书面保证。/ discharge one's ～履行自己的诺言

undertone / 'ʌnɪtəʊn / n. [C] ❶低音;低声:talk in ～s 低声细气地谈话 ❷内在的性质(或气质、因素等);潜在的情感(或意思);含意,意味:praise with an ～ of envy 带着妒忌的口气夸奖/ There was an ～ of sadness in her gaiety. 她活泼中透出丝丝忧伤。

underwater / ˌʌndə'wɔːtə(r) / Ⅰ adj. (在)水下的;水下生长的;水下使用(或进行)的:an ～ camera 水下照相机/ an ～ explosion 水下爆炸 Ⅱ adv. 在水下;在水中:live ～ 生活在水中

underwear / 'ʌndəweə(r) / n. [U]内衣 同 underclothes,underclothing

undesirable / ˌʌndɪ'zaɪərəbl / adj. 令人不快的;讨厌的;不合意的;不受欢迎的;～ tendencies 不良倾向/ Some of these drugs have ～ side effects. 这中间有些药会产生不良副作用。

undeveloped / ˌʌndɪ'veləpt / adj. 未(充分)开发的;未发展的;不发达的;an ～ area 未开发地区/ ～ countries 不发达国家

undistinguished / ˌʌndɪ'stɪŋgwɪʃt / adj. 普通的,平凡的;无特色的;平庸的;an ～ background 普通的背景/ The suspension bridge is of ～ design. 这座索桥的设计毫无特色。

undo / ʌn'duː / vt. (undid,undone) ❶解开;打开;松开;～ a button 解开纽扣/ ～ a parcel 打开包裹/ ～ the string 解开绳子 同 open,loosen 反 close,fasten ❷取消;消除;使

恢复原状:What is done cannot be undone. 事已成定局,无可挽回(覆水难收)。同 cancel 反 do,produce

undoubted / ʌn'daʊtɪd / adj. 确定的;无疑的 同 certain,sure 反 doubtful,uncertain 派 undoubtedly adv.

undress / ˌʌn'dres / v. ❶脱去衣服;除去覆盖物 ❷揭露;暴露 同 expose,reveal

uneasy / ʌn'iːzi / adj. (身体)不舒服的;不安的,焦虑的;feel ～ about sb.'s future 担心某人的前途/ We grew ～ at their long absence. 对他们的长期缺席,我们渐感焦虑。同 unpleasant,upset 反 pleasant,relaxed

unemployed / ˌʌnɪm'plɔɪd / adj. 未被雇用的;无工作的;失业的;～ men 失业者 同 idle,jobless 反 employed

unemployment / ˌʌnɪm'plɔɪmənt / n. [U] 失业;失业状态

unequal / ʌn'iːkwəl / adj. ❶不平等的;an ～ distribution of opportunity 机会的分配不均 ❷不相等的;planks of ～ length 长度不等的厚板/ classes of ～ size 不同规模的班级 ❸不合适的;不相称的;不能胜任的:We felt that he was ～ to the task. 我们觉得他不能胜任这项工作。

unexpected / ˌʌnɪk'spektɪd / adj. 意料不到的;意外的;an ～ guest 不速之客/ an ～ result 意外的结果 同 accidental,sudden 反 expected

unfair / ˌʌn'feə(r) / adj. 不公平的;～ treatment 不公平的待遇 同 unjust,unreasonable 反 fair

unfavo(u)rable / ʌn'feɪvərəbl / adj. ❶不利的;不顺利的:The weather is ～ to our plans for a holiday. 这种天气对于我们安排假期颇为不利。❷相反的;反对的,不赞同的;an ～ view of the film 对影片的批评意见 ❸不讨人喜欢的;令人不愉快的:I hear he's in an ～ position with his boss. 我听说他同老板关系不好。

unfit / ʌn'fɪt / Ⅰ adj. 不适当的;不能胜任的:He is ～ to be a doctor. 他不适合当医生。同 unsuitable,unqualified 反 fit,qualified Ⅱ v. (-fitted;-fitting)使不适当;使不胜任 同 disable,disqualify 反 fit,qualify

unfold / ʌn'fəʊld / v. 展开;使呈现:He ～ed the letter and found it was from his mother. 他展开信一看,发现是他母亲的来信。同

spread, reveal 反 fold

unforgettable / ˌʌnfəˈgetəbl / adj. 难忘的：It is really an ～ party. 那真是一次难忘的聚会。

unfortunate / ʌnˈfɔːtʃənət / adj. ❶不幸的；倒霉的：These students were ～ enough to fail in the exam. 这些学生很不幸，考试没有及格。同 unhappy, unlucky 反 fortunate, lucky ❷遗憾的：It is ～ that they lost the game. 很遗憾他们比赛输了。同 regretable, sorry 反 fortunate 派 unfortunately adv.；unfortunateness n.

unfriendly / ʌnˈfrendli / adj. ❶不友好的，不友善的；冷漠的，有敌意的：an ～ nation 敌对国家 / be ～ to reform 反对改革 ❷不利的；不顺利的；不祥的：the ～ environment 不利的环境

ungrateful / ʌnˈgreitfl / adj. 不表示感激的；忘恩负义的 同 unthankful 反 grateful

unhappy / ʌnˈhæpi / adj. ❶不愉快的 同 miserable, sad 反 happy ❷不幸的 同 unfortunate 反 fortunate

unidentified / ˌʌnaiˈdentifaid / adj. 未被认出（或识别）的；无法辨认的；来路不明的；身份不明的：an ～ flying object 不明飞行物/ The words had been spoken by an ～ Greek poet. 这些话是位不知姓名的希腊诗人所言。

uniform / ˈjuːnifɔːm / Ⅰ n. 制服，put on (take off) the ～ 穿上（脱下）制服 / school ～（学生）校服 Ⅱ adj. 一样的，一致的；始终如一的：～ in size 大小相同 / The classrooms are ～ in size. 教室的大小相同。同 alike, same 反 different, unlike 派 uniformly adv.

uniformity / ˌjuːniˈfɔːməti / n. [U]一样，一律；均匀 同 sameness, stability

unify / ˈjuːnifai / vt. 统一；使成一体；使一致：～ a country 统一国家/unified exam 统考 同 unite 反 divide, separate

unimportant / ˌʌnimˈpɔːtənt / adj. 不重要的；无价值的 同 insignificant 反 important

union / ˈjuːniən / n. ❶[U]联合；合并：the ～ of the three towns 三个镇的合并 同 joining, unity 反 division, separation ❷[C]同盟；协会：the Students' Union 学生会 / trade ～ 工会 同 federation, league

unique / juˈniːk / adj. 唯一的，独一无二的：This stamp is ～. 这张邮票是独一无二的。/ The custom is ～ to China. 这种风俗是中国特有的。同 singular, matchless 反 common, usual

unit / ˈjuːnit / n. [C] ❶（计量的）单位：～ area

单位面积/～ price 单价 / The metre is a ～ of length. 米是长度单位。同 measure ❷（指构成整体的）单位：a research ～ 科研单位 ❸（机械等的）部件，元件 同 part, element

unite / juˈnait / v. ❶（使）联合；（使）结合：the common interests that ～ our two countries 我们两国联合的共同利益 同 unify, combine 反 divide, separate ❷协力，团结；一致行动：Let us ～ in fighting poverty and diseases. 让我们团结起来战胜贫穷和疾病。同 cooperate

united / juˈnaitid / adj. 联合的；团结的；统一的：the ～ front 统一战线 / the United Kingdom 联合王国，英国 / the United Nation 联合国 / the United States of America 美国 同 combined, unified

unity / ˈjuːnəti / n. 联合，结合；统一；协调，一致：The figure on the left spoils the ～ of the painting. 左边那个人像破坏了那幅画的协调性。/ National ～ is essential in time of war. 举国一致在战争时是必要的。同 union, wholeness 反 disunity, independence

universal / ˌjuːniˈvɜːsl / adj. ❶宇宙的；全世界的：The writer made a ～ travel. 那位作家做了环球旅行。同 worldwide, international 反 local ❷普遍的；全体的：～ truth 普遍真理 / be of ～ significance 有普遍意义 同 general, whole 反 individual, limited ❸通用的；万能的：the ～ language 通用语

universe / ˈjuːnivɜːs / n. 宇宙

university / ˌjuːniˈvɜːsəti / n. [C]大学 同 college

unjust / ʌnˈdʒʌst / adj. ❶不公正的 同 unfair, prejudiced 反 just ❷不诚实的；不忠的 同 dishonest, disloyal 反 honest, loyal

unkind / ʌnˈkaind / adj. 不亲切的；缺乏同情心的 同 cruel, unfriendly 反 kind, friendly

unknown / ʌnˈnəun / adj. 不为人知的；不出名的：I often receive letters from persons ～. 我常常收到一些陌生人的来信。/ a man ～ to me 我不认识的人/ ～ number 未知数/ ～ term 未知项 同 undiscovered, unnoted 反 noted, well-known

unlawful / ʌnˈlɔːfl / adj. 非法的；不正当的 同 illegal 反 lawful, legal

unless / ənˈles / conj. 若不；除非：You will fail ～ you work hard. 如果你不努力，你就会失败。I shall go ～ it rains. 如果不下雨我就去。

用法

❶unless 引起的从句的动词用现在时,不用将来时(见上面例子)。❷unless 引起的从句的主语和动词 be 有时可以省略:I shall not go unless invited. 除非收到邀请,不然我就不去。(省略 I am。)

unlike /ˌʌn'laɪk/ Ⅰ *prep.* 不像 反 like Ⅱ *adj.* 不同的;不像的:The two books are quite ～. 这两本书完全不同。同 different, dissimilar 反 alike, similar

unlikely /ˌʌn'laɪkli/ *adj.* 未必的;不大可能的:～ event 不大可能的事件/～ winner 不可能取胜的人/ He is ～ to succeed. 他未必会成功。/ It is ～ that he will pass the exam. 他不大可能通过考试。同 improbable 反 likely, probable

unlimited /ʌn'lɪmɪtɪd/ *adj.* 无限的;不定的 同 infinite, indefinite 反 limited, definite

unload /ˌʌn'ləʊd/ *v.* 卸下;卸货:～ a truck 卸车/～ cargo from a ship 从船上卸货 同 discharge, empty 反 load

unlock /ˌʌn'lɒk/ *vt.* 开锁;开启 同 open, unfasten 反 lock

unlucky /ʌn'lʌki/ *adj.* 不幸的;不祥的;倒霉的 同 miserable, unfortunate 反 lucky

unmatched /ʌn'mætʃt/ *adj.* ❶无比的,无与伦比的:an ～ success 空前的成功/ The research provides a model quite ～ so far. 这项研究提供了一个前所未有的模式。❷不相配的;不匹配的;不配对的:～ socks 不配对的袜子

unnatural /ʌn'nætʃərəl/ *adj.* ❶不合乎自然规律的;违反常规的;不正常的:Her character becomes ～. 她的性格变得很反常。/ There is something ～ about this strange and sudden friendship between the two men. 这两个人之间突如其来的奇怪友谊是有些蹊跷。❷不自然的,做作的,虚假的:She began to cry, and it was an ～, tearless sort of weeping. 她哭了起来,但是装模作样,没有一滴泪水。

unnecessary /ʌn'nesəsəri/ *adj.* 不必要的;多余的 同 needless, excessive 反 necessary

unpaid /ˌʌn'peɪd/ *adj.* 未付的;未偿还的 同 owing, unsettled 反 paid

unpleasant /ʌn'pleznt/ *adj.* 不愉快的;令人讨厌的 同 nasty, offensive 反 pleasant

unqualified /ʌn'kwɒlɪfaɪd/ *adj.* ❶不合格的,不能胜任的;不够格的:She was ～ for the job. 她不能胜任这项工作。❷绝对的,完全的:an ～ denial 完全否定

unravel /ʌn'rævəl/ *v.* ❶解开;散开;拆散:I had to ～ both sleeves since they had been knitted too small. 因为两只袖子织得太小了,我只好把它们都拆掉。/The settlement began to ～ in an embarrassingly short time. 令人尴尬的是,该协议没过多久就开始土崩瓦解了。❷(被)弄清;(被)解决:～ the mysteries 解开谜团/ Now, if we swing back to the previous questions, the poem will begin to ～. 现在,如果我们再回到过去看前面的问题,那这首诗的含义就会慢慢清楚了。

unreal /ˌʌn'rɪəl/ *adj.* 假的;不真实的:The story is ～. 这故事不真实。同 false, untrue 反 real, true

unreasonable /ʌn'riznəbl/ *adj.* 不讲道理的;不合理的:It is ～ to demand employees of working on weekends. 要求雇员在周末加班是不合理的。同 irrational, senseless 反 reasonable, rational

unroll /ʌn'rəʊl/ *v.* ❶铺开,展开:～ the picture and hang it up. 请把画展开挂起来。❷显露,显示,展现,呈现:The pleasant memories of a Spanish summer ～ed in my mind 在西班牙度过的夏日里种种赏心乐事在我脑海中展现

unsatisfactory /ˌʌnˌsætɪs'fæktəri/ *adj.* 不能令人满意的;不恰当的 同 disappointing 反 satisfactory

unseen /ˌʌn'siːn/ *adj.* 未看见的;看不见的 同 undiscovered, invisible 反 seen, visible

unselfish /ʌn'selfɪʃ/ *adj.* 无私的;慷慨的;不谋取私利的:Lei Feng was an ～ man. 雷锋是一个无私的人。同 generous, liberal 反 selfish 派 unselfishly *adv.*; unselfishness *n.*

unsettled /ʌn'set(ə)ld/ *adj.* ❶未解决的;未确定的:Let's leave it ～. 咱们把问题先放一放。❷不稳定的;动荡的,动乱的:The late events in these two countries show that Africa is still ～. 这两个国家近来发生的事件说明非洲局势仍不稳定。❸未偿付的;未结算的:an ～ account 未结清的账目 ❹不安宁的;精神失衡的:be in an ～ mood 心神不定

unshakable /ʌn'ʃeɪkəbl/ *adj.* 不可动摇的;坚定不移的:The scientist is ～ in his faith. 科学家的信仰是坚定的。同 firm, steady 反 shakable

U

unstable / ʌn'steɪbl / *adj.* 不稳固的；不稳定的 同 unsteady, changeable 反 stable, steady

unsuitable / ʌn'sjuːtəbl / *adj.* 不合适的；不适宜的 同 unfit, improper 反 suitable, proper

unthinkable / ʌn'θɪŋkəbl / *adj.* 难以想象的；不可思议的：At that time, he was faced with ～ difficulties. 那时他面对的是难以想象的困难。同 unimaginable 反 thinkable, imaginable

untidy / ʌn'taɪdɪ / *adj.* 不整洁的；凌乱的：an ～ room 凌乱的房间 同 messy, disorderly 反 tidy

untie / ʌn'taɪ / *vt.* 解开；松开：～ a parcel 解开包裹 / ～ one's tie 解领带 同 unfasten, loose 反 tie, fasten

until / ən'tɪl / *conj.* & *prep.* 直到…时；到…为止 同 till

untouched / ʌn'tʌtʃt / *adj.* 原样的；未动过的

unusual / ʌn'juːʒʊəl / *adj.* 不常见的，不一般的；奇异的 同 singular, rare 反 usual

unveil / ʌn'veɪl / *vt.* ❶揭去…面纱：The bridegroom ～ed the bride's face. 新郎揭开新娘脸上的面纱。❷使公开；使暴露；揭示，揭露：～ the proposal 公布计划/ The government ～s the economic state of the country. 政府向公众透露了国家的经济状况。

unwilling / ʌn'wɪlɪŋ / *adj.* 不愿意的，不情愿的 同 reluctant, opposed 反 willing 派 unwillingly *adv.*

unworthy / ʌn'wɜːðɪ / *adj.* ❶不值得的；不配得到的：The phenomenon seems ～ of our attention. 这种现象似乎不值得我们关注。❷（与…）不相配的，不相称的，不合身份的：The books have been condemned as ～ of young children. 有人指责这些书不适合小孩子们看。❸卑鄙的，卑劣的，下作的，可耻的 派 unworthiness *n.*

unwrap / ʌn'ræp / *v.* (-wrapped;-wrapping)打开；解开 同 open, untie 反 wrap, tie

unzip / ʌn'zɪp / (-zipped;-zipping) *v.* 拉开（拉链）；拉开…的拉链：～ a jacket 拉开上衣拉链/ For about eight seconds earth's crust ～ed at more that two kilometers a second. 大约 8 秒钟的时间，地壳以每秒 2 千米以上的速度迸裂开来。

up / ʌp / Ⅰ *adv.* ❶向上：Lift your head ～. 抬起头来。The tide is ～. 潮水在上涨。Prices are still going ～. 物价仍在上涨。❷起床：He's already ～. 他已起床。She was ～ all

night with a sick child. 她整夜未睡陪伴一个病孩。❸完全；结束：We've eaten everything ～. 我们把所有食物都吃光了。Time is ～. 时间到了。～ **and down** 上上下下地；前后地；往返地：walking ～ and down the station platform 在车站月台上来回走动 ～ **till now** 直到现在为止 ～ **to date** 最新的；直到现在 ～ **to now** 到目前为止 Ⅱ *prep.* 向…的上端；向…的较高处：walk ～ stairs 上楼梯 / ～ **to** ①应由（某人）担任或负责：It's ～ to us to give them all the help we can. 我们理应给他们一切我们所能给予的帮助。②胜任：He is not ～ to his job. 他不能胜任工作。③正在做；正从事：What is he ～ to? 他在做什么？

update Ⅰ / ʌp'deɪt / *vt.* 更新，使不落后；使现代化：The software will need to be ～d regularly. 软件必须不断地更新。/ ～ the defensive weapons 使防御武器现代化 Ⅱ / 'ʌp,deɪt/ *n.* ❶[U;C]更新；修改 ❷[C]最新版本；最新报道；更新的内容（或数据）：What was the last news ～? 最后一条新消息是什么？

upgrade Ⅰ / ʌp'greɪd / *vt.* ❶ 提升，使升级：His job has been ～d from "assistant manager" to "manager". 他由"助理经理"升任"经理"。❷ 提高；改进，改善：～d the networks 改进网络系统 Ⅱ/'ʌp,greɪd/ *n.* ❶[U;C]提升；升级；提高 ❷[C]改进（或更新）的设施

uphold / ʌp'həʊld / *vt.* (upheld, upheld) ❶高举 同 raise ❷支持，赞成 同 support, approve 反 oppose

upon / ə'pɒn / *prep.* 在…上；…在身上：once ～ a time 从前 同 on, over

upper / 'ʌpə(r) / *adj.* 较高的；上面的：the ～ classes 上流阶层（社会）/ the ～ lip 上唇/ one of the ～ rooms 楼上的一个房间 同 higher, top / **get (have) the ～ hand of** 占上风，比…占优势

upright / 'ʌpraɪt / *adj.* 垂直的；笔直的：hold oneself ～ 笔直地站着 / set the pole ～ 把杆子竖直 同 vertical 反 horizontal 派 uprightly *adv.*

uprising / 'ʌp,raɪzɪŋ / *n.* [C] 起义；暴动，叛乱：put down an ～ 镇压起义

uproar / 'ʌp,rɔː(r) / *n.* [U] ❶骚动，骚乱：The news caused the public ～. 这条消息引发了公众骚乱。❷吵闹，喧嚣：This only increased the ～, when they heard him speak. 当人们一听到他这样说话，就更加起哄。

upset / ʌp'set / Ⅰ v. (upset, upset) ❶颠覆；推翻：Don't ~ the boat. 不要把船弄翻了。同 overturn ❷扰乱；使不安：~ the enemy's plan 破坏敌人的计划 / ~ one's stomach by eating too much rich food 因油腻的食物吃得太多而使胃不舒服 同 disturb Ⅱ n. [C]颠覆；扰乱；不安：have a stomach ~ 胃不舒服 同 overturn, nervousness Ⅲ adj. 难过的；不安的 同 worried, disturbed

upside / 'ʌpsaid / n. 上部；上边；上面

upside-down / 'ʌpsai'daʊn / adj. 倒转的，倒置的；乱七八糟的：The house was turned ~ by the burglars. 那房子被窃贼翻得乱七八糟。同 disorderly 反 orderly

upstairs / 'ʌp'steəz / Ⅰ adv. 向楼上；在楼上：go (walk) ~ 上楼 Ⅱ adj. 属于楼上的；位于楼上的：an ~ room 楼上的房间

up-to-date / 'ʌptə'deit / adj. 现代的；最新的：an ~ record 最近纪录 / an ~ store 最新式的店铺 同 modern, fashionable 反 old, outdated

upward / 'ʌpwəd / Ⅰ adj. 向上的；上升的：the ~ trend of prices 物价上升的趋势 同 rising 反 downward Ⅱ adv. (＝upwards) 向上地；上升地：The boat was on the beach, bottom ~. 那船搁置在海滩上，船底朝天。反 downward(s)

uranium / jʊ'reiniəm / n. [U]铀

urban / 'ɜːbən / adj. 城市的：~ construction 城市建设 / ~ inhabitants 城市居民 / exchange between ~ and rural areas 城乡交流 同 city 反 rural

urge / ɜːdʒ / vt. ❶劝；催促，敦促：The shopkeeper ~d me to buy a hat. 那店主极力劝我买一顶帽子。同 plead, request ❷极力主张：He ~d upon his pupils the importance of hard work. 他极力向学生讲解用功的重要。同 advise, support 反 oppose ❸推进；驱策 同 push, drive 反 prevent

【用法】
urge 作"力劝"讲时，常用句型是 urge sb. to do sth. 和 urge＋that 从句，其中 that 从句里谓语动词用虚拟语气：The teacher urged us to hand in our exercises. 老师催我们交作业。He urges that his son (should) do his best. 他劝告他的儿子要努力。

urgent / 'ɜːdʒənt / adj. ❶紧急的；急迫的：It's most ~ that the patient (should) be sent to hospital. 要紧的是病人应送医院。同 critical, important 反 uncritical, unimportant ❷催逼的；坚持要求的：They were ~ for the doctor to come. 他们急迫地催医生来。He was ~ to have more. 他坚持要多一些。同 earnest, demanding 反 indifferent

us / ʌs / pron. 我们(we 的宾格)

U. S. , US (＝United States)美国

U. S. A , USA (＝United States of America)美利坚合众国，美国

usage / 'juːzidʒ / n. ❶使用；用法 同 use, employment ❷习惯；习俗 同 custom, tradition

use Ⅰ / juːz / v. ❶用，使用；利用 同 apply, employ / ~ up 消耗；用尽：He has ~d up all his strength. 他已耗尽了所有的体力。❷惯常(只用过去时,后跟不定式)：You ~d to smoke a pipe, didn't you? 你过去要抽烟，是吗？Ⅱ / juːs / n. ❶[U]使用；应用；利用：the ~ of electricity for lighting 利用电力照明 同 service, usage 反 disuse, unemployment / **come into ~** 开始被使用：When did the word "transistor" come into ~? "transistor"一词何时开始使用的? **go (fall) out of ~** 已不再使用,废弃：The name has gone out of ~. 那名称已不再使用了。**in ~** 在使用中：The laboratory is in ~ until five o'clock. 实验室一直到 5 点钟都有人用。**make (good, the best) ~ of** 很好地利用；充分利用：You must make good ~ of any opportunity to practise English. 你应该好好利用一切机会练习英文。**put to ~** 投入使用：The new power station will be put to ~ next month. 这新发电厂下月投入使用。❷[C]用途；用处：a tool with many ~s 有多种用途的工具 / This big box is good ~. 这个大箱子很有用。同 function, utility ❸[U]价值；益处：It's no ~ complaining. 埋怨没有用。同 value, benefit

used / juːzd / adj. ❶用旧了的；二手的：a ~ car 旧汽车 ❷习惯于…的；惯常的：I'm quite ~ to speaking English. 我相当习惯讲英语。同 accustomed

【用法】
used to do 表示过去的习惯动作,现在已经结束或消失：The river used to be clean. 这条河以前是干净的。be used to doing, be used to sth. 意为"习惯于"：I'm not used to getting up early. 我不习惯早起。He is used to this kind of job. 他习惯干这种工作。

useful / ˈjuːsfl / *adj.* 有用的；有益的；有帮助的：a ~ tool 有用的工具 / It's ~ for one to know some English when traveling abroad. 懂点英语对在国外旅行的人是有好处的。Dictionaries are ~ to students. 词典对学生很有用。同 practical, helpful 反 useless 派 usefully *adv.* ; usefulness *n.*

useless / ˈjuːsləs / *adj.* 无用的，无价值的；无益的；无效的：It is ~ to discuss the problem at present. 目前讨论这个问题没有什么价值。同 valueless, worthless 反 useful

user / ˈjuːzə(r) / *n.* [C]用户；使用者

usual / ˈjuːʒʊəl / *adj.* 通常的；惯例的：Tea is the ~ drink of Chinese. 茶是中国人通常喝的饮料。同 common, regular 反 unusual, uncommon：as ~ 照例，照常：I went to bed at eleven as ~. 我照例 11 点睡觉。派 usually *adv.*

utensil / juːˈtensl / *n.* [C] 器皿；用具 同 tool, instrument

utility / juːˈtɪləti / *n.* ❶[U]效用；实用 同 usefulness, benefit ❷[C]有用之物 ❸[C]（常用 *pl.*）公用事业

utilize / ˈjuːtɪˌlaɪz / *vt.* (有效地)利用：~ the power of the wind 利用风力 / It is advantageous for employers to ~ higher paid employees for longer hours instead of hiring additional workers to increase output. 雇主给雇员加班加薪比另外雇人合算。

utmost / ˈʌtməʊst / Ⅰ *adj.* 极度的；最大的：with the ~ pleasure 极为高兴地 同 maximum, greatest 反 minimum, smallest Ⅱ *n.* 极限，极度；最大可能：at the ~ 至多 / do one's ~ 竭尽全力 同 maximum, ultimate 反 minimum

Utopia / juːˈtəʊpiə / *n.* 乌托邦；理想国

Utopian / juːˈtəʊpiən / *adj.* ❶乌托邦的 ❷理想的；空想的

utter¹ / ˈʌtə(r) / *adj.* 完全的，彻底的 同 complete, total 反 incomplete, partial

utter² / ˈʌtə(r) / *vt.* 发出(声音)；说；讲：~ a cry of pain 发出痛苦的叫声/ He ~ed only one word or two. 他只说了一两句话。同 express, speak 派 utterance *n.*

U

V v

vacancy / ˈveɪkənsi / n. ❶[U]空;空白;空间:
All was blackness and ～.四下里一团漆黑,
空空荡荡。❷[C]空缺;空职:His retirement
caused a ～ in the office. 他退休了,办公室有
个空职。/fill up the ～填补空缺 ❸[C](宾馆
等待租的)空房

vacant / ˈveɪkənt / adj. 空的;未占用的:a ～
room空房间 / apply for a ～ position 申请某空
缺职位 同 empty,unoccupied 反 full,occupied

vacation / vəˈkeɪʃn / n. [C]❶(大学的)假期;
(法庭的)休庭期:the summer (winter) ～ 暑
(寒)假 同 holiday,rest 反 term,work ❷休假:
You can't see the manager because he is on
～.经理在度假,你见不到他。The old couple
are going on ～ in Japan. 那对老年夫妇要去
日本度假。同 holiday,rest 反 work

vaccine / ˈvæksiːn / n. [C]❶疫苗,菌苗:
stamp out polio by using ～注射疫苗消灭小
儿麻痹症 ❷抗病毒软件

vacuum / ˈvækjuəm / Ⅰ n. [C]❶真空;封闭
状态;隔绝状态:Translation does not occur in
a ～.翻译不是在真空中进行的。❷真空;真
空度:perfect ～完全真空 ❸空白;空虚;沉
寂:His wife's death left a ～ in his life. 妻子
的去世使他的生活变得空虚起来。❹真空吸
尘器 Ⅱ vt. 用真空吸尘器打扫:The young lady is ～ing the carpets. 那位年轻女士正在用
真空吸尘器扫地毯。

vague / veɪɡ / adj. ❶含糊的,模糊的,不明确
的:To me all this explanation has been a ～
mystery. 我听这种解释真有些玄妙莫测。/
He remained ～ about when she would return
to Washington. 她什么时候返回华盛顿,对此
他一直含糊其词。❷没有表情的,茫然的:The
poor old man looked ～, not knowing what did
happened to him. 那可怜的老人一脸茫然,不
知发生了什么事。

vain / veɪn / adj. 无益的;无效的;无结果的 同
useless,fruitless 反 useful,fruitful / in ～无效

地,徒然:All our work was in ～. 我们的一切
工作都是徒然。

valid / ˈvælɪd / adj. 有效的;正当的:～ contract 有效合同 / ～ passport 有效护照 / ～
for one year (six months) 有效期一年(半年)/
One can sign up with ～ papers. 持有效证件
即能报名。同 legal,lawful 反 invalid,illegal
派 validly adv.

valley / ˈvæli / n. [C] (pl. valleys) 谷;山谷;
峡谷

valuable / ˈvæljuəbl / adj. 有价值的;贵重的;
有用的:a ～ discovery 有价值的发现 同 precious,useful 反 valueless,worthless

valuation / ˌvæljuˈeɪʃn / n. [U]评价;估价:It
is unwise to accept a person at his own ～.凭
一个人对自己的评价而相信他是不明智的。
同 assessment,estimate

value / ˈvæljuː / Ⅰ n. ❶[U]重要性;有用性 同
importance,use ❷[U](与他物比较时某物的)
价值:This book will be of great (little, some,
no) ～ to him for his studies. 这本书对他的研
究很有(几乎没有,有一些,没有)价值。同
worth ❸[U]价格;购买力:Is the ～ of the A-
merican dollar likely to decline? 美元可能贬值
吗? 同 price,cost ❹[C](常用 pl.)贵重物品:
You'd better keep your ～s in a safe. 你最好
把你的贵重物品锁进保险柜。Ⅱ vt. 尊重;重
视;评价:He ～d the house at half a million.
他估价这房子为 50 万。/ We ～ the
teacher's advice. 我们重视老师提出的意见。
同 respect,assess

valve / vælv / n.[C]阀门;safety ～ 安全阀

van / væn / n.[C]大篷车;运货车;luggage ～
行李车 同 truck

vanish / ˈvænɪʃ / vi. 突然不见;消失;～ from
sight 从眼前消失/～ into nothing 变得无影无
踪 / The moon ～ed behind the clouds. 月亮隐藏
到云后面去了。同 disappear,fade 反 appear

vanity / ˈvænəti / n. [U]虚荣心;虚夸 同 conceit 反 modesty

vapo(u)r / 'veɪpə(r) / n. [U](蒸)汽;雾:water ～ 水蒸气 / ～ bath 蒸汽浴 同 moisture,mist

variable / 'veərɪəbl / Ⅰ adj. 可变的,易变的,多变的:a specific disease in the ～ human body 人体随时变化的疾病/ His temper is ～. 他的脾气反复无常。Ⅱ n. ❶[C]易变的事物:the major ～ in risk assessment 对风险进行评估的主要因素 ❷[C]变量;变量符号:independent ～ 自变量/ dependent ～ 因变量

variation / ˌveərɪ'eɪʃn / n. ❶[U]变动,变更:Date of departure is subject to ～. 启程日期可能会有变更。❷[C]变体;变化了的东西:Today,more than 1,000 computer viruses and ～ are reportedly sweeping through the world. 据报道,目前有 1000 多种计算机病毒及其变种正席卷全球。

variety / və'raɪəti / n. ❶[U]变化;多样:～ dish 杂烩/ ～ show 综艺节目,杂耍/ ～ theatre 杂耍剧场/ We demanded more ～ of our food. 我们要求食物品种多样化。同 change,difference 反 sameness,likeness ❷(仅用单数)种类:for a ～ of reasons 由于种种原因 / a large ～ of patterns to choose from 可供选择的多种花样 同 kind,type

various / 'veərɪəs / adj. 不同的;各式各样的:at ～ times 在不同的时代 / a criminal who is known to the police under ～ names 为警察所知的以各种化名出现的罪犯 同 different,unlike 反 same,alike 派 variously adv.

vary / 'veəri / v. (使)不同;(使)变化:～ing prices 变动的物价 / You should ～ your diet. 你应该改变饮食。同 change,transform / ～ from ... to ... 从…变化到…:The ages in our class ～ from 12 to 15. 我们班同学的年龄从 12 岁到 15 岁不等。

辨析

vary 意为"使多种多样;不断地变化":The skyscrapers in the city vary in colour. 城市里林立的高楼颜色各不相同。**change** 是常用词,表示从一种状态转变到另一种状态:In autumn,leaves change from green to brown. 秋天树叶由绿变黄。

vase / vɑːz / n. [C]花瓶

vast / vɑːst / adj. 巨大的;广阔的:a ～ extension of desert 一大片沙漠 同 huge,wide 反 tiny,narrow

VCD (＝ video compact disc) [C]影碟;影碟机

vegetable / 'vedʒɪtəbl / n. ❶蔬菜 ❷(喻)植物人

vegetation / ˌvedʒɪ'teɪʃn / n. [U]植物;植被:～ zones 植被带/ hills covered to the top with luxuriant ～～一座座被郁郁葱葱的草木覆盖的小山

vehicle / 'viːɪkl,'viːəkl / n. [C]❶车辆;运载工具:heavy ～s 重型车辆 同 transport ❷传播工具;媒介:～ of propaganda 宣传工具 / Language is a ～ of human thoughts. 语言是人类思想的传播媒体。同 means,tool

veil / veɪl / n. ❶[C]面纱,面罩:put on the white ～ 戴上白面纱 ❷[C]遮盖物;借口,托词:under the ～ of friendship 在友谊的幌子下/ through a thin ～ of smoke in a black sky 透过黑色天空中的薄烟

vein / veɪn / n. [C]❶静脉;血管,脉 ❷趋势;气质;风格:a rich ～ of humor 颇有几分幽默/ The old man had a ～ of stubbornness. 这个老汉性格有点硬。

velocity / və'lɒsəti / n. [C]速率;速度:at a ～ of 30 meters per second 以每秒 30 米的速度/ initial (terminal,uniform) ～ 初(末,匀)速度 同 rate,speed

venture / 'ventʃə(r) / Ⅰ n. 冒险;冒险事业;投机:make a ～ 冒险 / a joint ～ 合资企业 同 risk,undertaking Ⅱ v. 冒险;大胆行事:I ～ to disagree. 我冒昧说不。/ Nothing ～, nothing gain (win, have). 不入虎穴,焉得虎子? 同 risk,dare

verb / vɜːb / n. 动词:auxiliary (link,modal) ～ 助动词(连系动词,情态动词) / regular (irregular) ～ 规则(不规则)动词 / transitive (intransitive) ～ 及物(不及物)动词

verbal / 'vɜːbl / adj. ❶用言辞的,用文字的;文字上的:～ abuse with consummate ～ dexterity 靠熟练的文字技巧谩骂/ This is a ～ trick. 这是玩弄字眼儿。❷口头的,非书面的:erect a ～ monument 树立起口碑/ a ～ contract 口头契约 ❸动词的;源自动词的;作动词的:～ inflexions 动词的曲折变化

verge / vɜːdʒ / n. [C]边缘;界线:界限 同 edge,boundary

verification / ˌverɪfɪ'keɪʃn / n. [U]证实;核实 同 confirmation

verify / 'verɪfaɪ / vt. ❶证实;查证;证明:Truth can be verified by practice. 真理可由实

践证明。同 confirm, prove 反 disprove ❷核实:～ a report (details, figures) 核实报告(细节, 数字)

versatile / 'vɜːsətail / adj. ❶多才多艺的, 有多种才能的:～ erudition 博学多才 / She was ～ at writing. 她是写作的多面手。❷(装置等)有多种用途的, 有多种功能的:a ～ chemical 有多种用途的化学品 / A pickup is ～ in function. 轻型货车有多种功能。派 versatility n.

verse / vɜːs / n. ❶[C; U]诗体作品, 诗歌; 诗句, 诗行, 歌词:compose ～作诗 / an extempore ～即兴诗 ❷[C](诗或韵文的)节, 诗节:quote a few ～s from sb. 引用某人的几句诗

version / 'vɜːʃn / n. ❶翻译; 译本:a new ～ of the Bible《圣经》的新版本 同 translation ❷叙述, 说法, 说明:There were contradictory ～s of what happened. 对所发生的事有矛盾的说法。同 account, explanation

versus / 'vɜːsəs / prep. ❶对, 以…为对手(略作 v., vs):The match is China ～ America. 比赛是中国队对美国队。❷与…相对, 与…相比:There's also something known as risk ～ benefit. 还存在权衡利弊的问题。

vertical / 'vɜːtikl / adj. 垂直的; 竖的:～ line 垂线 / ～ plane 垂面 同 upright 反 horizontal 派 vertically adv.

very / 'veri / Ⅰ adv. 很; 非常:～ amusing (interesting) 很好笑(有趣) / The book you lent me is ～ good. 你借给我的那本书很好。/ I like English ～ much. 我非常喜欢英语。/ Her daughter plays the violin ～ well. 她女儿的小提琴拉得非常好。同 extremely, quite Ⅱ adj. ❶同一的; 恰好的:At that ～ moment the telephone bell rang. 就在那时, 电话铃响了。同 same, exact ❷极端的:at the ～ end (beginning) 最终(最初) 同 extreme

vessel / 'vesl / n. [C] ❶容器; 器皿 同 container, utensil ❷船, 舰 同 ship, liner ❸脉管; 血管

辨析
vessel 指水能载动的各种中空构造物, 常指大型轮船:a merchant (passenger) vessel 商(客)船。**boat** 泛指大小水运工具, 尤指小型无篷船:The fishing boat left dock at dawn. 这条渔船黎明时就离开了码头。**ship** 指海上航行的载人或载物的较大轮船:Rough seas delayed the ship. 波涛汹涌的海水阻挡了船的航行。

vest / vest / n. [C]内衣; 汗衫; 背心

veteran / 'vetərən / Ⅰ n. [C] ❶老手; 老练的人; 有经验者 expert, master 反 beginner ❷老兵; 退役军人; disabled ～ 残疾老兵 / World War Ⅱ ～ 二战老兵 同 ex-serviceman Ⅱ adj. 老练的; 资格老的 同 experienced

veto / 'viːtəʊ / Ⅰ n. (pl. vetoes)否决; 否决权:exercise (use) a ～ 行使否决权 同 refusal, rejection 反 approval Ⅱ vt. 否决:～ a bill 否决一项议案 同 reject, prohibit 反 approve

via / 'vaiə / prep. 经过; 通过:They went to America ～ Japan. 他们途经日本去美国。/ We communicate ～ e-mail. 我们通过电子邮件交流。

vibrant / 'vaibrənt / adj. ❶震动的, 颤动的:He was ～ with emotion. 他激动得颤抖起来。❷充满生气的, 活跃的:a ～, enthusiastic person 一个活跃、热心的人 / a village ～ with life and energy 充满活力的山村

vibrate / vai'breit / v. (使)摆动; (使)摇动; (使)震动:The house ～ s whenever a heavy lorry passes. 大货车经过的时候, 这屋子总要发生震动。/ The strings of piano ～ when the keys are struck. 当钢琴的琴键受击时, 琴弦震动。同 swing, shake 派 vibration n.

vice / vais / n. ❶[C]缺点; 毛病:You must see the ～s of modern civilization. 你得看到现代文明的缺点。同 fault, flaw ❷[C]恶习:Too much drinking is a ～. 酗酒是一种恶习。❸邪恶; 邪恶行为 同 evil, wrongdoing 反 virtue

vice- / vais / (前缀) 副的:～-president 副总统; 副总裁; (大学的)副校长 / ～-chairman 副主席; 副会长 / ～-minister 副部长 / ～-premier 副总理

vicious / 'viʃəs / adj. ❶恶毒的, 狠毒的:It is ～ of her to make such an accusation. 她这么指责人真是恶毒。❷猛烈的, 剧烈的:a ～ headache 剧烈的头痛 ❸野蛮的; 残忍的:a ～ temper 性情残暴

victim / 'viktim / n. 受害者; 牺牲者:A fund was opened to help the ～s of the earthquake. 为了帮助地震受灾的灾民, 基金会开始募捐了。同 sufferer, sacrifice

victorious / vik'tɔːriəs / adj. 胜利的; 成功的; 凯旋的 同 triumphant, successful 反 conquered, defeated 派 victoriously adv.

victory / 'viktəri / n. 胜利; 成功:gain a ～ over the enemy 战胜敌人 / lead the troops to ～率领军队迈向胜利 同 triumph, conquest 反 defeat

video / 'vɪdɪəʊ / Ⅰ n. [C] (pl. videos) ❶电视；录像 ❷录像节目；录像机 Ⅱ adj. 电视的；录像的：～ tape 录像带 / ～ recorder 录像机

view / vju: / Ⅰ n. ❶[U]看；视力；眼界：The speaker stood in full ～ of the crowd. 演说者站在观众完全可以看见的地方。/ After you turn round the corner, the hospital will come into ～. 你转过那个街角就看得到医院了。同 sight, vision ❷景色；景物：a fine ～ in the valley 山谷中的优美景色 同 scene, prospect ❸意见；观点：He holds extreme ～s. 他持极端的见解。同 opinion, prospect / **in ～ of** 鉴于，由于：In ～ of the facts, he is believable. 鉴于事实，他是可信的。Ⅱ v. 看；观察：They ～ed the problem in different ways. 他们以不同的方式看这个问题。同 watch, observe

viewpoint / 'vju:pɔɪnt / n. [C]观点；见解：It is necessary to look at things with a mass ～. 看问题要有群众观点。同 view

vigilance / 'vɪdʒɪləns / n. [U]警戒；警戒性 同 watchfulness, caution

vigilant / 'vɪdʒɪlənt / adj. 警戒的 同 watchful, cautious

vigorous / 'vɪɡərəs / adj. 朝气蓬勃的；精力充沛的；健壮的；有力的：～ enforcement of law 执法有力 / The football player is ～. 这足球运动员精力充沛。同 strong, active 反 weak, inactive

vigo(u)r / 'vɪɡə(r) / n. [U]活力；精力：lose one's ～ 失去活力 / regain ～ 恢复活力 / He came back after the vacation, full of ～. 他度假回来后精力充沛。同 energy, spirit

village / 'vɪlɪdʒ / n. [C]村庄

villager / 'vɪlɪdʒə(r) / n. [C]村民

vine / vaɪn / n. [C]葡萄树；蔓，藤

vinegar / 'vɪnɪɡə(r) / n. [U] 醋

violate / 'vaɪəleɪt / vt. ❶违犯；违反；违背 同 break, disobey 反 respect, obey ❷妨碍；扰乱 同 invade, disturb ❸玷污 同 abuse, dishonor 反 honor, respect

violence / 'vaɪələns / n. [U] ❶猛烈；凶暴 同

force, fierceness 反 mildness, weakness ❷暴行 同 cruelty, wildness 反 gentleness

violent / 'vaɪələnt / adj. ❶暴力的；猛烈的；残暴的：a ～ attack 猛攻 / in a ～ temper 盛怒地 同 cruel, fierce 反 gentle, calm ❷剧烈的；厉害的 同 strong, severe 反 weak, mild

violet / 'vaɪələt / Ⅰ n. 紫罗兰 Ⅱ adj. 紫色的

violin / ˌvaɪə'lɪn / n. [C]小提琴

VIP (＝very important person)要人，大人物，贵宾

viral / 'vaɪərəl / adj. 病毒(性)的；病毒感染的，病毒引起的：as a result of a ～ infection 由于病毒感染

virgin / 'vɜːdʒɪn / Ⅰ n. [C] ❶童男，童女 ❷处女 ❸天真的人，不谙世事的人 Ⅱ adj. ❶未用过的，未开发的：～ land 生荒地 ❷纯洁的，未被玷污的：be arrayed in ～ white 打扮得一身纯白

virtual / 'vɜːtʃuəl / adj. ❶实际上的；实质上的 同 practical, essential ❷虚拟的：～ office 虚拟办公室 / ～ reality 虚拟现实

virtually / 'vɜːtʃuəli / adv. 实际上；事实上；几乎：They are ～ impossible to find out the secret. 事实上他们不可能发现这个秘密。

virtue / 'vɜːtʃu: / n. ❶善；德行；美德；优点：Patience is a ～. 忍耐是一种美德。同 morality, goodness 反 evil, vice / **by(in) ～ of** 由于，凭借：By ～ of his own effort he managed to finish the work. 凭自己的努力，他设法完成了工作。❷(尤指妇女的)贞操：a woman of ～ 贞洁的妇女 同 purity

virus / 'vaɪrəs / n. [C] ❶病毒：This ～ ruins the immune system. 这种病毒破坏人体免疫系统。❷计算机病毒

visa / 'viːzə / n. [C](护照的)背签；签证：apply for a ～ 申请签证 / get (receive) a ～ 获得签证

visibility / ˌvɪzə'bɪləti / n. [C]可见性；能见度 同 clearness, distinctness

visible / 'vɪzəbl / adj. 可见的；看得见的：The germs are not ～ to our naked eyes. 细菌是我们肉眼看不见的。同 observable, distinct 反 invisible

vision / 'vɪʒən / n. ❶[U]视力；想象力；远见；

the field of ～ 视野 / the ～ of a poet 诗人的想象力 / the ～ of a prophet 预言家的远见 同 sight, imagination 反 blindness ❷[C]景象；(尤指)幻想；梦想：We should not laugh at the romantic ～s of the young people. 我们不应该嘲笑年轻人不切实际的幻想。同 fancy, dream 反 fact, reality

visionary / 'vɪʒənəri / adj. ❶幻觉的, 幻想的 ❷有眼力的, 有预见的

visit / 'vɪzɪt / Ⅰ v. 访问, 拜访(某人)；游览, 参观(某地)：～ a friend 访友 / Rome 游览罗马 同 call on, drop in Ⅱ n.[C]访问；游览：pay a ～ to a friend 拜访朋友 / I paid a ～ to the writer out of my way. 我专程去拜访了那个作家。同 call, stay

visitor / 'vɪzɪtə(r) / n.[C]访问者；来访者；宾客：summer ～s 夏季游客 / the ～s' book 来宾签字簿；游客登记簿 同 caller, guest

visual / 'vɪzjuəl, 'vɪʒuəl / adj. 视觉的；视力的：a ～ defect 视力缺陷/ This test was as a basis for judging his ～ acuity. 根据这个测试可判断他视觉的敏锐程度.

vital / 'vaɪtl / adj. 生命力的；与生命有关的；维持生命必需的；精力充沛的：wounded in a ～ part 在要害处受伤 同 life, vigorous 反 dead, lifeless

vitality / vaɪ'tæləti / n.[U]活力；生命力；持久力 同 life, vigor

vitamin / 'vɪtəmɪn / n. 维生素

vivid / 'vɪvɪd / adj. ❶生动的；栩栩如生的：The novel gives a ～ description of the country life. 小说生动地描写了农村生活. 同 lively, vigorous 反 dull ❷鲜艳的：～ green 翠绿色 同 bright, colorful 反 dull, colorless 派 vividly adv.

vocabulary / və'kæbjələri / n. 词汇表；词汇

> **辨析**
> **vocabulary** 是一种语言的全部词汇或指词汇总量, 而 **word** 指单独的一个词：This word is not listed in the technical vocabulary. 这个词没有被列入技术词汇表.

vocal / 'vəukəl / Ⅰ adj. ❶嗓音的, 用嗓音的；歌唱的：～ tract 声道/ The strong contrasts between them extended well beyond mere ～

quality. 他们两人强烈的对比远远超出了音质的不同. ❷畅所欲言的, 自由表达的

vocation / və'keɪʃn / n.[C]职业；行业：choose (select) a ～ 挑选职业 / take up the ～ of 从事…的职业 同 career, occupation 派 vocational adj.

vogue / vəug / n.[U;C]时尚；流行事物；时髦人物：Garments of this fashion have gone out of ～. 这种式样的衣服已落伍了。/ The designs are in ～. 这些图案正在流行.

voice / vɔɪs / Ⅰ n. ❶人声；说话声：drop (lower) one's ～ 放低声音 / lift up (raise) one's ～ 提高嗓门 / lose one's ～ 嗓子哑了/ in a loud ～ 大声地 / I did not recognize her ～. 我没听出她的声音. 同 sound, speech / **give ～ to** 说出；发表(意见)；吐露 **with one ～** 一致地；异口同声地 ❷(语法)动词的语态：active (passive) ～ 主动(被动)语态 Ⅱ v. 说出来；表达；发出：The spokesman ～d the feelings of the crowd. 发言人说出了群众的心声. 同 utter, express

volcano / vɒl'keɪnəu / n.[C](pl. volcanoes) 火山：active ～ 活火山 / dormant ～ 休眠火山 / extinct ～ 死火山

volleyball / 'vɒlibɔːl / n. 排球运动；排球

volt / vəult / n.[C]伏特(电压单位)

voltage / 'vəultɪdʒ / n. 电压；伏特数

volume / 'vɒljuːm / n. ❶[C](尤指一部书中的)一册, 一卷：an encyclopaedia in 20 ～s 有20册的一部百科全书/a hardcover (paperback)～ 精(平)装本 / an out-of-print ～ 绝版书 ❷[U]体积；容积；容量：sails ～ 销售量 / the ～ of traffic 交通流量 / the ～ of water 水量 同 size, capacity ❸[U](指声音)有力；响度；音量：a voice of great ～ 音量大的声音 同 loudness, sound

voluntary / 'vɒləntri / adj. 自愿的；义务的：～ service 自愿服务(服役)同 willing, unforced 反 involuntary, unwilling

volunteer / ˌvɒlən'tɪə(r) / Ⅰ n.[C]❶志愿者 ❷志愿兵 Ⅱ v. 自愿提出；自愿效劳：He ～ed for the campaign. 他自愿参加这次战役. 同 propose, present

vomit / 'vɒmɪt / Ⅰ vt. ❶呕吐, 吐；He ～ed

up the foul water he had swallowed. 他将吞下去的脏水全部吐出。❷(火山、烟囱等)喷发,喷: The volcano is ～ing volumes of black smoke. 火山正在喷出滚滚黑烟。

vote / vəʊt / I n. ❶投票(权);表决(权);选举(权);Do women have the ～ in your country? 贵国的妇女有选举权吗? 同 poll, election ❷选票数: be beaten by one ～ 以一票之差落选/ pass ...by a majority ～ 以多数票通过…/ Will the Labour ～ increase or decrease at the next election? 在下届选举中,工党的票数将增加还是减少? Ⅱ v. ❶投票(与 for 或 against 连用,后接某物或某人;与 on 连用后接某问题):Fifteen ～d for and twelve (～d) a-gainst it. 15 票赞成,12 票反对。/ Now we will ～ on this question. 现在我们来对这个问题投票解决。❷投票表决:～ a sum of money for education 投票表决一笔教育经费

vow / vaʊ / I n. [C] ❶誓,誓约,誓言:break the ～ 违反诺言/ lovers' ～s 爱人的誓言 Ⅱ vt. 立誓给予;起誓做,发誓履行:If I do ～ a friendship, I'll perform it to the last article. 要是我发誓帮助一个朋友,我一定会帮到底。

vowel / 'vaʊəl / n. 元音;元音字母

voyage / 'vɔɪɪdʒ / I n. (尤指长途的)航行,航海:make (go on) a ～ 航行,航海 同 journey, trip Ⅱ vi. 航海;航行 同 sail

VS (＝versus)…对…

vulgar / 'vʌlgə(r) / adj. 粗俗的;庸俗的 同 rude, rough 反 elegant, polite

V

W w

wade / weɪd / vi. 过(河)；涉(水)：~ across a stream 过一条小溪

wag / wæg / Ⅰ v. (wagged；wagging)(使)摇摆；(使)摇动；上下移动：The dog ~ged its tail. 狗摇尾。同 shake，wave Ⅱ n. 摇摆，摇动 同 shake，wave

wage¹ / weɪdʒ / n. (常用 pl.)工资，薪水(通常按周计算)：His ~s are ￡80 a week. 他的工资是每周 80 英镑。同 pay，salary

wage² / weɪdʒ / vt. 开始；进行：The Chinese people ~d a national war against the Japanese aggression in 1937. 中国人民在 1937 年开始了一场抗击日本侵略的民族战争。同 engage，undertake

wag(g)on / ˈwægən / n. [C] ❶四轮运货马车 ❷(铁路)敞篷货车

waist / weɪst / n. 腰，腰部：measure 30 inches round the ~ 腰围 30 英寸 / let out (take in) the ~ of a dress 放大(收小)衣服的腰身

wait / weɪt / v. ❶等待，等候；期待：~ and see 等着瞧，观望 反 proceed / ~ **for** 等候：We are ~ing for the rain to stop. 我们在等雨停。~ **in line** 排队等候；~ in line for tickets 排队等候买票 **keep sb.** ~**ing** 让某人一直等候：His wife never keeps him ~ing. 他妻子从不让他等候。~ **until** 等到…才：She ~ed until her daughter was asleep. 她一直等到女儿入睡。❷伺候(进餐)：She couldn't get any other job except ~ing at table. 她除了端饭上菜外找不到别的工作了。同 serve，attend / ~ **on** (**upon**) sb. 服侍某人，伺候某人：They all ~ on the king. 他们都伺候国王。

辨析
❶**await** 比 **wait** 更书面化。❷**await** 是及物动词：I await your reply. 我等你的答复。wait 除在极个别场合(主要是口语中)可用作及物动词外，通常用作不及物动词。❸**await** 后面接名词作宾语，不可接不定式；

wait 后可接不定式作状语：He has awaited your coming for a week. 他期待你来已有一个星期了。I shall wait to hear from you. 我会等你的来信。

wake / weɪk / v. (woke /wəʊk/，woken /ˈwəʊkn/ 或 waked，waked) ❶(使)醒过来：~ out of a dream 从梦中醒来 / ~ up with a start 惊醒 / What time do you usually ~ (up)? 你通常什么时候醒来？/ The noise woke me (up). 那噪声把我吵醒了。同 awake，waken ❷认识到；激起；唤起：The event may ~ her up to the danger. 这件事可使她认识危险。同 arouse，stimulate 反 calm

wakeful / ˈweɪkf(ʊ)l / adj. ❶失眠的，无法入睡的：a ~ baby 醒着没有睡的婴儿 / Old age is always ~. 上年纪的人总是难以成眠。❷不眠的：We spent a ~ night worrying about where you were. 我们不知你的去向，忧心如焚，度过了一个不眠之夜。

waken / ˈweɪkən / v. 醒来；唤醒：The old man ~ed (up) at 4 in the morning. 老人早上四点钟就醒了。/ Don't forget to ~ me tomorrow morning. 别忘了明天早晨叫醒我。同 awake，wake

walk / wɔːk / Ⅰ v. ❶行走；步行 同 stroll，pace / ~ **about** (**around**)四处走动；散步；闲逛 ~ **away** 走开 ~ **on** 继续往走，不停地走：Walk on directly for about a hundred steps and turn right，and you'll see the post-office. 继续直走大约一百步向右转弯，你就会看到邮局了。~ **out** 走出；把(某人)带出：She ~ed the child out of the room. 她带着小孩走出房间。~ **over to** 向…走过去：The policeman ~ed over to the young man. 警察向那年轻人走过去。~ **up and down** 来回走动，走来走去：The old man ~ing up and down the path is Tom's father. 在小径上走来走去的那位老人是汤姆的父亲。~ **up to** 走近：Don't ~ up to the fire. 别走近火。❷使步行，使行走：Horses should be ～ed for a while after a race. 比赛后应让马慢走一会儿。Ⅱ n. [C] ❶步行；散步；徒步旅行：The station is ten minutes' ～ from my house. 从我家步行到车站需要十分钟。圊 stroll, pace / **go for a** ～ 去散步：He often goes for a ～ in the park. 他常去公园散步。**take（have）a** ～ 散步：Let's take a ～ along the river. 我们沿着河边散散步吧。❷ [U]步态；步法：I recognized him at once by his ～. 从步态上我立刻认出是他。圊 stop, pace

wall / wɔːl / Ⅰ n. [C]墙，壁：the Great Wall 万里长城 / She put up a beautiful picture on the ～. 她在墙上贴了一张很漂亮的画。圊 fence, enclosure / **hang（run）one's head against a** ～ 试图做不可能的事；碰壁 **drive（push）sb. to the** ～ 把某人逼到绝境 **go to the** ～（比赛等）败北；（事业等）失败，破产 **with one's back to the** ～ 陷入绝境；处于背水一战的形势 Ⅱ vt. 筑墙围住；用墙隔开 圊 enclose

wallet / ˈwɒlɪt / n. [C]钱夹；皮夹

wallop / ˈwɒləp / Ⅰ vt. ❶痛击，犯击；袭击：～ sb. hard on the shoulder 狠揍某人的肩膀 / The hurricane ～ed the whole island last night. 昨晚飓风袭击了整个岛屿。❷（在比赛中）轻取，彻底打败：She ～ed me at badminton. 羽毛球赛中她把我打得惨败。Ⅱ n. [C]痛击，犯击

wallpaper / ˈwɔːlˌpeɪpə(r) / Ⅰ n. [C; U]墙纸，壁纸：flowery ～花墙纸 / Ⅱ vt. 糊墙纸于：～ a room 给房间贴墙纸

walnut / ˈwɔːlnʌt / n. [C]胡桃；核桃树

wander / ˈwɒndə(r) / v. ❶漫游，漂泊，徘徊：～ up and down the road aimlessly 无目的地徘徊于路上 圊 ramble, stroll 反 settle, stay ❷走神；（精神）恍惚 ❸离题：～ from the subject 偏离主题

wane / weɪn / Ⅰ vi. ❶减少，缩小；衰退，衰落；减弱，消逝：The night was waning away. 夜色渐阑。/My interest in botany has ～d to extinction. 我对植物学已经毫无兴趣了。❷退潮；（月亮）亏缺Ⅱ n. [C] ❶减少，缩小；衰退，衰落，消逝 ❷衰退期；尾声 ❸月亏；月亏期：**on the** ～ ①（月）亏；月亮现在正值月亏。②日益衰落，逐渐败落：The patient's health is on the ～. 病人的健康状况正每况愈下。

want / wɒnt / Ⅰ v. ❶需要：These plants are drooping—they ～ water. 这些植物发蔫

了——它们需要浇水。/ Will you ～ anything more, sir? 先生，你还要别的东西吗？圊 need, demand ❷想要；希望，期望：She ～s to go to Italy. 她想到意大利去。圊 desire ❸贫乏，缺少：～ for 需要；缺少：They said that they ～ed for nothing. 他们说他们什么也不缺。圊 lack Ⅱ n. 缺少；需要：The plants died from ～ of water. 这些植物因缺水而死。/ The house is in ～ of repair. 那房子需要修理。/ If you need a waiter, you may place a ～ ad in the newspaper. 如果需要招服务员，你可以在报上登一则招聘广告。圊 lack, shortage 反 plenty, sufficiency 派 wanting adj.

用法

❶want 表示"需要"时与 need 意思相近，后面可接动名词或不定式。动名词用主动形式表示被动含义，用不定式则常用被动形式：The machine wants repairing. The machine wants to be repaired. 这机器需要修理。❷want 表示"想要；希望"时与 desire 意义相近，后面接名词或不定式，不能接动名词：The small girl wanted everything she saw. 这小女孩看见什么就要什么。I want to see him at once. 我要立即见他。

war / wɔː(r) / n. [C]战争：civil ～ 内战 / price ～ 价格战；star ～ 星球大战/ the First（Second）World War 第一次（第二次）世界大战 / They were at ～ with three great countries. 他们同三个大国交战。圊 fighting, conflict / **carry the** ～ **into the enemy's camp** 转为攻势；还击 **go to** ～ 诉诸武力；出征

ward / wɔːd / n. [C] ❶病房；病室：emergency ～ 急救病房 ❷监禁；拘留

warden / ˈwɔːdən / n. [C] ❶保管人；看护人；管理人 ❷监狱长，看守长 ❸监督人；监管人；监护人；监察：a fire ～ 消防官员/ traffic ～s 交通管理员

wardrobe / ˈwɔːdrəub / n. [C]衣柜；衣橱

ware / weə(r) / n. ❶（pl.）商品；货物：～house 仓库，货栈 圊 goods, merchandise ❷（总称）器皿

warfare / ˈwɔːfeə(r) / n. [C]战争；战争状态；交战：ban chemical（biological, germ）～ 禁止化学(生物、细菌)战争 圊 war

warm / wɔːm / Ⅰ adj. ❶暖的，温暖的；(指衣服)保暖的：Come and get ～ by the fire. 来炉火边取暖。圊 heated, hot 反 cool, col

❷热心的；热情的：give sb. a ～ welcome 热烈欢迎某人 同 earnest, hearty 反 cold-hearted Ⅱ v. 使暖和；使感到亲切 同 heat / ～ **up** ①使(变)温和；使(变)暖和：You'd better ～ up the milk before you drink it. 你喝牛奶之前最好把它热一热。②激动起来；兴奋起来；活跃起来：Having heard the good news, the children all ～ed up. 听到这个好消息，孩子们全都兴奋起来。③做热身(轻松)运动：All the players spend some minutes ～ing up before the game. 在比赛前，所有运动员都做几分钟热身运动。派 warmly adv.

warmth / wɔːmθ / n. [U]温暖；亲切；热烈：He was pleased with the ～ of his friends' welcome. 朋友们对他的热烈欢迎使他感到很高兴。/ They welcomed the delegation with ～. 他们热烈欢迎代表团。同 heat, kindness 反 chill, coldness

warn / wɔːn / vt. 警告；提醒；告诫；预先通知 同 caution, inform / ～ **sb. of sth.** (惊慌)某人…：The teacher ～ed us of possible failure in the experiment. 老师提醒我们实验可能会失败。～ **against** 警告；提醒；告诫(不要)：She ～ed me against eating and drinking too much. 她告诫我别暴饮暴食。/ He ～ed me against pickpockets. 他提醒我提防扒手。

warning / 'wɔːnɪŋ / Ⅰ adj. 警告的；预告的；预先通知的：He gave me a ～ look. 他向我递了一个警告的眼色。Ⅱ n. 警报；警告；预兆：He paid no attention to my ～s. 他忽视我的警告。同 alarm, caution

warranty / 'wɒrənti, 'wɔːrənti / n. ❶承诺，保证；担保：Your computer will be repaired without charge because it's still under ～. 你的计算机将免费修理，因为还在保修期内。❷[C]保证书，担保书；保(修或用)单：a ～ of quality for the goods 商品质量保证书/ a one-year ～ on a television set 电视机保用一年的保单

warrant / 'wɒrənt / n. [C]凭证；证件 同 permit, licence

wash / wɒʃ / Ⅰ v. 洗涤；洗去：He never ～es (himself) in cold water. 他从不用冷水洗澡。同 clean, mop / ～ **up** 洗餐具；洗手；洗脸：It's your turn to ～ up today. 今天轮到你洗碗碟了。Ⅱ n. 洗，洗涤：I must go and have a ～. 我得去洗个澡。同 cleaning

wastage / 'weɪstɪdʒ / n. [U]损耗量；损耗

waste / weɪst / Ⅰ v. 浪费；滥用：～ time and money 浪费时间和金钱 / ～ one's words (breath)白费唇舌 同 misuse, spoil 反 save, preserve Ⅱ [U] ❶浪费 同 misuse 反 economy ❷废物；垃圾：lay ～ to 使…荒废 同 refuse, rubbish Ⅲ adj. ❶(指土地)未利用的，废弃的，荒芜的：～ land 荒地 ❷无用的：～ paper 废纸 同 useless 反 useful

wasteful / 'weɪstfl / adj. 浪费的；挥霍的；不经济的：It's ～ to use so much water to wash a bowl. 用这么多水洗一个碗是很浪费的。同 extravagant 反 economical

watch[1] / wɒtʃ / n. [C]手表；挂表

watch[2] / wɒtʃ / Ⅰ v. 看，注视；警戒；守望；监视：She likes to ～ children play. 她喜欢看孩子们玩耍。/ Watch what I am doing. 细心看我做什么。/ The old couple usually ～es TV in the evening. 老夫妇通常在晚上看电视。/ Will you ～ over my clothes while I am swimming? 我去游泳时，你替我照看衣服好吗? 同 observe, guard 反 overlook, ignore / ～ **out** 当心，留神 / ～ **out for** 密切注意；提防 Ⅱ n. 看；注意；警戒；守望：keep ～ 守望，放哨 / keep (maintain) a close ～ on 对…进行严密的监视 同 observation, attention / **on** ～ 值班，值勤：Who is the man on ～ today? 今天谁值班?

watchful / 'wɒtʃfl / adj. 密切注意的；警惕的 同 cautious, careful 反 unguarded 派 watchfully adv.

water / 'wɔːtə(r) / Ⅰ n. 水；河水；湖水；海水：Water changes into steam by heat and into ice by cold. 水加热则变成蒸汽，冷却则结成冰。/ boiled ～ 开水 / mineral ～ 矿泉水 / by ～ 由水路，乘船 Ⅱ v. 浇水；灌溉：She is ～ing the flowers. 她正在给花浇水。同 splash, irrigate

waterfall / 'wɔːtəfɔːl / n. [C]瀑布

watermelon / 'wɔːtəmelən / n. [C;U]西瓜

waterproof / 'wɔːtəpruːf / Ⅰ adj. 防水的：～ material 防水材料 / ～ watch 防水手表 Ⅱ n. [C]雨衣：Put on your ～ before you go into the rain. 下雨时穿上雨衣出门。同 raincoat

watershed / 'wɔːtəʃed / n. ❶流域：～ of the Yellow River 黄河流域 ❷分水岭，分水线，分水界 ❸转折点；重要关头；决定性因素：the historic ～ of war 战争的历史性转折点

watertight / 'wɔːtətaɪt / adj. ❶防水的，不透水的：～ joints 不漏水的接头 / keep the submarine ～ 保持潜艇的不透水性 ❷严密的,无懈可击的;天衣无缝的:Their fire precautions are truly ～. 他们的火灾防范措施确实是滴水不漏。

watery / ˈwɔːtəri / adj. ❶水的;含水过多的 ❷湿的;湿润的 同 damp,wet 反 dry

watt / wɒt / n.[C]瓦(特)(功率单位)

wave / weɪv / Ⅰ v. ❶波动;飘扬;挥舞:flags waving in the wind 在风中飘扬的旗帜 同 flutter,shake ❷以挥动作为信号;挥手打招呼:～ goodbye to sb. 向某人挥手告别 / She ～d me a greeting. 她挥手给我打招呼。同 signal,gesture / ～ **aside** 挥走;挥退;排斥:His proposal was ～d aside. 他的建议被驳回。Ⅱ n.[C] ❶水波;波浪:long (medium, short) ～s 长(中、短)波 / light ～s 光波 / radio ～s 无线电波 / shock ～ (爆炸的)冲击波 / sound ～s 声波 ❷挥动:with a ～ of his hand 他挥动一下手

wavelength / ˈweɪvˌleŋθ / n.[C]波长:effective ～ 有效波长 / **on the same** ～ 相互协调;有相同观点(或兴趣):We seldom found ourselves on the same ～. 我们很难发现自己与琴瑟和谐的。

waver / ˈweɪvə(r) / vi. ❶摇摆;摇晃;摇曳:The boy ～s a little as he walks. 这孩子走路有点摇晃。同 sway,swing ❷犹豫;不决 同 hesitate

wavy / ˈweɪvi / adj. 波浪形的;波状的

wax / wæks / Ⅰ n. [U]蜡:～ cloth 蜡布 / ～ doll 蜡人 / ～ work 蜡制品;蜡像 Ⅱ vt. 给…上蜡:It is time to ～ the furniture and the floor. 该给家具和地板上蜡了。派 waxy adj.

way / weɪ / n.[C]❶路,通路;道路;街:a ～ across the forest 穿过森林的路 同 road,route ❷方法,方式;行动方针:the right ～ to do (of doing) a thing 做一件事情的正确方法/ Do it in your own ～ if you don't like mine. 如果你不喜欢我的方式,你可以按自己的方式做。同 method,means / **all the** ～ 一直,从头到尾;完全,全部 by **the** ～ By the ～, what are you doing now? 顺便问一问,你现在做什么? **by** ～ **of** 由,经过:He came by ～ of Dover. 他途经多佛来此。**give** ～ 让路,让步 **in a** ～ 在某种程度上,有点,有几分 **in any** ～ 不管怎样,好歹 **in every** ～ 在各方面;以各种方式 **in no** ～ 决不,一点也不:Study can in no

～ be separated from practice. 学习决不能与实践分离。**lead the** ～ 引路,带路;示范:A young girl led the ～ for us. 一位年轻姑娘为我们带路。**make** ～ 让路;腾出地方:You should make ～ for the old. 你应当给老人让路。**make one's** ～ 前进,前往 **on one's** ～ **to** 在路上:He is on his ～ to the station. 他在去车站的路上。**under** ～ 在进行中:A new project is under ～. 一个新的项目正在进行中。

WC (＝Water closet)盥洗室,厕所

we / wiː / pron. 我们

weak / wiːk / adj. ❶弱的,虚弱的;脆弱的;易破的:a ～ team 弱队 同 feeble,fragile 反 strong ❷(感官等)功能不佳的;衰弱的:The old lady is not ～ in hearing. 那老太太听力不差。/ a ～ heart 衰弱的心脏 同 unhealthy, delicate 反 healthy,vigorous ❸不精的;有欠缺的:(be) ～ **in** 在…方面差:Jack is a little ～ in Chinese. 杰克的汉语有点差。同 poor,unsatisfactory 反 good, excellent 派 weakly adv. ;weakness n.

weaken / ˈwiːkən / v. (使)变弱:The patient's heart was ～ing. 病人的心脏越来越衰弱。同 lessen,undermine 反 strengthen

wealth / welθ / n.[U]大量财产(的拥有);财富:a man of ～ 富人 同 fortune,riches 反 poverty,scarcity

wealthy / ˈwelθi / adj. (-ier, -iest)富有的;丰富的:～ in knowledge 知识丰富 / China is ～ in natural resources. 中国自然资源丰富。同 rich,prosperous 反 poor

weapon / ˈwepən / n.[C]武器,兵器:～s of mass destruction 大规模杀伤性武器 / A gun may be a ～ of offence or a ～ of defence. 枪可以是进攻武器,也可以是防卫武器。/ Are tears a woman's ～? 眼泪是女人的武器吗? 同 arms

wear / weə(r) / v. (wore /wɔː/, worn /wɔːn/) ❶穿,戴:He was ～ing a hat (a wristwatch,a ring on his finger). 他戴着一顶帽子(戴着手表,手指上戴着戒指)。同 dress in, put on ❷(面容)呈现出,显得:He ～s a troubled look. 他愁容满面。同 bear, display ❸(使)磨损;(使)变旧;用坏:I have worn my socks into holes. 我的袜子已经穿出洞来了。同 consume / ～ **away** 使磨损;磨平:The inscription has worn away. 那碑文已经磨平消失了。～ **ou**

① 使变坏：My shoes are worn out. 我的鞋穿坏了。② 使筋疲力尽；使耗尽：I am worn out with the hard work. 这些艰苦的工作使我疲乏不堪。

辨析

wear 一般用主动语态，指身上穿着某样衣服：He wears a new coat. 他穿着一件新外套。**dress** 多用被动语态，如果用主动语态，后紧接反身代词：She is dressed in green. 她穿着绿色的衣服。She could dress herself at four. 她四岁就会自己穿衣服了。

wearing / ˈweərɪŋ / adj. ❶使人疲倦的；令人厌倦的：It's a very ～ job. 那是很令人厌倦的工作。❷消耗性的，逐渐耗损的：Reading small print can be ～ on the eyes. 看小字体耗损人的视力。

weary / ˈwɪəri / Ⅰ adj. 疲倦的；厌烦的；war-～ 厌战的 同 tired, exhausted 反 refreshed / be ～ of 对…感到厌烦：People are ～ of the war. 人们对这场战争感到厌烦。Ⅱ vt. 使疲乏；使厌烦 同 tire, exhaust 反 refresh / ～ of 厌倦…：He wearies of living all alone. 他厌烦独居生活。～ sb. with 因…使某人厌烦：He wearied me with requests. 她的多次请求使我厌烦。

weather / ˈweðə(r) / n. [U]天气；气象：She stays indoors in wet ～. 雨天她待在家里。同 climate, temperature

用法

weather 作"天气"解时是不可数名词，但在 in all weathers 中 weathers 指"各种天气"：He has to go to work in all weathers. 无论什么天气他都得上班。

weave / wiːv / v. (wove/wəʊv/, woven /ˈwəʊvn/)编，织(纱、线)成布；纺织：be woven by hand 手工织的 / be woven of silk 用丝织成的/～ the flowers into a wreath 把一些花编成花环 / weave a metre of cloth 织一米布 同 knit, twist

web / web / n. [C]网络；蜘蛛网 同 net

website / ˈwebsaɪt / n. (计算机)网站

wed / wed / v. (wedded 或 wed; wedding)结婚，嫁，娶 同 marry

wedding / ˈwedɪŋ / n. 婚礼；结婚：attend a ～ 参加婚礼 / perform a ～ 主持婚礼/～ dress 结婚礼服/ ～ ring 结婚戒指 同 marriage

Wednesday / ˈwenzdi / n. 星期三

weed / wiːd / Ⅰ n. 杂草：My garden is running to ～s. 我的花园长满了杂草。Ⅱ v. 除去杂草：～ the garden 除去花园里的杂草

week / wiːk / n. 周，星期：There are a few weeks away from the final examination. 离期末考试还有几星期。

weekday / ˈwiːkdeɪ / n. [C]工作日：We have five ～s every week. 我们每周工作五天。

weekend / ˌwiːkˈend / n. [C]周末：at (during, over) the ～ 在周末 / on ～s 每个周末 / How do you usually spend your ～? 通常你们怎样度周末？

weekly / ˈwiːkli / Ⅰ adj. 每周一次的；一周的：a ～ wage of £150 周薪150英镑 Ⅱ n. 周刊；周报

weep / wiːp / v. (wept/wept/, wept)哭泣；流泪：～ over sb.'s misfortunes 为某人的不幸而流泪 / She wept herself to sleep. 她哭着睡着了。同 cry, sob 反 laugh, enjoy

weigh / weɪ / v. ❶称…的重量：He ～ed himself in the scales. 他在体重器上称体重。同 measure, balance ❷重(若干)：～ a ton 重一吨

weight / weɪt / n. ❶[U]重量；体重；重力：lose ～ 减少体重 / put on ～ 增加体重 / The man is twice my ～. 那人的体重是我的两倍。同 gravity, heaviness 反 weightlessness ❷砝码；秤砣 ❸重压；负担 同 load, burden

weightless / ˈweɪtlɪs / adj. 失重的；无重力的：carry out experiments in the ～ conditions 在失重条件下进行实验

welcome / ˈwelkəm / Ⅰ adj. ❶受欢迎的：a ～ visitor 受欢迎的来宾/～ news 佳音 同 accepted, wanted ❷被允许的：You are ～ to use my bicycle. 他们尽可以用我的自行车。同 acceptable, agreeable Ⅱ n. [C]欢迎；接待；款待：They gave us a warm ～. 他们对我们热情的欢迎。同 greeting, reception Ⅲ vt. 欢迎：We ～ criticisms. 我们欢迎批评。/ ～ sb. with open arms 热烈欢迎某人：Come soon. We'll ～ you with open arms. 快来吧！我们会热烈欢迎你们的。同 greet, receive

辨析

"You are welcome." 主要用于他人向你道谢时的答语：—Thank you very much. —谢谢你。—You are welcome. — 不用谢。**"Never mind."** 主要用于 ① 当某人要帮忙或为你做某事时的回答：—Let me carry that for you. — 我来替你拿吧。—Never mind. — 不用。② 当他人向你道歉时的回答：—Sorry, I kept you waiting. —对不起，让你久等了。— Never mind. —没关系。

weld / weld / I *vt.* 焊接：～ pieces into a unit 把部件焊接成整套装置 II *n.* 焊接

welfare / 'welfeə(r) / *n.* [U]福利；幸福：work for the ～ of the people 为人民的幸福而工作 / social ～ 社会福利 圓 benefit, happiness

well¹ / wel / I *adv.* (better, best) ❶ 好；对；满意地：They are ～ behaved children. 他们是乖孩子。/ Well done (played)! 做得好(表演得好)! ❷ 彻底地，完全；颇，甚：Examine the account ～ before you pay it. 付款之前要仔细核对账目。/ His name is ～ up in the list. 他的名字列在前面。圓 thoroughly, completely 反 incompletely **as ～ (as)** 除…之外；也：He gave me money as ～ as advice. 他除了给我忠告外还给我钱。**be ～ in** 在…方面做得好：Tom is always ～ in playing football. 汤姆踢球总是踢得很好。**be ～ off** 生活富裕：Although she is ～ off, she lives quite simply. 虽然她很富裕，但她生活十分简朴。/ a ～-off society 小康社会 II *adj.* (仅作表语)(身体)健康的：be (look, feel) ～ (看来是)健康的 圓 healthy, strong 反 unwell, sick III *interj.* (表示惊奇、同意等)哎呀；好；那么：Well, who would have thought it? 啊, 谁想得到是这样呢?

well² / wel / *n.* [C]井；drive (sink) a ～ 开(打)井 / ～ water 井水 / oil ～ 油井

well-being / 'wel;bi:ŋ / *n.* [U]健康；福利；幸福；康乐：sensation of ～幸福感 / Business executives believe that holidays are vital to their ～. 公司企业的经理们认为休假对他们的健康是至关重要的。

well-known / 'wel'nəʊn / *adj.* ❶著名的；出名的：A ～ scientist will come and give us a talk. 一位知名科学家要来给我们做报告。圓 famous, noted 反 unknown ❷众所周知的；熟悉的：a ～ voice 熟悉的声音/ It is a ～ fact.

那是众所周知的事实。圓 recognized, familiar 反 unknown, unfamiliar

wellspring / 'welsprŋ / *n.* [C]河源；泉源；(不断的)源泉：the ～s of the creative spirit 创造精神的源泉

west / west / I *n.* 西方，西部：The sun sets in the ～. 太阳从西边落下。the West 西方；西方各国(与亚洲相对而言)；(任何国家的)西部 II *adj.* 西方的；西部的：on the ～ coast 在西海岸 / the West Lake 西湖 III *adv.* 向西地：sail (travel) ～ 向西航行(旅行)

western / 'westən / *adj.* 西方的；来自西方的：the Western Hemisphere 西半球 / the ～ nations 西方国家

westward / 'westwəd / *adj. & adv.* 向西(的) 反 eastward

wet / wet / I *adj.* (wetter, wettest) ❶湿的，潮湿的：Her cheeks were ～ with tears. 眼泪顺着她的脸颊流下。圓 humid, soaked 反 dry / **be ～ through, be ～ to the skin** 全身湿透 ❷多雨的；下雨的：～ weather 雨天 圓 rainy II *vt.* (wet 或 wetted, wet 或 wetted)打(弄、淋)湿；尿湿：You should first ～ your hair before applying the shampoo. 你在抹洗发水前应先打湿头发。圓 damp, moisten

whale / weɪl / *n.* [C]鲸

what / wɒt / I *interj. & adj.* (疑问形容词)什么，哪些：Tell me ～ books you have read recently. 告诉我, 你近来读了些什么书。II *pron.* (疑问代词)什么，什么东西：What is he? 他是做什么的? / ～ about (用于询问人的意见或想法)…怎么样? What about going for a walk? 去散散步怎么样? ～ if ①万一…怎么办：What if she won't answer my letter? 她要是不回我的信怎么办? ②即使…又有什么关系：What if she gets angry? 即使她生气了又有什么关系? ❷(关系代词)…那样的事物或人：What he says is very important. 他所说的话很重要。/ Do ～ you think right. 按照你认为正确的做法去做。

whatever / wɒt'evə(r) / I *pron.* ❶无论什么；不管什么：Whatever you do, you must do it well. 无论你做什么事，一定要把它做好。/ Keep calm ～ happens. 无论发生了什么事情都要保持镇静。❷任何…的事物；凡是…的东西 II *adj.* 不管怎样的，无论什么样的：Whatever opinion you have, tell us, please. 不管你有什么意见，都请告诉我们。

what-if / ˈwɒtˌɪf / Ⅰ *adj.* 想象的；可能的；假定的：a ～ scenario 想象中的场景 Ⅱ *n.* [C]假定情况或事件；假定推测

whatnot / ˈwɒtˌnɒt / *n.* 诸如此类的东西：candies，crisps，cakes and ～ 糖果、薯片以及糕点之类的东西

wheat / wiːt / *n.* [C]小麦

wheel / wiːl / *n.* [C]轮；车轮；机轮：at the ～ ①开车的②掌握着支配权的 go on ～s 顺利进行

when / wen / *adv.* ❶(疑问副词)什么时候，何时：When does the train leave? 火车什么时候开？ ❷(关系副词)在那时：Sunday is the day ～ I am least busy. 星期天是我最不忙的日子。 ❸(连接副词)当…的时候，在…的时候：The pupils put up their hands ～ they know the answers. 当学生们知道答案时，他们全举手。

whenever / wenˈevə(r) / Ⅰ *conj.* ❶无论何时：I'll talk the matter with you ～ you come. 你无论什么时候来，我都愿意和你谈论这个问题。 ❷每当：Whenever I met with difficulties，he would come to help me. 每当我遇到困难的时候，他都会来帮助我。 Ⅱ *adv.* (口语)究竟何时：Whenever did I tell you such a thing? 我究竟何时告诉过你这样的事情？

where / weə(r) / *adv.* ❶(疑问副词)在哪里，在什么地方：Where are you going? 你往哪儿去？ ❷(关系副词)在那里，在该处：That's the place ～ the accident happened. 那就是出事的地点。 ❸(连接副词)在…的地方：Where there is no rain，farming is difficult or impossible. 没有雨水的地方，很难有农业，或者根本不可能有农业。 / Where there is smoke，there is fire. (谚语)无风不起浪。

whereabouts Ⅰ / ˌweərəˈbaʊts / *adv.* 在哪里，靠近什么地方；在某地附近，在某地周围：Whereabouts did you leave my umbrella? 你把我的雨伞放哪儿了？ /Whereabouts is your villa then? 您的别墅在什么地方？ Ⅱ / ˈweərəˌbaʊts / *n.* 位置；下落；行踪：Those children's ～ are unknown. 那些孩子们的下落不明。

whereas / ˌweərˈæz / *conj.* 但是，然而，反之：Some people like fat meat，～ others hate it. 有人喜欢肥肉，而有人讨厌肥肉。

wherever / ˌweərˈevə(r) / Ⅰ *conj.* 无论在哪里；无论到哪里：Sit ～ you like. 请随便坐。 Ⅱ *adv.* ❶无论什么地方，任何地方 ❷(口语)

究竟在哪里，究竟到哪里

whether / ˈweðə(r) / *conj.* ❶(常与 or 连用)是…还是…：I wonder ～ it will rain or snow. 我不知道天会不会下雨还是会下雪。 / Whether it rains or not，we'll go tonight. 无论天是不是下雨，我们今晚都要去。 ❷是否：Could you tell me ～ it's very hot in summer here? 你能否告诉我这儿夏天天气是不是很热？ 同 if

which / wɪtʃ / Ⅰ *pron.* ❶(疑问代词)哪一个；哪一些：Which do you prefer? 你喜欢哪一个？ ❷(关系代词)…的那个，…的那些：The house ～ is for sale is at the end of the street. 待售的房子在街的尽头。 The river ～ flows through London is called the Thames. 流经伦敦的那条河称为泰晤士河。 Ⅱ *adj.* 哪个；哪些：Which book would you like? 你喜欢哪一本书？

辨析

which 和 **what** 都含有选择之意，但 which 表示在一定范围内的选择，而 what 没有一定范围：Which book is he reading? (这几本书中间)他正在读哪一本？ What book is he reading? 他正在读什么书？

whichever / wɪtʃˈevə(r) / Ⅰ *pron.* 无论哪个；无论哪些：Choose ～ you like best. 你最喜欢哪个就选哪个。 Ⅱ *adj.* 无论哪个，无论哪些：Whichever method you use, the result is the same. 无论你用哪一种方法，结果都一样。

while / waɪl / Ⅰ *n.* (一段)时间：Where have you been all this ～? 这一阵子你在哪儿？ / **all the ～** 始终，一直：We stayed at home all the ～ yesterday. 昨天我们一直待在家里。 **in a (little) ～** 一会儿，不久：I'll be back in a little ～. 我很快就会回来。 **once in a ～** 偶尔，间或：Once in a ～ we go to a restaurant，but usually we eat at home. 我们偶尔下馆子，但一般都在家吃饭。 Ⅱ *conj.* ❶当…的时候；在…之时：He fell asleep ～ reading the grammar book. 他看语法书时睡着了。 / While there is life，there is hope. 只要有生命就有希望(留得青山在，不怕没柴烧)。 ❷而，然而，反之：Jane was dressed in brown ～ Mary was dressed in blue. 简穿褐色衣服，而玛丽穿蓝色衣服。 ❸尽管，虽然：While I admit that the problems are difficult，I don't agree that they cannot be solved. 虽然我承认这些问题很难，但我并不认为这些问题无法解决。 同 although，though

whip / wɪp / Ⅰ *n.* [C]鞭子 Ⅱ *v.* (whipped；whipping)鞭笞；抽打：～ a horse 用鞭打马

strike, beat

whirl / wɜːl / Ⅰ v. ❶(使)回旋；(使)旋转：
The wind ～ed the dead leaves about. 风吹得
枯叶四处飞旋。圆 turn, rotate ❷(指头)晕
眩；(指思绪)纷乱：His head ～ed. 他的头晕
了。圆 feel dizzy Ⅱ n.(仅用单数)旋转：His
brain was in a ～. 他的头晕了。圆 turn, rotation

whirlpool / wɜːlpuːl / n. [C]旋涡，涡流：be
caught in a ～ of the river 被卷入河水旋涡
之中。

whirlwind / wɜːlwɪnd / n. [C] ❶旋风，旋
流，龙卷风：The old church was seriously
damaged by a ～. 那座古老的教堂遭到了旋
风的严重破坏。❷旋风似的事物；猛烈的破坏
力量：a political ～一场政治风暴

whisker / ˈwɪskə(r) / n.(pl.)髯；胡须
圆 beard

whisky / ˈwɪski / n. [U]威士忌酒

whisper / ˈwɪspə(r) / Ⅰ v. ❶低语；耳语：
(a word) to sb. 低声对某人说；悄悄告诉某人
/ It is ～ed that he is heavily in debt. 据秘密
传闻他负债很多。圆 murmur, mutter 反 cry,
shout Ⅱ n. 耳语；私语：He answered in a ～.
他低声回答。/ Whispers are going round that
the firm is likely to go bankrupt. 据传闻，那家
商行可能倒闭。圆 murmur, mutter 反
cry, shout

whistle / ˈwɪsl / Ⅰ n. ❶哨子；汽笛：a
referee's ～ 裁判的哨子 ❷口哨声；汽笛声；
鸣叫声；啸叫声：We heard the ～ of a steam-
engine. 我们听到了蒸汽机的啸叫声。Ⅱ v. ❶吹
口哨；鸣笛：The driver ～d before reaching
the level-crossing. 司机在抵达水平交叉道之
前鸣汽笛。❷用口哨发信号：He ～d his dog
back. 他吹口哨唤狗回来。

white / waɪt / Ⅰ adj. ❶白色的；雪白的：as
～ as a sheet 苍白如纸 / Her hair has turned
～. 她的头发变白了。圆 snowy, gray 反 black
❷白肤色的：～ civilization 白色人种的文明
Ⅱ n. ❶白色：The girl (dressed) in ～ is the
famous singer. 穿白衣的女孩是著名的歌手。
❷白人 派 whiteness n.；whiten v.

white-collar / waɪtˈkɒlə(r) / adj. ❶白领阶层
的；脑力劳动的：～ workers 白领工作者

who / huː / pron. ❶(疑问代词)谁：Who are
those men? 那些人是谁？/ Do you know ～

broke the window? 你知道窗子是谁打破的
吗？❷(关系代词)那个人：This is the man ～
wanted to see you. 这就是要见你的那个人。

WHO(＝World Health Organization)世界卫生
组织

whoever / huːˈevə(r) / pron. ❶无论谁，不
管谁：Whoever made the mistake, he must correct it. 无论是谁犯的错，都得改正。❷(口语)
究竟是谁，到底是谁：Whoever did such a foolish thing? 究竟是谁做了这样一件傻事？

whole / həul / Ⅰ adj. 整个的；完整的；全体
的：I want to know the ～ truth about this
matter. 我要知道这件事的全部真相。圆 com-
plete, entire 反 partial, incomplete Ⅱ n. 完整的
东西；全部，全体 圆 body, total 反 part, por-
tion/ **as a** ～ 作为一个整体；整个看来 / **on
the** ～ 总的说来，大体上

wholesale / ˈhəulseɪl / Ⅰ n. [U]批发，趸售 Ⅱ
adj. ❶(有关)批发的，成批售出的；批发价
的：a ～ business 批发商店/～ prices are a-
bout twenty-five per cent off retail prices. 批发
价要比零售价约低 25%。❷大规模的；全部
的；不加区别的：the ～ application of the new
method 新方法的广泛应用 Ⅲ adv. ❶成批地；
以批发价：They only sell ～. 他们只搞批发销
售。❷大规模地，大量地；不加区别地；彻底地

wholly / ˈhəulli / adv. 完全地；完整地；整个
地：I ～ agree with you. 我完全同意你的意
见。圆 completely, entirely

whom / huːm / pron. ❶(疑问代词)谁(who
的宾格)：Whom did you see just now? 刚才你
看到了谁？❷(关系代词)…的那个人；…的
那些人：She is the girl ～ we met at the gate.
她就是我们在大门口遇到的那个女孩。

whose / huːz / pron. ❶(疑问代词)谁的(who
的所有格)：Whose house is that? 那是谁的
房子？❷(关系代词)那个的；那些的：The
boy ～ father complained to me is very stupid.
那个男孩非常愚笨，他的父亲曾向我诉苦。

why / waɪ / Ⅰ adv. ❶(疑问副词)何故，为什
么；有何目的：Do you know ～ he came here?
你知道他为什么来这里吗？❷(关系副词)…
的原因：That is the reason ～ he failed. 那就
是他失败的原因。Ⅱ interj. ❶(表示惊讶)：
Why, it's easy! A child could do it. 哎呀，那太
容易了！小孩也会做。❷(表示异议)：Why,
what's the harm? 嗨，难道有什么不对吗？

wicked / ˈwɪkɪd / adj. ❶邪恶的 圆 bad, evil
反 good, moral ❷淘气的；顽皮的：You ～

boy! 你这个淘气鬼! 同 naughty 反 well-mannered 派 wickedly *adv.* ; wickedness *n.*

wide / waɪd / Ⅰ *adj.* ❶宽广的;广阔的;的:a ～ river 宽阔的河流 / a road twelve feet ～ 12 英尺宽的道路 同 broad 反 narrow ❷广大的;广泛的,渊博的:a man with ～ interest 兴趣广泛的人 同 extensive 反 restricted ❸张大的: She stared at him with ～ eyes. 她睁大眼睛注视他。 同 expanded, open 反 closed, shut Ⅱ *adv.* 宽广地;充分地;张得很大地:He was ～ awake. 他是完全清醒的。 / The window was ～ open. 那窗子是大开着的。 派 fully, completely 反 narrowly, partially 派 widely *adv.*

widen / 'waɪdn / *v.* 加宽,放宽;变宽:The workers are ～ing the road. 工人们正在加宽道路。 同 broaden, extend 反 narrow, limit

widespread / 'waɪdspred / *adj.* 分布广的;普遍的:a ～ disease 流行病 / We cannot overlook the ～ influence of the book. 我们不能忽视该书的广泛影响。 同 extensive, prevalent 反 narrow, limited

widow / 'wɪdəʊ / *n.* [C]寡妇

widower / 'wɪdəʊə(r) / *n.* [C]鳏夫

width / wɪdθ / *n.* 宽阔;广度:A street of great ～ goes through the city. 一条很宽的大街穿过城市。 / The boy was known for ～ of mind. 那孩子心胸开阔是人所共知的。 / Leave a ～ of two meters here, please. 请在这里留下两米宽度。 同 broadness

wield / wiːld / *vt.* ❶手持(武器或工具等);使用,操纵(武器或工具等):soldiers ～ing swords 手持利剑的武士们 / ～ a new machine 操纵新机器 ❷运用,行使(权力或权威等);施加(影响等);支配,控制:He ～s a lot of power in the government. 他在政府中有很大的影响力。

wife / waɪf / *n.* [C](*pl.* wives /waɪvz/)妻子

wild / waɪld / *adj.* ❶(指动物)野性的;(指植物)野生的:～ flowers 野花 同 untamed, uncultivated 反 tame, cultivated ❷(指地方)荒凉的,无人居住的:～ mountain areas 荒凉的山区 同 uncivilized, uninhabited 反 civilized, inhabited ❸激动的;激昂的:She is ～ about music. 她酷爱音乐。 / He was ～ with anger. 他狂怒。 同 violent, unrestrained 反 gentle, quiet 派 wildly *adv.* ; wildness *n.*

will¹ / wɪl / *aux. v.* (would/wʊd, wəd/) ❶构成将来时(用于第二、三人称的肯定句及第三人称的疑问句):You ～ be in time if you hurry. 如果你快一点,就会及时赶到。 ❷表示愿意、同意、建议或应允(与第一人称连用):We said we would help him. 我们说过我们愿意帮助他。 ❸表示请求(用于第二人称的疑问句):Will you come in? 请进来好吗? ❹表示可能性:This ～ be the book you're looking for, I think. 我想,这可能就是你在寻找的那本书。 ❺表示假说,条件:They would have been killed if the car had gone over the cliff. 如果汽车当时从悬崖翻落,他们可能已丧命了。

will² / wɪl / *n.* ❶意志:the freedom of the ～ 意志的自由 ❷(仅用单数)决心:Where there is a ～, there's a way. (谚语)有志者事竟成。 同 determination, resolution ❸希望:She married him against the ～ of her parents. 她违背父母意愿与他结婚。 同 desire, wish / at ～ 随意:You may come and go at ～. 你可以随意来去。 ❹遗嘱:The old man's ～ is to build a school for the children. 老人的遗嘱是为孩子们修建一所学校。

willful / 'wɪlful / *adj.* ❶有意的,故意的,存心的:～ waste makes woeful want. 肆意挥霍,家徒四壁。 / It seemed ～. 这看来是故意的。 ❷固执的,执拗的,任性的:a ～ and difficult child 执拗而任性的孩子

willing / 'wɪlɪŋ / *adj.* 自愿的;乐意的:He was quite ～ to pay the price I asked. 他很愿付我要的价钱。 同 voluntary, ready 反 unwilling, reluctant 派 willingly *adv.* ; willingness *n.*

willow / 'wɪləʊ / *n.* [C]柳树

win / wɪn / *v.* (won/wʌn/, won)赢得,获胜,战胜:～ a race 在赛跑中获胜 同 triumph, succeed 反 lose, fail

wind¹ / wɪnd / *n.* 风:the north ～ 北风 / The ～ is rising (falling). 风势增强(减弱)。 派 windy *adj.*

wind² / waɪnd / *v.* (wound/waʊnd/, wound) ❶迂回前进;蜿蜒:The river ～s (its way) to the sea. 那条河蜿蜒流入大海。 同 curve, bend ❷给…上发条:If you forget to ～ up your clock, it will stop. 如果你忘记给钟上发条,它就会停走。

window / 'wɪndəʊ / *n.* [C]窗子;(计算机的)视窗

wine / waɪn / *n.* [C]酒;(尤指)葡萄酒

wing / wɪŋ / *n.* [C]翅膀,翼:on the ～ 在飞

行中；在活动中/ **under the ～ of sb. , under sb. 's ～** 在某人的保护之下

wink / wɪŋk / *vi.* ❶眨眼；眨眼示意 ❷闪烁；闪耀

winter / 'wɪntə(r) / *n.* [C]冬季

wipe / waɪp / *v.* 擦；抹；揩：～ the dishes 擦盘子 / ～ one's hands on a towel 在毛巾上擦手 / ～ the tears away 擦去眼泪 / ～ off the drawing from the blackboard 擦掉黑板上的图画 圓 rub , clean / ～ **out** 擦掉；除去；消灭；摧毁：The earthquake ～d out many buildings. 地震摧毁了许多建筑物。

wire / 'waɪə(r) / *n.* 金属线：telephone ～(s) 电话线 / copper ～ 铜丝

wisdom / 'wɪzdəm / *n.* [U]智慧 圓 intelligence

wise / waɪz / *adj.* 有判断力的；聪明的；明智的：He was ～ enough not to drive when he was feeling ill. 他很明智，在感到不舒服时便不开车。圓 intelligent 反 foolish, unwise

wish / wɪʃ / Ⅰ *v.* ❶意欲；想要：They ～ed the voyage at an end. 他们期望航程结束。/ She ～ed for an opportunity to go to school. 她希望有上学的机会。/ She ～es to be a-lone. 她想单独待着。圓 want, desire ❷但愿：She ～ed she had passed the exam. 她但愿自己通过考试。❸祝愿：～ sb. a pleasant journey 祝某人旅途愉快 Ⅱ *n.* 愿望，希望；祝愿：He disregarded his father's ～es. 他把他父亲的愿望置之度外。圓 want, desire

用法
❶wish 后面可接不定式或宾语加不定式，不接宾语加动名词：I wish to see him immediately. 我希望能立即见他。He wished someone else to take his place. 他希望有人来替他。❷wish 后接可引导的宾语从句应用虚拟语气。❸wish 后接双宾语用于祝福语中：I wish you a happy new year. 我祝你新年快乐。

wit / wɪt / *n.* ❶智力；才智；智能：A fall into the pit, a gain in your ～. 吃一堑，长一智。圓 brain, intelligence 反 foolishness / **at one's ～s'**(**～'s**)**end** 智穷才尽；不知所措 **out of one's ～s** 失去理智；发疯 ❷风趣：He is a man of ～. 他是一个风趣的人。圓 humor

with / wɪð / *prep.* ❶有；有…的特征：a coat ～ two pockets 有两个口袋的外衣 ❷用；借助

（表示使用的方法）：write ～ a pen 用笔写字 / ～ the help of your friends 在你朋友们的帮助下 ❸与…一起（表示陪伴）：to go for a walk with a friend 和朋友一起散步/He lives ～ his parents. 他和父母一起住。❹因为，由于（表示原因）：trembling ～ fear (rage) 因恐惧（愤怒）而颤抖 ❺以…，在…的情况下（表样子、做法）：do sth. ～ one's whole heart 全身心投入地做某事 / ease 轻易地；毫不费劲地 / He was standing ～ his hands in his pockets. 他双手插在口袋里站着。

withdraw / wɪð'drɔː / *v.* (withdrew/wɪð'druː/, withdrawn/ wɪð'drɔːn/) ❶取回：money from the bank 从银行取钱 圓 remove, extract ❷(使)撤退；收回：～ troops from an exposed position 让军队从暴露的阵地上撤退 圓 retire, retreat 反 arrive, appear 派 withdrawal *n.*

辨析
withdraw 和 **retreat** 都有"撤退"的意思。withdraw 指我方军队等出于战略目的而撤离，含褒义，它既是及物动词又是不及物动词；retreat 指敌方军队因战败或失去斗志而退却，含贬义，它只作不及物动词。

wither / 'wɪðə(r) / *v.* (使)枯萎；凋谢：The hot summer ～ed (up) the grass. 炎热的夏天使草枯萎了。圓 fade, droop

withhold /wɪð'həʊld/*vt.* (withheld, withheld) ❶保留，暂不给予：～ an announcement 暂不宣布 圓 hold back, reserve ❷压抑，抑制：I couldn't ～ my laughter. 我忍不住笑出来。圓 restrain ❸阻挡；隐瞒：～ the temptation of money 抵挡金钱的诱惑 圓 hinder; conceal

within / wɪ'ðɪn / Ⅰ *prep.* 在…之内，不出：～ an hour 在一小时内 / ～ a mile of the station 距离车站不到一英里 / live ～ one's income 量入为出 圓 inside Ⅱ*adv.* 在内，在里面 圓 inside

without / wɪ'ðaʊt / *prep.* 没有，不，无：You can't buy things ～ money. 没有钱你买不到东西。圓 lacking 反 with, within

withstand / wɪð'stænd / *vt.* (withstood /wɪð'stʊd/) 经受(住)，承受(住)；顶(得)住；抵住：I just couldn't ～ her taunts. 我就是受不了她的冷嘲热讽。/ Most ancient buildings have withstood the test of time. 大部分古建筑经受住了时间的考验。

witness / ˈwɪtnəs / Ⅰ v. ❶亲见；目击：~ an accident 目睹一次意外事件 同 see, notice ❷作证：~ against an accused person 作不利于被告的证明 同 verify, confirm Ⅱ n. ❶[C] 目击者；证人 同 observer ❷[U]证据；证明：give ~ on behalf of an accused person at his trial 在被告受审时替他作证 同 evidence, proof

wolf / wʊlf / n. [C] (pl. wolves/wʊlvz/) 狼：cry ~ 发虚假的警报：You've cried ~ too often. 你发虚假警报的次数太多了。

woman / ˈwʊmən / n. (pl. women /ˈwɪmɪn/)妇女，女性：International Women's Day 国际妇女节 / women's room 女厕所 / Women should enjoy equal rights with men. 妇女应当与男子享有同等的权利。同 female, lady 反 man

womb / wuːm / n. [C] ❶子宫 ❷发祥地，发源地，孕育处：the ~ of Judaism 犹太教的发祥地

wonder / ˈwʌndə(r) / Ⅰ n. ❶[U]惊奇，惊叹：They were filled with ~. 他们感到惊奇。同 amazement, astonishment ❷[C] 奇事；奇迹；奇观：work ~ s 创造奇迹 / It's a ~ (that) you didn't lose your way in the dark. 令人惊奇的是你在黑暗中竟未迷路。同 marvel, miracle Ⅱ v. ❶感到惊奇；感到惊讶：I ~ at her refusing to marry him. 对她拒绝跟他结婚，我感到惊奇。同 marvel ❷想知道：I ~ who he is (what he wants). 我不知道他是谁（他要什么，他为何迟到，他是否会来）。同 question, puzzle / no ~ (that...)难怪…，怪不得…：No ~ he came so early; he wanted to surprise all of us. 难怪他来得这么早，他是想让我们都感到吃惊。

wonderful / ˈwʌndəfl / adj. 惊人的；奇妙的，极好的；了不起的：~ weather 极好的天气 / ~ performance 精彩的演出 / ~ sight 奇妙的景象 / have a ~ time 过得非常愉快 / The girl has a ~ memory. 这女孩有惊人的记忆力。/ Edison made many ~ inventions. 爱迪生有许多了不起的发明。同 astonishing, excellent 派 wonderfully adv.

wood / wʊd / n. ❶[U]木，木材：Tables are usually made of ~. 桌子通常是木材做的。同 lumber, timber ❷[C](常用 pl.)树林：go for a walk in the ~ s 在树林中散步 同 forest, bush

wooden / ˈwʊdn / adj. 木制的：a ~ leg 木腿

woody / ˈwʊdi / adj. (-ier, -iest)多树木的；长满树木的：a ~ hillside 长满树木的山坡

woodpecker / ˈwʊdpekə(r) / n. [C]啄木鸟

wool / wʊl / n. 羊毛；驼毛；毛线；绒线；毛织品：wear ~ next to the skin 贴身穿羊毛衣 / the ~ trade 羊毛业

wool(l)en / ˈwʊlən / adj. 羊毛制的：~ blankets 毛毯

word / wɜːd / n. ❶[C]语；词；话：I have no ~s to express my gratitude. 我无法用言语来表达我的感激。同 expression, term / eat one's ~s 收回前言；认错；道歉 exchange angry ~s 发生口角 have a ~ with sb. 和某人说句话：Mr. Smith, can I have a ~ with you? 史密斯先生，我能与你说句话吗? get in a ~（get a ~ in）插话：She spoke so fast that I couldn't get a ~ in. 她说得很快，我插不上嘴。in a (one) ~ 总而言之 in other ~s 换句话说 ❷（单数，不加定冠词）消息，音讯：Please send me ~ of your safe arrival. 请把你平安到达的消息告诉我。同 message, news ❸(仅用单数，常与所有格连用)诺言，保证，信用 同 pledge, promise / be as good as one's ~ 信守诺言；说话算话 break one's ~ 失信；食言：Don't break your ~. You must come on time. 别失言，你一定得准时来。keep one's ~ 守信用，遵守诺言：You should keep your ~ and come to our meeting. 你应该遵守诺言来开会。❹文字：~ processor (计算机的)文字处理器

work / wɜːk / Ⅰ n. ❶[U]工作；劳动：I always found plenty of ~ in my garden. 在花园中我总能找到许多事情做。同 labor, toil 反 play, leisure / at ~ 在工作：He is at ~ now, but he'll be back at six. 他现在正在工作，不过六点钟会回来。out of ~ 失业：(机器)出毛病：His uncle has been out of ~ for three months. 他的叔叔已经失业三个月了。/ My computer is out of ~. 我的计算机出毛病了。❷作品；著作：the ~s of Beethoven 贝多芬的作品 / new ~ on modern art 关于现代艺术的新著 同 product, creation ❸(pl.)工厂；工场：a gas ~s 煤气厂 / a brick ~s 砖厂 同 factory, plant Ⅱ v. ❶工作；劳动：He's been ~ing hard all day. 他整天辛劳地工作。/ Most students ~ hard at English. 大多数学生都努力学习英语。同 labor, toil 反 play / ~ at 从事；致力于：We are ~ing at a new subject. 我

们正在从事新课题的研究。～ **for** 为…而工作：He is ～ing for a big company. 他在为一家大公司工作。～ **out** 算出；制订出：The total ～s out to ＄5000. 总数算出是 5000 美元。❷有效；成功：Will these new methods ～? 这些新方法有效吗？圊 effect，succeed ❸（使）工作；（使）运动：Don't ～ your poor wife to death. 不要累死你那可怜的妻子。The machines are ～ed by electricity. 机器是电动的。圊 make，move ❹ 做成；完成：～ miracles (wonders) 创造奇迹 圊 make，perform

worker / ˈwɜːkə(r) / n. [C]工人；工作者

working / ˈwɜːkɪŋ / adj. 工作的；劳动的：the ～ class 工人阶级

workmanship / ˈwɜːkmənʃɪp / n. [U]❶（成品的）做工，工艺；（工匠的）手艺，技艺：a bracelet of fine ～做工精细的手镯 ❷工艺品，作品：Is this teapot you ～? 这茶壶是你做的吗？

workshop / ˈwɜːkʃɒp / n. [C]车间；工场；作坊

world / wɜːld / n. ❶（the ～）地球；世界；领域：the animal (plant) ～ 动物(植物)世界／gambling ～ 赌场／ publishing ～ 出版界／the English-speaking ～ 讲英语的国家 圊 earth，universe ❷尘世；俗世；世事：renounce (give up) the ～ 弃绝尘世 圊 life，society／**in the ～** 究竟，到底；在世界上：Who in the ～ is that fellow? 那人究竟是谁？

worldwide / ˈwɜːldwaɪd / Ⅰ adj. 遍及全球的；世界范围的：The event has a ～ influence. 这事件有世界性的影响。圊 international Ⅱ adv. 遍及全球地：The scientist is famous ～.

那位科学家全球知名。圊 internationally

worm / wɜːm / n. [C]软体虫；蠕虫；（尤指）蚯蚓

worn / wɔːn / adj. ❶用过的；用坏的：a ～ suit 一套旧衣服 圊 decayed，shabby 圎 new ❷疲惫的；筋疲力尽的：a ～ look 面容疲惫／You look so ～. What's wrong with you? 你看起来那么疲惫。你怎么啦? 圊 exhausted，tired 圎 energetic

worried / ˈwʌrɪd / adj. 焦虑的；烦恼的：He looks ～. 他看起来很焦虑。圊 anxious 圎 calm

worry / ˈwʌri / Ⅰ v. 困扰；(使)不安；(使)烦恼：Her child has a bad cough and it rather worries her. 她的小孩咳得很厉害，她极为不安。／ Don't ～ about trifles. 别为小事烦恼。圊 distress，upset 圎 comfort，calm Ⅱ n. ❶烦恼，焦虑；担忧 圊 anxiety，distress 圎 comfort ❷烦恼事 圊 concern，care

worse / wɜːs / Ⅰ adj.（bad 和 ill 的比较级）更坏；更差；更糟：You are making things ～. 你把事情弄得更糟。Ⅱ n. 较坏或较差的人或事：She continued to tell us the ～. 她继续告诉我们更糟的情况。Ⅲ adv. 更糟地：He is behaving ～ than ever. 他的表现比任何时候都糟。／ **and** ～ 越来越糟：He has made the matter ～ and ～. 他已经把这事弄得越来越糟了。

worship / ˈwɜːʃɪp / Ⅰ n. [U]❶崇拜；崇敬 圊 admiration ❷敬慕；尊敬；hero ～ 英雄崇拜／She gazed at the film star with ～ in her eyes. 她注视着那电影明星，眼里充满着敬慕之意。圊 respect Ⅱ v. 崇拜；尊敬 圊 admire，respect

worst / wɜːst / Ⅰ adj.（bad 和 ill 的最高级）最坏的；最差的：the ～ storm in the past five years 五年来最厉害的暴风雨 Ⅱ adv. 最差地：I played basketball ～ in the class. 在班上我的篮球打得最差。Ⅲ n. 最坏的人或事：at the ～ 在最坏的情况下／ ～ of all 最坏的，最糟糕的 / You must prepare for the ～. 你必须做最坏的准备。

worth / wɜːθ / adj.（表语形容词）❶值；等于…的价值：I paid £600 for this used car, but it's ～ much more. 我仅付 600 英镑就买了这部旧车子，但它价值更高。❷值得；**be ～ do-ing sth.** 值得做某事：The novel Song of Youth is ～ reading. 小说《青春之歌》值得一读。/ He says life wouldn't be ～ living without friendship. 他常说无友谊的人生便没有活下去的价值。同 deserving

辨析
worth 后面必须接名词或动名词，以主动形式表示被动意义：The film is well worth seeing. 这电影很值得看。It's worth the time and effort we devoted to it. 我们在这件事上花时间和精力是值得的。worthy 后接 of十名词，of十动名词或不定式的被动式：His behaviour is worthy of great praise. 他的行为值得大加称赞。The deeds of these heroes are worthy of remembering. 这些英雄的事迹是值得纪念的。The novel is worthy to be ranked among the masterpieces of Chinese literature. 那小说被列为中国文学的杰作是值得的。worthwhile 作表语，句型用 It is worthwhile to do（doing）sth. 以上三个词中，worth 不能作定语。

worthless / 'wɜːθləs / *adj.* 无价值的；无用的 同 valueless, useless 反 worthy

worthwhile / ˌwɜːθ'waɪl / *adj.* 值得的：It is a ~ experiment. 这是一个值得做的实验。/ It is ~ to spend more time discussing the problem. 多花点时间讨论这件事是值得的。同 valuable, useful 反 worthless, useless

worthy / 'wɜːði / *adj.* ❶值得的：a cause ~ of support 值得支持的一项事业 同 worthwhile, deserving 反 unworthy, worthless ❷可敬的：a ~ gentleman 一位值得尊敬的绅士同 respectable 反 unworthy

wound / wuːnd / I *n.* 伤；创伤：a knife ~ in the arm 臂上的刀伤 / a bullet ~ 枪伤 同 injury, harm II *v.* 使受伤；伤害：Ten soldiers were killed and thirty ~ed. 10 名士兵阵亡，30 名受伤。同 injure, hurt 反 heal 派 wounded *adj.*

wrack / ræk / *n.* [U]毁灭；损毁；死亡：go to ~ and ruin 毁灭；灭亡

wrangle / 'ræŋɡl / I *n.* [C]争吵，吵架；争论，争辩：a legal ~法律纠纷 II *vi.* 争吵，吵架；争论，争辩：~ with sb. over sth. 为某事与某人争吵

wrap / ræp / *v.* (wrapped; wrapping) ❶卷，裹（与 in 连用）：~ oneself in a blanket 把自己裹在毯子里 / The mountain top was ~ped in mist. 山顶为雾所笼罩。同 fold, roll 反 unwrap ❷ 包裹；包装：Wrap it with plenty of paper. 用很多纸将它包起。同 bind, bundle 反 unwrap, unbundle

wreck / rek / I *n.* ❶[U]（指船等）失事，遭难；破坏：a ship ~ 船只失事 同 destruction, ruin ❷[C]失事船；残骸：Robinson Crusoe obtained food and supplies from the ~. 鲁滨孙·克鲁索从失事船上获得食物及其他物品。同 remains II *v.* 破坏；毁灭；失事：The ship was ~ed. 那船失事了。同 destroy, ruin 反 build, create 派 wreckage *n.*

wrench / rentʃ / I *v.* ❶拧 同 twist, wring ❷扭伤 同 strain II *n.* ❶拧 ❷扭伤 ❸扳手；扳钳

wrestle / 'resl / *n.* ❶摔跤 ❷斗争；搏斗 同 struggle, fight

wretched / 'retʃɪd / *adj.* 可怜的；不幸的；恶劣的：lead a ~ existence in the slums 在贫民窟里可怜地过活 / ~ weather 恶劣的天气 同 pitiful, unfortunate 反 fortunate, happy

wring / rɪŋ / *v.* (wrung /rʌŋ/, wrung)拧，扭；绞出（与 out 连用）：~ water out of one's swimming-suit 把游泳衣上的水拧出 / ~ one's neck 拧住某人的脖子 同 wrench, squeeze

wrinkle / 'rɪŋkl / I *n.* [C]皱纹 同 fold II *v.* (使)起皱纹 同 fold 派 wrinkly *adj.*

wrist / rɪst / *n.* 腕，手腕：He took me by the ~. 他握住我的手腕。

write / raɪt / *v.* (wrote /rəʊt/, written /'rɪtn/) ❶书写；写字：Are we to ~ in ink or in pencil? 我们用钢笔还是用铅笔书写呢？/ You'd better ~ down the address before you forget it. 你最好把这地址写下来，以免忘了。/ Can you ~ the new words we learned yesterday? 你能写出我们昨天学的新词吗？同 copy, record 反 say, speak ❷写信给（与 to 连用）：He promised to ~ to me every week. 他答应每周给我写信。/ He wrote me an account of his visit. 他写信给我讲他的访问情况。

writer / 'raɪtə(r) / *n.* [C]作者，作家；书写者：a fiction ~ 小说作家 /a popular ~ 受欢迎的作家 / Dickens was a famous English ~. 狄更斯是著名的英国作家。/ the ~ of this letter 写这封信的人 同 author 反 reader

辨析
writer 和 author 都有"作家"的意思，writer 多指以写作为职业的人，如作家、记者、编辑等；author 多指某部作品的写作人，不一定是以写作为职业。

writing / ˈraɪtɪŋ / *n.* ❶[U]书写；写作：busy with 〜 忙于写作 圆 handwriting ❷(*pl.*) 某专题的著述：the 〜s of Swift 斯威夫特的作品 圆 work, composition

wrong / rɒŋ / Ⅰ *adj.* ❶ 不正当的；不道德的；违法的：It is 〜 to steal. 偷窃是违法的。/ It was 〜 of you to use his bicycle without asking his permission. 你没得到他的允许就使用他的自行车是不对的。圆 immoral, evil 反 moral, right ❷ 错误的：We got into the 〜 train. 我们搭错了火车。圆 incorrect, false 反 correct, right ❸失常的；有毛病的；状况不佳的 圆 faulty, unfit 反 fit / **be 〜 with** 有毛病：There's something 〜 with my digestion. 我消化有点毛病。/ What's 〜 with the machine? 机器出了什么毛病? **go 〜** 发生故障，出毛病：Something has gone 〜 with her washing-machine. 她的洗衣机坏了。Ⅱ *n.* [U] ❶罪；不公正的事；邪恶：do 〜 违法；做坏事 / know the difference between right and 〜 知道是非之别 圆 immorality, evil 反 morality, goodness ❷不义的行为；不公正的事：She complained of the 〜s she had suffered. 她诉说她受过的委屈。圆 injustice, unfairness 反 justice, fairness / **do sb.** 〜 冤枉(委屈)某人 Ⅲ *adv.* 错误地，不正确，不对 圆 incorrectly, falsely 反 correctly Ⅳ *vt.* 冤枉；委屈：It's not his fault. Don't 〜 him. 那不是他的错，别冤枉他。圆 injure, abuse

WTO (＝World Trade Orgnization) 世界贸易组织

WWW (＝World Wide Web) 全球信息网；全球信息资讯网

W

X x

Xerox / ˈzɪərɒks / Ⅰ *v.* 影印,(用静电法)复印(常用 xerox) Ⅱ *n.* 静电复印;复印件

XO (＝extra old)(白兰地)特陈的(尤指法国的 XO 系列白兰地酒,贮藏年份至少在 40 年至 50 年)

Xmas (＝Christmas)圣诞节

X-ray / ˈeksreɪ / *n. & adj.* X 射线(的),X 光(的):～ diagnosis 用 X 光诊断

Y y

yacht / jɒt / n. [C]游艇；快艇

yap / jæp / Ⅰ n. 犬吠；急叫 Ⅱ vi. 狂吠；急叫

yard¹ / jɑːd / n. [C]院子；庭院 圊 courtyard

yard² / jɑːd / n. [C]码(英美长度单位，约等于 0.9144 米)

yarn / jɑːn / n. ❶纱，纱线；纺线；绳索股线：cotton ～棉纱线 ❷[C]故事；奇谈：adventure ～s 探险故事

yawn / jɔːn / Ⅰ vi. 打呵欠 Ⅱ n. 呵欠：John stretched himself with a ～. 约翰打着呵欠伸懒腰

year / jɜː(r), jɪə(r) / n. [C]❶太阳年(地球环绕太阳一周所用的时间，约为 365.25 天)❷年，历年：once a ～每年一次 / He made some progress in the last two ～s. 过去两年中他取得了一些进步。/ ～ after ～ 年年，每年 / all the ～ round 一年到头 / ～book n. 年鉴，年刊 ❸岁，年龄：a boy of ten ～s 一位 10 岁的男孩

yearly / ˈjɜːli / Ⅰ adj. 每年的：～ report 年报 / What is your ～ pay? 你的年薪是多少？圊 annual Ⅱ adv. 每年 圊 annually

yearn / jɜːn / vi. 渴望；向往；怀念；思慕：～ after letters from parents 切盼双亲的来信 / ～ to find a job soon 只想快快找到工作

yell / jel / vi. 叫喊：～ for help 大声呼救 圊 cry，shout

yellow / ˈjeləʊ / Ⅰ adj. 黄色的：the Yellow River 黄河 Ⅱ n. 黄色：bright ～ 鲜黄色 / pale ～ 淡黄色

yes / jes / adv. 是，对 / ～man n. 唯唯诺诺的人

yesterday / ˈjestədeɪ / Ⅰ n. 昨日：～ morning (afternoon, evening)昨天早上(下午、晚上) / Where's ～'s newspaper? 昨天的报纸在哪里？Ⅱ adv. 在昨天

yet / jet / Ⅰ adv. ❶(用于否定句及条件句中，且通常用于句末，也可紧跟在 not 之后)到此时，至今：They are not here ～. 他们尚未来此地。/ I wonder whether they have finished the work ～. 我不知他们到此时是否已完成了工作。/ You needn't do it just ～. 至今你们无须做那事。❷(用于肯定句中)仍，尚，还：Go at once while there is ～ time. 赶快去，还来得及。圊 still，but Ⅱ conj. 然而；可是：She is vain and foolish，～ people like her. 她自负而愚蠢，然而人们喜欢她。圊 however，nevertheless

yield / jiːld / Ⅰ v. ❶生产；出产：trees that ～ fruit 结果的树圊 bear，produce ❷让步；屈服；投降；放弃：～ to 屈服于；服从：～ to no remedy 无药可救 / ～ to none 不落人后，不让于人 / ～ to temptation 经不住诱惑：The disease ～ed to treatment. 疾病经过治疗而消除。圊 surrender 反 resist，attack Ⅱ n. 产量；收获量；收益：a good ～ of wheat 小麦的丰收 / total ～ 总产量 / yearly ～ 年产量 圊 harvest，interest

yielding / ˈjiːldɪŋ / adj. ❶易弯曲的；有弹性的 圊 flexible，plastic 反 stiff，rigid ❷顺从的；

不固执的 同 obedient 反 obstinate

yoga / 'jəugə / n. [U]瑜伽

yogurt, yoghurt, yoghourt / 'jəugət / n. [U]酸乳,酸奶

yoke / jəuk / n. ❶轭,牛轭 ❷枷锁;束缚

yolk / jəulk / n. [C;U]蛋黄:Separate the ～s from the whites. 把蛋黄和蛋清分开。

you / ju: / pron. ❶你;你们(人称代词主格和宾格):You are my friend. 你是我的朋友。Does he know ～? 他认识你们吗? ❷泛指任何人:It is much easier to cycle with the wind behind ～. 顺风骑自行车容易得多。

young / jʌŋ / Ⅰ adj. (-er /'jʌŋgə/,-est /'jʌŋgɪst/)年幼的;年轻的;幼小的:a ～ man 一个年轻人 / a ～ animal 幼兽 / She is two years ～er than her sister. 她比她姐姐小两岁。同 youthful, immature 反 old, senior Ⅱ n. 青年人;幼畜;幼禽:That music is popular with the ～. 那种音乐很受青年人的欢迎。/ The cat fought fiercely to defend its ～. 那猫凶狠地打斗以保护其幼仔。同 youths, offspring

youngster / 'jʌŋstə(r) / n. [C] ❶儿童;小孩 同 child, kid 反 adult ❷小伙子;年轻人 同 teenager, youth ❸幼小动物,幼小植物 同 young animal, young plant

your / jɔː(r), jur / pron. 你的;你们的(形容词性物主代词):Show me ～ hand. 把你的手伸

给我看看。

yours / jɔːz, jurz / pron. 你的;你们的(名词性物主代词):Yours was my favorite birthday present. 你送的东西是我最喜欢的生日礼物。/ That pen is ～. 那支钢笔是你的。

yourself / jɔː'self, jur'self / pron. 你自己:Did you hurt ～? 你伤了自己了吗?

> **用法**
>
> yourself 是反身代词,不能单独作主语,但可以作主语的同位语,如不能说:Yourself did it. 应说:You did it yourself. 或说:You yourself did it. 你自己做的这件事。

yourselves / jɔː'selvz, jur'selvz / pron. 你们自己

youth / juːθ / n. ❶[U]青春;青春期;青少年时代:give one's ～ to 把青春献给… / the friends of one's ～ 青少年时代的朋友/She lost(kept) her ～. 她青春不再(青春依旧)。同 childhood ❷[C](pl. youths/juːðz/)少年;青年:As a ～, he showed no promise of becoming a great pianist. 少年时,他未显出成为伟大的钢琴家的迹象。同 teenager, youngster ❸(集合名词)青年们:the ～ of the nation 全国的青年们 同 teenagers, youngsters

youthful / 'juːθfl / adj. ❶年轻的:～ cadres 年轻干部 同 young 反 elderly ❷富有青春活力的 同 vigorous 反 inactive

Y

Z z

zeal / ziːl / n. [U]热心；热情：show ～ for a cause 对事业表示热心 /work with great ～ 热情洋溢地工作 圖 enthusiasm, vigor 反 indifference

zealous / ˈzeləs / adj. 热心的；热情的：～ to please one's employer 热衷于讨好顾主 圖 enthusiastic, vigorous 反 indifferent

zebra / ˈziːbrə / n. [C]斑马

zero / ˈzɪərəʊ / n. ❶零 圖 nothing ❷零点；零位；零度：It was ten degrees below ～. 气温是零下十度。❸零分：The teacher put a ～ on his paper. 老师在他的考卷上打了零分。

zest / zest / n. [U]兴趣，兴味，兴致，热情：lose one's ～ for food 食欲不振 / He had a ～ for knowledge and for the distribution of knowledge. 他有强烈的追求知识、传播知识的欲望。

zigzag / ˈzɪɡzæɡ / Ⅰ n. [C] ❶曲折线条；之字形道路（或壕沟）；锯齿形凸出物（或图案）：The mountainous areas are full of ～s. 山区尽是曲曲折折的羊肠小道。❷曲折，拐弯 Ⅱ adj. 之字形的，锯齿形的；弯曲的；曲折的：a ～ coastline 锯齿状的海岸线 Ⅲ (-zagged; -zagging) vi. 呈之字形行走；曲折前进：The little child ～ged along the road. 这个小孩子左拐右拐地在路上走过。/ The lightening ～ged through the sky. 闪电呈之形划过天空。

zip / zɪp / Ⅰ (zipped; zipping) vt. 用拉链拉开（或扣上）：～ one's mouth 闭嘴 / It looks like the top of one of those plastic bags that ～ shut. 它有点像那种一拉就可以封口的塑料袋口子。反 unzip Ⅱ n. [C]拉链

zinc / zɪŋk / Ⅰ n. [U]锌 Ⅱ vt. 在…上镀锌

zone / zəʊn / n. ❶地区；区域：the war ～ 战区 / the danger ～ 危险地带 圖 area, region ❷（美国的）邮区；电话分区 ❸带，地带：frigid (temperate, torrid) ～ 寒带(温带、热带)

zoo / zuː / n. [C]动物园：take the children to the ～ 带孩子们去动物园 / go to the ～ 去动物园 / at the ～ 在动物园里

zoological / ˌzəʊəˈlɒdʒɪkl / adj. 动物的；动物学的

zoologist / zəʊˈɒlədʒɪst / n. [C]动物学家

zoology / zəʊˈɒlədʒi / n. [U]动物学

Chinese-English Dictionary

A a

a

阿 (ā) (a prefix used before pet names, monosyllabic surnames, or numbers denoting order of seniority in a family, to form terms of endearment)

另见 ē

【阿爹】〈方〉❶dad ❷granddad (on father's side)

【阿飞】Teddy boy; hooligan; young rowdy

【阿富汗】Afghanistan

【阿哥】〈方〉❶elder brother ❷an affectionate form of address between men of about the same age

【阿公】〈方〉❶grandpa; granddad ❷husband's father; father-in-law ❸a term of respect for any elderly man

【阿拉伯】Arabian; Arabic; Arab

【阿门】〈宗〉amen

【阿姨】❶one's mother's sister; aunt; auntie ❷a nurse in a family or in a nursery school or kindergarten

ai

哎 (āi)〈叹〉exclamation of surprise or regret

【哎呀】〈叹〉ah; damn

【哎哟】〈叹〉ouch; ow; hey

哀 (āi)❶grief; sorrow ❷mourning ❸pity

【哀愁】sad; sorrowful

【哀悼】grieve over sb.'s death: 深切～ profound condolence

【哀歌】a mournful song; dirge

【哀号】cry; wail

【哀怜】feel compassion for

【哀鸣】whine plaintively

【哀泣】weep plaintively

【哀求】entreat; implore

【哀伤】distressed; grieved; sad

【哀思】sad memories (of the deceased)

【哀叹】bewail; lament

【哀痛】deep sorrow; grief

【哀乐】funeral music; dirge

挨 (āi)❶get close to; be next to ❷in sequence; by turns

另见 ái

【挨次】in turn; one by one: ～入场 file in

【挨近】be close to; be near to: 我们家～商业区。Our house is close to the shopping center.

唉 (āi)❶(used to respond) right; yes ❷(expressing disappointment or regret) alas

【唉声叹气】heave deep sighs; sigh in despair; moan and groan

挨 (ái)❶suffer; endure ❷drag out ❸delay; play for time; stall

另见 āi

【挨打】take some beating; get a thrashing; come under attack

【挨批】be criticized

【挨整】be the target of criticism or attack

【挨揍】〈口〉❶take a beating; get a thrashing ❷come under attack

皑 (ái) pure white; snow white

【皑皑】pure white

癌 (ái)〈医〉cancer; carcinoma

【癌变】canceration

【癌细胞】〈医〉cancer cell

【癌症】cancer

矮 (ǎi)❶short (of stature) ❷low

【矮凳】a low stool

【矮胖】short and stout; dumpy; roly-poly

【矮人】❶a short person; dwarf ❷Pigmy (or Pygmy)

【矮小】short and small; low and small; undersized: 身材～ short and slight in figure | ～的帐篷 a small, low tent

蔼 (ǎi) friendly; amiable

A

【蔼蔼】〈文〉❶lush；luxuriant ❷dim；dark

【蔼然可亲】kindly；amiable；affable

爱（ài）❶love；affection ❷like；be fond of；be keen on ❸be apt to；be in the habit of ❹cherish；treasure；hold dear；take good care of

【爱抚】show tender care for

【爱国】be patriotic：～者 patriot|～主义 patriotism

【爱好】❶love；like；be fond of；be keen on ❷interest；hobby

【爱好者】lover（of art，sports，etc.）；enthusiast；fan：音乐～music-lover|体育～sports enthusiast；sports fan

【爱护】cherish；treasure

【爱怜】❶show tender affection for；show love or fondness for ❷love and pity

【爱恋】be in love with；feel attached to

【爱侣】lovers；sweethearts

【爱情】love（between man and woman）

【爱人】❶husband or wife ❷sweet-heart

【爱神】god of love；Cupid

【爱憎】love and hate

隘（ài）❶narrow ❷pass

【隘口】（mountain）pass

【隘路】defile；narrow passage

碍（ài）hinder；obstruct；be in the way of

【碍口】be too embarrassing to mention：这事有点～，不好说。It's rather embarrassing；I don't know how to bring it up.

【碍事】❶be in the way；be a hindrance ❷be of consequence；matter

【碍眼】be unpleasant to look at；be an eyesore；offend the eye

an

安（ān）❶peaceful；quiet；tranquil；calm ❷set（sb.'s mind）at ease ❸rest content；be satisfied ❹safe；secure；in good health ❺place in a suitable position；find a place for ❻install；fix；fit ❼bring（a charge against sb.）；give（sb. a nickname）❽harbour（an intention）❾〈电〉ampere

【安插】place in a certain position；assign to a job；plant：～亲信 put one's trusted followers in key positions

【安定】❶stable；quiet；settled：～团结 stability and unity ❷stabilize；maintain：～人心 reassure the public

【安顿】❶find a place for；help settle down；arrange for ❷undisturbed；peaceful

【安放】lay；place

【安分】❶be law-abiding ❷know one's place

【安抚】appease；pacify

【安好】safe and sound；well

【安家】settle down；set up a home

【安静】quiet；peaceful

【安康】peace and happiness

【安理会】the（U.N.）Security Council

【安谧】〈书〉（of a place）tranquil；quiet；peaceful

【安眠】sleep peacefully

【安宁】❶peaceful；tranquil：世界不～的根源 cause of world intranquillity ❷calm；composed；free from worry

【安排】arrange；plan；fix up

【安全】safe；secure：～设备 safety devices|～规则 safety regulations|～感 sense of security

【安然】❶safe ❷be free from worry；feel at ease

【安危】safety and danger：不顾个人～ heedless of one's personal safety

【安慰】comfort；console

【安稳】smooth and steady；safe and secure

【安息】❶rest；go to sleep ❷used to mourn

【安闲】enjoying leisure

【安详】composed；serene；unruffled

【安歇】rest；sleep；retire for the night

【安心】set one's mind to；keep one's mind on；not worried；set one's mind at rest

【安逸】easy and comfortable；leisurely：贪图～love comfort

【安葬】bury

【安置】place（a person）in certain post；find a place for；help settle down

【安装】install；fix；mount

氨（ān）〈化〉ammonia

【氨基】〈化〉amino；amino-group：～酸 amino acid

【氨水】〈化〉ammonia water；aqua ammonia

鞍（ān）saddle

【鞍架】saddletree

【鞍马】〈体〉pommelled horse；side horse

岸（àn）❶bank；coast；shore ❷〈书〉lofty

【岸然】in a solemn manner

按 (àn) ❶press;push down ❷according to;in the light of ❸shelve ❹restrain;control ❺ keep one's hand on

【按比例】pro rata;in proportion

【按成】according to percentage;proportionately:～计算 reckon in terms of percentages｜～分配红利 distribute the bonuses proportionately

【按次】in due order;in sequence:～发言 speak in due order

【按键】button

【按理】according to principle or reason;in the ordinary course of events;normally

【按脉】feel (or take) the pulse

【按摩】massage

【按钮】push button

【按期】on time;on schedule

【按时】on time;on schedule:～完成 meet the deadline;finish in time

【按说】in the ordinary course of events;ordinarily;normally

案 (àn) ❶an old-fashioned long,narrow table or desk ❷law case;case ❸a plan submitted for consideration;proposal

【案板】kitchen chopping board

【案犯】〈法〉criminals involved in a case

【案件】law case;legal case

【案卷】files of documents;files;archives

【案例】case;example of case

【案情】details of case;facts of a legal case

【案头】on the desk

暗 (àn) ❶dark;dim;dull ❷hidden;secret

【暗暗】secretly;inwardly

【暗藏】hide;conceal

【暗处】❶a dark place ❷a secret place;a covert place;cover

【暗沟】underground drainage ditch;underground drain

【暗害】❶kill secretly ❷stab in the back

【暗号】secret signal;secret sign

【暗合】be in complete agreement without prior consultation;(happen to) coincide

【暗河】underground river

【暗箭】an arrow shot from hiding;attack by a hidden enemy

【暗流】undercurrent

【暗码】secret code;private mark

【暗器】hidden weapon (as darts hidden inside sleeves)

【暗杀】assassinate

【暗伤】❶internal (or invisible) injury ❷indiscernible damage

【暗示】suggest;hint;drop a hint

【暗事】clandestine or illicit action:明人不做～。An honest man does nothing underhand.

【暗算】plot against:遭人～ fall a prey to a plot

【暗锁】built-in lock

【暗想】muse;ponder;turn over in mind

【暗笑】laugh up one's sleeve;sneer at

黯 (àn) dim;gloomy

【黯然】〈书〉❶dim;faint ❷dejected;downcast;low-spirited

ang

肮 (āng)

【肮脏】dirty;filthy:～的阴沟 a filthy sewer｜～的勾当 dirty work;a foul deed

昂 (áng) ❶hold (one's head) high ❷high;soaring

【昂藏】〈书〉tall and imposing:～七尺之躯 a tall strapping man;a manly man

【昂奋】(of spirits or enthusiasm) run high

【昂贵】(price) high;dear;expensive

【昂然】chin up and chest out;upright and unafraid:他～直入。He strode in,chin up and chest out.

【昂扬】high-spirited:斗志～ have high morale;be full of fight;be militant

盎 (àng) brimming,abundant

【盎然】abundantly;exuberantly:趣味～ full of interest｜春意～。Spring is in the air.

【盎司】ounce

ao

熬 (áo) ❶cook in water;boil ❷endure;hold out

【熬煎】endure,suffering

【熬夜】stay up all night;burn the midnight oil

鏖 (áo)〈书〉engage in fierce battle

【鏖兵】〈书〉fight hard;engage in fierce battle

【鏖战】〈书〉fight hard;engage in fierce battle

傲 (ào) ❶proud;haughty ❷refuse to yield to;brave;defy

A

【傲岸】〈书〉proud；haughty

【傲骨】lofty and unyielding character；self-esteem

【傲慢】arrogant；haughty；overbearing：态度～ put on airs

【傲气】❶ air of arrogance；haughtiness ❷ arrogant；haughty

【傲然】lofty and proud-looking；unyielding

【傲视】turn up one's nose at；show disdain for；regard superciliously

奥（ào）profound and difficult to understand；abstruse

【奥秘】mystery

【奥妙】mysterious；subtle；wonderful

懊（ào）❶ regretful；remorseful ❷ annoyed；vexed

【懊悔】repent；feel remorse；regret：我～没听他的忠告。I regretted having failed to take his advice.

【懊恼】displeased；annoyed；vexed：这门课没学完他心里很～。He was quite upset at not having completed the course.

【懊丧】dispirited；dejected；despondent；downcast

B b

ba

八 (bā) eight
【八方】the eight points of the compass;all directions;all quarters
【八哥】〈动〉myna
【八路军】the Eighth Route Army
【八月】❶August ❷the eighth month of the lunar year

巴 (bā) ❶hope earnestly;wait anxiously ❷cling to;stick to ❸be close to;be next to ❹〈物〉bar
【巴结】fawn on;curry favour with
【巴士】bus
【巴望】look forward to
【巴西】Brazil
【巴掌】palm;hand

扒 (bā) ❶hold on to;cling to ❷dig up;pull down ❸peel;strip off;take off ❹push aside
另见 pá
【扒车】climb onto a slow-going train,etc.
【扒拉】push lightly

芭 (bā)
【芭蕉】〈植〉banana
【芭蕾舞】ballet

吧 (bā)〈方〉〈口〉draw on (or pull at) one's pipe,etc.
另见 ba
【吧嗒】〈象〉smack one's lips (in surprise, alarm,etc.)

笆 (bā) basketry
【笆斗】round-bottomed basket
【笆篱】〈方〉bamboo or twig fence

拔 (bá) ❶pull out;pull up ❷draw;suck out ❸choose;pick;select ❹lift;raise ❺stand out among;surpass ❻capture;seize
【拔草】pull up weeds
【拔除】wipe out;remove
【拔萃】〈书〉stand out from one's fellows;be out of the common
【拔地】rise sheer (or steeply) from level ground; tower
【拔河】〈体〉tug-of-war
【拔举】select and propose sb. for an office; recommend
【拔群】stand head and shoulders above others
【拔丝】❶〈机〉wire drawing:～机 wire drawing bench (or machine) ❷candied floss：～山药 hot candied yam

把 (bǎ) ❶hold;grasp ❷guard;watch ❸control;dominate;monopolize ❹handle ❺〈量〉a handle of
另见 bà
【把柄】handle
【把持】control;dominate;monopolize
【把舵】hold the rudder;hold (or take,be at) the helm;steer
【把风】keep watch (for one's partners in a clandestine activity);be on the lookout
【把关】check on;guard a pass
【把揽】monopolize;take on everything;arrogate
【把理】〈方〉reasonable;sensible;right：说话～ give a reasonable statement
【把门】❶guard a gate：～很严。The gate was closely guarded. | 我说话嘴上缺个～的。I can't keep my mouth shut. ❷be a goalkeeper (in football,etc.)
【把式】❶〈口〉wushu ; martial arts ❷〈口〉a person skilled in wushu; a person skilled in a trade ❸〈方〉skill
【把守】guard
【把手】grip;handle;knob
【把稳】〈方〉trustworthy;dependable
【把握】❶grasp;hold ❷assurance;certainty
【把戏】❶acrobatics;jugglery ❷cheap trick; game

靶 (bǎ) target
【靶场】shooting range;range
【靶心】bull's-eye

把 (bà) ❶grip;handle ❷stem
另见 bǎ

B

罢 (bà) ❶cease;stop ❷dismiss ❸finish

【罢笔】 put down the pen and stop writing
【罢黜】 ❶dismiss from office ❷ban;reject
【罢工】 strike;go on strike
【罢官】 dismiss from office
【罢课】 students' strike
【罢了】 (used at the end of a declarative sentence) that's all;nothing else
【罢论】 abandoned idea:此事已作～。The idea has already been dropped.
【罢免】 recall
【罢手】 give up
【罢休】 give up;let the matter drop
【罢职】 remove from office;dismiss

霸 (bà) ❶chief of feudal princes;overlord ❷despot;tyrant;bully ❸hegemonist power;hegemonism;hegemony ❹dominate;lord it over;tyrannize over

【霸道】 high-handed;overbearing
【霸权】 hegemony;supremacy
【霸王】 overlord
【霸业】 achievements of a leader of feudal lords
【霸占】 forcibly occupy;seize:～土地 forcibly occupy the land
【霸主】 hegemon;overlord

吧 (ba) ❶indicating a suggestion, a request or a mild command ❷indicating consent or approval
　　另见 bā

bai

白 (bái) ❶white ❷clear ❸pure;plain;blank ❹in vain;to no purpose, for nothing ❺free of charge;gratis

【白白】 in vain;to no purpose;for nothing
【白班】 day shift
【白布】 plain white cloth;calico
【白菜】 Chinese cabbage
【白搭】〈口〉no use;no good
【白费】 waste
【白宫】 the White House
【白果】〈植〉ginkgo;gingko
【白鹤】〈动〉white crane
【白话】 ❶unrealizable wish or unfounded argument ❷the written form of modern Chinese
【白净】 (of skin)fair and clear
【白酒】 alcohol;spirit
【白卷】 a blank examination paper;an examination paper unanswered
【白兰地】 brandy

【白人】 white man or woman
【白色】 ❶white (colour) ❷white (as a symbol of reaction)
【白糖】 (refined) white sugar
【白天】 daytime;day
【白皙】〈书〉(of skin) fair and clear
【白细胞】〈生〉white blood cell;leucocyte
【白血病】〈医〉leukaemia
【白眼】 supercilious look
【白杨】〈植〉white poplar
【白夜】 white night
【白蚁】 termite;white ant
【白银】 silver
【白纸黑字】 (be) written in black and white;commit sth. to paper
【白昼】 daytime
【白字】 a character misused or mispronounced through confusion with one that sounds or looks like it

百 (bǎi) ❶hundred ❷numerous;all kinds of

【百般】 in every possible way;by every means
【百倍】 a hundred times;greatly
【百弊】 ❶all kinds of maladies or evils ❷many drawbacks or disadvantages
【百出】〈贬〉numerous;full of;plenty of:矛盾～ full of contradictions
【百分比】 percentage
【百合】〈植〉lily
【百货】 general merchandise
【百年】 ❶a hundred years;a century ❷lifetime
【百姓】 common people

摆 (bǎi) ❶put;place;arrange ❷lay bare;state clearly ❸put on;assume ❹〈物〉pendulum

【摆布】 order about;manipulate
【摆动】 swing;sway
【摆渡】 ferry
【摆放】 put;place;lay
【摆阔】 parade one's wealth
【摆弄】 ❶move back and forth;fiddle with ❷order about;manipulate
【摆平】 be fair to;be impartial to
【摆设】 furnish and decorate(a room)
【摆手】 ❶shake one's hand in admonition or disapproval ❷beckon;wave
【摆脱】 cast off;break away from;break loose;free oneself from
【摆尾】 wag the tail
【摆钟】 pendulum clock
【摆子】〈方〉malaria

B

败 (bài) ❶ be defeated;lose ❷ defeat;beat ❸ fail;failure ❹ spoil ❺ decay;wither ❻ counteract

【败北】suffer defeat;lose a battle

【败笔】❶ a faulty stroke in calligraphy or painting ❷ a faulty expression in writing

【败兵】a defeated army;an army in flight;defeated troops

【败毒】〈中医〉relieve internal heat or fever

【败坏】ruin;corrupt;undermine

【败绩】〈书〉be utterly defeated;be routed

【败局】lost game;losing battle

【败类】scum of a community;degenerate

【败露】fall through and stand exposed;be brought to light

【败落】decline(in wealth and position)

【败诉】〈法〉lose a lawsuit

【败退】retreat in defeat

【败兴】have one's spirits dampened;feel disappointed

拜 (bài) ❶ do obeisance ❷ make a courtesy call ❸ acknowledge sb. as one's master, godfather,etc.

【拜别】〈敬〉take leave of

【拜倒】prostrate oneself;fall on one's knees; grovel

【拜读】have the honor to read

【拜访】pay a visit;call on

【拜会】(usu. used on diplomatic occasions) pay an official call;call on

【拜见】❶pay a formal visit;call to pay respects ❷meet one's senior or superior

【拜年】pay a New Year call;wish sb. a Happy New Year

【拜上】(used in ending a letter,after the name of the writer) with my respectful bows

【拜师】formally acknowledge sb. as one's master;take sb. as one's teacher

【拜识】〈套〉have the pleasure of making sb. 's acquaintance

【拜寿】congratulate an elderly person on his birthday;offer birthday felicitations

【拜托】〈敬〉request sb. to do sth.

【拜望】〈套〉call to pay one's respects;call on

ban

扳 (bān) pull;turn(bar,switch,shift gears)

【扳机】trigger

【扳手】❶ spanner;wrench ❷ lever (on a machine)

班 (bān) ❶〈军〉squad ❷class;team ❸shift; duty ❹a measure word
(e. g. number of flight or bus)

【班车】regular bus (service)

【班次】❶ order of classes or grades at school ❷ number of runs or flights

【班底】❶ ordinary members of a theatrical troupe ❷core members of an organization

【班机】airliner;regular air service;scheduled flight

【班级】classes and grades in school

【班轮】regular passenger or cargo ship;regular steamship service

【班师】〈书〉withdraw troops from the front;return after victory

【班委会】class committee

【班长】class monitor;work team leader

【班主任】a teacher in charge of a class;the director of the class

【班子】❶〈古〉theatrical troupe ❷organized group

【班组】team;group

般 (bān) same as;just like

【般配】〈方〉well matched (in marriage,etc.); well suited

颁 (bān) promulgate;issue

【颁布】promulgate;issue;publish

【颁发】❶issue;promulgate ❷award

【颁行】issue for enforcement

斑 (bān) ❶spot;speck ❷spotted;striped

【斑白】grizzled;greying

【斑驳】〈书〉mottled;motley

【斑点】stain;spot;speckle

【斑马】zebra

【斑纹】stripe;streak

【斑竹】mottled bamboo

搬 (bān) ❶ take away; move; remove ❷ apply indiscriminately

【搬动】❶ move; remove; shift ❷ employ; draw on;dispatch

【搬家】move (house)

【搬弄】❶ move sth. about; fiddle with ❷ show off;display

【搬迁】move;transfer;remove

【搬运】carry;transport

板 (bǎn) ❶board;plank ❷shutter ❸bat ❹ an accented beat ❺hard ❻stiff;unnatural ❼stop smiling; look serious ❽〈音〉clappers ❾〈解〉lamina

B

【板材】plates;board

【板车】a flatbed cart

【板床】plank bed

【板凳】wooden bench or stool

【板斧】broad axe

【板结】harden

【板栗】Chinese chestnut

【板球】cricket

【板实】❶(of soil) firm and hard ❷(of dress material,etc.)smooth and stiff

【板书】writing on the blackboard

【板纸】paperboard;board:草～ strawboard|牛皮～ kraft board

【板子】❶board;plank ❷bamboo or birch for corporal punishment

版 (bǎn) ❶printing plate (*or* block) ❷edition;print ❸page (of a newspaper)

【版本】edition

【版次】the order in which editions are printed

【版画】print;woodcut

【版刻】carving;engraving

【版面】❶space of a whole page ❷layout of a printed sheet

【版权】copyright

【版式】format

【版税】royalty (on books);copyright royalty

【版图】domain;territory

办 (bàn) ❶do;handle;manage;tackle ❷set up;run ❸buy a fair amount of;get sth. ready ❹punish (by law);bring to justice

【办案】handle a legal case

【办报】run a newspaper

【办法】way;means;measure

【办公】handle official business;work (usually in an office)

【办公室】office

【办理】handle;conduct;transact

【办事】handle affairs;work

【办学】run a school

【办置】buy (durables);purchase

半 (bàn) ❶half; semi- ❷in the middle; half way ❸very little; the least bit ❹partly; about half

【半百】fifty

【半边】half of sth. ;one side of sth.

【半场】〈体〉❶half of a game or contest:上～ the first half (of a game) ❷half-court:～紧逼 half-court press(in basketball)

【半导体】semiconductor

【半岛】peninsula

【半点】the least bit:没有～慌张 not the least bit flurried

【半路】halfway;midway;on the way

【半票】half-price ticket;half fare

【半球】hemisphere

【半晌】〈方〉❶half of the day ❷a long time;quite a while:他想了～才想起来. It took him a long time to recall it.

【半生】half a lifetime:～戎马 led a soldier's life for many years

【半数】half the number;half:～以上 more than half;majority

【半死】half-dead

【半天】❶half of the day:前～ morning ❷a long time;quite a while:他～说不出话来. He remained tongue-tied for a long time.

【半头】❶half a head:高(矮)～ half a head taller (shorter) ❷half a piece

【半月刊】semimonthly;fortnightly

扮 (bàn) ❶play the part of;disguise oneself as ❷put on(an expression)

【扮戏】❶(of a traditional opera singer) put on makeup;make up ❷〈古〉put on a play;act in a play

【扮相】the appearance of an actor or actress in costume and makeup

【扮演】play the part of;act

【扮装】put on makeup;make up

伴 (bàn) ❶companion;partner ❷accompany

【伴唱】❶vocal accompaniment ❷accompany (a singer)

【伴侣】companion;mate

【伴陪】accompany;keep sb. company

【伴送】see sb. off;accompany

【伴随】accompany;follow

【伴舞】be a dancing partner

【伴奏】accompany(with musical instruments)

拌 (bàn) mix;mix in

【拌和】mix and stir;blend

【拌嘴】bicker;squabble;quarrel

bang

邦 (bāng) nation;state;country

【邦交】diplomatic relations

【邦联】confederation

帮 (bāng) ❶help;assist ❷side (of a boat, truck,etc.) ❸outer leaf(of cabbage, etc.) ❹gang;band

【帮办】❶assist in managing ❷deputy

【帮厨】 help in the mess kitchen
【帮扶】 help; assist; aid
【帮工】 ❶help with farm work ❷helper; servant
【帮会】 secret society; underworld gang
【帮忙】 help; give a hand; do a favour; do a good turn
【帮派】 faction
【帮腔】 speak in support of sb. ; echo sb. ; chime in with sb.
【帮手】 helper; assistant
【帮凶】 be an accomplice; accessory
【帮助】 help; assist

绑 (bǎng) tie; bind; fasten

【绑带】 ❶bandage ❷puttee
【绑匪】 kidnapper
【绑架】 ❶kidnap ❷〈农〉stake
【绑票】 kidnap(for ransom)
【绑腿】 leg wrappings; puttee; leggings
【绑扎】 ❶ wrap up; bind up ❷ tie up; bundle up; pack

榜 (bǎng) ❶a list of names posted up ❷announcement; notice

【榜首】 the first place on a list of successful candidates; the first place in a contest, etc.
【榜样】 example; model

膀 (bǎng) ❶upper arm ❷shoulder ❸wing

【膀臂】 ❶〈方〉upper arm; arm ❷ capable assistant; reliable helper; right-hand man

棒 (bàng) ❶ stick; club; ❷ good; fine; excellent; strong

【棒冰】〈方〉ice-lolly; popsicle; ice-sucker; frozen sucker
【棒球】 baseball
【棒子】 stick; club; cudgel

傍 (bàng) close to; near

【傍近】 be close to; near; ～身边 by one's side
【傍晚】 toward evening; at nightfall; at dusk
【傍午】 about noon

磅 (bàng) ❶pound ❷scales

【磅秤】 scales; platform scale

bao

包 (bāo) ❶ wrap ❷ bundle; package; pack; packet; parcel ❸ bag; sack; bundle ❹ surround; encircle; envelop ❺assure; guarantee ❻ hire; charter

【包办】 take sole charge of; do things or make decisions without consulting others

【包庇】 shield; harbour
【包藏】 contain; harbour; conceal
【包场】 book a whole theatre or cinema; make a block booking
【包抄】 outflank; envelop
【包饭】 ❶ get or supply meals at a fixed rate; board: 在附近的饭馆里 ～ board at a nearby restaurant ❷meals thus arranged
【包袱】 ❶ cloth-wrapper ❷ a bundle wrapped in cloth ❸load; weight; burden
【包工】 ❶undertake to perform work within a time limit and according to specifications; contract for a job ❷contractor
【包票】 guarantee slip; warranty
【包围】 surround; encircle
【包销】 ❶ have exclusive selling rights ❷ be the sole agent for a production unit or a firm
【包月】 make monthly payment
【包扎】 wrap up; bind up; pack: ～伤口 bind up (or dress) a wound
【包装】 pack; package

剥 (bāo) shell; peel; skin (limited to use in compound words and idiomatic phrases)
另见 bō

褒 (bāo) praise; honour; commend

【褒贬】 pass judgment on; appraise
【褒奖】 praise and honour; commend and award
【褒义】 commendatory

薄 (báo) ❶thin; flimsy ❷weak; light ❸lacking in warmth; cold ❹infertile; poor
另见 bó, bò

【薄饼】 thin pancake
【薄脆】 crisp fritter
【薄片】 slice; flake
【薄纸】 tissue paper

饱 (bǎo) ❶ have eaten one's fill; be full ❷ full; plump ❸fully; to the full ❹satisfy

【饱餐】 eat to one's heart's content
【饱读】 be well-read
【饱和】 saturation
【饱看】 watch to one's heart's content; take a good look at

宝 (bǎo) ❶treasure ❷precious; treasured

【宝贝】 ❶treasure ❷darling; baby
【宝刀】 a precious (or treasured) sword; a fine sword
【宝典】 a treasured book; a revered book
【宝贵】 ❶valuable; precious ❷value; treasure
【宝剑】 a double-edged sword

B

保 (bǎo) ❶protect;defend ❷keep;maintain; preserve ❸guarantee;ensure ❹stand guarantor for sb. ❺guarantor

【保安】❶ensure public security ❷ensure safety (for workers engaged in production)

【保镖】bodyguard;escort

【保藏】keep in store;preserve

【保持】keep;maintain;preserve

【保存】preserve;conserve;keep

【保单】guarantee slip;warranty

【保管】❶take care of ❷certainly;surely

【保护】protect;safeguard

【保健】health protection;health care

【保洁】keep a public place clean;do sanitation work

【保龄球】❶tenpin bowling;tenpins;bowling ❷ bowling ball

【保留】❶ continue to have;retain ❷ hold (or keep) back;reserve

【保密】maintain secrecy;keep sth. secret

【保命】save one's life;survive

报 (bào) ❶report;announce ❷reply;respond ❸recompense ❹ newspaper ❺ periodical; journal ❻bulletin;report ❼telegram;cable

【报案】report a case to the security authorities

【报表】forms for reporting statistics,etc.;report forms

【报偿】repay;recompense

【报仇】revenge;avenge

【报酬】reward;remuneration;pay

【报答】repay;requite

【报单】taxation form;declaration form

【报到】report for duty;check in register;enroll

刨 (bào) ❶plane sth. down;plane ❷plane; planer;planing machine
另见 páo

【刨冰】water ice (powdered or in shavings)

【刨床】planer;planing machine

【刨工】❶planing ❷planing machine operator; planer

【刨花】wood shavings

【刨子】plane (a carpenter's tool)

抱 (bào) ❶hold or carry in the arms;embrace;hug ❷ have one's first child or grandchild ❸adopt (a child) ❹〈方〉hang together ❺ cherish;harbour ❻ hatch (eggs);brood

【抱病】be ill;be in bad health

【抱不平】be outraged by an injustice (done to sb. else)

【抱负】aspiration;ambition

【抱恨】have a gnawing regret

【抱歉】be sorry;feel apologetic;regret

【抱屈】feel wronged

【抱养】adopt (a child)

【抱怨】complain;grumble

【抱罪】be conscious of one's guilt;be conscience-stricken

暴 (bào) ❶ sudden and violent ❷cruel;savage;fierce ❸short-tempered;hot-tempered ❹stick out;stand out

【暴病】sudden attack of a serious illness;得～ be suddenly seized with a severe illness

【暴跌】steep fall (in price);slump:股票价格～. There was a slump in share prices.

【暴动】insurrection;rebellion

【暴发】❶ break out ❷ suddenly become rich or important

【暴君】tyrant;despot

【暴力】violence;force

【暴利】sudden huge profits

【暴露】expose;reveal;lay bare;exposed to the open air

【暴乱】riot;rebellion;revolt

【暴怒】violent rage;fury

【暴虐】brutal;tyrannical

【暴晒】be exposed to the sun (for a long time)

【暴死】die of a sudden illness

【暴徒】ruffian;thug

【暴行】savage act;outrage;atrocity

【暴雨】torrential rain;rainstorm

【暴躁】irascible;irritable

【暴涨】(of floods,prices etc.) rise suddenly and sharply

【暴政】tyranny;despotic rule

爆 (bào) ❶ explode;burst ❷ quick-fry; quick-boil

【爆豆】❶pop beans:说话像～似的 chatter away like popping beans ❷popped beans

【爆发】erupt;burst into;burst out;break out

【爆裂】burst;crack

【爆满】❶(of a theatre,cinema,etc.) have a full house;house full ❷ (of a stadium,etc.) be filled to capacity

【爆破】blow up;demolish;dynamite;blast;explode

【爆炸】explode;blow up;detonate

bei

杯 (bēi) ❶cup ❷(prize) cup;trophy

【杯赛】cup (a competition):去年我们参加了那次～。We played in the cup last year.

【杯子】 cup;glass

卑 (bēi) ❶low ❷inferior ❸〈书〉modest; humble

【卑鄙】 base;mean;contemptible;despicable

【卑贱】 ❶lowly ❷mean and low

【卑劣】 base;mean;despicable

【卑陋】 ❶humble;mean:～的茅屋 a mean thatched cottage ❷lowly;degrading

【卑视】 look down upon;despise;scorn

【卑微】 petty and low

【卑下】 base;low

【卑职】 〈古〉〈谦〉(used by subordinate officials in addressing superiors) your humble subordinate;I

背 (bēi) ❶carry on the back ❷bear;shoulder
另见 bèi

【背包】 ❶knapsack;rucksack;infantry pack;field pack ❷〈军〉blanket roll

【背带】 braces;suspenders;sling;straps

【背债】 be in debt;be saddled with debts

悲 (bēi) ❶sad;sorrowful;melancholy ❷compassion

【悲哀】 grieved;sorrowful

【悲惨】 miserable;tragic

【悲恻】 〈书〉sad;grieved;sorrowful

【悲愤】 grief and indignation

【悲歌】 ❶sad melody;stirring strains ❷〈音〉elegy;dirge;threnody ❸sing with solemn fervour

【悲哽】 choke with grief:说到这里,她满眼泪花,声音～,不能说下去了。At this point her eyes filled with tears and her voice choked with sobs, she was unable to go on.

【悲观】 pessimistic

【悲剧】 tragedy

【悲苦】 grief;sorrow

【悲凉】 sad and dreary;forlorn;desolate

【悲伤】 sad;grieved;sorrowful

【悲痛】 grieved;sorrowful

碑 (bēi) an upright stone tablet;stele

【碑记】 a record of events inscribed on a tablet

【碑林】 forest of steles

【碑文】 an inscription on a tablet

北 (běi) north

【北半球】 the Northern Hemisphere

【北方】 ❶north ❷the northern part of a country

【北风】 north wind

【北纬】 north latitude

贝 (bèi) shellfish

【贝雕】 shell carving

【贝壳】 shell

【贝类】 shellfish;molluscs

备 (bèi) ❶be equipped with;have ❷prepare; get ready ❸provide against;prepare against ❹equipment ❺fully;in every possible way

【备案】 put on record;register;keep on record; enter(a case)in the records

【备办】 prepare (things needed)

【备查】 for future reference

【备耕】 make preparations for ploughing and sowing

【备荒】 prepare against natural disasters

【备考】 (an appendix,note,etc.)for reference

【备课】 (of a teacher)prepare lessons

【备料】 ❶get the materials ready ❷prepare feed (for livestock)

【备品】 spare parts;machine parts or tools kept in reserve

【备取】 be on the waiting list (for admission to a school)

【备用】 reserve;spare;alternate

【备战】 prepare for war;be prepared against war; war preparations

【备注】 notes;remarks

背 (bèi) ❶the back of the body ❷the back of an object ❸with the back towards ❹turn away ❺do sth. behind sb.'s back ❻learn by heart ❼act contrary to;break ❽hard of hearing ❾out of the way
另见 bēi

【背地里】 behind one's back;privately

【背后】 ❶behind;at the back ❷behind sb.'s back

【背景】 background

【背弃】 abandon;desert;renounce

【背诵】 recite;repeat from memory

【背心】 a sleeveless garment

倍 (bèi) ❶times;-fold ❷double;twice as much

【倍数】 〈数〉multiple

【倍增】 double;redouble

被 (bèi) ❶quilt ❷used in a passive sentence to introduce either the doer of the action or the action if the doer is not mentioned ❸used to form a set phrase with a passive meaning

【被单】 bed sheet

【被动】 passive

【被俘】 be captured;be taken prisoner

【被告】 〈法〉defendant;the accused

【被迫】 be compelled;be forced;be constrained

【被子】 quilt

辈 (bèi) ❶people of a certain kind the like ❷generation ❸lifetime

【辈出】come forth in large numbers

【辈分】seniority in the family or clan;position in the family hierarchy

【辈子】all one's life;lifetime

惫 (bèi) exhausted;fatigued

【惫懒】tired out;exhausted

【惫累】tired;weary

ben

奔 (bēn) ❶run quickly ❷hurry;hasten;rush ❸flee

另见 bèn

【奔波】rush about;be busy running about

【奔驰】run quickly;speed

【奔窜】run helter-skelter:敌军被打得四处～。The enemy forces were routed and fled in disorder.

【奔放】bold and unrestrained;untrammelled

【奔赴】hurry to (a place);rush to

【奔流】❶flow at great speed;pour:～入海 flow into the sea ❷racing current

【奔忙】be busy rushing about;bustle about:秋收季节,农民们一天到晚～着。During the autumn harvest,the farmers were busy working day and night.

【奔命】be in a desperate hurry

【奔跑】run

【奔腾】❶gallop ❷surge forward;roll on in waves

本 (běn) ❶the root or stem of a plant ❷foundation;basis ❸capital;principal ❹original ❺one's own;native ❻present;this;current ❼according to;based on ❽book ❾edition;version

【本部】headquarter

【本地】this locality

【本分】one's duty

【本行】one's line;one's own profession

【本届】current;this year's

【本金】capital;principal

【本科】undergraduate course; regular college course

【本来】❶original ❷originally;at first

【本领】skill;ability;capability

【本末】❶the whole course of an event from beginning to end;ins ad outs:详述～ tell the whole story from beginning to end ❷the fundamental and the incidental

【本能】instinct

【本钱】❶capital:没～做生意 have no capital to start a business ❷what is capitalized on;sth. used to one's own advantage

【本人】❶I (me,myself) ❷oneself;in person

【本色】true(or inherent) qualities;distinctive character

【本身】itself;in itself

【本事】❶source material;original story ❷skill;ability;capability

【本相】true colours;true features:～毕露 show one's true colours;be revealed for what one is

【本性】natural instincts(character, disposition);nature;inherent quality

【本义】〈语〉original meaning;literal sense

【本意】original idea;real intention

【本职】one's job (or duty)

奔 (bèn) ❶go straight towards;head for ❷approach;be getting on for

另见 bēn

【奔头儿】sth. to strive for;prospect

笨 (bèn) ❶ stupid;dull;foolish ❷clumsy;awkward ❸cumbersome;unwieldy

【笨蛋】fool;idiot

【笨重】heavy;cumbersome

【笨拙】clumsy;awkward;stupid

beng

崩 (bēng) ❶collapse ❷burst ❸be hit by sth. bursting ❹〈口〉execute by shooting;shoot

【崩溃】crumble;fall apart

【崩裂】break apart;crack

【崩塌】collapse; crumble:江堤～。The embankment along the river collapsed.

【崩陷】fall in;cave in

绷 (bēng) ❶stretch tight;draw tight ❷spring;bounce ❸swindle;cheat sb. out of money

【绷带】bandage

迸 (bèng) spout;spurt;burst forth

【迸发】burst forth;burst out

【迸裂】split;burst(open)

【迸射】strafe

bi

逼 (bī) ❶force;compel;drive ❷press for;extort ❸press on towards;close in on

【逼供】extort a confession

【逼近】press on towards;close in on;approach;draw near

B

【逼人】pressing；threatening
【逼问】❶force sb. to answer ❷question closely
【逼债】press for payment of debts；dun
【逼真】❶lifelike；true to life ❷distinctly；clearly

鼻 (bí) nose

【鼻孔】nostril
【鼻腔】nasal cavity
【鼻祖】the earliest（first）ancestor；founder；originator（of a tradition，school of thought，etc.）

比 (bǐ) ❶compare；contrast ❷emulate；compete；match ❸draw an analogy；be like；liken to；compare to ❹make a gesture；gesticulate ❺copy；model after ❻ratio；proportion ❼to（in a score）❽〈书〉close together；next to

【比方】analogy；instance
【比分】〈体〉score
【比画】gesture；gesticulate；他～着讲. He made himself understood with the help of gestures.
【比价】❶ price relations；parity；rate of exchange：工农业产品～ the price parities between industrial and agricultural products ❷compare bids or prices
【比肩】〈书〉shoulder to shoulder
【比较】❶ compare；contrast ❷ fairly；comparatively；rather；relatively；quite
【比例】proportion
【比率】ratio；rate
【比拟】❶compare；draw a parallel；match ❷analogy；comparison
【比如】for example；for instance；such as
【比赛】competition；race；contest；tournament；match
【比试】❶ have a competition ❷ measure with one's hand or arm；make a gesture of measuring
【比喻】metaphor；analogy；figure of speech
【比照】❶contrast ❷according to；in the light of
【比值】specific value；ratio
【比重】❶proportion ❷〈物〉specific gravity

彼 (bǐ) ❶that；those；the other；another ❷the other party

〖彼此〗each other；one another

笔 (bǐ) ❶pen，pencil or writing brush ❷technique of writing，calligraphy or drawing ❸write ❹stroke；touch

笔触】brush stroke in Chinese painting or calligraphy；brushwork；style of drawing or writing
笔调】（of writing）tone；style
笔端】〈书〉tip of the brush-style of writing or painting
笔锋】❶the tip of a writing brush ❷vigour of style in writing；stroke；touch

【笔记】notes
【笔记本】notebook
【笔迹】a person's handwriting；hand
【笔力】vigour of strokes in caligraphy or drawing；vigour of style in literary composition
【笔录】❶put down；take down ❷notes；record
【笔名】pen name；pseudonym
【笔墨】pen and ink；words；writing
【笔试】written examination
【笔顺】order of strokes observed in calligraphy
【笔挺】very straight；bolt upright；well-pressed；trim
【笔误】❶make a slip in writing ❷a slip of the pen
【笔者】the author；the present writer
【笔直】perfectly straight；bolt upright

鄙 (bǐ) ❶low；mean ❷〈书〉despise；disdain ❸〈谦〉my

【鄙薄】despise；scorn
【鄙贱】〈书〉❶lowly；humble ❷despise；disdain
【鄙陋】superficial；shallow
【鄙弃】disdain；loathe
【鄙人】〈谦〉your humble servant；I
【鄙视】disdain；look down on

币 (bì) money；currency

【币值】currency value
【币制】monetary standard；currency（or monetary）system

必 (bì) ❶certainly；surely；necessarily ❷must；have to

【必定】be bound to；be sure to
【必然】inevitable；certain
【必须】must；have to
【必需】essential；indispensable
【必要】necessary；indispensable

毕 (bì) ❶finish；accomplish；conclude ❷〈书〉fully；altogether；completely

【毕竟】after all；all in all；in the final analysis
【毕力】make every effort；do all one can；try one's best
【毕命】〈书〉end one's life；die a violent death；meet with a sudden death
【毕生】all one's life；lifetime
【毕肖】〈书〉resemble closely；be the very image of：画得神情～ paint a lifelike portrait of sb.
【毕业】graduate；finish school

闭 (bì) ❶shut；close ❷stop up；obstruct

【闭会】end a meeting
【闭门羹】usu. used in 饣以～ shut the door in

sb.'s face — refuse to receive sb.

B

【闭幕】❶the curtain falls ❷lower the curtain ❸close;conclude

【闭塞】❶stop up;close up ❷hard to get to;out-of-the-way

庇 (bì) shelter;protect;shield

【庇护】shelter;shield;take under one's wing

【庇荫】❶(of a tree etc.)give shade ❷shield

【庇佑】bless;prosper

毙 (bì) ❶die;get killed ❷〈口〉kill or execute by shooting;shoot

【毙命】meet a violent death

裨 (bì) benefit;advantage

【裨补】〈书〉❶make up;remedy ❷benefit;advantage;profit

【裨益】〈书〉profit

碧 (bì) ❶green jade ❷bluish green;blue

【碧蓝】dark blue

【碧绿】dark green

【碧落】〈文〉the green void;the blue empyrean;the blue sky

【碧血】blood shed in a just cause

【碧玉】jasper

蔽 (bì) cover;shelter;hide

【蔽匿】〈书〉hide;conceal

弊 (bì) ❶fraud;abuse;malpractice ❷disadvantage;harm

【弊病】❶malady;evil ❷drawback;disadvantage

【弊端】malpractice;abuse;corrupt practice

壁 (bì) ❶wall ❷sth. resembling a wall ❸cliff ❹rampart;breastwork

【壁报】wall newspaper

【壁橱】a built-in wardrobe or cupboard;closet

【壁灯】wall lamp;bracket light

【壁虎】〈动〉gecko;house lizard

【壁画】mural (painting);fresco

【壁垒】rampart;barrier;贸易～ trade barrier

【壁立】(of cliffs, etc.) stand like a wall;rise steeply:～千尺 a sheer rise of a thousand feet

【壁炉】fireplace

避 (bì) ❶avoid;evade;shun ❷prevent;keep away;repel

【避风】❶take shelter from the wind ❷lie low

【避讳】❶a word or phrase to be avoided as taboo;taboo ❷evade;dodge

【避开】avoid;evade;keep away from

【避免】avoid;refrain from;avert

【避难】take refuge;seek asylum

【避暑】❶be away for the summer holidays;spend a holiday at a summer resort ❷prevent sunstroke

【避嫌】avoid doing anything that may arouse suspicion;avoid arousing suspicion

璧 (bì) a round flat piece of jade with a hole in its centre (used for ceremonial purposes in ancient China)

【璧还】〈套〉❶return (a borrowed object) with thanks ❷decline(a gift)with thanks

bian

边 (biān) ❶side ❷margin;edge;brim;rim ❸border;frontier;boundary ❹bound ❺by the side of;close by

【边陲】〈书〉border area;frontier

【边防】frontier defence

【边际】bound;boundary

【边疆】border area

【边界】boundary;border

【边境】border;frontier

【边塞】〈军〉frontier fortress

【边沿】edge;fringe border;rim

【边缘】edge;fringe;verge;brink

【边远】far from the centre;remote;outlying

编 (biān) ❶weave;plait ❷organize;group;arrange ❸edit;compile ❹write;compose ❺fabricate;invent;make up;cook up

【编凑】fabricate;invent;make up;cook up:你可真会瞎～! You're quite good at making up stories!

【编导】❶write and direct ❷play wright-director (of a play);scenarist-director(of a film)

【编订】compile and edit

【编号】❶number ❷serial number

【编辑】❶edit;compile ❷(assistant)editor;compiler

【编剧】❶write a play scenario, etc. ❷playwright;screenwriter;scenarist

【编排】arrange;lay out

【编审】❶read and edit ❷senior editor

【编写】❶compile ❷write;compose

【编译】compile;translate and edit

【编者】editor;compiler

【编织】weave;knit;plait;braid

【编制】❶weave;plait;braid;～竹器 weav bamboo articles ❷work out;draw up;～教 大纲 draw up a teaching programme ❸author ized strength;establishment;部队～ establish ment (for army units)

【编撰】compile;write

B

鞭 (biān) ❶whip；lash ❷an iron staff used as a weapon in ancient China ❸sth. resembling a whip ❹a string of small firecrackers

【鞭策】spur on；urge on；encourage

【鞭打】whip；lash；flog；thrash

【鞭炮】firecrackers

贬 (biǎn) ❶demote；reduce；devalue（depreciate）❷censure

【贬低】belittle；play down

【贬价】reduce the price；mark down：～出售 sell at a reduced price

【贬值】〈经〉❶devalue；devaluate ❷lessen the value or price of sth.

扁 (biǎn) flat

【扁豆】〈植〉hyacinth bean

【扁圆】oblate

变 (biàn) ❶become different；change ❷transform；alter ❸changeable；changed ❹sell off(one's property) ❺an unexpected turn of events

【变成】change into；turn into；become

【变调】❶〈语〉modified tone ❷tonal modification

【变动】change；alteration

【变法】〈史〉introduce institutional reforms

【变革】transform；change；convert；reform

【变更】change；alter；modify；correct

【变故】unforeseen event；accident；misfortune

【变卦】go back on one's word；break an agreement

【变化】change；vary

【变幻】change irregularly；fluctuate

【变换】vary；alternate

【变价】appraise at the current rate：～出售 sell at the current price

【变节】make a political recantation；turn one's coat

【变脸】suddenly turn hostile

【变卖】sell off (one's property)

【变迁】changes；vicissitudes；change of fortunes；fluctuation

【变色】❶change colour；discolour ❷change countenance；show signs of displeasure；become angry

变速】〈机〉speed change；gearshift

变态】❶〈生〉metamorphosis ❷abnormal；anomalous

变通】be flexible；accommodate（or adapt）sth. to circumstances

变相】in disguised form；covert

变心】cease to be faithful

【变形】❶be out of shape；become deformed ❷〈物〉deformation；shape change；variant ❸〈数〉anamorphosis

【变异】variation

【变质】go bad；deteriorate

【变种】❶〈生〉mutation；variety ❷variety；variant

【变奏】〈音〉variation：～曲 variations（on a theme）

便 (biàn) ❶convenient；handy ❷when an opportunity arises；when it is convenient ❸informal；plain；ordinary ❹relieve oneself ❺piss or shit；urine or excrement

　另见 pián

【便当】convenient；handy

【便道】pavement；sidewalk

【便饭】a simple meal

【便服】❶everyday clothes；informal dress ❷civilian clothes

【便函】an informal letter sent by an organization

【便笺】notepaper；memo（pad）

【便捷】❶convenient ❷quick；nimble

【便利】❶convenient；easy ❷facilitate

【便秘】astriction；constipation

【便民】for the convenience of the people：～措施 facilities for the convenience of the people

【便人】somebody who happens to be on hand for an errand：如有～，请把那本书捎来。Please send the book by anyone who happens to come this way.

【便士】penny

【便条】(informal) note；memo

【便衣】civilian clothes；plain clothes

遍 (biàn) ❶all over；everywhere ❷〈量〉(for actions)once through；a time

【遍布】be found everywhere；spread all over

【遍地】all over the place；everywhere

【遍及】extend all over

辨 (biàn) differentiate；distinguish

【辨别】differentiate；discriminate

【辨明】make a clear distinction；distinguish

【辨认】identify；recognize

【辨析】differentiate and analyse；discriminate

【辨正】determine and rectify

辩 (biàn) argue；dispute；debate

【辩白】offer an explanation；plead innocence；try to defend oneself

【辩驳】dispute；refute

【辩才】〈书〉eloquence

【辩护】❶speak in defence of；argue in favour of；

B

defend ❷〈法〉plead;defend
【辩解】provide an explanation;try to defend one-self
【辩证】dialectical

biao

标 (biāo) ❶mark;sign ❷put a mark;label ❸ prize;award ❹tender;bid ❺triviality;su-perficiality;outward sign
【标榜】❶flaunt;parade;advertise ❷boost;ex-cessively praise
【标本】❶specimen;sample ❷〈中医〉the root cause and symptoms of a disease
【标兵】pace-setter;pioneer
【标杆】❶surveyor's pole ❷model;example
【标记】sign;flag;label;mark;symbol
【标价】❶mark a price ❷marked price
【标量】〈物〉scalar quantity
【标明】mark;indicate
【标签】label;tag
【标样】a trade sample
【标语】slogan;poster;label
【标志】sign;mark;symbol
【标致】pretty;beautiful;handsome
【标准】standard;criterion

表 (biǎo) ❶surface;outside;external ❷the relationship between the children or grand-children of a brother and a sister or of sisters ❸show;express ❹table;form;list ❺watch
【表白】show;assert;vindicate
【表册】statistical forms;book of tables or forms
【表层】surface layer
【表达】express;convey;voice;demonstrate
【表格】form;table
【表功】❶brag about one's deeds ❷〈书〉praise;commend
【表决】decide by vote;vote
【表面】surface;face;outside;appearance
【表明】make known;make clear;state clearly;indicate;declare
【表情】❶express one's feelings ❷expression
【表示】show;express;indicate
【表述】explain;state
【表率】example;model
【表态】make known one's position;declare where one stands
【表现】❶show;display;manifest ❷expres-sion;manifestation;display ❸behaviour;per-formance
【表演】❶perform;act;play ❷performance;exhi-bition ❸demonstrate
【表扬】praise;commend

bie

憋 (biē) ❶suppress;hold back ❷suffocate;feel oppressed
【憋闷】be depressed;be dejected
【憋气】feel suffocated;feel injured

别 (bié) ❶leave;part ❷other;another ❸ turn;change ❹differentiate;distinguish ❺ difference;distinction ❻classification;category ❼fasten with a pin or clip ❽（used in giving commands or advice)don't;had better not
另见 biè
【别称】another name;alternative name
【别管】no matter (who,what,etc.)：～是谁,一律按原则办事。No matter who he is,we'll act according to principle.
【别号】〈古〉another name;alias
【别离】take leave of;leave;depart
【别论】another or a different matter：又当～should be regarded as a different matter
【别名】another name;alternative name
【别人】other people;others;people
【别是】（used in expressing anxiety that sth. bad may happen)：他这时还没来,～不肯来吧? He hasn't come yet. I hope he is not unwilling to come.
【别墅】villa
【别说】to say nothing of;not to mention;let a-lone：～在下雨,你现在出去也太晚了。It's far too late for you to go out,not to mention the fact that it's raining.
【别提】〈口〉no need to mention;you can well i-magine
【别样】❶other;different ❷a different style
【别针】❶safety pin;pin ❷brooch
【别致】unique;unconventional

别 (biè) persuade sb. to change his opinion or give up his idea
另见 bié
【别扭】❶awkward;unnatural ❷cannot see eye to eye

bin

宾 (bīn) guest
【宾馆】guesthouse
【宾客】guests;visitors
【宾朋】friends and guests;guests
【宾语】〈语〉object
【宾主】host and guest：～频频举杯。Host and guests proposed repeated toasts.

B

濒 (bīn) ❶be close to;border on ❷be on the brink of;be on the point of

【濒近】close to;close on

【濒临】be close to;border on;be on the verge of

【濒危】❶ be in imminent danger ❷ be critically ill

【濒于】be on the brink of;be on the verge of

摈 (bìn)〈书〉discard;get rid of

【摈斥】〈书〉reject;dismiss;～异己 dismiss those who hold different opinions

【摈除】discard;get rid of;dispense with

【摈弃】abandon;discard;cast away

殡 (bìn)❶lay a coffin in a memorial hall ❷ carry a coffin to the burial place

【殡殓】encoffin a corpse

【殡仪馆】the undertaker's;mortuary house

【殡葬】funeral and interment

bing

冰 (bīng) ❶ice ❷put on the ice ❸feel cold

【冰雹】hail;hailstone

【冰川】glacier

【冰点】〈物〉freezing point

【冰雕】❶ice carving ❷carved ice;ice sculpture

【冰糕】〈方〉❶ice-cream ❷ice-lolly;Popsicle

【冰河】glacier

【冰窖】icehouse

【冰块】lump of ice;ice cube

【冰冷】ice-cold

【冰山】iceberg

【冰糖】crystal sugar;rock candy

【冰箱】icebox;refrigerator;freezer

【冰鞋】skating boots;skates

兵 (bīng) ❶weapons;arms ❷soldier;fighter ❸troops;army ❹military affairs

【兵法】art of war;military strategy and tactics

【兵家】❶military strategist in ancient China ❷military commander;soldier;～必争之地 a place contested by all strategists;strategic point

【兵精粮足】have well-trained troops and abundant supplies

【兵力】military strength;armed forces;troops

【兵马】troops and horses;military forces

【兵权】military power;military leadership

【兵士】ordinary soldier

【兵团】large military unit consisting of several armies;corps

【兵役】military service

【兵营】military camp;barracks

【兵种】arm of the services

秉 (bǐng) ❶〈文〉grasp;hold ❷〈书〉control;preside over

【秉承】〈书〉take (orders);receive (commands)

【秉持】adhere to (principles, etc.);hold onto;～公心,指摘是弊 castigate the error of the times out of unselfish motives

【秉公】justly;impartially

【秉正】〈书〉fair-minded;honest;upright

【秉政】〈书〉be at the helm of the state;be in power;be in office

饼 (bǐng) ❶a round flat cake ❷sth. shaped like a cake

【饼干】biscuit;cracker

【饼子】〈口〉(maize or millet)pancake

屏 (bǐng) ❶hold (one's breath) ❷get rid of;reject
另见 píng

【屏气】hold one's breath

【屏声】hold one's breath and keep quiet;～倾听 listen in rapt silence

禀 (bǐng) ❶report;petition ❷receive;be endowed with

【禀赋】natural endowment;gift

【禀告】〈书〉report (to one's superior or senior)

【禀性】natural disposition

并 (bìng) ❶ combine;merge;incorporate ❷ simultaneously;side by side ❸and;moreover

【并存】exist side by side

【并发】be complicated by;erupt simultaneously

【并肩】shoulder to shoulder;abreast

【并进】advance side by side

【并举】develop simultaneously

【并立】exist side by side;exist simultaneously

【并联】〈电〉parallel connection

【并列】stand side by side;be juxtaposed

【并排】side by side;abreast

【并且】and;besides;moreover

【并日】〈书〉❶on the same day ❷for days on end;day after day

【并入】merge into;incorporate into

【并世】of the time;of the day;～无第二人 the best of the time (or day);peerless;unrivalled

【并吞】swallow up;annex;absorb

【并行】❶walk abreast;run side by side ❷carry on (two things) at the same time

【并用】use two things simultaneously;手脚～ use both hands and feet

【并重】lay equal stress on;pay equal attention to

病 (bìng) ❶ill;sick ❷disease ❸fault;defect

【病变】 pathological changes
【病床】 ❶hospital bed ❷sickbed
【病倒】 be laid up
【病毒】〈医〉virus
【病房】 ward;sickroom
【病根】 ❶an incompletely cured illness;an old complaint ❷the root cause of trouble
【病故】 die of an illness
【病号】 sick personnel
【病患】 disease;illness;sickness
【病机】〈中医〉interpretation of the cause,onset and process of an illness;pathogenesis
【病假】 sick leave
【病句】 a faulty sentence (grammatically or logically)
【病菌】 pathogenic bacteria;germs
【病理】 pathology
【病历】 medical record;case history
【病例】 case(of illness)
【病魔】 serious illness
【病情】 state of an illness;patient's condition
【病人】 patient;invalid
【病势】 degree of seriousness of an illness; patient's condition:针灸以后,～略为减轻。The patient became a bit better after the acupuncture treatment.
【病态】 morbid state
【病痛】 slight illness;ailment
【病危】 be critically ill
【病因】 cause of disease
【病友】 a friend made in hospital or people who become friends in hospital;ward-mate
【病愈】 recover (from an illness)
【病员】 sick personnel;person on the sick list;patient
【病院】 a specialized hospital
【病症】 disease;illness

bo

拨 (bō) ❶move;turn;stir;poke ❷set side; allocate;appropriate
【拨款】 ❶allocate funds ❷appropriation
【拨拉】 move or adjust with the hand,the foot,a stick,etc.:～算盘子儿 move the beads on an abacus
【拨弄】 ❶fiddle with ❷stir up ❸manipulate
【拨冗】〈套〉find time in the midst of pressing affairs:务希～出席。Your presence is cordially requested.
【拨正】 set right;correct
波 (bō) ❶wave ❷〈物〉wave ❸an unexpected turn of events

【波长】 wavelength
【波动】 fluctuate;be unstable
【波段】 waveband
【波峰】 wave crest;peak;ridge
【波及】 spread to;involve;affect
【波兰】 Poland
【波浪】 wave
【波纹】 ripple
【波折】 twists and turns

玻 (bō)

【玻璃】 glass

剥 (bō) (meaning the same as 剥 bāo,limited to use in compound words and idiomatic phrases)
　　另见 bāo
【剥夺】 deprive;expropriate;strip
【剥离】 (of tissue,skin,covering,etc.) come off; peel off;be stripped
【剥落】 come off;peel off
【剥蚀】 denude;corrode;erode:由于风雨～,碑文已无法辨认。Owing to the ravages of wind and rain,the inscription on the stone tablet is already undecipherable.
【剥削】 exploit;exploitation

播 (bō) ❶sow;seed ❷broadcast ❸remove; go into exile
【播发】 broadcast
【播放】 ❶broadcast ❷broadcast a T. V. programme
【播弄】 ❶order sb. about ❷stir up
【播弄是非】 stir things up;stir up trouble;sow dissension;tell tales
【播撒】 spread;scatter;sprinkle
【播送】 broadcast;transmit;beam
【播音】 transmit;broadcast
【播种】 ❶sowing;seeding ❷sow seeds; sow

伯 (bó) ❶father's elder brother;uncle ❷the eldest among brothers ❸earl;count
【伯伯】 uncle
【伯父】 ❶father's elder brother;uncle ❷a term of address for a man of one's father's generation who is older than one's father;uncle
【伯乐】 ❶a legendary connoisseur of horses ❷a good judge of talent

驳 (bó) ❶transport by lighter ❷barge;lighter ❸extend or widen ❹refute;contradict; gainsay
【驳斥】 refute;denounce;deny;disprove;dispute
【驳倒】 demolish sb's argument;refute;outargue
【驳回】 reject;turn down;overrule;refute
【驳杂】 multifarious;heterogeneous

勃 (bó) suddenly

【勃勃】thriving;vigorous;exuberant
【勃发】〈书〉❶thrive;prosper ❷break out
【勃然】❶agitatedly ❷vigorously
【勃兴】〈书〉rise suddenly;grow vigorously

博 (bó) ❶rich;abundant;plentiful ❷erudite; well-informed ❸ loose;big ❹ win;gain ❺gamble

【博爱】universal fraternity (or brotherhood); universal love
【博大】broad;extensive
【博得】win;gain
【博古】❶conversant with things of the past ❷ paintings of ancient objects
【博览】read extensively
【博取】try to gain;court
【博识】learned;erudite
【博士】doctor
【博物】old general name for zoology, botany, mineralogy, physiology, etc.
【博弈】〈书〉play chess;have a game of chess

搏 (bó) ❶ wrestle; fight ❷ pounce on ❸ beat;throb

【搏动】pulsate;throb
【搏斗】struggle;wrestle with sb.
【搏击】strike;fight with hands
【搏杀】❶ fight with a weapon ❷ (in chess games) be locked in a fierce contest
【搏噬】(of an animal) pounce on and bite

薄 (bó) approach;near
另见 báo,bò

【薄待】treat sb. ungenerously
【薄酒】light wine (said by a host of his own wine)
【薄礼】gift
【薄利】small profits
【薄命】(usu. of women) born unlucky; born under an unlucky star
【薄膜】❶membrane ❷film
【薄情】inconstant in love;fickle
【薄弱】weak;frail
【薄雾】mist;haze
【薄晓】shortly before daybreak;before dawn
【薄行】❶frivolous conduct ❷frivolous;dissipated

跛 (bǒ) lame

【跛行】walk lamely;have a limp
【跛子】lame person;cripple

薄 (bò)
另见 báo,bó

【薄荷】〈植〉field mint;peppermint

bu

补 (bǔ) ❶ mend; repair ❷ fill; supply; make up for ❸nourish ❹help;benefit

【补报】❶make a report after the event;make a supplementary report:调查结果以后 ～。 Findings will be reported later. ❷repay a kindness
【补偿】❶compensate;make up;❷compensation
【补充】❶ replenish; supplement; complement; add ❷additional;complementary; supplementary
【补丁】patch
【补法】〈中医〉❶ treatment involving the use of tonics to restore the patient's health ❷reinforcing method (in acupuncture)
【补给】supply;provision
【补救】remedy
【补考】make-up examination
【补课】make up a missed lesson
【补票】buy one's ticket after the normal time
【补品】tonic
【补缺】fill a vacancy;supply a deficiency
【补税】❶pay a tax one has evaded ❷pay an overdue tax
【补贴】subsidy;allowance
【补习】take lessons after school or work
【补选】by-election
【补血】enrich the blood
【补牙】fill a tooth;have a tooth stopped
【补养】take a tonic or nourishing food to build up one's health
【补药】tonic
【补益】〈书〉❶benefit;help ❷be of help (or benefit)
【补助】❶help financially;subsidize ❷subsidy; allowance
【补足】bring up to full strength;make up a deficiency;fill (a vacancy,gap,etc.)

捕 (bǔ) catch;seize;arrest

【捕获】catch;capture;seize
【捕捞】fish for (aquatic animals and plants); catch
【捕猎】catch (wild animals);hunt
【捕杀】catch and kill
【捕食】catch and feed on;prey on
【捕捉】catch;seize

哺 (bǔ) ❶feed;nurse ❷the food in one's mouth

【哺乳】breast-feed;suckle;nurse
【哺育】〈书〉❶feed ❷nurture;foster

不 (bù) ❶ (used to express a negative statement) not; no ❷ (used to give a negative reply or response) no

【不安】 ❶intranquil; unpeaceful; unstable ❷sorry

【不安分】 discontented with one's lot

【不备】 ❶unprepared; off guard ❷〈书〉(used at the end of a letter) there is more than I can tell you in this letter

【不必】 need not; not have to

【不便】 inconvenient; inappropriate; unsuitable

【不测】 accident; mishap; contingency; unexpectedness

【不曾】 never (have done sth.)

【不成】 ❶won't do; 只说不做，那是～的。Mere talk and no action won't do. ❷ (used at the end of a rhetorical question beginning with)

【不错】 correct; right

【不但】 not only

【不惮】 not fear; not be afraid of; ～其烦 not mind taking the trouble; take great pains; be very patient

【不当】 unsuitable; improper; inappropriate; 处理～ not be handled properly

【不得了】 ❶desperately serious; disastrous ❷extremely

【不得已】 act against one's will; have no alternative but to

【不等】 ❶vary; differ ❷〈数〉unequal

【不定】 indefinite

【不端】 improper; dishonourable

【不断】 unceasing; uninterrupted; continuous; constant

【不对】 ❶incorrect; wrong ❷amiss; abnormal; queer

【不乏】〈书〉there is no lack of

【不法】 lawless; illegal

【不妨】 there is no harm in; might as well

【不分胜负】 tie; draw; come out even; 一场～的比赛 a drawn game

【不服】 refuse to obey (or comply); refuse to accept as final; remain unconvinced by; not give in to

【不甘】 unreconciled to; not resigned to

【不敢当】〈谦〉I really don't deserve this; you flatter me

【不够】 not enough; inadequate

【不顾】 in spite of; regardless of

【不关】 have nothing to do with

【不光】〈口〉❶not the only one ❷not only

【不过】 ❶only; merely ❷but

【不合】 not conform to; be unsuited to; be out of keeping with

【不和】 ❶not get along well; be on bad terms; be at odds ❷discord

【不会】 ❶ be unlikely; will not (act, happen, etc.) ❷ have not learned to; be unable to ❸ (used to express reproach for the non-performance of an action)

【不及】 ❶not as good as; inferior to ❷find it too late

【不见不散】 (let's) not leave without seeing each other (said when making an appointment)

【不见得】 not necessarily; not likely

【不解】 ❶not understand ❷indissoluble

【不禁】 can't help; can't refrain from

【不仅】 ❶not the only one ❷not only

【不经意】 carelessly; by accident

【不久】 ❶ soon; before long ❷ not long after; soon after

【不拘】 not stick to; not confine oneself to

【不倦】 tireless; untiring; indefatigable

【不可】 cannot; should not; must not

【不客气】 ❶impolite; rude; blunt ❷〈套〉(used to respond to other's thanks) you are welcome; don't mention it; not at all ❸〈套〉(used to appreciate other's kindness) please don't bother; I'll help myself

【不快】 ❶ be unhappy; be displeased; be in low spirits ❷ be indisposed; feel under the weather; be out of sorts

【不愧】 be worthy of; deserve to be called; prove oneself to be

【不理】 refuse to acknowledge; pay no attention to; take no notice of; ignore

【不力】 not do one's best; not exert oneself

【不利】 ❶ unfavourable; disadvantageous; harmful; detrimental ❷unsuccessful

【不良】 bad; harmful; unhealthy

【不料】 unexpectedly; to one's surprise

【不灵】 not work; be ineffective

【不论】 no matter

【不满】 resentful; discontented; dissatisfied

【不忙】 there is no hurry; take one's time

【不明】 ❶ not clear; unknown ❷ fail to understand

【不能】 must not; cannot

【不平】 ❶ injustice; unfairness; wrong; grievance ❷indignant; resentful

【不平衡】 disequilibria; out of balance

【不巧】 unfortunately; as luck would have it

【不求上进】 have no desire for progress; not seek to make progress

【不求甚解】not seek to understand things thoroughly; be content with superficial understanding

【不然】 ❶ not so; not the case; no ❷ if not so; otherwise; or else

【不人道】inhuman

【不忍】cannot bear to

【不容】not tolerate; not allow

【不如】 ❶ not equal to; not as good as; inferior to ❷ it would be better to

【不善】 ❶ bad; ill ❷ not good at

【不胜】 ❶ cannot bear; be unequal to ❷ very; extremely

【不时】 frequently; often; from time to time

【不适】unwell; indisposed; out of sorts

【不通】be obstructed; be blocked up; be impassable; not make sense; be illogical; be ungrammatical

【不同】not alike; different; distinct

【不妥】not proper; inappropriate

【不惜】 ❶ stint no effort; not spare ❷ not hesitate (to do sth.)

【不相容】incompatible

【不详】〈书〉❶ not in detail ❷ not quite clear

【不祥】ominous

【不像话】 ❶ unreasonable ❷ shocking; outrageous

【不孝】not in accordance with filiality

【不屑】 disdain to do sth. ; think sth. not worth doing

【不懈】untiring; unremitting; indefatigable

【不幸】 ❶ misfortune; adversity ❷ unfortunately ❸ unfortunate; sad

【不休】endlessly; ceaselessly

【不朽】immortal

【不要紧】 ❶ it's not serious; it doesn't matter; never mind ❷ it looks all right, but

【不要脸】〈讳〉have no sense of shame; shameless

【不一】differ; vary

【不依】 ❶ not comply; not go along with ❷ not let off

【不宜】not suitable; inadvisable

【不用】need not

【不争气】be disappointing; fail to live up to expectations

【不值】not worth

【不止】 ❶ without end; incessantly ❷ more than; not limited to

【不只】not only; not merely

【不准】not allow; forbid; prohibit

【不自在】uneasy; ill at ease; feel uncomfortable

【不足】 ❶ not enough; insufficient; inadequate ❷ less than ❸ not worth; be beneath ❹ can't; should not

布 (bù) ❶ cloth; fabric; textiles ❷ spread; disseminate ❸ declare; announce; publish; proclaim ❹ dispose; arrange; deploy

【布帛】cloth and silk; cotton and silk textiles

【布丁】pudding

【布告】notice; bulletin; proclamation

【布谷鸟】〈动〉cuckoo

【布局】 ❶ layout; distribution ❷ composition(of a picture, piece of writing, etc.)

【布匹】cloth; piece goods

【布衣】 ❶ cotton dress ❷ commoner

【布置】 ❶ fix up; arrange; decorate ❷ assign; make arrangements for

步 (bù) ❶ step; pace ❷ stage ❸ situation condition ❹ walk; go on foot ❺ move

【步兵】 ❶ infantry ❷ foot soldier

【步步登高】 ascend step by step; rise steadily in one's career

【步步为营】 consolidate at every step

【步调】pace; step

【步伐】step; pace

【步行】go on foot; walk

【步骤】step; move; measure

【步子】step; pace

部 (bù) ❶ part; section ❷ unit ❸ headquarters ❹ troops ❺ control; command ❻〈量〉used with books, films, etc.

【部队】army; armed forces; troops

【部分】part; section; share

【部件】parts; components; assembly

【部落】tribe

【部门】department; branch

【部首】radicals by which characters are arranged in traditional Chinese dictionaries

【部署】dispose; deploy

【部位】position; place

【部下】 ❶ troops under one's command ❷ subordinate

【部长】minister

簿 (bù) notebook; book

【簿册】books for taking notes or keeping accounts

【簿籍】account books, registers, records, etc.

C c

ca

擦 (cā) ❶rub ❷wipe ❸apply or spread sth. on ❹shave；brush

【擦边球】edge ball；touch ball

【擦去】wipe off

【擦伤】abrasion；gall；scratch

【擦身而过】pass each other so close that they almost rubbed each other

cai

猜 (cāi) guess；conjecture；speculate；suspect

【猜测】guess；conjecture；speculate

【猜度】surmise；conjecture：他心里在～，这位老人家是谁? He was wondering who that old man could be.

【猜忌】be suspicious and jealous of

【猜拳】a finger-guessing game；mora

【猜想】suppose；guess；suspect

【猜疑】harbour suspicious；be suspicious；have misgivings

【猜中】guess correctly；solve

才 (cái) ❶ability；talent ❷a capable person ❸ a moment ago；just ❹ (preceded by an expression of time)not until ❺ (followed by a numerical expression)only

【才德兼备】have both ability and moral integrity

【才干】ability；competence

【才高八斗】be endowed with unusual literary talents

【才华】literary or artistic talent

【才华横溢】brim with talent；have superb talent

【才略】ability and sagacity

【才貌双全】having both looks and real talent

【才能】ability；talent；〈心〉aptitude

【才气】literary talent

【才识】ability and insight

【才疏学浅】〈谦〉have little talent and less learning

【才思敏捷】have a facile imagination

【才学】talent and learning；(intelligence and) scholarship

【才智】ability and wisdom

【才子】gifted scholar

材 (cái) ❶ timber ❷ material ❸ ability；talent；aptitude ❹a capable person

【材料】❶material ❷data；material ❸makings；stuff

财 (cái) wealth；money

【财宝】money and valuables

【财产】property

【财富】wealth；riches

【财经】finance and economics

【财会】finance and accounting

【财力】financial resources；financial capacity

【财迷】moneygrubber；miser

【财权】❶ownership of property；property right ❷financial power；control over money matters

【财务】financial affairs

【财物】property；belongings

【财源】financial resources；source of revenue；finances

【财运】luck in making money

【财政】(public) finance

裁 (cái) ❶cut (paper, cloth, etc.) into parts ❷reduce；cut down；dismiss ❸judge；decide ❹check；sanction

【裁并】cut down and merge (organizations)：这个科已～到总务处。This section has been merged into the general affairs department.

【裁撤】dissolve (an organization)

【裁处】make arrangement after due consideration；make a decision after consideration and then deal with

【裁定】〈法〉ruling；holding；judge

【裁缝】tailor；dress-maker

【裁减】reduce；cut down

【裁剪】cut out

【裁决】ruling；adjudication

【裁军】disarmament

【裁判】❶〈体〉judgment ❷umpire；referee

【裁员】cut down the number of persons employed；reduce the staff

采（cǎi）❶pick；pluck ❷mine；extract ❸adopt；select ❹complexion；spirit

【采办】select and purchase on a considerable scale（esp. for a special occasion）

【采伐】fell；cut

【采访】gather material；cover

【采购】purchase

【采集】gather；collect

【采矿】mining

【采纳】accept；adopt

【采暖】〈建〉heating

【采取】take；adopt

【采样】sampling；take sample

【采用】use；employ

【采摘】pick（fruit，flowers，leaves，etc. ）；pluck

彩（cǎi）❶color ❷colored silk ❸applause；cheer ❹variety；splendor ❺prize ❻blood from a wound

【彩笔】colour pencil；crayon

【彩车】float（in a parade）

【彩带】coloured ribbon

【彩灯】coloured lights

【彩虹】rainbow

【彩礼】betrothal gifts

【彩排】dress rehearsal

【彩票】lottery ticket

【彩色】multicolour；colour

【彩霞】rosy clouds；pink clouds

踩（cǎi）step on；trample

【踩线】〈体〉❶foot fault ❷commit a foot fault；footfault

菜（cài）❶vegetable；greens ❷food ❸dish；course

【菜板】chopping board

【菜场】food（grocery；vegetable）market；market

【菜单】menu；bill of fare

【菜刀】kitchen knife

【菜地】vegetable plot

【菜豆】kidney bean

【菜花】❶cauliflower ❷rape flower

【菜篮子】❶ shopping basket（for food）；food basket ❷ food supply

【菜谱】recipe

【菜色】famished look

【菜市】food market；vegetable market

【菜肴】cooked food

【菜园】kitchen garden；vegetable farm（plot）

【菜籽】rapeseed

can

参（cān）❶join；enter；take part in ❷refer；consult ❸call to pay one's respects to ❹impeach an official before the emperor
　另见 cēn，shēn

【参拜】formally call on；pay a courtesy call；pay respects to

【参观】visit；look around

【参加】❶join；attend；take part in ❷give（advice；suggestion，etc. ）

【参见】❶see also ❷pay one's respects to（a superior，etc. ）

【参军】join the army；join up；enlist

【参看】❶see（used in references）❷read sth. for references；consult

【参考】❶consult；refer to ❷reference

【参谋】❶〈军〉staff officer ❷give advice

【参赛】participate in a match or contest

【参透】thoroughly understand

【参与】participate in；have a hand in

【参战】enter a war

【参照】consult；refer to

【参政】take part in politics or the government；participate in government and political affairs

餐（cān）❶eat ❷food；meal ❸regular meal

【餐车】restaurant car；dining car；diner

【餐风宿露】hardship of travel without shelter

【餐馆】restaurant

【餐巾】table napkin

【餐具】tableware；dinner service；dinner set

【餐厅】❶dining room；dining hall ❷restaurant

残（cán）❶incomplete；deficient ❷remnant；remaining ❸injure；damage

【残暴】cruel and ferocious；ruthless；brutal；savage

【残兵败将】remnants of a routed army

【残存】remnant；remaining；surviving

【残废】maimed；crippled；disabled

【残骸】remains；wreckage

【残害】cruelly injure or kill

【残疾】deformity

【残局】❶the final phase of a game of chess ❷the situation after the failure of an undertaking or after social unrest

【残酷】cruel；brutal；ruthless

【残留】remain；be left over

【残年】❶the last days of the year ❷the evening of life；declining years

【残缺】incomplete；fragmentary

C

【残忍】cruel；ruthless
【残杀】murder；massacre；slaughter
【残阳】the setting sun
【残余】remnants；remains；survivals；vestiges
【残渣】residual；residue；slag

蚕 ^(cán) silkworm

【蚕豆】broad bean (the plant，the pod or the seed)
【蚕食政策】the policy of nibbling at another country's territory
【蚕丝】natural silk；silk

惭 ^(cán) feel ashamed

【惭愧】be ashamed

惨 ^(cǎn) ❶miserable；tragic ❷cruel；brutal；merciless ❸to a serious degree；disastrously

【惨案】❶ massacre ❷ murder case；tragic case；tragedy
【惨白】deathly pale
【惨败】crushing defeat；disastrous defeat
【惨变】a tragic turn of fortune
【惨不忍睹】too horrible to look at
【惨淡】gloomy；dismal；bleak
【惨境】miserable condition；tragic circumstances；dire straits
【惨绝人寰】tragic beyond compare in this human world；extremely tragic
【惨痛】deeply grieved；painful；agonizing
【惨重】heavy；grievous；disastrous
【惨状】a miserable condition；a pitiful or horrible sight

灿 ^(càn)

【灿烂】magnificent；splendid；resplendent；bright

cang

仓 ^(cāng) storehouse；warehouse

【仓促】hurriedly；all of a sudden
【仓房】warehouse；storehouse
【仓皇】in a flurry；in panic
【仓皇失措】be scared out of one's wits；be panic-stricken
【仓库】warehouse；storehouse；depository

苍 ^(cāng) ❶dark green or blue ❷grey；ashen

【苍白】pale；pallid；wan
【苍苍】❶grey ❷vast and hazy
【苍翠】dark green；verdant
【苍劲】❶old and strong ❷vigorous；bold

【苍老】❶old (in appearance)；hoary；(of an old man's voice) hoarse ❷(of calligraphy or painting) vigorous；forceful
【苍凉】desolate；bleak
【苍茫】❶vast；boundless ❷indistinct
【苍天】Heaven
【苍鹰】goshawk
【苍蝇】fly；housefly

沧 ^(cāng) (of the sea)deep blue

【沧海】the deep blue sea；the sea
【沧海横流】the seas in turbulence — the country or the world in chaos
【沧海桑田】from seas into mulberry fields and from mulberry fields into seas — time brings great changes to the world
【沧海一粟】a drop in the ocean

舱 ^(cāng) ❶cabin (of an airplane or ship) ❷module (of a spacecraft)

【舱门】hatch door；cabin door
【舱面】deck
【舱室】cabin
【舱位】❶cabin seat or berth ❷shipping space

藏 ^(cáng) ❶hide；conceal ❷store；lay by

【藏龙卧虎】used esp. in ～之地 a place where dragons and tigers are hiding—a place where people of unusual ability are to be found
【藏匿】conceal；hide；go into hiding
【藏身】hide oneself
【藏书】collect books；collection of books；library

cao

操 ^(cāo) ❶grasp；hold ❷act；do ❸speak (a language or dialect) ❹ drill；exercise ❺conduct；behavior

【操办】manage affairs；make preparations or arrangements for
【操场】playground；sports ground
【操持】manage；handle
【操法】methods and rules for military drill or physical exercise
【操劳】❶work hard ❷take care
【操练】drill；practice
【操心】❶ worry about；take pains ❷ rack one's brains
【操行】behaviour or conduct of a student
【操纵】operate；control
【操纵杆】operating lever；control rod；control stick
【操作】operate；manipulate

嘈(cáo) noise;dim

【嘈杂】noisy

草(cǎo) ❶grass; straw ❷careless; hasty ❸draft ❹female

【草案】draft(of a plan,law,etc.)

【草本】herbaceous

【草草】carelessly;hastily

【草草收场】hastily wind up a matter

【草场】meadow;pasture;grassland

【草丛】a thick growth of grass

【草地】❶grassland ❷lawn

【草稿】rough draft

【草绿】grass green

【草莽】❶a rank growth of grass ❷uncultivated land;wilderness

【草帽】straw hat

【草莓】strawberry

【草拟】draw up;draft

【草皮】sod;turf

【草坪】lawn

【草食动物】plant-eating animal;herbivore

【草书】tachygraphy;cursive hand

【草率】careless;rash

【草堂】〈文〉grass hut; thatched hut; cottage (esp. as a poet's or recluse's retreat)

【草头王】king of the bushes—a bandit chief

【草图】sketch(map);draft

【草鞋】straw sandals

【草药】medicinal herbs

【草原】grasslands;prairie

【草纸】❶rough straw paper ❷toilet paper

ce

册(cè) ❶volume;book ❷copy

【册子】book;volume

厕(cè) lavatory;toilet;washroom;W. C.

【厕所】lavatory;toilet;W. C.

侧(cè) ❶side ❷incline;lean

【侧耳】incline the ear;strain one's ears

【侧击】flank attack;make a flank attack on

【侧门】side door

【侧面】side;aspect;flank

【侧目而视】look askance at sb. (with fear or indignation)

【侧身】lean to one side;on one's side;sideways

【侧卧】lie on one's side

【侧向】side direction

【侧影】silhouette;profile

【侧重】lay particular emphasis on

测(cè) ❶survey;fathom ❷conjecture;infer

【测定】determine

【测度】estimate;infer

【测绘】survey and draw;mapping

【测距】range (distance) finding; distance measurement;ranging

【测量】survey

【测试】❶test (a machine, meter or apparatus) ❷test (a student's proficiency)

【测算】measure and calculate

【测验】test

恻(cè) sorrowful;sad

【恻隐】〈书〉compassion;pity

策(cè) ❶plan;scheme ❷whip

【策动】instigate;engineer

【策反】instigate rebellion within the enemy camp;incite defection

【策划】plot;scheme

【策略】❶tactics ❷tactful

【策应】support by coordinated action;act in concert with each other; make supporting movement to cut off enemy

【策源地】source;place of origin

cen

参(cēn) 另见 cān,shēn

【参差】irregular;uneven

【参差不齐】uneven;not uniform

ceng

层(céng) ❶storey;floor ❷level ❸one on top of another;overlapping

【层层】layer upon layer

【层出不穷】emerge in an endless stream

【层次】❶administrative levels ❷arrangement of ideas

【层叠】one on top of another

【层见叠出】occur frequently;appear repeatedly

【层峦叠嶂】peaks rising one higher than another

曾(céng) (indicating that an action once happened or a state once existed)

【曾几何时】before long;not long after

【曾经沧海】have sailed the seven seas—have much experience of life; have seen much of the world

cha

叉（chā）❶ fork ❷ work with a fork; fork ❸cross

【叉车】forklift; fork truck; forklift truck

【叉腰】akimbo

【叉子】fork

差（chā）❶ difference; dissimilarity ❷ difference ❸only just; barely

另见 chà, chāi

【差别】difference; disparity

【差别阈限】〈心〉 difference limen (or threshold)

【差错】❶mistake; error; slip ❷mishap; accident

【差额】difference; balance; margin

【差价】price differences; gap between prices disparity

【差距】❶gap; disparity ❷〈机〉difference

【差强人意】just passable; barely satisfactory; fair

【差异】difference; divergence; discrepancy; diversity

插（chā）❶stick in; insert ❷interpose

【插班】join a class in the middle of the course

【插翅难飞】even if one had wings one could hardly fly away—no possible escape

【插话】❶interpose; chip in ❷digression; episode

【插曲】❶interlude ❷songs in a film or play ❸ episode; interlude

【插入】❶insert ❷〈电〉plug in

【插手】❶take part; lend a hand ❷have a hand in; poke one's nose into; meddle in; take a hand in

【插头】plug; plug contact; male plug

【插图】illustration; plate

【插秧】transplant rice seedlings (or rice shoots)

【插页】inset; insert

【插足】❶put one's foot in ❷participate

【插嘴】interrupt; chip in

【插座】〈电〉socket; outlet

茶（chá）❶tea(the plant or its leaves) ❷tea (the drink) ❸certain kinds of drink or liquid food

【茶杯】teacup

【茶匙】❶teaspoon ❷teaspoonful

【茶碟儿】saucer

【茶花】camellia

【茶话会】tea party

【茶几】tea table; teapoy; side table

【茶具】tea set; tea-things; tea service

【茶楼】a teahouse with two or more storeys

【茶盘】tea tray; tea-board

【茶色】dark brown

【茶树】tea tree

【茶水】tea water; boiled water

【茶亭】tea-booth; tea-stall; tea-kiosk

【茶叶】tea; tea-leaves

【茶余饭后】over a cup of tea or after a meal

【茶座】❶ tea-stall with seats ❷ seats in a teahouse or tea garden

查（chá）❶check; examine ❷look into; investigate ❸look up; consult

【查办】investigate and deal with accordingly

【查抄】make an inventory of a criminal's possessions and confiscate them

【查处】investigate and prosecute

【查对】check; verify

【查房】(of doctors, nurses, etc.) make (or go) the rounds of the wards

【查访】go around and make inquiries; investigate

【查封】seal up; close down

【查户口】check residence cards; check on household occupants

【查获】hunt down and seize; ferret out; track down

【查看】look over; examine

【查考】investigate; try to ascertain; do research on

【查明】prove through investigation; ascertain

【查票】examine (or check) tickets

【查实】check and verify

【查收】❶find sth. enclosed ❷check and accept

【查问】question; interrogate

【查无实据】investigation reveals no evidence (against the suspect)

【查询】inquire about

【查验】check; examine

【查阅】consult; look up

【查账】check (or audit) accounts

【查找】seek

【查证】verify

察（chá）examine; look into; scrutinize

【察访】make firsthand observations and inquiries; make an investigation trip

【察觉】be conscious of; become aware of; perceive

【察看】watch; observe

【察言观色】carefully weigh up a person's words and closely watch his expression

岔（chà）❶branching off；forked ❷turn off the main road

【岔开】❶branch off；diverge ❷diverge to（another topic）❸stagger

【岔口】fork(in a road)

【岔路】branch road；byroad；side road

【岔子】❶accident；trouble；something wrong ❷fault ❸branch road；byroad；side road

刹（chà）Buddhist temple；Buddhist monastery
　　另见 shā

【刹那】instant；split second

诧（chà）be surprised

【诧异】be astonished

差（chà）❶differ from；fall short of ❷wrong；mistake ❸wanting；short of ❹not up to standard；poor；bad
　　另见 chā，chāi

【差不多】❶almost；nearly ❷about the same；similar ❸just about right；not far off

【差点儿】❶not good enough ❷almost；nearly

【差劲】no good；disappointing；not up to the mark

姹（chà）〈书〉beautiful

【姹紫嫣红】brilliant purples and reds；beautiful flowers；gaily dressed maidens

chai

拆（chāi）❶tear open；take apart ❷pull down；dismantle

【拆除】demolish；dismantle；remove

【拆穿】expose；unmask

【拆封】seal off

【拆毁】pull down

【拆开】take apart；open；separate

【拆散】❶break（a set）❷break up(a marriage，family，etc.)

【拆台】cut the ground from under sb.'s feet；pull away a prop

【拆洗】wash after removing the padding or lining；take apart and clean

【拆卸】dismantle；dismount

【拆阅】open（a letter，document，etc.）and read

差（chāi）❶send on an errand；dispatch ❷errand；job
　　另见 chā，chà

【差遣】send sb. on an errand or mission；dispatch；assign

【差使】❶send；assign；appoint ❷official post

【差事】❶errand；assignment ❷official post

柴（chái）firewood

【柴草】faggot；firewood

【柴扉】〈书〉wicker gate

【柴油】diesel oil

豺（chái）〈动〉jackal

【豺狼成性】wolfish by nature；rapacious and ruthless

【豺狼当道】jackals and wolves stop the road — the cruel and the wicked are in power

chan

掺（chān）mix；mingle

【掺杂】mix；mingle；make impure

【掺假】adulterate

搀（chān）❶help by the arm；support sb. with one's hand ❷mix；mingle

【搀扶】support sb. with one's hand

谗（chán）backbite；slander

【谗害】calumniate sb. in order to have him persecuted

【谗言】slanderous talk；calumny

馋（chán）greedy；gluttonous

【馋涎欲滴】mouth drooling with greed

【馋嘴】❶gluttonous ❷glutton；a greedy eater

缠（chán）❶twine；wind ❷tangle；tie up；pester ❸deal with

【缠绵】melodious and moving

【缠绕】❶twine；bind；wind ❷pester；bother；harass

【缠手】troublesome；hard to deal with

蝉（chán）〈动〉cicada

【蝉联】continue to hold a title

【蝉翼】cicada's wings

潺（chán）

【潺潺】〈象〉murmur；babble；purl

蟾（chán）

【蟾蜍】❶〈动〉toad ❷the fabled three-legged toad in the moon ❸〈文〉the moon

产（chǎn）❶give birth to；be delivered of ❷produce；yield ❸product；produce ❹property；estate

【产地】place of production；producing area

【产房】delivery room

【产妇】lying-in woman

【产假】maternity leave

【产科】❶ obstetrical（maternity）department
❷obstetrics

【产量】output；yield

【产卵】lay eggs；spawn；oviposit

【产品】product；produce

【产权】property right

【产生】❶produce；engender ❷emerge；come into
being

【产物】outcome；result；product

【产销】production and marketing

【产业】❶estate；property ❷industry

【产值】value of output；output value

谄（chǎn） fawn on；curry favour with；
toady to

【谄媚】fawn on；toady to；curry favour with

铲（chǎn）❶ shovel ❷ lift or move with a
shovel；shovel

【铲除】root out；uproot；eradicate

【铲子】shovel

阐（chǎn）explain

【阐发】elucidate

【阐明】expound；clarity

【阐释】explain；expound；interpret

【阐述】expound；elaborate；set forth

【阐扬】expound and propagate

忏（chàn）repent

【忏悔】❶be penitent ❷〈宗〉confess(one's sins)

颤（chàn）tremble；shiver；shudder
另见 zhàn

【颤动】quiver

【颤抖】shake；shiver；tremble

【颤音】❶〈语〉trill ❷〈音〉trill；shake

【颤悠】flicker；shake；quiver

chang

昌（chāng） prosperous；flourishing

【昌盛】prosperous

猖（chāng） ferocious

【猖獗】be rampant；run wild

【猖狂】savage；furious

长（cháng）❶（of space or time）long ❷
length ❸strong point；forte ❹be good at；
be proficient in
另见 zhǎng

【长臂猿】〈动〉gibbon

【长波】long wave

【长城】the Great Wall

【长处】good qualities；strong(good) points

【长此以往】if things go on like this；if things
continue this way

【长存】live forever

【长笛】flute

【长度】length

【长短】❶length ❷accident；mishap ❸right and
wrong；strong and weak points

【长方体】cuboid；rectangular parallelepiped

【长方形】rectangle

【长歌当哭】compose and recite poems to vent
one's grief and indignation

【长工】〈旧〉farm labourer hired by the year；
long-term hired hand

【长话短说】to make a long story short

【长江】the Changjiang River；the Yangtze River

【长颈鹿】〈动〉giraffe

【长久】for a long time；permanently

【长久之计】a long-term plan；a permanent solution

【长空】vast sky

【长眠】〈婉〉have an eternal sleep；be dead

【长年】all the year round

【长年累月】year in year out；over the years

【长跑】long-distance race；long-distance run-
ning；long distance run

【长篇大论】a lengthy speech or article

【长期】over a long period of time；long-term

【长驱直入】drive straight in

【长生不老】live forever and never grow old

【长绳系日】use a long rope to tie the sun—try to
stop the passage of time

【长寿】long life；longevity

【长叹】deep sigh

【长途】long-distance

【长途跋涉】make a long，arduous journey；trudge
a long distance；trek a long way

【长途电话】long-distance telephone call

【长吁短叹】utter sighs and groans；moan and groan

【长于】be good at；be adept in

【长远】long-term；long-range

【长征】❶ long march；expedition ❷〈史〉the
Long March

【长治久安】a long period of peace and order；
lasting political stability

【长足进步】make great strides；make rapid progress

肠 (cháng) intestines

【肠胃】intestines and stomach; stomach and belly

尝 (cháng) ❶taste; try the flavour of ❷experience; come to know ❸ever; once

【尝试】attempt; try

【尝味】taste; savour

【尝鲜】have a taste of a delicacy; have a taste of what is just in season

【尝新】have a taste of what is just in season; taste a fresh delicacy

常 (cháng) ❶ordinary; common ❷constant; invariable ❸often; usually

【常常】frequently; often

【常规】convention; rule; common practice; routine

【常见】common

【常客】a frequent guest or customer; frequenter (of a theatre, restaurant, ballroom, etc.)

【常理】general rule; what is normal

【常绿植物】evergreen plant; evergreen

【常年】❶throughout the year; year in year out ❷an average year

【常情】reason; sense

【常人】ordinary person

【常任】permanent; standing: ～理事 standing member of a council

【常胜将军】an ever victorious general

【常识】❶general knowledge; elementary knowledge ❷common sense

【常数】〈数〉constant

【常态】normality; normal behaviours or conditions

【常温】❶ normal atmospheric temperature ❷〈动〉homoiothermy

【常务】day-to-day business; routine

【常务委员】member of the standing committee

【常用】in common use

【常驻】resident; permanent

偿 (cháng) ❶repay; compensate ❷meet; fulfill

【偿还】repay

【偿金】indemnity

【偿命】repay with one's life; a life for a life

【偿清】clear off

厂 (chǎng) ❶factory; mill; plant ❷yard; depot

【厂房】❶factory building ❷work-shop

【厂商】firm; factory owner

【厂长】factory director

【厂主】factory owner

场 (chǎng) ❶a place where people gather; ground ❷farm ❸sport ❹stage ❺scene ❻field

【场次】the number of showings of a film, play, etc.

【场地】space; place; site

【场合】occasion; situation

【场记】❶ log ❷ log keeper; script holder; script girl

【场面】❶scene (in drama, fiction, etc.); spectacle ❷occasion ❸appearance; front; facade

【场所】place; arena

敞 (chǎng) ❶spacious ❷open; uncovered

【敞怀】with one's coat or shirt unbuttoned

【敞开】open wide

【敞亮】❶ light and spacious ❷ clear (in one's thinking)

怅 (chàng) disappointed; sorry

【怅怅不乐】disconsolate; feeling gloomy; in low spirit

【怅恨】feel bitter at one's frustration; feel disappointed and resentful

【怅然】upset

【怅惘】distracted; listless

畅 (chàng) ❶smooth; unimpeded ❷free; uninhibited

【畅怀】to one's heart's content

【畅快】free from inhibitions; carefree

【畅所欲言】speak without any inhibitions; speak one's mind freely; speak out freely

【畅谈】talk freely and to one's heart's content; speak glowingly of

【畅通】unimpeded; unblocked

【畅销】be in great demand; sell well; have a ready market

【畅行无阻】pass unimpededly

【畅饮】drink one's fill

【畅游】❶have a good swim ❷enjoy a sightseeing tour

倡 (chàng) initiate; advocate

【倡导】initiate; propose

【倡言】propose; initiate

【倡议】propose; initiate

唱 (chàng) ❶sing ❷call; cry

【唱本】the libretto or script of a ballad-singer

【唱词】libretto; words of a ballad; the libretto (script) of a ballad-singer

【唱段】aria

【唱反调】sing a different tune; speak or act contrary to

【唱高调】mouth high-sounding words; say fine-sounding things; affect a high moral tone

【唱歌】sing

【唱空城计】perform The Stratagem of the Empty City—present a bold front to conceal a weak defence; have an absentee staff

【唱片】gramophone record; disc

【唱票】call out the names of those voted for while counting ballot-slips

【唱戏】〈口〉act in an opera

chao

抄 (chāo) ❶copy; transcribe ❷plagiarize; lift ❸search and confiscate; make a raid upon ❹take a shortcut ❺fold (one's arms) ❻grasp; take up

【抄本】transcript; copy; hand-copied book

【抄获】search out; ferret out

【抄家】search sb's house and confiscate his property

【抄录】make a copy of; copy

【抄送】make a copy for; send a duplicate to

【抄袭】❶plagiarize; lift ❷borrow indiscriminately from other people's experience ❸〈军〉launch a surprise attack on the enemy by making a detour

【抄写】copy; transcribe

超 (chāo) ❶exceed; surpass; overtake ❷ultra-; super; extra ❸transcend; go beyond

【超编】overstaff

【超产】overfulfil a production target (or quota)

【超常】be above average; be above the common run

【超车】overtake other cars on the road

【超出】overstep; go beyond; exceed

【超导】〈物〉superconduction

【超短波】ultrashort wave

【超短裙】miniskirt

【超额】above quota

【超负荷】excess load; overload

【超过】outstrip; surpass; exceed

【超级】super

【超龄】overage

【超然】aloof; detached

【超人】❶be out of the common run ❷superman

【超声波】ultrasonic (wave); supersonic (wave)

【超速】hypervelocity

【超脱】❶unconventional ❷be detached; stand aloof

【超越】overstep; surpass: ～前人 surpass one's predecessor

【超载】overload; excess freight; supercharge load (ing)

【超支】overspend

【超重】❶overload ❷overweight

【超自然】supernatural

朝 (cháo) ❶court; government ❷dynasty ❸an emperor's reign ❹have an audience with (a king, an emperor, etc.); make a pilgrimage to ❺facing; towards
另见 zhāo

【朝拜】pay respects to (a sovereign); pay religious homage to; worship

【朝代】dynasty

【朝奉】〈古〉a term of address for a rich man or a pawnshop assistant

【朝见】have an audience with (a king, etc.)

【朝圣】pilgrimage

【朝廷】❶royal court ❷royal government

【朝政】(in imperial times) court administration; affairs of state

嘲 (cháo) ridicule; deride

【嘲讽】sneer at; taunt

【嘲弄】〈俗〉mock; poke fun at

【嘲笑】laugh at; jeer at

潮 (cháo) ❶tide ❷(social) upsurge; current ❸damp; moist

【潮流】❶tide; tidal current ❷trend: 历史～ historical trend

【潮湿】moist; damp

【潮水】tide water; tidal water

【潮汐】morning and evening tides; tide

【潮汛】spring tide

吵 (chǎo) ❶make a noise ❷quarrel; wrangle; squabble

【吵架】quarrel; have a row

【吵闹】❶wrangle: ～不休 quarrel on and on ❷din; hubbub

【吵嘴】bicker; quarrel

炒 (chǎo) ❶stir-fry ❷roast while stirring ❸speculate (on the stock exchange, etc.)

【炒菜】❶stir-fry; sauté ❷a fried dish

【炒饭】❶fry rice ❷fried rice

【炒面】❶chow mein; fried noodles ❷parched flour

【炒勺】round-bottomed frying pan

【炒鱿鱼】〈口〉give sb. the sack; sack; fire

che

车 (chē) ❶vehicle ❷wheeled machine or instrument ❸machine ❹lathe ❺lift water by waterwheel

【车把】 handlebar (of a bicycle); shaft (of a wheelbarrow)

【车次】❶train number ❷motor coach number (indicating order of departure)

【车道】(traffic) lane; roadway

【车灯】 general name for lights on a vehicle (e. g. headlights, bicycle lamp, etc.)

【车队】 motorcade

【车费】 fare

【车夫】〈古〉carter; driver; rickshaw puller; chauffeur

【车祸】 traffic accident; road accident; automobile accident

【车间】 workshop; shop

【车库】 garage

【车辆】 vehicle; car

【车流】❶traffic ❷the rate of traffic flow

【车轮】 wheel (of a vehicle)

【车票】 train or bus ticket; ticket

【车水马龙】 incessant stream of horses and carriages; heavy traffic

【车速】 speed of a motor vehicle

【车胎】 tire

【车位】 parking spot; parking space

【车厢】 railway carriage; railroad car

【车站】 station; depot; stop

【车轴】 axletree; axle

扯 (chě) ❶pull ❷tear ❸buy ❹chat; gossip

【扯淡】〈方〉talk nonsense; nonsense

【扯谎】 tell a lie; lie

【扯皮】 dispute over trifles; argue back and forth; wrangle

【扯碎】 discerp

彻 (chè) thorough; penetrating

【彻底】 thorough; thoroughgoing

【彻骨】 to the bone

【彻头彻尾】 out and out; through and through; downright

【彻悟】 fully recognize the truth; come to understand thoroughly

【彻夜】 all night; all through the night

撤 (chè) ❶remove; take away ❷withdraw; e-vacuate

【撤除】 remove; dismantle

【撤换】 dismiss; recall; replace

【撤回】❶recall; withdraw ❷revoke; retract; withdraw

【撤军】 withdraw troops

【撤离】 withdraw from; leave; evacuate

【撤诉】 withdraw an accusation; drop a lawsuit

【撤退】 withdraw; pull out

【撤销】 cancel; rescind; revoke

【撤职】 dismiss sb. from his post; remove sb. from office

【撤走】 withdraw

chen

尘 (chén) ❶dust; dirt ❷this world

【尘埃】 dust

【尘封】 dust seal; be covered with dust; be dust-laden

【尘垢】 dirt

【尘俗】❶this world; this mortal life ❷mundane affairs

【尘土】 dust

【尘嚣】 hubbub; uproar

【尘缘】 the bonds of this world; carnal thoughts: ～未断 have not broken free the bonds of this world

沉 (chén) ❶sink ❷keep down; lower ❸deep; profound ❹heavy

【沉沉】❶heavy ❷deep

【沉甸甸】 heavy

【沉淀】 sediment; precipitate

【沉浮】❶sink and rise; bob on water ❷ups and downs of fortune; vicissitudes

【沉积】〈地〉deposit

【沉寂】 quiet; still

【沉浸】 immerse; steep

【沉静】 quiet; calm; serene; placid

【沉沦】 sink into(vice, degradation, depravity, etc.)

【沉闷】❶oppressive; depressing ❷depressed; in low spirits ❸not outgoing; withdrawn

【沉迷】 indulge; wallow

【沉没】 sink; founder

【沉默】❶reticent; taciturn; uncommunicative ❷silent

【沉溺】 indulge; wallow

【沉睡】 be sunk in sleep; be fast asleep

【沉思】 ponder; meditate; be lost in thought

【沉痛】❶deep feeling of grief or remorse ❷deeply felt; bitter

【沉稳】❶steady; staid; sedate ❷untroubled; sound

【沉渣】dregs；sediment
【沉重】❶heavy ❷serious；critical
【沉着】cool-headed；composed；steady；calm：～应战 meet an attack calmly｜勇敢～ brave and steady
【沉醉】get drunk；become intoxicated

陈 (chén) ❶lay out；put on display ❷state；explain ❸old；stale
【陈旧】outmoded；obsolete；old-fashioned；out-of-date
【陈列】display；set out；exhibit
【陈设】❶display；set out ❷furnishings
【陈述】state；declare

晨 (chén) morning
【晨操】morning exercises
【晨风】matinal；morning breeze
【晨光】the light of the early morning sun；dawn
【晨曦】the first rays of the morning sun

衬 (chèn) ❶line；place sth. underneath ❷lining；liner ❸provide a background for；set off；serve as a foil to
【衬衫】❶shirt ❷blouse
【衬托】set off；serve as a foil to
【衬衣】underclothes；shirt
【衬纸】slip sheet；interleaving paper；lining

称 (chèn) fit；match；suit
另见 chēng
【称心】find sth. satisfactory；be gratified
【称职】fill a post with credit；be competent

趁 (chèn) ❶take advantage of（time, opportunity, etc.）；avail oneself of ❷fit；suit
【趁便】when it is convenient；at one's convenience
【趁机】take advantage of the occasion；seize the chance：～溜走 seize the chance and sneak away
【趁热打铁】strike while the iron is hot
【趁势】take advantage of a favourable situation
【趁早】as early as possible；before it is too late；at the first opportunity

cheng

称 (chēng) ❶call ❷name ❸〈书〉say；state ❹〈书〉commend；praise ❺weigh
另见 chèn
【称霸】seek hegemony；dominate：～一方 ride roughshod over an area
【称臣】declare oneself a vassal or subject；acknowledge one's allegiance to a ruler

【称道】speak approvingly of；praise；acclaim
【称号】title；name
【称呼】❶call；address ❷form of address
【称快】express one's gratification
【称颂】praise；extol；eulogize
【称谓】appellation；title
【称谢】express one's thanks；thank
【称兄道弟】call each other brothers；be on intimate terms
【称雄】hold sway over a region；rule the roost
【称许】praise；commendation
【称赞】praise；commend

撑 (chēng) ❶prop up；support ❷push or move with a pole ❸maintain；keep up ❹open；unfurl ❺fill to the point of bursting ❻〈机〉brace；stay
【撑持】prop up；sustain
【撑竿】vaulting pole
【撑竿跳高】pole vault；pole jump
【撑腰】support；back up

瞠 (chēng)〈书〉stare
【瞠视】stare at

成 (chéng) ❶accomplish；succeed ❷become；turn into ❸achievement；result ❹fully developed；fully grown ❺established；ready made ❻in considerable numbers or amounts ❼all right；O. K. ❽able；capable ❾〈量〉one tenth
【成败】success or failure
【成本】cost
【成材】❶grow into useful timber ❷become a useful person
【成堆】form a pile；be in heaps
【成分】❶composition；component part；constituent；ingredient ❷one's class status
【成功】succeed；success
【成果】achievement；fruit；gain；positive result
【成活】survive
【成绩】result；achievement；success
【成家】get married
【成家立业】marry and embark on a career
【成见】preconceived idea
【成交】strike a bargain；conclude a transaction；clinch a deal
【成就】❶achievement；attainment；success ❷achieve
【成立】found；establish；set up
【成名】become famous
【成名成家】establish one's reputation as an authority in one's field
【成年】❶grow up；come of age ❷adult；grown-up

【成年累月】year in year out；for years on end

【成品】finished product

【成器】grow up to be a useful person

【成千上万】thousands and tens of thousands；thousands upon thousands：～的人 tens of thousands of people

【成全】help sb. to achieve his(or her) aim

【成群结队】in crowds

【成人】❶grow up；become full-grown ❷adult；grown-up

【成人之美】help sb. to fulfil his (or her) wish；aid sb. in doing a good deed

【成熟】ripe；mature

【成天】〈口〉all day long；all the time

【成为】become；turn into

【成文】❶existing writings ❷written

【成效】effect；result

【成心】intentionally；on purpose；with deliberate intent

【成形】❶take shape ❷shaping；forming

【成因】cause of formation

【成语】〈语〉set phrase；idiom

【成员】member

【成长】grow up；grow to maturity

呈 (chéng) ❶assume （form，colour，etc. ）❷submit or present （a report，etc. ）to a superior ❸petition；memorial

【呈报】submit a report；report a matter (to a superior)

【呈现】submit sth. to a higher authority for perusal

【呈请】apply (to the higher authorities for consideration or approval)

【呈文】a document submitted to a superior；memorial；petition

【呈现】present (a certain appearance)

【呈子】a petition (usu. from the common people) to the authorities

诚 (chéng) ❶sincere；honest ❷really；actually

【诚服】submit oneself willingly

【诚惶诚恐】with reverence and awe；in fear and trepidation

【诚恳】sincere

【诚然】❶truly；really ❷（used correlatively with 但是）no doubt；to be sure；it is true

【诚实】honest

【诚心】sincere desire；wholeheartedness

【诚心诚意】earnestly and sincerely

【诚意】good faith；sincerity

【诚挚】sincere；cordial

承 (chéng) ❶bear；hold；carry ❷undertake；contract (to do a job) ❸be indebted (to sb. for a kindness)；be granted a favour ❹continue；carry on

【承办】undertake

【承包】contract (with)

【承保】accept insurance；under writing acceptance

【承担】bear；undertake；assume

【承兑】〈商〉honor；accept

【承接】❶ hold out a vessel to have a liquid poured into it ❷continue；carry on ❸undertake the task of；contract to accept

【承诺】promise to undertake；undertake to do sth

【承认】❶admit；acknowledge；recognize ❷give diplomatic recognition；recognize

【承上启下】form a connecting link between what comes before and what goes after (as in a piece of writing，etc.)

【承受】❶bear；support；endure ❷inherit (a legacy，etc.)

【承袭】❶adopt；follow (a tradition，etc.) ❷inherit (a peerage，etc.)

【承先启后】inherit the past and usher in the future；serve as a link between past and future

【承允】agree；promise

【承重】load-bearing；bearing

城 (chéng) ❶city wall；wall ❷city ❸town

【城堡】castle

【城郊】outskirts of a town

【城里】inside the city；in town

【城区】the city proper

【城市】town；city

【城乡】town and country；city and countryside；urban and rural

【城镇】cities and towns：～居民 urban dwellers

乘 (chéng) ❶ride ❷bear；hold；carry ❸be indebted (to sb. for a kindness)；be granted a favour ❹multiply ❺take advantage of；avail oneself of

【乘便】when it is convenient；at one's convenience

【乘法】〈数〉multiplication

【乘方】〈数〉involution；power

【乘风破浪】ride the wind and cleave the waves；brave the wind and waves

【乘机】seize the opportunity

【乘客】passenger

【乘凉】enjoy the cool；relax in a cool place

【乘人之危】take advantage of sb. 's precarious po-

sition
【乘胜】 exploit a victory；follow up as victory
【乘数】〈数〉multiplier
【乘兴而来】 arrive in high spirits；set out cheerfully
【乘虚】 take advantage of a weak point in an opponent's defence；act when sb. is off guard
【乘虚而入】 break through at a weak point；act when one's opponent is off guard；exploit one's opponent's weakness

程 (chéng) ❶rule；regulation ❷order；procedure ❸journey；stage of a journey ❹distance
【程度】 level；degree
【程式】 form；pattern；formula
【程序】❶ order；procedure；course；sequence ❷〈自〉program

惩 (chéng) punish；penalize
【惩办】 punish；chastise
【惩处】 penalize；punish
【惩恶劝善】 punish evil-doers and encourage people to do good
【惩罚】 punish；penalize
【惩戒】 punish sb. to teach him a lesson；discipline sb. as a warning；take disciplinary action against
【惩治】 punish；mete out punishment to

澄 (chéng) ❶（of water，air，etc.）clear；transparent；limpid ❷clear up；clarify
【澄清】❶clear；transparent ❷clear up；clarify

橙 (chéng) ❶orange（the tree and the fruit）❷orange colour
【橙黄】 orange colour
【橙子】 orange（the fruit）

逞 (chéng) ❶show off；flaunt ❷carry out（an evil design）；succeed（in a scheme）❸indulge；give free rein to
【逞能】 show off one's skill；parade one's ability
【逞强】 flaunt one's superiority
【逞凶】 act violently

chi

吃 (chī) ❶eat；take ❷suffer；incur ❸annihilate；wipe out ❹ absorb；soak up ❺accept，take
【吃不消】 be unable to stand（exertion，fatigue，etc.）
【吃吃喝喝】〈贬〉indulge oneself in eating and drinking；wine and dine
【吃得开】 be popular；be much sought after

【吃饭】❶eat；have a meal ❷keep alive；make a living
【吃喝玩乐】 eat，drink and be merry-idle away one's time in pleasure-seeking
【吃惊】 be startled；be shocked；be amazed
【吃苦】 bear hardships
【吃苦耐劳】 bear hardships and stand hard work；work hard and endure hardships
【吃亏】❶ suffer losses；come to grief；get the worst of it；take（or get）a beating ❷at a disadvantage；in an unfavourable situation
【吃力】 entail strenuous effort；be a strain
【吃香】〈口〉be very popular；be much sought after；be well-liked

嗤 (chī) sneer
【嗤笑】 laugh at
【嗤之以鼻】 give a snort of contempt；despise

痴 (chī) ❶silly；idiotic ❷crazy about
【痴呆】 stupid
【痴迷】 infatuated；obsessed；crazy
【痴情】❶ unreasoning passion；infatuation ❷be infatuated
【痴人说梦】 idiotic nonsense；lunatic ravings
【痴想】 wishful thinking；illusion；fond dream
【痴心】 infatuation
【痴心妄想】 wishful thinking；fond dream

池 (chí) ❶pool；pond ❷an enclosed space with raised sides ❸stalls（in s theatre）；orchestra ❹〈书〉moat
【池鱼之殃】 a disaster for the fish in the moat—trouble not of one's own making
【池沼】 a large pond

迟 (chí) ❶slow；tardy ❷late
【迟迟】 slow；tardy
【迟到】 be（or come，arrive）late
【迟钝】 slow（in thought or action）；obtuse
【迟缓】 tardy；sluggish
【迟延】 delay；retard
【迟疑】 hesitate
【迟疑不决】 hesitate to make a decision；be irresolute；be undecided
【迟早】 sooner or later
【迟滞】❶slow-moving；sluggish ❷delaying（action）❸lag

持 (chí) ❶hold；grasp ❷support；maintain ❸manage；run ❹oppose
【持家】 run one's home
【持久】 lasting；enduring；protracted

【持平】unbiased;fair
【持枪】❶hold a gun ❷port arms
【持续】continued;sustained
【持有】hold
【持之以恒】persevere(in doing sth.)

尺 (chǐ) ❶rule;ruler ❷an instrument in the shape of ruler ❸〈量〉chi,a unit of length (3 chi ＝ 1 meter)

【尺寸】measurement;dimensions;size
【尺度】yardstick;measure
【尺幅千里】a thousand-mile view on a one-foot scroll—rich content within a small compass
【尺码】size;measures
【尺子】rule;ruler

齿 (chǐ) ❶tooth ❷a tooth-like part of anything ❸age ❹〈书〉mention

【齿轮】gear wheel;gear

耻 (chǐ) shame;disgrace

【耻骨】❶pubis; pubic bone ❷sidebone ❸pubio-;pubo
【耻辱】shame;disgrace;humiliation
【耻笑】hold sb. to ridicule;sneer at;mock

叱 (chì) 〈书〉loudly rebuke;shout at

【叱喝】shout at;bawl at
【叱骂】scold roundly;curse
【叱责】upbraid
【叱咤风云】commanding the wind and the clouds;shaking heaven and earth;all-powerful

斥 (chì) ❶upbraid;scold ❷repel;exclude

【斥力】repulsion;repulsive force
【斥骂】reproach
【斥责】rebuke;excoriate

赤 (chì) ❶red ❷loyal;sincere ❸bare

【赤膊】barebacked;be stripped to the waist
【赤诚】absolute sincerity
【赤胆忠心】utter devotion; whole-hearted dedication;ardent loyalty
【赤道】❶the equator ❷the celestial equator
【赤脚】barefoot
【赤脚医生】barefoot doctor (a nickname for part-time paramedical workers in rural areas trained in simple techniques of diagnosis and treatment)
【赤金】pure gold
【赤口毒舌】venomous tongue;vile language
【赤裸裸】❶ stark-naked ❷ undisguised; out-and-out

【赤贫】utterly destitute
【赤手空拳】barehanded; unarmed
【赤县神州】Red Territory and Divine Land (a poetic name for China)
【赤子】a newborn baby
【赤子之心】 the heart of a newborn baby—utter innocence
【赤字】〈经〉deficit

炽 (chì) flaming;ablaze

【炽烈】burning fiercely;blazing
【炽热】❶red-hot;blazing ❷passionate

翅 (chì) ❶wing ❷shark's fin

【翅膀】wing

chong

冲 (chōng) ❶ thoroughfare; important place ❷charge;rush ❸clash;collide ❹pour boiling water on ❺rinse;flush ❻〈摄〉develop

【冲淡】❶dilute ❷water down
【冲动】impulse
【冲锋】charge;assault
【冲锋陷阵】charge and shatter enemy positions; charge the enemy lines;charge forward
【冲毁】destroy by rush of water
【冲昏头脑】turn sb's head; have one's head turned
【冲击】❶lash;pound ❷charge;assault
【冲口而出】say sth. unthinkingly;blurt out
【冲破】break through;breach
【冲刷】erode;scour;wash out;wash away
【冲塌】cause to collapse;burst
【冲天】towering;soaring
【冲突】conflict;clash
【冲洗】wash;rinse;rinsing
【冲撞】❶ collide; bump; ram ❷ give offence; offend

充 (chōng) ❶sufficient;full ❷fill;charge ❸serve as;act as ❹pretend to be;pose as

【充斥】flood;congest
【充当】serve as;act as
【充电】〈电〉charge a battery;charge up
【充耳不闻】turn a deaf ear to
【充分】ample;abundant
【充饥】allay one's hunger
【充满】full of; brimming with; permeated with; imbued with
【充沛】plentiful;abundant;full of
【充实】❶ substantial; rich ❷ substantiate; enrich;replenish

【充数】 make up the number
【充裕】 abundant；ample；plentiful
【充足】 adequate；sufficient

憧 (chōng)

【憧憧】 flickering；moving
【憧憬】 long for；look forward to

虫 (chóng) insect or worm

【虫灾】 plague of insects
【虫子】 insect；worm

重 (chóng) ❶repeat；duplicate ❷again；once more ❸layer

另见 zhòng

【重播】 ❶ rebroadcast a programme (from the same station) ❷ resow (the same field)
【重操旧业】 return to one's old trade
【重唱】〈音〉 an ensemble of two or more singers，each singing one part
【重蹈覆辙】 follow the track of the overturned cart—follow the same old road to ruin
【重叠】 overlapping
【重返】 return
【重逢】 have a reunion；meet again
【重复】 repeat；duplicate
【重建】 rebuild；reconstruct；reestablish；rehabilitate
【重孙】 great-grandson
【重围】 tight encirclement
【重温】 rub up；brush up；review
【重现】 reappear
【重新】 again；anew；afresh
【重修旧好】 renew cordial relations；become reconciled；bury the hatchet
【重整旗鼓】 rally one's forces (after a defeat)
【重奏】〈音〉 an ensemble of two or more instrumentalists，each playing one part

崇 (chóng) ❶ high；lofty；sublime ❷esteem；worship

【崇拜】 worship；adore
【崇奉】 believe in (a religion)；worship
【崇高】 lofty；sublime；high
【崇敬】 esteem；respect；revere
【崇论闳议】 lofty and brilliant discourse
【崇山峻岭】 lofty ridges and towering mountains
【崇尚】 uphold；advocate
【崇信】 believe in；trust
【崇洋媚外】 worship foreign things and toady to foreign powers

宠 (chǒng) dote on；bestow favour on

【宠爱】 make a pet of sb.；dote on
【宠物】 pet (e. g. a cat or a dog)
【宠信】 be specially fond of and trust unduly (a subordinate)
【宠幸】 patronize；bestow favour on

chou

抽 (chōu) ❶ take out (from in between) ❷ take (a part from a whole) ❸ (of certain plants) put forth ❹obtain by drawing，etc. ❺lash；whip；thrash

【抽查】 selective examinations；spot check；spot test
【抽打】 lash；whip；thrash
【抽筋】 ❶pull out a tendon ❷〈口〉cramp
【抽空】 manage to find time
【抽泣】 sob
【抽签】 draw lots；cast lots
【抽屉】 drawer
【抽象】 abstract
【抽样】 sample；sampling

仇 (chóu) ❶enemy；foe ❷hatred；enmity

【仇敌】 foe；enemy
【仇恨】 hatred；enmity；hostility
【仇人】 personal enemy；foe；enemy
【仇视】 regard as an enemy；look upon with hatred；be hostile to
【仇怨】 grudge；hatred；spite

惆 (chóu)

【惆怅】 sad；disconsolate；melancholy

绸 (chóu) silk fabric；silk

【绸缎】 silks and satins
【绸缪】〈书〉 be sentimentally attached

酬 (chóu) ❶reward；payment ❷friendly exchange

【酬报】 reward；repay；recompense
【酬金】 monetary reward；remuneration
【酬劳】 recompense；reward
【酬谢】 thank sb. with a gift

稠 (chóu) ❶thick ❷dense

【稠密】 dense
【稠人广众】 a large crowd；a big gathering

愁 (chóu) worry；be anxious

【愁肠】 pent-up feelings of anxiety or sadness
【愁肠百结】 with anxiety gnawing at one's heart；weighed down with anxiety

【愁苦】anxiety;distress
【愁眉】knitted brows;worried look
【愁眉苦脸】wear a worried look;pull a long face
【愁闷】feel gloomy;be depressed
【愁容】anxious expression

筹 (chóu) ❶chip;counter ❷plan;prepare

【筹办】make preparations;make arrangements
【筹备】prepare;arrange
【筹措】raise（money）
【筹划】plan and prepare
【筹集】accumulate;raise（money）
【筹建】prepare to construct or establish sth.
【筹码】chip;counter
【筹募】collect（funds）

踌 (chóu)

【踌躇】hesitate;shilly-shally
【踌躇不前】hesitate to move forward;hesitate to make a move
【踌躇满志】enormously proud of one's success; smug;complacent

丑 (chǒu) ❶ugly;unsightly;hideous ❷disgraceful;shameful;scandalous

【丑恶】ugly;repulsive
【丑化】smear;uglify;defame
【丑角】clown;buffoon
【丑陋】ugly
【丑态】ludicrous performance;buffoonery
【丑态百出】act like a buffoon;cut a contemptible figure
【丑态毕露】be utterly shameless;be extremely nauseating
【丑闻】scandal

臭 (chòu) ❶smelly;foul;stinking ❷disgusting;disgraceful ❸smell;odor

【臭虫】bedbug;chinch
【臭名远扬】notorious
【臭名昭著】of ill repute;notorious
【臭气】bad smell;stink;offensive odour
【臭味相投】people of the same ilk like each other
【臭氧】〈化〉ozone

chu

出 (chū) ❶go or come out ❷exceed;go beyond ❸issue;put up ❹produce;turn out ❺arise;take place ❻put forth;vent ❼rise well（with cooking）❽put out;expend ❾〈量〉a dramatic piece

【出版】come off the press;publish;come out

【出殡】hold a funeral procession
【出兵】dispatch troops
【出操】go out for drill or a workout
【出差】be away on official business
【出产】produce;manufacture
【出场】❶come on the stage;appear on the scene ❷enter ❸enter the playing ground;enter the arena
【出车】❶dispatch a vehicle ❷be out driving a vehicle
【出丑】make a fool of sb. or oneself
【出处】source
【出错】make a mistake
【出动】set out;start off
【出尔反尔】go back on one's word;contradict oneself
【出发】❶set out;start off ❷start from; proceed from
【出风头】seek or be in the limelight
【出格】❶be out of the ordinary;be outstanding ❷overstep the bounds;exceed what is proper
【出轨】❶go off the rails;be derailed ❷overstep the bounds;exceed what is proper
【出国】go abroad
【出乎意料】exceeding one's expectations;contrary to one's expectations;unexpectedly
【出口】❶speak;utter ❷exit;outlet ❸export
【出口成章】words flow from the mouth as from the pen of a master;talk in literature
【出来】come out;emerge
【出类拔萃】stand out from one's fellows
【出路】way out;outlet
【出卖】❶offer for sale;sell ❷sell out;betray
【出面】appear personally
【出名】famous;well-known
【出没】appear and disappear;haunt
【出谋划策】give counsel;mastermind
【出纳】❶receipt and payment of money or bills ❷cashier;teller ❸lending and receiving books
【出品】produce;manufacture;make product
【出其不意】take sb. by surprise;catch sb. unawares
【出奇制胜】defeat one's opponent by a surprise move
【出勤】❶turn out for work ❷be or go out on business
【出人头地】rise head and shoulders above others;stand out among one's fellows
【出入】❶go out and come in ❷discrepancy;divergence;inconsistency
【出色】outstanding;remarkable;splendid

C

【出身】❶class origin; family background ❷one's previous experience or occupation

【出神】be spellbound; in a trance; be lost in thought

【出神入化】reach the acme of perfection; be superb

【出生】be born

【出生入死】go through fire and water; brave untold dangers; at the risk of life and limb

【出示】show; produce

【出事】meet with a mishap; have an accident

【出手不凡】make skilful (or masterly) opening moves (in wushu, chess, etc.)

【出逃】flee

【出头】❶hold up one's head; free oneself (from misery, persecution, etc.) ❷appear in public; come forward ❸(used after a round number) a little over, odd

【出头露面】appear in public; be in the limelight: ～的人物 a public figure

【出息】promise; prospects; future

【出席】attend

【出现】appear; arise; emerge

【出言不逊】make impertinent remarks; speak insolently

【出以公心】keep the public interest in mind; act without selfish considerations

【出院】leave hospital after recovery

【出众】be out of the ordinary; be outstanding

【出走】leave one's home or country under compulsion; run away; flee

【出租】hire; let; rent out

初 (chū) ❶at the beginning of; in the early part of ❷first (in order) ❸just; for the first time ❹elementary; rudimentary ❺original

【初版】first edition

【初步】initial; preliminary; tentative

【初出茅庐】just come out of one's thatched cottage—at the beginning of one's career; young and inexperienced

【初次】the first time

【初等】elementary; primary

【初犯】❶first offender ❷first offence

【初级】elementary; primary

【初恋】first love

【初露锋芒】display one's talent for the first time

【初露头角】begin to show ability or talent

【初期】initial stage; early days

【初试】❶first try ❷preliminary examination

【初选】primary election

【初学】begin to learn; be a beginner

【初中】junior middle school

【初衷】original intention

除 (chú) ❶get rid of; eliminate ❷except; but ❸besides; in addition to ❹〈数〉divide

【除暴安良】get rid of bullies and bring peace to good people

【除草】remove weeds; weed

【除恶务尽】one must be thorough in exterminating an evil

【除非】only if; unless

【除根】❶dig up the roots; root out; grub; stub ❷cure once and for all; eradicate

【除旧布新】get rid of the old to make way for the new; do away with the old and set up the new

【除了】❶except; except when ❷besides; in addition to

【除名】remove sb.'s name from the rolls

【除外】except; not counting; not including

【除夕】New Year's Eve

厨 (chú) kitchen

【厨房】kitchen

【厨师】cook; chef

锄 (chú) ❶hoe ❷do hoeing ❸uproot; eliminate; wipe out

【锄地】hoe the fields; do hoeing

【锄奸】eliminate traitors; ferret out spies

【锄强扶弱】suppress the strong and aid the weak

【锄头】❶pickaxe (used in southern China) ❷〈方〉hoe

雏 (chú) young

【雏鸟】squab; nestling; fledgling

【雏形】embryonic form

橱 (chú) cabinet; closet wardrobe

【橱窗】❶display window; showcase; shop window ❷glass-fronted billboard

【橱柜】❶cupboard ❷sideboard

处 (chǔ) ❶get along (with sb.) ❷be situated in; be in a certain condition ❸manage; deal with ❹punish; sentence
另见 chù

【处罚】penalize

【处方】〈医〉❶write out a prescription; prescribe ❷prescription

【处分】take disciplinary action against; punish

【处境】unfavourable situation; plight

【处决】put to death;execute
【处理】❶handle;deal with;dispose of ❷treat by a special process ❸treatment;treat by a special process
【处女】virgin;maiden
【处世】conduct oneself in society
【处事】handle affairs;deal with matters
【处心积虑】〈贬〉deliberately plan(to achieve evil ends);incessantly scheme
【处之泰然】take things calmly;remain unruffled
【处治】punish
【处置】❶handle;deal with ❷punish

储 (chǔ)store up
【储备】store for future use;lay in;lay up;reserve
【储藏】save and preserve;store;keep
【储存】lay in;lay up;keep in reserve;stockpile
【储户】depositor
【储量】reserves
【储蓄】save;deposit

处 (chù)❶place ❷point;part ❸department;office
　　另见 chǔ
【处处】everywhere;in all respects
【处所】place;location
【处长】the head of a department;section chief

触 (chù)❶touch;contact ❷strike;hit
【触电】get an electric shock
【触动】❶touch sth., moving it slightly ❷move sb.;stir up sb.'s feelings
【触发】detonate by contact;touch off; spark;trigger
【触犯】offend;violate;go against
【触及】touch
【触礁】run (up) on rocks;strike a reef (rock)
【触角】antenna;feeler;tentacle
【触景生情】the sight strikes a chord in one's heart
【触觉】tactile sensation;tactual sensation;sense of touch
【触类旁通】grasp a typical example and you will grasp the whole category;comprehend by analogy
【触目皆是】can be seen everywhere;be everywhere in evidence
【触目惊心】startling;shocking

矗 (chù)stand tall and upright
【矗立】stand tall and upright;tower over sth.

chuai

揣 (chuǎi)estimate;surmise;conjecture
【揣测】guess;conjecture
【揣摩】try to fathom;try to figure out

chuan

川 (chuān)❶river ❷plain ❸(Chuān)short for 四川(Sichuan Province)
【川流不息】flowing past in an endless str eam; never-ending

穿 (chuān)❶pierce through;penetrate ❷pass through;cross ❸wear;put on;be dressed in ❹string together
【穿插】❶alternate;do in turn ❷interweave; weave in;insert ❸trust deep into the enemy forces
【穿戴】apparel;dress
【穿过】go across or through;cross;penetrate
【穿孔】❶bore a hole;punch a hole ❷〈医〉perforation
【穿透】pierce through;run through
【穿越】pass through;cut across
【穿云裂石】cloud-piercing and rock-splitting——(of singing, the piping of a flute, etc.)penetrating
【穿凿附会】give strained inter-pretations and draw farfetched analogies
【穿针引线】act as a go-between
【穿着】dress;apparel;what one wears

传 (chuán)❶pass;pass on ❷hand down ❸spread ❹transmit;conduct ❺convey;express ❻infect;be contagious
　　另见 zhuàn
【传播】❶disseminate;propagate;spread ❷propagation
【传抄】make private copies of (a manuscript, document,etc. which is being circulated)
【传达】❶pass on;transmit ❷janitor
【传单】leaflet;handbill
【传导】〈物〉conduction
【传递】transmit(messages);deliver (a mail); transfer
【传奇】legend;romance
【传球】pass ball
【传染】infect;be contagious
【传人】❶pass on a skill or craft to others ❷〈书〉successor;exponent ❸summon sb. ❹be contagious;be infectious
【传神】vivid;lifelike

C

【传授】pass on（knowledge, skill）; instruct; impart

【传说】❶it is said; they say ❷legend; tradition

【传统】tradition

【传闻】❶it is said; they say ❷hearsay; rumour; talk

【传言】❶hearsay; rumour❷pass on a message

【传扬】spread（from mouth to mouth）

【传阅】pass round for perusal

【传真】❶portraiture ❷facsimile; fax

船 (chuán) boat; ship

【船舶】shipping; boats and ships

【船舱】❶ship's hold ❷cabin

【船员】(ship's) crew

【船闸】(ship) lock

【船长】captain; skipper

【船只】shipping; vessels

喘 (chuǎn) ❶ breathe heavily; gasp for breath; pant ❷〈医〉asthma

【喘气】❶breathe（deeply）; pant; gasp ❷take a breather

【喘息】❶ pant; gasp for breath ❷ breather; breathing spell; respite

【喘息未定】before catching one's breath; before one has a chance to catch one's breath

串 (chuàn) ❶ string together ❷conspire; gang up ❸go from place to place; run about; rove ❹play a part（in a play）; act ❺〈量〉string; bunch; cluster

【串换】exchange; change; swap

【串联】❶ establish ties; contact ❷〈电〉series connection

【串通】gang up; collaborate; collude with; be in collusion with

【串戏】(of an amateur actor) play a part in a professional performance

【串演】play the role of; act the role of; take part in a play

chuang

创 (chuāng) wound
另见 chuàng

【创痕】scar

【创巨痛深】badly injured and in great pain—in deep distress

【创口】cut

【创伤】〈医〉trauma

疮 (chuāng) ❶sore; skin ulcer ❷wound

【疮疤】scar

【疮口】the open part of a sore

【疮痍满目】everywhere a scene of devastation meets the eye

窗 (chuāng) window

【窗户】window; casement

【窗花】paper-cut for window decoration

【窗口】wicket; window

【窗帘】curtain

【窗纱】window screening

【窗台】apron; windowsill

床 (chuáng) ❶bed ❷sth. shaped like a bed

【床单】sheet

【床架】bedstead

【床头】the head of a bed; bedside

【床罩】bedspread; counterpane

闯 (chuáng) ❶rush; dash; charge ❷venture out into the world

【闯荡】make a living away from home

【闯祸】get into trouble; bring disaster

【闯将】daring general; pathbreaker

【闯路】blaze a trail; open a way; break a path

【闯入】burst into; intrude

创 (chuàng) ❶start（doing sth.）❷achieve （sth. for the first time）
另见 chuāng

【创办】establish; set up

【创见】original idea（view）; creative idea; brand-new idea

【创建】found; establish; set up

【创举】pioneering work

【创立】found; originate

【创设】found; create; set up

【创始】originate; initiate

【创新】bring forth new ideas; blaze new trails; make innovations

【创业】start an undertaking

【创造】create; produce

【创作】create; produce; creative work

chui

吹 (chuī) ❶blow; puff ❷boast; brag ❸break off; break up; fall through ❹flow; blow

【吹吹拍拍】boasting and toadying; 这个人～, 到处钻营。That man is given to boasting and flattering, trying to secure personal gain wherever he goes.

【吹风】❶ be in a draught; catch a chill ❷dry one's hair ❸let sb. in on sth. in advance; give a cue

【吹拂】sway;stir

【吹号】blow a bugle;blare the call

【吹灰之力】the effort needed to blow away a speck of dust;just a small effort

【吹毛求疵】find fault;pick holes;nitpick;cavil at

【吹牛】boast;brag;talk big

【吹捧】flatter;laud to the skies

【吹嘘】boast of;boast about

【吹奏】play（wind instruments）

炊 (chuī) cook a meal

【炊具】cooking utensils

【炊事员】a cook or the kitchen staff

【炊烟】smoke from kitchen chimneys

垂 (chuí) ❶hang down;droop;let fall ❷go down;hand down ❸nearing;approaching ❹(of one's elders or superiors)condescend

【垂爱】〈套〉(usu. used in correspondence) have gracious concern for (me)

【垂钓】go angling

【垂柳】weeping willow

【垂死】moribund;dying

【垂危】critically ill:生命～ dying

捶 (chuí) beat;thump;pound

【捶胸顿足】beat (or thump) one's breast and stamp one's feet (in deep sorrow,etc.)

锤 (chuí) ❶hammer ❷mace ❸hammer into shape ❹weight

【锤炼】❶hammer into shape ❷temper oneself; steel oneself ❸(of an artist,writer,etc.)try to perfect one's skill or technique by strenuous effort;hammer out;polish

chun

春 (chūn) ❶spring ❷love;lust ❸life;vitality

【春饼】spring pancake

【春播】spring sowing;spring seeding

【春风】spring breeze

【春耕】spring sloughing

【春光】sights and sounds of spring;spring scenery

【春季】spring;springtime

【春节】the Spring Festival

【春笋】bamboo shoots in spring

【春天】springtime

【春意】spring in the air;the beginning of spring

纯 (chún) ❶pure; unmixed ❷simple; pure and simple ❸skillful;practiced

【纯粹】pure

【纯洁】pure;clean and honest:心地～ (of a person) above any ultra intentions

【纯金】bullion

【纯朴】honest;simple

【纯真】sincere

【纯正】pure;unadulterated

【纯种】purebred;full blood

唇 (chún) lip

【唇膏】lipstick

【唇舌】words;argument

【唇音】labial (sound)

淳 (chún)〈书〉pure;honest

【淳厚】pure and honest;simple and kind;devoted

【淳朴】honest;simple;unsophisticated

蠢 (chǔn) ❶ stupid; foolish; clumsy ❷〈书〉wriggle

chuo

戳 (chuō) ❶jab;poke;stab ❷sprain;blunt ❸〈口〉stamp;seal

【戳穿】❶puncture ❷lay bare;expose

【戳记】stamp;seal

【戳子】stamp;seal;punch

绰 (chuò)〈书〉ample;spacious

【绰号】nickname

【绰约】〈书〉(of a woman) graceful

辍 (chuò)〈书〉stop;cease

【辍笔】stop in the middle of writing or painting

【辍学】discontinue one's studies

ci

疵 (cī) flaw;defect;blemish

【疵毛】defective wool

【疵品】defective goods

词 (cí) ❶〈语〉word; term ❷speech; statement ❸a Chinese poetic genre

【词典】dictionary

【词根】root;radical

【词汇】〈语〉vocabulary;words and phrases

【词句】words and phrases;expressions

【词类】〈语〉parts of speech

瓷 (cí) porcelain;china

【瓷器】porcelain;chinaware

【瓷砖】ceramic tile;glazed tile

C

辞 (cí) ❶ diction; phraseology ❷ a type of classical Chinese literature ❸ ballad; a form of classical poetry ❹ take leave ❺ dismiss; discharge ❻ resign ❼ shirk

【辞别】bid farewell
【辞典】dictionary
【辞令】language appropriate to the occasion
【辞书】lexicographical work
【辞退】dismiss; discharge

慈 (cí) ❶ kind; loving ❷〈书〉mother

【慈爱】love; affection; kindness
【慈悲】mercy; benevolence
【慈母】loving mother; mother
【慈善】charitable; benevolent
【慈祥】kindly

磁 (cí) ❶〈物〉magnetism ❷ porcelain; china

【磁带】(magnetic) tape
【磁化】〈物〉magnetization; magnetize
【磁力】〈物〉magnetic force
【磁石】magnetite; magnet
【磁性】magnetism; magnetic; magnetic performance

雌 (cí) female

【雌黄】flower
【雌雄】❶ male and female ❷ victory and defeat

此 (cǐ) ❶ this ❷ here and now

【此地】this place; here
【此后】after this; hereafter; henceforth
【此刻】this moment; now; at present

次 (cì) ❶ order; position in a series; place in a sequence ❷ second; next ❸ second-rate; inferior ❹〈量〉occurrence; time

【次等】second class
【次第】❶ order; sequence ❷ one after another
【次品】substandard products; defective goods
【次数】number of times; frequency
【次序】order; sequence
【次要】less important; secondary; subordinate
【次之】take second place

伺 (cì)
　另见 sì

【伺候】wait upon; serve

刺 (cì) ❶ thorn; splinter ❷ sting; stab; prick ❸ assassinate ❹ irritate; stimulate ❺ detect; spy ❻ criticize

【刺刺不休】talk incessantly; chatter on and on
【刺刀】bayonet
【刺耳】grating on the ear; jarring; ear-piercing; harsh
【刺骨】piercing to the bones; biting

赐 (cì) ❶ bestow; confer ❷ favour; grant ❸ gift

【赐福】blessing
【赐教】condescend to teach; grant instruction
【赐予】grant; bestow

cong

匆 (cōng) hastily; hurriedly

【匆匆】hurriedly; in a rush; in haste
【匆促】hastily; in a hurry
【匆忙】hastily; in a hurry; in haste

葱 (cōng) ❶ onion; scallion ❷ green

【葱翠】fresh green; luxuriantly green
【葱绿】pale yellowish green; light green; verdant
【葱郁】verdant; luxuriantly green

聪 (cōng) ❶ faculty of hearing ❷ acute hearing

【聪慧】bright; intelligent
【聪明】intelligent; bright; clever

从 (cóng) ❶ follow; comply with; obey ❷ join; be engaged in ❸ in a certain manner; according to a certain principle ❹ follower; attendant ❺ secondary; accessory ❻ from ❼ through; across; along ❽ ever

【从此】from this time on; from now on; from then on
【从而】thus; thereby
【从犯】accessory criminal
【从句】subordinate clause
【从来】always; at all times; all along
【从头】❶ from the beginning ❷ once again
【从小】from childhood

丛 (cóng) ❶ crowd together ❷ clump; thicket ❸ crowd; collection

【丛林】jungle; forest; 热带～ tropical forest
【丛生】❶ (of plants) grow thickly; 荆棘～ be infested with brambles ❷ (of disease, evils, etc.) break out
【丛书】series of books; collection

cou

凑 (còu) ❶ gather together; pool ❷ happen by chance; take advantage of ❸ move close to; come close to

【凑合】❶ collect; assemble ❷ make do (with) ❸ passable; not too bad
【凑巧】luckily; fortunately

【凑热闹】❶join in the fun ❷add trouble to
【凑手】at hand;within easy reach
【凑数】make up the number or amount

cu

粗 (cū) ❶wide;thick ❷coarse;crude;rough ❸gruff;husky ❹careless;negligent ❺rude;unrefined;vulgar
【粗暴】rude;rough;crude;brutal
【粗笨】clumsy;unwieldy
【粗糙】coarse;rough;crude
【粗细】❶(degree of) thickness ❷crudeness or fineness;degree of finish;quality of work
【粗心】careless;thoughtless

促 (cù) ❶(of time) short;hurried;urgent ❷urge;promote ❸close to;near
【促成】help to bring about;facilitate
【促进】promote;advance;accelerate
【促使】impel;urge;spur

醋 (cù) ❶vinegar ❷jealousy (as in a love affair)

簇 (cù) ❶〈书〉form a cluster;pile up ❷〈量〉cluster;bunch
【簇聚】gather in clusters;cluster
【簇新】brand new
【簇拥】cluster round

cuan

撺 (cuān)〈方〉❶throw;fling ❷do in a hurry ❸fly into a rage
【撺掇】〈口〉urge;egg on

窜 (cuàn) ❶flee;scurry ❷〈书〉exile;expel ❸change (the wording in a text,manuscript,etc.);alter
【窜改】alter;tamper with;falsify
【窜逃】flee in disorder;scurry off

篡 (cuàn) usurp;seize
【篡夺】usurp;seize
【篡改】distort;misrepresent
【篡位】usurp the throne

cui

催 (cuī) ❶urge;hurry ❷hasten;speed up
【催促】urge;hasten;press
【催化】catalysis
【催眠】lull(to sleep);hypnotize

摧 (cuī) break;destroy;ruin
【摧残】wreck;devastate

【摧毁】destroy;smash;wreck:猛烈的炮火～了敌人的阵地。Intense fire destroyed the enemy ramparts.

璀 (cuǐ)
【璀璨】〈书〉bright;resplendent

脆 (cuì) ❶fragile ❷crisp ❸clear;clear and sharp ❹〈方〉neat
【脆骨】gristle (as food)
【脆弱】fragile;frail;weak
【脆性】brittleness;shortness

翠 (cuì) ❶emerald green ❷kingfisher ❸jadeite
【翠绿】emerald green
【翠鸟】kingfisher

cun

村 (cūn) ❶village;hamlet ❷rustic;boorish
【村落】village hamlet
【村民】villager;village people
【村头】the edge of a village;entrance to a village
【村野】❶villages;countryside ❷rustic;countrified
【村镇】villages and small towns
【村庄】village;hamlet

存 (cún) ❶exist;live ❷store;keep ❸accumulate;collect ❹deposit ❺leave with;check ❻reserve;retain ❼remain on balance;be in stock ❽cherish;harbour
【存案】register with the proper authorities
【存储】〈计〉memory;storage
【存单】deposit receipt
【存档】keep in the archives
【存款】deposit;bank savings

忖 (cǔn) turn over in one's mind;ponder;speculate
【忖度】speculate;conjecture;surmise

寸 (cùn) ❶〈量〉cun,a unit of length(3 cun =1 decimeter) ❷very little;very short
【寸步不让】refuse to yield an inch;not budge an inch
【寸步不离】follow sb. closely;keep close to sb.;be always at sb.'s elbow
【寸步难行】difficult to move even none step;cannot move a single step
【寸草不生】not even a blade of grass grows
【寸土】an inch of land—a very small piece of land
【寸心】feelings

CUO

搓（cuō）❶ twist ❷ rub;scrub

【搓板】washboard

【搓弄】rub,knead,or twist idly

【搓手顿脚】wring one's hands and stamp one's feet—get anxious and impatient

磋（cuō） consult

【磋商】consult;exchange views

撮（cuō）❶〈书〉gather;bring together ❷ scoop up（with a dustpan or shovel）❸〈方〉pick up or hold（dust,powder,etc.）between the thumb and the first finger

【撮合】make a match;act as go-between

【撮要】❶ make an abstract;outline essential points ❷ abstract;synopsis;extracts

蹉（cuō）

【蹉跎】waste time

【蹉跎岁月】let time slip by accomplishing nothing;idle away one's time

挫（cuò）❶defeat;frustrate ❷subdue;lower

【挫败】frustrate;foil;defeat

【挫伤】❶contusion;bruise ❷dampen;blunt;discourage

【挫折】setback;reverse

措（cuò）❶ arrange;manage;handle ❷ make plans

【措辞】wording;diction

【措施】measure;step

【措手不及】be caught unprepared;be caught unawares

【措置裕如】handle with ease;manage very well

锉（cuò）❶ file ❷ make smooth with a file;file

错（cuò）❶interlocked and jagged;intricate;complex ❷alternate;stagger ❸uneven ❹ wrong; mistaken; erroneous ❺ fault; demerit;poor

【错爱】〈套〉undeserved kindness or favour

【错别字】wrongly written;mispronounced characters

【错彩镂金】elaborately carved and colourfully embellished—literary brilliance

【错处】fault;demerit

【错怪】blame sb. wrongly

【错过】miss;let slip

【错觉】illusion;misconception;wrong impression

【错开】stagger

【错乱】in disorder;in confusion;deranged

【错落】strewn at randon

【错落有致】in picturesque disorder

【错位】dislocation;malposition;misplacement

【错误】❶ wrong; mistaken; erroneous：～思想 wrong thinking;mistaken idea ❷mistake;error;blunder;fault;改正～ correct a mistake｜犯～ make a mistake;commit an error

【错综复杂】intricate;complex;very complicated

D d

da

耷（dā）〈书〉big-eared

【耷拉】droop；hang down

搭（dā）❶ put up；build ❷ hang over；put o-ver ❸ come into contact；join ❹ throw in more（people，money，etc.）；add ❺ lift sth. to-gether ❻ take（a ship，plane，etc.）；travel by

【搭伴】join sb. on trip；travel together

【搭档】❶cooperate；work together ❷partner

【搭伙】❶join as partner ❷ eat regularly in（a mess，canteen，etc.）

【搭救】rescue；go to the rescue of

【搭配】❶arrange in pairs or groups ❷〈语〉col-location

【搭腔】❶answer；respond ❷talk to each other

答（dā）
另见 dá

【答理】acknowledge（sb's greeting，etc.）；re-spond；answer

【答应】❶answer；reply；respond ❷agree；prom-ise；comply with

打（dá）〈量〉dozen
另见 dǎ

达（dá）❶ extend ❷ reach；amount to ❸ un-derstand thoroughly ❹ express；communi-cate ❺eminent；distinguished

【达标】reach a set standard

【达成】reach

【达到】achieve；attain；reach

【达观】take things philosophically；philosophi-cal；having broad perspective

【达官贵人】high officials and noble lords；VIPs

答（dá）❶ answer；reply ❷ return（a visit，etc.）；reciprocate
另见 dā

答案】answer；solution；key

答辩】reply（to a charge，query or an argument）

答复】answer；reply

答话】（usu. used in the negative）answer；reply

答谢】express appreciation（for sb.'s kindness

or hospitality）；acknowledge

打（dǎ）❶ strike；hit；knock ❷ break；smash ❸ fight；attack ❹ construct；build ❺ make （in a smithy）；forge ❻mix；stir；beat ❼tie up；pack ❽knit；weave ❾draw；paint；make a mark on
另见 dá

【打败】❶defeat；beat；worst ❷suffer a defeat；be defeated

【打扮】dress up；make up

【打抱不平】take up the cudgels for the injured party；defend sb. against an injustice；be the champion of the oppressed

【打草惊蛇】beat the grass and startle the snake—act rashly and alert the enemy

【打倒】overthrow

【打动】move；touch

【打赌】bet；wager

【打断】❶break ❷ interrupt；cut short

【打翻身仗】work hard to bring about a decisive turn for the better

【打躬作揖】bow and raise one's clasped hands in salute；fold the hands and make deep bows；bow and scrape

【打哈欠】yawn

【打鼾】snore

【打火机】lighter

【打击】hit；strike；attack

【打架】fight；scuffle

【打交道】come into contact with；have dealings with

【打搅】trouble；disturb；bother

【打劫】commit robbery；loot；plunder

【打开】❶ open ❷ turn on ❸ open up

【打捞】get；drag out of the water

【打量】look sb. up and down；size up；think；reckon

【打骂】beat and scold；maltreat

【打破】smash to pieces；break

【打气】inflate；pump up；bolster up the morale；cheer up

【打扰】trouble；disturb；bother

【打算】❶intend；plan；think；mean ❷ consideration；calculation

【打退】repulse；beat off

【打消】give up；dispel

【打针】give(have)an injection

【打中】hit the spot（target）

【打主意】seek；try to win sth.；scheme for

【打转】revolve；spin；move about

【打字】typewrite；type

大（dà）❶big；large；great ❷heavy；strong ❸ loud ❹ general；main；major ❺ size ❻ age ❼ greatly；fully ❽ eldest

【大白菜】Chinese cabbage

【大败】utterly be defeated；suffer a crushing defeat

【大半】more than half；greater part；very likely；most probably

【大本营】supreme headquarters；base camp

【大饼】large flat bread

【大伯】uncle

【大不列颠】Great Britain

【大步流星】at great strides；with big strides

【大材小用】large material put to small use；one's talent wasted on a petty job；not do justice to sb.'s talents

【大吃一惊】be greatly surprised；be quite taken aback

【大慈大悲】infinitely compassionate and merciful

【大错特错】completely mistaken；absolutely wrong

【大大咧咧】〈方〉careless；casual：别看他～的，什么事他都很在心。He seems unconcerned，but nothing escapes his attention.

【大刀阔斧】bold and resolute；drastic

【大地】earth；mother earth

【大典】grand ceremony；a body of classical writings；canon

【大动干戈】go to war；get into a fight

【大度包容】regard with kindly tolerance；be magnanimous and tolerant；be magnanimous

【大而无当】large but impractical；unwieldy

【大发雷霆】be furious；fly into a rage；bawl at sb. angrily

【大概】general idea；outline；approximate；most likely

【大纲】outline；synopsis

【大公无私】unselfish；selfless；impartial

【大功告成】accomplish(a project；work)successfully；be crowned with success

【大海捞针】fish for a needle in the ocean；look for a needle in a haystack

【大喊大叫】❶shout at the top of one's voice ❷ conduct vigorous propaganda

【大好河山】beautiful rivers and mountains（of a country）；one's beloved country

【大会】mass meeting；mass rally；plenary session；general membership meeting；convention；conference

【大祸临头】disaster is imminent；disaster is hanging over one

【大惑不解】be extremely puzzled；be unable to make head or tail of sth.

【大吉大利】good luck and great prosperity（an expression of good wishes）

【大计】matters of vital importance

【大家】all；everyone；great master；authority

【大家闺秀】a girl from a good family；a well-bred girl；lady

【大江】great river；the Changjiang River

【大将】senior officer；general；high-ranking officer

【大街】main street

【大街小巷】streets and lanes：～彩旗飘扬。The streets and lanes are decked with bunting.

【大捷】great success；victory

【大惊失色】turn pale with fright

【大惊小怪】make a fuss；much ado about nothing

【大举】（military operation）on a large scale；make a decisive move

【大军】army；military force；main force；large contingent

【大可不必】not at all necessary：其实这种担心～。As a matter of fact there's no need to worry about it at all.

【大快人心】（usu. of the punishment of an evildoer）affording general satisfaction；most gratifying to the people；to the immense satisfaction of the people

【大量】a large number；a big quantity；magnanimous

【大楼】tall building；multi-storied building

【大陆】mainland

【大略】roughly；briefly；general idea

【大门】gate

【大名鼎鼎】famous；celebrated；well-known

【大模大样】in an ostentatious manner；with a swagger

【大逆不道】treason and heresy；worst offence；greatest outrage

【大批】a large batch of；large quantities of；numbers of；an amount of

【大器晚成】great vessels take years to produce—great minds mature slowly

【大千世界】❶ the kaleidoscopic world ❷〈宗

the boundless universe

【大厦将倾】a great mansion on the point of collapse—the situation is hopeless

【大失所望】 greatly disappointed；to one's great disappointment

【大势】general trend；prevailing tendency of events

【大是大非】major issues of principle；wrong or right

【大手大脚】extravagant；wasteful

【大庭广众】（before）a big crowd；（on）a public occasion

【大同小异】much the same but with minor differences；alike except for slight differences；very much the same

【大西洋】the Atlantic（Ocean）

【大喜过望】be delighted that things are better than one expected

【大虾】prawn

【大显身手】display oneself to the full；distinguish oneself

【大显神通】give full play to one's remarkable skill（or abilities）

【大相径庭】totally different；entirely contrary

【大校】senior colonel

【大写】capital letter； capital form of a Chinese numeral

【大型】large-scale；large

【大选】general election

【大学】university；college

【大雪】❶heavy snow ❷Greater Snow（the 21st of the 24 solar terms）

【大言不惭】brag unblushingly；talk big

【大摇大摆】strutting；swaggering

【大义灭亲】place righteousness above loyalty to one's family；sacrifice ties of blood to righteousness

【大义凛然】inspiring awe by upholding justice；with stern righteousness

【大意】general idea；main points；gist；tenor；negligent；inattentive

【大有文章】there's something behind all this；there's more to this than meets the eye

【大有作为】have full scope for one's talents；be able to develop one's ability to the full；have great possibilities

【大雨】heavy rain

大雨如注】the rain is pouring down；it's raining cats and dogs

大院】courtyard；compound

大约】approximately；about；probably

【大张旗鼓】in a big way；on a large scale

大指】thumb

【大志】lofty ambition；high aim

【大治】great order

【大致】more or less；generally；about；roughly

【大智若愚】a man of great wisdom often seems slow-witted

【大自然】nature

【大宗】lots of；a large amount of

dai

呆（dāi）❶slow-witted；dull ❷blank；wooden ❸stay

【呆板】stiff and awkward；rigid；not natural；inflexible

【呆气】stupidity；foolishness

【呆若木鸡】dumb as a wooden chicken；dumbstruck

【呆账】bad debts

【呆滞】❶dull；lifeless ❷idle；sluggish

【呆子】idiot；simpleton；blockhead

待（dāi）stay
另见 dài

【待会儿】in a moment

歹（dǎi）bad；evil；vicious

【歹毒】sinister；vicious

【歹人】evil person；thieves or burglars

【歹徒】scoundrel；ruffian；evildoer

【歹意】malice；malicious intent；evil intention

逮（dǎi）〈书〉reach

【逮捕】arrest；take into custody

代（dài）❶ take the place of ❷ acting ❸ historical period ❹ generation

【代办】do sth. for sb.；be on sb.'s behalf；chargé d'affaires

【代表】represent；stand for；on behalf of；delegate；representative

【代词】〈语〉pronoun

【代号】code name

【代价】price；cost

【代理】❶ acting；agent；deputy；proxy ❷〈法〉procurator；attorney

【代名词】synonym；〈语〉pronoun

【代售】be commissioned to sell sth.

【代数】algebra

【代替】take the place of；substitute for；replace

【代谢】❶supersession ❷〈生〉metabolize

【代言人】spokesman；mouthpiece

带（dài）❶ belt；ribbon；band；tape；girdle；❷ zone；area；belt ❸ take；bring；carry；bear；have；lead；head；do sth

【带动】drive；spur on；bring along

【带劲】❶ energetic;forceful ❷ interesting;exciting

【带领】lead;guide

【带路】show the way;act as a guide

【带头】take the lead;be the first;set an example

贷 (dài) ❶loan ❷borrow or lend ❸shift(responsibility);shirk ❹pardon;forgive

【贷方】〈经〉credit side;credit

【贷款】❶ provide a loan;extend credit to ❷ loan;credit

待 (dài) ❶ treat;deal with ❷ entertain ❸ wait for;await ❹ need ❺ going to;about to
　　另见 dāi

【待价而沽】wait to sell at a good price;wait for the highest bid

【待命】await orders

【待续】to be continued

【待遇】❶ treatment ❷ pay;wages;salary

怠 (dài) ❶ lazy;idle;remiss;❷ slack

【怠惰】lazy;indolent

【怠工】slow down;go slow

【怠慢】cold-shoulder;slight

袋 (dài) bag;sack

【袋鼠】〈动〉kangaroo

【袋子】sack;bag;面～ flour bag

戴 (dài) ❶ put on;wear ❷ respect;honour

【戴高帽子】❶ flatter;lay it on thick ❷ wear a tall paper hat (as a mark of shame);wear a dunce's cap

【戴罪立功】atone for one's crimes by doing good deeds;redeem oneself by good service

dan

丹 (dān) ❶red ❷ pellet or power

【丹顶鹤】〈动〉red-crowned crane

【丹青妙笔】superb artistry (in painting);the superb touch of a great painter;the touch of a master

【丹田】the pubic region

【丹心】loyal heart;loyalty

担 (dān) ❶carry on a shoulder pole ❷ take on;undertake
　　另见 dàn

【担保】assure;guarantee;vouch for

【担当】take on;bear the burden;assume the responsibility

【担负】bear;shoulder;take on;be charged with

【担架】stretcher;litter

【担惊受怕】feel alarmed;be in a state of anxiety

【担任】assume the office of;～小组长 be a group leader

【担心】worry;feel anxious

【担忧】worry;be anxious

单 (dān) ❶ one;single ❷ odd ❸ singly;alone ❹ only;alone ❺ simple ❻ thin;weak ❼ unlined ❽ sheet ❾ bill;list

【单薄】❶ (of clothing) thin ❷ thin and weak;frail ❸ flimsy

【单程】one-way;(trip)single-pass

【单纯】❶simple;pure ❷alone;purely;merely

【单词】〈语〉individual word;word

【单打】〈体〉singles

【单单】only;alone

【单刀直入】come straight to the point;speak out without beating about the bush

【单调】monotonous;dull;drab

【单独】alone;by oneself

【单方面】one-sided;unilateral

【单杠】〈体〉❶ horizontal bar ❷ horizontal bar gymnastics

【单价】unit price

【单句】〈语〉simple sentence

【单枪匹马】single-handed;all by oneself;alone

【单身】❶unmarried;single ❷live alone

【单数】❶odd number ❷singular number

【单位】unit

【单项】〈体〉individual event

【单行线】〈交〉one-way traffic(road)

【单眼皮】eyelids that do not have a distinct fold along the edges

【单一】single;unitary

【单元】unit

耽 (dān) ❶delay ❷〈书〉abandon oneself to;indulge in

【耽搁】stop over;stay

【耽误】delay;hold up

【耽于】addict;indulge in

殚 (dān)〈书〉use up;exhaust

【殚竭】〈书〉use up;exhaust

【殚精竭虑】do one's utmost;go all out;use every ounce of one's energy

胆 (dǎn) ❶〈解〉gallbladder ❷courage;guts ❸a bladder-like inner container

【胆大包天】audacious in the extreme

【胆敢】dare;have the audacity to

【胆量】courage;pluck;spunk

【胆略】courage and resourcefulness

【胆怯】timid;cowardly;faint-hearted

【胆识】courage and insight

【胆小如鼠】as timid as a mouse;chicken- hearted

【胆战心惊】tremble with fear

【胆子】courage;nerve

掸 (dǎn) brush lightly;whisk

【掸子】duster（usu. made of chicken feathers or strips of cloth）

旦 (dàn) ❶〈书〉dawn;daybreak ❷day ❸the female character type in Beijing Opera,etc. ❹〈纺〉denier

【旦夕】〈书〉this morning or evening;in a short while

但 (dàn) ❶but;yet;still;nevertheless ❷only;merely

【但凡】without exception;as long as;in every case

【但求无过】seek only to avoid blame

【但是】but;yet;however

【但愿】if only;I wish

担 (dàn) ❶dan,a unit of weight（1 dan＝50 kilograms）❷a carrying（or shoulder）pole and the loads on it;load;burden ❸〈量〉shoulder-pole load

另见 dān

【担子】❶a carrying（or shoulder）pole and the loads on it;load;burden ❷task

诞 (dàn) ❶birth ❷absurd;fantastic

【诞辰】birthday

【诞生】be born;come into being;emerge

淡 (dàn) ❶thin;light ❷bland;tasteless;weak;without enough salt ❸light;pale ❹slack;dull

【淡泊】〈书〉not seek fame and wealth

【淡薄】❶（of cloud or fog）not dense;thin ❷weak ❸（of emotion,interest,etc.）cool down;lessen;abate

【淡淡】slight;light

【淡化】desalination

【淡季】slack season;off season

【淡漠】indifferent;nonchalant;dim;hazy

【淡然处之】treat coolly;take it easy

【淡水】fresh water

【淡忘】fade from one's memory

【淡雅】simple and elegant;quietly elegant

弹 (dàn) ❶ball;pellet ❷bullet;bomb

另见 tán

【弹尽粮绝】run out of ammunition and food supplies

【弹丸之地】a tiny area;a small bit of land

【弹药】ammunition

蛋 (dàn) ❶egg ❷an egg-shaped thing

【蛋白质】protein

【蛋糕】cake

【蛋黄】yolk

【蛋壳】eggshell

【蛋清】〈口〉egg white

dang

当 (dāng) ❶equal ❷ought to;should;must ❸in sb's presence;to sb's face ❹just at（a time or place）❺work as;serve as;be ❻bear;accept;deserve ❼direct;manage;be in charge of ❽〈象〉the sound of a gong or a bell

另见 dàng

【当班】be on duty

【当兵】serve in the army;be a soldier

【当场】on the spot;then and there

【当初】in the first place;originally

【当代】the present age;the contemporary

【当地】at the place in question;in the locality;local

【当机立断】decide quickly;make a prompt decision

【当家做主】be master in one's own house;be the master of one's own affairs（or destiny）

【当今】now;at present;nowadays

【当局】the authorities

【当面】to sb.'s face;in sb.'s presence

【当年】❶in those years ❷the prime of life

【当前】before one;facing one

【当然】of course;certainly

【当仁不让】not decline to shoulder a responsibility;not leave to others what one ought to do oneself;not pass on to others what one is called upon to do

【当时】at that moment

【当头棒喝】a blow and a shout—a sharp（or severe）warning

【当务之急】the most pressing matter of the moment;a top priority task;urgent matter

【当政】be in power;be in office

【当之无愧】fully deserve（a title, an honour, etc.）;be worthy of

【当众】in the presence of all;in public;before the public

挡 (dǎng) ❶keep off;ward off;block ❷block;get in the way of ❸fender;blind ❹gear（of a car）

【挡驾】〈婉〉turn away a visitor with some excuse;decline to receive a guest

党 (dǎng) ❶ political party;party ❷ clique;gang ❸ relatives;kinsfolk
【党籍】 party membership
【党纪】 party discipline
【党派】 political parties and groups;party groupings
【党同伐异】 defend those who belong to one's own faction and attack those who don't;be narrowly partisan
【党章】 party constitution

当 (dàng) ❶ proper;right;appropriate ❷ match;equal to ❸ treat as;regard as;take for ❹ think ❺ that very (day,etc.) ❻ pawn
　另见 dāng
【当成】 regard as;treat as;take for
【当年】 the same year;that very year
【当票】 pawn ticket
【当铺】 pawnshop
【当时】 right away;at once;immediately
【当天】 the same day;that very day
【当真】 ❶ take seriously ❷ (really) true ❸ really;sure enough
【当作】 treat as;regard as;look upon as

荡 (dàng) ❶ swing;sway;wave ❷ loaf about ❸ rinse ❹ clear away;sweep off
【荡船】 swing boat
【荡气回肠】 very touching;pathetic
【荡然无存】 all gone;nothing left
【荡漾】 ripple;undulate

档 (dàng) ❶ shelves (for files);pigeonholes ❷ files;archives ❸ grade
【档案】 files;archives;record;dossier
【档次】 grade

dao

刀 (dāo) ❶ knife;sword ❷ sth. shaped like a knife ❸ 〈量〉one hundred sheets(of paper)
【刀背】 the back of a knife
【刀兵之灾】 the calamities of war;war
【刀叉】 knife and fork
【刀耕火种】 slash-and-burn cultivation:那个偏僻山区,过去是～。In those remote mountains people used to farm by the slash-and-burn method.
【刀光剑影】 the glint and flash of daggers and swords
【刀口】 the edge of a knife;the crucial point
【刀片】 razor blade
【刀枪】 sword and spear;weapon
【刀山火海】 a mountain of swords and a sea of flames—most dangerous places;most severe trials

导 (dǎo) ❶ lead;guide ❷ transmit;conduct ❸ instruct;teach
【导弹】〈军〉guided missile
【导电】〈物〉electric conduction
【导火线】 ❶ (blasting) fuse ❷ a small incident that touches off a big one
【导师】 ❶ tutor;teacher ❷ guide of a great cause
【导体】〈物〉conductor
【导线】〈电〉(conducting) wire;conductor;traverse;harness
【导向】 steering;guiding;present
【导言】 introduction(to a piece of writing);introductory remarks
【导演】 ❶ direct(a film,play,etc.) ❷ director
【导游】 ❶ conduct a sightseeing tour ❷ guide
【导致】 lead to;bring about;result in;cause

岛 (dǎo) island
【岛国】 island country
【岛屿】 islands and islets

捣 (dǎo) ❶ pound with a pestle,etc.;beat with stick ❷ harass;disturb
【捣蛋】 make trouble
【捣鬼】 play tricks;do mischief
【捣毁】 smash up;demolish
【捣乱】 create a disturbance
【捣碎】 pound to pieces;stamp breaking;stamp crushing

倒 (dǎo) ❶ fall;topple ❷ collapse;fail ❸ close down;go bankrupt ❹ (of voice) become hoarse ❺ change;exchange ❻ move around
　另见 dào
【倒班】 change shifts;work in shifts
【倒闭】 close down;go bankrupt
【倒毙】 fall dead
【倒霉】 have bad luck;be in for hard times;meet with reverses
【倒塌】 collapse;topple down
【倒台】 fall from power
【倒胃口】 spoil one's appetite

祷 (dǎo) ❶ pray ❷ ask earnestly;beg
【祷告】 say one's prayers

蹈 (dǎo) ❶〈书〉tread;step ❷ skip;trip
【蹈常袭故】 go on in the same old way;get into a rut;follow a set routine
【蹈袭】 follow slavishly

到 (dào) ❶ arrive;reach ❷ go to;leave for ❸ up until;up to ❹ thoughtful;considerate
【到场】 be present;show up
【到处】 at all places;everywhere

【到达】arrive;get to;reach
【到底】to the end;to the finish
【到来】arrival;advent
【到期】become due;mature;expire
【到手】in one's possession;in one's hands

倒 (dào) ❶ upside down;inverse ❷ move backward;turn upside down ❸ pour;tip ❹ on the contrary
另见 dǎo

【倒背如流】know sth. thoroughly by heart
【倒车】❶back a car ❷astern
【倒立】❶stand upside down ❷〈体〉handstand
【倒退】go backwards;fall back
【倒影】inverted image;inverted reflection in water
【倒装】upside down mounting;upside-down charging

盗 (dào) ❶steal;rob ❷thief;robber

【盗匪】bandits;robbers
【盗卖】steal and sell
【盗窃】steal
【盗取】steal;embezzle
【盗用】embezzle;usurp
【盗贼】robbers;bandits

悼 (dào) mourn;grieve

【悼词】memorial speech
【悼念】mourn;grieve over

道 (dào) ❶road;way;path ❷channel;course ❸way;method ❹doctrine;principle ❺Taoism;Taoist ❻say;talk;speak ❼think;suppose ❽line

【道德】morals;morality;ethics
【道理】principle;truth;reason;argument
【道路】way;road;path
【道貌岸然】pose as a person of high morals;be sanctimonious
【道歉】apologize;make an apology
【道听途说】hearsay;rumour;gossip:这是～,不足为信。This is only hearsay, and is not to be taken seriously.
【道谢】express one's thanks;thank
【道义】morality and justice;moral principle

稻 (dào) rice;paddy

【稻草】rice straw
【稻草人】scarecrow

de

得 (dé) ❶get;obtain;gain ❷(of a calculation) result in ❸be finished;be ready ❹in-

dicating agreement or disagreement ❺used before other verbs to indicate permission
另见 děi

【得不偿失】the loss outweighs the gain
【得逞】〈贬〉succeed;have one's way:阴谋未能～。The plot fell through.
【得宠】〈贬〉find favor with sb.;win the favor of
【得出】reach a conclusion
【得寸进尺】reach for a yard after getting an inch;give him an inch and he'll take a yard (or a mile,an ell);be insatiable
【得当】proper;suitable:措词～ aptly worded;appropriate wording
【得到】get;obtain;receive
【得分】score
【得过且过】get by however one can;muddle along;drift along
【得奖】win a prize
【得力】❶ benefit from;get help from ❷ capable;competent
【得陇望蜀】covet Shu after getting Long —have insatiable desires
【得人心】be loved and supported by the people
【得胜】win a victory;triumph
【得失】❶gain and loss;success and failure ❷advantages and disadvantages;merits and demerits
【得天独厚】be richly endowed by nature;enjoy exceptional advantages
【得心应手】❶with facility;with high proficiency ❷serviceable;handy
【得意】 proud of oneself; pleased with oneself;complacent
【得意忘形】get dizzy with success;have one's head turned by success
【得志】achieve one's ambition;have a successful career
【得罪】offend;displease

德 (dé) ❶ virtue;morals ❷ heart;mind ❸ kindness;favour

【德才兼备】have both ability and political integrity;combine ability with character
【德高望重】be of noble character and high prestige
【德国】Germany
【德行】moral integrity;moral conduct
【德育】moral education

dei

得 (děi) need;must;have to
另见 dé

deng

灯 (dēng) ❶lamp；lantern；light ❷valve；tube
【灯标】〈交〉beacon；beacon light
【灯火辉煌】 brilliantly illuminated； blaze with lights
【灯谜】riddles；lantern riddles
【灯泡】bulb；light bulb
【灯塔】light house；beacon
【灯台】lampstand
【灯芯】lampwick；wick
【灯罩】lampshade；lamp-chimney
【灯座】lamp-socket

登 (dēng) ❶ascend；mount；scale（a height）❷publish；record；enter ❸step on；tread
【登岸】go ashore；land
【登场】come on stage
【登峰造极】reach the peak of perfection；reach the summit of achievement
【登广告】advertise(in a newspaper)
【登记】register；enter one's name
【登陆】land；disembark
【登山】〈体〉mountain-climbing；mountaineering
【登堂入室】pass through the hall into the inner chamber—reach a higher level in one's studies or become more proficient in one's profession

等 (dēng) ❶〈量〉class；grade；rank ❷wait；await ❸when；till ❹〈量〉equal ❺kind；sort ❻and so on；and so forth
【等边】equilateral
【等次】grade；rank
【等待】wait；await
【等到】when；until；by the time
【等等】❶ and so on；so on and so forth ❷wait a minute
【等候】wait；expect
【等级】grade；rank；social estate；social stratum
【等价】of equal value；equal in value
【等距离】equidistance
【等量齐观】equate；put on a par
【等式】equality
【等同】equate；be equal
【等闲视之】regard sth. as unimportant；treat sth. lightly (or casually)
【等于】❶equal to ❷amount to

凳 (dèng) stool or bench

瞪 (dèng) open(one's eyes) wide；stare；glare
【瞪眼】❶ open one's eyes wide；stare；glare ❷ glower and glare at sb. ；get angry with sb.

di

低 (dī) ❶low ❷let droop；hang down
【低潮】low tide；low ebb
【低沉】❶overcast；lowering ❷(of voice)low and deep ❸low-spirited；downcast
【低估】underestimate；underrate
【低级】lower；vulgar；elementary
【低廉】cheap；low
【低劣】inferior；poor in quality
【低落】downcast；low-spirited
【低烧】〈医〉low fever；slight fever
【低声】in a low voice；under one's breath；with bated breath
【低声下气】speak humbly and under one's breath；be meek and subservient；be obsequious
【低头】❶lower one's head；bow one's head；hang one's head ❷yield；submit
【低头认罪】hang one's head and admit one's guilt；plead guilty

堤 (dī) dyke；embankment
【堤岸】embankment
【堤坝】dykes and dams

提 (dī)〈方〉carry (in one's hand with the arm down)：～ 溜 carry
另见 tí
【提防】beware of；be on guard against；take precautions against

滴 (dī) ❶drip ❷drop
【滴答】〈象〉tick；ticktack
【滴管】dropper；pipette
【滴水不进】not take even a drop of water—unable to eat or drink
【滴水不漏】❶ watertight ❷ tightly packed or completely enclosed
【滴水穿石】water constantly dripping wears holes in stone；little strokes fell great oaks

的 (dí) true；really
【的当】〈书〉apt；appropriate；proper；suitable
【的确】indeed；really

敌 (dí) ❶enemy；foe ❷oppose；fight；resist ❸match；equal
【敌对】be hostile to；oppose；antagonistic
【敌军】enemy troops；hostile forces
【敌人】enemy；foe
【敌视】be hostile to；regard with hostility
【敌手】match；opponent；adversary；enemy hands
【敌意】hostility；enmity；animosity

笛 (dí) ❶ bamboo flute ❷ whistle

【笛子】 dizi, bamboo flute

嫡 (dí) ❶ of or by the wife (as distinguished from a concubine under the feudal-patriarchal system) ❷ of lineal descent; closely related

【嫡传】 be handed down in a direct line from the master

诋 (dǐ)〈书〉slander; defame

【诋毁】 vilify; calumniate

抵 (dǐ) ❶ support; prop ❷ resist; withstand ❸ compensate for; make good ❹ mortgage ❺ balance; set off ❻ be equal to ❼ reach; arrive at

【抵偿】 compensate for
【抵触】 conflict; contradict
【抵达】 arrive; reach
【抵挡】 keep out; ward off
【抵抗】 resist; stand up to
【抵赖】 deny; disavow
【抵消】 offset; cancel out
【抵制】 boycott
【抵罪】 be punished for a crime; bearing the crime; expiate

底 (dǐ) ❶ bottom; base ❷ the heart of a matter; ins and outs ❸ rough draft ❹ a copy kept as a record ❺ end ❻ ground; background

【底版】 original plate; photographic plate; negative
【底层】 ❶ ground floor; first floor ❷ bottom; the lowest rung
【底片】〈摄〉negative (film)
【底细】 exact details
【底下】 ❶ under; below; beneath ❷ next; later; afterwards
【底子】 ❶ bottom; base ❷ rough draft or sketch ❸ foundation
【底座】 lampstand; foundation; pedestal

砥 (dǐ)〈书〉whetstone

【砥柱】 baffle

地 (dì) ❶ the earth ❷ land; soil ❸ fields ❹ ground; floor ❺ place; locality ❻ position; situation ❼ background; ground ❽ distance

【地板】 ❶ floor board ❷ floor
【地步】 ❶ condition; plight ❷ extent ❸ room for action
【地层】〈地〉stratum; layer
【地产】 landed estate; real estate
【地大物博】 vast territory and abundant resources
【地带】 district; region; zone

【地道】 tunnel
【地地道道】 out-and-out; outright; hundred-per-cent; ～的伪君子 a thoroughgoing hypocrite
【地点】 site; local; place
【地动山摇】 earthshaking
【地洞】 burrow; hole in the earth
【地段】 sector of an area
【地方】 ❶ locality; local ❷ place; space; room; part; respect
【地广人稀】 a vast but thinly populated area; a vast territory with a sparse population
【地老天荒】 till the end of the world; for all eternity
【地理】 geography; geographical features
【地貌】 configuration of the earth's surface; landforms
【地面】 ground level; the earth's surface; area; territory
【地球】 the earth; the globe
【地球仪】 (terrestrial) globe
【地区】 area; district; zone; prefecture
【地势】 terrain; relief; topography
【地毯】 carpet; rug
【地铁】 underground (railway); subway
【地图】 map; atlas
【地位】 standing; ranking; status; place
【地下】 ❶ underground; subterranean ❷ secret (activities)
【地震】 earthquake; seism
【地址】 address
【地质】 geology
【地中海】 the Mediterranean (Sea)
【地主】 landlord

弟 (dì) young brother

【弟妹】 ❶ younger brother and sister ❷ one's younger brother's wife; sister-in-law
【弟兄】 brother
【弟子】 disciple; pupil; follower; student

帝 (dì) ❶ God ❷ emperor ❸ imperialism

【帝国】 empire
【帝国主义】 imperialism
【帝王】 monarch
【帝制】 monarchy

递 (dì) hand over; pass; give

【递加】 progressive increase; increase gradually
【递减】 decrease gradually; reduce
【递交】 hand over; present; submit
【递送】 send; deliver
【递增】 increase by degree

第 (dì) ❶ the first ❷〈古〉the residence of a high official

【第二】second; secondary

【第一】first; primary; foremost

【第一手】firsthand

【第一线】forefront; front line; first line

缔 (dì) form(a friendship); conclude(a treaty)

【缔交】❶ establish diplomatic relations ❷ contract a friendship

【缔结】conclude; establish

【缔约】conclude a treaty; sign a treaty

【缔造】found; create

dian

掂 (diān) weigh in the hand

【掂斤播两】engage in petty calculations; be calculating in small matters

【掂掇】〈方〉❶ weigh in the hand ❷ think over; weigh up

颠 (diān) ❶crown(of the head) ❷top; summit ❸ jolt; bump ❹ fall; turn over; topple down ❺run; go away

【颠簸】jolt; rock; bump; toss

【颠倒】❶ turn upside down; reverse; invert ❷ confused; disordered

【颠倒黑白】confound black and white; confuse right and wrong; stand facts on their heads

【颠覆】overturn; subvert; subversion

【颠来倒去】over and over; 就那么点事, 他却～说个没完。 It was only a small matter but he kept harping on it.

【颠沛流离】drift from place to place, homeless and miserable; wander about in a desperate plight; lead a vagabond life

【颠三倒四】incoherent; disorderly confused

癫 (diān) mentally deranged; insane

【癫狂】❶demented; mad ❷frivolous

典 (diǎn) ❶standard; law ❷standard work of scholarship ❸ allusion; literary quotation ❹ceremony ❺be in charge of ❻mortgage

【典当】pawn

【典范】model; example

【典故】〈语〉allusion

【典礼】celebration

【典型】❶typical case; model; type ❷typical

【典雅】(of diction, etc.)refined; elegant

点 (diǎn) ❶ drop(of liquid) ❷ spot; dot; speck ❸ point, place ❹ aspect; feature ❺ 〈量〉a little; a bit; some ❻ hint; point out ❼ light; burn; kindle ❽ select; choose ❾ embellish; decorate

【点播】❶ dibble seeding; dibbling ❷ request a programme from a radio station

【点菜】choose dishes from a menu; order dishes

【点火】light a fire; ignition; stir up trouble

【点名】❶call the roll ❷mention sb. by name

【点明】point out; put one's finger on

【点燃】light; kindle; ignite

【点石成金】touch a stone and turn it into gold— turn a crude essay into a literary gem

【点头】nod

【点头哈腰】〈口〉bow unctuously; bow and scrape

【点头之交】nodding (or bowing) acquaintance: 我和他只是～。 I have only a nodding acquaintance with him.

【点心】light refreshments; pastry; dessert

【点缀】adorn; ornament; embellish; show-up

【点子】drop; spot; speck; beat(percussion instruments); key point; to the point; idea; plan

碘 (diǎn) 〈化〉iodine (I)

跕 (diǎn) stand on tiptoe

电 (diàn) ❶ electricity ❷ give or get an electric shock ❸ telegram; cable

【电报】telegram; cable

【电表】electricity measuring meter; electricity meter

【电冰箱】refrigerator; fridge; icebox; freezer

【电波】electric wave

【电车】tram; streetcar; trolleybus; trolley

【电池】electric cell; battery

【电磁】electromagnetism

【电灯】electric lamp; light

【电动】motor-driven; power-operated

【电工】electric engineer; electrician

【电话】telephone; phone; phone call

【电汇】telegraphic money order; remittance by telegram; telegraphic transfer

【电机】electrical machinery

【电极】electrode

【电缆】cable; electric cable

【电疗】electrotherapy

【电炉】electric stove; electric furnace

【电路】circuit

【电门】switch

【电钮】push button; button

【电瓶】storage battery; accumulator

【电气】electric

【电器】electrical equipment(appliances)

【电视】television；TV

【电台】transmitter-receiver；broadcasting station

【电梯】lift；elevator

【电筒】torch；flashlight

【电线】wire

【电信】telecommunications

【电讯】（telegraphic）dispatch

【电压】voltage

【电影】film；movie；motion picture

【电源】power supply；mains

【电闸】electric brake；electromechanical brake；（electric）switch

【电子】electron

【电阻】resistance

店 （diàn）❶shop；store ❷inn

【店面】shop front

【店员】shop assistant；salesclerk；salesman or saleswoman

【店主】shopkeeper；storekeeper

玷 （diàn）❶a flaw in a piece of jade ❷blemish；disgrace

【玷辱】bring disgrace on

【玷污】stain；sully；tarnish

垫 （diàn）❶put sth. under sth. else to raise it or make it level；fill up ❷pad；cushion ❸pay for sb. and expect to be repaid later

【垫板】〈印〉make ready overlay

【垫付】pay for sb. and expect to be repaid later

【垫平】level up

【垫子】cushion；mat

淀 （diàn）❶form sediment；settle；precipitate ❷（usu. used as part of a place name）shallow lake

【淀粉】starch；amylum

惦 （diàn）remember with concern；be concerned about

【惦记】remember with concern

【惦念】be anxious about

奠 （diàn）❶establish；settle ❷make offerings to the spirits of the dead

【奠定】establish；settle

【奠都】establish a capital；found a capital

【奠基】lay a foundation

【奠仪】a gift of money made on the occasion of a funeral

殿 （diàn）❶hall；palace；temple ❷at the rear

【殿军】❶rearguard ❷a person who comes last in a contest or last among the winners；the last of the successful candidates

【殿试】the palace examination（the final imperial examination，presided over by the emperor）

【殿堂】❶palace or temple buildings ❷palace or temple halls

diāo

刁 （diāo）tricky；sly

【刁悍】cunning and fierce

【刁难】create difficulties

【刁钻】artful；wily

叼 （diāo）hold in the mouth

凋 （diāo）wither

【凋敝】❶（of life）hard；destitute ❷（of business）depressed

【凋零】withered，fallen and scattered about

【凋落】wither and fall

【凋谢】wither and fall

碉 （diāo）

【碉堡】pillbox；blockhouse

【碉楼】watch tower

雕 （diāo）❶carve；engrave ❷〈动〉vulture

【雕虫小技】insignificant skill（esp. in writing）；the trifling skill of a scribe；literary skill of no high order

【雕刻】carve；engrave

【雕栏玉砌】carved balustrades and marble steps—richly ornamented palace buildings

【雕塑】sculpture

【雕像】statue

【雕琢】❶cut and polish（jade）❷write in an ornate style

吊 （diāo）❶hang；suspend ❷lift up or let down with a rope，etc. ❸condole；mourn ❹put in a fur lining ❺revoke；withdraw ❻crane

【吊灯】pendent lamp

【吊环】〈体〉rings

【吊嗓子】train one's voice；exercise one's voice

【吊扇】ceiling fan

【吊销】revoke；withdraw

钓 （diào）fish with a hook and line；angle

【钓饵】bait

【钓竿】fishing pole；fishing rod；angling rod

【钓钩】fishhook；hook

【钓鱼】angle；go fishing

调 （diào）❶transfer；shift ❷accent ❸key ❹air；tune；melody ❺tone；tune

另见 tiáo

【调包】stealthily substitute one thing for another：～计 scheme of substitution

【调兵遣将】move troops；deploy forces

【调查】investigate；inquire into；look into；survey

【调查问卷】questionnaire

【调动】❶transfer；shift ❷move；muster ❸bring into play；arouse；mobilize

【调度】❶ dispatch（trains，buses，etc.）❷ dispatcher

【调虎离山】lure the tiger out of the mountains；lure the enemy away from his base

【调换】exchange；change

【调集】assemble；muster

【调令】transfer order

【调配】allocate；deploy

【调遣】assign；dispatch；听从～（be ready to）accept an assignment

【调运】allocate and transport

【调职】(diàozhí) be transferred to another post

【调子】❶tune；melody ❷tone(of speech)

掉 (diào) ❶ fall；come off ❷ lose；be missing ❸reduce ❹fall behind ❺turn ❻change；exchange ❼ used after certain verbs indicate removal

【掉队】drop out；fall behind

【掉泪】come to tears；tears falling

【掉色】lose colour；fade；discolour

【掉头】turn round；turn about

【掉转】turn round

die

爹 (diē)〈口〉father；dad；daddy；pa

【爹爹】〈口〉❶father；dad；daddy；pa❷grandfather

跌 (diē) ❶fall；tumble ❷drop；fall

【跌打损伤】injuries from falls，fractures，contusions and strains

【跌倒】fall；tumble

【跌跌撞撞】dodder along；stagger along

迭 (dié) ❶alternate；change ❷ repeatedly；again and again ❸ in time for

【迭次】repeatedly；again and again

【迭起】occur repeatedly；happen frequently

谍 (dié) ❶espionage ❷intelligence agent；spy

【谍报】information obtained through espionage；intelligence report；intelligence

喋 (dié)

【喋喋不休】chatter away；rattle on；talk endlessly

【喋血】bloodshed；bloodbath

叠 (dié) ❶ pile up；repeat ❷ fold

【叠床架屋】pile one bed upon another or build one house on top of another—needless duplication

【叠字】〈语〉reduplicated word；reduplication

碟 (dié) small plate；small dish

蝶 (dié) butterfly

【蝶泳】butterfly stroke

ding

叮 (dīng) ❶sting；bite ❷say or ask again to make sure

【叮嘱】urge again and again；warn；exhort

盯 (dīng) fix one's eyes on；gaze at；stare at

【盯梢】shadow sb. ；tail sb.

钉 (dīng) ❶nail；tack ❷follow closely；tail ❸urge；press
另见 dìng

【钉耙】rake

【钉鞋】spiked shoes；spikes

【钉子】nail；snag

顶 (dǐng) ❶the crown of the head ❷top ❸carry on the head ❹gore；butt ❺go against ❻retort；turn down ❼cope with；stand up to ❽ take the place of；substitute；replace ❾very；most；extremely

【顶点】zenith；pinnacle；vertex；apex

【顶多】at the most；at best

【顶风冒雨】brave wind and rain；be undeterred by wind and rain；in spite of wind and rain

【顶峰】top；summit；pinnacle

【顶尖】❶ tip ❷〈机〉centre

【顶角】〈数〉vertex angle

【顶礼膜拜】〈贬〉prostrate oneself in worship；make a fetish of；pay homage to

【顶梁柱】backbone；pillar

【顶替】take sb. 's place；replace

【顶天立地】indomitable；gigantic

【顶头上司】〈口〉immediate superior；one's direct superior

【顶针】thimble

【顶住】withstand；stand up to

【顶撞】contradict（one's elder or superior）

【顶嘴】〈口〉reply defiantly；answer back；talk back

鼎 (dǐng) ❶an ancient cooking vessel with two loop handles and three or four legs ❷

〈方〉pot ❸〈书〉enter upon a period of

【鼎沸】〈书〉like a seething cauldron; noisy and confused

【鼎力】〈套〉your kind effort

【鼎盛】in a period of great prosperity; at the height of power and splendour

【鼎足之势】tripartite balance of forces; triangular balance of power

订 (dìng) ❶ conclude; draw up ❷ subscribe to(a newspaper, etc.); book (seats, tickets, etc.) ❸ make corrections ❹ staple together

【订单】order for goods

【订购】order (goods); place an order for sth.

【订婚】be engaged (to be married); be betrothed

【订货】order goods

【订立】conclude (a treaty or an agreement); make (a contract, etc.)

【订阅】subscribe to(a newspaper, periodical, etc.)

【订正】make corrections; emend

钉 (dìng) ❶ nail ❷ sew on
另见 dīng

定 (dìng) ❶ calm; stable ❷ decide; fix; set ❸ fixed; settled; established ❹ subscribe to; book(seats, tickets, etc.); order ❺〈书〉surely; certainly; definitely

【定案】❶ decide on(or pass) a verdict; decision in a case; judgment ❷ verdict; final decision

【定夺】make a final decision

【定额】quota; norm

【定稿】❶ finalize a manuscript, text, etc. ❷ final version or text

【定购】order(goods); place an order for sth.

【定价】❶ fix a price ❷ fixed price

【定见】definite opinion; set view: 这事儿请你们讨论, 我没有～。Please discuss the matter among yourselves. I have no definite opinion about it.

【定金】〈经〉front money; bargain money; earnest money

【定居】settle down

【定局】inevitable outcome; irreversible situation; settle a situation finally

【定理】theorem

【定量】ration; fixed quantity

【定律】law

【定论】final decision

【定评】accepted opinion; final conclusion

【定期】regular; periodical; at regular intervals; fix a date

【定亲】engagement (usu. arranged by parents); betrothal

【定然】definitely; certainly

【定神】❶ collect oneself; compose oneself; pull oneself together ❷ concentrate one's attention

【定数】❶ fix a number or amount ❷ a fixed number or amount

【定位】❶ fixed position; location; orientation ❷ orientate; position

【定弦】❶ tune a stringed instrument ❷〈方〉make up one's mind

【定限】❶ a fixed limit (to quantity, or degree) ❷ a fixed time limit

【定语】〈语〉attribute

【定罪】convict sb. (of a crime); declare sb. guilty

diu

丢 (diū) ❶ lose; mislay ❷ throw; cast ❸ put aside; lay aside

【丢掉】❶ lose ❷ throw away; cast away; discard

【丢盔卸甲】throw away one's helmet and coat of mail; throw away everything in headlong flight

【丢脸】lose face; be disgraced

【丢弃】abandon; discard

【丢人】make a fool of oneself

【丢人现眼】make a fool of oneself; make a spectacle of oneself

【丢三落四】forgetful; scatterbrained

【丢失】lose

【丢卒保车】give up a pawn to save a chariot— sacrifice minor things to save major ones

dong

东 (dōng) east; master; owner; host

【东半球】the Eastern Hemisphere

【东北】northeast; northeast of China; the Northeast

【东奔西跑】rush about

【东窗事发】be exposed; come to the light

【东倒西歪】leaning; unsteady; tottering: 三间～的屋子 three tumbledown rooms

【东道主】host

【东方】east; the East; the Orient

【东海】the East China Sea

【东拉西扯】drag in irrelevant matters; talk at random; ramble

【东南】❶ southeast ❷ southeast China; the Southeast

【东南亚】Southeast Asia

【东跑西颠】rush here and hurry there; rush about

【东拼西凑】scrape together

【东山再起】stage a comeback; bob up like a cork

D

【东西】thing;creature
【东亚】East Asia
【东张西望】gaze around;peer around

冬 (dōng) ❶winter ❷〈象〉dub-a-dub;rat-tat

【冬季】winter
【冬眠】winter sleep;hibernation
【冬天】winter

董 (dǒng) ❶〈书〉direct;superintend;supervise ❷director;trustee

【董事】director;trustee
【董事长】chairman (*or* president) of the board of directors

懂 (dǒng) understand;know

【懂得】understand;know;grasp

动 (dòng) ❶move;stir ❷act;get moving ❸change;alter ❹use ❺touch;arouse ❻〈方〉eat or drink

【动笔】take up the pen
【动产】movable property;movables;personal property
【动词】〈语〉verb
【动荡】turbulence;upheaval
【动工】start building
【动画片】animated drawing;cartoon
【动机】motive;intention
【动静】❶the sound of sth. astir ❷movement;activity
【动力】❶ motive power;power ❷ motive force;impetus
【动人】moving;touching
【动人心弦】tug at one's heartstrings;be deeply moving
【动身】set out on a journey;leave(for a distant place)
【动手】❶start work;get to work ❷touch;handle ❸raise a hand to strike;hit out
【动态】trends;developments
【动听】interesting or pleasant to listen to
【动物】animal
【动物园】zoo;zoological garden
【动向】trend;tendency
【动心】one's mind is perturbed;one's desire, enthusiasm is aroused
【动摇】shake;waver
【动用】employ;use;draw on
【动员】mobilize;arouse
【动作】movement;action;motion

冻 (dòng) ❶freeze ❷jelly ❸feel very cold;be frostbitten

【冻疮】chilblain
【冻结】freeze
【冻伤】frostbite

栋 (dòng) ❶〈书〉ridgepole ❷〈量〉(for buildings)

【栋梁】ridgepole and beam—pillar of the state

洞 (dòng) ❶ hole;cavity ❷ penetratingly;thoroughly

【洞察】see clearly;have an insight into
【洞彻】understand thoroughly;see clearly
【洞房花烛】wedding festivities;wedding
【洞见症结】see clearly the crux of the matter;get to the heart of the problem
【洞若观火】see sth. as clearly as a blazing fire
【洞天福地】cave heaven and blessed region—fairyland;a heavenly abode
【洞悉】know clearly;understand thoroughly
【洞晓】have a clear knowledge of
【洞穴】cave;cavern

dou

都 (dōu) ❶all ❷even ❸already
另见 dū

兜 (dōu) ❶pocket; bag ❷wrap up in a piece of cloth, etc. ❸ move round ❹ take upon oneself;take responsibility for sth.

【兜风】❶catch the wind ❷go for a drive, ride or sail;go for a spin
【兜揽】❶ canvass; solicit ❷ take upon oneself (sb. else's work, etc.)
【兜圈子】❶go around in circles;circle ❷beat about the bush
【兜售】peddle;hawk

斗 (dǒu) ❶*dou*(=1 decalitre), a unit of dry measure for grain ❷ a *dou* measure ❸an object shaped like a cup or dipper
另见 dòu

【斗胆】〈谦〉make bold;venture
【斗笠】bamboo hat
【斗篷】❶cape;cloak ❷〈方〉bamboo hat

抖 (dǒu) ❶ tremble; shiver; quiver ❷ shake;jerk ❸ rouse;stir up ❹get on in the world

【抖动】shake;vibrate
【抖擞】enliven;rouse

陡 (dǒu) ❶steep;precipitous ❷suddenly;abruptly

【陡立】rise steeply
【陡坡】steep slope
【陡峭】precipitous
【陡然】suddenly

斗 (dòu) ❶fight; tussle ❷ struggle against;denounce ❸contest with; contend with ❹make animals fight(as a game) ❺fit together

另见 dǒu

【斗争】❶ struggle; fight; combat ❷ accuse and denounce at a meeting ❸ strive for; fight for

【斗志】will to fight; fighting will

【斗志昂扬】have high morale; be full of fight; be militant

【斗嘴】squabble; bicker

豆 (dòu) ❶ the bean or pea family ❷ anything in the form of a bean or pea

【豆瓣酱】thick broad-bean sauce

【豆豉】salted, fermented soya beans

【豆腐】bean curd; tofu

【豆浆】soy-bean milk

【豆蔻年华】marriageable age

【豆沙】sweetened bean paste

【豆芽】bean sprouts

【豆油】soy-bean oil

逗 (dòu) ❶ tease; play with ❷ provoke(laughter, etc.); amuse ❸ funny ❹ stay; stop

【逗号】comma(,)

【逗留】stay; stop

【逗弄】tease; make fun of

【逗引】tease

du

都 (dū) ❶ capital (of a country) ❷ big city; metropolis

另见 dōu

【都市】a big city; metropolis

【都市化】urbanization

督 (dū) superintend and direct

【督办】supervise and manage

【督察】superintend; supervise

【督促】supervise and urge: 已经布置了的工作, 应当认真～检查。(We) must supervise and accelerate fulfilment of the assignments.

毒 (dú) ❶ poison; toxin ❷ narcotics ❸ poisonous; noxious; poisoned ❹ malicious; cruel; fierce ❺ kill with poison

【毒害】poison (sb.'s mind)

【毒计】venomous scheme

【毒辣】sinister; diabolic

【毒品】narcotic drugs

【毒气】poisonous gas; poison gas

【毒杀】kill with poison

【毒蛇】poisonous snake

【毒手】murderous scheme

【毒素】〈生〉toxin; toxicant

【毒物】poisonous substance; poison

【毒药】poison; toxicant

独 (dú) ❶ only; single ❷ solely; only ❸ alone; by oneself; in solitude ❹ old people without offspring; the childless

【独霸】dominate exclusively; monopolize

【独白】soliloquy; mono-logue

【独步一时】have no equal in one's time: 她歌喉极佳, 演歌剧～。Gifted with a rare voice, she was an outstanding star among the opera singers.

【独裁】dictatorship; autocratic rule

【独唱】solo

【独出心裁】show originality; by original

【独创】original creation

【独当一面】take charge of a department or locality; assume responsibility for a certain sector

【独到之处】distinctive qualities; specific characteristics

【独断独行】make arbitrary decisions and take peremptory action; act arbitrarily

【独具匠心】show ingenuity; have originality

【独来独往】coming and going all alone—unsociable; aloof: 她老是～的。She kept pretty much to herself.

【独立】❶ stand alone ❷ independence ❸ independent; on one's own

【独立自主】maintain independence and keep the initiative in one's own hands

【独善其身】maintain one's own integrity

【独身】❶ separated from one's family ❷ unmarried; single

【独树一帜】fly one's own colours—develop a school of one's own

【独特】unique; distinctive

【独行其是】do what one thinks is right regardless of others' opinions

【独一无二】unique; unparalleled; unmatched

【独占鳌头】come out first; head the list of successful candidates; be the champion

【独自】alone; by oneself

【独奏】(instrumental) solo; pay a solo

读 (dú) ❶ read; read aloud ❷ attend school

【读本】reader; textbook

【读书】❶ read; study ❷ attend school

【读物】reading matter

【读音】pronunciation

【读者】reader

渎 (dú) ❶ show disrespect or contempt ❷ ditch; drain

【渎职】malfeasance; dereliction of duty

笃 (dú) ❶ sincere; earnest ❷ serious; critical

【笃实】❶honest and sincere ❷sound;solid
【笃信】sincerely believe in;be a devout believer in

堵 (dǔ) ❶ stop up;block up ❷ stiffed;suffocated ❸〈书〉wall
【堵截】intercept
【堵塞】stop up;block up

赌 (dǔ) ❶ gamble ❷ bet
【赌本】money to gamble with
【赌博】gambling
【赌场】gambling house
【赌气】feel wronged and act rashly
【赌徒】gambler
【赌注】stake

睹 (dǔ) see
【睹物思人】seeing the thing one thinks of the person—the thing reminds one of its owner

杜 (dù) ❶ birch-leaf pear ❷ shut out;stop;prevent
【杜鹃】❶〈动〉cuckoo ❷〈植〉azalea
【杜绝】stop(corrupt practices);put an end to (waste,etc.)
【杜撰】fabricate;make up

肚 (dù) belly;stomach;abdomen
【肚皮】〈方〉belly
【肚脐】navel;belly button
【肚子】belly

妒 (dù) be jealous of;be envious of;envy
【妒忌】be envious of(sb.'s success)
【妒贤嫉能】be jealous of the worthy and able

度 (dù) ❶ linear measure ❷ degree of intensity ❸〈量〉a unit of measurement for angles,temperature,etc.;degree ❹〈电〉kilowatt-hour(kwh) ❺limit;extent;degree ❻tolerance;magnanimity ❼consideration ❽〈量〉occasion;time ❾spend;pass
【度过】spend;live;tolerate
【度假】spend one's holidays;go vacationing
【度量】tolerance;magnanimity
【度日】subsist(in hardship);eke out an existence

渡 (dù) ❶ cross(a river,the sea,etc.) ❷ tide over;pull through ❸ ferry(people,goods,etc.)across
【渡船】ferryboat
【渡过】tide over
【渡口】ferry

镀 (dù) plating
【镀金】❶ gold-plating ❷ get gilded
【镀银】silvering

duan

端 (duān) ❶ end;extremity ❷ beginning ❸ point;item ❹ reason;cause ❺ upright;proper ❻hold sth. level with both hands;carry
【端详】❶details ❷dignified and serene ❸look sb. up and down
【端正】❶upright;regular:五官～ have regular features ❷proper;correct ❸rectify;correct:～学习态度 adopt a correct attitude towards study
【端庄】dignified;sedate

短 (duǎn) ❶short ❷lack;owe ❸weak point;fault
【短兵相接】fight at close quarters;engage in hand-to-hand fighting(or close combat)
【短波】short-wave
【短处】shortcoming;failing
【短见】❶shortsighted view ❷suicide
【短裤】shorts
【短命】die young;be short-lived
【短跑】dash;sprint
【短篇小说】short story
【短评】brief comment
【短期】short-term
【短缺】deficit;shortage
【短文】short essay
【短小】short
【短小精悍】❶not of imposing stature but strong and capable ❷short and pithy
【短语】〈语〉phrase
【短暂】of short duration

段 (duàn) ❶〈量〉section;segment;part ❷〈量〉paragraph;passage
【段落】❶paragraph ❷phase;stage

断 (duàn) ❶break;snap ❷break off;cut off;stop ❸give up;abstain from ❹judge;decide ❺〈书〉absolutely;decidedly
【断壁残垣】deserted ruins;dilapidated walls
【断定】conclude;form a judgment
【断断续续】off and on;intermittently
【断交】break off a friendship;sever diplomatic relations;break off diplomatic ties
【断句】punctuate
【断绝】break off;cut off;stop
【断线风筝】a kite with a broken string—gone beyond recall
【断言】say with certainty;assert categorically;

affirm

【断章取义】quote or interpret out of context

【断子绝孙】〈讳〉may you die sonless（or without sons）；may you be the last of your line

缎（duàn）satin

【缎纹】satin weave

【缎子】satin

煅（duàn）❶ forge ❷ calcine

【煅烧】calcine

锻（duàn）forge

【锻炼】❶ take exercise；have physical training：体育～ physical exercise ❷ temper；steel；toughen

dui

堆（duī）❶ pile up；heap up；stack ❷ heap；pile；stack

【堆放】pile up；stack

【堆积】pile up；heap up

【堆砌】❶load one's writing with fancy phrases：～辞藻 load with ornate phrases ❷pile up

队（duì）❶ a row of people；line ❷ team；group

【队列】formation

【队伍】〈军〉troops；ranks；contingent

【队形】formation

【队员】team member

【队长】captain

对（duì）❶answer；reply ❷treat；cope with；counter ❸be trained on；be directed at ❹ opposite；opposing ❺ compare；check；identify ❻right；correct ❼mix；add ❽ pair；couple ❾ at；to；toward

【对白】dialogue

【对半】half and half；fifty-fifty；double

【对不起】❶I'm sorry；sorry；excuse me；pardon me；I beg your pardon ❷let sb. down；be unworthy of；do a disservice to；be unfair to

【对策】countermeasure；countermove

【对称】symmetry

【对答】answer；reply

【对答如流】answer fluently；answer questions without hesitation

【对待】treat；approach；handle

【对调】exchange；swap

【对方】the opposite side；the other party

【对付】❶ deal with；cope with；counter；tackle ❷ make do

【对过】opposite；across the way

【对号】❶ check the number ❷ tally；fit；match ❸ check mark（√）；tick

【对话】dialogue

【对抗】❶ antagonism； confrontation ❷ resist；oppose

【对立】oppose；set sth. against；be antagonistic to

【对联】antithetical couplet

【对门】❶（of two houses）face each other ❷ the building or room opposite

【对面】❶ opposite ❷ right in fronts ❸ face to face

【对牛弹琴】play the lute to a cow；choose the wrong audience

【对手】❶adversary；opponent ❷match；equal

【对头】correct；right

【对头】❶enemy ❷opponent；adversary

【对外】external；foreign

【对外开放】（the policy of）opening to the outside world；the open policy

【对象】❶target；object ❷boy or girl friend

【对眼】❶ to one's liking；to one's taste ❷ cross-eye

【对应】corresponding

【对于】with regard to

【对照】contrast；compare

【对证】verify；check

【对症下药】suit the medicine to the illness；suit the remedy to the case；prescribe the right remedy for an illness

【对质】confrontation（in court）

【对峙】 stand facing each other；confront each other

【对准】aim at

兑（duì）❶ exchange；convert ❷ add

【兑付】cash

【兑换】exchange；convert

【兑现】❶ cash ❷ honor

dun

吨（dūn）ton

【吨位】tonnage

炖（dùn）❶stew ❷ warm sth. by putting the container in hot water

钝（dùn）❶ blunt；dull ❷ stupid；dull-witted

【钝角】〈数〉obtuse angle

顿（dùn）❶ pause ❷ arrange；settle ❸touch the ground（with one's head）❹ stamp（one's foot）❺ suddenly；immediately；at once

❻〈量〉time ❼fatigued;tired

【顿挫】pause and transition in rhythm or melody

【顿号】slight pause mark

【顿开茅塞】suddenly see the light;be suddenly enlightened:闻兄大教,～。You excellent advice has opened my eyes.

D 【顿时】immediately;at once

duo

多 (duō) ❶many;much;more ❷have(a specified amount) more or too much ❸(use in questions) to what extent ❹(used in exclamations) to what an extent ❺to an unspecified extent

【多边】multilateral

【多边形】〈数〉polygon

【多才多艺】versatile;gifted in many ways;master of trades

【多愁善感】sentimental;emotional;sensitive

【多此一举】make an unnecessary move

【多次】many times;time and again

【多多少少】more or less

【多多益善】the more,the better

【多方面】many-sided;in many ways

【多劳多得】more pay for more work

【多么】how;what

【多面手】a many-sided person;a versatile person;an all rounder

【多面体】〈数〉polyhedron

【多谋善断】resourceful and decisive;sagacious and resolute

【多幕剧】a full-length drama

【多如牛毛】as many as the hairs on an ox;countless;innumerable

【多少】number;amount;more or less;to some extent;some what;as much as

【多时】a long time

【多事】meddlesome;eventful

【多事之秋】an eventful period or year;troubled times

【多数】majority;most

【多云】cloudy;broken sky

【多种多样】varied;in varied forms;manifold

【多嘴】speak out of turn;long tongued;shoot off one's mouth

哆 (duō)

【哆嗦】tremble;shiver

夺 (duó) ❶take by force;seize;wrest ❷force one's way ❸contend for;compete for;strive for ❹deprive ❺decide

【夺标】win the first prize

【夺冠】carry off the first prize;win first place;win the championship

【夺回】recapture;take back;seize back

【夺门而出】force one's way out

【夺目】dazzle the eyes;strikingly attractive

【夺取】capture;seize;strive for

【夺去】take away from

【夺权】seize power

躲 (duó) ❶hide(oneself) ❷avoid;dodge

【躲避】avoid;dodge;elude;hide

【躲藏】hide oneself;conceal oneself

【躲闪】dodge;evade

【躲雨】take shelter from the rain

【躲债】avoid a creditor

堕 (duò) fall;sink

【堕落】degenerate;sink low

【堕入】sink into;lapse into;land oneself in

【堕胎】induced abortion;have an(induced) abortion

惰 (duò) lazy;indolent

【惰性】inertia

E e

e

阿 (ē) play up to; pander to
另见 ā
【阿谀】 fawn on; flatter
【阿谀奉承】 flatter and toady

婀 (ē)
【婀娜】 (of a woman's bearing) graceful

讹 (é) ❶erroneous; mistaken ❷extort; blackmail
【讹传】 false rumour
【讹诈】 extort under false pretences; blackmail

俄 (é) very soon; presently; suddenly
【俄而】 very soon; in a moment; in a little while; presently

鹅 (é) goose
【鹅卵石】 cobble; pebble
【鹅毛】 goose feather
【鹅绒】 goose down

额 (é) ❶ forehead ❷ a horizontal tablet ❸a specified number or amount
【额定】 specified (number or amount); rated
【额外】 extra; additional; added

恶 (ě)
另见 è, wù
【恶心】 ❶ feel sick; nausea ❷ nauseating; disgusting

厄 (è) ❶a strategic point ❷adversity; disaster; hardship
【厄境】 a difficult situation; adversity
【厄运】 adversity; misfortune; bad luck; ill luck; misfortune

扼 (è) ❶clutch; grip ❷guard; control
【扼杀】 strangle; smother
【扼守】 guard or hold (a strategic point)
【扼要】 to the point; main points of a statement or article; in brief summary
【扼制】 keep under control by force

恶 (è) ❶evil; vice; wickedness ❷fierce; ferocious ❸bad; evil
另见 ě, wù
【恶霸】 local tyrant
【恶毒】 malicious; venomous
【恶感】 ill feeling; malice
【恶棍】 ruffian; scoundrel
【恶狠狠】 fierce; ferocious
【恶化】 worsen; deteriorate; take a change (turn) for the worse
【恶劣】 odious; abominable; disgusting
【恶眉恶眼】 a very fierce expression
【恶魔】 ❶demon; devil; evil spirit ❷evil person
【恶习】 a bad habit
【恶意】 evil intentions; malice
【恶语中伤】 viciously slander
【恶作剧】 prank; mischief

饿 (è) ❶hungry ❷cause to starve; starve
【饿虎扑食】 like a hungry tiger pouncing on its prey

遏 (è) check; hold back
【遏止】 check; hold back
【遏制】 keep within limits; contain

噩 (è) shocking; upsetting
【噩耗】 sad news of the death of a beloved person
【噩梦】 a frightening (or horrible) dream; nightmare

鳄 (è)
【鳄鱼】〈动〉crocodile; alligator

en

恩 (ēn) kindness; favour
【恩爱】 conjugal love
【恩赐】 ❶ bestow (favours, charity, etc.) ❷favour; charity
【恩情】 loving-kindness
【恩人】 benefactor

【恩怨】❶ feeling of gratitude or resentment ❷ grievance

摁 (èn) press (with the hand or finger)

er

儿 (ér) ❶ child ❷ youngster; youth ❸ son ❹ male

【儿歌】children's song

【儿女】❶ sons and daughters; children ❷ young man and woman(in love)

【儿女情长】love between man and woman is long:英雄气短,～。Brief is the spirit of a hero, but love between man and woman is long (said of a man who turns from duty for the sake of love).

【儿孙】children and grandchildren; descendants; posterity

【儿童】children

【儿戏】trifling matter

而 (ér) ❶ but; while ❷ to

【而后】after that; then

【而今】at the present time

【而且】❶ and ❷ but

【而已】that is all

耳 (ěr) ❶ ear ❷ any ear-like thing; ear of a utensil ❸ on both sides; flanking; side

【耳垂】〈生理〉earlobe

【耳根清净】peace of heart or mind attained by staying away from, or shutting one's ears to, worldly discord

【耳光】a slap on the face; a box on the ear

【耳环】earrings

【耳机】earphone

【耳聋】deaf

【耳语】whisper in sb's ear; whisper

饵 (ěr) ❶ cakes; pastry ❷ (fish) bait ❸ 〈书〉entice

二 (èr) ❶ two ❷ different

【二胡】erhu fiddle, a two-stringed bowed instrument

【二月】❶ February ❷ the second month of the lunar year; the second moon

【二者】the two; both

F f

fa

发 (fā) ❶ send out; deliver ❷ utter; express ❸ discharge; shoot ❹ develop; expand ❺ (of foodstuffs) rise or expand when fermented or soaked ❻ come or bring into existence ❼ open up discover ❽ get into a certain state; become ❾ show one's feeling
另见 fà
【发表】 publish; issue
【发财】 get rich; make a fortune
【发愁】 worry; be anxious
【发出】 issue; give out
【发达】 developed; flourishing
【发呆】 stare blankly; be in a daze
【发电】〈电〉generate electricity (or electric power); furnish power; (electric) power generation
【发奋】 work energetically (hard); exert oneself; rouse oneself
【发愤】 make a firm resolution
【发挥】 ❶ bring into play ❷ develop; elaborate
【发货】 send out goods; deliver goods
【发烧】 have a fever; have a temperature
【发生】 happen; occur; take place
【发誓】 pledge; swear; vow
【发行】 issue; publish; distribute; put on sale
【发展】 ❶ develop; expand; grow; burgeon; ❷ recruit; admit
【发作】 break out; show effect; have a fit of anger

乏 (fá) ❶ lack ❷ tired; weary ❸ exhausted; worn-out
【乏味】 dull; insipid; drab; tasteless

罚 (fá) punish; penalize
【罚不当罪】 the punishment exceeds the crime; be punished too severely
【罚金】 fine; forfeit
【罚款】 ❶ impose a fine or forfeit; fine ❷ penalty; forfeit
◀【罚球】 penalty shot; penalty kick

阀 (fá)〈机〉valve
【阀门】〈机〉valve

筏 (fá) raft
【筏道】 log chute; logway
【筏子】 raft

法 (fǎ) ❶ law ❷ method; way; mode ❸ standard; model ❹ religious doctrine
【法案】 bill; proposed law
【法办】 deal with according to law; punish by law
【法宝】 a magic weapon
【法官】 judge; justice
【法律】 law; statute
【法盲】 a person ignorant of the law; one who lacks legal knowledge
【法人】〈法〉legal person; juridical person
【法庭】 court; tribunal
【法制】 legal system; legal institutions; legality
【法治】 rule by law; government by law; governed by law

发 (fà) hair
另见 fā
【发际】 hairline
【发夹】 hairpin; bobby pin
【发式】 hairstyle; hairdo; coiffure
【发型】 hairstyle; hairdo; coiffure

fan

帆 (fān) sail
【帆板】 windsurfer; sailboard
【帆布】 canvas; duck
【帆船】 sailing boat; sailing ship; junk; sailboat
【帆篷】 sail

番 (fān) ❶ aborigines ❷ foreign; barbarian ❸ (used in names for certain plants originally introduced from abroad)
【番邦】〈古〉a foreign (or barbarian) land
【番号】 the designation of a military unit
【番茄】 tomato
【番薯】〈方〉sweet potato

翻 (fān) ❶ turn upside down or inside out; turn over ❷ look through; search ❸ reverse ❹ cross; get over ❺ multiply; double ❻ translate ❼ fall out; break up

【翻案】 reverse a verdict

【翻版】 reprint; reproduction

【翻本】 win back all the money lost (in gambling)

【翻录】 pirate recordings

凡 (fán) ❶ ordinary ❷ this mortal world; the earth ❸ every; any; all ❹ altogether

【凡例】 notes on the use of a book etc.; guide to the use of a book, etc.

【凡人】 ❶〈书〉ordinary person ❷ mortal

【凡事】 everything

【凡是】 every; any; all

【凡响】 common music; ordinary music; 非同～ out of the ordinary

【凡庸】 (usu. of humans) commonplace; ordinary

烦 (fán) ❶ be vexed; be irritated; be annoyed ❷ be tired of ❸ superfluous and confusing ❹ trouble

【烦劳】 ❶ trouble (sb. to do sth.) ❷ depressed; feeling low

【烦闷】 be unhappy; be worried

【烦恼】 be vexed

【烦扰】 ❶ bother ❷ feel disturbed

【烦人】 annoying; vexing; troubling

【烦琐】 overelaborate; tedious

繁 (fán) ❶ in great numbers; numerous ❷ propagate

【繁多】 various

【繁复】 heavy and complicated; 有了计算机，～ 的计算工作在几秒钟之内就可以完成。A computer does complicated calculations in a few seconds.

【繁花】 full-blown flowers; flowers of different colours

【繁华】 bustling

【繁忙】 busy

【繁茂】 lush; luxuriant

【繁密】 dense; 林木～ densely wooded

【繁殖】〈生〉breed; reproduce; propagate

反 (fǎn) ❶ turn over ❷ in an opposite direction; in reverse; inside out ❸ on the contrary; instead ❹ revolt; rebel ❺ return; counter ❻ oppose; combat

【反比】 inverse relation; inverse proportion

【反比例】〈数〉inverse ratio; inverse proportion; 分数值与分母值成～。The value of a frac-

tion is inversely proportional to that of the denominator.

【反驳】 refute; retort

【反差】 contrast

【反常】 unusual; abnormal

【反衬】 set off by contrast; serve as a foil to

【反对】 oppose; be against; fight; combat

【反而】 on the contrary

【反复】 ❶ repeatedly; again and again ❷ reversal; relapse

【反光】 ❶ reflect light ❷ reflection of light

【反击】 strike back; beat back; counterattack

【反抗】 rebel; revolt; resist

【反馈】〈电〉feedback

【反胃】 have a gastric disorder; feel nauseated; feel queasy

【反问】 ❶ ask a question in reply ❷〈语〉rhetorical question

【反向】 opposite direction; reverse

【反省】 reflect on oneself; examine one's own conscience; introspection

【反义词】〈语〉antonym

【反应】 reaction; response; repercussion

【反映】 ❶ reflect; mirror ❷ report; make known

【反语】〈语〉irony

【反掌】 turn one's hand over—a most easy thing to do

【反正】 anyway; anyhow; in any case

返 (fǎn) return; come or go back

【返场】 (of a performer) give an encore

【返潮】 get damp

【返程】 return journey

【返工】 do poorly done work over again

【返航】 (of ships, planes, etc.) return to base or port

犯 (fàn) ❶ violate; offend ❷ criminal ❸ attack; assail; work against ❹ have a recurrence of (an old illness) ❺ commit (a mistake, crime, etc.)

【犯案】 (of a criminal) be found out and brought to justice

【犯病】 have an attack of one's old illness; 她妈 又～了。Her mother is ill again.

【犯愁】 worry; be anxious

【犯法】 break the law

【犯规】 ❶ break the rules ❷〈体〉foul

【犯急】 become impatient; get restless

【犯贱】 ❶ be perverse; act shamelessly ❷ feel languid (or listless)

【犯难】 feel embarrassed; feel awkward

【犯人】prisoner;convict

【犯傻】〈方〉❶pretend to be naive,ignorant,or stupid ❷do a foolish thing ❸be in a daze;stare blankly

【犯上作乱】defy one's superiors and start a rebellion;rebel

【犯事】commit a crime (*or* an offence)

【犯疑】become suspicious

【犯罪】commit a crime;offence

饭 (fàn) ❶cooked rice or other cereals ❷meal

【饭菜】❶meal;repast ❷dishes to go with rice,steamed buns,etc.

【饭店】❶hotel ❷〈方〉restaurant

【饭锅】❶pot for cooking rice;rice cooker ❷means of living;livelihood

【饭盒】lunch-box;mess tin;dinner pail

【饭粒】grains of cooked rice

【饭量】appetite

【饭票】meal ticket;mess card

【饭碗】❶rice bowl ❷〈口〉job

【饭桌】dining table

泛 (fàn) ❶float ❷be suffused with ❸flood ❹extensive;general

【泛读】extensive reading

【泛泛】general;not deep-going

【泛泛而谈】speak in generally;talk in generalities

【泛泛之交】a casual acquaintance

【泛览】read extensively

【泛滥】❶be in flood;overflow ❷spread unchecked

【泛论】a general survey or discussion

【泛溢】overflow;flood:江水～。The river overflowed.

【泛指】make a general reference

范 (fàn) ❶pattern ❷model;example;❸limits

【范本】model for calligraphy or painting

【范畴】category

【范例】example;model

【范围】scope;limits;range

【范文】model essay

贩 (fàn) ❶buy to resell ❷dealer;monger;peddler

【贩毒】traffic in narcotics

【贩卖】traffic;peddle;sell

【贩卖人口】traffic in human beings;human traffic;(specifically) traffic in women;the white-slave trade;white slavery

【贩运】transport goods for sale;traffic

【贩子】trader;monger

fang

方 (fāng) ❶square ❷involution;power ❸short for square metre or cubic metre ❹upright;honest ❺direction ❻side;party ❼place;region;locality ❽method;way ❾prescription ❿just;only

【方案】scheme;plan;program

【方便】convenient

【方便面】instant noodles

【方步】measured steps:迈～ walk with measured steps

【方才】just now

【方程】〈数〉equation

【方法】method;way;means

【方格】check

【方根】〈数〉root

【方今】now;nowadays

【方框】square frame

【方括号】square brackets

【方面】respect;aspect;side;field

【方式】way;fashion;pattern

【方术】medicine,divination,and similar arts

【方糖】cube sugar;lump sugar

【方外】❶beyond this world ❷〈方〉foreign lands

【方位】position;bearing;direction;placement

【方向】direction;orientation

【方兴未艾】be fast unfolding;be in the ascendant

【方形】square

【方言】dialect

【方圆】❶neighbourhood;vicinity ❷circumference

【方针】policy;guiding principle

【方正】❶upright and foursquare ❷straightforward;upright;righteous

【方桌】a square table

芳 (fāng) ❶sweet-smelling;fragrant ❷good reputation;virtuous

【芳草】fragrant grass

【芳龄】the age of a young woman

【芳香】fragrant;aromatic

【芳心】the heart of a young woman

防 (fáng) ❶guard against;provide against ❷defend ❸dyke

【防爆】flame-proof

【防备】guard against;take precautions against

【防病】prevent disease

【防潮】❶dampproof;moistureproof ❷protection

against the tide

【防尘】dustproof

【防除】prevent and kill off

【防磁】〈物〉antimagnetic

【防弹】bulletproof;shellproof

【防盗】guard against theft;take precautions against burglars

【防毒】gas defense

【防范】be on guard;keep a lookout

【防风】protect against the wind;provide shelter from the wind

【防腐】antiseptic;anticorrosive

【防旱】take precautions against drought

【防洪】prevent or control flood

【防护】protect;shelter

【防火】fire prevention;fireproof

【防空】air defence;antiaircraft

【防守】defend;guard

妨 (fáng) hinder;hamper;impede;obstruct

【妨碍】hinder;hamper;impede;obstruct

【妨害】impair;jeopardize;be harmful to

房 (fáng) ❶house ❷room ❸〈解〉chamber

【房产】house property

【房东】the owner of the house one lives in;landlord or landlady

【房间】room

【房契】title deed (for a house)

【房钱】house rent;room rent

【房屋】houses;buildings

【房檐】eaves

【房主】house-owner

【房柱】pillars of a house

【房子】❶house;building ❷room

【房租】rent (for a house,flat)

仿 (fǎng) ❶imitate;copy ❷resemble;be like

【仿佛】❶seem;as if ❷be more or less the same

【仿古】modelled after an antique;in the style of the ancients

【仿生学】bionics

【仿效】imitate;follow the example of

【仿行】follow an example;follow suit

【仿造】copy;be modelled on

【仿照】imitate;follow:这个办法很好,各地可以～办理。This is a good method. It might well be adopted by other localities.

【仿真】simulation;emulation;phantom

【仿制】be modelled on

访 (fǎng) ❶visit;call on ❷seek by inquiry or search;try to get

【访查】go about making inquiries;investigate

【访求】search for:～民间丹方 search for folk remedies

【访视】make a house call (to see a patient,lying-in woman,etc.)

【访问】visit

纺 (fǎng) ❶spin ❷a thin silk cloth

【纺车】spinning wheel

【纺绸】a soft plain-weave silk fabric

【纺锤】spindle

【纺纱】spin;spinning;yarn manufacture

【纺丝】〈化〉spinning:～泵 spinning pump

【纺织】spinning and weaving

【纺织品】textile;fabric

放 (fàng) ❶let go;set free;release ❷let off;give out ❸put out to pasture ❹let oneself go;give way to ❺lend(money) for interest ❻let out;expand ❼blossom;open ❽put;place ❾send away

【放大】enlarge;magnify;amplify

【放胆】act boldly and with confidence:你尽管～去干! Don't hesitate to forge ahead!

【放诞】wild in speech and behaviour

【放荡】❶dissolute;dissipated ❷unconventional

【放荡不羁】unconventional and unrestrained

【放风】❶let in fresh air ❷let prisoners out for exercise ❸leak certain information

【放工】get out of work;knock off;我们是下午六点钟放的工。We got out of work at six o'clock in the afternoon.

【放火】❶set fire to;set on fire;commit arson ❷create disturbances

【放假】have a holiday or vacation;have a day off

【放开】have a free hand in doing sth. :让外贸企业～经营 give foreign trade enterprises full authority over management

【放宽】relax; relax restrictions; liberalize; be more flexible

【放款】make loans;loan

【放牧】put out to pasture;herd

【放炮】❶fire a gun ❷set off firecrackers ❸blast ❹(of a tyre, etc.) blow out ❺shoot off one's mouth

【放弃】abandon;give up

【放晴】clear up (after rain)

【放热】〈化〉exothermic

【放任】 not interfere; let alone; let things

drift;noninterference

【放任自流】let things drift (or slide)

【放哨】stand sentry;be on sentry go

【放射】radiate

【放声痛哭】utter a stifled cry of agony

【放手】❶let go;let go one's hold ❷have a free hand;go all out ❸release one's control;hand over to sb. else

【放水】❶turn on the water ❷draw off some water (from a reservoir,etc.)

【放肆】unbridled; wanton：～ 的 行 为 unbridled behaviour

【放下】lay down;put down

【放心】set one's mind at rest;be at ease;rest assured;feel relieved

【放学】classes are over

【放眼】take a broad view;scan widely：～未来 look toward the future

【放养】put (fish,insects,etc.) in a suitable place to breed

【放映】show (a film);project

【放置】lay up;lay aside

【放纵】❶let sb. have his own way;connive at;indulge ❷self-indulgent;undisciplined

fei

飞 (fēi) ❶fly ❷hover or flutter in the air ❸swiftly ❹unexpected;accidental

【飞奔】dash;tear along

【飞车走壁】stunt cycling, driving or motorcycling on the inner surface of a cylindrical wall

【飞驰】speed along

【飞虫】winged insect

【飞船】airship

【飞弹】❶missile ❷stray bullet

【飞碟】❶〈体〉skeet shooting;skeet;trapshooting ❷flying saucer;UFO(unidentified flying object)

【飞短流长】spread embroidered stories and malicious gossip

【飞红】bright red;scarlet;crimson：她羞得满脸～。She was crimson with embarrassment.

【飞黄腾达】make rapid advances in one's career;have a meteoric rise

【飞机】aircraft;aeroplane;plane

【飞溅】splash

【飞快】❶very fast;at lightning speed ❷extremely sharp

【飞来横祸】unexpected disaster

【飞掠】fly past or over

【飞沫】flying particles of liquid;splattered drops

【飞盘】Frisbee disk;frisbee

【飞逝】(of time,etc.) slip by (or past);fly;elapse

【飞速】at full speed

【飞腾】fly swiftly upward

【飞艇】airship;dirigible

【飞舞】dance in the air

【飞翔】circle in the air;hover

【飞行】flight;flying

【飞行员】pilot;aviator;flyer

妃 (fēi) ❶imperial concubine ❷ the wife of a prince

【妃色】light pink

【妃子】imperial concubine

非 (fēi) ❶ wrong ❷ not conform to; run counter to ❸not;no ❹blame;censure ❺〈口〉have got to;simply must

【非常】❶extraordinary;unusual;special ❷very;extremely;highly

【非法】illegal;unlawful;illicit

【非凡】outstanding;extraordinary;uncommon

【非分】overstepping one's bounds; assuming;presumptuous

【非分之想】inordinate ambitions

【非公莫入】no admittance except on business

【非金属】nonmetal

【非晶体】amorphous body;noncrystal

【非卖品】not for sale

【非命】an unnatural death;a violent death

【非难】blame;censure;reproach

【非亲非故】be neither kith nor kin

【非人】❶〈书〉not the right person ❷inhuman

【非同小可】be no trivial (trifling) matter;be not usual

【非正式】unofficial;informal

【非洲】Africa

菲 (fēi) ❶ (of flowers and grass) luxuriant and rich with fragrance ❷chem phenanthrene ❸(Fēi) short for 菲律宾(the Philippines)

另见 fěi

【菲菲】❶luxuriant and beautiful ❷richly fragrant

【菲林】dial a roll of film;film

【菲律宾】the Philippines

绯 (fēi) red

【绯红】bright red;crimson

扉 (fēi)〈书〉door leaf

【扉页】〈印〉title page

霏（fēi）❶（of rain or snow）fall thick and fast ❷thin, floating clouds; mist

【霏霏】〈文〉（of rain, snow, mist, cloud, etc.）thick and fast; heavy

肥（féi）❶fat ❷fertile; rich ❸fertilizer; manure ❹loose-fitting; loose; large

【肥肠】pig's large intestines（used as food）

【肥大】❶loose; large ❷fat; plump; corpulent

【肥厚】❶plump; fleshy ❷thick and fertile

【肥料】fertilizer; manure

【肥美】❶ fertile; rich ❷ luxuriant; plump; fleshy; fat

【肥胖】fat; corpulent

【肥实】❶fat; stout ❷rich in fat

【肥瘦】❶the girth of a garment ❷the proportion of fat and lean

【肥土】fertile（*or* good）soil

【肥沃】fertile; rich

【肥皂】soap

【肥壮】stout and strong

匪（fěi）❶bandit; robber ❷〈书〉not

【匪帮】bandit gang; a felonious political gang

【匪首】bandit chieftain

【匪徒】gangster

诽（fěi）slander

【诽谤】calumniate; libel

菲（fěi）〈书〉〈谦〉poor; humble
另见 fēi

【菲薄】❶humble ❷belittle

悱（fěi）〈书〉be at a loss for words

【悱恻】〈书〉laden with sorrow; sad at heart; 缠绵～ lingering sorrow

斐（fěi）〈书〉（of literary talent）striking; brilliant

【斐济】Fiji

【斐然】〈书〉striking; brilliant; splendid

翡（fěi）

【翡翠】❶〈动〉halcyon（a bird）❷ jadeite（a mineral）

吠（fèi）bark; yap; yelp

【吠叫】（of a dog）bark; yap; yelp

肺（fèi）lung

【肺癌】lung cancer

【肺腑】the bottom of one's heart

【肺腑之言】words from the bottom of one's heart

【肺活量】vital capacity

【肺结核】pulmonary tuberculosis（TB）

【肺痨】〈口〉consumption; tuberculosis

【肺泡】〈生理〉pulmonary alveolus

【肺炎】pneumonia

废（fèi）❶give up; abandon; abolish ❷waste; useless ❸disabled; maimed

【废除】abolish; abrogate; annul; repeal

【废话】superfluous words; nonsense; rubbish

【废话连篇】pages of nonsense; reams of rubbish

【废旧】（of things）old and useless

【废票】❶ invalidated ticket ❷ invalidated ballot

【废品】waste product; reject; scrap

【废弃】discard; abandon; cast aside

【废寝忘食】lose sleep and forget to eat from anxiety, etc.

【废人】❶disabled person ❷good-for-nothing

【废铁】scrap iron

【废物】❶waste material; trash ❷good-for-nothing

【废墟】ruins; debris

【废渣】waste residue

【废止】abolish; annul; put an end to

【废纸】broke; wastepaper

沸（fèi）boil

【沸点】boiling point

【沸热】boiling hot; steaming hot

【沸腾】❶〈物〉boiling ❷ seethe with excitement; boil over

费（fèi）❶fee; dues; expenses; charge ❷cost; spend; expend

【费话】take a lot of talking or explaining

【费解】hard to understand; obscure; unintelligible

【费尽心机】rack one's brains in scheming

【费劲】〈口〉be strenuous

【费力】need or exert great effort; be strenuous

【费钱】cost a lot; be costly

【费神】❶need or exert great mental effort ❷〈套〉（used in making a request or giving thanks）may I trouble you（to do sth.）; would you mind（doing sth.）

【费时】take time; be time-consuming

【费事】give or take a lot of trouble

【费心】❶give a lot of care; take a lot of trouble ❷〈套〉（used in making a request or giving thanks）may I trouble you（to do sth.）; would you mind（doing sth.）

【费用】cost; expenses

痱^(fèi)

【痱子】〈医〉prickly heat
【痱子粉】prickly-heat powder

fen

分^(fēn) ❶divide；separate；part ❷distribute；assign；allot ❸distinguish；differentiate ❹branch(of an organization) ❺〈量〉one tenth (of certain units of the metric system) ❻fraction ❼point；mark
另见 fèn

【分崩离析】disintegrate；fall to pieces；come apart
【分辨】distinguish；differentiate
【分辩】defend oneself(against a charge)；offer an explanation
【分别】❶part；leave each other ❷distinguish；differentiate ❸difference ❹respectively；separately
【分布】be distributed；be scattered；be dispersed
【分册】a separately published part of a book；fascicle
【分成】divide into tenths
【分词】〈语〉participle
【分寸】proper limits for speech or action；sense of propriety；sense of proportion
【分担】share
【分道扬镳】go different ways；part company
【分店】branch (of a shop)
【分队】a troop unit corresponding to the platoon or squad；element
【分发】distribute；hand out；issue
【分隔】separate；divide
【分工】divide the work
【分管】be assigned personal responsibility for；be put in charge of
【分红】draw (or receive) dividends；share profits
【分化】❶become divided；break up ❷split up ❸〈生〉(of cells or tissues) differentiate
【分家】❶divide up family property and live apart；break up the family and live apart ❷separate；break up
【分解】❶〈物〉〈数〉resolve ❷〈化〉decompose；resolve ❸mediate ❹disintegrate；split up ❺explain (used in traditional novels)
【分居】(of members of a family) live apart
【分开】separate；part
【分类】classify
【分离】separate；sever
【分裂】❶〈生〉〈物〉split；divide；break up ❷division；fission

【分流】〈电〉by-pass；distributary；split-flow
【分路】❶go along separate routes or from several directions ❷〈电〉shunt
【分门别类】put into different categories；classify
【分娩】childbirth
【分秒】every minute and second；instant
【分秒必争】seize every minute and second；every second counts；not a second is to be lost
【分明】❶clearly demarcated；distinct ❷plainly；evidently
【分派】assign (to different persons)
【分配】distribute；allot；assign
【分批】in batches；group by group；in turn
【分期】by stages
【分歧】difference；divergence
【分清】distinguish；draw a clear line of demarcation between
【分散】disperse；scatter
【分手】part company
【分数】❶〈数〉fraction ❷mark；grade
【分送】send；distribute
【分庭抗礼】stand up to sb. as an equal；act independently and defiantly
【分析】analyse
【分一杯羹】take a share of the spoils or profits
【分忧】share sb.'s cares and burdens
【分赃】divide the spoils；share the booty (or loot)
【分支】branch；subfield；offtake
【分子】❶〈化〉molecule ❷〈数〉numerator(in a fraction)
【分组】❶divide into groups ❷grouping；subgroup；block sort；curtate

芬^(fēn) sweet smell；fragrance

【芬芳】❶sweet-smelling；fragrant ❷fragrance
【芬兰】Finland

吩^(fēn)

【吩咐】〈口〉❶tell；instruct ❷instructions

纷^(fēn) ❶confused；tangled；disorderly ❷many and various；profuse；numerous

【纷繁】numerous and complicated
【纷飞】(of thick-falling snowflakes, flowers, etc.) swirl in the air；fly all over
【纷纷】❶one after another；in succession ❷numerous and confused
【纷纷扬扬】(of snowflakes, flowers, leaves, etc.) flying or fluttering in profusion
【纷乱】numerous and disorderly

【纷扰】confusion；turmoil

【纷纭】diverse and confused

【纷杂】numerous and disorderly

【纷争】dispute；wrangle

【纷至沓来】come thick and fast；keep pouring in

氛 (fēn)

【氛围】atmosphere

F

坟 (fén) grave；tomb

【坟地】graveyard；cemetery

【坟墓】grave；tomb

【坟头】grave mound

焚 (fén) burn

【焚化】incinerate；cremate

【焚毁】destroy by fire；burn down

【焚烧】burn；set on fire

粉 (fěn) ❶ powder ❷ cosmetics in powder form ❸ noodles or vermicelli made from bean，etc. ❹ whitewash ❺ white ❻ pink

【粉笔】chalk

【粉刺】〈医〉acne

【粉底霜】foundation cream

【粉红】pink

【粉剂】powder；dust

【粉末】powder

【粉墨登场】make oneself up and go on stage—embark upon a political venture

【粉身碎骨】have one's body smashed to pieces and one's bones ground to powder；die the most cruel death

【粉饰太平】present a false picture of peace and prosperity

【粉丝】vermicelli made from bean starch，etc.

【粉碎】❶ smash；shatter；crush ❷ broken to pieces

【粉条】noodles made from bean or sweet potato starch

分 (fèn) ❶ component ❷ what is within one's rights or duty

另见 fēn

【分量】weight

【分内】one's job

【分外】❶ particularly；especially ❷ not one's job

【分子】member；element

份 (fèn) share；part；portion

【份儿】〈口〉degree extent：到这～上你该死心了。You should give up when things have come to this.

【份额】share；portion

【份子】❶ one's share of expenses for a joint undertaking as in buying a gift for a mutual friend ❷ a gift of money

奋 (fèn) ❶ exert oneself；act vigorously ❷ raise；lift

【奋不顾身】dash ahead regardless of one's safety

【奋斗】struggle；fight；strive

【奋发】rouse oneself；exert oneself

【奋发图强】make efforts；go all out to make the country strong

【奋击】strike out with great force；make a spirited attack

【奋袂而起】〈书〉throw up the sleeves and rise—get ready for action

【奋起直追】do all one can to catch up

【奋然】energetic animated

【奋勇】summon up all one's courage and energy

【奋战】fight bravely

粪 (fèn) ❶ excrement；faeces；dung；droppings ❷〈书〉apply manure ❸〈书〉clear away；wipe out

【粪便】excrement and urine；night soil

【粪池】manure pit

【粪土】dung and dirt；muck

愤 (fèn) indignation；anger；resentment

【愤恨】resent；detest

【愤激】excited and indignant；roused to indignation

【愤慨】〈书〉(righteous) indignation

【愤怒】anger；wrath

【愤然】angry；indignant

feng

丰 (fēng) ❶ abundant；plentiful ❷ great ❸ fine-looking；handsome

【丰碑】❶ monument ❷ monumental work

【丰产】high yield；bumper crop

【丰富】rich；abundant

【丰满】❶ plentiful ❷ full and round；well-developed ❸ chubby (cheeks，face)；plump (figure)

【丰茂】luxuriant；lush

【丰年】a bumper harvest year；a good year

【丰饶】rich and fertile

【丰润】plump and smooth-skinned

【丰盛】sumptuous

【丰收】bumper harvest

【丰足】abundant；plentiful

风 (fēng) ❶ wind ❷ put out to dry or air ❸ winnow ❹ style；practice；custom ❺ scene；

view ❻news；information ❼romoured；groundless

【风暴】windstorm；storm

【风波】disturbance

【风采】〈书〉graceful bearing

【风餐露宿】eat in the wind and sleep in the dew—endure the hardships of an arduous journey

【风潮】agitation；unrest

【风车】❶windmill ❷winnower；winnow ❸pinwheel（a child's toy）

【风尘】❶wind and dust—travel fatigue ❷hardships or uncertainties in an unstable society，esp. in the officials' circle ❸the life of a prostitute ❹〈书〉chaos caused by war

【风尘仆仆】have endured the hardships of a long journey；be travel-stained；be travel-worn and weary

【风驰电掣】swift as the wind and quick as lightning

【风吹草动】❶the rustle of leaves in the wind ❷a sign of disturbance or trouble

【风吹雨打】be buffeted by wind and rain；be exposed to the weather

【风度】demeanor；bearing

【风度翩翩】（of a young man）have an elegant and smart carriage

【风发】❶swift as the wind ❷energetic

【风风雨雨】❶difficulties and hardships ❷groundless gossip

【风干】air-dry：木材经过～可以防止腐烂。Airdrying can prevent wood rotting away.

【风格】style；manner；mode

【风光】scene；view；sight

【风寒】chill；cold

【风和日丽】a bright sun and a gentle breeze；warm and sunny weather

【风化】morals and manners；decency

【风景】scenery；landscape

【风景画】landscape painting

【风浪】❶stormy waves；storm ❷a stormy experience

【风凉】cool：大家坐在～的地方休息。All of us were sitting in a cool place for a rest.

【风流】❶distinguished and admirable ❷talented and romantic ❸dissolute；loose

【风貌】❶style and features ❷view；scene ❸elegant appearance and bearing

【风靡】fashionable

【风气】general mood；atmosphere；common（or established）practice

【风琴】organ：弹～ play the organ

【风趣】humour；wit

【风色】❶how the wind blows ❷how things stand

【风扇】electric fan；fan

【风势】❶the force or speed of the wind ❷situation；circumstances

【风俗】custom

【风土】natural conditions and social customs of a place

【风味】special flavour；local colour（or flavour）

【风险】risk；hazard

封

（fēng）❶confer（a little，territory，etc.）upon ❷seal ❸wrapper；envelope ❹for sth. envelope

【封闭】❶seal ❷seal off；close

【封底】〈印〉back cover

【封冻】（of a river，the ground，etc.）freeze

【封口】seal；heal

【封面】〈印〉front cover；the front and back cover of a book

【封皮】〈方〉paper wrapping

【封山】seal（or close）a mountain pass

【封锁】block；blockade；seal off

【封条】paper strip seal

【封印】seal；sealing stamp

【封装】seal and package

疯

（fēng）mad；insane；crazy

【疯话】mad talk；ravings；nonsense

【疯狂】❶insane ❷frenzied；unbridled

【疯子】lunatic；madman

峰

（fēng）❶peak；summit；crest ❷hump

【峰巅】mountain peak；summit

【峰回路转】the path winds through high peaks

【峰峦】ridges and peaks

烽

（fēng）beacon

【烽火】❶beacon-fire（used to give border alarm in ancient times）；beacon ❷flames of war

【烽火连天】flames of battle raging everywhere

【烽烟】beacon-fire；beacon

锋

（fēng）❶a sharp point or cutting edge（of a knife，sword，etc. ）❷vanguard ❸front

【锋快】❶（of a knife，sword，etc. ）sharp；keen ❷penetrating；incisive；sharp

【锋利】❶sharp；keen ❷incisive；sharp；poignant

【锋芒】❶cutting edge；spearhead ❷talent displayed；abilities

【锋芒逼人】trenchant；poignant

F

【锋芒毕露】make a display of one's abilities

【锋锐】❶（of a knife, sword, etc.）sharp; keen ❷penetrating; incisive; sharp ❸a person's impulsive force; drive; push

蜂 （fēng）❶wasp ❷bee ❸in swarms

【蜂巢】honeycomb

【蜂房】any of the six-sided wax cells in a honeycomb

【蜂蜜】honey

【蜂鸟】hummingbird

【蜂王】❶queen bee ❷queen wasp

【蜂王精】royal jelly

【蜂窝】honeycomb

【蜂箱】beehive; hive

【蜂拥】swarm; flock: 车门一开,乘客～而上。As soon as the door opened, passengers swarmed onto the bus.

【蜂拥而来】come swarming; swarm forward

逢 （féng）meet; come upon

【逢场作戏】join in the fun on occasion

【逢年过节】on New Year's Day or other festivals

【逢人说项】praise a person before everybody

【逢凶化吉】turn calamities into blessings; turn ill luck into good

【逢迎】fawn on; curry favour with: 阿谀～ flatter and toady

缝 （féng）stitch; sew 另见 fèng

【缝补】sew and mend: ～衣服 mend clothes

【缝合】〈医〉suture, sew up（a wound, an incision）

【缝纫】sewing; tailoring

【缝纫机】sewing machine

【缝线】〈医〉suture

【缝制】make（clothes, bedding, etc.）

讽 （fěng）❶satirize; mock ❷〈书〉chant; intone

【讽嘲】❶satirize; mock ❷〈书〉chant; intone

【讽刺】satirize

【讽刺画】caricature

【讽喻】parable; allegory

凤 （fèng）phoenix

【凤蝶】swallowtail butterfly; swallowtail

【凤凰】phoenix

【凤梨】pineapple（the plant and its fruit）

【凤毛麟角】rarity of rarities

奉 （fèng）❶give or present with respect ❷receive（orders, etc.）❸believe in ❹esteem ❺wait upon; attend to

【奉承】flatter; fawn upon; toady

【奉公守法】be law-abiding

【奉还】〈套〉return sth. with thanks

【奉命】act under orders

【奉陪】〈套〉keep sb. company

【奉劝】〈套〉offer a piece of advice

【奉送】〈套〉offer as a gift

【奉献】present with all respect

【奉行】pursue（a policy, etc.）

【奉养】support and wait upon（one's parents, etc.）

【奉旨】by order of the emperor; by imperial decree

俸 （fèng）pay; salary

【俸禄】〈古〉an official's salary; government salary

缝 （fèng）❶seam ❷crack; crevice 另见 féng

【缝隙】gap; slit; chink; crack; crevice

fo

佛 （fó）❶ Buddha ❷ Buddhism ❸ image of Buddha

【佛法】❶ Buddha dharma; Buddhist doctrine ❷ power of Buddha

【佛教】Buddhism

【佛寺】Buddhist temple

【佛像】statue of Buddha

【佛学】Buddhist

【佛祖】Buddhist patriarch

fou

缶 （fǒu）❶〈书〉a narrow-necked earthen jar ❷an ancient percussion instrument made of clay

否 （fǒu）❶ negate; deny ❷ turn down ❸ whether or not

【否定】negate; deny

【否决】veto; vote down; overrule

【否决权】veto power; veto

【否认】deny; repudiate

【否则】otherwise; if not; or else

fu

夫 （fū）❶husband ❷a manual worker ❸person pressed into service

【夫妇】husband and wife

【夫妻】husband and wife

【夫权】authority of the husband

【夫人】❶ Lady;Madam;Mrs. ❷ a lady of high rank ❸〈套〉wife

【夫子】❶〈古〉(a respectful term of address for a scholar or a teacher) master ❷〈古〉my husband ❸pedant

肤 (fū) skin

【肤浅】superficial;shallow

【肤色】colour of skin

孵 (fū) hatch;brood;incubate

【孵化】hatch;incubate

【孵育】hatch;incubate

敷 (fū) ❶ apply(powder,ointment,etc.) ❷ spread;layout ❸be sufficient for

【敷贴】apply ointment or plaster (to an affected part of the body)

【敷衍】〈书〉be perfunctory

伏 (fú) ❶lean over;bend over ❷lie prostrate ❸subside;go down ❹hide ❺admit ❻the hottest days of the year

【伏安】〈电〉volt-ampere

【伏笔】a hint foreshadowing later developments in a story essay,etc. ;foreshadowing

【伏兵】(troops in) ambush

【伏法】be executed

【伏击】ambush

【伏暑】the torrid weather of the year's hottest days

【伏天】the hottest summer days

【伏贴】fit perfectly

扶 (fú) ❶support with the hand;place a hand on sb. or sth. for support ❷ help;assist;support

【扶病】(do sth.) in spite of illness

【扶持】❶support sb. with one's hand;help sb. to stand or walk ❷help sustain;give aid to;support

【扶老携幼】holding the old by the arm and the young by the hand;bringing along the old and the young

【扶手】❶handrail;rail;banisters ❷ armrest

【扶危济困】help those in distress and aid those in peril

【扶养】provide for;support and assist

【扶植】foster;prop up

【扶助】help;assist;support

拂 (fú) ❶stroke ❷whisk;flick

【拂荡】sway gently;swing slightly;wave gracefully

【拂动】brush against;stroke;caress

【拂拭】whisk or wipe off

【拂晓】daybreak;dawn

【拂袖而去】leave with a flick of one's sleeve;go off in a huff

服 (fú) ❶clothes;dress ❷take(medicine) ❸ serve ❹ be convinced;obey ❺ by accustomed to

【服从】obey;submit (oneself) to;be subject to;be subordinated to

【服毒】take poison

【服法】submit to the law

【服气】be convinced

【服劲】be amenable to

【服丧】be in mourning (for the death of a kinsman,etc.)

【服饰】dress and personal adornment;dress

【服侍】wait upon;attend

【服输】admit defeat;acknowledge defeat

【服帖】❶docile;submissive ❷ be convinced;fitting;well arranged

【服务】give service to;be in the service of

【服务员】attendant

【服刑】serve a sentence

【服药】take medicine

【服役】enlist in the army;be on active service

【服用】take (medicine)

【服装】dress;clothing;costume

【服罪】plead guilty;admit one's guilt

俘 (fú) ❶capture;take prisoner ❷prisoner of war;captive

【俘获】capture;seize

【俘虏】❶ capture;take prisoner ❷ captive;captured personnel;prisoner of war (P. O. W.)

浮 (fú) ❶float ❷swim ❸on the surface;superficial ❹ shallow and frivolous;superficial ❺hollow;inflated ❻excessive;surplus

【浮标】buoy

【浮冰】floating ice

【浮尘】floating dust;surface dust

【浮沉】now sink,now emerge;drift along

【浮雕】relief sculpture

【浮动】❶float;drift ❷unsteady;fluctuate

【浮华】showy;ostentatious;flashy

【浮夸】be boastful;exaggerate

【浮力】〈物〉buoyancy

【浮浅】superficial;shallow

【浮桥】pontoon bridge;floating bridge

【浮生若梦】this fleeting life of ours is like an

empty dream
【浮水】swim
【浮现】appear before one's eyes
【浮想】❶thoughts flashing across one's mind ❷recollections
【浮云】floating clouds
【浮肿】〈医〉dropsy；edema

符〈fú〉❶a tally issued by a ruler to generals，envoys，etc．，as credentials in ancient China ❷symbol ❸tally with；accord with
【符号】symbol；mark；sign；insignia
【符合】accord with；tally with；conform to；be in keeping with：～事实 tally with the reality
【符节】a tally used in ancient times as credentials or a warrant
【符咒】Taoist magic figures or incantations

幅〈fú〉❶width of cloth ❷size ❸〈量〉for cloth，picture，etc．
【幅度】range；scope；extent
【幅面】width of cloth：～宽 double-width cloth
【幅员】the area of a country's territory；the size of a country
【幅员辽阔】（a country）with a vast expanse；（a country）with a vast territory

辐〈fú〉spoke（of a wheel）
【辐射】❶radiate（from a central point）❷〈物〉radiation
【辐射体】radiant body
【辐照】〈物〉irradiation

福〈fú〉good fortune；blessing；happiness
【福分】〈口〉good luck；good fortune；a happy lot：有～ fortunate；lucky
【福利】welfare；material benefits；well-being
【福气】happy lot；good fortune
【福相】a face showing good fortune
【福星】lucky star；mascot

抚〈fǔ〉❶comfort；console ❷nurture；foster ❸stroke
【抚爱】caress；fondle
【抚摩】stroke
【抚慰】comfort；console；soothe
【抚恤】comfort and compensate a bereaved family
【抚养】foster；bring up；raise
【抚育】foster；nurture；tend

斧〈fǔ〉axe；hatchet
【斧凿】❶hatchet and chisel ❷conscious artistry

（in literary works）
【斧正】〈套〉（please）make corrections
【斧子】axe；hatchet

俯〈fǔ〉bow（one's head）
【俯冲】dive
【俯瞰】look down at；overlook
【俯身】bend over；bend down
【俯视】look down at；overlook
【俯首】bow one's head（in submission）
【俯卧】lie prostrate；lie face down（on the ground）

辅〈fǔ〉assist；complement；supplement
【辅弼】〈书〉assist a ruler in governing a country
【辅车相依】as dependent on each other as the jowls and the jawbone；as close as the jowls and the jaws
【辅导】give guidance in study or training；coach
【辅料】subsidiary material；supplementary material
【辅音】〈语〉consonant
【辅助】❶assist ❷supplementary；auxiliary

腐〈fǔ〉❶rotten；stale；decayed ❷bean curd
【腐败】❶rotten；decayed；putrid（food）❷corrupt
【腐恶】corrupt and evil
【腐化】❶degenerate；corrupt；dissolute ❷rot；decay
【腐烂】decomposed；putrid
【腐蚀】〈化〉❶corrode；etch ❷corrupt
【腐刑】castration as a punishment
【腐朽】❶rotten；decayed ❷decadent；degenerate

父〈fù〉❶father ❷male relative of a senior generation
【父辈】elder generation
【父老】elders（of a country or district）
【父母】father and mother
【父兄】❶father and elder brothers ❷head of a family
【父子】father and son

付〈fù〉❶hand（or turn）over to；commit to ❷pay
【付出】pay；expend
【付方】credit side；credit
【付款】pay a sum of money
【付清】pay in full；pay off；clear（a bill）
【付息】pay interest
【付之一炬】commit to the flames

负 (fù) ❶carry on the back or shoulder;shoulder;bear ❷have at one's back;rely on ❸suffer ❹enjoy ❺owe ❻fail in one's duty,obligation,etc. ❼lose(a battle,game,etc.); be defeated ❽〈数〉minus;negative ❾〈电〉negative

【负担】 ❶ bear (a burden); shoulder ❷ burden;load

【负电子】electron;negatron

【负荷】〈书〉load

【负累】❶burden;load;encumbrance ❷〈古〉implicate;involve

【负伤】be wounded;be injured

【负心】ungrateful(esp. in love);untrue;heartless

【负责】be responsible for;be in charge of;负责人 person in charge;leading cadre

【负债】❶be in debt;incur debts ❷liabilities

【负重】bear a heavy burden

【负重致远】bear a heavy burden and go a long way—shoulder heavy responsibilities

妇 (fù) ❶woman ❷married woman ❸wife

【妇道】female virtues

【妇科】(department of) gynaecology

【妇女】woman

【妇人】married woman

【妇幼】women and children

附 (fù) ❶add;attach;enclose ❷get close to; be near ❸agree to

【附带】❶in passing ❷attach ❸subsidiary;supplementary

【附和】echo;chime in with

【附会】draw wrong conclusions by false analogy;strain one's interpretation

【附加】❶add;attach ❷additional;attached;appended

【附件】❶appendix;annex ❷enclosure ❸accessories;attachment;fitting;modification kit;❹ adnexa;adnexal

【附近】❶nearby;neighbouring ❷close to;in the vicinity of

【附录】appendix

【附设】have as an attached institution

【附身】(of an evil spirit, demon, etc.) possess a person

【附属】subsidiary;auxiliary

【附注】notes appended to a book,etc.; annotations

【附着】adhere to;stick to

赴 (fù) go to;attend

【赴会】attend a meeting; keep an appointment (to meet sb.)

【赴任】go to one's post; be on the way to one's post

【赴汤蹈火】go through fire and water

【赴宴】go to a feast;attend a banquet

【赴约】keep an appointment

复 (fù) ❶compound; complex ❷turn round; turn over ❸answer; reply ❹resume;recover ❺again

【复本】duplicate

【复辟】❶restoration of a dethroned monarch ❷ restoration of the old order

【复查】check;reexamine

【复仇】revenge;avenge

【复电】❶send a telegram in reply ❷a telegram in reply

【复返】return

【复方】〈中医〉❶ a prescription composed of two or more recipes of herbal medicines ❷ medicine made of two or more ingredients; compound

【复合】compound; complex; composite;〈语〉 compound (word)

【复核】❶ check ❷〈法〉(of the Supreme People's Court) review a case in which a death sentence has been passed by a lower court

【复活】bring back to life; revive

【复审】❶reexamine ❷〈法〉review a case;retrial

【复视】diplopia;double vision;ambiopia

【复述】repeat(an order); retell(a story)

【复苏】❶resuscitate ❷recovery

【复习】review; revise

【复现】reappear

【复写】make carbon copies;duplicate

【复信】❶write a letter in reply; reply ❷a letter in reply

【复兴】revive; rejuvenate

【复印】〈印〉duplicate

【复员】demobilize

【复杂】complicated;complex

【复职】resume one's post; be reinstated

【复制】duplicate;make a copy of

副 (fù) ❶deputy; assistant; vice ❷auxiliary; subsidiary;secondary ❸correspond to;fit

【副本】transcript; copy

【副标题】subheading; subtitle

【副产品】by-product

【副词】adverb

【副官】adjutant; aide-decamp

【副刊】supplement

F

【副品】substandard goods
【副食】non-staple food
【副手】assistant
【副题】subtitle；subheading
【副业】sideline；side occupation
【副职】deputy post
【副作用】side effect；by-effect

富 （fù）rich；wealthy；abundant

【富贵】riches and honour
【富国强兵】make the country rich and its military force efficient
【富豪】rich and powerful people
【富农】rich peasant
【富强】prosperous and strong
【富饶】fertile；abundant
【富人】the rich；rich people
【富翁】man of wealth
【富有】❶rich；wealthy ❷rich in；full of
【富裕】prosperous；well-off
【富源】natural resources

【富足】plentiful；rich

腹 （fù）belly；abdomen；stomach

【腹地】hinterland
【腹稿】a draft worked out in one's mind
【腹痛】abdominal pain
【腹心】❶vital organs；key parts ❷trusted subordinate；reliable agent ❸true thoughts and feelings

覆 （fù）〈书〉❶cover ❷overturn；upset

【覆盖】❶cover ❷plant cover；vegetation
【覆灭】destruction；collapse
【覆没】❶〈书〉capsize and sink ❷be overwhelmed；be annihilated
【覆亡】fall（of an empire，nation，etc.）

馥 （fù）〈书〉fragrance

【馥郁】〈书〉strongly fragrant；sweet-scented；sweet-smelling

G g

ga

夹 (gā)
另见 jiā,jiá

【夹肢窝】armpit

嘎 (gā)〈象〉a loud,high-pitched sound

【嘎嘎】〈象〉the quacking sound made by a duck; quack

【嘎吱】〈象〉(usu. reduplicated) the creaking sound of objects that are under great stress

gai

改 (gǎi) ❶ change; transform ❷ alter; revise ❸ correct; rectify; put right

【改编】❶ adapt; rearrange; revise ❷ reorganize; redesignate

【改变】change; alter; transform

【改朝换代】change dynasties (regime); substitute a new regime for the old

【改道】❶ change one's route ❷ (of a river) change its course

【改掉】give up; drop

【改动】change; alter; modify

【改革】reform

【改换】change over to; change

【改嫁】remarry

【改建】reconstruct; rebuild

【改进】improve; make better

【改良】❶improve; ameliorate ❷reform

【改善】improve; ameliorate

【改邪归正】give up vice and return to virtue; turn over a new leaf

【改写】rewrite; adapt

【改选】reelect

【改造】transform; reform

【改正】correct; amend; put right

【改装】❶ change one's costume or dress ❷ repack; repackage ❸modify; refit; reequip

【改组】reorganize; reshuffle

钙 (gài)〈化〉calcium (Ca)

【钙化】〈医〉calcify

盖 (gài) ❶ lid; cover ❷ shell ❸ put a cover on; cover ❹surpass; top ❺build

【盖棺论定】final judgment can be passed on a person only when the lid is on his coffin; no final verdict can be pronounced on a man until after his death

【盖世】〈书〉unparalleled; matchless; peerless

【盖世无双】unparalleled anywhere on earth; matchless throughout the world; peerless; unrivalled

【盖世英雄】a peerless (or matchless) hero

【盖章】affix one's seal; seal; stamp

【盖子】❶ lid; cover; cap; top ❷ shell (of a tortoise, etc.)

概 (gài) ❶general idea; broad outline ❷ generally; approximately ❸ without exception ❹the manner of carrying oneself; deportment

【概况】general situation; survey

【概括】❶ summarize; generalize; epitomize ❷ briefly; in broad outline

【概率】〈数〉probability

【概略】outline; summary

【概论】outline; introduction

【概貌】general picture

【概念】concept; conception; notion; idea

【概述】give a brief account of (an event, etc.)

【概要】(usu. used in book titles) essentials; outline

gan

干 (gān) ❶ shield ❷ offend ❸ have to do sth. ; be concerned with; be implicated in ❹ dry ❺empty; hollow ❻ take into nominal kinship ❼dried food
另见 gàn

【干巴巴】dull and dry; insipid; dryasdust; dull as ditchwater

【干杯】drink a toast

【干瘪】❶dry ❷ shrivelled; wizened ❸ (of writing) dull;drab;dryasdust

【干菜】dried vegetable

【干草】hay

【干脆】❶ clear-cut; straightforward; not mince one's words ❷ simply;just;altogether

【干戈】weapons of war;war

【干旱】(of weather or soil) dry

【干涸】dry up;run dry

【干净】❶ clean; neat and tidy ❷ completely;totally

【干咳】have a dry cough

【干枯】dried-up;withered;shrivelled;wizened

【干冷】dry and cold (weather)

【干粮】solid food(prepared for journey);rations for journey

【干裂】crack because of dryness; be dry and cracked

【干扰】❶disturb;interfere;obstruct ❷〈电〉interference;jam

【干涉】interfere;intervene;meddle

【干洗】dry-clean;dry cleaning

【干预】intervene;interpose;meddle

【干燥】❶dry;arid;❷dull;uninteresting

【干着急】be anxious but unable to do anything

甘 (gān) ❶ sweet; pleasant ❷ willingly; of one's own accord

【甘拜下风】candidly admit defeat (in friendly competition,etc.)

【甘苦】❶ sweetness and bitterness; weal and woe; joys and sorrows ❷ hardships and difficulties experienced in work

【甘露】❶sweet dew ❷〈药〉manna

【甘美】sweet and refreshing

【甘薯】sweet potato

【甘甜】sweet

【甘心】❶willingly;readily ❷resign oneself to

【甘于】be willing to

【甘愿】do sth willingly

【甘蔗】sugarcane

肝 (gān) liver

【肝胆】❶ open-heartedness; sincerity ❷ heroic spirit;courage

【肝胆相照】(of friends) treat each other with all sincerity; be devoted to each other heart and soul

【肝功能】liver function

【肝火】irascibility

【肝炎】hepatitis

【肝脏】liver

柑 (gān) mandarin orange

【柑橘】❶oranges and tangerines ❷citrus

竿 (gān) pole;rod

【竿子】bamboo pole

尴 (gān)

【尴尬】awkward;embarrassed

杆 (gān) ❶ the shaft or arm of sth. ❷〈量〉(for a long and thin cylindrical object)

【杆秤】steelyard

【杆菌】bacillus

赶 (gǎn) ❶catch up with;overtake ❷ hurry (or rush) through ❸ drive ❹ drive away; expel ❺happen to;find oneself in;avail oneself of

【赶场】〈方〉go to the village fair or market

【赶超】catch up with and surpass

【赶车】drive a cart

【赶集】go to market;go to a fair

【赶紧】hastily;without losing time

【赶快】at once;quickly

【赶忙】hurry;make haste

【赶上】❶overtake;catch up with;keep pace with ❷run into (a situation);be in time for

【赶时髦】follow the fashion;try to be in style

【赶早】do sth. as early as possible

敢 (gǎn) ❶ bold; courageous; daring ❷ be brave enough;dare ❸be certain;be sure ❹ make bold; venture ❺perhaps;I'm afraid

【敢于】dare to; be bold; have the courage to

【敢作敢为】bold and decisive in action

感 (gǎn) ❶ feel; sense ❷ move; touch; affect ❸be grateful; be obliged ❹ be affected ❺ feeling;impressions

【感触】thoughts and feelings

【感到】feel;sense

【感动】move;touch

【感恩戴德】be deeply grateful; be overwhelmed with gratitude

【感官】sense organ;sensory organ

【感光】sensitization

【感激】feel grateful;be thankful;feel indebted

【感激涕零】shed grateful tears;be moved to tears of gratitude

【感觉】❶sense;perception;sensation;feeling ❷ feel;perceive;become aware of

【感慨】sigh with emotion

【感冒】common cold

【感情】emotion；feeling；sentiment

【感情用事】give oneself over to blind emotions

【感染】❶infect ❷influence；affect

【感人】touching；moving

【感人肺腑】touch one deeply in the heart

【感叹号】exclamation mark

【感同身受】〈套〉I shall appreciate it as a personal favour（said when making a request on behalf of a friend）

【感悟】come to realize

【感想】impressions；reflections；thoughts

【感谢】thank；be grateful

【感性】perceptual

【感应】❶ response；reaction；interaction ❷
〈物〉induction

橄 (gǎn)

【橄榄】〈植〉❶Chinese olive（Canarium album）；
the fruit of the canary tree ❷olive

【橄榄球】〈体〉rugby；American football

干 (gàn) ❶trunk；main part ❷cadre ❸do；
work ❹capable；able
另见 gān

【干部】cadre

【干掉】〈口〉kill；get rid of

【干活】work on a job

【干将】capable person；go-getter

【干劲】drive；vigour；enthusiasm

【干练】capable and experienced

【干流】trunk stream；main stream

【干事】clerical worker in charge of sth.

【干线】main line；trunk line

gang

刚 (gāng) ❶ firm； strong； indomitable ❷
just；exactly ❸ barely；only；just ❹ only a
short while ago just

【刚愎自用】self-willed；headstrong；opinionated

【刚才】just now；a moment ago

【刚刚】❶ just；only；exactly ❷ a moment ago；
just now

【刚好】❶ just；exactly ❷ happen to；it so happened that

【刚劲】bold；vigorous；sturdy

【刚烈】fiery and forthright；upright and unyielding

【刚强】firm；staunch

【刚毅】resolute and steadfast

【刚正】upright；honourable

【刚正不阿】upright and above flattery

【刚直】upright and outspoken

肛 (gāng) anus

【肛门】anus

纲 (gāng) ❶the headrope of a fishing net ❷
key link；guiding principle ❸outline；pro-
gram ❹〈生〉class

【纲举目张】once the headrope of a fishing net is
pulled up，all its meshes open—once the key
link is grasped，everything falls into place

【纲领】programme；guiding principle

【纲目】（usu. used in book titles）detailed outline
（of a subject）；outline

【纲要】❶outline；sketch ❷essentials；compendi-
um

钢 (gāng) steel

【钢板】❶steel plate；plate ❷spring（of a motor-
car，etc.）❸stencil steel board

【钢笔】pen；fountain pen

【钢材】steel products；steels；rolled steel

【钢管】steel tube（or pipe）

【钢轨】rail

【钢筋】reinforcing bar

【钢锯】hacksaw

【钢盔】（steel）helmet

【钢琴】piano

【钢丝】（steel）wire

【钢铁】iron and steel；steel

缸 (gāng) ❶vat；jar；crock ❷a compound of
sand，clay，etc. for making earthenware ❸a
jar-shaped vessel

【缸盆】glazed earthen basin

【缸子】mug；bowl

岗 (gǎng) ❶hillock；mound ❷sentry；guard
❸ridge

【岗警】policeman on point duty

【岗楼】watchtower

【岗哨】❶lookout post ❷sentry

【岗亭】sentry box

【岗位】post；station

港 (gǎng) port；harbour

【港口】port；harbour

【港湾】harbour

杠 (gàng) ❶ a thick stick ❷ bar ❸ cross
out；delete

【杠棒】a stout carrying pole

【杠杆】lever

【杠铃】barbell

gao

高（gāo）❶ tall；high ❷ of a high level or degree；above the average ❸ high priced；dear；expensive

【高矮】height

【高昂】❶ hold high（one's head，etc.）❷ high；elated；exalted ❸ dear；expensive；exorbitant

【高傲】supercilious；arrogant；haughty

【高不可攀】too high to reach；unattainable

【高产】high yield；high production

【高潮】❶ high tide；high water ❷ upsurge；high tide ❸（of fiction，drama and films）climax

【高大】❶ tall and big；tall；❷ lofty

【高等】higher

【高低杠】〈体〉uneven（parallel）bars

【高地】❶ high-land；upland；elevation ❷ height

【高调】lofty tone；high-sounding words

【高度】❶ altitude；height ❷ a high degree

【高分子】〈化〉high polymer

【高峰】peak；summit；height

【高歌】sing heartily

【高贵】❶ noble；high ❷ highly privileged

【高级】❶ senior；high-ranking；high-level；high ❷ high-quality；advanced

【高价】high price

【高举】hold high；hold aloft

【高亢】loud and sonorous；resounding

【高考】college entrance examination

【高空】high altitude；upper air

【高利贷】usury；usurious loan

【高粱】kaoliang；Chinese sorghum

【高明】brilliant；wise

【高攀】make friends or claim ties of kinship with someone of a higher social position；a great gathering of distinguished guests

【高尚】noble；lofty

【高深】advanced；profound

【高深莫测】too profound to be understood

【高速】high speed

【高抬贵手】be magnanimous；be generous；not be too hard on sb.

【高谈阔论】indulge in loud and empty talk；talk volubly or bombastically

【高位】a high position

【高温】high temperature

【高下】relative superiority or inferiority

【高兴】glad；happy；cheerful

【高瞻远瞩】stand high and see far

【高涨】rise；upsurge

【高枕无忧】shake up the pillow and have a good sleep；sit back and relax

【高中】short for 高级中学（senior middle school）

【高姿态】lofty stance；magnanimous attitude

羔（gāo）lamb；kid；fawn

【羔羊】❶ lamb ❷ an innocent and helpless person or a scapegoat

膏（gāo）❶ fat；grease；oil ❷ paste；cream；ointment

【膏粱】〈文〉fat meat and fine grain；rich food

糕（gāo）cake；pudding

【糕点】cake；pastry

搞（gǎo）❶ do；carry on；be engaged in ❷ cause；make；produce；work out ❸ set up；start；organize ❹ get；get hold of；secure

【搞错】mistake

【搞法】way of doing or making a thing；method

【搞鬼】play tricks

【搞好】make a good job of；do well

【搞坏】damage；impair；spoil

【搞活】vitalize；enliven

【搞糟】mess up；make a mess（of）

稿（gǎo）❶ draft；sketch；❷ a rough draft（of a document）

【稿本】manuscript（of a book，etc.）

【稿费】payment for an article or book published；contribution fee；author's remuneration

【稿件】manuscript；contribution

【稿纸】standardized writing paper with squares or lines

【稿子】❶ draft；sketch；写～ draft an article ❷ manuscript；contribution ❸ idea；plan

告（gào）❶ tell；inform；notify ❷ accuse；go to law against；bring an action against ❸ ask for；request；solicit ❹ declare；announce

【告白】a public notice or announcement

【告别】❶ leave；part from ❷ bid farewell to；say good-bye to

【告辞】take leave（of one's host）

【告假】ask for leave

【告诫】warn；再三～ repeated exhortation

【告密】inform against sb.

【告示】official notice；bulletin；placard

【告诉】tell；let know

【告退】ask for leave to withdraw from a meeting

【告慰】❶ comfort；console ❷ feel relieved

【告知】inform；notify

【告终】come to an end;end up;conclude
【告状】〈口〉❶go to law against sb. ❷lodge a complaint against sb. with his superior

ge

戈（gē）dagger-axe

【戈壁】〈地〉❶Gobi ❷the Gobi Desert

疙（gē）

【疙瘩】❶pimple;lump ❷knot ❸a knot in one's heart

哥（gē）❶(elder)brother ❷a friendly term of address for male older acquaintances

【哥哥】(elder) brother
【哥伦比亚】Colombia
【哥特式】〈建〉Gothic

胳（gē）

【胳臂】arm
【胳膊】arm

鸽（gē）pigeon;dove

【鸽哨】a whistle tied to a pigeon

搁（gē）❶put ❷put aside;leave over;shelve

【搁笔】lay down the pen or brush;stop writing or painting
【搁浅】❶run aground;be stranded ❷reach a deadlock
【搁置】shelve;lay aside;pigeonhole

割（gē）cut;sever

【割爱】give up what one treasures
【割除】cut off;excise
【割地】cede territory
【割断】sever;cut off
【割据】set up a separatist regime by force of arms
【割裂】cut apart;separate
【割让】cede
【割舍】give up

歌（gē）❶song ❷sing

【歌本】songbook
【歌唱】sing
【歌词】words of a song
【歌喉】(singer's)voice;singing voice
【歌剧】opera
【歌谱】music score of a song;music of a song
【歌曲】song

【歌声】sound of singing;singing
【歌手】singer;vocalist
【歌颂】sing the praises of;extol;eulogize
【歌舞】song and dance
【歌舞升平】sing and dance to extol the good times—put on a show of peace and prosperity
【歌星】a singing star;accomplished vocalist
【歌谣】ballad;folksong;nursery rhyme
【歌咏】singing

革（gé）❶leather;hide ❷change;transform ❸remove sb. from office;expel

【革除】❶abolish;get rid of;～陋习 eliminate irrational practices ❷expel;dismiss;remove sb. from office
【革故鼎新】discard the old and introduce the new
【革命】revolution
【革命家】revolutionary;revolutionist
【革新】innovation
【革职】remove from office;cashier
【革制品】leather goods

阁（gé）❶pavilion（usu. two-storeyed）❷cabinet（of a government）❸old boudoir ❹〈书〉shelf

【阁楼】attic;loft;garret
【阁下】〈敬〉Your Excellency or His or Her Excellency

格（gé）❶squares formed by crossed lines;check ❷standard;pattern;style ❸character;quality;demeanor ❹fight

【格调】❶(literary or artistic) style ❷〈书〉one's style of work as well as one's moral quality
【格斗】grapple;wrestle;fistfight
【格格不入】incompatible with;out of tune with;out of one's element;like a square peg in a round hole
【格局】pattern;setup;structure
【格式】form;pattern
【格外】especially;all the more
【格物】investigate things;study the world
【格言】maxim;motto;aphorism
【格子】cell;lattice;check

隔（gé）❶separate;cut off;partition ❷be apart from;be at a distance from

【隔壁】next door
【隔断】cut off;separate;obstruct
【隔行】of different trades or professions
【隔绝】cut off;separate;obstruct
【隔离】keep apart;isolate;segregate
【隔膜】❶lack of mutual understanding ❷be un-

familiar with

【隔墙有耳】someone may be listening on the other side of the wall

【隔靴搔痒】scratch an itch from outside one's boot—fail to get to the root of the matter; fail to strike home; take totally ineffective measures

【隔夜】of the previous night

【隔音】give sound insulation

个 (gè) individual

【个别】❶ individual; specific ❷ very few; one or two

【个个】each and every one; all

【个人】individual (person)

【个体】individual

【个性】individuality; personality

【个子】height; stature; build

各 (gè) each; every; various different

【各奔前程】each pursues his own course

【各别】distinct; different

【各得其所】each is in his proper place; each is properly provided for; each has a role to play

【各个】❶ each; every; various ❷ one by one; separately

【各行各业】trades and professions; all walks of life

【各级】all or different levels

【各界】all walks of life; all circles

【各取所需】each takes what he needs

【各抒己见】each airs his own views

【各位】❶ everybody ❷ every

【各显神通】each showing his special prowess (skill)

【各行其是】each does what he thinks is right; each goes his own way

【各有所长】each has his own strong points

【各有所好】each has his likes and dislikes; each follows his own bent

【各执一词】each sticks to his own version or argument

【各自】each; respective

gei

给 (gěi) ❶ give; grant ❷ let; allow; make ❸ for the benefit of; for the sake of; for
另见 jǐ

【给脸】do sb. a favour; save sb.'s face

【给以】give; grant

gen

根 (gēn) ❶ root (of a plant) ❷〈化〉radical ❸ root; foot; base ❹ cause; origin; source ❺ thoroughly; completely ❻〈数〉root

【根本】❶ basic; fundamental; essential; cardinal ❷ at all; simply ❸ radically; thoroughly

【根除】root out; eliminate; eradicate

【根底】❶ foundation ❷ cause; root

【根基】❶ foundation; basis ❷ property accumulated over a long time; resources

【根据】〈介〉❶ on the basis of; according to; in the light of ❷ basis; grounds; foundation

【根深蒂固】deep-rooted; ingrained; inveterate

【根由】cause; origin

【根源】source; origin; root

【根治】effect a radical cure; cure once and for all; fundamental solution

【根子】〈口〉❶ root (of a plant) ❷ cause; origin; source; root

跟 (gēn) ❶ heel ❷ follow ❸ and

【跟差】〈古〉manservant of an official; attendant; footman

【跟前】in front of; close to

【跟人】〈口〉(of a woman) get married

【跟上】keep pace with; catch up with; keep abreast of

【跟随】follow

【跟头】❶ (have a) fall ❷ somersault

【跟踪】follow the tracks of; follow along behind sb.; track

geng

更 (gēng) ❶ change; replace ❷ experience ❸ one of the five two-hour periods into which the night was formerly divided; watch
另见 gèng

【更动】change; alter

【更夫】〈旧〉night watchman

【更改】change; alter

【更换】replace

【更名】change one's name

【更生】❶ regenerate; revive ❷ renew

【更替】replace

【更新】renew

【更衣】change one's clothes; change dresses

【更衣室】changeroom; locker room

【更正】make corrections (of errors in statements or newspaper articles)

耕 (gēng) plough；till

【耕地】❶plough；till ❷cultivated land

【耕牛】farm cattle

【耕田】plough；till

【耕耘】〈农〉sloughing and weeding；cultivation

【耕种】plough and sow；work on the farm；tillage

【耕作】tillage；farming

羹 (gēng) a thick soup

【羹匙】soup spoon；tablespoon

耿 (gěng) ❶honest and just；upright ❷bright ❸dedicated

【耿耿】❶devoted；dedicated ❷have sth. on one's mind

【耿直】honest and frank；straight forward

哽 (gěng) choke(with emotion)；feel a lump in one's throat

【哽咽】choke with sobs

梗 (gěng) ❶stalk；stem ❷a slender piece of wood or metal ❸straighten ❹obstruct；block

【梗概】broad outline；main idea

【梗塞】❶block；obstruct；clog ❷〈医〉infarction

【梗阻】❶block；obstruct；hamper ❷〈医〉obstruction

更 (gèng) ❶more；still more；even more ❷further；furthermore；what is more

另见 gēng

【更好】better

【更加】more；still more；even more

gong

工 (gōng) ❶worker；workman；the working class ❷work；labour ❸(construction) project ❹industry ❺skill；craftsmanship ❻exquisite；fine

【工兵】engineer (in an army)

【工厂】factory；mill；plant；works

【工场】workshop

【工程】engineering；project

【工程师】engineer

【工党】the Labour Party

【工地】building site；construction site

【工段】workshop section

【工蜂】worker (bee)

【工夫】❶time ❷workmanship；skill；art ❸work；labour；effort

【工会】trade union；labour union

【工件】workpiece；work

【工匠】craftsman；artisan

【工具】tool；means；instrument；implement

【工力】❶skill；craftsmanship ❷manpower (needed for a project)

【工龄】length of service；standing；seniority

【工钱】❶money paid for odd jobs；charge for a service ❷〈口〉wages；pay

【工人】worker；workman

【工人阶级】the working class

【工伤】injury suffered on the job；injury incurred while working；industrial injury

【工商界】industrial and commercial circles；business circles

【工事】fortifications；defence works

【工休日】day off；holiday

【工序】working procedure；process

【工业】industry

【工艺】technology；craft

【工整】carefully and neatly done

【工种】type of work in production

【工资】wages；job

【工作】work；job

【工作量】amount of work；work load

【工作日】workday；working day

弓 (gōng) ❶bow ❷bend；arch；bow

【弓背】❶back of a bow ❷stooping；hunchbacked

【弓箭】bow and arrow

【弓弦】bowstring

【弓腰】bend over；bend down

公 (gōng) ❶public；state-owned；collective ❷common；general ❸metric ❹make public ❺equitable；impartial；fair；just ❻public affairs；official business ❼duke ❽father-in-law ❾male (animal)

【公安】public security

【公安局】public security bureau

【公报】bulletin

【公报私仇】use one's position to get even with another person for a private grudge

【公倍数】〈数〉common multiple

【公布】promulgate；announce；publish；make public

【公差】❶〈数〉common difference ❷〈机〉tolerance

【公差】public errand；noncombatant duty

【公尺】metre；meter

【公道】❶justice ❷fair；just；reasonable；impartial

G

【公德】social morality;social ethics

【公敌】public enemy;common enemy

【公断】❶arbitrate ❷consider and decide impartially

【公而忘私】so devoted to public service as to forget private interests;selfless

【公费】at public expense

【公分】❶centimetre(cm.) ❷gram(g.)

【公愤】public indignation;popular anger

【公告】announcement; public announcement; proclamation

【公共】public;common;communal

【公海】open sea;high seas

【公害】social effects of pollution

【公会】trade council;trade association; guild

【公鸡】cock;rooster

【公斤】kilogram;kilo

【公开】❶ open; overt; public ❷ make public; make known to the public

【公款】public money

【公里】kilometre

【公理】❶generally acknowledged truth ❷axiom

【公路】highway;road

【公论】public opinion;verdict of the masses

【公民】citizen

【公亩】acre

【公平】fair;just;impartial;equitable

【公婆】❶husband's father and mother;parents-in-law ❷〈方〉husband and wife

【公仆】public servant

【公然】〈贬〉openly;undisguisedly;brazenly

【公式】formula

【公事】public affairs;official business

【公司】company;corporation;firm

【公务】public affairs;official business

【公物】public property

【公羊】ram

【公益】public good;public welfare

【公因子】〈数〉common factor

【公用】for public use;public;communal

【公有制】public ownership

【公寓】❶block of flats;apartment ❷〈古〉lodging house

【公元】the Christian era

【公园】park

【公约】❶convention;pact ❷joint pledge

【公债】(government) bonds

【公章】official seal

【公正】just;fair;impartial

【公证】notarization

【公之于众】make public

【公众】the public;～利益 public interest

【公主】princess

功 (gōng) ❶ meritorious service(or deed); merit;achievement ❷result;effect;success ❸skill

【功败垂成】fail on the verge of success

【功臣】meritorious statesman;a person who has rendered outstanding service

【功成名就】achieve success and win recognition

【功成身退】retire after winning merit

【功大于过】one's deeds outweigh one's faults

【功德无量】kindness knows no bounds; great service to man kind

【功绩】merits and achievements;contribution

【功课】schoolwork;homework

【功劳】contribution;meritorious service; credit

【功率】〈物〉power

【功能】function

【功效】efficacy;effect

【功勋】exploit;meritorious service

攻 (gōng) ❶attack;take the offensive ❷accuse;charge ❸study;specialize in

【攻打】attack;assault

【攻读】❶assiduously study;diligently study ❷specialize in

【攻关】❶ storm a strategic pass ❷ tackle key problems

【攻击】❶attack;assault;launch an offensive ❷accuse;charge;vilify

【攻克】capture;take

【攻破】make a breakthrough;breach

【攻其不备】strike where or when the enemy is unprepared;take sb. by surprise;catch sb. unawares

【攻势】offensive

【攻无不克】all-conquering;ever-victorious

【攻占】attack and occupy;storm and capture

供 (gōng) ❶supply;feed ❷provide to
另见 gòng

【供不应求】supply falls short of demand; demand exceeds supply

【供电】 supply electricity; power supply; current supply

【供给】supply;provide;furnish

【供暖】heating

【供求】supply and demand

【供销】supply and marketing

【供养】provide for;support

【供应】supply

宫 (gōng) ❶ palace ❷ temple ❸ a place for cultural activities and recreation ❹〈解〉womb; uterus
【宫殿】 palace
【宫禁】 ❶palace prohibitions ❷palace precincts
【宫女】〈古〉a maid in an imperial palace; maid of honour
【宫室】 palace
【宫廷】 ❶palace ❷court

恭 (gōng) respectful; reverent
【恭贺】 congratulate
【恭候】 await respectfully
【恭谨】 respectful and cautious
【恭敬】 respectful
【恭维】 flatter; compliment
【恭喜】〈套〉congratulations
【恭正】 ❶reverently ❷carefully and neatly

躬 (gōng) ❶〈书〉personally ❷ bend forward; bow
【躬亲】 attend to personally

巩 (gǒng) consolidate
【巩固】 ❶strengthen; solidify ❷strong; solid

汞 (gǒng)〈化〉mercury; hydrargyrum(Hg)

拱 (gǒng) surround; arch
【拱桥】〈建〉arch bridge
【拱手】 make an obeisance by cupping one hand in the other before the chest
【拱形】〈建〉arch

共 (gòng) ❶common; general ❷share ❸together ❹in all ❺ short for 共产党（the Communist Party）
【共产党】 the Communist Party
【共产主义】 communism
【共处】 coexist
【共存】 coexist
【共度】 spend（an occasion）together
【共和】 republicanism; republic; republican
【共和国】 republic
【共计】 amount to; add up to; total
【共鸣】 ❶〈物〉resonance ❷ sympathetic response
【共青团】 the Communist Youth League
【共事】 work together; be fellow workers
【共同】 ❶common ❷together; jointly
【共同体】〈政〉community
【共性】 general character; generality

【共振】 resonance
【共总】 altogether; in all; in the aggregate

贡 (gòng) tribute
【贡献】contribute; dedicate; devote

供 (gòng) ❶lay（offerings）❷ offerings ❸confess ❹confession
　另见 gōng
【供词】 a statement made under examination; confession
【供奉】 enshrine and worship; consecrate
【供品】 offerings
【供认】 confess
【供养】 make offerings to
【供职】 hold office
【供桌】 altar table

gou

勾 (gōu) ❶cancel; cross out; strike out; tick off ❷delineate; draw ❸induce; evoke; call to mind
　另见 gòu
【勾画】 draw the outline of; delineate; sketch
【勾魂】 captivate sb.'s soul—enchant; bewitch
【勾结】 collude with; collaborate with; gang up with
【勾勒】❶draw the outline of; sketch the contours of ❷give a brief account of; outline
【勾通】 collude with; work hand in glove with
【勾销】 liquidate; write off; strike out
【勾引】 tempt; entice; seduce

沟 (gōu) ❶ditch; channel; trench ❷groove; rut; furrow ❸gully; ravine
【沟壑】 gully; ravine
【沟坎】 ditch; trench
【沟堑】 ditch; trench
【沟渠】 irrigation canals and ditches
【沟通】 link up

钩 (gōu) ❶hook ❷hook stroke（in Chinese characters）❸ check mark; tick ❹secure with a hook; hook ❺crochet ❻sew with large stitches ❼ a spoken form for the numeral
【钩虫】 hookworm
【钩针】 crochet hook
【钩子】❶hook ❷a hook-like thing

篝 (gōu)〈书〉cage
【篝火】 bonfire; campfire

苟 (gǒu) ❶careless; negligent; indifferent（to right or wrong）❷ if

【苟且】❶ drift along; be resigned to circumstances ❷ perfunctory; careless ❸ illicit(sexual relation); improper

【苟全】aimlessly preserve (one's own life)：～性命 barely manage to survive

【苟同】〈书〉(usu. used in the negative) agree without giving serious thought; readily subscribe to(sb.'s view)

狗 (gǒu) ❶dog ❷damned; cursed

【狗急跳墙】〈口〉a cornered beast will do something desperate

【狗熊】❶black bear ❷coward

勾 (gòu) 另见 gōu

【勾当】〈贬〉(dirty) deal

构 (gòu) ❶construct; form; compose ❷fabricate; make up ❸literary composition

【构成】constitute; form; compose; make up

【构件】❶〈建〉(structural) member; component ❷〈机〉component

【构思】(of writers or artists) work out the plot of a literary work or the composition of a painting; conception; design

【构图】composition (of a picture)

【构想】an idea; a conception; a plan; a scheme

【构造】❶structure; construction ❷〈地〉tectonic; structural

【构筑】construct; build

购 (gòu) purchase; buy

【购办】buy (goods, supplies, etc.)

【购买】purchase; buy

【购销】purchase and sale; buying and selling

【购置】purchase (durables)

够 (gòu) ❶reach ❷enough; sufficient

【够本】make enough money to cover the cost; break even

【够格】be qualified; be up to standard

【够朋友】〈口〉deserve to be called a true friend

【够条件】reach the standard; be qualified

gu

估 (gū) estimate; appraise

【估产】❶estimate the yield ❷appraise the assets; assess

【估计】estimate; appraise

【估价】❶evaluate ❷appraised price

【估量】appraise; estimate; assess

咕 (gū)〈象〉the clucking of a hen; the cooing of a pigeon

【咕咚】〈象〉the sound of a heavy thing falling down; thud; splash; plump

【咕嘟】〈象〉bubble; gurgle

【咕噜】〈象〉rumble; roll

【咕哝】murmur; mutter; grumble

孤 (gū) ❶(of a child) fatherless; orphaned ❷solitary; isolated

【孤傲】proud and aloof

【孤本】the only copy extant; the only existing copy

【孤单】❶alone ❷lonely; friendless

【孤岛】an isolated island

【孤独】lonely; solitary

【孤儿】❶a fatherless child ❷orphan

【孤芳自赏】a solitary flower in love with its own fragrance; a lone soul admiring his own purity

【孤寡】orphans and widows

【孤寂】lonely

【孤家寡人】a person who is utterly isolated; a person who has no mass support

【孤军作战】fight in isolation; fight a lone battle

【孤苦伶仃】orphaned and helpless

【孤老】lonely old people

【孤立】❶isolated ❷isolate

【孤零零】solitary; lone; all alone

【孤陋寡闻】ignorant and ill-informed

【孤僻】unsociable and eccentric

【孤身】alone

【孤注一掷】stake everything on a single throw

姑 (gū) ❶father's sister; aunt ❷husband's sister; sister-in-law ❸nun ❹〈书〉tentatively; for the time being

【姑夫】the husband of one's father's sister, uncle

【姑姑】〈口〉father's sister; aunt

【姑娘】❶girl ❷〈口〉daughter

【姑婆】❶husband's aunt ❷paternal grandaunt

【姑且】tentatively; for the moment

【姑嫂】a woman and her brother's wife; sisters-in-law

【姑妄听之】see no harm in hearing what sb. has to say

【姑息】appease; indulge; tolerate

【姑息养奸】to tolerate evil is to abet it

轱 (gū)

【轱辘】❶〈口〉wheel ❷roll

辜 (gū) guilt; crime

【辜负】let down;fail to live up to;be unworthy of

箍 (gū) ❶bind round;hoop ❷ hoop;band

【箍子】〈方〉(finger)ring

古 (gǔ) ancient;age-old

【古板】old-fashioned and inflexible

【古代】ancient times;antiquity

【古典】classical

【古董】❶antique;curio ❷old fogey

【古怪】eccentric;odd;strange

【古迹】historic site;historic interest

【古今中外】ancient and modern, Chinese and foreign—at all times and in all lands

【古老】ancient;age-old

【古朴】(of art, architecture, etc.)simple and unsophisticated;of primitive simplicity

【古人】the ancients;our forefathers

【古往今来】throughout the ages;of all ages;since time immemorial

【古为今用】make the past serve the present

【古稀】seventy years of age

【古谚】old proverb;old saw

【古语】❶archaism ❷old saying

【古装】ancient costume

谷 (gǔ) ❶valley;gorge ❷millet ❸unhusked rice

【谷仓】granary;barn

【谷草】❶millet straw ❷〈方〉rice straw

【谷壳】husk (of rice)

【谷物】cereal;grain

汩 (gǔ)〈书〉(of running water)gurgle

【汩汩】gurgle

股 (gǔ) ❶thigh ❷section(of an office;enterprise, etc.) ❸strand;ply ❹share in a company or one of several equal parts of property

【股东】shareholder;stockholder

【股份】share;stock

【股票】share certificate;share;stock

【股息】dividend

骨 (gǔ) ❶ bone ❷ skeleton;framework ❸character;spirit

【骨干】❶〈生理〉diaphysis ❷backbone;mainstay;core member;key member

【骨骼】〈生理〉skeleton

【骨架】skeleton;framework

【骨牌】dominoes

【骨气】strength of character;moral integrity;backbone

【骨肉】flesh and blood;kindred

【骨瘦如柴】thin as a lath;worn to a shadow;a mere skeleton;a bag of bones

【骨髓】〈生理〉marrow

【骨折】〈医〉fracture

【骨子】frame

蛊 (gǔ) a legendary venomous insect

【蛊惑】poison and bewitch

【蛊惑人心】confuse and poison people's minds;resort to demagogy

鼓 (gǔ) ❶drum ❷beat;strike;sound ❸blow with bellows, etc. ❹rouse;agitate;pluck up ❺bulge;swell

【鼓吹】❶ advocate ❷〈贬〉preach;advertise;play up

【鼓动】❶agitate;arouse ❷instigate;incite

【鼓劲】rouse one's enthusiasm

【鼓励】encourage;urge

【鼓舞】inspire;hearten

【鼓乐】strains of music accompanied by drumbeats

【鼓掌】clap one's hands;applaud

固 (gù) ❶solid;firm ❷ solidify;consolidate;strengthen ❸firmly;resolutely ❹ originally;in the first place;as a matter of course

【固定】❶fixed;regular ❷fix;regularize

【固然】though of course;admittedly;no doubt;it is true

【固若金汤】strongly fortified;impregnable

【固有】intrinsic;inherent;inherence

【固执】❶ obstinate;stubborn ❷ persist in;cling to

【固执己见】stubbornly persist in one's opinions

故 (gù) ❶incident;happening ❷reason;cause ❸ on purpose;intentionally ❹ hence;therefore;so;for this reason ❺former;old ❻ friend;acquaintance ❼(of people)die;dead

【故步自封】stand still and refuse to make progress;be complacent and conservative

【故都】onetime capital

【故居】former residence(or home)

【故弄玄虚】purposely make a mystery of simple things;be deliberately mystifying

【故世】die;pass away

【故事】❶story;tale ❷plot

【故土】native land;native place;birthplace;hometown

【故乡】native place;hometown;birthplace

【故意】intentionally;willfully;on purpose

【故友】a departed friend
【故障】hitch; breakdown; stoppage; trouble
【故作姿态】strike a pose; put on airs; make a deliberate gesture

顾（gù）❶ turn round and look at; look at ❷ attend to; take into consideration ❸ but; however ❹ on the contrary; instead
【顾此失彼】cannot attend to one thing without neglecting the other; have too many things to take care of at the same time
【顾及】take into account; attend to; give consideration to
【顾忌】scruple; misgiving
【顾客】customer; shopper; client
【顾虑】misgiving; apprehension; worry
【顾面子】❶ save face; keep up appearances ❷ spare sb. 's feelings
【顾名思义】seeing the name of a thing one thinks of its function
【顾念】think about; be concerned about
【顾盼】〈书〉look around
【顾全】show consideration for and take care to preserve
【顾问】adviser; consultant
【顾影自怜】look at one's image in the mirror and pity oneself
【顾主】customer; client; patron

雇（gù）hire; employ
【雇工】❶ hire labour; hire hands ❷ hired labourer (or hand, worker)
【雇佣】employ; hire
【雇员】employee
【雇主】employer

痼（gù）chronic; inveterate
【痼疾】〈书〉chronic (or obstinate) illness
【痼弊】〈书〉age old malpractice; longstanding abuse
【痼习】confirmed habit

gua

瓜（guā）melon; gourd
【瓜分】carve up; divide up
【瓜葛】connection; implication
【瓜子】melon seeds

刮（guā）❶ scrape ❷ smear with (paste, etc.) ❸ plunder; fleece; extort ❹ blow
【刮脸】shave (the face)

【刮目相看】look at sb. with new eyes
【刮削】scrape

寡（guǎ）❶ few; scant ❷ tasteless ❸ widowed
【寡不敌众】be hopelessly outnumbered; fight against hopeless odds
【寡妇】widow
【寡头】oligarch
【寡言】of few words; taciturn; sparing of words
【寡欲】have few desires; be ascetic

挂（guà）❶ hang; put up ❷ hitch; get caught ❸ ring off ❹ call up; put sb. through to ❺〈方〉be concerned about ❻〈方〉covered with; be coated with ❼ register
【挂车】trailer
【挂斗】trailer
【挂钩】❶ couple (two railway coaches) ❷ link up with; establish contact with; get in touch with
【挂号】❶ register (at a hospital, etc.) ❷ send by registered mail
【挂记】worry about; be anxious about; keep thinking about
【挂面】fine dried noodles
【挂名】titular; nominal
【挂念】miss; worry about sb. who is absent
【挂失】report the loss of sth.
【挂帅】be in command; take command
【挂一漏万】for one thing cited, ten thousand may have been left out — the list is far from complete

褂（guà）a Chinese-style unlined garment; gown
【褂子】a Chinese-style unlined upper garment; short gown

guai

乖（guāi）❶ well-behaved (child); good ❷ clever; shrewd; alert
【乖乖】❶ well-behaved; obedient ❷ (to a child) little dear; darling ❸〈叹〉good gracious
【乖戾】perverse (behaviour); disagreeable (character)
【乖巧】❶ clever ❷ cute; lovely
【乖张】eccentric and unreasonable; perverse; recalcitrant

拐（guǎi）❶ turn ❷ limp ❸ crutch ❹ swindle; make off with ❺ abduct; kidnap
【拐棍】walking stick
【拐角】corner; turning
【拐卖】kidnap and sell; engage in slavery
【拐骗】❶ abduct ❷ swindle (money out of sb.)

【拐弯】❶turn a corner ❷turn round; pursue a new course
【拐杖】walking stick
【拐子】❶cripple ❷abductor ❸swindler

怪（guài）❶strange; odd; queer; bewildering ❷find sth. strange; wonder at ❸quite; rather ❹monster; demon; evil being ❺blame
【怪不得】no wonder; so that's why; that explains why
【怪诞】weird; strange
【怪话】cynical remark; grumble; complaint
【怪僻】eccentric; odd
【怪事】strange thing
【怪物】❶monster; monstrosity; freak ❷an eccentric person; a queer bird; oddball
【怪异】❶monstrous; strange; unusual ❷strange phenomenon; portent; prodigy
【怪罪】blame sb.

guan

关（guān）❶shut; close ❷turn off ❸shut in; lock up ❹close down ❺mountain pass; a graded passage ❻custom house ❼barrier; a critical juncture ❽concern; involve
【关闭】❶close; shut ❷(of a shop or factory) close down; shut down
【关怀】show loving care for; show solicitude for
【关键】hinge; key; crux
【关节】❶〈生理〉joint ❷a key (or crucial) link
【关联】be related; be connected
【关门】❶(of a shop, etc.) close ❷〈口〉(of a business) close down ❸refuse discussion or consideration; slam the door on sth. ❹be behind closed doors
【关切】❶considerate; thoughtful ❷be deeply concerned; show one's concern over
【关税】customs duty; tariff
【关头】juncture; key moment
【关系】❶relation; relationship ❷bearing; impact; significance ❸concern; have to do with
【关心】be concerned with; show solicitude for; be interested in; care for
【关押】lock up; put under detention; put in prison
【关于】about; on; with regard to; concerning
【关照】❶look after; keep an eye on ❷notify by word of mouth
【关注】follow with interest; pay close attention to; show solicitude for

观（guān）❶look at; watch; observe ❷sight; view ❸outlook; concept

【观测】observe; view
【观察】observe; watch; survey
【观点】point of view; viewpoint; standpoint
【观感】impressions
【观光】go sightseeing
【观看】watch; view
【观摩】inspect and learn from each other's work; view and emulate
【观念】sense; idea; concept
【观赏】view and admire; enjoy the sight of
【观望】wait and see; look on
【观象台】observatory
【观战】❶watch a battle; watch other people fight ❷watch a match or contest
【观众】spectator; audience

官（guān）❶government official; officer; officeholder ❷〈旧〉government-owned; government-sponsored; official; public ❸organ
【官兵】❶officers and men ❷〈古〉government troops
【官差】public errand
【官邸】official residence
【官方】of or by the government; official
【官府】〈古〉❶local authorities ❷feudal official
【官僚】bureaucrat
【官人】〈古〉wife's term of address for husband
【官司】〈口〉lawsuit
【官员】official
【官运】official career; fortunes of officialdom; ~亨通 have a successful official career
【官职】government post; official position

冠（guān）❶〈书〉hat ❷corona; crown
　　另见 guàn
【冠冕】royal crown; offcial hat
【冠心病】coronary heart disease
【冠子】crest; comb

棺（guān）
【棺材】coffin

馆（guǎn）❶accommodation for guests ❷embassy; legation or consulate ❸(of service trades) shop ❹a place for cultural activities ❺〈古〉an old-style private school
【馆藏】(of a library or a museum) ❶have a collection of ❷collection
【馆子】restaurant; eating house

管（guǎn）❶tube; pipe ❷wind instrument ❸manage; run; be in charge of ❹subject sb. to discipline ❺bother about ❻provide; guarantee ❼〈电〉valve; tube

【管保】guarantee;assure

【管道】pipeline;piping;conduit;tubing

【管教】subject sb. to discipline

【管教】〈方〉certainly;surely

【管理】❶manage;run;administer;supervise ❷take care of ❸look after

【管区】district

【管束】restrain;check;control

【管辖】have jurisdiction over

【管线】pipes and power lines

【管制】❶control ❷put under surveillance;交通～ traffic control

贯 (guàn) ❶be used to;be in the habit of ❷indulge;spoil

【贯彻】carry out;implement;put into effect

【贯穿】run through;penetrate

【贯串】spread through;run through;permeate

【贯通】❶have a thorough knowledge of;be well versed in ❷joined up

【贯注】concentrate on;be absorbed in

冠 (guàn) ❶〈书〉put on a hat ❷precede;crown with ❸first place;the best
另见 guān

【冠词】〈语〉article

【冠军】champ;champion;crown

惯 (guàn) ❶be used to;be in the habit of ❷indulge;spoil

【惯犯】habitual offender;repeater;old offender

【惯技】〈贬〉customary tactic;old trick

【惯例】convention;usual practice

【惯窃】hardened thief

【惯偷】hardened thief

【惯性】〈物〉inertia

【惯用】〈贬〉habitually practise;consistently use

灌 (guàn) ❶irrigate ❷fill;pour

【灌溉】irrigate

【灌输】instill into;inculcate;imbue with

【灌醉】make sb. drunk;inebriate;fuddle

鹳 (guàn) stork

罐 (guàn) ❶jar;pot;tin ❷coal tub

【罐车】tank car;tank truck;tanker

【罐头】〈方〉tin;can

【罐子】pot;jar;pitcher

guang

光 (guāng) ❶light;ray ❷brightness;lustre ❸honour;glory ❹scenery ❺smooth;

glossy;polished ❻used up;nothing left ❼bare;naked ❽solely;only;merely

【光彩】❶lustre;splendour;radiance ❷honourable;glorious

【光彩夺目】with dazzling brightness;brilliant;resplendent

【光复】recover (lost territory);restore (old glory,etc.)

【光顾】patronize

【光怪陆离】grotesque in shape and gaudy in colour;bizarre and motley

【光棍】❶ruffian;hoodlum ❷〈方〉a clever (or wise) person

【光华】brilliance;splendour

【光滑】smooth;glossy;sleek;not rough:皮肤～ smooth skin

【光环】❶a ring of light (round a planed) ❷halo (round the head of a holy person)

【光辉】❶radiance;brilliance;glory ❷brilliant;magnificent;glorious

【光洁】bright and clean

【光景】❶scene ❷circumstances;conditions ❸about;around

【光亮】bright;luminous;shiny

【光临】〈敬〉presence(of a guest;etc.)

【光溜溜】❶smooth;slippery ❷bare;naked

【光芒万丈】shining with boundless radiance;gloriously radiant;resplendent

【光面】plain noodles (without meat or vegetables)

【光明】❶light ❷bright;promising

【光明磊落】open and aboveboard

【光谱】〈物〉spectrum

【光圈】〈摄〉diaphragm;aperture

【光荣】honour;glory;credit

【光线】light;ray

【光学】optics

【光阴】time

【光源】〈物〉light source;illuminant

【光泽】lustre;gloss;sheen

【光照】〈植〉illumination

【光宗耀祖】make one's ancestors illustrious

广 (guǎng) ❶wide;broad;vast;extensive ❷numerous ❸expand;spread

【广播】broadcast;be on the air

【广博】(of a person's knowledge)extensive;wide

【广场】public square;square

【广大】vast;wide;extensive

【广度】scope;range

【广而言之】speaking generally;in a general

sense

【广泛】extensive；widespread

【广告】advertisement

【广阔】vast；wide；broad

【广厦】〈文〉a spacious mansion

【广义】❶broad sense ❷generalized

逛 (guàng) stroll；ramble；roam

【逛荡】〈贬〉loiter；loaf about

gui

归 (guī) ❶go back to；return ❷converge；come together ❸turn over to；put in sb's charge ❹give back to；return sth. to

【归案】bring to justice

【归并】❶incorporate into；merge into ❷lump together；add up

【归队】❶rejoin one's unit ❷return to the profession one was trained for

【归功于】give the credit to；attribute the success to

【归国】return to one's country

【归国华侨】returned overseas Chinese

【归还】return；revert

【归结】❶come to a conclusion；sum up；put in a nutshell ❷end (of a story，etc.)

【归来】return；come back；be back

【归类】sort out；classify

【归纳】induce；conclude；sum up

【归期】date of return

【归属】belong to；come under the jurisdiction of

【归顺】come over and pledge allegiance

【归宿】a home to return to

【归途】homeward journey；one's way home

【归于】❶belong to；be attributed to ❷result in；end in

【归罪】put the blame on；impute to

龟 (guī) tortoise；turtle

【龟甲】tortoise-shell

【龟缩】huddle up like a turtle drawing in its head and legs；withdraw into passive defence；hole up

规 (guī) ❶compasses；dividers ❷regulation ❸admonish；advise ❹plan；map out

【规避】evade；dodge；avoid

【规程】rules；regulations

【规定】❶stipulate；provide ❷fix；set

【规范】standard；norm；code

【规格】specifications；standards；norms

【规划】programme；plan

【规矩】❶rule；established practice；custom of the old routine way ❷well-behaved；well-disciplined

【规律】law；regular pattern

【规模】scale；scope；dimensions

【规劝】admonish；advise

【规行矩步】❶behave correctly and cautiously ❷stick to established practice；follow the beaten track

【规约】stipulations of an agreement

【规则】❶rule；regulation ❷regular

【规章】rules；regulations

闺 (guī) ❶〈古〉a small door ❷lady's chamber；boudoir

【闺房】lady's chamber；boudoir

【闺女】❶girl；maiden ❷〈口〉daughter

【闺秀】〈古〉a young lady

瑰 (guī)〈书〉rare；marvellous

【瑰宝】rarity；treasure；gem

【瑰丽】surpassingly beautiful；magnificent

轨 (guī) ❶rail；track ❷course；path

【轨道】❶track ❷orbit；trajectory ❸course；path

【轨范】standard；criterion

【轨迹】❶〈数〉locus ❷〈天〉orbit

【轨距】railway gauge

诡 (guī) ❶deceitful；tricky；cunning ❷weird；eerie

【诡辩】sophistry；sophism；quibbling

【诡称】falsely allege；pretend

【诡计】a crafty plot；a cunning scheme；trick；ruse

【诡诈】crafty；cunning；treacherous

鬼 (guī) ❶ghost；spirit；apparition ❷stealthy；surreptitious ❸terrible；damnable ❹〈口〉clever；smart；quick

【鬼聪明】clever in a shallow way

【鬼怪】ghosts and monsters；monsters of all kinds；forces of evil

【鬼鬼祟祟】sneaking；furtive；stealthy

【鬼话】lie；deceptive remark；nonsense

【鬼魂】ghost；spirit；apparition

【鬼混】lead an aimless or irregular existence；fool around

【鬼脸】❶funny face；wry face；grimace ❷mask used as a toy

【鬼神】ghosts and gods；spirits；supernatural beings

柜 (guī) ❶cupboard；cabinet ❷cashier's office in a shop；shop cashier

【柜台】counter;bar
【柜子】cupboard;cabinet

贵（guì）❶ expensive;costly;dear ❷ highly valued;valuable ❸of high rank;noble
【贵宾】honoured guest;distinguished guest
【贵妃】highest-ranking imperial concubine
【贵干】〈套〉honourable business;noble errand
【贵贱】❶the eminent and the humble ❷the expensive and the cheap:管它～,只要看中了,就买了来。Whatever the price is, if it caught my eyes I would buy it.
【贵重】valuable;precious
【贵族】noble;aristocrat

桂（guì）❶cassia ❷laurel;bay tree ❸sweet-scented osmanthus
【桂冠】laurel（as an emblem of victory or distinction）
【桂花】sweet-scented osmanthus
【桂圆】〈植〉longan

跪（guì）kneel
【跪拜】worship on bended knees;kowtow
【跪倒】throw oneself on one's knees;grovel
【跪姿】kneeling position

gun

滚（gǔn）❶roll;trundle ❷get away;beat it
【滚刀】〈机〉hobbing cutter;hob
【滚动】roll;trundle
【滚翻】〈体〉roll
【滚瓜烂熟】(recite;etc.)fluently;(know sth.)pat
【滚开】get away;get out
【滚热】piping hot;burning hot;boiling hot
【滚水】boiling water
【滚圆】round as a ball

棍（gùn）❶rod;stick ❷scoundrel;rascal
【棍棒】❶club;cudgel;bludgeon ❷a stick or staff used in gymnastics

guo

聒（guō）noisy
【聒耳】grate on one's ears
【聒噪】〈方〉noisy;clamorous

锅（guō）❶pot;pan,boiler,caldron,etc. ❷bowl(of a pipe,etc.)
【锅巴】crust of cooked rice;rice crust
【锅铲】slice (a kitchen utensil)

【锅盖】the lid of a cooking pot
【锅炉】boiler
【锅台】the top of a kitchen range
【锅子】❶〈方〉pot;pan ❷bowl:烟袋～ bowl of a pipe ❸chafing dish;hotpot

蝈（guō）
【蝈蝈儿】〈动〉katydid;long-horned grasshopper

国（guó）❶country;state;nation ❷of the state;national ❸of our country;Chinese
【国宝】national treasure
【国本】the foundation of a nation
【国宾】state guest
【国策】national policy
【国产】made in our country;made in China
【国耻】national humiliation
【国粹】the quintessence of Chinese culture
【国都】(national)capital
【国度】country;state;nation
【国法】(national)law
【国防】national defence
【国歌】national anthem
【国花】national flower
【国画】traditional Chinese painting
【国徽】national emblem
【国会】Congress;Parliament
【国籍】nationality
【国计民生】the national economy and the people's livelihood
【国际】international
【国家】country;state;nation
【国界】national boundaries
【国境】national territory;national border or boundary
【国内】internal;domestic;home
【国旗】national flag
【国庆】National Day
【国色】〈文〉reigning beauty;a woman of matchless beauty
【国色天香】ethereal colour and celestial fragrance (said of the peony or a beautiful woman)
【国泰民安】The country is prosperous and the people are at peace.
【国体】❶state system ❷national prestige
【国土】territory;land
【国外】external;overseas;abroad
【国王】king
【国务卿】(in the U. S.)Secretary of State
【国务院】❶the State Council ❷(in the U. S.) the State Department

【国营】state-operated；state-run

【国语】❶ national language ❷〈旧〉Chinese taught in schools

果（guǒ）❶fruit ❷result；consequence ❸resolute；determined ❹ really；as expected；sure enough ❺if indeed；if really

【果断】resolute；decisive

【果脯】preserved fruit；candied fruit

【果敢】courageous and resolute；resolute and daring

【果酱】jam

【果皮】the skin of fruit；peel；rind

【果品】fruit

【果然】❶ really；as expected；sure enough ❷ if indeed

【果肉】pulp

【果实】❶fruit；❷gains；fruits

【果树】fruit tree

【果糖】〈化〉fructose；levulose

【果园】orchard

【果汁】fruit juice

裹（guǒ）❶ bind；wrap ❷ carry off ❸ suck（milk）

【裹胁】force to take part(in bad things)；coerce

【裹足不前】hesitate to move forward

过（guò）❶ cross；pass ❷ across；past；through；over ❸spend(time)；pass（time）❹after；past ❺undergo a process；go through；go over ❻exceed；go beyond ❼excessively；unduly ❽fault；mistake

【过程】course；process

【过秤】weigh（on the steelyard）

【过错】fault；mistake

【过道】passageway；corridor

【过冬】pass the winter；winter

【过度】excessive；undue；over

【过渡】transition；interim

【过多】too many or much；more than enough；excessive

【过分】excessive；undue；over

【过关】❶pass a barrier；go through an ordeal ❷ pass a test；reach a standard

【过后】afterwards；later

【过活】make a living；live

【过火】go too far；go to extremes；overdo

【过境】pass through the territory of a country；be in transit

【过来】come over；come up

【过路】pass by on one's way

【过路人】passerby

【过滤】filter；filtrate

【过敏】❶〈医〉allergy：皮肤～ skin allergy

【过年】❶ celebrate the New Year；spend the New Year ❷next year

【过期】be overdue

【过去】❶in or of the past；formerly；previously ❷go over；pass by

【过日子】live；get along

【过剩】excess；surplus

【过失】❶fault；slip；error ❷〈法〉negligence

【过时】out-of-date；outmoded；obsolete；antiquated；out of fashion

【过世】die；pass away

【过往】❶ come and go ❷ have friendly intercourse with；associate with

【过问】concern oneself with；take an interest in；bother about

【过眼云烟】like floating smoke and passing clouds

【过夜】pass the night；put up for the night；stay overnight

【过瘾】satisfy a craving；enjoy oneself to the full；do sth. to one's heart's content

【过犹不及】going too far is as bad as not going far enough

【过于】too；unduly；excessively

【过誉】〈套〉overpraise；unearned praise

【过重】（of luggage, letters, etc.）overweight

H h

ha

哈 (hā) ❶ blow one's breath; breathe out (with the mouth open) ❷〈象〉ha; ha-ha; aha

【哈欠】yawn

【哈腰】〈口〉❶ bend one's back ❷ bow:点头～ bow and scrape; bow unctuously

蛤 (há)

【蛤蟆】❶frog ❷toad

hai

咳 (hāi) expressing sadness, regret or surprise
　　另见 ké

还 (hái) yet; still; even
　　另见 huán

【还好】❶not bad; passable ❷fortunately

【还是】❶still; yet ❷expressing a preference for an alternative ❸no matter what, how

孩 (hái) child

【孩童】child

【孩子】❶child ❷son or daughter

骸 (hái) ❶ bones of the body; skeleton ❷body

【骸骨】bones of the dead

海 (hǎi) ❶sea; big lake ❷a great number of people or things coming together ❸ extra large; of great capacity

【海岸】seacoast; seashore

【海拔】elevation

【海报】playbill

【海豹】seal

【海滨】seaside

【海带】kelp

【海岛】island (in the sea)

【海盗】pirate; sea rover

【海防】coast defence

【海风】sea breeze; sea wind

【海港】seaport; harbour

【海关】customs; customhouse

【海龟】green turtle (Chelonia mydas)

【海军】navy

【海枯石烂】(even if) the seas run dry and the rocks crumble

【海阔天空】as boundless as the sea and sky; unrestrained and far-ranging

【海里】nautical mile; sea mile

【海量】〈套〉❶magnanimity ❷great capacity for liquor

【海绵】❶sponge ❷foam rubber or plastic

【海面】sea surface

【海内】within the four seas; throughout the country

【海鸥】〈动〉seagull

【海平面】sea level

【海上】at sea; on the sea

【海誓山盟】(make) a solemn pledge of love

【海滩】beach; sea beach

【海图】sea chart

【海豚】〈动〉dolphin

【海外】overseas; abroad

【海湾】bay; gulf

【海味】seafood

【海峡】strait; channel

【海洋】seas and oceans; ocean

【海员】seaman; sailor

【海运】sea transportation; ocean shipping

【海藻】marine alga; seaweed

【海战】sea warfare; naval battle

【海蜇】jellyfish

骇 (hài) be astonished; be shocked

【骇然】gasping with astonishment; struck dumb with amazement

【骇人听闻】shocking; appalling

【骇异】be shocked; be astonished

害 (hài) ❶evil; harm ❷harmful; destructive ❸ do harm to; impair ❹kill; murder ❺suffer from ❻feel (ashamed, afraid, etc.)

【害病】fall ill:害了一场大病 have been seriously ill

【害虫】injurious (or destructive) insect; pest

【害处】harm：吸烟过多对身体有～。Excessive smoking is harmful to one's health.

【害命】murder

【害怕】be afraid；be scared

【害群之马】black sheep

【害臊】〈口〉feel ashamed

【害羞】be bashful；be shy

han

酣 (hān)（drink, etc.）to one's heart's content

【酣畅】❶merry and lively（with drinking）❷sound（sleep）❸with ease and verve；fully

【酣畅淋漓】heartily；to one's heart's content

【酣然】❶merrily（drunk）❷sound（asleep）

【酣睡】sleep soundly；be fast asleep

【酣战】hard-fought battle

【酣醉】be dead drunk

憨 (hān)❶foolish；silly ❷straightforward；native

【憨痴】idiotic

【憨厚】simple and honest；straightforward and good-natured

【憨实】simple and honest；straightforward and good-natured

【憨笑】smile fatuously；simper；smirk

【憨直】honest and straightforward

鼾 (hān) snore

【鼾声】sound of snoring

【鼾声如雷】snore thunderously

【鼾睡】sound, snoring sleep

含 (hán)❶keep in the mouth ❷contain ❸nurse；cherish；harbour

【含苞未放】still in bud

【含恨】nurse a grievance or hatred

【含糊】❶ambiguous；vague ❷careless；perfunctory

【含糊其词】talk ambiguously；equivocate

【含量】content：牛奶的乳糖～ the lactose content of the milk

【含情脉脉】（soft eyes）exuding tenderness and love

【含沙射影】attack by innuendo

【含笑】have a smile on one's face

【含辛茹苦】endure suffering；bear hardships

【含羞】with a shy look；bashfully

【含蓄】❶ contain；embody ❷ implicit；veiled ❸reserved

【含血喷人】make slanderous accusations；make vicious attacks

【含义】meaning；implication

【含冤】suffer a wrong；be the victim of a false or unjust charge

【含怨】bear a grudge；nurse a grievance

函 (hán)❶〈书〉case；envelope ❷letter

【函电】letters and cables

【函购】purchase by mail；mail order

【函件】letters；correspondence

【函授】teach by correspondence

【函数】〈数〉function

涵 (hán)❶contain ❷culvert

【涵养】❶ability to control oneself；self restraint ❷conserve

寒 (hán)❶cold ❷tremble(with fear)

【寒潮】〈气〉cold wave

【寒窗】a cold window the difficulties of a poor student

【寒带】〈地〉frigid zone

【寒风】cold wind：～凛冽 a piercing wind

【寒假】winter vacation

【寒噤】shiver or shudder（with cold or fear）；tremble：打～ have the shivers

【寒冷】cold；icy；frigid

【寒流】〈气〉cold current

【寒毛】fine hair on the human body

【寒舍】〈谦〉my humble home（or abode）

【寒暑表】thermometer

【寒暄】exchange of greetings

【寒衣】winter clothing

【寒意】a nip（or chill）in the air

【寒战】shiver（with cold or fear）；chill

罕 (hǎn) rarely；seldom

【罕见】seldom seen；rare

【罕事】a rare event

【罕闻】seldom heard of

【罕物】a rare thing

【罕有】very rare

喊 (hǎn)❶shout；cry out；yell ❷call（a person）

【喊话】❶ propaganda directed to the enemy at the front line ❷ communicate by tele-equipment

【喊叫】shout；cry out

【喊冤叫屈】cry out about one's grievances；complain loudly about an alleged injustice

汉 (hàn)❶the Han Dynasty ❷the Han nationality ❸Chinese(language) ❹man

【汉白玉】white marble

【汉堡包】hamburger

【汉奸】traitor (to China)

【汉语】Chinese (language)

【汉字】Chinese character

【汉族】the Han nationality;China's main nationality

汗 (hàn) sweat;perspiration

【汗背心】sleeveless undershirt;vest;singlet

【汗脚】〈口〉feet that sweat easily;sweaty feet

【汗孔】〈生理〉pore of a sweat gland

【汗流浃背】sweat streaming down and drenching one's back;soaked with sweat

【汗马功劳】❶distinctions won in battle;war exploits ❷ one's contributions in work;render great services

【汗毛】fine hair on the human body

【汗如雨下】sweat profusely;The sweat runs down like raindrops.

【汗衫】undershirt;T-shirt

【汗水】sweat

【汗腺】sweat gland

【汗液】sweat;perspiration

【汗渍】❶sweat stain ❷be soaked with sweat

旱 (hàn) ❶dry spell;drought ❷dryland ❸on land

【旱冰场】roller rink

【旱稻】upland rice;dry rice

【旱地】nonirrigated farmland;dry land

【旱路】overland route

【旱情】damage to crops by drought;ravages of a drought

【旱田】dry farmland;dry land

【旱灾】drought

捍 (hàn) defend;guard

【捍拒】〈书〉resist;fight back

【捍卫】guard;protect

悍 (hàn) ❶brave;bold ❷fierce;ferocious

【悍然】outrageously;brazenly;flagrantly

【悍然不顾】in flagrant disregard of; in defiance of

焊 (hàn) weld;solder

【焊工】❶welding;soldering ❷welder;solderer

【焊接】welding

【焊油】soldering paste

撼 (hàn) shake

【撼动】shake;vibrate

【撼天动地】shake heaven and earth

憾 (hàn) regret

【憾事】a matter for regret

瀚 (hàn)〈书〉vast

【瀚海】〈书〉big desert

hang

行 (háng) ❶line;row ❷seniority among brothers and sisters ❸trade;profession;line of business ❹business firm
另见 xíng

【行辈】seniority in the family or clan;position in the family hierarchy

【行话】jargon;cant

【行会】〈古〉guild

【行家】expert;connoisseur

【行间】❶〈书〉in the ranks ❷between lines ❸between rows

【行距】〈农〉row spacing

【行列】ranks

【行情】quotations(on the market);prices

【行业】trade;profession;industry

【行长】president (of a bank)

航 (háng) ❶boat;ship ❷navigate

【航班】scheduled flight;flight number

【航标】navigation mark

【航程】voyage;passage;range;distance travelled

【航船】boat that plies regularly between inland towns

【航道】channel;lane;course

【航海】navigation

【航空】aviation

【航路】air or sea route

【航天】spaceflight

【航线】air or shipping line;route;course

【航向】course(of a ship or plane)

【航行】❶navigate by water;sail ❷navigate by air;fly

【航运】shipping

hao

号 (háo) ❶howl;yell ❷wail
另见 hào

【号叫】howl;yell

【号哭】wail

毫 (háo) ❶fine long hair ❷writing brush ❸in the least;at all ❹milli

【毫不】not at all

【毫发不爽】not deviating a hair's breadth;without the slightest error

【毫克】milligram (mg)

【毫厘】the least bit

【毫毛】soft hair on the body

【毫米】millimeter（mm）

【毫升】millilitre（ml.）

【毫无二致】without the slightest difference;just the same

豪（háo）❶a person of extraordinary powers of endowments ❷bold and unconstrained;forthright;unrestrained ❸despotic;bullying

【豪宕】〈书〉bold and unconstrained

【豪放】bold and unconstrained

【豪富】❶ powerful and wealthy ❷ the rich and powerful

【豪华】luxurious;sumptuous

【豪杰】person of exceptional ability;hero

【豪迈】bold;heroic;bold and generous

【豪门】rich and powerful family;wealthy and influential clan

【豪气】heroism;heroic spirit

【豪强】❶despotic tyrannical ❷despot;bully

【豪情】lofty sentiments

【豪爽】forthright

【豪言壮语】brave words;proud remarks;heroic words

【豪壮】grand and heroic

好（hǎo）❶good;fine;nice ❷friendly;kind ❸be in good health;get well ❹be easy（to do）;be convenient ❺so as to;so that
另见 hào

【好比】can be compared to;may be likened to;be just like

【好处】❶good;benefit;advantage ❷gain;profit ❸be easy to get along with

【好歹】❶ good and bad ❷ what's good and what's bad ❸ mishap;disaster ❹ in any case;anyhow

【好多】❶a good many;a good deal;a lot of ❷how many;how much

【好感】good impression

【好汉】brave man;true man;hero

【好话】❶ a good word;words of praise ❷ fine words

【好价】a good（selling）price

【好看】❶ good-looking;nice ❷ interesting ❸ honoured;proud ❹in a embarassing situation;on the spot

【好脸】〈口〉（usu. used in the negative）a smiling face

【好人】❶a good（or fine）person ❷a healthy person ❸a soft person who tries to get along with everyone（often at the expense of principle）

【好事】good deed;good turn

【好事多磨】❶ the road to happiness is strewn with setbacks ❷the course of true love never did run smooth

【好手】good hand;past master

【好似】seem;be like

【好听】pleasant to hear

【好戏】good play

【好像】seem;be like;appear as if;as though

【好笑】laughable;funny;ridiculous

【好心】good intention;kindhearted

【好意】kindness;good intention

【好运】luck

【好在】fortunately;luckily

【好转】take a turn for the better;take a favourable turn;improve:局势～逐渐。The situation took a favourable turn gradually.

【好自为之】conduct oneself well

号（hào）❶name ❷assumed name;alternative name ❸mark;sign;signal ❹number ❺size ❻date
另见 háo

【号兵】bugler;trumpeter

【号称】❶be known as ❷claim to be

【号角】❶horn;bugle ❷bugle call

【号令】command;order

【号码】number

【号脉】feel the pulse

【号手】trumpeter;bugler

【号外】extra（of a newspaper）;extra issue

【号召】call;appeal

好（hào）❶like;love;be fond of ❷be liable to
另见 hǎo

【好客】be hospitable;keep open house

【好奇】be curious

【好强】eager to do well in everything

【好色】love woman's beauty;be fond of women

【好学】be fond of learning;be eager to learn

【好战】bellicose;warlike

耗（hào）❶consume;cost ❷waste time;dawdle ❸bad news

【耗费】consume;expend:～时间 expend time

【耗竭】exhaust;use up

【耗尽】exhaust;use up

【耗损】consume;waste;lose:～ 精神 take up one's energy

【耗资】cost（a large sum of money）

【耗子】〈方〉mouse;rat

浩（hào）great;vast;grand

【浩博】extensive;wide-embracing

【浩大】very great;huge;vast

【浩荡】vast and mighty

【浩瀚】vast
【浩劫】great calamity
【浩气】noble spirit
【浩叹】❶heave a deep sigh; sigh deeply ❷be greatly touched

皓 ^(hào) ❶white ❷bright; luminous

【皓白】white; pure white

he

呵 ^(hē) ❶breathe out (with the mouth open) ❷scold

【呵斥】berate; excoriate
【呵护】〈书〉bless
【呵欠】yawn

喝 ^(hē) ❶drink ❷drink alcoholic liquor 另见 hè

禾 ^(hé) standing grain (esp. rice)

【禾苗】seedlings of cereal crops

合 ^(hé) ❶close; shut ❷join; combine ❸whole ❹suit; agree ❺be equal to; add up to

【合办】operate or run jointly
【合编】❶compile in collaboration with ❷merge and reorganize (army units, etc)
【合并】merge; amalgamate
【合唱】chorus
【合成】❶compose; compound ❷synthesize
【合法】legal; lawful; legitimate; rightful
【合格】qualified; up to standard
【合乎】conform with; correspond to; accord with; tally with
【合伙】form a partnership
【合计】amount to; add up to; total
【合计】think over; figure out
【合家】the whole family
【合理】rational; reasonable; equitable
【合流】❶flowing together; confluence ❷collaborate; work hand in glove with sb. ❸different schools (of thought, art, etc.) merge into one
【合谋】conspire; plot together
【合群】❶get on well with others; be sociable ❷be gregarious
【合身】fit
【合时】fashionable; in vogue
【合适】suitable; appropriate
【合算】❶paying; worthwhile ❷reckon up
【合同】contract
【合眼】close one's eyes; sleep
【合意】suit; be to one's liking(or taste)
【合营】jointly owned; jointly operated
【合影】group photo (or picture)

【合用】❶share ❷of use
【合资】joint stock
【合奏】instrumental ensemble
【合作】cooperate; work together

何 ^(hé) what; which; how; why

【何必】there is no need; why
【何不】why not
【何尝】(used in rhetorical questions) ever so
【何等】❶what kind ❷(used in exclamations) what; how
【何苦】why bother; is it worth the trouble
【何况】much less; let alone
【何其】(indicating disagreement)how; what
【何谓】〈书〉what is meant by
【何许】〈书〉what kind of; what
【何以】〈书〉❶how ❷why
【何止】far more than

和 ^(hé) ❶gentle; mild; kind ❷harmonious; on good terms ❸draw; tie ❹indicating relationship, comparison, etc. ❺and ❻sum

【和蔼】kindly; good-natured; affable; amiable
【和风】soft breeze
【和好】become reconciled
【和缓】❶gentle; mild; ❷ease up; relax
【和会】peace conference
【和解】become reconciled
【和局】drawn game; draw; tie
【和乐】happy and harmonious
【和美】harmonious
【和睦】harmony; amity
【和暖】pleasantly warm; genial
【和盘托出】reveal everything; hold nothing back
【和平】peace
【和气】gentle; kind; polite; amiable; friendly; in a friendly way; good-natured
【和洽】harmonious; on friendly terms
【和蔼】kind and gentle; genial
【和尚】Buddhist monk
【和顺】gentle and amiable
【和谈】peace talks
【和祥】kindly; affable; amiable
【和谐】harmonious
【和煦】pleasantly warm; genial
【和颜悦色】a (pleasant) benign countenance
【和议】peace talks
【和约】peace treaty
【和悦】kindly; affable; amiable

河 ^(hé) river

【河岸】river bank
【河川】rivers and creeks

【河床】river bed
【河道】river course
【河堤】dike
【河谷】river valley
【河口】river mouth；stream outlet
【河流】rivers
【河马】hippopotamus；hippo；river horse
【河泥】river silt；river mud
【河渠】rivers and canals；waterways
【河山】rivers and mountains；territory
【河塘】river embankment
【河蟹】river crab
【河沿】river bank；riverside
【河运】river transport

荷 (hé) lotus

【荷包】❶small bag ❷pocket(in a garment)
【荷花】lotus
【荷兰】the Netherlands；the Holland
【荷叶】lotus leaf

核 (hé) ❶ pit；stone ❷ nucleus ❸ examine；check

【核爆炸】nuclear explosion；nuclear burst；atomic blast
【核导弹】nuclear missile
【核电站】nuclear power station
【核定】check and ratify；appraise and decide
【核对】check；check up
【核辐射】nuclear radiation
【核火箭】nuclear rocket
【核计】assess；calculate
【核能】nuclear energy
【核潜艇】nuclear-powered submarine
【核燃料】nuclear fuel
【核仁】kernel (of a fruit-stone)
【核实】check；verify
【核算】business accounting
【核桃】walnut
【核武器】nuclear weapon
【核销】cancel after verification
【核心】core；kernel
【核准】examine and approve；check and approve

盒 (hé) box；case

【盒饭】box lunch
【盒子】box；case；casket

贺 (hè) congratulate

【贺电】message of congratulation
【贺礼】congratulatory gift
【贺年】extend New Year greetings；pay a New Year call

【贺年片】New Year card
【贺喜】congratulate sb. on a happy occasion
【贺信】congratulatory letter

喝 (hè) shout loudly
另见 hē

【喝彩】acclaim；cheer
【喝令】shout an order
【喝问】shout a question to

赫 (hè) ❶conspicuous；grand ❷〈电〉hertz

【赫赫】illustrious；very impressive
【赫赫有名】distinguished；illustrious
【赫然】❶ impressively；awesomely ❷ terribly (angry)

褐 (hè)〈书〉❶ coarse cloth or clothing ❷brown

鹤 (hè) crane

【鹤发童颜】white hair and ruddy complexion；healthy in old age；hale and hearty

hei

黑 (hēi) ❶black ❷dark ❸secret；shady ❹wicked；sinister

【黑暗】dark
【黑白】black and white；right and wrong
【黑白分明】with black and white sharply contrasted；in sharp contrast
【黑板】blackboard
【黑帮】reactionary gang；sinister gang；cabal
【黑沉沉】(of the sky) gloomy；overcast
【黑道】❶ dark road ❷ dark deeds (as of robbers)
【黑点】stain；blemish；smirch
【黑光】black light
【黑幕】inside story of a plot，shady deal，etc.
【黑钱】ill-gotten money
【黑人】Black people；Negro
【黑色】black (colour)
【黑市】black market
【黑天】night；nightfall
【黑土】black earth；black soil
【黑心】black heart；evil mind
【黑夜】night
【黑云】black clouds；dark clouds

hen

痕 (hén) mark；trace

【痕迹】mark；trace；vestige

很 (hěn) very；very much；quite

【很好】quite well

狠 (hěn) ❶ ruthless；relentless ❷ suppress (one's feelings)；harden (the heart) ❸ firm；resolute

【狠毒】vicious；venomous；malicious

【狠心】cruel-hearted；heartless

恨 (hèn) ❶hate ❷regret

【恨不得】one wishes one could；one would if one could；be dying to

【恨之入骨】hate sb. to the marrow of one's bones；bear a bitter hatred for sb.；bitterly hate

heng

亨 (hēng) go smoothly

【亨利】〈电〉henry

【亨通】go smoothly；be prosperous

哼 (hēng) ❶groan；snort ❷hum；croon

【哼哧】〈象〉puff hard

恒 (héng) ❶ permanent；lasting ❷ perseverance ❸usual；common；constant

【恒等】〈数〉identically equal；identical

【恒温】constant temperature

【恒心】constancy of purpose

【恒星】〈天〉(fixed) star

【恒性】perseverance；persistence

【恒言】common saying

横 (héng) ❶horizontal；transverse ❷across；sideways ❸move crosswise；traverse ❹unrestrainedly；turbulently ❺violently；fiercely
另见 hèng

【横冲直撞】push one's way by shoving or bumping；jostle and elbow one's way；dash around madly；barge about

【横穿】cross

【横渡】cross(a river；etc.)；sail across；traverse

【横断面】cross section

【横幅】❶horizontal scroll of painting or calligraphy ❷banner；streamer

【横亘】lie across；span

【横祸】unexpected calamity；sudden misfortune

【横跨】stretch over or across

【横扫】sweep away；make a clean sweep

【横生】❶grow wild ❷be overflowing with；be full of ❸happen unexpectedly

【横向】crosswise

【横心】steel one's heart；become desperate

【横行】run wild be on a rampage

【横行霸道】ride roughshod (over)；play the tyrant

【横征暴敛】extort excessive (or heavy) taxes and levie

衡 (héng) ❶the graduated arm of a steelyard ❷ weighing apparatus ❸ weigh；measure；judge

【衡量】weigh；measure；judge

【衡器】weighing apparatus

横 (hèng) ❶harsh and unreasonable；perverse ❷unexpected
另见 héng

【横暴】perverse and violent

【横财】ill-gotten wealth (or gains)：发～ get rich by foul means；have a windfall

【横蛮】rude and unreasonable

【横事】an untoward accident

【横死】die a violent death；meet with a sudden death

【横恣】〈书〉perverse and wanton

hong

轰 (hōng) 〈象〉❶ bang；boom ❷ rumble；bombard；explode ❸shoo away；drive off

【轰动】cause a sensation；make a stir

【轰赶】shoo away；drive off

【轰轰烈烈】on a grand and spectacular scale；vigorous；dynamic

【轰击】bombard；bombardment；shell

【轰隆】〈象〉rumble；roll

【轰鸣】thunder；roar

【轰然】with a loud crash (or bang)

【轰响】roar；rumble

【轰炸】bomb

哄 (hōng) 〈象〉❶roars of laughter ❷hubbub
另见 hǒng

【哄传】(of rumours) circulate widely

【哄闹】(of a crowd of people) make a lot of noise；make a racket

【哄然】boisterous；uproarious

【哄抬】drive up (prices)

【哄堂大笑】the whole room rocking with laughter

【哄笑】(of a crowd of people) break into loud laughter；roar with laughter

烘 (hōng) ❶dry or warm by the fire ❷set off

【烘干】❶dry over heat ❷〈化〉stoving

【烘烤】toast；bake

【烘漆】baking finish；stoving finish

【烘托】❶(in Chinese painting) add shading around an object to make it stand out ❷set off by contrast；throw into sharp relief

【烘箱】oven

【烘云托月】paint clouds to set off the moon; provide a foil for a character or incident in a literary work

弘 (hóng) ❶great; grand; magnificent ❷enlarge; expand

【弘扬】carry forward; develop; enhance

红 (hóng) ❶red ❷symbol of success ❸bonus; dividend

【红榜】honour roll (or board)

【红茶】black tea

【红光满面】one's face glowing with health; in the pink

【红红绿绿】in gay colours

【红火】〈方〉flour-shing; prosperous

【红军】❶short for 中国工农红军 (the Chinese Workers' and Peasants' Red Army, 1928—1937); the Red Army ❷the Red Army man

【红利】bonus; extra dividend

【红脸】❶blush ❷flush with anger; get angry ❸red face, face painting in Beijing opera, etc., traditionally for the heroic or the honest

【红领巾】❶red scarf ❷Young Pioneer

【红绿灯】traffic light; traffic signal

【红扑扑】flushed

【红旗】red flag; red banner

【红润】ruddy; rosy

【红色】red

【红烧】braise in soy sauce

【红外线】〈物〉infrared ray

【红眼】❶become infuriated; see red ❷〈方〉be envious; be jealous of

【红晕】blush; flush

【红涨】(of one's face) be swelled with blood

【红肿】red and swollen

宏 (hóng) great; grand; magnificent

【宏博】extensive; wide

【宏大】grand; great

【宏观】❶〈物〉macroscopic ❷macro

【宏丽】magnificent; grand; majestic

【宏论】informed opinion; intelligent view

【宏图】great plan; grand prospect

【宏伟】magnificent; grand

【宏愿】great aspirations; noble ambition

洪 (hóng) ❶big; vast ❷flood

【洪大】loud

【洪恩】great kindness; great favour

【洪福】great blessing

【洪亮】loud and clear

【洪流】mighty torrent; powerful current

【洪水】flood; floodwater

【洪灾】a big flood; inundation

鸿 (hóng) ❶swan goose ❷〈书〉letter ❸great; grand

【鸿沟】wide gap; chasm

【鸿鹄】❶swan ❷a person of noble aspirations; a person with lofty ideals

【鸿毛】〈书〉a goose feather; something very light or insignificant

【鸿雁】swan goose

【鸿运】good luck

哄 (hǒng) ❶fool; humbug ❷coax; humour 另见 hōng

【哄逗】keep (esp. a child) in good humour; coax

【哄弄】〈方〉cheat; humbug; hoodwink

【哄骗】cheat

hou

喉 (hóu) larynx; throat

【喉结】〈生〉Adam's apple

【喉咙】throat

【喉舌】mouthpiece

【喉头】larynx; throat

猴 (hóu) ❶monkey ❷clever boy; smart chap

【猴子】〈动〉monkey

吼 (hǒu) roar; howl

【吼叫】roar; howl; shout

后 (hòu) ❶behind; back; rear ❷after; afterwards; later ❸last ❹offspring ❺empress; queen

【后备】reserve

【后背】❶back (of the body) ❷〈方〉at the back; in the rear

【后辈】❶younger generation ❷posterity

【后步】room for manoeuvre

【后尘】〈书〉footsteps

【后代】❶later periods (in history); later ages ❷later generations; descendants; posterity ❸〈生〉progeny

【后灯】taillight (of a car); tail lamp

【后盾】backing; backup force

【后方】rear; behind

【后夫】second husband

【后顾】❶turn back (to take care of sth.) ❷look back (on the past)

【后果】consequence; aftermath

【后患】future trouble

【后悔】regret; repent

【后记】postscript

【后继】succeed; carry on

【后脚】❶the rear foot (in walking) ❷close behind

【后进】❶lagging behind; less advanced; backward ❷juniors

【后劲】❶delayed effect; aftereffect ❷reserved strength

【后来】afterwards; later

【后路】❶communication lines to the rear; route of retreat ❷room for manoeuvre

【后面】❶at the back; in the rear; behind ❷later

【后脑】hindbrain; rhombencephalon

【后年】the year after next

【后期】later stage; later period

【后勤】rear service; logistics

【后人】future generations; posterity; descendants

【后晌】〈方〉afternoon

【后身】❶the back of a person ❷the back of a garment ❸the back of a building ❹reincarnation ❺sth. deriving from an earlier form; descendant

【后生】〈方〉❶young man; lad ❷having a youthful appearance

【后世】❶later ages ❷later generations

【后台】❶backstage ❷backstage supporter; behind-the-scenes backer

【后天】❶the day after tomorrow ❷postnatal; acquired

【后退】draw back; fall back; retreat

【后卫】❶〈军〉rear guard ❷football full back; defender ❸basketball guard

【后行】carry out as a second step; carry out later

【后遗症】sequelae

【后援】reinforcements; backup force; backing

【后院】backyard

【后缀】〈语〉suffix

厚 (hòu) ❶thick ❷deep; profound ❸kind; magnanimous ❹large; generous ❺rich or strong in flavour ❻favor; stress

【厚爱】〈套〉your kind thought; your kindness

【厚薄】thickness

【厚道】honest and kind

【厚度】thickness

【厚恩】〈套〉your great kindness

【厚礼】generous gifts

【厚实】thick and solid

【厚望】great expectations

【厚味】savoury; rich (or greasy) food

【厚颜无耻】impudent; brazen; shameless

【厚意】kind thought; kindness

【厚重】❶thick and heavy ❷rich and generous ❸〈书〉kind and dignified

候 (hòu) ❶wait; await ❷inquire after ❸time; season

【候补】be a candidate (for a vacancy); be an alternate

【候车】wait for a train, bus, etc.

【候鸟】migratory bird; migrant

【候审】〈法〉await trial

【候选人】candidate

【候诊】wait to see the doctor

【候诊室】waiting room (in a hospital)

hu

呼 (hū) ❶breathe out; exhale ❷shout; cry out ❸call

【呼风唤雨】❶summon wind and rain; control the forces of nature ❷stir up trouble

【呼喊】call out; shout

【呼号】❶wail; cry out in distress ❷call sign; call letters ❸catchword

【呼吼】whistle; roar

【呼唤】call; shout to

【呼叫】❶call out; shout ❷〈讯〉call

【呼救】call for help

【呼噜】〈口〉snore

【呼哨】whistle

【呼声】cry; voice

【呼天抢地】lament to heaven and knock one's head on earth

【呼吸】breathe; respire

【呼啸】whistle; scream; whizz

【呼应】echo; work in concert

【呼吁】appeal; call on

忽 (hū) ❶neglect; overlook ❷suddenly

【忽地】suddenly; all of a sudden

【忽略】neglect; overlook; lose sight of

【忽然】suddenly; all of a sudden

【忽闪】(of a light) flash

【忽视】ignore; neglect

【忽悠】〈方〉flicker

囫 (hú)

【囫囵】whole

【囫囵吞枣】swallow dates whole; read without understanding

狐 (hú) fox

【狐狸】fox

【狐朋狗友】evil associates

【狐疑】doubt; suspicion

弧 (hú) 〈数〉arc

【弧度】〈数〉radian
【弧线】pitch arc
【弧形】arc;curve

胡 (hú) ❶〈史〉non-Han nationalities living in the north and west in ancient times ❷ introduced from the northern and western nationalities or from abroad ❸ recklessly;wantonly;outrageously ❹〈书〉why ❺moustache, beard or whiskers

【胡扯】（talk）nonsense
【胡吹】boast outrageously;talk big
【胡搞】❶mess things up;meddle with sth. ❷carry on an affair with sb.;be promiscuous
【胡话】ravings;wild talk
【胡椒】pepper
【胡来】❶fool with sth. ❷run wild
【胡噜】〈方〉❶rub ❷sweep（away）;scrape together
【胡乱】carelessly;casually
【胡萝卜】carrot
【胡闹】run wild
【胡说】❶talk nonsense ❷nonsense;twaddle
【胡思乱想】go off into wild flights of fancy
【胡同】lane;alley
【胡言乱语】talk nonsense;rave
【胡诌】cook up;fabricate wild tales
【胡子】beard,moustache or whiskers
【胡作非为】commit all kinds of outrages

壶 (hú) ❶kettle;pot ❷bottle;flask

蝴 (hú)

【蝴蝶】butterfly
【蝴蝶花】fringed iris
【蝴蝶结】bowknot;bow

糊 (hú) ❶be burnt;be singed ❷paste

【糊料】thickener
【糊涂】muddled;confused
【糊涂虫】blunderer;bungler

虎 (hǔ) ❶tiger ❷brave;vigorous

【虎背熊腰】giant knotweed
【虎将】a brave general
【虎劲】dauntless drive;dash
【虎口】tiger's mouth—jaws of death
【虎视眈眈】glare like a tiger eyeing its prey;eye with hostility
【虎头虎脑】（usu. of a boy）looking strong and good-natured
【虎头蛇尾】in like a lion,out like a lamb;fine start and poor finish

【虎威】（of a military officer）valiant and awe-inspiring
【虎穴】tiger's den—a danger spot

琥 (hǔ)

【琥珀】amber

互 (hù) mutually;each other

【互访】exchange visits
【互换】exchange
【互惠】mutually beneficial;reciprocal
【互见】❶cross-reference ❷（of two contrasting things）exist side by side
【互敬互爱】mutually respect and love
【互利】mutually beneficial;of mutual benefit
【互让】yield to each other;give in to each other
【互相】mutual;each other;mutually
【互训】mutual glossing
【互助】help each other

户 (hù) ❶door ❷household;family ❸account ❹family status

【户籍】❶census register;household register ❷registered permanent residence
【户口】number of households and total population
【户头】（bank）account
【户外】outdoor
【户主】head of a household

护 (hù) ❶protect;guard;shield ❷be partial to;shield from censure

【护兵】（an official's）bodyguard;guard
【护城河】city moat
【护持】shield and sustain
【护短】shield a shortcoming or fault;attempt to justify one's mistakes
【护发素】hair conditioner
【护理】nurse;tend and protect
【护身符】amulet
【护士】nurse
【护守】guard;defend
【护送】convoy
【护卫】❶protect;guard ❷bodyguard
【护膝】〈体〉kneepad
【护养】❶cultivate;nurse;rear ❷maintain
【护照】passport
【护罩】guard shield;hood shield

hua

花 (huā) ❶flower;blossom;bloom ❷fireworks ❸pattern;design ❹multicoloured;coloured;variegated ❺blurred;dim ❻fancy;florid;flowery;showy ❼cream;essence ❽ wound ❾spend;expend

【花白】grey

【花斑】piebald:～马 a piebald horse

【花瓣】petal

【花苞】bud

【花边】❶decorative border;floral border ❷lace

【花草】❶ flowers and plants ❷〈方〉Chinese milk vetch

【花茶】scented tea

【花插】crisscross

【花车】festooned vehicle

【花丛】flowering shrubs

【花缎】figured satin;brocade

【花朵】flower

【花房】greenhouse

【花费】❶ spend; expend; cost; use up; take ❷ money spent;expenditure;expenses

【花粉】〈植〉pollen:～管 pollen tube

【花好月圆】blooming flowers and full moon; perfect conjugal bliss

【花红柳绿】red flowers and green willows—beautiful spring scene

【花花公子】dandy;coxcomb;playboy;a fine gentleman;a loose fish;a sad dog

【花花绿绿】brightly coloured;colourful:穿得～的 be colourfully dressed|～的招贴画 poster in colour

【花环】garland;floral hoop;torse

【花卉】❶flowers and plants ❷traditional Chinese Painting of flowers and plants

【花会】flower fair

【花甲】a cycle of sixty years

【花匠】gardener

【花椒】Chinese prickly ash

【花轿】bridal sedan chair

【花篮】❶ basket of flowers ❷ gaily decorated basket

【花里胡哨】❶gaudy;garish;showy ❷without solid worth

【花露水】toilet water;perfumed toilet water

【花苗】flower seedling

【花名册】register (of names); member roster; muster roll

【花木】flowers and trees

【花农】flower grower

【花盆】flowerpot

【花前月下】amidst flowers and in the moonlight—an ideal setting for amorous dalliance

【花腔】❶coloratura ❷guileful talk;crafty talk

【花圈】wreath

【花容月貌】flower-like features and moon-like face a great beauty

【花色】❶design and colour ❷(of merchandise) variety of designs,sizes,colours,etc.:新的～ latest designs

【花生】peanut;groundnut

【花市】flower market

【花天酒地】indulge in dissipation; lead a life of debauchery

【花筒】tube-shaped fireworks

【花团锦簇】bouquets of flowers and piles of silks — rich multicoloured decorations

【花纹】decorative pattern;figure:各种～的地毯 carpets of different patterns

【花絮】titbits(of news);interesting sidelights

【花言巧语】 flowery and deceiving words; sweet words

【花眼】❶presbyopia ❷be dazzled:挑来挑去挑～了 be dazzled by so many varieties to choose from

【花样】❶kind;variety;pattern ❷trick

【花样游泳】water ballet;synchronized swimming

【花园】garden;flower garden

【花枝招展】(of women)be gorgeously dressed

划 (huá) scratch;cut the surface of
另见 huà

【划不来】be not worth it;do not pay:为这点儿小事跑那么远的路～. It doesn't pay to walk such a long way for a trifle.

【划得来】be worth it;pay

【划水】strike water with one's arms in swimming

【划算】❶ calculate; weigh ❷ be to one's profit;pay

【划艇】canoe:～运动 canoeing

【划子】small rowboat

华 (huá) ❶magnificent;splendid ❷prosperous;flourishing ❸best part;cream ❹flashy;extravagant ❺China ❻Chinese

【华灯】colourfully decorated lantern;light

【华而不实】flashy and without substance;superficially clever

【华尔兹】waltz

【华发】〈书〉grey hair

【华贵】luxurious;costly

【华丽】resplendent;gorgeous

【华年】〈文〉youth;tender years

【华侨】overseas Chinese

【华人】Chinese:美籍～ an American Chinese

【华语】Chinese (language)

哗 (huá) noise;clamour

【哗变】mutiny

【哗然】in an uproar;in commotion

滑(huá)❶slippery;smooth ❷slip;slide ❸cunning;crafty

【滑冰】ice-skating;skating

【滑道】chute;slide

【滑动】〈物〉slide

【滑竿】a kind of litter

【滑稽】❶funny;amusing;comical ❷comic talk

【滑坡】❶landslide;landslip ❷be on the slippery slope;decline;come down;drop

【滑润】smooth;well-lubricated

【滑石】talcum;talc

【滑水】〈体〉water skiing

【滑梯】(children's) slide

【滑翔】glide

【滑行】slide;coast

【滑雪】〈体〉ski;skiing

化(huà)❶change;turn;transform ❷convert;influence ❸melt;dissolve ❹digest ❺burn up ❻〈化〉chemistry ❼beg alms ❽〈宗〉die

【化除】eliminate;dispel;remove:～成见 dispel prejudices

【化冻】thaw;melt

【化肥】chemical fertilizer

【化工】chemical industry

【化合物】chemical compound

【化名】assumed name;alias

【化脓】fester;suppurate

【化身】incarnation;embodiment

【化石】fossil

【化食】help(or aid) digestion

【化为乌有】come to nothing;bring to naught;come to naught

【化险为夷】turn danger into safety;head off a disaster

【化学】chemistry

【化验】chemical examination;laboratory test

【化妆】put on makeup;make up

【化装】❶(of actors)make up ❷disguise oneself

划(huà)❶delimit;differentiate ❷transfer;assign ❸plan ❹draw;mark;delineate ❺stroke
另见 huá

【划分】❶divide ❷differentiate

【划归】put under;in corporate into

【划价】have a prescription priced (in a hospital dispensary)

【划清】draw a clear line of demarcation;make a clear distinction:～是非 make a clear distinction between right and wrong

【划一】❶standardized;uniform:～的模式 a uniform model ❷standardize

画(huà)❶draw;paint ❷drawing;painting;picture ❸be decorated with paintings or pictures ❹stroke (of a Chinese character)

【画板】drawing board

【画报】pictorial

【画笔】painting brush;brush

【画饼充饥】draw cakes to allay hunger;feed on illusions

【画册】an album of paintings;picture album

【画法】technique of painting or drawing:～新颖 a novel technique in painting or drawing

【画幅】❶picture;painting ❷size of a picture

【画家】painter;artist

【画绢】silk for drawing on;drawing silk

【画面】❶tableau ❷(of a film) frame

【画图】❶draw designs,maps,etc. ❷picture(fig)

【画像】❶draw a portrait ❷portrayal

【画页】page with illustrations (in a book or magazine);plate

【画展】art exhibition

【画字】〈方〉make one's cross;sign

话(huà)❶word;talk ❷talk about;speak about

【话别】say good-bye

【话锋】thread of discourse;topic of conversation

【话旧】talk over old times;reminisce

【话剧】modern drama;stage play

【话题】topic of conversation

【话筒】❶microphone ❷telephone transmitter ❸megaphone

【话头】thread of discourse:打断～ interrupt sb.;cut sb. short

【话音】one's voice in speech

【话语】discourse;speech

huái

怀(huái)❶bosom ❷mind ❸keep in mind;cherish ❹think of;yearn for ❺conceive (a child)

【怀抱】bosom

【怀表】pocket watch

【怀恨】nurse hatred

【怀旧】remember past times or old acquaintances (usu. with kindly thoughts)

【怀恋】think fondly of (past times,old friends, etc.);look back nostalgically

【怀念】cherish the memory of

【怀想】think about with affection (a faraway person,place,etc.);yearn for

【怀疑】doubt;suspect

【怀孕】conception; in the family way; be pregnant

踝 (huái) ankle

【踝骨】anklebone

坏 (huài) ❶bad ❷go bad; spoil ❸badly; awfully; very ❹evil idea; dirty trick

【坏处】harm; disadvantage

【坏蛋】〈口〉bad egg; bastard

【坏话】malicious remarks; unpleasant words; vicious talk

【坏人】bad person; evildoer

【坏事】❶had thing; evil deed ❷ruin sth; make things worse

【坏死】〈医〉necrosis; 局部～ local necrosis

huan

欢 (huān) ❶joyous; merry; jubilant ❷vigorously; with great drive; in full swing

【欢蹦乱跳】healthy-looking and vivacious

【欢畅】thoroughly delighted; elated

【欢唱】sing merrily

【欢度】spend (an occasion) joyfully

【欢呼】hail; cheer; acclaim

【欢聚】happy get-together; happy reunion

【欢快】happily; light-hearted; lively

【欢乐】happy; joyous; merry; gay

【欢庆】celebrate joyously

【欢声雷动】cheers resound like peals of thunder

【欢声笑语】happy laughter and cheerful voices

【欢送】see off; send off (usu. referring to a collective affair)

【欢腾】great rejoicing

【欢天喜地】wild with joy; overjoyed

【欢慰】be gratified

【欢喜】joyful; happy; delighted

【欢笑】laugh heartily

【欢心】joyous; liking; love

【欢欣】joyous; elated

【欢宴】entertain sb. to dinner on some happy occasion

【欢迎】welcome; greet

【欢悦】happy; joyous

【欢跃】jump for joy

还 (huán) ❶go(or come) back ❷give back; return; repay
　　另见 hái

【还击】fight back; return fire; counterattack

【还价】counter-offer; counter-bid; abate a price

【还口】answer back; retort

【还礼】❶return a salute ❷〈方〉send a present in return; present a gift in return

【还清】pay off

【还手】strike (or hit) back

【还乡】return to one's native place

【还原】❶return to the original condition or shape; restore ❷〈化〉reduction; ～剂 reducing agent; reductant

【还愿】❶redeem a vow to a god ❷fulfil one's promise

【还债】pay one's debt; repay a debt

【还嘴】〈口〉answer (or talk) back; retort

环 (huán) ❶ring; hoop ❷link ❸surround; encircle; hem in

【环抱】surround; encircle

【环城】around the city; ～赛跑 round-the-city race | ～公路 ring road; belt highway; beltway

【环顾】〈书〉look about; look round

【环节】link

【环境】environment; surroundings; circumstances

【环球】❶round the world ❷the earth; the whole world

【环绕】surround; encircle; revolve around

【环山】❶around a mountain; ～公路 a road circumscribing(or going around) a mountain ❷be surrounded by mountains

【环视】look around

【环卫】〈书〉imperial guards; guards

【环行】going in a ring

【环形】annular; ringlike

【环游】tour around (a place): ～世界 take a round-the-world tour

缓 (huǎn) ❶slow; unhurried ❷delay; postpone; put off ❸not tense; relaxed ❹recuperate; revive; come to

【缓步】walk unhurriedly

【缓冲】buffer, cushion

【缓和】❶relax; ease up ❷calm down

【缓急】❶pressing or otherwise; of greater or lesser urgency ❷emergency

【缓解】relieve; alleviate

【缓慢】slow

【缓期】postpone a deadline; suspend

【缓气】get a breathing space; have a respite; take a breather

幻 (huàn) ❶unreal; imaginary; illusory ❷magical; changeable

【幻灯】❶slide show ❷slide projector

【幻景】illusion; mirage

【幻境】dreamland; fairyland

【幻觉】〈心〉hallucination

【幻灭】vanish into thin air

【幻听】〈医〉phonism

【幻想】fancy
【幻象】mirage; phantom; phantasm
【幻影】unreal image

换 (huàn) ❶exchange; barter ❷change

【换班】❶change shifts ❷relieve a person on duty ❸changing of the guard
【换车】change trains or buses
【换代】replace; regenerate: 产品更新～ replace the older generations of products by new ones
【换挡】〈机〉shift gears
【换岗】relieve a sentry(or guard)
【换货】exchange goods; barter: ～和付款协定 goods exchange and payments agreement
【换季】change garments according to the season; wear different clothes for a new season
【换毛】moult
【换气】take a breath (in swimming)
【换取】exchange sth. for
【换算】conversion
【换洗】change clothes (for washing)
【换药】change bandage; use fresh dressing for a wound
【换约】exchange of notes (or letters)

唤 (huàn) call out

【唤起】arouse; call; recall
【唤醒】wake up; awaken

涣 (huàn) melt; vanish

【涣然】(of misgivings, doubts, etc.) melt away; disappear; vanish
【涣散】lax; slack

患 (huàn) ❶trouble; peril; disaster ❷anxiety; worry ❸contract; suffer from

【患病】suffer from an illness; fall ill; be ill
【患处】affected part of a patient's body
【患得患失】worry about personal gains and losses
【患难与共】go through thick and thin together; share weal and woe
【患难之交】friends in adversity; tested friends
【患者】sufferer; patient

焕 (huàn) shining; glowing

【焕发】shine; glow; irradiate
【焕然一新】take on an entirely new look (or aspect); look brand new

huang

荒 (huāng) ❶waste ❷desolate; barren ❸famine ❹neglect; be out of practice ❺absurd

【荒草】weeds
【荒诞】absurd; preposterous; fantastic; incredible
【荒岛】a desert(or uninhabited)island
【荒废】❶leave uncultivated; lie waste ❷waste
【荒瘠】wild and barren; desolate and infertile
【荒郊】desolate place outside a town; wilderness
【荒凉】bleak and desolate; wild
【荒乱】in great disorder; in turmoil
【荒谬】absurd; preposterous
【荒漠】❶desolate and boundless: ～的草原 desolate and boundless grasslands ❷bleak and boundless desert; wilderness
【荒弃】leave uncultivated; lie waste
【荒时暴月】a time of dearth; a lean year; hard times
【荒唐】❶absurd; fantastic; preposterous ❷dissipated; loose; interoperate
【荒无人烟】desolate and uninhabited
【荒芜】lie waste; go out of cultivation
【荒野】wasteland; wilderness; the wilds
【荒原】wasteland; wilderness

慌 (huāng) ❶flurried; flustered; confused ❷awfully; unbearably

【慌乱】in a hurry; in a rush; alarmed and bewildered
【慌忙】in a great rush; hurriedly
【慌手慌脚】in a rush; in a flurry
【慌张】flustered; confused

皇 (huáng)〈书〉❶grand; magnificent ❷emperor; sovereign

【皇朝】feudal dynasty
【皇帝】emperor
【皇宫】(imperial) palace
【皇冠】imperial crown
【皇后】empress
【皇权】imperial power (or authority)
【皇上】❶the emperor; the throne; the reigning sovereign ❷Your Majesty; His Majesty
【皇族】people of imperial lineage; imperial kinsmen

黄 (huáng) ❶yellow; sallow ❷short for the Huanghe River ❸〈口〉fizzle out; fall through

【黄灿灿】bright yellow; golden: ～的稻子 golden rice
【黄道】〈天〉ecliptic
【黄澄澄】glistening yellow; golden
【黄瓜】cucumber
【黄河】the Huanghe River; the Yellow River
【黄褐色】yellowish-brown; tawny

【黄花】❶chrysanthemum ❷day lily ❸〈口〉virgin

【黄昏】dusk

【黄金】gold

【黄牛】❶ox;cattle ❷〈方〉scalper of tickets,etc.

【黄泉】the Yellow springs; the world of the dead;the underworld;the nether world

【黄色】❶ yellow ❷ decadent; obscene; pornographic

【黄鼠狼】yellow weasel

【黄糖】〈方〉brown sugar

【黄铜】brass;～管 brass pipe(or tube)

【黄土】〈地〉loess

【黄种】the yellow race

惶 (huáng) fear;anxiety;trepidation

【惶惶】in a state of anxiety; on tenterhooks; a-larmed

【惶惑】perplexed and alarmed

【惶恐】terrified

蝗 (huáng) locust

【蝗虫】locust

【蝗灾】plague of locusts

簧 (huáng)〈音〉❶reed ❷spring

【簧风琴】reed organ;harmonium

【簧片】〈音〉reed

【簧乐器】reed instrument

恍 (huǎng) all of a sudden;suddenly

【恍惚】❶ in a trance; absentminded ❷ dimly;faintly

【恍然大悟】suddenly see the light; suddenly realize what has happened

晃 (huǎng) ❶dazzle ❷flash past
　　另见 huàng

【晃眼】❶dazzle ❷twinkling

谎 (huǎng) lie;falsehood

【谎报】lie about sth.; give false information; start a canard

【谎称】falsely claim to be;pretend to be

【谎话】lie;falsehood:～连篇 a pack of lies

【谎骗】deceive;cheat;dupe

【谎言】lie;falsehood:戳穿～ expose a lie

幌 (huǎng)〈书〉heavy curtain

【幌子】❶ shop sign; signboard ❷ pretence; cover;front

晃 (huàng) shake;sway
　　另见 huǎng

【晃荡】rock;shake

【晃动】rock;sway

【晃悠】wobble;stagger;shake from side to side

hui

灰 (huī) ❶ash ❷dust ❸lime;(lime) mortar ❹grey ❺disheartened;discouraged

【灰暗】murky grey;gloomy

【灰白】greyish white;ashen;pale:～的鬓发 greying temples

【灰尘】dust;dirt

【灰沉沉】gloomy; leaden:天空～的 a gloomy sky;a leaden sky

【灰飞烟灭】flying ashes and smouldering smoke

【灰烬】ashes

【灰溜溜】❶dull grey ❷gloomy;dejected; crestfallen

【灰蒙蒙】dusky; overcast:～的夜色 a dusky night scene

【灰色】❶grey;ashy ❷pessimistic;gloomy ❸obscure;ambiguous

【灰心】lose heart; be discouraged; be disheartened

诙 (huī)

【诙谐】humorous;jocular

【诙谐曲】〈音〉humoresque

挥 (huī) ❶ wave; wield ❷ wipe off ❸ command (an army) scatter;disperse

【挥斥】〈书〉bold and unrestrained;untrammelled

【挥动】wave;brandish

【挥发】volatilize

【挥汗如雨】dripping with sweat

【挥霍】spend freely;squander

【挥洒】❶sprinkle(water);shed(tears) ❷write or paint freely and easily

【挥手】wave one's hand;wave

【挥舞】wave;brandish;wield

恢 (huī) extensive;vast

【恢复】❶ renew; resume (diplomatic relation, etc.) ❷ recover (one's health, consciousness, etc.) ❸restore;reinstate

【恢恢】〈书〉extensive

辉 (huī) ❶brightness;splendour ❷shine

【辉煌】brilliant;splendid;glorious

【辉耀】shine;illuminate

【辉映】shine;reflect

徽 (huī) ❶ emblem; badge; insignia ❷ fine;glorious

【徽记】sign;mark

【徽章】badge;insignia

回 (huí) ❶circle;wind ❷return;go back ❸turn round ❹answer;reply ❺decline;refuse;cancel;dismiss ❻time;occasion

【回报】❶report back ❷repay;reciprocate ❸pay sb. back in his own coin

【回避】avoid (meeting sb.);evade

【回禀】report back (to one's superior)

【回肠】〈书〉worried;agitated;anxious

【回潮】❶(of dried things) get damp again ❷resurgence;reversion

【回程】❶ return trip ❷〈机〉 return (or back) stroke

【回春】❶return of spring ❷bring back to life

【回答】answer;reply;response

【回荡】resound

【回电】❶wire back ❷a telegram in reply

【回访】pay a return visit

【回复】reply (to a letter)

【回顾】look back;review

【回锅】❶heat up(a cooked dish)❷cook again

【回航】return to base or port

【回合】round

【回击】fight back;return fire;counterattack

【回教】Islam

【回绝】decline;refuse

【回扣】sales commission;rebate

【回来】return;come back;be back

【回落】(water levels,priced,etc.)fall after a rise

【回请】give a return banquet

【回去】❶(used after a verb to indicate returning to where sth. came from) back ❷return;go back;be back

【回升】rise again;pick up

【回生】bring back to life

【回声】echo

【回收】retrieve;recover;reclaim

【回手】❶turn round and stretch out one's hand ❷hit back;return a blow

【回首】❶ turn one's head;turn round ❷ look back;call to mind

【回头】❶turn one's head; turn round ❷repent ❸later

【回味】❶aftertaste ❷call sth. to mind and ponder over it

【回乡】return to one's home village:～探亲 go home to visit one's family and relatives

【回响】reverberate;echo;resound

回想】think back;recall;recollect

回心转意】change one's views;come around

回信】❶write in reply;write back ❷a letter in reply ❸a verbal message in reply;reply

【回旋】❶circle round;round and round ❷(room for) manoeuvre

【回忆】call to mind;recollect;recall

【回音】❶echo ❷reply:立候～ hoping for an immediate reply ❸〈音〉turn

【回应】answer;respond

【回赠】send a present in return;present a gift in return

【回转】turn round:～马头 turn the horse round

悔 (huǐ) regret;repent

【悔改】repent and mend one's ways

【悔过】repent one's error;be repentant

【悔过自新】repent and turn over a new leaf;repent and make a fresh start

【悔恨】regret deeply

【悔悟】realize one's error and show repentance

【悔罪】show repentance;show penitence

毁 (huǐ) ❶destroy;ruin;damage ❷burn up ❸defame;slander ❹〈方〉make over

【毁谤】slander;malign;calumniate

【毁害】destroy;damage

【毁坏】destroy;damage

【毁灭】exterminate

【毁弃】scrap;annul

【毁容】disfigure one's face

【毁损】damage;impair

【毁誉】praise or blame;praise or condemnation

【毁约】❶break one's promise ❷scrap a contract or treaty

汇 (huì) ❶converge ❷gather together ❸things collected; assemblage; collection ❹remit

【汇报】report;give an account of

【汇编】compilation;collection

【汇兑】remittance

【汇费】remittance fee

【汇合】converge;join

【汇集】❶collect;compile ❷come together;converge;assemble

【汇寄】remit:通过邮局～款项 remit(or send) money by post

【汇款】❶remit money;make a remittance ❷remittance

【汇流】converge;flow together

【汇拢】❶come together;gather;assemble ❷collect;compile

【汇率】exchange rate

【汇票】draft;bill of exchange;money order

【汇算】settle accounts;wind up an account

【汇总】gather;collect;pool

H

会 (huì) ❶get together；assemble ❷meet；see ❸meeting；gathering；party；get-together；conference ❹association；society；union ❺chief city；capital ❻opportunity；occasion ❼understand；grasp ❽know ❾can；be able to

【会餐】dine together；have a dinner party

【会操】hold a grand parade；hold a joint drill exercise

【会场】meeting-place；conference(or assembly) hall

【会费】membership dues

【会合】join forces；meet；assemble

【会话】conversation(as in a language course)

【会徽】emblem of a sports meet，etc.

【会见】meet with

【会聚】assemble；flock together

【会客】receive a visitor (or guest)

【会面】meet；come together

【会齐】get together；assemble

【会旗】the banner of a meeting

【会审】❶joint hearing (or trial) ❷make a joint checkup

【会师】join forces

【会水】know how to swim

【会说】have the gift of the gab；be a glib talker

【会谈】talks

【会堂】assembly hall；hall

【会同】(handle an affair)jointly

【会悟】〈书〉understand；comprehend

【会晤】meet

【会心】understanding；knowing：～的微笑 an understanding smile

【会演】joint performance(by a number of theatrical troupes，etc.)

【会议】meeting；conference

【会员】member

【会诊】〈医〉consultation of doctors

【会址】❶the site of an association or society ❷the site of a conference or meeting

荟 (huì)〈书〉luxuriant growth (of plants)

【荟萃】(of distinguished people or exquisite objects) gather together；assemble

绘 (huì) draw；paint

【绘画】drawing；painting

【绘声绘色】vivid；lively

【绘图】mapping

【绘制】draw(a design，etc.)

贿 (huì) ❶wealth ❷bribe

【贿赂】❶bribe ❷bribery

【贿买】buy over；suborn

【贿选】practise bribery at an election；get elected by bribery

彗 (huì) broom

【彗星】〈天〉comet

晦 (huì) ❶the last day of a lunar month ❷dark；obscure；gloomy ❸night

【晦暗】dark and gloomy

【晦迹】〈书〉live in seclusion；withdraw from society and live in solitude

【晦气】unlucky

【晦涩】(of literary writing，music，etc.) hard to understand；obscure

秽 (huì) ❶dirty ❷ugly；abominable

【秽迹】〈书〉dirty business；scandalous affair

【秽气】stink；bad (or offensive) smell：～冲天 stink to high heaven

【秽语】obscene words；lewd speech

【秽浊】foul；filthy；dirty

惠 (huì) ❶favour；kindness；benefit ❷kind；gracious

【惠存】〈敬〉please keep；to so-and-so

【惠顾】your patronage

【惠书】〈套〉your kind letter

慧 (huì) intelligent；bright

【慧心】wisdom

【慧眼】mental discernment (or perception)；insight；acumen

hun

昏 (hūn) ❶dusk ❷dark；dim ❸confused；muddled ❹lose consciousness；faint

【昏暗】dim；dusky

【昏沉】❶murky ❷dazed；befuddled

【昏黑】dark

【昏花】dim-sighted

【昏黄】pale yellow；faint；dim：月色～faint moonlight

【昏厥】faint；faint away

【昏君】a fatuous and self-indulgent ruler

【昏乱】dazed and confused

【昏迷】coma

【昏眩】dizzy

【昏庸】stupid

婚 (hūn) ❶wed；marry ❷wedding；marriage

【婚假】marriage leave

【婚嫁】marriage

【婚礼】wedding ceremony；wedding

【婚配】married

【婚期】wedding day

【婚事】marriage；wedding：操 办 ～ prepare a wedding

【婚书】〈古〉marriage certificate

【婚姻】marriage

【婚约】marriage contract；engagement

浑 (hún) ❶muddy；turbid ❷foolish；stupid ❸ simple and natural ❹whole；all over

【浑厚】❶simple and honest ❷(of writing，painting，etc.) simple and vigorous

【浑话】impudent remark

【浑然一体】one integrated mass；a unified entity；an integral whole

【浑身】from head to foot；all over

【浑水摸鱼】fish in troubled waters

【浑圆】perfectly round：～ 的 珍珠 a perfectly round pearl

【浑浊】muddy；turbid

混 (hún) ❶muddy；turbid ❷foolish；stupid ❸ simple and natural；unsophisticated ❹ whole；all over
另见 hùn

魂 (hún) ❶soul ❷mood；spirit ❸ the lofty spirit of a nation

【魂不附体】as if the soul had left the body；scared out of one's wits

【魂不守舍】one's mind is somewhat unhinged

【魂飞魄散】be frightened out of one's wits (senses)

【魂灵】〈口〉soul

【魂魄】soul

混 (hùn) ❶mix；confuse ❷pass for；pass off as ❸muddle along；drift along
另见 hún

【混纺】blending

【混合】mix

【混合物】mixture

【混乱】confusion；chaos

【混凝土】concrete

【混日子】drift along aimlessly

【混同】confuse；mix up

【混为一谈】confuse sth. with sth. else

【混淆】confuse；mixed up

【混杂】mix

【混战】tangled warfare

【混账】scumbag

【混浊】muddy

huo

豁 (huō) ❶slit；break；crack ❷give up；sacrifice
另见 huò

【豁出去】go ahead regardless；be ready to risk everything

【豁口】break；breach

【豁子】〈方〉❶opening；break；breach ❷a harelipped person

【豁嘴】❶〈口〉harelip ❷a harelipped person

活 (huó) ❶live ❷alive；living ❸vivid；lively ❹save ❺movable；moving ❻exactly；simply ❼work ❽product

【活宝】a bit of a clown；a funny fellow

【活便】〈口〉❶dexterous；nimble；agile：手脚 ～ dexterous and quick in action ❷convenient

【活动】❶move about；exercise ❷shaky；unsteady ❸movable；mobile；flexible ❹activity；manoeuvre ❺use personal influence or irregular means ❻〈心〉behaviour

【活该】〈口〉it serve sb. right

【活化】〈化〉activation

【活话】indefinite words；vague promise

【活活】while still alive

【活计】❶handicraft work；manual labour ❷handiwork；work

【活力】vigour；vitality；energy

【活路】❶means of subsistence；way out ❷workable method

【活命】❶earn a bare living；scrape along；eke out an existence ❷〈书〉save sb.'s life ❸life

【活泼】lively；vivacious；vivid

【活期】current

【活水】flowing water；running water

【活页】loose-leaf；leaflet

【活跃】❶brisk；active；dynamic ❷enliven；animate

【活捉】capture alive

【活罪】❶living hell；untold suffering ❷living punishment

火 (huǒ) ❶fire ❷firearms；ammunition ❸〈中医〉internal heat ❹fiery；flaming ❺urgent；pressing ❻anger；temper

【火把】torch

【火柴】match

【火车】train

【火光】flame；blaze

【火锅】chafing dish

【火海】a sea of fire

【火红】red as fire；flaming；fiery

【火候】❶duration and degree of heating，cooking，smelting，etc. ❷level of attainment ❸a crucial moment

【火花】spark

【火化】cremation

【火鸡】〈动〉turkey

【火急】urgent；pressing

【火箭】rocket

【火井】〈方〉gas well

【火警】fire alarm

【火炬】torch

【火坑】fiery pit；pit of hell；abyss of suffering

【火辣辣】burning

【火力】〈军〉firepower；fire

【火笼】〈方〉hand-held bamboo basket brazier

【火炉】stove

【火冒三丈】fly into a rage

【火苗】a tongue of flame；flame

【火炮】cannon；gun

【火盆】fire pan；brazier

【火气】❶〈中医〉internal heat(as a cause of illness) ❷anger；temper

【火枪】firelock

【火热】❶burning hot；fiery ❷intimate

【火山】volcano

【火伤】burn (caused by fire)

【火势】the intensity of a fire

【火速】at top speed；posthaste

【火炭】burning charcoal or faggot

【火腿】ham

【火险】fire insurance

【火线】❶battle (or firing，front) line ❷〈电〉live wire

【火性】〈口〉bad temper；hot temper

【火焰】flame

【火药】gunpowder；powder

【火灾】fire；conflagration

【火葬】cremation

【火种】❶kindling material；kindling；tinder ❷live cinders kept for starting a new fire

伙 (huǒ) ❶mess；board；meal ❷partnership；company ❸partner；mate ❹group；crowd；band ❺combine；join

【伙伴】partner；companion

【伙房】kitchen(in a school，factory，etc.)

【伙计】❶partner ❷〈口〉fellow；mate

【伙食】mess；food；meals

【伙同】in league with；in collusion with

或 (huò) ❶perhaps；maybe；probably ❷or；either ...or ...

【或然】probable

【或许】perhaps；maybe

【或者】❶perhaps；maybe ❷or；either ...or ...

货 (huò) ❶goods；commodity ❷money

【货币】money；currency

【货场】goods (or freight)yard

【货车】❶goods train ❷goods van；freight car ❸truck

【货船】freighter；cargo ship

【货单】manifest；bill；shipping list

【货机】cargo aircraft (or plane)；air freighter

【货价】commodity price；price of goods

【货款】payment for goods

【货品】kinds or types of goods

【货色】❶goods ❷〈贬〉stuff；trash；rubbish

【货物】goods；commodity

【货箱】packing box

【货样】sample(goods)

【货源】source of goods

【货运】〈交〉freight transport

【货主】owner of cargo

获 (huò) ❶capture；catch ❷obtain；win；reap ❸harvest；gather in

【获得】gain；obtain；acquire；win；achieve

【获奖】win a prize；be awarded a prize

【获救】be rescued

【获利】make a profit；reap profits

【获取】procure；obtain；gain；reap

【获胜】win victory；be victorious；triumph

【获释】be released；be set free；get off

【获悉】learn (of an event)

【获致】gain；obtain；acquire；achieve

【获准】get (or obtain) permission

祸 (huò) ❶misfortune；disaster；calamity ❷bring disaster upon；ruin

【祸根】the root of the trouble；the cause of ruin；bane

【祸害】❶disaster；course；scourge ❷damage；destroy

【祸患】disaster；calamity

【祸乱】disastrous disorder；turmoil；social upheaval

【祸事】disaster；calamity；mishap

【祸殃】disaster；calamity；catastrophe

【祸种】the root of the trouble；the cause of ruin；bane

惑 (huò) ❶be puzzled；be bewildered ❷delude；mislead

【惑乱】delude and confuse

豁 (huò) ❶clear；open；open-minded；generous ❷exempt；remit
　　另见 huō

【豁达】sanguine；optimistic

【豁朗】high-spirited；broad-minded

【豁亮】❶roomy and bright ❷sonorous；resonant

【豁免】exempt；remit

J j

jī

几 (jī) ❶ a small table ❷ nearly; almost
另见 jǐ

【几乎】 almost; nearly; practically

【几近】 be close to; be on the verge of

讥 (jī) ridicule; mock; satirize

【讥讽】 ridicule; satirize

【讥诮】〈书〉sneer at; deride

【讥笑】 jeer; sneer at; deride

击 (jī) ❶ beat; hit; strike ❷ attack; assault ❸ come in contact with; bump into

【击败】 defeat; beat; vanquish

【击毙】 shoot dead

【击沉】 bombard and sink; send (a ship) to the bottom

【击穿】〈电〉puncture; breakdown

【击发】❶ pull the trigger (of a gun) ❷〈军〉percussion

饥 (jī) ❶ be hungry; starve; famish ❷ famine; crop failure

【饥饿】 hunger; starvation

【饥寒交迫】 suffer from hunger and cold; live in hunger and cold; be poverty-stricken

【饥荒】 famine; crop failure

【饥民】 famine victim; famine refugee

机 (jī) ❶ machine; engine ❷ aircraft; aeroplane; plane ❸ crucial point ❹ chance; occasion; opportunity ❺ flexible; quick-witted

【机舱】❶ engine room (of a ship) ❷ passenger compartment (of an airplane); cabin

【机场】 airport; airfield; aerodrome

【机车】 locomotive; engine

【机船】 motor vessel

【机动】❶ power-driven; motorize ❷ flexible; expedient; mobile ❸ keep in reserve; for emergency use

【机组】 aircrew; flight crew;〈机〉unit; set

肌 (jī) muscle; flesh

【肌肤】〈书〉(human) skin

【肌腱】 tendon

【肌肉】 flesh; muscle

【肌体】 human body; organism

鸡 (jī) chicken

【鸡蛋】 egg

【鸡公】〈方〉cock; rooster

【鸡冠】 cockscomb

【鸡毛】 chicken feather

【鸡婆】 hen

【鸡肉】 chicken

【鸡汤】 chicken broth

奇 (jī) ❶ odd (number) ❷〈书〉a fractional amount (over that mentioned in a round number); odd lost
另见 qí

【奇数】〈数〉odd number

积 (jī) ❶ amass; store up; accumulate ❷ longstanding; long-pending; age-old ❸ product

【积案】 a long-pending case

【积弊】 age-old malpractice; long-standing abuse

【积储】 store up; lay up; stockpile

【积存】 store up; lay up; stockpile

【积肥】 collect (farmyard) manure

【积分】〈数〉integral

【积极】❶ active; positive ❷ active; energetic; vigorous

【积蓄】❶ store up; put aside; save; accumulate ❷ savings

【积雪】 accumulated snow

【积压】 overstock; keep long in stock

基 (jī) ❶ base; foundation ❷ basic; key; primary; cardinal ❸ radical; base; group

【基本】❶ basic; fundamental; elementary ❷ main; essential ❸ basically; in the main; on the whole

【基本功】 basic training; basic skill; essential technique

【基层】 basic level; primary level; grassroots unit

【基础】 foundation; base; basis

【基地】 base

【基点】 basic point

【基肥】 base manure; base fertilizer

【基价】base price
【基金】fund
【基因】〈生〉gene
【基于】because of; in view of

缉 (jī) seize; arrest

【缉捕】seize; arrest
【缉拿】arrest
【缉私】suppress smuggling

畸 (jī) ❶lopsided; unbalanced ❷irregular; abnormal

【畸变】distortion
【畸形】❶〈医〉deformity ❷unbalanced; abnormal

稽 (jī)

【稽查】❶check (to prevent smuggling, tax evasion, etc.) ❷an official engaged in such work; customs officer
【稽核】check; examine
【稽考】〈书〉ascertain; verify

激 (jī) ❶swash; surge; dash ❷arouse; stimulate; excite ❸sharp; fierce; violent ❹excitement; stimulation

【激昂】roused; aroused; excited and indignant; be emotionally wrought up
【激荡】agitate; rage
【激动】❶stir; heat; excite; agitate; inspire ❷excitement; emotion ❸excitedly
【激发】❶arouse; stimulate; set off ❷excite
【激奋】rouse sb. to action
【激愤】wrathful; indignant: 心情～ be filled with indignation
【激光】laser
【激化】sharpen; intensify
【激进】radical
【激励】encourage; urge; stimulate; inspire; impel
【激烈】intense; sharp; fierce; fiery; violent; acute
【激流】torrent; rapids; turbulent current

及 (jí) ❶reach; come up to ❷in time for ❸and; as well as

【及格】pass a test or examination; pass
【及龄】reach a required age
【及时】❶timely; in time; seasonable; at the right time ❷promptly; without delay
【及早】at an early date; as soon as possible; before it is too late
【及至】up to; until

吉 (jí) lucky; auspicious; propitious

【吉利】lucky; auspicious; propitious
【吉他】〈音〉guitar

【吉祥】lucky; auspicious; propitious
【吉凶】good or ill luck
【吉兆】good omen; propitious sign

级 (jí) ❶level; rank; grade ❷grade ❸course; class; form ❹step; stage ❺〈语〉degree

【级别】rank; level; grade; scale
【级联】〈电〉cascade
【级数】〈数〉progression; series

极 (jí) ❶the utmost point; extreme ❷pole ❸extremely; exceedingly

【极大】〈数〉maximum
【极地】polar region: ～航行 arctic navigation; polar air navigation
【极点】the limit; the extreme
【极度】extreme; to the utmost
【极端】extreme; exceeding
【极光】〈天〉aurora; polar lights
【极口】in highest terms
【极力】do one's utmost; spare no effort
【极品】〈书〉highest grade; best quality
【极其】most; extremely; exceedingly
【极限】❶the limit; the maximum ❷〈数〉limit
【极夜】polar night

即 (jí) ❶approach; reach; be near ❷assume; undertake ❸at present; in immediate future ❹prompted by the occasion

【即便】even; even if
【即或】even; even if; even though
【即将】be on the point of
【即景】〈文〉(of a literary or artistic work) be inspired by what one sees
【即刻】at once; immediately
【即令】even; even if; even though
【即日】〈书〉❶this or that very day ❷within the next few days; within a few days
【即若】〈书〉even; even if; even though
【即时】immediately
【即使】even if; even though
【即事】write out of inspiration
【即位】〈书〉ascend the throne
【即席】〈书〉❶impromptu; extemporaneous ❷take one's seat at a dinner table, etc.
【即兴】impromptu; extemporaneous

急 (jí) ❶impatient; anxious ❷worry ❸irritated; annoyed ❹fast; rapid; violent ❺urgent; pressing ❻urgency; emergency

【急巴巴】anxious; impatient
【急病】acute disease
【急不可待】too impatient to wait; extremely anxious
【急促】❶hurried; rapid ❷short; pressing
【急电】urgent telegram; urgent cable (message)

【急风暴雨】violent storm;hurricane;tempest

【急件】an urgent document or dispatch

【急救】first aid;give first-aid treatment

【急剧】rapid;sharp;sudden

【急流勇进】forge ahead against a swift current;press on in the teeth of difficulties

【急忙】in a hurry;in haste

【急难】〈书〉❶ misfortune;grave danger ❷ be anxious to help(those in grave danger):扶危～ be eager to help(those in need or in danger)

【急迫】pressing;urgent;imperative

【急切】❶ eager;impatient;urgent;imperative;anxious ❷in a hurry;in haste

【急弯】sharp turn:拐了个～made a sharp turn

【急性】acute:～阑尾炎 acute appendicitis

【急需】❶be badly in need of ❷urgent need

【急用】urgent need

【急于】eager;anxious

【急躁】impatient;rash;impetuous

【急诊】emergency case;emergency call;emergency treatment

【急症】sudden attack(of illness);acute disease;emergency case

【急骤】hurried;flurried:～的脚步声 the sound of hurried footsteps

疾 (jí) ❶ disease; sickness; illness ❷ suffering;pain;difficulty ❸ hate;abhor ❹ fast;quick ❺vigorous;strong

【疾病】disease;illness;sickness;trouble

【疾步】walking quickly;at a fast pace:～上前 go forward quickly

【疾恶如仇】hate evil like an enemy

【疾风】❶strong wind;gale ❷〈气〉moderate gale

【疾患】〈书〉illness;disease

【疾苦】sufferings;hardships;difficulties

【疾驶】(of vehicles) speed along

集 (jí) ❶gather;collect ❷country fair;market ❸collection;anthology ❹volume;part

【集成电路】integrated circuit

【集股】collect capital;form a stock company

【集合】❶gather up;assemble;muster;call together ❷Fall in!(word of command)

【集会】assembly;meeting;conference;rally;gathering;

【集结】(esp. of troops) mass;concentrate;build up:～军队 mass troops;concentrate forces

【集市】country fair;market

【集体】collective:～生活 collective life

【集团】group;bloc;clique;community;circle;an organization;a body of people;a faction

【集训】assemble for training

【集邮】stamp collecting;philately

【集运】transport sth. containerized

【集中】concentrate;centre;centralize;focus;amass;put together:精神～ concentrate one's mind

【集中营】concentration camp

【集资】raise funds;collect money;pool resources;fund raising

嫉

【嫉妒】be jealous;be envious ❷hate

【嫉妒】be jealous of;envy

【嫉恨】hate out of jealousy

籍 (jí) ❶book;record ❷registry;roll ❸native place;home town;birthplace ❹membership

【籍贯】the place of one's birth or origin;native place

几 (jǐ) ❶how many ❷a few;several;some 另见 jī

【几多】〈方〉how many;how much

【几分】a bit;somewhat;rather

【几个】several;some;a few

【几何】❶〈书〉how many;how much ❷geometry

【几经】several times;time and again

【几时】what time;when

【几许】〈文〉how much;how many

己 (jǐ) ❶oneself;one's own;personal ❷the sixth of the ten Heavenly Stems

【己方】one's own side

【己任】〈书〉one's duty

挤 (jǐ) ❶squeeze;press ❷jostle;push against ❸crowd;pack;cram

【挤兑】a run on a bank

【挤对】〈方〉❶force into submission ❷ push aside;push out;squeeze out;elbow out ❸make fun of;poke fun at

【挤奶】milk (a cow,etc.)

【挤压】〈冶〉extruding

【挤眼】wink

济 (jǐ) 另见 jì

【济济】(of people) many;numerous

【济济一堂】gather together under the same roof

给 (jǐ) ❶supply;provide ❷ample;well provided for 另见 gěi

【给水】❶〈建〉watersupply:～工程 watersupply engineering ❷〈机〉feed water:锅炉～ boiler feed water

【给养】provisions；rations；victuals
【给予】〈书〉give；render；offer

脊 (jǐ) ❶spine；backbone；vertebra ❷ridge

【脊背】back（of a human being）
【脊梁】〈方〉back(of the human body)
【脊髓】spinal cord
【脊柱】〈解〉spinal column
【脊椎】vertebra

计 (jì) ❶count；compute；calculate；number ❷haggle over ❸idea；ruse；stratagem；plan

【计策】stratagem；plan；scheme；device；trick；trap
【计程表】taximeter
【计酬】work out or calculate payment：按件～ pay by the piece
【计划】❶plan；project；program ❷map out；plan
【计价】valuate
【计件】reckon by the piece
【计较】❶bother about；haggle over；mind；care；fuss about ❷argue；dispute；discuss；talk it over；negotiate
【计量】measure；calculate；estimate
【计谋】stratagem；plot；scheme；trick
【计时】reckon by time
【计数】count
【计算】❶count；compute；calculate；reckon ❷consideration；planning
【计算机】computer；calculating machine
【计算器】calculator
【计议】deliberate；talk over；consult

记 (jì) ❶remember；bear in mind ❷write down；record；jot down；take down ❸notes；record ❹mark；sign ❺birthmark

【记仇】bear grudges；harbour bitter resentment
【记得】remember
【记工】record workpoint
【记功】record a merit
【记挂】〈方〉be concerned about；keep thinking about；miss
【记过】record a demerit
【记号】mark；sign；symbol
【记恨】bear grudges
【记录】❶take notes；keep the minutes；record ❷minutes；notes；record
【记起】recall；recollect
【记取】remember；bear in mind
【记事】❶keep a record of events；make a memorandum；刻书结绳～ keep records by notching wood or tying knots ❷account；record of events；chronicles
【记述】record and narrate
【记下】note；put down；take down；make out

【记性】memory
【记叙】narrate
【记忆】❶remember；recall ❷memory ❸storage
【记载】put down in writing record；account
【记账】❶keep accounts ❷charge to an account
【记者】reporter；correspondent
【记住】remember；learn by heart；bear in mind

伎 (jì) ❶skill；ability；trick ❷a professional female dancer or singer in ancient China

【伎俩】trick；intrigue；manoeuvre

纪 (jì) ❶discipline ❷put down in writing；record ❸age；epoch ❹〈地〉period

【纪检】inspect discipline
【纪律】discipline
【纪年】❶a way of numbering the years ❷chronological record of events；annals
【纪念】commemorate；mark
【纪念碑】monument；memorial；人民英雄～ the Monument to the People's Heroes
【纪念册】autograph book；autograph album
【纪念品】souvenir；keepsake；memento
【纪念日】commemoration day；red-letter day
【纪念堂】memorial hall；commemoration hall
【纪元】❶the beginning of an era ❷epoch；era
【纪传体】history presented in a series of biographies

技 (jì) skill；ability；trick

【技工】❶skilled worker ❷mechanic；technician
【技能】technical ability
【技巧】skill；technique；craftsmanship
【技师】technician
【技术】technology；skill；technique
【技术性】technical；of a technical nature：～问题 technical matters
【技艺】skill；artistry；feat

忌 (jì) ❶be jealous of；envy ❷fear；dread；scruple ❸avoid；shun；abstain from ❹quit；give up

【忌惮】dread；fear；scruple
【忌妒】be jealous of；envy
【忌讳】taboo

际 (jì) ❶border；boundary；edge ❷between；among；inter ❸inside ❹occasion；time ❺on the occasion of ❻one's lot；circumstances

【际遇】favourable turns in life；spells of good or bad fortune

季 (jì) ❶season ❷the last month of a season ❸the fourth or youngest among brothers

【季冬】last month of winter
【季度】quarter（of a year）
【季风】〈气〉monsoon

【季节】season：农忙～ a busy farming season
【季军】the third prize winner
【季刊】quarterly；quarterly publication
【季夏】last month of summer

迹（jì）❶mark；trace ❷remains；ruins；vestige ❸an outward sign；indication
【迹象】sign；indication

济（jì）❶cross a river ❷aid；relieve；help ❸be of help；benefit
　　另见 jǐ
【济贫】aid the poor；relieve the poor
【济世】benefit mankind；do good to society
【济事】(usu. used in the negative) be of help (or use)

既（jì）❶already ❷since；as；now that ❸both … and …；as well as
【既定】set；fixed；established
【既而】〈书〉afterwards；subsequently；later
【既然】since；as；now that
【既是】since；as；now that

继（jì）❶continue；succeed；follow ❷then；afterwards
【继承】inherit；carry on
【继父】stepfather
【继母】stepmother
【继女】stepdaughter
【继任】succeed sb. in a post
【继位】succeed to the throne
【继续】❶continue；go on (with)；keep on；proceed ❷continuation
【继子】stepson

祭（jì）❶hold a memorial ceremony for ❷offer a sacrifice to ❸wield
【祭奠】hold a memorial ceremony for
【祭礼】❶ sacrificial rites ❷ memorial ceremony ❸sacrificial offerings
【祭品】sacrificial offerings；oblation
【祭祀】offer sacrifices to gods or ancestors
【祭文】funeral oration；elegiac address

寄（jì）❶send；post；mail ❷entrust；deposit；place ❸depend on；attach oneself to
【寄出】send off
【寄存】deposit；leave with；check
【寄放】leave with；leave in the care of
【寄费】postage
【寄父】foster father
【寄居】live away from home
【寄卖】consign for sale on commission
【寄宿】❶lodge；put up ❷board
【寄托】❶entrust to the care of sb.；leave with sb. ❷place(hope, etc.)on；pin one's hopes on；find sustenance in；repose

【寄信】send a letter；post a letter
【寄养】entrust one's child to the care of sb.；ask sb. to bring up one's child
【寄意】send one's regards
【寄予】❶place(hope, etc.)on ❷show；give；express

寂（jì）❶ quiet；still；silent ❷ lonely；lonesome；solitary
【寂静】quiet；still
【寂寥】〈文〉still；silent；lonely；desolate
【寂寞】lonely
【寂然】〈文〉silent；still；～无声 quiet and still

jiā

加（jiā）❶add；plus ❷increase；augment ❸put in；append
【加班】work overtime
【加倍】double；redouble
【加餐】snack
【加车】(put on) extra buses or trains
【加法】〈数〉addition
【加工】❶process ❷〈机〉machining；working
【加固】reinforce；consolidate
【加害】injure；do harm to
【加号】plus sign(＋)
【加紧】step up；intensify
【加劲】put more energy into；make a greater effort
【加快】quicken；speed up
【加宽】broaden；widen
【加拿大】Canada
【加强】strengthen；enhance；argument；reinforce
【加热】heating
【加入】❶add；mix；put in ❷join；accede to
【加上】❶add；give ❷moreover；in addition
【加深】deepen
【加数】〈数〉addend
【加速】quicken；speed up；accelerate
【加油】❶oil；lubricate ❷refuel ❸make an extra effort：～干 work with added vigour
【加重】❶make or become heavier；increase the weight of ❷make or become more serious；aggravate ❸ aggravation；exacerbation；weighting；bodiness

夹（jiā）carry sth. under one's arm
　　另见 gā，jiá
【夹板】❶ boards for pressing sth. or holding things together ❷〈医〉splint
【夹层】double layer
【夹带】❶carry secretly；smuggle ❷notes smuggled into an examination hall
【夹道】❶a narrow lane；passageway ❷line both

sides of the street

【夹缝】a narrow space between two adjacent things; a crack; crevice

【夹攻】attack from both sides; converging attack; pincer attack

【夹心】with filling

【夹杂】be mixed up with; be mingled with

【夹子】❶clip; tongs❷folder; wallet

佳 (jiā) good; fine; beautiful

【佳话】a deed praised far and wide; a story on everybody's lips; a much-told tale

【佳节】festival

【佳句】beautiful line (in a poem); wellturned phrase

【佳偶】〈书〉a happily married couple

【佳品】excellent product; famous produce

【佳期】wedding (or nuptial) day

【佳肴】delicacies

【佳音】〈书〉good news; good tidings; favourable reply

【佳作】a fine piece of writing; an excellent work

枷 (jiā) cangue

【枷锁】yoke; chains; shackles; fetters

家 (jiā) ❶family; household ❷home ❸a person or family engaged in a certain trade ❹a specialist in a certain field ❺a school of thought; school

【家产】family property

【家常】the daily life of a family; domestic trivia

【家丑】family scandal; the skeleton in the cupboard(or closet)

【家畜】domestic animal; livestock

【家传】handed down from the older generations of the family

【家伙】〈口〉❶tool; utensil; weapon ❷fellow; guy

【家教】family education; upbringing

【家居】stay idle at home; be unemployed

【家具】furniture

【家谱】family tree; genealogical tree; genealogy

【家禽】poultry; domestic fowl

【家人】❶family members ❷servant

【家史】family history

【家属】family; family members

【家庭】family; household

【家务】housework; household duties; 〜劳动 household chores

【家乡】hometown; native place

【家业】family property

【家长】❶the head of a family; patriarch ❷the parent or guardian of a child; parents

【家族】clan; family

嘉 (jiā) ❶good; fine ❷praise; commend

【嘉宾】honoured guest; welcome guest

【嘉奖】commend; cite

【嘉勉】praise and encourage

【嘉许】praise; approve

夹 (jiá) double-layered; lined
另见 gā; jiā

甲 (jiǎ) ❶first ❷shell; carapace ❸nail ❹armour ❺the first of the ten Heavenly Stems ❻ formerly, a unit of civil administration consisting of 10 households ❼(used for an unspecified person or thing)

【甲板】deck

【甲兵】〈书〉❶armour and weaponry ❷soldier in armour

【甲虫】beetle

【甲壳】crust

【甲鱼】soft-shelled turtle

假 (jiǎ) ❶false; fake; sham; phony; artificial ❷if; in case ❸suppose; assume; grant; presume ❹borrow; avail oneself as
另见 jià

【假扮】dress up as; disguise oneself as

【假充】pretend to be; pose as

【假道】via; by way of

【假定】❶suppose; assume; grant ❷hypothesis

【假发】wig

【假花】artificial flower

【假话】lie; falsehood; 说〜 tell lies

【假借】❶make use of; 〜外力 make use of outside forces ❷〈语〉phonetic loan characters, characters adopted to represent homophones, e. g.

【假冒】counterfeit; imitate; pass oneself off as

【假名】pseudonym

【假如】if; on condition that; in case; supposing

【假山】rockery

【假设】❶suppose; assume; grant ❷hypothesis

【假使】if; in case; in the event that

【假释】〈法〉release on parole (or on probation)

【假托】❶ on the pretext of ❷ under sb. else's name ❸by means of; through the medium of

【假想】❶imagination; hypothesis; supposition ❷imaginary; hypothetical; fictitious

【假象】false appearance; 制造〜 create a false impression; put up a false front

【假意】❶ unction; insincerity; hypocrisy ❷pretend; put on

【假造】❶forge; counterfeit ❷invent; fabricate

【假装】pretend; feign; simulate; make believe

价 (jià) ❶price ❷value

【价格】price

【价款】money paid for sth. purchased or received for sth. sold; cost

【价目】marked price; price

【价钱】price; 讲～ haggle over the price; bargain

【价值】value; value in use

驾 (jià) ❶harness; draw ❷drive; pilot; sail

【驾驶】drive; pilot; sail

【驾驭】❶drive ❷control; master; dominate

架 (jià) ❶frame; rack; shelf; stand ❷put up; erect ❸fend off; ward off; withstand ❹support; prop; help ❺kidnap; take sb. away forcibly ❻fight; quarrel

【架空】❶built on stilts; be without foundations ❷fanciful; impracticable; unpractical ❸make sb. a mere figurehead; render unfeasible

【架设】set up; put up; erect

【架势】〈方〉posture; manner

【架子】❶frame; stand; rack; shelf ❷framework; skeleton; outline ❸airs; haughty manner ❹posture; stance

假 (jià) ❶holiday; vacation ❷leave of absence; furlough
另见 jiǎ

【假期】vacation; period of leave

【假日】holiday; day off

【假条】❶application for leave ❷leave permit

嫁 (jià) ❶marry ❷shift; transfer

【嫁祸于人】put the blame on sb. else

【嫁接】〈植〉graft

【嫁妆】dowry; trousseau

jian

尖 (jiān) ❶point; tip; top ❷pointed; tapering ❸shrill; piercing ❹sharp; acute ❺the best of its kind; the pick of the bunch; the cream of the crop

【尖刀】sharp knife; dagger

【尖顶】pinnacle

【尖端】❶pointed end; acme; peak ❷most advanced

【尖刻】caustic; biting

【尖利】sharp; keen; cutting; shrill; piercing

【尖锐】❶sharp-pointed ❷penetrating; incisive; sharp; keen

【尖酸】acrid; acrimonious; tart

奸 (jiān) ❶wicked; evil; treacherous ❷traitor ❸self-seeking and wily

【奸臣】treacherous court official

【奸猾】treacherous; crafty; deceitful

【奸计】an evil plot

【奸商】unscrupulous merchant; profiteer

【奸细】spy; enemy agent

【奸险】wicked and crafty; treacherous; malicious

【奸笑】sinister(or villainous) smile

【奸贼】traitor; conspirator

【奸诈】fraudulent; crafty; treacherous

歼 (jiān) annihilate; wipe out; destroy

【歼击】attack and wipe out

【歼灭】annihilate; wipe out; destroy

坚 (jiān) ❶hard; solid; firm; strong ❷solid things ❸firmly; stead fastenly; resolutely

【坚不可摧】indestructible; impregnable

【坚持】insist on; persist in; stick to; adhere to; keep up

【坚持不懈】consistently; unremitting; persistent

【坚持不渝】persistent; persevering

【坚定】firm; staunch; stead fast

【坚固】sturdy; strong

【坚决】firm; resolute; determined

【坚苦】steadfast and assiduous

【坚牢】strong; solid

【坚强】❶strong; firm; staunch ❷strengthen

【坚忍不拔】firm and indomitable; stubborn and unyielding

【坚如磐石】solid as a rock; rock firm

【坚实】solid; substantial

【坚守】stand fast; hold fast to; stick to

【坚信】be fully confident of; firmly believe; be firmly convinced

【坚毅】firm and persistent; with unswerving determination; with inflexible will

【坚硬】solid; hard

【坚贞】faithful; constant

【坚贞不屈】remain faithful and unyielding

【坚执】insist on; persist in

间 (jiān) ❶between; among ❷within a definite time or space ❸room
另见 jiàn

【间不容发】not a hair's breadth apart or away—extremely critical

【间量】〈方〉the area of a room; floor space

【间奏曲】〈音〉❶entr'acte ❷intermezzo

肩 (jiān) ❶shoulder ❷take on; undertake; shoulder; bear

【肩膀】shoulder

【肩负】take on; undertake; shoulder; bear

【肩头】❶〈书〉on the shoulders ❷〈方〉shoulders

【肩章】❶shoulder loop; shoulder strap ❷epaulet

艰 （jiān）difficult；hard

【艰巨】arduous；formidable
【艰苦】difficult；hard；tough；arduous
【艰苦奋斗】hard struggle
【艰难】difficult；hard；arduous
【艰涩】involved and abstruse；intricate and obscure
【艰深】difficult to understand；abstruse
【艰险】hardships and dangers；perilous
【艰辛】hardships

监 （jiān）❶ supervise；inspect；watch ❷ prison；jail

【监测】monitor
【监测器】〈物〉monitor
【监察】supervise；control
【监场】invigilate
【监督】❶ supervise；superintend；control ❷ supervisor
【监犯】prisoner；convict
【监工】❶ supervise work；oversee ❷ overseer；supervisor
【监管】supervise；keep watch on
【监护】〈法〉guardianship；tutelage
【监禁】take into custody
【监考】invigilate；monitor examinations
【监牢】〈口〉prison；jail
【监票】scrutinize balloting
【监视】keep watch on
【监守】have custody of；guard
【监狱】prison；jail

兼 （jiān）❶ double；twice ❷ simultaneously；concurrently

【兼备】have both...and...
【兼并】annex（territory，property，etc.）
【兼程】travel at double speed
【兼而有之】have both at the same time
【兼顾】give consideration to two or more things
【兼任】❶ hold a concurrent post ❷ part-time
【兼容】TV compatible
【兼旬】twenty days
【兼之】〈书〉furthermore；in addition；besides
【兼职】❶ hold two or more posts concurrently ❷ concurrent post；part-time job

缄 （jiān）seal；close

【缄口】〈书〉keep one's mouth shut；hold one's tongue；say nothing
【缄默】keep silent；be reticent

俭 （jiǎn）thrifty；frugal

【俭朴】frugal；simple；thrifty and simple；economical
【俭省】economical；thrifty
【俭约】〈书〉thrifty；economical

捡 （jiǎn）pick up；collect；gather

检 （jiǎn）❶ check up；inspect；examine ❷ restrain oneself；be careful in one's conduct

【检测】test；examine；check up
【检查】❶ check up；inspect；examine ❷ self-criticism
【检察】procuratorial work
【检点】❶ examine；check ❷ be cautious（about what one says or does）
【检举】report（an offence）to the authorities；inform against（an offender）
【检阅】review；inspect

减 （jiǎn）❶ subtract ❷ reduce；decrease；cut

【减产】reduction of output；drop in production
【减低】lower；reduce；cut；bring down
【减法】〈数〉subtraction
【减肥】reduce（weight）
【减号】〈数〉minus sign（一）
【减缓】retard；slow down
【减价】mark down
【减免】❶ mitigate or annul（a punishment）❷ reduce or remit（taxation，etc.）：申请～所得税 apply for a reduction of or exemption from income tax
【减轻】ease；lighten
【减弱】weaken
【减色】lose lustre；impair the excellence of；detract from the merit of
【减少】lessen；reduce；decrease；cut down
【减速】slow down；decelerate；retard
【减缩】reduce；cut down；retrench：～开支 reduce expenditure
【减退】go down；come down；decrease；drop
【减压】reduce pressure；decompress：～器 pressure reducer；decompressor
【减震】shock absorption；damping：～器 shock absorber；damper

剪 （jiǎn）❶ scissors；shears；clippers ❷ cut；clip；trim

【剪裁】❶ cut out（a garment）；tailor ❷ cut out unwanted material（from a piece of writing）；prune
【剪彩】cut the ribbon at an opening ceremony
【剪除】wipe out；annihilate；exterminate
【剪刀】scissors；shears；一把～ a pair of scissors
【剪辑】❶ 〈影〉montage ❷ editing and rearrange-

ment

【剪票】punch a ticket

【剪影】❶paper-cut;silhouette ❷outline; sketch

简 (jiǎn) ❶simple;simplified; brief ❷bamboo slips(used for writing on in ancient times) ❸letter ❹select;choose

【简报】briefing;bulletin

【简本】concise edition

【简称】❶abbreviation；shorter form ❷be called sth. for short;known as sth. for short

【简单】❶ simple; brief; uncomplicated ❷ over-simplified;casual

【简短】short;brief

【简介】brief introduction;synopsis

【简历】biographical notes

【简练】terse;succinct; pithy;内容丰富,文字～ rich in content and succinct in style

【简陋】simple and crude

【简讯】news in brief

【简要】brief;concise and to the point

【简直】simply;at all

见 (jiàn) ❶see;catch sight of ❷show evidence of;appear to be ❸refer to; see; vide ❹meet;call on;see ❺view;opinion

【见报】appear in the newspapers

【见怪】mind;take offence

【见鬼】〈口〉❶fantastic; preposterous; absurd ❷go to hell

【见机】as the opportunity arises; as befits the occasion;according to circumstances

【见解】opinion;view;point of view;idea; understanding

【见面】meet;see

件 (jiàn) ❶〈量〉(for matters in general) ❷〈量〉(for clothing,furniture,luggage,etc.) ❸ single item ❹ letter; correspondence; paper;document

间 (jiàn) ❶space in between;opening ❷separate ❸sow discord

　　另见 jiān

【间接】indirect;secondhand

【间日】〈书〉every other day

【间隙】interval;gap;space

【间歇】intermittence;intermission

【间杂】be intermingled;be mixed

建 (jiàn) ❶build; construct; erect ❷establish;set up;found

【建都】found a capital;make (a place) the capital

【建国】build up a country

【建交】establish diplomatic relations

【建立】build;establish;set up;found

【建设】build;construct

【建议】❶propose; suggest ❷proposal; suggestion

【建造】build;construct;make

【建制】organizational system;部队～ the organizational system of the army

荐 (jiàn) ❶ recommend ❷grass; straw ❸〈书〉straw mat

【荐举】propose sb. for an office;recommend

【荐头】〈方〉employment agent

【荐引】〈书〉recommend;introduce

贱 (jiàn) ❶low-priced; inexpensive; cheap ❷lowly; humble ❸ low-down; base; despicable ❹〈谦〉my

剑 (jiàn) sword;sabre

【剑客】chivalrous swordsman (in old novels)

【剑眉】straight eyebrows slanting upwards and outwards;dashing eyebrows

【剑术】swordsmanship;fencing skill

健 (jiàn) ❶ healthy; strong ❷ strengthen;toughen

【健步】walk with vigorous strides;～登上主席台 mount the rostrum in vigorous strides

【健将】master sportsman;topnotch player

【健康】❶health; physique ❷ sound

【健美】strong and handsome; vigorous and graceful

【健全】❶sound;perfect ❷improve; strengthen

【健身操】bodybuilding exercises

【健身房】gymnasium;gym

【健谈】talkative; be a good talker; be an eloquent talker; be a brilliant conversationalist

【健忘】forgetful;liable to forget;have a poor memory

【健在】〈书〉(of a person of advanced age) be still living and in good health

【健壮】healthy and robust; healthy and strong; strong and vigorous

舰 (jiàn) warship;naval vessel;man-of-war

【舰队】fleet;naval force

【舰艇】naval ships and boats;naval vessels

【舰载】carrier-borne; carrier-based; ship-based

【舰长】captain (of a warship)

渐 (jiàn) gradually; step by step; little by little;by degrees

【渐变】gradual change

【渐渐】gradually;little by little

【渐进】advance gradually;progress step by step

践 (jiàn) ❶trample; tread ❷act on;carry out

【践踏】tread on; trample underfoot

【践约】keep a promise; keep an appointment

溅 (jiàn) splash; spatter

【溅落】(of a space vehicle; etc.) splash down

鉴 (jiàn) ❶ancient bronze mirror ❷reflect; mirror ❸warning; object less on ❹inspect; scrutinize; examine

【鉴别】distinguish

【鉴定】❶appraisal ❷appraise; identify

【鉴戒】warning; object lesson

【鉴赏】appreciate

【鉴于】in view of; seeing that

键 (jiàn) key

【键盘】keyboard; fingerboard

箭 (jiàn) arrow

【箭步】a sudden big stride forward

【箭杆】arrow shaft

【箭头】❶arrowhead ❷arrow

jiang

江 (jiāng) ❶river ❷the Changjiang River

【江河日下】go from bad to worse; be on the decline

【江湖】❶rivers and lakes ❷all corners of the country ❸itinerant entertainers ❹trade of such people

【江畔】river bank; beside the river

【江山】state power; national territory

将 (jiāng) ❶incite sb. to action; challenge; prod ❷with; by means of; by ❸be going to; be about to; will; shall ❹certainly; no doubt 另见 jiàng

【将才】just now; a moment ago

【将功赎罪】atone for a crime by good deeds; expiate one's guilt by good deeds

【将计就计】beat sb. at his own game

【将近】close to; nearly; almost

【将就】make do with; put up with; make the best of

【将军】❶〈军〉general ❷〈体〉(Chinese chess) check ❸embarrass; challenge; put sb. on the spot

【将来】future; in the future

【将养】rest; recuperate

【将要】be going to; be about to

姜 (jiāng) ginger

僵 (jiāng) ❶stiff; numb ❷deadlocked

【僵持】(of both parties) refuse to budge

【僵化】become rigid; ossify

【僵局】deadlock; impasse; stalemate

【僵尸】corpse

【僵死】dead; ossified

【僵硬】❶stiff ❷rigid; inflexible

缰 (jiāng) reins; halter

【缰绳】reins; halter

疆 (jiāng) boundary; border

【疆场】battlefield

【疆界】boundary; border

【疆土】territory

【疆域】territory; domain

讲 (jiǎng) ❶speak; say; tell; talk about ❷explain; make clear; interpret ❸discuss; negotiate

【讲法】❶the way of saying a thing; wording ❷statement; version; argument

【讲稿】❶the draft or text of a speech ❷lecture notes

【讲故事】tell stories

【讲和】make peace; settle a dispute; become reconciled

【讲话】❶speak; talk; address; make a speech ❷talk; speech

【讲价】bargain; haggle over the price

【讲解】explain; expound; interpret

【讲究】❶be particular; pay attention to; stress; strive for ❷tasteful; elegant; exquisite

【讲课】teach; lecture

【讲理】reason with sb.; argue; be sensible; be reasonable

【讲明】explain; make clear; state explicitly

【讲评】comment on and appraise：～学生的作业 comment on the students'work

【讲情】intercede; plead for sb.：为他～ plead for him

【讲求】be particular about; pay attention to; stress; strive for.：～效率 strive for efficiency

【讲师】lecturer

【讲述】tell about; give an account of

【讲台】platform; rostrum

【讲堂】lecture room; classroom

【讲题】topic of a lecture

【讲演】❶make a speech ❷lecture; speech; address

【讲义】teaching materials

【讲座】a course of lecture

奖 (jiǎng) ❶encourage;praise;reward ❷award;prize;reward

【奖杯】cup

【奖惩】rewards and punishments;rewards and penalties

【奖金】bonus;prize;premium

【奖励】encourage;commend;reward;award

【奖牌】medal

【奖品】prize;award

【奖券】lottery ticket

【奖赏】award;reward

【奖售】encourage sales to the state

【奖学金】scholarship;exhibition

【奖章】medal

【奖状】certificate of award;honorary credential;diploma

桨 (jiǎng) oar;scull;paddle

匠 (jiàng) artisan;craftsman

【匠心】〈书〉ingenuity

【匠心独运】consummate craftsmanship

降 (jiàng) fall;drop;lower
另见 xiáng

【降低】reduce;drop;lower

【降级】❶reduce to a lower rank;demote ❷send (a student) to a lower grade

【降价】reduce(or lower) the prices

【降临】befall;arrive;come

【降落】descend;land

【降旗】lower a flag

【降生】〈书〉(of the founder of a religion,etc.) be born

【降水】〈气〉precipitation

【降温】❶lower the temperature ❷drop in temperature;cool down

【降压】❶step-down;reduction voltage ❷bring high blood pressure down ❸depressurization;pumpdown;decompression

【降雨量】rainfall

将 (jiàng) ❶general ❷commander in chief,the chief piece in Chinese chess ❸command;lead
另见 jiāng

【将领】general

【将门】the family of a general

【将士】〈书〉officers and men

【将帅】commander-in-chief

强 (jiàng) stubborn;unyielding
另见 qiáng;qiǎng

【强嘴】reply defiantly;answer back;talk back

酱 (jiàng) ❶thick sauce made from soybeans,flour,etc. ❷cooked or pickled in soy sauce ❸sauce;paste;jam

【酱菜】pickles

【酱肉】pork cooked in soy sauce

【酱色】dark reddish brown

【酱油】soy sauce;soy

jiao

交 (jiāo) ❶hand in;hand over;give up;deliver ❷meet;join ❸cross ❹associate with ❺deal;bargain;business transaction ❻friend;acquaintance;friendship;relation;relationship ❼fall

【交班】hand over to the next shift

【交叉】❶intersect;cross;crisscross ❷alternate;stagger

【交差】report to the leadership after accomplishing a task

【交出】surrender;hand over;～武器 surrender one's weapons

【交错】❶interleave;interlace ❷〈机〉staggered

【交代】❶hand over(work to one's successor) ❷make clear;brief;tell;explain(policy,etc.) ❸account for;justify oneself ❹confess(a crime,etc.)

【交锋】cross swords;engage in a battle or contest

【交付】❶pay ❷hand over;deliver;consign

【交好】(of people or states) be on friendly terms

【交还】give back;return

【交换】exchange;swop

【交货】delivery

【交际】social intercourse;communication

【交加】〈书〉(of two things) accompany each other;occur simultaneously

【交接】transfer;hand over;take over

【交界】have a common border;have a common boundary;border on

【交卷】❶hand in an examination paper ❷fulfil one's task;carry out an assignment

【交流】❶exchange;interflow;interchange;communication ❷〈电〉alternating

【交纳】pay;hand in

【交配】mating;copulation

【交情】friendship;friendly relation

【交融】blend;mingle

【交涉】negotiate;make representations;take up with

【交手】fight hand to hand;be engaged in a hand-to-hand fight;come to grips

【交谈】talk with each other;converse;chat;have

a conversation

【交替】❶ supersede; replace ❷ alternately; take place by turn; in turn

【交通】traffic; communications

【交通事故】traffic (or road) accident

【交通阻塞】traffic jam(or block)

【交头接耳】speak in each other's ears; whisper to each other

【交往】association; contact

【交尾】mating; pairing; coupling

【交响乐】symphony; symphonic music

【交易】business; deal; trade; transaction

【交织】interweave; intertwine; mingle

郊（jiāo）suburbs; outskirts

【郊区】suburban district; suburbs; outskirts

【郊外】the countryside around a city; outskirts

【郊游】outing; excursion

浇（jiāo）❶ pour liquid on; sprinkle water on ❷ irrigate; water ❸〈印〉cast ❹〈书〉straw mat〈书〉degenerate; depraved

【浇灌】❶ water; irrigate ❷ pour

【浇注】❶ pour (melted metal, cement mixed with water; etc.)into a mould ❷ devote (one's energies; etc.)to

娇（jiāo）❶ tender; lovely; charming ❷ fragile; frail; delicate ❸ squeamish ❹ pamper; spoil

【娇惯】pamper; coddle; spoil：～孩子 pamper a child

【娇贵】❶ spoiled; coddled ❷ delicate and fragile

【娇客】❶ son-in-law ❷ a pampered person

【娇嫩】tender and lovely; delicate; fragile

【娇妻】a beloved wife; a pretty young wife

【娇气】squeamish; finicky

【娇生惯养】brought up in clover

【娇声娇气】speak in a seductive tone

【娇小玲珑】delicate and exquisite; petite and dainty

骄（jiāo）proud; arrogant; conceited

【骄傲】❶ arrogant; conceited ❷ be proud; take pride in ❸ pride

【骄傲自满】conceited and self-satisfied; arrogant and complacent

【骄横】arrogant and imperious; overbearing

【骄慢】arrogant; haughty

【骄气】overbearing airs

【骄阳】blazing sun：～似火 a scorching sun beating down

【骄纵】arrogant and wilful

胶（jiāo）❶ glue; gum ❷ stick with glue; glue ❸ gluey; sticky; gummy ❹ rubber

【胶版】offset plate

【胶卷】film; roll film

【胶囊】capsule

【胶水】mucilage; glue

【胶鞋】❶ rubber overshoes; galoshes; rubbers ❷ rubber-soled shoes; tennis shoes; sneakers

【胶靴】high rubber overshoes; galoshes

【胶着】deadlocked; stalemated：～状态 deadlock; stalemate; impasse

教（jiāo）teach; instruct
另见 jiào

【教书】teach

焦（jiāo）❶ burnt; scorched; charred ❷ coke ❸ worried; anxious

【焦点】❶〈物〉focal point; focus ❷ central issue; point at issue

【焦黑】burned black

【焦黄】sallow; brown

【焦急】anxious; worried

【焦渴】terribly thirsty; parched

【焦枯】shrivelled; dried up; withered

【焦虑】feel anxious; have worries and misgivings

【焦煤】coking coal

【焦心】〈方〉feel terribly worried

【焦躁】restless with anxiety; impatient

【焦灼】〈书〉deeply worried; very anxious

角（jiāo）❶ horn; bugle ❷ cape; promontory; headland ❸ corner; angle ❹ a fractional unit of money in China
另见 jué

【角尺】angle square

【角度】❶〈数〉angle ❷ point of view; angle

【角楼】a watchtower at a corner of a city wall; corner tower; turret

【角落】corner

【角门】side gate

【角球】〈体〉(soccer) corner (kick)

侥（jiāo）

【侥幸】by luck; by a fluke; lucky; chancy

狡（jiāo）crafty; foxy; cunning

【狡辩】quibble; indulge in sophistry

【狡猾】sly; crafty; cunning; tricky

【狡计】crafty trick; ruse

【狡黠】〈书〉sly; crafty; cunning

【狡诈】deceitful; crafty; cunning

饺（jiāo）

【饺子】dumpling

绞（jiǎo）❶ twist；wring；entangle ❷〈量〉hank ❸ hang by the neck

【绞架】gallows

【绞尽脑汁】rack one's brains

【绞索】(the hangman's) noose

【绞痛】angina

【绞刑】death by hanging

矫（jiǎo）❶ rectify；straighten out；correct ❷ strong；brave

【矫健】strong and vigorous

【矫捷】vigorous and nimble；brisk

【矫揉造作】artificial；unnatural；affected

【矫饰】feign in order to conceal sth.；dissemble

【矫正】correct；put right

皎（jiǎo）clear and bright

【皎皎】very clear and bright；glistening white

【皎洁】(of moonlight) bright and clear

脚（jiǎo）❶ foot ❷ foot；base

【脚本】script；scenario

【脚步】step；pace

【脚灯】footlights

【脚夫】porter

【脚心】the underside of the arch（of the foot）；arch

【脚印】footprint；footmark；track

【脚掌】sole（of the foot）

【脚爪】〈方〉claw；paw；talon

【脚趾】toe

【脚注】footnote

搅（jiǎo）❶ stir；mix ❷ disturb；annoy

【搅拌】stir；mix

【搅动】mix；stir：拿棍子～灰浆 stir the plaster with a stick

【搅混】mix；blend；mingle；muddy

【搅和】〈口〉❶ mix；blend；mingle ❷ spoil；mess up

【搅乱】confuse；throw into disorder；mess up

【搅扰】disturb；annoy；bother

【搅匀】mix up

缴（jiǎo）❶ pay；hand over；hand in ❷ capture

【缴获】capture；seize

【缴销】hand in for cancellation：～营业执照 hand in the business licence for cancellation

【缴械】❶ disarm ❷ surrender one's weapons；lay down one's arms：～投降 lay down one's arms and surrender

叫（jiǎo）❶ cry；shout ❷ call；greet ❸ hire；order ❹ name ❺ ask；order ❻ allow

【叫喊】cry；shout(at)；yell；call out

【叫号】call out the numbers（of waiting patients，etc.）

【叫唤】❶ cry out；call out ❷（of animals，birds，insects，etc.）cry；call

【叫苦】complain of hardship of suffering；moan and groan

【叫卖】cry one's wares；peddle

【叫屈】complain of being wronged；protest against an injustice

【叫嚷】shout；howl；clamour

【叫嚣】clamour；raise a hue and cry

【叫醒】wake up；awaken

【叫作】be called；be known as

觉（jiào）sleep
另见 jué

校（jiào）check；proofread；collate
另见 xiào

【校订】check against the authoritative text

【校对】❶ proofread；❷ proofreader

【校改】read and correct proofs

【校勘】collate criticism

【校样】proof sheet；proof

【校阅】read and revise

【校正】proofread and correct；rectify

【校准】〈机〉calibration；方位～ bearing calibration

轿（jiào）sedan (chair)

【轿车】❶（horse-drawn）carriage ❷ bus or car

【轿夫】〈古〉sedan-chair bearer

较（jiào）❶ compare；as compared with；in comparison with ❷ comparatively；relatively；fairly；quite；rather ❸ clear；obvious；marked

【较劲】〈方〉match strength

【较量】❶ have a contest；have a test of strength ❷ argue；dispute

【较真】〈方〉serious；earnest

教（jiào）❶ teach；instruct ❷ religion
另见 jiāo

【教案】teaching plan；lesson plan；piece-by-piece plan

【教本】textbook

【教鞭】(teacher's) pointer

【教材】teaching material

【教程】❶ course of study ❷（published）lectures

【教导】❶ instruct；teach ❷ teaching；guidance

【教父】godfather

【教官】〈古〉drillmaster；instructor

【教规】〈宗〉canon

【教会】(the Christian) church

【教诲】〈书〉teaching；instruction

【教具】teaching aid

【教练】❶train;drill ❷coach

【教师】teacher;schoolteacher

【教士】priest;clergyman;Christian missionary

【教室】classroom;schoolroom

【教授】❶professor ❷instruct;teach

【教唆】instigate;abet

【教堂】church;cathedral

【教条】dogma;doctrine;creed;tenet

【教务】educational administration

【教务处】Dean's Office

【教学】education;teaching

【教学相长】teaching benefits teacher and student alike; teaching benefits teachers as well as students

【教训】chide;admonish;give sb. a talking-to; give sb. a piece of one's mind;give sb. a dressing down;moral

【教研组】teaching and research group

【教养】❶bring up;train;educate ❷breeding;upbringing;education;culture

【教育】❶teach;educate ❷education

【教员】teacher;instructor

【教长】religion imam;dean

窖 (jiào) ❶cellar or pit for storing things ❷store sth. in a cellar or pit

【窖藏】store sth. in a cellar or pit

jiē

阶 (jiē) ❶steps;stairs ❷rank

【阶层】(social) stratum

【阶级】❶〈书〉steps;stairs ❷〈古〉rank ❸(social) class

【阶级斗争】class struggle

【阶级矛盾】class contradictions

【阶级社会】class society

【阶梯】a flight of stairs;ladder

【阶下囚】prisoner;captive

皆 (jiē) all;each and every

【皆大欢喜】everybody is happy; to the satisfaction of all

结 (jiē) bear (fruit);form (seed);produce 另见 jié

【结巴】❶stammer ❷stammerer

【结果】bear fruit;fructify

【结实】❶solid;durable ❷strong

接 (jiē) ❶come into contact with;come close to ❷connect;join;put together ❸catch; take hold of ❹receive;take ❺meet;welcome ❻take over

【接班】take one's turn on duty; take over from;

succeed;carry on

【接触】❶come into contact with; get in touch with ❷engage(the enemy) ❸〈电〉contact

【接待】receive;admit

【接风】give a dinner of welcome (to a visitor from afar)

【接骨】set a (broken) bone;set a fracture

【接管】take over control;take over;～产业 take over the estate

【接见】receive sb.;grant an interview to

【接近】be close to;near;approach

【接力】relay;work by relays

【接连】on end; in a row;in succession

【接纳】admit(into);take in

【接洽】take up a matter with;arrange(business, etc.) with;consult with

【接生】deliver a child;practise midwifery

【接收】❶receive ❷take over;expropriate ❸admit

【接受】accept

【接替】take over;replace

【接通】put through

【接头】❶ connect; join; joint ❷ contact; get in touch with; meet ❸ have knowledge of; know about

【接吻】kiss

【接线员】(telephone) operator

【接应】❶come to sb.'s aid;coordinate with;reinforce ❷supply

【接着】❶follow;carry on;go on(with);proceed ❷then;after that ❸catch

【接种】have an inoculation;inoculate

【接住】catch

揭 (jiē) ❶tear off;take off ❷uncover;lift ❸expose; show up; bring to light ❹raise;hoist

【揭穿】expose;lay bare;show up

【揭底】reveal the inside story;揭了他的老底 exposed his old secret;dragged the skeleton out of his closet

【揭发】expose;unmask;bring to light;lay bare

【揭开】uncover;reveal;open;～宇宙的奥秘 reveal the secrets of the universe

【揭露】expose;unmask;disclose;show up;bring to light

【揭幕】unveil (a monument,etc.);inaugurate

【揭破】expose;lay bare

【揭示】reveal;disclose;bring to light

【揭晓】announce;make known;publish

街 (jiē) street;country fair;market

【街道】❶ street ❷ residential district; neighbourhood

【街坊】〈口〉neighbour

【街垒】street barricade

【街门】a gate or door facing the street

【街区】block

【街市】downtown streets

【街头】street

子 (jié)〈书〉lonely; all alone

【孑然】solitary; lonely; alone

【孑然一身】all alone in the world

【孑身】〈书〉all by oneself; all alone

节 (jié) ❶joint; node; knot ❷division; part ❸ section; length ❹ festival; red-letter day; holiday ❺economize; save ❼item ❽ moral integrity; chastity

【节假日】festivals and holidays

【节俭】thrifty; frugal

【节减】save and economize

【节目】program; item (on a program); number

【节能】save energy

【节日】festival; red-letter day; holiday

【节省】economize; save; cut down on

【节食】be moderate in eating and drinking; be (or go) on a diet

【节衣缩食】economize on food and clothing; live frugally

【节余】surplus(as a result of economizing)

【节约】practise thrift; save

【节制】❶control; check; be moderate in ❷temperance; abstinence

【节奏】rhythm

劫 (jié)〈书〉❶rob; plunder; raid ❷coerce; compel ❸calamity; disaster; misfortune

【劫持】kidnap; hijack

【劫机】hijack a plane

【劫掠】plunder; loot

【劫狱】break into a jail and rescue a prisoner

杰 (jié) ❶ outstanding; prominent ❷ outstanding person; hero

【杰出】outstanding; remarkable; prominent; distinguished

【杰作】masterpiece

洁 (jié) clean

【洁白】pure white

【洁净】clean; spotless

【洁癖】an unhealthy obsession with cleanliness; mysophobia

结 (jié) ❶tie; knit; knot; weave ❷congeal; form; forge; cement ❸settle; conclude

另见 jiē

【结案】close a case; wind up a case

【结疤】become scarred

【结拜】become sworn brothers or sisters

【结伴】go with：～而行 go or travel in a group

【结冰】freeze; ice up

【结彩】adorn (or decorate) with festoons

【结成】form：～ 同 盟 form an alliance; become allies

【结仇】start a feud; become enemies; breed enmity with

【结存】❶ cash on hand; balance ❷ goods on hand; inventory

【结发】❶〈古〉bind up one's hair; come of age ❷〈古〉first wife

【结构】structure; composition; construction

【结果】❶result; outcome ❷finally; at last

【结合】❶combine ❷marry

【结核】〈医〉tuberculosis

【结汇】settlement of exchange

【结婚】marry; get married

【结伙】gang

【结集】❶ concentrate; mass ❷ collect articles, etc. into a volume：～付印 compile a collection of writings and send it to the press

【结交】make friends with; associate with

【结晶】❶crystallize ❷crystal ❸crystallization：智慧的～ a crystallization of wisdom

【结局】outcome; final result; ending

【结论】conclusion

【结欠】balance due

【结清】settle; square up：～账目 square accounts （with sb.）

【结识】get acquainted with sb.; get to know sb.

【结束】finish; end; conclude; close; wind up

【结算】settle accounts; close an account; wind up an account; clear

【结尾】ending; winding-up stage

【结业】complete a course; wind up one's studies

【结余】cash surplus; surplus; balance

【结账】settle accounts; balance the books

捷 (jié) ❶ prompt; nimble; quick ❷ victory; triumph

【捷报】news of victory; report of a success

【捷径】shortcut

【捷足先登】the swift-footed arrive first; the race is to the swiftest; the early bird catches the worms

睫 (jié) eyelash; lash

【睫毛】eyelash; lash

截 (jié) ❶cut; sever ❷stop; check; stem; intercept ❸〈量〉section; chunk; length ❹by; up to

【截断】❶cut off; block ❷interrupt; cut short

【截获】intercept and capture

【截留】❶hold back; retain for one's own use ❷interception; entrapment

【截流】locking of the river

【截取】cut off a section of sth.

【截然】completely; sharply

【截止】end; close

【截至】by (a specified time); up to

竭 (jié) ❶deplete; exhaust ❷exert

【竭诚】wholeheartedly; with all one's heart

【竭尽】use up; exhaust; spare no effort

【竭尽全力】spare no effort; do one's utmost; do all one can

【竭力】do one's utmost; 尽心～ try one's best

【竭泽而渔】drain the pond to get all the fish; kill the goose that lays the golden eggs

姐 (jiě) elder sister; sister

【姐夫】elder sister's husband; brother-in-law

【姐姐】elder sister; sister

【姐妹】❶sisters ❷brothers and sisters

解 (jiě) ❶separate; divide ❷untie; undo ❸lay; alleviate; dispel; dismiss ❹explain; interpret; solve ❺understand; comprehend

【解馋】satisfy a craving for good food

【解除】remove; relieve; get rid of

【解答】answer; explain

【解冻】❶thaw; unfreeze ❷unfreeze (funds, assets, etc.)

【解法】〈数〉solution

【解放】liberate; emancipate

【解放军】liberation army

【解雇】discharge; dismiss; fire; give the sack

【解恨】vent one's hatred; have one's hatred slaked

【解惑】〈书〉resolve (or remove, dispel)

【解救】save; rescue; deliver

【解决】solve; resolve; settle

【解开】untie; undo; ～头巾 untie a kerchief

【解渴】quench one's thirst

【解囊相助】help sb. generously with money

【解剖】analyse; dissect

【解散】❶dismiss ❷dissolve; disband (an organization, etc.)

【解释】explain; expound; interpret

【解说】explain orally; comment

【解题】solve a (mathematical, etc.) problem

【解脱】extricate oneself (from a predicament, etc.)

【解围】❶(force an enemy to) raise a siege ❷save sb. from embarrassment

【解约】terminate an agreement; cancel (or rescind) a contract

【解职】dismiss from office; discharge; relieve sb. of his post

介 (jiè) ❶be situated between; interpose ❷take seriously; take to heart; mind

【介入】intervene; get involved

【介绍】❶introduce; present ❷let know; brief ❸recommend; suggest

【介绍信】letter of introduction; reference

【介意】take offence; mind

戒 (jiè) ❶guard against; avoid ❷exhort; admonish; warn ❸give up; drop; stop ❹Buddhist monastic discipline ❺(finger) ring

【戒备】guard; take precautions

【戒尺】teacher's ruler for beating pupils

【戒除】give up; drop; stop

【戒忌】❶taboos; don'ts ❷be wary of violating a taboo

【戒骄戒躁】guard against arrogance and rashness; be on one's guard against conceit and impetuosity

【戒酒】give up drinking; swear off drinking

【戒律】religious discipline; commandment

【戒心】vigilance; wariness; 对某人怀有～ be on one's guard against someone; keep a wary eye on someone

【戒烟】swear off smoking; give up smoking

【戒严】enforce martial law; impose a curfew; cordon off an area

【戒指】(finger) ring

届 (jiè) ❶fall due ❷session

【届满】at the expiration of one's term of office

【届期】when the day comes; on the appointed date

【届时】on the occasion

界 (jiè) ❶boundary ❷scope; extent ❸circles ❹primary division; kingdom

【界碑】boundary tablet; boundary marker

【界标】sign (mark)

【界河】boundary river

【界面】interface

【界限】limits; bounds

【界线】boundary line

借 (jiè) ❶borrow ❷lend ❸make use of; take advantage of ❹use as a pretext

【借出】lend

【借贷】❶borrow or lend money ❷debit and credit sides

【借刀杀人】kill sb. by another's hand；make use of one person to get rid of another

【借调】temporarily transfer；loan

【借读】study at a school on a temporary basis

【借方】debtor

【借风使船】sail the boat with the help of the wind — achieve one's purpose through the agency of sb. else

【借古讽今】use the past to disparage the present

【借故】find an excuse

【借花献佛】present Buddha with flowers given by another—make a gift of sth. given by another

【借鉴】draw lessons from

【借酒浇愁】drown one's sorrows in liquor

【借口】excuse；pretext

【借款】❶borrow or lend money；ask for or offer a loan ❷loan

【借题发挥】make use of the subject under discussion to put over one's own ideas；seize on an incident to exaggerate matters

【借条】receipt for a loan(IOU)

【借用】borrow

【借债】borrow money；raise（or contract）a loan；～度日 live by borrowing

【借支】ask for an advance on one's pay

【借助】have the aid of；draw support from；with the help of

【借住】stay at sb. else's place

jīn

巾 （jīn）a piece of cloth（as used for a towel，scarf，kerchief，etc.）

【巾帼】❶ancient woman's headdress：～丈夫 heroine ❷woman

【巾帼英雄】a heroic woman；heroine

斤 （jīn）〈量〉❶Chinese weight measurement ❷used as weight

【斤斤计较】haggle over every ounce

【斤两】weight

今 （jīn）❶modern；present-day；nowadays；now ❷today ❸this（year）；of this year

【今晨】this morning

【今番】this time

【今非昔比】no comparison between past and present；the past cannot be compared with the present

【今后】from now on；henceforth；hereafter；in future

【今年】this year

【今日】❶this day；today ❷present；now

【今生】this life

【今世】❶this life ❷this age；the contemporary age

【今是昨非】today right，yesterday wrong（i. e. what I do today is right，what I did yesterday was wrong；said of repentance and reformation）

【今岁】this year

【今天】❶today ❷the present；now

【今昔对比】contrast the past with the present

【今夜】this evening；tonight

【今朝】❶〈口〉today ❷the present；now

金 （jīn）❶metals ❷money ❸ancient metal percussion instruments ❹gold ❺highly respected；precious

【金杯】gold cup

【金币】gold coin

【金黄色】golden

【金库】treasury；national(state) treasury

【金牌】gold medal

【金钱】money

【金钱豹】〈动〉spotted leopard

【金融】finance；banking

【金色】golden：～的朝阳 golden rays of the morning sun；golden dawn

【金属】metal

【金条】gold bar

津 （jīn）❶saliva ❷sweat ❸ferry crossing；ford

【津津乐道】talk with great relish；take delight in talking about

【津津有味】with relish；with gusto；with keen pleasure

【津贴】subsidy；allowance

【津液】❶〈中医〉body fluid ❷saliva

筋 （jīn）❶muscle ❷tendon；sinew ❸vein

【筋斗】❶somersault ❷fall；tumble(over)

【筋骨】bones and muscles-physique

【筋疲力尽】worn out；tired out；exhausted

【筋肉】muscles

禁 （jīn）❶bear；stand；endure ❷contain（or restrain）oneself
另见 jìn

【禁不起】be unable to stand

【禁不住】❶be unable to bear of endure ❷can't help（doing sth.）；can't refrain from

【禁受】bear；stand；endure

仅 （jǐn）only；merely；barely；simply；solely；alone

【仅供参考】just for reference；for reference only

【仅见】rarely seen；世所～ have no parallel any-where

【仅仅】only；merely；barely

【仅只】only；merely

尽 (jǐn) ❶to the greatest extent ❷within the limits of；no more than ❸give priority to；first ❹at the furthest end of
另见 jìn

【尽管】❶feel free to；not hesitate to ❷though；even though；in spite of；despite

【尽快】as quickly (or soon，early)as possible

【尽量】to the best of one's ability；as far as possible

【尽先】give first priority to；～照顾孩子们 look after the children first

【尽自】〈方〉always；all the time

紧 (jǐn) ❶tight；taut；close ❷tighten ❸ur-gent；pressing；tense ❹strict；stringent ❺hard up；short of money

【紧巴巴】❶tight ❷hard up；short of money：日子过得～的 be in financial straits

【紧逼】press hard；close in on：步步～ press on at every stage

【紧凑】terse；well-knit；tight；compact

【紧跟】follow closely(on sb.'s heels)；keep in step with；keep up with

【紧急】urgent；critical；pressing；emergent

【紧接】next

【紧密】❶close together；inseparable：～团结 be closely united ❷rapid and intense

【紧迫】pressing；urgent；imminent

锦 (jǐn) ❶brocade ❷bright and beautiful

【锦标赛】championships

【锦缎】brocade

【锦旗】silk banner

【锦绣】as beautiful as brocade；beautiful；splen-did

谨 (jǐn) ❶careful；cautious；circumspect ❷solemnly；sincerely

【谨防】beware of；be cautious of；guard against

【谨慎】careful；cautious；prudent

【谨严】careful and precise：治学～ careful and exact scholarship

尽 (jìn) ❶exhausted；finished ❷to the ut-most；to the limit ❸use up；exhaust ❹try one's best；put to the best use ❺all；exhaustive
另见 jǐn

【尽力】do one's best

【尽量】(drink or eat) to the full

【尽其所有】give everything one has；give one's all

【尽情】to one's heart's content

【尽然】(usu. used in the negative) entirely so：也不～ not exactly so；not exactly the case

【尽是】full of；all；without exception

【尽数】total number；whole amount

【尽头】end

【尽孝】fulfil one's duty to one's parents；display filial piety towards one's parents

【尽心】with all one's heart

【尽兴】enjoy oneself to the full

【尽责】do one's duty；discharge one's responsi-bility

【尽职】fulfill one's duty

【尽忠】❶be loyal to ❷sacrifice one's life for

进 (jìn) ❶advance；move forward；move ahead ❷enter；come into；go into；get into ❸re-ceive ❹eat；drink；take

【进步】❶advance；progress；improve ❷progres-sive

【进城】❶go into town；go to town ❷enter the big cities (to live and work)

【进程】course；process

【进出】❶pass in and out ❷(business) turnover

【进度】❶rate of progress ❷planned speed；schedule

【进而】and then；after that

【进发】set out；start

【进犯】intrude into；invade

【进攻】attack；assault；offensive

【进化】evolution

【进货】stock (a shop) with goods；lay in a stock of merchandise；replenish one's stock

【进军】march；advance

【进口】❶enter port ❷import ❸entrance

【进来】come in；enter

【进取】be eager to make progress；be enterpris-ing

【进去】go in；enter

【进入】get into；enter

【进食】take food；have one's meal

【进退两难】find it difficult to advance or to re-treat；be in a dilemma

【进行】❶go on；be on；be under way；go ahead；be in progress ❷carry on；make；conduct；carry out

【进行曲】〈音〉march

【进修】take a refresher course；pursue further studies

【进言】offer a piece of advice or an opinion：大胆～ make so bold as to offer an opinion

【进展】make progress；make headway

【进站】(of a train) get into (*or* draw into, pull into) a station

【进账】income; receipts

近 (jìn) ❶near; close ❷approaching; approximately; close to ❸intimate; closely related ❹easy to understand

【近便】close and convenient

【近处】vicinity; neighbourhood

【近代】modern times

【近海】coastal waters; inshore; offshore

【近郊】outskirts of a city; suburbs; environs

【近景】〈摄〉close shot

【近况】recent developments; how things stand

【近来】recently; of late; lately

【近邻】near neighbour

【近路】shortcut：走～ take a shortcut

【近年】recent years；～来 in recent years

【近亲】close relative

【近日】❶recently; in the past few days ❷within the next few days

【近世】modern times

【近视】myopia; nearsightedness; shortsightedness

【近水楼台】waterside pavilion a favourable position

【近似】approximate; similar

【近义词】〈语〉near synonym

【近在咫尺】close at hand; well within reach

劲 (jìn) ❶strength; energy ❷vigour; spirit; drive; zeal ❸air; manner; expression
另见 jìng

晋 (jìn) ❶enter; advance ❷promote ❸(Jìn) the Jin Dynasty (265—420)

【晋级】〈书〉rise in rank; be promoted

【晋见】have an audience with

【晋升】〈书〉promote to a higher office

浸 (jìn) soak; steep; immerse

【浸染】steep; disseminate; impregnation; tincture

【浸入】immersion; infiltration

禁 (jìn) ❶prohibit; forbid; ban ❷imprison; detain
另见 jīn

【禁闭】confinement (as a punishment)

【禁地】forbidden area; restricted area; out-of-bounds area

【禁忌】❶taboo ❷avoid

【禁令】prohibition; ban

【禁区】restricted zone

【禁书】banned book

【禁烟】ban on opium-smoking and the opium trade

【禁止】prohibit; ban; forbid

【禁阻】prohibit; ban; forbid; prevent; stop

jing

京 (jīng) ❶ the capital of a country ❷ (Jīng) Beijing

【京城】〈古〉the capital of country

【京剧】Peking opera

经 (jīng) ❶wrap ❷channels ❸longitude ❹manage; deal in; engage in ❺pass through; undergo; experience ❻ as a result of; after; through ❼stand, bear; endure

【经办】handle; deal with

【经常】often; frequently; constantly; regularly

【经典】classics

【经度】longitude

【经费】funds; expenditure; outlay

【经过】❶pass through; go by; pass by ❷after; through ❸course; process

【经纪人】broker; agent; middleman

【经济】❶〈经〉economy; economic ❷financial ❸economical, thrifty

【经久】prolonged

【经理】manager

【经历】❶experience; go through; undergo ❷experience; past; story

【经年累月】for years and years; year in year out

【经商】be in business; be engaged in trade; go in to business

【经手】handle; deal with：～公款 handle public money

【经受】undergo; experience; withstand; stand; weather

【经天纬地】have heaven and earth under one's control have great ability

【经心】careful; mindful; conscientious

【经学】study of Confucian classics

【经验】experience

【经营】manage; operate; run; engage in

【经营权】power of management; managerial authority

荆 (jīng) chaste tree; vitex

【荆钗布裙】thornwood hairpins and hemp skirts—the plain, simple dress of a poor woman

【荆条】twigs of the chaste tree (used for weaving baskets, etc.)

旌 (jīng) an ancient type of banner hoisted on a featherdecked mast

【旌旗】banners and flags

惊（jīng）❶ start；be frightened ❷ surprise；shock；alarm ❸ shy；stampede

【惊诧】surprised；amazed；astonished

【惊动】disturb；bother

【惊愕】〈书〉stunned；stupefied

【惊风】〈中医〉infantile convulsions：急～ acute infantile convusions

【惊弓之鸟】a bird that starts at the mere twang of a bow-string—a badly frightened person

【惊呼】cry out in alarm

【惊慌】alarmed；scared

【惊慌失措】frightened out of one's wits；seized with panic；panic-stricken

【惊魂】the state of being frightened：～未定 not yet recovered from a fright；still badly shaken

【惊叫】exclaim；scream

【惊恐】frightened；terrified；in alarm

【惊奇】astonish；wonder；surprise；in surprise

【惊人】astonishing；amazing；striking；wonderful；alarming

【惊人之举】masterstroke；a shocking action

【惊涛骇浪】（often fig.）terrifying waves；a stormy sea

【惊天动地】shaking heaven and earth；earth-shaking；world-shaking

【惊喜】pleasantly surprised

【惊吓】frighten；scare

【惊险】alarmingly dangerous；breathtaking；thrilling

【惊心动魄】soul-stirring；profoundly affecting

【惊醒】❶ wake up with a start ❷ rouse suddenly from sleep；awaken

【惊讶】surprised；amazed；astonished；astounded

【惊疑】surprised and bewildered

【惊异】surprised；amazed；astonished；astounded

晶（jīng）❶ brilliant；glittering ❷ quartz；（rock）crystal ❸ any crystalline substance

【晶体】crystal

【晶莹】sparkling and crystal-clear

兢（jīng）

【兢兢业业】cautious and conscientious

精（jīng）❶ refined；picked；choice ❷ meticulous；fine；precise ❸ skilled；conversant；proficient ❹ extract；essence ❺ sharp；clever；shrewd

【精兵】picked troops；crack troops

【精彩】brilliant；splendid；wonderful

【精诚】〈书〉absolute sincerity；good faith

【精粹】succinct；pithy；terse

【精打细算】careful calculation and strict budgeting

【精到】precise and penetrating

【精雕细刻】work at sth. with the care and precision of a sculptor；work at sth. with great care

【精耕细作】intensive and meticulous farming；intensive cultivation

【精光】❶ with nothing left ❷ bright and clean；shiny

【精悍】❶ capable and vigorous ❷ pithy and poignant

【精华】essence；cream；soul

【精简】simplify；reduce；cut；retrench

【精力】energy；vigour

【精力充沛】full of vim and vigour；vigorous；energetic

【精练】concise；succinct；terse：语 言 ～ succinct language

【精良】excellent；superior；of the best quality

【精美】delicate；elegant；exquisite

【精密】precise；accurate

【精妙】exquisite：书法～ write a beautiful hand

【精明】astute；shrewd

【精疲力竭】exhausted；worn out

【精辟】penetrating

【精巧】ingenious

【精确】crack；picked

【精锐】pick；crack

【精深】profound

【精神】❶ spirit；mind ❷ essence；gist；spirit

【精神病】mental disease；mental disorder；psychosis

【精神抖擞】full of energy（or vitality）；vigorous：～ 地 迈 着 大 步 walk with long, vigorous strides

【精神文明】cultural and ideological progress

【精神污染】spiritual contamination；cultural contamination；ideological pollution

【精通】be proficient in；master

【精细】meticulous；fine；careful：手 工 十 分 ～ show fine workmanship

【精心】meticulously；painstakingly；elaborately

【精选】❶ concentration ❷ carefully chosen；choice

【精益求精】constantly improve

【精制】make with extra care；refine：～品 highly finished products；superfines

【精致】fine；exquisite

【精忠报国】serve one's country with unreserved loyalty

【精装】（of books）clothbound；hardback；hardcover

【精子】〈生理〉sperm；spermatozoon

鲸（jīng）whale

【鲸波】ocean waves
【鲸吞】swallow like a whale
【鲸须】baleen；whalebone
【鲸鱼】whale

井（jǐng）❶well ❷sth. in the shape of a well ❸neat；orderly
【井底】❶the bottom of a well ❷shaft bottom；pit bottom
【井底之蛙】a frog in a well a person with a very limited outlook
【井灌】well irrigation
【井井有条】in perfect order；well-arranged
【井口】❶the mouth of a well ❷pithead ❸well-head；～气 wellhead gas；casinghead gas
【井然有序】in good order；orderly；methodical
【井绳】a rope for drawing water from a well
【井水】well water
【井水不犯河水】well water does not intrude into river water—I'll mind my own business，you mind yours
【井下】in the pit；under the shaft；～作业 operation in the pit；underpit operation

颈（jǐng）neck

【颈项】neck
【颈椎】cervical vertebra

景（jǐng）❶view；scenery；scene ❷situation；condition ❸scenery（of a play or film）
【景观】landscape
【景况】situation；circumstances
【景气】boom；prosperity
【景色】view；scene；scenery；landscape；outlook
【景物】scenery
【景象】scene；sight
【景仰】respect and admire；hold in deep respect
【景遇】〈书〉circumstances；one's lot
【景致】view；scenery；scene

警（jǐng）❶alert；vigilant ❷warn；alarm ❸alarm ❹police
【警报】alarm；alert
【警备】guard；garrison；～森严 be heavily guarded
【警察】police；policeman
【警车】police car；police van
【警告】warn；caution；admonish
【警官】police officer
【警棍】policeman's baton；truncheon
【警戒】❶warn；admonish ❷be on guard against sth.
【警句】aphorism；epigram

【警觉】vigilance；alertness
【警犬】police dog
【警惕】be on guard against
【警卫】（security）guard
【警钟】alarm bell；tocsin

劲（jìng）strong；powerful；sturdy 另见 jìn
【劲吹】（of the wind）blow hard
【劲敌】formidable adversary；strong opponent（or contender）
【劲风】a strong wind
【劲旅】strong contingent

径（jìng）❶footpath；path；track ❷way；means ❸straight；directly ❹diameter
【径迹】〈物〉track
【径情直遂】as smoothly as one would wish
【径赛】〈体〉track
【径直】straight；directly；straightaway
【径自】without leave；without consulting anyone

净（jìng）❶clean ❷make clean ❸completely ❹net ❺all；all the time ❻only；merely；nothing but
【净额】net amount
【净化】purify
【净价】net price
【净尽】completely used up；with nothing left
【净身】（of a man）be castrated
【净收入】net income
【净增】net increase；net growth：人口～率 net growth rate of population
【净值】net worth；net value：出口～ net export value
【净重】net weight
【净赚】net earnings

竞（jìng）compete；contest；vie

【竞渡】❶boat race ❷swimming race
【竞技】sports；athletics
【竞赛】contest；competition；emulation；race
【竞相】compete；vie
【竞选】enter into an election contest；campaign for（office）；stand for；run for
【竞争】compete；vie；contend
【竞走】〈体〉heel-and-toe walking race

竟（jìng）❶finish；complete ❷throughout；whole
【竟敢】actually dare；have the audacity；have the impertinence
【竟然】❶unexpectedly；to one's surprise；actually ❷go to the length of；have the impudence to
【竟日】the whole day；all day long
【竟自】unexpectedly；to one's surprise；actually

敬 (jìng) ❶respect；honour ❷respectfully

【敬爱】 respect and love
【敬辞】 term of respect；polite expression
【敬而远之】 stay at a respectful distance from sb.
【敬奉】 ❶piously worship ❷offer respectfully；present politely
【敬老爱幼】 respect the aged and cherish the young
【敬老院】 home of respect for the aged；old folks' home
【敬老尊贤】 respect the aged and honour the worthy
【敬礼】 ❶salute ❷extend
【敬慕】 respect and admire
【敬佩】 esteem；admire
【敬请】〈套〉invite respectfully
【敬仰】 revere；venerate
【敬意】 respect；tribute；regards
【敬重】 highly esteem；look up to with great respect；deeply respect；revere；honor
【敬祝】〈套〉（used at the end of a letter）I wish you

静 (jìng) still；quiet；calm

【静电】〈物〉static electricity
【静观】 watch quietly
【静默】 ❶become silent ❷mourn in silence；observe silence
【静穆】 solemn and quiet
【静悄悄】 very quiet
【静态】〈物〉static state
【静养】 rest quietly to recuperate；convalesce
【静止】 motionless；static；at a standstill
【静坐】 sit-in

境 (jìng) ❶border；boundary ❷place；area；territory ❸ condition；situation；circumstances

【境地】 condition；circumstances
【境界】 ❶boundary ❷state；realm
【境况】 circumstances；condition
【境域】 ❶condition；circumstances ❷area；realm
【境遇】 circumstances；one's lot

镜 (jìng) ❶looking glass mirror ❷lens；glass

【镜花水月】 flowers in a mirror or the moon in the water—an illusion
【镜框】 ❶picture frame ❷spectacles frame
【镜片】 lens
【镜台】 dressing table
【镜头】 ❶〈摄〉camera lens ❷shot；scene
【镜子】 mirror；looking glass

jiong

迥 (jiǒng)〈书〉❶far away ❷widely different

【迥别】 totally different
【迥然】 far apart
【迥然不同】 utterly different；not in the least alike
【迥异】 totally different

炯 (jiǒng) bright；shining

【炯炯】 bright
【炯炯有神】 (of eyes) bright and piercing

窘 (jiǒng) ❶in straitened circumstances；hard up ❷ awkward；embarrassed ❸ embarrass；disconcert

【窘境】 awkward situation；plight；predicament：摆脱～ extricate oneself from a predicament
【窘况】 awkward situation；predicament；plight
【窘迫】 ❶very poor；hard up；poverty-stricken ❷ embarrassed；in a predicament
【窘态】 embarrassed look
【窘相】 an embarrassed look

jiu

纠 (jiū) ❶entangle ❷gather together ❸correct；rectify；put right

【纠察】 ❶maintain order at a public gathering ❷picket
【纠缠】 ❶get entangled；be in a tangle ❷nag；worry
【纠缠不清】 too tangled up to unravel
【纠纷】 dispute；issue
【纠葛】 entanglement；dispute
【纠集】〈贬〉get together；muster
【纠正】 correct；put right；set right

究 (jiū) ❶study carefully；go into；investigate ❷actually；really；after all

【究办】 investigate and deal with
【究诘】〈书〉interrogate，cross examine
【究竟】 ❶outcome；what actually happened ❷actually

揪 (jiū) ❶hold tight；seize ❷pull；tug；drag；give a hard tug

【揪辫子】 seize sb.'s queue；seize upon sb.'s mistakes or shortcomings；capitalize on sb.'s vulnerable point
【揪出】 uncover；ferret out
【揪心】〈方〉❶anxious；worried ❷heartrending；agonizing；gnawing

九 (jiǔ) ❶nine ❷many；numerous

【九九表】 multiplication table

【九九归一】when all is said and done; in the last analysis; after all

【九牛一毛】a single hair out of nine ox—hides a drop in the ocean

【九泉之下】down in the Nine Springs in the nether regions; after death

【九十】ninety

【九死一生】a narrow escape from death; survival after many hazards

【九五之尊】the imperial throne

【九霄云外】beyond the highest heavens—far, far away

【九月】September

【九州】❶the nine divisions of China in remote antiquity ❷a poetic name for China

久（jiǔ）❶for a long time; long ❷of a specified duration

【久别】long separation

【久别重逢】meet again after a long separation; reunite after a long parting

【久病成医】prolonged illness makes a doctor of a patient

【久等】wait for a long time

【久而久之】as time passes; in the long run

【久后】long afterwards; in the future

【久经考验】long-tested; seasoned

【久久】for a long, long time

【久留】stay long

【久已】for a long time; long since

【久远】remote; far back; ages ago

韭（jiǔ）fragrant-flowered garlic;（Chinese）chives

【韭菜】fragrant-flowered garlic;（Chinese）chives

【韭黄】hotbed chives

酒（jiǔ）alcoholic drink; wine; liquor; spirits

【酒吧】bra; barroom

【酒杯】wine glass; wine bowl

【酒店】pub; wineshop

【酒饭】food and drink

【酒馆】public house; pub

【酒会】cocktail party

【酒家】restaurant; wineshop

【酒精】alcohol

【酒量】capacity for liquor; one's drinking capacity

【酒窝】dimple

旧（jiù）❶past; bygone; old ❷used; worn; old ❸former; onetime ❹old friend ship; an old friend

【旧案】❶a court case of long standing ❷old regulations; former practice

【旧病】old complaint

【旧好】〈书〉❶old friendship ❷an old friend

【旧货】junk; secondhand goods

【旧交】an old acquaintance; an old friend

【旧居】former residence; old home

【旧年】❶the lunar New Year ❷〈方〉last year

【旧情】old or former friendship; former affection

救（jiù）❶rescue; save ❷save sb. from; relieve（distress, etc.）

【救出】rescue; help out

【救国】save the country; national salvation

【救护】give first-aid; rescue

【救活】bring sb. back to life; resuscitate

【救火】fight the fire

【救急】help sb. to cope with an emergency; help meet an urgent need

【救济】relieve

【救命】save sb.'s life

【救生】save life（esp. through the prevention of drowning）

【救灾】provide disaster relief; send relief to a disaster area

【救治】treat and cure

【救助】help sb. in danger or difficulty; succour

就（jiù）❶come near; move towards ❷go to; take up; undertake; engage in; enter upon ❸accomplish; make ❹go with ❺with regard to; concerning; on; in the light of; as far as ❻only; merely; just ❼exactly; precisely ❽even if; even

【就便】at sb.'s convenience; while you're at it

【就餐】〈书〉have a meal; eat; dine

【就此】at this point; here and now; thus

【就地】on the spot

【就读】〈书〉attend school

【就范】submit; give in

【就教】go to sb. for advice or instructions

【就近】nearby; without having to go far

【就擒】be seized; be captured

【就寝】retire for the night; go to bed

【就事论事】consider sth. in isolation or out of context; deal with a matter on its merits

【就是】quite right; exactly; precisely

【就手】while you're at it

【就算】even if

【就位】take one's place

【就绪】be in order

【就学】go to school; attend school

【就要】be about to; be going to; be on the point of

【就业】❶obtain employment; get a job ❷be provided with employment

【就医】seek medical advice；go to a doctor

【就义】die a martyr

【就职】assume office

【就座】take one's seat；be seated

舅 (jiù) ❶ mother's brother；uncle ❷ wife's brother；brother-in-law ❸〈书〉husband's father

【舅父】mother's brother；uncle

【舅舅】〈口〉mother's brother；uncle

【舅妈】〈口〉wife of mother's brother；aunt

【舅子】〈口〉wife's brother；brother-in-law

ju

拘 (jū) ❶ arrest；detain ❷ restrain；restrict；limit

【拘捕】arrest

【拘谨】overcautious；reserved

【拘禁】take into custody

【拘礼】be punctilious；stand on ceremony

【拘留】detain；hold in custody；intern；detention；provisional apprehension

【拘泥】be a stickler for；rigidly adhere to

【拘票】arrest warrant；warrant

【拘束】❶ restrain；restrict ❷ constrained；awkward；ill at ease

【拘押】take into custody；detain

【拘执】rigid；inflexible

居 (jū) ❶ reside；dwell；live ❷ residence；house ❸ be (in a certain position)；occupy (a place) ❹ claim；assert ❺ storeup；lay by ❻ stay；put；be at a standstill

【居安思危】think of danger in times of safety；be vigilant in peace time

【居多】be in the majority

【居功】claim credit for oneself

【居功自傲】become arrogant because of one's achievements；claim credit and put on airs

【居家】live at home；run a household

【居留】reside

【居民】resident；inhabitant

【居奇】hoard and speculate

【居然】❶ surprisingly；to one's surprise；factually；unexpectedly ❷ go so far as to；have

【居心不良】harbour evil intentions

【居心叵测】with hidden intent；with ulterior motives

【居中】❶ (mediate) between two parties ❷ be placed in the middle

【居住】live；reside；dwell

鞠 (jū) rear；bring up

【鞠躬】bow

【鞠躬尽瘁】bend oneself to a task and exert oneself to the utmost

【鞠养】〈书〉rear；bring up

局 (jú) ❶ office；bureau ❷ game；set；innings ❸ situation；state of affairs ❹ gathering ❺ ruse；trap

【局部】part

【局促】❶ (of place) narrow；cramped ❷ (of time) short ❸ feel or show constraint

【局度】〈书〉tolerance；forbearance

【局面】aspect；phase；situation

【局骗】swindle

【局势】situation

【局外人】a person not in the know；outsider

【局限】limit；confine

【局限性】limitations

菊 (jú)

【菊花】〈植〉chrysanthemum

咀 (jǔ) chew

【咀嚼】❶ masticate ❷ mull over；ruminate；chew the cud

沮 (jǔ)〈书〉stop；prevent

【沮遏】〈书〉prevent

【沮丧】dejected；depressed；dispirited；disheartened

矩 (jǔ) ❶ carpenter's square；square ❷ rules；regulations ❸〈物〉moment

【矩尺】carpenter's square

【矩形】rectangle

举 (jǔ) ❶ lift；raise；hold up ❷ act；deed；move ❸ start ❹ elect；choose ❺ cite；take；give ❻ whole；entire

【举案齐眉】holding the tray level with the brows — husband and wife treating each other with courtesy

【举办】conduct；hold；run

【举报】report (an offender)；inform against

【举步】〈书〉take a step

【举措】behave；move；act

【举动】movement；move；act；activity

【举发】report (an offender)；inform against

【举国】whole nation；entire nation；throughout the country

【举荐】recommend

【举例】give an example；cite an instance

【举目无亲】be away from all one's kin；be a stranger in a strange land；have no one to turn to (for help)

【举棋不定】hesitate about (or over) what move to make；be unable to make up one's mind；vacillate;shilly-shally

【举世】all over the world;universally

【举世瞩目】attract worldwide attention;become the focus of world attention

【举事】〈书〉stage an uprising;rise in insurrection

【举手】put up or raise one's hand or hands

【举头】raise the head

【举行】hold;give;take place

【举一反三】draw inferences about other cases from one instance

【举止】manner;mien

【举重】weight-lifting

【举足轻重】play a decisive role

【举坐】all those present

巨 (jù) huge;tremendous;gigantic

【巨变】great change

【巨大】tremendous;enormous;huge;gigantic; immense

【巨额】a huge sum

【巨富】❶immense wealth ❷a man of immense wealth;multimillionaire

【巨匠】〈书〉great master;consummate

【巨款】a huge sum of money

【巨人】giant;colossus

【巨著】monumental work

【巨子】magnate;tycoon;giant

句 (jù) sentence

【句法】❶sentence structure ❷〈语〉syntax

【句号】full stop;full point

【句型】sentence pattern

【句子】sentence

拒 (jù) ❶resist;repel ❷refuse;reject

【拒捕】resist arrest

【拒谏饰非】reject representations and gloss over errors; reject criticisms and whitewash one's mistakes

【拒绝】❶refuse ❷reject;decline

具 (jù) ❶utensil;tool;implement ❷possess; have ❸provide;furnish

【具备】have;possess;be provided with

【具结】〈古〉sign an undertaking

【具体】concrete;specific;particular

【具体而微】small but complete;miniature

【具文】mere formality;dead letter

【具有】have;possess;be provided with

俱 (jù) all;complete

【俱乐部】club

【俱全】complete in all varieties

剧 (jù) ❶theatrical work; drama; play; opera ❷acute;severe;intense

【剧本】play;drama;script

【剧变】a violent change

【剧场】theatre

【剧毒】hypertoxic

【剧烈】severe;violent;fierce

【剧目】a list of plays or operas

【剧情】plot;story

【剧坛】theatrical circles

【剧团】(theatrical)troupe;opera troupe

【剧院】theatre

【剧终】the end;curtain

【剧作】drama;play

【剧作家】playwright;dramatist

据 (jù) ❶occupy;seize;take possession of;lay hold of ❷rely on;depend on ❸according to; on the grounds of ❹ evidence; proof;grounds

【据称】it is said;they say;allegedly

【据点】strongpoint

【据实】according to the facts;according to the actual situation

【据守】guard;be entrenched in

【据说】it is said;they say

【据为己有】take forcible possession of; appropriate

【据悉】it is reported

距 (jù) in between;remote from

【距离】❶distance ❷be away from

惧 (jù) fear;dread

【惧怕】fear;dread

【惧色】a look of fear

飓 (jù)

【飓风】hurricane

锯 (jù) ❶saw ❷cut with a saw;saw

【锯齿】sawtooth

【锯床】sawing machine

【锯末】sawdust

【锯条】saw blade

聚 (jù) assemble;gather;get together

【聚餐】have a dinner party

【聚赌】group gambling

【聚合】❶get together ❷〈化〉polymerization

【聚会】❶get together;meet ❷party; meeting

【聚积】accumulate;collect;build up

【聚集】gather;collect;assemble
【聚精会神】be all attention;be concentrated;be intent on;attentively
【聚居】inhabit a region (as an ethnic group);live in a compact community
【聚拢】gather together
【聚星】〈天〉multiple star
【聚众】assemble a crowd;gather a mob

踞（jù）❶crouch;squat ❷sit ❸occupy

juan

捐（juān）❶ relinquish; abandon ❷ contribute;donate;subscribe ❸tax
【捐款】❶ contribute money ❷ donation; subscription
【捐躯】〈书〉sacrifice one's life;lay down one's life (for one's country)
【捐税】taxes and levies
【捐献】contribute;donate;present
【捐赠】offer;contribute;donate
【捐助】offer (financial or material assistance);contribute;donate

涓（juān）a tiny stream
【涓滴】〈书〉a tiny drop;dribble;driblet
【涓滴归公】every bit goes to the public treasury;turn in every cent of public money
【涓涓】〈文〉trickling sluggishly

娟（juān）beautiful;graceful
【娟娟】〈文〉beautiful;graceful
【娟秀】〈书〉beautiful;graceful

镌（juān）engrave
【镌刻】〈书〉engrave

卷（juǎn）❶ roll up;coil;curl ❷ sweep off;carry along ❸cylindrical mass of sth.;roll ❹roll;spool;reel
另见 juàn
【卷笔刀】pencil sharpener
【卷尺】tape measure;band tape
【卷发】curly hair;wavy hair
【卷入】be drawn into(a whirlpool,etc.)
【卷逃】abscond with valuables
【卷土重来】stage a comeback
【卷心菜】cabbage
【卷轴】reel

卷（juàn）❶ book ❷ volume ❸ examination paper ❹file;dossier
另见 juǎn
【卷子】examination paper

【卷宗】❶folder ❷file;dossier

倦（juàn）weary;tired
【倦怠】languid;sluggish
【倦容】a tired look
【倦意】a feeling of tiredness
【倦游】〈书〉weary of wandering and sightseeing

绢（juàn）thin,tough silk
【绢花】silk flower
【绢丝】spun silk(yarn)

圈（juàn）
另见 quān
【圈肥】barnyard manure

眷（juàn）❶ family dependant ❷〈书〉have tender feeling for
【眷爱】regard with affection;love
【眷恋】be sentimentally attached to
【眷念】〈书〉think fondly of;feel nostalgic about
【眷属】family dependants

jue

撅（juē）❶stick up ❷break;snap

决（jué）❶decide;determine ❷(used before a negative word) definitely; certainly; under any circumstances ❸ execute a person ❹ be breached;burst
【决策】❶make policy ❷policy decision
【决出】contest (prizes);fight for
【决堤】breach a dyke
【决定】❶decide;resolve;make up one's mind ❷decision;resolution
【决斗】❶duel ❷decisive struggle
【决断】❶ make a decision ❷ resolve; decisiveness;resolution
【决计】❶have decided;have made up one's mind ❷definitely;certainly
【决口】(of a dyke,etc.) be breached; burst
【决然】absolutely;completely
【决赛】〈体〉finals
【决胜】decide the issue of the battle;determine the victory
【决死】life-and-death
【决算】final accounts;final accounting of revenue and expenditure
【决心】❶make up one's mind;be determined ❷determination;resolution
【决一雌雄】fight to see who is the stronger;fight it out
【决一死战】fight to the death;fight to a finish
【决议】resolution

【决意】have one's mind made up；be determined
【决战】decisive battle

诀 (jué) ❶rhymed formula ❷knack；tricks of the trade ❸bid farewell；part
【诀别】bid farewell；part
【诀窍】secret of success；tricks of the trade；knack

抉 (jué) pick out；single out
【抉择】choose

角 (jué) ❶role；part；character ❷actor or actress
　另见 jiǎo
【角斗】wrestle
【角力】have a trial of strength；wrestle
【角色】role；part
【角逐】contend；tussle；enter into rivalry

觉 (jué) ❶sense；feel ❷wake (up)；awake ❸become aware；become awakened
　另见 jiào
【觉察】sense；read；find；perceive；become aware of
【觉得】❶feel ❷think；feel；find
【觉悟】❶consciousness；awareness ❷come to understand；become aware of
【觉醒】awaken；awake；rouse

绝 (jué) ❶cut off；sever ❷exhausted；used up；finished ❸desperate；hopeless ❹unique；superb；matchless ❺extremely；most ❻absolutely；in the least；by any means；on any account ❼leaving no leeway；making no allowance；uncompromising；definitive
【绝版】out of print
【绝笔】❶last words written before one's death ❷the last work of an author or painter
【绝唱】the peak of poetic perfection
【绝代】〈书〉unique among one's contemporaries；peerless
【绝顶】❶extremely；utterly ❷〈书〉peak；summit
【绝对】❶absolute ❷absolutely；perfectly；definitely
【绝后】❶without offspring ❷never to be seen again
【绝技】unique skill
【绝迹】disappear；vanish；be stamped out
【绝交】break off relations
【绝境】hopeless situation；blind alley
【绝口】❶stop talking ❷keep one's mouth shut
【绝路】❶block the way out；leave no way out ❷road to ruin；blind alley；dead end；impasse
【绝密】top-secret；most confidential
【绝妙】extremely clever；ingenious；excellent

【绝情】heartless；cruel
【绝食】go on a hunger strike；fast
【绝望】give up all hope；despair
【绝无仅有】the only one of its kind；unique

掘 (jué) dig
【掘墓人】grave-digger

崛 (jué) rise abruptly
【崛起】❶rise abruptly；suddenly appear on the horizon ❷rise (as a political force)

矍 (jué)
【矍铄】〈书〉hale and hearty

攫 (jué) seize；grab
【攫取】seize；grab

倔 (juè) gruff；surly
【倔头】a stubborn and surly person；a difficult customer

jun

军 (jūn) armed forces；army；troops

【军备】armament；arms
【军部】army headquarters
【军车】military vehicle
【军刀】soldier's sword；sabre
【军队】army；troops；military forces；armed forces
【军阀】warlord
【军官】officer
【军国主义】militarism
【军号】bugle
【军徽】army emblem
【军火】arms and ammunition；munitions
【军籍】military status；one's name on the army roll
【军纪】military discipline
【军舰】warship；naval vessel
【军区】military area command；military region
【军权】military leadership；military power
【军人】armyman；soldier
【军师】〈古〉war counsellor；military adviser
【军事】military affairs
【军团】army group
【军务】military affairs；military task
【军衔】military rank
【军校】military school；military academy
【军训】military training
【军医】medical officer；military surgeon
【军营】military camp；barracks
【军装】military uniform；uniform

均（jūn）❶ equal; even ❷ without exception; all

【均等】equal; fair

【均分】share out equally; divide equally

【均衡】balanced; even

【均势】balance of power; equilibrium of forces; equilibrium; parity：保持～ keep a balance of power

【均摊】share equally; share alike

【均匀】even; uniform; well-distributed; evenly

君（jūn）❶ monarch; sovereign; supreme ruler ❷〈书〉(used as a title) Mr. ❸〈书〉(used in direct address) you; sir

【君权】monarchical power; royal prerogative

【君王】monarch; sovereign; emperor

【君主】monarch; sovereign

【君主制】monarchy

【君主专制】autocratic monarchy; absolute monarchy

俊（jùn）❶ handsome; pretty ❷ of outstanding talent

【俊杰】a person of outstanding talent

【俊美】pretty

【俊俏】pretty and charming

【俊秀】pretty; of delicate beauty

【俊雅】〈书〉refined and elegant

峻（jùn）❶ high ❷ harsh; severe; stern

【峻拒】〈书〉refuse sternly

【峻峭】high and steep

骏（jùn）fine horse; steed

【骏马】fine horse; steed

竣（jùn）complete; finish

【竣工】(of a project) be completed

【竣事】(of a task) be completed

K k

ka

咖 (kā)

【咖啡】coffee

【咖啡因】caffeine

卡 (kǎ) ❶block；check ❷calorie ❸card
另见 qiǎ

【卡车】truck；lorry

【卡片】card；资料～ reference cards

【卡塔尔】Qatar

【卡通】cartoon

kai

开 (kāi) ❶open；turn on；be on ❷make an o-pening；open up；reclaim ❸start；operate；drive；pilot；run；work ❹set out；move ❺set up；run ❻begin；start ❼hold ❽write out；make out；draw ❾boil

【开采】extract；exploit

【开车】❶drive or start a car, train, etc. ❷set a machine going

【开初】〈方〉at first；at the outset

【开除】expel；discharge；fire；sack

【开动】start；set in motion

【开发】❶develop；open up；exploit ❷exploitation

【开饭】serve a meal

【开放】❶lift a ban, restriction, etc. ❷open to traffic or public use ❸be open（to the public, to the outside world）coastal cities

【开心】❶happy；joyous；elated ❷amuse oneself at sb.'s expense；make fun of sb.

【开学】school opens；term begins

【开业】❶（of a shop, etc.）start business ❷（of a lawyer, doctor, etc.）open a private practice

【开展】❶develop；launch；unfold ❷open-minded；politically progressive

【开张】❶ open a business；begin doing business ❷ conduct the first transaction of a day's business ❸（of certain activities）begin；start

【开账】❶ make out a bill ❷ pay the bill（at a restaurant, hotel, etc.）

【开支】❶pay expense ❷expense ❸pay wages or salaries

【开罪】offend

凯 (kǎi) ❶triumphant strains ❷triumphant；victorious

【凯歌】a song of triumph；paean

【凯旋】triumphant return

铠 (kǎi)

【铠甲】(a suit of) armour

慨 (kǎi) ❶indignant ❷deeply touched ❸generous

【慨然】❶with deep feeling ❷generously

【慨叹】sigh with regret

楷 (kǎi) pattern；model

【楷模】model；pattern

【楷书】regular script

kan

刊 (kān) ❶print；publish ❷periodical；publication

【刊登】publish in a newspaper or magazine；carry

【刊头】masthead of a newspaper or magazine

【刊物】publication

【刊误】correct errors in printing

【刊行】print and publish

【刊印】❶ cut blocks and print ❷ compose and print

【刊载】publish；carry

看 (kān) ❶look after；take care of；tend ❷keep under surveillance；keep an eye on
另见 kàn

【看护】❶ nurse；～病人 nurse the sick ❷〈古〉a hospital nurse

【看家】❶look after the house；mind the house ❷outstanding（ability）

【看门】❶ guard the entrance；act as doorkeeper ❷ look after the house

【看守】❶watch；guard ❷jailer；warder

【看押】take into custody；detain；～俘虏 detain prisoners-of-war

勘 (kān) ❶read and correct the text of; collate ❷investigate; survey

【勘测】survey

【勘察】reconnaissance：～地形 topographical survey

【勘探】exploration; prospecting

【勘误】correct errors in printing

坎 (kǎn) ❶bank; ridge ❷〈书〉pit; hole

【坎肩】sleeveless jacket

【坎坷】❶bumpy; rough ❷full of frustrations

【坎子】mound; rise

砍 (kǎn) ❶cut; chop; hack; hew ❷cut(down)

【砍刀】chopper

【砍伐】fell(trees)

【砍头】chop off the head; behead

看 (kàn) ❶see; look at; watch ❷read ❸think; consider ❹call on visit; go to see ❺treat ❻look after ❼depend on

另见 kān

【看报】read newspapers

【看病】❶(of a doctor) see a patient ❷(of a patient) see or consult a doctor

【看出】make out; see

【看穿】see through

【看待】look upon; regard; treat

【看到】catch sight of; see

【看好】have a good prospect

【看见】catch sight of; see

【看破】see through

【看轻】to look down upon

【看清】see clearly; see through; understand

【看书】read books

【看头】〈口〉sth. worth seeing or reading

kang

康 (kāng) well-being; health

【康复】restored to health

【康健】healthy; in good health

【康乐】happy and peaceful

【康乃馨】carnation

慷 (kāng)

【慷慨】❶vehement; fervent ❷generous; liberal

扛 (káng) carry on the shoulder; shoulder

【扛竿】acrobatics on a bamboo pole

【扛活】work as a farm labourer

亢 (kàng) ❶high; haughty ❷excessive; extreme

【亢奋】stimulated; excited

【亢旱】severe drought

【亢进】〈医〉hyperfunction

【亢直】〈书〉upright and outspoken; upright and unyielding

伉 (kàng)

【伉俪】〈书〉married couple; husband and wife

抗 (kàng) ❶resist; combat; fight ❷refuse; defy ❸contend with; be a match for

【抗癌】anticancer

【抗辩】❶contradict ❷〈法〉counterplea; demurrer

【抗旱】fight or combat a drought

【抗命】defy orders; disobey

【抗体】〈医〉antibody

【抗议】protest

【抗灾】fight natural calamities

【抗争】make a stand against; resist

炕 (kàng) ❶kang, a heatable brick bed ❷〈方〉bake or dry by the heat of a fire

【炕洞】the flue of a kang

【炕席】a kang mat

【炕沿】〈口〉the edge of a kang

kao

考 (kǎo) ❶give or take an examination; test or quiz ❷check; inspect ❸study; investigate; verify

【考查】examine; check

【考察】inspect; make an on-the-spot investigation

【考场】examination hall (or room)

【考订】examine and correct; do textual research

【考核】examine; check; assess

【考问】examine orally

拷 (kǎo) flog; beat; torture

【拷贝】copy

【拷打】flog; beat; torture

【拷问】torture sb. during interrogation; interrogate with torture

烤 (kǎo) ❶bake; boast; toast ❷scorching

【烤火】warm oneself by a fire

【烤炉】oven

【烤肉】roast meat; roast

【烤箱】oven

【烤鸭】roast duck

犒 (kào) reward with food and drink

【犒劳】reward with food and drink

【犒赏】reward a victorious army, etc. with bounties

靠 (kào) ❶lean against; lean on; rest against ❷keep to; get near; come up to ❸near ❹depend on; rely on ❺trust

【靠岸】pull in to shore; draw alongside
【靠把】wearing or featuring stage armour
【靠背】back(of a chair)
【靠边】keep to the side(of the road, etc.)
【靠山】backer; patron
【靠实】〈方〉❶ indeed; really ❷ dependable; reliable ❸ feel relieved; be at ease
【靠手】armrest

ke

苛 (kē) severe; exacting

【苛待】treat (inferiors) harshly
【苛刻】harsh (terms, etc.)
【苛求】be overcritical
【苛杂】exorbitant taxes and levies
【苛责】castigate; denounce strongly
【苛政】tyranny

科 (kē) ❶a branch of academic or vocational study ❷section; department ❸family ❹impose a punishment; pass a sentence

【科幻】science fiction
【科技】science and technology
【科目】subject in a curriculum; course; headings in an account book
【科学】science; scientific knowledge
【科研】scientific research
【科员】a member of an administrative section; section member
【科长】section chief

颗 (kē)

【颗粒】❶pellet ❷grain

磕 (kē) ❶knock ❷rap

【磕巴】〈口〉stutter; stammer
【磕打】knock out
【磕碰】❶collide with; bump against ❷clash; squabble
【磕头】kowtow

瞌 (kē)

【瞌睡】sleepy; drowsy

蝌 (kē)

【蝌蚪】tadpole

咳 (ké) cough
另见 hāi

【咳嗽】cough

可 (kě) ❶ approve ❷ can; may ❸ need (do-); be worth(doing) ❹ but; yet; however ❺fit; suit

【可爱】lovable; likable; lovely
【可好】as luck would have it; by a happy coincidence
【可见】it is thus clear or evident, obvious that
【可敬】worthy of respect; respected
【可靠】reliable; dependable; trustworthy
【可可】cocoa
【可口】good to eat; nice; tasty; palatable
【可乐】cola
【可怜】pitiful; pitiable; poor; have pity on; meagre; wretched; miserable
【可亲】amiable; affable; genial
【可取】desirable; advisable
【可惜】it's a pity; it's too bad
【可喜】gratifying; heartening
【可笑】laughable; ridiculous; ludicrous; funny
【可以】❶can; may ❷be worth ❸ passable; pretty good; not bad ❹terrible; awful
【可憎】hateful; detestable

渴 (kě) ❶thirsty ❷yearningly

【渴求】ask earnestly
【渴望】thirst for; long for; yearn for
【渴想】long for; miss sb. very much
【渴仰】admire; look up to

克 (kè) ❶can; be able to ❷restrain ❸overcome; subdue; capture ❹digest ❺gram

【克服】❶ surmount; overcome; conquer ❷〈口〉put up with (hardships, inconveniences, etc.)
retake; recapture; recover
【克食】help digestion
【克制】restrain; exercise restraint

刻 (kè) ❶ carve; engrave; cut ❷ quarter ❸ moment ❹ unkind; harsh ❺ in the highest degree

【刻板】❶cut blocks for printing ❷mechanical; stiff; inflexible
【刻版】cut blocks for printing; carve printing blocks
【刻本】block-printed edition
【刻薄】unkind; harsh; mean
【刻骨】deeply ingrained; deep-rooted
【刻画】depict; portray
【刻苦】assiduous; hardworking; painstaking

恪 (kè) scrupulously and respectfully

【恪守】scrupulously abide by(a treaty, promise, etc.)

K

客 (kè) ❶visitor;guest ❷traveller;passenger ❸customer ❹settle or live in a strange place;be a stranger ❺a person engaged in some particular pursuit
【客舱】passenger cabin
【客车】passenger train;bus
【客船】passenger ship (or boat)
【客人】❶visitor;guest ❷guest(at a hotel,etc.)
【客商】travelling trader

课 (kè) ❶subject;course ❷class ❸〈量〉lesson ❹levy
【课本】textbook
【课表】school timetable
【课程】course;curriculum
【课时】class hour;period
【课室】classroom;schoolroom

ken

肯 (kěn) ❶agree;consent ❷be willing to;be ready to
【肯定】❶affirm;confirm;approve ❷positive;affirmative ❸definite;sure ❹certainly;undoubtedly;definitely

垦 (kěn) cultivate;reclaim
【垦荒】reclaim wasteland;open up virgin soil
【垦区】reclamation area
【垦殖】reclaim and cultivate wasteland

恳 (kěn) ❶earnestly;sincerely ❷request;beseech;entreat
【恳辞】sincerely decline;earnestly beg off
【恳切】earnest;sincere
【恳请】earnestly request
【恳求】implore;entreat;beseech
【恳挚】〈书〉earnest;sincere

keng

坑 (kēng) ❶hole;pit;hollow ❷tunnel ❸entrap;cheat
【坑害】lead into a trap;entrap
【坑骗】entrap;cheat
【坑人】❶cheat;entrap ❷〈方〉be upset (by a heavy loss)

铿 (kēng)〈象〉the sound of clanging or clattering
【铿锵】(of sound produced by the gong, piano, cymbals, etc.)rhythmic and sonorous
【铿然】〈书〉loud and clear

kong

空 (kōng) ❶empty;hollow;void ❷sky;air ❸for nothing;in vain

另见 kòng
【空喊】loud empty talk
【空话】empty talk;idle talk
【空口】eat dishes without rice or wine
【空旷】open;spacious
【空阔】open;spacious
【空论】empty talk;idle talk;hollow words
【空名】❶empty title;empty name ❷undeserved reputation
【空难】air disaster;aviation accident
【空气】❶air ❷atmosphere
【空前】unprecedented
【空袭】air raid;air attack
【空想】idle dream;fantasy
【空心】become hollow inside

孔 (kǒng) hole;opening;aperture
【孔洞】opening or hole in a utensil,ect
【孔雀】〈动〉peacock;peafowl
【孔穴】hole;cavity

恐 (kǒng) ❶fear;dread ❷I'm afraid
【恐怖】terror:～主义 terrorism|～分子 terrorist
【恐吓】threaten;intimidate:～信 threatening letter
【恐慌】panic;panic-stricken
【恐惧】fear;dread:～不安 be frightened and restless
【恐龙】dinosaur
【恐怕】❶I'm afraid ❷perhaps;I think

空 (kòng) ❶leave empty;leave blank;vacate ❷vacant;unoccupied;blank ❸empty space;room ❹free time;spare time;leisure

另见 kōng
【空白】blank space
【空地】opening;blank;open space;unused land
【空额】vacancy
【空格】blank space
【空余】free;vacant;unoccupied

控 (kòng) ❶accuse;charge ❷control;dominate ❸turn upside down to let the liquid trickle out
【控告】charge;accuse;complain;indict
【控诉】denounce;condemn
【控制】control;dominate;command

kou

口 (kǒu) ❶mouth ❷opening;entrance ❸cut;hole ❹edge;blade
【口岸】port
【口才】eloquence
【口风】one's intention or view as revealed in

what one says
【口福】gourmet's luck
【口角】quarrel;bicker;wrangle
【口述】give an oral account
【口水】saliva
【口算】do a sum orally

叩 (kòu) ❶knock ❷kowtow ❸inquire;ask

【叩拜】kowtow
【叩见】visit（one's superior）;call on
【叩头】kowtow
【叩谢】kowtow in thanks;offer earnest thanks

扣 (kòu) ❶button up;buckle ❷detain;take into custody;arrest ❸deduct ❹smash or spike（a ball）❺knot

【扣除】deduct
【扣留】detain;arrest;hold in custody
【扣押】❶detain;hold in custody ❷〈法〉distrain
【扣子】❶button ❷buckle ❸knot;tache;tach; hasp ❹a sudden break in a story（to create suspense）

ku

枯 (kū) ❶(of a plant, etc.）withered ❷（of a well, river, etc.）dried up ❸dull;uninteresting

【枯竭】dried up;exhausted
【枯燥】dull and dry;uninteresting

哭 (kū) cry;weep

【哭泣】cry;weep;sob
【哭诉】complain tearfully

苦 (kǔ) ❶bitter ❷hardship;suffering;pain; bitterness ❸cause sb. suffering;give sb. a hard time

【苦楚】suffering;misery;distress
【苦处】❶suffering;hardship ❷difficulty
【苦干】work hard
【苦工】hard work
【苦水】❶bitter water ❷gastric secretion, etc. rising to the mouth
【苦笑】forced smile;wry smile
【苦衷】difficulties

库 (kù) ❶warehouse;storehouse;depository; depot ❷library

【库存】stock;reserve

裤 (kù) trousers;pants

【裤脚】bottom of a trouser leg
【裤腿】trouser legs
【裤腰】waist of trousers
【裤子】trousers;pants

酷 (kù) ❶cruel;brutal;oppressive ❷very;extremely;exceedingly

【酷爱】ardently love
【酷热】extremely hot（weather）;scorching;sultry
【酷暑】the intense heat of summer
【酷似】be the very image of;be exactly like
【酷刑】cruel torture

kua

夸 (kuā) ❶exaggerate;overstate;boast ❷praise

【夸大】overstate;magnify
【夸奖】praise;commend
【夸口】boast;talk big;brag

跨 (kuà) ❶step;stride ❷bestride;straddle; ride astride

【跨度】span
【跨越】stride across;leap over

kuai

会 (kuài)
另见 huì

【会计】❶accounting ❷bookkeeper;accountant
【会计师】certified accountant; chief accountant;treasurer

块 (kuài) ❶piece;lump;chunk ❷〈量〉piece; lump ❸〈量〉〈口〉（for gold or silver dollars,Renminbi,and certain paper money）

【块头】〈方〉（physical）build

快 (kuài) ❶fast;quick;rapid;swift ❷hurry up;make haste ❸speed ❹soon;before long ❺quick-witted;nimble;clever ❻sharp ❼straightforward;forthright;plainspoken ❽pleased;happy;gratified

【快报】bulletin
【快餐】quick meal;fast food
【快车】express train or bus
【快活】happy;merry;cheerful
【快乐】happy;joyful;cheerful
【快慢】speed
【快门】shutter
【快速】fast;high-speed

脍 (kuài) 〈书〉❶meat chopped into small pieces;minced meat ❷chop meat or fish into small pieces

【脍炙人口】（of a piece of good writing, etc.） win universal praise;enjoy great popularity

筷 (kuài) chopsticks

【筷子】chopsticks

kuan

宽（kuān）❶wide；broad ❷width；breadth ❸ relax；relieve ❹extent ❺generous；lenient ❻comfortably off；well-off
【宽敞】spacious；roomy
【宽大】❶spacious；roomy ❷lenient；magnanimous
【宽待】treat with leniency；be lenient in dealing with；treat liberally
【宽度】breadth；width
【宽广】tolerance；broad
【宽心】feel relieved

款（kuǎn）❶sincere ❷receive with hospitality；entertain ❸section of an article in a legal document，etc．；paragraph ❹a sum of money；fund ❺leisurely；slow
【款待】treat；treat cordially；entertain
【款式】style
【款项】fund；a sum of money

kuang

狂（kuáng）❶mad；crazy ❷violent ❸wild；unrestrained ❹arrogant；overbearing
【狂暴】frantic；frenzied；furious；violent；wild；outrageous；ungoverned
【狂飙】hurricane
【狂风】whole gale；fierce wind
【狂欢节】carnival
【狂乱】hysteria
【狂怒】furious；mad

旷（kuàng）❶vast；spacious ❷free from worries and petty ideas ❸neglect or waste ❹loose-fitting
【旷课】be absent from school without leave；cut school
【旷日持久】long-drawn-out；protracted；prolonged
【旷野】wilderness

况（kuàng）❶condition；situation ❷compare ❸moreover；besides ❹much less；let alone
【况且】moreover

矿（kuàng）❶ore（or mineral）deposit ❷ore ❸mine
【矿藏】mineral resources
【矿产】mineral products
【矿床】ore deposit
【矿工】miner；mine worker；pitman
【矿井】mine
【矿坑】pit
【矿脉】mineral vein；lode；vein
【矿区】ore district

【矿泉】mineral spring
【矿山】mine

框（kuàng）❶frame；circle；case ❷draw a frame round ❸restrict；restrain；bind
【框架】frame；framework

kui

亏（kuī）❶lose（money，etc．）；have a difficulty ❷short of；deficient ❸treat unfairly ❹wane
【亏本】lose money in business
【亏待】treat shabbily
【亏空】❶be in debt ❷debt；deficit
【亏欠】be in debt；be in arrears
【亏损】❶loss；deficit ❷general debility
【亏心】have a guilty conscience

窥（kuī）peep；spy
【窥测】spy out
【窥见】catch a glimpse of
【窥视】peep at；spy on
【窥伺】lie in and wait for；be on watch for
【窥探】pry about

葵（kuí）certain herbaceous plants with big flowers
【葵花】sunflower

魁（kuí）❶chief；head ❷of stalwart build
【魁首】a person who is head and shoulders above others；the first
【魁伟】big and tall；majestic；strongly-built
【魁梧】big and tall；stalwart

睽（kuí）go against；run counter to
【睽睽】stare；gaze
【睽异】（of views）be in disagreement

馈（kuì）make a present
【馈赠】present；make a present of sth．

溃（kuì）❶burst ❷break through ❸be defeated；be routed ❹fester；ulcerate
【溃败】be defeated
【溃烂】fester；ulcerate
【溃灭】crumble and fall
【溃散】be defeated and dispersed
【溃逃】escape in disorder

愧（kuì）❶ashamed ❷embarrassed；uneasy
【愧色】ashamed look；sign of shame

kun

昆（kūn）❶elder brother ❷〈书〉offspring

【昆虫】insect
【昆曲】❶ Kunqu opera ❷ melodies for Kunqu opera

捆 (kǔn) ❶tie; bind; bundle up; truss ❷bundle; sheaf; truss
【捆绑】truss up; bind; tie up
【捆扎】tie up; bundle up; bind up

困 (kùn) ❶be stranded; be hard pressed; be distressed; be beset ❷surround; pin down; besiege; hem in; encircle ❸tired; weary; fatigued
【困乏】tired; fatigued
【困惑】perplexed; puzzled
【困境】predicament
【困倦】sleepy
【困苦】(live) in privation
【困难】❶difficulty ❷financial difficulties
【困守】stand a siege

kuo

扩 (kuò) expand; enlarge; extend

【扩充】strengthen; augment; expand(forces, etc.)
【扩大】enlarge; expand; extend
【扩建】extend (factory, mine, etc.)
【扩军】arms expansion
【扩散】spread; diffuse
【扩展】expand; spread; develop
【扩张】expand; enlarge

括 (kuò) ❶draw together (muscles, etc.); contract ❷include
【括号】bracket
【括弧】parentheses

阔 (kuò) ❶wide; broad; vast ❷wealthy; rich
【阔别】long separated; long parted
【阔步】take big strides
【阔气】luxurious; extravagant

廓 (kuò) ❶wide; extensive ❷outline
【廓落】〈书〉spacious and still
【廓张】〈书〉expand; enlarge; extend; spread

L l

la

垃 (lā)

【垃圾】 rubbish; garbage; refuse
【垃圾堆】 rubbish heap; refuse dump
【垃圾箱】 dustbin; garbage can; ash can

拉 (lā) ❶pull; draw; tug; drag ❷move ❸play ❹drag out; draw out; space out ❺give (or lend) a helping hand; help ❻drag in; implicate ❼draw in; win over; canvass ❽empty the bowels
【拉扯】 ❶drag; pull ❷take great pains to bring up ❸drag in; implicate ❹chat
【拉家常】 talk about everyday matters; engage in small talk; chit-chat
【拉交情】〈贬〉try to form ties with; cotton up to
【拉力】〈物〉pulling force
【拉链】 zip-fastener; zipper
【拉拢】 draw sb. over to sb. 's side; rope in

喇 (lǎ)

【喇叭】 ❶suona ❷loudspeaker ❸ trumpet

落 (là) ❶leave out; be missing ❷forget to bring
另见 luò

腊 (là) ❶an ancient sacrifice which took place each (lunar) year shortly after the winter solstice ❷the twelfth lunar month ❸cured
【腊肠】 sausage
【腊梅】〈植〉wintersweet
【腊肉】 cured meat; bacon

蜡 (là) ❶wax ❷candle
【蜡笔】 wax crayon
【蜡黄】 wax yellow; waxen; sallow
【蜡纸】 ❶waxed paper ❷stencil paper; stencil
【蜡烛】 candle

辣 (là) ❶peppery; hot ❷(of smell or taste) burn; bite; sting ❸vicious; ruthless
【辣酱】 thick chilli sauce

【辣椒】 hot pepper; chilli
【辣手】 ❶ruthless method; vicious device ❷〈方〉vicious; ruthless ❸〈口〉thorny; troublesome; knotty

lai

来 (lái) ❶come ❷cause to come; send here; bring ❸in order to ❹future; coming; next ❺approximately; about; around ❻hither; here
【来宾】 guest; visitor
【来到】 arrive; come
【来访】 come to visit; come to call
【来回】 make a round trip; make a return trip; back and forth; to and fro
【来件】 communication or parcel received
【来历】 origin; source; antecedents background; past history

赖 (lài) ❶rely; depend ❷rascally; shameless ❸hang on in a place; hold on to a place ❹deny one's error or responsibility ❺blame sb. wrongly; put the blame on sb. else ❻blame
【赖皮】〈口〉rascally; shameless; unreasonable
【赖账】 repudiate a debt

lan

兰 (lán)(used in ancient texts) lily magnolia
【兰草】 fragrant thoroughwort (Eupatorium fortunei)
【兰闺】 boudoir
【兰花】 cymbidium; orchid

拦 (lán) bar; block; hold back
【拦挡】 block; obstruct
【拦劫】 intercept and rob
【拦截】 intercept
【拦路】 block the way

栏 (lán) ❶fence; railing; balustrade; hurdle ❷pen; shed ❸column
【栏杆】 fence; railing; banisters
【栏目】 the heading or title of a column (in a magazine, etc.)

蓝 (lán) ❶blue ❷indigo plant

【蓝宝石】sapphire

【蓝本】❶chief source ❷original version(of a literary work)

【蓝天】blue sky

【蓝图】blueprint

篮

(lán) basket;goal

【篮球】basketball

【篮子】basket

揽

(lǎn) ❶pull sb. into one's arms; take into one's arms ❷fasten with a rope, etc. ❸take on; take upon oneself; canvass ❹grasp;monopolize

【揽笔】〈书〉take up one's pen;write

【揽活】take on work

【揽总】assume overall responsibility; take on everything

缆

(lǎn) ❶hawser; mooring rope ❷thick rope;cable

【缆车】cable car

【缆绳】hawser

懒

(lǎn) ❶lazy; indolent; slothful ❷sluggish;languid

【懒得】not feel like (doing sth.); not be in the mood to

【懒惰】lazy

【懒汉】idler;lazybones

【懒散】negligent;indolent

【懒洋洋】listless

烂

(làn) ❶sodden; mashed; pappy ❷rot; spoil; fester; decay ❸messy

【烂泥】mud;slush

【烂熟】❶overripe; thoroughly cooked ❷know sth. thoroughly

【烂醉】dead drunk

滥

(làn) ❶overflow; flood ❷excessive; indiscriminate

【滥捕】heavy fishing

【滥调】hackneyed tune;worn-out theme

lang

郎

(láng) ❶an official title in imperial times ❷(used in forming nouns designating certain classes of persons)❸(used by a woman in addressing her husband or lover)my darling

【郎君】〈古〉(used in addressing one's husband)you

【郎中】a physician trained in herbal medicine; doctor

狼

(láng)〈动〉wolf

琅

(láng)

【琅琅】〈象〉a tinkling or jingling sound; the sound of reading aloud

廊

(láng) porch;corridor;veranda

【廊庙】〈书〉imperial court

【廊檐】the eaves of a veranda

【廊腰】the corner of a corridor

朗

(lǎng) ❶light;bright ❷loud and clear

【朗读】read aloud;read loudly and clearly:～课文 read the text loudly

【朗声】in a clear loud voice:～大笑 laugh loudly

【朗爽】hearty

【朗诵】read aloud with expression; recite; declaim:诗歌～会 poem recital party

浪

(làng) ❶wave; billow; breaker ❷unrestrained;dissolute ❸stroll;roam

【浪潮】tide;wave:改革的～ tide of reform

【浪荡】❶loiter about; loaf about ❷dissolute;dissipated

【浪费】waste;run through;squander

【浪花】❶the foam of breaking waves ❷〈喻〉episodes in one's life

【浪迹】wander about;roam about

【浪子】prodigal;loafer;wastrel

lao

捞

(lāo) ❶drag for; dredge up; fish for; scoop up from the water ❷get by improper means;gain

【捞本】win back lost wagers

【捞钱】make money (by quick or improper means)

【捞取】fish for;gain

劳

(láo) ❶work; labour ❷put sb. to the trouble of ❸fatigue; toil ❹meritorious deed; service ❺express one's appreciation; reward

【劳保】❶labour insurance ❷labor protection

【劳动】❶work; labour ❷physical labour; manual labour

【劳动力】labour force;labour

【劳工】〈旧〉labourer;worker

【劳驾】excuse me;may I trouble you (to do sth.)

牢

(láo) ❶jail;prison ❷firm

【牢不可破】unbreakable;indestructible

【牢房】cell;ward

【牢记】keep firmly in mind;remember well

【牢靠】❶firm; strong; sturdy ❷dependable; reliable

【牢笼】❶cage ❷bonds

【牢骚】discontent;grievance;complaint

老（lǎo）❶ old；aged ❷ old people ❸ of long standing；old ❹ outdated ❺ overdone；tough ❻ overgrown ❼ always；constantly ❽ dark

【老百姓】 common people；civilians

【老板】 boss；shop keeper；proprietor

【老伴】〈口〉(of an old married couple) husband or wife

【老辈】 one's elders；old folks

【老本】 principal；capital

【老成】 experienced；steady

姥（lǎo）

【姥姥】〈方〉grandmother；grandma

烙（lào）❶ brand；iron ❷ bake in a pan

【烙饼】 a kind of pancake

【烙铁】 ❶ flatiron；iron ❷ soldering iron

【烙印】 brand

涝（lào）water logging；waterlogged

【涝灾】 damage or crop failure caused by water logging

le

乐（lè）❶ happy；cheerful；joyful ❷ be glad to；find pleasure in；enjoy ❸ laugh；be amused
　　另见 yuè

【乐观】 optimistic；hopeful

【乐趣】 delight；pleasure；joy；interest

【乐事】 pleasure；delight

【乐天】 carefree；happy-go-lucky

【乐意】 ❶ be willing to；be ready to ❷ pleased；happy

【乐于】 be happy to；take delight in

【乐园】 paradise

勒（lè）❶ rein in ❷ force；coerce

【勒令】 compel(by legal authority)；order

【勒索】 blackmail

lei

累（léi）❶ tie；bind；truss up ❷ rope；cord
　　另见 lěi，lèi

【累赘】 ❶ burdensome ❷ wordy；verbose ❸ burden；nuisance

雷（léi）❶ thunder ❷ mine

【雷暴】〈气〉thunderstorm

【雷达】 radar

【雷电】 thunder and lightning

累（lěi）
　　另见 léi，lèi

【累积】 accumulate

【累及】 involve；drag in；implicate

【累计】 ❶ add up ❷ accumulative total；grand total

【累累】 ❶ again and again；many times ❷ innumerable

肋（lèi）❶ rib ❷ costal region

【肋骨】 rib

【肋窝】 armpit

泪（lèi）tear；teardrop

【泪痕】 tear stains

【泪花】 tears in one's eye

【泪水】 tear；teardrop

【泪眼】 tearful eyes

【泪珠】 teardrop

类（lèi）❶ kind；type；class；category ❷ resemble；be similar to

【类比】 analogy

【类别】 classification；category

【类似】 similar；analogous

【类推】 analogize

【类型】 type

累（lèi）❶ tired；weary；fatigued ❷ tire；wear out；strain ❸ work hard；toil
　　另见 léi，lěi

【累死累活】 tire oneself out with backbreaking toil；work oneself to death

擂（lèi）beat(a drum)

【擂台】 ring(for martial contests)；arena

leng

棱（léng）❶ edge ❷ corrugation；ridge

【棱角】 ❶ edges and corners ❷ edge；pointedness

【棱镜】 prism

【棱柱体】〈数〉prism

冷（lěng）❶ cold ❷ (of food) cool ❸ cold in manner；frosty ❹ unfrequented；deserted；out-of-the-way ❺ strange；rare

【冷餐】 buffet

【冷藏】 refrigeration；cold storage

【冷场】 awkward situation

【冷淡】 ❶ cheerless；desolate ❷ cold；indifferent

li

厘（lí）❶ centi- ❷ a unit of Chinese currency ❸ a very small amount；a fraction，the least ❹ regulate；rectify

【厘米】 centimeter

离 (lí) ❶leave; part from; be away from ❷from(in giving distances) ❸without; independent of

【离别】part(for a long time); leave; depart; farewell

【离婚】divorce

【离间】sow discord; drive a wedge between

【离境】leave a country or a place

【离开】leave; depart from; go off

梨 (lí)〈植〉pear

【梨涡】〈文〉dimple (of a female)

犁 (lí) ❶plough ❷work with a plough; plough

【犁牛】〈方〉farm cattle

【犁头】❶ploughshare ❷plough

黎 (lí)〈书〉multitude; host

【黎民】the common people; the multitude

【黎明】dawn; daybreak

篱 (lí) hedge; fence

【篱笆】bamboo or twig fence

礼 (lǐ) ❶ceremony; rite ❷courtesy; etiquette; manners ❸gift; present

【礼拜】❶〈宗〉religious service ❷〈口〉week

【礼服】full dress; formal attire

【礼花】fireworks display

【礼节】courtesy; etiquette; protocol

里 (lǐ) ❶lining; inside ❷inner ❸hometown ❹li (= 1/2 kilometre), a Chinese unit of length ❺in; inside

【里边】inside; in; within

【里程】mileage

理 (lǐ) ❶texture; grain (in wood, skin, etc.) ❷reason; logic; truth ❸natural science, esp. physics ❹manage; run ❺put in order; tidy up ❻pay attention to; acknowledge

【理财】manage money matters

【理睬】show interest in

【理发】haircut; hairdressing

鲤 (lǐ)〈动〉carp

【鲤鱼】〈动〉carp

力 (lì) ❶force ❷power; strength; ability ❸physical strength ❹do all one can; make every effort

【力臂】〈物〉arm of force

【力量】❶ physical strength ❷ power; force; strength

【力图】try hard to; strive to

【力学】〈物〉mechanics

历 (lì) ❶go through; undergo; experience ❷all previous ❸covering all; one by one

【历程】course

【历次】all previous

【历来】always; constantly; all long; all through the ages

【历年】over the years

【历时】last; take

【历史】history; past records

厉 (lì) ❶strict; rigorous ❷stern; severe

【厉行】strictly enforce; make great efforts to carry out

立 (lì) ❶stand ❷erect; set up ❸upright; erect; vertical ❹found; establish; setup

【立场】position; stand; standpoint

【立春】Beginning of Spring

【立法】legislation

【立功】render meritorious service; do a deed of merit; win honor

【立即】immediately; at once; promptly

【立刻】immediately; at once; right away

利 (lì) ❶sharp ❷favourable; smooth ❸advantage; benefit ❹profit; interest ❺do good to; benefit

【利害】❶fierce; terrible ❷strict; stern; harsh ❸intense; severe; terrible

【利率】〈经〉rate of interest; interest rate

【利落】❶agile; nimble; dexterous ❷neat; orderly ❸settled; finished

例 (lì) ❶example; instance ❷precedent ❸rule; regulation ❹regular; routine

【例会】regular meeting

【例假】❶official holiday ❷〈口〉(menstrual) period

【例句】illustrative sentence

【例如】for instance; for example; such as

隶 (lì) ❶be subordinate to; be under ❷a person in servitude

【隶属】be subordinate to; be under the command of

荔 (lì)

【荔枝】〈植〉litchi; lychee; lichee

俪 (lì) ❶paired; parallel ❷husband and wife; married couple

【俪辞】a form of literary writing marked by antitheses

【俪句】parallel sentences

砾 (lì) gravel; shingle

【砾石】gravel whetstone

【砾岩】〈地〉conglomerate

lian

连 (lián) ❶ link; join; connect ❷ in succession; one after another; repeatedly ❸ include ❹ company ❺ even
【连词】〈语〉conjunction
【连队】company
【连贯】❶ link up; piece together; hang together ❷ coherent; consistent
【连环】chain of rings
【连接】join; link
【连累】implicate; involve

怜 (lián) ❶ sympathize with; pity ❷ love
【怜爱】love tenderly; have tender affection for
【怜悯】pity; take pity on; have compassion for
【怜惜】take pity on; have pity for

帘 (lián) ❶ flag as a shop sign ❷ (hanging) screen; curtain
【帘子】〈口〉screen; curtain

莲 (lián) lotus
【莲花】lotus flower; lotus
【莲藕】the lotus plant, or esp. its root
【莲心】the heart of a lotus seed
【莲子】lotus seed

涟 (lián)〈书〉❶ ripples ❷ continuous flow (of tears)
【涟漪】〈文〉wavelet; ripples

联 (lián) ❶ ally oneself with; unite; join ❷ antithetical couplet
【联邦】federation; commonwealth
【联防】joint defence
【联合】❶ unite; ally ❷ alliance; union ❸ joint; combined

廉 (lián) ❶ honest and clean ❷ low-priced; inexpensive; cheap
【廉耻】sense of honour
【廉价】low-priced; cheap
【廉洁】honest

镰 (lián) sickle
【镰刀】sickle

敛 (liǎn) ❶ hold back; restrain ❷ collect
【敛步】check one's steps; hold back from going
【敛财】accumulate wealth by unfair means
【敛足】〈书〉check one's steps; hold back from going

脸 (liǎn) ❶ face; countenance ❷ front
【脸面】face; self-respect; sb. 's feelings

【脸盆】washbasin
【脸皮】face; cheek
【脸谱】types of facial makeup in operas
【脸色】❶ complexion; look ❷ facial expression

练 (liàn) ❶ white silk ❷ boil and scour raw silk ❸ practice; train; drill
【练兵】(troop) training
【练功】do exercises in gymnastics, acrobatics, etc.; practise one's skill
【练习】❶ practise ❷ exercise

炼 (liàn) ❶ smelt; refine ❷ temper (a metal) with fire ❸ polish
【炼乳】condensed milk; evaporated milk
【炼油】❶ oil refining ❷ extract oil by heat ❸ heat edible oil

恋 (liàn) ❶ love ❷ long for; feel attached to
【恋爱】love; love affair
【恋人】a sweetheart; a lover

链 (liàn) ❶ chain ❷ cable length (= 1/10 of a nautical mile)
【链钩】chain hook; sling
【链锯】chain saw
【链轮】chain wheel; sprocket (wheel)
【链条】❶ chain ❷ roller chain (of a bicycle)
【链子】❶ chain ❷ roller chain (of a bicycle)

liang

良 (liáng) ❶ good; fine ❷ good people ❸ very; very much
【良策】good plan; sound strategy
【良好】good; well
【良机】good (or golden) opportunity
【良久】〈书〉a good while; a long time: 沉思～ ponder for a long time
【良师】good teacher

凉 (liáng) ❶ cool; cold ❷ discouraged; disappointed
【凉菜】cold dish
【凉快】❶ nice and cool ❷ cool oneself; cool off
【凉爽】nice and cool
【凉台】balcony
【凉亭】summer house
【凉席】summer sleeping mat
【凉鞋】sandals

梁 (liáng) ❶ roof beam ❷ bridge ❸ purlin
【梁龙】diplodocus (a dinosaur)
【梁桥】beam bridge

量 (liáng) ❶ measure ❷ appraise; evaluate; estimate
　　另见 liàng

【量度】measurement
【量具】measuring tool

粮

（liáng）grain；food；provisions

【粮仓】barn
【粮草】army provisions
【粮店】grain shop
【粮食】grain；food

两

（liǎng）❶two ❷both；either end ❸a few；some ❹〈量〉a traditional unit of weight

【两倍】twofold；double；twice as much
【两面】❶two sides；two aspects ❷dual；double
【两面派】〈贬〉double-dealer
【两难】be in a dilemma
【两旁】both sides；either side

亮

（liàng）❶ bright；light ❷ enlightened ❸show

【亮度】brightness；brilliance
【亮光】light
【亮堂】❶light；bright ❷clear；enlightened
【亮相】❶make a pose on the stage ❷state one's views

谅

（liàng）❶forgive；understand ❷I think；I suppose；I expect

【谅解】understand；make allowance for

量

（liàng）❶ capacity ❷ quantity；amount；volume ❸estimate；measure
　另见 liáng

【量变】quantitative change
【量力】estimate one's own strength or ability （and act accordingly）

晾

（liàng）❶dry in the air；air ❷dry in the sun；sun ❸neglect sb.

【晾干】dry by airing
【晾烟】❶air-curing of tobacco leaves ❷air-cured tobacco

liao

辽

（liáo）❶distant；faraway ❷（Liáo）the Liao Dynasty（907—1125）

【辽阔】vast；extensive；幅员～ vast territory
【辽远】distant；faraway

疗

（liáo）treat；cure

【疗程】course of treatment；period of treatment
【疗法】treatment；therapy
【疗效】curative effect
【疗养】recuperate

嘹

（liáo）

【嘹亮】resonant；loud and clear

潦

（liáo）

【潦草】❶hasty and careless ❷sloppy
【潦倒】be frustrated；be down and out

缭

（liáo）❶entangled ❷sew with slanting stitches

【缭乱】confused
【缭绕】curl up；wind around

燎

（liáo）burn

【燎原】set the prairie ablaze

了

（liǎo）❶finish；conclude；settle；dispose of ❷to a finish ❸in the least ❹understand
【了】❶know；understand ❷find out；inquire ❸knowledge；understanding

【了然】understand；be clear
【了事】get sth. over；dispose of a matter；get things done carelessly
【了无惧色】not show a trace of fear；look completely undaunted

料

（liào）❶suppose，expect；anticipate ❷material；stuff ❸feed

【料到】foresee；expect
【料酒】cooking wine
【料理】arrange；manage；take care of；deal with
【料想】expect；think；presume

瞭

（liào）watch from a height or a distance

【瞭望】❶ look far out from a height ❷ watch from a height or a distance；keep a lookout
【瞭望台】observation tower；lookout tower

lie

咧

（liē）
　另见 liě

【咧咧】❶talk nonsense；blabber ❷（of a child）cry

咧

（liě）
　另见 liē

【咧嘴】draw back the corners of the mouth；grin

列

（liè）❶arrange；line up ❷list；enter in a list ❸ row；file；rank ❹ various；each and every

【列兵】〈军〉private
【列车】train
【列举】enumerate；list；～事实 cite facts
【列强】big powers
【列席】attend（a meeting）as a nonvoting delegate

劣

（liè）bad；inferior；of low quality

【劣等】of inferior quality；low-grade；poor
【劣迹】misdeed

【劣绅】evil gentry
【劣势】inferior strength or position
【劣种】inferior strain

烈 (liè) ❶ strong; violent; intense ❷ fiery; staunch; upright
【烈火】raging fire
【烈日】burning sun; scorching sun
【烈士】martyr
【烈属】members of a revolutionary martyr's family
【烈性】❶spirited ❷strong

猎 (liè) hunt
【猎狗】hound
【猎奇】hunt for novelty; seek novelty
【猎枪】shotgun; hunting rifle
【猎取】❶hunt ❷pursue; seek
【猎犬】hunting dog
【猎人】hunter

裂 (liè) split; crack; rend
【裂变】〈核〉fission
【裂缝】rift; crevice; crack; fissure
【裂痕】rift; crack; fissure
【裂口】❶breach; gap; split ❷〈地〉vent
【裂纹】crackle
【裂隙】crack; fissure; crevice

趔 (liè)
【趔趄】stagger; reel

lin

拎 (līn)〈方〉carry; lift
【拎包】〈方〉handbag; shopping bag; bag

邻 (lín) ❶ neighbour ❷ neighbouring; near; adjacent
【邻邦】neighbouring country
【邻接】border on; be next to
【邻近】near; close to
【邻属】neighbour

林 (lín) ❶forest; woods ❷a group of persons or things ❸forestry
【林场】forestry centre
【林带】forest belt
【林地】forest land; woodland

临 (lín) ❶face; overlook ❷arrive; be present ❸on the point of; just before; be about to ❹copy
【临别】at parting; just before departure
【临床】clinical
【临近】close to; close on

淋 (lín) pour; drench

【淋巴】〈医〉lymph
【淋漓】❶dripping; 大汗～ dripping with sweat; sweating all over ❷(of writing or speech) free from inhibition
【淋湿】be soaked; splashed wet
【淋雨】get wet in the rain; be exposed to the rain
【淋浴】shower bath; shower

琳 (lín) beautiful jade
【琳琅】beautiful jade; gem

鳞 (lín) scale (of fish, etc.)
【鳞甲】scale and shell
【鳞片】scale

凛 (lǐn) ❶ cold ❷ strict; stern; severe ❸ afraid; apprehensive
【凛冽】piercingly cold
【凛凛】❶cold ❷stern; awe-inspiring
【凛然】stern

吝 (lìn) stingy; mean; closefisted
【吝啬】niggardly; miserly
【吝惜】grudge; stint

ling

伶 (líng) actor or actress
【伶仃】left alone without help; lonely
【伶俐】clever; bright

灵 (líng) ❶quick; clever; sharp ❷efficacious; effective ❸ spirit; intelligence ❹ fairy; elf ❺bier
【灵便】❶nimble; agile ❷easy to handle; handy
【灵车】hearse
【灵感】inspiration
【灵魂】soul; spirit

玲 (líng)
【玲珑】❶ingeniously and delicately wrought; exquisite ❷clever and nimble

铃 (líng) ❶bell ❷anything in the shape of a bell ❸boll; bud
【铃铛】small bell

凌 (líng) ❶ insult ❷ approach ❸ rise high; tower aloft ❹ice
【凌晨】in the small hours; before dawn
【凌驾】place oneself above; override
【凌空】❶be high up in the air; soar or tower aloft ❷volley

陵 (líng) ❶ hill; mound ❷ imperial tomb; mausoleum
【陵墓】mausoleum; tomb

【陵园】tombs surrounded by a park

聆 (líng) listen;hear

【聆听】listen(respectfully)

菱 (líng) ling;water chestnut;water caltrop

【菱角】〈植〉ling;water chestnut;water caltrop
【菱形】diamond;rhombus;lozenge

羚 (líng) 〈动〉antelope

【羚羊】〈动〉antelope;gazelle

零 (líng) ❶zero sign(0);naught ❷odd;with a little extra ❸naught;zero;nil ❹zero ❺fractional;part ❻wither and fall ❼〈体〉nil;love

【零点】❶〈物〉zero point ❷zero hour;0：00 a. m.
【零分】zero;no marks;scoreless
【零工】❶odd job ❷odd-job man
【零花】❶incidental expenses ❷pocket money

领 (líng) ❶neck ❷collar;neckband ❸outline;main point ❹〈量〉for mats ❺lead;usher ❻have jurisdiction over,be in possession of ❼receive;draw;get ❽understand;comprehend;grasp

【领带】tie;necktie
【领导】❶ lead; exercise leadership ❷ leadership;leader
【领地】territory

另 (lìng) other;another;separate

【另外】in addition;moreover
【另行】separately

令 (lìng) ❶command;order;decree ❷make;cause ❸season ❹your

【令出如山】orders are like a mountain (i. e. compel obedience)
【令行禁止】strict execution of orders and prohibitions

liu

溜 (liū) ❶slide;glide ❷smooth ❸sneak off;slip away

【溜冰】slide on the ice;skating
【溜达】〈口〉stroll;saunter;go for a walk
【溜号】sneak away;slink off

留 (liú) ❶remain;stay ❷reside in a foreign country to study ❸ask sb. to stay;keep sb. where he or she is ❹pay attention to ❺reserve;keep;save ❻let grow;grow;wear ❼accept;take ❽leave behind

【留级】repeat the year's work

【留恋】be reluctant to part (from sb. or with sth.) can't bear to part
【留念】accept or keep as a souvenir
【留情】show mercy or forgiveness
【留神】be careful;take care

流 (liú) ❶(of liquid) flow ❷moving from place to place; drifting; wandering ❸spread;circulate ❹banish; send into exile ❺stream of water ❻current ❼class;rate;grade

【流产】❶ miscarriage; abortion ❷ miscarry; fall through
【流畅】smooth
【流程】technological process
【流传】spread;circulate;hand down
【流动】❶flow ❷going from place to place; on the move; mobile

硫 (liú) 〈化〉sulphur(S)

【硫酸】sulphuric acid
【硫酸盐】sulphate

榴 (liú) pomegranate

【榴弹】high explosive shell
【榴莲】〈植〉durian

柳 (liǔ) willow

【柳条】willow twig;osier;wicker
【柳絮】catkin

六 (liù) six

【六神无主】all six vital organs failing to work properly distracted;out of one's wits;at a loss what to do
【六一国际儿童节】the International Children's Day
【六月】June

long

龙 (lóng) ❶dragon ❷imperial ❸a huge extinct reptile

【龙船】dragon boat
【龙卷风】tornado
【龙头】tap;cock
【龙王】the Dragon King

聋 (lóng) deaf;hard of hearing

【聋哑】deaf-mute
【聋子】a deaf person

笼 (lóng) ❶cage;coop ❷(food) steamer
　　另见 lǒng

【笼屉】food steamer

隆（lóng）❶ grand ❷ prosperous; thriving ❸ intense; deep ❹ swell; bulge

【隆冬】midwinter
【隆隆】〈象〉rumble (of thunder, gunfire, etc.)
【隆起】❶ rise; swell ❷〈解〉eminence
【隆重】grand; solemn

拢（lǒng）❶ approach; reach ❷ add up; sum up ❸ hold (or gather) together ❹ (used after verbs) bring together ❺ comb (hair)

【拢共】altogether; all told; in all
【拢头】comb hair

垄（lǒng）❶ ridge (in a field) ❷ raised path between fields ❸ a thing like a ridge

【垄断】monopolize

笼（lǒng）❶ envelop; cover ❷ a large box or chest; trunk
另见 lóng

【笼络】win sb. over by any means; draw over; rope in
【笼统】general; sweeping
【笼罩】envelop; shroud

lou

楼（lóu）❶ a storied building tower ❷ storey; floor ❸ superstructure

【楼板】floor
【楼道】corridor; passage away
【楼房】a building of two or more stories
【楼上】upstairs
【楼梯】stairs; staircase
【楼下】downstairs

搂（lǒu）hold in one's arms; hug; embrace

【搂抱】embrace; hug

陋（lòu）❶ plain; ugly ❷ humble; mean ❸ vulgar; corrupt; ❹ limited; shallow

【陋规】objectionable practices
【陋俗】undesirable customs
【陋习】corrupt customs; bad habits

漏（lòu）❶ leak ❷ water clock; hourglass ❸ divulge; leak ❹ be missing; leave out by mistake

【漏洞】❶ leak ❷ flaw; hole; loophole
【漏斗】funnel
【漏勺】strainer
【漏税】evade taxation

露（lòu）reveal; show
另见 lù

【露丑】make a fool of oneself in public
【露风】divulge a secret; leak out information
【露面】show one 's face; make an appearance; appear or reappear on public occasions
【露头】❶ show one's head ❷ appear; emerge

lu

芦（lú）reed

【芦笋】asparagus
【芦苇】reed; ditch reed

庐（lú）hut; cottage

【庐舍】〈书〉house; farmhouse

炉（lú）❶ stove; furnace ❷〈量〉heat

【炉顶】〈冶〉furnace top; furnace roof
【炉灶】kitchen range; cooking range

颅（lú）cranium; skull

【颅骨】cranial bones
【颅腔】cranial cavity

虏（lǔ）❶ take prisoner ❷ captive; prisoner of war ❸〈古〉slave ❹〈古〉〈贬〉enemy

【虏获】capture (men or arms)

鲁（lǔ）❶ stupid; dull ❷ rash; rough; rude

【鲁钝】dull-witted; obtuse; stupid
【鲁莽】crude and rash; rash; ～从事 act rashly; act without thought

陆（lù）land

【陆地】dry land
【陆军】ground force; land force; army
【陆路】land route
【陆续】in succession

录（lù）❶ record; write down; copy ❷ employ; hire ❸ tape-record ❹ record; register; collection

【录取】enroll; recruit; admit
【录音】sound recording
【录音机】videocorder; video tape recorder
【录用】employ

鹿（lù）deer

【鹿死谁手】who will win the prize; who will gain supremacy

碌（lù）❶ commonplace ❷ busy

【碌碌】❶ busy with miscellaneous work ❷ mediocre; commonplace

路（lù）❶ road; path; way ❷ journey; distance route ❸ sequence; line; logic ❹ sort; grade; class

【路标】❶ road sign ❷ route sign
【路程】route; path; way; journey; distance travelled

【路灯】street lamp
【路段】a section of a highway or railway
【路费】railway expense

露 (lù) ❶dew ❷beverage distilled from flowers, fruit or leaves; syrup ❸ show; reveal; betray
　　另见 lòu

【露地】〈书〉❶open country ❷an open or uncovered vegetable plot ❸(of roots, etc.) show above the ground
【露水】dew
【露宿】sleep in the open
【露天】in the open; outdoors

lǚ

侣 (lǚ) companion; associate

旅 (lǚ) ❶travel; stay away from home ❷brigade; troops

【旅伴】travelling companion; fellow traveller
【旅差费】travelling expenses on a business trip
【旅程】route; trip; journey
【旅店】inn
【旅费】travelling expenses
【旅馆】hotel
【旅客】passenger; hotel guest; traveller
【旅途】journey; trip; 踏上～ start one's journey
【旅行】travel; journey; tour; trip

铝 (lǚ)〈化〉aluminium (Al)

【铝箔】aluminium foil
【铝合金】aluminium alloy

屡 (lǚ) time and again; repeatedly

【屡次】time and again; repeatedly

履 (lǚ) ❶shoe ❷tread on; walk on ❸footstep ❹carry out; honor; fulfill

【履历】personal details; antecedents
【履新】〈书〉❶celebrate the New Year ❷take up a new post
【履行】perform; fulfill; carry out
【履约】keep a promise; pledge, agreement, appointment

律 (lǜ) ❶law ❷〈法〉restrain; keep under control

【律师】lawyer; solicitor

率 (lǜ) rate; proportion; ratio
　　另见 shuài

绿 (lǜ) green

【绿茶】green tea
【绿灯】green light
【绿豆】green gram
【绿化】afforest

氯 (lǜ)〈化〉chlorine (Cl)

滤 (lǜ) strain; filter

【滤器】filter
【滤液】filtrate
【滤纸】filter paper

luan

孪 (luán) twin

【孪生】twin

卵 (luǎn) ovum; egg; spawn

【卵白】white of an egg; albumen
【卵巢】ovary
【卵黄】yolk
【卵石】cobble; pebble; shingle

乱 (luàn) ❶in disorder; in a mess; in confusion ❷be confused; be upset; be disturbed ❸confuse; upset; throw sb. into chaos ❹indiscriminate; random; arbitrary ❺ promiscuous sexual behavior; promiscuity

【乱码】error codes
【乱世】troubled times
【乱弹琴】act or talk like a fool; talk nonsense

lüe

掠 (lüè) ❶ plunder; pillage; sack ❷ sweep past; brush past; skim over; graze

【掠地飞行】minimum-altitude flight; treetop flight; hedgehopping
【掠夺】rob; pillage
【掠取】seize; grab

略 (lüè) ❶brief; sketchy ❷slightly; a little; somewhat ❸summary; brief account; outline ❹omit; delete; leave out ❺strategy; plan; scheme ❻capture; seize

【略去】omit; leave out
【略胜一筹】a notch (or cut) above; slightly better
【略识之无】know only a few simple characters
【略图】sketch map
【略微】slightly; a little; somewhat
【略语】abbreviation; shortening

lun

伦 (lún) ❶human relations ❷logic; order ❸peer; match

【伦比】rival；equal

【伦理】ethics；moral principles

沦 (lún) ❶sink ❷fall；be reduced to

【沦落】fall low；come down in the world；be reduced to poverty

【沦没】❶sink；submerge ❷(of humans) die

【沦亡】(of a country) be annexed (or subjugated)

【沦陷】❶(of territory,etc.) be occupied by the enemy；fall into enemy hands ❷〈书〉submerge；inundate；flood；drown

轮 (lún) ❶wheel ❷steamer ❸take turns

【轮班】in rotation；by turns；in shifts

【轮船】ship；steamer；steamship；steamboat

【轮次】❶ order of turns ❷ number of turns or rounds

【轮番】take turns

【轮换】rotate；take turns

论 (lùn) ❶discuss；talk about ❷view；opinion；statement ❸dissertation；essay ❹theory ❺mention；regard；consider ❻determine

【论点】thesis

【论调】view；argument

【论断】judgment

luo

啰 (luō)

【啰唆】❶talkative；long-winded；wordy ❷fussy ❸over-elaborate；troublesome

罗 (luó) ❶a net for catching birds ❷catch birds with a net ❸collect；gather together ❹display；spread out ❺sieve；sift ❻a kind of silk gauze ❼〈量〉twelve dozen；a gross

【罗锅】arched

【罗列】❶spread out；set out ❷enumerate

【罗网】net；trap

萝 (luó) trailing plants

【萝卜】radish

逻 (luó) patrol

【逻辑】logic

锣 (luó) gong

【锣鼓】gong and drum

箩 (luó) a square-bottomed bamboo basket

【箩筐】a large bamboo or wicker basket

骡 (luó)〈动〉mule

【骡马店】〈古〉an inn with sheds for carts and animals

【骡子】〈动〉mule

螺 (luó) spiral shell；snail

【螺钉】screw

【螺母】(screw) nut

【螺栓】〈机〉(screw) bolt；gudgeon

【螺丝】screw

【螺旋】❶spiral；helix ❷screw

裸 (luǒ) bare；naked；exposed

【裸露】uncovered

【裸体】naked；nude

【裸线】bare conductor；bare wire；naked wire

骆 (luò) a white horse with a black mane (mentioned in ancient texts)

【骆驼】〈动〉camel

落 (luò) ❶fall；drop ❷go down；set ❸lower ❹decline；come down；sink ❺lag behind；fall behind ❻ leave behind；stay behind ❼settlement ❽fall onto；rest with ❾get；have；receive

另见 là

【落榜】flunk

【落差】〈水〉❶drop ❷head

【落潮】ebb tide

【落成】completion (of a building,etc.)

M m

ma

妈 (mā)〈口〉❶ma; mum; mummy; mother ❷a form of address for a married woman or a married woman of the elder generation

【妈妈】〈口〉ma; mum; mummy; mother

麻 (má) ❶ fibre of hemp; flax ❷ sesame ❸ rough; coarse ❹ pocked; pitted; spotty ❺ tingling; numb

【麻痹】❶〈医〉paralysis ❷be numb; blunt; lull

【麻布】linen

【麻袋】gunny-bag; burlap sack

马 (mǎ) ❶horse ❷horse; one of the pieces in Chinese chess

【马车】❶(horse-drawn)carriage ❷cart

【马虎】careless; casual

【马脚】sth. that gives the game away

【马厩】stable

【马具】harness

码 (mǎ) ❶a sign or thing indicating number ❷an instrument used to indicate number ❸pile up; stack

【码头】wharf; dock; quay; pier

蚂 (mǎ)

【蚂蚁】ant

骂 (mà) ❶abuse; curse; swear; call names ❷condemn; rebuke; reprove; scold

【骂街】shout abuses in the street; call people names in public

【骂名】bad name; infamy

mai

埋 (mái) cover up; bury
另见 mán

【埋藏】lie hidden in the earth; bury

【埋伏】ambush

【埋名】conceal one's identity; keep one's identity hidden

【埋没】❶bury; cover up ❷neglect; stifle

【埋头】be engrossed in

买 (mǎi) buy; purchase

【买单】pay the bill

【买价】buying price

【买卖】business; trade; deal; bargain; transaction

【买通】bribe; buy over; buy off

【买主】buyer; customer

迈 (mài) ❶step; stride ❷advanced in years; old ❸mile

【迈步】step forward; forge ahead

【迈进】stride forward; forge ahead; advance with big strides

麦 (mài) ❶general name for wheat; barley; etc. ❷wheat

【麦秆】straw

【麦浪】rippling wheat; billowing wheat fields

【麦苗】wheat seeding

【麦片】oatmeal

【麦秋】wheat harvest season

【麦收】wheat harvest

【麦穗】ear of wheat; wheat head

【麦子】wheat

卖 (mài) ❶sell ❷betray ❸exert to the utmost ❹show off

【卖唱】sing for a living

【卖掉】sell off

【卖方】the selling party (of a contract, etc.)

【卖乖】show off one's cleverness

【卖光】sell out

【卖国】betray one's country; turn traitor to one's country

【卖好】curry favour with; ingratiate oneself with; play up to; fawn on

【卖价】selling price

【卖老】flaunt one's seniority; put on the airs of a veteran

脉 (mài) ❶〈解〉arteries and veins ❷pulse ❸vein
另见 mò

【脉搏】pulse

【脉冲】〈物〉pulse; impetus; impulse; impulsion

【脉络】❶arteries and veins ❷vein (of a leaf,

etc.）❸thread of thought；sequence of ideas
【脉象】pulse condition；type of pulse

man

埋 (mán)
另见 mái
【埋怨】blame；complain；grumble

蛮 (mán) ❶rough；fierce；reckless；unreasoning ❷〈方〉quite；pretty
【蛮干】act rashly；be foolhardy
【蛮横】crude and unreasonable；arbitrary；peremptory
【蛮劲】sheer animal strength

馒 (mán)
【馒头】steamed bun

瞒 (mán) hide the truth from
【瞒哄】deceive；pull the wool over sb.'s eyes

满 (mǎn) ❶full；filled；packed ❷fill ❸expire；reach the limit ❹completely；entirely；perfectly ❺satisfied ❻complacent；conceited ❼(Mǎn) the Man nationality
【满额】fulfill the (enrolment，etc.）quota
【满分】full marks；full score
【满贯】❶reach the limit ❷(in mahjong，card games，etc.）perfect score；slam
【满怀】have one's heart filled with；be imbued with
【满口】(speak) unreservedly or profusely；be full of

曼 (màn) ❶graceful ❷prolonged；long-drawn-out
【曼延】stretch；trail；draw out

谩 (màn) disrespectful；rude
【谩骂】abuse；swear at

蔓 (màn)
【蔓延】spread

幔 (màn) curtain；screen
【幔帷】heavy curtain
【幔帐】curtain；screen；canopy

漫 (màn) ❶overflow；brim over；flood；inundate ❷be all over the place；be everywhere ❸free；unrestrained；casual
【漫笔】(usu. used as title of an essay) literary notes
【漫步】stroll；ramble
【漫长】very long；endless
【漫道】do not say or talk

【漫画】cartoon；caricature
【漫话】chat freely；have an informal discussion
【漫骂】use bad language against sb.；fling abuse
【漫漫】very long；boundless

慢 (màn) ❶slow ❷postpone；defer ❸supercilious；rude
【慢车】slow train
【慢待】treat rudely or discourteously
【慢慢】❶slowly；leisurely ❷gradually
【慢性】❶chronic ❷slow

mang

芒 (máng) awn；beard；arista
【芒果】〈植〉mango

忙 (máng) ❶busy；fully occupied ❷hurry；hasten；make haste
【忙活】be busy with sth.
【忙碌】be busy；bustle about：忙忙碌碌 as busy as a bee
【忙乱】be in a rush and a muddle；tackle a job in a hasty and disorderly manner
【忙人】busy person

盲 (máng) blind
【盲肠】〈生理〉caecum
【盲从】follow blindly
【盲点】blind spot；blackspot；scotoma
【盲干】act aimlessly or rashly
【盲目】blind
【盲人】blind person
【盲文】Braille

茫 (máng) ❶boundless and indistinct ❷ignorant；in the dark
【茫茫】vast
【茫然】in the dark；at a loss

莽 (mǎng) ❶rank grass ❷rash
【莽汉】a boorish fellow；boor
【莽莽】❶luxuriant；rank ❷vast
【莽原】wilderness overgrown with grass
【莽撞】rude and impetuous

mao

猫 (māo) 〈动〉cat
【猫熊】〈动〉panda
【猫眼】cat's eye；cat eye；peephole

毛 (máo) ❶hair；feather；down ❷wool ❸mildew ❹semifinished ❺gross ❻little；small ❼careless；crude；rash ❽panicky；scared；flurried ❾(of currency) be no longer worth its face value;depreciate

【毛笔】writing brush

【毛病】trouble;mishap

【毛发】hair

【毛巾】towel

矛 (máo) lance;pike;spear

【矛盾】contradiction;contradictory

【矛头】spearhead

茅 (máo)〈植〉cogongrass

【茅草】〈植〉cogongrass

【茅屋】thatched cottage

卯 (mǎo) ❶ mortise ❷ the fourth of the twelve Earthly Branches

【卯时】the period of the day from 5 a.m. to 7 a.m.

茂 (mào) ❶ luxuriant;exuberant;profuse ❷ rich and splendid

【茂密】dense;thick

【茂盛】exuberant;flourishing

冒 (mào) ❶ emit;send out;give off ❷ risk; brave ❸ boldly;rashly ❹ falsely;fraudulently

【冒充】pretend to be;pass off as;assume

【冒顶】roof fall

【冒渎】bother or annoy a superior

贸 (mào) trade

【贸然】rashly;without careful consideration

【贸易】trade;commerce

帽 (mào) headgear;hat;cap

【帽子】❶hat;cap ❷label;tag;brand

貌 (mào) ❶small;petty ❷slight;despise ❸ looks;appearance

【貌不惊人】look mediocre

【貌合神离】(of two persons or parties) be seemingly in harmony but actually at variance

【貌似】seemingly;in appearance

mei

没 (méi) ❶not have;be without ❷be not so as ❸less than ❹have not or did not have
另见 mò

【没救】incurable;incorrigible;beyond remedy or hope

【没脸】feel ashamed;feel embarrassed

【没命】❶lose one's life;die ❷recklessly;desperately;like nad;for all one's worth

【没趣】feel put out

玫 (méi) rose

【玫瑰】〈植〉rugosa rose;rose

眉 (méi) ❶eyebrow;brow ❷the top margin of a page

【眉睫】(as close to the eye as) the eyebrows and eyelashes

【眉毛】eyebrow;brow

【眉目】❶looks;features ❷logic;sequence of ideas ❸essential ❹sign of a positive outcome; prospect of a solution

【眉梢】the tip of the brow

【眉头】brows;～紧锁 frown severely

【眉心】between the eyebrows

【眉宇】〈书〉forehead

梅 (méi)〈植〉plum

【梅花】plum blossom

【梅花鹿】〈动〉sika (deer)

【梅雨】plum rains

【梅子】plum

媒 (méi) ❶match maker;go-between ❷intermediary

【媒介】medium;vehicle

【媒人】〈旧〉woman matchmaker

【媒体】media

煤 (méi) coal

【煤矿】coal mine

【煤气】gas

【煤球】briquette

【煤炭】coal

霉 (méi) mold;mildew

【霉菌】〈微〉mold

【霉烂】mildew and rot

每 (měi) ❶every;each;per ❷on each occasion;each time

【每每】often

【每人】each one;every one

【每天】each day;every day

美 (měi) ❶beautiful;pretty ❷very satisfactory;good ❸be pleased with oneself

【美餐】❶tasty food;table delicacies ❷eat and drink one's fill;have an excellent

【美差】cushy job

【美称】good name;laudatory title

【美德】virtue;moral excellence

【美感】aesthetic feeling;sense of beauty

【美工】❶art designing ❷art designer

妹 (mèi) younger sister;sister

【妹夫】younger sister's husband;brother-in-law

【妹妹】younger sister;sister

M

媚 (mèi) ❶ fawn on; favor with; toady to ❷ charming; fascinating; enchanting

【媚骨】obsequiousness

【媚态】coquetry; subservience

魅 (mèi) evil spirit; demon

【魅力】glamour; charm; enchantment; fascination

men

闷 (mēn) ❶ stuffy; close ❷ cover tightly ❸ (of a sound) muffled ❹ shut oneself or sb. indoors
另见 mèn

【闷热】hot and suffocating; stuffy

门 (mén) ❶ door; gate; entrance ❷ valve; switch ❸ way to do sth.; knack ❹ sect; school ❺ class; category

【门把】door knob; door handle

【门道】❶gateway ❷way to do sth. ❸social connections

【门第】family status

M

【门房】gatekeeper; doorman; janitor; porter

【门风】ethics and moral standards that a family or a clan keeps

【门户】❶door ❷gateway; important passage way

闷 (mèn) ❶ bored; depressed; in low spirits ❷tightly closed; sealed
另见 mēn

【闷气】stuffy; close

meng

蒙 (mēng) ❶cheat; deceive; swindle ❷make a wild guess ❸unconscious; senseless
另见 méng

【蒙蒙亮】first glimmer of dawn; daybreak

【蒙骗】delude

萌 (méng) sprout; shoot forth; bud

【萌发】〈植〉germinate; sprout; shoot

【萌生】produce; conceive

【萌芽】❶ sprout; germinate; shoot; bud ❷ rudiments; seed; germ

蒙 (méng) ❶cover ❷receive; meet with ❸ignorant; illiterate
另见 mēng

【蒙蔽】hoodwink; deceive; pull the wool over sb.'s eyes

【蒙混】mislead (people)

【蒙昧】❶uncivilized; uncultured ❷ignorant; benighted; unenlightened

【蒙难】（of a revolutionary）be confronted by danger; fall into the clutches of the enemy

【蒙太奇】〈电影〉montage

盟 (méng) ❶alliance ❷league ❸sworn brothers

【盟国】allied country; ally

【盟军】allied forces; allied armies; allies

【盟友】ally

朦 (méng)

【朦胧】❶dim moonlight ❷obscure; dim; hazy

猛 (měng) ❶fierce; violent; energetic; vigorous ❷suddenly; abruptly

【猛烈】fierce; violent

【猛然】suddenly; abruptly

【猛士】brave warrior

【猛兽】beast of prey

孟 (mèng) ❶the first month of a season ❷the eldest among brothers

【孟春】the first month of spring

【孟秋】the first month of autumn

梦 (mèng) dream

【梦话】❶words uttered in one's sleep; somniloquy ❷daydream; nonsense

【梦幻】illusion; reverie

【梦见】see in a dream; dream about

【梦境】dreamland

【梦寐】dream; sleep

mi

弥 (mí) ❶ full; overflowing ❷ cover; fill ❸more

【弥补】make up; remedy; make good

【弥封】seal the examinee's name on an exam paper so as to prevent fraudulence

【弥留】be dying

【弥漫】fill the air; spread all over the place

【弥散】scatter

迷 (mí) ❶be confused; be lost ❷be fascinated by; be crazy about ❸fan; enthusiast; fiend ❹confuse; perplex; fascinate

【迷航】（of a plane, ship, etc.）drift off course; lose one's course; get lost

【迷糊】❶misted; blurred; dimmed ❷dazed; confused

【迷惑】puzzle; confuse; baffle

【迷离】blurred; misted

【迷恋】be infatuated with; madly cling to

【迷路】❶lose one's way; get lost ❷〈解〉labyrinth; inner ear

谜 (mí) ❶riddle; conundrum ❷enigma; mystery; puzzle
【谜底】answer to a riddle
【谜语】riddle; conundrum

米 (mǐ) ❶rice ❷shelled seed; husked seed ❸meter; metre
【米饭】rice
【米粉】ground rice; rice flour
【米酒】rice wine
【米面】❶rice and wheat flour ❷ground rice; rice flour ❸〈方〉rice-flour noodles
【米色】cream-coloured
【米汤】rice water
【米制】the metric system
【米粥】congee; rice gruel

觅 (mì) look for; hunt for; seek
【觅取】look for; hunt for; seek

秘 (mì) secret; mysterious
【秘方】secret recipe
【秘诀】secret recipe; secret formula; secret trick of the trade
【秘密】secret; confidential; underground; private
【秘史】secret history (as of a feudal dynasty); inside story
【秘书】secretary

密 (mì) ❶close; dense; thick ❷intimate; close ❸fine; meticulous ❹secret
【密报】❶secretly report; inform against sb. ❷a secret report
【密布】densely covered
【密电】❶cipher telegram; restricted message ❷secretly telegraph sb.
【密度】density
【密封】seal up; seal hermetically; seal airtight

蜜 (mì) ❶honey; honey-like thing ❷honeyed; sweet
【蜜蜂】〈动〉bee; honeybee
【蜜饯】sweetmeats; preserved fruit

miao

眠 (mián) ❶sleep ❷〈动〉dormancy

绵 (mián) ❶silk floss ❷continuous ❸soft
【绵延】be continuous; stretch long and unbroken
【绵羊】sheep

棉 (mián) ❶general name for cotton and kapok ❷cotton ❸cotton-padded; quilted
【棉袄】cotton-padded coat(jacket)
【棉被】wadded quilt

【棉花】cotton
【棉毛衫】cotton (interlock) jersey (worn as underwear)

免 (miǎn) ❶excuse sb. from; exempt; dispense with ❷remove from office; dismiss; relieve ❸avoid; avert; escape ❹be not allowed
【免除】❶remove; prevent; avoid ❷remit; excuse; exempt; relieve
【免得】so as not to; so as to avoid
【免费】free; free of charge; for nothing; gratis
【免冠】❶take one's hat off (in salutation) ❷without a hat on; bareheaded

勉 (miǎn) ❶exert oneself; strive ❷encourage; urge; exhort ❸strive to do what is beyond one's power
【勉力】exert oneself; try hard; make great efforts
【勉励】encourage; urge
【勉强】❶manage with an effort; do with difficulty ❷reluctantly; grudgingly ❸force sb.

缅 (miǎn) remote; far back
【缅甸】Myanmar; Burma
【缅怀】cherish the memory of; recall

腼 (miǎn)
【腼腆】shy; bashful

面 (miàn) ❶face ❷surface; top ❸personally; directly; face to face ❹side; aspect ❺entire area ❻extent; range; scale ❼powder; wheat flour; flour ❽noodles
【面包】bread
【面对】face; confront
【面粉】flour
【面积】area
【面颊】cheek; chap
【面具】mask
【面孔】face

miao

苗 (miáo) ❶young plant; seedling ❷the young of some animals ❸vaccine ❹sth. resembling a young plant
【苗木】〈林〉nursery-grown plant; nursery stock
【苗圃】nursery (of young plants)
【苗条】slender; slim
【苗头】symptom of a trend
【苗子】❶〈方〉young plant; seedling ❷young successor ❸〈方〉symptom of a trend; suggestion of a new development

描 (miáo) ❶trace; copy ❷touch up; retouch
【描红】trace in black ink over characters printed

M

in red (in learning to write with a brush)

【描画】draw;paint

【描绘】depict;portray

【描金】〈工艺〉trace a design in gold

【描摹】delineate

【描述】describe

【描图】tracing

【描写】describe;depict

瞄 (miáo) concentrate one's gaze on;take aim

【瞄准】take aim;train on;lay; sight

秒 (miǎo) (of time)second; (of degree)second

【秒表】chronograph;stopwatch

【秒针】second hand

渺 (miǎo) ❶ vast; distant and indistinct; vague ❷tiny;insignificant

【渺茫】❶distant and indistinct; vague ❷uncertain

【渺无人烟】uninhabited; without a trace of human habitation

藐 (miǎo) ❶despise slight;ignore;look down ❷very small

【藐视】despise;look down upon

【藐小】tiny;negligible;insignificant;paltry

妙 (miào) ❶wonderful; excellent; fine ❷ingenious;clever;subtle

【妙不可言】too wonderful for words; most intriguing

【妙计】an excellent plan;a brilliant scheme

【妙诀】a clever way;an ingenious method

【妙论】an ingenious remark; a very clever remark

庙 (miào) ❶temple;shrine ❷temple fair

【庙会】temple fair

【庙堂】❶ the Imperial Ancestral Temple ❷imperial court

【庙祝】temple attendant in charge of incense and religious service;acolyte

mie

灭 (miè) ❶go out ❷extinguish; put out;turn off ❸submerge;drown ❹destroy; exterminate;wipe out

【灭此朝食】will not have breakfast until the enemy is wiped out—be anxious to finish off the enemy immediately

【灭火】❶put out a fire ❷cut out an engine

【灭迹】destroy the evidence

【灭绝】become extinct

【灭口】do away with a witness or accomplice

【灭亡】be destroyed; become extinct;die out

蔑 (miè) 〈书〉❶slight; disdain ❷nothing; none ❸smear

【蔑视】despise; show contempt for;scorn

min

民 (mín) ❶the people ❷a person of a certain occupation ❸a member of a nationality ❹of the people; folk ❺civilian

【民办】run by people; run by community; privately-run

【民兵】❶ militiaman; people's militia; militia ❷militiaman ❸Minuteman

【民不聊生】the people have no means of livelihood;the masses live in dire poverty; the people are destitute

【民船】a junk or small boat for civilian use

【民法】civil law

【民愤】popular indignation; the people's wrath

【民歌】folk song

【民航】civil aviation

【民间】❶among the people;popular;folk ❷nongovernmental;people-to-people

【民居】local style dwelling houses

抿 (mǐn) smooth (hair, etc.)with a wet brush

泯 (mǐn) vanish;die out

【泯灭】die out;disappear;vanish

【泯没】vanish; sink into oblivion; become lost

悯 (mǐn) ❶commiserate; pity ❷〈书〉sorrow

【悯惜】take pity on;have pity for

【悯恤】feel compassion for;pity

敏 (mǐn) quick; nimble;agile

【敏感】sensitive;susceptible

【敏捷】quick; agile; nimble;smart;quick- witted

【敏锐】sharp;acute;keen

ming

名 (míng) ❶name ❷excuse; false pretences ❸fame; reputation; renown ❹famous; celebrated; well-known;noted ❺express;describe

【名册】register;roll

【名称】name;title

【名城】a famous city

明 (míng) ❶bright; brilliant; light ❷clear; distinct ❸ open; overt; explicit ❹ sharpeyed; clear-sighted ❺ aboveboard; honest ❻sight ❼understand; know ❽immediately following in time

【明摆着】obvious;clear;plain

【明白】❶clear;plain ❷frank;explicit ❸sensible;reasonable ❹know;realize

【明畅】clear and lucid;lucid and smooth

【明澈】bright and limpid;transparent

【明处】in the open;in public

【明断】〈书〉pass (fair) judgement

鸣 (míng) ❶the cry of birds,animals or insects ❷ring;sound ❸express;voice;air

【鸣不平】complain of unfairness;cry out against injustice

【鸣笛】whistle

【鸣放】❶fire a shot ❷air one's views (through meetings,newspapers and other media)

【鸣礼炮】fire a salute

【鸣枪】fire a shot

【鸣谢】express one's thanks formally;express gratitude

【鸣冤】voice grievances;complain of unfairness: 击鼓～ beat the drum to call for redress

冥 (míng) ❶dark;obscure ❷deep;profound ❸ dull; stupid ❹ underworld; the nether world

【冥思苦想】 think long and hard; cudgel one's brains

【冥顽不灵】dull and stupid;impenetrably thickheaded

【冥想】deep thought

铭 (míng) ❶inscription ❷engrave

【铭感】〈书〉be deeply grateful

【铭记】bear firmly in mind;always remember

【铭刻】❶inscription ❷engrave on one's mind; always remember

【铭文】epigraph

【铭心】be engraved on one's heart be remembered with gratitude;刻骨～ deeply engraved in one's heart

瞑 (míng)

【瞑目】close one's eyes in death;die content

命 (mìng) ❶life ❷lot;fate;destiny ❸order; command ❹assign

【命案】homicide case

【命不该绝】not be destined to die (said of a person who has had a narrow escape)

【命定】be determined by fate;be predestined

【命令】order;command;instructions

【命脉】lifeblood;lifeline

【命题】assign a topic;set a question

【命运】destiny;fate;lot

【命中】hit the mark

miu

谬 (miù) wrong;false;erroneous;mistaken

【谬传】a false report

【谬论】fallacy;absurd theory

【谬误】error;mistake

mo

摸 (mō) ❶touch;feel;stroke ❷feel for;grope for;fumble ❸ get to know; find out; sound out

【摸底】❶know the real situation ❷sound sb. out

【摸哨】steal up to an enemy sentinel in the dark and get rid of him

【摸索】❶grope;feel about;fumble ❷try to find out(laws,secret,etc.)

【摸头】get to know sth. ;begin to understand

【摸透】get to know sb. or sth. very well

摹 (mó) copy;trace

【摹本】facsimile

【摹刻】❶carve a reproduction of an inscription or painting ❷a carved reproduction of an inscription or painting

【摹写】❶copy;imitate ❷describe

【摹印】❶copy and print ❷a style of characters or lettering on ancient imperial seals

模 (mó) ❶ pattern; standard ❷ imitate ❸model

另见 mú

【模本】calligraphy or painting

【模范】model;fine example

【模仿】imitate;copy;model oneself on

【模糊】❶dim;vague;indistinct;obscure ❷blur; obscure;confuse;mix up

膜 (mó) ❶membrane ❷film

【膜拜】prostrate oneself;worship

摩 (mó) ❶rub;scrape;touch ❷study;mull over

【摩擦】❶rub ❷〈物〉friction ❸clash;conflict

【摩登】modern;fashionable

【摩电灯】dynamo-powered lamp (on a bicycle, etc.)

【摩天】sky scraping

【摩托】motor

【摩托车】motorcycle;motorbike

磨 (mó) ❶rub; wear ❷grind; polish; sharpen ❸wear down; wear out ❹trouble; pester; worry ❺ dawdle; waste time ❻ obliterate; die out

M

另见 mò

【磨蹭】move slowly;dawdle
【磨刀】sharpen the sword (or knife, ect.)
【磨光】rub;polish;ground finish
【磨炼】temper oneself;steel oneself
【磨灭】wear away;obliterate
【磨难】tribulation;hardship
【磨损】wear and tear
【磨牙】❶grind one's teeth (in sleep) ❷〈方〉indulge in idle talk;argue pointlessly

蘑 (mó)

【蘑菇】〈植〉mushroom

魔 (mó) ❶ devil;demon;evil spirit ❷ magic;mystic

【魔法】magic;wizardry;sorcery;witch craft
【魔怪】demons and monsters;fiends
【魔鬼】devil
【魔力】magic power;charm

抹 (mǒ) ❶put on;apply;plaster ❷wipe off ❸erase;strike out;blot out;cross out
另见 mò

【抹黑】blacken sb.'s name;throw mud at;bring shame on
【抹杀】blot out;obliterate

末 (mò) ❶tip;end ❷nonessentials;minor details ❸end;last stage ❹powder;dust
【末减】〈书〉leniently convict sb.; lighten a punishment
【末了】last;finally;in the end
【末路】dead end;impasse
【末期】last phase;final period

没 (mò) ❶sink;submerge ❷overflow;rise beyond ❸disappear;hide ❹confiscate;take possession of ❺till the end
另见 méi

【没落】decline;wane
【没收】confiscate;expropriate

抹 (mò) ❶daub;plaster ❷skirt;bypass
另见 mǒ

【抹不开】feel embarrassed

茉 (mò)

【茉莉】〈植〉jasmine

沫 (mò) foam;froth

【沫子】foam;froth

陌 (mò) ❶a path between fields (running east and west) ❷road

【陌生】strange;unfamiliar

脉 (mò)
另见 mài

【脉脉】affectionately;lovingly:含情～ full of tenderness and love

莫 (mò) ❶no;not ❷don't

【莫不】there's no one who doesn't or isn't
【莫大】greatest;utmost
【莫非】can it be that;is it possible that

蓦 (mò) suddenly

【蓦地】unexpectedly;all of a sudden

漠 (mò) ❶desert ❷indifferent;unconcerned

【漠漠】❶misty ❷vast and lonely
【漠然】indifferently;apathetically
【漠视】treat with indifference;ignore;overlook

墨 (mò) ❶ink;inkstick ❷handwriting and painting ❸learning ❹black;dark

【墨迹】ink mark
【墨镜】sunglasses
【墨绿】blackish green;dark green
【墨水】ink
【墨汁】prepared Chinese ink

默 (mò) ❶silent;tacit ❷write from memory

【默哀】stand in silent tribute
【默读】read silently;silent reading:～课文 read a text silently
【默记】memorize
【默默】quietly;silently;in silence:～无言 silently;without saying a word
【默念】❶ read silently ❷ think back;recollect;recall
【默契】❶tacit agreement;tacit understanding ❷secret agreement
【默认】acquiesce in; tacitly accept; tacitly approve;give tacit consent to
【默诵】read silently
【默算】❶do mental arithmetic;do sums in one's heart ❷calculate;figure;plan
【默写】write from memory;dictation
【默许】tacitly consent to;acquiesce in

磨 (mò) ❶ mill; millstones ❷ grind; mill ❸ turn round

【磨盘】❶nether (or lower) millstone ❷〈方〉mill;millstones
【磨棚】grinding shed;mill shed
【磨子】〈方〉mill;millstones

mou

牟 (móu) try to gain;seek;obtain

【牟利】seek profit

【牟取】try to gain;seek

谋 (móu) ❶stratagem;plan;scheme ❷work for;seek ❸consult

【谋反】plot a rebellion

【谋害】❶plot to murder ❷plot a frame-up against

【谋划】plan;scheme

【谋利】profit;turn something to profit

某 (mǒu) ❶certain ❷some

【某某】so-and-so

【某些】certain;a few

mu

模 (mú) mold;pattern;matrix
另见 mó

【模具】mould;matrix;pattern;die

【模样】❶appearance;look ❷about;around

【模子】mould;matrix;pattern

母 (mǔ) ❶mother ❷one's female elders ❸female ❹origin;parent

【母爱】mother love

【母亲】mother

【母线】❶〈数〉generating line;generator;generator ❷〈电〉bus;bus line;bus bar

牡 (mǔ) male

【牡丹】〈植〉tree peony;peony

【牡蛎】〈动〉oyster

拇 (mǔ)

【拇指】❶thumb ❷big toe

木 (mù) ❶tree ❷timber;wood ❸made of wood;wooden ❹coffin ❺numb;wooden

【木偶】❶puppet;marionette ❷wooden image;carved figure

【木板】block

【木材】wood;timber;lumber

【木耳】an edible fungus

【木兰】〈植〉lily magnolia

【木料】timber;lumber

【木乃伊】mummy

【木炭】charcoal

【木头】wood;log;timber

【木已成舟】the wood is already into a boat—what is done cannot be undone

目 (mù) ❶eye ❷look;regard ❸item ❹order ❺catalogue;table of contents;a list of things

【目标】❶target;objective;object ❷goal;aim;end

【目的】aim;purpose;end;goal

【目睹】witness;see(with one's own eyes)

【目光】❶sight;vision;view ❷gaze;look

沐 (mù) wash one's hair

【沐猴而冠】a monkey with a hat on—a worthless person in imposing attire

【沐浴】❶take a bath ❷bathe

牧 (mù) herd;tend

【牧草】herbage;forage grass

【牧场】grazing land;pasture

【牧歌】❶pastoral song ❷madrigal

【牧民】herdsman

募 (mù) raise;collect;enlist;recruit

【募集】raise;collect

【募捐】solicit contributions;collect donations

墓 (mù) grave;tomb;mausoleum

【墓碑】tombstone;gravestone

【墓地】graveyard;cemetery

【墓志铭】inscription on the memorial tablet within a tomb;epitaph

幕 (mù) ❶curtain;screen ❷act

【幕后】behind the scenes;backstage

暮 (mù) ❶dusk;evening;sunset ❷towards the end;late

【暮霭】evening mist

【暮春】late spring (the third month of the lunar year)

【暮景】❶sunset scene;twilight ❷life in old age;evening of one's life

【暮年】declining years;old age;evening of one's life

【暮色】dusk;twilight;gloaming

穆 (mù) solemn;reverent

【穆斯林】Moslem;Muslim

M

N n

na

拿 (ná) ❶ hold; take; bring; fetch ❷ seize; capture ❸ be sure of; be able to do ❹ put sb. in a difficult position ❺ with

【拿获】apprehend (a criminal)

【拿开】take away

【拿捏】〈方〉❶ be affected bashful ❷ make things difficult for; put pressure on; threaten

【拿手】adept; expert; good at

哪 (nǎ) ❶ which; what ❷ any

【哪个】❶ which ❷ who

【哪里】❶ where ❷ wherever

【哪怕】even; even if

【哪些】which; who; what

【哪样】❶ what kind of ❷ any kind of

【哪知】who would have thought

那 (nà) ❶ that ❷ then

【那边】that place; there; over there

【那里】there; that place

【那么】so; to such a degree; like that; in that way

【那时】at that time; in those days

【那些】those

【那样】so; in such a manner; to such a degree

呐 (nà)

【呐喊】shout loudly; cry out

纳 (nà) ❶ receive; admit ❷ accept; take in ❸ enjoy; take delight or pleasure in life ❹ pay; offer ❺ sew close stitches

【纳粹】Nazi

【纳闷】feel puzzled; wonder

【纳入】bring into; fit into; ～正轨 set something on the right track

【纳税】pay taxes

捺 (nà) press down; restrain

nai

奶 (nǎi) ❶ breasts ❷ milk ❸ suckle; breast-feed

【奶茶】tea with milk

【奶粉】milk powder

【奶奶】〈口〉grandmother; grandma; granny

【奶牛】milk cow; cow

【奶瓶】nursing bottle; feeding bottle

【奶糖】toffee; toffy

【奶油】cream

奈 (nài) ❶ what; how; but ❷ bear; endure

【奈何】❶ (used in a rhetorical question) what alternative is there; what's to be done ❷ 〈书〉how; why ❸ do sth. to (a person); cope with; deal with

耐 (nài) be able to bear or endure

【耐穿】durable; stand wear and tear

【耐烦】have patience; be patient

【耐寒】cold-resistant

【耐久】lasting long; durable

nan

男 (nán) ❶ man; male ❷ son; boy

【男方】the bridegroom's or husband's side

【男女】men and women

【男人】❶ man ❷ menfolk

【男生】boy student; schoolboy

【男性】male

南 (nán) south

【南边】❶ south; the southern side ❷ 〈口〉the southern part of the country, esp. the area south of the Chang jiang River; the South

【南部】southern part; south

【南方】south; the southern part (of a country)

【南风】south wind

【南瓜】〈植〉pumpkin

【南海】the Nanhai Sea；the South China Sea

【南极】the Antarctic Pole

难 (nán) ❶difficult；hard；troublesome ❷put sb. into a difficult position ❸hardly possible ❹bad；unpleasant

另见 nàn

【难办】hard to do

【难保】❶there is no guarantee；one cannot say for sure；it's hard to say ❷difficult to preserve，protect，defend，etc.

【难辨】difficult to discriminate

【难处】difficult to deal with；hard to get along with

【难处】difficulties，troubles；disaster，predicament

【难道】（used to give force to a rhetorical question）

【难得】❶hard to come by；rare ❷seldom；rarely

【难点】a difficult point；difficulty；a hard nut to crack

难 (nàn) ❶catastrophe；disaster；calamity ❷blame；reproach

另见 nán

【难民】refugee

【难友】fellow sufferer

nao

挠 (náo) ❶scratch ❷hinder ❸yield；flinch

【挠头】❶scratch one's head ❷difficult to tackle

恼 (nǎo) ❶angry；irritated；annoyed ❷unhappy；worried

【恼恨】resent；hate

【恼火】irritated；vexed

【恼怒】angry；indignant

【恼人】irritating；annoying

脑 (nǎo) ❶brain；mind；head ❷essence

【脑袋】head

【脑海】brain；mind

【脑浆】brains

【脑筋】mind；brain；intelligence；mental ability

【脑力】mental power；intelligence

【脑力劳动】mental work

【脑震荡】〈医〉cerebral concussion；concussion

【脑子】❶〈口〉brain ❷brains；mind；head

闹 (nào) ❶noisy；make a noise；stir up trouble ❷give vent ❸suffer from，be troubled by ❹go in for；do，make

【闹病】fall ill；be ill

【闹场】a flourish of gongs and drums introducing a theatrical performance

【闹翻】fall out with sb.

【闹荒】（of peasants in former times）start famine riots

【闹剧】farce

【闹热】〈方〉lively；bustling with noise and excitement

nei

内 (nèi) ❶inside；inner；within ❷one's wife or her relatives

【内白】words spoken by an actor from offstage

【内宾】domestic guest

【内部】internal；interior；inside

【内地】inland；interior；hinterland

【内定】（of an official appointment）decided at the higher level but not officially announced

【内行】an expert

【内脏】viscera；splanchna；internal organs

【内战】civil war

【内政】internal affairs；domestic affairs；home affairs

nen

嫩 (nèn) ❶tender；delicate ❷light ❸inexperienced；unskilled

【嫩红】pink；apricot pink

【嫩黄】light yellow

【嫩绿】light green；soft green

【嫩气】❶delicate looks；youthfulness ❷daintylooking；youthful-looking

【嫩生生】very tender；very delicate

neng

能 (néng) ❶ability；capacity；skill ❷energy ❸able；capable ❹can；be able to；be capable of

【能动】active；dynamic；vigorous

【能干】able；capable；competent

【能够】can，be able to；be capable of

【能事】what one is particularly good at

【能手】dab；expert；a good hand

【能源】energy

ni

尼 (ní) Buddhist nun

【尼姑】nun;Buddhist nun
【尼古丁】nicotine
【尼龙】nylon

泥 (ní) ❶ mud;mire ❷ mashed vegetable or fruit
【泥垢】dirt;grime
【泥滑】muddy and slippery
【泥浆】slurry;mud
【泥坑】mud pit;morass

霓 (ní)〈气〉secondary rainbow
【霓虹灯】neon light

拟 (nǐ) ❶ draw up;draft ❷ intend;plan ❸ imitate
【拟订】draw up;work out
【拟稿】make a draft
【拟人】〈语〉personification
【拟议】❶ proposal;recommendation ❷ draw up
【拟作】a work done in the manner of a certain author

你 (nǐ) ❶ you (second person singular) ❷ you (second person plural) ❸ you (indefinite pronoun);one;anyone
【你的】❶ your ❷ yours
【你好】how do you do;how are you;hello
【你们】you

逆 (nì) ❶ contrary;counter ❷ go against;disobey;defy ❸ traitor ❹〈数〉inverse;converse
【逆差】trade deficit;unfavourable balance
【逆耳】grate on the ear;unpleasant to hear
【逆风】❶ against the wind ❷ head wind;contrary wind;adverse wind
【逆光】〈摄〉against the light
【逆境】adverse circumstances;adversity
【逆时针】anticlockwise
【逆事】❶ untoward incidents;mishaps ❷ rebellious acts
【逆水】against the current
【逆转】reverse;become worse;deteriorate

匿 (nì) hide;conceal
【匿藏】conceal;hide;go into hiding
【匿名】anonymous

溺 (nì) ❶ drown ❷ be addicted to
【溺爱】spoil;dote on
【溺水】drowning;sinking

nian

蔫 (niān) ❶ shrivel up,wither;wilt;fade ❷ droopy;listless;spiritless

年 (nián) ❶ year ❷ annual;yearly ❸ age ❹ New Year ❺ a period of one's life ❻ a period in history ❼ harvest
【年报】annual report;annual
【年初】the beginning of the year
【年代】age;years;time;era
【年底】the end of the year
【年度】year
【年份】❶ a particular year ❷ age;time
【年糕】New Year pudding (made of glutinous rice flour)
【年关】the end of the year (formerly time for settling accounts)
【年号】reign title
【年华】passage of time,age or youth:虚度～ idle away one's time
【年会】annual meeting
【年货】special shopping for the Spring Festival
【年级】grade;year
【年纪】age
【年鉴】yearbook;almanac
【年景】the year's harvest:好～ year of good harvest
【年历】single-page calendar
【年龄】age:入学～ school age
【年轮】〈植〉growth ring;annual ring
【年迈】old;aged
【年年】year after year
【年轻】young
【年少】❶ young ❷ youngster;a young man
【年时】❶〈方〉years;a long time ❷〈书〉former years
【年岁】❶ age ❷ years
【年息】annual interest
【年限】fixed number of years
【年薪】yearly salary
【年幼】young;under age
【年月】days;years:漫长的～ long years;aeon
【年终】the end of the year;year-end

黏 (nián) sticky;glutinous
【黏虫】armyworm
【黏胶】〈化〉viscose
【黏米】❶ glutinous rice ❷〈方〉broomcorn millet

撵 (niǎn) ❶drive out ❷catch up

碾 (niǎn) ❶ roller ❷ grind or husk with a roller ❸crush,grind ❹flatten

【碾坊】grain mill

【碾碎】pulverize

念 (niàn) ❶think of;miss ❷thought;idea ❸read aloud ❹attend school;study

【念叨】always talking about

【念旧】keep old friendship in mind constantly

【念诵】read aloud;chant

【念头】thought;idea;intention

niang

娘 (niáng) ❶ma;mum;mother ❷a form of address for an elderly married woman ❸a young woman

【娘家】a married woman's parents' home

【娘胎】mother's womb

酿 (niàng) ❶make（wine）;brew（beer）❷make（honey）❸lead to;result in ❹wine

【酿酒】make wine;brew beer

【酿造】make（wine,vinegar,etc.）;brew（beer,etc.）

niao

鸟 (niǎo) bird

【鸟巢】bird's nest

【鸟瞰】❶ look down from above ❷ a bird's eye view

【鸟瞰图】a bird's-eye view;an aerial view

【鸟类】bird

【鸟笼】birdcage

【鸟兽】birds and beasts

【鸟篆】bird script, an ancient form of Chinese written characters,resembling birds' footprints

【鸟嘴】beak;bill

袅 (niǎo) slender and delicate

【袅袅】❶ curl upwards ❷ wave in the wind ❸linger

【袅娜】〈文〉❶(of plants) soft and slender ❷ (of a female figure) delicate and graceful;willowy

尿 (niào) ❶urine❷urinate;make water;piss

【尿布】diaper;napkin;nappy

【尿床】bed-wetting

【尿道】〈生理〉urethra

【尿素】〈化〉urea;carbamide

nie

捏 (niē) ❶hold between the fingers;pinch ❷knead with the fingers;mould ❸fabricate;make up

【捏把汗】be breathless with anxiety or tension;be keyed up;be on edge

【捏合】mediate;act as go-between

【捏弄】❶ play with;fiddle with ❷ order about;manipulate

【捏造】fabricate;concoct;fake

镊 (niè) ❶tweezers❷pick up sth. with tweezers

【镊子】tweezers

蹑 (niè) ❶lighten one's step;walk on tiptoe ❷step on;walk with

【蹑手蹑脚】sneak;tiptoe

【蹑足】❶walk with light steps ❷〈书〉participate in;join

ning

宁 (níng) peaceful;tranquil
另见 nìng

【宁静】tranquil;quiet

狞 (níng) (of facial expression) ferocious;hideous

【狞视】stare fiercely at;fix one's sinister eyes on

【狞笑】grin hideously

柠 (níng)

【柠檬】〈植〉lemon

凝 (níng) ❶congeal;curdle;condense;coagulate ❷with fixed attention

【凝固】solidify

【凝华】〈气〉sublimate

【凝集】〈化〉agglutinate

【凝结】coagulate;congeal;condense

【凝练】concise;condensed;文笔～ write in a laconic style

【凝神】with fixed attention;～思索 be deep in contemplation

【凝重】❶ dignified;imposing ❷ (of sound or voice) deep and forceful ❸deep;dense;thick

宁 (nìng) rather;would rather;better
另见 níng

【宁可】would rather;better

【宁肯】would rather

【宁愿】would rather;better

N

niu

牛 （niú）ox；cattle
【牛车】ox cart
【牛顿】〈物〉newton（the standard metre-kilogram-second unit of force, named after Isaac Newton）
【牛劲】❶tremendous effort；great strength ❷stubbornness；tenacity
【牛栏】cattle pen
【牛马】oxen and horses；beasts of burden

扭 （niǔ）❶turn round ❷twist；wrench ❸sprain；wrench ❹roll；swing ❺seize；grapple with
【扭摆】（of one's body）sway
【扭打】wrestle；grapple
【扭结】twist together；tangle up
【扭力】〈物〉twisting force
【扭捏】be affectedly bashful
【扭伤】sprain；wrench

纽 （niǔ）❶handle；knob ❷button ❸bond；tie
【纽带】link；tie；bond
【纽扣】button

拗 （niù）stubborn；obstinate
另见 ào
【拗不过】unable to dissuade sb.；fail to talk sb. out of doing sth.

nong

农 （nóng）❶ agriculture；farming ❷peasant；farmer
【农场】farm
【农村】rural area；countryside；village
【农夫】farmer
【农妇】peasant woman
【农户】peasant household

浓 （nóng）❶dense, thick；concentrated ❷strong, rich ❸great；keen
【浓度】consistency；concentration；density
【浓厚】❶ dense；thick ❷ deep；strong；pronounced ❸strong
【浓烈】strong；thick；heavy
【浓眉】heavy eyebrows；thick eyebrows
【浓密】dense；thick
【浓缩】〈化〉concentrate；enrich

弄 （nòng）❶play with；food with；trifle with ❷do；make；handle ❸get；fetch
【弄错】make a mistake；misunderstand
【弄好】do well
【弄坏】ruin；put out of order
【弄通】get a good grasp of
【弄脏】stain；soil；pollute
【弄糟】make a mess of

nu

奴 （nú）❶slave；bondservant ❷enslave
【奴才】flunkey；lackey
【奴隶】slave
【奴仆】servant；lackey
【奴役】enslave

驽 （nú）❶an inferior horse；jade ❷（of a person）dull；incompetent
【驽钝】dull；stupid
【驽马】an inferior horse；jade

努 （nǔ）❶put forth；exert ❷protrude；bulge
【努力】strive；endeavour；make great efforts
【努嘴】pout one's lips as a signal

怒 （nù）❶anger；rage；fury ❷forceful；vigorous；dynamic
【怒潮】❶（tidal）bore ❷angry tide；raging tide
【怒斥】fulminate；angrily rebuke
【怒冲冲】in a great rage

nü

女 （nǚ）❶woman；female ❷daughter；girl
【女方】the bride's side；the wife's side
【女将】❶woman general ❷a female dab, expert or mastermind
【女朋友】girlfriend
【女强人】a strong woman；a woman of exceptional ability
【女人】women；womenfolk
【女色】woman's beauty；feminine charms
【女子】woman；female

nuan

暖 （nuǎn）❶warm；genial ❷warm up
【暖调】warm colour tone；warm tone
【暖房】green house；hothouse
【暖风】genial breeze；〈气〉warm braw
【暖和】warm
【暖气】heating；warm air

【暖色】warm colour
【暖水瓶】thermos（flask）

nüe

虐（nüè）cruel；tyrannical

【虐待】maltreat；ill-treat
【虐杀】cause sb.'s death by maltreating him；kill sb. with maltreatment
【虐政】tyrannical government

nuo

挪（nuó）move；shift

【挪动】move；shift
【挪借】get a short-term loan

【挪开】move away
【挪威】Norway
【挪用】❶divert ❷misappropriate；embezzle

诺（nuò）❶promise；assent；nod ❷yes；yep

【诺贝尔奖】Nobel Prize
【诺言】promise

懦（nuò）cowardly；weak

【懦夫】coward；craven
【懦弱】cowardly；weak in character；easily swayed by others

糯（nuò）glutinous（cereal）

【糯米】polished glutinous rice

N

O o

ou

讴 (ōu) ❶sing ❷folk songs；ballads

【讴歌】〈书〉sing the praises of；eulogize；celebrate in song

欧 (ōu) short for Europe

【欧美】Europe and America；Western；the west
【欧亚大陆】Eurasia
【欧元】Euro
【欧洲】Europe

殴 (ōu) beat up；hit

【殴打】beat up；hit

鸥 (ōu) gull

呕 (ǒu) vomit；throw up

【呕吐】vomit；throw up；be sick
【呕心】exert one's utmost effort
【呕心沥血】shed one's heart's blood；take infinite pains；work one's heart out
【呕血】〈医〉haematemesis；spitting blood

偶 (ǒu) ❶image；idol ❷even；in pairs ❸mate；spouse

【偶尔】once in a while；occasionally
【偶发】accidental；chance；fortuitous

【偶犯】casual offence
【偶感】❶random thoughts (often used in titles of articles) ❷suddenly feel；occasionally feel
【偶合】coincidence
【偶或】occasionally；now and then；sometimes；once in a while
【偶然】accidental；fortuitous；chance
【偶然性】〈哲〉contingency；fortuity；chance
【偶数】〈数〉even number；even
【偶像】image；idol
【偶一为之】do sth. once in a while；do sth. accidentally or by way of exception

藕 (ǒu) lotus roots

【藕断丝连】the lotus root snaps but its fibres stay joined (of lovers, etc.) still in contact though apparently separated—separated but still in each other's thoughts
【藕粉】❶lotus root starch ❷lotus root paste (a semifluid food)

沤 (òu) soak；macerate；steep

【沤肥】❶make compost ❷wet compost；waterlogged compost

怄 (òu) 〈方〉❶irritate；annoy ❷be irritated

【怄气】be difficult and sulky

P p

pa

趴 (pā) ❶lie on one's stomach; lie prone ❷bend over; lean over; lean on

扒 (pá) ❶gather up; rake up ❷stew; braise 另见 bā

【扒拉】〈方〉rake rice into one's mouth with chopsticks

【扒窃】pilfer; pick sb.'s pocket; steal

【扒手】pickpocket; shoplifter：政治～ political swindler; political trickster

爬 (pá) ❶crawl; creep ❷climb; scramble

【爬高】climb

【爬犁】sledge; sleigh

【爬行】crawl; creep

耙 (pá) ❶rake ❷make smooth with a rake

【耙子】rake

帕 (pà) handkerchief

怕 (pà) ❶fear; dread; be afraid of ❷I suppose; perhaps ❸feel anxious about; feel concerned for or about

【怕人】❶be afraid of people ❷spooky; eerie

【怕生】(of young child) be shy with strangers

【怕事】be afraid of getting into trouble

【怕死】fear death

【怕死鬼】〈口〉coward

【怕羞】coy; shy; bashful

pai

拍 (pāi) ❶clap; pat; beat ❷bat; racket ❸beat; time ❹take; shoot ❺send ❻flatter; fawn on

【拍打】pat; slap

【拍马】fawn：逢迎～ go out of one's way to curry favour with sb.

【拍卖】❶auction ❷selling off goods at reduced prices; sale

【拍摄】take (a picture); shoot

【拍手】clap one's hands; applaud

排 (pái) ❶arrange; put in order ❷row; line ❸platoon ❹rehearse ❺exclude; reject; discharge ❻push ❼raft ❽pie

【排版】〈印〉composing; typesetting

【排比】〈语〉parallelism

【排场】❶grand style; ostentation; extravagance：～大 of a grand scale | 讲～ be given to doing things in a grandiose way ❷extravagant ❸dignified; respectable

【排斥】repel; exclude; reject

【排解】❶mediate; reconcile ❷divert oneself from a bad mood, etc.

【排练】rehearse

【排列】❶arrange; range; put in order ❷〈数〉permutation

【排名】ranking

【排球】volleyball

【排水】drain off water

【排头】the person at the head of a procession, file leader; the person at the head of a row

【排外】exclusive; antiforeign

【排尾】the last person in row; the person at the end of a row

徘 (pái)

【徘徊】❶pace up and down; walk back and forth ❷hesitate; waver; hover

牌 (pái) ❶plate; tablet ❷brand ❸cards; dominoes

【牌匾】board (fixed to a wall or the lintel of a door)

【牌价】list price; market quotation：零售～ retail sales price | 批发～ wholesale price

【牌示】bulletin; public notice

【牌照】license plate; license tag

派 (pài) ❶political group; school of thought or art ❷style; manner and air ❸send; dispatch; assign; appoint

【派别】group school;faction
【派遣】send;dispatch
【派生】derive
【派头】style;manner
【派性】factionalism
【派驻】accredit;garrison;dispatch sb. to stay at

pan

攀（pān）❶climb;clamber ❷seek connections in high places ❸involve;implicate
【攀比】compare unrealistically with sb. better than oneself;互相～ make unrealistic comparison with each other
【攀扯】implicate(sb. in a crime)
【攀登】climb; scale: ～科学高峰 scale new heights of science
【攀附】❶(of a plant) climbing;trailing ❷cotton up to sb. in power in search of a promotion:～权贵 seek affiliation with the rich and powerful
【攀亲】❶claim kinship ❷arrange a match
【攀谈】engage in small talk
【攀缘】climb;clamber
【攀折】pull down and break off(twigs, etc.)

盘（pán）❶tray;plate ❷sth. shaped like or used as a tray, plate, etc. ❸coil;wind ❹build ❺check;examine ❻transfer ❼game;set
【盘查】interrogate and examine
【盘缠】〈口〉travelling expenses; money for the journey
【盘点】make an inventory of:～库存 take stock

蹒（pán）
【蹒跚】walk haltingly;limp

判（pàn）❶distinguish; discriminate ❷obviously (different) ❸appraise; give a mark ❹judge;decide ❺sentence; condemn
【判处】condemn sb. to a certain penalty:～有期徒刑一年 sentenced to one year's imprisonment
【判定】judge;decide;determine
【判断】decide; determine;〈法〉court decision;judgment
【判决】〈法〉court decision;judgment
【判刑】pass a sentence on (a convict);sentence (a convict) to (death,imprisonment,etc.)
【判罪】declare guilty;convict

盼（pàn）❶hope for; long for; expect; yearn for;look forward to ❷look
【盼头】sth. hoped for and likely to happen; good prospects
【盼望】hope for;long for;look forward

叛（pàn）betray;rebel against
【叛变】turn traitor
【叛离】desert
【叛乱】armed rebelling
【叛徒】apostate;deserter;defector

pang

滂（pāng）rushing;gushing;pouring
【滂湃】roaring and rushing
【滂沱】torrential

庞（páng）❶huge ❷innumerable and disordered ❸face
【庞大】huge creature; enormous; colossal; gigantic
【庞杂】numerous and jumbled

旁（páng）❶side ❷other;else
【旁白】aside (in a play)
【旁边】side
【旁观】look on;be on-looker

磅（páng）
另见 bàng
【磅礴】boundless;majestic

螃（páng）
【螃蟹】〈动〉crab

胖（pàng）fat;stout;plump
【胖墩儿】〈口〉(esp. referring to children) roly-poly;fatty
【胖子】fatty;fat person

pao

抛（pāo）❶throw;toss;fling ❷leave behind; cast aside
【抛锚】❶drop anchor; cast anchor ❷break down;be out of order
【抛弃】abandon;forsake;cast away;cast aside
【抛售】undersell;dump;sell sth in big
【抛掷】throw;cast,toss

刨（páo）❶dig;excavate ❷excluding;not counting

另见 bào

【刨根问底】get to the root (or bottom) of things

咆 (páo) (of beast of prey) roar; howl

【咆哮】roar; thunder: ～如雷 in a thundering rage

炮 (páo) 〈中医〉prepare herbal medicine by roasting or parching (in a pan)

另见 pào

【炮炼】〈中医〉parch and refine medicinal herbs

【炮制】❶〈中医〉the process of preparing Chinese medicine, as by parching, roasting, baking, steaming, etc. ❷〈贬〉concoct; cook up

跑 (páo) ❶run ❷run away; escape ❸run about doing sth.; run errands ❹evaporate ❺away; off

【跑遍】go around; travel all over

【跑表】〈体〉stop watch

【跑步】run; march at the double

【跑车】❶racing bike ❷roadster

【跑道】❶runway; airstrip; pared strip on which planes land take off ❷racing track; skating rink

【跑题】(of talk, writing, etc.) irrelevant; beside the point

【跑账】〈古〉(of a shop assistant) run around collecting credits

【跑辙】〈方〉run off the track digress from the subject; stray from the point

泡 (páo) ❶bubble ❷sth. shaped like a bubble ❸steep; soak ❹dawdle; dillydally

【泡菜】pickles

【泡饭】❶soak cooked rice in water ❷cooked rice reheated in boiling water

【泡沫】foam; froth

【泡汤】〈方〉come to naught; fizzle out; miscarriage

【泡影】visionary hope, plan, scheme, etc; bubble

炮 (pào) ❶big gun; cannon; artillery ❷bombard ❸firecracker ❹a blasthole filled with dynamite

另见 páo

【炮兵】artillery; artilleryman

【炮弹】(artillery) shell

【炮火】artillery fire; gunfire

【炮击】bombard; shell

【炮声】thunder of guns; report of artillery; roar of guns

疱 (pào)

【疱疹】❶bleb ❷herpes

pei

陪 (péi) accompany; keep sb. company

【陪伴】accompany; keep sb. company

【陪衬】❶serve as a contrast or foil; set off ❷foil; set off

【陪嫁】〈方〉dowry

【陪客】sb. invited to a dinner party to help entertain a guest

【陪送】❶give as a dowry ❷dowry

【陪同】accompany

培 (péi) ❶bank up with earth; earth up ❷foster; train

【培训】cultivate; train

【培养】❶ foster; train; develop ❷〈生〉culture; cultivate

【培育】cultivate; foster; breed

【培植】cultivate; foster; train

赔 (péi) ❶make good a loss; compensate; pay for ❷stand a loss

【赔本】sustain losses in business; run a business at a loss

【赔偿】compensate; pay for

【赔款】❶pay an indemnity; pay reparations ❷indemnity; reparations

【赔礼】make (or offer) an apology; apologize

【赔笑】smile obsequiously, apologetically or appeasingly; smile an apologetic or obsequious smile

【赔账】❶pay for the loss of cash or goods entrusted to one ❷〈方〉lose money in business

【赔罪】apologize (for a wrong done to sb.); ask forgiveness for one's wrongdoing

佩 (pèi) ❶wear (at the waist, etc) ❷admire

【佩带】wear

【佩戴】wear (a badge, insignia, etc.) on the chest, arm, or shoulder

【佩服】admire

【佩剑】〈体〉sabre

配 (pèi) ❶join in marriage ❷mate ❸compound; mix ❹apportion ❺find sth. to fit or replace sth else ❻subordinate; supplementary ❼match; harmonize with ❽deserve; suit; be qualified

【配备】❶allocate; provide; fit out ❷dispose; deploy ❸outfit; equipment

【配搭】❶supplement ❷collocate
【配电】distribution
【配对】❶pair ❷〈口〉(of animals)mate
【配额】quota
【配方】prescription
【配合】coordinate;cooperate;concert
【配件】❶fittings(of a machine,etc) ❷a replacement

pen

喷 (pēn)〈口〉❶spurt;spout ❷spray;sprinkle

另见 pèn

【喷灌】spray irrigation
【喷壶】sprinkling can
【喷漆】spray paint
【喷泉】fountain
【喷洒】spray;sprinkle:～农药 spray insecticide
【喷射】spray;spurt;jet
【喷嚏】sneeze
【喷头】❶shower nozzle ❷sprinkler head
【喷雾】atomizing;mist spray

盆 (pén)❶basin;round utensil with a large opening and small bottom for use as a receptacle or for washing ❷sth. akin to a basin

【盆地】basin;plain area skirted by mountains or highland
【盆花】potted flower
【盆浴】tub bath;bath in a tub
【盆子】tub

喷 (pèn)〈口〉❶in season ❷crop

【喷红】crimson
【喷香】fragrant;delicious

peng

抨 (pēng) attack(in speech or writing);assail;lash out at

【抨击】attack(in speech or writing);assail (with words);lash out at

烹 (pēng)❶boil;cook ❷fry quickly;in hot oil and stir in sauce

【烹饪】cooking
【烹调】cook(dishes)

朋 (péng) friend

【朋比为奸】act in collusion;conspire;collude; gang up
【朋党】clique;cabal

【朋友】❶friend ❷boy friend or girl friend

棚 (péng)❶canopy or awning of reed mats, etc. ❷shed;shack

【棚车】❶box wagon;boxcar ❷covered truck
【棚圈】covered pen(for animals)
【棚子】〈口〉shed;shack

蓬 (péng)❶〈植〉bitter fleabane ❷fluffy;dishevelled

【蓬荜增辉】lustre lent to a humble house (said in thanks for a visit or a gift such as a scroll)
【蓬勃】vigorous;flourishing
【蓬乱】(of grass, hair, etc.) dishevelled；unkempt
【蓬门荜户】(a house with) a wicker door—a humble abode
【蓬松】puffy
【蓬头垢面】with dishevelled hair and a dirty face;unkempt

鹏 (péng) roc

【鹏程万里】(make) a roc's flight of 10,000 li — have a bright future

澎 (péng) splash;spatter

【澎湃】surge

篷 (péng)❶covering or awning on a car, boat, etc. ❷sail (of a boat)

【篷布】tarpaulin
【篷帐】tent
【篷子】awning (for protection from the sun, rain, wind, etc.)

膨 (péng)

【膨大】expand;inflate
【膨胀】expand;swell;dilate;inflate

捧 (péng)❶hold or carry in both hands ❷boost;exalt

【捧杯】(of sports competition) win the cup;win a championship
【捧场】❶be a member of a claque ❷boost;sing the praises of;flatter
【捧腹】split
【捧腹大笑】be convulsed with laughter;split one's sides with laughter

碰 (pèng)❶touch;bump ❷meet;run into ❸take one's chance

【碰杯】clink glasses
【碰壁】run up against a stone wall;be rebuffed
【碰见】meet unexpectedly;run into

【碰巧】by chance；by coincidence

pi

批 (pī) ❶slap ❷refute；criticize ❸write comments on ❹wholesale ❺batch；lot；group

【批驳】refute；criticize；rebut

【批斗】criticize and denounce sb.（at a public meeting）

【批发】❶wholesale ❷（of an official document）be authorized for dispatch

【批复】give an official，written reply to a subordinate body

纰 (pī) ❶become unwoven or untwisted ❷be spoilt

【纰漏】small accident；make a slip

坯 (pī) ❶base；semifinished product ❷unburned brick；earthen brick

【坯布】〈纺〉unbleached and undyed cloth；grey cloth；grey

【坯模】mold

披 (pī) ❶drape over；wrap around；throw on；spread ❷open；unroll；spread out ❸split open；crack；break

【披风】cloak

【披肩】❶cape ❷shawl

【披露】publish；announce

【披靡】❶be swept by the wind ❷be routed；flee

【披散】hang down loosely

【披阅】open and read（a book）；peruse

砒 (pī) arsenic

【砒霜】（white）arsenic

劈 (pī) ❶split；chop ❷right against（one's face，etc.）❸strike
　　另见 pǐ

【劈柴】firewood

霹 (pī)

【霹雷】〈口〉thunderbolt；thunderclap

【霹雳】thunderbolt；thunderclap

皮 (pí) ❶skin ❷leather；hide ❸fur ❹cover；wrapper ❺surface ❻a broad，flat piece（of some thin material）；sheet ❼become soft and soggy ❽naughty ❾casehardened ❿rubber

【皮包】leather handbag；briefcase；portfolio

【皮鞭】leather-thronged whip

【皮尺】tape（measure）

【皮带】（leather）belt

【皮蛋】preserved egg

【皮肤】skin

毗 (pí) adjoin；be adjacent to

【毗邻】join；border on；be adjacent to

疲 (pí) tired；weary；exhausted

【疲惫】tired out；exhausted

【疲敝】（of manpower，material resources，etc.）be running low；become inadequate

【疲乏】weary；tired

【疲倦】tired；weary

【疲困】❶tired ❷（of economic situation，etc.）weaken：～不振 sluggish

【疲劳】tired；weary；fatigued

【疲软】fatigued and weak

啤 (pí)

【啤酒】beer

脾 (pí)

【脾气】❶temperament；disposition ❷temper

【脾胃】taste

【脾性】〈方〉temperament；disposition；nature

匹 (pǐ) be equal to；be a match for

【匹敌】be equal to；be well matched

【匹夫】❶ordinary man ❷an ignorant person

【匹配】❶〈方〉mate；marry ❷（of components，parts，etc.）matching

劈 (pǐ) ❶divide；split ❷break off；strip off ❸injure one's legs or fingers by opening them too wide
　　另见 pī

【劈叉】do the splits

【劈账】share out proceeds according to a certain rate

癖 (pǐ) addiction；weakness for

【癖好】favourite hobby

【癖性】natural inclination

屁 (pì) wind（from bowels）；fart

【屁股】❶〈口〉buttocks；bottom ❷〈动〉rump ❸end

【屁话】〈口〉nonsense；rubbish

辟 (pì) ❶open up（territory，land etc.）；break（ground）❷penetrating；incisive ❸refute；repudiate

【辟谣】refute a rumour

媲^(pì)

【媲美】compare favourably with;rival

僻^(pì)

❶ out-of-the-way; secluded ❷ eccentric ❸ rare

【僻静】secluded;lonely

【僻壤】a place of seclusion

譬^(pì) example;analogy

【譬解】try to persuade;try to talk sb. round

【譬如】for example;for instance;such as

【譬若】〈书〉for example;for instance;such as

【譬喻】metaphor;simile;analogy;figure of speech

pian

偏^(piān)

❶ inclined to one side; slanting; leaning ❷ partial; prejudiced ❸ insistently;persistently

【偏爱】have partiality for sth.

【偏差】deviation;error

【偏方】folk prescription

【偏护】be partial to and side with; be biased and shield

【偏激】extreme

【偏见】prejudice;bias

【偏离】deviate;diverge

篇^(piān)

❶a piece of writing ❷sheet of paper ❸piece;leaf

【篇幅】❶length (of a piece of writing) ❷space (on a printed page)

【篇目】table of contents;contents;list of articles

【篇章】sections and chapters

翩^(piān)

【翩翩】❶dance lightly ❷elegant smart

【翩然】lightly;trippingly

【翩跹】lightly;trippingly

便^(pián)

另见 biàn

【便便】bulging;swelling

【便宜】❶cheap ❷small advantages:占～ gain extra advantage by unfair means ❸let sb. off lightly

片^(piàn)

❶a flat; thin piece; slice; flake ❷part of a place ❸cut into slices ❹incomplete; fragmentary; partial; brief ❺slice;stretch

【片段】part;passage;extract;fragment

【片刻】a short while;an instant;a moment

【片面】unilateral;one-sided

【片言】a few words; brief words:～只字 (in) only a few words

骗^(piàn)

❶ deceive; fool; hoodwink ❷ cheat;swindle

【骗局】fraud;hoax;swindle

【骗取】gain sth by cheating;defraud

【骗人】deceive people

【骗术】deceitful trick;ruse;hoax

【骗子】swindler;impostor;cheat

piao

剽^(piāo)

❶rob ❷nimble;swift

【剽悍】agile and brave

【剽窃】plagiarize;lift

漂^(piāo) float;drift

另见 piǎo,piào

【漂泊】lead a wandering life;drift

【漂浮】❶ float ❷ (of style of work) superficial;showy

【漂流】drift about

缥^(piāo)

【缥缈】dimly dissemble;misty

飘^(piāo) wave to and fro;float;flutter

【飘荡】drift;wave;flutter

【飘动】float (in the air or upon the waves);flutter;drift

【飘拂】float slowly

【飘忽】❶float (of wind, cloud, etc.) ❷swing; sway;rock:情绪～不定 in uncertain mood

【飘零】❶faded and fallen ❷wandering;drifting; homeless

【飘落】drift and fall slowly

瓢^(piáo) gourd ladle;wooden dipper

【瓢虫】〈动〉ladybug;ladybird

漂^(piǎo)

❶bleach ❷rinse

另见 piāo,piào

【漂白】bleach

【漂洗】rinse:～衣裳 rinse clothes

瞟^(piǎo) look sidelong at;glance sideways at

票^(piào)

❶ticket ❷ballot

【票额】the sum, stated on a check or bill;denomination

【票房】❶booking office ❷box office

【票根】counterfoil;stub

【票价】the price of a ticket; admission fee; entrance fee

【票据】❶bill;note ❷voucher;receipt

漂 (piào) come to nothing; fall through
另见 piāo,piǎo

【漂亮】❶handsome; good-looking; pretty; beautiful ❷remarkable; brilliant; splendid; beautiful

pie

撇 (piē) ❶ cast aside; throw overboard ❷skim
另见 piě

【撇开】leave aside;bypass

【撇弃】cast away;abandon

瞥 (piē) shoot a glance at; dart a look at

【瞥见】get a glimpse of; catch sight of

【瞥眼】〈书〉in the twinkling of an eye; in an instant; in a flash

撇 (piě) ❶ throw; cast ❷ left-falling stroke (in Chinese characters)
另见 piē

【撇嘴】curl one's lip;twitch one's mouth

pin

拼 (pīn) ❶put together; piece together ❷be ready to risk one's life (in fighting,work, etc.);go all out in work

【拼版】〈印〉makeup

【拼搏】struggle hard; exert oneself to the utmost;go all out

【拼刺】❶bayonet drill; bayonet practice ❷bayonet charge

【拼音】❶ combine sounds into syllables ❷ spell;phoneticize

贫 (pín) ❶poor ❷be poor in; be deficient in ❸garrulous

【贫乏】short;lacking

【贫寒】poverty-stricken

【贫瘠】barren

【贫苦】poor;poverty-stricken

【贫困】in straitened circumstances

频 (pín) ❶frequently; repeatedly ❷frequency

【频传】keep pouring in

【频道】frequency channel

【频繁】frequently;often

【频率】〈物〉frequency

品 (pǐn) ❶ article; product ❷ grade; class; rank ❸character; quality ❹taste sth. with discrimination;sample; savour

【品尝】taste;sample;savour

【品德】moral character

【品格】one's character and morals

【品级】❶official rank in feudal times ❷grade (of products,commodities,etc.)

聘 (pìn) ❶ engage ❷ betroth ❸〈口〉(of a girl)get married or be married off

【聘金】betrothal money for the bride's family

【聘礼】betrothal gifts;bride-price

【聘请】engage;invite

【聘任】engage;appoint to a position

【聘书】letter of appointment

【聘用】employ;engage; appoint to a position

ping

乒 (pīng) table tennis;ping-pong

【乒乓球】〈体〉❶table tennis; ping-pong ❷table tennis ball;ping-pong ball

【乒赛】table tennis match or tournament

平 (píng) ❶flat; level; even ❷tie, draw ❸equal;fair, impartial ❹calm, peaceful; quiet ❺put down;suppress ❻average,common

【平安】safe and sound;without mishap; well

【平白】for no reason;gratuitously

【平辈】of the same generation

【平常】ordinary;common;general

【平川】level land; plain;～广野 flat, open wilderness|一马～ wide expanse of flat land

【平淡】dull;insipid;prosaic

评 (píng) ❶comment; criticize review ❷judge appraise

【评比】compare and assess

【评定】evaluate;assess

【评断】judge; arbitrate:～是非 judge between right and wrong

【评分】mark (student's papers,etc.)

【评述】commentary;comment and depiction

【评说】comment on; appraise; evaluate:～古人 comment on the ancients

【评选】choose through public appraisal

苹 (píng)

【苹果】〈植〉apple

凭 (píng) ❶ lean on; lean against ❷ rely on; depend on ❸ evidence; proof ❹ go by; base on ❺ no matter (what, how, etc.)

【凭单】 bill or document of warrant

【凭借】 rely on; depend on

【凭据】 evidence; proof

【凭证】 proof; evidence; certificate

屏 (píng) ❶ screen ❷ a set of scrolls ❸ shield sb. or sth.; screen

另见 bǐng

【屏风】 screen

【屏门】 screen door (between the outer and inner courtyards of an old-style Chinese residence)

【屏幕】 screen

【屏条】 a set of vertically hung scrolls (usu. four in a row) of painting or calligraphy; a set of wall scrolls

瓶 (píng) bottle; vase; flask

【瓶胆】 glass liner (of a thermos flask)

【瓶子】 bottle

po

坡 (pō) ❶ slope ❷ sloping; slanting

【坡地】 hillside fields; sloping fields

【坡度】 slope

【坡田】 sloping field

泼 (pō) ❶ sprinkle; splash ❷ rude and unreasonable; shrewish

【泼冷水】 pour (or throw) cold water on; dampen the enthusiasm (or spirits) of

【泼妇】 shrew; virago; rude and unreasonable woman

【泼辣】 ❶ rude and unreasonable; shrewish ❷ pungent; forceful ❸ bold and vigorous

【泼皮】 knave; gangster; blackguard

【泼洒】 spill (liquid); splash

婆 (pó) ❶ old woman ❷ a woman in a certain occupation ❸ husband's mother; mother-in-law

【婆家】 husband's family

【婆婆】 husband's mother; mother-in-law

迫 (pò) ❶ compel; force ❷ urgent; pressing ❸ approach; go towards (near)

【迫不得已】 have no alternative (but to); be forced to

【迫不及待】 unable to hold

【迫得】 force; compel

【迫害】 persecute

【迫降】 forced landing; distress landing

【迫近】 approach; get close to; draw near

【迫切】 urgent; pressing; imperative

【迫使】 make sb. do sth. with pressure; force; press; compel; oblige; coerce: ～ 对方让步 force one's opponent to make concessions

破 (pò) ❶ broken; damaged; torn; worn-out ❷ break; split; cut ❸ destroy ❹ defeat; capture ❺ expose the truth of ❻ poor; paltry; shabby

【破案】 solve (or clear up) a case; crack a criminal case

【破败】 ❶ ruined; dilapidated; run down ❷ decline; wane; be at the wane: ～的家庭 family on the decline

【破产】 ❶ go bankrupt; become insolvent; become ❷ come to naught; fall through; be bankrupt

【破除】 do away with; get rid of; eradicate; break with

【破费】 spend money

【破获】 unearth; uncover

【破旧】 old and shabby; worn-out; dilapidated: ～衣服 worn-out clothes

魄 (pò) ❶ soul ❷ vigour; spirit

【魄力】 daring and resolution

pou

剖 (pōu) ❶ cut open; rip open ❷ analyse; examine

【剖白】 explain oneself; vindicate oneself: ～心迹 lay one's heart bare

【剖腹】 lay open the bowel; disembowel: ～自尽 lay open the bowel and commit suicide; hara-kiri

【剖解】 analyse (reasons, etc.): ～细密 make a minute analysis

【剖面】 section

pu

扑 (pū) ❶ throw oneself on; pounce on ❷ devote ❸ rush at; attack ❹〈方〉flap; flutter

【扑鼻】 (of strong scent) assail the nostrils: 香气～. A sweet smell greeted us.

【扑打】 ❶ swat ❷ beat; pat

【扑救】 put out a fire to save life and property

【扑克】 ❶ playing cards ❷ poker

【扑空】fail to get or achieve what one wants
【扑面】blow on one's face

铺 (pū) ❶spread; extend ❷pave; lay
另见 pù

【铺床】make the bed
【铺垫】bedding; foreshadowing

仆 (pú)

【仆从】footman; retainer; henchman; servant
【仆仆】travel-stained; travel-worn and weary: 风尘～ endure the hardship of travel
【仆人】servant

菩 (pú)

【菩萨】❶Bodhisattva ❷Buddha
【菩提】〈佛教〉bodhi, supreme wisdom or enlightenment, necessary to the attainment of Buddhahood

朴 (pǔ) simple; plain

【朴实】❶simple; plain ❷guileless: 言行～ sincere and honest in words and deeds ❸earnest; down-to-earth
【朴素】simple; plain
【朴直】honest and straightforward: 语言～ speak in an honest and straightforward way | 文笔～simple and straightforward writing

【朴质】simple and unadorned; natural

普 (pǔ) general; universal

【普遍】universal; general; widespread
【普查】general survey
【普及】❶popularize; spread ❷universal; popular
【普通话】putonghua; common speech(of the Chinese language); standard Chinese pronunciation
【普选】general election

谱 (pǔ) ❶a register or record for easy reference (in the form of charts, tables, lists, etc.)❷manual; guidebook❸music score; music ❹set to music; compose(music)

【谱曲】set(words) to music; compose music for
【谱写】compose(music)

铺 (pù) ❶shop; store ❷plank bed
另见 pū

【铺板】bed board
【铺面】shop front
【铺位】bunk; berth

瀑 (pù) waterfall

【瀑布】waterfall; falls

曝 (pù)〈书〉expose to the sun

【曝露】〈书〉expose to the open air

Q q

qi

七 (qī) seven

【七颠八倒】 at sixes and sevens; all upside down; topsy-turvy

【七老八十】 in late seventies and early eighties; very old

【七零八落】 scattered here and there; in disorder

【七巧板】 seven-piece puzzle; tangram

【七窍生烟】 fume with anger; foam with rage; be outraged

【七十】 seventy

【七手八脚】 with everyone lending a hand

【七月】 July

妻 (qī) wife

【妻儿老小】 parents, wife and children — a married man's entire family

【妻子】 wife

栖 (qī) ❶perch ❷dwell; stay

【栖身】 stay; sojourn

【栖息】 perch; rest

凄 (qī) ❶chilly; cold ❷bleak and desolate ❸ sad; wretched; miserable

【凄惨】 wretched; miserable; tragic

【凄厉】 sad and shrill

【凄凉】 dreary; desolate; miserable

【凄迷】〈书〉❶(of scenes and sights) fuzzy and dreary ❷ grief-stricken: 神 情 ～ woebegone looks

【凄清】 ❶sombre; cheerless: ～的月光 cheerless moonlight ❷sad; lamentable: 琴声～ plaintive tune of a zither

【凄然】 sad; mournful

【凄婉】 ❶doleful ❷(of sound) plaintively melodious: ～的笛声 heartrending notes of a flute

戚 (qī) ❶relative ❷sorrow; woe

【戚戚】 sad; worried, anxious

【戚友】 friends and relatives

期 (qī) ❶a period of time; phase; stage ❷ scheduled time ❸expect ❹make an appointment

【期待】 expect; await; look forward to

【期货】 futures; forward

【期间】 time; period; course

【期刊】 periodical

【期考】 end-of-term examination; final (or terminal) examination

【期满】 expire; run out; come to an end

【期末考试】 terminal examination; the final examination of a school term; the final

【期盼】 expect; await; look forward to

【期票】 promissory note; term bill

【期期艾艾】 stammer; stutter

【期望】 hope; expectation

【期限】 allotted time, time limit; deadline

【期许】 ardently hope or expect (usu. used of one's juniors)

【期中考试】 midterm examination

欺 (qī) ❶deceive ❷bully; take advantage of sb.

【欺负】 bully; treat sb. high-handedly

【欺哄】 hoodwink; fool

【欺凌】 bully and humiliate: ～百姓 run roughshod over the people

【欺瞒】 hoodwink; dupe; pull the wool over sb.'s eyes

【欺骗】 deceive; cheat; dupe

【欺人太甚】 what a beastly bully; that's going too far; push people too hard

【欺辱】 humiliate; insult: 受尽～ have one's fill of insult

【欺侮】 bully and humiliate; treat sb. high-handedly

【欺压】 run roughshod over; ～百姓 oppress the people

【欺诈】 cheat; swindle

漆 (qī) ❶lacquer; paint ❷coat with lacquer; paint

【漆工】 ❶lacquering; painting ❷lacquerer; lacquer man; painter

【漆黑】 pitch-dark; pitch-black

【漆画】lacquer painting
【漆匠】❶lacquerware worker ❷lacquerer；lacquer man；painter

齐 (qí) ❶neat；even；uniform ❷be level with ❸even up at one point or along one line ❹together；simultaneously ❺all ready；all present ❻alike；similar

【齐备】complete；all ready：货色～ commodities of complete specifications
【齐唱】〈音〉chorus；group singing；sing in unison
【齐集】congregate；assemble；gather
【齐全】complete；all in readiness
【齐声】in unison
【齐头并进】advance side by side；do two or more things at once
【齐心】be of one mind
【齐整】neat；uniform
【齐奏】playing (instruments) in unison；unison

其 (qí) ❶his (or her，its，their) ❷he(or she，it，they) ❸that；such

【其次】next；secondly；then
【其间】❶between；among；amidst；in the midst of ❷during this or that period；in the intervening years
【其实】actually；in fact；as a matter of fact
【其他】other；else
【其余】the others；the rest；the remainder
【其中】among；in

奇 (qí) ❶strange；queer；rare ❷remarkable；wonderful ❸be surprised；be astonished ❹very；extremely
　　另见 jī

【奇才】a rare talent；a genius
【奇耻大辱】galling shame and deep humiliation；deep disgrace
【奇怪】strange；surprising；odd
【奇观】marvellous spectacle；wonder
【奇幻】❶fantastic；visionary：～的遐想 fantastic imagination ❷dreamlike；kaleidoscopic
【奇迹】miracle；wonder；marvel
【奇妙】marvelous；wonderful
【奇巧】ingenious；exquisite
【奇特】peculiar；queer；singular
【奇闻】sth. unheard-of；a thrilling，fantastic story
【奇袭】surprise attack；raid
【奇异】❶queer；strange ❷curious；amazed
【奇遇】adventure

歧 (qí) ❶fork branch ❷divergent；different

【歧路】branch road；forked road
【歧视】discriminate against：种族～ racial discrimination；racism
【歧途】wrong road
【歧义】different meanings；various interpretations
【歧异】difference；discrepancy

祈 (qí) ❶pray ❷entreat

【祈祷】pray；say one's prayers
【祈请】request；beseech
【祈求】earnestly hope；pray for
【祈望】hope；wish

骑 (qí) ❶ride；sit on the back of ❷horse or horse rider

【骑兵】cavalryman
【骑士】knight；cavalier
【骑手】good rider；horseman
【骑术】horsemanship；equestrian skill

棋 (qí) chess

【棋迷】chess fan；chess enthusiast
【棋盘】chessboard；checkerboard
【棋谱】chess manual
【棋手】chess player
【棋子】piece (in a board game)；chessman

旗 (qí) flag；banner；standard

【旗鼓相当】be matched in strength；be well-matched
【旗开得胜】win victory the moment one's standard is raised；win victory in the first battle；win speedy success
【旗帜】❶banner；flag ❷stand；colours
【旗子】flag；banner；pennant

乞 (qǐ) beg；supplicate

【乞丐】beggar
【乞怜】beg for pity or mercy
【乞求】beg for；supplicate；implore
【乞讨】beg；go begging
【乞援】ask for aid：四处～ seek high and low for assistance

岂 (qǐ) 〈书〉(used to ask a rhetorical question)

【岂但】not only
【岂非】(used to ask a rhetorical question)
【岂敢】〈套〉you flatter me；I don't deserve such praise or honour
【岂有此理】preposterous；outrageous；absurd

企 (qǐ) ❶stand on tiptoe ❷anxiously expect sth；look forward to

【企鹅】penguin
【企及】hope to attain：难以～ unattainable
【企盼】hope for；yearn for：～合家欢聚 yearn for a happy family reunion

【企求】desire to gain;seek for;hanker after

【企图】attempt;try;seek

【企望】hope for;look forward to

【企业】enterprise;business

启 (qǐ) ❶ open ❷ start;initiate ❸ enlighten;awaken ❹ state;inform

【启齿】open one's mouth; start to talk about sth.

【启迪】〈书〉open and enlighten;awaken

【启动】start(a machine etc.);switch on

【启发】arouse;inspire;enlighten

【启封】❶ unseal;break(or remove)the seal ❷ open an envelop or wrapper

【启蒙】impart rudimentary knowledge to beginners

【启示】enlightenment;inspiration;revelation

【启事】notice;announcement

【启用】start using(an official seal,etc.)

起 (qǐ) ❶ rise;get up;stand up ❷ remove;extract;pull ❸ appear;raise ❹ rise;grow ❺ draft;work out ❻ build;set up ❼ start;begin ❽ draw;get ❾ case;instance

【起兵】dispatch troops;launch an armed struggle;～造反 rise in a revolt

【起步】❶ start ❷ make a beginning

【起草】draft;draw up

【起程】leave;set out;start on a journey

【起初】originally;at first;at the outset

【起床】get up;get out of bed

【起点】starting point

【起飞】take off

【起伏】rise and fall,undulate

【起航】set sail

【起哄】❶(of a crowd of people)create a disturbance ❷(of a crowd of people)jeer;boo and hoot;tease clamorously

【起火】flare up;catch fire

【起家】build up;grow and thrive

【起劲】energetic; enthusiastic(in work,games,etc.)

【起居】daily life

【起来】❶ stand up;sit up;rise to one's feet ❷ get up;get out of bed ❸ rise;arise;revolt

【起落】rise and down;up and down

【起码】❶ minimum;elementary ❷ at least

【起锚】weigh anchor;set sail

【起跑】(of runners in a race)get ready and start;on your marks

【起跑线】starting line

【起身】❶ get up;get out of bed ❷ leave,set out;get off

【起誓】vow;对天～ swear by God

【起诉】sue;prosecute;～ 状 indictment;bill of complaint

【起先】at the outset;in the beginning

【起义】uprising;revolt

【起因】cause;origin

【起源】❶ origin ❷ originate from;stem from;come from

【起早贪黑】start work early and knock off late;work from dawn to dusk

【起止】beginning and end;～日期 dates of beginning and end

绮 (qǐ) ❶ figured woven silk material;damask ❷ beautiful;gorgeous

【绮丽】beautiful;gorgeous

【绮年】〈书〉young;youthful

【绮思】〈书〉beautiful thoughts(in literature)

气 (qì) ❶ gas ❷ air ❸ breath ❹ weather ❺ smell;odor ❻ spirit;morale ❼ airs;manner;style ❽ make ❾ get angry;be enraged

【气昂昂】full of dash;雄赳赳，～ valiantly and spiritedly

【气冲冲】furious;beside oneself with rage

【气喘】〈医〉asthma

【气窗】transom(window)

【气垫】air-cushion

【气度】deportment;spirit;～不凡 or unusual verve

【气氛】atmosphere

【气愤】indignant;furious

【气概】lofty quality;mettle spirit

【气功】qi gong,a system of deep breathing exercises;breathing exercises

【气鼓鼓】fuming with anger;foaming with rage;furious

【气贯长虹】filled with a spirit as lofty as the rainbow spanning the sky;full of noble aspiration and daring

【气候】❶ climate ❷ situation

【气呼呼】in a huff

【气急败坏】flustered and exasperated;utterly discomfited

【气节】moral integrity;unyielding quality in the face of an enemy or pressure;民族～ moral integrity of a patriot

【气量】tolerance

【气流】❶ air current ❷〈语〉breath

【气闷】❶ unhappy;worried;in low spirits ❷ feel suffocated(or oppressed)

【气恼】take offence;be ruffled

【气派】manner;style;air

【气魄】boldness of vision;breadth of spirit;daring

【气球】balloon

【气色】complexion;colour

【气势】momentum;imposing manner

【气势磅礴】of great momentum;powerful

【气势汹汹】in a (very) threatening manner; an aggressive posture fierce;overbearing

【气态】gas state;gaseity;gaseousness

【气体】gas

【气团】〈气〉air mass

【气吞山河】imbued with a spirit that conquers mountains and rivers;full of daring

【气味】❶smell;odor;flavour ❷smack；taste

【气味相投】congenial to each other；be two of a kind

【气温】air temperature

【气息】❶breath ❷flavour;smell

【气息奄奄】be breathing feebly；be at one's last gasp；be at the point of death；be sinking fast

【气象】❶ meteorological phenomena ❷ atmosphere;scene

【气象卫星】meteorological satellite weather satellite

【气呼呼】pant;gasp for breath

【气焰】arrogance;bluster

【气焰嚣张】be puffed up with pride

【气宇轩昂】have an impressive bearing

【气质】❶ temperament; disposition ❷ qualities;makings

【气壮山河】with a heroic spirit that conquers mountains and rivers

迄 (qì) ❶up to；till ❷so far；all along

【迄今】up to now；so far；until now

弃 (qì) throw away;abandon

【弃暗投明】forsake darkness for light; leave the reactionary side and cross over to the side of progress

【弃儿】abandoned child;foundling

【弃旧图新】turn over a new leaf

【弃权】❶abstain from voting ❷〈体〉waive the right (to play)

【弃世】pass away;die

【弃学】drop out of school；become a school dropout；～经商 abandon school to start a business

【弃置】discard;throw aside

汽 (qì) vapor;steam

【汽车】automobile;motor;car

【汽水】aerated water;soft drink；soda water

【汽艇】motorboat

【汽油】petrol;gasoline;gas

泣 (qì) ❶snivel；sob；哭～ in tears ❷tears：饮～ swallow one's own tears

【泣不成声】choke with sobs；feel extremely sad

【泣诉】give a tearful account；呜咽～ tell what has happened between sobs

契 (qì) ❶contract; deed ❷agree; get along well ❸〈书〉engrave

【契合】agree with；correspond to

【契据】deed；contract；receipt

【契友】close friend；bosom friend

【契约】contract；deed；charter

砌 (qì) build by laying bricks or stones

器 (qì) ❶implement；utensil ❷organ ❸capacity;talent

【器材】equipment；material

【器官】organ；apparatus

【器件】parts of an apparatus or appliance

【器具】utensil;implement;appliance

【器量】tolerance

【器皿】household utensils；containers esp. for use in the house

【器使】give sb. work suited to his abilities；assign jobs to people according to their abilities

【器物】implements;utensils

【器械】apparatus;appliance;instrument

【器宇轩昂】have a dignified appearance

【器重】think highly of sb. ；regard highly

qia

掐 (qiā) ❶pinch;nip ❷clutch

【掐断】nip off;cut off

【掐算】count sth. on one's fingers

【掐头去尾】break off both ends；do away with unnecessary parts (details) at both ends

卡 (qiǎ) ❶jam;cram;lodge ❷withhold;hold back ❸hold sth. in place with part of the hand between the thumb and the index finger：～脖子 seize sb. by the throat

另见 kǎ

洽 (qià) ❶be in harmony；agree ❷consult；arrange with

【洽商】make arrangements with；talk over with

【洽谈】make arrangement with；talk over with

【洽妥】have made an arrangement

恰 (qià) ❶appropriate；proper ❷just；exactly

【恰当】proper；suitable；fitting；appropriate

【恰到好处】just right

【恰好】happen to;just right
【恰恰】just;exactly;precisely
【恰巧】by chance;fortunately
【恰如】just as;just like
【恰如其分】apt;appropriate;just right

qian

千 (qiān) ❶thousand ❷a great amount of;a great number of
【千变万化】ever-changing
【千差别别】differ in thousands of ways
【千锤百炼】❶thoroughly tempered ❷(of literary works) be polished again and again
【千刀万剐】(usu. used in a curse) be hacked to pieces;be made mincemeat of
【千恩万谢】express a thousand thanks;be eternally indebted
【千方百计】in a thousand and one ways;by every(all) possible means
【千古罪人】one who stands condemned through the ages
【千呼万唤】a thousand calls;a thousand entreaties
【千回百转】full of twists and turns
【千家万户】innumerable households or families;ever family
【千娇百媚】(of a woman) bewitchingly charming
【千金】❶a thousand pieces of gold;a lot of money ❷〈敬〉daughter
【千钧重负】a grave responsibility
【千钧一发】a hundredweight hanging by a hair
【千里】a thousand li a long distance or a vast expanse
【千里迢迢】from a thousand *li* away;from afar
【千篇一律】stereotyped;following the same pattern
【千奇百怪】all sorts (kinds) of strange things;exceedingly strange
【千万】ten million;millions upon millions
【千辛万苦】innumerable trials and tribulations;untold hardships
【千言万语】thousands and thousands of words
【千载难逢】occurring only once in a thousand years
【千真万确】(be) absolutely true;really and truly;that's only too true

迁 (qiān) ❶move ❷change
【迁就】accommodate oneself to;yield to
【迁居】move;change residence
【迁怒】vent one's anger on sb. who's not to blame;take it out on sb.
【迁徙】move;migrate;change one's residence
【迁延】procrastinate;delay:～时日 cause a long delay;become long-drawn-out
【迁移】move;remove;migrate

牵 (qiān) ❶lead along;pull ❷involve
【牵缠】involve sb.;get sb. entangled:家事～ bogged down by family affairs
【牵肠挂肚】feel deep anxiety;be very worried;be on tenterhooks
【牵扯】involve;implicate;drag in
【牵掣】hold up;impede:互 相 ～ hold each other up
【牵动】❶produce a change in sb. or sth.;affect;influence:～全局 have an impact on the overall situation ❷touch;move
【牵挂】worry;care
【牵累】❶weigh down;tie down:家务～ be weighed down by family chores ❷implicate;involved:～无辜 implicate the innocent
【牵连】involve;implicate;tie up with
【牵强】forced;farfetched
【牵强附会】draw a forced analogy;make a farfetched (*or* irrelevant) comparison;give a strained interpretation
【牵涉】concern;drag in;involve
【牵头】take the lead;be the first to do sth.
【牵制】(usu. used with reference to military operations) pin down;tie up;check;contain

铅 (qiān) lead;black lead
【铅笔】pencil
【铅笔刀】a small knife for sharpening pencils;pen-knife
【铅球】shot
【铅字】type;letter

谦 (qiān) modest
【谦卑】humble;modest
【谦辞】self-depreciatory expression
【谦恭】modest and courteous
【谦和】modest and amiable:为人～ be amiable towards people
【谦谦君子】a modest gentleman
【谦让】modestly decline
【谦虚】❶modest;self-effacing ❷make modest remarks
【谦逊】modest;unassuming

签 (qiān) ❶sign;autograph ❷make brief comments on a document ❸bamboo slips used for divination or drawing lots ❹label; sticker ❺a slender pointed piece of bamboo or wood ❻tack

【签到】register one's attendance at a meeting or at an office; sign

【签订】conclude and sign(a treaty)

【签发】sign and issue (a document, certificate, etc.)

【签名】sign one's name; autograph

【签收】sign after receiving sth. ; sign to acknowledge the receipt of sth.

【签署】sign

【签约】sign a treaty or agreement

【签证】visa; vise

【签注】❶attach a slip of paper to a document with comments on it; write comments on a document (for a superior to consider) ❷write comments or points for attention on a certificate, book of tables, etc.

【签字】sign; affix one's signature

前 (qián) ❶front ❷forward; ahead ❸ago; before ❹preceding ❺former; formerly ❻first ❼future

【前半夜】the first half of the night

【前辈】senior (person); elder; the older generation

【前边】❶in front; ahead ❷above; preceding

【前车之鉴】warning taken from the overturned cart ahead; lessons drawn from others' mistakes

【前尘】〈书〉what happened in the past: 回首～ look back on the past

【前程】future; prospect

【前额】forehead

【前方】❶ahead ❷the front

【前锋】❶vanguard ❷〈体〉forward

【前赴后继】advance wave upon wave

【前功尽弃】waste all the previous efforts; waste the efforts already made; all labour lost

【前后】❶around (a certain time); about ❷from beginning to end; altogether ❸in front and behind

【前呼后拥】with a large retinue

【前进】advance; go forward; forge ahead

【前景】❶〈摄〉foreground ❷prospect; vista; perspective

【前倨后恭】first supercilious and then deferential; change from arrogance to humility

【前例】precedent; case that can be cited or referred to by later generations: 史无～ unprecedented in history; without any parallel in history

【前列】front row(or rank); forefront; van

【前面】❶in front; at the head; ahead; forward ❷above; preceding; above-mentioned; forepart

【前年】year before last

【前期】earlier stage; early days

【前前后后】the whole story; ins and outs

【前人】forefathers; predecessors

【前任】predecessor

【前日】the day before yesterday

【前哨】outpost; advance guard

【前身】predecessor

【前思后想】think over again and again

【前所未闻】never heard of before

【前所未有】never existed before; hitherto unknown; unprecedented

【前提】❶〈逻〉premise ❷prerequisite; presupposition

【前天】the day before yesterday

【前途】future; prospect

【前途无量】have boundless prospects; have unlimited possibilities

【前途渺茫】have a bleak future; have gloomy prospects

【前往】go to; leave for; proceed to

【前无古人】without parallel in history; unprecedented

【前夕】eve

【前线】front; frontline

【前言】preface; foreword; introduction

【前兆】omen; forewarning; premonition

【前者】the former

【前奏】prelude

虔 (qián) pious; sincere

【虔诚】pious; devout

【虔敬】reverent

【虔心】❶pious; sincere; devout: 一片～ a pious heart ❷devout; sincere; pious; reverent: ～忏悔 repent sincerely

钱 (qián) ❶coin; cash ❷money; wealth ❸fund; sum

【钱包】wallet; purse

【钱币】coin

【钱财】wealth; money

钳 (qián) ❶hold or grip with pincers ❷clamp; restrain

【钳制】clamp down on; pin down; suppress: ～住敌人的兵力 pin down the enemy's armed forces

【钳子】pliers; pincers; forceps; tool used to hold or cut things

乾 (qián)

【乾坤】heaven and earth;the universe

潜(qián) ❶latent;hidden ❷secretly;on the sly

【潜藏】hide;go into hiding

【潜伏】hide;conceal;lie low

【潜力】latent capacity;potential

【潜入】❶slip into;steal in ❷dive

【潜水】go under water;dive

【潜水员】diver;frogman

【潜逃】abscond;flee secretly:～在外 abscond

【潜艇】submarine

【潜望镜】periscope

【潜心】❶with great concentration ❷devote one-self to

【潜行】❶ move under water ❷ move stealthily;slink

【潜意识】subconsciousness;the subconscious

【潜泳】underwater swimming

【潜在】latent;potential

浅(qiǎn) ❶shallow ❷simple,easy ❸super-ficial ❹not intimate;not close ❺light ❻not long in time

【浅薄】shallow;superficial;meagre

【浅见】superficial view;humble opinion:～寡闻 superficial views and meagre knowledge

【浅陋】shallow;meagre;mean;deficient in knowledge;narrow-minded

【浅色】light colour

【浅滩】shoal;shallows

【浅显】plain;easy to read and understand

【浅易】simple and easy

遣(qiǎn) ❶send;dispatch ❷dispel

【遣词造句】choice of words and building of sen-tences;wording and phrasing

【遣返】repatriate

【遣散】disband;dismiss;send away

【遣送】send back;repatriate

谴(qiǎn) condemn;denounce;censure

【谴责】condemn;denounce;censure;reproach

欠(qiàn) ❶owe;be behind with ❷not e-nough;lacking;wanting ❸raise slightly

【欠款】money that is owing;arrears;balance due;debt

【欠缺】❶be deficient in;be short of ❷shortcom-ing;deficiency

【欠条】a bill signed in acknowledgement of debt

【欠妥】not proper

【欠债】be in debt;owe money

纤(qiàn) a rope for towing a boat;tow line
另见 xiān

【纤夫】boat tracker

【纤绳】towline;towrope

倩(qiàn) 〈书〉 beautiful; pretty;attractive;handsome

【倩影】(usu. of a woman) beautiful figure;well-proportioned from

堑(qiàn) moat;ditch;chasm;trench that cuts off a road:～壕 trench;entrenchment

歉(qiàn) ❶poor harvest ❷apology;sorry

【歉年】lean year

【歉收】poor harvest

【歉意】apology;regret

qiang

枪(qiāng) ❶rifle;gun ❷spear

【枪靶】target;mark

【枪毙】execute by shooting

【枪刺】bayonet

【枪弹】❶cartridge ❷bullet

【枪法】marksmanship

【枪击】shoot with a gun:遭～身亡 be shot dead

【枪杀】shoot dead;kill by firearm;gun fatality:惨遭～ be gunned down in cold blood

【枪声】report of a gun;shot;crack

【枪手】marksman;gunner

【枪战】gun battle;shoot-out:激烈的～ fierce shoot-out

【枪支】firearms

戕(qiāng)〈书〉kill:自～（自杀）kill one-self;commit suicide;take one's own life

【戕害】damage;ruin;injure:～健康 ruin one's health

【戕贼】harm;injure;undermine:～身体 under-mine or ruin one's health

腔(qiāng) ❶cavity ❷speech ❸tune;pitch ❹accent

【腔调】❶tune ❷accent

【腔骨】〈方〉spinal joints of pigs,sheep,etc. (for food)

强(qiáng) ❶strong;powerful ❷by force ❸better ❹slightly more than;plus
另见 jiàng,qiǎng

【强暴】❶violent;brutal;ferocious:～的行为 act of violence ❷ferocious adversary;brute force;despotic strength:不畏～ defy brute force

【强大】big and powerful;powerful;formidable

【强盗】robber;bandit

【强调】stress;emphasize;underline

【强攻】storm;attack violently and force one's

way into：～敌营 storm the enemy camp

【强国】powerful nation；power

【强横】brutal and unreasonable；tyrannical；overbearing；despotic：～无理 overbearing and unreasonable；unruly

【强化】strengthen；intensify；consolidate

【强加】impose；force

【强奸】rape；violate

【强健】strong and healthy

【强劲】powerful；forceful；vigorous：～的对手 powerful opponent

【强力】❶great force：～夺取 seize by great force ❷power of resistance；strength

【强烈】strong；intense；violent

【强权】power；might

【强人】❶strong man；person who is powerful，strong and capable ❷bandit；robber

【强身】keep fit by physical exercise or taking tonics：～术 way to keep fit

【强盛】powerful and prosperous

【强似】be better than；be superior to

【强行】force

【强有力】strong；vigorous；force-ful

【强硬】strong；tough；unyielding

【强占】❶seize；forcibly take；occupy by violence：～地盘 forcibly occupy turf ❷occupy by force of arms

【强者】the strong

【强制】force；compel；coerce

【强壮】❶（of a body）strong，robust；sturdy；powerful：～的体魄 of strong build；of robust construction ❷strengthen；build up：～剂 tonic；roborant

墙 （qiáng）wall

【墙报】wall newspaper

【墙角】corner

【墙纸】wallpaper

蔷 （qiáng）

【蔷薇】〈植〉rose

抢 （qiǎng）❶rob；loot ❷snatch；grab ❸vie for；scramble for ❹rush ❺scrape；scratch

【抢答】hurry to answer a question before others；race to be the first to answer a question

【抢夺】snatch；wrest；seize

【抢购】rush to purchase

【抢劫】rob；loot；plunder

【抢救】rescue；save；salvage

【抢手】（of goods）in great demand

【抢险】rush to deal with an emergency

【抢修】rush to repair；do rush repairs

强 （qiǎng）make an effort；strive

另见 jiàng，qiáng

【强逼】compel；force

【强辩】defend oneself by sophistry

【强迫】force；compel

【强求】insist on；impose

【强使】compel；force：～服从 force or compel sb. to obey

qiao

悄 （qiāo）

【悄悄】❶ quietly；on the quiet ❷without being noticed

跷 （qiāo）❶lift up；hold up ❷on tiptoe ❸stilts

【跷蹊】fishy；dubious

敲 （qiāo）❶knock；beat；strike ❷over charge；fleece sb.

【敲打】❶beat；rap；tap ❷〈方〉say sth. to imitate sb.

【敲定】settle；decide finally；make a final decision

【敲击】beat；rap；tap

【敲诈】extort；blackmail；racketeer

乔 （qiáo）❶tall ❷disguise ❸（Qiáo）a promotion

【乔木】〈植〉arbor；tree

【乔迁】move to a better place or have a promotion

【乔装】disguise（oneself as）

侨 （qiáo）❶live abroad ❷a person living abroad

【侨胞】countrymen residing abroad

【侨居】live abroad

【侨民】national of a particular country residing abroad

【侨务】affairs concerning nationals living abroad

桥 （qiáo）bridge

【桥洞】〈口〉bridge opening

【桥墩】pier

【桥拱】〈建〉bridge arch

【桥梁】bridge

【桥牌】bridge

翘 （qiáo）❶raise or lift up（one's head）：～首 raise or lift up one's head and look；crane one's neck ❷（of wood，paper，etc.）become warped or bent（when drying）

另见 qiào

憔 （qiáo）

Q

【憔悴】 wan and sallow；thin and pallid

瞧 (qiáo)〈口〉look；see

【瞧不起】 look down upon
【瞧见】〈口〉see；catch sight

巧 (qiǎo) ❶skillful；ingenious；clever ❷cunning；deceitful；artful ❸opportune；coincidental

【巧夺天工】 wonderful workmanship（or superb craftsmanship）excelling nature
【巧合】 coincidence
【巧计】 clever device；artful scheme；smart trick；artifice
【巧克力】 chocolate
【巧立名目】 invent all sorts of excuses；concoct various pretexts
【巧妙】 ingenious；clever
【巧取豪夺】 secure（sb.'s belongings，rights，etc.）by force or trickery
【巧遇】 encounter by chance

俏 (qiào) ❶pretty；smart-looking；handsome ❷sell well；be in great demand

【俏丽】 handsome；pretty
【俏皮】 ❶ good-looking； smart-looking ❷ witty；clever

峭 (qiào) ❶high and steep；precipitous ❷severe；stern

【峭壁】 cliff；precipice

窍 (qiào) ❶aperture ❷a key to sth.

【窍门】 key；knack

翘 (qiào) stick up；hold up
另见 qiáo

【翘辫子】〈诙〉kick the bucket

qie

切 (qiē) ❶cut；slice ❷tangency
另见 qiè

【切除】 excision；resection
【切磋】 learn from each other by exchanging views；compare notes
【切磋琢磨】 carve and polish — learn from each other by exchanging views
【切点】 point of tangency；point of contact
【切断】 cut off
【切割】 cut；carve up
【切开】 cut apart；cut open
【切入点】 penetrating（or breakthrough）point
【切碎】 cut up

茄 (qié)〈植〉eggplant；aborigine

【茄子】〈植〉eggplant；aborigine

且 (qiě) ❶〈书〉even ❷both...and...

【且慢】 wait a moment；not so soon；not so fast

切 (qiè) ❶correspond to；be close to ❷eager；anxious ❸be sure to
另见 qiē

【切齿】 gnash one's teeth
【切肤之痛】 pain of cutting one's body；a deep sorrow；an acute pain
【切合】 suit；fit in with correspond to；accord with；～实际 fit in with the reality；be practical
【切记】 be sure to keep in mind；must always remember
【切忌】 must guard against；avoid by all means
【切身】 ❶of immediate concern to oneself ❷personal
【切实】 ❶ feasible； practical ❷ conscientiously；earnestly
【切题】 keep to the point；be relevant to the subject；stick to the topic
【切勿】 never
【切要】 vital；essential；indispensable：～的知识 essential knowledge
【切中】 hit（the mark）

怯 (qiè) timid；cowardly；nervous

【怯步】 draw back；hang back
【怯场】 have stage fright
【怯懦】 timid and overcautious
【怯生】 shy with strangers
【怯声怯气】 speak in a timid manner；speak haltingly
【怯头怯脑】 uncouth；lumpish；countrified

窃 (qiè) ❶steal；pilfer ❷secretly；furtively

【窃据】 usurp；seize
【窃密】 steal secret information
【窃取】 steal；grab
【窃听】 eavesdrop；wiretap；bug
【窃贼】 thief；burglar

惬 (qiè) be satisfied

【惬意】 be pleased；be satisfied

qin

钦 (qīn) ❶ admire；respect ❷ by the emperor himself

【钦差】 imperial envoy
【钦慕】 admire and respect；hold in esteem
【钦佩】 admire；esteem
【钦羡】 admire and respect：～的目光 admiring look
【钦仰】〈书〉revere；venerate；esteem

侵（qīn）❶invade；intrude into ❷approaching

【侵犯】infringe upon；encroach on；violate

【侵害】encroach on；make inroads on

【侵略】aggression；invasion

【侵权】tort；violate or infringe upon others' lawful rights or interests

【侵扰】invade and harass

【侵入】invade；intrude into；make incursions into

【侵蚀】corrode；erode

【侵吞】❶misappropriate ❷swallow up；annex

【侵袭】make inroads on；hit

【侵占】seize

亲（qīn）❶parent ❷blood relation；next of kin ❸relative；kinsfolk ❹marriage；match ❺bride ❻close；intimate；dear ❼in person；oneself ❽kiss

【亲笔】in one's own handwriting

【亲骨肉】one's own flesh and blood（i. e. parents and children，brothers and sisters）

【亲近】be close to；be on intimate terms with

【亲口】（say sth. ）personally

【亲临】come or go to a place personally

【亲密】close，intimate

【亲密无间】be on intimate terms

【亲昵】intimate；affectionate；attached

【亲戚】relative

【亲切】cordial；kind

【亲情】emotional attachment among family members；父女～ affection between father and daughter

【亲热】affectionate；intimate

【亲人】one's parents，spouse，children，etc. ；one's family members

【亲如一家】as dear to each other as members of one family

【亲善】goodwill（between countries）

【亲生】one's own（children，parents）

【亲事】marriage

【亲手】with one's own hands；personally；oneself

【亲疏】（of relationships）close and distant

【亲属】kinsfolk；relatives

【亲吻】kiss

【亲信】❶be close with and trust：～小人 be close with and trust villains ❷trusted follower；confidant

【亲眼】with one's own eyes

【亲友】relatives and friends；kith and kin

【亲缘】affinity；blood relations；consanguinity

【亲自】personally；in person

【亲嘴】kiss

琴（qín）❶general name for certain musical instruments❷qin，a seven-stringed plucked instrument in some ways similar to the zither

【琴剑飘零】（of a scholar）wander from place to place

【琴键】key（on a musical instrument）

【琴书】story-telling，mainly in song，with dulcimer accompaniment

【琴弦】string（of a musical instrument）

禽（qín）birds

【禽兽】birds and beasts

勤（qín）❶diligent；industrious ❷often；frequently ❸duty；attendance

【勤奋】diligent；assiduous

【勤工俭学】study under a work-study programme；part-work and part-study

【勤俭】hardworking and thrifty

【勤恳】diligent and conscientious

【勤快】〈口〉diligent；hardworking；industrious：手脚～ quick and industrious

【勤劳】diligent；industrious；hardworking

【勤勉】diligent；assiduous

【勤学苦练】study diligently and train hard

擒（qín）capture；catch；seize

【擒获】catch；capture；arrest：～歹徒 capture a scoundrel

【擒拿】arrest；catch

寝（qǐn）❶sleep ❷bedroom ❸coffin chamber

【寝具】bedding

【寝食】sleeping and eating

【寝室】bedroom；dormitory

沁（qìn）❶ooze；seep；exude❷〈方〉let one's head droop downward；hang❸〈方〉put sth. into water

【沁人心脾】gladdening the heart and refreshing the mind；mentally refreshing；refreshing

【沁润】（of liquid，aroma，etc. ）soak into；permeate through；penetrate to

qing

青（qīng）❶blue and green ❷black ❸green grass or young crops ❹young

【青菜】greens；green vegetables

【青草】green grass

【青春】youth；youthfulness

【青翠】verdant；fresh and green

【青黄不接】green and yellow have not joined；a new crop has not yet come

【青睐】favour；good graces

【青绿】dark green
【青年】youth;young people
【青山】green hill
【青山绿水】blue mountains and green waters — beautiful scenery
【青少年】teenagers;youngsters
【青天】blue sky
【青蛙】frog;common pond frog

轻 (qīng) ❶of little weight;light ❷small in number,degree,etc. ❸not important ❹not serious;relaxing;light ❺gentle;soft ❻rashly ❼belittle;make light of
【轻便】light;portable
【轻薄】frivolous;flirtatious;态度～ frivolous attitude
【轻敌】take the enemy lightly;underestimate the enemy
【轻而易举】easy to do
【轻放】put down gently
【轻浮】frivolous;flippant;flighty
【轻歌曼舞】soft music and graceful dances
【轻工业】light industry
【轻捷】spry and light;nimble;springy;agile;～的脚步 brisk steps
【轻快】❶brisk;spry ❷light hearted;lively
【轻狂】extremely frivolous;举止～ extremely frivolous in behaviour
【轻慢】treat sb. without proper respect;slight;～失礼 act impolitely by slighting sb.
【轻描写】mention casually
【轻蔑】scornful;disdainful;contemptuous
【轻巧】❶light and ingenious;handy ❷nimble;agile;动作～ nimble in movement ❸simple;easy
【轻取】romp;rout;win without difficulty;win hands down;beat one's opponent easily
【轻柔】soft;gentle;pliable
【轻伤】slight wound;flesh wound
【轻生】make light of one's life;commit suicide
【轻视】despise;look down on;underestimate
【轻率】rash;hasty;indiscreet
【轻松】light;relaxed
【轻微】light;slight;trifling;to a small extent
【轻信】be credulous;readily believe
【轻易】easily;lightly;rashly
【轻音乐】light music
【轻盈】slim and graceful;lithe;lissom
【轻重】❶weight ❷degree of seriousness;relative importance

氢 (qīng)〈化〉hydrogen(H)

【氢气】〈化〉hydrogen

倾 (qīng) ❶incline;lean;bend ❷deviation;tendency ❸collapse ❹overturn and pour out;empty ❺do all one can
【倾巢出动】(of the enemy or bandits,etc.) turn out in full force (or strength)
【倾城】the whole city and town
【倾倒】❶topple over;tumble;collapse ❷greatly admire;adore;prostrate oneself
【倾倒】tip;dump;empty;pour out
【倾覆】overturn;topple;capsize
【倾国倾城】(of a woman) lovely enough to cause the fall of a city or a state;devastatingly beautiful;exceedingly beautiful
【倾家荡产】lose a family fortune
【倾慕】adore
【倾囊相助】empty one's purse to help;give generous financial assistance
【倾盆大雨】heavy downpour;torrential rain
【倾诉衷肠】pour out one's heart,reveal one's innermost feelings
【倾听】listen attentively to;lend an attentive ear to
【倾向】tendency;trend;inclination
【倾销】dump;sell goods at a very low price
【倾斜】tilt;incline;slope;slant
【倾泻】come down in torrents
【倾心】❶ admire; fall in love with ❷ cordial;heart-to-heart
【倾注】❶pour into ❷throw (energy,etc.)into

清 (qīng) ❶unmixed;clear ❷distinct;clarified ❸quiet ❹completely ❺clean up ❻settle;clear up ❼count
【清白】pure;clean;unblemished;unsullied;innocent;sinless;clean-handed; blameless
【清查】❶check ❷uncover;comb out;ferret out
【清澈】limpid;clear
【清晨】early morning
【清除】clear away;eliminate;get rid of;sweep away
【清楚】❶clear;distinct ❷clear;lucid ❸be clear about;understand
【清纯】❶pretty and pure;～秀丽 pretty and innocent ❷ fresh and pure; 泉 水 ～ fresh spring water
【清脆】clear and melodious
【清单】list of items;checklist;stock list;bill;databook;muster;开～ make an inventory
【清淡】❶light;weak;delicate ❷dull;slack
【清点】make an inventory;sort through and check;～物资 make an inventory of materials

【清风】cool breeze

【清高】aloof from politics and material pursuits; self-contained; pure and lofty

【清歌妙舞】clear singing, exquisite dancing

【清官】〈书〉honest and upright officials; clean-handed officials

【清还】clean up and pay off; discharge (a debt)

【清寂】cold and quiet

【清洁】clean

【清净】peace and quiet

【清静】quiet

【清冷】❶chilly: ～的秋夜 chilly autumn night ❷deserted; empty

【清理】put in order; check up

【清廉】(of officials) honest and clean; clean-handed; incorruptible; fair and disinterested: 为政～ be an incorruptble official

【清凉】cool and refreshing

【清亮】clear and sonorous; resonant; ringing: 嗓音～ have a resonant voice

【清贫】be poor

【清爽】❶fresh and cool; brisk; refreshing ❷easy; light; relieved; relaxed

【清算】❶settle; clear; square; pay off; liquidate: ～账目 settle accounts; balance accounts ❷call or bring to account: ～恶霸的罪恶 expose and condemn the crimes of a local tyrant

【清晰】distinct; clear

【清洗】❶clean; wash; launder; rinse ❷purge; ferret out; eliminate; get rid of

【清闲】at leisure; idle

【清香】delicate fragrance; faint scent; refreshing fragrance

【清新】pure and fresh

【清醒】❶clear-headed ❷come to; come round regain consciousness

【清秀】delicate and pretty

【清雅】elegant; refined

【清账】settle accounts; square or clear an account

【清正】honest and upright: 为官～ be an honest and upright official

蜻 (qīng)

【蜻蜓】dragonfly

【蜻蜓点水】like a dragonfly skimming the surface of the water—touch on sth.

情 (qíng) ❶feeling; affection ❷favor; kindness ❸love; passion ❹situation; circumstance

【情爱】❶(esp. between a man and a woman) love; affection ❷caring love

【情报】intelligence; information

【情不可却】it would be ungracious not to accept (an invitation, etc.)

【情不自禁】be overcome by one's feelings; be seized with a sudden impulse

【情操】moral integrity; character: 高尚的～ noble character

【情场】arena of love; love affair; love relationship: ～失意 be frustrated in love; be a failure in love

【情敌】rival in a love triangle

【情调】emotional appeal

【情窦初开】(of a young girl) first awakening (or dawning) of love

【情分】mutual affection

【情夫】fancy man; paramour

【情妇】ladylove; paramour

【情感】emotion; feeling

【情歌】love song; ballad; madrigal

【情话】lovers' prattle; whispered sweet talk

【情怀】emotions; sentiments; feelings: 抒发～ express one's feelings and thoughts

【情急智生】hit on an idea in a moment of desperation

【情节】plot; story

【情结】complex; love knot: 浓重的思乡～ strong nostalgia

【情景】scene; sight; circumstances

【情况】circumstances; situation; condition, state of affairs

【情郎】woman's lover; spark; beau; inamorato

【情理】reason; sense

【情侣】sweethearts; lovers

【情面】favour; feelings: 不讲～ no place for sentiment

【情趣】❶temperament and interest ❷interest; appeal; delight

【情人】sweetheart; lover

【情势】trend of events

【情书】love letter

【情丝】affection; tender feelings: ～万缕 a wealth of tender love

【情随事迁】feeling change with circumstances

【情态】spirit; mood

【情同手足】like brothers; with brotherly love for each other

【情投意合】agree in opinion; be closely allied in opinion and feelings; be (work) hand in glove with

【情网】snares of love; net of love; web of love: 坠

入～ fall in love; be caught in the snares of love

【情味】 sentiment; taste; overtone; flavour

【情文并茂】 (of writing) excellent in both content and language

【情形】 condition; situation

【情绪】 ❶morale; feeling; emotion ❷depression; the sulks

【情义】 ties of friendship, comradeship etc.

【情谊】 friendly feelings: 深厚的～ deep friendship

【情意】 affection; goodwill

【情由】 the hows and whys

【情有可原】 excusable; pardonable

【情缘】 predestined love between a man and woman: ～已断。Their love is over.

【情愿】 ❶be willing to ❷would rather; prefer

【情致】 interest; taste; 别有～ of special appeal

晴 (qíng) fine; clear

【晴和】 clear and warm

【晴空万里】 a clear and boundless sky; the vast clear skies

【晴朗】 fine; sunny

【晴天】 fine day, sunny day

【晴天霹雳】 a bolt from the blue

请 (qǐng) ❶request; ask ❷invite; engage ❸〈敬〉please

【请安】 pay respects to sb. ; wish sb. good health

【请便】 do as you wish; please yourself

【请功】 ask a superior to record a merit for sb.

【请假】 ask for leave

【请柬】〈书〉invitation card

【请教】 ask for advice; consult

【请客】 stand treat; invite sb. to dinner; entertain guests

【请求】 ask; request

【请示】 ask for instruction

【请帖】 invitation card

【请问】 excuse me; please

【请罪】 ❶admit one's error and ask for punishment ❷apologize; humbly apologize

庆 (qìng) ❶celebrate; congratulate ❷occasion for celebration

【庆典】 celebration; a ceremony to celebrate

【庆贺】 congratulate; celebrate

【庆幸】 rejoice

【庆祝】 celebrate

qiong

穷 (qióng) ❶poor; poverty stricken ❷limit; end ❸thoroughly ❹extremely

【穷愁】 poverty-stricken and woeful

【穷当益坚】 the greater the adversity, the stronger the will

【穷光蛋】 pauper; poor wretch; penniless vagrant

【穷极无聊】 ❶be utterly bored ❷absolutely senseless; disgusting

【穷家富路】 one should be frugal at home but well equipped for a journey

【穷尽】 limit; end

【穷究】 make a thorough (or exhaustive) inquiry into sth.

【穷寇】 hard-pressed enemy; tottering foe

【穷苦】 impoverished

【穷困】 destitute; in straitened circumstances

【穷忙】 be pointlessly busy; be busy for nothing

【穷目】 look as far as the eye can see

【穷年累月】 for years on end; year after year

【穷人】 poor people; the poor

琼 (qióng)〈书〉fine jade

【琼浆】〈文〉jadelike wine; good wine

【琼脂】 agar-agar; agar

qiu

丘 (qiū) ❶mound; hillock ❷grave

【丘陵】 hills

【丘疹】 papule; pimple

秋 (qiū) ❶autumn; fall ❷harvest time ❸year ❹time; period

【秋播】 autumn sowing

【秋高气爽】 the autumn sky is clear and the air is bracing (a set phrase for describing fine autumn weather)

【秋耕】 autumn ploughing

【秋毫之末】 the tip of an autumn hair a minute, almost indiscernible particle

【秋季】 autumn; fall

【秋景】 ❶autumn scenery; autumnal scenes ❷autumn harvest

【秋千】 swing

【秋收】 autumn harvest

【秋游】 autumn outing

蚯 (qiū)

【蚯蚓】〈动〉earthworm; anglworm

囚 (qiú) ❶imprison ❷prisoner ❸convict

【囚车】 prison van

【囚犯】 convict

【囚禁】 imprison; put in jail

【囚牢】 prison; jail

【囚笼】(wooden) prisoner's cage used in imperial China

【囚徒】convict; prisoner

求 (qiú) ❶ ask; beg ❷ strive for; seek ❸ demand

【求告无门】have nowhere to turn to for help

【求过于供】demand exceeds supply

【求和】❶ sue for peace ❷ (in ball games or chess) try to equalize the score; try for a draw

【求见】request an interview

【求解】find the solution (of a mathematical problem); solve a problem

【求救】ask sb. to come to the rescue; cry for help

【求情】plead; ask for a favor

【求饶】beg for mercy; beg for one's life; ask for pardon

【求人】ask for help

【求生】seek survival; keep oneself alive

【求实精神】matter-of-fact attitude; realistic approach

【求索】explore; seek; grope for; search for; quest after

【求学】❶ go to school; attend school ❷ pursue one's studies; seek knowledge

【求援】request reinforcements

【求证】seek to prove; seek evidence or verification

【求知】seek knowledge

【求职】job wanted

【求助】turn to sb for help

球 (qiú) ❶ sphere; globe ❷ ball ❸ the globe; the earth ❹ anything shaped like a ball

【球场】court; field

【球队】(ball game) team

【球风】sportsmanship shown in ball games

【球门】goal

【球迷】(ball game) fan

【球赛】ball game; match

【球鞋】gym shoes; tennis shoes; sneakers

qu

区 (qū) ❶ area; district; region ❷ an administrative division ❸ distinguish; classify ❹ zone

【区别】distinguish; differentiate

【区分】differentiate; distinguish

【区划】division into districts

【区间】interval

【区区】trivial; trifling

【区域】region; area

曲 (qū) ❶ bent; crooked ❷ bend (of a river, etc.) ❸ wrong; unjustifiable

另见 qǔ

【曲解】misinterpret; twist

【曲尽其妙】bring out (a quality, point, etc.) in a subtle and skilful way

【曲径通幽】a winding path leads to quiet seclusion

【曲线】curve

【曲折】❶ tortuous; winding ❷ complications

【曲直】right and wrong

【曲衷】〈书〉heartfelt emotion; inner feelings

驱 (qū) ❶ drive ❷ expel; disperse ❸ run quickly

【驱车】drive; ride (oft. in a car)

【驱除】drive out; get rid of

【驱散】disperse; dispel; break up

【驱使】❶ order about ❷ prompt; urge; spur on

【驱邪】exorcise (or drive out) evil spirits

【驱逐】drive out; expel; banish

屈 (qū) ❶ bend; bow ❷ subdue; submit ❸ wrong; injustice ❹ in the wrong

【屈从】submit to; yield to; knuckle under to

【屈服】surrender; yield; knuckle under to

【屈驾】〈套〉condescend (or be kind enough) to make the journey

【屈就】condescend to take a post offered

【屈居】be forced to accept a place or position

【屈理】unreasonable; unfair; unjust

【屈膝】go down on one's knees; bend one's knees

【屈指】count on one's fingers

【屈尊】condescend

祛 (qū) dispel; remove; drive away

【祛除】dispel; get rid of; drive out

【祛风】〈中医〉dispel the wind; relieve rheumatic pains, colds, etc.

【祛暑】drive away summer heat

【祛淤活血】〈中医〉remove blood stasis and promote blood circulation

躯 (qū) the human body

【躯干】trunk; torso

【躯壳】the body (as opposed to the soul); outer form

【躯体】body

趋 (qū) ❶ hasten; hurry along ❷ tend towards; tend to become

【趋附】ingratiate oneself with; curry favour with: ～权贵 attach oneself to bigwigs

【趋势】trend; tendency

【趋向】❶ tend to; incline to; ❷ trend; direction

渠 (qú) canal; ditch; channel

【渠道】❶irrigation ditch ❷medium of communi-cation

曲 (qǔ) ❶song;tune ❷music (of a song)
另见 qū

【曲调】tune (of a song);melody

【曲高和寡】highbrow songs find few singers;too highbrow to be popular

【曲目】number; items of song or performance;repertoire

【曲艺】qu yi, folk art forms including ballad singing,story telling,comic dialogues,clapper talks,cross talks,etc.

【曲终奏雅】a grand finale

【曲子】song;tune;melody

取 (qǔ) ❶take;get;fetch ❷aim at;seek ❸a-dopt;assume;choose

【取保】〈法〉go bail for one

【取材】draw materials

【取长补短】learn from others' strong points to offset one's own weaknesses

【取偿】get reimbursement or compensation

【取代】replace

【取道】by way of;through;via

【取得】gain;acquire;obtain

【取缔】prohibit; ban; suppress; clamp down; put the lid on;～无照商贩 clamp down on unli-censed vendors

【取而代之】replace sb.;supersede sb.

【取景】find a view

【取决】be decided by;depend on;hinge on

【取乐】seek pleasure; find amusement; amuse oneself;make merry

【取闹】❶kick up a row;make trouble ❷amuse oneself at sb.'s expense;make fun of

【取暖】warm oneself

【取巧】resort to trickery to serve oneself

【取舍】accept or reject;make one's choice

【取胜】win victory;score a success

【取消】cancel;call off;abolish

【取笑】ridicule;make fun of;poke fun at

【取信】win the confidence (or trust) of the oth-ers

【取样】sampling

【取悦】try to please;ingratiate oneself with sb.

【取证】take the evidence

娶 (qǔ) marry (a woman);take to wife

【娶亲】(of a man)get married

龋 (qǔ)

【龋齿】❶dental caries ❷decayed tooth

去 (qù) ❶go ❷remove;get rid of ❸be apart from ❹of last year

【去处】place to go;whereabouts

【去火】〈中医〉reduce internal heat; relieve in-flammation or fever

【去路】the way along which one is going;outlet

【去年】last year

【去世】(of grown-up people)die;pass away

【去向】the direction in which sb. or sth. has gone

【去职】no longer hold the post

趣 (qù) ❶interest;delight ❷interesting

【趣事】amusement; fun; joke; funny thing;逸闻～ anecdotes;episodes;jokes

【趣味】❶interest;delight ❷taste;liking;prefer-ence

【趣闻】interesting hearsay or news

quan

圈 (quān) ❶circle;ring ❷circle;group ❸en-close;encircle ❹mark with a circle
另见 juàn

【圈点】❶punctuate ❷mark words and phrases for special attention

【圈套】snare;trap

【圈子】circle ring

权 (quán) ❶right ❷power; authority ❸ad-vantageous position ❹weigh ❺tentatively; for the time being ❻expediency

【权贵】influential officials;bigwigs

【权衡】weigh;balance

【权力】power;authority

【权利】right

【权略】political choice;diplomacy

【权谋】(political) tactics;trickery

【权能】powers and functions

【权势】power and influence

【权术】political trickery; shifts in politics; in-trigue

【权威】❶authority;authoritativeness ❷a person of authority;authority

【权位】power and status

【权限】limits of authority (or powers); power;authority

【权宜之计】an expedient measure; makeshift (device);stopgap

【权益】rights and interests

【权欲熏心】be overcome with a lust for power

【权责】power and responsibility; rights and du-ties

【权诈】trickery;craftiness

【权杖】staff of authority (as carried by political

全（quán）❶ complete ❷ whole; entire; full; total ❸ entirely; completely ❹ make perfect or complete; keep intact

【全部】whole; complete; total; all
【全才】a versatile person; all-rounder
【全场】❶ the whole audience; all those present ❷〈体〉full-court; all-court
【全称】full name; unabbreviated form
【全程】whole journey; whole course
【全国】the whole nation (or country); nationwide; countrywide; throughout the country
【全会】plenary meeting; plenary session
【全景】panorama; full view; whole scene
【全局】the overall situation; the situation as a whole
【全军】❶ the whole (or entire) army ❷〈书〉preserve military strength
【全力】with all one's strength; all-out; sparing no effort
【全力以赴】spare no effort
【全貌】complete picture; full-view
【全面】overall; comprehensive; all-round
【全民】the whole people; all the people
【全能】〈体〉all-round
【全年】annual; yearly
【全勤】full work attendance (without a single day off during a specified period)
【全球】the whole world
【全权】❶ full powers; plenary powers ❷ full responsibility
【全然】completely; entirely
【全身】all over (the body); from head to foot; from tip to toe
【全神贯注】be absorbed (or engrossed) in; be preoccupied with
【全胜】❶ complete victory ❷〈体〉win every match; be all-victorious
【全始全终】see (or carry) sth. through; stick to sth. to the very end
【全数】total number; whole amount
【全速】full speed; maximum speed; full split; full tilt
【全体】❶ all; wholeness; total number:～会员 all the members ❷ all over (the body)
【全文】full text
【全线】❶ all along the frontline (of a war):～出击 launch an attack on all fronts ❷ whole line; entire length
【全心全意】whole-heartedly; heart and soul
【全知全能】omniscient and omnipotent

泉（quán）❶ spring ❷ an ancient term for coin
【泉水】spring water
【泉眼】the mouth of a spring; spring
【泉源】❶ springhead ❷ source (of wisdom, strength, etc.)

拳（quán）❶ fist ❷ boxing; pugilism
【拳击】boxing; pugilism
【拳术】❶ Chinese boxing ❷ pugilistic art
【拳套】a series of skills and tricks in Chinese boxing
【拳头】fist

痊（quán）recover from an illness
【痊愈】be fully recovered

蜷（quán）curl up; huddle up
【蜷伏】lie with the knees
【蜷曲】coil; twist
【蜷缩】roll up; curl up

颧（quán）
【颧骨】cheekbone

犬（quǎn）dog
【犬齿】canine tooth
【犬马之劳】serve like a dog or a horse
【犬牙】❶ canine tooth ❷ fang (of a dog)

劝（quàn）❶ advise; urge; try to persuade ❷ encourage
【劝导】induce; talk sb. round
【劝告】urge; advise
【劝和】try to persuade two parties to become reconciled; mediate
【劝架】try to reconcile parties to a quarrel or to stop people from fighting each other; mediate
【劝解】mediate
【劝诫】dissuade; admonish; exhort; expostulate
【劝勉】admonish and encourage:互相～ encourage each other
【劝说】persuade; advise
【劝慰】comfort; console; soothe
【劝阻】dissuade sb from; advise sb not to

que

缺（quē）❶ be short of; lack ❷ incomplete; imperfect ❸ be absent ❹ vacancy; opening
【缺德】wicked; rotten; mean
【缺点】shortcoming; defect; weakness; drawback
【缺额】vacancy

【缺乏】be short of；lack；be out of stock
【缺货】be in short supply；be out of stock
【缺课】be absent from school；miss a class
【缺口】❶ gap；breach；nick；indentation；jag ❷ (of funds，materials，etc.) gap；shortfall
【缺漏】gaps and omissions；弥缝～ fill in gaps and supple omissions
【缺勤】absence from duty（or work）
【缺少】lack；be short of
【缺损】❶damaged；worn；torn ❷〈医〉physiological defect；physiological deficiency
【缺席】absent（from a meeting，etc.）
【缺陷】defect；drawback；flaw；blemish；physical defect
【缺嘴】〈方〉❶harelip ❷fail to satisfy one's appetite or hunger

瘸（qué）be lame；limp

【瘸腿】〈口〉lame
【瘸子】〈口〉a lame person；cripple

却（què）❶step back；fall back ❷drive back；repulse ❸decline；refuse ❹ but；yet

【却步】step back（in fear or disgust）；hang back
【却敌】repulse the enemy

雀（què）sparrow

【雀鹰】sparrow hawk
【雀跃】jump for joy
【雀噪】〈贬〉enjoy loud fame

确（què）❶true；reliable ❷firmly

【确保】ensure；guarantee
【确当】fitting；proper；appropriate
【确定】define；fix；determine
【确立】establish
【确切】definite；exact
【确认】affirm；confirm；acknowledge

【确实】❶true；reliable ❷really；indeed
【确信】firmly believe；be convinced；be sure
【确凿】conclusive；authentic
【确诊】make a definite diagnosis；diagnose
【确证】❶ prove conclusively or positively ❷ proof positive；conclusive or irrefutable evidence

qun

裙（qún）skirt

【裙带】❶ belt（as a decoration for a skirt or dress）❷connected through one's female relatives
【裙子】skirt

群（qún）〈量〉❶crowd；group ❷herd；flock

【群策群力】pool the wisdom and efforts of everyone
【群芳】❶ beautiful and fragrant flowers ❷ a group of beauties or artists
【群芳之冠】the queen of flowers—the reigning beauty
【群峰】connected mountain peaks
【群集】get together；assemble；mass；congregate；throng；troop together；swarm
【群聚】bunching
【群龙无首】a host of dragons without a head—a group without a leader
【群情】public sentiment；popular feelings；of the masses：～激奋。The public is aroused and excited.
【群言堂】a conference hall where everyone is allowed to have his say rule by the voice of the many
【群英】galaxy of talents or heroes
【群众】crowd；the masses

R r

ran

然（rán）❶ right; correct ❷ so; like that ❸ but; nevertheless

【然而】yet; but; however

【然后】then; after that

【然则】〈书〉in that case; then

燃（rán）❶burn ❷ignite ❸light

【燃点】❶ignite; kindle; set fire to; light ❷〈化〉ignition(or burning, kindling)point

【燃放】set off (fireworks)

【燃料】fuel

【燃烧】❶burn; kindle ❷inflammation

冉（rǎn）slowly

【冉冉】〈书〉❶(of hair, twigs, etc.) hang down softly ❷slowly; gradually

染（rǎn）❶dye ❷catch (a disease) ❸acquire (a bad habit, etc.)

【染病】catch(or contract) an illness; be infected with a disease

【染料】dyestuff; dye

【染色】dyeing; colouring

【染指】take a share of sth. one is not entitled to; encroach on

rang

壤（rǎng）❶soil ❷earth ❸area

【壤地】〈书〉territory; land

【壤界】boundary; border

【壤土】〈农〉loam

嚷（rǎng）〈口〉❶shout; yell; make an uproar ❷make widely known

【嚷叫】shout; yell; make an uproar

【嚷嘴】〈方〉quarrel; bicker

让（ràng）❶give way; give ground ❷invite ❸let; allow ❹let sb. have sth at a fair price

【让步】make a concession; give in

【让价】(of a seller) agree to reduce the price asked

【让路】give way; make way for

【让位】❶abdicate ❷yield to

【让贤】relinquish one's post in favour of sb. better qualified

【让座】❶offer (give up) one's seat to sb. ❷invite guests to be seated

rao

饶（ráo）❶ rich; plentiful; ❷ have mercy on; let sb. off ❸ give sth. extra; let sb. have sth. into the bargain ❹although; in spite of the fact that

【饶命】spare sb. 's life

【饶舌】❶ too talkative; garrulous ❷ say more than is proper; shoot off one's mouth

【饶恕】forgive; pardon; spare sb. punishment

【饶头】〈口〉a small item given away free (in business transactions) ; extra

【饶裕】〈书〉richly endowed; fertile; abundant

扰（rǎo）❶harass; trouble ❷trespass on sb. 's hospitality

【扰动】be in turmoil; be turbulent

【扰害】disturb and harm; cause trouble

【扰乱】disturb; create confusion

【扰攘】hustle and bustle; noisy confusion; tumult

【扰扰】〈书〉disorderly; confused; chaotic

绕（rào）❶wind; coil ❷move round; circle ❸make a detour; bypass ❹confuse; baffle

【绕道】make a detour; go by a roundabout route

【绕口令】tongue twister

【绕圈子】circle; go round and round

【绕腾】talk in a roundabout way; beat about the bush

【绕弯子】beat about the bush

【绕行】❶ make a detour; bypass ❷ move round; circle

【绕嘴】be difficult to articulate

re

惹（rě）❶invite or ask for (sth. undesirable) ❷offend; provoke ❸attract; cause

【惹祸】court disaster

【惹恼】make sb. angry；offend

【惹气】get angry

【惹事】stir up trouble

【惹是非】provoke a dispute；stir up trouble

【惹眼】〈方〉conspicuous；showy

热（rè）❶heat ❷hot ❸heat up；warm up ❹fever；temperature ❺ardent；warmhearted ❻in great demand；popular ❼craze；fad ❽envious；eager ❾thermal；thermo-

【热爱】ardently love；have deep affection for

【热潮】great mass fervour；upsurge

【热忱】zeal；warm-heartedness；enthusiasm and devotion

【热诚】enthusiastic；ardent；earnest；cordial

【热带】the tropics

【热点】hot spot

【热度】❶degree of heat；heat ❷fever；temperature

【热功当量】〈物〉mechanical equivalent of heat

【热火朝天】buzzing (or bustling) with activity；in full swing

【热浪】〈气〉❶heat wave；hot wave ❷craze

【热泪】hot tears；tears of joy, sorrow or gratitude

【热泪盈眶】one's eyes brimming with tears

【热恋】be passionately in love

【热量】quantity of heat

【热烈】ardent；passionate；fervent

【热流】❶〈气〉thermal current ❷warm current

【热门】cause of popular interest：～货 commodity in short demand

【热闹】lively；animated；noisy

【热气腾腾】❶steaming hot ❷seething with activity

【热切】fervent；earnest

【热情】enthusiasm；zeal；warmth

【热情奔放】bubbling with enthusiasm

【热情洋溢】permeated (or brimming) with warm feeling；gloving with enthusiasm

【热身】warm-up

【热汤面】noodles in soup

【热天】sweltering weather；summer

【热望】ardently wish

【热线电话】(telephone) hot line

【热心】enthusiastic；zealous；earnest

【热心肠】〈口〉❶warmheartedness ❷a warm-hearted (or sympathetic) and helpful person

【热血动物】warm-blooded animal；warm blood

【热血沸腾】one's blood boils；burning with righteous indignation

【热衷】hanker for；be fond of

ren

人（rén）❶human being；person；people ❷adult ❸other people ❹person considered as a worker or employee ❺personality；character ❻everybody；each；all

【人才】talent；a talented person

【人才外流】brain drain

【人才出众】a person of exceptional ability or striking appearance

【人才荟萃】a galaxy of talent

【人才济济】an abundance of capable people；a galaxy of talent

【人才流动】flow (or mobility) of trained personnel

【人才辈出】people of talent coming forth in large numbers

【人潮】stream of people

【人称】〈语〉person

【人道】humanity

【人道主义】humanitarianism

【人地生疏】be unfamiliar with the place and the people；be a complete stranger

【人丁兴旺】have a growing family；have a flourishing population

【人定胜天】man can conquer nature；man will triumph over nature

【人非木石】man is not made of wood or stone — man is not feelingless

【人浮于事】more staff (or hands) than needed；overstaffed

【人格】personality；character；moral quality

【人工】man-made；artificial

【人工呼吸】artificial respiration

【人工授粉】〈农〉artificial pollination

【人工智能】artificial intelligence

【人工繁殖】〈农〉artificial propagation

【人欢马叫】people bustling and horses neighing — a busy, prosperous country scene

【人迹罕至】without human trace；uninhabited；untraversed

【人间天堂】heaven on earth

【人杰地灵】the greatness of a man lends glory to a place

【人尽其才】make the best possible use of men

【人均】per capita

【人口】population；all the members of a family

【人困马乏】the men weary, their steeds spent tired out；exhausted

【人类】mankind；humanity

【人力】manpower

【人满为患】overcrowded with people；overstaffed

【人面桃花】her face and the peach-blossoms— the pinings of a lover

【人面兽心】the face of a man but the heart of a beast—a beast in human form

【人民】the people

【人命关天】a case involving human life is one of supreme importance

【人莫予毒】no one dare harm me—be supercilious

【人品】personal character; moral quality

【人强马壮】both men and horses are strong— ❶ a strong, combat effective army ❷ a strong working force

【人情】human feeling; human sympathy

【人情世故】worldly wisdom

【人情冷暖】social snobbery

【人情练达】experienced in the ways of the world

【人穷志短】poverty chills ambition

【人权】human rights

【人群】crowd; throng; multitude

【人人】everybody

【人山人海】huge crowds of people; a sea of people

【人身自由】freedom of person; personal freedom

【人神共愤】(of a great outrage) arouse the great indignation of both men and gods

【人生】life

【人生观】one's outlook on life

【人声鼎沸】a hubbub of voices; a babel of voices

【人士】personage; public figure

【人世】this world; the world

【人世沧桑】tremendous changes in this world of ours

【人事】❶ human affairs; occurrences in human life ❷ personnel matters ❸ way of the world ❹ consciousness of the outside world

【人事处】personnel division

【人微言轻】the words of the lowly carry little weight

【人物】personage; figure

【人心】❶ popular feeling; public feeling; the will of the people ❷ human feelings; human reason

【人心惶惶】popular anxiety

【人心不古】public morality is not what it used to be (i. e. has degenerated)

【人心叵测】man's heart is incomprehensible; harbour an evil heart; one's heart is past finding out

【人心所向】popular sentiment; the feelings of the people

【人心向背】whether the people are for or against; the feelings of the people

【人行横道】pedestrian crossing; zebra crossing

【人性】human nature; humanity

【人员】personnel; staff

【人云亦云】repeat word for word what others say; echo the views of others; follow another's lead in voicing opinions

【人造】man-made; artificial; synthetic

【人证】testimony of a witness

【人之常情】what is natural and normal (in human relationships)

【人质】hostage

【人种】ethnic group; the human species; race

仁 (rén) ❶ benevolence; humanity ❷ sensitive ❸ kernel

【仁爱】charity

【仁慈】kindness; tender mercy; benevolent

【仁德】kindheartedness; benevolence; humanity

【仁厚】kind-hearted and tolerant：～待人 treat people with generosity

【仁义】amiable; kind; reasonable

【仁义道德】humanity, justice and virtue; virtue and morality

【仁至义尽】be most perfectly fulfilled both in love and duty

忍 (rěn) ❶ bear; endure; tolerate; put up with ❷ be hard hearted enough to

【忍不住】cannot help (doing sth)

【忍饥挨饿】endure the torments of hunger

【忍俊不禁】cannot help laughing

【忍耐】exercise patience; exercise restrain

【忍气吞声】swallow an insult; submit to humiliation; stifle one's indignation

【忍让】exercise forbearance; be forbearing and conciliatory：互相～ be mutually accommodating

【忍辱含垢】bite the dust; eat humble pie

【忍受】bear; endure; stand

【忍痛割爱】part reluctantly with what one treasures

【忍心】have the heart to; be hardhearted enough to

认 (rèn) ❶ recognize; know; make out; identify ❷ adopt ❸ admit; recognize; own ❹ undertake to do sth

【认出】recognize; make out; identify

【认错】acknowledge a mistake

【认定】❶ firmly believe; maintain; hold ❷ set one's mind on

【认购】subscribe; offer to buy

【认可】approve; give legal force to

【认领】❶ claim ❷ adopt

【认命】accept fate; resign oneself (or be resigned) to fate

R

【认亲】❶become related by marriage ❷claim a family connection

【认清】see clearly; recognize

【认识】❶ know; understand ❷knowledge; understanding

【认输】throw in the towel; admit defeat

【认同】❶identify oneself with ❷approve of; recognize

【认为】think; consider; hold; deem

【认贼作父】take the foe for one's father; regard the enemy as kith and kin

【认账】acknowledge a debt; admit (or confess) what one has said or done

【认真】take seriously

【认证】legalize; attest

【认罪】confess one's guilt

任 (rèn) ❶appoint ❷assume a post; take up a job ❸official post; office ❹undertake; bear ❺let; allow; give free reign to ❻ no matter (how, what, etc.)

【任便】as you see fit; as you like

【任何】any; whatever

【任教】teach; be a teacher

【任课】be a lecturer; teach class

【任劳任怨】bear responsibility without grudge

【任免】appoint and dismiss

【任命】appoint

【任凭】despite; no matter (what, how, etc.)

【任期】tenure of office, a tour of duty

【任务】task; mission

【任性】willful; self-willed; wayward

【任意】wanton; arbitrary; willful

【任用】assign sb. to a post; appoint

【任职】assume office

纫 (rèn) ❶thread a needle ❷sew; stitch ❸ 〈书〉usu. used in a letter expressing one's thanks

【纫佩】〈书〉feel gratefulness and admiration towards sb.

韧 (rèn) pliable but strong; tenacious; tough

【韧带】ligament

【韧性】toughness; tenacity

妊 (rèn)〈书〉be pregnant

【妊妇】a pregnant woman

【妊娠】gestation; pregnancy

reng

扔 (rēng) ❶throw; toss; cast ❷throw away; cast aside

【扔掉】throw away;

【扔弃】abandon; discard; cast aside

【扔下】abandon; put aside

仍 (réng) ❶remain ❷still; yet

【仍旧】as usual; still; yet

【仍然】still; yet

ri

日 (rì) ❶sun ❷daytime; day ❸daily; every day; with each passing day ❹time

【日班】day shift

【日报】daily; daily paper

【日本】Japan

【日不暇给】be fully occupied every day; be pressed for time

【日常】usual; usually; daily

【日程】daily schedule; agenda

【日出】sunrise

【日光】sunlight

【日后】in the days to come; in the future

【日积月累】by slow accumulation

【日记】diary

【日渐】day by day

【日久天长】after a considerable period of time

【日理万机】attend to numerous affairs of state every day; be occupied with a myriad of state affairs

【日历】calendar

【日落】sunset

【日暮】evening; nightfall; dusk

【日期】date

【日益】change with each passing day; day by day；～繁荣 become prosperous on a daily basis

【日托】part-time nursery; day care

【日新月异】change rapidly; alter from day to day; bring about new changes

【日薪】daily wage; per diem

【日趋】day and night; round the clock

【日以继夜】day and night

【日用】daily expenses

【日月】life; livelihood

【日月星辰】the sun, the moon and the stars; the heavenly bodies

【日月重光】the sun and the moon shining again back to peace and prosperity after a dark period

【日月如梭】the sun and the moon shuttle back and forth—how time flies

【日照】sunshine

【日子】day; date

rong

荣 (róng) ❶grow luxuriantly;flourish ❷honour;glory

【荣归】 return in glory

【荣华富贵】 glory, splendour, wealth and rank; high position and great wealth

【荣获】 have the honour to get or win

【荣枯】 ❶(of plants) flourishing and withering ❷rise and fall (or decline)

【荣辱】 honour or disgrace

【荣辱与共】 (of friends) share honour or disgrace, weal or woe

【荣幸】 be honoured

【荣耀】 honour;glory

【荣誉】 honour;credit;glory

容 (róng) ❶hold; contain ❷tolerate ❸permit; allow ❹facial expression ❺appearance;looks

【容积】 volume

【容量】 capacity

【容留】 provide shelter to;take sb. in

【容貌】 appearance looks

【容纳】 hold; have a capacity of accommodate

【容器】 container vessel

【容情】 show mercy;tolerate

【容人】 tolerant:心胸狭隘，容不得人 narrow-minded and intolerant

【容忍】 tolerate;put up with;condone

【容身】 take shelter

【容许】 ❶permit; allow ❷possibly perhaps

【容颜】 appearance;looks;facial appearance

【容易】 ❶easy ❷easily likely; liable; apt

溶 (róng) dissolve

【溶化】 dissolve;melt

【溶解】 dissolve

【溶媒】 menstruum;resolver

熔 (róng) melt;fuse

【熔点】 melting point

【熔化】 melt

【熔炉】 ❶furnace ❷crucible

【熔融】 melt

融 (róng) ❶melt; thaw ❷blend; fuse; be in harmony

【融合】 mix together;merge:文化～ cultural ferment

【融化】 melt;thaw

【融会】 mix together;fuse;merge

【融解】 melt;thaw

【融洽】 harmonious; on friendly terms:关系～ congenial relations

冗 (rǒng) ❶superfluous; redundant ❷full of trivial details ❸busyness

【冗笔】 superfluity in writing or painting; unnecessary touches or strokes

【冗长】 tediously long;lengthy

【冗词】 superfluous words (in a piece of writing)

【冗繁】 (of affairs) many and diverse; miscellaneous

【冗员】 redundant personnel:裁减～ cut down on surplus personnel

【冗杂】 ❶(of writing) lengthy and jumbled ❷(of affairs) miscellaneous

【冗赘】 verbose;diffuse

rou

柔 (róu) ❶ soft; supple ❷ soften ❸ gentle; yielding

【柔肠】 tender heart; tender feelings:～寸断 lovelorn;heartbroken|～百折 broken-hearted

【柔道】 judo

【柔和】 soft;gentle;mild

【柔滑】 soft and smooth

【柔美】 soft and graceful

【柔媚】 gentle and lovely;genial; lovable

【柔嫩】 tender;delicate

【柔能克刚】 the soft can overcome the hard

【柔情】 tender feelings;tenderness

【柔情似水】 tender feelings like water be deeply attached; be passionately devoted

【柔韧】 pliable and tough

【柔软】 soft;lithe

【柔润】 soft and smooth;delicate

【柔弱】 weak

【柔顺】 gentle and agreeable;meek

【柔荑】〈书〉 ❶sprout; shoot ❷(of a woman's hands) slender and white ❸a woman's hands

【柔细】 soft and fine

揉 (róu) rub;knead

【揉搓】 rub;knead

【揉磨】〈方〉 torment

肉 (ròu) ❶meat; flesh ❷pulp; flesh (of fruit)

【肉饼】 ground-meat pie;meat pie

【肉搏】 fight hand to hand

【肉搏战】 hand-to-hand fight (or combat); bayonet fighting (or charge)

【肉食】 carnivorous:～动物 carnivorous animal;carnivore

【肉体】 human body;flesh

R

ru

如 (rú) ❶in compliance with; according to ❷ like; as ❸can compare with; be as good as ❹for instance; such ❺ if

【如臂使指】have a perfect command of sth.

【如出一口】as if from one mouth with one voice; unanimously

【如出一辙】be exactly the same; be no different from each other; be cut from the same cloth

【如初】as always; as of old; as before

【如此】so; such; in this way; like that

【如此而已】that's what it all adds up to

【如此这般】thus and thus; thus and so

【如此等等】and so on; and so forth

【如故】as before

【如果】if; in case; in the event of

【如何】how; what

【如获至宝】as if one had found a priceless treasure

【如饥似渴】as if thirsting or hungering for sth.; with great eagerness

【如胶似漆】stick to each other like glue or lacquer; remain glued to each other; be deeply attached to each other

【如狼似虎】as ferocious as wolves and tigers; like cruel beasts of prey

【如雷贯耳】reverberate like thunder

【如临大敌】as if faced with a formidable foe

【如梦初醒】as if awakening from a dream beginning to see the light

【如期】on schedule; on time; 〜抵达目的地 arrive on time

【如日中天】like the sun at high noon — at the apex (or zenith) of one's power, career, etc.

【如日方升】rising like the morning sun — have bright and boundless prospects

【如丧考妣】(look) as if one had lost one's parents, (look) utterly wretched

【如实】go strictly by facts

【如释重负】(feel) as if relieved of a heavy load

【如同】like; as

【如下】as follows

【如一】identical; consistent; 始终〜 remain the same from beginning to the end

【如意】as one wishes

蠕 (rú) wriggle; squirm

【蠕虫】worm; helminth

【蠕动】❶wriggle; squirm ❷〈生理〉peristalsis ❸ 〈地〉creep

乳 (rǔ) ❶ breast ❷ milk ❸ any milk-like liquid ❹give birth to ❺newborn

【乳白】milky white

【乳牙】deciduous teeth; primary teeth; milk teeth

【乳汁】milk

【乳制品】dairy products

辱 (rǔ) ❶ disgrace; dishonour ❷ bring disgrace to; insult ❸be indebted

【辱骂】abuse; call sb. names; hurl insults

【辱命】disgrace a commission; fail to accomplish a mission

【辱没】bring disgrace to; be unworthy of

入 (rù) ❶go into; enter ❷income ❸join; be admitted into ❹conform to; agree with

【入场】go in; admission

【入党】join a political party

【入耳】pleasant to the ear; 不堪〜 offensive to the ear

【入股】become a share holder

【入伙】join in partnership

【入境】enter a country

【入口】entrance

【入门】be initiated into a subject

【入迷】fascinated; enchanted

【入魔】completely bewitched

【入侵】invade; intrude

【入神】be entranced; be enthralled

【入时】be modish; fashionable

【入手】start with; proceed from

【入睡】fall asleep

【入托】start going to a nursery

【入伍】enlist; enroll

【入学】enter a school

【入座】take one's seat

褥 (rù) cotton-padded mattress

【褥单】bed sheet

【褥套】quilt cover; mattress cover

【褥子】cotton-padded mattress; bedding

ruan

软 (ruǎn) ❶ soft; flexible; supple; pliable ❷ mild; gentle ❸weak; feeble ❹poor in quality, ability, etc. ❺easily moved or influenced

【软化】❶soften ❷change from steadfast to wavering; from being stiff to being compliant; 态度逐渐〜 softening attitude ❸soften; 〜血管 soften the blood vessels

【软和】soft; fluffy; 〜羊毛 fluffy wool

【软件】software

【软禁】keep sb. under detention; put sb. under house arrest

【软弱】❶ feeble; weak; sickly ❷ effete; wishy-washy; prissy

rui

蕊 (ruǐ) stamen; pistil：雄 ～ stamen | 雌 ～ pistil

锐 (ruì) ❶ sharp; keen; acute ❷ vigour; fight spirit ❸ rapid; sudden

【锐利】sharp-edged

【锐敏】(of perception) discerning; shrewd；(of eyesight) keen; sharp

【锐气】fortitude; dauntless courage

【锐意】firm; resolute; determined; be bent on

瑞 (ruì) propitious; opportune：祥 ～ auspicious

【瑞雪】timely snowfall：～兆丰年。A timely snow bodes well for a year of abundance.

run

闰 (rùn) intercalation

【闰年】leap year

【闰月】leap month

润 (rùn) ❶ moist; smooth; sleek ❷ lubricate ❸ polish; embellish ❹ profit; benefit

【润笔】❶ (of a writing brush) dip in ink ❷〈古〉remuneration for a writer, painter or calligrapher

【润色】polish a piece of writing; touch up

【润燥】〈中医〉moisten the respiratory tract, skin, etc.

【润泽】❶ moist; smooth; sleek ❷ moisten; lubricate

ruo

若 (ruò) ❶ like; seem; as if ❷〈书〉if ❸〈书〉you

【若非】if not; were it not for

【若干】a certain number or amount

弱 (ruò) ❶ weak; feeble ❷ young ❸ inferior ❹〈书〉lose (through death) ❺ a little less than

【弱不禁风】too weak to withstand a gust of wind; extremely delicate; fragile

【弱不胜衣】(of a woman) too frail to bear the weight of one's clothes

【弱点】weakness; weak point

【弱肉强食】the weak will stand as an easy prey to (or of) the strong; jungle justice

【弱视】weak-sighted

【弱小】small and weak; puny

R

S s

sa

撒（sā）❶cast；let go ❷throw off all restraint；let oneself go

另见 sǎ

【撒谎】tell a lie

【撒娇】act like a spoiled child

【撒赖】make a scene；raise hell

【撒泼】be unreasonable and make a scene；～放刁 act in a rascally manner

【撒气】❶（of a ball，tyre，etc.）leak；go soft；get a flat ❷vent one's anger or ill temper

【撒手】let go one's hold；let go

【撒野】act wildly；behave atrociously

洒（sǎ）sprinkle；spray

【洒泪】shed tears

【洒洒】in great numbers：洋洋～ prolific

【洒扫】sprinkle water and sweep the floor；sweep

【洒脱】free and easy

撒（sǎ）❶scatter（granules）；sprinkle；spread：～种 sowing ❷spill；drop

另见 sā

【撒播】broadcast sowing

飒（sà）

【飒然】〈书〉soughing；whistling

【飒飒】〈象〉sough；rustle

【飒爽】〈书〉of martial bearing；valiant

sai

腮（sāi）cheek

【腮颊】cheek

【腮腺】〈生理〉parotid gland

塞（sāi）❶fill in；stuff ❷stopple；plug：软木～ cork｜瓶～ bottle stopper

另见 sài

【塞车】traffic jam；traffic congestion

【塞子】stopper；plug；spigot；cork

塞（sài）a place of strategic importance

【塞外】north of the Great Wall；beyond the Great Wall

【塞翁失马】the old frontiersman losing his horse—a blessing in disguise

赛（sài）❶match；game；contest ❷have a competition ❸be comparable to；surpass

【赛车】cycle racing；automobile race

【赛过】overtake；be better than；exceed

【赛马】horse racing

【赛区】venue

【赛艇】〈体〉❶rowing ❷racing boat；shell

san

三（sān）❶three ❷several；many

【三八妇女节】March 8，International Working Women's Day

【三岔路口】a fork in the road；a junction of three roads

【三长两短】unexpected misfortune；sth. unfortunate，esp. death

【三朝元老】minister to three emperors—an official who stays in power under different regimes

【三重】triple

【三番五次】time and again

【三更半夜】in the dead of night

【三姑六婆】women of dubious character making a living by dishonest means（e. g. women matchmakers，sorceresses，etc.）

【三顾茅庐】make three calls at the thatched cottage（as Liu Bei did when he sought the aid of Zhuge Liang，a master strategist then living in seclusion）—repeatedly request sb. to take up a responsible post

【三角】❶triangle ❷〈数〉trigonometry

【三令五申】repeatedly give injunctions

【三人成虎】the testimony of three men creates a

tiger in the market—repeated false reports will lead one astray

【三三两两】in twos and threes

【三生有幸】consider oneself most fortunate (to make sb.'s acquaintance,etc.)

【三思而行】look before you leap

【三心二意】be of two minds; shilly-shally; hesitate

【三言两语】in a few words; in one or two words

【三月】March

【三战两胜】〈体〉the best of three games

伞 (sǎn) ❶umbrella ❷ umbrella-like: 降落～ parachute

【伞降】parachuting; chuting

【伞投】drop by parachute; parachute; chute

散 (sǎn) ❶come loose; fall apart ❷scattered ❸medicinal powder
另见 sàn

【散架】fall apart; fall to pieces; collapse, disband; dissolve

【散乱】in disorder

【散漫】❶undisciplined; careless and sloppy ❷scattered; unorganized

【散文】essay; prose

【散装】unpackaged; loose packed; in bulk

散 (sàn) ❶break up; disperse ❷distribute; disseminate; give out ❸let out; dispel
另见 sǎn

【散播】spread

【散布】spread; disseminate; scatter; diffuse

【散步】stroll; walk; take a walk; go for a walk

【散发】send out; send forth; diffuse emit

【散会】(of a meeting) be over; break up

【散伙】❶(of a group, body or organization) dissolve; disband ❷〈口〉(of lovers or a married couple) break up

【散开】spread out or apart; disperse; scatter

【散落】❶fall scattered ❷be scattered

【散闷】divert oneself from boredom: ～消愁 seek diversion from one's worries

【散热】❶dissipate heat ❷radiate heat

【散失】❶be missing; be lost ❷(of moisture) be lost; dissipate; vaporise

【散心】drive away one's cares; relieve boredom; ease up

sang

丧 (sāng) funeral; mourning
另见 sàng

【丧服】mourning apparel

【丧家】family of the deceased

【丧礼】obsequies; funeral

【丧事】funeral arrangements

【丧葬】burial: ～费 funeral expenses

桑 (sāng) white mulberry; mulberry

【桑拿浴】sauna bath

【桑蚕】silkworm

【桑树】white mulberry; mulberry

嗓 (sǎng) ❶throat; larynx ❷voice

【嗓音】voice

【嗓子】throat; voice

丧 (sàng) lose
另见 sāng

【丧胆】be terror-stricken

【丧命】meet one's death; get killed

【丧气】feel disheartened; lose heart

【丧气】〈口〉be unlucky; be out of luck; have bad luck

【丧生】lose one's life; get killed

【丧失】lose; forfeit

【丧志】dispirited; demoralized; dejected: 玩物～ sap one's aspiration by seeking pleasure

sao

骚 (sāo) disturb; upset

【骚动】❶disturbance; commotion; ferment ❷be in a tumult

【骚乱】riot

【骚扰】harass

扫 (sǎo) ❶sweep ❷pass quickly along or over; sweep ❸put all together
另见 sào

【扫除】❶cleaning; clean up ❷clear away; wipe out: ～障碍 remove an obstacle

【扫荡】❶mop up ❷root out; do away with thoroughly

【扫地】❶sweep the floor ❷be dragged in the dust

【扫盲】wipe out illiteracy

【扫描】scanning

【扫平】quell; crack down on

【扫视】(of eyes) glance

【扫尾】wind up; round off

【扫兴】have one's spirits dampened; feel disappointed

嫂 (sǎo) elder brother's wife；sister-in-law

【嫂子】〈口〉elder brother's wife；sister-in-law

扫 (sào) 另见 sǎo

【扫帚】broom

【扫帚星】〈天〉comet

se

色 (sè) ❶colour ❷look；countenance；expression ❸kind；description ❹scene；scenery ❺quality ❻feminine charms

【色彩】colour；hue；tint；shade

【色调】❶tone；hue；shade of colour ❷ideological or sentimental appeal

【色厉内荏】fierce of mien but faint of heart；threatening in manner but cowardly at heart

【色盲】〈医〉achromatopsia；colour blindness

【色情】sexual urge：～小说 erotic fiction

【色泽】colour and lustre：～鲜明 bright and lustrous

涩 (sè) ❶puckery；astringent ❷unsmooth；hard-going ❸hard to understand；obscure

【涩滞】(of style of writing) not smooth

sen

森 (sēn) ❶full of trees ❷multitudinous；in multitudes ❸dark；gloomy

【森林】forest

【森罗万象】all-embracing；all-inclusive

【森严】stern；strict；forbidding

seng

僧 (sēng) Buddhist monk；monk

【僧道】Buddhist monks and Taoist priests

【僧院】Buddhist temple；Buddhist monastery

sha

杀 (shā) ❶kill；slaughter ❷fight；go into battle ❸weaken；reduce ❹extremely；to death

【杀害】murder；kill

【杀戮】massacre；slaughter

【杀伤】kill and wound；inflict casualties on：～力 antipersonnel capacity

【杀手】killer：职业～ assassin；murderer

沙 (shā) ❶sand ❷powdered ❸hoarse；husky

【沙包】❶sand dune ❷sandbag

【沙暴】sandstorm

【沙发】sofa

【沙拉】salad

【沙砾】grit

【沙丘】(sand) dune

【沙滩】sandy beach；sand beach；sea beach

【沙哑】hoarse；husky；raucous

【沙子】❶sand；grit ❷small grains；pellets：铁～ iron pellets；shot

纱 (shā) ❶yarn ❷gauze；sheer

【纱厂】cotton mill

【纱窗】screen window；screen

【纱罩】❶gauze or screen covering (over food) ❷mantle (of a lamp)

刹 (shā) put on the brakes；stop；check 另见 chà

【刹车】❶put on the brakes ❷turn off a machine ❸brake

砂 (shā)

【砂布】emery cloth；abrasive cloth

【砂矿】placer deposit；placer

【砂轮】〈机〉emery wheel；grinding wheel；abrasive wheel

【砂土】sandy soil；sand

傻 (shǎ) ❶stupid；muddleheaded ❷tactless

【傻乎乎】simple-minded；silly；foolish

【傻瓜】fool；blockhead；simpleton

【傻笑】laugh foolishly；smirk

【傻眼】〈口〉be dumbfounded；be stunned

【傻样】〈口〉a foolish look

【傻子】fool；blockhead；simpleton

煞 (shà) ❶evil spirit；goblin ❷very

【煞白】deathly pale；pallid

【煞气】(of anything with air inside) leak

【煞神】demon；fiend

霎 (shà) a very short time；moment

【霎时间】in a twinkling；in a split second；in a jiffy

【霎眼】in a moment；in a twinkling

shai

筛 (shāi) ❶sieve；sifter ❷sift；sieve

【筛管】〈植〉sieve tube
【筛号】screen size；screen mesh；mesh number
【筛选】preparation by screen
【筛子】sieve，sifter screen

晒

（shài）❶shine upon ❷dry in the sun；bask

【晒场】sunning ground（for drying grain，etc.）
【晒台】flat roof（for drying clothes，etc.）

shan

山

（shān）hill；mountain

【山崩】landslide
【山崩地裂】mountains collapsing and the earth cracking up（said of a cataclysm or of deafening noises）
【山川】landscape；mountains and rivers
【山村】mountain village
【山顶】peak；hilltop；the summit of a mountain
【山峰】mountain peak
【山高水远】the mountains are high and the rivers are far away—a long distance
【山沟】gully；ravine；valley
【山谷】valley；gulch
【山河】mountains and rivers the land of a country
【山洪】mountain torrents；swollen mountain
【山岭】mountain ridge
【山麓】piedmont；the foot of a mountain
【山峦】chain of mountain；multipeaked mountain
【山脉】mountains；mountain range；mountain chain
【山南海北】❶south of the mountains and north of the seas far away；far and wide ❷discursive；rambling
【山坡】mountain slope；hillside；versant；mountainside
【山清水秀】green hills and clear waters—a picturesque scenery
【山穷水尽】the end of hills and rivers；be at（on）one's last shift（shifts）
【山区】mountain，mountain area
【山水】❶water from a mountain ❷mountains and rivers；scenery with hills and waters ❸traditional Chinese painting of mountains and waters；landscape painting；landscape
【山水相连】be linked by common mountains and rivers
【山外有山】there's always a mountain beyond a

mountain；there's always something better；nothing can be perfect
【山岳冰川】mountain glacier；alpine glacier
【山珍海味】table delicacies from land and sea；a feast of fat things；all kinds of costly foods

删

（shān）delete；leave out

【删除】delete；cancel；cut（or cross）out
【删掉】expunge；strike out
【删改】delete and change；revise
【删节】abridge；abbreviate
【删略】leave out；omit
【删削】delete；cut out；strike out

姗

（shān）see below

【姗姗来迟】be slow in coming；be late

珊

（shān）

【珊瑚】coral
【珊瑚虫】coral polyp；coral insect
【珊瑚岛】coral island

扇

（shān）❶fan ❷slap ❸incite；instigate；fan up；stir up
　　另见 shàn

【扇风耳】protruding ears；flappy ears

煽

（shān）

【煽动】flap；instigate；excite；incite；whip；stir up；blow
【煽风点火】fan the flames；inflame and agitate people；stir up trouble
【煽惑】incite；agitate

闪

（shǎn）❶dodge；get out of the way ❷twist；sprain ❸lightning ❹flash；sparkle ❺leave behind

【闪避】dodge；sidestep
【闪电】lightning
【闪动】flash；twinkle；flicker
【闪躲】dodge；evade：～不开 too late or slow to dodge
【闪光】❶a flash of light ❷gleam；glisten；glitter
【闪光灯】❶〈摄〉flash lamp；flashlight；photoflash ❷flashlight（used for signals）
【闪开】get out of the way；jump aside
【闪亮】sparkling；glittering；glistening
【闪念】an idea which flashes through one's mind
【闪闪】sparkling；glistening；glittering：～发光 glowing
【闪射】glitter；shine；radiate

【闪身】❶dodge ❷move sideways
【闪失】mishap;accident
【闪烁】twinkle;glimmer;glisten;evasive vague
【闪烁其词】speak evasively;hedge
【闪现】flash before one
【闪耀】glitter;shine;radiate

讪 （shàn） ❶mock; ridicule ❷embarrassed;awkward

【讪谤】〈书〉slander;malign;calumniate
【讪讪】embarrassed;awkward;shamefaced
【讪笑】deride

扇 （shàn）fan leaf
另见 shān

【扇贝】〈动〉scallop;fan shell
【扇车】winnowing machine;winnower
【扇骨子】the ribs (*or* mount) of a folding fan
【扇形】❶fan-shaped ❷sector
【扇坠】fan pendants
【扇子】fan

善 （shàn）❶good ❷satisfactory good ❸make a success of;perfect ❹kind; friendly ❺be good at;be expert in ❻well ❼be apt to

【善罢甘休】(usu. used in the negative) leave the matter at that;let it go at that
【善本】reliable text;good edition
【善变】be apt to change;be changeable
【善处】〈书〉deal discreetly with;conduct oneself well
【善待】treat sb. well
【善感】(of a person) sensitive
【善果】good fruit—the rewards of good deeds
【善后】deal with problems arising from an accident,etc.
【善良】good and honest;kind-hearted
【善男信女】Buddhist devotees
【善事】charitable deeds;good deeds
【善忘】be forgetful;have a short memory
【善心】mercy;benevolence
【善意】good will
【善于】be good at;be adept in
【善终】❶die a natural death;die in one's bed ❷end well

缮 （shàn）❶repair;mend:修～ repair ❷copy;write

擅 （shàn）❶arrogate to oneself;do sth. on one's own authority ❷be good at;be expert in

【擅便】〈书〉act on one's own authority
【擅长】be good at;be expert in;be skilled in

【擅场】〈书〉dominate the scene be the supreme arbiter
【擅权】monopolize power;have sole power;arrogate all authority to oneself
【擅自】do sth. without authorization

膳 （shàn）meals;board

【膳费】board expenses
【膳食】meals;food
【膳宿】board and lodging

嬗 （shàn）

【嬗变】❶evolution ❷transmutation

赡 （shàn）❶support;provide for ❷〈书〉sufficient;abundant

【赡养】support;provide for

shang

伤 （shāng）❶wound;injury ❷injure;hurt ❸distressed ❹get sick of sth. ;develop an aversion to sth. ❺be harmful to;hinder

【伤疤】scar
【伤悲】to regret;be regretful;to grieve over
【伤财】suffer financial loss
【伤残】invalidism;disability
【伤风】cold;common cold;have a cold
【伤风败俗】offend public decency; corrupt public morals;harmful (or offensive) to society's morals
【伤感】anguish;sick at heart;sentimental
【伤害】injure;harm;hurt
【伤寒】❶typhoid fever;typhoid ❷〈中医〉diseases caused by harmful cold factors;febrile diseases;fevers
【伤号】(usu. used among army personnel) the wounded
【伤痕】scar;bruise;hack
【伤怀】〈书〉sad;grieved;brokenhearted
【伤口】wound;cut;bite
【伤气】❶〈书〉feel frustrated;feel disheartened ❷〈中医〉sap one's vitality
【伤情】❶the condition of an injury or wound ❷sick at heart;sentimental
【伤神】❶overtax one's nerves;be nerve-racking ❷sad;grieved
【伤势】the condition of an injury (or wound)
【伤痛】❶grieved;distressed ❷the pain of an injury or wound
【伤亡】casualties;destruction;injuries and deaths
【伤心】grieve;grief

【伤员】the wounded

商 (shāng) ❶discuss; consult ❷trade; commerce; business ❸merchant; trader; businessman; dealer

【商标】mark; trade mark

【商场】market; bazaar

【商船】merchant ship; merchantman

【商店】shop; store

【商定】decide through consultation; agree

【商贩】small retailer; pedlar

【商港】commercial port

【商行】trading company; commercial firm; trade

【商界】business circles

【商量】consult; discuss; talk over

【商品】commodity; goods; merchandise

【商榷】discuss; deliberate

【商人】businessman; merchant; trader; tradesman; middleman; handler

【商谈】confer; discuss; negotiate; exchange views

【商讨】discuss; deliberate over

【商务】commercial affairs

【商业】business; commerce; trade

【商议】confer; discuss

【商约】commercial treaty

【商酌】discuss and consider deliberate; berate over

晌 (shǎng) ❶part of the day ❷noon

【晌饭】❶midday meal; lunch ❷extra meal in the daytime during the busy farming season

【晌午】midday; noon

赏 (shǎng) ❶grant a reward ❷reward; award ❸view and admire; delight in viewing; feast ones eyes on ❹recognize; appreciate

【赏赐】grant (or bestow) a reward; award bestow

【赏罚】reward and punishments

【赏光】〈套〉(used when requesting sb. to accept an invitation)

【赏脸】〈套〉honour me with your presence

【赏识】appreciate

【赏玩】delight in; enjoy; fondle: ～山景 enjoy mountain scenery

【赏雪】enjoy a beautiful snow scene

【赏月】enjoy the moon

上 (shàng) ❶above ❷up; upward ❸upper; higher; better; superior ❹most recent; last; former ❺first (part) preceding previous ❻go to; leave for ❼go up; get on ❽set; fix ❾apply; paint; smear

【上半场】first half (of a game, concert, etc.)

【上班】go to work; start work; be on duty; work; employment

【上策】the best plan; the best way out; the best thing to do

【上层】upper strata; upper levels; superior

【上层社会】upper strata of society; upper-class society

【上场】❶appear on the stage; enter ❷〈体〉enter the court or field; join in a contest

【上蹿下跳】run around on sinister errands

【上当】be taken in; be fooled; be duped

【上等】elegant; first-class; first-rate; superior

【上帝】❶the Lord on Hight ❷God

【上吊】hang oneself

【上告】complain to the higher authorities

【上工】go to work; start work

【上钩】get hooked; take; hook; bite

【上级】higher level; higher authorities

【上交】hand in (or over) to sb. above oneself; pass on to the higher authorities

【上缴】turn over (revenues, etc.) to the higher authorities

【上街】go to street; go shopping

【上进】go forward; make progress; ascend

【上课】attend class; go to class; conduct a class; give a lesson (or lecture); be at school

【上空】in the sky; overhead; over

【上列】the above-listed; the above

【上流】upper reaches; upper-class

【上路】start off

【上任】take up an official post; assume office; entrance into office

【上上下下】high and low; old and young; everybody

【上升】rise; go up; ascend

【上述】above mentioned; aforementioned; aforesaid

【上税】pay taxes

【上司】superior; boss

【上诉】〈法〉appeal (to higher court)

【上台】assume power; come or rise to the power

【上吐下泻】throw up on top and purge down below; suffer from vomiting and diarrhoea; have loose bowels and vomit

【上下其手】practise fraud; manoeuvre for some evil end; get up to tricks

【上行】up; unbound; upgoing; 〈航〉upriver; upstream

S

【上行下效】those below follow the（usu. bad）example of those above；if a leader sets a bad example，it will be followed by his subordinates

【上演】put on a stage；perform；play；stage；offer

【上瘾】be addicted（to sth.）；get into the habit（of doing sth.）

【上映】show（a film）；screen；project

【上游】upstream；upward；upper reaches（of a river）；advanced position

【上涨】rise；go up；move up；move upward；mount

【上肢】upper limb

尚（shàng）❶esteem；value；set great store by ❷still；yet

【尚存】extant

【尚待】remain

【尚书】〈古〉❶a high official in ancient China ❷minister（in the Ming and Qing Dynasties）

shao

捎（shāo）take along sth. to or for sb；bring to sb.

【捎带】incidentally；in passing

【捎话】take a message to sb.

【捎脚】pick up passengers or goods on the way；give sb. a lift

【捎手】〈方〉conveniently；without extra trouble

烧（shāo）❶burn ❷cook；bake ❸stew after frying or fry after stewing ❹roast ❺run a fever；have a temperature ❻fever

【烧饭】do the cooking；cook food；prepare a meal

【烧化】❶cremate ❷burn（paper，etc. as an offering to the dead）

【烧荒】burn the grass on waste land

【烧毁】burn out；burn down

【烧火】make a fire；light a fire

【烧酒】spirit usually distilled from sorghum or maize；colourless spirit

【烧伤】burn（an injury）

【烧香】burn joss sticks（before an idol）

【烧灼】burn；scorch；singe

稍（shāo）a little；a bit
另见 shào

【稍微】slightly；a trifle

勺（sháo）spoon；ladle

【勺子】ladle；scoop

少（shǎo）❶few；little；less ❷be short；lack ❸lose；be missing ❹a little while

另见 shào

【少而精】smaller quantity，better quality；fewer but better

【少见】❶I haven't seen you for a long time；I have seen very little of you ❷seldom seen；infrequent；rare

【少见多怪】the less a man has seen the more he has to wonder at；ignorant people are easily surprised

【少刻】after a little while；a moment later

【少量】a little；a few

【少陪】〈套〉（an apology for taking leave of sb.）if you'll excuse me；I'm afraid I must be going now

【少顷】〈书〉after a short while；after a few moments；presently

【少数】small number；few；minority

【少数民族】minority nationality；national minority

【少许】a little；a few

【少有】rare；few and far between

少（shào）❶young ❷son of a rich family；young master
另见 shǎo

【少白头】❶be prematurely grey ❷a young person with greying hair

【少妇】young married woman

【少男】unmarried young man：～少女 young men and young women

【少年】❶early youth ❷juvenile young person

【少女】young girl

【少先队】Young Pioneers

哨（shào）❶sentry post；post ❷warble；chirp ❸whistle

【哨兵】sentry；guard

【哨岗】sentry post（where a sentinel is posted）

【哨卡】a frontier sentry post or a strategic sentry post

【哨所】sentry post；post

【哨子】whistle

稍（shào）
另见 shāo

【稍息】〈军〉stand at ease

she

奢（shē）❶luxurious；extravagant ❷excessive；inordinate

【奢侈】extravagant；wasteful

【奢华】sumptuous

【奢求】extravagant claims；excessive demands；

unreasonable demands

【奢望】extravagant hopes；wild wishes

赊 (shē) buy or sell on credit

【赊购】buy on credit
【赊欠】give or get credit
【赊销】sell on credit
【赊账】〈经〉open account

舌 (shé) ❶tongue ❷sth. shaped like a tongue

【舌根】the root of the tongue
【舌苔】〈中医〉coating on the tongue
【舌头】tongue
【舌战】❶have a verbal battle with；argue heatedly with ❷a hot dispute；a verbal battle

折 (shé) ❶break；snap ❷lose money in business

另见 zhē, zhé

【折本】lose money in business
【折秤】damage and loss to goods（such as vegetables, fruits, etc.）in the course of reweighing
【折耗】damage and loss（to goods during transit, storage, etc.）

舍 (shě) ❶give up；abandon ❷give alms；dispense charity

另见 shè

【舍得】be willing to part with；not grudge
【舍己救人】sacrifice oneself to save sb. else
【舍己为人】sacrifice one's own interests for the sake of others
【舍弃】give up；abandon
【舍身】give one's life；sacrifice oneself

设 (shè) ❶set up；establish ❷work out ❸〈数〉given；suppose ❹if；in case

【设备】equipment；installation；facilities
【设法】think of a way；try；do what one can
【设防】set up defences；fortify；garrison
【设伏】lay an ambush；～擒敌 lay an ambush to take enemy soldiers
【设计】design；plan
【设立】establish；set up；found
【设身处地】put oneself in sb. else's position
【设施】installation；facilities
【设想】❶ imagine；conceive；assume ❷ tentative plan
【设宴】give a banquet
【设置】set up；put up；install

社 (shè) ❶organized body；agency ❷the god of the land, sacrifices to him or altars for such sacrifices

【社会】society
【社会关系】❶human relations in society；social relations ❷one's social connections；relatives and friends
【社交】social intercourse；social contact
【社论】editorial；leading article；leader
【社区】community
【社团】mass organizations；body of persons；corporation
【社戏】village theatrical performance given on religious festivals in old times
【社员】a member of a society, club, etc.

舍 (shè) house；shed；hut

另见 shě

【舍间】my humble abode；my house；my place
【舍利】Buddhism relics left after the cremation of Buddhas or saintly monks（deposited in stupas for worship）
【舍亲】〈谦〉my relative；a relative of mine
【舍下】〈谦〉 my humble abode；my house；my place

射 (shè) ❶shoot；fire ❷discharge in a jet ❸send out ❹allude to sth. or sb.

【射程】range
【射击】shoot；fire
【射线】ray

涉 (shè) ❶wake；ford ❷go through；experience ❸involve

【涉笔】wet the brush start writing or painting
【涉及】involve, relate to；touch upon
【涉猎】do desultory reading；read cursorily
【涉世】gain life experience
【涉外】concerning foreign affairs or foreign nationals
【涉嫌】be suspected of being involve；be a suspect
【涉险】go through dangers
【涉足】set foot in

赦 (shè) remit（a punishment）；pardon

【赦令】order of pardon or amnesty
【赦免】remit(a punishment)；pardon
【赦罪】absolve sb. from guilt；pardon sb.

摄 (shè) ❶absorb；assimilate ❷take a photograph of；shoot ❸conserve（one's health）❹act for

【摄取】absorb；take in
【摄像】make a video recording（with a video

camera or TV camera)

【摄像机】pickup camera；video camera

【摄影】❶take a photograph ❷shoot a film

【摄影机】camera

【摄制】produce

慑（shè）fear；be awed

【慑服】❶submit in fear；succumb ❷cow sb. into submission

shen

申（shēn）❶state；express ❷the ninth of the twelve Earthly Branches

【申办】bid for hosting sth.：～下届运动会 bid for the next sports meet

【申报】❶report to a higher body ❷declare sth. (to the customs)

【申辩】defend oneself；argue one's case

【申斥】rebuke；reprimand

【申明】declare；avow

【申请】apply for

【申时】the period of the day from 3 p.m. to 5 p.m.

【申述】state；explain in detail

【申诉】appeal

【申讨】openly condemn；denounce

【申谢】acknowledge one's indebtedness；express one's gratitude

【申冤】❶redress an injustice；right a wrong ❷appeal for redress of a wrong

【申奏】submit a memorial to the emperor

伸（shēn）stretch；extend

【伸手】stretch out one's hand

【伸缩】❶stretch out and draw back；expand and contract；lengthen and shorten ❷flexible；elastic；adjustable

【伸展】spread；extend；stretch；tend；lead；reach；expansion

【伸张】uphold；promote

【伸张正义】uphold justice

【伸直】straighten；extend；untangle

身（shēn）❶body ❷life ❸oneself；personally ❹one's moral character and conduct ❺the main part of a structure

【身边】at (or by) one's side；(have sth.) on one；with one

【身不由己】involuntarily；under compulsion；in spite of oneself

【身材】stature；figure

【身份】status；capacity；identity；dignity；legitimacy

【身高】height(of a person)；stand

【身上】❶on one's body ❷on one；with one

【身世】one's life experience；one's lot

【身手】skill；talent；好～ good skill

【身首异处】be beheaded

【身受】experience personally：感同～ feel as if one experiences sth. personally

【身体】body；health

【身体素质】physique；constitution

【身心】body and mind

【身影】person's silhouette；form；figure

【身孕】pregnancy

参（shēn）❶ginseng ❷the twenty-first of the twenty-eight constellations into which the celestial sphere was divided in ancient Chinese astronomy 另见 cān，cēn

【参商】〈文〉shen and shang，two stars that never appear in the same sky—two friends or relatives who are separated and can never meet again or who have become estranged and irreconcilable

深（shēn）❶deep ❷depth ❸hard to understand；difficult；abstruse；profound ❹thorough-going；penetrating；profound ❺close；intimate ❻late；dark；rich ❼very；greatly；deeply

【深奥】abstruse；profound；recondite

【深层】❶depth；deeper layers ❷deep-going；thorough；incisive：～原因 deep-seated cause

【深长】profound

【深沉】❶dark；deep；(of sound of voice) deep ❷undemonstrative；reserved

【深仇大恨】bitter and deep-seated hatred；profound hatred

【深度】degree of depth；depth；profundity；depth；intensity

【深更半夜】at dead of night；in the depth (or dead) of night；in the middle of the night

【深沟高垒】deep trenches and high ramparts；strong defence

【深广】deep and broad

【深厚】deep；profound

【深化】deepen

【深交】❶deep friendship ❷close contact

【深刻】deep；profound；deepgoing

【深浅】depth

【深切】heartfelt；deep；profound

【深情】deep feeling；deep love

【深情厚谊】profound sentiments of friendship; profound friendship

【深入】go deep into; penetrate into; thorough; deepgoing

【深入人心】strike root in the hearts of the people

【深入浅出】explain the profound in simple terms

【深深】deeply; keenly; profoundly

【深思】think deeply about

【深信】be deeply convinced; firmly believe

【深夜】last at night

【深渊】abyss

【深远】profound and lasting

【深造】take up advanced studies; take a more advanced course of study or training; pursue advanced studies

【深重】very grave; extremely serious

什 (shén)
另见 shí

【什么】what; whatever; anything; nothing; what's

神 (shén) ❶god; deity; divinity ❷supernatural; magical; miraculous ❸spirit; mind ❹expression; look ❺smart; clever

【神不守舍】be out of one's wits; be distracted

【神采】demeanour; mien; countenance

【神话】mythology; myth; fairy tale

【神机妙算】a superb strategy, a miracle of foresight; wonderful foresight in military operations, etc.

【神经】nerve

【神秘】mysterious; mystical

【神妙】wonderful; marvellous; ingenious：～莫测 wonderful; marvellous

【神奇】magical; mystical; miraculous

【神气】❶expression; air; manner ❷spirited; vigorous ❸overweening

【神气十足】looking very dignified; putting on grand airs; looking triumphant

【神气活现】very cocky; high and mighty

【神情】expression; look

【神色】expression; look：～匆忙 look in a hurry

【神色自若】be perfectly calm and collected; show composure and presence of mind

【神圣】sacred; holy：～的使命 sacred mission

【神思恍惚】be distracted; be distraught; be in a trance

【神算】❶accurate prediction ❷miraculous scheme

【神态】expression; manner; bearing

【神通广大】have vast magic powers; possess un-

usual powers; be infinitely resourceful

【神童】child prodigy

【神往】be carried away; be rapt; be charmed：心驰～ yearn after as if one's mind were already there

【神仙】❶supernatural being; celestial being; immortal ❷person who has the power of clairvoyance ❸person free from worldly cares

【神效】magical effect; miraculous effect

【神勇】extraordinarily brave; superhumanly brave：～无敌 extraordinarily brave and invincible

【神韵】romantic charm

【神志】consciousness; senses; mind：～不清 be unconscious

审 (shěn) ❶careful; meticulous ❷examine; go over ❸interrogate; try

【审查】examine; investigate

【审处】❶try and punish ❷deliberate and decide

【审订】examine and revise

【审定】examine and approve

【审度】study and weigh

【审改】examine and revise (a manuscript); revise

【审核】examine and verify

【审计】audit

【审理】try; hear：依法～ try a case according to law

【审美】appreciation of the beautiful

【审判】bring to trial; try; judge

【审批】examine and approve

【审慎】cautious; careful; circumspect

【审时度势】judge the hour and size up the situation

【审视】look at carefully

【审问】interrogate; question

【审讯】〈法〉interrogate; try

【审议】consideration; deliberation; discussion

【审阅】examine carefully and critically

婶 (shěn) aunt; auntie

【婶娘】〈方〉wife of father's younger brother; aunt

肾 (shèn) kidney

【肾脏】kidney

甚 (shèn) ❶very; extremely ❷more than ❸what; whatever

【甚而】even; (go) so far as to; so much so that

【甚或】〈书〉❶even to the extent that ❷(go) so far as to; so much so that

【甚为】very;extremely

【甚嚣尘上】cause a great clamour

【甚至】❶even to the extent that ❷(go) so far as to;so much so that

渗 (shèn) ooze;seep

【渗出】effusion;seep sweat;strain

【渗入】permeate;seep into;infiltrate

【渗透】〈物〉osmosis;permeate;seep

慎 (shèn) careful;cautious

【慎独】be careful of oneself when alone try to be blameless in one's private life

【慎言慎行】be cautious in speech and conduct

【慎重】cautious;careful;prudent;discreet

sheng

升 (shēng) rise;hoist;go up;ascend;promote;litre

【升沉】the ups and downs of official career

【升幅】increase;margin of increase

【升格】promote;upgrade

【升官发财】win promotion and get rich;(be out for) power and money

【升华】sublimation;distillation

【升级】go up(one grade,etc.);escalate

【升降】go up and down

【升平】peace;～气象 peaceful atmosphere;peaceful life

【升旗】hoist(or raise) a flag;～仪式 flag-raising ceremony

【升堂入室】pass through the hall into the inner chamber—have profound scholarship;become highly proficient

【升腾】(of flames,gas,etc.) leap up;rise

【升值】revalue;appreciate

生 (shēng) ❶give birth to;bear ❷be born;come into existence ❸grow ❹life;living ❺alive ❻be afflicted with;get;have ❼light ❽unripe;green ❾raw;uncooked

【生病】fall ill

【生财】to make money

【生财有道】know how to make money;have the knack of making money

【生产】produce;manufacture;give birth to a child

【生成】come or bring into being

【生词】new word

【生存】subsist;exist;live

【生动】lively;vivid

【生而知之】be born wise;be born with knowledge;have innate knowledge

【生花妙笔】a brilliant pen;a brilliant style of writing

【生还】emerge unscathed;come back alive;survive

【生活】❶life 日常～ daily life ❷live ❸livelihood ❹survive;do;get along

【生机】❶lease of life ❷life;vitality;～勃勃 vibrate with life;imbued with vitality

【生计】means of livelihood;livelihood;另谋～ try to find some other means of livelihood

【生就】be born with;be gifted with

【生来】from birth;since childhood

【生老病死】birth and old age,sickness and death —the lot of man

【生离死别】part never to meet again;part for ever

【生理】physiology

【生灵涂炭】the people are plunged into an abyss of misery

【生命】life

【生怕】be afraid of;fear

【生僻】uncommon

【生平】all one's life

【生气】vim;vitality

【生气勃勃】dynamic;vigorous;full of vitality

【生擒活捉】capture alive;take prisoner

【生日】birthday

【生身】give birth to;～父母 biological parents

【生生世世】generation after generation;for generations

【生事】make trouble;create a disturbance;造谣～ spread a rumour to stir up trouble

【生手】sb. new to a job;green hand

【生疏】❶not familiar;人地～ be a complete stranger ❷out of practice;rusty;技艺～ be impaired in skill by inaction or neglect ❸getting distant;感情～ feel not as close as before

【生死】life and death

【生死与共】share a common destiny;go through thick and thin together

【生死之交】friends that are ready to die for each other

【生态】ecology

【生吞活剥】swallow sth. raw and whole accept sth. uncritically

【生物】living things;living beings;organisms;life

【生效】go into effect；become effective

【生性】natural disposition：～活泼 have a lively disposition

【生涯】career；profession

【生疑】be suspicious

【生意】business；trade

【生硬】stiff；rigid；harsh

【生育】give birth to；bear

【生长】grow；grow up

【生殖】reproduction

声（shēng）❶sound；voice ❷make a sound ❸initial consonant ❹tone ❺reputation

【声辩】argue；justify；explain away

【声波】〈物〉sound wave；acoustic wave

【声称】profess；claim；assert

【声调】tone；note

【声东击西】make a feint to the east and attack in the west

【声浪】many voices；clamour

【声泪俱下】shedding tears while speaking；in a tearful voice

【声名】reputation

【声明】❶state；declare；announce ❷statement；declaration

【声情并茂】(of a singer) be remarkable for both voice and expression

【声势】momentum；impetus

【声讨】denounce；condemn

【声望】popularity

【声威】❶renown；prestige：～大震 gain great fame and high prestige ❷power；strength；momentum

【声息】❶sound；voice；noise ❷information；message

【声音】sound；voice

【声誉】reputation；fame；prestige：～卓著 be famous；enjoy high reputation

【声援】express support for

【声张】make public；disclose

牲（shēng）❶domestic animal ❷animal sacrifice

【牲畜】livestock；domestic animal

【牲口】draught animals

甥（shēng）sister's son；nephew

【甥女】sister's daughter；niece

绳（shéng）❶rope；cord；string ❷restrict；restrain

【绳锯木断】a rope can cut through a log；little

strokes fell great oaks

【绳捆索绑】truss up；bind；tie up

【绳趋尺步】conform to every rule and regulation；toe the line

【绳索】rope；cord

【绳梯】rope ladder

【绳之以法】prosecute and punish according to law；bring to justice

【绳子】cord；rope；string

省（shěng）❶economize，save ❷omit；leave out ❸province
　　另见 xǐng

【省城】〈口〉provincial capital

【省吃俭用】skimp and save；live frugally

【省份】province

【省略】❶leave out；omit ❷ellipsis

【省事】save trouble；simplify matters

【省视】❶call upon；pay a visit to ❷inspect

【省心】save worry

【省治】〈古〉the seat of a provincial government；provincial capital

圣（shèng）❶sage；saint ❷holy；sacred ❸emperor

【圣诞】the birthday of Jesus Christ

【圣诞树】Christmas tree；Xmas tree

【圣地】sacred place；shrine

【圣洁】holy and pure

【圣经】the Bible

【圣母】〈宗〉❶a female deity；goddess ❷the (Blessed) Virgin Mary；Madonna

【圣人】sage

【圣贤】sages and men of virtue

胜（shèng）❶victory；success ❷surpass；be superior to ❸superb；wonderful ❹be equal to；can bear

【胜败】victory or defeat

【胜地】famous scenic spot

【胜负】victory or defeat；success or failure

【胜过】be better than；be superior to

【胜局】victory；success

【胜利】❶victory；triumph；win ❷successful

【胜任】competent；qualified

【胜于】be better than；be superior to

【胜仗】victory；triumph

盛（shèng）❶flourishing；prosperous ❷vigorous；energetic ❸magnificent；grand ❹abundant；plentiful ❺popular；common ❻greatly；deeply
　　另见 chéng

【盛产】abound in；teem with

【盛传】be circulated extensively；be widely known；be widely rumoured

【盛大】grand；magnificent

【盛典】grand；magnificent a grand ceremony (or occasion)

【盛会】grand meeting；distinguished gathering

【盛极一时】be in fashion (or vogue) for a time；be all the rage

【盛举】grand occasion (or activity)；great undertaking (or enterprise)

【盛况】spectacular event

【盛况空前】an exceptionally (or unprecedentedly) grand occasion

【盛名】great reputation

【盛怒】rage；fury

【盛气凌人】domineering；arrogant；overbearing

【盛情难却】it would be ungracious not to accept your kindness

【盛世】flourishing age；time of prosperity；heyday；太平～ times of peace；times of peace and prosperity

【盛事】grand occasion；great event

【盛衰荣辱】prosperity and decline，glory and humiliation；rise and fall；ups and downs；vicissitudes of life

【盛夏】midsummer；the height of summer

【盛行】be current；be in vogue

【盛宴】grand banquet；sumptuous dinner

【盛誉】great fame；high reputation

【盛赞】highly praise

【盛装】splendid attire；rich dress

剩 (shèng) surplus；remnant

【剩下】be left (over)；remain

【剩余】surplus；remainder

shi

尸 (shī) corpse；dead body；remains

【尸骨】skeleton

【尸横遍野】a field littered with corpses

【尸体】corpse；carcass；body；subject；dead body；remains

失 (shī) ❶lose ❷miss；let slip ❸not act according to；neglect；violate ❹lose control of ❺err；have a slip；be defective in ❻slip；mistake；defect；mishap

【失败】be defeated；lose(a war，etc.)；fail；miss

【失策】unwise；inexpedient；mis-step；mistake

【失常】off；not normal；odd

【失宠】〈贬〉fall into disfavour；be out of favour

【失传】not be handed down from past generations；be lost；misplaced

【失聪】become deaf；双耳～ deaf in both ears

【失措】lose one's head

【失当】inappropriate；improper；indiscreet；处理～ not properly handled

【失道寡助】an unjust cause finds scant (or little) support

【失掉】lose；miss；fail to grasp；dissolve；shed；strip

【失衡】lose balance；unbalance；out-of-balance；比例～ unbalanced proportions

【失悔】regret；repent；be remorseful

【失魂落魄】be out of one's wits

【失火】catch fire；be on fire

【失控】runaway；物价～ runaway prices

【失礼】❶impoliteness；discourtesy ❷express regrets to sb. for one's impropriety；lack of manners，etc.

【失利】suffer a setback(defeat)；reverse

【失恋】be disappointed in love；be jilted

【失灵】be ineffective；be out of order

【失落】lose；drop

【失眠】(suffer from) insomnia

【失明】lose one's sight；go blind

【失窃】be burgled or burglarized；have one's property stolen

【失去】lose

【失散】be separated from and lose touch with each other；become scattered

【失神】❶ inattentive；absent-minded ❷ out of sorts；in low spirits

【失慎】❶not cautious；careless ❷〈书〉cause a fire through carelessness

【失声】cry out involuntarily；lose one's voice

【失实】inconsistent with the facts；unfounded

【失势】lose power and influence；be out of power；fall into disgrace

【失事】have an accident；meet with a disaster or misfortune；飞机～ plane crash；aviation accident

【失手】❶ accidentally drop；have a slip of the hand；～伤人 hurt sb. accidentally ❷〈喻〉loss or defeat

【失守】(of a defensive area) fall；be taken

【失算】miscalculate；misjudge；misread

【失态】forget oneself; be not one's usual self: 酒后～ forget oneself in drink

【失调】❶ imbalance; lose balance; dislocation: 供求～ imbalance of supply and demand ❷ lack of proper care and rest

【失望】lose hope; disappointed

【失物】lost article; lost property

【失误】fault; muff; lapse; miscarriage; error

【失陷】(of cities, territory, etc.) fall; fall into enemy hands

【失效】lose efficacy; lose effectiveness; cease to be effective; (of a treaty; an agreement, etc.) be no longer in force; become invalid disable; extinguish; expire

【失修】(of houses, etc.) be in bad repair; fall into disrepair

【失学】drop out of school; be a school dropout

【失言】slip

【失业】lose one's job; be out of work; be unemployed; workless

【失宜】inappropriate; improper: 决策～ make an inappropriate policy decision

【失意】be frustrated; be disappointed: 情场～ be disappointed in love; be unlucky in love

【失约】fail to keep an appointment; break one's promise

【失之交臂】just miss the person or opportunity

【失职】neglect one's duty; dereliction of duty

【失主】owner of lost property

【失踪】be missing; untraced; disappear

【失足】lose one's footing; slip; take a wrong step in life

师 (shī) ❶ teacher; tutor; master ❷ model; example ❸ a person skilled in a certain profession ❹ of one's master or teacher ❺ division ❻ troops; army

【师出无名】dispatch troops without just cause

【师道尊严】dignity of the teaching profession

【师范】teacher-training

【师傅】master

【师老兵疲】an army worn-down and war-weary

【师直为壮】an army fighting for a just cause has high morale

【师资】teachers: 培养～ cultivate teachers

诗 (shī) poetry; verse; poem

【诗歌】poetry; poesy

【诗集】collection of poems; poetry anthology

【诗句】verse; line

【诗礼之家】a highly cultured household; a family of scholars

【诗情画意】idyllic

【诗人】poet muse

【诗意】poetry; poetic quality or flavour

虱 (shī)〈动〉louse

狮 (shī)〈动〉lion

施 (shī) ❶ bring into effect; execute; carry out ❷ bestow; grant; hand out ❸ exert; impose ❹ use; apply

【施恩】bestow favours

【施放】discharge; fire; lay

【施肥】fertilize; manure

【施工】construction

【施惠】oblige

【施加】impose; exercise; bear; exert; bring to bear on

【施礼】salute

【施舍】give alms; give in charity

【施行】put into force; implement

【施展】put to good use; give free play to

【施主】❶ alms giver; benefactor ❷〈物〉an electron donor

湿 (shī) wet; damp; humid

【湿度】humidity

【湿冷】damp and chilly; dank; clammy

【湿气】moisture; dampness

【湿润】moist

【湿透】wet through; drenched

十 (shí) ❶ ten ❷ topmost

【十步芳草】fragrant grass is to be found within ten paces—talent is close at hand

【十二月】December

【十分】very; fully

【十行俱下】take in ten lines at a glance; read rapidly

【十拿九稳】ninety per cent sure; practically certain; in the bag

【十年寒窗】ten years' study at a cold window—a student's long years of hard study

【十全十美】be perfect in every way; be the acme of perfection; leave nothing to be desired

【十室九空】nine houses out of ten are stripped bare—the aftermath of war, natural calamities, etc.

S

【十万八千里】a distance of one hundred and eight thousand li；poles apart

【十万火急】most urgent；posthaste；express

【十一月】November

【十月】October

【十字架】cross

【十字路口】crossroads

【十足】full；solid

什（shí）❶assorted；varied ❷〈书〉ten
另见 shén

【什锦】〈食〉assorted；mixed

【什物】articles for daily use；odds and ends；sundries

石（shí）❶stone；rock ❷stone inscription

【石拱桥】stone arch bridge

【石碑】stone tablet；stele

【石沉大海】like a stone dropped into the sea disappear for ever；never to be seen or heard of again

【石雕】❶stone carving ❷carved stone

【石墩】a block of stone used as a seat

【石膏】gypsum；plaster stone

【石工】❶rockwork；masonry ❷stonemason；mason

【石灰】lime

【石级】stone stairs or steps

【石匠】stonemason；mason

【石窟】rock cave；grotto

【石榴】pomegranate

【石磨】graphite

【石器】❶stone artifact ❷stone vessel

【石笋】stalagmite

【石头】stone；rock

【石英】quartz

【石油】petroleum；oil

时（shí）❶time；times ❷fixed time ❸hour ❹season ❺current；present ❻opportunity；chance ❼now and then；occasionally ❽now...now...；sometimes... sometimes... ❾〈语〉tense

【时不我待】time and tide wait for no man

【时差】time difference

【时常】often；frequently

【时代】times；age；era；epoch

【时而】from time to time

【时光】❶time ❷times；years

【时过境迁】things have changed with the lapse of time

【时候】❶（the duration of）time ❷（a point in）time；moment

【时机】opportunity

【时间】time；hour

【时节】season；time

【时局】the current political situation

【时刻】❶time；moment；hour ❷constantly；always

【时空】time and space

【时令】season

【时髦】fashionable

【时期】period

【时区】time zone

【时尚】fashion；fad；vogue：不合～ out of fashion

【时时】often；constantly

【时势】the current situation；the trend of the times；the way things are going

【时事】current events

【时态】tense

【时下】currently；at present；right now

【时限】deadline；time limit：～紧迫 pressed for time

【时效】❶effectiveness for a given period of time ❷prescription ❸ageing

【时兴】fashionable；in vogue；popular

【时宜】what is appropriate to the occasion；what suits the occasion：不合～ be not appropriate for the occasion；be inappropriate

【时运】luck；fortune

【时运不济】have bad luck；be down on one's luck

【时针】❶hands of a clock or watch ❷hour hand

【时至今日】at this late hour；at the present time；even to this day

【时钟】clock

【时装】fashionable dress

识（shí）❶know ❷knowledge

【识别】distinguish；discern；spot

【识破】see through；penetrate

【识趣】be judicious

【识相】〈方〉be sensible；showing good sense；be tactful

【识羞】feel ashamed；have a sense of shame：好不～ so shameless

【识字】learn to read；become literate：读书～ read and write

实（shí）❶solid ❷true；real；honest ❸reality；fact ❹fruit；seed

【实逼处此】be forced to do so by the circumstances；there's no alternative under the circumstances

【实测】survey

【实处】where it really matters

【实词】〈语〉notional word

【实弹】❶be loaded：荷枪～ carry a loaded rifle ❷live shell；live ammunition：演习～ practise with live ammunition

【实地】on the spot

【实感】true or genuine feelings；real sentiments：真情～ true feelings

【实干】get right on the job；do solid work；be steadfast in one's work：～家 person of action

【实话】truth

【实话实说】speak frankly；talk straight；not mince matters

【实惠】❶material benefit ❷substantial，solid

【实际】❶reality；practice ❷practical；realistic ❸real；actual；concrete

【实践】❶practice ❷put into practice；carry out；live up to

【实据】substantial evidence；actual proof：真凭～ ironclad evidence

【实况】what is actually happening

【实况转播】televise live；live broadcast；live telecast

【实力】strength

【实例】living example；example

【实情】the true state of affairs；the actual situation；truth

【实情实理】the actual situation and the real reason

【实施】put into effect；implement；carry out

【实事求是】seek truth from facts；be practical and realistic

【实物】material object

【实习】practice；fieldwork；field trip

【实现】❶realize；achieve；bring about ❷fulfill；execute；enforce effect；accomplish；come true ❸achievement；performance；actualization

【实效】actual effect；substantial results；practical results

【实心】sincere；solid

【实心眼儿】❶honest and serious-minded ❷an honest and serious-minded person

【实行】put into practice（or effect）；carry out；practise；implement；exercise；perform；execution；works

【实学】real learning；sound scholarship：真才～

real ability and learning

【实验】experiment；test

【实用】practical；pragmatic；functional

【实在】❶true；real；honest ❷indeed；really；honestly

【实质】❶ substance；essence ❷ stuff；thing；content

拾（shí）❶ pick up；collect ❷ tidy up；put in order

【拾掇】tidy up；put in order；repair；fix；〈口〉settle with；punish

【拾金不昧】not pocket the money one picks up

【拾零】news in brief；tidbits；sidelights：赛场～ sidelights from the competitive arena

【拾取】pickup；collect

【拾人牙慧】pick up phrases from sb. and pass them off as one's own

【拾物】(lost) articles found：～招领处 lost and found（bureau）；lost-property office

【拾遗补阙】make good omissions and deficiencies

食（shí）❶ eat ❷ meal；food ❸ food for animal；feed ❹for cooking；edible

【食不果腹】have not enough food in one's belly；go hungry

【食不甘味】eat without relish

【食而不化】 eat without digesting； read without understanding

【食粮】grain；food

【食量】capacity for eating；appetite

【食品】foodstuff；food；provisions：罐头～ tinned or canned food

【食谱】recipes；cookbook

【食堂】dining room；mess hall；canteen

【食糖】sugar

【食物】food；eatables；edibles

【食言】break one's promise

【食用】edible；use for food

【食油】edible oil；cooking oil

【食欲】appetite

【食欲不振】❶have a jaded appetite；have a poor appetite ❷〈医〉anorexia

【食指】index finger

蚀（shí）❶lose ❷erode；corrode

【蚀本】lose one's capital

史（shǐ）❶ history ❷ official historian in ancient China

【史不绝书】history is full of such instances

【史册】history;annals
【史籍】historical records;history
【史迹】historical site or relics
【史料】historical data;historical materials
【史前】prehistoric:～时代 prehistoric age
【史诗】epic;heroic poetry
【史实】historical facts;history
【史书】history;historical records
【史无前例】unprecedented
【史学】science of history;historical science;historiography

矢 (shǐ) arrow

【矢口】state categorically;insist emphatically;assert positively
【矢口狡赖】quibble and prevaricate,refusing to admit one's guilt;persistently quibble and deny one's errors
【矢志不渝】vow to adhere to one's chosen course

使 (shǐ) ❶send;tell sb. to do sth ❷use;employ;apply ❸make cause;enable ❹if;supposing ❺envoy;messenger

【使馆】diplomatic mission;embassy
【使坏】be up to mischief;play a dirty trick;create trouble:暗中～ play a dirty trick in secret
【使唤】❶order about or around;have sb. do sth. ❷use;handle;manage
【使节】diplomatic envoy;envoy
【使劲】exert one's strength
【使命】mission
【使团】diplomatic mission
【使性】lose one's temper;fly off the handle;throw a tantrum:任情～ throw a tantrum wilfully
【使用】make use of;use;employ;apply
【使用权】the right of use
【使者】emissary;envoy;messenger

始 (shǐ) ❶begin;start ❷only then;not until

【始料】originally expected
【始乱终弃】(of a man) seduce and then abandon
【始末】beginning and end;the whole story
【始终】from beginning to end;from start to finish;all along;throughout
【始终不渝】unswerving;consistent;steadfast
【始终如一】constant;consistent;persistent
【始祖】first ancestor
【始作俑者】the man who first made tomb fig-

ures;the creator of a bad precedent (from Confucius' condemnation of the use of tomb figures because of their resemblance to men)

屎 (shǐ) ❶excrement;faeces;stool;dung;droppings:拉～ shit;empty the bowels ❷secretion (from the eye,ear,etc.):眼～ eye discharge;gum in the eyes|耳～ earwax

士 (shì) ❶scholar ❷noncommissioned officer ❸a person trained in a certain field ❹(commendable)person ❺bodyguard,one of the pieces in Chinese chess

【士兵】rank-and-file soldiers
【士气】morale

氏 (shì) ❶family;clan ❷(used after a married woman's maiden name)

【氏族】clan

示 (shì) show;notify

【示范】set an example;demonstrate
【示警】give a warning;warn
【示例】give typical examples;give a demonstration
【示人】show sth. to others;let others have a look at sth.
【示弱】give the impression of weakness;take sth. lying down
【示威】❶demonstrate;hold a demonstration ❷display one's strength
【示意】signal;hint
【示众】publicly expose;put before the public

世 (shì) ❶lifetime;life ❷generation ❸age;era ❹world ❺〈地〉epoch

【世传】be handed down through generations
【世代】for generations;generation
【世代相传】pass on from generation to generation
【世道人心】the ways of the world and public sentiment
【世故】❶(versed in) the ways of the world ❷worldly-wise
【世纪】century
【世间】world;society
【世交】❶friendship spanning two or more generations ❷old family friends
【世界】world
【世界观】〈哲〉world ideology;world outlook
【世界语】〈语〉Esperanto
【世局】world situation;international situation;～动荡 turbulent international situation

【世面】society；world；life

【世情】ways of the world：不懂 ～ ignorant of the ways of the world；inexperienced in life

【世人】common people；people at large

【世上】in the world；on earth

【世事】affairs of human life

【世俗】❶ common customs ❷ secular；worldly

【世态】the ways of the world

【世态炎凉】warmth or coldness is the way of the world—people are friendly or unfriendly, depending on whether one is successful or not

【世外桃源】the Land of Peach Blossoms—a fictitious land of peace, away from the turmoil of the world；a haven of peace

【世袭】hereditary

【世子】the eldest son of the emperor by his·empress or of a feudal prince by his princess

仕 (shì) ❶ be an official ❷ bodyguard, one of the pieces in Chinese chess

【仕宦】〈书〉be an official：～之家 official's family

【仕女】❶ a maid in an imperial palace；maid of honour ❷ traditional Chinese painting of beautiful women

【仕途】official career

市 (shì) ❶ market ❷ city；municipality

【市场】marketplace；market；bazaar

【市集】fair

【市郊】suburb；outskirts

【市侩】sordid merchant

【市民】residents of a city；townspeople

【市区】city proper；urban district

【市容】appearance of a city

【市长】mayor

【市镇】towns

【市政】municipal administration

式 (shì) ❶ type；style ❷ pattern；form ❸ ceremony；ritual ❹ formula ❺ mood；mode

【式样】style；type；model

【式子】❶ posture ❷ formula

势 (shì) ❶ power；force；influence ❷ momentum，tendency ❸ situation；circumstance ❹ circumstance ❺ sign；gesture

【势必】certainly will；be bound to

【势不可挡】be a（general）trend which cannot be halted；advance irresistibly；carry all before one

【势不两立】be mutually exclusive；be extremely antagonistic；be irreconcilable

【势成骑虎】like riding a tiger—a situation from which it is hard to extricate oneself

【势均力敌】match each other in strength

【势利】snobbish

【势力】force；power；influence

【势如破竹】like splitting a bamboo；like a hot knife cutting through butter；with irresistible force

【势态】position；situation：～严重 in a serious situation

【势在必行】be imperative（under the circumstances）

事 (shì) ❶ matter；affair；thing；business ❷ trouble；audient ❸ job；work ❹ responsibility ❺ be engaged in

【事半功倍】get twice the result with half the effort

【事倍功半】get half the result with twice the effort

【事变】incident；emergency；exigency；the course of events；events

【事出有因】there is good reason for it；it is by no means accidental

【事到临头】when things come to a head；when the situation becomes critical；at the last moment

【事端】disturbance；incident

【事故】accident；mishap

【事过境迁】when the incident（or matter）is over，the circumstances will be different（or change）

【事后】after the event；afterwards

【事机】❶ affairs that should be kept secret：～败露 leak out a secret；expose ❷ situation；the right time to act；opportunity：延误～ miss an opportunity because of a delay

【事迹】deed；achievement

【事假】leave of absence；compassionate leave

【事件】incident；event

【事理】reason；logic：明白 ～ be reasonable；be sensible

【事例】example；instance

【事前】before the event；in advance；beforehand：～一无所知 with no preparation at all

【事情】affair；matter；thing；business；instance；occasions；occupation；employment；pursuit

【事实】fact

【事态】state of affairs；situation

S

【事务】work；routine；general affairs

【事物】thing；object

【事先】in advance；beforehand；prior

【事项】item；matter

【事业】cause；undertaking；enterprise； facilities

【事宜】matters concerned；arrangements

【事由】the origin of an incident；particulars of a matter

【事与愿违】things turn out contrary to one's wishes

【事在人为】human effort is the decisive factor；human effort can achieve anything

侍（shì）wait upon；attend upon；serve

【侍奉】support and wait upon (one's elders)；～父母 support and wait upon one's parents

【侍候】wait upon；look after；attend to

【侍弄】〈方〉tend with care (crops，domestic animals，etc.)

【侍卫】imperial bodyguard

【侍养】support and wait upon (one's elders)

【侍应生】attendant

【侍者】attendant；servant；waiter

饰（shì）❶decorations；ornaments ❷adorn；dress up；polish；cover up ❸play the role of；act the part of；impersonate

【饰物】articles for personal adornment；jewelry；ornaments；decorations

【饰演】play the role of

试（shì）❶try；test；attempt ❷examination；test

【试管】test tube

【试题】examination questions；test questions

【试图】attempt；try

【试销】trial marketing；trial sale

【试行】try out

【试验】trial；experiment；test

【试样】sample

【试用】on trial；try out；on probation

【试纸】test paper

视（shì）❶look at ❷regard；look upon ❸inspect；watch

【视察】inspect；visitation；inspection； visit

【视而不见】look but see not，turn a blind eye to；close (or shut) one's eyes to

【视觉】〈生理〉visual sense；vision；sense of sight

【视力】vision；sight

【视频】video frequency

【视同等闲】regard sb. or sth. as unimportant；treat lightly or casually

【视线】line of vision；view

【视野】field of vision；ken

拭（shì）wipe away；wipe

【拭目以待】wait and see；wait expectantly (for sth. to happen)

是（shì）❶correct；right ❷yes；right ❸be

【是非】right and wrong；quarrel；dispute

【是非曲直】rights and wrongs；truth and falsehood

【是否】whether or not；whether；if

【是古非今】praise the past and condemn the present

适（shì）❶fit；suitable；proper ❷just；right ❸comfortable；well ❹to；follow；pursue

【适当】suitable；proper；appropriate；adequacy；措辞～ appropriately worded

【适得其反】run counter to one's desire；be just the opposite to what one wished

【适度】appropriate measure；moderate degree；繁简～ neither too simple nor too elaborate

【适逢其会】happen to be present at the right moment (or on the occasion)

【适合】suit；fit；suit with；part to；be suited to；frame

【适可而止】stop before going too far；know when or where to stop；not overdo it

【适口】be agreeable to the taste；be palatable

【适量】an appropriate amount or quantity

【适龄】of right age

【适时】at the right moment；in good time

【适销】salable

【适宜】suitable；appropriate

【适应】suit；adapt；fit

【适用】suit；be applicable

【适者生存】〈生〉survival of the fittest

【适中】❶moderate；proper ❷ well situated

恃（shì）rely on；depend on

【恃才傲物】be inordinately proud of one's ability；be conceited and contemptuous

【恃强凌弱】use one's strength to bully the weak

室（shì）

【室内】indoor；interior

【室外】outdoor；outside

逝

逝（shì）❶pass ❷die,pass away

【逝世】pass away,die

释

释（shì）❶explain;elucidate ❷clear up;dispel
❸let go;be relieved of ❹release;set free

【释放】release;set free

【释怀】(usu. used in the negative) dispel from one's bosom;dismiss from one's mind

【释然】〈书〉feel relieved;feel at ease

【释疑】clear up (or remove) doubts;dispel suspicion

【释义】explain the meaning (of a word, sentence,etc.)

嗜

嗜（shì）have a liking for;be addicted to

【嗜好】hobby addiction;habit

【嗜杀成性】bloodthirsty;sanguinary

【嗜血】bloodthirsty;bloodsucking

誓

誓（shì）❶swear;vow;pledge ❷oath;vow

【誓不罢休】swear not to stop;swear not to rest

【誓不两立】swear not to coexist with sb. ; resolve to destroy sb. or die in the attempt;be irreconcilable

【誓词】oath;pledge

【誓死不二】pledge to be true to death

【誓言】oath;pledge:立下～ swear an oath

【誓愿】vow

【誓约】vow;pledge;solemn promise

shou

收（shōu）❶receive; accept ❷put away; take in ❸collect ❹money received; receipts ❺harvest;gather in ❻close ❼bring to an end; stop ❽restrain;control

【收兵】❶withdraw (or recall) troops;call off a battle:鸣金～ beat the gongs and withdraw the army ❷〈喻〉wind up

【收藏】collect;store up

【收场】❶wind up;end up;stop ❷end

【收车】return the vehicle to the garage, terminal,etc. and knock off

【收成】harvest;crop

【收存】receive and keep

【收到】receive;get;achieve;obtain

【收发】❶receive and dispatch ❷dispatcher

【收费】collect fees;charge

【收服】subdue;reduce to submission

【收复】recover

【收割】gather in;reap;harvest

【收工】stop work for the day;knock off;pack up

【收购】purchase;buy

【收回】❶take back;call in;regain ❷withdraw

【收获】❶ gather in the crops; harvest ❷results;gains

【收集】collect;gather

【收缴】take over;capture

【收据】receipt

【收敛】❶weaken or disappear ❷restrain oneself

【收殓】lay a body in a coffin

【收留】take sb. in;have sb. in one's care

【收录机】radio recorder

【收罗】collect; gather; enlist:～人才 recruit qualified personnel

【收买】❶purchase;buy in ❷buy over; bribe

【收纳】receive;take in:如数～ accept a sum of money as indicated

【收取】get payment; receive; collect:～手续费 collect service (or handling) charges

【收容】take in;accept;house

【收入】❶income; revenue; receipts; earnings ❷take in;include

【收拾】❶put in order;tidy;clear away ❷pack

【收拾残局】clear up the mess;pick up the pieces

【收受】receive;accept;take

【收缩】contract;shrink

【收听】listen to (the radio):～天气预报 listen to a weather forecast

【收尾】❶bring to a conclusion;wind up ❷ending (of an article,etc.)

【收效】yield results; produce effects; bear fruit:～显著 bring notable results

【收养】adopt

【收益】income;profit;earnings;gains

【收音】❶ reception ❷(of an auditorium, etc.) have good acoustics

【收支】income and expenses

【收支逆差】balance of payments deficit

手

手（shǒu）❶hand ❷have in one's hand;hold ❸handy;convenient ❹personally

【手臂】❶arm ❷〈喻〉reliable helper

【手边】on hand;at hand

【手表】wrist watch

【手柄】arm;handle

【手不释卷】be never seen without a book in hand; always with a book in one's hand

【手册】handbook;manual

【手到病除】illness departs at a touch of the hand

S

（said as a tribute to a doctor or a trouble-shooter）

【手到擒来】 just stretch the hand and bring it back very easy

【手段】 ❶means; medium; measure; method ❷trick; artifice

【手感】 handle; feel

【手稿】 manuscript

【手工】 ❶handwork ❷by hand; manual

【手工业】 handicraft

【手疾眼快】 quick of eye and deft of hand

【手巾】 towel

【手锯】 handsaw

【手绢】 handkerchief

【手铐】 handcuffs

【手快】 deft of hand: 眼疾～ quick of eye and deft of hand

【手榴弹】 hand grenade; grenade

【手锣】 small gong

【手忙脚乱】 in a rush; in a flurry

【手枪】 pistol

【手巧】 skillful with one's hands; nimble-fingered; deft; dexterous: 心灵～ clever and deft

【手勤】 diligent; industrious; hard-working: ～脚快 hard-working

【手球】 handball

【手势】 gesture; sign; signal

【手术】 operation

【手套】 ❶gloves; ❷baseball gloves; mitts

【手提包】 handbag; bag

【手提箱】 suitcase

【手腕】 ❶trick; artifice ❷skill; finesse; tactics

【手舞足蹈】 dance for joy

【手下败将】 one's vanquished foe; one's defeated opponent

【手下留情】 show mercy; be lenient; make allowances for (when dealing out punishment to sb.)

【手心】 ❶centre of the palm ❷〈喻〉scope of control

【手续】 procedures; formalities

【手眼通天】 exceptionally adept in trickery

【手艺】 craftsmanship; workmanship; handicraft; trade; art

【手语】 sign language; dactylology

【手掌】 palm

【手杖】 walking stick; stick

【手纸】 toilet paper

【手镯】 bracelet; bangle

【手足】 brothers

【手足无措】 disconcerted; at a loss as to what to do

守 （shǒu） ❶guard; defend ❷keep watch ❸observe; abide by ❹close to; near

【守财奴】 miser

【守备】 perform garrison duty; be on garrison duty; garrison

【守法】 abide by (or observe) the law; be law-abiding

【守恒】 conservation: 能量～ conservation of energy

【守候】 wait for; expect; keep watch

【守护】 guard; defend: ～仓库 guard the storehouse

【守旧】 adhere to past practices; stick to old ways; be conservative

【守口如瓶】 keep one's mouth shut; breathe not a single word; be tight-mouthed; be tight-lipped

【守门员】 goalkeeper

【守身如玉】 keep oneself as pure as jade; preserve one's honour or integrity

【守望】 keep watch

【守望相助】 (of neighbouring villages, etc.) keep watch and help defend each other; give mutual help and protection

【守卫】 guard; defend

【守信】 keep one's word

【守则】 rules; regulations

【守职】 stand fast at one's post; be faithful in the discharge of one's duties: ～尽责 be committed to one's duties

【守株待兔】 stand by a stump waiting for more hares to come and dash themselves against it—trust to chance and strokes of luck

首 （shǒu） ❶head ❷first ❸leader; head; chief ❹bring charges against sb

【首创】 initiate; originate; pioneer

【首次】 for the first time

【首当其冲】 be the first to bear the brunt; bear before others the brunt of an attack; bear the brunt of doing sth.

【首都】 capital (of a country)

【首届】 the first time

【首肯】 nod approval; nod assent; approve; consent

【首脑】 head: 政府～ head of government

【首屈一指】 come first on the list; be second to none

【首饰】(woman's personal) ornaments; jewelry

【首鼠两端】be in two minds; shilly-shally

【首尾】❶ head and tail; beginning and end ❷ from beginning to end

【首位】the first place

【首席】seat of honour; chief

【首先】first; in the first place; first of all; above all

【首相】prime minister

【首选】first choice

【首要】of the first important

【首战告捷】win in the very first battle or game

【首长】leading cadre; senior officer

寿 (shòu) ❶ long life; old age ❷ life; age ❸ birthday ❹ funerary

【寿辰】birthday (of an elderly person): 八十～ the 80th birthday

【寿诞】birthday anniversary

【寿命】lifespan; life

【寿桃】❶ peaches offered as a birthday gift ❷ peach-shaped birthday cake

【寿险】life insurance

【寿星】❶ the god of longevity ❷ an elderly person whose birthday is being celebrated

【寿终正寝】die in one's bed; die a natural death; die in bed of old age

受 (shòu) ❶ receive; accept ❷ suffer; be subjected to ❸ stand; endure; bear ❹ be pleasant

【受潮】be affected with damp

【受宠若惊】be overwhelmed by an unexpected favour; be overwhelmed by a special favour

【受挫】be foiled; be baffled; be thwarted; suffer a setback

【受罚】be punished

【受过】bear the blame (for sb. else): 代人～ take the blame for sb.

【受害】suffer injury; fall victim; be affected

【受贿】accept (or take) bribes

【受奖】be rewarded

【受惊】be frightened; be startled

【受苦】suffer (hardships); have a rough time

【受苦受难】live in misery; have one's fill of sufferings

【受累】get involved on account of sb. else; be put to much trouble

【受理】❶ accept and handle ❷ (of the court) accept and hear (a case)

【受凉】catch cold

【受命】receive instructions or assignments

【受难】suffer calamities or disasters; be in distress

【受骗】be deceived (or fooled, cheated, taken in)

【受聘】accept an appointment (to a post)

【受气】be bullied; suffer wrong

【受穷】suffer poverty; live in poverty: 吃苦～ live in hardship and poverty

【受权】be authorized

【受辱】be insulted; be disgraced; be humiliated: 当场～ be insulted on the spot

【受伤】be injured; be wounded; sustain an injury

【受赏】be awarded

【受审】stand trial; be tried; be on trial: 到庭～ be tried in a court of law

【受益】benefit from; profit by

【受用】benefit from; profit by; enjoy

【受灾】be hit by a natural disaster (or calamity): ～地区 disaster area; stricken (or affected) area

【受之有愧】I don't deserve it; I am not worthy of it

【受阻】be obstructed; meet with obstruction

【受罪】endure hardship, torture, etc. ; (in a broad sense) have a hard time; have an unpleasant experience

狩 (shòu) hunting

【狩猎】hunting

授 (shòu) ❶ award; vest; confer; give ❷ teach; instruct

【授奖】award a prize

【授课】give lessons; give instruction

【授命】give orders

【授权】empower; authorize; warrant

【授予】confer; award; grant; endow

售 (shòu) ❶ sell ❷〈书〉make (one's plan, trick, etc.) work; carry out (intrigues)

【售货员】shop assistant; salesclerk

【售票口】wicket

【售票员】ticket seller; (bus, tram, etc.) conductor; booking-office clerk; box-office clerk

兽 (shòu) ❶ beast; animal ❷ beastly; bestial

【兽环】animal-head knocker (on doors of old-type houses)

【兽行】❶ brutal act; brutality ❷ act of lust

【兽性】brutish nature; barbarity

【兽医】veterinary surgeon; veterinarian; vet

S

瘦 (shòu) ❶thin; emaciated ❷lean ❸tight ❹ not fertile; poor

【瘦长】 long and thin; tall and thin; lanky: ～脸 thin face | ～个儿 lanky

【瘦弱】 thin and weak

【瘦小】 thin and small

shu

书 (shū) ❶write ❷style of calligraphy; script ❸book ❹letter ❺document

【书包】 satchel; schoolbag

【书不尽言】 I have much more to say than I can write in this letter (used at the end of a letter)

【书橱】 bookcase

【书店】 bookshop; bookseller's

【书法】 penmanship; calligraphy

【书房】 a study

【书稿】 manuscript

【书柜】 bookcase

【书籍】 books; works; literature

【书记】 ❶secretary ❷clerk

【书家】 calligrapher; calligraphist

【书架】 bookshelf

【书局】 publishing house; press

【书刊】 books and periodicals

【书库】 stack room

【书眉】 top of a page; top margin

【书面】 written; in written form

【书面语】 written language; literary language

【书目】 booklist; title catalogue

【书皮】 cover; jacket

【书签】 bookmark

【书亭】 bookstand

【书信】 letter

【书页】 page

【书桌】 desk

抒 (shū) express; give expression to

【抒发】 express; voice; give expression to

【抒怀】 pour out one's heart; unburden one's heart

【抒情】 express one's emotion

【抒写】 express in writing; write of; describe

枢 (shū)

【枢纽】 pivot; hub; axis; key position

叔 (shū) ❶father's younger brother; uncle ❷ (a form of address for a man about one's father's age) uncle ❸husband's younger broth-er

【叔伯】 relationship between cousins of the same grandfather or great-grandfather

【叔叔】 ❶father's younger brother; uncle ❷ (a child's form of address for any young man one generation its senior) uncle

殊 (shū) ❶different ❷outstanding; special ❸ very much; extremely

【殊不知】 little imagine; hardly realize

【殊荣】 special honours

【殊死】 desperate; life-and-death: ～战 fight to the death; fight a last-ditch battle; put up a desperate fight

候 (shū) swiftly

【倏地】 suddenly; quickly

【倏尔】〈书〉 suddenly; quickly

【倏然】〈书〉 suddenly; abruptly

梳 (shū) comb

【梳理】〈纺〉 carding

【梳头】 comb one's hair

【梳洗】 wash and dress

【梳子】 comb

淑 (shū) kind and gentle, fair

【淑德】 female virtue

【淑静】 (of a woman) refined and gentle

【淑美】 virtuous and beautiful; refined and beautiful

【淑女】 a fair maiden; a virtuous maiden; a noble lady

舒 (shū) ❶stretch; unfold ❷easy; leisurely

【舒畅】 happy; entirely free from worry

【舒服】 ❶comfortable ❷be well

【舒缓】 ❶slow and unhurried; leisurely: 节拍～ 的歌声 singing in a slow tempo ❷relaxed; mild: 语调～ in a mild tone

【舒眉展眼】 smiling eyes; a beaming face

【舒散】 ❶stretch and flex ❷shake off one's fatigue or cares: ～心中的郁闷 shake off a gloomy mood

【舒适】 cosy; comfortable; snug

【舒心】 comfortable; happy

【舒展】 ❶unfold; extend; smooth out ❷limber up; stretch

【舒张】 diastole

疏（shū）❶ dredge（a river，etc.）❷ thin；sparse ❸(of family or social relations)distant ❹not familiar with ❺neglect ❻scanty ❼disperse；scatter

【疏导】❶dredge ❷persuade

【疏忽】carelessness；negligence

【疏解】❶mediate ❷ease up；mitigate

【疏漏】careless omission；slip；oversight

【疏落】sparse；scattered：～的晨星 sparse morning stars

【疏散】❶sparse；scattered；dispersed ❷evacuate

【疏松】loose

【疏通】mediate between two parties

【疏远】drift apart

输（shū）❶transport；convey ❷lose；beaten；be defeated

【输出】❶send out ❷export ❸output

【输掉】lose

【输入】put into；input

【输送】transport；convey；carry；infuse；wheel；send；feed；provide；conduction

【输血】blood transfusion

【输氧】oxygen therapy

【输液】infusion

【输赢】❶victory or defeat ❷winnings and losses cin gambling

蔬（shū）

【蔬菜】vegetables；greens；greenstuff

赎（shú）❶redeem；ransom ❷atone for

【赎金】ransom money；ransom

【赎买】redeem；buy out

【赎身】（of slaves，prostitutes）redeem oneself；buy back one's freedom

【赎罪】atone for one's crime

熟（shú）❶ripe ❷cooked；done ❸processed ❹familiar ❺skilled；experienced；practised ❻deeply；thoroughly

【熟谙】〈书〉be familiar with；be good at

【熟练】skilled；practised；proficient；neat；expert

【熟门熟路】a familiar road and a familiar door — things that one knows well

【熟能生巧】skill comes from practice；practice makes perfect

【熟人】acquaintance；friend

【熟识】be well acquainted with；know well

【熟手】old hand；practised hand

【熟睡】sleep soundly；be fast asleep

【熟思】ponder deeply；consider carefully；deliberate

【熟悉】know sb. or sth. well；be familiar with

暑（shǔ）heat；hot weather

【暑假】summer vacation（or holidays）

【暑期】summer vacation time

【暑热】hot summer weather：～难耐 intolerably hot summer weather

【暑天】hot summer days；dog days

属（shǔ）❶category ❷genus ❸be under；be subordinate to ❹belong to ❺family members

【属下】subordinate

【属性】attribute；property

【属于】belong to；be one part of

署（shǔ）❶government office ❷make arrangement for；arrange ❸handle by proxy；act as deputy ❹put one's signature to；sign

【署名】sign；put one's signature to

鼠（shǔ）mouse；rat

【鼠辈】scoundrel；nobody：无名～ a nobody

【鼠窜】〈喻〉scamper off like a rat：抱头～ scurry away like a frightened rat

【鼠疫】plague

数（shǔ）❶count ❷be reckoned as exceptionally（or good，bad，etc.）❸enumerate；list 另见 shù，shuò

【数不清】countless

【数不胜数】innumerable；incalculable；countless

【数典忘祖】give all the historical facts except those about one's own ancestors；forget one's own origins；be ignorant of the history of one's own country

【数九寒天】the coldest days of the year

【数米而炊】count the grains of rice before cooking them — fuss over small things；be miserly

【数一数二】count as one of the very best；rank very high

曙（shǔ）daybreak；dawn

【曙光】the first light of morning；dawn

术（shù）❶art；skill；technique ❷method；tactics

【术语】technical terms；terminology

束（shù）❶bind；tie ❷bundle；bunch；sheaf ❸control；restrain

【束缚】tie；bind up；fetter

S

【束手就擒】allow oneself to be seized without putting up a fight

【束手待毙】fold one's hands and await destruction；helplessly wait for death；resign oneself to extinction

【束手无策】be at a loss what to do；feel quite helpless；be at one's wit's end

【束之高阁】put (lay) on the shelf；have (sth.) shelved and forgotten；brush sth. aside

述（shù）state；relate；narrate

【述评】review；commentary

【述说】state；recount；narrate

树（shù）❶tree ❷plant；cultivate ❸set up；establish；uphold

【树碑立传】erect a monument to sb. and write his biography；build up sb.'s public image

【树丛】grove；thicket

【树大招风】a tall tree catches the wind—a person in a high position is liable to be attacked

【树大根深】a big tree with deep roots (said of an influential person or a huge organization)

【树干】tree trunk；trunk

【树根】tree stump；root

【树冠】crown (of a tree)

【树立】set up；establish

【树林】woods；grove

【树苗】sapling

【树木】trees

【树皮】bark

【树液】sap

竖（shù）❶vertical；upright；perpendicular ❷set upright；erect；stand ❸vertical stroke

【竖立】erect；set upright；stand

【竖起】hold up；erect

数（shù）❶number；finger ❷number ❸several；a few

另见 shǔ，shuò

【数词】〈语〉numeral

【数额】a fixed number；a definite amount

【数据】data

【数量】quantity；amount

【数码】numeral

【数目】number；amount

【数学】mathematics

【数值】numerical value

【数字】❶numeral；figure；digit ❷quantity

漱（shù）rinse (the mouth)；gargle

【漱口】rinse the mouth；gargle

【漱口剂】gargle

shua

刷（shuā）❶brush ❷brush；scrub ❸daub；paste up ❹〈口〉eliminate；remove ❺〈象〉swish；rustle

【刷洗】scrub

【刷新】❶renovate；refurbish ❷break

【刷牙】brush one's teeth

【刷子】brush；scrub

耍（shuǎ）❶〈方〉play ❷play with；flourish ❸play (tricks)

【耍花招】play tricks

【耍赖】act shamelessly

【耍弄】make fun of；make a fool of；deceive

【耍笑】❶joke；have fun ❷make fun of

shuai

衰（shuāi）decline；wane

【衰败】decline；wane；be at a low ebb

【衰减】weaken；fail；diminish：功能～weaken function

【衰竭】failure；exhaustion：心力～heart failure

【衰老】old and feeble；decrepit

【衰落】decline；be on the wane

【衰弱】weak；feeble

【衰颓】weak and degenerate

【衰退】fail；decline

【衰亡】become feeble and die；decline and fall

摔（shuāi）❶fall；tumble；lose one's balance ❷hurtle down；plunge ❸cause to fall and break；break ❹cast；throw；fling

【摔打】❶beat；knock ❷rough it；temper oneself

【摔跤】❶tumble ❷come a cropper ❸〈体〉wrestling

甩（shuǎi）❶move backward and forward；swing ❷throw；fling ❸leave sb. behind；throw off

【甩卖】disposal of goods at reduced prices；off a clearance sale

【甩手】❶swing one's arms ❷refuse to do；wash one's hands

帅（shuài）❶commander in chief ❷beautiful；graceful；smart

【帅印】the seal of a commander in chief

率（shuài）❶lead；command ❷rash；hasty ❸frank；straightforward ❹generally；usually

另见 lǜ

【率领】lead；head；command：～队伍 command a troop

【率先】take the lead in doing sth.；be the first to do sth.：～表态 take the lead in making public one's position

【率直】straightforward；unreserved：说话～ speak frankly

shuan

闩（shuān）❶bolt；latch ❷fasten with a bolt or latch

拴（shuān）tie；fasten

【拴绑】tie up；bind up

涮（shuàn）swill；rinse

【涮羊肉】❶instant-boil slices of mutton in a chafing dish ❷instant-boiled mutton；Mongolian fire pot

shuang

双（shuāng）❶two；twin；both；dual ❷pair ❸even ❹double；two-fold

【双胞胎】twins

【双边】bilateral

【双层】double deck

【双重】double；dual；twofold

【双方】both sides；the two parties

【双杠】parallel bars

【双关】having a double meaning

【双管齐下】paint a picture with two brushes at the same time—work along both lines

【双全】complete in both respects；possessing both：文武～ be well versed in both literary and martial arts

【双喜临门】a double blessing has descended upon the house

【双向】two-way；bidirectional：～贸易 two-way trade

霜（shuāng）❶frost ❷frostlike ❸white；hoar

孀（shuāng）widow

【孀居】〈书〉be a widow；live in widowhood

爽（shuǎng）❶bright；clear；crisp ❷frank；straightforward；openhearted ❸feel well ❹deviate

【爽身粉】talcum powder

【爽口】tasty and refreshing

【爽快】❶refreshed；comfortable ❷frank；straightforward；outright

【爽朗】❶bright and clear ❷hearty；candid

【爽然若失】not know what to do；be at a loss

【爽约】fail to keep an appointment；break an appointment

【爽直】straightforward：性情～ straightforward disposition

shui

谁（shuí）who

水（shuǐ）❶water ❷river ❸general term for rivers；lakes，seas，etc. ❹a liquid

【水坝】dam

【水泵】water pump

【水表】water meter

【水兵】seaman；sailor；blue jacket

【水波】wave；ripple

【水产】aquatic product

【水到渠成】when water flows，a channel is formed

【水稻】paddy；rice

【水滴石穿】dripping water wears through a stone

【水貂】mink

【水分】❶moisture content ❷〈喻〉exaggeration

【水果】fruit

【水火】❶fire and water—two things diametrically opposed to each other ❷extreme misery

【水火无情】〈口〉floods and fires have no mercy

【水晶】crystal

【水井】well

【水库】reservoir

【水雷】〈军〉（submarine）mine

【水力】waterpower；hydraulic power

【水利】waterpower；hydraulic power；water conservancy

【水流】❶general term for rivers and streams ❷current；flow

【水龙头】stop；faucet；bibcock

【水路】waterway；water route

【水落石出】when the water subsides the rocks emerge

【水面】surface of water

【水泥】cement

【水牛】（water）buffalo

【水平】horizontal；level；standard

【水乳交融】as well blended as milk and water—in complete harmony

S

【水深火热】deep water and scorching fire — an a-byss of suffering;extreme misery

【水天一色】the water and the sky blended in one colour (said of a vast body of water)

【水田】paddy field

【水土流失】soil erosion

【水位】water level

【水文】hydrology

【水系】river system;hydrographic net

【水泄不通】not even a drop of water could trick-le through;be watertight

【水星】〈天〉Mercury

【水银】〈化〉mercury;quicksilver

【水域】waters;water area;body of water

【水源】the source of a river;headwaters;water-shed

【水蒸气】steam;water vapour

【水质】water quality

税 （shuì）tax;duty

【税金】tax payment;taxation

【税款】tax payment;taxation

【税率】tax rate;rate of taxation;tariff rate

【税收】tax revenue

【税种】categories of taxes;items of taxation;tax categories

睡 （shuì）sleep

【睡袋】sleeping bag

【睡觉】sleep

【睡梦】sleep;slumber

【睡眠】sleep

【睡醒】wake up

【睡衣】night-clothes;pajamas

shun

顺 （shùn）❶in the same direction as;with ❷along ❸arrange;put in order ❹obey;yield to;act in submission to ❺fall in with;suit;a-gree with ❻in sequence ❼conveniently

【顺便】conveniently;by the way

【顺差】favourable balance

【顺畅】smooth and easy;unhindered

【顺次】in order;in succession;in proper sequence

【顺从】be obedient to;submit to;yield to

【顺带】in passing

【顺耳】pleasing to the ear

【顺风】have a tail wind;favourable wind

【顺风转舵】trim one's sails;take one's cue from changing conditions

【顺理成章】(of a statement,argument,etc.) logical;well reasoned

【顺利】smoothly;successfully;without a hitch

【顺路】❶on the way ❷direct route;regular route

【顺势】take advantage of an opportunity (as pro-vided by as opponent's reckless move)

【顺遂】(of things) to one's way;to well;go smoothly

【顺心】satisfactory;诸事～all is well

【顺序】❶sequence;order ❷in proper order;in turn

【顺延】postpone;put off

【顺眼】be an eyeful;pleasing to the eye

【顺意】satisfactory;as one wishes

【顺应】comply with;conform to

瞬 （shùn）wink;twinkling

【瞬时】instantaneous

【瞬息】twinkling

shuo

说 （shuō）❶speak;talk;say ❷explain ❸the-ory;teachings ❹scold

【说长道短】indulge in idle gossip;backbite peo-ple

【说大话】brag;boast;talk big

【说定】settle;agree on

【说服】persuade;convince;prevail on;talk sb. o-ver

【说和】mediate a settlement;patch up a quarrel

【说话】❶speak;talk;say ❷chat;talk ❸gossip;talk

【说谎】tell a lie

【说理】❶persuasive article:～的文章 persua-sive article ❷listen to reason;be reasonable

【说明】❶explain;illustrate;show:～原因 ex-plain the reasons ❷explanation;directions;caption

【说明文】expository writing

【说明书】❶directions ❷manual;technical man-ual ❸synopsis

【说一不二】say one and it never becomes two — one never changes his words

烁 （shuò）shining;bright

【烁烁】glitter;sparkle

朔（shuò）❶new moon ❷the first day of the lunar month ❸north

【朔日】〈天〉the first day of the lunar month

【朔望】syzygy

【朔月】〈天〉new moon

硕（shuò）large

【硕果】rich fruits；great achievements

【硕士】Master

数（shuò）frequently；repeatedly 另见 shǔ，shù

【数见不鲜】be a common occurrence；be nothing new

【数脉】〈中医〉rapid pulse（of more than 90 beats per minute）

sī

司（sī）❶take charge of；attend to ❷department

【司法】administration of justice；judicature

【司机】driver

【司令】commander；commanding officer

【司仪】master of ceremonies

丝（sī）❶silk ❷a threadlike thing ❸a tiny bit；trace

【丝绸】silk cloth；silk

【丝带】silk ribbon

【丝瓜】〈植〉dishcloth gourd；towel gourd

【丝毫】bit；the slightest amount or degree：～不差 tally in every detail；be just right

【丝巾】silk scarf

【丝绒】velvet；velour

【丝丝入扣】（mostly of a writing or artistic performance）（done）with meticulous care and flawless artistry

【丝袜】silk stockings

【丝织品】silk fabric

私（sī）❶personal；private ❷selfish ❸secret ❹illicit；illegal

【私奔】elopement

【私弊】corrupt practices

【私产】private property

【私仇】personal enmity

【私愤】personal spite

【私交】personal friendship

【私情】personal relationships

【私人】private；personal

【私生活】private life

【私下】private；in secret

【私心杂念】selfish ideas and personal considerations；selfish considerations

【私营】privately owned；privately operated

【私有】privately owned；private

【私语】whisper

【私自】privately；secretly；without permission

思（sī）❶think；consider；deliberate ❷think of；long for ❸thought；thinking

【思潮】trend of thought；ideological trend

【思考】think deeply；ponder over；reflect on

【思量】consider；turn sth. over in one's mind

【思路】train of thought；thinking

【思虑】consider carefully；contemplate；deliberate

【思念】long for；miss

【思索】think deeply；ponder

【思维】thought；thinking

【思想】thought；idea

【思绪】❶train of thought；thinking：～万千 myriad of thoughts well up in one's mind ❷feeling：～不宁 feel perturbed

【思议】conceive；think；imagine：不可～ inconceivable；unimaginable；unthinkable

斯（sī）❶this ❷then；thus

【斯文】refined；gentle

【斯文扫地】scholarly dignity swept into the dust

厮（sī）〈古〉❶male servant ❷fellow；guy

【厮缠】pester

【厮打】wrestle；grapple；tussle

【厮混】fool around（or about）with sb.；play around（or about）with sb.

【厮杀】fight at close quarters（with weapons）

撕（sī）tear；rip

【撕毁】tear up；tear to shreds

【撕裂】laceration；tearing

【撕碎】tear into pieces

嘶（sī）〈书〉❶neigh ❷hiss ❸hoarse

【嘶哑】hoarse

死（sī）❶die；be dead ❷to the death ❸extremely ❹implacable；deadly ❺fixed；rigid ❻impassable；closed ❼stubbornly

【死对头】deadly enemy

【死而后已】until one's dying day；to the end of one's days

【死规矩】inflexible rule and regulations

【死胡同】blind alley；dead end

【死火山】 extinct volcano

【死板】 rigid;inflexible;stiff

【死党】 sworn followers;diehard followers

【死敌】 deadly enemy; mortal enemy; implacable foe

【死活】 ❶life or death;fate ❷anyway; simply

【死记】 memorize mechanically; learn by rote; learn without comprehending:～硬背 memorize without comprehending

【死寂】〈书〉deathly stillness;absolute silence

【死结】 a fast knot

【死局】 hopeless game of chess

【死牢】 death cell;condemned cell

【死路】 blind alley;the road to ruin(or destruction)

【死命】 doom;death;desperately

【死难】 die in an accident of a political incident (esp. for a revolutionary cause)

【死气沉沉】 lifeless;spiritless;stagnant

【死去活来】 hovering between life and death;extremely sad and painful

【死人】 dead man or women;corpse;dead body

【死伤】 the dead and the wounded;casualties:～惨重 suffer heavy casualties

【死神】 Death

【死尸】 corpse;dead body

【死水】 stagnant water

【死亡】 death;doom:～率 death rate;mortality|～线 verge of death

【死心塌地】 be dead set;be hell-bent

【死刑】〈法〉death penalty; death sentence; capital punishment

【死硬】 ❶stiff;in flexible ❷very obstinate:～分子 diehard

【死有余辜】 one's crime deserves more than death

【死于】 die of;dic from

【死于非命】 die an untimely (or unnatural) death; die a premature death; die a violent death

四 (sì) four

【四边】 (on) four sides

【四边形】 quadrilateral

【四处】 all around;in all directions;everywhere

【四分五裂】 fall apart;be rent by disunity;be all split up;disintegrate

【四顾】 look around (or about):～无人 look around and see no one

【四海】 the four seas; the whole country; the whole world

【四海之内皆兄弟】 within the four seas all men are brothers

【四合院】 a courtyard;quadrangle

【四季】 the four seasons

【四邻】 one's near neighbours:街坊～ neighbours

【四面】 (on) four sides;(on) all sides;all round

【四面八方】 all directions; all quarters; all around;far and near

【四肢】 the four limbs;arms and legs;all fours

【四周】 all round

寺 (sì) temple;monastery

【寺院】 temple;monastery

似 (sì) ❶similar;like ❷seem;appear

【似曾相识】 seem to have met before

【似乎】 it seems;as if;seemingly

【似是而非】 apparently right but actually wrong

【似水流年】 time passes swiftly like flowing water

伺 (sì) watch;await
另见 cì

【伺机】 watch for one's chance;wait for an opportunity to

饲 (sì) raise;rear

【饲料】 forage;fodder;feed

【饲养】 raise;rear;feeding

【饲养员】 stockman;breeder;raiser

肆 (sì) ❶ wanton; unbridled ❷ four ❸〈书〉shop

【肆虐】 indulge in wanton massacre or persecution;wreak havoc

【肆无忌惮】 brazen;unscrupulous

【肆意】 recklessly;willfully

song

松 (sōng) ❶pine ❷loose; slack ❸loose; relax;slacken ❹not be hard up ❺light and flaky; soft ❻untie; unfasten; release ❼dried meat floss;dried minced meat

【松弛】 limp;flabby;slack;lax

【松动】 ❶become less crowded ❷not hard up ❸(of teeth,screws) loose ❹show flexibility

【松紧】 ❶degree of tightness ❷elasticity

【松劲】 relax one's efforts;slacken(off)

【松快】 ❶feel relieved:感觉～ feel relieved ❷be

less crowded

【松软】soft；spongy；loose

【松散】❶loose ❷inattentive

【松手】loosen one's grip；let go

【松鼠】squirrel

【松树】pine tree

【松涛】soughing of the wind in the pines

【松懈】relax；slack

【松脂】rosin

【松子】pine nut

怂（sǒng）

【怂恿】instigate(sb. to do sth.)；incite；egg sb. on；abet

耸（sǒng）❶towering；lofty ❷alarm；shock

【耸动】❶ shrug (one's shoulders) ❷ create a sensation

【耸肩】shrug one's shoulders

【耸立】tower aloft

【耸人听闻】deliberately exaggerate so as to create a sensation

讼（sòng）❶ bring a case to court ❷argue；dispute

【讼案】a case in court；lawsuit

【讼事】lawsuit；litigation

【讼状】a legal plaint

送（sòng）❶delivery；carry ❷give as a present；give ❸ see sb. off or out；accompany；escort

【送报】deliver newspaper

【送别】see sb. off

【送殡】attend a funeral；take part in a funeral procession

【送还】give back；return

【送货】deliver goods

【送交】deliver；hand over

【送客】to send a visitor off

【送礼】give sb. a present；present a gift to sb.

【送命】lose one's life；get killed；go to one's

【送行】❶see sb. off ❷give a send-off party

【送葬】take part in a funeral procession

【送终】attend upon a dying parent or other senior member of one's family；bury a parent

诵（sòng）❶read aloud；chant ❷recite

【诵读】read aloud；chant

【诵习】〈书〉chant and study

颂（sòng）❶praise；extol；eulogize；laud ❷song；ode；paean；eulogy ❸ express good wishes cin letters

【颂词】panegyric

【颂歌】song；ode

【颂古非今】eulogize the past and condemn the present

【颂扬】praise；laud；extol

sou

搜（sōu）search

【搜捕】track down and arrest

【搜查】ransack；rummage

【搜刮】extort；plunder

【搜集】collect

【搜剿】track down and exterminate：～残敌 track down and exterminate all traces of the enemy

【搜缴】search for and capture：～凶器 search for and capture a lethal weapon

【搜罗】collect；gather；recruit：～人才 recruit qualified persons；scout for talent

【搜身】frisk；search the person；make a body search

【搜索】hunt for；scout around

【搜索枯肠】rack one's brains (for fresh ideas or apt expressions)

【搜寻】search for；look for

嗖（sōu）whiz

馊（sōu）sour；spoiled

【馊主意】a stupid suggestion；a lousy idea

su

苏（sū）❶revive；come to ❷(Sū)Soviet

【苏打】〈化〉soda

【苏联】the Soviet Union(1917—1990)

【苏醒】revive；regain consciousness；come to (oneself)；come to one's senses

酥（sū）❶crisp；short ❷short pastry；shortbread ❸limp；weak

【酥脆】crisp

【酥麻】limp and numb

【酥软】limp；weak；soft

【酥油】butter

俗（sú）❶custom；convention ❷popular；common ❸vulgar ❹secular；lay

【俗称】commonly called

S

【俗话】common saying;proverb
【俗气】vulgar;in poor taste
【俗套】convention;conventional pattern
【俗语】common saying

夙（sù）〈书〉❶early in the morning❷long-standing;old
【夙仇】❶a long-time enemy❷long-standing enmity
【夙敌】an old enemy
【夙愿】a long-cherished wish

诉（sù）❶tell;relate ❷complain;accuse ❸appeal to;resort to
【诉苦】vent one's grievances
【诉说】tell;relate;recount
【诉讼】〈法〉lawsuit;litigation

肃（sù）❶respectful ❷solemn ❸eliminate;clean up;mop up
【肃静】solemn silence
【肃立】stand as a mark of respect
【肃穆】solemn and quiet
【肃清】eliminate;clean up;mop up

素（sù）❶white;unbleached and undyed ❷plain;simple;quiet ❸vegetable ❹native ❺basic element;element ❻usually;habitually;always
【素材】source material（of literature and art）;material
【素菜】vegetable dish
【素餐】❶vegetarian meal;be a vegetarian ❷not work for one's living
【素淡】plain;quiet;颜色～ quiet colour
【素净】plain and neat;quiet;衣着～ be plainly and neatly dressed
【素来】always;usually
【素昧平生】have never met before
【素描】sketch;literary sketch
【素雅】simple but elegant;plain and in good taste:衣着～ be tastefully dressed in a simple style
【素质】❶quality ❷diathesis ❸disposition;timber

速（sù）❶fast;rapid;quick;speedy ❷speed;velocity
【速成】speeded-up educational program
【速冻】quick-freeze
【速度】〈物〉speed;velocity;〈音〉tempo
【速记】shorthand;stenography
【速溶】instant
【速效】quick result
【速写】sketch;literary sketch

宿（sù）❶lodge for the night;stay over night ❷long-standing;old ❸veteran;old
另见 xiǔ
【宿仇】feud
【宿舍】hostel;living quarters;dormitory
【宿营】camp

粟（sù）foxtail millet;millet

塑（sù）model;mould
【塑胶】plastics;polyester
【塑料】plastics
【塑像】statue
【塑造】model;mould;portray

溯（sù）❶go against the stream ❷trace back;recall
【溯源】trace to the source

簌（sù）
【簌簌】❶〈象〉rustle ❷(of tears)streaming down

suan

酸（suān）❶acid ❷sour;tart ❸sick at heart;grieved;distressed ❹tingle;ache
【酸菜】pickled Chinese cabbage;Chinese sauerkraut
【酸楚】grieved;distressed
【酸涩】sad
【酸痛】ache

蒜（suàn）garlic
【蒜泥】mashed garlic

算（suàn）❶calculate;reckon;compute;figure ❷include;count ❸plan;calculate ❹guess;think;suppose ❺consider;regard as;count as ❻carry weight;count ❼at long last;in the end;finally ❽let it be;let pass
【算法】〈数〉arithmetic
【算计】❶calculate;reckon ❷consider;plan ❸expect;figure ❹scheme;plot;被人～ be plotted against by others
【算盘】abacus
【算式】equation
【算术】arithmetic
【算数】count;hold;stand
【算账】do（or work out）accounts;balance the books;make out bills;square（or settle）accounts with sb.;get even with sb.

sui

虽 （suī）though;although

【虽然】though;although

【虽死犹生】live on in spirit

绥 （suí）〈书〉❶peaceful ❷pacify

【绥靖】pacify;appease

【绥靖政策】policy of appeasement

随 ❶follow ❷comply with;adapt to ❸ let(sb. do as he likes) ❹along with ❺〈方〉look like;resemble

【随笔】informal essay;jottings

【随便】❶casual;random;informal ❷careless; slipshod

【随波逐流】drift with the tide (*or* current);go with the stream

【随处】everywhere;anywhere

【随从】❶accompany (one's superior);attend ❷ retinue;suite

【随地】anywhere;everywhere;随时～ at any time and in any place

【随和】amiable;obliging

【随机应变】do as the changing circumstances demand;suit one's actions to changing conditions;act according to circumstances

【随即】soon after that;immediately;presently

【随口】speak thoughtlessly or casually;blurt out whatever comes into one's head;～附和 casually echo

【随人俯仰】be at sb. 's beck and call;follow sb. servilely

【随身】(carry) on one's person;(take) with one; ～携带 carry on one's person

【随声附和】echo what others say;chime in with others

【随时】❶ at any time;at all time ❷ whenever necessary;as the occasion demands

【随同】be in company with;accompany

【随乡入乡】wherever you are, follow local customs;when in Rome do as the Romans do

【随心】after one's own heart;to one's liking

【随意】at will;as one pleases;to one's liking;～ 出入 come in and out at will

岁 （suì）❶year ❷year (of age) ❸year (for crops)

【岁月】years

遂 （suì）❶ satisfy; fulfill ❷ succeed ❸〈书〉 then;thereupon

【遂心】after one's own heart;to one's liking;～ 如意 be perfectly satisfied

【遂愿】have one's wish fulfilled;称心～ perfectly satisfied;be highly satisfied

碎 （suì）❶ break into pieces; smash ❷ broken;fragmentary ❸garrulous; gabby

【碎米】broken rice

【碎石】crushed stones;broken stones

隧 （suì）

【隧道】tunnel

邃 （suì）❶remote ❷deep;profound

【邃密】❶deep ❷profound

sun

孙 （sūn）❶ grandson ❷ generations below that of the grandchild ❸ second growth of plants

损 ❶decrease;lose ❷harm;damage ❸ 〈方〉sarcastic;caustic

【损兵折将】suffer heavy casualties

【损公肥私】seek private gain at public expense; feather one's nest at public expense

【损害】harm;damage;injure

【损耗】❶loss;wear and tear ❷wastage

【损坏】damage;injure

【损毁】damage or destroy

【损人利己】harm others to benefit oneself;benefit oneself at the expense of others

【损伤】harm;damage

【损失】❶lose ❷damage ❸loss

笋 （sǔn）bamboo shoot

【笋尖】tender tips of bamboo shoots

榫 （sǔn）tenon

【榫头】tenon

【榫眼】mortise

suo

唆 （suō）instigate;abet

【唆使】instigate

梭 （suō）shuttle

S

【梭巡】〈书〉move around to watch and guard; patrol to and fro

缩（suō）❶ contract；shrink ❷ draw back；withdraw

【缩短】cut down；shorten；curtail

【缩短战线】contract the front—narrow the scope of an activity

【缩减】reduce；cut

【缩手缩脚】❶ shrink with cold ❷ be overcautious

【缩水】shrink

【缩头缩脑】❶recoil in fear；be timid；be faint-hearted ❷shrink from responsibility

【缩小】reduce；lessen；narrow；shrink

【缩写】❶abbreviation ❷abridge

【缩印】reprint books in a reduced format

【缩影】epitome；miniature

所（suǒ）place

【所得税】income tax

【所向无敌】be all-conquering；be ever-victorious；break all enemy resistance

【所向披靡】（of troops）carry all before one；sweep away all obstacles；send the enemy fleeing helter-skelter

【所以】so；therefore；as a result

【所以然】the reason why；the whys and wherefores

【所有】❶own；possess ❷possession ❸all

【所有权】proprietary rights；ownership；title

【所有制】ownership；system of ownership

【所在】❶place；location ❷where

【所致】be caused by；be the result of

【所作所为】one's behaviour or conduct

索（suǒ）❶a large rope ❷search ❸demand；ask；exact ❹ all alone；all by oneself ❺ dull；insipid

【索道】cableway；rope way

【索价】ask（or demand）a price；charge：～过高 demand an exorbitant price

【索赔】claim damages；claim an indemnity

【索求】seek

【索取】ask for；demand；exact；extort

【索然】dull；dry；insipid

【索性】simply；just；might as well

【索引】index

唢（suǒ）

【唢呐】suona horn，a woodwind instrument

琐（suǒ）trivial；petty

【琐事】trifles；trivial matters

【琐碎】trifling；trivial

锁（suǒ）❶lock ❷lock up ❸lock and chains；chains ❹lock-stitch

【锁国】close the country

【锁紧】locking

【锁链】chain；shackles；fetters

T t

ta

他 (tā) he; him

【他方】the other party; other places
【他们】they
【他人】other people; others

它 (tā) it

【它们】they

她 (tā) she; her

【她们】they

塌 (tā) ❶collapse; fall down ❷sink; droop ❸ calm down; settle down

【塌方】landslide; landslip
【塌台】collapse; fall from power
【塌陷】subside; sink; cave in

踏 (tā)
另见 tà

【踏实】dependable; steady and sure; free from anxiety

塔 (tǎ) ❶pagoda ❷tower

【塔楼】❶tower; high-rise building ❷turret
【塔钟】tower clock; turret clock

踏 (tà) ❶ step on; tread; stamp ❷ go to the spot
另见 tā

【踏板】treadle; footboard; footrest
【踏步】mark time; march in place

tai

胎[1] (tāi) ❶foetus; embryo❷birth❸padding; stuffing; wadding ❹ roughcast (in the making of china, cloisonné, etc.)❺ tyre

【胎儿】❶(human) foetus❷foetus (of a domestic animal)
【胎教】antenatal instruction (i. e. influencing the development of the foetus by maternal impressions)
【胎盘】〈生理〉placenta

台 (tái) ❶ platform; stage; terrace ❷ stand; support ❸ table; desk ❹ broadcasting station ❺special telephone service

【台布】table cloth
【台秤】platform scale; platform balance
【台词】actor's lines
【台灯】desk lamp; table lamp; reading lamp
【台风】typhoon
【台阶】a flight of steps; chance to extricate oneself from an awkward position
【台历】desk calendar
【台球】billiards; billiard ball

抬 (tái) ❶lift; raise ❷carry

【抬杠】argue for the sake of arguing; bicker; wrangle
【抬高】raise; lift
【抬价】force up commodity prices
【抬举】praise or promote sb. to show favor; favor sb.
【抬头】raise one's head; look up; rise

太 (tài) ❶ highest; greatest ❷ remotest ❸ more and more senior ❹excessively; too; over ❺very

【太仓一粟】a grain of millet in a granary—a drop in the ocean
【太监】eunuch
【太空】outer space
【太平】peace and tranquility
【太平洋】the Pacific (Ocean)
【太甚】too far; to the extreme; 欺人～ go too far in insulting people
【太太】Mrs; madam
【太阳】the sun; solar; sunshine; sunlight
【太阳镜】sunglasses
【太阳穴】the temples
【太医】imperial physician (or doctor)
【太子】crown prince

态 (tài) ❶form; appearance; condition ❷state ❸voice

【态度】manner; bearing; how one conducts oneself; attitude; approach
【态势】state; posture

泰（tài）❶safe；peaceful ❷extreme；most

【泰然处之】take something calmly；bear sth. with equanimity

【泰然自若】behave with perfect composure；be self-possessed

tan

贪（tān）❶embezzle；practise graft；be corrupt ❷have an insatiably desire for ❸covet；hanker after

【贪财】be greedy for money

【贪得无厌】be insatiably avaricious

【贪官污吏】corrupt officials；venal officials

【贪婪】avaricious；greedy；rapacious

【贪恋】cling to；hate to leave

【贪求】seek；hanker after；～富贵 lust for riches and honour

【贪色】be fond of women；be a womanizer

【贪图】seek；hanker after；covet

【贪污】corruption；graft

【贪心】greed；avarice；rapacity；insatiable

【贪赃】take bribes；practise graft；～枉法 practise graft and bend the law

【贪嘴】be greedy for food；gluttonous

摊（tān）❶spread out ❷vendor's stand；booth；stall ❸fry batter in a thin layer ❹befall；happen to ❺take a share in

【摊点】stand；booth

【摊贩】street pedlar

【摊开】spread out；unfold

【摊牌】lay one's cards on the table；have a showdown

【摊派】apportion；quotas

【摊位】vendors' stand；booth：固定～ fixed vendors' stands

滩（tān）❶beach；sands ❷shoal

瘫（tān）be physically paralysed

【瘫痪】paralysis；palsy；be paralysed；break down；be at a standstill

【瘫软】become weak and limp

昙（tán）cloudy；overcast

【昙花】〈植〉broad-leaved epiphyllum

【昙花一现】flower briefly as the broad-leaved epiphyllum；last briefly；be a flash in the pan

谈（tán）❶talk；chat；discuss ❷what is said or talked about

【谈到】speak of；talk about；refer to

【谈得来】get along well（with sb.）

【谈话】conversation；talk；chat；statement

【谈恋爱】fall in love with each other；be lovers

【谈论】discuss；talk about

【谈判】negotiations；talks

【谈起】mention；speak of

【谈天】chat；make conversation

【谈吐】style of conversation

【谈心】heart-to-heart talk

弹（tán）❶shoot；send forth ❷spring；leap ❸flick；flip ❹fluff；tease ❺play（a stringed musical instrument）；pluck ❻elastic ❼accuse；impeach
另见 dàn

【弹唱】sing while playing a stringed instrument

【弹劾】impeach（a public official）

【弹簧】spring

【弹泪】shed tears；cry in sorrow

【弹力】elastic force；elasticity；spring

【弹跳】bounce；spring

【弹匣】box magazine；magazine

【弹性】elasticity；resilience；spring

【弹奏】play；pluck

坦（tǎn）❶level；smooth ❷open；candid ❸calm；composed

【坦白】❶honest；frank；candid ❷confess；make a confession；own up

【坦诚】frank and sincere；心地～ open-hearted｜相见～ treat sb. with sincerity

【坦荡】magnanimous；big-hearted

【坦克】tank

【坦然】calm；unperturbed

【坦率】candid；frank；straightforward

袒（tǎn）❶leave uncovered；be stripped to the waist or have one's shirt unbuttoned ❷give unprincipled protection to；shield

【袒护】give unprincipled protection to；shield

【袒露】expose；bare；leave uncovered

叹（tàn）❶sigh ❷exclaim in admiration

【叹词】〈语〉interjection

【叹服】gasp in admiration

【叹气】（heave a）sigh

【叹息】〈书〉heave a sigh；sigh

【叹惜】moan in regret

探（tàn）❶try to find out；explore ❷visit；pay a call on ❸stretch out；stretch forward ❹scout；spy

【探测】survey；sound；probe

【探查】look over；examine；scout；剖腹～ dissect the paunch for diagnosis

【探察】observe；look carefully at；～地形 survey

the terrain

【探访】❶search;look into:～新闻 look for the leads of a news story ❷visit;call on:～亲友 visit relatives and friends

【探戈】tango

【探监】visit a prisoner

【探究】probe into

【探秘】explore the mysteries;probe the secrets:宇宙～ probe the secrets of the universe

【探亲】go home to visit one's family or go to visit one's relatives

【探求】pursue;search for:～真理 seek truth

【探身】lean forward

【探视】❶visit;call on:～病人 drop in on a patient ❷observe:向窗外～ look out of a window

【探索】explore;probe

【探讨】inquire into;probe into

【探听】try to find out;make inquiries

【探望】❶look about ❷visit

【探问】❶ make cautious inquiries about ❷inquire after

【探悉】ascertain;learn;find out

【探险】explore;make explorations:～队 exploring team

【探寻】seek;pursue;search for:～真理 search for truth

tang

汤 (tāng) ❶hot water;boiling water ❷hot springs ❸soup;broth

【汤匙】soup-spoon

【汤盘】soup plate

堂 (táng) ❶a hall for a specific purpose ❷the main room of a house ❸relations between cousins

【堂堂正正】❶impressive or dignified ❷open and above-board

【堂皇】grand;stately;magnificent

塘 (táng) pool;pond

搪 (táng) ❶ward off;keep out ❷evade;doing sth. perfunctorily

【搪瓷】enamel;porcelain

【搪塞】stall sb. off;do sth. perfunctorily

糖 (táng) ❶sugar ❷sweets;candy

【糖葫芦】sugar-coated haws on a stick

【糖果】confectionery;candy

螳 (táng) mantis

【螳螂】mantis

倘 (tǎng) if;supposing;in case

【倘若】if;supposing;in case

躺 (tǎng) lie;recline

【躺倒】lie down

【躺椅】deck chair;sling chair

烫 (tàng) ❶scald;burn ❷heat up in hot water;warm ❸iron;press ❹very hot;scalding;boiling hot ❺ perm; have one's hair permed

【烫发】give or have a permanent wave;perm

【烫金】bronzing

【烫伤】scald

【烫手】〈喻〉troublesome;sticky;knotty

tao

掏 (tāo) ❶draw out;pull out ❷dig;scoop out ❸steal from sb. 's pocket

【掏腰包】〈口〉❶pay out of one's own pocket;foot a bill ❷pick sb. 's pocket

【掏心】from the bottom of one's heart

滔 (tāo) inundate;flood

【滔滔】surging;billowy;keeping up a constant flow of words

【滔滔不绝】pouring out words in a steady flow

【滔天】a terrible disaster

逃 (táo) ❶run away;escape;flee ❷evade;dodge;shirk

【逃避】escape;evade;shirk

【逃兵】army deserter;deserter

【逃窜】run away;flee in disorder

【逃遁】flee;escape:仓皇～ flee in panic

【逃犯】escaped criminal;escaped convict

【逃荒】flee from famine;get away from a famine-stricken area

【逃命】run (or flee)for one's life

【逃难】flee from a calamity;be a refugee

【逃匿】go into hiding:～山林 go into hiding in a wooded mountain

【逃跑】run away;flee;take to one's heels

【逃生】flee for one's life;escape with one's life

【逃税】evade a tax;tax evasion

【逃脱】❶ escape; make good one's escape ❷shirk;evade:～罪责 evade one's responsibility for an offence

【逃亡】become a fugitive;flee from home

【逃学】cut class;play truant

【逃逸】escape;run away

【逃债】dodge or avoid a creditor

陶 (táo) ❶pottery;earthenware ❷make pottery ❸cultivate;mould ❹contented;happy

【陶瓷】pottery and porcelain;ceramics

【陶器】pottery;earthenware

【陶土】pottery clay

淘 (táo) ❶wash in a pan ❷clean out;dredge ❸tax ❹〈方〉naughty

【淘金】panning

【淘气】naughty;mischievous

【淘神】get on one's nerves;taxing

【淘汰】❶eliminate through selection or competition ❷die out;fall into disuse;be obsolete

【淘汰赛】knock-out rounds;elimination game

讨 (tǎo) ❶ send armed forces to suppress; send a punitive expedition against ❷demand;ask for ❸marry ❹incur;invite ❺discuss;study

【讨伐】send a punitive expedition against

【讨饭】beg for food;be a beggar

【讨好】❶fawn on;toady to ❷be rewarded with a fruitful result

【讨价】ask a price

【讨教】consult;ask for advice

【讨论】discuss;talk over

【讨饶】beg for mercy;ask for forgiveness

【讨厌】❶disagreeable;disgusting;repugnant ❷troublesome ❸ dislike; loathe; be disgusted with

【讨债】demand repayment of a debt

套 (tào) ❶sheath;case;cover;sleeve ❷cover with;slip over;encase ❸that which covers (other garments,etc.) ❹overlap;interlink ❺traces;harness (for a draught animal) ❻harness (an animal);hitch up ❼knot;loop;noose ❽put a ring,etc. round;tie ❾model on;copy

【套话】❶polite formula;conventionality ❷stereotyped expressions

【套间】❶a small room opening off an- other;inner room ❷apartment;flat

【套衫】pullover;男～ man's pullover

【套用】apply mechanically;copy：～公式 apply the formula

【套语】polite remarks;pleasantries

【套种】interplanting

【套装】suit

te

特 (tè) ❶special;particular;unusual;exceptional ❷for a special purpose;specially ❸secret agent;spy

【特别】special;out of the ordinary;specially;particularly

【特产】special local product

【特长】strong point; specialty; what one's skilled in

【特出】outstanding;prominent：～的人才 outstanding talent

【特大】specially big;the most

【特等】special grade;top grade

【特地】for a special purpose;specially

【特点】characteristic;distinguishing feature

【特定】❶specially designated (or appointed)：～的人选 person specially designated for a post ❷specific;specified;given；～环境 specific environment(s);specific surroundings

【特工】secret service：～人员 special agent;secret service personnel

【特惠】indulgence;preference;odds

【特急】extra urgent

【特价】special offer;bargain price：～出售 sell at a bargain price

【特刊】special issue;special

【特快】express

【特例】special case

【特派】specially appoint for a special assignment：～记者 special correspondent

【特区】special zone

【特权】privilege;prerogative

【特色】characteristic;distinguishing feature

【特赦】special pardon

【特使】special envoy

【特殊】special;particular;exceptional

【特务】special (or secret) agent;spy

【特效】specially good effect;special efficacy：～药 specific drug;specific;effective cure

【特性】specific property or characteristic：民族～ national characteristic

【特许】special permission

【特异】❶distinct;exceptionally good;excellent;superfine ❷peculiar;distinctive

【特意】specially

【特有】peculiar;characteristic

【特征】characteristic;feature;trait

【特制】specially made

【特种】special type;particular kind：～兵 special force;special technical troops

teng

疼 (téng) ❶ ache; pain ❷ love dearly; be fond of

【疼爱】be very fond of;love dearly

【疼痛】pain;ache;soreness

腾（téng）❶gallop；jump ❷rise；soar ❸make room；clear out

【腾达】〈书〉❶rise；soar ❷make rapid advances in one's career；rise to power and position

【腾飞】❶fly swiftly upward；soar ❷make rapid advance；develop rapidly：经济～ rapid economic development

【腾空】soar；rise to the sky；rise high into the air

【腾挪】❶ transfer（funds, etc.）to other use ❷ move sth. to make room

【腾腾】steaming；seething；rise of gases：热气～ steaming hot；piping hot

【腾越】jump over

誊（téng）transcribe（by hand）；copy out

【誊录】transcribe（by hand）；copy out

藤（téng）❶cane；rattan ❷vine

【藤条】rattan

【藤子】〈口〉❶cane；rattan ❷vine

tī

剔（tī）❶ clean with a pointed instrument；pick ❷pick out and throw away；reject

【剔除】get rid of；reject

梯（tī）ladder；steps

【梯田】terraced fields；terrace

【梯形】trapezoid

提（tí）❶carry ❷lift；raise；promote ❸shift to an earlier time；move up a date ❹bring up；raise；put forward ❺draw out；extract ❻ mention；refer to；bring up

另见 dī

【提案】motion；proposal；draft resolution

【提拔】promote

【提包】hand bag；shopping bag；valise

【提倡】advocate；promote；encourage；recommend

【提成】deduct a percentage

【提出】put forward；advance；pose；raise

【提纯】purify；refine

【提单】bill of lading（B/L）

【提法】formulation；wording

【提纲】outline

【提高】raise；heighten；enhance；improve；increase

【提供】provide；supply；furnish；offer

【提货】pick up goods；take delivery of goods

【提交】submit to；refer to

【提炼】extract and purify；abstract；refine

【提名】nominate

【提前】shift to an earlier date；move up；advance；in advance；ahead of time；before hand

【提琴】the violin family

【提请】submit sth. to

【提取】❶draw；pick up；collect ❷ extract；abstract；recover

【提神】refresh oneself；give oneself a lift

【提升】❶promote；advance ❷hoist；elevate

【提示】point out；prompt

【提问】put questions to；quiz

【提醒】remind；warn；call attention to

【提选】select；choose

【提要】summary；abstract；epitome

【提议】propose；suggest

题（tí）❶ topic；subject；title；problem ❷inscribe

【题材】subject matter；theme

【题词】❶ write an inscription ❷ inscription ❸foreword

【题目】title；subject；topic

【题字】❶inscription；autograph ❷inscribe

蹄（tí）hoof

【蹄筋】tendons of beef, mutton or pork

【蹄膀】〈方〉the upper part of a leg of pork

体（tǐ）❶body；part of the body ❷substance；state of a substance ❸style；form ❹aspect（of a verb）❺ personally do or experience sth.；put oneself in another's position ❻system

【体裁】types or forms of literature

【体操】gymnastics

【体察】experience and observe：～民情 be aware of the condition of the people

【体尝】have personal experience of；experience personally：仔细品味～ taste carefully

【体罚】physical punishment

【体格】physique；build

【体会】know（or learn）from experience；realise；knowledge；understand

【体积】volume；bulk

【体检】physical examination

【体力】physical strength

【体例】stylistic rules and layout；style

【体谅】show understanding and sympathy for；make allowances for

【体貌】one's figure and features；general physical appearance：～特征 characteristics of one's figure and appearance

【体面】❶dignity；face ❷honorable；creditable

【体魄】physique；锻炼～ go in for

physical training

【体腔】body cavity

【体态】posture;carriage

【体坛】sports world;sports circles:～精英 elite of the sports world;top athletes

【体贴】give every care to

【体统】decorum;propriety;decency:不成～ most improper;downright outrageous

【体味】appreciate;savour

【体温】temperature

【体系】system

【体现】embody;reflect

【体形】bodily form;build

【体验】learn through practice;learn through personal experience

【体液】body fluid;humour

【体育】physical culture;physical training;sports

【体育馆】gymnasium;gym

【体制】system of organization

【体质】physique;constitution

【体重】weight

替 (tì) ❶take the place of ❷for;on behalf of

【替补】substitute for

【替代】substitute for;replace;supersede

【替换】replace;substitute for;displace;take the place of

【替身】substitute;replacement;stand-in

【替天行道】right wrongs in accordance with heaven's decree (a slogan often used by leaders of peasant uprisings)

【替罪羊】scapegoat

tian

天 (tiān) ❶sky;heaven ❷day ❸overhead ❹time;a period of time in a day ❺season ❻weather ❼nature;elements ❽God;Heaven

【天边】horizon;the ends of the earth

【天才】genius;talent;gift

【天成】be wrought as if through the invisible hands of nature;springing from nature:美丽～ natural beauty

【天敌】natural enemy

【天地】❶heaven and earth;world;universe ❷〈喻〉field of activity;scope of operation ❸〈方〉pass;plight

【天地不容】a towering crime or a sinner that neither god nor men can forgive

【天地良心】can say in all honesty;must point out in all fairness

【天鹅】swan

【天赋】inborn;innate;endowed by nature;natural gift;talent;endowments

【天高地厚】as high as the heavens and as deep as the earth—❶(of kindness) profound;deep ❷complexity of things

【天高气爽】the sky is clear and the air is crisp—fine autumn weather

【天河】the Galaxy

【天花乱坠】as if it were raining flowers

【天昏地暗】❶a murky sky over a dark earth;dark all round;gloomy above and dark below ❷in a state of chaos and darkness;total absence of justice

【天机】❶nature's mystery;sth. inexplicable ❷God's design;secret

【天经地义】(be regarded) as unalterable principles

【天井】❶small yard;courtyard ❷skylight

【天空】sky;heavens:仰望～ look up into the sky

【天蓝】sky blue;azure

【天理】❶heavenly principles-feudal ethics as propounded by the Song Confucianists ❷justice

【天良】conscience:丧尽～ conscienceless;heartless

【天亮】daybreak;dawn

【天南地北】❶far apart ❷from different places or areas

【天南海北】❶all over the country ❷discursive;rambling

【天平】balance;scales

【天气】weather

【天桥】overlying bridge;platform bridge

【天穹】vault of heaven

【天然】natural:～景色 natural scenery

【天然气】natural gas

【天生】born;inborn;inherent;innate:～丽质 born beautiful;naturally beautiful

【天使】angel

【天堂】❶paradise;heaven ❷〈喻〉paradise

【天文馆】planetarium

【天文台】observatory

【天文学】astronomy

【天下第一】the first under heaven—unequalled;peerless

【天下太平】peace reigns under heaven;the world (or the country) is at peace

【天下无敌】invincible;ever-victorious;all-conquering

【天线】aerial;antenna

【天性】natural instincts;nature:～善良 be good and kind by nature

【天旋地转】(feel as if) the sky and earth were spinning round；dizzy

【天衣无缝】a seamless heavenly robe — flawless

【天灾】natural disaster (or calamity)；act of God

【天灾人祸】natural and man-made calamities

【天造地设】created by nature；heavenly；ideal

【天真】innocent；artless；naive

【天职】bounden duty；vocation

【天资】natural gift；talent

【天姿国色】reigning beauty；a woman of matchless beauty

【天尊】celestial worthy (the title of some deities in the Taoist pantheon)

添 (tiān) ❶add；increase ❷〈方〉have a baby

【添补】replenish；get more

【添加】add to；increase

【添加剂】additive

【添置】add to one's possessions；acquire

田 (tián) ❶field；farmland；cropland ❷an open area abounding in same natural product；field

【田产】real estate

【田地】❶field；farmland；❷plight；wretched situation

【田间】field；farm；countryside

【田径】track and field

【田野】field；open country

【田园】fields and gardens；countryside

恬 (tián) ❶quiet；tranquil；calm ❷not care at all；remain unperturbed

【恬不知耻】not feel ashamed；have no sense of shame；be shameless

【恬淡】❶indifferent to fame or gain；心怀～ remain indifferent ❷quiet；tranquil；peaceful

【恬静】quiet；peaceful；tranquil

【恬美】quiet and happy

【恬然】unperturbed；calm；nonchalant

甜 (tián) ❶ sweet；honeyed ❷ (of sleep)sound

【甜菜】beet；beetroot

【甜点】sweet；honeyed

【甜瓜】muskmelon

【甜美】❶sweet；luscious❷pleasant；refreshing

【甜蜜】sweet；happy

【甜品】sweet snacks；sweets

【甜润】sweet；melodious；嗓音～ sweet voice；melodious voice

【甜食】sweet food；sweets

【甜头】❶sweet taste；pleasant flavour ❷benefit

填 (tián) ❶fill；stuff ❷write；fill in

【填报】fill in a form and submit it to the leadership

【填补】fill

【填充】fill in the blanks；fill up；stuff

【填词】compose a poem

【填空】fill a vacant position

【填平】fill and level up

tiao

挑 (tiāo) ❶choose；select ❷pick；find ❸carry on the shoulder with a pole；shoulder 另见 tiǎo

【挑拣】pick and choose

【挑食】be very choosy about what one eats

【挑选】choose；select；pick out

条 (tiáo) ❶twig ❷a long narrow piece；strip ❸item；article ❹order

【条件】❶condition；term；factor ❷requirement

【条款】clause；article；provision

【条理】proper arrangement or presentation；orderliness；method；～分明 well-organized

【条例】regulations；rules；ordinances

【条令】regulations

【条目】clauses and subclauses；entry

【条文】clause；article

【条约】treaty；pact

调 (tiáo) ❶suit well；fit in perfectly ❷mix；adjust ❸mediate ❹provoke；tease；tantalize ❺incite；instigate；sow discord 另见 diào

【调羹】spoon

【调和】mediate； reconcile； compromise； make concessions

【调剂】make up a prescription；adjust；regulate；provide physical and mental relaxation

【调价】readjust prices

【调焦】focusing

【调节】regulate；adjust

【调解】mediate；make peace

【调侃】ridicule；jeer at；deride

【调理】nurse one's health；recuperate；take care of；subject sb. to discipline

【调料】condiment；seasoning；flavouring

【调弄】❶make fun of ❷fix；arrange；adjust；～琴弦 adjust the strings ❸instigate；stir up；～是非 stir up a trouble

【调皮】 naughty； mischievous； unruly； tricky；play tricks

【调频】frequency modulation

【调试】debug

【调停】mediate；intervene；act as an intermediary

【调味】flavor；season

【调匀】mix well
【调整】adjust;regulate;revise

挑 (tiāo) ❶push sth. up with a pole or stick; raise ❷poke;pick ❸stir up;instigate ❹ rising stroke
另见 tiāo

【挑拨】instigate;incite;sow discord
【挑动】provoke;stir up;incite
【挑逗】provoke;tease;tantalize
【挑明】no longer keep it back;let it all out;bring it out into the open
【挑头】take the lead;be the first to do sth.
【挑衅】provoke
【挑战】challenge to battle

眺 (tiào) look into the distance from a high place
【眺望】look into the distance from a high place

跳 (tiào) ❶jump;leap;bounce ❷move up and down;beat ❸skip over;make omissions
【跳板】gangplank;springboard;diving board
【跳槽】abandon one occupation in favor of another
【跳动】move up and down;pulsate
【跳高】high jump
【跳栏】hurdle race
【跳马】vaulting horse
【跳棋】Chinese checkers;Chinese draughts
【跳伞】parachute;bale out
【跳绳】rope skipping
【跳水】diving
【跳台】diving tower
【跳舞】dance
【跳远】long jump;broad jump

tie

贴 (tiē) ❶paste;stick;glue ❷keep close to; nestle closely to ❸subsidize;help(out) financially ❹subsidies;allowance
【贴补】subsidize;help financially
【贴近】press close to;nestle up against
【贴切】apt;suitable;appropriate;proper
【贴心】intimate;close

铁 (tiě) ❶iron ❷arms;weapon
【铁饼】〈体〉❶discus throw ❷discus
【铁道】railway;railroad
【铁轨】rail
【铁匠】blacksmith
【铁锹】spade;shovel

ting

厅 (tīng) ❶hall ❷office ❸department

听 (tīng) ❶listen;hear ❷heed;obey ❸〈书〉allow;let ❹〈方〉tin;can
【听便】as one pleases;please yourself
【听从】obey;heed;comply
【听话】heed what an elder or superior says;be obedient
【听见】hear
【听讲】listen to a talk;attend a lecture
【听觉】sense of hearing
【听力】hearing
【听命】take orders from
【听任】allow;let
【听说】be told;hear of
【听筒】receiver;headphone;earphone
【听写】dictation
【听信】hear and believe rumors
【听诊】auscultation
【听众】audience;listeners

庭 (tíng) ❶front courtyard;front yard ❷law court
【庭园】flower garden;grounds
【庭院】courtyard

停 (tíng) close down;stop;cease
【停泊】anchor;berth
【停产】stop production
【停车】stop;pull up;stall;stop working
【停当】ready;settled
【停电】power cut;power failure
【停放】park (a vehicle);place (a coffin)
【停火】cease fire
【停刊】stop publication
【停靠】(of a train) stop;(of a ship) berth
【停课】suspend classes
【停留】stay for a time;stop;remain
【停水】cut off the water
【停息】stop;cease
【停业】stop doing business;close down
【停战】ceasefire;armistice
【停职】suspend sb. from his duties
【停止】stop;cease;halt;suspend;call off
【停滞】stagnate;bog down;be at a standstill

挺 (tǐng) ❶straight;erect ❷straighten up; stick out ❸endure;stand ❹very;rather
【挺拔】❶tall and straight ❷forceful
【挺好】good;very good
【挺进】boldly drive on;press onward;push forward;～队 advancing vanguard units
【挺立】❶stand upright ❷stand firm
【挺身】straighten one's back
【挺直】straight and upright

tong

通 (tōng) ❶open；through ❷open up or clear out by poking or jabbing ❸lead to；go to ❹connect；communicate ❺notify；ell ❻understand；know ❼authority；expert ❽logical；coherent ❾general；common

【通报】❶circulate a notice（of commendation，criticism，etc.）❷circular（on the situation，etc.）❸bulletin；jornal

【通病】common mistake；common fault；common failing

【通常】general；usual；normal

【通畅】❶unobstructed；clear ❷easy and smooth

【通达】understand things；be sensible or be reasonable：～人情 be understanding and considerate

【通道】thoroughfare；passageway；passage

【通风】ventilate

【通告】give public notice；announce；notify；public notice；an announcement；circular

【通共】in all；altogether；all told

【通观】viewed overall；viewed in an overall way；take an overall view：～全局 take the whole situation into consideration

【通过】❶pass through；get past；carry；pass；adopt；ask the consent or approval of ❷by means of；by way of；by；through

【通红】very red；red through

【通货】currency；current money

【通缉】order the arrest of a criminal at large；list as wanted

【通力】concerted effort

【通例】❶general rule；usual practice ❷〈书〉universal law

【通亮】well-illuminated；brightly lit

【通路】thoroughfare；highway；route；passage across

【通明】well-illuminated；brightly lit：灯火～ be ablaze with lights；be brightly lit

【通盘】overall；all-round；comprehensive：～筹划 overall planning

【通气】ventilate；be in touch with each other；have communication with

【通窍】understand things；be sensible or reasonable

【通商】have trade relations；have commercial intercourse

【通史】comprehensive history；general history

【通顺】clear and coherent；smooth

【通俗】popular；common

【通宵】all night；the whole night

【通晓】thoroughly understand；be proficient in；be perfectly familiar with；be well versed in

【通信】correspondence；communications

【通信员】messenger

【通行】pass through；current；general

【通讯】communication

【通用】in common use；current；general；interchangeable

【通邮】accessible by postal communication

【通则】general rule；general provision

【通知】❶notify；inform；give notice；let know ❷notice；circular；notification

同 (tóng) ❶same；alike；similar ❷be the same as ❸together；in common ❹with ❺and

【同案犯】an accomplice

【同班】be in the same class：～同学 classmate

【同伴】companion

【同胞】❶born of the same parents ❷fellow countryman

【同步】synchronism

【同窗】schoolmate

【同等】of the same class；on an equal basis

【同感】the same feeling

【同行】❶of the same trade or occupation ❷people of the same trade or occupation

【同化】assimilate；assimilation

【同伙】be in partnership；collude with；partner；associate；confederate

【同居】❶live together ❷cohabit；a common-law（or companionate）marriage；shack up with

【同类】of the same kind；similar

【同龄】of the same age or about the same age

【同路】go the same way

【同盟】alliance；league

【同谋】conspire；be of complicity；accomplice；confederate

【同年】the same year；of the same age

【同期】the corresponding period；the same term；the same year

【同情】sympathize with；show sympathy for

【同人】colleague

【同时】at the same time；simultaneously；meanwhile；in the meanwhile；moreover；besides；furthermore

【同事】work together；colleague；fellow worker

【同行】travel together：一路～ travel together all the way

【同姓】of the same surname

【同性恋】homosexuality

【同学】❶classmate；schoolmate ❷be in the same

school ❸a form of address used in speaking to a student

【同样】same；equal

【同义词】〈语〉synonym

【同意】agree；approve

【同志】comrade

铜（tóng）copper

【铜匠】coppersmith

【铜像】bronze statue

童（tóng）❶ child ❷ unmarried；virgin ❸ page；page boy ❹bare；bald

【童工】❶child labourer ❷child labour

【童话】children's stories；fairy tales

【童年】childhood

【童心】childlike innocence：～未泯 retain a childlike heart

【童谣】children's folk rhyme or song

【童装】children's garment

统（tǒng）❶interconnected system ❷all；to-gether ❸gather into one；unite ❹any tube-shaped part of an article of clothing，etc.

【统称】be called by a joint name

【统筹】plan as a whole

【统共】altogether；in all

【统管】centralized control；unified management：～家务 unified management of household chores

【统计】❶statistics ❷add up；count

【统考】uniform examination：全国～ nationwide unified examinations

【统领】❶lead；command：～各路人马 command a joint force ❷leader；commander

【统属】subordination：～关系 relations of subor-dination

【统帅】❶ commander in chief；commander ❷command

【统率】command；lead：～全军 command or lead the whole army

【统一】❶unify；unite；integrate ❷centralized

【统制】control

【统治】rule；dominate

筒（tǒng）❶ a section of thick bamboo ❷ a thick tube-shaped object❸any tube-shaped part of an article of clothing，etc.

恸（tòng）〈书〉deep sorrow；grief

【恸哭】wail；cry one's heart out

痛（tòng）❶ache；pain ❷sorrow；sadness ❸ extremely；deeply；bitterly

【痛斥】bitterly attack

【痛楚】pain；anguish；suffering；distress：内心～万分 be overwhelmed by grief；be greatly grieved

【痛悼】mourn deeply；grieve over：～死难烈士 deeply mourn the martyrs

【痛恨】hate bitterly

【痛苦】pain；suffering

【痛快】❶very happy；delighted；joyful ❷to one's heart's content；to one's great satisfaction

【痛惜】deeply regret；deplore

tou

偷（tōu）❶ steal；pilfer ❷stealthily；secretly ❸find（time）

【偷盗】steal；pilfer

【偷工减料】use inferior materials and turn out substandard goods

【偷懒】loaf on the job；be lazy：从不～ never loaf on the job

【偷情】carry on a clandestine love affair；have a love affair stealthily

【偷税】evade taxes；tax dodging；tax evasion

【偷袭】sneak attack；dawn raid

头（tóu）❶head ❷hair ❸top；end ❹begin-ning or end ❺remnant；end ❻chief；head ❼side；aspect ❽first ❾leading

【头版】front page

【头部】head

【头等】first class；first rate

【头发】hair

【头号】size one；number one

【头昏】dizzy；giddy

【头巾】scarf；kerchief

【头领】chief；leader；commander：土匪～ chief of the bandits

【头目】head of gang；ringleader；chieftain

【头脑】brains；mind

【头皮】❶scalp；epicranium ❷dandruff；scurf

【头饰】head ornaments

【头痛】headache

【头衔】title

【头屑】dandruff；scurf

【头绪】main threads

【头晕】dizzy；giddy

投（tóu）❶ throw；fling；hurl ❷ put in；drop ❸ throw oneself into ❹ project；cast ❺ send；deliver ❻go to；join ❼fit in with；agree with；cater to

【投案】give oneself up to the police

【投保】insure；take out an insurance policy

【投奔】go to for shelter；seek employment or

protection from somebody
【投标】submit a tender; enter a bid
【投产】go into operation; put into production; commission
【投弹】drop a bomb or firebomb; throw a hand grenade
【投敌】go over to the enemy; defect; surrender to the enemy: 叛变～ go over to the enemy and turn traitor
【投递】deliver
【投稿】submit a piece of writing for publication; contribute
【投机】❶agreeable; congenial: 话不～ disagreeable conversation ❷speculate; be a profiteer
【投靠】go and seek refuge with sb.
【投篮】shoot
【投票】vote; cast a vote
【投入】put into; throw into
【投射】throw; cast; project
【投身】throw oneself into
【投诉】appeal
【投宿】seek temporary lodging; put up for the night
【投降】surrender; capitulate
【投缘】agreeable; congenial
【投掷】throw; hurl; cast; fling: ～标枪 throw a javelin
【投资】invest; investment

透 (tòu) ❶ penetrate; pass through; seep through ❷ tell secretly; let out; reveal ❸ fully; completely; thoroughly ❹appear; show
【透彻】penetrating; thorough
【透顶】thoroughly; downright; in the extreme; through and through
【透风】let in air; ventilate; divulge a secret; leak
【透话】hint; drop or give a hint; tip off
【透镜】lens
【透亮】❶ bright; transparent ❷ obvious; (perfectly) clear
【透露】divulge; leak; disclose; reveal: ～风声 leak (or disclose) information
【透明】transparent; diaphanous
【透气】❶ventilate ❷breathe freely ❸leak information
【透视】perspective; fluoroscopy; roentgenoscopy
【透支】❶overdraw ❷expenditure exceeds revenue; overspend

tu

凸 (tū) protruding; raised

【凸面镜】convex mirror
【凸透镜】convex lens

秃 (tū) ❶bald; bare ❷bare ❸blunt; without a point ❹incomplete; unsatisfactory
【秃顶】bald; be going bald

突 (tū) ❶charge; dash forward ❷sudden; abrupt ❸projecting
【突出】❶sudden change ❷prominent ❸stress
【突进】charge; march forward; press onward
【突破】❶break through; make a breakthrough: ～封锁 break through a blockade ❷surmount (difficulty); break (limit): ～难关 overcome a difficulty
【突起】❶break out ❷rise high; tower ❸swelling; protuberance
【突然】abruptly; suddenly; unexpectedly
【突袭】surprise attack; strike

图 (tú) ❶ picture; drawing; map ❷ scheme; plan; attempt ❸pursue; seek
【图案】pattern; design
【图版】plate
【图表】chart; diagram; graph
【图画】drawing; picture; painting
【图景】view; prospect
【图例】legend (of a map, etc.)
【图片】picture; photograph
【图书】book
【图书馆】library
【图像】picture; image
【图形】graph; figure
【图样】pattern; design; draft; drawing; mold
【图章】seal; stamp
【图纸】blueprint; drawing sheet; drawing

徒 (tú) ❶ on foot ❷ empty; bare ❸ only; merely ❹ in vain; to no avail ❺ apprentice; pupil
【徒步】on foot: ～旅行 hike; travel on foot
【徒弟】apprentice; disciple
【徒劳】futile effort; fruitless labor
【徒然】❶ in vain; for nothing; to no avail ❷ merely; only

途 (tú) way; road
【途径】way; channel

涂 (tú) ❶spread on; apply ❷scribble; scrawl ❸cross out
【涂改】alter
【涂料】coating; paint
【涂抹】daub; smear; scribble
【涂饰】❶cover with paint, lacquer, color wash, etc. ❷daub on a wall; whitewash
【涂写】scribble; scrawl; doodle

屠

（tú）❶slaughter ❷massacre; slaughter

【屠夫】butcher

【屠戮】slaughter; massacre

【屠宰】butcher; slaughter (livestock)

土

（tǔ）❶ soil; earth ❷ land; ground ❸ local; native

【土产】local product

【土地】land; soil; ground

【土豆】potato

【土匪】bandit; brigand

【土木】building; construction: 大兴～ go in for large-scale construction

【土坯】sun-dried mud brick; adobe

【土气】❶rustic style; cloddish manner ❷rustic; countrified; uncouth; unfashion-able

【土壤】soil

【土色】ashen; pale; 面如～ turn deathly pale

【土星】〈天〉Saturn

吐

（tǔ）❶spit ❷put ❸say; tell; pour out
　　另见 tù

【吐露】reveal; tell

吐

（tù）❶vomit; throw up; spit ❷give up unwillingly; disgorge
　　另见 tǔ

【吐血】spitting blood; haematemesis

【吐赃】disgorge ill-gotten gains

兔

（tù）〈动〉hare; rabbit

tuan

湍

（tuān）

【湍急】rapid; torrential

【湍流】❶swift current; rushing waters ❷turbulent flow; turbulence

团

（tuán）❶ round; circular; roundish ❷ roll ❸group; society; organization

【团队】group; team; corps; collective with some property: 体育～ sports team

【团伙】gang; ring

【团结】unite; rally

【团聚】reunite

【团体】organization; group; team

【团员】League member

【团圆】reunion

tui

推

（tuī）❶push; shove ❷turn a mill or grindstone; grind ❸cut; pare ❹ push forward; promote; advance ❺infer; deduce ❻ push away; shirk; shift ❼put off; postpone ❽elect;

choose ❾hold in esteem; praise highly

【推测】infer; conjecture; guess

【推车】push a cart

【推陈出新】weed through the old to bring forth the new

【推迟】postpone; defer; delay; put off

【推崇】extol; hold in esteem; praise highly

【推辞】decline (an appointment; invitation)

【推导】deduce; infer; derive

【推动】push forward; promote; give impetus to

【推断】infer; deduce

【推广】popularize; spread; extend

【推及】spread; extend; analogize; extend by analogy: ～其余 generalize; extend to the rest

【推进】push on; carry forward; advance; give impetus to; move forward; push; drive

【推举】elect; choose; press

【推理】inference; reasoning

【推力】thrust

【推论】inference; deduction; corollary

【推敲】weigh; deliberate

【推却】refuse; decline

【推让】submit; yield

【推算】calculate; reckon

【推托】offer as an excuse; plead

【推脱】evade; shirk

【推想】imagine; guess; reckon

【推销】promote sales; market; peddle

【推卸】shirk; ～职责 shirk or evade one's duty

【推行】carry out; pursue; practice: ～新方案 carry out a new work plan

【推选】elect; choose: ～代表 choose representatives

【推移】elapse; pass: 日月～ as time passes

【推知】infer; reckon; deduce

颓

（tuí）❶ruined ❷declining; decadent ❸dejected; dispirited

【颓败】decay; decline; become corrupt; 荒凉～的景象 scene of desolation and decay

【颓废】dispirited

【颓丧】listless; dejected

【颓势】declining tendency

【颓唐】declining fortune

腿

（tuǐ）❶leg ❷a leg-like support ❸ham

【腿脚】ability to walk

退

（tuì）❶ move back; retreat ❷ cause to move back; withdraw ❸ withdraw from; quit ❹ decline; recede ❺ fade ❻ return; give back ❼cancel

【退避】withdraw and keep off; keep out of

the way

【退步】❶lag behind；retrogress ❷room for maneuver；leeway

【退潮】ebb（tide）

【退出】withdraw from；secede

【退化】❶degeneration ❷deteriorate

【退还】return：原物～ return the original

【退换】exchange a purchase

【退回】❶return；send back ❷go back

【退款】reimburse

【退路】❶route or line of retreat ❷room for manoeuvre；leeway：留个～ leave some leeway

【退却】retreat；withdraw；hang back；shrink back；flinch

【退让】make a concession；yield；give in

【退烧】bring down a fever

【退缩】shrink back；flinch；cower

【退位】give up the throne；abdicate

【退席】leave a banquet；walk out

【退休】retire

【退学】leave school；discontinue one's schooling

蜕（tuì）❶slough off；exuviate；moult ❷exuviate

【蜕变】transform；transmute

【蜕化】slough off；exuviate；degenerate

褪（tuì）❶take off（clothes）；shed（feathers）❷（of colour）fade

【褪色】colour fading

tun

吞（tūn）❶swallow；gulp down ❷take possession of；annex

【吞并】annex；gobble up

【吞灭】conquer and annex；gobble up

【吞没】embezzle；misappropriate；swallow up；engulf

【吞咽】swallow；gulp down

屯（tún）❶collect；store up ❷station（troops）；quarter（troops）❸village

【屯兵】station troops

【屯集】assemble；collect

【屯聚】gather together；assemble（troops or forces）

【屯垦】station troops to open up wasteland

囤（tún）store up；hoard

【囤积】hoard for speculation；corner the market

tuo

托（tuō）❶hold in the palm；support with the hand or palm ❷sth. serving as a support ❸serve as foil；set off ❹ask；entrust ❺plead；give as a pretext ❻rely upon；owe to

【托福】❶thanks to you ❷TOEFL（Test of English as a Foreign Language）

【托付】entrust

【托故】make an excuse；give a pretext：～不来 give an excuse for not coming

【托管】trusteeship

【托架】bracket

【托盘】tray

【托收】collection

【托运】consign for shipment；check

【托嘱】entrust

拖（tuō）❶pull；drag；haul ❷delay；drag on；procrastinate

【拖把】mop

【拖车】trailer

【拖船】tugboat；tug；towboat

【拖拉机】tractor

【拖累】❶encumber；be a burden on ❷implicate；involve

【拖欠】be in arrears；default

【拖沓】dilatory；sluggish；laggard：工作～ dilatory in work

【拖鞋】slippers

【拖延】delay；pay off

脱（tuō）❶（of hair skin）shed；come off ❷take off；cast off ❸escape from；get out of ❹miss out

【脱产】be released from production or one's regular work to take on other duties

【脱发】alopecia

【脱稿】be derailed

【脱轨】be derailed

【脱节】come apart；be disjointed；be out of line with

【脱口而出】say sth'；unwittingly；blurt out；let slip

【脱离】separate oneself from；break away from；be divorced from

【脱落】❶drop；fall out or come away；fall off：毛发～ lose one's hair ❷omit：字句～ omission of words and sentences（in an article）

【脱皮】exuviate；peel

【脱贫】quit poverty；shake off poverty

【脱身】get away；get free；extricate oneself；slip away

【脱手】slip out of the hand；get off one's hands；dispose of；sell

【脱水】deprivation of body fluids；dehydration

【脱俗】be cleansed of vulgarity；refined：超凡～ stand out from the general run of people

【脱逃】run away；escape；flee；break free：临阵

～ flee from battle

【脱险】escape or be out of danger：虎口～ escape mortal danger

【脱销】out of stock；sold out

【脱鞋】take off one's shoes

陀 (tuó)

【陀螺】top (a toy)

驼 (tuó) camel；humpbacked

【驼背】hunchbacked；humpbacked

【驼峰】hump (of a camel)

妥 (tuǒ) ❶appropriate；proper ❷ready

【妥当】appropriate；proper

【妥靠】reliable；dependable；trustworthy：为人～ be reliable or trustworthy

【妥善】proper；well arranged

【妥实】appropriate；proper；well arranged；practical and reliable

【妥帖】appropriate；proper；fitting

【妥协】come to terms；compromise

拓 (tuò) open up；develop

【拓荒】reclaim wasteland

【拓宽】extend；broaden：～视野 broaden one's view

唾 (tuò) ❶saliva；spittle ❷spit

【唾骂】spit on and curse；revile

【唾弃】cast aside；spurn

【唾液】saliva；spittle

T

W w

wā

挖 (wā) dig；excavate

【挖补】patch up
【挖掘】excavate；unearth
【挖苦】ridicule；satirize；speak sarcastically or ironically

洼 (wā) hollow；low-lying

【洼地】low-lying land
【洼陷】sunken；depressed

娃 (wá) ❶baby；child ❷〈方〉newborn animal

【娃娃鱼】〈动〉giant salamander
【娃娃】baby；child

瓦 (wǎ) ❶tile ❷made of baked clay

【瓦房】tile-roofed house
【瓦解】disintegrate；collapse；fall into pieces；crumble
【瓦块】fragments of tiles；broken tiles
【瓦砾】rubble；debris
【瓦斯】gas

wai

歪 (wāi) ❶askew；crooked；inclined；slanting ❷devious；underhand；crooked ❸recline to take a rest ❹domineering；bossy

【歪缠】nag；drive one up the wall；get on one's nerves
【歪打正着】hit the mark by a fluke；but harvest exactly what one wishes；do sth. unintentionally
【歪道】❶evil ways；depraved life；vice ❷bad ideas
【歪风】evil wind；unhealthy trend
【歪风邪气】evil winds and noxious influences；unhealthy trends and evil practices
【歪理】false reasoning
【歪扭】twisted；awry
【歪七扭八】crooked；askew；shapeless and twisted

【歪曲】twist；distort
【歪斜】askew；aslant

外 (wài) ❶outer；outward；outside ❷other ❸foreign；external ❹（relatives）of one's mother；sisters or daughters ❺not of the same organization，class，etc.；not closely related ❻in addition；beyond ❼unofficial

【外币】foreign currency
【外边】❶outside；out；exterior ❷a place other than where one lives or works
【外表】outward appearance；surface；exterior
【外宾】foreign guest；foreign visitor
【外出】go out
【外传】❶spread；leak ❷it is said；they say
【外地】other place；～人 settler
【外观】outward appearance；exterior
【外国】foreign country
【外行】❶amateurish；nonprofessional ❷amateur；outsider
【外号】nickname
【外患】foreign aggression：内忧～ home unrest and foreign aggression
【外汇】foreign exchange
【外籍】foreign nationality
【外加】extra；in addition
【外交】diplomacy；foreign affairs
【外界】the external world；outside
【外景】outdoor scene
【外科】surgical department
【外壳】outer covering；shell；case
【外寇】invaders：抗击～ resist foreign invaders
【外快】extra income：捞～ make some extra money
【外力】outside force；〈物〉external force
【外流】outflow；drain
【外露】show；be an extrovert：凶相～ look fierce
【外贸】foreign trade
【外貌】appearance；exterior；looks
【外面】outside；out
【外婆】grandmother
【外人】stranger；outside
【外伤】injury；wound

【外商】foreign business
【外事】foreign affairs
【外孙】grandson
【外围】❶periphery ❷peripheral
【外文】foreign language
【外向】〈心〉extroversion
【外形】appearance; external form; contour
【外延】denotation; extension
【外扬】spread; publicize
【外衣】coat
【外溢】❶outflow; drain: 资金～ drain of fund
　❷spill; overflow
【外语】foreign language
【外援】outside help
【外在】external; extrinsic: ～因素 external factor
【外债】external debt; foreign debt
【外资】foreign capital

wan

弯 (wān) ❶curved; crooked straight ❷bend ❸turn; curve
【弯度】curvature
【弯曲】winding; meandering; zigzag; crooked; curved

湾 (wān) ❶gulf; bay ❷moor

蜿 (wān)
【蜿蜒】❶wriggle ❷wind; zigzag; meander

完 (wán) ❶intact; whole ❷exhaust; use up ❸finish; be over
【完备】complete; perfect
【完毕】complete; end; be done
【完璧归赵】return the jade intact to the State of Zhao—return sth. to its owner in perfect condition
【完成】complete; bring to success
【完蛋】be done for; be finished
【完工】complete a project; finish doing sth.
【完好】intact; whole; in good condition
【完结】end; finish: 工作～ finish one's work; get a job done
【完满】come to fruition; come to a full cycle
【完美】perfect; consummate
【完全】complete
【完善】perfect; consummate
【完事】be settled; finish doing sth.
【完整】complete; integrated

玩 (wán) ❶play; have fun; amuse oneself ❷employ; resort to ❸trifle with; toy with ❹enjoy; find pleasure in

【玩忽】neglect; trifle with; ignore
【玩具】toy
【玩乐】play around; make merry
【玩弄】❶play with; juggle with ❷resort to; employ
【玩偶】doll
【玩赏】enjoy; take pleasure in
【玩耍】play; have fun; amuse oneself
【玩味】ponder; ruminate
【玩笑】joke; jest

顽 (wán) ❶stupid; dense; insensate ❷stubborn; obstinate ❸naughty; mischievous
【顽固】obstinate; stubborn; headstrong
【顽抗】be recalcitrant: 负隅～ put up a desperate struggle
【顽劣】stubborn and stupid: ～异常 be unusually obstinate
【顽皮】naughty; mischievous
【顽强】indomitable; staunch; tenacious
【顽童】urchin; naughty boy
【顽症】chronic and stubborn disease; persistent ailment

宛 (wǎn) ❶winding; tortuous ❷〈书〉as if
【宛然】as if
【宛如】just like

挽 (wǎn) ❶draw; pull ❷roll up ❸lament sb.'s death ❹coil up
【挽歌】dirge; elegy
【挽回】retrieve; redeem
【挽救】save; remedy; rescue
【挽留】urge sb. to stay; persuade sb. to stay

晚 (wǎn) ❶evening; night ❷far on in time; late ❸younger; junior
【晚安】good night
【晚班】night shift
【晚报】evening paper
【晚辈】the younger generation; one's juniors
【晚餐】supper; dinner
【晚点】late; behind schedule
【晚饭】supper; dinner
【晚会】evening party: 联欢～ get-together party
【晚婚】marry late; late marriage
【晚间】in the evening; (at) night
【晚礼服】night wear; night dress
【晚年】old age; one's later years: 度过幸福的～ lead a happy life in old age
【晚期】later period
【晚秋】late autumn
【晚上】at night; in the evening
【晚霞】sunset glow; evening glow

惋 （wǎn） sigh

【惋伤】 heave a sign of grief

【惋惜】 feel sorry for sb. or about sth.；sympathize with

婉 （wǎn） ❶gentle；gracious；tactful ❷beautiful；graceful；elegant

【婉辞】 euphemism

【婉言】 tactful persuasion：～拒绝 tactful refusal

【婉转】 mild and indirect，tactful；sweet and agreeable；歌声～ sweet and melodious notes of a song

万 （wàn） ❶ten thousand ❷a very great number；myriad ❸absolutely

【万般】 all the different kinds；utterly；extremely

【万端】 (of moods) multifarious：感慨～ a turmoil of feelings wells up in one's mind

【万恶】 extremely evil；absolutely vicious

【万分】 very much；extremely

【万古长青】 remain fresh forever；be everlasting

【万古流芳】 leave a good name that will live forever；achieve immortal fame

【万古千秋】 through unnumbered ages；for eons

【万家灯火】 a myriad twinkling lights (of a city)

【万里长城】 the Great Wall

【万马奔腾】 ten thousand horses galloping ahead—all going full steam ahead

【万能】 ❶all-powerful ❷universal；all-purpose

【万年】 eternity：遗臭～ be consigned to an eternity of notoriety

【万念俱灰】 all thoughts (or ambitions) are blasted；all hopes dashed to pieces

【万千】 ❶countless；innumerous；myriad ❷multifarious：变化～ constant changes

【万全】 perfectly sound；surefire

【万全之计】 a completely safe plan

【万人空巷】 the whole town turns out (to celebrate or to welcome sb.)

【万事】 every thing；all the things

【万无一失】 no danger of anything going wrong；no risk at all；perfectly safe

【万象更新】 all things take on a new aspect；everything looks new and fresh

【万幸】 by sheer luck

【万一】 ❶just in case；if by any chance ❷eventuality

【万有引力】 〈物〉gravitation

【万丈】 lofty；bottomless；infinite：光芒～ shine in full splendour

【万众】 millions of people；the multitude

腕 （wàn） wrist

【腕子】 wrist

wang

汪 （wāng） ❶ (of a body of water) deep and vast ❷ (of liquid) collect；accumulate ❸pond；pool

【汪洋】 vast；boundless：一片～ a vast stretch of water

【汪洋大海】 a vast (or boundless) ocean

亡 （wáng） ❶flee；run away ❷lose；be gone ❸die；perish ❹deceased ❺conquer；subjugate

【亡故】 die；pass away；decease

【亡国奴】 a conquered people

【亡魂】 soul；ghost

【亡灵】 soul of a deceased person；ghost；specter

【亡命】 flee；seek refuge；go into exile；desperate

王 （wáng） ❶king；monarch ❷duke；prince ❸grand；great ❹best or strongest of it's kind

【王朝】 ❶imperial court；royal court ❷dynasty

【王储】 crown prince

【王国】 ❶kingdom ❷realm；domain

【王牌】 trump card

【王位】 throne

【王族】 persons of royal lineage；imperial kinsmen

网 （wǎng） ❶net ❷network

【网罗】 ❶clapnet ❷enlist：～人才 enlist talented people

【网络】 network；electric network

【网球】 tennis

枉 （wǎng） ❶crooked ❷twist；pervert ❸treat unjustly；wrong ❹in vain；vainly

【枉法】 pervert the law

【枉费】 waste；try in vain；be of no avail

【枉然】 in vain；to no purpose；futile

【枉自】 futile；in vain；to no purpose

往 （wǎng） ❶go ❷in the direction of；toward ❸former；past

【往常】 as usual

【往返】 to and fro：～奔走 on the run back and forth

【往复】 ❶repeat；back and forth：～运动 reciprocate ❷contact；exchange

【往来】 ❶to and fro ❷visit each other；in contact

【往年】 before；former years

【往事】 past events；the past

【往昔】 in the past；in former times

惘 （wǎng） feel frustrated；feel disappointed

【惘然】 frustrated；disappointed

妄 (wàng) ❶absurd ❷presumptuous

【妄动】(take) rash action
【妄断】jump to a conclusion
【妄念】wild fancy；improper thought
【妄求】inappropriate request
【妄说】talk irresponsibly；talk nonsense：无知～ ignorance and absurdity
【妄图】in a vain attempt
【妄为】act audaciously
【妄想】vain hope；wishful thinking
【妄语】❶tell lies；talk nonsense ❷delusive talk

忘 (wàng) ❶forget ❷overlook；neglect

【忘本】forget one's past suffering
【忘掉】forget；lose sight of
【忘恩负义】be devoid of gratitude；be ungrateful
【忘怀】forget；cannot remember
【忘记】forget；overlook；neglect
【忘情】❶ callous，apathetic；detached ❷ let oneself go；abandon oneself to
【忘我】oblivious of oneself；selfless：～ 的精神 spirit of selflessness
【忘性】poor memory；forgetfulness

旺 (wàng) prosperous；flourishing；vigorous

【旺季】peak period；busy season
【旺盛】vigorous；exuberant
【旺销】sell briskly；sell like hot cakes：～ 商品 commodities in big demand

望 (wàng) ❶gaze into the distance；look far ahead ❷call on；visit ❸hope；expect；look forward to ❹reputation；prestige
【望远镜】telescope
【望族】long-established and distinguished family；prominent family：名门～ family of the rich and powerful

wei

危 (wēi) ❶danger；peril ❷endanger ❸dying ❹proper
【危房】unsafe building
【危害】harm；jeopardize；endanger；do damage to
【危机】crisis
【危及】endanger；compromise：～生命 endanger life
【危急】critical；in imminent danger
【危局】desperate situation：扭转～ turn the table and avert a dangerous situation
【危难】dire peril；calamity
【危亡】in peril；at stake

【危险】dangerous；perilous
【危重】mortally ill：抢救～病人 rescue the critically ill

威 (wēi) ❶impressive strength；might；power ❷by force
【威逼】threaten by force
【威风】❶ power and prestige ❷ imposing；impressive
【威吓】threaten
【威力】power；might
【威名】fame based on might or military exploits；mighty reputation：～ 远扬 the fame of sb. spreads far and wide
【威权】authority；power
【威慑】deter；terrorize sb. with force：～ 力量 deterrent force
【威士忌】whisky
【威望】prestige
【威武】❶might；force；power ❷powerful；mighty
【威胁】threaten；menace
【威信】prestige；high reputation
【威严】dignified；stately；majestic

微 (wēi) ❶minute；tiny；slight ❷profound；abstruse ❸decline
【微波】〈电〉microwave
【微薄】little；scanty；meagre
【微风】〈气〉gentle breeze
【微观】microcosmic
【微积分】〈数〉calculus
【微利】small profit；low profit：蝇头～ petty benefit；petty profit
【微妙】delicate；subtle
【微弱】faint；weak
【微生物】microorganism
【微微】slight；faint
【微小】small；little
【微笑】smile
【微型】miniature；mini

为 (wéi) ❶do；act ❷act as；serve as ❸become ❹be；mean ❺by
另见 wèi
【为力】put forth one's strength；exert oneself：无能～ can do nothing about it
【为难】feel embarrassed；feel awkward
【为期】for a certain period of time；by a definite date：～不远 be drawing near
【为人】behave；conduct oneself：～ 忠厚 honest and tolerant；sincerely and kindly
【为生】eke oneself through a living：捕鱼～ make a living as a fisherman
【为时】in terms of time：～ 过早 premature；too

early；too soon

【为首】with sb. as the leader；headed (or led) by

【为数】amount to；number

【为伍】associate with：羞与～ feel ashamed to be associated with sb.

【为止】up to；till

违 (wéi) ❶disobey；violate ❷be separated

【违背】violate；go against

【违法】break the law；be illegal

【违反】violate

【违犯】violate (laws，regulations，etc.)；infringe；act contrary to

【违禁】violate a ban

【违抗】disobey；defy

【违心】against one's will

【违约】❶ break a contract；violate a treaty ❷ break one's promise；break off an engagement；breach；infringement

【违章】break rules and regulations

围 (wéi) ❶enclose；surround ❷all round

【围捕】surround and seize；round up：～逃犯 hunt down a fugitive

【围城】encircle or besiege a city：～战 battle of besiegment

【围攻】jointly attack；besiege

【围观】watch；look on

【围剿】encircle and suppress：～残匪 roundup a remnant bandit force

【围巾】scarf

【围困】besiege；hem in；pin down

【围拢】close in；surround from all sides

【围棋】weiqi，a game played with black and white pieces on a board of 361 crosses

【围墙】enclosing wall；enclosure

【围裙】apron；pinafore；daidle

【围绕】❶move around ❷centre on；focus on

桅 (wéi) mast

【桅灯】❶mast head light；range light❷barn lantern

【桅杆】mast

唯 (wéi) only；alone 另见 wěi

【唯独】only；alone

【唯恐】for fear that；lest

【唯心论】〈哲〉idealism

【唯物论】〈哲〉materialism

【唯一】only；sole

帷 (wéi) bed-curtain

【帷幕】heavy curtain

【帷帐】bed-curtain

【帷子】curtain

惟 (wéi) ❶only；alone ❷but

【惟妙惟肖】absolutely lifelike

维 (wéi) ❶tie up；hold together ❷maintain；safeguard；preserve

【维持】keep；maintain；preserve

【维护】safeguard；defend；uphold

【维修】keep in (good) repair；service；maintain

伟 (wěi) big；great

【伟岸】tall and sturdy；stalwart：身材～ of tall and sturdy stature

【伟大】great；mighty

【伟绩】great feats；great exploits；brilliant achievements

【伟人】a great man

【伟业】great cause

伪 (wěi) ❶false ❷puppet

【伪钞】counterfeit banknote

【伪劣】(of goods) fake or of low quality：～商品 shoddy goods

【伪善】hypocritical

【伪造】forge；falsify；fabricate；counterfeit

【伪证】perjury；false witness；false evidence

【伪装】❶pretend；feign ❷guise；mask ❸camouflage

尾 (wěi) ❶tail ❷end〈反〉❸remaining part；remnant

【尾巴】tail

【尾灯】tail light

【尾骨】〈生理〉coccyx

【尾迹】wake；jet trace

【尾欠】❶owe a small balance ❷small part of a balance due

【尾声】❶coda ❷epilogue ❸end

【尾数】❶ number after a decimal point ❷odd amount in addition to the round number of settled accounts ❸last number of a multidigit figure

【尾随】tail behind；tag along after

【尾追】in hot pursuit

纬 (wěi) ❶weft；woof ❷latitude

【纬度】latitude

【纬纱】weft

【纬线】❶parallel ❷weft

委 (wěi) ❶entrust；appoint ❷ throw away；cast aside ❸shift ❹indirect；roundabout ❺〈书〉end ❻listless；dejected ❼committee

【委顿】tired;weary:精神～ in low spirits

【委靡】dispirited;dejected:神志～ look spiritless

【委派】appoint;delegate;designate

【委曲】winding;tortuous

【委屈】❶feel wronged;nurse a grievance ❷put sb. to great inconvenience

【委任】appoint

【委实】really;indeed:～不容易 by no means easy

【委托】entrust;trust

【委婉】❶mild and roundabout ❷tactful

【委员】committee member;member of a committee

萎（wěi）wither;wilt

【萎落】❶wither;fade ❷weaken

【萎缩】shrink;shrivel;wither

唯（wěi）
　另见 wéi

【唯唯诺诺】be a yesman;be subservient

猥（wěi）❶numerous;multifarious❷base;obscene;salacious;indecent

【猥辞】obscene words;dirty language

【猥劣】〈书〉base;mean

【猥琐】(of appearance,deportment) uncouth

【猥亵】❶obscene;salacious❷act indecently towards（a woman）

卫（wèi）defend;guard;protect

【卫兵】guard;bodyguard

【卫队】squad of bodyguards;armed escort

【卫护】protect;guard

【卫生】health;sanitation

【卫生间】toilet;washroom;room with sanitary equipment in hotel,inn,house,etc.

【卫士】bodyguard

【卫戍】garrison

【卫星】satellite;moon

为（wèi）❶for;for the benefit of;in the interests of ❷for;for the sake of ❸because;on account of
　另见 wéi

【为何】why;for what reason

【为了】for,for the sake of;in order to:学习是～工作 study for the sake of work

未（wèi）❶have not;did not;not yet ❷not;no

【未必】may not

【未卜】〈书〉cannot be anticipated;cannot be foreseen;unpredictable;unforeseen

【未卜先知】know without consulting an oracle;can foretell things;foresee

【未曾】have not;did not

【未来】❶coming;approaching;near future ❷future;tomorrow

【未了】unfinished;outstanding

【未免】rather;a bit too;truly

【未能】fail to;cannot;haven't been able to

【未然】not yet become a fact

【未遂】not accomplished;abortive

位（wèi）❶place;location ❷position ❸〈数〉place;figure;digit

【位觉】sense of balance

【位移】displacement;difference between the later position and the original position

【位于】be located;be situated;lie

【位置】seat;place;position

【位子】seat;place;position

味（wèi）❶taste;flavour ❷smell;odour ❸interest;delight ❹distinguish the flavour of

【味道】taste;flavour

畏（wèi）❶fear ❷respect

【畏避】shrink from;recoil from

【畏忌】have scruples;fear;dread

【畏惧】fear;dread;无所～ be fearless

【畏难】be afraid of difficulty;flinch from difficulty

【畏怯】cowardly;timid;chicken-hearted

【畏缩】recoil;shrink;finch;dare not go forward because of fear

【畏罪】dread punishment for one's crime

胃（wèi）stomach

【胃口】❶appetite ❷liking

【胃痛】stomachache

【胃腺】gastric gland

【胃液】gastric juice

谓（wèi）❶say ❷call;name ❸meaning;sense

【谓词】predicate

【谓语】〈语〉predicate

喂（wèi）〈象〉❶hello;hey ❷feed;spoon-feed

【喂奶】breastfeed;nurse

【喂食】feed (a person or an animal)

【喂养】feed;raise;keep

蔚（wèi）❶luxuriant;grand ❷colourful

【蔚蓝】sky blue;azure

慰（wèi）❶console;comfort ❷be relieved 【慰劳】bring gifts and greetings to

【慰勉】comfort and encourage
【慰问】express sympathy and solicitude for;convey best wishes to
【慰唁】condole with (family of a deceased)

wen

温 (wēn) ❶warm;lukewarm ❷temperature; ❸warm up ❹review;revise
【温饱】dress warmly and eat one's fill
【温差】different in temperature range of temperature
【温床】hotbed;breeding ground
【温存】❶be attentive to ❷gentle;kind
【温带】temperate zone
【温度】temperature
【温和】❶ temperate; mild; moderate ❷gentle;mild
【温厚】gentle and kind;good-natured:为人～ kind and sincere
【温良】gentle and kindhearted
【温暖】warm
【温情】tender feeling
【温泉】hot spring
【温柔】gentle and soft
【温室】hothouse;greenhouse;glasshouse
【温顺】meek;docile
【温习】review;revise
【温馨】cosy;warm:～的家 warm and sweet home
【温煦】❶warm ❷kind and cordial
【温驯】(of animals) docile;meek;tame

瘟 (wēn) ❶〈中医〉acute communicable diseases ❷(of traditional opera) dull and insipid
【瘟疫】pestilence

文 (wén) ❶character;script;writing ❷language ❸literary composition;writing ❹literary language ❺culture ❻formal ritual ❼civilian; civil ❽ gentle; refined ❾ certain natural phenomena
【文本】text;version
【文笔】style of writing
【文采】❶ rich and bright colours ❷ literary grace;literary talent;aptitude for writing
【文辞】language;diction
【文法】grammar
【文风】style of writing
【文稿】manuscript;draft
【文告】proclamation;statement;message
【文官】civil official
【文豪】great writer;literary giant
【文化】❶civilization;culture ❷literacy
【文集】collected works

【文件】documents;papers
【文教】culture and education
【文静】(of character, manners, etc.) gentle and quiet
【文句】sentences of an article
【文具】writing materials;stationery
【文科】liberal arts
【文明】civilization;culture of mental labour
【文凭】diploma
【文人】man of letters;scholar;literati
【文书】❶ document; official dispatch ❷ copy clerk in an organization or in the army
【文体】type of writing;literary form;style
【文武】❶civil and military skills ❷〈书〉statecraft and military exploits
【文献】document;literature of historical value:历史～ historical documents
【文选】selected works;literary selections
【文学】literature
【文艺】literature and art
【文娱】entertainment
【文摘】abstract;digest
【文章】❶ essay; article ❷ literary works;writings ❸hidden meanings;implied meaning
【文职】civilian post;civil service
【文字】❶ characters; script; writing ❷ written language

纹 (wén) lines;veins;grain
【纹理】veins;grain
【纹路】lines or grain of an object

闻 (wén) ❶hear ❷news; story ❸wellknown; famous ❹ repute; reputation ❺smell
【闻名】❶famous;well known;renowned ❷be familiar with sb's name
【闻人】well-known figure;famous man;celebrity:社会～ social celebrities

吻 (wěn) ❶lips ❷kiss ❸an animal's mouth
【吻合】be identical;coincide

紊 (wěn) disorderly;confused
【紊乱】disorder;chaos;confusion

稳 (wěn) ❶steady;firm ❷sure;certain
【稳步】with steady steps
【稳产】stable yields
【稳当】❶reliable;secure;safe ❷steady; stable
【稳定】❶stable;steady ❷stabilize
【稳固】firm;stable
【稳健】❶ firm; steady ❷ steady; sure; reliable;

not rash;not reckless

【稳练】steady and proficient

【稳妥】safe;reliable

【稳重】(of speech , behaviour) steady;staid;sedate

问 (wèn) ❶ask ❷ask after;inquire after ❸interrogate;examine ❹hold responsible

【问安】wish sb. good health

【问答】questions and answers:～题 problems to be answered

【问号】question mark

【问候】send one's respects to;extend greetings to

【问津】ask for the ferry

【问世】(of a work) be published;come out

【问题】❶question;problem ❷trouble

【问心】examine one's conscience

【问讯】inquire;ask;send one's regards to

【问诊】inquiry; interrogation, one of the four methods of diagnosis;diagnose through interrogation

【问罪】denounce;condemn

WO

涡 (wō) whirlpool;eddy

【涡流】❶ the circular movement of a whirling fluid;eddy ❷〈物〉eddy current;vortex fluid;eddying flow

窝 (wō) ❶nest ❷lair;den ❸a hollow part of the human body;pit ❹harbour;shelter ❺litter;brood

【窝藏】harbour

【窝点】lair;den;hideout

【窝工】hold up in the work through poor organization

【窝囊】❶ feel vexed; be annoyed ❷ good-for-nothing;hopelessly stupid;worthless wretch

【窝棚】shack;shed;shanty

【窝头】steamed bread of corn,sorghum,etc.

【窝赃】harbour stolen goods;conceal booty

我 (wǒ) ❶I ❷we ❸self ❹my ❺our

【我们】we

卧 (wò) ❶lie ❷crouch;sit

【卧病】be confined to bed;be laid up

【卧车】❶sleeping car; sleeping carriage; sleeper ❷automobile;car;sedan

【卧床】lie in bed;～不起 become bed-ridden

【卧铺】sleeping berth;sleeper

【卧室】bedroom

握 (wò) hold;grasp

【握别】shake hands at parting

【握力】grip

【握拳】make a fist;clench one's fist

【握手】shake hands;clasp hands

WU

乌 (wū) ❶crow ❷black;dark

【乌龟】tortoise

【乌亮】glossy black;jet-black

【乌鸦】crow

【乌有】nothing;naught

【乌鱼】snakehead

【乌云】black clouds;dark clouds

【乌贼】cuttlefish;inkfish

污 (wū) ❶dirt;filth ❷dirty;filthy ❸corrupt ❹defile;smear

【污点】spot;stains;blemish;smirch

【污垢】dirt;filth

【污秽】〈书〉❶filthy;foul ❷dirt;filth

【污迹】smudge

【污蔑】❶slander ❷sully

【污泥】mud;mire;sludge

【污染】pollute

【污辱】❶ humiliate; insult ❷ defile; sully; tarnish

【污浊】dirty;muddy;foul;filthy

【污渍】stain;smear;grease sticking to an object

巫 (wū) shaman;witch

【巫婆】witch;sorceress

【巫师】wizard;sorcerer

【巫医】witch doctor

鸣 (wū)〈象〉toot;hoot;zoom

【鸣呼】〈象〉❶〈书〉alas; alack ❷die ❸all is lost

【鸣咽】sob;whimper

诬 (wū) accuse falsely

【诬告】bring a false charge against

【诬害】calumniate;malign

【诬赖】falsely incriminate

【诬蔑】slander;vilify

【诬陷】frame sb.

【诬栽】calumniate and frame; fabricate a charge against sb.

屋 (wū) ❶house ❷room

【屋顶】roof;housetop

【屋脊】ridge (of a roof)

【屋架】roof truss
【屋面】roofing;materials that cover a roof
【屋檐】eaves
【屋宇】〈书〉house
【屋子】room

无 (wú) ❶nothing;nil;not have;without ❷not ❸regardless of

【无比】incomparable;matchless
【无边】boundless
【无补】of no help;of no avail
【无不】all without exception;invariable
【无产者】proletarian
【无常】variable;changeable
【无偿】free;gratis;gratuitous
【无成】accomplish nothing:一事～ accomplish nothing
【无耻】shameless;impudent
【无从】have no way (of doing sth.);not be in a position (to do sth.)
【无度】immoderate;excessive
【无端】for no reason at all
【无法】unable;incapable;no way
【无妨】there's no harm;may (or might) as well
【无非】nothing but;no more than;simply;only
【无干】have nothing to do with
【无辜】innocent
【无关】have nothing to do with;be unconcerned
【无害】harmless;do no harm to
【无华】simple and unadorned
【无稽】unfounded;fantastic;absurd
【无几】very few;very little;hardly any
【无际】boundless;limitless;vast
【无价】priceless;invaluable
【无尽】endless;inexhaustible;infinite; limitless
【无愧】feel no qualms;have a clear conscience
【无赖】rascally;scoundrelly;blackguardly
【无礼】rudeness
【无理】unreasonable;unjustifiable
【无力】unable;incapable;powerless
【无聊】❶bored ❷senseless;silly;stupid
【无论】regardless of
【无能】❶incompetent ❷incapable
【无情】merciless;ruthless;heartless
【无穷】infinite;endless
【无色】colourless;transparent
【无声】noiseless;silent;still
【无视】ignore;disregard;defy
【无数】countless;innumerable
【无双】unparalleled;unrivalled;matchless
【无损】cannot harm;be harmless;will not lessen
【无条件】unconditional;without preconditions
【无望】hopeless

【无味】❶tasteless;unpalatable ❷dull;insipid;uninteresting
【无畏】fearless;dauntless
【无物】empty;devoid of substance
【无误】no mistake;errorless
【无暇】have no time;be too busy
【无限】infinite;limitless;boundless;immeasurable
【无效】of no avail;to no avail;invalid;null and void
【无心】❶not be in the mood for ❷not intentionally;unwittingly;inadvertently
【无须】need not;not have to
【无业】be out of work;be unemployed;～游民 vagrant
【无遗】nothing left
【无疑】beyond doubt;undoubtedly
【无益】unprofitable;useless;no good
【无垠】〈书〉boundless;vast
【无用】useless;of no use
【无缘】have no chance or luck (to do sth.)
【无知】ignorant
【无阻】without hindrance;unimpeded; unobstructed
【无罪】innocent;not guilty

五 (wǔ) five

【五彩】five colours of blue, yellow, red, white and black
【五官】five sense organs (ears,eyes,mouth,nose and tongue);facial features
【五角星】five-pointed star
【五金】hardware
【五月】May
【五洲】the five continents;the whole world

午 (wǔ) noon;midday

【午饭】lunch;midday meal
【午后】afternoon
【午睡】take (or have) a nap after lunch
【午休】noon break;midday rest;noontime rest;lunch hour
【午夜】midnight

武 (wǔ) ❶military ❷connected with boxing skill;sword play ❸valiant;fierce

【武备】〈书〉military preparations;armed forces and weaponry (or armaments)
【武打】acrobatic fighting in Chinese opera or motion picture
【武断】❶make an arbitrary decision;make a subjective conclusion ❷(of speech, act) arbitrary;subjective

【武功】❶〈书〉military accomplishments（or a-chievements，exploits）❷martial arts skills
【武将】military officer；general
【武力】❶force ❷military force；armed might
【武器】❶ weapon；arms ❷ tool used to wage struggle：思想～ ideological weapon
【武术】wushu，martial arts such as shadowbox-ing swordplay，etc.
【武侠】knight；swordsman
【武装】❶arms；military equipment；battle outfit ❷arm；equip；provide troops with arms ❸ar-my；armed forces

侮 （wǔ）insult；bully

【侮骂】abuse；call sb. names；hurl insults
【侮蔑】despise；look down on
【侮辱】insult；humiliate；subject sb. to indignities

舞 （wǔ）❶dance ❷move about as in a dance ❸dance with sth. in one's hands ❹flour-ish；wield；brandish
【舞伴】dancing partner
【舞弊】irregularities；embezzlement；fraudulent
【舞步】dancing step：～ 轻 盈 graceful dancing steps
【舞场】dance hall；ballroom
【舞蹈】dance
【舞动】wave；brandish
【舞会】dance；ball
【舞曲】dance music；dance
【舞台】stage
【舞厅】ballroom；dance hall
【舞艺】dancing skill
【舞姿】dancer's posture and movements

兀 （wù）〈书〉❶rising to a height；towering ❷bald
【兀傲】〈书〉supercilious；arrogant；haughty
【兀立】stand upright
【兀自】〈方〉still

务 （wù）❶affair；business ❷be engaged in；devote one's efforts to ❸must；be sure to
【务必】must；be sure to
【务农】be engaged in agriculture
【务期】must；be sure to

【务求】must；be sure to have sth. done
【务实】deal with concrete matter relating to work；be pragmatic
【务须】must；be sure to：～准时到达 be sure to arrive in good time

物 （wù）❶thing；matter ❷the outside world as distinct from oneself ❸content；sub-stance
【物产】products；produce
【物价】prices
【物件】thing；article
【物理】innate laws of things；physics
【物力】material resources
【物品】article；goods
【物色】look for；seek out；choose
【物体】body；object
【物证】material evidence
【物质】matter；substance；material
【物种】〈生〉species
【物资】goods and materials

误 （wù）❶mistake；error ❷miss ❸hinder；impede ❹by mistake；be accident
【误差】error
【误场】（of an actor）fail to turn up for a per-formance
【误导】mislead；lead astray
【误点】late；behind schedule
【误工】❶delay one's work ❷loss of working time
【误会】❶misunderstand ❷misunderstanding
【误解】misunderstand；misread
【误期】exceed the time limit；be behind schedule
【误伤】❶accidentally injure ❷accidental injury
【误事】hold things up；cause delay in work or business
【误诊】❶ make a wrong diagnosis ❷ miss the chance for diagnosis and treatment

恶 （wù）loath；dislike；hate 另见 ě，è

悟 （wù）realize；awaken

【悟彻】understand thoroughly；realise completely
【悟性】power of understanding；comprehension

W

X x

xī

夕 (xī) ❶sunset ❷evening; night

【夕烟】evening mist
【夕阳】the setting sun
【夕照】the glow of the setting sun; evening glow

西 (xī) ❶west ❷occidental; western

【西班牙】Spain
【西半球】the Western Hemisphere
【西餐】the Western-style food; European food
【西方】❶ the west; westward ❷ the West; the Occident
【西风】❶west wind; westerly wind ❷Western social mores and culture
【西服】Western-style clothes; suit
【西瓜】watermelon
【西式】Western style: ～糕点 Western pastry
【西洋】the West; Western world
【西药】Western medicine
【西医】❶ Western medicine（as distinguished from traditional Chinese medicine）❷a doctor trained in Western medicine
【西装】Western-style clothes

吸 (xī) ❶inhale; breathe in; draw ❷suck(liquids) ❸ absorb; suck up ❹ attract; draw to oneself

【吸尘器】vacuum-cleaner; dust collector
【吸毒】take drugs
【吸附】absorb
【吸力】suction; attraction
【吸取】absorb; draw
【吸食】suck; take in（liquid foods, narcotic drugs, etc.）
【吸收】❶ absorb; suck up; draw ❷ enroll; admit; recruit
【吸吮】suck; absorb
【吸引】attract; draw; fascinate

希 (xī) ❶hope ❷rare; scarce

【希冀】〈书〉hope for; wish for

【希腊】Greece
【希求】❶hope for ❷wish; desire
【希望】prospect; hope; wish; expect

昔 (xī) former times; the past

【昔年】〈书〉in years gone by; in the past
【昔日】former days

析 (xī) ❶divide; separate ❷analyse

【析居】〈书〉(of family members) live separately
【析疑】〈书〉resolve a doubt; clear up a doubtful point

牺 (xī) sacrifice

【牺牲】❶ sacrifice; lay down one's life; sacrifice oneself ❷sacrifice; give up; do sth. at the expense of

息 (xī) ❶breath ❷news ❸cease; stop ❹rest ❺grow; multiply ❻interest

【息怒】don't be angry; calm one's anger
【息止】cease

奚 (xī)

【奚落】scoff at; taunt; gibe

悉 (xī) ❶all; entirely ❷know; learn; be informed of

【悉心】devote all one's attention; take the utmost care

淅 (xī) 〈书〉wash rice

【淅沥】〈象〉the sound of a light rain, a breeze, falling leaves, etc.
【淅淅】〈象〉the sound of gentle wind, light rain or snow

惜 (xī) ❶cherish; value highly; use sparingly; care for tenderly ❷spare; grudge stint ❸ have pity on; feel sorry for

【惜别】be reluctant to part; hate to see sb. go
【惜阴】cherish every minute of one's life

稀 (xī) ❶rare; scarce; uncommon ❷sparse; scattered ❸watery; thin

【稀薄】thin; rare
【稀饭】porridge; rice or millet gruel

【稀罕】❶scarce；uncommon ❷value as a rarity；cherish；treasure

【稀客】rare visitor

【稀烂】❶completely mashed；pulpy ❷smashed to smithereens

【稀奇】strange；curious：～古怪 eccentric

【稀少】rare；few；scarce

【稀世】rare on earth：～珍宝 rare treasure

【稀疏】sparse；thin；here and there；few and far between

【稀松】❶sloppy；lax：作风～ sloppy style of work ❷no good；bad

【稀有】rare

溪（xī）small stream；brook；rivulet

【溪涧】mountain stream

【溪流】brook；rivulet

熄（xī）extinguish；put out

【熄灯】turn off the light

【熄火】extinction

【熄灭】go out；die out

嬉（xī）〈方〉play；sport

【嬉闹】laugh and frolic

【嬉戏】〈书〉play；sport

【嬉笑】be laughing and play

习（xí）❶practice；exercise；review ❷get accustomed to；be used to ❸habit；custom；usual practice

【习惯】❶be accustomed to；be used to；be inured to ❷custom；habit

【习俗】custom；convention

【习题】exercises (in school work)

【习艺】learn a trade，skill，handicraft，etc.

【习用】habitually use：～语 idiom

【习字】practise penmanship；do exercises in calligraphy

【习作】❶do exercises in composition ❷an exercise in composition，drawing，etc.

席（xí）❶ mat ❷ seat；place ❸ feast；banquet；dinner

【席地】on the ground

【席卷】❶roll up like a mat；take away everything ❷sweep across；engulf

【席面】dishes served at a feast

【席位】seat

袭（xí）❶make a surprise attack on；raid ❷follow the pattern of；carry on as before

【袭击】raid

【袭取】take over (sth. long been in use in the past)

【袭用】take over；follow

【袭占】take (a place) by surprise

媳（xí）daughter-in-law

【媳妇】❶son's wife；daughter-in-law ❷the wife of a relative of the younger generation

檄（xí）〈书〉❶a call to arms (in ancient time) ❷announce or denounce in such a call

【檄文】❶an official call to arms ❷an official denunciation of the enemy

洗（xǐ）❶wash；bathe ❷baptize ❸redress；right ❹kill and loot；sack ❺develop；process ❻clear；erase ❼shuffle

【洗尘】give a dinner to greet a visitor from afar

【洗涤】wash；cleanse

【洗劫】loot；sack

【洗礼】❶baptism ❷a severe test

【洗脸】wash one's face

【洗钱】money laundering

【洗手】❶wash one's hands of sth. ❷quit a job

【洗漱】wash one's face and rinse one's mouth

【洗刷】❶ wash and brush；scrub ❷ wash off；clean oneself of

【洗衣机】washing machine

【洗印】develop and print photos；process

【洗澡】take a bath；have a bath

喜（xǐ）❶happy；delighted；pleased ❷happy event；occasion for celebration ❸pregnancy ❹like

【喜爱】like；love；be fond of

【喜报】bulletin of glad tidings

【喜出望外】 be overjoyed (at an unexpected gain，good news，etc.)；be pleasantly surprised

【喜从天降】a heaven-sent for tune；a heavenly blessing—an unexpected piece of good fortune；a gift from the gods

【喜好】be fond of；be keen on；love

【喜欢】like；love；be fond of；be keen on

【喜酒】drinks offered to guests at a wedding

【喜剧】comedy

【喜乐】happiness

【喜气】cheerful countenance or atmosphere

【喜庆】joyous；jubilant

【喜人】heartening；gratifying

【喜色】happy expression；joyful look

【喜事】a happy event；a joyous occasion

【喜糖】wedding sweets or candies

【喜帖】wedding invitation card

【喜幸】〈书〉delighted；rejoicing

【喜讯】happy news；good news

【喜悦】happy；joyous

【喜滋滋】feeling greatly pleased；filled with joy

戏 (xì) ❶play；sport ❷make fun of；joke ❸drama；play；show

【戏法】conjuring；jugglery；tricks；magic

【戏剧】drama；play；theatre

【戏剧家】playwright；dramatist

【戏迷】theatre fan

【戏弄】make fun of；play tricks on；tease；kid

【戏台】stage

【戏谑】banter；crack jokes

【戏言】❶joke；joking remarks；一句～ a joking remark ❷jest；banter；～身后事 jest about arrangements after one's death

【戏院】theatre

【戏装】theatrical costume；stage costume

【戏子】〈古〉actor；actress；opera singer

系 (xì) ❶system ❷department(in a college)；faculty ❸relate to；bear on ❹feel anxious；be concerned ❺tie；fasten ❻be

【系列】series；set

【系念】〈书〉be anxious about；worry about；feel concerned about

【系数】coefficient；ratio；modulus

【系统】❶system ❷systematic

细 (xì) ❶thin；slender ❷in small particles；fine ❸thin and soft ❹fine；delicate ❺careful；detailed ❻minute

【细胞】cell

【细别】❶fine distinction；fine difference ❷make (or draw) fine distinctions between

【细布】muslin

【细发】〈方〉fine；smooth

【细工】fine handcraft work

【细节】details；particulars

【细菌】germ；bacterium

【细密】❶fine and closely woven；close ❷meticulous

【细目】detailed catalogue；specific item；detail

【细嫩】delicate；tender

【细腻】❶fine and smooth ❷minute；exquisite

【细情】details

【细软】❶valuables；jewelry；expensive clothing and other valuables；收拾～ take stock of one's valuables ❷fine and soft

【细弱】thin and delicate；slim and fragile

【细碎】in small，broken bits

【细微】fine；subtle

【细小】very small；tiny；fine

【细心】careful；attentive

【细账】itemized account

【细致】careful；meticulous painstaking

【细作】spy；secret agent

xia

瞎 (xiā) ❶blind ❷aimlessly；groundlessly；foolishly

【瞎扯】gabble；prattle；matter；waffle；talk nonsense

【瞎话】untruth；lie；说～ tell a lie；tell a fib

【瞎闹】act senselessly；mess about；fool around；be mischievous

【瞎说】talk groundlessly or irresponsibly；talk nonsense；～一通 talk rubbish

【瞎眼】blind；lose one's eyesight

【瞎子】❶blind person ❷〈方〉blind seed；blind ear of grain

匣 (xiá) a small box；a small case；casket

【匣子】small box or case with a lid；casket

侠 (xiá) ❶a person adept in martial arts and given to chivalrous conduct（in olden times）❷having a strong sense of justice and ready to help the weak；chivalrous

【侠骨】〈书〉chivalry

【侠义】having a high sense of justice and ready to help the down and under：～心肠 chivalrous temperament

狭 (xiá) narrow

【狭隘】narrow

【狭长】long and narrow：～的山谷 long and narrow valley

【狭小】cramped；房屋～ narrow and small house

【狭义】narrow sense

【狭窄】❶contracted；cramped；narrow ❷（of mind，knowledge，etc.）narrow；limited；心地～ intolerant；narrow-minded

遐 (xiá) ❶far；distant ❷lasting；long

【遐迩】〈书〉far and near

【遐龄】advanced age；venerated age

【遐想】daydream

瑕 (xiá) ❶flaw in a piece of jade ❷flaw；defect；shortcoming

【瑕疵】flaw；blemish

辖 (xiá) have jurisdiction over；administer；govern

【辖区】area under one's jurisdiction

【辖制】〈书〉control

霞 (xiá) rosy clouds；morning or evening glow

【霞光】rays of morning or evening sunlight：～

万道 a myriad of sun rays

下 (xià) ❶ below；down；under ❷ lower；inferior ❸ next；latter ❹ downward；down ❺ descend；get off ❻ (of rain，snow，etc.) fall ❼ issue；deliver；send ❽ go to ❾ put in；cast

【下巴】❶ the lower jaw ❷ chin

【下摆】 lower hem of a gown，jacket or shirt

【下班】 off duty；knock off；come off work

【下辈】❶ children and grandchildren；offspring ❷ younger generation of a family

【下笔】 put pen to paper；begin to write or paint：～千言 finish writing a thousand words at one go

【下操】❶ have drills ❷ finish drilling

【下策】 a bad plan (or advice)；an unwise decision (or move)；the worst thing to do

【下层】 (of organization，social ladder，etc.) lower levels：～社会 lower rung of the social ladder

【下场】 end；fate

【下车】 get off

【下沉】❶ sink；submerge ❷ go down；cave in

【下船】❶ go ashore；disembark ❷〈方〉get down into a junk；board；go aboard

【下垂】 hang down；droop

【下次】 next time

【下达】 make (an order，instruction，etc.) known (or transmit) to subordinates

【下蛋】 (of a bird or reptile) lay eggs

【下等】 low grade；inferior：～货 low-grade goods

【下地】 go to the fields：～劳动 work in the fields

【下跌】 (of water level，price，etc.) fall；drop；plunge

【下饭】❶ (of dishes) go with rice ❷ go well with the rice

【下放】 (of power) be decentralized；delegate power to lower level

【下岗】 come or go off sentry duty

【下海】❶ go to sea ❷ (of fisherman) go fishing on the sea

【下级】 subordinate；lower level：～组织 lower level organization

【下贱】❶ of humble origin；low in social status ❷ abject；low；mean；degrading

【下降】 descend；go or come down；drop；fall；decline：气温～ drop in the temperature

【下酒】❶ go with wine ❷ go well with wine

【下课】 finish class；class is dismissed or over

【下来】 come down

【下令】 send down an order；issue an order；order：～解散 issue an order to disband an organization

【下流】❶ lower reaches (of a river) ❷ lowdown；mean；off colour；near the bone

【下落】 where-about；drop；fall

【下水】 downstream；downriver：～船 downriver boat

【下台】❶ step down from the stage or platform ❷ fall out of power；leave office

【下头】❶ below；lower level ❷ subordinate

【下文】❶ the sentence，paragraph or chapter that follows；context ❷ further development；follow-up

【下午】 afternoon；part of day from 12 a. m. to 12 p. m. but often from noon until sunset

【下陷】 sunken；hollow；眼眶～ sunken eyes

【下泻】❶ (of water) flow down：～不畅 impeded flow ❷ have loose bowels

【下雪】 snow

【下药】❶ prescribe medicine；对症～ suit the medicine to the illness ❷ put poison on or into sth.

【下游】❶ low reaches ❷ backward position；不可甘居～。Don´t resign yourself to backwardness.

【下雨】 rain

吓 (xià) frighten；scare

【吓唬】 frighten；scare；intimidate

【吓人】 spooky；frightening

夏 (xià) summer

【夏令营】 summer camp

【夏眠】 aestivation

【夏收】 summer harvest

【夏天】 summer

【夏装】 summer clothing；summer wear

罅 (xià)〈书〉crack；rift；chink

【罅漏】〈书〉crack；chink；〈喻〉loophole；shortcoming

【罅隙】〈书〉crack；rift；chink

xiān

仙 (xiān) celestial being；immortal

【仙境】 fairyland；wonderland；paradise

【仙女】 female celestial；fairy maiden

【仙人】 celestial being；immortal

【仙人球】〈植〉ball cactus

【仙人掌】〈植〉cactus

先 (xiān) ❶ early; before; first; advance ❷ ancestor

【先辈】elder generation; ancestors

【先导】guide; forerunner

【先锋】vanguard; van

【先后】❶ being early or late; priority; order ❷ successively; one after another

【先进】❶ advanced: ~工作者 advanced worker ❷ advanced individual or unit: 后进赶~ those behind trying to catch up with those ahead

【先决】prerequisite: ~条件 prerequisite; precondition

【先例】precedent

【先烈】martyr

【先令】shilling

【先前】before; previously

【先人】❶ ancestor; forefather ❷ my late father

【先行】❶ go ahead of the rest; start off before the others ❷ beforehand; in advance

【先兆】omen; portent; sign; indication

【先哲】〈书〉a great thinker of the past; sage

【先知】❶ a person of foresight ❷ prophet

纤 (xiān) fine; minute
另见 qiàn

【纤巧】dainty; delicate

【纤柔】soft and slender; delicate and soft

【纤弱】slim and fragile

【纤维】fiber; staple

【纤悉】〈书〉extremely detailed

【纤细】very thin; slender

【纤纤】〈书〉long and slender

【纤小】tenuous

掀 (xiān) lift (a cover, etc.)

【掀风鼓浪】raise a storm; stir up trouble

【掀起】❶ lift; raise ❷ surge ❸ set off (a movement)

鲜 (xiān) ❶ fresh ❷ bright-colored; bright ❸ delicious; tasty ❹ delicacy
另见 xiǎn

【鲜果】fresh fruit

【鲜红】bright red; scarlet

【鲜花】(fresh) flowers

【鲜货】❶ fresh fruit or vegetables ❷ fresh aquatic foods ❸ fresh medicinal herbs

【鲜丽】bright-coloured and beautiful: 衣着色彩~ be beautifully dressed in bright colours

【鲜亮】〈方〉pretty; beautiful; handsome: 长得~ look pretty

【鲜美】delicious; tasty

【鲜明】❶ bright ❷ distinct; clear-cut

【鲜嫩】fresh and tender: ~的藕 fresh and tender lotus roots

【鲜血】blood

【鲜艳】bright-colored; gaily-colored

闲 (xián) ❶ not busy; idle ❷ not in use; unoccupied; lying idle ❸ spare time; free time; leisure

【闲扯】chat; engage in chitchat

【闲逛】saunter; stroll; loaf

【闲话】❶ digression ❷ complaint; gossip

【闲居】stay at home idle; lead a quiet life

【闲空】free time; spare time; leisure

【闲聊】chat

【闲钱】spare cash; spare money

【闲人】unoccupied person; idler

【闲暇】leisure

【闲心】leisurely mood; free, unburdened mind

贤 (xián) ❶ virtuous; worthy; able ❷ a worthy person; an able and virtuous person

【贤德】❶ virtue and kindheartedness ❷ virtuous: ~女子 virtuous and kindhearted woman

【贤惠】virtuous

【贤良】〈书〉able and virtuous

【贤明】sagacious

【贤能】❶ virtuous and able: ~之士 virtuous and talented person ❷ virtuous and talented person

【贤哲】good and wise man

咸 (xián) salted; salty

【咸菜】salted vegetable; pickles

【咸盐】〈方〉table salt; salt

衔 (xián) ❶ hold in the month ❷ harbour; bear ❸ link up; join ❹ rank; title

【衔接】join; link up

【衔命】〈书〉carry out an order; be ordered to; receive an order

【衔冤】have a simmering sense of injustice

舷 (xián) board

【舷窗】porthole

【舷梯】❶ gangway ladder; accommodation ladder ❷ (boarding) ramp

嫌 (xián) ❶ suspicion ❷ ill will; resentment; enmity; grudge ❸ dislike; mind; complain of

【嫌弃】dislike and avoid; cold-shoulder

【嫌恶】disgust; loathe; detest

【嫌疑】suspicious: ~犯 suspect | 不避~ unafraid of other people's suspicion

【嫌怨】grudge; resentment; enmity

【嫌憎】be disgusted with; dislike intensely

显 (xiǎn) ❶ be apparent; be obvious; be noticeable ❷ show; display; manifest ❸ illustrious and influential

【显达】illustrious and influential

【显得】look；seem；appear

【显贵】❶occupying a distinguished position；of high position；illustrious：～人物 illustrious person of high position ❷high officials (in former times)

【显露】become visible；appear；manifest itself

【显明】obvious；manifest；distinct；marked：～的对照 sharp contrast；striking contrast

【显能】show off one's talent or competence

【显然】obviously；evidently；clearly

【显示】show；demonstrate；manifest

【显微镜】microscope

【显现】appear；show

【显像管】kinescope；picture tube

【显效】produce or show effect

【显形】show one's (true) colours；betray oneself

【显眼】showy；conspicuous

【显要】powerful and influential

【显著】marked；remarkable；noticeable；striking；outstanding

险 (xiǎn) ❶place difficult of access；a narrow pass ❷danger；peril；risk ❸vicious；venomous ❹by a hair's breadth；by inches；nearby

【险隘】strategic pass；defile

【险地】❶strategic vantage point ❷perilous situation；dangerous circumstances

【险恶】❶dangerous；perilous ❷vicious；sinister

【险峰】perilous peak

【险关】a strategic pass；difficult of access

【险境】dangerous situation

【险峻】dangerously steep；precipitous

【险情】dangerous state or situation

【险胜】win by a narrow margin

【险象】dangerous sign；dangerous symptom

【险阻】(of roads)dangerous and difficult

鲜 (xiǎn) little；rare
另见 xiān

【鲜见】rarely seen；seldom met with

县 (xiàn) county

【县城】county town；county seat

【县令】county magistrate

【县治】seat of a county government；county seat

现 (xiàn) ❶present；current；existing ❷in time of need ❸(of money)on hand ❹cash；ready money ❺show；appear；visible

【现场】❶scene (of an accident) ❷site；spot

【现成】ready-made

【现存】in stock；extant

【现货】〈商〉merchandise on hand；spots

【现今】nowadays；these days

【现金】cash

【现款】cash；ready money

【现年】present age

【现任】at present hold the office of；current in office

【现时】now；at present

【现实】❶reality；actuality ❷realistic；practical；real；actual

【现世】this life：～报 retribution in this life

【现势】current situation；trend of the times

【现象】phenomenon；appearance

【现行】in force；in operation

【现形】reveal one's true features；betray oneself

【现役】❶active service；active duty ❷on active service

【现有】now available；existing

【现在】now；today；at present

【现职】incumbent；present position (or job，post)

【现状】present situation；existing state of affairs；current situation

限 (xiàn) ❶limit；bounds ❷set a limit；restrict

【限定】restrict；set a limit to

【限度】limit；limitation

【限额】norm；quota

【限价】❶fix the official price ❷the (officially) fixed price

【限量】set bound to；limit the quantity of

【限令】orders to be executed within a time limit

【限期】❶set a time limit ❷time limit；deadline

【限于】be limited to；be confined

【限制】restrict；limit；confine

线 (xiàn) ❶thread；string；wire ❷line；route ❸brink；verge ❹clue；thread

【线段】line segment

【线路】line；circuit

【线圈】coil

【线索】clue；thread

【线条】line；contour；figure

【线头】❶end of a thread ❷an odd piece of thread

【线性】〈数〉linear

【线装本】thread-bound edition

【线装书】thread-bound Chinese book

宪 (xiàn) ❶statute ❷constitution

【宪兵】military police；military policeman

【宪法】constitution；charter

【宪警】gendarme and police

【宪章】charter

陷（xiàn）❶ pitfall；trap ❷ get stuck or bogged down ❸ sink；cave in ❹ frame（up）❺（of a town, etc.）be captured；fall ❻ defect；deficiency

【陷害】frame(up)

【陷阱】pit；snare；trap；pitfall

【陷落】❶ subside；sink in；cave in ❷ fall into enemy's hands ❸ sink (or fall) into；land oneself in；foundering；depression

【陷入】❶ sink (or fall) into；land oneself on；be caught in ❷ be absorbed in；be deep in；be lost in

【陷身】fall into；land in

【陷阵】break through enemy lines：冲锋～ charge against the enemy lines；fight bravely in battles

献（xiàn）❶ offer；present；dedicate；donate ❷ show；put on；display

【献策】offer advice；make suggestions

【献词】congratulatory message：新年～ New Year message

【献技】show one's skill (in a performance)

【献礼】present a gift

【献媚】butter up；make up to；try to ingratiate oneself with：～取宠 curry favour with

【献身】devote oneself to；dedicate oneself to；give one's life for

【献艺】show one's skill；give a performance

xiang

乡（xiāng）❶ country；countryside；village；rural area ❷ native place；home village or town ❸ township

【乡愁】homesickness

【乡村】village；countryside；rural area

【乡间】village；country

【乡里】❶ home village or town：荣归～ return to one's home village in glory ❷ fellow villagers or townspeople：看望～ pay a visit to one's fellow villagers

【乡亲】fellow villager；villagers；folks；local people

【乡情】affection for one's home village or home town

【乡曲】〈书〉remote countryside

【乡思】homesickness

【乡俗】local customs；village customs

【乡土】native soil；one's native land；local

【乡下】countryside；village

【乡音】accent of one's native place；local accent：～未改 one's local accent remains unchanged

【乡镇】❶ villages and towns ❷ small towns

相（xiāng）each other；one another；mutually 另见 xiàng

【相安】get along in peace：～无事 live in peace with each other

【相比】compare

【相称】match；suit

【相成】complement each other

【相持】be locked in a stalemate：意见～不下 each side sticks to his own stand

【相处】get along

【相传】❶ hand down or pass on from one to another ❷ tradition has it that...

【相当】❶ match；balance；correspond to；be equivalent to；be equal to ❷ suitable；fit；appropriate

【相等】be equal

【相对】❶ opposite ❷ relative

【相反】opposite；contrary

【相仿】similar；much alike；more or less the same

【相逢】meet (by chance)；come across

【相符】conform to；tally with；correspond to

【相隔】be separated by；be apart；be at a distance of

【相关】be interrelated

【相好】❶ be on intimate terms ❷ intimate friend

【相互】mutual；each other

【相继】in succession；one after another

【相间】alternate with

【相交】❶ intersect ❷ make friends with

【相近】close；near：年岁～ about the same age

【相距】apart；away from

【相看】❶ look at each other ❷ regard；treat

【相连】be linked together；be joined

【相配】be suited to each other；be well-matched；be a good match

【相亲】size up a prospective mate in an arranged meeting

【相劝】persuade

【相让】❶ exercise forbearance；give in；make concessions ❷ defer to each other politely

【相商】consult each other

【相识】be acquainted with each other

【相似】resemble；be similar；be alike

【相通】communicate with each other；be interlinked

【相同】identical；the same；alike

【相投】be congenial；agree with each other：气味～ be birds of a feather

【相向】❶ in opposite directions：～而行 go in opposite directions ❷ face to face；facing

each other

【相像】resemble;be similar;be alike

【相信】believe in;be convinced of

【相依】be interdependent

【相应】corresponding;relevant

【相映】reflect each other;set each other off;form a contrast：～生辉 set each other off wonderfully

【相与】❶get along with sb.;deal with sb. ❷each other;mutually;together：～议论 talk with each other;discuss together

【相知】❶be well acquainted with each other ❷bosom friend;great friend

【相助】come to sb.'s help;aid;彼此～help each other

香（xiāng）❶fragrant;sweet-smelling;scented ❷savory;appetizing;delicious

【香槟酒】champagne

【香波】shampoo

【香肠】sausage

【香醇】fragrant and mellow；～的美酒 mellow wine

【香菇】mushroom

【香花】fragrant flowers

【香蕉】banana

【香水】perfume;scent

【香烟】cigarette

【香油】sesame oil

【香皂】perfumed soap

箱（xiāng）box;case;trunk

【箱笼】boxes and baskets;luggage;baggage

【箱子】box;case;trunk

详（xiáng）❶detailed;minute ❷details;particulars ❸know clearly

【详备】detailed and all-inclusive

【详尽】detailed

【详明】full and clear

【详情】detailed information

【详实】full and accurate

【详悉】❶know the details ❷detailed and complete

【详细】detailed;minute

降（xiáng）❶surrender;capitulate ❷subdue;vanquish;tame

　　另见 jiàng

【降敌】surrender to the enemy

【降伏】yield;surrender and acknowledge allegiance

【降服】yield;surrender;break in（a wild horse）

【降顺】yield and pledge allegiance to

享（xiǎng）enjoy

【享福】enjoy a happy life

【享乐】lead a life of pleasure;indulge in creature comforts

【享年】die at the age of：～七十四 die at the age of 74

【享受】❶enjoy ❷enjoyment

【享用】fruition;enjoy the use of;enjoy

【享有】enjoy（rights,prestige,etc.）

响（xiǎng）❶sound;noise ❷make a sound;ring ❸noisy;loud ❹echo

【响彻】resound through

【响动】sound of movement;sound of sth. astir

【响亮】loud and clear;resounding

【响声】sound;noise

【响头】resonant kowtow;knock one's head on the floor with a bang

【响应】respond;answer

想（xiǎng）❶think;ponder ❷suppose;reckon;consider ❸want to;would like to ❹remember with longing;miss

【想必】most probably

【想法】idea;opinion;what one has in mind

【想见】know from supposition;gather

【想念】miss;long to see again

【想起】remember;recollect

【想象】imagine;fancy

【想要】be going to;want

向（xiàng）❶direction ❷face;turn towards ❸take sb's part;side with;be partial to ❹to;towards;in the directions of

【向背】support and oppose

【向导】guide

【向火】〈方〉warm oneself in front of a fire：围炉～warm oneself in front of a fireplace

【向来】always;all along

【向前】forward;ahead

【向上】upward;up

【向外】outward

【向往】yearn for;look forward to

【向阳】be exposed to the sun;have a southern exposure

【向右】towards the right

【向隅】stand in a corner;feel left out

项（xiàng）❶nape（of the neck）❷sum（of money）❸term

【项背】person's background

【项链】necklace

【项目】item

相 (xiàng) ❶ looks；appearance ❷ bearing；posture ❸ look at and appraise ❹ photograph ❺ phase
另见 xiāng
【相册】photo album
【相机】camera
【相貌】looks；appearance
【相片】photograph；photo
【相声】comic dialogue；cross-talk
【相书】book about physiognomy
【相术】physiognomy
【相位】phase
【相纸】photographic paper；printing paper

象 (xiàng) ❶ elephant ❷ appearance；shape；image ❸ resemble ❹ look as if；seem ❺ such as；like
【象鼻】trunk
【象棋】(Chinese) chess
【象形】pictograph
【象牙】ivory
【象征】❶ symbolize；signify；stand for ❷ symbol

像 (xiàng) ❶ be like；resemble；take after ❷ look as if；seem ❸ such as；like ❹ likeness；portrait；picture ❺ image
【像样】up to the mark；presentable
【像章】badge with sb's likeness on it

橡 (xiàng) ❶ oak ❷ rubber tree
【橡胶】rubber
【橡皮】rubber；eraser

xiao

枭 (xiāo) ❶ owl ❷ brave；valiant ❸ smuggler
【枭将】〈书〉a brave general
【枭雄】a fierce and ambitious person；a formidable man

骁 (xiāo) valiant；brave；spirited
【骁将】〈书〉a valiant general
【骁骑】〈书〉a brave cavalryman
【骁勇】〈书〉brave；valiant

逍 (xiāo)
【逍遥】free and unfettered

消 (xiāo) ❶ disappear；vanish ❷ cause to disappear；eliminate；dispel remove ❸ pass (time) in a leisurely way；while away(time)
【消沉】low-spirited；downhearted；depressed
【消除】eliminate；remove；dispel；clear up
【消毒】disinfect；sterilize
【消防】fire control；fire fighting

【消费】consume
【消耗】consume；use up；expend
【消化】digest
【消极】❶ negative ❷ passive；inactive
【消减】diminish；decrease：食 欲 ～ decrease in appetite
【消灭】❶ perish；pass away；become extinct；die out ❷ eliminate；abolish；wipe out
【消磨】idle away
【消气】calm one's anger；cool down；be mollified
【消失】disappear；vanish；die away
【消食】help digestion
【消逝】fade away；elapse
【消受】❶ enjoy；benefit from：无福 ～ have no luck to enjoy ❷ stand；endure；bear
【消退】abate；subside；decrease
【消亡】wither away；die out
【消息】news；information
【消夏】spend summer in a leisurely way
【消闲】❶ while away one's leisure time；fill one's spare time ❷ easy；at leisure
【消炎】diminish inflammation；reduce inflammation；dephlogisticate

萧 (xiāo)
【萧墙】〈书〉screen wall facing the gate of a house
【萧飒】〈书〉desolate；bleak and chilly
【萧瑟】❶ rustle in the air ❷ bleak；desolate
【萧条】❶ desolate；bleak ❷ depression
【萧萧】〈书〉❶ sound of a neighing horse or a whistling wind, etc. ❷ grizzled and sparse

硝 (xiāo) ❶ nitre；saltpetre ❷ taw (animal skin)
【硝石】nitre；saltpetre
【硝酸】〈化〉nitric acid
【硝酸铵】ammonium nitrate
【硝酸盐】nitrate
【硝烟】smoke of gunpowder

销 (xiāo) ❶ melt ❷ cancel；annul ❸ sell；market ❹ expend；spend
【销案】close a case
【销毁】destroy by melting or burning
【销魂】be so distressed or happy that one's soul departs from one's body
【销假】report back (to one's superior) after a leave of absence
【销路】sale；market
【销售】sale；market
【销赃】❶ sell stolen goods ❷ dispose of stolen goods
【销账】cancel or remove from an account；

write off

潇 (xiāo)〈书〉❶(of water) deep and clear ❷ Xiao River,a tributary of the Xiang River

【潇洒】(of a person's appearance, demeanour, carriage, etc.)natural and unrestrained

【潇潇】❶(of wind and rain) driving; whistling and pattering ❷drizzling; drizzly

霄 (xiāo)❶clouds ❷sky; heaven

【霄壤】heaven and earth

嚣 (xiāo) clamour; hubbub; din

【嚣杂】noisy

【嚣张】rampant; arrogant; aggressive

小 (xiǎo)❶small ❷young

【小百货】small articles of daily use

【小班】junior kindergarten

【小半】less than half; the lesser (or smaller) half

【小报】tabloid

【小辈】junior members of a family

【小便】(of humans) urinate; piss; void; pass (or make) water

【小刀】pocket knife

【小队】maniple

【小贩】pedlar; vendor

【小节】small matter

【小结】preliminary summary; brief sum-up

【小姐】miss; young lady

【小康】relatively comfortable life

【小麦】wheat

【小卖】snack

【小米】millet

【小跑】trot; jog

【小朋友】❶ children ❷ little friend; little boy or girl

【小憩】take a short rest

【小气】❶stingy, mean, miserly ❷(方) narrow minded; petty

【小钱】❶copper coin; copper ❷ small amount of money

【小巧】small and delicate; 身体～ (of the body) be small and delicately shaped

【小巧玲珑】small and exquisite

【小人】❶ person of low social status ❷ mean man; base person; vile character; villain; ～得志 small man intoxicated by success

【小人物】unimportant person; nobody; cipher; nonentity

【小时】hour

【小事】trifle; minor matter

【小视】look down upon; underestimate; slight

【小睡】nap; short sleep

【小说】novel; fiction

【小偷】petty thief; sneak; pilferer

【小写】small letter

【小心】take care; be careful; be cautious

【小型】small-sized; small-scale; miniature; ～会议 small-scale meeting

【小学】primary school; elementary school

【小指】little finger or toe

【小传】brief biography

【小子】〈书〉❶younger male generation; 后生～ young greenhorns ❷ term of address used by those elder to their juniors

【小组】group

【小坐】sit for a short while; ～片刻 sit for a short while

晓 (xiǎo)❶dawn; daybreak ❷ know ❸tell; let sb. know

【晓得】know

【晓示】explicitly tell; notify; ～众人 explicitly tell everybody

【晓市】morning market

孝 (xiào)❶filial piety ❷mourning

【孝服】mourning (dress)

【孝敬】give presents (to one's elders or superiors)

【孝顺】show filial; obedience

【孝心】filial sentiments; filial devotion; 一片～ one's filial devotion

【孝子】❶dutiful son ❷son in mourning

肖 (xiào) resemble; be like

【肖像】portrait; portraiture

校 (xiào)❶ school ❷ field officer; field grade officer

　　另见 jiào

【校风】school spirit; atmosphere of a school

【校官】field officer; field grade officer

【校规】school regulations

【校花】campus belle

【校徽】school badge

【校刊】school magazine; college journal

【校庆】anniversary of the founding of a school or college

【校舍】school building

【校训】school motto

【校友】alumnus or alumna

【校园】campus; school yard

【校长】❶ headmaster; principal ❷

president；chancellor

【校址】the location of a school or a college

哮（xiào）❶ heavy breathing；wheeze ❷ roar；howl

【哮喘】〈医〉asthma

笑（xiào）❶smile；laugh ❷ridicule；laugh at

【笑柄】butt；laughingstock；joke

【笑哈哈】with a laugh；laughingly

【笑话】❶joke；jest ❷laugh at；ridicule

【笑脸】smiling；～相迎 greet with a genial smile

【笑料】sth. funny or laughable；laughing stock；joke

【笑貌】smiling face；smiling expression

【笑容】smiling expression；smile

【笑声】laugh；laughter

【笑语】cheerful talk interspersed with hearty laughter；欢声～ cheerful chatting and laughter

效（xiào）❶ effect ❷imitate；follow the example ❸ devote（one's energy or life）to；render

【效法】follow the example of

【效仿】imitate；follow the example of

【效果】effect；result

【效劳】work in the service；work for

【效力】❶render a service to；serve ❷effect

【效率】efficiency

【效能】efficacy；useful functions contained inside sth.

【效益】beneficial result；benefit

【效应】〈物〉effect

【效用】effective and useful；effectiveness；usefulness

【效忠】pledge loyalty to；devote oneself heart and soul to；fealty

xie

些（xiē）some

【些个】some；several；a few

【些微】slightly；a little；a bit

【些须】a little；a few：～识得几字 know a few words

【些许】a little；a few：～小利 some small benefits

歇（xiē）❶have a rest ❷stop；knock off

【歇班】be off duty；have time off

【歇乏】have a rest in order to relieve fatigue after working

【歇脚】stop on the way for a rest

【歇气】stop and take a break

【歇手】stop doing sth.

【歇息】❶have a rest ❷put up for the night；go to bed

【歇业】close a business；go out of business

协（xié）❶joint；common ❷assist

【协办】do sth. in assistance；assist in handling

【协定】agreement；accord

【协和】coordinate；harmonize

【协会】association；society

【协商】consult；be in consultation with；talk things over

【协调】harmonize；bring into line；coordinate

【协同】cooperate with；work in coordination with

【协议】agreement

【协约】sign a treaty after negotiations：～国 the Entente countries

【协助】assist；help；give assistance；provide help

【协作】cooperate；coordinate；combine

邪（xié）evil；heretical；weird；irregular

【邪道】evil ways；infamous behaviour；vice

【邪恶】evil；wicked；vicious

【邪念】wicked idea；evil thoughts

【邪气】perverse trend or style；evil influence

【邪说】heresy；heretical ideas；fallacy

【邪行】evil deed；wicked conduct

胁（xié）❶the upper part of the side of the human body ❷coerce；force

【胁持】force sb. to submit

【胁从】be an accomplice under duress

【胁迫】force

挟（xié）❶hold sth. under the arm ❷coerce；force sb. to submit to one's will ❸harbor

【挟持】❶seize sb. on both sides by the arms ❷hold sb. under duress

【挟制】force sb. to do one's bidding

偕（xié）together with；in the company of

【偕老】live together to a ripe old age

【偕同】in the company by；along with

斜（xié）slanting；inclined

【斜度】degree of inclination；gradient

【斜晖】〈书〉slanting rays of the setting sun

【斜路】wrong path

【斜率】slope

【斜面】oblique plane

【斜坡】slope

【斜射】cast oblique rays（or beams）on an object

【斜视】strabismus
【斜眼】wall-eye;cross-eye
【斜阳】setting sun

谐 (xié) ❶in harmony;in accord ❷come to an agreement ❸humorous
【谐和】harmonious;concordant
【谐趣】wit and humour
【谐调】harmonious;concerted
【谐谑】banter
【谐音】❶homophony ❷〈音〉partials

携 (xié) ❶carry;take along ❷take sb. by the hand;hold sb. by the hand
【携带】carry;take along
【携手】hand in hand

鞋 (xié) shoe
【鞋帮】uppers of a shoe;the two sides of a shoe
【鞋带】shoelace;shoestring
【鞋底】sole
【鞋垫】shoe-pad;insole
【鞋粉】shoe powder;powder for polishing shoes
【鞋跟】heel
【鞋匠】shoemaker;cobbler
【鞋油】shoe polish (or cream)

写 (xiě) ❶write ❷compose ❸describe;depict ❹paint;draw
【写法】❶style of writing;literary style ❷style of handwriting;penmanship
【写景】describe scenery
【写生】paint or sketch from nature;do a painting of an object or a landscape:静物～ still-life painting
【写信】write letters
【写照】portrayal;portraiture
【写真】❶portray a person ❷portrait
【写作】writing

泄 (xiè) ❶let out;discharge ❷leak ❸give vent to;vent
【泄底】reveal or expose what is at the bottom of sth.
【泄愤】give vent to one's pent-up anger:借端～ give vent to one's anger on an excuse
【泄洪】discharge flood water
【泄劲】lose heart;lose confidence
【泄漏】leak;divulge;give away
【泄露】let out;reveal
【泄密】divulge a secret;let out (or give away) a secret;betray confidential matters
【泄气】❶lose heart ❷disappointing

泻 (xiè) ❶flow swiftly;rush down;pour out ❷have loose bowels;have diarrhoea

卸 (xiè) ❶unload;discharge ❷remove;strip ❸get rid of;shirk
【卸车】unload (goods,etc.)from a vehicle
【卸货】discharge cargo;disburden;breaking bulk
【卸肩】❶lay down one's load ❷shirk one's responsibility;resign from one's office
【卸任】be relieved of one's office;be removed from one's office
【卸载】unload the cargo from a vehicle or a ship
【卸责】shirk responsibility and shift the blame onto others:推诿～ shift blame onto another person
【卸妆】remove ornaments and formal dress
【卸装】remove stage makeup and costume

亵 (xiè) ❶treat with irreverence;be disrespectful ❷obscene;indecent
【亵渎】blaspheme;profane;pollute
【亵慢】〈书〉show disrespect:言语～ salacious words

谢 (xiè) ❶thank ❷apologize;make an apology ❸decline ❹wither
【谢忱】gratitude;thankfulness
【谢词】thank-you speech;short address expressing thanks at a ceremony
【谢恩】express gratitude for a favour
【谢绝】politely refuse;decline:婉言～ decline politely
【谢客】❶decline to receive visitors;not be seeing any visitors ❷thank a guest for his visit
【谢帖】note of thanks;thank-you note
【谢谢】thanks;thank you
【谢意】gratitude;thankfulness
【谢罪】apologize for an offence;offer one's apology for a fault:登门～ call someone to make an apology

懈 (xiè) slack;lax
【懈怠】sluggish;lax;slack
【懈气】relax one's exertions;lose one's drive;slack off

xin

心 (xīn) ❶heart;mind ❷center
【心爱】love
【心肠】❶heart;intention ❷state of mind
【心潮】tidal surge of emotion;surging thoughts and emotions:～澎湃 feel an upsurge of emotion
【心胆】❶heart and gall bladder ❷determination and courage
【心得】what one has learned from work,study,etc.

【心底】❶ the bottom of one's heart ❷〈方〉intention

【心地】❶ person's mind, character, moral nature, etc.: ～坦白 candid; open ❷ state of mind: ～轻松 have an ease of mind; relax

【心毒】wicked; vicious; malignant

【心烦】❶ be vexed; go hot and cold; be perturbed; vexation; ❷ dyspeptic

【心服口服】be sincerely convinced

【心腹】❶ trusted subordinate; henchman; reliable agent; bosom friend ❷ confidential ❸ chest and abdomen

【心甘】willing

【心肝】conscience; sense of justice

【心狠】cruel; merciless

【心机】thinking; scheming: 枉费 ～ rack one's brains in vain

【心急】impatient; short-tempered: ～如焚 burning with impatience

【心计】calculation; scheming; planning

【心间】in one's mind; in one's heart

【心焦】anxious; worried

【心境】state (or frame) or mind; mental state; mood

【心宽】broad-minded; tolerant of anything undesirable

【心理】psychology; mentality

【心里】in the heart; at heart; in (the) mind

【心力】mental and physical efforts

【心灵】❶ clever; intelligent ❷ heart; soul; spirit

【心领】understand tacitly: ～ 神会 understand tacitly; readily take a hint

【心律】rhythm of the heartbeat

【心目】❶ memory; mood; mind's eye ❷ mind; view

【心切】eager; impatient; anxious: 求胜 ～ be anxious to gain victory

【心情】state of mind; mood

【心软】be softhearted; be tenderhearted

【心神】mind; state of mind

【心声】heartfelt wishes; aspirations; thinking

【心思】❶ thought; idea ❷ thinking; thoughts

【心酸】be grieved; feel sad

【心算】mental arithmetic

【心态】mentality

【心疼】❶ love dearly ❷ make one's heart ache; feel sorry; be distressed

【心跳】palpitation

【心头】mind; heart: 记在 ～ bear (or keep) in mind

【心细】careful; scrupulous

【心胸】breadth of mind

【心虚】be afraid of being found out; with a guilty conscience

【心血】thoughts and energies; painstaking care (or effort); painstaking labour: 花费 ～ expend one's thoughts and energies

【心意】❶ regard; kindly feelings ❷ meaning; intention; purpose

【心硬】hard-hearted; stone-hearted; callous; unfeeling

【心愿】wish; aspiration; cherished desire

【心脏】the heart

【心醉】be enchanted or fascinated

辛 (xīn) ❶ hot (in taste, flavour, etc.); pungent ❷ hard; laborious ❸ suffering

【辛苦】hard; laborious; hardworking; undergo; go to a great troubles

【辛辣】❶ pungent; hot; bitter ❷ sharp, bitter or pungent language: ～的讽刺 bitter irony; biting sarcasm

【辛劳】pains; toil

【辛勤】diligent; industrious; hardworking

【辛酸】❶ hot and sour ❷ sad; bitter; miserable: ～泪 sad tears; hot and bitter tears

欣 (xīn) glad; happy; joyful

【欣然】joyful; with pleasure

【欣赏】enjoy; appreciate; admire

【欣慰】be grateful

【欣喜】glad; joyful; happy

【欣羡】〈书〉admire

新 (xīn) ❶ new; fresh; up-to-date ❷ newly; freshly; recently ❸ brand-new; unused

【新版】new edition

【新兵】new recruit; recruit

【新潮】❶ new trend; new fashion: 文艺 ～ new trends in literature and art ❷ fashionable; modish: ～发型 new hair style; modish hairdo

【新义】new meaning of a word

【新意】new meaning; new conception

【新风】new custom; new trend; new practice: 校园～ trend on the campus

【新欢】new sweetheart (esp. a woman): 另有 ～ have a new sweetheart; be taken up with another woman

【新婚】newly-married: ～ 夫妇 newly-married couple; newly-weds

【新交】❶ make a new acquaintance; make a new friend ❷ new friends

【新近】recently; lately; in recent times

【新居】new house; new residence

【新郎】bridegroom

【新年】New Year

【新娘】bride

【新奇】strange；novel；new

【新人】❶people of new ethic standards；people of a new type：～新事 new people and new things ❷new talent；new personality：文艺～ new people in the literature and art circles ❸ new comer；new recruit ❹reformed person

【新任】newly appointed：～局长 newly appointed bureau director

【新生】newborn；newly born

【新手】newcomer；new hand；greenhorn；raw recruit

【新闻】news

【新鲜】❶fresh ❷new；novel；strange

【新兴】newly emerging；new and developing

【新雅】fresh and elegant；诗句～ fresh and elegant lines

【新颖】nascent；new and original；novel：题材～ original in choice of subject (or theme)

【新作】new literary or art work：新人～ new work by a new author

信 (xìn) ❶true；real ❷confidence；trust；faith ❸believe ❹profess faith in；believe ❺at will；at random；without plan ❻sign；evidence ❼letter；mail ❽message；word；information

【信步】take a leisure stroll；walk aimlessly

【信从】trust and follow the advice of：盲目～ trust blindly

【信贷】credit

【信风】trade wind；trade

【信封】envelop

【信服】completely accept；be convinced

【信函】letters；私人～ personal letters

【信号】signal

【信汇】mail transfer(M/T)

【信笺】letter paper；writing paper

【信件】mail；letter

【信赖】trust；have faith in；depend on

【信念】faith；belief；conviction

【信任】trust；have confidence in；have trust in；believe in

【信实】❶trustworthy；honest；reliable：为人～ be honest and reliable ❷true and reliable：史料～ true and reliable historical data

【信使】messenger；courier

【信守】abide by；stand by

【信条】article of faith

【信简】pillar-box；mailbox

【信徒】believer；disciple；follower

【信托】trust；entrust

【信物】authenticating object；token；keep sake；定情～ keepsake for engagement；object confirming one's engagement

【信息】❶information；news；message ❷〈数〉information

【信箱】❶letter box；mailbox ❷post-office box (P. O. B.)

【信心】confidence；faith

【信仰】faith；belief；conviction

【信义】good faith；faith

【信意】at random；at will；as one pleases：～胡闹 be given to making trouble

【信用】trustworthiness；credit

【信誉】prestige；reputation；credit

【信纸】letter paper；writing paper

xing

兴 (xīng) prosper；rise；prevail 另见 xìng

【兴办】initiate；set up

【兴奋】be excited

【兴奋剂】dope；excitant

【兴国】rejuvenate a country：科学～ make a country strong by developing sciences；rejuvenate a country through science

【兴建】build；construct

【兴隆】prosperous；thriving；flourishing

【兴起】rise；spring up；be on the upgrade

【兴盛】prosperous；in the ascendant

【兴师】〈书〉send an army；dispatch troops：～问罪 send a punitive expedition

【兴衰】rise and decline；rise and fall

【兴叹】〈书〉heave a sigh；lament；bemoan

【兴亡】rise and fall

【兴旺】prosper；flourish；thrive

【兴修】start construction

【兴许】perhaps；maybe

星 (xīng) ❶star ❷heavenly body

【星光】starlight

【星火】spark

【星际】interplanetary；interstellar：～空间 interplanetary space

【星空】starry sky；star-studded sky；starlit sky

【星期】week

【星期日】Sunday

【星期一】Monday

【星体】celestial body

【星系】galaxy

【星星】tiny spot；speck：～点点 tiny spots；

bits；pieces

【星夜】starlit（*or* starry）night

【星云】〈天〉nebula

猩（xīng）〈动〉orangutan

【猩红】scarlet；bloodred

【猩猩】〈动〉orangutan

惺（xīng）

【惺忪】not yet fully open on waking up

【惺惺】❶〈书〉clear-headed；awake ❷ wise；intelligent

腥（xīng）❶ raw meat or fish ❷ having the smell of fish，seafood，etc.

【腥臭】stinking smell（as of rotten fish）；stench

【腥气】❶offensive smell of fish，seafood，etc. ❷ stinking；fishy

刑（xíng）❶ punishment ❷ torture；corporal punishment

【刑场】execution ground

【刑罚】〈法〉penalty；punishment

【刑法】penal code

【刑期】〈法〉term of imprisonment；prison term

【刑事】〈法〉criminal；penal

【刑讯】inquisition by torture；extort a confession by torture

【刑侦】criminal investigation

【刑种】categories of punishment

行（xíng）❶go ❷travel ❸do；perform ❹behavior；conduct ❺all right；ok
另见 háng

【行车】drive a vehicle：～执照 driving license or driver's license

【行程】❶route or distance of travel ❷course：历史发展～ course of historical development

【行船】sail a boat；navigate

【行道】preach one's political doctrine：立身～ conduct oneself by preaching one's political doctrine

【行动】❶move about；get about ❷act；take action ❸action；operation

【行好】act charitably；be merciful；be charitable

【行贿】bribe；offer a bribe；resort to bribery

【行迹】whereabouts；tracks（of a person）；traces：～无定 wander about；lead a vagrant life；have no fixed whereabouts

【行将】〈书〉be about to；be just going to；be the verge of：～就道 be about to set out on a journey

【行劫】commit robbery；rob：拦路～ waylay and rob

【行进】march forward；advance：～路线 march route

【行径】act；action

【行乐】〈书〉indulge in pleasures；seek amusement；make merry

【行礼】salute（bow，raise hand，etc.）

【行李】luggage；baggage

【行猎】〈书〉go hunting

【行旅】traveller；wayfarer：～往来 stream of travellers coming and going

【行囊】〈书〉travelling bag carried for a trip

【行期】date of departure

【行窃】steal；thieve

【行人】pedestrian

【行使】exercise；perform；wield

【行驶】go；ply；travel

【行事】❶behaviour；conduct：言谈～ speech and conduct ❷ act；handle matters：～谨慎 act prudently

【行为】action；behavior；product

【行文】❶ style or manner of writing；organization and expression of ideas：～简练 succinctly write ❷（of a government office）send an official communication to other organizations

【行星】planet

【行刑】carry out a death sentence；execute

【行凶】commit physical assault or murder；do violence：持刀～ assault a person with a knife

【行医】practise medicine：挂牌～ practise medicine with a license

【行政】administrative：～单位 administrative unit

【行装】luggage

【行踪】whereabouts；track

【行走】walk；go on foot

形（xíng）❶form；shape ❷body；entity ❸appear；look ❹compare；contrast

【形成】take shape；form

【形迹】❶ person's movements and expression：～可疑 of suspicious appearance；suspicious-looking ❷ trace；mark；sign：不留～ betray nothing in one's expression and movements ❸ manners；formality；etiquette：不拘～ without formality；not standing on ceremony

【形容】describe

【形容词】〈语〉adjective

【形式】form；shape

【形势】❶terrain ❷ situation；circumstance

【形似】likeness in from or appearance；formal likeness

【形态】❶form；shape；pattern ❷formation
【形体】❶figure；body；shape of the body ❷form and structure；文字的～ form and structure of Chinese characters
【形象】image；figure
【形状】form；appearance；shape

型 (xíng) ❶mold ❷model；type；pattern
【型号】model；type
【型心】core；part of a mould which forms the interior of a hollow casting

省 (xǐng) ❶examine oneself critically ❷visit ❸become conscious；be aware
另见 shěng
【省察】examine oneself critically；examine one's thoughts and conduct
【省亲】pay a visit to one's parents or elders
【省视】call upon；pay a visit to；～双亲 pay a visit to one's parents

醒 (xǐng) ❶regain consciousness；sober up；come to ❷wake up；be awake ❸clear in mind ❹be striking；catch one's attention
【醒豁】clear；explicit
【醒酒】dispel the effects of alcohol；sober up
【醒来】wake up
【醒目】be striking；attract attention
【醒悟】come to realize the truth；suddenly see the light

兴 (xìng) mood or desire to do sth.；interest；excitement
另见 xīng
【兴会】sudden flash of inspiration；brain wave
【兴趣】interest；taste
【兴味】interest；饶有～ with keen interest
【兴致】interest；mood to enjoy

杏 (xìng)〈植〉apricot
【杏仁】apricot kernel；almond

幸 (xìng) ❶good fortune；good luck ❷rejoice ❸luckily；luckily
【幸存】survive
【幸而】luckily；fortunately
【幸福】❶happiness；well-being ❷happy
【幸好】luckily；fortunately
【幸亏】fortunately；luckily
【幸免】escape by sheer luck；have a narrow escape
【幸事】a piece of good fortune；a stroke of luck；blessing
【幸喜】fortunately；luckily
【幸运】good fortune；good luck

性 (xìng) ❶nature；character；disposition ❷property；quality ❸sex
【性别】sexual distinction；sex
【性感】sex appeal；sexiness
【性格】nature；disposition；temperament
【性急】impatient；short-tempered
【性价比】performance-to-price patio
【性命】life
【性能】function；performance；property
【性情】disposition；temperament；temper
【性质】quality；nature；character
【性状】shape and properties；properties；character
【性子】❶temper ❷strength；potency

姓 (xìng) surname；family name；clan name
【姓名】surname and personal name；full name
【姓氏】surname

悻 (xìng)
【悻然】enraged
【悻悻】angry；resentful

xiong

凶 (xiōng) ❶inauspicious；ominous ❷bad for crops ❸fierce；ferocious ❹terrible；fearful ❺act of violence；murder
【凶案】murder case
【凶暴】fierce and brutal
【凶残】savage and ruthless
【凶恶】fierce；ferocious；fiendish
【凶犯】murderer
【凶狠】fierce and malicious；fierce and cruel
【凶横】fierce and arrogant；rude and ferocious
【凶狂】fierce；savage；ferocious
【凶猛】violent；ferocious
【凶气】fierce manner；ferocious expression
【凶器】a tool or weapon for criminal purposes；a lethal weapon
【凶杀】homicide；murder
【凶神】demon；fiend
【凶手】murder；assassin
【凶险】dangerous and dreadful
【凶相】ferocious features；fierce look
【凶兆】ill omen；boding of evil

兄 (xiōng) elder brother
【兄弟】brother
【兄长】respectful form of address for one's male friend.

汹 (xiōng)

【洶洶】 sound of turbulent waves

【洶涌】 surging; turbulent; tempestuous

胸 (xiōng) ❶thorax; chest; breast; bosom ❷ mind; heart

【胸部】 chest; breast

【胸怀】❶ mind; heart ❷ keep in the mind

【胸襟】 breadth of mind; mind

【胸口】 pit of the stomach; chest

【胸脯】 chest

【胸围】 chest measurement

【胸针】 brooch

雄 (xióng) ❶male ❷grand; imposing ❸powerful; mighty

【雄辩】 convincing argument

【雄大】 full of power and grandeur

【雄风】❶〈书〉strong wind ❷ awe-inspiring bearing; stately appearance

【雄厚】 rich; solid; abundant

【雄浑】 vigorous and firm; forceful

【雄健】 powerful; vigorous

【雄劲】 vigorous; robust; powerful

【雄威】 full of power and grandeur; strong and imposing; awe-inspiring

【雄伟】 grand; magnificent; imposing

【雄心】 great ambition; lofty aspiration

【雄壮】 strong; majestic; powerful

【雄姿】 majestic appearance; heroic posture

熊 (xióng)〈动〉bear

【熊猫】〈动〉panda

【熊熊】 flaming; ablaze; raging：～ 的 烈 火 raging flames

【熊掌】 bear's paw

xiu

休 (xiū) ❶stop; cease; end ❷rest

【休会】 adjourn

【休假】 have a holiday; take a vacation

【休克】 shock

【休眠】 dormancy

【休戚】 weal and woe; joys and sorrows

【休憩】 have (or take) a rest; rest

【休息】 have a rest; take a rest

【休闲】 have a leisure life

【休想】 don't imagine (that it's possible)

【休学】 suspend one's schooling without losing one's status as a student

【休养】 recuperate; convalesce

【休业】❶ suspend business ❷ come to an end; wind up

【休战】 truce; ceasefire; armistice

【休整】 rest and reorganization

【休止】 stop; cease; measured

修 (xiū) ❶ decorate; embellish ❷ repair; mend; overhaul ❸write; compile

【修补】 mend; patch up; repair; revamp

【修长】 tall and thin

【修辞】〈语〉rhetoric

【修订】 revise

【修短】〈书〉length

【修复】 restore; repair

【修改】 revise; correct; alter; makeover; modify

【修盖】 build (houses)

【修好】〈书〉foster cordial relations between states

【修剪】 prune; trim

【修建】 build; construct

【修理】 repair; mend; fix

【修面】〈方〉shave; have a shave

【修女】 nun; sister

【修身】 cultivate one's moral character

【修饰】❶decorate; adorn; embellish ❷make up and dress up ❸polish (a piece of writing) ❹ qualify; modify ❺〈语〉modifier

【修书】❶compile a book ❷write a letter

【修行】 practice Buddhism or Taoism

【修养】❶ accomplishment; training; mastery ❷ self-cultivation

【修业】 study at school

【修正】 revise; amend; correct

【修筑】 build; construct; put up

羞 (xiū) ❶shy; bashful ❷shame; disgrace

【羞惭】 shamed; 满面～ be shamefaced

【羞耻】 shame; sense of shame

【羞愤】 ashamed and resentful

【羞愧】 ashamed; abashed

【羞怯】 shy; timid; sheepish

【羞人】 feel embarrassed or ashamed

【羞辱】❶shame; humiliation; dishonor ❷ humiliation; put sb. to shame

【羞涩】 shy; embarrassed

【羞恶】〈书〉feel ashamed of and disgusted at sth. or sb.

朽 (xiǔ) ❶rotten; decayed ❷senile

【朽败】 decayed; rotten

【朽坏】 decayed; rotten

【朽烂】 rotten

【朽木】❶rotten wood or tree ❷a hopeless case; a good-for-nothing

宿 (xiǔ) (used for counting nights)
另见 sù

秀 (xiù) ❶elegant;beautiful ❷excellent

【秀才】〈古〉scholar;intellectual;skillful writer
【秀丽】pretty;beautiful
【秀美】graceful;elegant
【秀媚】pretty and charming
【秀气】❶delicate;elegant;fine ❷delicate and well-made
【秀色】beautiful scenery or appearance
【秀雅】tasteful and refined;graceful;elegant

袖 (xiù) sleeve

【袖手旁观】put the hands in the sleeves and look on —have nothing to do with a thing
【袖章】armband;sleeve badge
【袖珍】pocket-size;pocket
【袖子】sleeve

绣 (xiù) ❶embroider ❷embroidery

【绣房】〈古〉a young lady's bedchamber
【绣工】❶embroidery worker ❷embroidery;embroidery work
【绣花】embroider;do embroidery
【绣像】❶tapestry portrait;embroidered portrait ❷exquisitely drawn portrait
【绣鞋】embroidered shoes

XU

须 (xū) ❶must;have to ❷wait;await ❸beard;mustache ❹palpus;feeler

【须发】beard and hair
【须根】fibrous root
【须眉】beard and eyebrows
【须要】must;have to

虚 (xū) ❶emptiness;void ❷empty;unoccupied ❸different;timid ❹in vain ❺false;nominal ❻humble;modest ❼weak;in poor health ❽abstract;theory;guiding principles

【虚报】make a false report
【虚词】〈语〉function word;form word
【虚辞】〈书〉exaggerations;empty words
【虚度】waste;spend time in vain
【虚浮】impractical;superficial
【虚构】fairy;make up;fabricate
【虚汗】abnormal sweating due to general debility or nervousness
【虚幻】unreal;illusory
【虚假】false;sham
【虚惊】false alarm
【虚空】hollow;void
【虚夸】exaggerative;bombastic;boastful
【虚名】false reputation;undeserved reputation

【虚拟】❶invented;fictitious ❷suppositional
【虚荣】false pride;vanity
【虚弱】weak;feeble
【虚设】existing in name only;nominal
【虚实】false or true;the actual situation (as of the opposing side)
【虚伪】two-faced;hypocritical
【虚心】open-minded;modest
【虚造】fabricate

需 (xū) ❶need;want;require ❷necessaries;need

【需求】requirement;demand
【需要】need;want;require;demand

徐 (xú) slowly;gently

【徐步】〈书〉walk slowly (or leisurely);stroll
【徐缓】slowly
【徐徐】〈书〉slowly;gently

许 (xǔ) ❶praise ❷promise ❸allow;permit ❹maybe;perhaps

【许多】many;much;a lot of;a great deal of;lots of;a great many;a number of;dozens of
【许久】for a long time;for ages;for long
【许可】❶permit;allow ❷consent;permission
【许诺】make a promise;promise
【许配】betroth one's daughter to;be betrothed to
【许愿】❶make a vow (to a god) ❷promise sb. a reward for some service

栩 (xǔ)

【栩栩】vivid;lively

旭 (xù) brilliance of the rising sun

【旭日】the rising sun

序 (xù) ❶order;sequence ❷arrange in order ❸introductory;initial ❹preface

【序列】alignment;〈数〉sequence
【序目】preface and table of contents
【序幕】prologue
【序曲】overture
【序数】ordinal number
【序文】preface;foreword
【序言】preface;foreword;introduction

叙 (xù) ❶talk;chat ❷narrate;relate ❸assess;appraise ❹introductory;initial

【叙别】have a farewell talk
【叙功】assess sb.'s services
【叙旧】talk about the old days
【叙事】narrate;recount
【叙述】recite;narrate;recount;relate
【叙说】tell;narrate
【叙谈】chat;chitchat

畜 (xù) raise (domestic animals)

【畜产】livestock products
【畜牧】raise livestock or poultry
【畜牧业】animal husbandry; livestock husbandry; livestock farming
【畜养】raise(domestic animals)

绪 (xù) ❶ thread ❷ order in sequence or arrangement ❸ mental or emotional state ❹ task; cause

【绪论】introduction
【绪言】introduction

续 (xù) ❶ continuous; successive ❷ continue; extend; join

【续订】renew one's subscription
【续航】continue (or pursue) a journey without refueling
【续集】continuation; sequel
【续假】extend leave
【续借】renew
【续篇】continuation of a book (or an article); sequence
【续聘】continue to engage sb.; continue to employ sb.
【续弦】remarry after the death of one's wife

絮 (xù) ❶ (cotton) wadding ❷ sth. resembling cotton ❸ wad with cotton ❹ long-winded

【絮叨】garrulous; long-winded
【絮烦】tired; bored
【絮棉】cotton for wadding
【絮窝】do up a nest or lair with withered grass, feathers, etc.
【絮语】〈书〉❶ prattle on ❷ endless chatter

蓄 (xù) ❶ store up; save up ❷ grow ❸ entertain (ideas); harbor

【蓄洪】store flood water
【蓄积】store up; save up
【蓄谋】premeditate
【蓄念】harbour an idea
【蓄水】retain water
【蓄养】build up; accumulate
【蓄意】premeditated; deliberate

xuan

宣 (xuān) ❶ declare; proclaim; announce ❷ lead off (liquids); drain

【宣布】proclaim
【宣称】assert; declare; profess
【宣传】conduct propaganda; give publicity to
【宣读】read out (in pubic)
【宣告】declare proclaim

【宣讲】❶ explain and publicise (a policy, decree, etc.) ❷ preach (a religious doctrine)
【宣判】pronounce judgment
【宣示】declare openly; make publicly known
【宣誓】take an oath; swear an oath; make a vow; make a pledge
【宣言】declaration; manifesto
【宣扬】publicize; advocate
【宣战】declare war
【宣召】summon sb. to court; summon an audience

喧 (xuān) noisy

【喧哗】confused noise; uproar
【喧闹】bustle; racket
【喧嚷】clamour; din; hubbub
【喧扰】stir up a disturbance; make a commotion
【喧腾】noise and excitement; hubbub
【喧嚣】❶ noisy ❷ clamour; hullabaloo; din

玄 (xuán) ❶ black; dark ❷ profound ❸〈口〉unreliable; incredible

【玄奥】profound
【玄机】arcane truth
【玄妙】mysterious; abstruse
【玄想】fancy; imagination
【玄虚】deceitful trick

悬 (xuán) ❶ hang; suspend ❷ outstanding; unresolved ❸ feel anxious; be solicitous ❹ imagine ❺ far apart

【悬案】❶ pending criminal case; unsettled law case; a case of pendency ❷ outstanding issue; unsettled question
【悬垂】overhang
【悬浮】suspension
【悬挂】hang
【悬空】hang in the air
【悬赏】offer a reward (for)
【悬殊】great disparity
【悬想】imagine; fancy
【悬心】be worried about; be on tenterhooks
【悬崖】steep cliff; precipice

旋 (xuán) ❶ revolve; spin ❷ return; come back ❸〈书〉soon

【旋即】soon; before long; quickly
【旋律】〈音〉melody
【旋绕】curl up; wind around
【旋涡】whirlpool; vortex; eddy
【旋翼】rotor (wing)
【旋转】revolve; gyrate; rotate

选 (xuǎn) ❶ select; choose; pick ❷ elect ❸ selection; anthology

【选拔】select; choose

X

【选本】anthology; selected works
【选材】select suitable material
【选调】recruit
【选读】selected readings
【选段】aria
【选集】anthology; selected; works
【选辑】select and compile
【选举】elect
【选刊】❶select and publish❷periodicals exclusively carrying selected writings
【选录】select
【选民】voter; elector
【选派】select; detail; draft
【选票】vote; ballot
【选取】select; choose
【选任】select a suitable person for a post
【选手】contestant; player
【选送】select and recommend sb. (for a position or for admission to a school, etc.)
【选修】take as an elective course
【选样】sampling; sample
【选用】select and use; choose and apply
【选择】select; choose; opt
【选种】seed selection
【选中】pick on; decide on; settle on

炫 (xuàn) ❶dazzle ❷show off; display

【炫目】dazzling
【炫弄】show off; display; parade
【炫耀】make a display; show off; flaunt

绚 (xuàn) gorgeous

【绚烂】splendid; gorgeous
【绚丽】gorgeous; magnificent

xue

削 (xuē) pare; cut

【削壁】precipice; cliff
【削发】tonsure
【削价】cut the price; lower the price
【削减】cut (down); reduce
【削平】〈书〉wipe out; suppress; subdue
【削弱】weaken

学 (xué) ❶study; learn ❷imitate; mimic ❸learning; knowledge ❹subject of study ❺school; college

【学报】journal (of a college)
【学潮】student strike; a class boycott
【学费】tuition fee; tuition; school fee
【学分】credit
【学风】style of study

【学府】institution of higher learning; seat of learning
【学好】learn from a good example; emulate good
【学会】❶learn; master ❷academy; institute; association; society; learning society
【学籍】one's status as a student; one's name on the school roll
【学监】proctor
【学界】educational circles; field of education
【学科】discipline; subject; branch of learning
【学力】educational level; knowledge
【学历】educational background; a written account of one's education
【学龄】school age
【学年】school year; academic year
【学派】school; school of thought
【学期】term; semester; quarter
【学生】pupil; student
【学时】class hour; period
【学识】learning; knowledge; scholarly attainments
【学士】❶scholar ❷bachelor
【学塾】private school; family school
【学术】academic research; learning; science
【学说】theory; doctrine; teaching
【学童】pupil; primary school student
【学徒】trainee; apprentice
【学位】academic degree
【学问】study; learn; knowledge
【学习】study; learn; emulate
【学校】school
【学业】one's studies; school work
【学员】student; trainee
【学院】college; academy; institute
【学长】respectful term of address for a classmate
【学者】scholar; 青年～ young scholar
【学制】❶educational system; school system ❷length of schooling

雪 (xuě) ❶snow ❷wipe out; clean

【雪白】snow-white; snowy white; ～的墙壁 snow-white wall
【雪暴】snowstorm
【雪崩】snow slide; avalanche
【雪耻】avenge an insult
【雪糕】ice-cream
【雪恨】avenge
【雪花】snowflake
【雪茄】cigar
【雪亮】bright as snow; shiny
【雪片】flying snowflakes
【雪人】snowman; snow piled up in the shape of a

human being

【雪山】snow capped mountain

【雪线】snow line

【雪原】snowfield

血（xuè）❶blood ❷related by blood

【血案】murder case; bloody incident

【血仇】blood feud

【血管】blood vessel; vascullum; vessel

【血汗】sweat and blood; hard toil

【血红】blood red; as red as blood

【血迹】bloodstain

【血浆】blood plasma

【血泪】shed tears of blood when one cries with grief

【血亲】relatives by blood

【血球】〈医〉blood cell; blood corpuscle

【血肉】blood and flesh

【血色】redness of the face; colour

【血水】watery blood flowing out from a part of the body

【血统】blood relationship; blood lineage; descent

【血污】bloodstain

【血腥】reeking of blood; bloody

【血型】blood type

【血性】courageous and upright

【血压】blood pressure

【血液】lifeblood; lifeline

【血缘】ties of blood; consanguinity; relationship by birth

【血债】debt of blood; crime of slaughter

【血战】bloody battle; extremely fierce fight

【血渍】bloodstain

xun

勋（xūn）merit; meritorious service; achievement

【勋绩】meritorious service; outstanding contribution

【勋爵】❶a feudal title of nobility conferred for meritorious service ❷(in Great Britain) Lord

【勋劳】meritorious service

【勋业】〈书〉meritorious service; great achievements

【勋章】medal; decoration

熏（xūn）❶expose to smoke or fume; fumigate ❷treat (meat, fish, etc.) with smoke; smoke

【熏染】exert a gradual, corrupting influence on

【熏陶】nurture; edify

【熏蒸】sultry

【熏制】smoking

旬（xún）❶a period of ten days ❷a period of ten years in a person's age (applied only to old persons)

【旬刊】a publication appearing once every ten days

【旬日】ten days

寻（xún）look for; search; seek

【寻查】search; look for; seek

【寻常】ordinary; usual; common

【寻访】look for; try to locate; make inquiries about

【寻根】get to the bottom of sth.; investigate deeply into

【寻机】look for or seek an opportunity

【寻觅】seek; look for

【寻求】explore; go inquest of

【寻事】invite trouble; seek a quarrel; pick a fight on purpose

【寻味】chew sth. over; ruminate

【寻衅】pick a quarrel

【寻找】seek; look for: ～真理 seek truth

巡（xún）❶patrol; make one's rounds ❷round of drinks

【巡查】make one's rounds

【巡逻】patrol

【巡视】make an inspection tour

询（xún）ask; enquire; inquire

【询查】enquire about; demand; make enquiries

【询问】ask about

循（xún）follow; abide by

【循环】circulate; cycle

【循序】in proper order or sequence

训（xùn）❶instruct; admonish; give sb. a lecture ❷instructions; teachings ❸standard; model; example ❹critical explanation or interpretation of a text

【训斥】rebuke; dress down

【训导】instruct and guide

【训迪】〈书〉instruct and enlighten

【训话】give a dressing-down to one's subordinates

【训诲】〈书〉instruct; teach

【训诫】❶lesson; advise ❷rebuke

【训练】train; drill

【训示】allocution

讯（xùn）❶interrogate; question ❷information; news; message; dispatch

【讯号】radio signal; signal

【讯实】prove sth. to be true through interrogation

【讯问】❶ interrogate; question ❷ ask about; inquire

汛 (xùn) flood; high water

【汛期】flood season; high-water season

【汛情】flood situation; water level in flood season

迅 (xùn) fast; swift

【迅即】immediately; at once

【迅急】very fast; rapidly; at high speed

【迅疾】swiftly; rapidly

【迅捷】fast; agile; quick

【迅猛】swift and violent

【迅速】rapid; swift; speedy; prompt

驯 (xùn) ❶ tame and docile ❷ tame

【驯服】❶ docile; tame; tractable ❷ break; domesticate

【驯化】domestication; taming

【驯良】tractable; docile; tame and gentle

【驯顺】tame and docile; submissive

【驯养】raise and train (animals)

徇 (xùn) give into; submit to; comply with

【徇情】〈书〉act wrongly out of personal considerations

【徇私】bend the law to help one's friends or relatives

殉 (xùn) sacrifice one's life for

【殉国】give one's life for one's country

【殉节】die out of loyalty to one's country; commit suicide to defend her chastity

【殉难】die for (a just cause); die a martyr

【殉情】die for love

【殉葬】be buried alive with the dead

【殉职】die at one's post

X

Y y

yā

丫 (yā) bifurcation; fork

【丫鬟】 slave girl; servant girl

【丫头】 ❶〈方〉girl ❷slave girl

压 (yā) ❶press; weigh down ❷keep under control; control; quell ❸suppress; intimidate ❹approach; be getting near ❺pigeonhole; shelve ❻risk on sth.; stake

【压宝】 stake

【压倒】 overwhelm; overpower

【压低】 keep down; lower; reduce

【压顶】 bear down on one; weigh heavily on one

【压价】 force prices down; demand a lower price

【压垮】 collapse under pressure; overwhelm

【压力】 ❶〈物〉pressure ❷overwhelming force

【压迫】 ❶oppress; repress ❷constrict

【压气】 calm sb.'s anger

【压强】 intensity of pressure

【压缩】 compress; condense; cut down

【压抑】 ❶constrain; inhibit; depress; hold back ❷oppressive; stifling

【压制】 ❶suppress; stifle; inhibit ❷〈机〉pressing

押 (yā) ❶give as security; mortgage; pawn ❷detain; take into custody ❸escort ❹signature; mark in lieu of signature

【押解】 escort

【押金】 cash pledge; deposit; security

【押款】 ❶borrow money on security ❷a loan on security

【押送】 escort; send (a prisoner or captive) under escort

【押运】 escort (goods) in transportation

【押租】 rent deposit

鸦 (yā) crow

【鸦片】 opium

鸭 (yā) duck

【鸭蛋】 ❶duck's egg ❷〈口〉zero (as a score or mark)

【鸭黄】〈方〉duckling

【鸭绒】 duck's down; eiderdown; down

【鸭舌帽】 peaked cap

牙 (yá) tooth

【牙齿】 tooth

【牙雕】 ivory carving

【牙膏】 toothpaste

【牙刷】 toothbrush

芽 (yá) bud; sprout; shoot

崖 (yá) precipice; cliff

【崖画】 cliff painting

【崖刻】 cliff inscription

涯 (yá) margin; limit

【涯际】 limit; boundary

哑 (yǎ) ❶mute; dumb ❷hoarse; husky

【哑巴】 a dumb person; mute

【哑剧】 dumb show; pantomime

【哑谜】 riddle; puzzling remark; enigma

【哑语】 sign language; dactylology

雅 (yǎ) ❶standard; proper; correct ❷refined; elegant

【雅观】 refined; seemly; in good taste

【雅静】 ❶tasteful and quiet ❷gentle and quiet

【雅量】 ❶broad-mindedness; magnanimity; generosity ❷great capacity for liquor

【雅趣】 refined taste

【雅兴】 an aesthetic mood

【雅意】 kindly consideration; tender regards

【雅致】 refined; tasteful

【雅座】 private room; comfortable seats (of a restaurant, etc.)

轧 (yà) ❶roll; run over ❷oust; squeeze out; push out

　另见 zhá

亚 (yà) inferior; second

【亚军】 second place; runner-up

【亚麻】〈植〉flax
【亚热带】subtropical zone; subtropics
【亚运会】Asian Games
【亚洲】Asia

yan

咽 （yān）pharynx
另见 yàn
【咽喉】❶ pharynx and larynx; throat ❷ key point; strategic passage

恹 （yān）
【恹恹】weak and weary through illness; run-down

胭 （yān）
【胭脂】rouge
【胭脂红】❶carmine ❷famille rose

烟 （yān）❶ smoke ❷ mist; vapour ❸ tobacco ❹cigarette ❺opium
【烟波】mist-covered waters
【烟草】tobacco
【烟尘】smoke and dust
【烟囱】chimney; funnel; stovepipe
【烟斗】(tobacco) pipe
【烟海】foggy or misty sea-vast and voluminous
【烟火】❶smoke and fire ❷cooked food ❸firework
【烟具】smoking paraphernalia
【烟头】cigarette end (or stub, but, stump)
【烟雾】smoke; mist; vapour; smog; smoke and vapour
【烟瘾】crave for smoking
【烟雨】misty rain
【烟云】smoke, mists and clouds

淹 （yān）flood; submerge; inundate
【淹灌】basin irrigation
【淹没】drown; submerge; flood; inundate
【淹死】be drowned

腌 （yān）preserve in salt, sugar, etc.; pickle; salt
【腌制】make by pickling or salting

嫣 （yān）〈书〉handsome; beautiful
【嫣红】〈书〉bright red
【嫣然】〈书〉beautiful; sweet：～一笑 give a winsome smile

延 （yán）❶prolong; extend; protract ❷postpone; delay ❸engage
【延长】prolong; extend; lengthen
【延迟】delay; defer; postpone
【延搁】delay; procrastinate
【延缓】delay; postpone; put off
【延绵】extend uninterruptedly; be continuous
【延聘】〈书〉engage; invite
【延期】postpone; defer; put off
【延伸】extend; stretch; elongate
【延展】extend; stretch

严 （yán）❶tight ❷strict; severe; stern; rigorous
【严办】deal with severely; punish with severity
【严惩】punish severely
【严词】strong terms; stern words
【严冬】severe winter; hard winter
【严防】strictly guard against; take strict precautions against
【严格】strict; rigorous; rigid; stringent
【严寒】bitter cold; severe cold
【严谨】rigorous; careful and precise
【严禁】strictly forbid
【严峻】stern; severe; grim; rigorous
【严酷】❶harsh; bitter; grim ❷cruel; ruthless
【严厉】stern; severe
【严令】give strict orders
【严密】tight; close
【严明】strict and impartial
【严师】demanding teacher
【严师诤友】a strict teacher and a friend who will give unpalatable advice
【严实】〈方〉hide sth. carefully so that it is hard to find
【严守】observe strictly
【严丝合缝】fit together perfectly; join tightly; dovetail
【严肃】serious; earnest; solemn; grave
【严刑】cruel torture; severe punishment
【严阵以待】in full battle array; in combat readiness
【严正】solemn and just; serious and principled; stern
【严重】serious; grave; critical：问题～ the gravity of a problem

言 （yán）❶speech; word ❷say; talk; speak ❸character; word
【言传】explain in words
【言传身教】teach by personal example as well as verbal instruction; teach by precept and example
【言辞】one's words; what one says
【言和】make peace; become reconciled; bury the hatchet
【言欢】chat amiably; talk and laugh
【言简意赅】concise and comprehensive; compendious

【言教】teach by word of mouth; give verbal directions
【言论】opinion on public affairs; expression of one's political view; speech
【言情】romantic
【言说】put into words; say
【言谈】the way one speaks; what one says
【言行】words and deeds; statement and actions
【言近旨远】simple words but deep meaning; simple in language but profound in meaning
【言行不一】the deeds do not match the words; one's actions do not square with one's promises
【言犹在耳】the words still ring (or reverberate) in one's ears
【言语】spoken language; speech
【言喻】〈书〉describe
【言状】describe or depict sb. or sth. in words

岩(yán) ❶rock ❷cliff; crag

【岩洞】grotto
【岩浆】magma
【岩溶】karst
【岩穴】cavern; cave; grotto

炎(yán) ❶scorching; burning hot ❷inflammation

【炎黄子孙】descendants of Yan Di and Huang Di—the Chinese people
【炎凉】hot and cold
【炎热】scorching; blazing; burning hot
【炎日】burning (or scorching) sun
【炎暑】hot summer; sweltering summer days
【炎夏】torrid or scorching summer

沿(yán) ❶along ❷follow ❸trim ❹edge; border

【沿岸】along the bank or coast; littoral; riparian
【沿海】along the coast; coastal
【沿街】along the street
【沿路】along the road; on the roadside; on the way
【沿途】on the way; throughout a journey
【沿袭】carry on as before; follow; inherit
【沿线】along the line
【沿用】continue to use

研(yán) ❶grind; pestle ❷study

【研读】delve into; study carefully
【研究】study; research; consider; discuss
【研讨】discuss; deliberate
【研习】study; research
【研制】prepare; develop; devise and manufacture

盐(yán) salt

【盐分】salt content
【盐湖】salt lake
【盐井】salt well; brine pit
【盐田】salt pan; salina; saltworks
【盐业】salt industry

颜(yán) ❶face; countenance ❷prestige; face ❸colour

【颜料】pigment
【颜面】face; prestige
【颜容】facial expression; complexion; countenance
【颜色】❶colour ❷countenance; facial expression

奄(yǎn) ❶cover; include ❷all of a sudden; suddenly

【奄然】suddenly; quickly
【奄奄】feeble; breathing feebly

俨(yǎn)〈书〉majestic; solemn; dignified

【俨然】〈书〉❶solemn; dignified ❷neatly arranged ❸just like
【俨如】just like

衍(yǎn)〈书〉❶spread out; develop; amplify ❷redundant; superfluous ❸low-lying flatland ❹marsh; swamp; bog

【衍变】develop; evolve
【衍文】redundancy due to misprinting or miscopying

掩(yǎn) ❶cover; hide ❷shut; close ❸get squeezed while shutting a door, lid, etc. ❹attack by surprise

【掩蔽】shelter; cover; masking; screen
【掩藏】hide; conceal
【掩盖】cover; conceal
【掩护】cover; shield; screen; guise
【掩埋】bury
【掩饰】❶cover up; gloss over; put a good face on; conceal ❷deception

眼(yǎn) ❶eye ❷small hole; aperture ❸key point

【眼见】soon; in no time
【眼界】field of view; outlook
【眼镜】glasses; spectacles
【眼睛】eye
【眼泪】tears

演(yǎn) ❶develop ❷elaborate ❸perform; play; act

【演变】develop; evolve
【演播】telecast a television program
【演唱】sing (in a performance)
【演出】perform; show; put on a show
【演化】evolution
【演技】acting

【演讲】give a lecture
【演练】drill：～场 drill ground
【演示】demonstrate
【演说】❶deliver a speech；make an address ❷speech
【演算】perform mathematical calculations
【演习】maneuver；exercise；drill；practice
【演戏】❶put on a play；act in a play ❷play-act；pretend
【演义】historical romance
【演绎】deduction
【演员】actor or actress；performer
【演奏】play a musical instrument

厌（yàn）❶be disgusted with；detest ❷be bored with；be tired of ❸be satisfied
【厌烦】be fed up with
【厌恨】abhor；loathe
【厌倦】be weary of
【厌弃】spurn；turn one's nose up at
【厌食】loss of appetite；anorexia
【厌世】be world-weary；be pessimistic
【厌恶】detest；abominate；be disgusted with
【厌战】be weary of war；be war-weary

砚（yàn）inkstone；ink slab
【砚台】inkstone；brick ink slab

咽（yàn）swallow
另见 yān
【咽气】die；breath one's last

艳（yàn）bright；fresh and attractive
【艳福】man's good fortune in love affairs
【艳情】erotic
【艳阳】❶bright sun ❷sunny sky；spring day

唁（yàn）extend condolences
【唁电】telegram（or cable）of condolence；message of condolence
【唁函】letter（or message）of condolence

宴（yàn）❶entertain at a banquet ❷feast；banquet
【宴会】feast；dinner party
【宴请】entertain；fete
【宴席】banquet；feast

验（yàn）❶examine；check ❷prove effective；produce the expected result
【验光】optometry
【验看】examine；inspect
【验尸】postmortem；autopsy
【验收】acceptance examination；check upon delivery
【验算】checking computations

【验证】verify

雁（yàn）wild goose
【雁行】swan geese flying in a line
【雁阵】flying formation of wild geese

焰（yàn）flame；blaze
【焰火】fireworks
【焰心】flame core

燕（yàn）swallow
【燕麦】oats
【燕窝】edible bird's nest
【燕子】swallow

赝（yàn）〈书〉spurious；fake；counterfeit
【赝本】spurious edition
【赝币】〈书〉counterfeit currency
【赝品】sham；counterfeit

yang

央（yāng）❶center ❷entreat
【央告】beg；ask earnestly
【央求】beg；plead
【央托】entreat sb. to do sth.

殃（yāng）❶calamity；disaster；misfortune ❷bring disaster to
【殃及】bring disaster to

秧（yāng）❶seedling；sprout ❷rice seedling ❸vine；stem ❹young；fry
【秧歌】yangge（dance），a popular rural folk dance
【秧苗】rice seedling；rice shoot
【秧田】rice seedling bed

扬（yáng）❶raise ❷throw up and scatter；winnow ❸spread；make known
【扬长避短】show one's strong points and hide one's weaknesses；maximize favourable factors and minimize unfavourable ones
【扬长而去】stalk off；swagger off
【扬场】winnow
【扬帆】hoist the sails；set sail
【扬名】make a name for oneself；become famous
【扬威】make a show of force
【扬言】threaten（that one is going to take action）

羊（yáng）sheep
【羊羔】lamb
【羊绒】cashmere
【羊肉】mutton

【羊水】amniotic fluid

阳 (yáng) ❶ the sun ❷ south of a hill or north of a river ❸ in relief ❹ open;overt ❺ 〈物〉positive

【阳春】spring
【阳沟】open drain;ditch
【阳光】sunlight;sunshine
【阳历】solar calendar
【阳伞】parasol;sunshade
【阳台】balcony

杨 (yáng) poplar

【杨柳】❶ poplar and willow ❷ (in a broad sense) willow
【杨树】poplar

佯 (yáng) pretend;feign

【佯狂】〈书〉feign madness;pretend to be mad
【佯言】〈书〉allege falsely;tell lies
【佯装】〈书〉pretend;feign

洋 (yáng) ❶ vast ❷ ocean ❸ foreign ❹ modern

【洋葱】onion
【洋行】foreign firm
【洋货】foreign goods;imported goods
【洋流】ocean current
【洋洋】numerous;copious
【洋溢】be permeated with;brim with

仰 (yǎng) ❶ face upward ❷ admire;respect; look up to ❸ rely on;depend on

【仰角】angle of elevation
【仰面】face upward
【仰慕】admire;look up to
【仰视】look up
【仰望】❶ look up at ❷ 〈书〉respectfully seek guidance or help from;look up to
【仰卧】lie on one's back;lie supine;supination
【仰泳】backstroke;back crawl;crawl backstroke
【仰仗】rely on;look to sb. for backing;look to sb. for support

养 (yǎng) ❶ support; provide for ❷ raise; keep;grow ❸ give birth to ❹ foster; adoptive ❺ form; acquire; cultivate ❻ rest; convalesce; recuperate one's health; heal ❼ maintain; keep in good repair

【养兵千日,用兵一时】maintain an army for a thousand days to use it for an hour
【养病】take rest and nourishment to regain one's health
【养分】nutrient
【养父】foster father
【养护】❶ maintain;conserve ❷ curing

【养活】❶ support;feed ❷ raise ❸ give birth to
【养家】raise a family;support one's family
【养料】aliment;nutriment;nourishment
【养母】foster mother
【养气】〈书〉❶ foster the spirit of nobility (by moral cultivation or through a moral life, as advocated by Confucianists) ❷ conserve one's vital powers (by avoiding conflict with the unchangeable laws of nature,as practised by Taoists)
【养伤】nurse one's injuries or wounds
【养神】rest to attain mental tranquility; repose
【养育】bring up;rear
【养殖】breed

氧 (yǎng) oxygen

【氧化】oxidize
【氧气】oxygen

痒 (yǎng) itch;tickle

样 (yàng) ❶ appearance; shape ❷ sample; model;pattern ❸ 〈量〉kind;type

【样板】sample plate;template;model;prototype
【样本】sample book
【样稿】sample manuscript
【样品】sample;specimen
【样式】pattern;type;style
【样张】❶ specimen page ❷ pattern
【样子】❶ appearance;shape ❷ manner;air

yāo

夭 (yāo) ❶ die young ❷ 〈书〉tender and luxuriant

【夭亡】die young;short-lived
【夭折】❶ die young ❷ come to a premature end

妖 (yāo) ❶ goblin; demon; evil spirit ❷ evil and fraudulent ❸ seductive

【妖怪】monster;bogy;demon
【妖精】evil spirit;alluring woman
【妖媚】seductively charming;bewitching; sexy
【妖娆】〈书〉enchanting;fascinating; bewitching
【妖物】evil spirit;monster
【妖艳】pretty and coquettish
【妖冶】seductive;bewitching

要 (yāo) ❶ demand; ask ❷ force coerce ❸ same as
另见 yào

【要求】ask;demand;require;claim
【要挟】coerce;put pressure on;threaten; blackmail

腰 (yāo) ❶ waist; the small of the back ❷ waist (of a garment) ❸ middle

【腰包】purse;pocket
【腰带】belt;girdle
【腰身】waistline;waist;waist measurement of a robe,coat,etc.;girth
【腰围】❶waistline ❷girdle
【腰椎】lumbar vertebra

邀（yāo）❶invite;ask ❷solicit;seek ❸intercept
【邀功】take credit for someone else's achievements
【邀击】intercept (the enemy);waylay
【邀集】invite to meet together;call together
【邀请】invite
【邀约】invite;send an invitation to

谣（yáo）❶ballad;rhyme ❷rumour
【谣传】rumour;hearsay;it is rumoured that
【谣言】rumour;groundless allegation

摇（yáo）shake;wave;rock;turn
【摇摆】swing;sway;rock;vacillate
【摇荡】rock;sway
【摇动】shake;wave
【摇撼】give a violent shake to (a tree, building,etc.)
【摇晃】rock;sway;shake
【摇惑】❶waver and confuse ❷resort to demagoguery
【摇篮】cradle
【摇手】handle on a machine
【摇头】shake one's head
【摇曳】flicker;sway

遥（yáo）distant;remote;far
【遥测】telemetering
【遥控】remote control;telecontrol;remote operate
【遥望】look into the distance
【遥想】imagine;fancy;visualize
【遥遥】❶far away;a long way off：～领先 be far ahead ❷for a long time
【遥远】distant;remote;faraway：路途～ a long journey;a long way to go ｜ ～ 的将来 distant future

杳（yǎo）〈书〉distant and out of sight

咬（yǎo）❶bite;snap at ❷grip;bite ❸of a dog bark ❹pronounce;articulate ❺be nit-picking (on words)
【咬耳朵】whisper in sb.'s ear
【咬定】assert emphatically;insist：一口～ assert

positively;state categorically

舀（yǎo）ladle out;spoon up (or out); scoop up
【舀子】dipper;ladle;scoop

药（yào）❶medicine;drug;remedy ❷certain chemicals ❸cure with medicine ❹kill with poison
【药材】medicinal materials;crude drugs
【药店】drugstore;pharmacy
【药房】drugstore;pharmacy
【药费】charges for medicine;expenses for medicine
【药剂】medicament;drug
【药酒】medicinal liquor
【药力】efficacy of a drug
【药棉】absorbent cotton
【药片】tablet
【药品】medicine and chemical reagents
【药铺】herbal medicine shop
【药水】liquid medicine;medicinal liquid; lotion
【药丸】pill
【药物】pharmaceuticals;material medica
【药效】efficacy of a drug
【药性】property of a medicine
【药皂】medicated soap

要（yào）❶important;essential ❷want;ask for;wish;desire ❸ask sb. to do sth. ❹want to;wish to ❺must;should;it is necessary ❻shall;will;be going to ❼need;take ❽if; suppose;in case
另见 yāo
【要隘】strategic pass
【要案】important case
【要道】❶thoroughfare;main road ❷important ways or methods
【要得】〈方〉good;fine;desirable
【要地】important place;strategic point
【要点】main points;essentials;gist;key strongpoint
【要犯】important or principal criminal
【要害】❶ vital part; crucial point ❷ strategic point
【要好】❶be on good terms;be close friends ❷be eager to improve oneself
【要价】charge;ask a price
【要件】❶an important document ❷an important condition
【要紧】❶vital;important;essential ❷be critical; be serious;matter
【要领】main points;essentials;gist
【要略】outline;summary
【要命】❶drive sb. to his death;kill ❷confoundedly;

extremely;awfully;terribly

【要目】important clauses or contents

【要强】be eager to excel;be anxious to outdo others

【要人】very important person(V. I. P.);important personage

【要塞】fort;fortress;fortification

【要事】important matter

【要死】extremely;awfully;terribly

【要素】essential factor;key element

【要图】important plan

【要闻】important news;front page story

【要务】important affairs

【要职】important post

【要旨】main idea;gist

钥 (yào)

【钥匙】key

耀 (yào)

❶shine;illuminate;dazzle ❷boast of;laud ❸honour;credit

【耀眼】dazzling

ye

椰 (yē) coconut palm;coconut

【椰丝】shredded coconut meat (used as a topping for cakes)

【椰子】coconut palm;coconut tree

爷 (yé) 〈方〉grandfather;grandpa

【爷爷】〈口〉❶(paternal) grandfather ❷grandpa (a respectful form of address for any old man)

也 (yě) ❶also;too;either ❷as well as ❸even

【也许】perhaps;probably;maybe

冶 (yě) smelt (metal)

【冶金】metallurgy

【冶炼】smelt

【冶容】〈书〉❶be seductively made up ❷seductive looks

【冶艳】〈书〉seductive and bewitching

野 (yě) ❶open country;the open ❷limit;boundary ❸not in power;out of office ❹wild;uncultivated;undomesticated;untamed ❺rude;rough ❻unrestrained;abandoned;unruly

【野菜】edible wild herbs

【野餐】picnic

【野炊】cook in the open air

【野地】wilderness

【野火】prairie fire

【野鸡】(ring-necked) pheasant

【野景】wild scenery

【野马】untamed horse

【野蛮】❶uncivilized;savage ❷barbarous;cruel;brutal

【野猫】stray cat

【野生】wild;uncultivated

【野兽】wild beast;wild animal

【野兔】hare

【野外】open country;field

【野味】game (as food)

【野心】wild ambition;careerism

【野性】wild nature;unruliness

【野战】field operations

业 (yè) ❶line of business;trade;industry ❷occupation;profession;employment;job ❸course of study ❹cause;enterprise ❺estate;property ❻engage in ❼already ❽〈佛教〉karma;deed;action

【业绩】outstanding achievement

【业经】already

【业务】vocational work;professional work;business

【业余】spare time;after-hours;amateur

【业主】owner;proprietor;business entrepreneur

叶 (yè) ❶leaf;foliage ❷leaf-like thing ❸page;leaf ❹part of a historical period

【叶脉】leaf vein

【叶肉】mesophyll

【叶枝】leafy branch

【叶子】foliage

页 (yè) ❶leaf;sheet ❷page

【页码】page number

夜 (yè) night;evening

【夜班】night shift

【夜半】in the middle of the night;midnight;12 o'clock at night

【夜餐】midnight snack

【夜场】evening show;evening performance

【夜车】night train

【夜饭】〈方〉supper;dinner

【夜空】the night sky

【夜阑】〈书〉late at night

【夜阑人静】in the dead of night;in the still (or quiet) of the night

【夜里】at night;the time from dusk to dawn

【夜幕】the curtain (or veil) of night;gathering darkness

【夜色】the dim light of night

【夜市】night fair;night market

【夜晚】night

【夜宵】refreshments taken late at night; midnight snack

【夜校】night school; evening school

【夜战】night fighting; night work

【夜总会】nightclub

液 (yè) liquid; fluid; juice

【液化】liquefaction

【液泡】vacuole

【液态】liquid state

【液体】liquid

yī

一 (yī) ❶ one ❷ same ❸ whole; all ❹ concentrated; wholehearted ❺ every; each; per

【一把手】❶ party to an undertaking; a member; a hand ❷ a very capable person ❸ (of an institution) first in command; head

【一败涂地】fail completely; suffer a crushing defeat; be routed

【一般】same as; just like

【一般见识】(lower oneself to) the same level as sb.

【一板一眼】following a prescribed (or set) pattern in speech or action; scrupulous and methodical

【一半】one half; half; in part

【一本正经】in all seriousness; in dead earnest

【一笔勾销】write off at one stroke; cancel

【一笔抹杀】blot out at one stroke; condemn out of hand; totally negate

【一臂之力】a helping hand

【一表人才】a man of striking appearance

【一病不起】take to one's bed and never leave it again; fall ill and die

【一波三折】full of twists and turns or ups and downs

【一倡百和】when one starts singing, the others join in—meet with general approval

【一唱一和】sing a duet; aing the same tune; echo each other

【一成不变】immutable and frozen; invariable; unalterable

【一筹莫展】can find no way out; be at one's wits' end; be at the end of one's tether

【一触即溃】collapse at the first encounter

【一次】once

【一刀两断】sever at one stroke—make a clean break

【一道】together; side by side; alongside

【一得之功】just an occasional, minor success

【一定】❶ fixed; specified; certain; regular ❷

surely; necessarily ❸ must; certainly

【一动】easily; frequently; at every turn

【一度】once

【一发千钧】a hundredweight hanging by a hair—in imminent peril

【一帆风顺】plain sailing; smooth sailing

【一概】one and all; without exception; totally; categorically

【一概而论】(usu. used in the negative) treat (different matters) as the same

【一干二净】thoroughly; completely

【一共】altogether; in all

【一鼓作气】press on to the finish without letup; get sth. done in one sustained effort

【一贯】consistent; persistent

【一哄而起】(of a group of people) be roused to precipitate action; rush headlong into mass action

【一呼百应】hundreds respond to a single call

【一己】oneself; personal

【一技之长】proficiency in a particular line (or field); professional skill; speciality

【一家之言】a distinctive doctrine or theory; an original system of thought

【一见钟情】fall in love at first sight

【一箭双雕】hit two hawks with one arrow; kill two birds with one stone

【一箭之仇】the wrong of an arrow shot—a loss or defeat to be retrieved

【一箭之地】as far as the arrow flies—a short distance

【一举一动】every act and every move; every action

【一举两得】gain two ends at once; kill two birds with one stone

【一蹶不振】collapse after a single setback; be unable to recover after a setback

【一刻】a short while; an instant

【一刻千金】one moment is worth a thousand pieces of gold—time is gold

【一孔之见】a peephole view; a narrow view; a very limited outlook

【一口咬定】state categorically; assert positively; insist emphatically

【一来二去】in the course of frequent contact; in the course of time

【一劳永逸】by one supreme effort gain lasting repose—settle a matter once and for all

【一了百了】all troubles end when the main trouble ends

【一路】all the way; throughout the journey

【一路平安】have a pleasant journey; have a

good trip

【一路货色】the same sort of stuff;one of a kind; birds of a feather

【一律】❶same;alike;uniform ❷all;without exception

【一落千丈】drop a thousand zhang in one fall— suffer a drastic decline

【一马当先】gallop at the head—take the lead;be in the forefront

【一毛不拔】unwilling to give up even a hair— very stingy

【一门心思】heart and soul;wholeheartedly

【一面】❶ one side;one aspect ❷ at the same time;simultaneously

【一面之词】the statement of only one of the parties

【一面之缘】having met once（as ordained by fate）

【一鸣惊人】（of an obscure person）amaze the world with a single brilliant feat;set the world on fire

【一命呜呼】die; kick the bucket; give up the ghost

【一模一样】exactly alike;as like as two peas

【一目了然】be clear at a glance

【一目十行】take in ten lines at a glance— read rapidly

【一年四季】throughout（the four seasons of）the year;all the year round

【一年半载】in a year or so;in about a year

【一年到头】throughout the year; all the year round

【一念之差】a wrong decision made in a moment of weakness; a momentary slip with serious consequences

【一诺千金】a promise worth a thousand pieces of gold—a promise that can be counted on

【一拍即合】fit in readily;chime in easily

【一盘散沙】a sheet of loose sand—a state of disunity（formerly said of a country）

【一贫如洗】penniless;utterly destitute

【一平二调】equalitarianism and indiscriminate transfer of resources

【一曝十寒】have one day's sun and then ten day's cold—work by fits and starts

【一起】❶in the same place ❷together;in company

【一气之下】in a fury;in a fit of anger

【一钱不值】not worth a penny;utterly worthless;mere trash

【一切】all;every;everything

【一清二楚】perfectly clear

【一日千里】a thousand li a day—at a tremendous pace;with giant strides

【一如既往】just as in the past; as before; as always

【一扫而光】make a clean sweep of;clear off;finish off;get rid of sth. lock,stock and barrel

【一身】❶all over the body ❷a suit

【一身两役】hold two jobs at the same time; serve in a dual capacity

【一身是胆】one's whole body is all pluck—know no fear;be absolutely fearless

【一生】all one's life;throughout one's life

【一生一世】all one's life;throughout one's life

【一声不响】not say a word;not utter a sound

【一视同仁】treat equally without discrimination

【一手包办】keep everything in one's own hands; take everything on oneself

【一手遮天】shut out the heavens with one hand—hide the truth from the masses;hoodwink the public

【一丝不苟】not be the least bit negligent; be scrupulous about every detail; be conscientious and meticulous

【一丝不挂】not have a stitch on;be stark naked

【一丝一毫】a tiny bit;an iota;a trace

【一潭死水】a pool of stagnant water—a stagnant or lifeless condition

【一天到晚】from morning till night;from dawn to dusk;all day long

【一条道儿跑到黑】follow one road until it's dark — cling obstinately to one course

【一通百通】master one and you'll master a hundred;grasp this and you'll grasp everything

【一同】together;at the same time and place

【一吐为快】cannot rest until one has one's say

【一团和气】keep on good terms with everyone（at the expense of principle）;keep on the right side of everyone

【一网打尽】catch the whole lot in a dragnet; round up the whole gang at one fell swoop

【一往无前】press forward with an indomitable will

【一往情深】be deeply attached; be passionately devoted;be head over heels in love

【一望无际】stretch as far as the eye can see; stretch to the horizon

【一文不值】not worth a farthing; utterly worthless;mere trash

【一无可取】have nothing to recommend one; be worthless

【一无所有】not own a thing in the world; not have a thing to one's name

【一无是处】without a single redeeming feature; devoid of any merit; having no saving grace

【一无所知】know nothing about; not have the least inkling of; be absolutely ignorant of

【一息尚存】so long as one still has a breath left; till one's last gasp

【一厢情愿】one-sided wish; one's own wishful thinking

【一些】〈量〉a number of; certain; some; a few; a little

【一心】❶ wholeheartedly; heart and soul ❷ of one mind; at one

【一心一意】heart and soul; wholeheartedly

【一样】the same; equally; alike; as ... as ...

【一月】January

【一再】time and again; repeatedly

【一张一弛】tension alternating with relaxation

【一朝一夕】in one morning or evening; overnight; in one day

【一针见血】pierce to the truth with one pertinent remark; hit the nail on the head

【一阵】a burst; a fit; a peal

【一知半解】have a superficial knowledge of; a smattering of knowledge; half knowledge

【一直】❶ straight ❷ continuously; always; all along; all the way

【一致】fit; showing no difference; identical

伊 (yī) she; he

【伊甸园】the Garden of Eden; paradise

【伊斯兰教】Islam; Islamism

【伊始】〈书〉beginning

衣 (yī) ❶ clothing; clothes; garment ❷ coating; covering

【衣橱】wardrobe; clothes press

【衣服】clothing; clothes

【衣架】coat hanger; clothes-rack

【衣料】material for clothing; dress material

【衣衫褴褛】shabbily dressed; out at elbows; in rags

【衣裳】〈口〉clothes; clothing

【衣物】clothing and other articles of daily use

【衣装】❶dress; attire ❷clothes and luggage

【衣着】clothing, headgear and footwear

医 (yī) ❶doctor; physician ❷medical service; medical science ❸cure; treat

【医术】medical skill; art of healing

【医务】medical matters

【医学】medical science; medicine

【医院】hospital

【医治】cure; treat; heal

依 (yī) ❶depend on ❷comply with; yield to ❸according to; in the light of; judging by

【依次】in proper order; successively

【依从】comply with; yield to

【依存】depend on sb. or sth. of existence

【依法】according to law; by operation of law; in conformity with legal provisions

【依附】be attached to

【依归】❶ starting point and destination ❷ dependence; reliance

【依旧】still; as before

【依据】❶according to; on the basis of ❷foundation; basis

【依靠】rely on; depend on; backing

【依赖】rely on; be dependent on

【依恋】be reluctant to leave; feel regret at parting from

【依凭】❶rely on; depend on ❷evidence; certificate; voucher

【依然】still; as before

【依顺】be obedient; comply with

【依随】agree to; yield to; comply with

【依托】❶rely on; depend on ❷pretext; excuse

【依偎】snuggle up to; lean close to

【依稀】vaguely; dimly

【依允】assent; consent

【依照】cata; according to; in the light of

仪 (yí) ❶ appearance ❷ ceremony; rite ❸ present; gift ❹apparatus; instrument

【仪表】❶appearance; bearing ❷meter

【仪器】instrument; apparatus

【仪容】looks; appearance

【仪式】ceremony; rite; function

【仪态万方】(of a beauty)appear in all her glory

【仪仗】insignia carried before the emperor

怡 (yí) happy; joyful; cheerful

【怡然】happy and contented

【怡然自得】be happy and pleased with oneself; feel a glow of happiness

宜 (yí) ❶ suitable; appropriate; fitting ❷ should; ought to

【宜人】pleasant; delightful

贻 (yí) 〈书〉❶make a gift of sth. ; present ❷ bequeath; leave behind; hand down

【贻害无穷】entail untold troubles; involve endless trouble

【贻人口实】provide one's critics with a handle; give occasion for talk

【贻误】affect adversely; bungle

姨 (yí) ❶one's mother's sister; aunt ❷one's wife's sister; sister-in-law

【姨夫】husband of mother's sister (or maternal aunt); uncle

【姨父】uncle

【姨母】aunt

移 (yí) ❶ move; remove; shift ❷ change; alter

【移动】move; shift

【移交】turn over; transfer; hand over one's job to a successor

【移居】migrate

【移民】migrate; emigrate; immigrate

【移易】〈书〉change; alter; transform

【移用】divert from one use to another

【移栽】transplant

【移植】transplant

遗 (yí) ❶ lose ❷ something lost ❸ omit ❹ leave behind; keep back; not give ❺ leaving behind at one's death; bequeath; hand down ❻ involuntary

【遗产】legacy; inheritance; heritage

【遗传】〈生〉heredity; inheritance

【遗毒】evil legacy; harmful tradition

【遗风】traditions and customs handed down from a certain age

【遗稿】a manuscript left unpublished by the author at his death

【遗憾】regret; pity

【遗恨】eternal regret; lifelong regret

【遗患】leave a legacy of trouble

【遗祸】leave a legacy of trouble

【遗迹】historical remains; vestiges

【遗老】adherent of a former dynasty; old fogy; old diehard

【遗留】leave over; hand down

【遗漏】omit; leave out

【遗民】adherent of a former dynasty; survivor of a great upheaval

【遗弃】abandon; forsake; desert

【遗缺】vacancy

【遗容】❶ remains ❷ a portrait of the deceased; portrait of a dead person

【遗失】lose

【遗书】❶ posthumous papers ❷ a letter of note left by one immediately before death

【遗孀】widow; relict

【遗体】❶ remains ❷ remnants of animals and plants after they die

【遗忘】forget

【遗闻】tales of old times

【遗物】things left behind by the deceased

【遗像】photograph or portrait of the deceased

【遗言】words of the deceased; (a person's) last words

【遗愿】unfulfilled wish of the deceased

【遗志】unfulfilled wish; behest

【遗嘱】make a will orally or in writing; leave one's last words

【遗著】writings of a dead author; posthumous work (of an author)

疑 (yí) ❶ doubt; disbelieve; suspect ❷ doubtful; uncertain

【疑案】doubtful case; open question; mystery

【疑点】doubtful points

【疑忌】be suspicious

【疑惧】apprehensive, worried and nervous

【疑虑】misgivings; doubt

【疑难】difficult; knotty

【疑似】doubtful

【疑团】doubts and suspicions

【疑问】query; question; doubt

【疑心】suspicion

【疑义】doubt; doubt point; doubtful argument

【疑云】misgivings or suspicions clouding one's mind

已 (yǐ) ❶ stop; cease; end ❷ already ❸ thereafter; afterwards ❹ too

【已故】deceased; late

【已经】already

【已往】before; previously; in the past

【已知数】〈数〉known number

以 (yǐ) ❶ with; by means of ❷ according to ❸ because of ❹ in order to; so as to

【以暴易暴】replace one tyranny by another

【以备不虞】be prepared for any contingency

【以便】so that; in order to; so as to

【以点带面】fan out from point to area; use the experience of selected units to promote work in the entire area

【以毒攻毒】fight poison with poison; use poison as an antidote for poison

【以讹传讹】incorrectly relay an erroneous message (so that it becomes increasingly distorted); spread an error or a falsehood

【以耳代目】rely upon hearsay instead of seeing for oneself

【以防万一】be prepared for all contingencies; be ready for any eventuality

【以攻为守】use attack as a means of defence; attack in order to defend

【以古非今】disparage the present by extolling the past

【以寡敌众】pit few against many; fight against heavy odds

【以观后效】(lighten a punishment and) see how

the offender behaves

【以后】after;afterwards;later;hereafter

【以及】as well as;along with;and

【以己度人】judge others by oneself; measure others' corn with one's own bushel

【以假乱真】mix the false with the true;mix the spurious with the genuine

【以解倒悬】so as to relieve sb.'s distress

【以来】since

【以礼相待】treat sb. with due respect

【以免】so as not to;lest;in order to avoid

【以内】within;less than;inside of

【以偏概全】take a part for the whole

【以前】before;formerly;previously

【以求】in order to;in an attempt to

【以上】❶ more than; over; above ❷ the above; the foregoing;the above-mentioned

【以外】beyond;outside;other than;except

【以往】before;formerly;in the past

【以为】think;believe;consider

【以逸待劳】wait at one's ease for an exhausted enemy

【以怨报德】return evil for good;repay good with evil; requite kindness with ingratitude; bite the hand that feeds one

【以正视听】in order to ensure a correct understanding of the facts

【以至】❶ down to; up to ❷ to such an extent as to …;so …that …

【以致】so that; as a result; with the result that;consequently

倚 (yǐ) ❶ lean on or against; rest on or against ❷ rely on; count on ❸ 〈书〉 biased;partial

【倚靠】❶ rely on; depend on ❷ lean on or against;rest on or against

【倚仗】rely on;count on

【倚重】rely heavily on somebody's service

椅 (yǐ) chair

旖 (yǐ)

【旖旎】〈文〉charming;enchanting

亿 (yì) a hundred million

【亿万】hundreds of millions;millions upon millions

义 (yì) ❶ justice; righteousness ❷ righteous; just ❸ human ties; relationship ❹ adopted; adoptive ❺ meaning;significance

【义不容辞】be duty-bound; have an unshirkable duty

【义地】cemetery

【义愤】moral indignation

【义愤填膺】be filled with indignation

【义举】a magnanimous act undertaken for the public good

【义气】personal loyalty

【义务】❶ duty; obligation ❷ volunteer; voluntary

【义演】benefit performance

【义勇】righteous and courageous

艺 (yì) skill;art

【艺人】❶ actor or entertainer (in local drama, storytelling, acrobatics, etc.) ❷ artisan; handicraftsman

【艺术】❶ art ❷ skill; art; craft ❸ conforming to good taste

【艺术家】artist

【艺术品】work of art;usually work of plastic art

忆 (yì) recall;recollect;remember

【忆苦】recall one's suffering in the old society

【忆念】cherish the memory of;think of

【忆想】recall;recollect;call to mind

议 (yì) ❶ opinion; view ❷ discuss; exchange views on;talk over

【议案】proposal;motion

【议程】agenda

【议定】decide through consultation;agree on

【议会】parliament;legislative assembly

【议价】negotiate a price; negotiated price; negotiable price

【议论】comment;talk;discuss

【议事】discuss official business

【议题】item on the agenda; subject under discussion

【议席】seat in a legislative assembly

【议员】member of a legislative assembly

【议院】legislative assembly; parliament; congress

【议长】speaker;president

【议政】discuss affairs of government

屹 (yì) 〈书〉 towering like a mountain peak

【屹立】stand towering like a giant;stand erect

【屹然】towering;majestic

异 (yì) ❶ identical; different ❷ strange; unusual ❸ surprise ❹ other; another ❺ separate

【异常】❶ unusual;abnormal ❷ extremely

【异地】place far away from home;strange land

【异端】heterodoxy; heresy; ～邪说 heresies; heretical beliefs;unorthodox opinions

【异国】foreign country (or land)

【异乎】different from：～寻常 unusually；extraordinarily

【异趣】❶different in taste and interest ❷peculiar taste

【异日】❶some other day ❷(in) former days

【异同】similarities and differences

【异外】unusual；exceptional

【异味】❶a rare delicacy ❷a peculiar smell

【异物】❶foreign matter；a foreign body ❷〈书〉a dead person；ghost ❸a rare object

【异乡】foreign land；strange land；客居～ live in a foreign land

【异香】unusually sweet smell；rare perfume

【异心】infidelity；disloyalty

【异性】❶the opposite sex ❷different in nature

【异姓】different family names

【异言】dissenting words

【异样】❶difference ❷unusual；peculiar

【异议】objection；dissent

【异域】❶a foreign country ❷an alien land；a strange land

抑 (yì) ❶press down；restrain；repress；curb ❷or ❸but

【抑扬】(of sound) rise and fall；modulate

【抑郁】depressed；despondent；gloomy

【抑制】restrain；control；inhibition

呓 (yì) talk in one's sleep

【呓语】❶talk in one's sleep ❷crazy talk；ravings

役 (yì) ❶labour；service ❷use as a servant ❸servant ❹battle；campaign

【役龄】❶enlistment age ❷years of military service

【役使】work (an animal)；use

译 (yì) translate；interpret

【译本】translated version (of a book)；translation

【译电】❶encode；encipher ❷decode；decipher

【译码】decode；decipher

【译名】translated term or name

【译述】translate (or render) freely

【译文】translated text；translation

【译员】interpreter；translator

【译制】dub

【译注】translate and annotate：～古籍 translate and annotate ancient books

【译作】translations

易 (yì) ❶easy ❷amiable ❸change ❹exchange

【易如反掌】as easy as turning one's hand over；as easy as falling off a log

【易手】change hands

【易于】be easy to

驿 (yì) post

【驿道】post road

【驿使】courier；post

【驿站】post (where formerly couriers changed horses or rested)

奕 (yì) grand；great

【奕奕】〈书〉❶grand；great ❷radiating power and vitality

疫 (yì) epidemic disease；pestilence

【疫病】epidemic disease

【疫苗】〈医〉vaccine

【疫情】epidemic situation

益 (yì) ❶benefit；profit；advantage ❷beneficial

【益虫】beneficial insect

【益处】good；benefit；profit

【益鸟】beneficial bird

【益友】friend and mentor

逸 (yì) ❶toil ❷escape；flee ❸be lost ❹excel all others

【逸乐】comfort and pleasure

【逸事】anecdote

【逸闻】anecdote

【逸豫】〈书〉idleness and pleasure

肄 (yì) study

【肄业】study in school or at college

意 (yì) ❶meaning；idea；thought ❷wish；desire；intention ❸anticipate；expect ❹suggestion；hint；trace

【意大利】Italy

【意会】perceive by intuition；sense；只可～，不可言传 can be sensed, but not explained in words

【意见】❶idea；view；opinion；suggestion ❷objection；differing opinion；complaint

【意境】mood of a literary work or a work of art；artistic conception；artistic mood

【意料】anticipate；expect

【意念】idea；thought

【意气】❶will and spirit ❷temperament and interest ❸personal feelings or prejudice

【意识】❶consciousness ❷be aware of；be conscious of

【意思】❶meaning；idea ❷opinion；wish；desire ❸a token of affection, appreciation, gratitude, etc. ❹look like；seem ❺interest；fun

【意图】intention；intent

【意外】unexpected;unforeseen;accident;mishap
【意味】meaning;significance;implication
【意味深长】having deep meaning;pregnant with meaning;of profound significance
【意下】❶in the mind;in the hearted ❷opinion;idea;view
【意想】expect;imagine
【意向】intention;purpose
【意象】images;imagery
【意兴】interest;enthusiasm
【意义】meaning;sense;significance;importance
【意译】free translation
【意愿】wish;desire;aspiration
【意蕴】meaning;implication;connotation
【意在言外】the meaning is implied
【意旨】intention;wish;will
【意志】will;determination;will-power
【意中人】the person one is in love with;the person of one's heart;the beloved one

溢 (yì) ❶overflow;spill ❷excessive
【溢出】overflow;spill
【溢流】overflow;brim over
【溢于言表】(of feelings) show clearly in one's words and manner

毅 (yì) firm;resolute;staunch
【毅力】willpower;will;stamina
【毅然】resolutely;firmly;determinedly

臆 (yì) ❶chest ❷subjectively
【臆测】conjecture;surmise
【臆断】assume;suppose
【臆见】a subjective view
【臆说】assumption;supposition
【臆想】a wishful imagination
【臆造】fabricate(a story,reason,etc.);make up

翼 (yì) ❶the wings of a bird,an insect,etc. ❷the wings of an airplane ❸flank wing
【翼翅】wing
【翼护】shield sb. with one's own body
【翼翼】〈书〉❶serious and cautious ❷in orderly array;in neat formation ❸thriving;abundant

yin

因 (yīn) ❶follow;carry on ❷rely on;accord with ❸cause;reason ❹because of;as a result of ❺because
【因此】therefore; for this reason;consequently;hence
【因而】as a result;therefore;thus
【因果】cause and effect

【因式】〈数〉factor
【因素】factor;element
【因为】because;for;on account of
【因小失大】try to save a little only to lose a lot;penny wise and pound foolish;spoil the ship for a haporth of tar
【因循】❶follow;continue in the same old tracks ❷procrastinate
【因循守旧】stick to old ways;follow the beaten track
【因噎废食】give up eating for fear of choking— refrain from doing what one should for fear of running a risk
【因由】reason;cause;origin

阴 (yīn) ❶the moon ❷overcast ❸shade ❹in intaglio ❺hidden;secret ❻of the nether world ❼negative ❽private parts ❾the back side
【阴暗】dark;gloomy
【阴沉】cloudy;overcast;gloomy
【阴毒】insidious;sinister and ruthless
【阴风】❶cold wind ❷ill wind;wind from a dark place
【阴干】be placed in the shade to dry
【阴沟】sewer;covered drain
【阴魂】ghost;spirit of the dead
【阴魂不散】the ghost lingers on —the evil influence remains
【阴极】negative pole;negative electrode
【阴间】netherworld
【阴冷】gloomy and cold;sombre;glum
【阴历】lunar calendar
【阴凉】shady and cool
【阴面】shady side;back side
【阴谋】plot;scheme;conspiracy
【阴森】gloomy;gruesome;ghastly
【阴天】overcast sky;cloudy day
【阴险】sinister;insidious;treacherous
【阴影】shadow

荫 (yīn) arbour
【荫蔽】❶shade or hide ❷ cover;conceal

音 (yīn) ❶sound ❷news;tidings ❸〈物〉tone
【音带】audio tape;cassette (tape);magnetic sound-recording tape
【音调】tone;the pitch of a sound
【音阶】scale
【音节】〈语〉syllable
【音量】volume of sound
【音律】temperament
【音频】〈物〉audio frequency

【音区】range
【音容】voice and facial expression
【音色】tone colour；timbre
【音位】phoneme
【音问】news；tidings
【音响】sound；acoustics
【音像】audiovisual；sound and video recording
【音信】mail；message；news：杳无～ have not been heard from（sb.）since
【音译】transliteration
【音域】〈音〉range；compass
【音乐】music
【音质】tone quality

姻（yīn）❶marriage ❷relation by marriage

【姻亲】relation by marriage
【姻缘】the happy fate that brings lovers together

殷（yīn）❶ abundant；rich ❷ eager；ardent ❸hospitable

【殷富】wealthy；well-off；家道～ wealthy family
【殷切】eager；～的期望 ardent expectations
【殷勤】eagerly attentive
【殷殷】❶ ardent；sincere ❷〈书〉distressed；be laden with sorrow
【殷忧】great worries；deep anxieties

吟（yín）❶chant；recite ❷ song ❸the cry of certain animals

【吟风弄月】sing of the moon and the wind—write sentimental verse
【吟诵】chant；recite
【吟咏】recite（poetry）with a cadence；chant

银（yín）❶silver（Ag）❷relating to currency；relating to money ❸silver-colored

【银白】silvery white
【银杯】silver cup（of sport games）
【银币】silver coin
【银发】silver（or silvery）hair：满头～ silver-haired
【银行】bank
【银河】〈天〉Milky Way
【银红】pale rose colour；the colour of a mixture of pink pigment and vermilion
【银灰】silver grey
【银婚】silver wedding
【银匠】silversmith
【银幕】screen
【银圆】silver dollar

淫（yín）❶ licentious；lewd；lascivious ❷ obscene；pornographic

【淫荡】loose in morals；lascivious；licentious；lewd

【淫妇】a wanton woman；adulteress
【淫棍】libertine；womanizer；wolf
【淫秽】obscene；risque；salacious；bawdy
【淫乱】（sexually）promiscuous；licentious
【淫威】abuse of power；despotic power
【淫雨】excessive rains

引（yǐn）❶draw；stretch ❷lead；guide ❸leave ❹lure；attract ❺cause；make ❻quote；cite ❼a unit of length

【引爆】ignite；detonate；cause（a fuel mixture）to burn by a lighting device
【引导】guide；lead
【引动】cause；arouse；stir up（feelings）
【引逗】tease；lure；entice
【引渡】lead sb. across（water）；direct
【引发】initiate；trigger；spark of；touch off
【引吭高歌】sing joyfully in a loud voice；sing heartily
【引号】quotation marks（" "）
【引河】❶irrigation channel；water course dug for irrigation ❷diversion canal
【引火】light fuel with sth. burning
【引见】introduce and get people acquainted with one another
【引荐】recommend
【引进】introduce from elsewhere；import
【引领】❶lead；guide ❷〈书〉crane one's neck to look into the distance—eagerly look forward to sth.
【引路】lead the way
【引起】give rise to；touch off；cause
【引人入胜】（of scenery，literary works，etc.）fascinating；enchanting；bewitching
【引人注目】noticeable；conspicuous；spectacular
【引申】extend（the meaning of a word，etc.）
【引述】quote（sb.'s words or writing）：～专家的评论 quote an expert's comments
【引退】retire from an official position；resign
【引文】quoted passage；quotation
【引线】❶ wire-like fuse ❷go-between ❸〈方〉sewing needle
【引言】foreword；introduction；preface
【引以为荣】regard it as an honour；take it as an honour
【引用】cite；quote
【引诱】lure；seduce
【引证】quote or cite a truth，speech，or literary work as proof or evidence

饮（yǐn）❶ drink ❷ drinks ❸ keep in the heart；nurse

【饮恨】cherish a grievance
【饮恨吞声】swallow one's resentment and choke

back one's sobs；endure insults and injuries

【饮料】drink；beverage

【饮泣】〈书〉weep in silence

【饮食】food and drink；diet

【饮食业】catering service

【饮水】drinking water；potable water

【饮誉】enjoy a sterling reputation

隐（yǐn）❶ hidden from view ❷ secret；latent；dormant

【隐蔽】conceal；take cover

【隐避】evade and conceal

【隐藏】hide；conceal；remain under cover

【隐伏】lie concealed；lie hidden

【隐患】hidden trouble；snake in the grass

【隐晦】obscure；veiled

【隐居】live in seclusion；be a hermit

【隐瞒】conceal；hide；hold back；cover up

【隐没】hide and gradually disappear；immerge

【隐情】facts or circumstances one wishes to hide；secret

【隐士】hermit；recluse

【隐私】one's secrets；private matters one wants to hide

【隐痛】❶ secret anguish ❷ indistinct pain；dull pain；obtuse pain

【隐退】go and live in seclusion；retire from political life

【隐喻】metaphor

【隐约】indistinct；faint

印（yìn）❶ seal；stamp；chop ❷ print；mark；trace ❸ print；engrave ❹ tally；conform

【印度】India

【印发】print and distribute

【印痕】mark of print；trace

【印花】printing

【印迹】trace；mark；vestige

【印染】printing and dyeing

【印刷】printing

【印象】impression；深刻的～ deep impression

【印章】seal；signet；stamp

【印证】confirm；verify；corroborate

ying

应（yìng）❶ answer；respond ❷ agree ❸ should；ought to
　　另见 yìng

【应分】be part of one's job (or duty)

【应该】should；ought to；must

【应声】answer；respond

【应许】❶ agree (to do sth.)；promise ❷ permit；allow

【应有】due；proper；deserve

【应允】assent；consent

英（yīng）❶〈书〉flower ❷ hero；outstanding person ❸ Britain ❹ English

【英镑】pound sterling

【英才】person of outstanding ability

【英尺】foot

【英寸】inch

【英豪】hero；outstanding figure

【英魂】spirit of the brave departed；spirit of a martyr

【英杰】hero；outstanding figure

【英俊】❶ eminently talented；brilliant ❷ handsome；smart

【英里】mile

【英烈】❶ heroic and fiery；valiant ❷ martyr

【英灵】spirit of the brave departed；spirit of a martyr

【英明】wise；～果断 wise and determined

【英模】heroes and model workers

【英亩】acre

【英气】heroic spirit

【英武】of soldierly bearing

【英雄】hero

【英勇】valiant；brave；gallant

【英语】English (language)

【英姿】heroic bearing；heroic posture；bright and valiant look

婴（yīng）baby；infant

【婴儿】baby；infant

樱（yīng）❶ cherry ❷ oriental cherry

【樱花】oriental cherry

【樱桃】cherry

鹦（yīng）

【鹦鹉】parrot

鹰（yīng）hawk；eagle

【鹰犬】falcons and hounds — lackeys；hired thugs

迎（yíng）❶ go the meet；greet；welcome ❷ move towards；meet face to face

【迎风】❶ against the wind ❷ downwind；with the wind

【迎合】cater to

【迎候】await the arrival of (a guest) at a place

【迎击】repulse enemy's attacks；counterattack against an approaching enemy

【迎接】meet；welcome；greet

【迎面】head-on；in one's face

【迎娶】(of a man) get married

【迎新】welcome new arrivals：～晚会 evening party to welcome newcomers

【迎战】meet an approaching enemy head-on

荧 （yíng）❶ glimmering；shimmering；twinkling ❷ dazzled；perplexed

【荧光屏】fluorescent screen

【荧荧】starlight，lamplight，or candlelight：明星～ twinkling stars

盈 （yíng）❶ be full of；be filled with ❷ have a surplus of

【盈亏】profit and loss

【盈利】profit；gain

【盈盈】❶clear；limpid：春水～ clear spring water ❷(of one's manner) delicate；dainty

【盈余】surplus；profit

营 （yíng）❶seek ❷operate；run ❸camp；barracks ❹battalion

【营部】battalion headquarters

【营地】encampment；campsite

【营房】barracks

【营火】campfire；bonfire used esp. during camping

【营建】construct；build：～宿舍楼 construct a dormitory building

【营救】rescue；manage to save：～遇险船员 rescue the sailors in danger

【营利】seek profits

【营区】camping area；location of a military camp

【营私】seek private gain；feather one's nest：结党～ gang up for selfish interests

【营养】nutrition；nourishment

【营业】do business；business：～额 turnover；volume of business

【营运】business and operation

【营造】construct；build

【营长】battalion commander

【营帐】tent (esp. for military or fieldwork purposes)

萦 （yíng）entangle；encompass

【萦回】hover；linger

【萦绕】linger on

【萦系】worry；miss

【萦纡】〈书〉linger；wind around

蝇 （yíng）fly；housefly

【蝇头】very small；tiny

赢 （yíng）❶win；beat ❷gain (profit)

【赢得】gain；win；obtain；attain：～信任与支持 obtain trust and support

【赢家】winner；winning party in gambling or a competition

【赢利】profit；gain

颖 （yǐng）❶ glume；grain husk ❷ tip；point ❸clever

【颖慧】〈书〉bright；intelligent

【颖异】〈书〉❶ be extraordinarily clever ❷ novel；strange：构思～ novel design

影 （yǐng）❶ shadow ❷ reflection；image ❸ vague impression；sign ❹ photograph；picture ❺film；movie

【影集】photo album

【影迷】〈影〉movie fan；movie goer

【影片】film；movie

【影评】film review；article devoted to commentary on a film

【影射】allude to；hint obliquely at

【影视】film and television：～圈 show business；film and television circles

【影响】❶effect；impact ❷affect；influence

【影像】an image；a portrait

【影印】photo-offset process

【影院】cinema；movie theatre

【影子】❶ shadow；reflection ❷ trace；sign；vague impression

应 （yìng）❶answer；respond；echo ❷comply with；grant ❸suit；respond to ❹deal with；cope with
　　另见 yíng

【应变】cope with an emergency (or contingency)：随机～ act according to circumstances

【应承】agree (to do something)；promise；consent

【应酬】have special intercourse with；treat with courtesy

【应从】assent to；comply with

【应答】reply；answer

【应付】❶deal with；cope with；handle ❷do sth. perfunctorily；do sth. after a fashion

【应和】echo each other：同声～ echo simultaneously

【应急】meet an urgent need；meet an emergency；meet a contingency

【应考】take (or sit for) an entrance examination

【应力】stress

【应募】respond to a call for recruits；enlist；join up

【应诺】agree (to do sth.)；promise；undertake

【应聘】accept an offer of employment

【应声】happen right at the sound of sth.

【应验】come true；be confirmed；be fulfilled；tally

with what later actually happens

【应邀】at sb.'s invitation;on invitation

【应用】apply;use

【应用文】practical writing

【应战】❶engage the enemy ❷accept (*or* take up) a challenge

【应招】respond to a call for recruits or candidates

【应诊】(of a doctor) see patients and offer treatment

【应征】❶be recruited;enlist ❷answer to calls;answer to requests

映 (yìng) reflect;mirror;shine

【映衬】set off

【映射】shine upon;cast light upon

【映像】image

【映照】shine upon;cast light upon;晚霞～ glory of the dusk shines upon (sth.)

硬 (yìng) ❶hard;stiff ❷strong

【硬币】coin;specie

【硬度】hardness;rigidity

【硬朗】〈口〉hale and hearty

【硬面】hard dough

【硬木】hardwood

【硬实】〈方〉strong;sturdy;robust

【硬挺】force oneself to go on doing (sth.);endure with all one's will

【硬卧】hard berth;hard sleeper (on a train)

【硬性】rigid;stiff;inflexible

【硬座】hard seat (on a train)

yong

佣 (yōng) ❶hire (a labourer) ❷servant

另见 yòng

【佣妇】woman servant;maid

【佣工】hired labourer;servant

【佣人】servant

拥 (yōng) ❶hold in one's arms;embrace;hug ❷gather around;wrap around ❸crowd;throng;swarm ❹support ❺have;possess

【拥抱】embrace;hug;hold in one's arms

【拥戴】support

【拥护】support;uphold;endorse

【拥挤】crowd;push and squeeze

【拥塞】jam;congest

【拥有】possess;have;own

庸 (yōng) ❶commonplace;mediocre ❷inferior;second-rate

【庸才】〈书〉mediocre person;person of mediocre

ability;mediocrity

【庸碌】mediocre and unambitious

【庸人】mediocre person

【庸俗】vulgar;philistine;low

【庸医】quack;charlatan

永 (yǒng) perpetually;forever;always

【永别】part forever

【永不】never

【永存】eternal;lasting forever

【永恒】eternal;perpetual

【永久】permanent;perpetual;everlasting;forever

【永生】❶eternal life ❷all one's life;for life

【永世】forever;for life;～长存 live forever;be everlasting;be immortal

【永逝】❶pass away;be gone forever ❷die

【永远】forever;always;ever;to perpetuate

咏 (yǒng) ❶chant;intone ❷express or narrate in poetic form

【咏唱】chant;sing

【咏怀】singing from one's heart;express one's feelings and aspirations in poetic form

【咏叹】intone;chant;sing

泳 (yǒng) swim

【泳程】swimming distance

【泳道】lane (in a swimming race)

勇 (yǒng) brave;valiant;courageous

【勇敢】brave;courageous

【勇悍】brave and fierce

【勇力】courage and strength;～过人 exceptional courage and strength

【勇猛】bold and powerful;full of valour and vigour;～冲杀 rush ahead and fight fiercely

【勇气】courage;nerve

【勇士】warrior

【勇于】be brave in;be bold in;have the courage to

涌 (yǒng) ❶gush;pour;surge ❷rise;spring;well;emerge

【涌流】flow rapidly;pour

【涌现】emerge in large numbers;spring up

踊 (yǒng) leap up;jump up

【踊跃】leap;jump

用 (yòng) ❶use;apply ❷expenses ❸usefulness;use ❹need ❺〈敬〉eat;drink;take

【用处】use

【用法】use;usage

【用饭】have a meal

【用费】expense;cost
【用工】recruit and use（workers）
【用功】diligent;studious
【用户】consumer;user
【用具】utensil;apparatus;appliance
【用力】exert oneself（physically）;put forth one's strength
【用品】articles for use
【用人】❶choose and use personnel ❷need hands
【用事】〈书〉be in power
【用途】use
【用武】use military force;resort to arms
【用心】diligently;attentively;with concentrated attention:学习～ concentrate on one's studies;study diligently
【用意】intention;purpose
【用语】❶wording ❷term
佣（yòng）commission
另见 yōng
【佣金】commission;brokerage;middleman's fee

you

优（yōu）❶ inferior ❷〈旧〉 actor or actress valour
【优待】give favoured treatment
【优等】high-class;first-rate;excellent
【优点】merit;advantage;virtue
【优厚】munificent;liberal;favourable
【优化】optimize:～组合 optimization grouping or regrouping
【优惠】〈经〉preferential;favourable
【优良】fine;good
【优美】graceful;fine;exquisite
【优柔】❶leisurely;unhurried ❷〈书〉gentle;amiable ❸weak in character;hesitant
【优生】give birth to healthy babies
【优胜】winning;superior
【优势】superiority;preponderance
【优先】have priority;take precedence（in treatment）
【优秀】excellent;splendid
【优选】select the best
【优雅】❶ graceful;exquisite;elegant;in good taste ❷beautiful and elegant
【优异】outstanding;exceedingly good
【优游】〈书〉leisurely and carefree ❷have leisurely fun;amuse oneself in a leisurely way
【优裕】affluent;abundant
【优越】superior;advantageous
【优质】high quality
忧（yōu）❶worry;be worried ❷sorrow;anxiety

【忧愁】sad;depressed
【忧烦】worried;vexed;dejected
【忧愤】worried and indignant
【忧患】suffering;misery;hardship
【忧虑】anxious;concerned
【忧闷】depressed;feeling low;weighed down with cares
【忧伤】weighed down with sorrow;laden with grief
【忧心】❶〈书〉anxiety ❷care-laden
【忧郁】melancholy
幽（yōu）❶ deep and remote;secluded ❷secret;hidden ❸quiet;tranquil ❹imprison ❺of the nether world
【幽暗】dim;gloomy
【幽愤】hidden resentment
【幽谷】deep and secluded valley
【幽会】a lovers' rendezvous;tryst
【幽魂】soul of a deceased;ghost;spectre
【幽寂】secluded and lonely
【幽静】quiet and secluded
【幽灵】spectre;spirit
【幽美】secluded and beautiful:景色～ secluded and beautiful sights
【幽明】〈书〉nether world and this world
【幽默】humorous
【幽情】exquisite feelings
【幽深】deep and serene;deep and quiet
【幽微】❶faint;weak ❷〈书〉profound and exquisite
【幽香】delicate（or faint）fragrance:～四溢 give out a delicate fragrance;delicate fragrance permeate the air
【幽雅】（of a place）quiet and tastefully laid out
【幽怨】hidden bitterness（of a young woman thwarted in love）
悠（yōu）❶remote in time or space ❷leisurely ❸〈口〉swing
【悠长】long;long-drawn-out
【悠荡】swing
【悠久】long;long-standing;age-old
【悠然】carefree and leisurely
【悠闲】leisurely and carefree
【悠扬】rising and falling;melodious
【悠远】❶long time ago;long ago;distant ❷far off（or away）;remote;distant
尤（yóu）❶particularly ❷especially ❸fault;mistake ❹have a grudge against;blame
【尤其】especially;particularly
【尤异】〈书〉excellent;outstanding
由（yóu）❶cause;reason ❷pass through;go by way of ❸be up to sb.;rest with sb. ❹

by；through；via ❺ by sb. ❻ because of；due to ❼ by means of ❽ from

【由不得】❶ not be up to sb. to decide；be beyond the control of ❷ cannot help

【由此】thus；there from；from this

【由此可见】thus it can be seen；this shows；that proves

【由得】be up to；allow；permit

【由来】origin

【由于】owing to；thanks to；as a result of；in virtue of

【由衷】from the bottom of one's heart；heartfelt；sincere

邮 (yóu) ❶ post；mail ❷ postal

【邮包】postal parcel；parcel

【邮差】postman

【邮船】ocean liner；liner

【邮戳】postmark

【邮递】post delivery

【邮递员】postman；mailman

【邮费】postage

【邮购】mail order

【邮汇】remit money by post

【邮集】stamp album

【邮寄】send by post；post

【邮件】postal matter；post；mail

【邮局】post office

【邮票】stamp；postage stamp

【邮箱】postbox；mailbox

【邮政】postal service

【邮政局】post office

【邮资】postage

犹 (yóu) ❶ just；just as before ❷ still

【犹然】still；just as before

【犹如】as；just as；like

【犹豫】hesitate；be irresolute

【犹自】still

油 (yóu) ❶ oil；fat；grease；petroleum ❷ apply tung oil；vanish or paint ❸ oily；greasy；stained or smeared with oil or grease ❹ oily；glib

【油饼】oil cake

【油布】oilcloth；oilskin

【油灯】oil lamp；lamp using vegetable oil as its fuel

【油光】glossy；shiny；varnished

【油滑】slippery；foxy；slick

【油画】oil painting

【油矿】❶ oil deposit ❷ oilfield

【油亮】glossy；shiny

【油腻】❶ greasy；fatty；oily ❷ greasy food；fatty food；oily food

【油漆】❶ paint ❷ cover with paint

【油然】❶ spontaneously；involuntarily ❷（of clouds）gathering

【油田】oilfield

【油污】greasy dirt

【油性】oiliness；greasiness

【油脂】grease

【油纸】oil paper

【油渍】grease stains on clothes, etc.

【油嘴】spray nozzle；spray head

游 (yóu) ❶ swim ❷ rove around；saunter；stroll；travel；tour ❸ moving about；roving；floating ❹ associate with ❺ part of a river；reach

【游程】❶ distance of swimming ❷ route of travel

【游船】pleasure boat

【游荡】loiter；loaf about；wander

【游逛】go sight-seeing；stroll about

【游记】travel notes

【游客】visitor；tourist；sightseer；excursionist

【游览】go sight-seeing；visit；tour

【游乐】make merry；amuse oneself

【游历】travel for pleasure；travel；tour

【游民】vagrant；vagabond

【游目骋怀】look as far as one's eyes can see and give free rein to one's thoughts and feelings

【游人】visitor；tourist；sightseer

【游水】swim

【游说】go canvassing；go about selling an idea

【游艇】yacht；pleasure-boat

【游玩】amuse oneself；play；stroll about；go sightseeing

【游戏】recreation；game；play

【游行】❶ rove about ❷ parade；march

【游移】❶ float ❷ waver；vacillate；wobble

【游泳】swim

【游泳池】swimming pool

【游泳衣】swimwear；bathe；swimsuit

【游园】visit a garden or park

友 (yǒu) ❶ friend ❷ friendly

【友爱】friendly affection；fraternal love

【友邦】friendly nation

【友好】❶ close friend；friend ❷ friendly；amicable

【友情】friendly sentiments

【友人】friend：国际～ foreign friend

【友善】amicable

【友谊】friendship

有 (yǒu) ❶ have; possess ❷ there is; exist ❸ as...as... ❹ one; some

【有偿】 with compensation; compensated; paid

【有待】 remain (to be done); await

【有底】 know how things stand and feel confident of handling them

【有点】 a bit; some; a little

【有关】 have something to do with; have a bearing on; relate to; concern

【有救】 can be saved; can be cured

【有口皆碑】 win universal praise; be universally acclaimed

【有理】 reasonable; justified; in the right

【有力】 strong; powerful; might; energetic; vigorous; 领导～ strong leadership

【有利】 advantageous; beneficial; favourable

【有利无弊】 have every advantage and not a single disadvantage; be advantageous in every respect

【有利可图】 have good prospects of profit; stand to gain; be profitable

【有名】 well-known; famous; celebrated

【有名无实】 in name but not in reality; merely nominal; titular

【有名有姓】 identifiable by both given name and surname—of established identity

【有目共赏】 have a universal appeal; appeal to all alike

【有凭有据】 fully substantiated; well-documented

【有气无力】 feeble; weak; faint; listless

【有求必应】 respond to every plea; grant whatever is requested

【有去无还】 gone never to return; gone forever

【有趣】 interesting; fascinating; amusing

【有如】 just like; as if; as though

【有生以来】 since birth

【有声有色】 full of sound and colour—vivid and dramatic

【有识之士】 a person with breadth of vision; a man of insight

【有史以来】 since the beginning (or dawn) of history; throughout history

【有始有终】 carry sth. through to the end

【有恃无恐】 when one has something to fall back upon one has nothing to fear; feel secure in the knowledge that one has strong backing

【有喜】 be pregnant; be expecting; be in a family way

【有隙可乘】 there is a crack to squeeze through—there is a loophole to exploit

【有限】 limited; finite

【有效】 effective; valid

【有些】 ❶ some ❷ somewhat; rather

【有心】 ❶ have a mind to; set one's mind on ❷ intentionally; purposely

【有形】 tangible; visible; physical

【有幸】 be lucky to; have the good fortune to

【有益】 profitable; beneficial; useful

【有意】 ❶ have a mind to; be inclined (or disposed) to ❷ intentionally; deliberately; purposely

【有意识】 consciously; purposely; in a planned way

【有意思】 ❶ significant; meaningful ❷ be attracted sexually; take a fancy to

【有余】 have a surplus; have enough to spare; have more than enough

【有缘】 be predetermined by fate; be predestined; have a bond; have an affinity

【有朝一日】 someday

【有种】 have guts; be plucky; be gritty

右 (yòu) the right side; the right

【右边】 right (or right-hand) side; right

【右手】 right hand

幼 (yòu) ❶ young ❷ child; the young

【幼苗】 seedling; young plants after seeds sprout and grow

【幼年】 childhood; infancy

【幼体】 the young; larva

【幼小】 immature

【幼芽】 budlet

【幼稚】 ❶ young ❷ childish

【幼子】 the youngest son

诱 (yòu) ❶ guide; lead ❷ lure; seduce

【诱捕】 trap (animals)

【诱导】 guide; lead; induce

【诱饵】 bait anything used as a lure

【诱发】 bring out induce; cause to happen

【诱拐】 abduct; kidnap

【诱惑】 ❶ entice; tempt; seduce; lure ❷ attract; allure

【诱骗】 coax; cajole; trap; decoy

【诱杀】 trap and kill; lure to destruction

【诱致】 lead to; cause (negative result)

yu

迂 (yū) ❶ winding; roundabout ❷ clinging to outworn rules and ideas; pedantic

【迂腐】 pedantry

【迂缓】 slow; dilatory

【迂回】 ❶ roundabout ❷ outflank

【迂阔】high-sounding and impracticable
【迂执】pedantic and obstinate

淤 (yū) ❶become silted up ❷silt

【淤积】silt up;deposit
【淤泥】sludge;silt;ooze
【淤塞】silt up;be choked with silt
【淤血】extravasated blood
【淤滞】be retarded by silt;silt up

于 (yú) ❶in;at;on ❷for;to ❸from ❹than

【于今】❶up to the present;since ❷nowadays;
　today;now
【于是】thereupon;hence;consequently;as a re-
　sult

予 (yú) (formal) I;me
　另见 yǔ

【予取予求】take from me whatever you please—
　make unlimited demands

余 (yú) ❶surplus;spare ❷more than;over ❸
　beyond;after

【余波】repercussions
【余存】balance;remainder
【余党】remnants of an overthrown clique (or
　gang);remaining confederates
【余地】leeway;margin;room;latitude
【余毒】residual poison
【余额】❶vacancies yet to be filled ❷remaining
　sum ❸balance
【余晖】twilight at sunset;afterglow
【余悸】lingering fear
【余烬】ashes
【余力】surplus energy or strength
【余粮】surplus grain
【余年】one's remaining years
【余热】surplus energy
【余生】❶remainder of one's life;evening years;
　one's remaining years ❷survival
【余剩】surplus;remainder
【余数】remainder
【余威】remaining prestige or influence
【余味】agreeable aftertaste;pleasant impression
【余暇】spare time;leisure time;leisure
【余下】remaining
【余弦】cosine
【余音】lingering sound
【余裕】enough and to spare;ample
【余韵】remaining grace
【余震】aftershock

鱼 (yú) fish

【鱼刺】fishbone,which is thin and pointed

【鱼饵】bait;killer
【鱼缸】fishbowl;fish globe;fish jar
【鱼群】shoal of fish
【鱼水】fish and water
【鱼塘】fish pond
【鱼子】roe

娱 (yú) ❶ give pleasure to; amuse ❷ joy;
　pleasure;amusement

【娱乐】amusement;entertainment;recreation

渔 (yú) fishing

【渔产】aquatic products
【渔场】fishery;fishing ground
【渔船】fishing vessel;fishing boat
【渔村】fishing village;village where fishermen
　live
【渔夫】fisherman
【渔竿】fishing rod;fish pole
【渔港】fishing port;fishing harbor
【渔歌】fisherman's song
【渔火】lights on fishing boats
【渔家】fisherman's family
【渔民】fisherman;fisherfolk
【渔网】fishnet;fishing net
【渔业】fishery

逾 (yú) ❶exceed;go beyond ❷even more

【逾常】out of the ordinary;unusual
【逾分】excessive;undue
【逾期】exceed the time limit
【逾越】exceed;go beyond

愉 (yú) pleasure;happy;joyful;cheerful

【愉快】happy;joyful;cheerful
【愉悦】joyful;cheerful;delighted

愚 (yú) ❶ foolish; stupid ❷ make a fool
　of;fool

【愚笨】foolish;stupid;clumsy
【愚痴】stupid;idiotic;folly;silly
【愚蠢】stupid;clumsy
【愚钝】slow-witted;stupid
【愚昧】ignorant
【愚弄】deceive;dupe;make a fool of
【愚懦】stupid and timid
【愚顽】ignorant and stubborn
【愚妄】 ignorant but self-important; stupid
　but conceited

与 (yǔ) ❶give;offer ❷with;against ❸and;
　together with
　另见 yù

【与共】together;生死～ share a common desti-
　ny;go through thick and thin together|荣辱～

share honour and dishonour (*or* disgrace)

予 (yǔ) give;grant;bestow
另见 yú

【予人口实】give people a handle
【予以】give;grant

屿 (yǔ) small island;islet

宇 (yǔ) ❶eaves ❷house ❸space;universe

【宇航】space navigation;astronavigation
【宇航员】astronaut;cosmonaut
【宇宙】universe;cosmos

羽 (yǔ) feather;plume

【羽冠】crest
【羽毛】feather;plume
【羽毛球】❶badminton ❷shuttlecock
【羽绒】fine soft feathers;eiderdown;down
【羽翼】❶wing ❷assistant

雨 (yǔ) rain

【雨点】raindrop
【雨季】rainy season
【雨脚】thick and fast raindrops
【雨量】rainfall;precipitation
【雨林】rainforest
【雨露】❶rain and dew ❷favour;grace;bounty:
　～之恩 favour and kindness
【雨披】waterproof cape;rain cape
【雨伞】umbrella
【雨水】rainwater;rainfall
【雨丝】very light rain;drizzle;fine rain
【雨雾】misty rain
【雨鞋】galoshes;rubbers
【雨靴】rubber or plastic boots;rain boots;water-
　proof boots
【雨衣】raincoat;waterproof
【雨意】signs of approaching rain

语 (yǔ) ❶language; tongue ❷speak; say ❸
　set phrase;proverb;saying
【语病】faulty wording or formulation
【语词】words and phrases
【语调】intonation
【语法】grammar
【语感】instinctive feel for the language
【语汇】vocabulary
【语句】sentence;～不通 incoherent sentence
【语库】language data bank
【语录】quotation
【语气】❶tone;manner of speaking ❷mood
【语文】❶Chinese ❷language and literature
【语言】language

【语义】semanteme;semantics
【语意】meaning of words
【语音】speech sounds;pronunciation; voice

与 (yù) take part in;participate in
另见 yǔ

【与会】participate in a conference
【与闻】have a participant's knowledge of

玉 (yù) ❶jade ❷pure; fair; handsome; beauti-
　ful
【玉米】maize;corn
【玉佩】jade pendant
【玉器】jade article;jade object;jadeware;jade ar-
　tworks
【玉色】〈方〉jade green; light bluish green
【玉石】jade

郁 (yù) ❶strongly fragrant ❷luxuriant; lush
　❸gloomy;depressed
【郁愤】worried and indignant
【郁积】pent-up
【郁结】smouldering; pent-up; unable to vent
　what's building up in one's heart
【郁闷】depressed;gloomy;oppressive

育 (yù) ❶give birth to ❷rear; raise; bring
　up;bread
【育才】cultivate talent;train people
【育雏】raise young birds;feed young birds
【育林】plant trees;cultivate woods;afforest
【育龄】child-bearing age
【育秧】raise rice seedlings
【育养】❶bring up;rear ❷breed (aquatics); cul-
　tivate
【育种】breeding

狱 (yù) prison;jail

【狱警】prison guard;jailer
【狱卒】〈古〉prison guard;turnkey

浴 (yù) bath;bathe

【浴场】outdoor bathing place
【浴池】public bathhouse
【浴巾】bath towel
【浴室】❶bathroom;shower room ❷public bath-
　house;public baths
【浴血】bathed in blood;bloody;sanguinary
【浴衣】bathrobe;bathing-gown;bathing-wrap

预 (yù) in advance;beforehand

【预报】forecast
【预备】prepare;get ready
【预测】forecast;calculate
【预订】subscribe;book;place an order
【预定】fix in advance;schedule; predetermine

【预断】prejudge;predict;anticipate
【预防】prevent; take precautions against; guard against
【预付】pay (money) in advance
【预感】have a premonition;premonition
【预告】announce in advance;herald;advance notice
【预购】purchase in advance
【预计】calculate in advance;estimate
【预见】foresee;predict;foresight;prevision
【预警】early-warning;forewarning
【预料】anticipate;expect;predict as expected
【预谋】plan beforehand
【预期】expect;anticipate
【预赛】〈体〉preliminary contest;trial match
【预审】preliminary hearing
【预示】betoken;indicate;presage;forebode
【预收】collect (money) in advance
【预售】open to booking;advance-booking
【预算】budget
【预习】prepare lessons before class
【预先】in advance;beforehand
【预想】anticipate;expect;envisage
【预行】carry out ahead of schedule
【预言】prophesy;predict;foretell
【预约】make an appointment
【预兆】omen;presage;sign
【预支】advance
【预祝】congratulate beforehand

域 (yù) territory;region
【域外】outside the country
【域中】inside the country

欲 (yù) ❶desire;longing ❷wish;want;desire ❸about to;just going to;on the point of
【欲罢不能】unable to stop even though one wants to; try to stop but cannot; cannot refrain from going on
【欲望】desire;wish;lust

遇 (yù) ❶meet ❷treat;receive ❸chance;opportunity
【遇刺】be attacked by an assassin
【遇到】run into;come across;encounter;meet
【遇害】be murdered
【遇合】❶meet and hit it off; meet and get on well ❷come across;run into;encounter
【遇见】meet;come across
【遇救】be rescued;be saved;～脱险 be rescued out of danger
【遇难】die in an accident;be murdered
【遇险】meet with a mishap; be in danger; in distress

御 (yù) ❶drive(a carriage) ❷manage;control ❸of an emperor;imperial
【御笔】imperial brush
【御赐】bestowed by the emperor
【御道】a road for the imperial carriage
【御寒】keep out the cold
【御医】imperial physician;court physician
【御用】❶hired by the emperor;for the use of an emperor ❷serve as a tool for reactionary forces;be in the pay of

寓 (yù) ❶reside;live ❷residence;abode ❸imply;contain
【寓所】residence;dwelling place;abode
【寓言】fable;allegory;parable
【寓意】implied meaning;import

愈 (yù) ❶heal;recover ❷excel
【愈合】heal
【愈加】increasingly;even more;all the more
【愈益】all the more;even more;further; increasingly

yuan

冤 (yuān) ❶wrong;injustice ❷feeling of bitterness; hatred; enmity ❸ kid; fool ❹ bad luck;loss;disadvantage
【冤案】case of injustice
【冤仇】rancor;enmity
【冤家】enemy;foe
【冤情】grievance;facts of an injustice
【冤屈】wrong;treat unjustly;wrongful treatment
【冤枉】wrong; treat unjustly; not worthwhile

渊 (yuān) ❶a deep pool ❷deep
【渊博】broad and profound;erudite
【渊海】abyss and ocean
【渊源】origin;source

元 (yuán) ❶first;primary ❷chief;principal ❸basic fundamental ❹unit;component
【元旦】New Year's Day
【元件】element;component;cell
【元老】senior statesman;founding member
【元配】the first wife
【元气】vitality
【元首】head of state
【元帅】marshal;supreme commander
【元素】element
【元宵节】Lantern Festival
【元凶】crime;culprit
【元音】〈语〉vowel
【元月】January;first month of the lunar calendar

园 (yuán) ❶ an area of land for growing plants ❷ a place for public recreation park

【园地】 garden plot; field; scope
【园丁】 gardener
【园林】 gardens; park
【园田】 vegetable garden
【园艺】 gardening; horticulture

员 (yuán) a person engaged in some field

【员工】 staff; personnel

原 (yuán) ❶ primary; original; former ❷ unprocessed; raw ❸ excuse; pardon ❹ open country; plain; level

【原版】 original edition
【原本】 master copy; the original
【原初】 originally; formerly; at first
【原材料】 raw and processed materials
【原产地】 country of origin
【原稿】 original manuscript; master copy
【原告】 〈法〉 plaintiff; prosecutor
【原籍】 ancestral home
【原价】 original price; former price
【原件】 original manuscript
【原来】 ❶ original; former ❷ turn out to be; so
【原理】 principle
【原谅】 excuse; pardon; forgive
【原料】 raw material
【原貌】 original appearance
【原煤】 raw coal
【原始】 original; firsthand
【原委】 whole story; all the details
【原文】 original text; the original
【原先】 former; original
【原形】 original shape
【原型】 model; prototype
【原样】 original appearance or state; same old way
【原野】 open country; champaign
【原意】 original intention
【原因】 cause; reason
【原则】 principle; tenet
【原址】 former address
【原主】 original owner
【原著】 original; original work
【原装】 ❶ factory-assembled; factory-packed ❷ original packing
【原状】 original state; previous condition; status quo ante
【原子】 atom
【原作】 original work

圆 (yuán) ❶ round; circular; spherical ❷ circle ❸ tactful; satisfactory ❹ make plausible; justify ❺ the monetary unit of china

【圆场】 mediate; help to effect a compromise
【圆鼓鼓】 round and bulging; rotund
【圆规】 compasses
【圆弧】 arc
【圆滑】 slick and sly
【圆浑】 ❶ rich; mellow ❷ natural and smooth
【圆满】 satisfactory
【圆梦】 oneiromancy; divination by dreams
【圆盘】 disc
【圆球】 globe; ball
【圆圈】 circle; ring
【圆润】 ❶ mellow and full ❷ fluid; smooth
【圆实】 round and solid; plump
【圆熟】 ❶ skilful; proficient; dexterous ❷ astute; tactful; flexible
【圆形】 circular; round
【圆周】 circumference; boundary of a circle
【圆珠笔】 ball-pen; ball-point pen
【圆柱】 cylinder
【圆锥】 circular cone; taper
【圆桌】 round table

援 (yuán) ❶ pull by hand; hold ❷ quote; cite ❸ help; aid

【援兵】 relief troops; reinforcements
【援救】 rescue; save
【援军】 reinforcements; relief troops
【援例】 quote or cite a precedent
【援外】 aid to another country; aid a foreign country
【援引】 ❶ quote; cite ❷ promote; recommend or appoint sb. to a post
【援用】 ❶ quote; cite; invoke ❷ recommend and appoint sb.
【援助】 help; support; aid

缘 (yuán) ❶ reason ❷ edge; brink ❸ predestined relationship ❹ along

【缘故】 cause
【缘起】 ❶ cause; origin ❷ account of the reasons for sponsoring sth.
【缘由】 reason; cause

猿 (yuán) ape

【猿猴】 apes and monkeys
【猿人】 ape-man

源 (yuán) ❶ source; fountainhead ❷ cause

【源流】 source and course of a river
【源泉】 source; fountainhead; well-spring
【源头】 fountainhead; source

辕（yuán）❶shafts of a cart or carriage ❷the outer gate of a government office in ancient times❸a government office in ancient times
【辕马】horse in the shafts; shaft-horse
【辕门】the outer gate of a government office in ancient times

远（yuǎn）far
【远程】long-range; long-distance
【远大】long-range; broad
【远道】long way; long journey
【远东】the Far East
【远方】distant place
【远房】distantly related（kinsman）; remote（kinsfolk）
【远海】distant seas; high or open seas
【远航】take a long voyage
【远见】foresight; vision
【远郊】outer suburbs; outskirts; exurbs
【远近】far and near; distance
【远景】❶distant view; long-range perspective; prospect ❷future; prospects
【远虑】foresight; long view
【远略】long-term strategy
【远门】❶travel far away from home; go on a long journey ❷distantly related
【远谋】long-term plan
【远视】long sight; hyperopia
【远扬】spread far and wide: 臭名～ be notorious
【远洋】ocean; sea waters that are far away from the continent
【远征】expedition
【远志】lofty ideal; noble aspiration; great ambition: 胸怀～ cherish high aspirations
【远足】excursion; outing; hike; pleasure trip on foot

怨（yuàn）❶resentment; enmity ❷blame; complain
【怨不得】cannot blame; no wonder
【怨仇】hatred; enmity
【怨敌】foe; enemy
【怨毒】〈书〉enmity; hatred; animosity
【怨愤】discontent and indignation
【怨恨】❶hate ❷resentment; grudge; enmity
【怨气】grievance; complaint; resentment; indignant expression or mood
【怨望】〈书〉resentment; grudge; enmity
【怨言】complaint; grumble

院（yuàn）courtyard; yard
【院士】academician
【院子】courtyard; yard; compound

愿（yuàn）❶hope; desire; wish ❷be willing; be ready ❸vow
【愿望】wish; aspiration: 主观～ wishful thinking; subjective desire
【愿心】(in a broad sense) desire; hope; wish
【愿意】❶be willing; be ready ❷wish; like; want

yue

约（yuē）❶make an appointment ❷ask or invite in advance
【约定】agree on; appoint; arrange
【约分】reduction of a fraction
【约会】appointment; engagement; date
【约集】invite to meet; call together; gather
【约计】count roughly; come roughly to
【约见】make an appointment to meet
【约略】rough; approximate
【约莫】about; roughly; approximately
【约期】❶fix a date; appoint a time❷appointment or engagement; the appointed time ❸the term or duration of an agreement
【约请】invite; ask
【约束】restrain; bind
【约数】approximate number
【约同】ask sb. to go together
【约言】promise; word; pledge: 履行～ fulfil one's promise; redeem one's promise
【约制】keep within bounds; restrain; bind

月（yuè）❶the moon ❷month ❸monthly ❹full-moon-shaped; round
【月白】bluish white; pale blue
【月饼】mooncake
【月城】〈书〉barbican entrance to a city
【月底】end of a month
【月度】monthly
【月份】month
【月光】moonlight; moonbeam
【月季】〈植〉Chinese rose
【月刊】monthly magazine
【月历】monthly calendar
【月票】monthly ticket
【月钱】monthly allowance
【月色】moonlight; moonshine; moonbeam: 荷塘～ the moon over a lotus pond
【月食】〈天〉lunar eclipse

乐（yuè）music
另见 lè
【乐队】orchestra; band
【乐歌】❶music and songs ❷song with musical accompaniment
【乐谱】music score; music
【乐器】musical instrument

【乐曲】music；musical composition

【乐师】musician；musical player

【乐坛】music circles

【乐团】philharmonic society or orchestra

【乐舞】dance with musical accompaniment

【乐章】〈音〉movement

阅 （yuè）❶ read；go over ❷ review；inspect ❸ experience；pass through

【阅兵】review troops

【阅读】read

【阅卷】go over examination papers and give grades；read and mark examination papers

【阅览】read（books and newspapers）

【阅历】experience

【阅世】〈书〉see the world

悦 （yuè）❶ happy；pleased；delighted ❷ please；delight

【悦耳】pleasing to the ear；sweet-sounding

【悦服】admire from the bottom of one's heart

【悦目】good-looking；pleasing to the eye

跃 （yuè）leap；jump

【跃进】make a leap；leap forward

【跃然】show forth in one's writing；appear vividly

越 （yuè）❶ get over；jump over ❷ exceed；o-verstep ❸ the more …，the more …

【越发】all the more；even more

【越轨】exceed the bounds；transgress

【越过】cross；surmount；negotiate

【越级】bypass the immediate leadership and go directly to higher levels

【越界】overstep the boundary；cross the border

【越境】cross the boundary illegally；sneak in or out of a county

【越野】cross-country

yun

晕 （yūn）❶ dizzy；giddy ❷ swoon；faint
另见 yùn

【晕倒】fall in a faint；pass out

【晕厥】syncope；faint

云 （yún）❶ say ❷ cloud

【云鬓】〈书〉thick，beautiful hair over the temples of a woman

【云彩】cloud

【云层】cloud layer

【云端】high in the clouds

【云朵】fluffy cloud；mass of cloud；cloud

【云海】sea of clouds；stretch of clouds that look like a sea from far above

【云气】thin，floating cloud

【云雀】skylark

【云梯】scaling ladder

【云天】sky；welkin

【云头】cloud cluster；cloud；heap of clouds

【云雾】cloud and mist；mist；〈喻〉veil；coverage；blockade；hindrance

【云霄】sky；heaven

【云烟】cloud and mist；mist

匀 （yún）❶ even ❷ even up；divide evenly ❸ spare

【匀称】well-balanced；well-proportioned；symmetrical

【匀和】❶ even；equal；uniform ❷ even up；divide evenly

【匀净】uniform；even；neat

【匀实】even；neat；uniform

【匀整】neat and well-spaced；tidy；even and orderly

允 （yǔn）❶ permit；allow；consent ❷ fair；just

【允当】proper；suitable

【允诺】promise；consent

【允许】permit；allow

陨 （yǔn）fall from the sky of outer space

【陨落】（of a meteorite，etc.）fall from the sky or outer space

【陨灭】❶ （of objects）fall from the sky or outer space，and burn up ❷ meet one's death；perish；die

【陨石】〈天〉aerolite；stony meteorite

殒 （yǔn）perish；die

【殒命】〈书〉meet one's death；perish

【殒身】〈书〉be killed；perish；meet one's death

孕 （yùn）❶ pregnant ❷ pregnancy

【孕妇】pregnant woman

【孕期】pregnancy；gestation

【孕育】be pregnant with；breed

运 （yùn）❶ motion；movement ❷ carry；transport；ship ❸ use；wield；utilize ❹ fortune；luck；fate

【运笔】wield the pen（to write or paint）；start writing

【运动】❶ motion；movement ❷ sports；athletics；exercise ❸ movement；campaign；drive

【运动场】sports venue；athletic ground；playground；stadium

【运动会】sports meet；games

【运动员】sportsman；athlete；player

【运费】transportation expense; freight; carriage

【运输】transport; carriage; conveyance

【运送】transport; ship; convey

【运算】operation; solving a math problem according to mathematical rules

【运行】move; be in motion

【运营】be in operation; open for service; put into operation

【运用】utilize; wield; apply; put to use

【运作】be in operation; operate; run

晕（yùn）❶dizzy; giddy ❷〈气〉halo
另见 yūn

【晕场】have stage fright; feel dizzy due to excessive nervousness or other reasons

【晕车】car sickness

【晕船】sea sickness

【晕机】suffer from airsickness; be airsick

愠（yùn）〈书〉angry; irritated

【愠恼】angry; indignant; furious

【愠怒】be inwardly angry

韵（yùn）❶ musical sound; sweet tone ❷ rhyme ❸charm

【韵调】musical tone

【韵律】❶metre (in verse) ❷rules of rhyming; rhyme scheme

【韵母】〈语〉simple or compound vowel

【韵事】romantic or anecdotal event: 风流～ romantic affair; love affair

【韵味】❶charm or appeal implied by sound and rhythm; implicit richness ❷ charm; appeal; interest

【韵文】verse

【韵致】grace; charm; appeal

蕴（yùn）〈书〉accumulate; contain

【蕴藏】hold in store; contain

【蕴涵】implication

【蕴蓄】lie hidden and undeveloped; be latent; be implicit

熨（yùn）iron; press

【熨斗】iron; flatiron

Y

Z z

zā

扎 (zā) tie；bind
另见 zhā

杂 (zá) ❶sundry；mixed ❷mix；mingle

【杂草】weeds；rank grass；hogweed

【杂处】live in one area

【杂凑】together at random；jumble up；knock together

【杂费】❶ incidental expenses；incidentals ❷ sundry fees

【杂感】❶random thoughts ❷a type of literature recording such thoughts

【杂货】sundry goods；groceries

【杂记】❶miscellanies ❷jottings；notes：学习～ study notes

【杂技】acrobatics

【杂交】hybridize；crossbreed

【杂粮】coarse cereals

【杂品】odds and ends for daily use；groceries；sundry goods

【杂食】❶ omnivorous；eating different kinds of both meat and plants ❷〈书〉snack；between-meal nibbles

【杂事】trivial matters；sundry matters

【杂税】miscellaneous levies；sundry taxes：苛捐～ exorbitant taxes and levies

【杂文】essay

【杂务】odd jobs；sundry duties；chore

【杂音】noise；heart murmur

【杂志】magazine

【杂质】impurity

【杂种】hybrid；crossbreed；intercross

砸 (zá) ❶ pound；tamp ❷ break；smash ❸〈方〉fail；fall through；be bungled

【砸碎】break into pieces；smash

zai

灾 (zāi) ❶calamity；disaster ❷personal misfortune；adversity

【灾害】calamity；disaster

【灾患】calamity；disaster；mischance；catastrophe

【灾荒】famine due to crop failures

【灾祸】disaster；calamity；catastrophe

【灾民】victims of a natural calamity

【灾难】suffering

【灾年】famine (or lean) year

【灾情】the condition of a disaster

【灾区】disaster area

【灾殃】suffering；calamity；disaster

栽 (zāi) ❶plant；grow ❷stick in；insert；plant ❸force sth. on sb. ；impose ❹tumble；fall

【栽培】❶cultivate；grow：～水稻 cultivate rice ❷foster；train；educate

【栽赃】frame sb. ；fabricate a charge against sb.

【栽植】plant；transplant：～葡萄 transplant grapes

【栽种】plant；grow

【栽子】young plant；seedling

仔 (zǎi) young
另见 zǐ

载 (zǎi) ❶year ❷put down in writing；record
另见 zài

宰 (zǎi) ❶slaughter；butcher ❷govern；rule

【宰割】invade，oppress and exploit

【宰相】prime minister

再 (zài) ❶another time；again；once more ❷come back；return

【再版】second edition；reprint

【再次】second time；once more；once again：～获奖 win awards once again

【再度】once more；a second time

【再会】〈套〉good-bye；see you again

【再婚】remarry；marry again

【再见】〈套〉good-bye；see you again

【再三】over and over again

【再生】❶revive；rise again ❷regenerate；reproduce ❸recycle；regenerate

【再世】❶next life ❷〈书〉reappear；reincarnate；revive

【再现】reappear；be reproduced；playback

【再造】give sb. a new lease of life

在 (zài) ❶exist；be living ❷be ❸at；in ❹rest with；depend on

【在编】be on the payroll；be on the permanent staff

【在册】registered；on the name list：登记～ registered

【在场】be on the scene；be on the spot

【在行】be an expert at；know well；be a professional；be adept in

【在乎】care about；mind；take to heart

【在即】very soon；in the near future

【在家】be at home；be in

【在理】reasonable；sensible；right

【在内】included

【在世】alive；be living

【在逃】be at large；have escaped；be on the run

【在望】be within the range of vision；be in sight；be in view；be visible

【在位】❶be on the throne；reign；be a monarch ❷hold an official post；be a leader

【在握】be in one's hands；be within one's grasp；be under one's control

【在业】be employed；be on the job

【在意】take notice of；care about；mind；take to heart

【在于】❶depend on；rest on；be determined by ❷lie in；consist in

【在职】be on the job；be employed

【在座】be present(at a meeting，banquet，etc.)

载 (zài) carry；hold；be loaded with
另见 zǎi

【载客】carry passengers

【载运】convey by vehicles，ship，etc.

【载重】load；carrying capacity

zan

暂 (zàn) ❶of short duration ❷temporarily；for the time being；for the moment

【暂缓】put off；defer；postpone

【暂且】for the moment；for the time being；for the present

【暂时】temporary；transient

【暂停】suspend

【暂行】provisional；temporary；interim

赞 (zàn) ❶support；favor；assist ❷praise；commend

【赞成】approve of；favor；agree with；endorse

【赞歌】paean；hymn；song or poem in praise of a person or a thing

【赞美】praise；eulogize

【赞佩】esteem；admire；hold in esteem

【赞赏】appreciate；admire

【赞颂】extol；eulogize；sing the praises of

【赞叹】gasp in admiration；highly praise

【赞同】approve of；agree with；endorse；consent；accede

【赞许】speak favourably of；praise；commend

【赞扬】speak highly of；praise；commend；applaud

【赞誉】praise；acclaim；commend

【赞助】support；assistance

zang

赃 (zāng) ❶stolen goods；booty；spoils ❷bribes

【赃官】corrupt official；dishonest official

【赃款】embezzled money；accepted bribes；stolen money；illicit money

【赃物】❶stolen goods ❷bribes

脏 (zāng) dirty；filthy

【脏话】obscene（or dirty，foul）language；obscenities

【脏乱】dirty and messy

葬 (zàng) bury；inter

【葬礼】funeral rites；funeral

【葬埋】entomb；bury；inter

【葬送】ruin；spell an end to

藏 (zàng) ❶storing place；depository ❷Buddhist or Taoist scriptures
另见 cáng

【藏蓝】purplish blue

【藏青】dark blue

zao

遭 (zāo) meet with；suffer

【遭到】meet with；suffer；encounter

【遭逢】meet with；come across；encounter

【遭际】〈书〉circumstances；lot

【遭劫】meet with catastrophe；come face to face with calamity

【遭难】meet with misfortune；suffer disaster；be killed in an accident；be murdered

【遭受】suffer；be subjected to；sustain；undergo

【遭殃】suffer disaster；suffer

【遭遇】❶meet with；run up against；encounter ❷bitter experience；fate

【遭罪】have a difficult time

糟 (zāo) ❶distillers' grains ❷be pickled with grains or in wine ❸rotten；poor ❹in the terrible state；in a mess

【糟糕】terrible；too bad

【糟害】spoil；damage；lay waste to；make havoc of

【糟践】spoil；lay waste to；ruin；waste；befool；trample on；insult

早 (zǎo) ❶(early) morning ❷long ago；for a long time ❸early；beforehand ❹good morning

【早安】good morning

【早餐】breakfast

【早操】morning exercises

【早茶】morning tea

【早场】morning show

【早晨】morning；early morning

【早春】early spring

【早稻】early (season) rice

【早点】breakfast

【早年】❶many years ago；in the past ❷when one is young；at a tender age

【早期】early period；early days；early stage；early phase

【早日】at an early date；early；soon

【早上】morning；early morning

【早熟】❶precocity；paedogenesis；acceleration ❷early-maturing；early-ripe

【早退】leave early

【早晚】❶morning and evening ❷sooner or later

【早先】previously；before；in the past

【早已】❶long ago；for a long time ❷〈方〉previously；before；in the past

枣 (zǎo) jujube；(Chinese) date；tsao

【枣红】purplish red；claret

【枣泥】jujube paste

【枣树】jujube tree

皂 (zào) ❶black ❷soap

【皂白】black and white

【皂片】soap flakes

灶 (zào) ❶kitchen range；cooking stove ❷kitchen；mess；canteen

【灶火】〈口〉❶kitchen range；cooking stove ❷kitchen

【灶具】〈口〉cooking utensils

【灶台】the top of a kitchen range

【灶头】〈口〉kitchen range；cooking stove

造 (zào) ❶make；build；create ❷invent；cook up；concoct ❸train；educate

【造成】make；create；cause

【造次】〈书〉❶hurried；hasty ❷rash；impetuous；impertinent

【造反】rebel；revolt；rise in rebellion

【造访】pay a visit；call on

【造福】benefit；bring benefit to

【造价】cost of building

【造句】make a sentence

【造林】afforestation

【造像】statue

【造型】moulding；modelling

【造诣】attainment or accomplishment

【造纸】paper making

【造作】affected；artificial

噪 (zào) ❶(of birds, insects, etc.) chirp ❷confusion of voices

【噪声】noise；din；discordant sound in certain environments

【噪音】noise

燥 (zào) dry

【燥热】hot and dry

躁 (zào) rash；impetuous；restless

【躁动】move restlessly

【躁急】restless；uneasy

ze

则 (zé) ❶standard；norm；criterion ❷rule；regulation

【则声】make a sound；utter a word

责 (zé) ❶duty；responsibility ❷demand；require ❸question closely；call sb. to account ❹reproach；blame；reprove ❺punish

【责备】reproach；blame

【责打】punish by beating

【责罚】punish；fine

【责怪】blame

【责令】instruct；order

【责骂】scold；rebuke；dress down

【责难】censure；blame

【责任】duty；responsibility；obligation

【责问】bring sb. to account

择 (zé) select；choose；pick

【择交】choose friends

【择偶】choose a spouse

【择期】select a day or time

【择优】select the superior ones

zei

贼 (zéi) ❶thief ❷traitor；enemy ❸crooked；wicked；evil；furtive ❹craftily；sly；cunning；deceitful ❺injure；harm；murder

【贼寇】robber；bandit；housebreaker；invader；aggressor

【贼心】evil design；evil intention

【贼眼】shifty eyes;furtive glance
【贼赃】stolen goods;booty;spoils

zen

怎 (zěn) why;how
【怎么】❶why;how;what ❷in a certain way;in any way;no matter how ❸ very;much;quite too

zeng

增 (zēng) increase;gain;add
【增补】supplement;augment
【增产】increase production
【增订】revise and enlarge
【增多】increase
【增幅】increasing range;growth rate
【增高】❶get higher;rise;increase ❷improve;elevate;heighten;increase
【增光】do credit to;win honour for
【增加】increase;raise;add
【增进】promote;enhance;improve
【增刊】supplementary issue
【增强】strengthen;enhance
【增设】establish an additional or new
【增收】increase income
【增援】reinforce
【增长】increase;add;raise;rise
【增值】〈经〉rise in value;appreciation

憎 (zēng) hate;detest;abhor
【憎称】term of condemnation
【憎恨】hate;detest
【憎恶】abhor;loathe;abominate

赠 (zèng) give as a present;present as a gift
【赠别】present a friend with gifts, poems, etc. at parting
【赠礼】gift;present:接受～ accept a gift
【赠品】giveaway;gift
【赠送】give as a present;present as a gift
【赠言】words of advice given at parting
【赠与】favour;gift;grant
【赠阅】given free by polisher

zha

扎 (zhā) ❶prick;run or stick into ❷plunge into;get into ❸be stationed;be quartered
另见 zā
【扎根】❶take root ❷make a foundation
【扎实】❶ sturdy;strong;robust ❷ solid;firm;

down-to-earth
【扎手】❶prick the hand ❷difficult to handle;thorny
【扎眼】❶ dazzling;offending to the eye;loud;garish ❷offensively conspicuous
【扎营】pitch a camp;camp
【扎针】give (or have) acupuncture treatment

札 (zhá) ❶thin pieces of wood used for writing on in ancient China ❷〈书〉letter
【札记】reading notes

轧 (zhá) ❶run;run over ❷oust;squeeze out;push out
另见 yà
【轧伤】run over and injure
【轧死】run over and kill

闸 (zhá) ❶ floodgate;sluice gate ❷ dam up water ❸brake ❹〈口〉switch
【闸口】〈水〉water-gate
【闸门】❶sluice gate ❷〈机〉throttle valve

眨 (zhǎ) blink;wink;bat
【眨巴】〈方〉blink
【眨眼】very short time;twinkle

诈 (zhà) ❶cheat;swindle ❷pretend;feign ❸bluff sb. into giving information
【诈唬】bluff;bluster
【诈骗】defraud:～钱财 cheat or swindle sb. out of his or her money and property
【诈降】pretend to surrender;feign surrender
【诈语】lie;falsehood;fabrication;deceit

炸 (zhà) ❶explode;burst ❷blow up;blast;bomb ❸〈口〉fly into a rage;flare up ❹〈方〉flee in terror
【炸弹】bomb
【炸雷】〈方〉loud thunderbolt
【炸窝】❶flee in fright ❷be thrown into panic;be in disarray
【炸药】explosive(charges);dynamite

榨 (zhà) press;extract
【榨菜】mustard tuber
【榨取】squeeze;extort

zhai

摘 (zhāi) ❶ pick;pluck ❷select;make extracts from
【摘编】extract and compile
【摘除】excise;remove
【摘登】publish excerpts or extracts of something
【摘记】❶take notes ❷excerpts
【摘借】borrow money when in urgent need
【摘录】❶make extracts ❷extracts

【摘要】❶make a summary ❷summary
【摘引】quote

宅 (zhái) residence；house

【宅第】a large house；mansion
【宅基】the foundations of a house；the site of a house
【宅门】❶gate of a large old-style house ❷family living in a mansion with spacious courtyards
【宅院】a house with a courtyard；house
【宅子】residence；house；abode；dwelling

债 (zhài) debt

【债户】debtor
【债款】loan
【债利】interest on loans
【债权】〈法〉creditor's rights
【债券】bond；debenture
【债务】debt；liabilities；amount due
【债主】creditor

zhan

沾 (zhān) ❶ moisten；wet；soak ❷ be stained with

【沾边】❶touch on (or upon) only lightly ❷be close to what it should be；be relevant
【沾光】benefit from association with sb. or sth.
【沾亲】be somewhat related
【沾染】❶be infected with ❷be contaminated by
【沾手】❶ touch with one's hand ❷ have a hand in

粘 (zhān) glue；stick；paste

【粘连】adhesion
【粘贴】paste；stick
【粘住】stick；adhere

瞻 (zhān) look up or forward

【瞻顾】〈书〉look ahead and behind
【瞻念】think of；look ahead：～前途 think of the future
【瞻望】look forward；look far ahead
【瞻仰】look at with reverence

斩 (zhǎn) ❶chop；cut ❷behead

【斩决】execute by decapitation
【斩首】behead；decapitate

展 (zhǎn) ❶ spread out；unfold ❷ give free play to ❸ postpone；prolong ❹ exhibition

【展播】broadcast for publicity purposes
【展出】put on display；be on show；exhibit
【展开】❶spread out；unfold；open up；roll out；

unroll ❷launch；develop；carry out
【展宽】expand；broaden；widen：～马路 widen the road
【展览】put on display；exhibit；show：～馆 exhibition hall｜～会 exhibition
【展品】exhibit；item on display
【展示】show；lay bare
【展望】❶look into the distance ❷look ahead
【展现】unfold before one's eyes；emerge；show；appear

崭 (zhǎn) ❶ towering (over) ❷ 〈方〉fine；swell

【崭齐】perfectly uniform；perfectly even
【崭然】〈书〉towering；outstanding
【崭新】brand-new；completely new

占 (zhàn) ❶ occupy；seize ❷ constitute；account for ❸ take (up)

【占据】occupy；hold
【占领】capture；seize
【占先】take precedence；take the lead；get ahead of
【占线】the line(of a telephone) is busy
【占用】occupy and use
【占有】❶own；possess；have ❷occupy；hold

栈 (zhàn) ❶warehouse ❷inn；hostel ❸shed；pen

【栈道】a plank roadway built along perpendicular rock-faces by means of wooden brackets fixed into the cliff
【栈房】❶warehouse；storehouse ❷inn
【栈桥】landing stage (in a port)；loading bridge (at a railway station)

战 (zhàn) ❶ war；warfare；battle；fight ❷ fight ❸shiver；tremble；shudder

【战败】❶be defeated；suffer a defeat；lose ❷defeat
【战备】war preparedness；combat readiness；preparation for war
【战场】battlefield；battleground；battlefront
【战地】battlefield；battleground；combat zone
【战斗】fight；battle；combat
【战犯】war criminal
【战俘】prisoner of war (P. O. W.)
【战歌】battle song；fighting song
【战果】victory；results of battle
【战壕】trench；entrenchment
【战后】postwar
【战火】flames of war
【战祸】disaster of war；scourge of war
【战绩】military successes or exploits
【战局】war situation in a certain period or area
【战具】weapon；arms

Z

【战例】specific example of a battle (in military science)

【战栗】tremble; shiver

【战乱】chaos caused by war; war turmoil

【战略】strategy

【战区】war zone; theatre of operations; theatre of war

【战胜】defeat; overcome

【战事】war; hostilities

【战士】soldier

【战术】military tactics

【战线】battle lines; battlefront; front; frontline

【战役】campaign; battle

【战友】battle companion; comrade-in-arms

【战争】war; warfare

站 (zhàn) ❶stop; halt ❷station; stop ❸station or centre for rendering certain services ❹stand; be on one's feet; take a stand

【站队】line up; queue up; stand in line

【站岗】stand or mount guard; stand sentinel

【站立】stand; rise; be on one's feet

【站票】ticket for standing room only; standing ticket

【站台】platform

【站稳】❶stand firm; take a firm stand ❷come to a stop

绽 (zhàn) split; burst

【绽放】(of flowers)burst forth; burst into bloom

【绽裂】split open; burst open

湛 (zhàn) ❶profound; deep❷crystal clear

【湛蓝】(of the sky, the sea, a lake, etc.) azure blue; azure

【湛清】limpid; clear

颤 (zhàn) quiver; tremble

另见 chàn

zhang

张 (zhāng) ❶open; spread; stretch ❷magnify; exaggerate

【张榜】put up a notice; post a notice; put up a proclamation

【张大】〈书〉magnify; exaggerate; publicize widely

【张挂】hang up

【张皇】alarmed; scared

【张口】open one's mouth (to say sth.)

【张狂】insolent

【张目】❶open one's eyes wide ❷inflate sb.'s arrogance

【张贴】put up

【张望】look around

【张嘴】❶open one's mouth ❷ask for a loan or a favour

章 (zhāng) ❶chapter; section ❷order ❸rules; regulations ❹seal; stamp ❺badge; medal

【章程】rules; regulations; constitution

【章节】chapters and sections

【章则】rules and regulations

长 (zhǎng) ❶older; elder; senior ❷eldest; oldest ❸chief; head ❹grow; develop ❺come into being; begin to grow; form

另见 cháng

【长辈】senior; elder

【长大】grow up; be brought up

【长官】senior officer or official; commanding officer

【长进】progress

【长年】〈方〉owner of a ship

【长上】❶elder member of a family; elder; senior ❷superior; boss

【长势】the way a crop is growing

【长孙】eldest son's eldest son; eldest grandson

【长相】looks; features; appearance

【长者】senior; elder

【长子】eldest son

涨 (zhǎng) (of water, prices, etc.)rise; go up

【涨潮】rising tide; flood tide

【涨幅】margin or rate of rise; rise

【涨价】rise in price

【涨落】(of water, prices, etc.) rise and fall; fluctuate

掌 (zhǎng) ❶palm ❷strike with the palm of the hand; slap ❸hold in one's hand; be in charge of ❹shoe sole or heel ❺horseshoe

【掌厨】chef

【掌灯】❶hold a lamp in one's hand ❷light an oil lamp

【掌故】anecdotes

【掌管】be in charge of; administer

【掌柜】❶shopkeeper; manager (of a shop) ❷〈方〉form of address of a landlord by tenant farmers ❸〈方〉husband

【掌权】be in power; wield power

【掌声】clapping; applause

【掌纹】friction ridge; palm print

【掌握】grasp; master; know well

【掌心】the centre (hollow) of the palm

【掌印】❶keep the seal ❷take control; be in power

【掌子】face; work; horseshoe area

丈 (zhàng) ❶ a unit of length (= 3 $\frac{1}{3}$ metres) ❷ senior; elder

【丈夫】husband

【丈量】measure

【丈人】❶ a respectful form of address for an old man ❷ wife's father; father-in-law

仗 (zhàng) ❶ weaponry; weapons ❷ hold (a weapon) ❸ depend on ❹ battle; war

【仗势】take advantage of one's own or others's power

【仗恃】rely on

【仗义】❶〈书〉uphold justice ❷ be loyal to (one's friends)

杖 (zhàng) cane; stick

【杖子】(usu. used as part of a place name) hedge

帐 (zhàng) ❶curtain; canopy ❷account ❸account book ❹debt; credit

【帐篷】tent

账 (zhàng) ❶account book weaponry; weapons ❷bill

【账簿】account book

【账单】bill; check

【账户】account

【账面】items of an account

【账目】account

障 (zhàng) ❶hinder; obstruct ❷barrier

【障碍】❶hinder ❷obstruction impediment

【障蔽】block; obstruct; shut out

【障子】a barrier made of reeds, sorghum stalks or closely planted shrubs; hedge

zhao

招 (zhāo) ❶ beckon ❷ recruit; enlist ❸ attract; incur ❹ provoke; tease ❺ confess ❻ trick; device

【招标】invite tenders (or public bidding); call for tenders

【招兵】recruit soldiers; raise troops

【招待】receive; serve

【招风】catch the wind

【招呼】❶call ❷greet; say hello to ❸notify; tell ❹take care of

【招魂】call back the spirits of the dead;〈喻〉revive

【招集】call together; convene

【招架】ward off blows; hold one's own

【招考】give public notice of an entrance examination

【招领】announce the finding of lost property

【招牌】shop sign; signboard

【招聘】invite applications for a job; give notice of a vacancy to be filled

【招惹】❶provoke; incur; court ❷tease

【招认】confess one's crime(s); plead guilty

【招收】recruit; take in

【招手】beckon; wave

【招贤】summon people of worth to serve their country

【招降】summon sb. to surrender

【招摇】act ostentatiously; show off

【招引】attract; induce

【招灾】court disaster; invite trouble

【招展】move to and fro; flutter; wave

【招致】❶recruit ❷bring about; lead to

昭 (zhāo) clear; obvious

【昭布】make known to the public

【昭示】make clear to all; declare publicly

【昭雪】exonerate; rehabilitate

【昭彰】clear; manifest; evident

【昭昭】〈书〉❶bright; light; well-lit ❷clear; obvious; plain

【昭著】clear; evident; obvious

着 (zhāo) ❶a move in chess ❷trick; device; move ❸put in; add ❹all right; O. K.
另见 zháo, zhuó

【着数】❶ a move in chess ❷ a movement in wushu ❸trick; device

朝 (zhāo) ❶early morning; morning ❷day
另见 cháo

【朝晖】morning sunlight

【朝令夕改】issue an order at dawn and rescind it at dusk

【朝露】〈书〉morning dew; ephemeral; transitory

【朝气】youthful spirit; vigor; vitality

【朝夕】❶morning and evening; from morning till night; day and night; daily ❷ shortly; very short time

【朝霞】rosy clouds of dawn; rosy dawn

着 (zháo) ❶ touch ❷ feel; be affected by ❸ burn; light
另见 zhāo, zhuó

【着慌】get alarmed; become flustered

【着火】catch fire; be on fire

【着急】feel anxious

【着凉】catch cold

【着忙】be in a hurry

【着迷】be fascinated; be captivated

【着魔】be bewitched; be possessed; be entranced

爪 (zhǎo) claw; talon
另见 zhuǎ

【爪牙】talons and fangs—lackeys;underlings

找（zhǎo）❶ look for;seek ❷ want to see; call on

【找病】look for illness

【找补】make up a deficiency

【找齐】❶ make uniform; even up; balance ❷ make complete

【找钱】give change

【找事】❶look (or hunt)for a job ❷pick a quarrel

【找死】court death

【找头】change

【找寻】look for;seek

沼（zhǎo）natural pond

【沼气】marsh gas;fire damp;methane

【沼泽】marsh;swamp;bog

召（zhào）call together;convene;summon

【召唤】call;summon

【召回】recall

【召集】call together;convene

【召见】call in;summon

【召开】convene; hold; convoke (a meeting or conference)

兆（zhào）❶ sign; omen; portent ❷ million;mega

【兆头】sign;omen;portent

照（zhào）❶shine;light up ❷reflect;mirror ❸ take a picture; photograph ❹ photograph;picture ❺license;permit ❻take care of; look after ❼notify ❽contrast ❾understand

【照搬】indiscriminately imitate;copy

【照办】act accordingly; act upon; follow; comply with

【照常】as usual

【照发】❶ approved for distribution ❷ be paid as usual

【照顾】❶give consideration to; make allowance for ❷look after;care for

【照管】look after;tend;be in charge of

【照护】look after

【照旧】as before;as usual;as of old

【照看】look after;attend to;keep an eye on

【照理】❶in the ordinary course of events; normally ❷〈方〉look after;attend to

【照例】as a rule; as usual; usually

【照料】take care of; attend to:～病人 look after patients

【照明】illumination;lighting

【照片】photograph;picture

【照射】shine;illuminate;light up

【照实】according to the facts

【照说】ordinarily;generally;as a rule

【照相】take a picture;take photos

【照样】in the same old way; as before; all the same;as usual

【照耀】shine;illuminate;enlighten

【照应】❶look after;take care of;互相～ be well coordinated ❷coordinate;correlate

【照直】❶ (go) straight on ❷straightforward;direct

罩（zhào）❶ cover; wrap ❷ cover; casing; hood;shade

【罩袍】overall;dustrobe

【罩衣】dustcoat

zhe

折（zhē）〈口〉❶ roll over; turn over ❷ pour back and forth between two containers
　　另见 shé,zhé

【折腾】〈口〉❶turn from side to side;toss about ❷do sth. over and over again ❸get sb. down

遮（zhē）❶hide from view;cover ❷block;obstruct ❸cover up

【遮蔽】❶cover;screen ❷obstruct; block

【遮藏】hide;conceal;cover up

【遮丑】gloss over one's blemishes; hide one's shame;cover up one's defects

【遮挡】shelter from;keep out

【遮盖】❶overspread ❷hide;conceal;cover up

【遮光】irising;dodging;diaphragmation

【遮拦】block;obstruct;impede

【遮羞】hush up a scandal;cover up one's embarrassment;conceal one's disgrace

【遮掩】❶ cover; overspread; envelope ❷ cover up;hide;conceal

【遮阳】sunshade

折（zhé）❶break;snap ❷suffer the loss of; lose ❸bend;twist ❹turn back;change direction ❺be convinced;be filled with admiration ❻convert into;amount to ❼discount;rebate ❽an act of ❾turning stroke
　　另见 shé,zhē

【折半】reduce by half

【折变】sell off

【折尺】folding ruler

【折叠】fold

【折断】break

【折服】❶subdue;bring into submission;convince ❷be convinced;be filled with admiration

【折光】❶refract light ❷refracted light

【折合】be equivalent to;convert into;amount to

【折回】turn back (halfway)

【折价】convert into money;evaluate in terms

of money

【折旧】〈经〉depreciation

【折磨】cause physical or mental suffering；torment

【折扇】folding fan

【折算】convert

【折腰】〈书〉bend one's back；bow in obeisance；cringe

【折账】pay a debt in kind

【折中】compromise

哲 （zhé）❶wise；sagacious ❷wise man；sage

【哲理】philosophic theory；philosophy：人生～ philosophy of life

【哲人】sage；philosopher

【哲学】philosophy

这 （zhè）❶this ❷now

【这边】this side；here

【这次】this time；present；current

【这个】❶this one；this ❷〈口〉so；such

【这里】over here；here

【这些】these

【这样】so；such；like this；this way

zhen

贞 （zhēn）❶loyal；faithful ❷chastity or virginity

【贞操】❶chastity or virginity ❷loyalty；moral integrity

【贞洁】chaste and undefiled

【贞烈】(of a woman) would rather die than lose one's chastity

【贞淑】〈书〉chaste and gentle

针 （zhēn）needle

【针对】be directed against；be aimed at；be targeted at；take into consideration

【针管】needle tube

【针剂】〈药〉injection

【针尖】pinpoint；the point of a needle

【针脚】❶line of stitches ❷stitch

【针灸】acupuncture and moxibustion

【针线】needlework

【针眼】❶eye of a needle；needle's eye ❷pinprick

【针织】knitting

侦 （zhēn）detect；scout；investigate

【侦办】investigate and handle (a case)

【侦查】investigate

【侦察】reconnoitre；scout

【侦获】investigate and crack

【侦破】investigate and uncover；detect；solve

【侦探】detective；spy

珍 （zhēn）❶treasure ❷precious；valuable；rare ❸value highly；treasure

【珍爱】be very fond of；treasure；love dearly

【珍宝】jewellery；treasure；riches

【珍本】rare edition；rare book

【珍藏】collect

【珍贵】valuable；precious

【珍品】treasure

【珍奇】rare

【珍视】value；prize；cherish；treasure

【珍玩】rare curios

【珍闻】news titbits；fillers

【珍惜】treasure；value；cherish

【珍稀】rare and precious

【珍重】highly value；treasure；set great store by

【珍珠】pearl；gem；margarite

真 （zhēn）❶true；real；genuine ❷really；truly；indeed ❸clear；unmistakable

【真才实学】real ability and learning；genuine talent

【真诚】sincere；genuine；true

【真谛】true essence；true meaning

【真假】true or false；genuine or sham

【真空】〈物〉vacuum

【真理】truth

【真切】❶vivid；clear；distinct；graphic ❷sincere；genuine

【真情】❶real or true situation；facts；actual state of affairs；truth ❷true feelings；real sentiments

【真实】true；real；actual；authentic

【真是】really；indeed

【真率】sincere；candid；unaffected；straight forward

【真相】the real situation；the true facts；truth

【真心】wholehearted；heartfelt；sincere；from the bottom of one's heart

【真性】❶true；genuine ❷〈书〉nature；natural instincts

【真正】genuine；true；real

【真知】genuine knowledge；correct under standing

【真挚】cordial；sincere

【真主】〈宗〉Allah

诊 （zhěn）examine (a patient)

【诊察】examine (a patient)

【诊断】diagnose

【诊疗】make a diagnosis and give treatment

【诊脉】feel the pulse

【诊室】consulting room
【诊所】clinic
【诊治】make a diagnosis and give treatment

枕 (zhěn) pillow

【枕木】(of railway) sleeper; tie
【枕套】pillowcase
【枕头】pillow
【枕席】❶〈书〉bed ❷mat used to cover a pillow; pillow mat
【枕芯】pillow

阵 (zhèn) ❶battle array ❷front; position ❸a period of time

【阵地】position; front
【阵容】❶battle array (or formation) ❷strength displayed by and army
【阵势】situation; position
【阵痛】❶labour pains; throes (of childbirth) ❷birth pangs
【阵亡】be killed in action; fall in battle
【阵线】front; ranks; alignment
【阵雪】snow shower
【阵营】group of people who pursue a common interest; camp
【阵雨】shower

振 (zhèn) ❶shake; flap ❷rise with force and spirit; brace up

【振臂】raise one's arm
【振荡】generation; oscillating; oscillation
【振动】vibration
【振奋】❶rouse oneself; be inspired with enthusiasm ❷inspire; stimulate
【振兴】promote
【振作】bestir oneself; display vigor

赈 (zhèn) relieve; aid

【赈济】relieve; aid
【赈款】relief fund
【赈灾】provide relief to people in stricken areas

震 (zhèn) ❶shake; shock; vibrate ❷greatly excited; deeply astonished

【震波】seismic wave; earthquake wave
【震颤】tremble; quiver
【震荡】shake; shock; vibrate; quake
【震动】shake; shock; vibrate; quake
【震感】seismesthesia
【震撼】shake; shock; vibrate
【震惊】amaze; astonish; ～世界 shock the world
【震怒】be enraged; be furious
【震慑】awe; frighten
【震悚】〈书〉tremble with fear; be terrified; be frightened

【震源】focus
【震中】epicentre

镇 (zhèn) ❶press down; keep down ❷calm; tranquil ❸ town ❹ guard ❺garrison post ❻cool with cold water or ice

【镇定】calm; cool
【镇反】suppress counter-revolutionaries
【镇静】composed; unruffled
【镇守】guard; garrison
【镇压】suppress; repress; put down

zheng

争 (zhēng) ❶contend; strive ❷argue; dispute ❸〈方〉short of

【争辩】argue; debate; contend
【争吵】quarrel; squabble
【争持】refuse to give in; stick to one's guns
【争宠】strive for sb.'s favour
【争斗】fight; struggle; strife
【争端】issue; dispute; conflict
【争夺】fight (or contend, scramble)
【争光】win honor for
【争论】argument; controversy; dispute; debate
【争鸣】contend
【争气】try to make a good showing; try to win credit
【争取】strive for; fight for
【争胜】compete for first place
【争先】try to be the first to do sth.
【争议】dispute; controversy
【争战】fight; war; 两军～ war between two armies
【争执】disagree; dispute
【争嘴】〈方〉❶scramble for a bit to eat ❷quarrel; row

征 (zhēng) ❶go on a journey ❷go on expedition

【征兵】conscription; draft; call-up
【征程】journey
【征调】call up; requisition
【征订】solicit subscriptions
【征发】(of government) make requisition for supplies and personnel
【征伐】go on a punitive expedition
【征服】conquer; subdue
【征稿】solicit contributions
【征购】government purchase (of agricultural products, land, etc.)
【征婚】marriage seeking
【征集】❶collect; gather ❷call up; draft
【征聘】invite applications for a job
【征求】solicit; seek; ask for

Z

【征收】levy;collect;impose
【征税】levy taxes;taxation
【征途】journey
【征文】solicit essays
【征象】sign;symptom;indication
【征询】consult;seek the opinion of
【征引】quote;cite
【征用】requisition;commandeer
【征战】go on an expedition (*or* a campaign)
【征召】❶ call up;enlist;draft;conscript ❷〈书〉appoint to an official position
【征兆】sign;omen;portent

挣 (zhēng) 另见 zhèng
【挣扎】struggle

蒸 (zhēng) ❶ evaporate ❷ steam

【蒸发】evaporate
【蒸锅】steamer;a pot for steaming food
【蒸饺】steamed dumpling food
【蒸笼】food steamer
【蒸气】vapour
【蒸汽】steam
【蒸食】steamed wheaten foods
【蒸腾】rising

拯 (zhěng) save;rescue;deliver

【拯救】save;deliver;rescue

整 (zhěng) ❶ whole;complete;full;entire ❷ in good order;neat;tidy ❸ put in order;rectify ❹ repair;mend;renovate ❺ make sb. suffer;punish;fix ❻ do;make;work
【整备】reorganize and outfit (troops)
【整队】get (*or* bring) the ranks into orderly alignment;line up
【整顿】reorganize;rectify;consolidate
【整改】reform and consolidate
【整个】whole;entire
【整洁】clean and tidy;neat
【整理】arrange;put in order;sort out
【整齐】❶ in good order;neat;tidy ❷ regular;even
【整套】complete (*or* whole) set of
【整体】whole;entirely
【整形】reshaping;shaping;plastic
【整修】rebuild;renovate;repair
【整整】whole;full
【整治】❶ renovate;repair;dredge (a river, etc.) ❷ punish;fix;make to suffer

正 (zhèng) ❶ straight;upright ❷ situated in the middle;main ❸ punctually;sharp ❹ honest;upright ❺ correct ❻ pure;light ❼ principal;chief ❽ regular ❾ positive
【正本】❶ original ❷ reserved copy
【正比】direct proportion
【正步】parade step;goose step
【正常】normal;regular
【正大】upright;honest;aboveboard
【正当】just when;just the time for
【正道】❶ right way (*or* course);correct path ❷ correct principle;correct way
【正点】on schedule;on time;punctually
【正反】positive and negative
【正告】earnestly admonish;sternly warn;warn in all seriousness
【正规】regular;standard;conforming to a recognized standard
【正轨】the right path
【正好】❶ just in time;just right;just enough ❷ happen to;chance to
【正理】correct principle
【正路】right way (*or* course);correct path
【正面】❶ front;facade;frontage ❷ the right side ❸ directly;openly ❹ positive
【正派】upright;decent;honest
【正片】positive
【正品】quality products;quality goods
【正巧】happen to;chance to;as it happens;just in time;in the nick of time
【正确】correct;right
【正式】formal;regular
【正事】one's proper business
【正视】face up to;look in the face
【正题】subject
【正文】text
【正误】correct errors
【正项】main project;regular project
【正义】❶ justice ❷ just;righteous
【正在】in process of;in course of
【正直】honest;upright;fair-minded
【正中】middle;centre
【正宗】orthodox school
【正座】central seats that directly face the stage;stalls

证 (zhèng) ❶ prove;demonstrate ❷ evidence;proof;testimony ❸ certificate;card
【证词】testimony
【证婚】witness a wedding
【证件】credentials;paper;certificate
【证据】evidence;proof;testimony
【证明】❶ prove;testify;bear out;certify ❷ certificate;identification;testimonial
【证人】〈法〉witness
【证实】confirm;verify

Z

【证书】certificate;credentials
【证物】exhibit
【证言】testimony
【证验】❶verify ❷real results;efficacy
【证章】badge

政 (zhèng) ❶politics;political affairs ❷certain administrative aspects of government
【政变】coup
【政策】policy
【政党】political party
【政敌】political opponent
【政法】politics and law
【政府】government
【政工】political work
【政纪】government discipline
【政绩】achievements in one's official career
【政见】political view
【政界】political circles;movement circles
【政局】political situation;political scene
【政客】politician
【政论】political comment
【政权】political power;regime
【政事】movement affairs
【政务】government affairs;government administration
【政治】politics
【政治学】political science

挣 (zhèng) ❶ struggle to get free;try to throw off ❷earn;make
另见 zhēng
【挣钱】earn money

症 (zhèng) disease;illness

zhi

支 (zhī) ❶prop up;put up ❷protrude;raise ❸support;sustain;bear ❹send away;put sb. off ❺pay or draw (money) ❻branch;offshoot
【支撑】prop up;shore up;sustain
【支持】❶support;back;stand by ❷sustain;hold out;bear
【支出】❶ pay; expend ❷ expenses; expenditure;outlay
【支点】❶ fulcrum; pivot about which a lever turns ❷strongpoint;fortified point;stronghold
【支队】detachment
【支付】pay
【支行】subbranch(of a bank)
【支架】support;stand
【支离】❶ fragmented; broken; disorganised ❷ trivial and jumbled;incoherent

【支流】❶tributary;affluent ❷minor aspects;nonessentials
【支派】branch;sect;offshoot
【支配】❶arrange;allocate;budget ❷control;determine
【支票】cheque;check
【支渠】branch (irrigation) canal
【支取】draw
【支使】order about;send away;put sb. off
【支吾】equivocate;hum and haw
【支援】support;assist;help
【支柱】pillar;prop;mainstay

汁 (zhī) juice
【汁水】〈方〉juice

芝 (zhī)
【芝麻】❶sesame ❷sesame seed
【芝麻油】sesame-seed oil;sesame oil

枝 (zhī) branch;twig
【枝权】branch;twig
【枝节】branches and knots;minor matters;minor aspects;side problems
【枝蔓】branches and tendrils
【枝条】branch;twig
【枝丫】branch;twig
【枝叶】❶ branches and leaves ❷ nonessentials;minor details
【枝子】branch;twig

知 (zhī) ❶know;realize;be aware of ❷inform;notify;tell ❸knowledge
【知道】know;realize;be aware of
【知底】know the inside story;know the background;be in the know
【知会】tell
【知己】❶ intimate; understanding ❷ intimate;friend
【知觉】❶consciousness ❷perception
【知名】well-known;noted;famous
【知名度】popularity;fame
【知情】know the facts of a case or the details of an incident;be in the know
【知趣】know how to behave in a delicate situation;be sensitive;be tactful
【知识】knowledge
【知悉】learn;be informed of
【知晓】know;be aware of
【知心】intimate;understanding:～朋友 intimate (or bosom) friend
【知友】close friend;intimate friend
【知照】inform;notify;tell

【知足】be content with one's lot

肢 (zhī) limb

【肢体】❶limbs ❷limbs and trunk

织 (zhī) weave;knit

【织补】darning;invisible mending
【织布】weaving cotton cloth;weaving
【织品】textile;fabric

脂 (zhī)

【脂肪】fat

蜘 (zhī)

【蜘蛛】spider

执 (zhí) ❶hold;grasp ❷take charge of;direct manage ❸stick to;persist ❹carry out

【执笔】write;do the actual writing
【执法】enforce the law
【执教】be a teacher or coach;teach
【执拗】stubborn;willful;headstrong
【执勤】be on duty
【执行】carry out;implement
【执意】insist on;be determined to
【执友】〈书〉intimate friend;bosom friend
【执掌】wield;be in control of
【执照】license;permit
【执政】be in power;be in office
【执着】persistent; persevering; inflexible; rigid; work unflaggingly

直 (zhí) ❶straight ❷straighten ❸vertical; perpendicular ❹just; upright ❺frank; straight forward ❻directly

【直拨】direct dialing
【直肠】〈生理〉rectum
【直尺】straightedge
【直达】through;nonstop
【直到】until
【直根】taproot
【直观】direct perception
【直角】right angle
【直接】direct;immediate
【直径】diameter
【直觉】intuition
【直立】stand erect;stand upright
【直面】look sb. in the eye; face squarely; look squarely at
【直抒】express freely;state frankly
【直属】❶directly under;directly subordinate to; affiliated to ❷under the jurisdiction
【直爽】straightforward;forthright
【直辖】directly under the jurisdiction of

【直线】straight line
【直性】straightforward;downright; forthright
【直言】speak bluntly;state outright

伫 (zhí) nephew

【伫女】niece
【伫孙】grandnephew
【伫子】nephew

值 (zhí) ❶value ❷be worth ❸happen to ❹be on duty;take one's turn at sth.

【值班】be on duty
【值得】be worth;deserve
【值钱】costly;valuable
【值勤】be on duty;be on point duty
【值日】be on duty for the day;be one's turn to be on duty
【值夜】be on night duty;be on the night shift

职 (zhí) ❶duty;job ❷post;office

【职别】official rank
【职称】the title of a technical or professional post
【职工】staff and workers
【职能】function
【职权】powers (or authority) or office
【职守】post;duty;擅离～ be away without leave
【职位】position
【职务】post;duties;job
【职衔】post and rank
【职业】occupation;profession;vocation
【职员】office worker;staff member;functionary
【职责】duty;obligation;responsibility

植 (zhí) ❶plant;grow ❷set up;establish

【植苗】transplant seedlings
【植树】tree planting
【植物】plant;flora
【植物人】(of a human being) vegetable

殖 (zhí) breed;multiply

【殖民】establish a colony;colonize
【殖民地】colony

止 (zhǐ) ❶stop; cease; discontinue ❷to; till ❸only

【止步】halt;stop;go no further
【止境】end;limit
【止息】cease;stop

只 (zhǐ) only;merely;just

【只得】have no alternative but to;be obliged to; have to
【只顾】be absorbed in

Z

【只管】by all means；feel free to

【只好】cannot but；have to；be forced to

【只是】❶ only；just；merely ❷ except that；only；but

【只消】all one has to do is；you only need to

【只要】if only；as long as；provided

【只有】❶ only；alone ❷ have to；be forced to

旨 (zhǐ) ❶purpose；aim ❷decree

【旨趣】main purpose；objective

【旨意】decree；order

纸 (zhǐ) paper

【纸板】paperboard

【纸币】paper money；paper currency；note

【纸浆】pulp

【纸张】paper

指 (zhǐ) ❶finger ❷point to；point at ❸indicate；point out；refer to

【指标】target；quota；index

【指导】guide；direct

【指点】give directions

【指挥】❶command；direct；conduct ❷〈音〉conductor

【指挥棒】baton

【指挥员】commander

【指甲】nail

【指教】❶give directions or guidance；instruct；teach；indoctrinate；coach ❷〈套〉used to ask sb. to give advice or comments

【指控】accuse；charge

【指令】instruct；order

【指名】mention by name；designate

【指派】send a assign；appoint；designate；name；call on

【指认】point out and affirm；identify；recognize

【指使】incite；instigate

【指示】❶indicate；point out ❷instruct；order ❸order；instruction

【指头】finger

【指望】❶ look forward to；count on；expect ❷hope

【指纹】fingerprint

【指引】lead；show the way；direct；guide：～航向 steer a ship along the right course；direct the course of a ship

【指责】criticize；find fault with

【指摘】pick fault and criticize

【指正】❶point out mistakes so that they can be corrected ❷〈套〉used to invite sb. to make comments or critical remarks

咫 (zhǐ)

【咫尺】very close

趾 (zhǐ) ❶toe ❷foot

至 (zhì) ❶ arrive；reach ❷ to；until ❸ extremely；most

【至诚】sincerity

【至此】❶here and now；at this point；up to here；hereto；here-unto；thus far ❷until now；up to this time；be now

【至多】at（the）most

【至高无上】most lofty；paramount；supreme

【至极】attaining the greatest or highest degree；to the utmost point；extremely；exceedingly

【至交】best friend

【至今】up to now；so far；to date

【至亲】very close relative；close kin

【至上】supreme；sovereign；paramount

【至少】at（the）least

【至死】till death

【至于】❶as far；as to ❷go so far as to

【至尊】❶ most honoured and revered：～无上 most distinguished ❷emperor

志 (zhì) ❶will；ideal ❷keep in mind ❸mark；sign

【志哀】expression of mourning

【志气】ambition；aspiration

【志趣】inclination

【志士】person of ideals and integrity

【志向】ideal；ambition

【志愿】❶ideal；wish ❷volunteer

制 (zhì) ❶make；manufacture ❷work out ❸restrict；control ❹system

【制版】plate making

【制备】(in chemical industry) preparation

【制裁】sanction；punish

【制订】work out

【制定】lay down；draw up

【制度】system；institution

【制服】uniform

【制剂】preparation

【制冷】refrigeration

【制片】produce

【制品】products；goods

【制胜】gain or get the upper hand

【制药】pharmacy

【制约】restrict；restrain

【制造】❶make；manufacture ❷create；fabricate

【制止】check；curb；prevent；stop

【制作】make；manufacture

Z

质（zhì）❶nature；character ❷quality ❸simple；plain ❹question

【质变】qualitative change

【质地】texture

【质点】particle

【质量】quality

【质朴】plain；unaffected

【质数】〈数〉prime number

【质问】question

【质询】address inquiries

【质疑】query；call in question

【质证】question the witness；cross-examine；challenge the witness

【质子】proton

治（zhì）❶rule；govern；administer；manage ❷order；peace ❸treat（a disease）；cure ❹control；harness ❺study；research

【治安】public order or security

【治本】effect a permanent cure

【治理】❶govern；administer ❷harness；bring under control

【治疗】treat；cure

【治丧】make funeral arrangements

【治水】dredge a watercourse to prevent floods；water control

【治学】study and research；pursue one's studies：～严谨 be a rigorous scholar；seek precision in one's studies

【治罪】bring sb. to justice for a crime；punish

挚（zhì）〈书〉sincere；earnest

【挚爱】sacred fire；affections；true love；deep love；profound love；flame of passion

【挚诚】sincere；earnest

【挚友】intimate friend；bosom friend

致（zhì）❶send；deliver ❷devote ❸incur；result in ❹fine；delicate ❺manner or style that engages attention or arouses interest

【致辞】make a speech

【致富】become rich；make a fortune；acquire wealth

【致敬】salute；pay one's respects to

【致力】devote one's efforts to sth.；work for

【致密】fine and close；compact

【致命】fatal；mortal

【致使】cause；result in

【致死】lethal；deadly

【致谢】express one's gratitude

【致意】give one's regards；give one's best wishes

秩（zhì）〈书〉❶order；rank ❷decade

【秩序】order；sequence

掷（zhì）throw；cast

【掷还】〈套〉please return

窒（zhì）〈书〉stop up；obstruct；block

【窒塞】stop up；block

【窒息】stifle；suffocate

智（zhì）wisdom

【智慧】wisdom

【智力】intelligence

【智龄】intelligence age

【智略】resourcefulness and talent；wisdom and ability

【智谋】resourcefulness

【智能】aptitude；brainpower；capacity；intelligence

【智商】intelligence quotient

【智育】intellectual education；intellectual development；mental development

【智者】wise man or woman

滞（zhì）stagnant；sluggish

【滞洪】flood detention

【滞留】be detained；be held up

置（zhì）❶place；put ❷set up；install ❸buy

【置办】buy；purchase

【置备】purchase

【置换】displacement

【置身】place oneself；stay

【置身事外】keep oneself out of it；stay out of it；stay aloof from sth.

【置信】believe；give credit to

【置疑】doubt

稚（zhì）young；childish

【稚嫩】❶young and tender ❷immature

【稚气】childishness

【稚弱】childish and tender

zhong

中（zhōng）❶center；middle ❷China ❸in；among ❹middle；mid- ❺medium；intermediate ❻mean；halfway between two extremes ❼intermediary ❽fit for；good for ❾in the process of；in the course of
另见 zhòng

【中层】middle-level；middle-ranking

【中档】of middling quality or price

【中等】❶secondary ❷medium；moderate；middling

【中国】China

【中级】intermediate;mid-level

【中坚】nucleus;hare core;backbone

【中间】❶among;between ❷middle;intermediate

【中立】neutrality

【中流】midstream

【中路】of middling quality;mediocre

【中年】middle age

【中期】mid-term;medium-term

【中听】pleasant to the ear;agreeable

【中途】halfway;midway

【中外】China and foreign countries

【中文】Chinese language

【中心】center;heart;core

【中型】medium-sized;medium

【中性】neutral

【中央】❶centre;middle ❷central authorities

【中医】❶traditional Chinese medical science ❷ practitioner of traditional Chinese medicine

【中用】of use;useful

【中游】middle reaches (of a river)

【中原】Central Plains

【中正】〈书〉equity;impartiality;justice

【中止】discontinue;suspend;interrupt; break off

【中指】middle finger;medius;long finger

【中子】neutron

忠 (zhōng) loyal;devoted

【忠诚】loyal;faithful;staunch

【忠告】sincerely advise

【忠厚】honest and sincere

【忠良】❶faithful and upright ❷person of good faith and integrity

【忠实】faithful;reliable

【忠顺】wholeheartedly obedient;loyal and meek

【忠心】loyalty;devotion

【忠言】sincere advice;earnest advice

【忠义】❶loyalty; righteousness ❷〈古〉loyal court official

【忠勇】loyal and brave;faithful and courageous; staunch and valiant

【忠于】be true to;be loyal to

【忠贞】loyal and steadfast

终 (zhōng) ❶end; finish ❷death; end ❸e- ventually;in the end ❹whole;entire;all

【终场】end of a performance (or show,sports e- vent,etc.)

【终点】❶terminal point;end point;destination ❷ 〈体〉finish

【终端】terminal

【终古】〈书〉forever

【终归】eventually;in the end;after all;～无效 eventually prove useless

【终极】final;ultimate;～目的 ultimate aim

【终结】end;conclusion;final stage

【终究】after all;in the end;eventually

【终局】ending;finale

【终了】(of a period) come to an end;学期～ end of the (school term)

【终年】❶throughout the year;all the year round ❷the age at which one dies

【终日】all the day;all day long;all day

【终身】lifelong;all one's life

【终身大事】a great event in one's life (usu. re- ferring to marriage)

【终审】❶last instance; final judgement;～判决 final judgement ❷final censoring

【终生】all one's life

【终于】at last;in the end;finally

【终止】stop;put an end to;terminate

钟 (zhōng) ❶ bell ❷ clock ❸ time·as meas- ured in hours and minutes

【钟爱】cherish

【钟摆】pendulum

【钟表】clocks and watches;timepiece

【钟点】❶ time at which sth. happens or gets done ❷hour

【钟情】be deeply in love

【钟头】hour

衷 (zhōng) inner feelings;heart

【衷肠】〈书〉words from one's heart;倾吐～ pour out one's feelings

【衷情】heartfelt emotion;inner feelings

【衷心】heartfelt;wholehearted

肿 (zhǒng) swelling;swollen

【肿瘤】tumour

【肿胀】swelling;tumescence

种 (zhǒng) ❶species ❷race ❸seed; strain; breed ❹kink;sort;tape 另见 zhòng

【种畜】stock male or female domestic animal; stud stock

【种蛋】breeding egg

【种类】category;pattern;type;kind

【种群】population

【种种】all sorts of;a variety of

【种子】seed

【种族】race

中 (zhòng) ❶hit; fit exactly ❷be hit by;be affected by;suffer 另见 zhōng

【中标】get the bid or tender
【中毒】poisoning
【中计】fall into a trap
【中奖】win lottery
【中肯】apropos；pertinent；to the point
【中伤】slander；malign
【中暑】❶suffer sunstroke ❷sunstroke
【中选】be chosen；be selected
【中意】be to one's liking

仲 (zhòng) ❶the second mouth of a season ❷the second among brothers ❸middle；intermediate
【仲裁】arbitrate

众 (zhòng) ❶many；numerous ❷crowd；multitude
【众多】multitudinous；numerous
【众怒】public wrath
【众人】everybody
【众生】all living creatures；all flesh；mouse and man；芸芸～ mouse and man；common herd
【众说】public opinion；different versions of (an event)
【众望】people's expectations；popular confidence

种 (zhòng) grow；plant；cultivate
另见 zhǒng
【种花】grow flowers
【种植】plant；grow

重 (zhòng) ❶ weight ❷ heavy；weighty ❸ considerable in amount or value ❹deep；serious ❺attach importance to
另见 chóng
【重工业】heavy industry
【重办】severely punish
【重兵】large number of forces：～把守 be heavily guarded
【重彩】strong colours (used in painting)：浓墨～ (paint in) dark ink and rich colours
【重创】heavy losses on；maul heavily；plaster
【重大】great；major；significant
【重担】heavy burden；difficult task
【重地】important location：工程～ construction site
【重点】key；emphasis
【重负】heavy load；heavy burden
【重话】harsh words；offensive remarks
【重活】heavy work
【重价】high price
【重奖】❶ handsome reward ❷ highly reward sb.；offer rich rewards to sb.
【重金】huge sum of money；high price
【重力】〈物〉gravity；gravitational force

【重利】❶heavy interest；high rate of interest；usury ❷great profit；huge profit ❸〈书〉value material gains：～轻义 put material gains above justice
【重量】weight
【重任】important task；heavy responsibility
【重伤】severe injury；grievous bodily harm
【重视】pay attention to；attach importance to
【重听】hard of hearing
【重托】great trust
【重心】❶centre；centre of mass ❷median point；intersection of the three medians of a triangle ❸heart；focus；core；crux
【重型】heavy：～汽车 heavy vehicle
【重要】important；significant；major：～问题 big issue；major problem
【重用】put sb. in an important position
【重责】❶ heavy responsibility：身负 ～ bear heavy responsibilities ❷ severely reprimand or punish
【重镇】town of military importance
【重资】large sum of money；great deal of capital
【重子】baryon；heavy particle

zhou

周 (zhōu) ❶circumference；periphery ❷make a circuit；move in a circular course ❸all over；all around ❹thoughtful；attentive ❺week
【周报】weekly(publication)
【周长】girth；circumference；perimeter
【周到】attentive and satisfactory；considerate：服务～ offer good service
【周刊】weekly；weekly publication
【周六】Saturday
【周密】careful；thorough
【周末】weekend
【周年】anniversary
【周期】period；cycle
【周全】❶thorough；comprehensive ❷help sb. to fulfil their wishes
【周身】all over the body；all over；at every pore；from head to foot
【周岁】one full year of life；exactly one year in age
【周围】around；round；about
【周旋】❶ whirl；circle around；convolve；hover；orbit；whorl ❷ engage in social intercourse；deal with；interact with；mix with (sb.)
【周游】travel round；journey round
【周章】〈书〉❶ scared；startled；frightened；in a panic；in a fluster ❷ setbacks；pains

taking;trouble

【周折】 twists and turns;setbacks;a complicated (*or* troublesome) course of development

【周正】 〈方〉 straight;regular

【周转】 turnover

轴 (zhóu) ❶axle;shaft ❷spool;rod

【轴承】 bearing

【轴线】 spool thread;spool cotton

【轴心】 axis

肘 (zhǒu) elbow

【肘窝】 crook of the arm

【肘腋】 〈书〉 close at hand

咒 (zhòu) ❶incantation ❷curse;damn

【咒骂】 curse;swear;abuse

zhu

朱 (zhū) cinnabar

【朱红】 vermilion;bright red

【朱漆】 red paint;red lacquer

珠 (zhū) ❶pearl ❷bead

【珠宝】 pearls and jewels;jewelry

【珠算】 reckoning by the abacus;calculation with an abacus

【珠子】 ❶pearl ❷bead

株 (zhū) 〈量〉 ❶ trunk of a tree;stem of a plant ❷individual plant

【株连】 involve(others) in a criminal case;implicate

【株守】 〈书〉 hold on stubbornly to

诸 (zhū) all;various

【诸多】 a good deal;a lot of

【诸侯】 dukes or princes under an emperor

【诸如】 such as

【诸位】 ladies and gentlemen

猪 (zhū) pig;hog;swine

【猪倌】 swineherd

【猪圈】 pigsty;pigpen;hogpen

【猪猡】 〈方〉 pig;swine;hog

【猪肉】 pork

竹 (zhú) bamboo

【竹编】 bamboo basketry

【竹材】 bamboo wood

【竹竿】 bamboo pole

【竹排】 bamboo raft

【竹器】 bamboo ware

【竹笋】 bamboo shoots

逐 (zhú) ❶pursue;chase ❷expel;drive out ❸one by one

【逐步】 progressively;step by step

【逐个】 one by one

【逐渐】 gradually;by degrees

【逐年】 on a yearly or annual basis;year by year; year after year

【逐日】 day by day;every day

【逐字】 word for word;verbatim

烛 (zhú) ❶candle ❷illuminate;light up

【烛光】 candlepower;candle

【烛花】 snuff;charred end of a candlewick

【烛台】 candlestick

主 (zhǔ) ❶ host ❷ owner;master ❸ person concerned;party concerned ❹ 〈宗〉 God; Lord ❺ 〈宗〉 Allah ❻ main;primary ❼ manage;be in charge of ❽stand for;be in favor of ❾indicate;signify

【主办】 sponsor;direct

【主编】 chief editor

【主持】 ❶take charge manage;direct ❷uphold; stand for:～公道 uphold justice

【主次】 primary and secondary

【主从】 principal and subordinate:～关系 relationship between the principal and the subordinate

【主导】 leading;dominating;guiding

【主动】 initiative

【主妇】 housewife;hostess

【主干】 trunk

【主根】 main root;taproot

【主攻】 main attack

【主顾】 customer;client

【主观】 subjective

【主管】 be in charge of;be responsible for

【主婚】 preside over a wedding ceremony

【主见】 ideas or thoughts of one's own;one's own judgment

【主讲】 be the speaker;give a lecture

【主将】 ❶chief commander;commanding general ❷one who plays the main role in a certain field of endeavour

【主角】 leading role;lead;protagonist

【主考】 chief examiner

【主力】 principal strength;main force

【主流】 ❶main stream ❷main trend;essential aspect

【主脑】 ❶control centre;centre of operations ❷leader;chief

【主权】sovereign rights;sovereignty
【主人】❶master;owner ❷host
【主任】director;head;办公室～ office director
【主食】staple food
【主事】be in charge;take charge
【主题】theme;subject
【主体】main body;main part
【主席】chairman
【主线】main threads
【主刑】principal penalty
【主演】act the leading role
【主要】main;major;chief;principal
【主意】idea;plan;decision
【主宰】❶dominate;dictate;decide ❷force that controls and governs the destiny of mankind or the development things
【主张】❶hold;maintain;advocate ❷view stand

嘱 (zhǔ) enjoin;advise;urge

【嘱咐】enjoin;tell;exhort
【嘱托】entrust

瞩 (zhǔ) gaze;look steadily

【瞩目】〈书〉fix one's eyes upon;focus one's attention upon
【瞩望】〈书〉❶look forward to ❷gaze at;look long and steadily upon

助 (zhù) help;assist;aid

【助教】(of a college faculty)assistant
【助理】assistant
【助手】assistant;helper;aide;person who helps others at work
【助威】boost the morale of;cheer (for)
【助兴】liven things up;add to the fun

住 (zhù) ❶live;reside;stay ❷stop;cease ❸firmly;to a stop

【住持】abbot;abbess;highest
【住处】residence;lodging
【住地】dwelling (place);lodging
【住房】housing;lodgings
【住户】household;resident
【住家】❶live;reside in ❷household;resident
【住居】live;reside;inhabit
【住手】stay one's hand;stop
【住宿】accommodate;put up;lodge
【住所】residence;dwelling place
【住院】be hospitalized;be in hospital
【住宅】residence;dwelling
【住址】address

贮 (zhù) store;save;lay aside

【贮备】lay aside;store up
【贮藏】store up;lay in keep
【贮存】stock;store;keep in storage

注 (zhù) ❶pour;fill ❷concentrate;fix ❸stakes(in gambling) ❹annotate;notes ❺record;register

【注册】register
【注定】be doomed;be destined
【注解】❶explanatory note ❷explain with notes
【注明】give clear indication of
【注目】gaze at;fix one's eyes on
【注射】inject
【注视】look attentively at;gaze at
【注销】cancel;write off
【注意】pay attention to
【注重】emphasize;lay stress on;attach importance to

驻 (zhù) ❶halt;stay ❷be stationed

【驻地】place where troops,etc.,are stationed
【驻防】be on garrison duty;garrison
【驻军】station troops;garrison
【驻守】garrison;defend
【驻扎】be stationed;be quartered
【驻足】halt;stop;go no further

柱 (zhù) post;upright;pillar;column

【柱石】pillar and its foundation
【柱子】post;pillar

祝 (zhù) express good wishes;wish

【祝祷】pray;say one's prayers
【祝福】blessing;benediction
【祝告】pray;say one's prayers
【祝贺】congratulate
【祝捷】celebrate a victory
【祝酒】a toast;toast
【祝寿】congratulate(an elderly or old person)on his or her birthday
【祝颂】express good wishes
【祝愿】wish

著 (zhù) ❶marked;outstanding ❷show;prove ❸write ❹book;work

【著称】celebrated;famous
【著录】put down in writing;record
【著名】famous;celebrated;well-known
【著者】author;writer
【著作】❶write;to express one's opinion knowledge,thinking,or emotion in writing ❷work;book;writings

zhua

抓 (zhuā) ❶ grab; seize ❷ scratch ❸ arrest; catch ❹ stress; pay special attention to ❺ take charge of; be responsible for ❻ attract; grip

【抓获】catch; capture; seize

【抓紧】firmly grasp; pay close attention to

【抓举】snatch

【抓瞎】find oneself at a loss; be in a rush and a muddle; be thrown off balance

爪 (zhuǎ) claw; talon; paw
另见 zhǎo

zhuan

专 (zhuān) ❶ concentrate ❷ monopolize ❸ special; specialize ❹ expert

【专长】speciality; speciality skill or knowledge

【专场】❶ special performance ❷ performance of a certain type of programme

【专程】special trip：～看望 make a special trip to visit sb.

【专断】make an arbitrary decision; act arbitrarily

【专访】❶ special coverage; interview with sb. on a certain topic ❷ special article

【专家】expert; specialist

【专刊】monograph

【专科】speciality; special field of study; specialized subject：～医生 medical specialist

【专款】special fund; fund earmarked for a special purpose：教育～ education fund

【专栏】special column

【专卖】monopoly

【专门】special; specialized

【专任】full-time; regular：～教员 full-time teacher

【专书】monograph; book on a specific topic

【专项】special item：～训练 specialized training

【专心】be absorbed; concentrate one's attention

【专修】major in; specialize in

【专业】❶ specialized subject; special field of study; speciality; discipline ❷ specialized trade or profession; special line

【专业课】specialized course

【专一】single-mind; concentrated

【专用】for a special purpose or a person：～电话 telephone for special use

【专政】dictatorship

【专职】full-time (position)：～工会干部 full-time trade union cadre

【专制】autocratic

【专注】concentrate one's attention on; be absorbed in; devote one's mind to

【专著】monograph; treatise

砖 (zhuān) brick

【砖头】〈方〉brick

【砖窑】brick kiln

转 (zhuǎn) ❶ turn; change ❷ pass on; transfer
另见 zhuàn

【转变】change; transform

【转播】relay

【转车】change trains or buses; transfer to another train or bus

【转达】pass on; convey; communicate

【转道】make a detour; go by way of

【转调】modulation; transposition

【转动】turn; turn round; revolve; rotate

【转发】❶ transmit ❷ republish ❸ relay

【转告】pass on (word); communicate; transmit

【转轨】❶ switch to another track; orbital transfer ❷ change the original operation mechanism

【转行】❶ change one's profession ❷ move to the next line

【转化】change; transform

【转换】change; transform：～方向 change direction

【转机】favourable turn of events; turn a corner

【转嫁】❶ marry again; remarry ❷ shift; transfer

【转交】pass on; transmit

【转角】street corner; corner

【转借】❶ lend a borrowed thing to someone else ❷ lend one's personal certificate to sb. else

【转口】transit; entrepot

【转脸】❶ turn one's face ❷ in no time; in the twinkling of an eye

【转卖】resell；倒手～ sell what one has bought

【转念】have second thoughts; think better of

【转让】transfer the ownership of; make over：～房屋 transfer the ownership of real estate

【转身】turn round; face about

【转手】pass on; sell on what one has bought

【转述】report; relate sth. as told by another

【转送】❶ pass on; transmit onwards ❷ make a present of what one has been given

【转弯】turn a corner; make a turn

【转向】❶ change direction ❷ change one's political stand

【转学】(of a student) transfer from one school to another

【转眼】in the twinkling of an eye; in an instant; in a flash

【转业】change one's profession

【转移】❶shift;transfer;divert ❷change;transform

【转院】(of a patient) transfer from one hospital to another

【转运】❶(superstition) have a change of luck;luck takes a turn in one's favour ❷transport;transfer;trans-ship:～站 transfer post

【转战】fight in one place after another:～千里 fight successively for a thousand li

【转账】transfer money from one account to another

【转折】❶a turn in the course of events ❷transition

传 (zhuàn) ❶commentaries on classics ❷biography ❸a novel or story written in historical style
另见 chuán

【传记】biography

【传略】biographical sketch;profile

转 (zhuàn) ❶turn;revolve ❷〈量〉revolution
另见 zhuǎn

【转动】turn;revolve;rotate;turn around a central point or axis

【转门】revolving door

【转圈】circle;go round and round

【转台】revolving stage

【转椅】❶swivel chair;chair whose seat revolves horizontally from a pivot at its base ❷roundabout

【转悠】❶turn;move from side to side ❷stroll;take a leisurely walk

【转子】rotor

赚 (zhuàn) ❶make a profit;gain ❷〈方〉earn

【赚头】profit

撰 (zhuàn) write;compose

【撰述】❶write;compile:～文章 write articles ❷book;work:～甚多 have written many books

【撰写】write;compose:～碑文 write an inscription for a tablet

【撰著】write;compose

zhuang

庄 (zhuāng) village

【庄户】peasant household:～人 peasant

【庄家】banker (in a gambling game)

【庄稼】crops

【庄田】field;farmland;cropland

【庄严】solemn;dignified;stately

【庄园】manor

【庄重】serious;grave;solemn

【庄子】❶village;hamlet ❷country estate

桩 (zhuāng) stake;pile

【桩子】stake;pile

装 (zhuāng) ❶dress up;attire ❷outfit;clothing ❸stage makeup and costume ❹pretend;make believe ❺load;pack ❻install;fit

【装扮】❶attire;deck out ❷disguise

【装备】equip;fit out

【装船】shipment

【装点】decorate;dress;deck:～门面 put on a facade;keep up appearances

【装订】binding;book binding

【装裹】❶dress a corpse;wrap (a corpse) in a shroud ❷shroud;burial clothes

【装潢】mount;mounting;packaging

【装甲】armoured

【装假】pretend;feign

【装配】assemble;fit together

【装腔】behave affectedly;be artificial

【装饰】decorate;adorn;ornament;deck

【装束】dress;attire

【装相】pretend;put on an act

【装运】shipment;loading

【装载】load;put (goods or passengers) into or upon a carrier

【装置】❶install;fit ❷installation;unit;device;plant

壮 (zhuàng) ❶strong;robust ❷strengthen;make better ❸magnificent;grand

【壮大】grow in strength;expand;strengthen

【壮胆】build up sb.'s courage;boost sb.'s courage

【壮观】grand sight

【壮怀】〈书〉great aspiration;lofty ideal

【壮健】healthy and strong;robust

【壮举】magnificent feat;heroic undertaking

【壮阔】❶vast;magnificent;grandiose:波澜～ surging forward with grand momentum;unfolding on a magnificent scale ❷great;grand:规模～ grand in scale

【壮丽】majestic;glorious

【壮烈】heroic;brave

【壮士】brave man;heroic man;hero;warrior

【壮实】sturdy;robust

【壮心】high aspirations;lofty (or noble) ideal

【壮志】lofty ideal

状 (zhuàng) ❶ form; shape ❷ describe ❸ written complaint; plaint ❹ state; condition ❺ certificate

【状况】 condition

【状态】 state; condition; state of affairs

【状语】 adverbial modifier; adverbial

【状元】 Number One Scholar

【状子】 written complaint; indictment

撞 (zhuàng) ❶ bump against; run into ❷ meet by chance; bump into ❸ dash; barge

【撞车】 traffic collision

【撞击】 ram; dash against

【撞见】 meet or discover by chance; run across; catch sb. in the act

【撞骗】 swindle

【撞墙】 run up against a wall; be rebuffed

zhui

追 (zhuī) ❶ chase after; pursue ❷ trace; look into ❸ seek; go after

【追补】 ❶ add to (the original amount): ～预算 supplement a budget ❷ make up; remedy; make good: 不可～的遗憾 irremediable regret

【追捕】 pursue and capture

【追查】 investigate; trace; find out

【追悼】 mourn over a person's death

【追访】 make a follow-up visit

【追肥】 topdress

【追赶】 run after; pursue

【追怀】 call to mind; recall; reminisce: ～往事 reminisce about the old days

【追回】 recover

【追悔】 repent; regret

【追击】 pursue and attack; follow up: 乘胜～ follow up a victory with a pursuit that routs the enemy

【追记】 ❶ posthumously ❷ record re-troactively

【追加】 add to (the original amount)

【追究】 look into; find out; investigate

【追求】 ❶ seek; pursue ❷ court (a woman); woo

【追述】 talk about events from the past; relate; recount

【追思】 recall; reminisce: ～往事 recall the past

【追诉】 prosecute

【追溯】 trace back to; date from

【追随】 follow

【追尾】 tailgate; run into the back of the preceding car

【追问】 question closely; make a detailed inquiry; examine minutely

【追想】 recall; reminisce

【追叙】 tell about the past; relate; recount

【追寻】 pursue; search; track down: ～走散的同伴 search for lost companions

【追忆】 recollect; recall; look back

【追赃】 order the return of stolen money or goods

【追逐】 ❶ pursue; chase; run after ❷ seek; quest

【追踪】 follow the trail of; track; trace

坠 (zhuì) ❶ fall; drop ❷ weigh down ❸ weight; a hanging object

【坠地】〈书〉(of a child) be born

【坠毁】 (of a plane, etc.) fall

【坠落】 fall; drop

【坠子】〈方〉 weight; plummet; pendant; eardrop

缀 (zhuì) ❶ sew; stitch ❷ put words together correctly; compose ❸ embellish; decorate

【缀合】 put together; make up; compose

赘 (zhuì) superfluous; redundant

【赘述】 give unnecessary details; say more than is needed

【赘言】 ❶ give unnecessary details; say more than is needed ❷ superfluous words; redundancy

zhun

谆 (zhūn)

【谆谆】 earnestly and tirelessly

准 (zhǔn) ❶ allow; grant ❷ standard; norm ❸ in accordance with; follow ❹ accurate; exact ❺ definitely; certainly

【准保】 certainly; for sure

【准备】 prepare; get ready

【准点】 on time; on the dot

【准话】 definite message or information

【准确】 accurate; exact; precise

【准绳】 criterion; yardstick

【准时】 punctual; on time; on schedule

【准许】 permit; allow

【准予】 grant; approve; permit

【准则】 norm; standard; criterion

zhuo

拙 (zhuō) clumsy; awkward; dull

【拙笨】 clumsy; dull; unskilful

【拙笔】〈谦〉 my (poor) writing, painting or calligraphy

【拙劣】 clumsy; inferior: 文笔～ poor writing

【拙涩】 clumsy and obscure

【拙直】 straightforward and good-natured; simple and frank

捉 (zhuō) ❶clutch; hold; grasp ❷catch; capture

【捉摸】ascertain; fathom

【捉拿】arrest; catch

【捉弄】make fun of; tease

桌 (zhuō) table; desk

【桌布】tablecloth

【桌灯】desk or table lamp

【桌面】top of a table; tabletop (including fixed and movable ones)

【桌子】table; desk

灼 (zhuó) ❶burn; scorch ❷bright; luminous

【灼见】profound view; penetrating insight：真知～ profound knowledge and penetrating insight

【灼热】scorching hot

【灼灼】〈书〉shining; brilliant

苗 (zhuó) thriving

【苗实】〈方〉sturdy; robust; healthy and strong

【苗长】grow up strong and sturdy

【苗壮】healthy and strong; sturdy

卓 (zhuó) ❶tall and erect ❷eminent; outstanding

【卓见】brilliant idea; excellent understanding or view

【卓绝】outstanding; unsurpassed

【卓然】outstanding; remarkable; eminent; brilliant：成绩～ outstanding achievements; remarkable achievements

【卓识】outstanding insight

【卓异】out of the ordinary; outstanding; remarkable; unique

【卓越】outstanding; excellent; brilliant

【卓著】distinguished; outstanding; eminent

浊 (zhuó) ❶turbid muddy ❷deep and thick ❸chaotic; confused

【浊世】〈书〉corrupt world; chaotic or turbulent world

【浊音】voiced sound; sound articulated by vibrating the vocal chords

酌 (zhuó) ❶pour out (wine); drink ❷a meal with wine ❸consider; think over

【酌量】deliberate; use one's judgment

【酌情】take into consideration the circumstances; use one's discretion

着 (zhuó) ❶wear ❷touch; come into contact with ❸apply; use ❹whereabouts ❺send 另见 zhāo, zháo

【着笔】set pen to paper; begin to write or paint

【着陆】(of airplane) land; touch down

【着落】❶whereabouts ❷assured source; source that one may depend or count on ❸fall on; rest with ❹lay; settle：～停当 properly laid

【着墨】describe in writing

【着实】❶really; truly; indeed ❷severely; sharply weighty; great in strength

【着手】set about; begin

【着想】consider

【着眼】have sth. in mind

【着意】❶strive; take pains; spare no pains; exert oneself ❷take seriously; mind

【着重】stress; emphasize

琢 (zhuó) chisel; carve

【琢磨】❶carve and polish ❷improve (literary works); polish; refine; turn sth. over in one's mind; ponder

zǐ

孜 (zī)

【孜孜】diligent; industrious; hardworking

咨 (zī) consult; take counsel

【咨询】seek advice; consult

姿 (zī) ❶looks; appearance ❷gesture; carriage; posture

【姿容】looks; appearance：～秀美 good-looking; pretty

【姿色】(of a woman) good looks; charm

【姿势】gesture; position

【姿态】❶carriage; posture ❷attitude

资 (zī) ❶money; expenses ❷subsidize; support ❸provide; supply ❹endowment; natural ability ❺qualifications; record of service

【资本】capital

【资材】materials and equipment

【资财】funds and goods; capital and goods; assets：清点～ make an inventory of the assets

【资产】assets; property; capital

【资方】those representing capital (in private industry and commerce); capitalist; owner of a private enterprise

【资格】qualifications

【资金】fund

【资力】financial strength

【资历】qualifications; seniority; record of service：～浅 have little previous experience

【资料】data; information; material

【资源】natural resources

【资质】(of a person) aptitude; natural endowments; intelligence; credentials：～ 高 highly intelligent

【资助】subsidize; aid financially

滋 (zī) ❶ grow; multiply ❷ more ❸ spurt; burst

【滋补】nourish

【滋蔓】〈书〉grow and spread; grow vigorously; grow quickly

【滋润】moist; moisten

【滋生】❶ multiply; breed; grow; propagate ❷ cause; create; provoke; bring

【滋事】make or cause trouble; provoke a dispute：酗酒～ make trouble under the influence of alcohol

【滋味】taste; flavor

【滋养】❶ nourish; supplying nutriment：～ 品 nutriment; nourishment; nourishing food ❷ nutriment; nourishment：吸收～ assimilate nutriment

【滋长】grow; develop; engender

子 (zǐ) ❶ son; child ❷ person ❸ seed ❹ egg ❺ young; tender; small ❻ something small and hard ❼ copper coin; copper

【子弹】bullet

【子弟】❶ younger brothers, sons, nephews, etc.：职工～ children of the workers and staff (of a factory, etc.) ❷ younger generation; children; juniors：～兵 army made up of the sons of the people; people's own army

【子粒】seed; grain; kernel; bean

【子女】children

【子孙】children and grandchildren; (in a broad sense) descendants：～ 万 代 generation after generation

【子夜】midnight

仔 (zǐ) 另见 zǎi

【仔细】careful; attentive

籽 (zǐ) seed

紫 (zǐ) purple; violet

【紫红】purplish red; dark red touched with purple

自 (zì) ❶ self; oneself; one's own ❷ certainly; of course; naturally ❸ from; since

【自爱】regard for oneself; self-respect

【自拔】free oneself (from pain or evil-doing); extricate oneself

【自白】make clear one's meaning or position; vindicate oneself

【自卑】abject; feel oneself inferior (to others); be self-abased：～感 sense of inferiority; inferiority complex

【自备】provide for oneself

【自裁】〈书〉kill oneself; commit suicide; take one's own life

【自残】injure oneself; kill each other (in the same group); autotomy

【自沉】〈书〉drown oneself; commit suicide by throwing oneself into a river, well, etc.

【自称】claim to be; profess

【自从】since; from

【自大】self-important; arrogant; conceited; feeling proud of oneself：自高～ conceited; arrogant

【自得】contented; self-satisfied; self-complacent

【自动】❶ voluntarily; of one's own accord ❷ automatic

【自发】spontaneous

【自费】at one's own expense

【自焚】burn oneself to death; self-immolation

【自荐】proclaim oneself

【自奉】〈书〉provide the necessities of life for oneself

【自负】be conceited

【自供】confess; confess on one's own to a crime

【自古】since ancient times; since antiquity; from time immemorial

【自豪】be proud of

【自己】❶ referring to the person mentioned earlier in the sentence ❷ oneself ❸ closely related; own

【自给】self-sufficient; self-supporting

【自家】〈方〉oneself

【自荐】recommend oneself

【自尽】commit suicide; take one's own life

【自咎】blame oneself

【自救】save oneself; support oneself; provide for and help oneself：～生产 support oneself by engaging in production

【自居】consider oneself to be; pose as

【自决】self-determination; matter decided by oneself

【自觉】conscious; aware

【自绝】alienate oneself

【自夸】sing one's own praises; build oneself up; blow one's own trumpet

【自来】from the beginning; originally; in the first place; from the outset

【自来水】tap water; running water

【自理】provide for oneself; be at one's own expense

【自立】self-supporting；earn one's own bread

【自量】estimate one's own actual ability or strength

【自满】self-satisfied

【自命】regard oneself as；consider oneself（to have some character, identity, etc.）：～清高 profess to be above worldly considerations

【自强】strive to become stronger：～不息 make unremitting efforts to improve oneself

【自然】❶ natural world；nature ❷ unaffected；natural ❸naturally

【自如】freely；smoothly；with facility

【自杀】commit suicide；take one's own life

【自上而下】from above to below；from top to bottom

【自身】oneself；self

【自首】❶（of a criminal）voluntarily surrender oneself；confess one's crime；give oneself up（to law）❷ make a political recantation；surrender to the enemy

【自述】an account in one's own words；recount or narrate by oneself

【自私】selfish；self-centred；self-seeking

【自诉】private prosecution

【自卫】self-defence

【自刎】commit suicide by slitting one's throat；cut one's throat

【自问】❶ask oneself；examine oneself：反躬～ examine oneself；examine one's conscience ❷ reach a conclusion after weighing a matter

【自我】self；oneself

【自习】study by oneself

【自新】turn over a new leaf；make a fresh start

【自信】self-confident

【自行】by oneself

【自行车】bicycle；bike

【自修】study by oneself

【自学】study independently；teach oneself

【自用】❶〈书〉obstinately holding to one's own views ❷for private use；personal

【自由】❶freedom；liberty ❷free；unrestrained

【自愿】voluntary；of one's own accord；of one's own free will；on a voluntary basis：自觉～ voluntarily

【自在】free；unrestrained；comfortable；at ease

【自治】exercise autonomy；autonomous rule；self-rule

【自重】❶ conduct oneself with dignity；be self-possessed；be self-dignified ❷ dead-weight；dead load

【自传】autobiography

【自尊】self-respect；self-esteem；proper pride

字（zì）❶ word；character ❷ pronunciation ❸ form of a written or printed character；style of handwriting；printing type ❹ scripts；writings ❺receipt；written pledge

【字典】dictionary

【字调】tones of Chinese characters

【字幅】horizontal or vertical scroll of calligraphy

【字号】❶name of a shop ❷shop；store

【字画】calligraphy and painting

【字迹】handwriting；writing

【字句】words and expressions；writing

【字据】written pledge

【字谜】a riddle about a character or word

【字面】literal；superficial meaning of words or phrases

【字模】matrix

【字母】letter

【字母表】alphabet

【字幕】captions

【字条】brief note；note

【字帖】copybook（for calligraphy）

【字形】character pattern；font：标准～ standard font

【字眼】wording；diction

【字样】❶model of written characters ❷printed or written words or phrases

【字义】meaning of a word：解释～ interpret or explain the meaning of a word

【字音】pronunciation：注明～ marked with phonetic symbols

zong

宗（zōng）❶ancestor ❷clan ❸sect；faction；school ❹purpose；principal aim

【宗教】religion

【宗派】faction，sect

【宗仰】〈书〉hold in esteem；海内～ be held in esteem throughout the country

【宗旨】aim；purpose

【宗族】clansman

综（zōng）put together；sum up

【综观】make a comprehensive survey：～全局 take a broad view of the whole situation

【综合】synthesize；comprehensive

【综计】sum up；add up

【综括】sum up；in a word

【综述】summarize；sum up

棕（zōng）palm

【棕榈】palm
【棕毛】palm fibre
【棕色】brown

踪 (zōng) footprint; track; trace

【踪迹】trace; track
【踪影】trace; sign

总 (zǒng) ❶ assemble; put together; sum up ❷ general; overall; total ❸ chief; head; general ❹ always; invariably ❺ anyway; after all; eventually; sooner or later ❻ surely; certainly; probably

【总产值】gross output value
【总部】general headquarters
【总得】must; have to; be bound to
【总督】governor-general; governor
【总队】general detachment; army unit corresponding to a regiment or division
【总额】total; 存款～ total deposits
【总而言之】in a word; in short; in brief; to make a long story short
【总纲】general programme; general principles
【总攻】general offensive; ～令 order for a general offensive
【总共】in all; altogether; in the aggregate
【总管】❶ take overall responsibility; be in full charge of ❷ person in full charge; manager
【总归】anyway; after all; eventually
【总合】sum up; add up
【总和】sum; total
【总汇】❶ come or flow together ❷ confluence; concourse; aggregate
【总机】telephone exchange; switchboard
【总计】total; amount to
【总结】❶ sum up; summarize ❷ summary; summing up
【总括】sum up; ～起来说 to sum up; to state succinctly
【总览】overview; take an overall view; ～全局 make an overall survey of the whole situation
【总评】general comment
【总数】total
【总体】overall; total
【总统】president
【总务】general affairs; general services; ～科 general affairs section
【总则】general rules; general principles
【总账】general ledger; general account
【总之】in a word; in short; in brief
【总支】general branch
【总装】❶ process of putting all parts together; general assembly; final assembly ❷ fit parts into a whole; ～空间站 final assembly of a space station

纵 (zòng) ❶ from north to south ❷ vertical; longitudinal ❸ release; set free ❹ indulge; let loose ❺ jump up; jump into the air ❻〈书〉even if

【纵步】❶ stride; ～向前走去 stride forward ❷ jump; bound
【纵队】column; file
【纵横】❶ length and breadth; vertically and horizontally; ～交错 criss-cross ❷ with great ease; freely; 笔意～ write with great ease ❸ sweep over; march over unhindered
【纵横驰骋】(of an army) move about freely and quickly; sweep through the length and breadth of
【纵火】set on fire; commit arson
【纵览】look far and wide; scan; ～四周 look all round
【纵目】look as far as one's eyes can see; ～四望 look far into the distance in all directions
【纵情】to one's heart's content; as much as one likes; ～快乐 indulge in unbridled joy
【纵然】even if; even though
【纵容】connive; wink at
【纵身】jump; leap; ～上马 leap on to a horse
【纵深】depth
【纵使】even if; even though
【纵向】❶ vertical; longitudinal; lengthwise; ～比较 vertical comparison ❷ from north to south

ZOU

走 (zǒu) ❶ walk; go ❷ run; move ❸ leave; go away ❹ visit; call on

【走笔】〈书〉write rapidly; ～疾书 write rapidly (or swiftly)
【走避】flee; escape
【走道】pavement; sidewalk; path; walk; footpath
【走动】❶ walk about; stretch one's legs ❷ (of relatives and friends) visit each other
【走读】attend a day school
【走访】❶ interview; have an interview ❷ pay a visit to; go and see
【走风】let out a secret; leak out
【走狗】hunting dog;〈喻〉person who is paid to do evils
【走红】❶ have good luck; be in luck ❷ in favour; in demand
【走火】❶ (of firearms) discharge accidentally ❷ go too far in what one says; put sth. too

strongly; overstate ❸ sparking; fire caused by the leakage of electricity due to to damaged wire

【走廊】corridor; passage; passageway

【走漏】❶leak out; divulge：～风声 divulge a secret; leak information ❷smuggling and tax evasion ❸things stolen out of a bulk

【走路】❶walk; go on foot ❷leave; go away

【走马】gallop or trot along on horseback：平原～ ride a horse across the plain

【走禽】cursorial birds

【走人】go away; leave

【走神儿】wander; be absent-minded

【走失】❶wander away; be lost; be missing ❷fail to keep; lose

【走时】❶tick; keep time ❷〈方〉have good luck; be in luck

【走势】❶trend; tendency ❷direction; alignment：勘察山谷的～ survey the run of a valley

【走兽】four-footed animals; quadrupeds; beasts：飞禽～ birds and beasts

【走水】❶leak water ❷flow; run：渠道～通畅 water runs well in the canal

【走私】smuggle

【走向】❶run; trend; alignment ❷move towards; head for; be on the way to ❸strike

【走形】be out of shape

【走眼】mistake for

【走样】lose shape; go out of form; be different from what is expected or intended

【走运】have good luck; be in luck

【走账】enter a sum in the account book; charge a sum to account

【走嘴】make a slip of the tongue; let slip an inadvertent remark

奏（zòu）play; perform; strike up

【奏捷】win a battle; score a success

【奏凯】sing a song of victory; win victory; be victorious; triumph

【奏鸣曲】sonata

【奏效】prove effective; be successful; get the desired result

【奏乐】play music; strike up a tune

【奏章】memorial to an emperor (or the throne)

【奏折】memorial to the throne

ZU

租（zū）❶rent; hire ❷rent out; let out

【租户】❶tenant; lessee; leaseholder ❷hirer

【租价】rent; rental

【租界】concession

【租借】rent; hire; lease

【租金】rent; rental

【租赁】❶rent; lease; hire ❷lease

【租用】rent; hire; take on lease

【租约】lease

足（zú）❶foot; leg ❷sufficient; enough ❸full; as much as

【足赤】pure gold; solid gold

【足够】enough; ample; sufficient

【足迹】footmark; foot print

【足见】it serves to show; one can well perceive

【足球】soccer; football

【足岁】actual age

【足下】polite term of address between friends

【足以】enough; sufficiently

卒（zú）❶soldier ❷finish; end ❸finally; at last ❹die

【卒岁】〈书〉get through the year

【卒业】graduate; finish a course of study

族（zú）❶clan ❷race; nationality

【族谱】family tree; genealogical tree

【族人】clansman; members of the same clan or family

诅（zǔ）

【诅咒】curse; swear; wish sb. evil; imprecate

阻（zǔ）hinder; block

【阻碍】block; impede

【阻挡】stem; resist; obstruct

【阻隔】separate; cut off

【阻击】block; check

【阻截】stop; obstruct; bar the way

【阻绝】block; obstruct; clog：交通～ traffic jam

【阻拦】stop; obstruct; bar the way; stymie

【阻力】❶resistance; drag ❷obstruction; resistance

【阻难】thwart; obstruct; make things difficult for sb.

【阻挠】thwart; stand in the way

【阻塞】❶block; obstruct; clog; stop ❷barrage; barricade

【阻止】prevent; stop

组（zǔ）❶organize; form ❷group ❸〈量〉set

【组办】organize

【组成】composition

【组稿】commission authors to write on given topics; contributions

【组合】❶make up; compose; constitute ❷association; solicit combination

【组建】put together (a group)；form：～剧团 put together a theatrical troupe

【组团】form or organize an art troupe or delegation：～出国访问 form an art troupe for a foreign tour

【组织】❶organize；form ❷tissue

【组装】put together；assemble

【组装线】assembly line

祖 (zǔ) ❶grandfather ❷ancestor

【祖辈】ancestors；forefathers；ancestry

【祖产】property handed down from one's ancestors；ancestral estate

【祖传】hand down from one's ancestors

【祖坟】ancestral grave

【祖父】grandfather

【祖国】one's country；homeland；motherland

【祖籍】original family home；ancestral home

【祖母】grandmother

【祖上】ancestors；forefathers；forebears

【祖师】❶guru；founder of a school of learning, a craft, etc. ❷founder of a sect of Buddhism or Taoism ❸originator of a superstitious sect or a secret society

【祖先】ancestry；ancestors；forbears；forefathers

【祖业】❶property handed down from ancestors；ancestral estate ❷ ancestors' meritorious achievements

【祖宗】forefathers；ancestry；forbears

zuan

钻 (zuān) ❶drill；bore ❷get into；go through ❸study intensively；dig into
另见 zuàn

【钻牛角尖】split hairs；get into a dead end (or a blind alley)

【钻探】drilling：～机 drilling machine

【钻心】unbearable：痒得～ itch unbearably

【钻研】dig into；study intensively：刻苦～ study hard｜～理论 dig into theories

【钻营】curry favour with sb. in authority for personal gain；secure personal gain

钻 (zuàn) ❶drill；bore ❷drill；auger ❸diamond；jewel
另见 zuān

【钻戒】diamond ring

【钻井】well drilling

【钻石】❶diamond ❷jewel

【钻台】drilling platform

zui

嘴 (zuǐ) mouth

【嘴巴】slap one in the face

【嘴笨】inarticulate；clumsy of speech

【嘴刁】❶be choosy about what one eats；be particular about food ❷〈方〉cunning；tricky

【嘴乖】clever and pleasant when speaking to elders

【嘴角】corners of the mouth

【嘴快】have a loose tongue

【嘴脸】face；features；countenance：丑恶～ hideous face

【嘴碎】loquacious；garrulous

【嘴损】〈方〉sharp-tongued；sarcastic：～不饶人 be sharp-tongued and pick on someone

【嘴甜】ingratiating in speech；smooth-tongued；honeymouthed

【嘴稳】able to keep a secret；discreet in speech

【嘴硬】stubborn and reluctant to admit mistakes or defeats

【嘴直】outspoken；plainspoken

最 (zuì) most

【最初】initial；first

【最大】greatest；biggest；maximum

【最多】most；at the most；maximum

【最好】❶best；first-rate ❷had better；it would be best

【最后】final；last；ultimate

【最佳】❶optimum ❷the best

【最近】❶recently；lately of late ❷nearest

【最少】least；at the least；minimum

罪 (zuì) ❶crime；guilt ❷fault；blame ❸suffering；hardship ❹put the blame on

【罪案】case

【罪恶】crime；evil

【罪犯】criminal

【罪过】fault；sin

【罪魁】chief criminal；culprit；arch-criminal

【罪名】charge；accusation

【罪孽】sin；wrong-doing

【罪人】guilty person；offender；sinner

【罪行】crime；guilt；offence

【罪责】❶responsibility for an offence：～难逃 cannot escape the responsibility for the offence (or crime) ❷〈书〉penal punishment：免于～ exempt from punishment

【罪证】evidence of crime；proof of one's guilt

【罪状】facts about a crime；charges in an indictment

醉 (zuì) ❶ drunk；intoxicated ❷ steeped in liquor

【醉汉】drunkard；drunken man

Z

【醉人】❶intoxicate；make drunk ❷intoxicating；enchanting；fascinating：春意～ enchanting springtime

【醉生梦死】lead a befuddled life as if drunk or in a dream

【醉心】be bent on；be dead gone on sth.；be immersed in；be wrapped up in

【醉眼】〈书〉eyes showing the effects of drink

【醉意】signs or feeling of getting drunk

zun

尊（zūn）❶senior；of a senior generation ❷respect；venerate

【尊称】❶a respectful form of address；honorific title ❷address sb. respectfully

【尊崇】worship；revere

【尊贵】honourable；respectable

【尊敬】respect；esteem

【尊亲】❶one's senior relatives ❷your relatives

【尊严】dignity；honor

【尊长】elders and betters：尊重～ respect the elders and betters

【尊重】respect；value；esteem

遵（zūn）abide by；obey

【遵从】defer to；follow

【遵命】comply with your wish；obey your command：～照办 act in compliance with your instructions

【遵守】observe；abide by；comply with

【遵行】act on；follow

【遵循】follow；abide by；adhere to

【遵照】follow；conform to；comply with；act in accordance with

zuo

作（zuō）workshop
另见 zuó,zuò

【作坊】workshop

作（zuó）
另见 zuō,zuò

【作践】〈口〉❶spoil；waste ❷run sb. down；disparage ❸humiliate

【作料】〈口〉condiments；seasoning

昨（zuó）yesterday

【昨天】yesterday

左（zuǒ）❶the left side；the left ❷queer；unorthodox ❸wrong；incorrect ❹different；contrary ❺the Left ❻east

【左不过】〈方〉❶ anyway；anyhow；in any event ❷only；merely；just

【左边】the left；the left side

【左手】left hand

【左右】❶the left and right sides ❷about；or so ❸master；control；influence ❹those in close attendance；retinue

佐（zuǒ）❶assist ❷assistance

【佐餐】be eaten together with rice or bread；go with rice or bread；～之佳品 go well with rice or bread

【佐证】evidence；proof

作（zuò）❶ do；make ❷write；compose ❸writings；work ❹pretend；affect ❺regards as ❻feel；have ❼act as；be
另见 zuō,zuó

【作案】commit a crime

【作罢】give up

【作保】be sb.'s guarantor；vouch for

【作弊】cheat；practise fraud

【作别】〈书〉bid farewell；take one's leave：拱手～ bid farewell by cupping one hand in another before one's chest

【作答】answer；reply

【作对】oppose

【作恶】do evil

【作法】way of doing things；method；practice

【作风】style；way

【作怪】do mischief；make trouble：兴妖～ make trouble；conjure up demons to make trouble

【作家】writer

【作假】❶ pretend；put up a show to deceive ❷falsify

【作客】〈书〉sojourn：～他乡 sojourn in an alien land

【作乐】make merry；enjoy oneself；have a good time：寻欢～ seek pleasure and make merry

【作乱】stage an armed rebellion：犯上～ rebel against the authority

【作难】〈书〉start a revolt；rise in revolt

【作孽】do evil；commit a sin

【作弄】tease；make a fool of；play a trick on；poke fun at

【作呕】❶feel sick；feel like vomiting；be overcome by nausea ❷be utterly disgusted by sb. or sth.：令人～ be nauseating

【作陪】help entertain a guest of honour；be invited along with the guest of honour

【作品】works

【作曲】compose；write music

【作色】show signs of anger；get worked up：愤然～ flush with indignation

【作势】assume a posture；attitudinize：装腔～ be pretentious；strike a posture

【作数】count；be valid

【作速】lose no time；hasten：～处理 deal with the matter as soon as possible；settle the matter quickly

【作痛】have a pain；ache

【作为】❶ conduct；deed；action ❷ accomplishment；achievement ❸ regard as；look on as；take as ❹ in the capacity（or character，role）of；as

【作文】❶write a composition ❷a composition

【作物】crop

【作息】work and rest

【作业】❶ assignment；homework ❷ work；task；operation

【作用】❶role；function ❷action；effect

【作战】fight；fight a battle

【作者】author；writer

【作证】testify；give witness

【作准】❶ count；be valid；be authentic ❷ approve；recognize；acknowledge

坐 （zuò）❶sit；take a seat ❷travel by or on（any conveyance except those which one straddles）❸ have its back towards ❹ put（a pan，pot，etc.）on a fire ❺（of a building）sink；subside ❻（of rifles，guns，etc.）recoil；kick back

【坐班】usually. referring to sitting in one's office hours：～制 office hour system

【坐标】coordinate

【坐待】sit back and wait：～胜利 sit and wait for victory

【坐等】sit back and wait

【坐地】❶stay at a fixed place ❷on the spot

【坐垫】cushion

【坐牢】be in prison；be in jail；be imprisoned

【坐落】be situated；be located

【坐视】sit by and watch；sit tight and look on；sit by idly and remain indifferent

【坐误】let slip（an opportunity）：因循～ pro-

crastinate until it is too late

【坐席】❶take one's seat at a banquet table；attend a banquet ❷seat

座 （zuò）❶seat；place ❷stand；pedestal；base

【座次】order of seats；seating arrangements：～表 seating chart

【座谈】have an informal discussion

【座位】seat；place

【座右铭】maxim；motto

【座钟】desk clock

做 （zuò）❶do；make；produce；manufacture ❷cook；prepare ❸do；act；engage in ❹be；become ❺write；compose ❻be used as ❼form or contract a relationship

【做伴】keep sb.'s company

【做操】do exercises

【做东】play the host；stand treat

【做法】way of doing or making a thing method of work；practice

【做工】❶do manual work；work ❷workmanship

【做鬼脸】make faces

【做活儿】work；do manual labour

【做客】be a guest

【做买卖】do business；carry on trade：～的 businessman；trader；merchant

【做媒】be a matchmaker（or go-between）

【做梦】have a dream；dream

【做派】acting；stage business；business

【做亲】❶become related by marriage ❷get married；be united in marriage；take a wife

【做人】behave

【做声】make a sound

【做事】❶do work；do a deed；handle affairs ❷work；have a job

【做学问】engage in scholarship；do research

【做贼心虚】have a guilty conscience like a thief；have sth. on one's conscience

【做主】❶decide ❷back up；support

【做作】affected；artificial

汉语拼音音节索引
Phonetic Index

A

a

阿　395

ai

哎　395
哀　395
挨　395
唉　395
挨　395
皑　395
癌　395
矮　395
蔼　396
霭　396
爱　396
隘　396
碍　396

an

安　396
氨　396
鞍　396
岸　396
按　397
案　397
暗　397
黯　397

ang

肮　397
昂　397
盎　397

ao

熬　397
鏖　397
傲　397
奥　398
懊　398

B

ba

八　399
巴　399
扒　399
芭　399
吧　399
笆　399
拔　399
把　399
靶　399
把　399

罢　400
霸　400
吧　400

bai

白　400
百　400
摆　400
败　401
拜　401

ban

扳　401
班　401
般　401
颁　401
斑　401
搬　401
板　401
版　401
办　402
半　402
扮　402
伴　402
拌　402

bang

邦　402
帮　403
绑　403
榜　403
膀　403
棒　403
傍　403
磅　403

bao

包　403
剥　403
褒　403
薄　403
饱　403
宝　404
保　404
报　404
刨　404
抱　404
暴　404
爆　404

bei

杯　404
卑　405
背　405

悲　405
碑　405
北　405
贝　405
备　405
背　405
倍　405
被　405
辈　406
惫　406

ben

奔　406
本　406
奔　406
笨　406

beng

崩　406
绷　406
迸　406

bi

逼　406
鼻　407
比　407
彼　407
笔　407
鄙　407
币　407
必　407
毕　407
闭　408
庇　408
毙　408
裨　408
碧　408
蔽　408
弊　408
壁　408
避　408
壁　408

bian

边　408
编　408
鞭　409
贬　409
扁　409
变　409
便　409
遍　409
辨　409

辩　409

biao

标　410
表　410

bie

憋　410
别　410

bin

宾　410
濒　411
摈　411
殡　411

bing

冰　411
兵　411
秉　411
饼　411
屏　411
禀　411
并　411
病　411

bo

拨　412
波　412
玻　412
剥　412
播　412
伯　412
驳　413
勃　413
博　413
搏　413
薄　413
跛　413
薄　413

bu

补　413
捕　413
哺　413
不　414
布　415
步　415
部　415
簿　415

C

ca

擦　416

cai		豺	421	诚	427	**chuai**	
猜	416	**chan**		承	427	揣	433
才	416	掺	421	城	427	**chuan**	
材	416	搀	421	乘	427	川	433
财	416	谗	421	程	428	穿	433
裁	416	馋	421	惩	428	传	433
采	417	缠	421	澄	428	船	434
彩	417	蝉	421	橙	428	喘	434
踩	417	潺	421	逞	428	串	434
菜	417	蟾	421	**chi**		**chuang**	
can		产	422	吃	428	创	434
参	417	谄	422	嗤	428	疮	434
餐	417	铲	422	痴	428	窗	434
残	418	阐	422	池	428	床	434
蚕	418	忏	422	迟	428	闯	434
惭	418	颤	422	持	428	创	434
惨	418	**chang**		尺	429	**chui**	
灿	418	昌	422	齿	429	吹	434
cang		猖	422	耻	429	炊	435
仓	418	长	422	叱	429	垂	435
苍	418	肠	423	斥	429	捶	435
沧	418	尝	423	赤	429	锤	435
舱	418	常	423	炽	429	**chun**	
藏	418	偿	423	翅	429	春	435
cao		厂	423	**chong**		纯	435
操	418	敞	423	冲	429	唇	435
嘈	419	怅	423	充	429	淳	435
草	419	畅	423	憧	430	蠢	435
ce		倡	423	虫	430	**chuo**	
册	419	唱	423	重	430	戳	435
厕	419	**chao**		崇	430	绰	435
侧	419	抄	424	宠	430	辍	435
测	419	超	424	**chou**		**ci**	
恻	419	朝	424	抽	430	疵	435
策	419	嘲	424	仇	430	词	435
cen		潮	424	惆	430	瓷	435
参	419	吵	424	绸	430	辞	436
ceng		炒	424	酬	430	慈	436
层	419	**che**		稠	430	磁	436
曾	419	车	425	愁	430	雌	436
cha		扯	425	筹	430	此	436
叉	420	彻	425	踌	431	次	436
差	420	撤	425	丑	431	伺	436
插	420	**chen**		臭	431	刺	436
茶	420	尘	425	**chu**		赐	436
查	420	沉	425	出	431	**cong**	
察	420	陈	426	初	432	匆	436
岔	421	晨	426	除	432	葱	436
刹	421	衬	426	厨	432	聪	436
诧	421	称	426	锄	432	从	436
差	421	趁	426	雏	432	丛	436
姹	421	**cheng**		橱	432	**cou**	
chai		称	426	处	432	凑	436
拆	421	撑	426	储	433	**cu**	
差	421	瞠	426	处	433	粗	437
柴	421	成	426	触	433	促	437
		呈	427	矗	433	醋	437

第一列

簇　437

cuan
撺　437
窜　437
篡　437

cui
催　437
摧　437
璀　437
脆　437
翠　437

cun
村　437
存　437
忖　437
寸　437

cuo
搓　438
磋　438
撮　438
蹉　438
挫　438
措　438
锉　438
错　438

D

da
耷　439
搭　439
答　439
打　439
达　439
答　439
打　440

dai
呆　441
待　441
歹　441
逮　441
代　441
带　442
贷　442
待　442
怠　442
袋　442
戴　442

dan
丹　442
担　442
单　442
耽　442
殚　442
胆　442
掸　443
旦　443

第二列

但　443
担　443
诞　443
淡　443
弹　443
蛋　443

dang
当　443
挡　443
党　444
当　444
荡　444
档　444

dao
刀　444
导　444
岛　444
捣　444
倒　444
祷　444
蹈　444
到　445
倒　445
盗　445
悼　445
道　445
稻　445

de
得　445
德　445
得

dei
445

deng
灯　446
登　446
等　446
凳　446
瞪　446

di
低　446
堤　446
提　446
滴　446
的　446
敌　447
笛　447
嫡　447
诋　447
抵　447
砥　447
地　447
弟　447
帝　447
递　447
第　448
缔　448

第三列

dian
掂　448
颠　448
癫　448
典　448
点　448
碘　448
踮　449
电　449
店　449
垫　449
淀　449
惦　449
奠　449
殿　449

diao
刁　449
叼　449
凋　449
碉　449
雕　449
吊　449
钓　449
调　449
掉　450

die
爹　450
跌　450
迭　450
谍　450
喋　450
叠　450
碟　450
蝶　450

ding
叮　450
盯　450
钉　450
顶　450
鼎　450
订　451
钉　451
定　451

diu
丢　451

dong
东　451
冬　452
董　452
懂　452
动　452
冻　452
栋　452
洞　452

dou
都　452

第四列

兜　452
斗　452
抖　452
陡　452
斗　452
豆　453
逗　453

du
都　453
督　453
毒　453
独　453
读　453
渎　453
笃　453
堵　454
赌　454
睹　454
杜　454
肚　454
妒　454
度　454
渡　454
镀　454

duan
端　454
短　454
段　454
断　454
缎　455
煅　455
锻　455

dui
堆　455
队　455
对　455
兑　455

dun
吨　455
炖　455
钝　455
顿　455

duo
多　456
哆　456
夺　456
躲　456
堕　456
惰　456

E

e
阿　457
婀　457
讹　457
俄　457
鹅　457

额	457	绯	463	扶	469	杠	475
恶	457	扉	463	拂	469	**gao**	
厄	457	霏	464	服	469	高	476
扼	457	肥	464	俘	469	羔	476
恶	457	匪	464	浮	469	膏	476
饿	457	诽	464	符	470	糕	476
遏	457	菲	464	幅	470	搞	476
噩	457	悱	464	辐	470	稿	476
鳄	457	斐	464	福	470	告	476
en		吠	464	抚	470	**ge**	
恩	457	肺	464	斧	470	戈	477
摁	458	废	464	俯	470	疙	477
er		沸	464	辅	461	哥	477
儿	458	费	465	腐	464	胳	477
而	458	痱	465	父	464	鸽	477
耳	458	**fen**		付	465	搁	477
饵	458	分	465	负	465	割	477
二	458	芬	465	妇	465	歌	477
F		吩	465	附	465	革	477
fa		纷	466	赴	466	阁	477
发	459	氛	466	复	466	格	477
乏	459	坟	466	副	471	隔	477
罚	459	焚	466	富	471	个	478
阀	459	粉	466	腹	471	各	478
筏	459	分	466	覆	471	**gei**	
法	459	份	466	馥	472	给	478
发	459	奋	466			**gen**	
fan		粪	466	**G**		根	478
帆	459	愤	466	**ga**		跟	478
番	459	**feng**		夹	473	**geng**	
翻	460	丰	466	嘎	473	更	478
凡	460	风	466	**gai**		耕	479
烦	460	封	467	改	473	羹	479
繁	460	疯	467	钙	473	耿	479
反	460	峰	467	盖	473	哽	479
返	460	烽	467	概	473	梗	479
犯	460	锋	467	**gan**		更	479
饭	461	蜂	468	干	473	**gong**	
泛	461	逢	468	甘	474	工	479
范	461	缝	468	肝	474	弓	479
贩	461	讽	468	柑	474	公	479
fang		凤	468	竿	474	功	480
方	461	奉	468	尴	474	攻	480
芳	461	俸	468	杆	474	供	480
防	462	缝	468	赶	474	宫	481
妨	462	**fo**		敢	474	恭	481
房	462	佛	468	感	475	躬	481
仿	462	**fou**		橄	475	巩	481
访	462	缶	468	干	475	汞	481
纺	462	否	468	**gang**		拱	481
放	462	**fu**		刚	475	共	481
fei		夫	468	肛	475	贡	481
飞	463	肤	469	纲	475	供	481
妃	463	孵	469	钢	475	**gou**	
非	463	敷	469	缸	475	勾	481
菲	463	伏	469	岗	475	沟	481
				港	475	钩	481

				hao		hu	
篝	481	龟	487				
苟	481	规	487	号	492	呼	498
狗	482	闺	487	毫	492	忽	498
勾	482	瑰	487	豪	493	囫	498
构	482	轨	487	好	493	狐	498
购	482	诡	487	号	493	弧	498
够	482	鬼	487	好	493	胡	499
	gu	柜	487	耗	493	壶	499
估	482	贵	488	浩	493	蝴	499
咕	482	桂	488	皓	494	糊	499
孤	482	跪	488		he	虎	499
姑	482		gun	呵	494	琥	499
轱	482	滚	488	喝	494	互	499
辜	482	棍	488	禾	494	户	499
箍	483		guo	合	494	护	499
古	483	聒	488	何	494		hua
谷	483	锅	488	和	494	花	499
汩	483	蝈	488	河	495	划	500
股	483	国	488	荷	495	华	500
骨	483	果	489	核	495	哗	500
蛊	483	裹	489	盒	495	滑	501
鼓	483	过	489	贺	495	化	501
固	483			喝	495	划	501
故	484	**H**		赫	495	画	501
顾	484		ha	褐	495	话	501
雇	484	哈	490	鹤	495		huai
痼	484	蛤	490		hei	怀	501
	gua		hai	黑	495	踝	502
瓜	484	咳	490		hen	坏	502
刮	484	还	490	痕	495		huan
寡	484	孩	490	很	495	欢	502
挂	484	骸	490	狠	496	还	502
褂	484	海	490	恨	496	环	502
	guai	骇	490		heng	缓	502
乖	484	害	490	亨	496	幻	502
拐	484		han	哼	496	换	503
怪	485	酣	491	恒	496	唤	503
	guan	憨	491	横	496	涣	503
关	485	鼾	491	衡	496	患	503
观	485	含	491	横	496	焕	503
官	485	函	491		hong		huang
冠	485	涵	491	轰	496	荒	503
棺	485	寒	491	哄	496	慌	503
馆	485	罕	491	烘	496	皇	503
管	485	喊	491	弘	497	黄	503
贯	486	汉	491	红	497	惶	504
冠	486	汗	492	宏	497	蝗	504
惯	486	旱	492	洪	497	簧	504
灌	486	捍	492	鸿	497	恍	504
鹳	486	悍	492	哄	497	晃	504
罐	486	焊	492		hou	谎	504
	guang	撼	492	喉	497	幌	504
光	486	憾	492	猴	497	晃	504
广	486	瀚	492	吼	497		hui
逛	487		hang	后	497	灰	504
	gui	行	492	厚	498	诙	504
归	487	航	492	候	498	挥	504

恢 504
辉 504
徽 504
回 505
悔 505
毁 505
汇 505
会 506
荟 506
绘 506
贿 506
彗 506
晦 506
秽 506
惠 506
慧 506

hun
昏 506
婚 507
浑 507
混 507
魂 507
混 507

huo
豁 507
活 507
火 507
伙 508
或 508
货 508
获 508
祸 508
惑 508
豁 508

J
ji
几 509
讥 509
击 509
饥 509
机 509
肌 509
鸡 509
奇 509
积 509
基 510
缉 510
畸 510
稽 510
激 510
及 510
吉 510
级 510
极 510
即 510
急

疾 511
集 511
嫉 511
籍 511
几 511
己 511
挤 511
济 512
脊 512
计 512
记 512
伎 512
纪 512
技 512
忌 512
际 512
季 513
迹 513
济 513
既 513
继 513
祭 513
寄 513
寂

jia
加 513
夹 514
佳 514
枷 514
家 514
嘉 514
夹 514
甲 515
假 515
价 515
驾 515
架 515
假 515
嫁

jian
尖 515
奸 515
歼 515
坚 515
间 516
肩 516
艰 516
监 516
兼 516
缄 516
俭 516
捡 516
检 516
减 516
剪 516
简 517

见 517
件 517
间 517
建 517
荐 517
贱 517
剑 517
健 517
舰 517
渐 518
践 518
溅 518
鉴 518
键 518
箭 518

jiang
江 518
将 518
姜 518
僵 518
缰 518
疆 518
讲 519
奖 519
桨 519
匠 519
降 519
将 519
强 519
酱

jiao
交 520
郊 520
浇 520
娇 520
骄 520
胶 520
教 520
焦 520
角 520
侥 520
狡 520
饺 521
绞 521
矫 521
皎 521
脚 521
搅 521
叫 521
觉 521
校 521
轿 521
较 521
教 522

jie
阶 522

皆 522
结 522
接 522
揭 522
街 522
孑 523
节 523
劫 523
杰 523
洁 523
结 523
捷 523
睫 523
截 524
竭 524
姐 524
解 524
介 524
戒 524
届 524
界 524
借 524

jin
巾 525
斤 525
今 525
金 525
津 525
筋 525
禁 525
仅 526
尽 526
紧 526
锦 526
谨 526
尽 526
进 526
近 527
劲 527
晋 527
浸 527
禁 527

jing
京 527
经 527
荆 527
旌 527
惊 528
晶 528
兢 528
精 528
鲸 529
井 529
颈 529
景 529
警 529
劲 529
径 529

净	529	决	534	咳	539	愧	542
竞	529	诀	535	可	539	**kun**	
竟	529	抉	535	渴	539	昆	542
敬	530	角	535	克	539	捆	543
静	530	觉	535	刻	539	困	543
境	530	绝	535	恪	539	**kuo**	
镜	530	掘	535	客	540	扩	543
jiong		崛	535	课	540	括	543
迥	530	矍	535	**ken**		阔	543
炯	530	攫	535	肯	540	廓	543
窘	530	倔	535	垦	540		
jiu		**jun**		恳	540	**L**	
纠	530	军	535	**keng**		**la**	
究	530	均	536	坑	540	垃	544
揪	530	君	536	铿	540	拉	544
九	531	俊	536	**kong**		喇	544
久	531	峻	536	空	540	落	544
韭	531	竣	536	孔	540	腊	544
酒	531			恐	540	蜡	544
旧	531	**K**		空	540	辣	544
救	531	**ka**		控	540	**lai**	
就	531	咖	537	**kou**		来	544
舅	532	卡	537	口	540	赖	544
ju		**kai**		叩	541	**lan**	
拘	532	开	537	扣	541	兰	544
居	532	凯	537	**ku**		拦	544
鞠	532	铠	537	枯	541	栏	544
局	532	慨	537	哭	541	蓝	544
菊	532	楷	537	苦	541	篮	545
咀	532	**kan**		库	541	揽	545
沮	532	刊	537	裤	541	缆	545
矩	533	看	537	酷	541	懒	545
举	533	勘	538	**kua**		烂	545
巨	533	坎	538	夸	541	滥	545
句	533	砍	538	跨	541	**lang**	
拒	533	看	538	**kuai**		郎	545
具	533	**kang**		会	541	狼	545
俱	533	康	538	块	541	琅	545
剧	533	慷	538	快	541	廊	545
据	533	扛	538	脍	541	朗	545
距	533	亢	538	筷	541	浪	545
惧	533	伉	538	**kuan**		**lao**	
飓	533	抗	538	宽	542	捞	545
锯	533	炕	538	款	542	劳	545
聚	534	**kao**		**kuang**		牢	545
踞	534	考	538	狂	542	老	546
juan		拷	538	旷	542	姥	546
捐	534	烤	538	况	542	烙	546
涓	534	犒	538	矿	542	涝	546
娟	534	靠	538	框	542	**le**	
镌	534	**ke**		**kui**		乐	546
卷	534	苛	539	亏	542	勒	546
倦	534	科	539	窥	542	**lei**	
绢	534	颗	539	葵	542	累	546
圈	534	磕	539	魁	542	雷	546
眷	534	瞌	539	睽	542	累	546
jue		蝌	539	馈	542	肋	546
撅	534			溃	542	泪	546

类	546		
累	546		
擂	546		
leng			
棱	546		
冷	546		
li			
厘	546		
离	547		
梨	547		
犁	547		
黎	547		
篱	547		
礼	547		
里	547		
理	547		
鲤	547		
力	547		
历	547		
厉	547		
立	547		
利	547		
例	547		
隶	547		
荔	547		
俪	547		
砾	547		
lian			
连	548		
怜	548		
帘	548		
莲	548		
涟	548		
联	548		
廉	548		
镰	548		
敛	548		
脸	548		
练	548		
炼	548		
恋	548		
链	548		
liang			
良	548		
凉	548		
梁	548		
量	548		
粮	548		
两	549		
亮	549		
谅	549		
量	549		
辌	549		
liao			
辽	549		
疗	549		
嘹	549		
潦	549		
缭	549		
燎	549		
了	549		
料	549		
瞭	549		
lie			
咧	549		
列	549		
劣	550		
烈	550		
猎	550		
裂	550		
趔	550		
lin			
拎	550		
邻	550		
林	550		
临	550		
淋	550		
琳	550		
鳞	550		
凛	550		
吝	550		
ling			
伶	550		
灵	550		
玲	550		
铃	550		
凌	551		
陵	551		
菱	551		
羚	551		
零	551		
领	551		
另	551		
令	551		
liu			
溜	551		
留	551		
流	551		
硫	551		
榴	551		
柳	551		
六	551		
long			
龙	551		
聋	551		
笼	552		
隆	552		
拢	552		
垄	552		
笼	552		
lou			
楼	552		
娄	552		
陋	552		
漏	552		
露	552		
lu			
芦	552		
庐	552		
炉	552		
颅	552		
虏	552		
鲁	552		
陆	552		
录	552		
鹿	552		
碌	552		
路	552		
露	553		
lü			
侣	553		
旅	553		
铝	553		
屡	553		
履	553		
律	553		
率	553		
绿	553		
氯	553		
滤	553		
luan			
孪	553		
卵	553		
乱	553		
lüe			
掠	553		
略	553		
lun			
伦	553		
沦	554		
轮	554		
论	554		
luo			
啰	554		
罗	554		
萝	554		
逻	554		
锣	554		
笸	554		
骡	554		
螺	554		
裸	554		
骆	554		
落	554		

M

ma			
妈	555		
麻	555		
马	555		
码	555		
蚂	555		
骂	555		
mai			
埋	555		
买	555		
迈	555		
麦	555		
卖	555		
脉	555		
man			
埋	556		
蛮	556		
馒	556		
瞒	556		
满	556		
曼	556		
漫	556		
蔓	556		
幔	556		
漫	556		
慢	556		
mang			
芒	556		
忙	556		
盲	556		
茫	556		
莽	556		
mao			
猫	556		
毛	556		
矛	557		
茅	557		
卯	557		
茂	557		
冒	557		
贸	557		
帽	557		
貌	557		
mei			
没	557		
玫	557		
眉	557		
梅	557		
媒	557		
煤	557		
霉	557		
每	557		
美	557		
妹	557		
媚	558		
魅	558		
men			
闷	558		
门	558		
闷	558		
meng			
蒙	558		
萌	558		
蒙	558		
盟	558		

朦	558	魔	562	nen		nuo	
猛	558	抹	562	嫩	565	挪	569
孟	558	末	562	neng		诺	569
梦	558	没	562	能	565	懦	569
mi		抹	562	ni		糯	569
弥	558	茉	562	尼	565	**O**	
迷	558	沫	562	泥	566	ou	
谜	559	陌	562	霓	566	讴	570
米	559	脉	562	拟	566	欧	570
觅	559	莫	562	你	566	殴	570
秘	559	漠	562	逆	566	鸥	570
密	559	墨	562	匿	566	呕	570
蜜	559	默	562	溺	566	偶	570
mian		磨	562	nian		藕	570
眠	559	mou		蔫	566	沤	570
绵	559	牟	562	年	566	怄	570
棉	559	谋	563	黏	566	**P**	
免	559	某	563	撵	567	pa	
勉	559	mu		碾	567	趴	571
缅	559	模	563	念	567	扒	571
腼	559	母	563	niang		爬	571
面	559	牡	563	娘	567	耙	571
miao		拇	563	酿	567	帕	571
苗	559	木	563	niao		怕	571
描	559	目	563	鸟	567	pai	
瞄	560	沐	563	袅	567	拍	571
秒	560	牧	563	尿	567	排	571
渺	560	募	563	nie		徘	571
藐	560	墓	563	捏	567	牌	571
妙	560	幕	563	镊	567	派	571
庙	560	穆	563	蹑	567	pan	
mie				ning		攀	572
灭	560	**N**		宁	567	盘	572
蔑	560	na		狞	567	蹒	572
min		拿	564	柠	567	判	572
民	560	哪	564	凝	567	盼	572
抿	560	那	564	宁	567	叛	572
泯	560	呐	564	niu		pang	
悯	560	纳	564	牛	568	滂	572
敏	560	捺	564	扭	568	庞	572
ming		nai		纽	568	旁	572
名	560	奶	564	拗	568	磅	572
明	560	奈	564	nong		螃	572
鸣	561	耐	564	农	568	胖	572
冥	561	nan		浓	568	pao	
铭	561	男	564	弄	568	抛	572
瞑	561	南	564	nu		刨	572
命	561	难	565	奴	568	咆	573
miu		nao		驽	568	炮	573
谬	561	挠	565	努	568	跑	573
mo		恼	565	怒	568	泡	573
摸	561	脑	565	nü		炮	573
摹	561	闹	565	女	568	疱	573
模	561	nei		nuan		pei	
膜	561	内	565	暖	568	陪	573
摩	561			nüe		培	573
磨	561			虐	569		
蘑	562						

赔		573	pie		岂		581	巧	588
佩		573	撇	577	企		581	俏	588
配		573	瞥	577	启		582	峭	588
	pen		撇	577	起		582	窍	588
喷		574	pin		绮		582	翘	588
盆		574	拼	577	气		582	qie	
喷		574	贫	577	迄		583	切	588
	peng		频	577	弃		583	茄	588
抨		574	品	577	汽		583	且	588
烹		574	聘	577	泣		583	切	588
朋		574	ping		契		583	怯	588
棚		574	乒	577	砌		583	窃	588
蓬		574	平	577	器		583	惬	588
鹏		574	评	577		qia		qin	
澎		574	苹	578	掐		583	钦	588
篷		574	凭	578	卡		583	侵	589
膨		574	屏	578	洽		583	亲	589
捧		574	瓶	578	恰		583	琴	589
碰		574	po			qian		禽	589
	pi		坡	578	千		584	勤	589
批		575	泼	578	迁		584	擒	589
纰		575	婆	578	牵		584	寝	589
坯		575	迫	578	铅		584	沁	589
披		575	破	578	谦		584	qing	
砒		575	魄	578	签		585	青	589
劈		575	pou		前		585	轻	590
霹		575	剖	578	虔		585	氢	590
皮		575	pu		钱		585	倾	590
毗		575	扑	578	钳		585	清	590
疲		575	铺	579	乾		586	蜻	591
啤		575	仆	579	潜		586	情	591
脾		575	菩	579	浅		586	晴	592
匹		575	朴	579	遣		586	请	592
劈		575	普	579	谴		586	庆	592
癖		575	谱	579	欠		586	qiong	
屁		575	铺	579	纤		586	穷	592
辟		575	瀑	579	倩		586	琼	592
媲		576	曝	579	堑		586	qiu	
僻		576			歉		586	丘	592
譬		576	**Q**			qiang		秋	592
	pian		qi		枪		586	蚯	592
偏		576	七	580	戕		586	囚	592
篇		576	妻	580	腔		586	求	593
翩		576	栖	580	强		587	球	593
便		576	凄	580	墙		587	qu	
片		576	戚	580	蔷		587	区	593
骗		576	期	580	抢		587	曲	593
	piao		欺	580	强		587	驱	593
剽		576	漆	580		qiao		屈	593
漂		576	齐	581	悄		587	祛	593
缥		576	其	581	跷		587	躯	593
飘		576	歧	581	敲		587	趋	593
瓢		576	祈	581	乔		587	渠	593
漂		576	骑	581	侨		587	曲	594
瞟		576	棋	581	桥		587	取	594
票		577	旗	581	翘		587	娶	594
漂		577	乞	581	憔		588	龋	594
					瞧		588	去	594

趣		594	融冗	601	sha		shen	
	quan			601	杀	606		612
圈		594		rou	沙	606	申	612
权		594			601	纱	606	伸	612
全		595	柔	601	刹	606	身	612
泉		595	揉	601	砂	606	参	612
拳		595	肉	601	傻	606	深	613
痊		595		ru	煞	606	什	613
蜷		595	如	602	霎	606	神	613
颧		595	蠕	602		shai	婶	613
犬		595	乳	602	筛	606	肾	613
劝		595	辱	602	晒	607	甚	613
	que		入	602		shan	渗	614
缺		595	褥	602	山	607	慎	614
瘸		596		ruan	删	607		sheng
却		596	软	602	姗	607	升	614
雀		596		rui	珊	607	生	614
确		596	蕊	603	扇	607	声	615
	qun		锐	603	煽	607	牲	615
裙		596	瑞	603	闪	607	甥	615
群		596		run	讪	608	绳	615
			闰	603	扇	608	省	615
R			润	603	善	608	圣	615
	ran			ruo	缮	608	胜	615
然		597	若	603	擅	608	盛	615
燃		597	弱	603	膳	608	剩	616
冉		597				嬗	608		shi
染		597	**S**		赡	608	尸	616
	rang			sa		shang	失	616
壤		597	撒	604	伤	608	师	617
嚷		597	洒	604	商	609	诗	617
让		597	撒	604	晌	609	虱	617
	rao		飒	604	赏	609	狮	617
饶		597		sai	上	609	施	617
扰		597	腮	604	尚	610	湿	617
绕		597	塞	604		shao	十	618
	re		赛	604	捎	610	什	618
惹		597		san	烧	610	石	618
热		598	三	604	稍	610	时	618
	ren		伞	605	勺	610	识	618
人		598	散	605	少	610	实	619
仁		599		sang	哨	610	拾	619
忍		599	丧	605	稍	610	食	619
认		599	桑	605		she	蚀	619
任		600	嗓	605	奢	610	史	620
纫		600	丧	605	赊	611	矢	620
妊		600		sao	舌	611	使	620
	reng		骚	605	折	611	始	620
扔		600	扫	605	舍	611	屎	620
仍		600	嫂	606	设	611	士	620
	ri		扫	606	社	611	氏	620
日		600		se	舍	611	示	620
	rong		色	606	射	611	世	621
荣		601	涩	606	涉	611	仕	621
容		601		sen	赦	611	市	621
溶		601	森	606	摄	611	式	621
熔		601		seng	慑	612	势	621
			僧	606				

事	621	shuai		su		泰 638
侍	622	衰 628	苏 633			tan
饰	622	摔 628	酥 633			贪 638
试	622	甩 628	俗 634			摊 638
视	622	帅 628	夙 634			滩 638
拭	622	率 628	诉 634			瘫 638
是	622	shuan	肃 634			昙 638
适	622	闩 629	素 634			谈 638
恃	622	拴 629	速 634			弹 638
室	622	涮 629	宿 634			坦 638
逝	623	shuang	粟 634			祖 638
释	623	双 629	塑 634			叹 638
嗜	623	霜 629	溯 634			探 638
誓	623	孀 629	簌 634			tang
shou		爽 629		suan		汤 639
收	623	shui	酸 634			堂 639
手	623	谁 629	蒜 634			塘 639
守	624	水 629	算 634			搪 639
首	624	税 630		sui		糖 639
寿	625	睡 630	虽 635			螳 639
受	625	shun	绥 635			倘 639
狩	625	顺 630	随 635			躺 639
授	625	瞬 630	岁 635			烫 639
售	625	shuo	遂 635			tao
兽	625	说 630	碎 635			掏 639
瘦	626	烁 630	隧 635			滔 640
shu		朔 631	邃 635			逃 640
书	626	硕 631		sun		陶 640
抒	626	数 631	孙 635			淘 640
枢	626	si	损 635			讨 640
叔	626	司 631	笋 635			套 640
殊	626	丝 631	榫 635			te
倏	626	私 631		suo		特 640
梳	626	思 631	唆 635			teng
淑	626	斯 631	梭 636			疼 640
舒	627	厮 631	缩 636			腾 641
输	627	撕 631	所 636			誊 641
蔬	627	嘶 631	索 636			藤 641
赎	627	死 631	唢 636			ti
熟	627	四 632	琐 636			剔 641
暑	627	寺 632	锁 636			梯 641
属	627	似 632				提 641
署	627	伺 632	**T**			蹄 641
鼠	627	肆 632	ta			体 641
数	627	song	他 637			替 642
曙	627	松 632	它 637			tian
术	627	怂 633	她 637			天 642
束	628	耸 633	塌 637			添 643
述	628	讼 633	踏 637			田 643
树	628	送 633	塔 637			恬 643
竖	628	颂 633	踏 637			甜 643
数	628	sou		tai		填 643
漱	628	搜 633	胎 637			tiao
shua		嗖 633	台 637			挑 643
刷	628	馊 633	抬 637			条 643
耍	628		太 637			调 643
			态 637			

挑	644	妥	650	猥	656	奚	661
眺	644	拓	650	卫	656	悉	661
跳	644	唾	650	为	656	淅	661
tie				未	656	惜	661
贴	644	**W**		位	656	稀	661
铁	644	**wa**		畏	656	溪	662
ting		挖	651	胃	656	熄	662
厅	644	洼	651	谓	656	嬉	662
听	644	娃	651	喂	656	习	662
庭	644	瓦	651	蔚	656	席	662
挺	644	**wai**		慰	656	袭	662
tong		歪	651	**wen**		媳	662
通	645	外	651	温	657	檄	662
同	645	**wan**		瘟	657	洗	662
铜	646	弯	652	文	657	喜	662
童	646	湾	652	纹	657	戏	663
统	646	蜿	652	闻	657	系	663
筒	646	完	652	吻	657	细	663
恸	646	玩	652	紊	657	**xia**	
痛	646	顽	652	稳	657	瞎	663
tou		宛	652	问	658	匣	663
偷	646	挽	652	**wo**		侠	663
头	646	晚	653	涡	658	狭	663
投	646	惋	653	窝	658	遐	663
透	647	婉	653	我	658	瑕	663
tu		万	653	卧	658	辖	663
凸	647	腕	653	握	658	霞	663
秃	647	**wang**		**wu**		下	664
突	647	汪	653	乌	658	吓	664
图	647	亡	653	污	658	夏	664
徒	647	王	653	巫	658	罅	664
途	647	枉	653	呜	658	**xian**	
涂	648	往	653	诬	658	仙	664
屠	648	惘	654	屋	659	先	665
土	648	妄	654	无	659	纤	665
吐	648	忘	654	五	659	掀	665
兔	648	旺	654	午	659	鲜	665
tuan		望	654	武	659	闲	665
湍	648	**wei**		侮	660	贤	665
团	648	危	654	舞	660	咸	665
tui		威	654	兀	660	衔	665
推	648	微	654	务	660	舷	665
颓	648	为	655	物	660	嫌	665
腿	648	违	655	误	660	显	666
退	649	围	655	恶	660	险	666
蜕	649	桅	655	悟	660	鲜	666
褪	649	唯	655			县	666
tun		帷	655	**X**		现	666
吞	649	惟	655	**xi**		限	666
屯	649	维	655			线	666
囤	649	伟	655	夕	661	宪	667
tuo		伪	655	西	661	陷	667
托	649	尾	655	吸	661	献	667
拖	649	纬	655	希	661	**xiang**	
脱	650	委	656	昔	661	乡	667
陀	650	萎	656	析	661	相	667
驮	650	唯	656	牺	661	香	668
				息	661	箱	668

详 668
降 668
享 668
响 668
想 668
向 668
项 668
相 668
象 669
像 669
橡 669

xiao
枭 669
骁 669
逍 669
消 669
萧 669
硝 669
销 669
潇 670
霄 670
嚣 670
小 670
晓 670
孝 670
肖 670
校 671
哮 671
笑 671
效 671

xie
些 671
歇 671
协 671
邪 671
胁 671
挟 671
偕 671
斜 672
谐 672
携 672
鞋 672
写 672
泄 672
泻 672
卸 672
亵 672
谢 672
懈 672

xin
心 672
辛 673
欣 673
新 673
信 674

xing
兴 674
星 674

猩 675
惺 675
腥 675
刑 675
行 675
形 675
型 676
省 676
醒 676
兴 676
杏 676
幸 676
性 676
悻 676

xiong
凶 676
兄 676
汹 676
胸 677
雄 677
熊 677

xiu
休 677
修 677
羞 677
朽 677
宿 677
秀 678
袖 678
绣 678

xu
须 678
虚 678
需 678
徐 678
许 678
栩 678
旭 678
序 678
叙 679
畜 679
绪 679
续 679
絮 679
蓄 679

xuan
宣 679
喧 679
玄 679
悬 679
选 679
炫 680
绚 680

xue
削 680
学 680

雪 680
血 681

xun
勋 681
熏 681
旬 681
寻 681
巡 681
询 681
循 681
训 682
讯 682
汛 682
迅 682
驯 682
徇 682
殉 682

Y

ya
丫 683
压 683
押 683
鸦 683
鸭 683
牙 683
芽 683
崖 683
涯 683
哑 683
雅 683
轧 683
亚 683

yan
咽 684
恹 684
胭 684
烟 684
淹 684
腌 684
嫣 684
延 684
严 684
言 684
岩 685
炎 685
沿 685
研 685
盐 685
颜 685
奄 685
俨 685
衍 685
掩 685
眼 685
演 685
厌 685
砚 686

咽 686
艳 686
唁 686
宴 686
验 686
雁 686
焰 686
燕 686
赝 686

yang
央 686
殃 686
秧 686
扬 686
羊 686
阳 687
杨 687
佯 687
洋 687
仰 687
养 687
氧 687
痒 687
样 687

yao
夭 687
妖 687
要 687
腰 688
邀 688
遥 688
摇 688
遥 688
杳 688
咬 688
舀 688
药 688
要 688
钥 689
耀 689

ye
椰 689
爷 689
也 689
冶 689
野 689
业 689
叶 689
页 689
夜 689
液 690

yi
一 690
伊 692
衣 692
医 692
依 692
仪 692

怡 692
宜 692
贻 692
姨 692
移 693
遗 693
疑 693
已 693
以 693
倚 694
椅 694
旖 694
亿 694
义 694
艺 694
忆 694
议 694
屹 694
异 695
抑 695
呓 695
役 695
译 695
易 695
驿 695
奕 695
疫 695
益 695
逸 695
肄 695
意 696
溢 696
毅 696
臆 696
翼 696

yin

因 696
阴 696
荫 696
姻 697
殷 697
吟 697
银 697
淫 697
引 697
饮 697
隐 698
印 698

ying

应 698
英 698
婴 698
樱 698
鹦 698
鹰 698
迎 698
荧 699

盈 699
营 699
萦 699
蝇 699
赢 699
颖 699
影 699
应 699
映 700
硬 700

yong

佣 700
拥 700
庸 700
永 700
咏 700
泳 700
勇 700
涌 700
踊 700
用 700
佣 701

you

优 701
忧 701
幽 701
悠 701
尤 701
由 701
邮 702
犹 702
油 702
游 702
友 703
有 703
右 703
幼 703
诱 703

yu

迂 703
淤 704
于 704
予 704
余 704
鱼 704
娱 704
渔 704
逾 704
愉 704
愚 704
与 704
予 705
屿 705
宇 705
羽 705
雨 705
语 705
与 705

玉 705
郁 705
育 705
狱 705
浴 705
预 705
域 706
欲 706
遇 706
御 706
寓 706
愈 706

yuan

冤 706
渊 706
元 706
园 707
员 707
原 707
圆 707
援 707
猿 707
源 708
辕 708
远 708
怨 708
院 708
愿 708

yue

约 708
月 708
乐 709
阅 709
悦 709
跃 709
越 709

yun

晕 709
云 709
匀 709
允 709
陨 709
殒 709
孕 709
运 709
晕 710
愠 710
韵 710
蕴 710
熨 710

Z

za

扎 711
杂 711
砸 711

zai

灾 711
栽 711
仔 711
载 711
宰 711
再 711
在 712
载 712

zan

暂 712
赞 712

zang

赃 712
脏 712
葬 712
藏 712

zao

遭 712
糟 712
早 713
枣 713
皂 713
灶 713
造 713
噪 713
燥 713
躁 713

ze

则 713
责 713
择 713

zei

贼 713

zen

怎 714

zeng

增 714
憎 714
赠 714

zha

扎 714
札 714
轧 714
闸 714
眨 714
诈 714
炸 714
榨 714

zhai

摘 714
宅 715
债 715

zhan

沾 715
粘 715
瞻 715
斩 715

展	715	蒸	721	种	727	灼	733	
崭	715	拯	721	重	727	苗	733	
占	715	整	721			卓	733	
栈	715	正	721	**zhou**		浊	733	
战	715	证	722	周	727	酌	733	
站	716	挣	722	轴	728	着	733	
绽	716	症	722	肘	728	琢	733	
湛	716			咒	728			
颤	716	**zhi**				**zi**		
		支	722	**zhu**				
zhang		汁	722	朱	728	孜	733	
张	716	芝	722	珠	728	咨	733	
章	716	枝	722	株	728	姿	733	
长	716	知	722	诸	728	资	733	
涨	716	肢	723	猪	728	滋	734	
掌	716	织	723	竹	728	子	734	
丈	717	脂	723	逐	728	仔	734	
仗	717	蜘	723	烛	728	籽	734	
杖	717	执	723	主	728	紫	734	
帐	717	直	723	嘱	729	自	734	
账	717	侄	723	瞩	729	字	735	
障	717	值	723	助	729			
		职	723	住	729	**zong**		
zhao		植	723	贮	729	宗	735	
招	717	殖	723	注	729	综	735	
昭	717	止	723	驻	729	棕	735	
朝	717	只	723	柱	729	踪	736	
着	717	旨	724	祝	729	总	736	
爪	717	纸	724	著	729	纵	736	
找	718	指	724					
沼	718	咫	724	**zhua**		**zou**		
召	718	趾	724	抓	730	走	736	
兆	718	至	724	爪	730	奏	737	
照	718	志	724					
罩	718	制	724	**zhuan**		**zu**		
		质	725	专	730	租	737	
zhe		治	725	砖	730	足	737	
折	718	挚	725	转	730	卒	737	
遮	718	致	725	传	731	诅	737	
折	719	秩	725	转	731	阻	737	
哲	719	掷	725	赚	731	组	737	
这	719	窒	725	撰	731	祖	738	
		智	725					
zhen		滞	725	**zhuang**		**zuan**		
贞	719	置	725	庄	731	钻	738	
针	719	稚	725	桩	731			
侦	719			装	731	**zui**		
珍	719	**zhong**		壮	731	嘴	738	
真	719	中	725	状	732	最	738	
诊	719	忠	726	撞	732	罪	738	
枕	720	终	726			醉	738	
阵	720	钟	726	**zhui**				
振	720	衷	726	追	732	**zun**		
赈	720	肿	726	坠	732	尊	739	
震	720	种	726	缀	732	遵	739	
镇	720	仲	727	赘	732			
		众	727			**zuo**		
zheng				**zhun**		作	739	
争	720			谆	732	昨	739	
征	720			准	732	左	739	
挣	721					佐	739	
				zhuo		作	739	
				拙	732	坐	740	
				捉	733	座	740	
				桌	733	做	740	